Essential Forms For Self Advocacy

NAVIGATING

PUBLIC

SCHOOL

A Guide To Education Law

A Kelly Neal, Esq.
Neal Student Support Advocacy & Disability, LLC

Library of Congress Control Number: 2025911415

ISBN No: 979-8-9929441-3-6
Cover design by A. Kelly Neal, Esq.
Printed in the United States of America
For more information, visit www.SSAdisability.org

Disclaimer:
This book is intended for informational and educational purposes only. It does not constitute legal advice or establish an attorney-client relationship. Readers should consult a qualified attorney for legal guidance regarding specific situations. While every effort has been made to ensure accuracy, the author and publisher assume no responsibility for errors or omissions.

The information contained in this book is provided for informational purposes only, and should not be construed as legal advice on any subject matter. This book is similarly not intended as a solicitation for or advertisement of A. Kelly Neal, Esq.'s legal services. Transmission of the information contained in this book is not intended to create, and receipt does not constitute, an attorney-client or business relationship between the sender and receiver. An attorney-client relationship between A. Kelly Neal, Esq. and any reader of this book does not exist unless and until an agreement has been reached between you and A. Kelly Neal, Esq. to handle a particular matter. Receipt of unsolicited confidential information by A. Kelly Neal, Esq. will not disqualify the firm from representing another party in any matter to which the information relates. Laws differ by jurisdiction, and the information in this book may not apply to every reader. No recipients of content from this book should act or refrain from acting on the basis of any content included in the book without seeking the appropriate legal or other professional advice on the particular facts and circumstances at issue from an attorney licensed in the recipient's state. A. Kelly Neal, Esq. expressly disclaims all liability in respect to actions taken or not taken based on any or all the contents of this book. A. Kelly Neal, Esq. is licensed to practice law only in the State of Georgia.

Law is constantly evolving. The information in this book is intended for general informational purposes and may not reflect the most current legal developments. This book provides an overview of the subject matter covered and is sold with the understanding that neither the publisher nor the author is providing legal or other professional services. For legal advice regarding a specific situation, you should consult a qualified attorney.

This book is a battle cry. A call to expose the failures, the indifference, and the willful neglect that have stolen futures and shattered spirits. It is dedicated to every educator who has looked away instead of stepping up, who has denied services for convenience, who has hidden behind bureaucracy instead of doing what is right. You know exactly who you are. Your inaction has forced parents into exhausting, merciless fights for the bare minimum—the rights their children are both legally and morally owed.

To the parents who have been dismissed, manipulated, and told to 'trust the process' while watching their child suffer—this book is your weapon. Use it to tear through the excuses, to shine a glaring light on the system's failures, to demand what should never have been denied. Because if they refuse to fight for your child, you will. And you will win.

Power to Our Pupils.

To everyone who contributed to this book, thank you from the bottom of my heart. Your support, insights, and efforts have been invaluable, and I am deeply grateful. Your contributions have not gone unnoticed—they have made this book possible, and I appreciate each and every one of you.

IV.C <u>Evolution of the War</u> (26 Vols.)
Direct Action: The Johnson Commitments, 1964-1968
(16 Vols.)
6. U.S. Ground Strategy and Force Deployments: 1965-1967
(3 Vols.)
a. Volume I: Phase II, Program 3, Program 4

UNITED STATES - VIETNAM RELATIONS

1945 - 1967

VIETNAM TASK FORCE

OFFICE OF THE SECRETARY OF DEFENSE

SET # 13

0205

IV.C.6.(a)

U.S. GROUND STRATEGY
AND FORCE DEPLOYMENTS
1965--1967

VOLUME I

IV.c.6

U.S. GROUND STRATEGY AND FORCE DEPLOYMENTS
1965 -- 1967

CHRONOLOGY

18 Jun 65	Memo from McGeorge Bundy to SecDef	Bundy passes on President's desires that "we find more dramatic and effective action in South Vietnam."
1 Jul 65	Draft Memo for the President	SecDef recommends 44 battalions (34 U.S.) to Vietnam in next few months. Says Westmoreland is not sure about requirements for 1966.
2 Jul 65	Memo for General Goodpaster from ASD(ISA) McNaughton	Secy McNaughton suggests questions to be addressed by JCS study on assurance of winning the war.
7 Jul 65	SecDef message to Saigon 072352Z Jul 65	SecDef gives Westmoreland questions he will want answered on his trip - includes probable requirements for additional forces in 1966.
12 Jul 65	Memo for the Record, Subj: 63 Battalion Plan	SecDef memorandum for the record calls for building up the armed forces by 63 battalions.
14 Jul 65	Intensification of the Military Operations in Vietnam - Concept and Appraisal	JCS study on concept and appraisal of assurance of winning goes to SecDef.
16-20 Jul 65		SecDef in Saigon, receives Westmoreland's requirements.
17 Jul 65	Message from Secy Vance to SecDef McNamara 072042Z Jul 65	Vance informs McNamara that President has approved 34 Battalion Plan and will try to push through reserve call-up.
20 Jul 65	Memo for the President, Subj: Recommendations of Additional Deployments to Vietnam	SecDef recommends 34 U.S. battalions to SVN in 1965 (Phase I) with possible need for 100,000 additional troops in 1966 (Phase II).
22 Jul 65	MACV message 220625Z Jul 65	MACV recommends 101,712 personnel and 27 battalions for Phase II.

i

5

13 Dec 65	SecDef Multi-Addressee Memo	SecDef disseminates tables showing Phase IIA deployments, bringing U.S. strength to 75 battalions and 367,800 by December 1966, 393,000 personnel by June 1967.
16 Dec 65	CINCPAC Letter Ser: 000473	CINCPAC sends revised requirements for Phase IIA, desires 75 battalions and 443,000 by December 1966.
1 Jan 66		173rd Airborne Brigade begins Operation MARAUDER in Hau Nghia Province near Cambodia border.
8 Jan 66		173rd Airborne Brigade units and 1st US Infantry Division launch Operation CRIMP in Hau Nghia and Binh Tuong Provinces.
15 Jan 66	Memo for SecDef	Guidelines for assumptions on availability of forces for SE Asia. Case 3 assumes availability of CONUS forces and activations only. Case 2 adds drawdowns from overseas areas. Case 1 further adds callup of selected reserve units and extension of terms of service.
19 Jan 66		1st Brigade, 101st Airborne Division, begins Operation VAN BUREN, in Phu Yen Province.
24 Jan 66		3rd Brigade, 1st Cavalry, launches Operation MASHER/WHITE WING near Bong Son in Binh Dinh Province.
24 Jan 66	Memo for the President	SecDef estimates U.S. strength at end of 1966 at 75 battalions and 367,800 troops.
28 Jan 66		U.S. Marine Corps units launch DOUBLE EAGLE in Quang Ngai Province.
7-9 Feb 66		Honolulu Conference with Ky and President Johnson.
12 Feb 66	CINCPAC 3010 Ser: 00055	CINCPAC forwards revised version of requirements for SE Asia, and deployment plans under the assumptions of Cases, 1, 2, and 3.

TOP SECRET - Sensitive

17 Feb 66	SecDef Multi-Addressee Memo, Subj: SE Asia Planning Assumptions	SecDef directs Military Departments and the JCS to study possible ways of meeting Case 1 deployment schedule without calling reserves or extending tours of duty.
21 Feb 66		1st Brigade, 101st Airborne Division, begins Operation HARRISON, in Phu Yen Province.
1 Mar 66	JCSM 130-66	JCS reply they cannot meet Case I deployment schedule without calling up reserves. Recommend stretch out of deployment into 1967.
7 Mar 66		1st Brigade, 1st Infantry Division, and 173d Airborne Division launch Operation SILVER CITY, a 17-day search and destroy operation in the Bien Duong and Long Khanh Provincial border area.
9 Mar 66		Estimated NVA regiment overwhelms Ashau Special Forces camp at Thua Thien Province.
10 Mar 66	SecDef Memo to CJCS	SecDef directs planning on the basis of Case I schedule without call-up of reserves or extension of terms of service.
10 Mar 66		GVN National Leadership Committee votes to remove Lt Gen Thi from his post as I Corps Commander. Demonstrations protesting Thi's ouster signalled the start of long political turbulence.
19 Mar 66		USMC units launch Operation TEXAS in Quang Ngai Province.
4 Apr 66	JCSM 218-66	JCS reply to SecDef giving a program reflecting the Services "current estimate of their capabilities to provide forces required...(and meeting) as closely as feasible the program for South Vietnam prescribed" by the SecDef on 10 March.

TOP SECRET - Sensitive

TOP SECRET - Sensitive

11 Apr 66	SecDef Multi-Addressee Memo, Subj: SE Asia Deployment Plan	SecDef approves Deployment Plan recommended by JCS in JCSM 218-66.
12 Apr 66	SecDef Memo for CJCS	SecDef requests an explanation of differences between JCSM 218-66 and the Case I Deployment Plan.
24 Apr 66		Elements of 1st Infantry Division launch Operation BIRMINGHAM. The 24-search and destroy operation involving the deepest friendly penetration in 5 years into War Zone C in Tay Ninh Province.
10 May 66		Elements of 3d Brigade, 25th Infantry Division, launch Operation PAUL REVERE, an 82-day border screening area control operation in Pleiku Province.
16 May 66		Elements of 1st Cavalry Division launch 22-day Operation CRAZY HORSE in Binh Dinh Province.
2 Jun 66		Elements of 1st Infantry Division begin Operation EL PASO II. 41-search and destroy operation in Binh Long Province.
2 Jun 66		1st Brigade, 101st Airborne Division, launches Operation HAWTHORNE, a 19-search and destroy operation in Kontum Province.
10 Jun 66	ASD(SA) Memo for SecDef, Subj: Report on Deployments to SEA	ASD Enthoven reports that a large number of adjustments to deployment plan have been proposed by the Army.
13 Jun 66	ASD(SA) Memo for SecDef, Subj: Deployments to SE Asia	Enthoven explains major bookkeeping changes in deployment schedules.
18 Jun 66	CINCPAC 3010 Ser: 000255	CINCPAC's CY 66 and CY 67 requirements based upon a concept which now emphasizes restricting access to the land borders of RVN and increased efforts in the highlands and along the western RVN border. CINCPAC envisions a rise to 90 maneuver battalions and 542,588 personnel by end of CY 67.

v

TOP SECRET - Sensitive

28 Jun 66	President's Memo for SecDef	Requests SecDef and JCS to see if any more acceleration of deployment is possible.
30 Jun 66	ASD(SA) Memo for SecDef, Subj: SE Asia Deployment Plan	Revised version of 10 April plan indicates acceleration of deployment of 2 brigades of the 9th Division to December 1966, and deployment of 196th Infantry Brigade in August 1966.
2 Jul 66	SecDef Multi-Addressee Memo, Subj: SE Asia Deployment Plan	Revised 10 April Plan, now named "Program #3," is published.
7 Jul 66		USMC units launch Operation HASTINGS, a 27-day search and destroy operation against the 324B NVA Division south of the DMZ.
8 Jul 66	JCSM 450-66, Subj: CINCPAC Calendar Year Deployments	JCS report that further acceleration is unlikely.
15 Jul 66	SecDef Memo for the President, Subj: Schedule of Deployments to South Vietnam	SecDef reports to the President on the acceleration achieved since the beginning of the year.
16 Jul 66		Operation DECK HOUSE in eastern Quang Tri Province is conducted in support of HASTINGS.
1 Aug 66		1st Cavalry Division units launch 25-day search and destroy operation, PAUL REVERE II in Pleiku.
3 Aug 66	SAIGON 2564	Lodge quotes Westmoreland as agreeing with him on urgent desirability of hitting pacification hard while other things are going well.
5 Aug 66	JCSM 506-66	JCS forwards CINCPAC's requirements for CY 66 and 67. Recommend that almost all of them be accepted.
5 Aug 66	SecDef Memo to CJCS	SecDef directs JCS to evaluate CINCPAC's requirements and also Issue Papers referred for SecDef by Systems Analysis.

8 Aug 66	SAIGON 2934 to Secy of State	Lodge reports an upsurge of enemy infiltration thru the DMZ and passes on Westmoreland's KANZUS recommendation.
10 Aug 66	MACV 27578	Westmoreland passes on his evaluation of the requirements forwarded by CINCPAC. "I cannot justify a reduction in requirements submitted."
10 Aug 66	SAIGON 3129	Lodge points out the need for making a strong effort now to make sure "the smell of victory" is in the air. He reemphasizes the need for pacification.
17 Aug 66	SAIGON 3670	Porter in Saigon informs Komer of anti-inflationary measures and points out possible problem areas, including US military piaster budget.
23 Aug 66		CINCPAC sends MACV its draft strategy for 1966 and 1967. The proposed strategy emphasizes pacification and nation building.
24 Aug 66	Interagency Roles and Missions Study Group Final Report	Roles and Missions Study Group report points out need for pacification. Makes several recommendations to improve pacification effort.
26 Aug 66	MACV 29797	Westmoreland in cable to CINCPAC describes his concept of operations for the rest of the year. He describes his strategy during the period 1 May to 1 November 1966 that of containing the enemy through offensive tactical operations; describes his strategy for 1 November 1966 to 1 May 1967 as increasing momentum of operations in a general offensive with maximum practical support to area and population security in further support of revolutionary development. He visualizes that significant numbers of US/FW maneuver battalions will be involved in pacification. In addition to emphasizing pacification, Westmoreland emphasizes need to fight against enemy main forces.

31 Aug 66	SAIGON 4923	Lodge points out efforts being taken in Saigon to emphasize pacification. He begins to express reservations on need for more troops.
2 Sep 66	SecDef Memo for CJCS	SecDef asks CJCS to explore carefully all desirable tradeoffs between piaster funding of GVN and US armed forces in SVN.
7 Sep 66	JCS 1975 to CINCPAC	JCS informs CINCPAC of Jason Plan for aerial supported anti-infiltration barrier.
11 Sep 66		GVN elections.
13 Sep 66	Cite Unknown	CINCPAC comments on anti-infiltration barrier proposed by Jason study. Doubts practicality of scheme.
13 Sep 66	MACV 41191 to CINCPAC	Westmoreland discusses build-up in Quang Tri Province. Requests authority to use B-52 strikes.
13 Sep 66		1st Cavalry Division launches 40-day search and destroy Operation THAYER I in Binh Dinh Province.
14 Sep 66		196th Infantry Brigade begins 72-day search and destroy Operation ATTLEBORO in Tay Ninh Province, which grows into largest operation of war to date. Other US units involved included all three brigades of the 1st Infantry Division, the 2nd Brigade of the 25th Division, the 3rd Brigade of the 4th Infantry Division, and 1 battalion of the 173rd Airborne Brigade.
15 Sep 66	SAIGON 6100	Embassy gives their latest data on inflation in SVN; forecast a 44.1 billion piaster inflationary gap in CY 67.
16 Sep 66	MACV 41676	Westmoreland discusses Slam concept designed to impede enemy infiltration thru Laos.
20 Sep 66	MACV 8212	Westmoreland conveys his concern over enemy forces in sanctuaries to Admiral Sharp.

22 Sep 66	CM-1774-66	Chairman of the Joint Chiefs of Staff tells SecDef that piaster costs per man of US forces are several times those of GVN forces. However, he does not see any piaster advantages from feasible exchanges.
23 Sep 66	State 53541 to Saigon	State calls news of size of inflationary gap in Saigon's 15 September message very disturbing.
24 Sep 66	MACV 8371 to Sharp and Wheeler	Westmoreland reviews VC/NVA's recent campaign and assesses the effectiveness of US campaigns. Does not mention pacification.
24 Sep 66	JCSM 613-66	JCS forward their final evaluation of CINCPAC's 18 June submission and the results of their evaluation of the SecDef's Issue Papers, from 5 August.
29 Sep 66	ASD(SA) Memo for SecDef	Enthoven tells SecDef he is reviewing JCSM-613-66 and forwards some new deployment Issue Papers to Secretary of Defense.
1 Oct 66	SAIGON 7332	Lodge, in a message to Rusk, McNamara and Komer, sets forth his proposal on piaster ceilings. Sets a piaster ceiling of 42 billion on military spending in South Vietnam.
2 Oct 66	MACV 43926	MACV recommends to CINCPAC and JCS deployment of Caltrop for operational tests ASAP.
5 Oct 66	MACV 44378	Westmoreland submits his reclama to Lodge's proposal for a piaster budget ceiling.
5 Oct 66	ASD(SA) Memo for SecDef	Dr. Enthoven analyzes Lodge's message of 1 Oct for SecDef. Points out differences in spending associated with different deployments small relative to other uncertainties. Terms Lodge's estimates on holding inflation down optimistic.
6 Oct 66	SecDef Memo for CJCS	SecDef forwards another set of deployment Issue Papers to the Joint Chiefs of Staff.

TOP SECRET - Sensitive

7 Oct 66	JCSM-646-66	Joint Chiefs of Staff forward their evaluation of world-wide military posture and the effects which deployments to SVN will have upon same.
10 Oct 66		the 3rd US Marine Division assumes control of Operation PRAIRIE in Quang Tri Province. This is the first Division-controlled operation in I CTZ.
14 Oct 66	Draft Presidential Memo, Trip Report, Actions Recommended for Vietnam	SecDef recommends force levels stabilize at 470,000, that US stabilize ROLLING THUNDER, deploy a barrier and gird itself for a long haul.
14 Oct 66	JCSM-672-66	Joint Chiefs of Staff submit their comments on SecDef's memorandum for the President. Do not agree with 470,000-man limitation. Are doubtful on feasibility of the barrier, reserve judgment until they receive detailed programs being prepared by CINCPAC.
18 Oct 66		Elements of 4th Infantry Division, 25th Infantry Division and 1st Cavalry Division, launch 74-day Operation PAUL REVERE IV, in Pleiku Province.
20 Oct 66	CINCPAC 3010 Ser: 000438	CINCPAC forwards results of the Honolulu Planning Conference. Recommend a build-up to 91 maneuver battalions and 493,969 personnel by end of CY 67. Total strength after filling out will be 94 battalions and 555,741 personnel.
23 Oct 66	CINCPAC Ser: 000455	CINCPAC forwards three alternative deployment plans and their associated piaster costs.
23-25 Oct 66		Manila Conference
26 Oct 66	ASD(ISA) Memo for SecDef, Subj: "McNaughton in Manila"	McNaughton gives his report of conversations with Westmoreland on force levels and ROLLING THUNDER. Says Westmoreland is thinking of an end-CY 67 strength of 480,000.

x   TOP SECRET - Sensitive

13

4 Nov 66	JCSM 702-66, "Deployment of Forces to Meet CY 67 Requirements"	Joint Chiefs of Staff forward report of Honolulu Planning Conference.
7 Nov 66	AB 142, Combined Campaign Plan, 1967	MACV and RVNAF JGS set forth campaign plan for 1967. Plan emphasizes pacification.
9 Nov 66	ASD(SA) Memo for SecDef	Enthoven outlines his "Program 4," bringing strength to 87 battalions and 469,000 troops by June 1968.
11 Nov 66	SecDef Memo for CJCS, "Deployments to SEA"	SecDef responds to JCS recommendations in JCSM 702-66, and sets forth guidelines for Program 4 essentially as recommended by Enthoven.
17 Nov 66	Draft Presidential Memo, "Recommended FY 67 SEA Supplemental Appropriation"	SecDef sets forth in some detail his reasoning behind the deployment plan now called "Program 4."
18 Nov 66	SecDef Memo for Secys of Military Departments, C/JCS, Asst Secys of Def	Transmits tables of deployments which were authorized on 11 November 1966.
2 Dec 66	JCSM 739-66, "Deployments to SEA and other PACOM Areas"	JCS asked direct substitution of units to provide "balanced forces".
9 Dec 66	Memo for CJCS from Sec Def, Subj: "Deployments to SEA and other PACOM Areas"	Approves direct substitution within 470,000 man ceiling.
22 Dec 66	DCPG memo for SecDef, Subj: "Plan for Increased Anti-Infiltration Capability for SEA"	Established intent and guidance for planning barrier concept.
2 Jan 67	COMUSMACV 00610	MACV's year-end assessment of enemy situation and strategy.
8 Jan 67		Operation CEDAR FALLS. Begins longest operation of war to date in terms of forces employed.

21 Feb 67	Memo from DepSecDef to Under Sec State, Subj: "Military Action Programs for SEA"	Forwarded DOD input to analysis of alternative strategies prepared for the President. Incorporated various separate proposals made by JCS over past two months.
22 Feb 67	JCSM 97-67, Subj: MACV Practice Nine Requirements Plan	JCS forwards and coments on MACV manpower and logistics requirements to implement barrier plan. Recommends plan not be approved.
22 Feb 67	CM-2134-67, "PRACTICE NINE Requirements Plan, dated 26 Jan 1967"	CJCS forwards his dissent to JCSM 97-67. Recommends implementation of plan.
18 Mar 67	COMUSMACV message 09101	MACV analysis of current force requirements submitted to CINCPAC. "Optimum force" of 4-2/3 divisions; "minimum essential force" of 2-1/3 divisions.
20-21 Mar 67		Guam Conference. Bunker, Locke, Komer introduced to Vietnamese leaders.
24 Mar 67	JCS message 59881	Requested CINCPAC/MACV detailed analysis and justification for additional forces.
28 Mar 67	COMUSMACV 10311	Forwarded MACV detailed justification and planning calculations to JCS.
7 Apr 67		Task Force OREGON formed, posted to Quang Ngai Province.
14 Apr 67	JCSM-208-67, Subj: Marine Corps Reinforcement of I Corps Tactical Zone	Proposed 2 brigades from 9th MAB be stationed off Vietnamese coast to be committed when required by COMUSMACV, remainder of MAB placed on 15-day call in Okinawa.
20 Apr 67	JCSM-218-67	Formally reported to SecDef the MACV force requirements.
25-27 Apr 67		General Westmoreland returns to US, consults with President.
1 May 67	OASD(ISA) Memo for SecDef, Subj: Increase of SEA forces	Detailed analysis of MACV force request. Recommended against adding more US combat forces.

9 May 1967	NSAM 362	All pacification efforts placed under MACV. Komer named Deputy for Pacification to COMUSMACV.
19 May 1967	Draft Memorandum for President, Subject: Future Actions in Vietnam	ASD(ISA) reviews situation in Vietnam, analyzes alternative military courses of action, argues against force level increases, proposes strategy of "slow progress."
20 May 1967	JCSM 286-67, "Operations Against North Vietnam"	JCS seriously concerned at the prospective introduction by the USSR into NVN of new weapons. Proposed neutralization of Hanoi-Haiphong complex by attacking all elements of the import system of NVN, "shouldering out" foreign shipping, mining port.
20 May 1967	JCSM 288-67, "US Worldwide Military Posture"	JCS recommend selective callup of reserves so US could more effectively fulfill worldwide commitments.
23 May 1967	Memo for CJCS, Subject: Combat Service Support Staffing in SVN	SecDef requested JCS to prepare detailed study analyzing in depth CSS staffing levels in SVN.
24 May 1967	CM 2278-67, "Alternative Courses of Action"	JCS reply to 26 April memo by DepSecDef. Concluded that (a) force levels recommended in JCSM 218-67 should be deployed; (b) a more effective air/naval campaign against NVN should be conducted as recommended in JCSM 218-67.
29 May 1967	CM 2381-67, Future Actions in Vietnam	Identifies certain factual corrections and annotations in COMUSMACV 18 March "minimum essential force" request.
1 June 1967	JCSM 306-67, Draft Memorandum for the President on Future Actions in Vietnam	JCS reply to 19 May DPM, expressed strong objections to basic orientation as well as specific recommendations and objectives. Saw "alarming pattern" which suggested a major realignment of US objectives and intentions in SEA, recommended that DPM "not be considered further."
2 June 1967	JCSM-312-67, Air Operations Against NVN	JCS response to SecDef memo of 20 May. Concluded that original recommendation of 20 May represented the most effective way to prosecute air/naval campaign against NVN.

2 June 1967	Note, Wm. P. Bundy to Mr. McNaughton	Comments on 19 May DPM. Expressed general agreement with basic objectives as stated in DPM, but agreed with JCS that DPM displayed a negative turn to our strategy and commitment in SVN.
8 June 1967	Memorandum for Under SecDef (sic) Vance from UnderSecState Katzenbach, Subject: Preliminary Comments on DOD Draft of 19 May.	Comments on 19 May DPM. Recommended increase of 30,000 men in small increments over 18 months, get GVN more fully involved and effective, concentrate bombing LOCs in the north.
12 June 1967	ASD(ISA) Draft Memorandum for the President, Subject: Alternative Military Actions Against NVN	Revised DPM incorporated views of JCS, CIA, State. Opposed JCS program, recommended concentrating bulk of bombing on infiltration routes south of 20th parallel, skirted question of ground force increase.
13 June 1967	Memo for CJCS from SecDef, Subj: Increased Use of Civilians for US Troop Support (C)	Requested JCS to determine which logistical requirements could be met by increased use of SVN civilians for US troop support.
5 July 1967	Memo for SecDef from ASD(SA), subject: Current Estimate of Additional Deployment Capability	Update of original estimate of what Army could provide. Approx. 3-2/3 DE could be provided to MACV by 31 Dec 68 without calling reserves.
7-8 July 1967		SecDef in SVN receives MACV justification.
13 July 1967	Memo for Record, Subj: Fallout from SecDef Trip to SVN	ASD(ISA) memo for the record indicates decision in Saigon to increase forces to 525,000 limit.
13 July 1967	Memo for SecDef from Richard C. Steadman, DASD, Subject: Additional Third Country Forces for Vietnam	Provided series of letters to Manila countries making clear the need for additional forces.
14 July 1967	Memo for Record, Subj: SEA Deployments	ASD(SA) outlined the decisions made in Saigon and directed work priorities and assignments for OASD(SA) to flesh out the 525,000 troop limit.

17

20 July 1967	JCSM 416-67, Subject: US Force Deployments - Vietnam.	JCS provide detailed troop list within 525,000 ceiling. Reaffirmed force requirements as set forth in JCSM 288-67.
26 July 1967	Memo from DepSecDef to CJCS, Subj: Operations Against NVN	Comments on JCSM 286-67.
22 Jul - 5 Aug 1967		General Taylor, Mr. Clifford tour troop contributing countries, seek additional third-country forces.
14 Aug 1967	ASD(SA) Memo for Secys of Mil Depts, CJCS, ASDs, Subject: SEA Deployment Program #5	Formally approved forces for deployment in Program 5. Established civilianization scheduled, approved additional 5 destroyers for gunfire support.
9 Sept 1967	DJCSM 1118-67, Subj: Examination of Speed-Up in Program 5 Deployments	Joint Staff examined possible actions to speed up Program 5 deployments.
12 Sept 1967	CM 2640-67	Joint Staff requested by President to indicate actions which would increase pressure on NVN.
15 Sept 1967	JCSM-505-67	JCS forward refined troop list for Program 5.
16 Sept 1967	SecArmy Memo for SecDef, Subject: Deployment Schedule for 101st Airborne Division (-)	Div(-) could be deployed to close in VN prior to Christmas.
22 Sept 1967	SecDef Memo for SecArmy, Subj: Deployment of 101st Airborne Division (-).	Approves accelerated deployment of 101st Airborne Div(-).
28 Sept 1967	MACV message 31998	MACV plan for reorienting in-country forces.
4 Oct 1967	SecDef Memo for the President	SecDef indicated actions taken on MACV recommendations contained in message 31998.
5 Oct 1967	SecDef memo for Secys of Mil Depts, CJCS, ASDs, Subject: FY 68 U.S. Force Deployments, Vietnam.	SecDef approves force deployments listed in JCSM 505-67.

16 Oct 1967	SecArmy memo for SecDef, Subj: Deployment of 101st Airborne Division (-)	SecArmy indicates that remainder of 101st Airborne Division can be accelerated to close in Vietnam by 20 December 1967.
17 Oct 1967	JCSM-555-67	JCS forward to President through SecDef their reply to questions raised on 12 September.
21 Oct 1967	SecDef memo for SecArmy, Subject: Deployment of the 101st Division (-)	SecDef approves accelerated deployment of remainder of 101st Airborne Division.
31 Oct 1967	SecArmy memo for SecDef, Subject: Deployment of 11th Infantry Brigade.	SecArmy indicates that Brigade could be deployed on or about 10 December.
6 Nov 1967	SecDef memo for SecArmy, Subject: Deployment of the 11th Infantry Brigade.	SecDef approves early deployment of the 11th Infantry Brigade.
7 Nov 1967	CM-2743-67	CJCS directs Joint Staff to explore what further foreshortening of deployment dates could be accomplished.
10 Nov 1967	CM-2752-67	CJCS directs Joint Staff to recommend military operations in SEA for next four months.
21 Nov 1967	DJSM-1409-71	Joint Staff reply to CJCS request of 7 Nov to explore foreshortening of deployment dates.
27 Nov 1967	JCSM-663-67	JCS provide SecDef their recommendations for conduct of military operations in SEA over next four months.
22 Dec 1967	ASD(ISA) memo to CJCS.	Forwards SecDef and SecState comments on JCSM 663-67.
26 Jan 1968	MACV message 61742	COMUSMACV year-end assessment.
31 Jan 1968		TET offensive begins.
12 Feb 1968	JCSM-91-68	JCS examine plans for emergency augmentation of MACV, recommended deployment of reinforcements be deferred.

TOP SECRET - Sensitive

13 Feb 1968	JCS Message 9926	Directs deployment of brigade task force of 82nd Airborne Division to SVN.
13 Feb 1968	JCS Message 9929	Directs deployment of one Marine regimental landing team to SVN.
13 Feb 1968	JCSM-96-68	JCS forward to SecDef recommendations for actions to be taken relative to callup of reserves.
23-26 Feb 68		CJCS visit to SVN.
27 Feb 1968	Report of CJCS on Situation in SVN and MACV Force Requirements	CJCS reports on his trip to SVN and furnishes MACV Program 6 force requirements.
1 Mar 1968		Clark Clifford sworn in as Secretary of Defense.
4 Mar 1968	Draft Memorandum for the President	Forwards recommendations of SecDef Working Group to the President.
8 Mar 1968	CM-3098-68	JCS forward COMUSMACV comments on DPM.
11-12 Mar 68		SecState testifies before Senate Foreign Relations Committee
14 Mar 1968	DepSecDef memo for CJCS, Subject: SEA Deployments	DepSecDef informs CJCS of Presidential decision to deploy 30,000 additional troops.
14 Mar 1968	SecArmy memo to SecDef	SecArmy indicated requirement for 13,500 additional men to support emergency reinforcement.
16 Mar 1968	ASD(SA) Memo for Record	Summarizes decision to deploy 43,500 additional troops and plans for reserve call-up.
22 Mar 1968		Gen. Westmoreland to be new Chief of Staff of the Army.
23 Mar 1968	OASD(SA) Memo for SecDef, Subj: Program #6 Summary Tables (Tentative)	Forwarded to SecDef for approval Program 6, based on manpower ceiling of 579,000.

TOP SECRET - Sensitive

26-27 Mar 68		General Abrams in Washington, confers with President.
30 Mar 1968	Dept of State msg 139431	Announces Presidential decision to US Ambassadors in troop contributing countries.
31 Mar 1968	Remarks of President to the Nation	President announces partial bombing halt, deployment of 13,500 additional troops.
3 Apr 1968	White House Press Release	Hanoi declares readiness to meet. U.S. accepts.
4 Apr 1968	DepSecDef memo for Secys of Mil Depts, CJCS, ASD's, Subj: SEA Deployment Program #6	DepSecDef establishes Program #6, placed new ceiling of 549,500 on U.S. forces in SVN.

TOP SECRET - Sensitive

VOLUME I
U.S. GROUND STRATEGY AND FORCE DEPLOYMENTS, 1965--1967

TABLE OF CONTENTS and OUTLINE

I. PHASE II

I. PHASE II

IV.C.6.

U.S. GROUND STRATEGY AND FORCE DEPLOYMENTS
1965 - 1967

I. PHASE II

A. Prelude to Phase II

The story of the Phase II build-up begins near the end of the chain
of events which led to the decision, announced on 28 July 1965, on a
Phase I build-up to 44 Free World battalions. Sparked by the news that
the Viet Cong were building up their strength, that ARVN was doing badly
on the battlefield, and that the President desired "that we find more
dramatic and effective actions in South Vietnam," 1/ Secretary of
Defense McNamara prepared to decide what forces would be necessary to
achieve the goals of the United States in Vietnam. The history of the
decision on the size and composition of the forces to be deployed during
the time remaining in 1965, termed Phase I forces, is the subject of
another study in this series. 2/ However, there were some events and
decisions taken in this period which were to influence the decisions on
Phase II forces. While Secretary McNamara was preparing for his 16-20
July trip to Saigon to discuss the build-up of American forces in
Vietnam, he asked General Wheeler, Chairman of the Joint Chiefs of Staff
for an assessment of "the assurance the U.S. can have of winning in South
Vietnam if we do everything we can." The results of the study, which
General Wheeler directed to be prepared by an ad hoc study group with
representation from the Office of the Chairman, the Chairman's Special
Studies Group, DIA, J-3, and the Joint War Games Agency, were given to
Secretary McNamara on 14 July. 3/ The study group's assessment was a
conditional affirmative. 4/ "Within the bounds of reasonable assumptions...there appears to be no reason we cannot win if such is our will
-- and if that will is manifested in strategy and tactical operations."

At the same time, Secretary McNamara asked Assistant Secretary
McNaughton to work with the study group to suggest some of the questions
that occurred to him. McNaughton's memorandum to General Goodpaster is
included in full.

MEMORANDUM FOR GENERAL GOODPASTER
              Assistant to the Chairman, JCS

SUBJECT: Forces Required to Win in South Vietnam

Secretary McNamara this morning suggested that General Wheeler
form a small group to address the question, "If we do everything
we can, can we have assurance of winning in South Vietnam?"
General Wheeler suggested that he would have you head up the
group and that the group would be fairly small. Secretary

McNamara indicated that he wanted your group to work with me
and that I should send down a memorandum suggesting some of the
questions that occurred to us. Here are our suggestions:

1. I do not think the question is whether the 44-battalion
program (including 3d-country forces) is sufficient to do the
job, although the answer to that question should fall out of the
study. Rather, I think we should think in terms of the 44-
battalion build-up by the end of 1965, with added forces -- as
required and as our capabilities permit -- in 1966. Furthermore,
the study surely should look into the need for forces other than
ground forces, such as air to be used one way or another in-
country. I would hope that the study could produce a clear
articulation of what our strategy is for winning the war in
South Vietnam, tough as that articulation will be in view of
the nature of the problem.

2. I would assume that the questions of calling up reserves
and extending tours of duty are outside the scope of this study.

3. We must make some assumptions with respect to the number
of VC. Also, we must make some assumptions with respect to what
the infiltration of men and material will be especially if there
is a build-up of US forces in South Vietnam. I am quite concerned about the increasing probability that there are regular
PAVN forces either in the II Corps area or in Laos directly
across the border from II Corps. Furthermore, I am fearful that,
especially with the kind of build-up here envisioned, infiltration of even greater numbers of regular forces may occur. As a
part of this general problem of enemy build-up, we must of course
ask how much assistance the USSR and China can be expected to give
to the VC. I suspect that the increased strength levels of the
VC and the more "conventional" nature of the operations implied
by larger force levels may imply that the often-repeated ratio of
"10 to 1" may no longer apply. I sense that this may be the case
in the future, but I have no reason to be sure. For example, if
the VC, even with larger forces engaged in more "conventional"
type actions, are able to overrun towns and disappear into the
jungles before we can bring the action troops to bear, we may
still be faced with the old "ratio" problem.

4. I think we might avoid some spinning of wheels if we
simply assumed that the GVN will not be able to increase its
forces in the relevant time period. Indeed, from what Westy
has reported about the battalions being chewed up and about their
showing some signs of reluctance to engage in offensive operations,
we might even have to ask the question whether we can expect them
to maintain present levels of men -- or more accurately, present
levels of effectiveness.

5. With respect to 3d-country forces, Westy has equated
the 9 ROK battalions with 9 US battalions, saying that, if he
did not get the former, he must have the latter. I do not
know enough about ROK forces to know whether they are in all
respects "equal to" US forces (they may be better in some
respects and not as good in others). For purposes of the
study, it might save us time if we assumed that we would get
no meaningful forces from anyone other than the ROKs during
the relative time frame. (If the Australians decide to send
another battalion or two, this should not alter the conclusions
of the study significantly.)

6. I would hope that we can minimize the amount of the
team's creative effort that must go into analyzing the ROLLING
THUNDER program or such proposals as the mining of the DRV
harbors. Whether we can or not, of course, depends a good
deal on the extent to which we believe that the ROLLING THUNDER
program makes a critical difference in the level of infiltration (or perhaps the extent to which it puts a "ceiling" on
logistical support) and the time lag in the impact of such
things as a quarantine of DRV harbors. My suggestion is we
posit that the ROLLING THUNDER program will stay at approximately the present level and that there will be no mining of
the DRV harbors. My own view is that the study group probably
should not invest time in trying to solve the problem by cutting
off the flow of supplies and people by either of these methods.
I do not know what your thoughts are about the wisdom of invest-
ing time in the proposal that ground forces be used to produce
some sort of an anti-infiltration barrier.

7. Is it necessary for us to make some assumption with
respect to the nature of the Saigon government? History does
not encourage us to believe that Ky's government will endure
throughout the time period relevant to the study. Ky's beha-
viour is such that it is hard to predict his impact -- he could,
by his "revolutionary" talk and by his repressive measures generate either a genuine nationalist spirit or a violent reaction
of some sort. I would think that the study must make some observation, one way or the other, as to things which might happen to
the government which would have a significant effect on the conclusions of the study. My own thought is that almost anything
within the realm of likelihood can happen in the Saigon government, short of the formation of a government which goes neutral
or asks us out, without appreciably affecting the conduct of the
war. The key point may be whether the Army rather than the
government holds together.

8. One key question, of course, is what we mean by the words
"assurance" and "win." My view is that the degree of "assurance"
should be fairly high -- better than 75% (whatever that means).

3

With respect to the word "win," this I think means that we
succeed in demonstrating to the VC that they cannot win; this,
of course, is victory for us only if it is, with a high degree
of probability, a way station toward a favorable settlement in
South Vietnam. I see such a favorable settlement as one in
which the VC terrorism is substantially eliminated and, obviously, there are no longer large-scale VC attacks; the central
South Vietnamese government (without having taken in the
Communists) should be exercising fairly complete sovereignty
over most of South Vietnam. I presume that we would rule out
the ceding to the VC (either tacitly or explicitly) of large
areas of the country. More specifically, the Brigadier
Thompson suggestion that we withdraw to enclaves and sit it
out for a couple of years is not what we have in mind for purposes of this study.

9. At the moment, I do not see how the study can avoid
addressing the question as to how long our forces will have to
remain in order to achieve a "win" and the extent to which the
presence of those forces over a long period of time might, by
itself, nullify the "win." If it turns out that the study cannot
go into this matter without first getting heavily into the political side of the question, I think the study at least should
note the problem in some meaningful way.

10. I believe that the study should go into specifics --
e.g., the numbers and effectiveness and uses of the South
Vietnamese forces, exactly where we would deploy ours and
exactly what we would expect their mission to be, how we would
go about opening up the roads and providing security for the
towns as well as protecting our own assets there, the time frames
in which things would be done, command relationships, etc. Also,
I think we should find a way to indicate how badly the conclusions might be thrown off if we are wrong with respect to key
assumptions or judgments.

As to timing, the Secretary said he would like to have a "quick
answer" followed by a "longer-term answer." He set no specific
dates; I gather that he expects your team to work as fast as you
reasonably can.

General Vogt and General Seignious of ISA are available to work
with you on this project, as am I.

Copies to: Sgd: JOHN T. McNAUGHTON
  General Vogt
  General Seignious   5/

The McNaughton memorandum is of interest because it demonstrates several
important items. First, the fact that the question about assurance of

winning was asked indicates that at the Secretary of Defense level there
was real awareness that the decisions to be made in the next few weeks
would commit the U.S. to the possibility of an expanded conflict. The
key question then was whether or not we would become involved more deeply
in a war which could not be brought to a satisfactory conclusion.

Secondly, the definition of "win," i.e., "succeed in demonstrating to the VC that they cannot win," indicates the assumption upon which
the conduct of the war was to rest -- that the VC could be convinced in
some meaningful sense that they were not going to win and that they would
then rationally choose less violent methods of seeking their goals. But
the extent to which this definition would set limits of involvement or
affect strategy was not clear.

Thirdly, the assumptions on the key variables (the infiltration
rates, the strength of GVN forces, the probable usefulness of Third
Country Forces, the political situation in South Vietnam) were rightfully
pessimistic and cautious. If they were to be taken seriously, the conclusions of the Study Group were bound to be pessimistic. If the Study
Group was to take a "positive attitude," they were bound to be ignored.
The latter inevitably happened.

The study outlined the strategy as follows:

4. Concept:

a. Presently organized and planned GVN forces, except
for present GVN national reserve battalions, possibly augmented
by a limited number of ranger and infantry battalions, retain
control over areas now held, extend pacification operations and
area control where possible, defend critical installations and
areas against VC attack and seek out and destroy Viet Cong
militia units.

b. US and Allied forces, in conjunction with the GVN
national reserve, by offensive land and air action locate and
destroy VC/PAVN forces, bases and major war-supporting organizations in South Vietnam.

5. a. Under this concept the RVNAF, now hard-pressed by
the Viet Cong summer offensive, would continue to regroup
battle-damaged units and build up total strengths. For the
most part they would be relieved, except for the national reserve (6 Airborne Battalions, 5 Marine Battalions), of offensive actions against main force units and would concentrate
their efforts on maintaining and extending the present GVN
area control. They would defend important installations from
attack and would conduct offensive operations against local VC
militia units. As the situation might allow, selected units

5

would participate with the national reserve battalions in
operations against VC main force units in order to engender
the buildup of an offensive spirit within the RVNAF.

      b. US and Allied forces would occupy and secure
bases at which their major items of heavy equipment, such as
aircraft, would be stationed. Thereafter they would operate
in coordination with the RVNAF reserve battalions to seek out
and destroy major Viet Cong units, bases and other facilities.
Individual units would rotate between security tasks and
mobile offensive operations. Secure base areas would be
expanded by deep patrolling. 6/

The JCS Study Group estimated that this strategy would have the following
results:

    <u>Military operations in SVN</u>. Presently organized and
planned GVN forces, except for reserve battalions (possibly
including a limited number of ranger and infantry battalions),
would retain control over areas now held, extend pacification
operations and area control where permitted by the progress of
major offensive operations, defend critical installations and
areas against VC attack and seek out and eliminate VC militia
units. US, SVN, and Third-Country forces, by offensive land
and air action, would locate and destroy VC/DRV forces, bases
and major war-supporting organizations in SVN. The cumulative
effect of sustained, aggressive conduct of offensive operations,
coupled with the interdiction of DRV efforts to provide the
higher level of support required in such a combat environment,
should lead to progressive destruction of the VC/DRV main force
battalions. 7/

As can be seen, the strategy was essentially that which has governed the
conduct of the war ever since. However, it did not take escalatory reactions into account nor did it address the problems of pacification or
rural development.

    The strategic concept which the JCS developed was predicated on their
estimate of what strength was available to the Viet Cong and North Vietnamese, and on their judgment about what the enemy was trying to do with
his forces. The estimate of enemy strength given in the Study Group's
14 July 1965 report was that the Viet Cong organized combat units consisted of 10 regimental headquarters, 65 battalions, 188 companies, for
a total strength of approximately 48,500. The 101st Regiment, 325th PAVN
Division, with its subordinate battalions, is included in this total. In
addition, 17,600 personnel were considered to be engaged in combat support
type operations. At that time, the Viet Cong were continuing to expand
their control in rural areas and had succeeded in isolating several provincial and district towns from the bulk of the rural population. Their

apparent willingness to accept large casualties in offensive engagements indicated the manpower shortage did not currently exist. Intelligence estimates of PAVN's capability of intervening overtly in South Vietnam across the Demilitarized Zone was that PAVN could do so with approximately three divisions against moderate opposition. If PAVN were to try to introduce units into South Vietnam covertly through the Laotian Corridor, it is estimated he would be able to introduce 1 to 2 additional divisions by the end of 1965. The estimate admitted that the purpose and role of PAVN units were not certain and might well have changed since their initial deployment. Perhaps Hanoi had wanted a PAVN force on the spot in the eventuality that the Saigon government collapsed, and perhaps Hanoi wanted to assure itself the VC would not collapse in the face of the US military commitment, or, more likely, Hanoi may have wanted to assist the VC in increasing the tempo of its campaign and in hastening a victory. At that time, it appeared that there was no intention of employing the PAVN units as a division; rather, they would assist the recurrent VC strategy of widespread harassment and terrorism punctuated with multi-battalion spectaculars.

The manner in which the probable requirements for additional forces were derived is of interest. The critical assumption was "that the VC/NVA can mount simultaneous attacks in each GVN corps area not to exceed one reinforced regimental (4 battalions) attack and one single battalion attack at any given time." From this, a simple numerical calculation, based upon the assumption that a 4 to 1 superiority would provide a high probability of victory, resulted in the requirement for Free World offensive maneuver battalions. When added to the number needed for base defense, the result was the total of required Free World battalions. If U.S. forces were to be placed in all four Corps Tactical Zones, a total of 35 additional battalions would be needed to secure bases and gain the 4 to 1 advantage desired. If the U.S. effort were limited to the area north of Saigon, only 7 additional battalions would be needed. It would seem that this requirement was very sensitive to rates of infiltration and recruitment by the VC/NVA, but very little analysis was, in fact, given to the implications of the capabilities of the VC/NVA in this regard.

B. McNamara Goes to Saigon - A Decision on II

1. Westmoreland Proposals

On 7 July 1965, Secretary McNamara cabled Westmoreland to lay out the purpose of his visit to Saigon and some of the questions which he would like to have answered.

The main purpose of our visit will be to receive from you your recommendations for the number of U.S. combat battalions, artillery battalions, engineering battalions, helicopter companies, tactical aircraft, and total military personnel to be

assigned to South Vietnam between now and the end of this
year;... /and/ the probable requirements for additional forces
next year. 8/

This request for "probable requirements for additional forces next year"
seemed to be an attempt to improve the quality of planning figures for
1966. In his 1 July Draft Memorandum for the President, McNamara quoted
Westmoreland as saying that he "cannot now state what additional forces
may be required in 1966 to gain and maintain the military initiative...
Instinctively, we believe that there may be substantial U.S. Force Requirements." The memorandum went on to comment that "He /COMUSMACV/
has a study underway, with a fairly solid estimate due in early August.
The number of battalions ultimately required could be double the 44
mentioned above. 9/

According to the MACV Command History of 1965, General Westmoreland
answered Secretary McNamara's question about forces required in 1966
during the Secretary's Saigon visit. 10/ General Westmoreland "anticipated that a need would exist for an increase of 24 maneuver battalions,
14 artillery battalions; 3 air defense (Hawk) battalions; 8 engineer
battalions; 12 helicopter companies; 6 helicopter battalions, and additional support units." 11/ As reconstructed by the MACV Command History,
this requirement was predicated upon a concept of operations in South
Vietnam and upon a three phased plan:

CCMUSMACV's objective was to end the war in RVN by convincing the enemy that military victory was impossible and
to force the enemy to negotiate a solution favorable to the
GVN and the US. To secure these objectives, US/FWMA forces
would be built up and then employed to wrest the initiative
from the enemy, secure vital areas and support the GVN in
expanding its control over the country.

The overall concept was based on three assumptions:

(1) That the VC would fight until convinced that
military victory was impossible and then would not be willing
to endure further punishment.

(2) That the CHICOM's would not intervene except to
provide aid and advice.

(3) That friendly forces would maintain control of the
air over RVN.

The concept visualized a three-phase operation:

Phase I - The commitment of US/FWMA forces necessary
to halt the losing trend by the end of 1965.

33

Phase II - The resumption of the offensive by US/FWMA forces during the first half of 1966 in high priority areas necessary to destroy enemy forces, and reinstitution of rural construction activities.

Phase III - If the enemy persisted, a period of a year to a year and a half following Phase II would be required for the defeat and destruction of the remaining enemy forces and base areas.

Specific military tasks were associated with the objective of each phase.

Phase I:

(1) Secure the major military bases, airfields and communications centers.

(2) Defend major political and population centers.

(3) Conduct offensive operations against major VC base areas in order to divert and destroy VC main forces.

(4) Provide adequate reserve reaction forces to prevent the loss of secure and defended areas.

(5) Preserve and strengthen the RVNAF.

(6) Provide adequate air support, both combat and logistic.

(7) Maintain an anti-infiltration screen along the coast and support forces ashore with naval gunfire and amphibious lift.

(8) Provide air and sea lifts as necessary to transport the necessary but minimum supplies and services to the civil populace.

(9) Open up necessary critical lines of communication for essential military and civil purposes.

(10) Preserve and defend, to the extent possible, areas now under effective governmental control.

Phase II:

(1) All Phase I measures.

(2) Resume and/or expand pacification operations. Priority will be given to the Hop Tac area around Saigon, to that part of the Delta along an east-west axis from Go Cong to Chau Doc, and in the provinces of Quang Nam, Quang Tri, Quang Ngai, Binh Dinh and Phu Yen.

(3) Participate in clearing, securing, reserve reaction and offensive operations as required to support and sustain the resumption of pacification.

Phase III:

(1) All Phase I and II measures.

(2) Provide those additional forces necessary to extend and expand clearing and securing operations throughout the entire populated area of the country and those forces necessary to destroy VC forces and their base areas. 12/

2. McNamara's Recommendations

Secretary McNamara's 20 July 1965 Memorandum for the President spelled out the troop requirements for Vietnam as follows: The forces for 1965 should be brought up to about 175,000, and "It should be understood that the deployment of more men (perhaps 100,000) may be necessary in early 1966, and that the deployment of additional forces thereafter is possible but will depend on developments." 13/

This 100,000-man possible addition was broken down in a cable from COMUSMACV to CINCPAC as providing 27 maneuver battalions with associated combat and service support elements, bringing the total number of maneuver battalions to 61 sometime in 1966. 14/ The question arises as to how this 100,000-man 27-battalion figure was reached. In the absence of documentary evidence, it seems simplest to assume that Westmoreland was given pretty much what he asked for. However, the 61 battalion figure comes very close to the number of battalions the Secretary of Defense was thinking about earlier in July, when a memorandum for the record dated 12 July shows a proposal to strengthen U.S. forces by 63 battalions through a combination of calling up reserves, extending tours of duty, and increasing the draft. 15/ In fact, the 63 battalion figure appears again in the Secretary's 20 July memorandum to the President, allowing one to speculate that the size of the build-up had already been fixed in early July prior to the trip.

In either case, the result was that Phase II was recommended to the President at a level of roughly 100,000 which when added to the then current estimates for Phase I of 175,000 gave a total estimate of 275,000 by the end of 1966.

Secretary McNamara envisioned that the employment of U.S. forces
would be as follows:

...Use of forces. The forces will be used however they
can be brought to bear most effectively. The US/third-country
ground forces will operate in coordination with South Vietnamese forces. They will defend their own bases; they will
assist in providing security in neighboring areas; they will
augment Vietnamese forces, assuring retention of key logistic
areas and population centers. Also, in the initial phase they
will maintain a small reserve-reaction force, conducting nui-
sance raids and spoiling attacks, and opening and securing
selected lines of communication; as in-country ground strength
increases to a level permitting extended US and third-country
offensive action, the forces will be available for more active
combat missions when the Vietnamese Government and General
Westmoreland agree that such active missions are needed. The
strategy for winning this stage of the war will be to take the
offensive -- to take and hold the initiative. The concept of
tactical operations will be to exploit the offensive, with the
objects of putting the VC/DRV battalion forces out of operation
and of destroying their morale. The South Vietnamese, US and
third-country forces, by aggressive exploitation of superior
military forces, are to gain and hold the initiative -- keeping
the enemy at a disadvantage, maintaining a tempo such as to
deny them time to recuperate or regain their balance, and
pressing the fight against VC/DRV main force units in South
Vietnam to run them to ground and destroy them. The operations
should combine to compel the VC/DRV to fight at a higher and
more sustained intensity with resulting higher logistical consumption and, at the same time, to limit his capability to
resupply forces in combat at that scale by attacking his LOC.
The concept assumes vigorous prosecution of the air and sea
anti-infiltration campaign and includes increased use of air
in-country, including B-52s, night and day to harass VC in
their havens. Following destruction of the VC main force units,
the South Vietnamese must reinstitute the Program of Rural
Reconstruction as an antidote to the continuing VC campaign of
terror and subversion. 16/

He evaluated the probable results in the following manner:

...Evaluation. ARVN overall is not capable of successfully
resisting the VC initiatives without more active assistance
from more US/third-country ground forces than those thus far
committed. Without further outside help, the ARVN is faced with
successive tactical reverses, loss of key communication and
population centers particularly in the highlands, piecemeal
destruction of ARVN units, attrition of RVNAF will to fight,

and loss of civilian confidence. Early commitment of additional US/third-country forces in sufficient quantity, in general reserve and offensive roles, should stave off GVN defeat.

The success of the program from the military point of view turns on whether the Vietnamese hold their own in terms of numbers and fighting spirit, and on whether the US forces can be effective in a quick-reaction reserve role, a role in which they are only now being tested. The number of US troops is too small to make a significant difference in the traditional 10-1 government-guerrilla formula, but it is not too small to make a significant difference in the kind of war which seems to be evolving in Vietnam -- a "Third Stage" or conventional war in which it is easier to identify, locate and attack the enemy.

The plan is such that the risk of escalation into war with China or the Soviet Union can be kept small. US and South Vietnamese casualties will increase -- just how much cannot be predicted with confidence, but the US killed-in-action might be in the vicinity of 500 a month by the end of the year. The South Vietnamese under one government or another will probably see the thing through and the United States public will support the course of action because it is a sensible and courageous military-political program designed and likely to bring about a success in Vietnam.

It should be recognized, however, that success against the larger, more conventional, VC/PAVN forces could merely drive the VC back into the trees and back to their 1960-64 pattern -- a pattern against which US troops and aircraft would be of limited value but with which the GVN, with our help, could cope. The questions here would be whether the VC could maintain morale after such a set-back, and whether the South Vietnamese would have the will to hang on through another cycle. 17/

3. The President's Decision

The President accepted the recommendation of building up to 175,000, but disapproved the call up of reserves, and made no decision (since none was really necessary at the time) on the full Phase II strength. In a backgrounder, following his announcement of the troop increase on 28 July 1965, the President explained that the reserves, if called, would have taken several months before they were equipped to be effective in Vietnam, so he decided to use the Airmobile Division and Battalions on Okinawa which were ready to go. 18/ The disapproval of the reserve call up appears to have been the President's decision and

was probably based more on considerations of political feasibility. As
late as the 17th of July, Deputy Secretary of Defense Vance had cabled
McNamara that the President had OK'd the 34 Battalion Phase I Plan and
would try to "bull" the reserve call up through Senator Stennis whom he
saw as his chief obstacle on this issue. 19/   The President's decision
was evidently a difficult one to make. Prior to McNamara's departure
for Saigon, both he and the President had hinted at press conferences
that a reserve call-up and higher draft calls were a distinct possibility.
This, of course, triggered the predictable response from some members of
Congress in opposition to a reserve call up. Upon McNamara's return from
Saigon, President Johnson waited over a week before he publicly announced
his Vietnam decisions. Since Vance's cable to McNamara of the 17th of
July indicated that the President had approved the 34 battalion deployment, it is probably reasonable to assume that the President spent much
of the week assessing the political variables of the situation. The
consensus in the press was that the announced measures were not as great
a leap as had been expected and that perhaps the attitude of influential
Senate Democrats had restrained Johnson from taking stronger action.
The issue was not that pressing as far as Phase I was concerned because,
as the President pointed out, there were active Army units already
available to cover the short term needs.

C. Development of a Concept

   1. Concept for Vietnam

       By late August 1965, the JCS had developed and coordinated a
Concept for Vietnam which was set out in JCSM 652-65 dated 27 August.
The heart of the concept is summarized as follows:

       a. The objective in Vietnam, as stated by NSAM 288,
   dated 17 March 1964, is a stable and independent noncommunist government.

       b. The major problems to be dealt with in the conduct
   of the war are:

       (1) The continued direction and support of Viet
   Cong operations by the DRV, infiltration from the north,
   and the apparent attendant Viet Cong capability to provide materiel support and to replace heavy personnel
   losses.

       (2) The continued existence of a major Viet Cong
   infrastructure, both political and military, in the RVN.

       (3) The greater growth rate of Viet Cong strength
   as compared to that of the South Vietnamese ground
   forces.

(4) The continued loss of LOCs, food-producing areas, and population to Viet Cong control.

(5) The lack of a viable politico/economic structure in the RVN.

(6) The threat of CHICOM intervention or aggression in Southeast Asia and elsewhere in the Western Pacific.

c. The basic military tasks, of equal priority, are:

(1) To cause the DRV to cease its direction and support of the Viet Cong insurgency.

(2) To defeat the Viet Cong and to extend GVN control over all of the RVN.

(3) To deter Communist China from direct intervention and to defeat such intervention if it occurs.

d. The US basic strategy for accomplishing the above tasks should be: to intensify military pressure on the DRV by air and naval power; to destroy significant DRV military targets, including the base of supplies; to interdict supporting LOCs in the DRV; to interdict the infiltration and supply routes into the RVN; to improve the combat effectiveness of the RVNAF; to build and protect bases; to reduce enemy reinforcements; to defeat the Viet Cong, in concert with RVN and third country forces; and to maintain adequate forces in the Western Pacific and elsewhere in readiness to deter and to deal with CHICOM aggression. By aggressive and sustained exploitation of superior military force, the United States/Government of Vietnam would seize and hold the initiative in both the DRV and RVN, keeping the DRV, the Viet Cong, and the PL/VM at a disadvantage, progressively destroying the DRV war-supporting power and defeating the Viet Cong. The physical capability of the DRV to move men and supplies through the Lao Corridor, down the coastline, across the DMZ, and through Cambodia must be reduced to the maximum practical extent by land, naval, and air actions in these areas and against infiltration-connected targets. Finally, included within the basic US military strategy must be a buildup in Thailand to ensure attainment of the proper US-Thai posture to deter CHICOM aggression and to facilitate placing US forces in an advantageous logistic position if such aggression occurs. 20/

It continued:

...In order to gain the offensive and to seize and hold the initiative in the RVN, a major effort must be made not only

in terms of direct combat action to expand the areas under
US/GVN control but also to support the GVN in its rural reconstruction program and to assist that government in the
creation of new military units and the rehabilitation of its
depleted units as rapidly as possible. A psychological
climate must be created that will foster RVN rural reconstruction progress. 21/

The strategic concept envisioned that during...

...the build-up phase US-Third Country and GVN forces should
strengthen military and civilian control in present areas of
the RVN...As the force build-up is achieved, a principal
offensive effort within the RVN of US-Third Country forces
should be to participate with the RVNAF in search and destroy
operations while assisting the RVNAF in clearing and securing
operations in support of the rural reconstruction effort. 22/

The document went on to explain that:

Friendly control of population and resources is essential
to success in countering guerrilla warfare. In this regard,
the RVN areas of major military significance are: the Saigon
area and the Mekong Delta; the coastal plain; and the central
highlands. It is imperative that the US/GVN have the support
of the people and the control of resources in those areas.
Elimination of the Viet Cong from these areas must be vigorously undertaken in order to provide adequate security for
the people. Of particular importance is the need for friendly
control of the main food-producing areas in order that the GVN
may gain control of rice, feed the people under its control,
enable exports of rice to bolster the economy, and cause the
Viet Cong to import or to fight for food. A paramount requirement under this concept is the building and maintaining of a
series of secure bases and secure supporting LOCs at key
localities along the sea coast, and elsewhere as necessary,
from which offensive operations can be launched and sustained,
with the subsequent enlargement and expansion of the secure
areas. 23/

Assistant Secretary McNaughton, in a memorandum for Secretary
McNamara, gave the following evaluation of the JCS plan. "The concept
includes certain generalized courses of action about which there would
be little or no dispute and a number of other courses that are clearly
controversial and raise far-reaching policy issues (e.g., blockade and
mining of DRV, U.S. build-up in Thailand, intensified RT)." He recommended that since "an overall approval...is not required at this time...
the concept proposed not be specifically approved." 24/ Acting along
these lines, Secretary McNamara agreed "that recommendations for future
operations in SEA should be formulated," but went no further. 25/

2. Westmoreland's Concept

This concept of operations was interpreted by General Westmoreland in his MACV Directive 525-4 of 20 September 1965, in which he set forth the tactics and techniques for employment of US forces in the Republic of Vietnam. General Westmoreland's strategy consisted of three successive steps:

1. First, to halt the VC offensive -- to stem the tide,

2. Second, to resume the offensive -- to destroy VC and pacify selected high priority areas,

3. Third, to restore progressively the entire country to the control of the GVN. 26/

The tasks which he saw necessary included the defense of military bases, the conduct of offensive operations against VC forces and bases, the conduct of clearing operations as a prelude to pacification, provision of permanent security for areas earmarked for pacification, and the provision for reserve reaction forces. Most of the document is concerned with the conduct of offensive operations against VC base areas and forces. The conduct of clearing operations were given little attention since these were planned to be primarily accomplished by RVN regional forces and popular forces.

3. The JCS on Future Operations and Force Deployments

By early November, the Joint Chiefs had further refined their "Concept for Vietnam" and in JCSM 811-65, dated 10 November, 27/ submitted their recommendations to the Secretary of Defense. Although it was billed as establishing a basis for determining the Phase II force requirements, it achieved little more than explicating in some detail the tasks to be accomplished in Phase II, and evaluating the degree to which the forces already programmed for Phase II would accomplish these goals. However, the figures used were close to those discussed in July. The new figures were 112,430 personnel and 28 battalions, most of which would be in Vietnam by the end of 1966. These figures were still being used as late as 20 November 1965. 28/

The JCS did manage to capture the essence of the Phase II concept by pointing out that "Phase I...was designed to stop losing the war. Phase II...is then the phase needed to start winning it." Their concept still included the three basic military tasks of pressuring North Vietnam, defeating the VC and extending GVN control over South Vietnam, and deterring Communist China. However, the memorandum went on to spell out in which areas of Vietnam the JCS and presumably MACV felt were the "militarily and economically significant areas in Vietnam." These were listed as Saigon, the Mekong Delta, Coastal Plain, and the Central

Highlands. The role of the US forces was to assist the GVN in expanding
its control over these areas. However, primary emphasis was placed upon
providing "heavy assault strength against VC forces and bases. The
division of effort between RVNAF and US/Third Country forces clarified
as follows:

> The overall concept...visualizes the employment of US,
> Third Country and RVNAF forces for the basic mission of
> search and destroy, and participation in clearing and secur-
> ing operations and civic actions plus the defense of govern-
> mental centers and critical areas.

> US/Third Country forces will not ordinarily be employed
> throughout securing operations except in areas contiguous to
> their bases. The Vietnamese JGS is in general agreement with
> this concept and with the concept of weighting the effort
> wherein the bulk of operations against the VC forces and bases
> outside the secure areas will be undertaken by US/Third Country
> and RVNAF general reserve forces, while the bulk of RVN forces
> will be committed to the defense of GVN installations and
> securing operations. 29/

Interestingly enough, a note of growing disenchantment with the
Vietnamese capabilities appeared in this memorandum, when it was explained
that "complex, detailed US conceived programs may not be picked up and
executed by the Vietnamese /therefore/ COMUSMACV now deals with them in
terms of simple tasks and short step by step objectives."

D. Overall Strategy Reviewed as Conflict in SVN Steps Up

Meanwhile in November two other things were taking place which would
have a significant effect on Phase II.

1. McNamara's DPM on Increasing the Pressure

In early November a Draft Memorandum for the President was in the
works which addressed the problem of how best to conduct the overall effort
in Vietnam. 30/ In this memorandum, Mr. McNamara discussed the relative
merits of varying combinations of a pause in the air war against North
Vietnam, gradual intensification of the ROLLING THUNDER program, and
carrying out Phase II deployments. This memorandum seems to mark one of
the key decision points in the growing involvement of U.S. in Vietnam.
The Phase I deployments appeared to have arrested the deterioration of the
situation in Vietnam, and it now became feasible to consider what kind of
outcome we might be able to get from the present situation. The analysis
in the memorandum was that roughly sticking with the present situation
would lead to a "compromise outcome" which would very likely be unstable,
difficult to sell domestically, and damaging to "U.S. political effectiveness on the world scene." Therefore, the course of action to follow was

to step up the pressure both in the North, i.e., increase the tempo of
ROLLING THUNDER, and in the South, i.e., move ahead with Phase II deployments. However, a pause in bombing would be inserted prior to the
increased pressure. The arguments for the pause were four: (1) It
would offer the DRV and VC a chance to move toward a solution if they
should be so inclined...(2) It would demonstrate to domestic and international critics that our efforts to settle the war are genuine. (3)
It would probably tend to reduce the dangers of escalation after we
resumed the bombing...And (4) it would set the stage for another pause
perhaps in late 1966, which might produce a settlement. The conclusion
to this draft, which was discussed with the President on 7 November, was
the warning that "none of these actions assures success...the odds are
even that despite our effort, we will be faced in early 1967 with stag-
nation at a higher level and with a need to decide whether to deploy
Phase III forces, probably in Laos as well as in South Vietnam."

While the pros and cons of a pause or a cease-fire were being
debated in a series of drafts and memoranda which were prepared and
circulated between Defense and State, the situation in Vietnam was undergoing a change.

2. NVA Infiltration Increases

By November 1965, the infiltration of units from North Vietnam
had begun to increase. By 17 November, six confirmed, two probable, and
one possible, PAVN regiments had been identified in South Vietnam. The
Viet Cong regimental-size units had increased from five in July of 1965
to twelve. The total strength of the PAVN/VC army was estimated at
27 PAVN infantry battalions and a total of 110 PAVN/VC battalions. The
accepted strength was 63,500 in combat units, and 17,000 in combat support units, with 53,600 in the militia. The VC/PAVN build-up rate was
estimated to be 15 battalions per quarter during 1967.

The implications of the build-up were made abundantly clear by the
bloody fighting in the Ia Drang Valley in mid-November. 31/

In mid-October, the Viet Cong attack on Plei Me Special Forces Camp
in Pleiku Province, had triggered a month-long campaign by both RVN and
U.S. forces. Operation SILVER BAYONET, conducted by the 1st Cavalry
Division was designed to provide security and artillery support to RVN
forces around Plei Me. On 27 October, the 1st Brigade of the 1st Cavalry
Division, was given a search and destroy mission between Plei Me and the
Cambodian border. By 1 November, the brigade, having contacted a large
enemy force, began to pursue VC/NVA forces west of the Plei Me camp,
moving along the South Vietnamese/Cambodian border. Then, on 14 November,
after the 3rd Brigade of the 1st Cavalry Division had relieved the 1st
Brigade in the vicinity of Plei Me and Pleiku, the most significant phase
of SILVER BAYONET began. Airmobile search and destroy operations were
initiated which resulted in very heavy and intense contacts within the

43

direction of VC/NVA forces. COMUSMACV requested a series of B-52 strikes
to support ground operations in the vicinity of Chu Pong Mountain. These
strikes were delivered on 16 November. Three U.S. infantry battalions
were closely engaged, supported by tactical air sorties and artillery.
The VC/NVA forces, which exceeded division strength, continued active
resistance to the U.S. forces from well-entrenched position. The battle
of the 3rd Brigade against numerically superior VC/NVA forces continued
until 18 November in the vicinity of Chu Pong Mountain and Ia Drang Valley.
Fighting was often hand to hand with many small units temporarily cut off
from their parent organization.

On 20 November, the 2d Brigade, 1st Cavalry Division, flew to Pleiku
to relieve the 3d Brigade. The VC/NVA had lost over 1,200 killed in
action while the U.S. losses were over 200. 32/

According to the MACV Command History, 1966:

"The overall NVN political strategy was aimed at the demoralization of the RVN and the collapse of resistance in the south,
as well as the closely related contingency of US withdrawal from
Vietnam. In their planning to accomplish this strategy the NVN
leaders were influenced by their experience during the Indochina
War, when the Viet Minh had relied on the unwillingness of the
French people to continue to support a long and costly "dirty war."
Although the US was a more formidable enemy, NVN leaders apparently believed that the same political strategy would succeed
again, and that their own will to fight would outlast that of the
Americans. The enemy expected that the high financial cost, the
loss of American lives, international pressures, and domestic
dissension inevitably would force the US Government to withdraw
military forces from RVN. The enemy's long-range plan of military
strategy had three phases. The first phase called for the creation
of a political organization and a guerrilla capability, and the
initiation of guerrilla warfare. The second phase called for the
establishment of larger bases from which a "strategic mobility"
effort could be launched. The third phase called for the initiation of the final large-scale attacks that would annihilate the
opposing forces. During the first phase of the NVN plan the Lao
Dong Party established a firm party organization by the creation
of the NLF. Concurrently, NVN began guerrilla-type operations,
established secure bases for larger operations, and began to force
the RVN into a defensive posture. Infiltration routes from NVN
were established and a system of logistic support for the base
areas was set up. In order to accelerate the transition to the
final phase of annihilation, NVN began to move regular NVA troops
into the RVN. This activity was first indicated in April 1964,
when the 325th NVA Div began accelerated training in preparation
for deployment to the RVN.

An important facet of the second phase was to attain "strategic mobility" in order to counter the tactical mobility of RVN and FW forces. The object of a "strategic mobility" was to mass a large number of maneuver battalions in several widely-scattered areas. These maneuver battalions would tie large numbers of Allied forces to static defense roles, and permit the NVA/VC to attack specific positions at times of their own choosing. The buildup in the number of battalions, and particularly the infiltration of larger NVA units, would be done covertly with the object of initiating the larger-sized attacks by surprise. The version of "strategic mobility" implemented by Gen Vo Nguyen Giap was a "defensive/offensive" strategy which had the following objectives:

1) to develop strong multi-division forces in dispersed areas that were secure and accessible to supplies; 2) to entice FW forces into prepared enemy positions so that the entrenched communist forces could inflict heavy casualties on them; and 3) to continue country-wide guerrilla action to tie down Allied forces, destroy small units, and extend control.

The NVN and VC emphasized in guidance put out to their people that the war would be won in the highlands of MR5, an area that the enemy envisioned as a "killing zone." The mountainous and jungled terrain favored VC operations in that the highlands were closer to the NVA buildup areas near the DMZ and to the secure base areas in Laos and Cambodia. These factors made the highlands a much more favorable battle area for the NVA/VC than for the FW forces. The enemy would also be able to place sizeable forces on the entrance routes to the heavily populated coastal areas. In order to use the highlands as the killing zone in the war for RVN, the enemy hoped first to establish an "equilibrium of forces" in the highlands, and then to launch an offensive in one or more districts. The enemy had thus hoped in 1966 to launch ever-larger attacks in the highlands, to concentrate his troops and firepower, and, with improved command and control, to attack and hold important objectives.

During the same enemy time-frame that the highlands were being exploited as the killing zone, the enemy had other plans for the Delta area and for Saigon. The Delta was to be the support area and as such was to continue to provide manpower and fill logistic requirements for the other operational regions, particularly MR5. Insofar as possible, it was planned that the Delta should move also toward the second phase of larger-unit "strategic mobility." The Delta, being the seat of the old revolutionary political organization, was to be the originating point of new political organizations sent out to support the offensive

45

in the highlands. In his plans concerning Saigon and the surrounding areas, the enemy intended to dominate all routes
leading into the city, to isolate the city economically, and
to create an atmosphere of insecurity in and around the city.
It appeared that the enemy intended to capture and hold important areas in an arc above the Capital Military District
(CMD). For this purpose several special units had been formed
and were operating in the area of Saigon. 33/

On 23 November, General Westmoreland analyzed the impact of the
increased infiltration upon his Phase II requirements as follows:

* * * * *

2. The VC/PAVN buildup rate is predicated to be double that
of U.S. Phase II forces. Whereas we will add an average of
seven maneuver battalions per quarter the enemy will add fifteen.
This development has already reduced the November battalion
equivalent ratio from an anticipated 3.2 to 1, to 2.8 to 1, and
it will be further reduced to 2.5 to 1 by the end of the year.
If the trend continues, the December 1966 battalion equivalent
ratio, even with the addition of Phase II, will be 2.1 to 1.

3. Thus far the PAVN increase has been concentrated in the
central highlands and the Viet Cong increases have largely been
in the northern part of III Corps. There is little evidence so
far that there is any appreciable enemy increase south of the
Mekong, and in fact it appears that the local forces in the lower
delta may have lost some capability as a result of the movement
of guerrillas to Tay Ninh for training and organization into
battalions.

4. MACV must, as an absolute minimum, free at least one US
division for mobile operations against new PAVN units in the
general area of II Corps. In addition, there is a vital need to
open Highway 15 from Vung Tau to Saigon to utilize the port
capacity there and to project US forces into the delta at least
as far as My Thiem, this will strengthen the GVN hand in this
critical population and food producing area and interdict the
main infiltration route from the delta to War Zone C. The addition of a ROK division (or US division) to II Corps, for location
at coastal bases near Duc My, Nha Trang, Cam Ranh and Phan Rang,
will permit the entire 4th Infantry Division (with its bases protected by the coastal division) to be used for sustained combat
against the new PAVN forces. The opening of Highway 15 to Vung
Tau would be facilitated by adding a brigade to the 1st Infantry
Division to be located in the Ba Ria area and additional brigade
for the 25th Division to be located at Tan Hiep would provide

46

protection necessary for the area north of My Tho. Besides the requirement for an additional division and two brigades, operations by the 1st Air Cavalry Division have shown that this unit needs one more infantry battalion (airmobile) and an additional air cavalry squadron so that it can sustain operations over a long period of time. Because of the tactical problems involved in conducting combat reconnaissance over vast areas to find and fix PAVN/VC it would be highly desirable to have one of the brigades of the 4th Infantry Division composed of three Airmobile Infantry Battalions and provide for the division one Air Cavalry Squadron. A ROK RCT to fill out the capital division would permit deployment of the ROK Marine Brigade to I Corps for operations with III MAF.

5. The additional units described above are essential to meet the immediate threat and certain immediate problems. However, even these additional forces will not match the enemy buildup. To reach the level of force required to make significant progress toward accomplishment of Phase II tasks will ultimately require much larger deployments.

6. Unfortunately certain physical restrictions and the time required to establish a suitable logistics base limit the rate of buildup in RVN CY 66. If the deployment of logistics forces can be further accelerated and if construction programs meet the increased requirements we might be able to squeeze two additional brigades into SVN in CY 66 over and above Phase II forces AFD the minimum add-ons which we have described in paragraph 4 above. We should program these additional logistics and combat forces against the maximum build-up rate because we need them to match the PAVN/VC buildup. With two more brigades we would have three US divisions in the area around Saigon and the 4th Division in the II Corps area would have three infantry brigades plus an airmobile brigade and an air cavalry squadron.

7. Because of current problems regarding port and support facilities, no major deployments other than currently requested Phase II deployments can be accepted in the 1st Qtr of CY 66. Thereafter, the buildup should be incremental. If ROK units were made available (with both the RVN and the ROK providing a portion of the support, reinforced by additional US support) a division could be handled in the second quarter, and an additional division equivalent in each quarter thereafter, provided appropriate US logistics forces are available.

8. Tactical air support would amount to three tactical fighter squadrons for the first deployment alternative and four squadrons for the second. Eventually, this might require construction of another airfield, in addition to Tuy Hoa.

47

9. One of the most pressing needs is to improve the logistics situation in RVN. Phase I logistic units are stretched out through CY 66 and into CY 67. It was determined at the Honolulu Conference in September that the preferred schedule for deployment of major Phase II combat units could not be met because the essential logistics units would not be available in the time frame required. Nevertheless, we accepted marginal logistic support in order to deploy combat units as rapidly as possible. Therefore the logistics system in SVN cannot accept the even greater burden represented by the required additional combat forces without significant augmentation early in CY 66. We appreciate the fact that this may require extraordinary measures. It has been determined that the ports can accommodate the force buildup if the critical through-put capability can be provided in the form of added logistics units and related facilities. MACV is prepared to specify the quantity, type and time phasing of logistics units required to support the buildup.

10. Undoubtedly the detailed development of these added force requirements and their integration into existing programs and schedules will require another set of conferences. The initial development should take place here with assistance from the PACOM components as required. Subsequently a final conference in Honolulu appears necessary to check requirements against availability, make adjustments and work out the detailed scheduling.

11. ....

g. We estimate that our minimum course of action (a ROK division and RCT and two US brigades as major units) will require a total add-on strength of approximately 48,000 (23,000 ROK), which includes 35,300 combat and combat support and 12,700 service support. Our preferred course of action (a ROK div and RCT and a US div and brigade as major units) will add approximately 64,500 (23,000 ROK), which includes 47,200 combat and combat support and 17,300 service support.

* * * * *   34/

This assessment of the VC/PAVN buildup appears to be consistent with the retrospective evaluation found in the intelligence community's National Intelligence Estimate 14.3-66, published on 7 July 1966. According to this later estimate, the infiltration for the months of September and October 1965 totaled approximately 10,000 which was only 1,000 less than the total for the preceding 8 months, from January through August 1965. The estimated rate of the buildup given in NIE 14.3-66 was one or two infantry regiments per month which fits the earlier MACV estimate of 15 battalions per quarter.

Westmoreland's recommendation for an additional 41,500 U.S. forces
would have raised the Phase II deployment to approximately 154,000 bringing total U.S. troop strength in the area to nearly 375,000 by mid-1967.

E. McNamara Goes to Saigon - A Decision on IIA

　　1. McNamara Visits Saigon

　　　　Faced with this changed enemy situation, Secretary of Defense
McNamara diverted his return from a NATO meeting in Paris to allow him
to visit Saigon on 28-30 November. As outlined in the Secretary of
Defense's 23 November cable to Saigon, the purpose of the trip was
"further discussion of Phase II requirements." 35/　　Specifically, he
asked: "Will it not be necessary to add one or two divisions to the 28
battalions proposed in order to provide forces for the Delta; will even
more forces be required in 1966 if the number of PAVN regiments continues
to increase?"

　　2. Westmoreland's Recommended Add-Ons

　　　　According to the MACV Command History, when Secretary McNamara
arrived in Saigon, "COMUSMACV expressed a need for an additional division
(which could be ROK) for deployment along the coastal plain in II CTZ,
thereby freeing the 4th Infantry Division...for operations further
inland. Another USA division was needed for employment in the Upper
Delta in the area contiguous to Saigon, for a total of three USA divisions around the capital city. A separate brigade for FFORCEV was
necessary to reinforce the 1st Cavalry Division (AM)...Two air cavalry
squadrons were needed to support the 4th Infantry Division and the
1st Cavalry Division (AM), as was another airmobile infantry battalion
for the 1st Cavalry Division (AM) to give that division a balanced force
of three 3-battalion brigades." This revised deployment plan was referred
to as Phase IIA (add-on). 36/

　　　　Secretary McNamara was told that the Free World battalions requested
for the end of CY 1966 and ARVN would be used for the major tasks in the
following proportions:

	FWMAF	ARVN	
Defense of Major U.S. Bases	29	1	
Defense of Government Centers and 　Critical Installations	--	68	
Security for Expansion of Government Control	22	22	
Offensive Operations and Major Reactions	46	71	
Total	97	162	37/

49

3. McNamara's Recommendations to the President

Upon his return from Saigon, Secretary McNamara drafted a Memorandum for the President, outlining the changed military situation in Vietnam, and commenting that in view of the communist build-up, "the presently contemplated Phase I forces will not be enough...Nor will the originally contemplated Phase II addition of 28 more U.S. battalions (112,000 men) be enough...Indeed it is estimated that, with the contemplated Phase II addition of 28 U.S. battalions we would be able only to hold our present geographical positions." 39/

In order to "provide what it takes in men and materiel...to stick with our stated objectives and with the war," Secretary McNamara recommended the deployment of one Korean division plus another brigade, an additional Australian battalion, and 40 U.S. combat battalions, bringing the total of U.S. maneuver battalions to 74, and the total of U.S. personnel in Vietnam to approximately 400,000 by the end of 1966 with the possible need for an additional 200,000 in 1967.

In the 7 December version of his Memorandum for the President, McNamara added the information that "although the 1966 deployments to South Vietnam may require some shift of forces from other theaters, it is believed that they can be accomplished without calling up reserve personnel; however, the Joint Chiefs of Staff do not believe additional forces can be deployed to Southeast Asia or elsewhere unless reserves are called." 40/

In evaluating this course of action, the Secretary warned that it "will not guarantee success." He estimated the odds to be about even that the NVA/VC will match the U.S. buildup and that "even with the recommended deployments, we will be faced in early 1967 with a military standoff at a much higher level, with pacification still stalled, and with any prospect of military success marred by the chance of an active Chinese intervention."

4. Phases I, II, and IIA Are Published

On 13 December, the Secretary of Defense sent out a Draft Memorandum for the President, which included tables outlining the planned deployments to Southeast Asia under Phases I, II and IIA. This December Plan projected the total strength for Phases I, II and IIA to be 367,800 by the end of 1966 and 393,900 by the end of June 1967. The number of U.S. maneuver battalions would reach 75 by the end of 1966.

Meanwhile, the requirements which Secretary McNamara had brought back from Saigon with him were being reviewed by CINCPAC in preparation for a planning conference scheduled for 17 January to 6 February 1966 at which the refined requirements would be presented and recommended deployment schedules prepared.

F. Phase IIA is Revised

1. CINCPAC's Requirements

The results of the review were forwarded to the Secretary of Defense on 16 December. CINCPAC's new requirements were summarized by ASD Enthoven as follows:

The CINCPAC request involves a deployment to RVN of 443,000 personnel by December 1966, vice 368,000 in the December plan...In addition he wants to increase Thailand strength from the approved December 1966 total of 26,800 to 57,100 of which 33,000 is available. While CINCPAC still wants 75 US maneuver battalions by December, his request involves an earlier deployment, approximately 711 battalion months in CY 1966 vs 654 in the December plan or 693 Service capability.

The increase and acceleration of Combat Support Battalions is more serious, involving over 82 battalions as compared with less than 60 in the December plan; 13 battalions of this increase are HAWK and Air Defense guns, neither of which are readily available. Similarly CINCPAC wants over 68 battalions of engineers by December, 22 more than in the December plan, and similarly unavailable.

The helicopter problem would be further compounded by the CINCPAC request for 2,884 by December versus 2,391 in the December plan and 2,240 said to be available by the Services.... 42/

With the revised CINCPAC requirements in hand, the services began to estimate their capability of meeting them. This exercise surfaced the problem of assumptions to be made about sources of manpower available to meet the requirements.

2. Assumptions for Planning

These assumptions were grouped into three sets or cases:

CASE 1: Meeting these requirements by providing forces from CONUS current force structure including activations, plus feasible draw-downs from overseas areas, call-up of selected reserve units and individuals, and extending terms of service.

CASE 2: Meeting these requirements by providing forces from CONUS current force structure including activations, plus feasible draw-downs from overseas areas.

51

      CASE 3: Meeting these requirements by providing forces
             from CONUS current force structure including
             activations.

A fourth case was considered by the JCS. It assumed:

      ...provision of forces from CONUS current force
      structure including activations, call-up of
      select reserve units and individuals, and ex-
      tension in terms of service, but no draw-down
      from overseas areas.

Assistant Secretary Enthoven added that:

      The JCS deleted Case 4 from the agenda largely because
they estimate that the President is more reluctant to call
up reserve units and extend terms of service than he is to
take forces out of Europe. If they are correct, I think
that the agenda as they have laid it out makes a great deal
of sense and will provide us with much useful information.
If, on the other hand, willingness to activate reserves and
extend terms of service has been underestimated, I think we
should recommend to the JCS that they restore Case 4 to the
agenda.

      Significantly, the guidance the JCS received was to study only the
first three cases, indicating that the JCS had not underestimated the
"willingness to activate reserves and extend terms of service."

      Meanwhile, Secretary McNamara, in a Memorandum for the President,
dated 24 January 1966, gave, as his best estimate of force levels for
the next twelve months, the following:

      1. By December 1966, the U.S. would have 75 battalions
         and 367,800 men in Vietnam.

      2. Allied nations would have 23 battalions and 44,600. 43/

He noted, however, that the JCS believed that "it would be necessary to
have a selective call-up of reserves and a selective extension of terms
of service to achieve the personnel strengths shown at the times indicated." He noted that the U.S. figures would rise substantially above
those shown if CINCPAC estimates were accepted.

      He also included General Westmoreland's estimate that such a deploy-
ment would:

      "a. Result in destruction of one-third of the enemy's base
areas, i.e., in-country resources.

b. Permit friendly control of just under one-half, as compared with the present one-third, of the critical roads and railroads.

c. Attrite VC/PAVN forces at an increasing rate, leading to the leveling off of enemy forces at the 150+ battalion level...(provided the Chinese do not supply volunteers).

d. Ensure that friendly bases and government centers are defended under any foreseeable circumstances (though some district towns may be overrun and have to be retaken).

e. Lead to government control of an estimated 50 per cent of the population."

3. The Honolulu Conference

However, by 28 January, the CINCPAC/MACV requirements had risen to 102 Free World battalions (79 U.S. including 4 tank battalions...) 44/ An intermediate evaluation was that "it appears that the MACV-CINCPAC requirements (102 battalions...) are valid, and required to meet the military objective on which the Secretary of Defense has been previously briefed. The information brought back by Secretary of Defense in late November as to combat and support force requirements was incomplete."

During the CINCPAC Conference, the top American and Vietnamese leaders also met at Honolulu, primarily to "permit the leaders of the United States and South Vietnam to get to know each other better and to discuss non-military programs."

Upon his return, Secretary McNamara assembled his key subordinates. The summary of this conference follows:

DRAFT
9 Feb 66

SUMMARY FOR RECORD

A meeting was held in the Conference Room of the Secretary of Defense from 1:45 to 3:00 p.m., February 9, 1966 following the return of the Secretary of Defense from Honolulu. At the conference table were the Secretary and Deputy Secretary of Defense, the Service Secretaries, and the members of the Joint Chiefs of Staff minus the Chairman. Also present were Mr. Anthony, Mr. Ignatius, Mr. McNaughton, Mr. Morris, Dr. Enthoven, Mr. Glass, and the undersigned. This memorandum will summarize the major points of the meeting.

1. The Honolulu Conference. Mr. McNamara opened with a general report on the events in Honolulu. The meetings in general were highly successful. The primary purpose of the Honolulu conference was as indicated in the press, namely to permit the leaders of the United States and South Vietnam to get to know each other better and to discuss non-military programs. The top South Vietnamese handled themselves superbly and made a fine impression. They have a non-military program which, if it can be put into effect, should greatly strengthen the government and the country. Most of the discussions concentrated on the non-military programs. The Vice President is going to Saigon to assist on this. McGeorge Bundy is also going there to help the American Embassy organize so as to further the non-military efforts.

Mr. McNamara brought back with him a great deal of material prepared by General Westmoreland and Admiral Sharp. He will have this material reproduced and copies sent to the Service Secretaries and the Chiefs of Staff. No significant military decisions were taken with the exception of one which he will now discuss.

2. The Case 1 Decision. Mr. McNamara reminded the group of the three cases which have been under discussion involving various assumptions. Briefly, Case 1 assumes that the Reserves will be called up, tours will be extended, and units will be re-deployed from other overseas areas. Case 2 is the same as Case 1 but does not involve calling up the Reserves. Case 3 involves no Reserve call-up and no overseas re-deployment. One of the big differences between these cases is in the number of support units available, with the resulting effect on the number of combat units that can be deployed. For example, under Case 1, some 102 maneuver battalions would be deployed by the end of the year as opposed to 80 such battalions under Case 3. This is in comparison to approximately 50 deployed at present.

General Westmoreland, in his deployment planning, is proceeding on the important assumption that on balance any proposed
deployments must increase his overall combat effectiveness; that is,
before he deploys a combat unit he must be sure that he has adequate
support for it. This does not mean, however, that he will deploy a
unit only when he can get 100 percent combat effectiveness for the unit.

Both General Westmoreland and Admiral Sharp put to McNamara
the critical question: In our future planning, which of the three cases
shall we assume will be followed? McNamara told them that it was simply
not possible yet to decide, but for the present, they should plan on combat
unit deployments equal to those in Case 1. (In this regard, it should be
noted that the combat unit deployments under Case 1 and Case 3 do not
differ significantly for the first 6 months of 1966, although the logistics
deployments do differ for that period.) Likewise the Department of
Defense is to:

(1) Assume and act to deploy combat units as provided
under Case 1, but without a reserve call-up. (This does not prejudice
the still-open question whether or not the Reserves will be called up.)

(2) Assume and act on the basis that we are authorized to
deploy up to 260,000 personnel through March 31, 1966. (This is in lieu
of the existing authorization of 220,000 through February 28, 1966.)
However, it should be understood that if we need to go above 260,000,
we will not hesitate to request further authorizations.

This contemplates the deployment by the end of the year of 102
combat maneuver battalions (including third country forces) and related
forces amounting to 429,000 U.S. military personnel.

There was discussion of extensions of tours. With respect to
the possible reserve call-up, this is to be subjected to intense critical
analysis over the next several weeks. It must be studied on a world-
wide basis. Furthermore General Westmoreland and Admiral Sharp
have done a good deal of work on alternatives under Case 1 to call-up
of the reserves. Mr. McNamara has these studies. Dr. Enthoven
will reproduce them and distribute them to the Service Secretaries
and the Chiefs of Staff.

55

3. <u>Southeast Asia Program Office</u>. It is essential that the
Department of Defense has at all times a readily available and centralized bank of information with respect to the Southeast Asia build-up.
To this end, Dr. Enthoven is to establish a Southeast Asia Program
Office which is to be able to furnish Mr. McNamara and Mr. Vance
all information that may be required with respect to Southeast Asia.
Among other things, this unit is to be able to provide immediate
information on what overseas units are being depleted in order to
accommodate Southeast Asia needs. If there is any draw-down anywhere, Mr. McNamara wants to know it promptly. We must know the
full price of what we are doing and propose to do.

Mr. McNamara suggested that each Service Secretary establish
a similar Southeast Asia Program Unit to bring together and keep current
data relating to that Service involving Southeast Asia, and that the Joint
Staff might establish a similar set-up.

Mr. McNamara said that it was mandatory that the situation be
brought under better control. For example, the Southeast Asia construction program was $1.2 billion in the FY 66 Supplement; yesterday at
Honolulu the figure of $2.5 billion was raised. Yet there is only the
vaguest information as to how these funds will be spent, where, on what,
and by whom. This is part of the bigger problem that there is no proper
system for the allocation of available resources in Vietnam. McGeorge
Bundy is to help organize the country team to deal with this problem,
including reconciling military and non-military demands.

4. <u>Manpower Controls</u>. Mr. McNamara designated Mr. Morris as
the person to be responsible for the various manpower requirements. He
is either to insure that the requirements are met or to let Mr. McNamara
know if they are not being met. Mr. McNamara wants a written statement whenever we have been unable to do something that General Westmoreland says he needs for full combat effectiveness. (In this regard,
General Westmoreland recognizes that it is not possible to have 100
percent combat effectiveness for all the 102 battalions. For example,
there are not sufficient helicopter companies. Roughly, he estimates
he will get 96 battalion combat effectiveness out of the 102 battalions.)

56

At this point there was a brief discussion concerning the use of U.S. troops for pacification purposes. Mr. Nitze indicated that in his view the Marines were doing this to some degree. The point was disputed. At any rate, Mr. McNamara said that the 102 combat battalions contemplated under Case 1 were not to be used for pacification but only for defense of base areas and offensive operations. Mr. McNamara outlined briefly the South Vietnamese Government's plan for pacification. It will affect some 235,000 people in the whole country. The major allocation of resources and personnel will be to four very limited areas, one of which is near Danang. There will also be a general program extending throughout the country involving some 900 hamlets.

5. Call-Up of Reserves. Mr. McNamara said that it was important that everyone understand why a Reserve call-up is receiving such careful study. There are at least two important considerations. First, the problem is a very complicated one and we do not yet have all the facts. Mr. Morris and others will amass the necessary data as soon as possible. Second, the political aspects of a Reserve call-up are extremely delicate. There are several strong bodies of opinion at work in the country. Look, for example, at the Fulbright Committee hearings. One school of thought, which underlies the Gavin thesis, is that this country is over-extended economically and that we cannot afford to do what we are doing. Another school of thought feels that we plain should not be there at all, whether or not we can afford it. A third school of thought is that although we are rightly there, the war is being mismanaged so that we are heading straight toward war with China. Furthermore, there is no question but that the economy of this country is beginning to run near or at its capacity with the resulting probability of a shortage of certain skills and materiel. If this continues we may be facing wage and price controls, excess profits taxes, etc., all of which will add fuel to the fire of those who say we cannot afford this. With all these conflicting pressures it is a very difficult and delicate task for the Administration to mobilize and maintain the required support in this country to carry on the war properly. The point of all this is to emphasize that a call-up of the Reserves presents extremely serious problems in many areas and a decision cannot be made today.

General Johnson said he wished to add three additional considerations. First, a Reserve call-up might be an important factor

32

in the reading of the North Vietnamese and the Chinese with respect to our determination to see this war through. Second, Reserve call-ups are traditionally a unifying factor. Third, as a larger problem, a hard, long-term look should be taken at the degree to which we as a government are becoming committed to a containment policy along all the enormous southern border of China. Mr. McNamara said he would ask for a JCS study of this last point and discussed it briefly.

During the course of the meeting, General Johnson also pointed out that with respect to overseas deployment, the Army is already shortchanging certain overseas areas so as to increase the training cadres in CONUS. He pointed out that because of the effect on the strategic reserve of deployments already made, the quality of new units will be lower than at present. He raised certain additional points affecting the Army. Mr. McNamara, Mr. Vance, Mr. Resor and General Johnson will discuss these problems further.

6. _Deployment Schedule._ Dr. Brown asked whether there is any single authoritative document which now sets forth the planned deployment schedule. Mr. McNamara said for the time being everyone should operate off of the schedule in the December 11 Draft Memorandum to the President. By Monday evening, February 14, Dr. Enthoven will have a revised deployment schedule which will be distributed and then become the official one. (Mr. McNaughton mentioned that people should keep in mind that Phase II-A in the Draft Memorandum to the President is not quite the same as Case I.) A procedure will be worked out for changing the deployment schedule in an official and orderly way, probably through the use of a procedure similar to that of Program Change Proposals.

It should be kept in mind that the deployment schedule referred to covers only deployments to South Vietnam (and not to Thailand or elsewhere in Southeast Asia), and that it is a planning deployment schedule. Actual deployment authorizations will continue to be required from Mr. McNamara or Mr. Vance in writing, as at present.

Attachment
a/s

John M. Steadman
The Special Assistant   45/

Two important items as far as the build-up was concerned were the
guidance to "assume and act to deploy combat units as provided under
Case 1, but without a reserve call-up," and the emphasis on the serious
problems which a reserve call-up would present (in spite of the insistence that the reserve call-up was a "still-open question").

4. Results of the CINCPAC Planning Conference

On 12 February, the results of the CINCPAC Conference were
published. 46/

The concept of operations for 1966 had been more completely
spelled out. The three basic military objectives had by this time grown
to four. Now there were two separate objectives,

1. To extend GVN dominion, direction, and control over
    SVN, and

2. To defeat the VC and PAVN forces in ARVN and force
    their withdrawal,

instead of the old task which combined both of these. In achieving the
objective for extending GVN domination, US forces' tasks were very carefully spelled out as "assisting the RVNAF in the conduct of clearing and
securing the civic action operations...assist and reinforce other US
mission agencies, and assist the RVNAF to defend major political, economic, food producing population centers." The object of defeating the
VC and PAVN forces required more direct action such as conducting sustained coordinated offensive operations against the enemy, conducting
air offensives, raids and special operations against enemy war zones and
base areas to render them unusable. In general, "US military operations
are aimed at creating operation environment and opportunity for the GVN
to gain control and establish security of main food producing areas in
order to feed the people, deny food to the enemy, bolster the economy,
to cause the enemy to import or fight for food." In explaining the US
emphasis on search and destroy, the memorandum stated that such operations "against VC/PAVN forces and base areas attrite VC/PAVN main forces
and destroy VC base areas and in-country supplies. These operations,
although contributory to, are not a part of the rural construction effort,
per se, but are constituted concomitantly with it. It is clear that a
known and expected VC/PAVN build-up, the prime focus of combat capable
units of US/FWMAF and RVNAF forces must be directed to the search and
destroy effort."

CINCPAC conceded that:

This concept of employment of forces is of long standing;
however, the lack of sufficient ARVN regular forces for offensive operations plus the increasing VC strength have resulted

in local RVN military commanders utilizing the security forces
(primarily RF, PF) in offensive actions against hard core VC
units. The introduction of US/FWMA forces into key areas has
reestablished the balance of force in these areas in favor of
the GVN. These deployments allow RVNAF forces to be employed
in the roles for which they were originally conceived and
equipped, and permit the RF and PF to function in their proper
role. 47/

The CINCPAC/MACV submission included the following estimates of
MACV's requirements and the deployments to Vietnam possible under the
assumptions of Cases 1, 2, and 3.

Strength at End of CY '66

Maneuver Bns	Requirement	Case 1	Case 2	Case 3
U.S.	79	79	70*	61
Allied	23	23	23	23
Total	102	102	93	84
Equivalent Strength	102	96	88	72

Personnel

U.S.	459,000	422,517

* Other 9 battalions available in Jan 67   48/

The difference in the programs in Case 1 and Case 2 was the degree
to which helicopter and combat service support could be provided. The
support required for the 102 battalion force would not be completely
provided in either case, which would result according to MACV estimates
in a reduction in the effectiveness of the 102 battalion force to the
equivalent of 96 fully supported battalions under Case 1 and to the
equivalent of 88 under Case 2.

Case 3 provided a total of only 84 maneuver battalions.

The CINCPAC requirements also included 20 battalions for reconstitution of the PACOM reserve. Case 1 provided for the full 20 battalions,
Case 2 for 10, and Case 3 for 13 battalions.

CINCPAC's evaluation of the impact of the three cases upon military
objectives was:

    (1) Case 3:

        (a) Provides for the security of the US/FWMAF command
            at the projected rate of VC/PAVN build up.

60

(b) The principal deficiencies of the Case 3 forces are:

    1. Inadequate mobility.

    2. Inadequate artillery support.

    3. There are no ground forces provided for stationing in the Delta.

    4. Insufficient force and mobility to guarantee defense of all provinces and districts now under GVN control.

(2) Case 2:

    (a) Provides for the safety of the US/FWMAF command.

    (b) Provides the required number of maneuver battalions.

However, shortfalls in combat and service support restrict the capabilities of the force and produce the following deficiencies:

    1. Inadequate mobility.

    2. Limited offensive capability, resulting in an inability to produce enemy casualties faster than the enemy can produce replacements, thereby prolonging the war at a high level of casualties on both sides.

    3. A high rate of equipment loss and deadline resulting from maintenance deficiencies.

    4. The acceptance of a high risk in the event of escalation because the force is not supported adequately for sustained operations of the kind which could be expected.

    5. Insufficient forces for desired level of sustained offensive operations to offset VC/PAVN build-up.

    6. A shortage of maneuver units, the adverse effects of which are cumulative and project into CY 67.

    7. Insufficient logistic support forces to provide desired level of support for US forces in SVN. The adverse effects caused by the shortage of logistic units are cumulative and project into CY 67.

61

(3) Case 1:

    (a) Generally adequate when measured against CINCPAC
        objectives and capabilities except that there is
        a continuing deficiency in helicopter mobility. 49/

Having received CINCPAC's requirement, the Secretary of Defense
directed a series of studies to identify and evaluate the options which
appeared to be open. The scope of these studies is indicated by a
partial listing of projects compiled by Assistant Secretary for Manpower, Thomas D. Morris:

Views on Army and Marine Corps PACOM reserve forces;

Acceptable draw-down on Europe;

Recommendations on use of third country forces;

Posture paper on strategic reserves and reconstitution
of draw-downs;

Analyze rotation base requirements;

Study possibilities for further expansion of Army
training base;

Recommend temporary draw-downs on Army CONUS and overseas forces to support deployments, activations and
training-rotation base;

Evaluate use of resources of Army temporary forces
(9th Division and 2 add-on brigades) to meet other
MACV requirements. ... 50/

One key question asked was the latest date at which a decision on
use of reserves must be made. 51/

Part of the answer -- the dates by which reserves would have to be
called in lieu of forming the 9th Division and the 198th Brigade -- was
15 June for the brigade and 26 June for the division. 52/

With this time to work in, the Secretary of Defense directed the

    ...Military Departments and the JCS to assume that this
    /the Case 1 deployment schedule/ is the requirement we will
    try to meet, to study all possible ways of meeting it short
    of calling reserves or extending terms of service, and until
    further notice, in so far as possible, to plan to deploy
    forces to SVN on this schedule (forces to other SEA areas

will continue to be deployed on the basis of the "December 11, 1965 Plan"). I would like to urge that you use all the ingenuity you can in developing suggested ways of meeting these conditions by use of suitable substitutes, civilian contractor personnel, etc. In this connection, General Westmoreland and Admiral Sharp have made a list of suggestions which is being analyzed by the JCS J-4 and my staff. Every effort should be made to carry out these and similar suggestions.

The fourth line in the tables is my understanding of the current Service estimates of their capabilities to meet these requirements under the assumption that only cadres are taken from Europe, and that no Reserves or extensions of terms of service are utilized. Would you please study these estimates, improve upon them, and find ways to bring our effective combat capability into equality with the Case 1.

I would like by February 28 the individual Service and JCS comments on our capabilities to meet Case 1 requirements. 53/

G. Phase IIA(R) Presented

1. The JCS Recommendation

On 1 March 1966, the Joint Chiefs of Staff forwarded their recommendation for Phase IIA(R) and their plan to reconstitute the draw-downs on our strategic reserve. 54/ The JCS recommended that the 43-2/3 battalion U.S. force be deployed to Vietnam in CY 1966, which would require a "selective call-up of reserve units and personnel and extension of terms of service." They also considered, at the request of the Secretary of Defense, a variation of Case 1, in which reserve call-up and extension of terms of service were excluded. They recommended against this plan because of the severe effects upon our combat effectiveness in Europe. If the reserves were not to be called or terms of service extended, the JCS recommended that the deployments for Phase IIA(R) be extended into 1967 rather than attempt to complete them by the end of 1966. Their plan was basically to delay the deployment of 13 of the scheduled 37 Army maneuver battalions until the first half of 1967 (7 the first quarter and 6 the second quarter). The battalions themselves would be ready for deployment by 1 January 1967, but the necessary combat service support units would not be.

2. McNamara Directs Another Try

However, the JCS's recommendations were not bought by the Secretary of Defense and on 10 March he stated, "I have reviewed JCSM 130-66 and the related memorandums from the Secretary of the Military Departments. All of these require more study and review. However, until such studies are completed, you should plan to deploy forces to SVN in accordance

63

with...Case 1...all necessary actions are to be taken to meet these deployment dates without call-up of reserves or extension of terms of service. Troop movements from Europe will be made only by written approval of Mr. Vance or myself." 55/

3. The JCS Try Again

Accordingly, the JCS submitted their plan on 4 April 1966 which provided for placing all 37 Army maneuver battalions in SVN by January 1967. 56/ The end of year strength for 1966 was projected to be 376,350, while the strength at the end of CY 67 was to be 438,207.

Although Secretary McNamara still had questions about the discrepancy between the JCS plan laid out on 4 April 1966 and the Case 1 capabilities, he apparently accepted the reasoning expressed by Assistant Secretary of Defense Alain Enthoven in his memorandum of 9 April 1966, "that there is not much to be gained by insisting on a more rapid deployment of maneuver battalions." 57/

4. McNamara Acquiesces

Accordingly, on 11 April 1966 Secretary McNamara, "with the exceptions noted.../approved/...the deployment plan proposed by the Joint Chiefs of Staff in JCSM 218-66." 58/

Attached to his approval memorandum was a set of tables entitled "April 10 Deployment Plan." These showed planned U.S. strength at the end of December 1966 to be 70 maneuver battalions and 383,500 personnel. The remaining 9 maneuver battalions would arrive in January 1967 and by the end of June 1967 total strength was scheduled to be 425,000. This plan, called the "10 April Plan" by Systems Analysis and the Secretary of Defense's office represented the approved version of what the Services called the Deployment Plan for Phase IIA(R).

Apparently however, even this was not close enough to the original Case 1 deployment capabilities schedule to suit Secretary McNamara, and in a memorandum dated 12 April 1966 he asked why the difference between the revised JCS figure for end of '66 strength and the Case 1 figure for end '66 strength of 413,557. 59/

The Acting Chairman of the JCS answered as follows:

*   *   *   *   *

3. (TS) JCSM-218-66 reflects a projected and calendar year 1966 strength of 376,350 compared to the Case I strength of 413,557 -- a shortfall of 37,207. However, due to adjustments since Case I capabilities were developed, including changes in requirements and refinements in strengths, the

64

actual net shortfall reflected in the Appendices hereto amounts
to 47,731....

4. (S) The basic difference in the two capability plans,
as viewed by the Joint Chiefs of Staff, is that Case I was based
upon the call up of Reserve forces, extension of terms of service, and a firm decision by 1 February 1966. The JCSM-218-66
plan represented a changed set of assumptions in that it did not
have access to the skilled resources available from the Reserves
and from extended terms of service. Furthermore, JCSM-218-66
represented a two-month delay in certain basic decisions. Despite extraordinary actions being taken to improve the availability of combat support and combat service support units, no
means have been found to eliminate certain skill shortages and
to create these skills in the time available. Another fundamental difference is that Case I would have deployed largely
units in being, whereas the current deployment plan will depend
primarily on activation of new units.

5. (S) Despite the shortcomings apparent in the 10 April
1966 plan, the Services are taking positive actions to bring
this plan, which is based essentially upon Case II rules, in
line with the Case I deployment capabilities insofar as possible.
Such extraordinary actions have resulted in significant improvements.

6. (S) In consideration of the above, the current approved
deployment program in JCSM-218-66 meets as closely as feasible
the program for South Vietnam prescribed in your directive to
plan, for an interim period, to deploy forces in accordance with
Case I. However, this program as well as the Case I capability
plan falls short of the total calendar year 1966 CINCPAC force
requirements submitted by CINCPAC to the Joint Chiefs of Staff.
Although there will be a delay in meeting the total requirement,
the Joint Chiefs of Staff and the Services will continue their
efforts to fulfill the total requirements as close to CINCPAC's
schedule as practicable. 60/

The question of where the numbers for Phases II, IIA, and IIA(R)
came from provokes much speculation. It can be hypothesized that from
the outset of the American build-up, some military men felt that winning
a meaningful military victory in Vietnam would require something on the
order of one million men. Knowing that this would be unacceptable
politically, it may have seemed a better bargaining strategy to ask for
increased deployments incrementally. At the outset, the limiting factor
on the build-up was the speed with which units could be readied for
deployment, and the speed with which logistical support facilities could
be provided in Vietnam (the later constraint being heavily influenced by

65

the scarcity of dock facilities and the shipping jam up in Saigon). Once these problems had been surmounted, the barrier then became the level at which the reserves would have to be called up. This barrier became very real in early '66 when General Westmoreland's desires for numbers of men and rates of deployments began to exceed the capabilities of the services to provide them without a reserve call up. In this speculative explanation of military bargaining strategy, the reserve call-up could have been viewed as a barrier that should be breached in order to fight the conflict in South Vietnam along more rational-professional lines.

An alternative explanation is that no one really foresaw what the troop needs in Vietnam would be and that the ability of the DRV/VC to build up their effort was consistently underrated. During the period under review this explanation seems with some exceptions, to be reasonable. The documents from the period around July 1965 seem to indicate that MACV had not given much thought to what he was going to do in the year or years after 1965. The words of the MACV History for 1965 indicate something of this. "The President's 28 July announcement that the U.S. would commit additional massive military forces in SVN necessitated an overall plan clarifying the missions and deployment of the various components. COMUSMACV's Concept of Operations was prepared to fulfill this need." If this is a true reflection of what happened it would indicate the MACV's plan of what to do was derived from what would be available rather than the requirements for manpower being derived from any clearly thought out military plan.

A compromise explanation of the origins of the numbers is that the military may have had a visceral feeling that a large (somewhere above 500,000) number of troops would be needed to win the war, but were unable to justify their requirements in terms clear or strong enough to persuade the President, who had an interest in keeping the domestic effects of war as small as possible.

FOOTNOTES

1. Memorandum from McGeorge Bundy to SecDef, dated 18 Jun 65.

2. Phase I in the Build-up of U.S. Forces: The Debate, March-July 1965.

3. Intensification of the Military Operations in Vietnam--Concept and Appraisal, Report of Ad Hoc Study Group, 14 July 1965.

4. Ibid., p. ii.

5. Memo for General Goodpaster, Subj: "Forces Required to Win in South Vietnam," dated 2 July 1965.

6. Intensification of the Military Operations in Vietnam--Concept and Appraisal, op. cit.

7. Ibid., p. J-3.

8. SecDef 072352Z Jul 65.

9. Draft Memorandum for the President dated 7/1/65, Subject: Program of expanded military and political moves with respect to Vietnam. Secretary McNamara has inserted "Rev'd" before the typed date, 7/1/65, and written the date 6/26/65 above it.

10. Command History, United States Military Assistance Command, Vietnam, 1965, p. 42.

11. Ibid.

12. Ibid., pp. 141-148.

13. Memo for the President from SecDef, dtd 20 Jul 65, Subj: Recommendations of Additional Deployments to Vietnam, pp. 4-5.

14. MACV 220625Z Jul 65.

15. Memo for the Record, dtd 12 Jul 65, Subj: "63 Battalion Plan," signed by Col Moody, Military Assistant to the Secretary of Defense. The same figures, in McNamara's handwriting, are in his notebook for the Saigon trip.

16. Op. Cit., 20 Jul 65, Memo for the President from the Secretary of Defense.

17. Ibid.

18. Notes on background briefing given by President Johnson on 28 Jul 65, taken by ASD(PA) Goulding.

19. Message from DepSecDef Vance to Secretary McNamara, 172043E Jul 65, Back Channel.

20. JCSM 652-65 dated 27 August 1965, Subj: Concept for Vietnam, pp. 1-3.

21. _Ibid._, pp. 6-7.

22. _Ibid._, p. 8.

23. _Ibid._

24. Memo for SecDef, dtd 8 Sep 65, Subj: Concept for Vietnam, signed McNaughton.

25. Memo for CJCS, Subj: Concept for Vietnam, dtd 11 Sep 65, signed McNamara.

26. MACV Directive 525-4, 20 Sep 65, p. 2.

27. JCSM 811-65, dtd 10 Nov 65, Subj: Future Operations and Force Deployments with Respect to the War in Vietnam.

28. ASD(SA) Memo for Secys of Military Departments, Chmn JCS, Subj: Southeast Asia Deployment Assumptions for Planning, dtd 20 Nov 65, signed Enthoven.

29. JCSM 811-65, 10 Nov 65.

30. 1st Rough Draft of Memorandum for the President, dtd 3 Nov 65, Subj: Courses of Action in Vietnam. Secretary McNamara has written "a copy of this was sent to the President by courier thru Mac's office on 11/7 and discussed with him by me, Dean, George, & Mac on 11/7."

31. MACV 40748, 17 Nov 65, to DIA, Subj: VC and PAVN Forces Build-up.

32. MACV Command History, 1965, p. 168.

33. MACV Command History, 1966, pp. 20-21.

34. COMUSMACV 41485 to CINCPAC, 23 Nov 65. Add-On to Phase II Deployments.

35. SecDef 4539-65 to Saigon, 23 Nov 65.

36. MACV Command History, 1965, pp. 44-45.

37. J-3 Briefing given to McNamara while in Saigon.

38. MACV Command History, 1965, p. 45.

39. Draft Memorandum for the President, dtd 30 Nov 65.

40. Memorandum for the President, dated 7 December, Subject: Military and Political Actions Recommended for South Vietnam, p. 3.

41. Draft Memo for President, Subject: Recommended FY 1966 Southeast Asia Supplemental Appropriation (U), dated December 11, 1965 (transmitted by multiaddress memo signed by DepSecDef dated 13 Dec 65).

42. ASD Memorandum for Secretary of Defense, Subject: Southeast Asia Deployments, dated 14 Jan 66.

43. Memorandum for the President dated 24 Jan 66, Subj: The Military Outlook in South Vietnam.

44. Notes on Honolulu Visit, dated 1/28/66, unsigned but marked "Mr. Vance has seen."

45. Summary for Record, dated 9 Feb 66, signed by John T. Steadman.

46. CINCPAC 3010, Ser: 00055, 12 Feb 66, to JCS, Subj: Calandar Year 1966 Capabilities Programs (U).

47. Ibid.

48. Ibid.

49. Ibid.

50. ASD(M) Memorandum for Secretary McNamara and Secretary Vance, dated 16 Feb 66.

51. ASD(M) Memorandum for Record, Subject: Studies of CINCPAC Requirements as of 2/16/66, dated 14 Feb 66, signed by Thomas D. Morris.

52. ASD(M) Memorandum for Secretary Vance, Subject: Decision Dates Required to Call Reserve Units in Lieu of Forming the 9th Division and one of the Temporary Brigades, dated 16 Feb 66, signed by Thomas D. Morris.

53. SecDef Memo for Secys of the Mil Depts, CJCS, Subj: Southeast Asia Deployment Planning Assumptions (U), dtd 17 Feb 66, signed Robert S. McNamara.

54. JCSM-130-66, dated 1 March 1966, Subject: CY 1966 Deployments to Southeast Asia and World Wide Military Posture.

55. JCSM 218-66, 4 Apr 66, Deployment Program for Southeast Asia and Other PACOM Areas.

56. JCSM 218-66, 4 Apr 66, Deployment Program for Southeast Asia and Other PACOM Areas.

57. Memorandum for SecDef, Subject: Deployments to Southeast Asia (U), dtd 9 April 1966, from Alain Enthoven.

58. Secretary of Defense Memorandum for Secretaries of the Military Departments, Chairman of the Joint Chiefs of Staff, Assistant Secretaries of Defense, Assistants to the Secretary of Defense, Subject: SEA Deployment Plan, dated 11 April 1966, signed Robert S. McNamara.

59. Memorandum to the Chairman, Joint Chiefs of Staff, dated 12 April 1966, Subject: JCSM 218-66, dated 4 April 1966.

60. JCSM-274-66, 28 April, Subject: Deployment Program for South Vietnam.

II. PROGRAM NO. 3

71

II. PROGRAM No. 3

A. Interlude

As far as the actual conduct of ground operations in Vietnam was concerned, the period of time from 1 May 1965 to 1 November 1965 was spent in building up combat and logistical forces and learning to employ them effectively. This was followed by a period from 1 November 1965 to 1 May 1966, in which the deployment of U.S. forces was extended toward the frontiers, logistical support was exercised in furnishing support to troops in sustained combat, and commanders were indoctrinated on the techniques of sustained ground combat.

The NVA/VC avoided initiating actions which might result in large and unacceptable casualties from the firepower of Allied forces. During the year the enemy became increasingly cautious in the face of increased Allied strength. The enemy tended to attack only when he had overwhelming superiority of numbers, such as during the attack in March on the Special Forces outpost at A Shau. VC tactics were designed to conserve main force strengths for the most opportune targets. The NVA/VC avoided attacking large Allied units of regiment or brigade size, but did attack isolated battalions and companies using sufficient strength to insure great numerical superiority. It was typical of the enemy to attack with one-third of his available force and to employ the remaining two-thirds of the units to set up an ambush of the Allied relief column. During attacks the NVA/VC used a hugging tactic as a means of protecting themselves from Allied artillery and air strikes. The enemy often withdrew by small squad-sized increments, using multiple routes. To defend against surveillance and artillery and air strikes, the enemy dispersed into the jungle in small units, moved frequently, and made maximum use of darkness and periods of low visibility... 1/

It is interesting to note, however, the pattern formed by MACV's operations during 1966. In the I Corps area, the large-scale operations conducted by the Marines in the spring of the year were for the most part located along the coast of the southern part of the area, in the Provinces of Quang Tin and Quang Ngai.

Beginning with Operation DOUBLE EAGLE I (28 January to 17 February), they progressed through DOUBLE EAGLE II (19 February to 1 March); Operation UTAH (4 March); Operation TEXAS (18 March); and Operation HOT SPRINGS on 21 April. All of these operations were keyed on intelligence of an enemy build-up in and around Quang Ngai. Contact on these operations ranged from sporadic to contact with a NVA regiment on Operation UTAH. The major exception to the location of operations in this area was Operation OREGON which was conducted in the vicinity of Thua Thien in late March.

TOP SECRET - Sensitive

Another significant activity during the period, although not one
initiated by the United States forces, was the fall of the Special
Forces camp at A Shau, on the 10th of March.

Operations in the II Corps Tactical Zone in 1966 displayed a similar pattern. The two key areas of concern in II Corps were the coastal
plains in Binh Dinh Province and near Tuy Hoa, and the Central Highland
Plateau area around Pleiku. Although General Westmoreland appeared to
be impatient to find the enemy and defeat him in the relatively sparsely
populated plateau area, most of the operations in the first half of the
year which resulted in significant contact with the enemy took place
near the Coastal Plains. The first operation of the year, which ran
from 28 January to 4 February, was Operation MASHER, renamed Operation
WHITE WING because of the concern over public reaction to the image
portrayed by the name "MASHER."

Operation WHITE WING continued until 6 March. This operation in
the Bong Son and An Lao Valley region made heavy contact with 1 VC and
1 NVA regiment. It was followed by DAVEY CROCKETT (4-16 May) and
CRAZY HORSE (17 May to 5 June), both in the same area.

Other significant operations in the spring of the year were Operations VAN BUREN and HARRISON which, together, ran from 19 January through
24 March in the area around Tuy Hoa. These operations, conducted by the
1st Brigade of the 101st Airborne Division, were designed to protect the
rice harvest in that area.

Operations in the III Corps area began with Operation MARAUDER in
Hau Nghia and Long An Provinces on 7 January; Operation CRIMP, along the
Hau Nghia/Binh Duong border; and Operation BUCKSKIN near ChuChi on
11 January.

In February, Operation MASTIFF into the Michelin Plantation, and
Operation MALLET in Phouc Tuy Province, were carried out. Neither
Operation produced substantial enemy kills, but hopefully they were
instrumental in breaking up VC supply and command and control facilities.
By 10 February, however, Operation ROLLING STONE had been kicked off and
by 20 September it had encountered a 1,000-man VC force in Binh Duong.
On 7 March, another search and destroy operation in Binh Duong, Operation
SILVER CITY, triggered a four-hour attack by the enemy against 173rd Airborne Brigade, one of the participating units. On 24 April, the center
of operations moved further north when BIRMINGHAM began a thrust into
Tay Ninh. The most significant part of BIRMINGHAM was the capture of
vast quantities of enemy supplies and facilities despite the small number
of enemy killed. By May of 1966, the 1st Cavalry Division was operating
in the Central Highlands, the 1st Infantry Division was in operation
north of Saigon, while the 25th Infantry Division had one brigade operating with the 1st Cavalry Division on the Central Plateau, with the other
brigades engaged in the III Corps area.

As far as the pattern which American forces in Vietnam followed, there seemed to be an initial preoccupation in the spring of 1966 with the Viet Cong and NVA units located in the populated areas, Quang Ngai in the I Corps, Binh Dinh and Phu Yen in the II Corps and Hau Nghia and Binh Duong in the III Corps.

B. Phase IIA(R) Becomes Program No. 3

1. Bookkeeping Changes

Reflecting the relatively low level of combat and the preoccupation with the build-up of U.S. forces, only minor changes and adjustments to the figures in the plan were made during the two months following the publication of Phase IIA(R). By June, however, the number of changes had begun to build up. Assistant Secretary Enthoven, in his 10 June 1966 memorandum to Secretary McNamara, reported that there had been "a large number of changes proposed by the Army...This package of deployment adjustments is the result of detailed CONARC studies of unit availability based upon equipment inventories, personnel training outputs, etc. These changes affect virtually every month and type of unit." 2/

Assistant Secretary Enthoven then followed this with a memorandum on 13 June 1966 providing copies of the current statistical summary of deployments and an explanation of the major changes. Most of these were bookkeeping in nature, having to do with changes in the base from which future strengths were computed and certain other adjustments such as eliminating transients from the totals. This made no change in battalion strengths but brought the December 1966 and June 1967 totals to 378,000 and 427,000, respectively. 3/

On 16 June, Secretary McNamara, in a handwritten note in the margin of this latest Enthoven memorandum, directed Dr. Enthoven to make some changes in strengths to be included and to issue the revised plan as a separate document, not as part of the statistical summary.

By 30 June, when Enthoven sent the revised plan back to McNamara for approval, two changes had occurred which brought the totals for December 66 and June 67 to 391,000 and 431,000. These changes were the acceleration of the deployment of two brigades of the 9th Infantry Division from January 67 to December 66, and the availability of the 196th Infantry Brigade for deployment in August of 1966. This brigade was originally scheduled for deployment to Dominican Republic, but was diverted to Vietnam. These changes brought the total of U.S. maneuver battalions scheduled to be in Vietnam by the end of 1966 to 79 and the total by June 67 to 82. 4/

2. The Pen is Quicker Than The Eye

The question arises here as to why this revision of the plan became Program No. 3 rather than "change x" to the 10 April Plan. The

difference in the December 66 strengths of the 10 April Plan (later
retroactively designated Program No. 2) was 7,500 while the difference
in the June 1967 strengths was 5,900 -- hardly very large changes.

An explanation may lie in an exchange of memoranda which took place
between 28 June and 15 July. On 28 June, the President wrote Secretary
McNamara as follows:

                        THE WHITE HOUSE
                          Washington

                                    Tuesday, June 28, 1966
                                    5:05 p.m.

MEMORANDUM FOR THE SECRETARY OF DEFENSE

        As you know, we have been moving our men to Viet Nam on a
schedule determined by General Westmoreland's requirements.

        As I have stated orally several times this year, I should
like this schedule to be accelerated as much as possible so that
General Westmoreland can feel assured that he has all the men he
needs as soon as possible.

        Would you meet with the Joint Chiefs and give me at your
early convenience an indication of what acceleration is possible
for the balance of this year.

                            Sgd: Lyndon B. Johnson   6/

Secretary McNamara passed the question on to the Joint Chiefs of Staff,
who replied on 8 July, 7/ that the present revised schedule did meet
the CINCPAC requirements of 79 maneuver battalions by December 1966, and
that "it appears that no significant acceleration of supportable combat-
ready forces beyond those indicated will be attained." McNamara then
replied to the President on 15 July that the Department of Defense had
been "making strenuous efforts to accelerate deployments." 8/   He added,

        I am happy to report that this effort has been successful,
        and we will be able to provide more troops and equipment during
        the remainder of this calendar year than we had though possible
        last spring...To illustrate the degree of acceleration already
        achieved, we now plan to have 79 Army and Marine Corps maneuver
        battalions in South Vietnam by December 1966, as compared to the
        70 battalions we thought could be safely deployed only four months
        ago. We now expect to have 395,000 personnel in South Vietnam
        by the end of this year compared to 314,000 estimated last March.

The whole exchange may have a purpose other than simply requesting
information or directing acceleration. Presumably, the President and

McNamara frequently conferred on the conduct of the Vietnam war and there would seem to be little need for such a request or directive to be placed in writing unless it was to act as some sort of record which could be easily pulled out and displayed in order to demonstrate that the President had been sending troops to Vietnam as rapidly as Westmoreland needed them.

This makes sense if it is recalled that at this particular time the President was just in the process of publicly turning up the pressure on North Vietnam by ordering the bombing of the POL supplies. This effort to step up the pace in the aftermath of the disruption caused by the Buddhist struggle movement probably also included a desire to increase the pace of the ground war in an effort to convince the DRV that we could and would do whatever was necessary to defeat them in the South.

At the same time, there began to be some comment in the news, particularly by Hanson W. Baldwin of the New York Times that top military men were beginning to feel that the policy of a gradual build-up was becoming outmoded and that what was needed was a sharp increase in the application of force.

Seen in this context, the exercise of naming the last change to Phase IIA(R), "Program 3," and the exchange of memoranda between the Secretary of Defense and the President can be interpreted as follows. The President, impatient at being held back by the internal strife in South Vietnam in his effort to convince the North of our will to win the war, was anxious to get on with the war in an attempt to get it over with quickly. The implication, from a writer reputed to have close ties with the Joint Chiefs of Staff, that the military felt that the President was not doing enough, prompted the President to write a memorandum to the Secretary of Defense asking him specifically to see if the JCS could think of some way to accelerate the deployments of ground forces. When the JCS wrote back that the present plan did meet Westmoreland's requirements and that additional acceleration was unlikely, the President had in effect secured the agreement of his senior military men that he was doing all that was needed and possible.

The ploy of naming the latest change "Program #3" can be seen to have two effects in this effort. First, it gave the illusion of progress. Second, it neatly wrapped up the changes since the beginning of the year, making the very real progress since December readily apparent, but obscuring the fact that most of the increase in the plan had occurred by 10 April.

FOOTNOTES

1.   MACV Command History 1966, pp. 20-21.

2.   Asst SecDef (Systems Analysis) Memo for SecDef, Subj: Report on
     Deployments to SEA (U), dtd 10 Jun 66.

3.   ASD(SA) memorandum for SecDef, Subj: Deployments to Southeast
     Asia (U), dtd 13 Jun 66.

4.   ASD(SA) Memorandum for SecDef, Subj: Southeast Deployment Plan (U),
     dtd 30 Jun 66.

5.   SecDef Memorandum for Secretaries of the Military Departments,
     Chairman of the Joint Chiefs of Staff, Assistant Secretaries of
     Defense, Subj: Southeast Asia Deployment Plan, dtd 2 Jul 66.

6.   President's Memorandum for the SecDef, June 28, 1966.

7.   JCSM 450-66, Subj: CINCPAC Calendar Year Deployments dtd 8 Jul 66.

8.   SecDef Memorandum for the President, Subj: Schedule of Deployments
     to South Vietnam (U), dated 15 July 1966.

78

III. PROGRAM No. 4

A. Planning Begins for CY 67

1. CINCPAC's 18 June Request

However, even before the Secretary of Defense published Program No. 3, CINCPAC had submitted his Calendar Year 1966 adjusted requirements and Calendar Year 1967 requirements. 1/

CINCPAC's requirements were based on a new concept for Vietnam. The four basic objectives remained as they had been set forth in CINCPAC's February concept. A new item in the June concept was that US/FWMAF and RVNAF general reserves and ARVN corps reserve forces would conduct sustained and coordinated operations with increased effort in the Highlands and along the western ARVN border. This was in line with the generally increased emphasis given in the concept to restricting NVA/VC forces' access to the coastal and land borders of ARVN through effective land, sea, and air interdiction operations.

During this time, two slightly different estimates of enemy strength were available. The figures used by CINCPAC in their 18 June submission were 125 confirmed, 7 probable, and 18 possible battalions in South Vietnam. It was estimated that the enemy was capable of infiltrating up to 15 battalion equivalents (9,000 personnel) per month into South Vietnam unless denied capability to do so. It was also estimated that the enemy could train 7 VC battalion equivalents (3,500 personnel) per month under the current existing situation. However, the best estimate of his intentions was that he would attempt to reinforce at the rate of 18.5 battalion equivalents (11.5 NVA, and 7 VC) per month, which would give him a maximum build-up total of 180 battalion equivalents by March 1967, at which time losses would exceed inputs and total VC strength would begin to decline.

The estimate of VC strength given in NIE 14.3-66, 2/ was as follows: The total Communist force in South Vietnam was estimated to be between 260,000 and 280,000. The major combat elements included some 38,000 North Vietnamese troops, approximately 63,000 regular main and local forces and from 100 - 200,000 guerrillas. The North was estimated to have a capability to infiltrate from 75,000 to 100,000 individual replacements, but present evidence suggested that the probable infiltration would be between 55,000 and 75,000. The estimate of VC recruiting in the South was from 7,000 to 10,000 a month. A projection of strength for end of 1966 was 125,000 in the Communist regular forces, but this could grow by the end of 1967 to over 150,000. The estimated strength for 1 January 1967, in terms of battalions, was between 170 and 190.

7?

The requirements for 1966 had been adjusted to 474,786 bringing the year-end totals for 1966 and 1967 to 395,269 and 436,406, although the maneuver battalion strength remained at 79 U.S. battalions (this did not include the windfall of the 3 battalions of the 196th Brigade). The CINCPAC submission also reiterated the request made in February for 20 battalions to reconstitute the PACOM reserve.

The requirements for CY 1967 were basically considered to be "rounding out forces." This force package basically consisted of: 5 tactical strike squadrons; 11 U.S. maneuver battalions of infantry/ armored cavalry/tank configuration; a 4th rifle company for each of the 61 U.S. infantry battalions, and 7 FWMAF battalions, 6 of which were to round out the ROK Marine Brigade to a Division, and 1 additional battalion for the Australian Task Force to round it out to a full regiment. After all of the deployments recommended in the plan were carried out, the strength of U.S. forces in Vietnam would be 90 maneuver battalions and 542,588 personnel.

2. JCS Recommendations

These requirements were forwarded to the Secretary of Defense by the JCS in JCSM 506-66, on 5 August. 3/

The memorandum noted that the JCS felt that with a few exceptions the requirements and proposed force additions were valid, and that a capabilities planning conference was scheduled for early October to "correlate this planning into a comprehensive program."

3. Secretary of Defense Directs Studies

On the same day, the Secretary of Defense sent a memorandum to the Chairman of the Joint Chiefs of Staff as follows:

5 August 1966

MEMORANDUM FOR CHAIRMAN OF THE JOINT CHIEFS OF STAFF

SUBJECT: CINCPAC CY 1966 Adjusted Requirements & CY 1967
          Requirements (U)

As you know, it is our policy to provide the troops, weapons, and supplies requested by General Westmoreland at the times he desires them, to the greatest possible degree. The latest revised CINCPAC requirements, submitted on 18 June 1966, subject as above, are to be accorded the same consideration: valid requirements for SVN and related tactical air forces in Thailand will be deployed on a schedule as close as possible to CINCPAC/COMUSMACV's requests.

TOP SECRET - Sensitive

Nevertheless, I desire and expect a detailed, line-by-line analysis of these requirements to determine that each is truly essential to the carrying out of our war plan. We must send to Vietnam what is needed, but only what is needed. Excessive deployments weaken our ability to win by undermining the economic structure of the RVN and by raising doubts concerning the soundness of our planning.

In the course of your review of the validity of the requirements, I would like you to consider the attached Deployment Issue Papers which were prepared by my staff. While there may be sound reasons for deploying the units questioned, the issues raised in these papers merit your detailed attention and specific reply. They probably do not cover all questionable units, particularly for proposed deployments for the PACOM area outside of SVN. I expect that you will want to query CINCPAC about these and other units for which you desire clarification.

I appreciate the time required to verify the requirements and determine our capability to meet them, but decisions must be made on a timely basis if units are to be readied and equipment and supplies procured. Therefore I would appreciate having your recommended deployment plan, including your comments on each of the Deployment Issue Papers, no later than 15 September 1965.

Enclosures   Sgd: ROBERT S. McNAMARA 4/

The items questioned in the Issue Papers totalled approximately 70,000 troops with artillery and air defense providing the two largest single items.

4. The "Quick Fix"

While the JCS were beginning their review of the items questioned by the Secretary of Defense, they attempted to secure a "quick fix" in the form of a message from General Westmoreland. General Westmoreland evaluated the 1966 and 1967 force requirements as follows:

...Continuous study of the situation indicates that past and current developments reinforce my appraisal of the war on which the CY 66-67 force requirements were based. There are no indications that the enemy has reduced his resolve. He has increased his rate of infiltration, formed Division size units, introduced new weapons into his ranks, maintained lines of communications leading into South Vietnam, increased his use of Cambodia as a safehaven, and recently moved a combat division through the DMZ.

TOP SECRET - Sensitive

81

These and other facts support earlier predictions and suggest
that the enemy intends to continue a protracted war of attrition. We must not underestimate the enemy nor his determination.

The war can continue to escalate. Infiltration of enemy troops
and supplies from NVN can increase and there is no assurance
that this will not occur.

If, contrary to current indications, Hanoi decides not to escalate further, some modification of the forces which I have
requested probably could be made. Under such circumstances, I
conceive of a carefully balanced force that is designed to fight
an extended war of attrition and sustainable without national
mobilization.

I recognize the possibility that the enemy may not continue to
follow the pattern of infiltration as projected. Accordingly,
my staff is currently conducting a number of studies with the
objective of placing this command and the RVN in a posture that
will permit us to retain the initiative regardless of the
course the enemy chooses to pursue. These include:

   A. A study which considers possible courses of action by
the enemy on our force posture and counteractions to maintain
our superiority.

   B. An analysis of our requirements to determine a balanced
US force that can be employed and sustained fully and effectively in combat on an indefinite basis without national mobilization.

   C. A study to determine the evolutionary steps to be taken
in designing an ultimate GVN security structure.

   D. A study to determine the optimum RVNAF force structure
which can be attained and supported in consideration of recent
experience and our estimate of the manpower pool.

Ref B /The CINCPAC submission/ establishes and justifies minimal
force requirements, emphasizing the requirement for a well
balanced, sustainable force in SVN for an indefinite period.
Consequently, at this point in time I cannot justify a reduction in requirements submitted. 49/

B. Events in the Summer

   1. Emphasis on Pacification

      In the meantime, other things were happening which would have a
significant effect on U.S. strategy in Vietnam and force requirements for

supporting that strategy. First of these was the growing emphasis on pacification. The story of this growing emphasis is the subject of another study in this series. However, a few of the highlights and their implications for U.S. force requirements may be useful. Although the war between U.S. and enemy battalions progressed satisfactorily during the spring and early summer of 1966, it became increasingly apparent that the pacification effort was not keeping pace. Urged on by Komer's visits to Vietnam, both Ambassador Lodge and General Westmoreland turned their attention increasingly towards the problem of pacification. On August 3, Ambassador Lodge in his weekly report to the President mentioned that he "conferred with General Westmoreland about the Vietnamese Regular Army -- the ARVN -- contributing more to pacification. He agrees on the urgent desirability of hitting pacification hard at this time when other things are going quite well." 5/

By 10 August, Lodge was putting even more emphasis upon the pacification effort. This 10 August weekly report to the President gives an indication of the atmosphere in Saigon at this time. Lodge's cable opened with the following:

> In the struggle of the independence of Vietnam, the following can be said: we are not losing; we cannot lose in the normal sense of the word; never have things been going better; indeed, never have things been going so well. We are "on the track" with regard to almost every aspect of the war and we are winning in several...but all of this is still not called "victory." Indeed, however much they disagree about many things everyone -- in Washington and Hanoi and in Saigon -- seems to agree that what we have now is not victory. In truth we do not need to define "victory" and then go ahead and achieve it 100%. If it becomes generally believed that we are sure to win (just as it is now generally believed that we cannot lose) all else would be a mopping up. If there is "the smell of victory" we will be coasting. 6/

Lodge followed this up by listing a number of things which would psychologically mean "victory." Among these were "smashing results" in the criminal war of terrorism, subversion and local guerrilla action, movement towards constitutional democracy, spectacular success in the Chieu Hoi program and the opening of the roads in Vietnam. Lodge estimated that none of these things were "just around the corner." Therefore, it seemed to him that we had quite a stretch of time ahead of us. His questions then were "Could we shorten the time? Should we shorten the time? and if so, How? It was Lodge's judgment that a quick victory as the result of a relatively big, fast offensive might be easier to obtain than a victory achieved through a relatively moderate, slow offensive. He observed that,

> ...Maybe the Vietnamese can last indefinitely -- although it may be dangerous to assume it. But certainly it would be

helped by a quick end to the war, assuming always that a satisfactory outcome was achieved. At present, U.S. military forces
must help the Vietnamese actively in order to get the Vietnamese
pacification effort moving -- let alone the war against the big
units. We have high hopes that eventually they can undertake
it all themselves and our soldiers have already expressed appreciation for the newly created Vietnamese political action
teams and have recognized that they render the kind of service
no American can render. Nonetheless, our help is at present
indispensable in the field of criminal-terrorist war as it is
on the purely military side. 7/

To back up his feeling that now was the time for a big push, he quoted
General Eisenhower's saying that if you desire to conquer one well readied
organized and entrenched battalion with two battalions, you may succeed,
but it will take a long time and many casualties. However, if you use a
Division, you will do the job quickly and the losses will be slight.

Ambassador Lodge then went on to discuss the newest proposals for
pacification. He said that MACV had explained that:

In the past ARVN had been so hard pressed by VC main forces
and North Vietnamese army units that it had had no choice but
to concentrate on major offensive and defensive operations against
these forces, leaving regional and popular forces with primary
responsibility for providing local security in hamlets and villages.
The latter had not been adequate to this mission. Now the build-up
in US and Free World military forces makes it feasible to release
a major part of ARVN from its former primary task of search and
destroy operations and direct its main attention to pacification.
This new concept of ARVN support of pacification operations will
mean that US tactical forces will be carrying the main burden of
search and destroy operations against the VC main force in North
Vietnamese army units, while ARVN will be concentraing on pacification. 8/

This new interest was picked up as far away as CINCPAC where a draft
military strategy to accomplish the U.S. objectives for Vietnam had been
prepared. This draft was sent to MACV for his comments on 23 August
1966. 9/ This draft strategy broke down our concept for Vietnam into
three inter-dependent undertakings. The first being U.S. actions against
North Vietnam, the second, by actions against Communist forces in the
South, and third, "nation building." In the section on nation building,
draft strategy stated:

Military operations will provide a steady improvement in
security throughout the country permitting extension of government control in creating an environment in which RD can proceed.
The RD program is vital to the attainment of military success
in South Vietnam. Our forces will vigorously support and

participate in the program in such areas as logistics, sanitation, medical care, construction, and resources and population control. Military personnel having the necessary skills would be employed in political, economic and social development programs until they can be replaced by qualified civilians. 10/

On 24 August, the Roles and Missions Study Group in Saigon had completed its study and gave its recommendations to the Ambassador. 11/ Among their recommendations were several which had implications for the deployment of U.S. forces. One of these was that "as the increase of FWMAF strength permits, these forces engage with RVNAF in clearing up operations in support of RD with the primary objective of improving the associated GVN forces." They also recommended that ARVN be the principal force in RVNAF to provide the security essential for RD. To accomplish this, they recommended that the bulk of ARVN divisional combat battalions be assigned to sector commanders, that the ARVN division be removed from RD chain of command, and that the province chief be upgraded. They further recommended that Ranger units be disbanded because of their frequently intolerable conduct toward the population and that the RF and PF become provincial and district constabulary under the control of the ministry of RD. Also recommended was that the national police (special branch) assume primary responsibility with the identification and destruction of VC infra-structure.

As far as the U.S. advisory effort was concerned, they recommended that USAID/Field Operations, USAID/Office of Public Safety, JUSPAO/Field Operations, OSA/Cadre Division and OSA/Liaison Branch have one responsibility in each province at a minimum. In MACV, they recommended that a Deputy for RD be established at the division advisory, corps advisory, and COMUSMACV levels.

General Westmoreland, on 26 August, 2 days after the Roles and Missions Study was published, sent a message to CINCPAC, information copies going to the White House and State Department, Secretary of Defense, the JCS, and CIA. He opened by saying that:

> In order to promote a better understanding of the role which military operations play in the overall effort in South Vietnam I discern a need at this time to review the military situation in South Vietnam as relates to our concepts; past, present, and future. This is an appropriate time in light of the fact we are on the threshold of a new phase in the conflict resulting from our battlefield successes and from the continuing US/FWMAF build-up. 12/

He went on to describe the enemy's infiltration and build-up in his effort to gain control in South Vietnam. After characterizing his efforts from 1 May 1965 to 1 May 1966, as being basically to build up our combat and logistical forces and to learn how to employ them effectively, he went on

to describe his strategy for the period from 1 May to November 1966.
This SW monsoon season had been spent seeking to:

> ...contain the enemy through offensive tactical operations
> (referred to as "spoiling attacks" because they catch the
> enemy in the preparation phases of his own offensive), force
> him to fight under conditions of our choosing, and deny him
> attainment of his own tactical objectives. At the same time,
> we had utilized all forces that could be made available for
> area and population security in support of RD...the threat of
> enemy main forces has been of such magnitude that fewer
> friendly forces devoted to general area security and support
> of RD envisualized at the time our plans were prepared for the
> period. 13/

General Westmoreland visualized his strategy for the period 1 November
1966 to 1 May 1967 -- the NE monsoon season -- as being one of maintaining and increasing the momentum of operations. The strategy would be
one of

> ...a general offensive with maximum tactical support to area
> and population security in further support of RD. The essen-
> tial tasks of RD in nation building cannot be accomplished if
> enemy main forces can gain access to population centers and
> destroy our efforts. US/FW forces, with their mobility and
> coordination with RVNAF, must take the fight to the enemy by
> attacking his main forces and invading his base areas. Our
> ability to do this is improving steadily...The growing strength
> of US/FW forces will provide the shield that will permit ARVN
> to shift its weight of effort to an extent not heretofore feasi-
> ble, to direct support of RD. Also, I visualize that a signi-
> ficant number of the US/FW maneuver battalions will be committed
> to tactical areas of responsibility (TAOR) missions. These
> missions encompass base security and at the same time support
> RD by spreading security radially from the bases to protect more
> of the population...At the same time, ARVN troops will be avail-
> able if required to reinforce offensive operations and to serve
> as reaction forces for outlying security posts and government
> centers under attack...The priority effort of ARVN forces will
> be in direct support of the RD program. In many instances,
> province chiefs will exercise operational control over these
> units. This fact notwithstanding, the ARVN division structure
> must be maintained and it is essential that the division com-
> mander enthusiastically support RD. Our highly capable US
> division commanders who are closely associated with correspond-
> ing ARVN commanders are in a position to influence them to do
> what is required. We intend to employ all forces to get the
> best results measured, among other things, in terms of population

security; territory cleared of enemy influence; VC/NVA bases
eliminated; and enemy guerrillas, local forces, and main forces
destroyed. Barring any unforeseen change in enemy strategy, I
visualize our strategy for South Vietnam will remain essentially
the same throughout 1967...In summation, the MACV mission,which
is to assist GVN to defeat the VC/NVA forces and extend GVN
control throughout South Vietnam, prescribes our two principal
tasks. We must defeat the enemy through offensive operations
against his main forces and bases. We must assist the GVN to
gain control of the people by providing direct support of revolutionary development...Simultaneous accomplishment of these
tasks is required to allow the people of SVN to get on with the
job of nation building. 14/

Westmoreland closed his message by adding that Ambassador Lodge concurred
with the following comment:

I wish to stress my agreement with the attention paid to
this message to the importance of military support for RD.
After all, the main purpose of defeating the enemy through
offensive operations against his main forces and bases must
be to provide the opportunity through RD to get at the heart
of the matter, which is the population of South Vietnam. 15/

A possible interpretation of this message is that it is a reaction
both to a growing tendency to focus almost all attention on the pacification effort, and to the on-going battle over who would control the RD
effort. General Westmoreland seemed to be saying that, while he fully
recognized the essential importance of pacification effort, we should not
lose sight of the importance of the mission performed by US/FW forces in
keeping the enemy main force units away from the areas undergoing pacification. However, he did not want to restrict MACV only to fighting the
war against main force units. He indicated that some US/FW forces would
be used in direct support of RD activities, and recommended that the
ARVN division be left in the RD chain of command, keeping the RD effort
"militarized," and more susceptible to control through MACV. The
military's coolness to many of the recommendations of the Roles and
Missions Study is indicated by the fact that MACV did not forward the
study to CINCPAC until 26 September, while CINCPAC did not forward the
study to the JCS until 26 October.

However, Ambassador Lodge, on August 31, felt that he had finally 16/
achieved "the biggest recent American effort affecting Vietnam...giving
pacification the highest priority which it has ever had -- making it,
in effect, the main purpose of all our activities." He pointed to
Westmoreland's "concept of military operations in South Vietnam," a
MACV proposal to put ARVN in support of pacification, and the report of
the Inter-Agency Roles and Missions Study Group as evidence. He did,

however, begin to back away from the implication of his earlier cable
(in which he felt that now was the time for a big push) by quoting
General DePuy as saying that

> ...As a general rule, he does not undertake pacification
> operations until RD personnel are ready to put in. Other-
> wise, he says, the effort is wasted and ground is covered
> which simply returns to the enemy if no organized formations
> exist which can be left behind. This statement could influ-
> ence the question of how much to increase the number of US
> troops in Vietnam. If US troops assigned to pacification
> are limited by the availability of RD personnel, and RD per-
> sonnel are presently being trained at the rate of about
> 16,000 to 20,000 a year, then this fact (unless offset by
> others such as increased NVN infiltration) must have a limit-
> ing effect on the number of US troops which can profitably
> be used in Vietnam. 17/

Ambassador Lodge then quoted General Westmoreland as believing that
we had "reached a crossover point where the rate of enemy losses equals
the rate of infiltration," raising the question whether a certain number
of US troops should be pared off of one task (the fighting of main force
units) to go to the other (pacification).

He next modified his earlier quotation of General Eisenhower's to
read:

> There were advantages in having overwhelmingly superior
> military forces which would cut the time and cut the casual-
> ties -- if conditions at the specific time and place warranted
> it. Clearly, this limit on producing RD personnel is a new
> and big "if." 18/

Lodge finally rounded out his appeals to authority by quoting an article
by Sir Robert Thompson in the 12 August _Spectator_ which advised that
American military strategy

> ...should be rather to commit the minimum forces against the
> enemy's purely military forces, sufficient only to keep the
> Viet Cong dispersed and off balance. Thus the remainder of
> the American troops could then be committed to providing the
> punch and protection without which the pacification program
> still left almost entirely in Vietnamese hands will not gather
> momentum. 19/

Lodge closed by claiming that the new stress on pacification was consistent with Thompson's advice.

2. Westmoreland's Attention Turns to the Sanctuaries

However, in spite of Ambassador Lodge's belief that the attention of General Westmoreland had been turned toward pacification, and that pacification was now to receive first priority, events were occurring which began to divert COMUSMACV's attention:

The NVA/VC had planned to shift into the final annihilation phase as far back as early 1965. The buildup of US forces in particular in late 1965 and early 1966 inhibited the shift by the VC into their final phases. As an alternative the enemy attempted to build up larger forces in certain areas in accordance with Giap's version of "strategic mobility." The areas wherein the enemy attempted these buildups were Quang Tri Province in the I CTZ, and the border areas opposite the highlands in the II CTZ. In July it appeared that the enemy might also attempt to create a holding area between the highlands and the Delta by the use of sufficient forces to prevent the US and FW forces from reinforcing the main threat in the highlands.

During late June and early July the NVA attempted to move the 324B Div across the DMZ without detection and establish a base area complete with underground shelters and supply caches. At the same time the NVA/VC attempted to establish a base for a two or three division force in the southwestern part of Kontum Province. In addition, it appeared that in War Zone C an attempt would be made to train and re-equip the 9th VC Div and reinforce it with a regiment of the NVA, and to establish a base area east of Tay Ninh. With the advent of the northeast monsoon season in October the NVA/VC had planned to launch attacks from the base area into Quang Tri and Thua Thien. The NVA 2d Div was to make diversionary attacks along the coast between Quang Tri and Quang Ngai. From the base area in southern Kontum an attack to the east would be made in coordination with the NVA 3d Div in Binh Dinh. The objective was to control the Pleiku-Qui Nhon axis, a classic element of strategy which long has been of interest to the NVA and VC. The main effort in the III CTZ was an attack from the base east of Tay Ninh by the 9th VC Div and the 101st NVA Regt. The aim of this attack was to control Tay Ninh, Bien Quong, and Hau Nghia, the three provinces northwest of Saigon. In the Delta the VC continued random attacks on outposts and isolated units. Toward the end of the year the enemy disposition of one division in Quang Ngai, one in Binh Dinh and one in Phu Yen indicated a possible intention to retain control over large population centers and LOC's and to increase his access to rice, fish, and salt. The enemy dispositions also made it possible for him to threaten to isolate the I CTZ. 20/

By July, the focus of operations had shifted. In I Corps during early July, Operation HASTINGS, the largest combined operation of the

war to that date, began. This operation took place in the area south
of the DMZ. As the operation continued, heavy contact was made with the
NVA 325B Division, which had infiltrated through the DMZ with the suspected purpose of attacking and seizing Quang Tri Province. Operation
HASTINGS was followed by Operation PRAIRIE, which began on 3 August,
when one battalion was retained south of the DMZ to keep track of the
NVA 324B and 341st Divisions which had been driven back into the DMZ in
Operation HASTINGS. Contact with the enemy began immediately and continued to increase. The Marine Corps forces were redistributed and
Operation PRAIRIE continued until the end of the year. During this
period of time, amphibious Operation DECK HOUSE IV was launched against
enemy units which had been detected trying to infiltrate from the DMZ
southward along the coast. 21/

In II Corps, General Westmoreland set forth his strategy for the
highlands in the immediate future. It was apparent that, although the
enemy had begun his final SW monsoon campaign, the US SW monsoon campaign was proceeding admirably and had only to continue to keep the
enemy off balance. General Westmoreland envisioned a series of operations in which the 1st Brigade, 101st Airborne Division, the 3rd Brigade
of the 25th Infantry Division, and a brigade of the 1st Cavalry Division
would provide surveillance and a screen to the west of Kontum and
Pleiku. 22/

Late in the spring, on 10 May, the 3rd Brigade of the 25th Infantry
Division had initiated Operation PAUL REVERE along the Cambodian border
near Chupong Mountains. This operation was to be evaluated by MACV 23/
as "probably the single most significant Allied action in keeping the
enemy from mounting his vaunted SW monsoon offensive." By July, when
the NVA infiltration appeared to have become too much for them to handle,
the 1st Air Cavalry was called in to assist. When the 1st Cavalry Division
became involved the operation was renamed PAUL REVERE II. It continued
for another 25 days when the major threat seemed to abate, at which time
the operation was again redesignated, this time, PAUL REVERE III.

In III Corps, BIRMINGHAM was followed by EL PASO II, which ran
from 2 June through July. This search and destroy operation marked
the entrance of the 1st Infantry Division into the War Zone C. The
results of this operation included killing of over 800 enemy, destruction of a substantial quantity of rice, salt, and fish, and the engagement of three VC regiments, the 271st, 272nd, and 273rd -- the regiments
of the 9th VC Division. 24/

By August, Operations HASTINGS south of the DMZ in I Corps, PAUL
REVERE II along the Cambodian border in the Central Highlands of II Corps,
and EL PASO II along the Cambodian border in III Corps had indicated to
COMUSMACV that infiltration was increasing from sanctuaries outside the
boundaries of South Vietnam. The most pressing of these infiltration
routes appeared to be the one through the DMZ. On 8 August, Ambassador
Lodge sent a message to the Department of State.

The recent upsurge of enemy infiltration thru the DMZ is
causing a complete re-evaluation of Allied military posture
in Quang Tri Province. If, as is strongly indicated, the
enemy has made the decision to increase the tempo of his
operations thru the DMZ, additional steps must be taken to
block that approach effectively. 25/

Ambassador Lodge quoted General Westmoreland as advancing the suggestion, with which he agreed, that there might be merit in giving these
measures the greatest possible international flavor by constituting a
multi-national organization to help block enemy's infiltration through
the DMZ.

The organization would be known as the KANZUS Force from
its national components: Korean, Australian, New Zealand, and
US. As presently visualized, the organization would be
brigade size, with 2 US Marine and 1 ROK battalion as the
combat elements. Individual battalions would retain their
national identity. Formation of the command headquarters supporting structure would provide a place for incorporating token
remaining national contributions from Australia and New Zealand
and others such as the Philippines, should this become suitable
...The organization, commanded by a USMC officer, possibly a
brigadier general, would operate in the US tactical chain of
command in close coordination with and in support of the ARVN. 26/

Ambassador Lodge foresaw that:

The establishment of such a force might eventually provide
us with a basis for suggesting the presence of an international
force of different composition under UN or Asian regional
sponsorship which could inherit the anti-infiltration role of
KANZUS. An eventual successor would function obviously as a
political and psychological cordon sanitaire and not, of course,
as a military Maginot Line. However, a physical barrier is a
possible future development. 27/

On 10 August, General Westmoreland, in a message for Admiral Sharp
and General Wheeler, 28/ pointed out that the enemy "has increased his
rate of infiltration, formed division-size units, introduced new weapons
into his ranks, maintained lines of communication into South Vietnam,
increased his use of Cambodia as a safe haven, and recently moved a
combat division through the DMZ."

The KANZUS suggestion was only the first of a series of ideas pro-
posed by various people and agencies to limit infiltration through the
DMZ. On 16 August, Lodge forwarded to the Secretary of State
General Westmoreland's proposal that:

91

We consider defoliation of the southern portion of the DMZ
as a possible means to prevent enemy infiltration through that
area...In the event defoliation of the DMZ is not acceptable,
MACV staff has drawn up an alternate plan which would call for
defoliation of a large area just south of DMZ running east from
Laos border to fringe of coastal lowlands. Target would be
sufficiently south to insure against accidental spread into
DMZ itself. I see no serious political objections. 29/

On September 7th, the JCS sent to CINCPAC, with an information copy
to COMUSMACV, a proposal which had resulted from a Jason summer study on
an air supported anti-infiltration barrier. 30/

This study suggested that an air supported barrier system specifically designed against the North Vietnamese infiltration system through
Laos, based on further development of components that in the main were
available, might be obtainable in about a year after the decision to go
ahead. The barrier would have two somewhat different parts, one designed
for foot traffic and one against vehicles. The proposed location for
the foot traffic barrier was the region along the southern edge of the
DMZ to the Laotian border, then north to Tchepone, and then to the
vicinity of Muong Sen. The location for the anti-vehicle part of the
system was further to the west where the road network was more open to
traffic.

The anti-troop infiltration system (which would also
function against supply porters) would operate as follows.
There would be a constantly renewed minefield of non-
sterilizing Gravel (and possibly button bomblets) distributed in patterns covering interconnected valleys and slopes
over the entire barrier region...There would also be a
pattern of acoustic detectors to locate mine explosions
indicating an attempted penetration. The minefield is intended to deny opening of alternate routes for troop infiltrators and should be emplaced first. On the trails currently being used from which mines may -- we tentatively
assume -- be cleared without great difficulty, a more dense
pattern of sensors would be designed to locate groups of
infiltrators. Air strikes using Gravel and SADEYES would
then be called against these targets. The sensor patterns
would be monitored 24 hours a day by patrol aircraft. The
struck area would be reseeded with new mines.

The anti-vehicle system would consist of acoustic detectors distributed every mile or so along all truckable roads
in the interdicted area, monitored 24 hours a day by patrol
aircraft with vectored strike aircraft using SADEYE to
respond to signals that trucks or truck convoys are moving. 31/

The Gravel mines were small mines designed to damage the enemy's feet and legs. These mines were to sterilize (become non-effective) after a given period of time. The button bomblets were small mines (aspirin size) designed to give a loud report but not to injure when stepped on by a shod foot. Their purpose was to make a noise, indicating pedestrian traffic, which could be picked up by the acoustic sensors. The SADEYE was a bomblet cluster, dropped from aircraft, which was exceedingly effective against personnel.

This was not the first barrier proposed against infiltration from North Vietnam. Earlier in the year, in April, CINCPAC had replied to a suggestion to construct a conventional barrier, utilizing mines, and wire with troops to monitor and back it up, which would run from the coast across the northern portion of South Vietnam through the panhandle of Laos, to Thailand. CINCPAC and MACV had argued against this barrier because of the tremendous strain it placed upon the logistical facilities in both South Vietnam and Thailand, and because of the large number of troops which it required. 32/ The CINCPAC reply to the Jason proposal was sent to the JCS on 13 September 1966. Although CINCPAC conceded that "any measure which will effectively impede, disrupt flow of men and materiel from North Vietnam into South Vietnam merits consideration." Their judgment was that even "if we were to invest the time, effort and resources in a barrier project, it is doubtful that it would improve US position in South Vietnam." CINCPAC expressed doubt whether the barrier suggested would impede infiltration. He contended that a barrier system must be tended; if not, it could be breached with ease, while the flow of men and materiel to the VC/NVA continued. An aerial delivered obstacle would not be expected to supplant the need for soldiers on the ground, and the time, effort and resources of men and materiel required to establish a ground barrier would be tremendous. Also, he expressed his misgivings over the reliability and practicality of the electronic and other type gadgetry which would be in the barrier.

However, General Westmoreland was interested in another anti-infiltration device which was under development by the Army. This was a Caltrop -- a non-explosive device designed to penetrate enemy footwear to inflict wounds. On 24 September 1966, General Westmoreland had indicated that a 30-90 days sterilization time for the Caltrop would be acceptable, 33/ and on 2 October, he recommended to CINCPAC and JCS that the Caltrop be deployed for operational tests as soon as possible. 34/

Unfortunately, all of these ideas for halting or slowing the infiltration through the DMZ were to become effective sometime in the future. General Westmoreland's problem was very much in the present. On September 13, he sent Admiral Sharp a message on the threat to the I Corps Tactical Zone. 35/ In this message, Westmoreland laid out what he considered to be the nature of the threat posed by the enemy sanctuaries; in this case, the Demilitarized Zone and North Vietnam immediately above the DMZ.

93

The current enemy build-up...constitutes a direct threat
to US/FW GVN forces in I CTZ and to the security of Quang Tri
and Thua Thien Provinces. The seriousness of this threat
underscores the importance and urgency of utilizing all practicable means to prevent the enemy from generating a major
offensive designed to 'liberate' the provinces in question
and to inflict maximum casualties on US/FW/GVN forces....The
enemy is consolidating his position in northern I CTZ and,
according to my J-2, the 324th B Division is reinforced by the
341st Division and being further reinforced by possibly two
additional divisions, one now in the vicinity of the DMZ and
one on the move south. He continues to use the DMZ as a troop
haven and as a supply head for his forces moving into northern
I CTZ....The size of his build-up, disposition of forces, forward
stockage of supplies, AA weapons systems being deployed southward,
and depth of patrol penetrations indicate by all accepted standards that the enemy is developing an offensive as opposed to
defensive posture. By October, the weather in Laos will be
clearing and the enemy may be expected once again to move personnel and supporting materiel in quantity through the area, thus
permitting him to engage our flank in Quang Tri Province from
the west. Conversely, worsening weather in the coastal plain
of I and II CTZ's would work to the enemy's advantage in attacks
on friendly positions in these areas. Utilizing traditional
routes through the Laos panhandle he will be able to reinforce
large-scale diversionary attacks further south in coordination
with a main assault through the DMZ and against the Western
flank. The success of our efforts in coping with enemy initiatives has been based upon spoiling attacks by ground and air
forces to disrupt the plans before he is capable of completing
preparations for attack. He has thus been kept off balance from
mounting a successful offensive. It now would appear, however,
that because of our approach the enemy is employing a new tactic
entailing use of sanctuaries in the DMZ and north thereof in an
effort to prevent spoiling attacks. Since we are unable to
exercise the initiative in moving ground forces into the DMZ or
NVN we are left with fire power alone as the instrument for attack.
I consider it imperative in this regard that we utilize aerial
delivered fire power and naval gun fire in this situation if we
are to thwart the enemy's pending offensive as discussed above."

He concluded by requesting employment of B-52's against the North
Vietnamese forces infiltrating through the DMZ.

On 16 September General Westmoreland sent a message to Admiral
Sharp 36/ in which he presented his concept for handling infiltration
through the Laotian panhandle. As General Westmoreland put it, "With
the arrival of the NE monsoon season weather in Laotian panhandle will
be clearing and enemy is expected to infiltrate personnel and supporting

materiel in quantity through that area. The requirement to carry this
threat is evident. If allowed to go unchecked, it will permit enemy to
engage our flank in Quang Tri Province from the west and will permit
large-scale diversionary attacks further south. The seriousness of
this thrust led us to development of a new concept to block, deny, spoil
and disrupt the infiltration of enemy personnel and supplies through
Laos during the forthcoming dry season." The concept hinged upon two
basic principles. "First, we will intensify around-the-clock surveillance
and interdiction of known infiltration routes. This process will stress
attack of selected interdiction points as well as strikes against targets
of opportunity. Second, we will concentrate our resources on successive
key target areas to be known as 'slams.'" Once an area was designated as
a slam it would be hit with B-52 and Tactical Air Strikes to neutralize
it. This action would be followed by visual and photo air reconnaissance
and/or ground reconnaissance patrols and, if appropriate, exploitation
forces. Upon their withdrawal they would leave mines and booby traps,
and the Air Force would follow with air delivered land mines. In special
instances, General Westmoreland planned to leave stay-behind reconnaissance
parties. The term 'slam' itself came from "seek, locate, annihilate, and
monitor."

On 20 September 1966, General Westmoreland followed this up with
yet another message to Admiral Sharp. 37/

Subject: Containment of Enemy Forces in Sanctuaries

1. The threat to South Vietnam of large enemy forces in
the sanctuaries of Laos, Cambodia and North Vietnam has now
clearly emerged and is of increasing concern to me. Particularly vulnerable to enemy attacks from these sanctuaries are
the Special Forces Camps of Khe Sanh, Duc Co, Du Dop, Loc Ninh
and Song Be. We are therefore compelled to seek ways of containing the enemy forces in their sanctuaries and preventing
a major ingress of these forces in South Vietnam.

2. The problem is now under active study by my staff.
Redeployment of available forces to counter this threat may
be necessary and could seriously jeopardize other important
undertakings. Moreover, additional forces already requested
may not be sufficient to contain the enemy forces in their
sanctuaries and still accomplish other essential tasks.
Studies are now underway to determine what additional forces
will be required.

3. The above is submitted for your information in connection with the force requirements and capabilities actions now
in progress. You will be advised of the results of our current
studies.

3. Lodge's Attention Turns to Inflation

While General Westmoreland's attention was being increasingly drawn towards the problems of infiltration from sanctuaries outside the borders of Vietnam, Ambassador Lodge's attention was being increasingly drawn towards the problem of inflation inside the borders. As Ambassador Porter in Saigon wrote to Komer on 17 August:

> Fiscal year 1966 was a year of inflation. Money supply rose by 72% and Saigon working class cost of living index by 92%. Near of end of year (June 18) the piaster was devalued from 60 piasters per dollar to 118 piasters per dollar and six weeks later at time of writing, prices had begun to stabilize....It appears at this writing (Aug 11, 1966) that devaluation of June 18 has been successful surgical operation. It has increased by nearly 100% the number of piasters withdrawn from circulation for each dollar of imports, and this has sopped up enough demand to stabilize prices and actually reduce the total monetary circulation. Retail price indices have shown little change for last five weeks. Black market price of green dollars appears to have levelled off at a level of about 185-195, and price of gold also declining. There remain, however, number of threats to this newly established and so far fragile stability. 38/

He then listed five primary threats: The first was wage stability. There had been a general round of wage increases since devaluation, but it was not yet certain that labor demands had been satisfied.

Second was mounting U.S. expenditure:

> US military build-up has tendency to generate continuously greater piaster expenditure, both by US DOD officially, and by our troops as individuals. Current total rate of expenditure around 36 billion piasters a year. In US, DOD programming rise to rate of over 47 billion piasters was originally foreseen for fiscal year 1967. This order of increase would tend very definitely to upset the stabilization effort. Budget of 36 billion piasters for total DOD generated expenditure in FY 1967 has now been ordered, but this may prove very difficult to implement.

The third danger was seen to be an increased GVN budget. The total GVN civil and military expenditures were about 55 billion piasters in FY 1966, and they might rise to 70 billion or more in FY 67.

On 15 September the Saigon Embassy 39/ forwarded their latest computation of the inflationary gap, based upon programs and budgets which had been submitted for CY 67.

The GVN military budget was estimated at 57 billion piasters, while the GVN civil budget was estimated at 40.1 billion piasters. The U.S. expenditures were estimated to be as follows: US Military Personal Expenditures, 16.9 billion piasters; US Military Official Purchases, 28.7 billion; Wage Increase for Local Personnel, 2.4 billion; US Mission Civilian Housing, 1 billion; US Military Cantonments, 3 billion; Expenditures of other US Agencies, 8 billion; and Non-Official Purchases, 1 billion. With credit expansion and exports added in the total, monetary creation projected for year 1967 was 175.9 billion piasters. Total monetary absorption was estimated to be 131.8 billion piasters which left an inflationary gap of 44.1 billion piasters. The message concluded:

> We consider a gap of this magnitude to be unacceptable in light of current U.S. policies. Mission currently studying ways to reduce gap.

In answer to this news, the Department of State sent back a message on 23 September. 40/ It stated that the size of the inflationary gap was "very disturbing," and tersely indicated that:

> ...much work needs to be done on policy side to get US house in order in preparation for discussions with GVN ....Official US piaster spending estimated to be 45 billion piasters. However /according to your message, U.S. expenditures/, total 59.8 piasters, of which military expenditures alone total 48.6 excluding US civilian housing project and any portion 2.4 billion for wage increase for local military hire. This would appear to represent 50% increase over present level official US spending (including over 1/3 increase in military spending) which is certainly way out of line with stabilization. Military spending figures also gross variance with quarterly ceilings imposed for the first half of CY 67 of 9 billion piasters. 41/

Apparently, at this time Secretary McNamara was also becoming interested in the piaster situation in Vietnam. On 22 September, the JCS answered 42/ a question given them on 2 September by Secretary of Defense with regard to a preliminary examination of the piaster cost per man for the U.S. forces in Vietnam compared to those of GVN forces. Their reply indicated that "the piaster costs per man for U.S. forces /were/ several times the magnitude of the joint support piaster costs per man for GVN armed forces. /However,/ since available indicators /did/ not support a comparable ratio of combat effectiveness per man, consideration purely on a piaster cost basis might suggest increasing GVN armed forces strength in relation to U.S." On the other hand, other considerations had indicated that "we may be near the upper manpower limit on GVN armed forces strength." The Joint Chiefs indicated they would "include appropriate consideration of potential piaster cost tradeoffs in future recommendations with respect to the strength of both US and GVN armed forces in Vietnam," but did not "foresee significant piaster advantages as becoming available through feasible exchanges."

99

C. Conflicting Inexorables

1. Lodge's Piaster Ceiling

On 1 October 1966, Ambassador Lodge sent back his reply to the State Department's earlier message. 43/

A. SUMMARY

1. REPEATED ATTEMPTS TO OBTAIN MISSION COUNCIL CONCURRENCE ON PIASTER BUDGETS FOR THE CALENDAR YEAR OF 1967 HAVE NOT PROVEN SUCCESSFUL. AFTER CONSIDERABLE STUDY OF THIS ENTIRE MATTER, I, NEVERTHELESS, PROPOSE THAT WASHINGTON ACCEPT A U.S. PIASTER EXPENDITURE CEILING FOR 1967 OF 42 BILLION FOR THE U.S. MILITARY AND 16 FOR THE U.S. CIVILIAN ELEMENTS. THIS TOTAL OF 58 BILLION FOR 1967 COMPARES WITH 42 BILLION IN 1966. THESE SPENDING LEVELS, WHEN OFFSET BY ANTI-INFLATIONARY MEASURES, GIVE AN ESTIMATED SO-CALLED "INFLATIONARY GAP" OF 10 BILLION PIASTERS FOR 1967. IN MY JUDGMENT, HIGHER U.S. PIASTER SPENDING LEVELS WOULD CAUSE AN ACCELERATION OF INFLATION WHICH WOULD JEOPARDIZE OUR POLITICAL AND MILITARY PROGRESS.

B. STAFF STUDIES

2. DURING THE USAID PRESENTATION TO THE MISSION COUNCIL OF ITS 1967 PROGRAM IT BECAME APPARENT THAT A DECISION ON THE USAID PROGRAM COULD BE MADE ONLY IN CONJUNCTION WITH A REVIEW OF ALL U.S. AGENCY PROGRAMS IN TERMS OF THEIR PIASTER AND MANPOWER REQUIREMENTS. I REQUESTED A REVIEW OF PLANNED PROGRAMS AND SPENDING LEVELS OF U.S. AGENCIES AND RECEIVED REQUESTS TOTALLING 75 BILLION PIASTERS (REF. A), OF WHICH ABOUT 49 BILLION PIASTERS WERE FOR US MILITARY AND 26 BILLION FOR U.S. CIVILIAN PURPOSES. THIS COMPARES TO A TOTAL U.S. PIASTER SPENDING THIS YEAR OF ABOUT 42 BILLION PIASTERS, OF WHICH THE MILITARY CONSTITUTES 30 AND THE CIVILIAN 12. THE INCREASE REQUESTED BY THE MILITARY OF 19/BILLION IS OBVIOUSLY CLOSELY RELATED TO THE PROPOSED INCREASE IN TROOP STRENGTH WHICH LATEST REPORTS AVAILABLE TO ME SHOW LILLIGO FROM ABOUT 386,000 BY THE END OF 1966 TO ABOUT 519,000 OR SO BY THE END OF 1967. THE INCREASE REQUESTED BY THE CIVILIAN SECTOR OF 14 BILLION IS TO FINANCE THE SHARPLY EXPANDING OF "THE OTHER WAR" ACTIVITIES. TOGETHER THESE SUGGESTED BUDGET LEVELS WOULD REQUIRE AN INCREASE OF 33 BILLION PIASTERS, WHICH WHEN PLACED ON TOP OF AN ALREADY TAUT ECONOMY WOULD CERTAINLY CAUSE SERIOUS INFLATION. THE QUESTION IS NOT HOW MUCH WE MUST CUT, BUT WHERE.

3. I ASKED FOR A STAFF STUDY TO REDUCE THESE PIASTER REQUESTS TO
A LEVEL WHICH IS CONSISTENT WITH REASONABLE ECONOMIC STABILITY
DURING 1967 AND YET WHICH DOES NOT JEOPARDIZE OUR MILITARY
PROGRESS AND OUR CIVILIAN PROGRAMS. THE STAFF RECOMMENDED
A LEVEL OF 33 BILLION PIASTERS FOR THE U.S. MILITARY FORCES.
MACV STATED THAT THIS WAS TOO LOW TO ALLOW FOR EXPANSION OF
FORCES IN 1967 AND I AGREED. A SECOND STAFF STUDY WAS PREPARED
WHICH SET 39 BILLION AS A MAXIMUM FIGURE FOR THE U.S.
MILITARY FORCES. THIS TOO WAS TURNED DOWN BY GENERAL
WESTMORELAND AS BEING INADEQUATE TO MEET THE NEEDS OF
MACV DURING 1967. AGAIN, I AGREE.
4. ON THE CIVILIAN SIDE THE FIRST STAFF STUDY RECOMMENDED
A LEEL OF 18 BILLION PIASTERS OF WHICH USAID WOULD RECEIVE
12 BILLION. THIS IS 3 BILLION LESS THAN USAID REQUESTED.
THE SECOND STAFF STUDY PROPOSED 16 BILLION PIASTERS OF WHICH
USAID WOULD RECEIVE 10 BILLION. HIS REDUCTION WAS NOT
AGREED TO BY MR. MCDONALD OF USAID WHO SAID HE DID NOT
REGARD THIS REDUCED AMOUNT SUFFICIENT FINANCING FOR
ESSENTIAL GVN/US BUILD-UP ON THE CIVILIAN SIDE.
C. THE DANGER OF INFLATION
5. FAILING AGREEMENT AMONG U.S. AGENCIES, I HAVE REVIEWED
BOTH THE VARIOUS PIASTER REQUESTS AND THE ECONOMIC OUTLOOK AND
AM HERE PRESENTING FOR WASHINGTON CONSDERATION MY PROPOSAL
FOR PIASTER SPENDING CEILINGS IN CALENDAR YEAR 1967. BEFORE
PGESENTING THIS PROPOXSAL, IT IS IMPORTANT TO GET CLEARLY IN MIND
WHY AN INCREASE IN SPENDING BY U.S. AGENCIES OF 33 BILLION
PIASTERS DURING 1967 IS INTOLERABLE AND MUST BE REDUCED
LET US FOR THE SAKE OF ARGUMENT CONSIDER THIS LHOLE SUBJECT
IN THE LIGHT OF THE AMERICAN SOLDIER'S LIFE. CLEARLY, HIS LIFE
CAN BE IMPERILED SEVERAL WAYS:
A) THE MOST OBVIOUS IS BY DEFEAT IN BATTLE.
B) BUT IN THIS COUNTRY, A WILDCAT, SOUL DESTROYING INFLATION
WHICH MEANS THAT VIETNAMESE MILITARY PERSONNEL CANNOT MAKE
BOTH ENDS MEET AND THEREBY THE VIETNAMESE ARMED FORCES LOSE
FIGHTING QUALITY COULD ALSO JEOPARDIZE OUR OWF TROOPS.
C) ALSO, AN INFLATION WHICH RESULTS IN THOUSANDS OF ADULTS
DEMONSTRATING IN THE STREETS (WHERE FORMRLY WE HAVE HAD ONLY
ROCK-THROWING TEENAGERS),/ WITH THERESULTING POLITICAL
INSTABILITY LEADING TO THE OVERTHROW OF THE GOVERNMENT, COULD
BE AN EVEN MORE PRESSING DANGER--MORE SO EVEN THAN DEFEAT IN
BATTLE. INDEED, RAND REPORTS INDICATE VIET CONG PRISONERS NO
LONGER BELIEVE THAT THEY CAN BE VICTORIOUS IN BATTLE, BUT ARE
COUNTING ON OVERTHROWING THE GOVERNMENT IN SAIGON. THIS IS THE
POLITICAL DANGER WHICH INFLATION CAN CAUSE.
6. THEREFORE, IF WE LOOK AT THIS PROPOSITION SOLELY FROM THE
STANDPOINT OF THE LIFE AND DEATH OF THE SOLDIER, WE FIND OUR-
SELVES CAUGHT BETWEEN VARIOUS INEXORABLES: THE INEXORABLES
OF BATTLE, OF INFLATION, AND OF POLITICS
7. LET US NOW CONSIDER THESE VARIOUS, APPARENTLY CONFLICTING,
INEXORABLES, TAKING THE MILITARY FIRST.

8. I BELIEVE THAT WE SHOULD BRING AS MASSIVE AN AMERICAN MILITARY FORCE TO BEAR IN VIET-NAM AS WE CAN AND THAT WE SHOULD DO SO AS QUICKLY AS WE CAN--SO LONG AS THIS CAN BE DONE WITHOUT A WILDCAT INFLATION AND WITHOUT OTHER LETHAL POLITICAL EFFECTS. I BELIEVE THAT WHEN ONE HAS RECOURSE TO FORCE, OVERWHELMING STRENGTH BRINGS A QUICKER RESULT, A SHORTER WAR AND THUS FEWER CASUALTIES.

9. THE POLITICAL AND INFLATIONARY DANGERS WHICH THE PRESENCE OF TROOPS CREATES MUST BE CONSTANTLY WATCHED. WE HAVE, CLEARLY, FOR EXAMPLE, ALREADY GONE TOO FAR IN PUTTING AMERICANS--MILITARY OR CIVILIAN--INTO VIETNAMESE COMMUNITIES, JOSTLING THE VIET-NAMESE, SQUATTING ON AFTER LEASES HAVE EXPIRED, AND IN EFFECT TELLING THEM TO MOVE OVER.

10. I UNDERSTAND THAT TODAY SOME 40 PERCENT OF U.S. TROOPS ARE ASSIGNED UNDER THE GENERAL HEADING OF "GUARDING BASES" AND THAT THE REMAINING 60 PERCENT IS ENGAGED IN SO-CALLED "OFFENSIVE OPERATIONS" AGAINST MAIN FORCE UNITS. IT NOW APPEARS THAT TROOPS ARE GOING TO BE NEEDED FOR AN ENTIRELY NEW KIND OF WORK--THAT IS CONTAINMENT OF THE SANCTUARIES" IN COUNTRIES ADJACENT TO VIET-NAM WHICH ARE BECOMING VERY BIG. THE TROOPS ENGAGED IN SUCH WORK WOULD BE IN RELATIVELY UNPOPULATED COUNTRY AND THEY SHOULD NOT HAVE SERIOUS POLITICAL CONSEQUENCE.

11. IF, ON THE OTHER HAND, TROOPS ARE STATIONED IN THE DELTA, WHICH IS BOTH THICKLY POPULATED AND A GREAT RICE PRODUCING COUNTRY, THE POLITICAL AND ECONOMIC DANGERS COULD BE GREAT. THESE THINGS CANNOT BE FORETOLD AHEAD OF TIME AND MUST BE WATCHED ON A DAILY BASIS.

D. RECOMMENDATIONS

12. TURNING NOW TO THE CIVIL SIDE, I FEEL IT IS NOTEWORTHY THAT USAID EXPENDITURES FOR 1966 ARE 7.6 BILLION AND I BELIEVE WE COULD DO THE ABSOLUTELY VITAL THINGS IN 1967 WITH SOMEWHERE AROUND THAT AMOUNT. THIS IS BECAUSE OF MY BELIEF, AS REGARDS CIVIL EXPENDITURES, THAT THE PROBLEM IS NOT SO MUCH

O DO MORE AS IT IS TO DO WHAT WE DO BETTER AND MORE SKILL-FULLY, THEREBY DEVELOPING AND ENCOURAGING VIETNAMESE SELF HELP AND SKILL DEVELOPMENT. INSTEAD OF GOING TO THE 1966 LEVEL OF 7.6, I PROPOSE AN INCREASE OF UP TO 10. WITH OTHER CIVILIAN EXPENDITURES I THUS PROPOSE AN OVERALL CIVILIAN CEILING OF 16 BILLION PIASTERS. HAVING IN MIND THE FACT THAT IN THIS PAINFUL CONTEMPLATION THE IMMOVEABLE FORCE IS UP AGAINST THE IRRESIST-IBLE OBJECT, I BELIEVE THIS WILL BE THE BEST THING TO DO -- DIFFICULT THOUGH IT IS.

13. THE U.S. MILITARY IS THUS ASSIGNED A CEILING OF 42 BILLION PIASTERS FOR 1967. THIS PROPOSED MILITARY CEILING OF 42 BILLION PIASTERS IS 12 BILLION HIGHER THAN THE SPENDING LEVEL FOR 1966. IT CONSTITUTES AN INCREASE OF 9 BILLION PIASTERS ABOVE THE FIRST STAFF STUDY RECOMMENDATION OF 33 BILLION. IT RE-PRESENTS AN INCREASE OF 3 BILLION ABOVE THE SECOND STAFF STUDY. THE LEVEL OF 42 BILLION PIASTERS APPEARS TO BE REASONABLE IN

LIGHT OF OUR SERIOUS INFLATIONARY PROBLEM. THIS REPRESENTS AN
INCREASE OF 6 BILLION PIASTERS ABOVE THE CURRENT PIASTER
CEILING FOR THIS FISCAL YEAR OF 36 BILLION PIASTERS. WHILE IT
IS CLEAR THAT SOME INCREASE OVER THE CURRENT CEILING IS
NECEUSARY IN VIEW OF THE TROOP BUILDUP, I FEEL THAT AN INCREASE
ABOVE 42 BILLION WOULD BE DANGEROUS. SUCH AN INCREASE WOULD
CONFRONT US WITH A CHOICE BETWEEN STILL FURTHER REDUCING CIVILIAN
VROGRAMS OR FACING DANGEROUS INFLATION DURING 1967. NEITHER
OF THESE ALTERNATIVES IS ACCEPTABLE.
14. I, THEREFORE, RECOMMEND THAT WASHINGTON APPROVE MY
PROPOSAL FOR U.S. PIASTER SPENDING WHICH, WHEN ADDED TO
VIETNAMESE SPENDING, WOULD GIVE THE FOLLOWING GRAND TOTAL:
A MILITARY SENIOR BUDGET OF 92BILLION PIASTERS OF WHICH 50
WOULD BE FOR VNAF AND 42 FOR MACV, AND A CIVILIAN PIASTER
BUDGET OF 41 BILLION, OF WHICH 25 WOULD BE FOR GVN CIVIL BUDGET,
10 FOR USAID, AND 6 FOR NON-USAID U.S. MOHER EXPENDITURES
TOTAL 15 BILLION, OF WHICH CREDIT EXPANSION AMOUNTS TO 12.
THIS MAKES A TOTAL OF PIASTER EXPENDITURES OF 148 BILLION.
FACTORS WHICH DECREASE THE MONEY SUPPLY, SUCH AS IMPORTS
AND TAXES, ARE ESTIMATED TO TOTAL 138 BILLION PIASTERS, LEAVING
A SO-CALLED "GAP" OF 10 BILLION (SEPARATE TELEGRAM WILL FOLLOW
GIVING FURTHER DETAILS).
. WEAKNESSES OF THE GVN
15. QLEASE NOTE TWO POINTS WHICH REINFORCE THE NECESSITY FOR
KEEPING OUR PLANNED "INFLATIONARY GAP" TO 10 BILLION PIASTERS
OR LESS.
16. FIRST, I DOUBT WHETHER ANY STABILIZATION AGREEMENT HERE
CAN DO SO MUCH OR SO WELL AS DESCRIBED IN REF C. VIETNAMESE
OFFICIALS WILL PROBABLY TRY TO OBLIGE US BY AGREEING TO A NUMBER
OF THINGS, SIMPLY IN ORDER TO BE POLITE. BUT WHEN IT COMES TO
MEASURES WHICH REALLY HAVE SOVE TEETH, I AM NOT OPTIMISTIC.
WHAT MADE KY'S MEASURES ON DEVALUATION AND PORT OPERATIONS
VALUABLE IS THAT THEY WERE THINGS WHICH WERE CLEARCUT AND WHICH
HE COULD CARRY OUT. I FEAR A MUCH LARGER U.S.-SPONSORED PROGRAM
IN VIET-NAM BECAUSE I BELIEVE THAT THE GVN IS ADMINISTRATIVELY
TOO WEAK TO KARRY THEM OUT AND SPECIAL INTERESTS ARE STILL
VERY STRONG. IT IS A BIT LIKE A FLYWHEEL BELT WHICH CAN BE
TIGHTENED SO MUCH THAT TRACTION IS LOST AND THE MOTOR MERELY
SPINS WITHOUT GETTING THE FLYWHEEL TO VOVE. AS I HAVE SAID
IN PREVIOUS TELEGRAMS, I BELIEVE THERE IS A RATE AT WHICH
THESE PEOPLE CAN GO AHEAD AND ANYTHING BEYOND THAT RATE
TENDS TO BE LIP SERVICE. THE GOVERNMENT CONTINUES, IN MY
MIND, TO RESEMBLE LITTLE EVA, JUNPING FROM ICE FLOE TO ICE
FLOE. THIS MAKES THE SEPTEMBER 11 ELECTION A PARTICULARLY
WELCOME MIRACLE, BUT SOMEWHAT OF A VIRACLE NEVERTHELESS.
THE GOVERNMENT'S POSITION IS TENUOUS AND PRECARIOUS.
17. SECOND, OUR GAP ESTIMATES ARE ON THE OPTIMISTIC SIDE. I
DOUBT WHETHER THE GVN CAN RAISE DOMESTIC TAX REVENUES FROM
ABOUT 13.5 BILLION PIASTERS THIS YEAR TO 20 BILLION PIASTERS
NEXT YEAR. FURTHERMORE, GIVEN THE PRESENT LULL IN THE MARKET

AND CONTINUING PORT CONGESTION, IT IS DOUBTFUL THAT IMPORTS WILL REACH THE ASSUMED LEVEL OF $725 MILLION DURING 1967. TO THE EXTENT THEY DO NOT AND CUSTOMS COLLECTION ARE LESS THAN PLANNED, WE WILL BE FACED WITH A LARGER GAP AND HENCE MORE INFLATION THAN WE NOW ANTICIPATE IN OUR PLANNING FIGURES.

F. KEY ASSUMPTIONS

18. BASED ON THE ABOVE THINKING, WE MADE AS STRINGENT A BUDGET PLAN AS WE COULD, CONSISTENT WITH OUR OTHER MILITARY AND CIVILIAN OBJECTIVES. OUR PROPOSED BUDGET PLAN IS BASED ON THE FOLLOWING ASSUMPTIONS.

A. VIETNAMESE ARMED FORCES ARE ASSUMED TO HOLD DURING 1967 AT A FORCE LEVEL EQUAL TO THAT REACHED AT THE END OF OCTOBER 1966. I FEEL THAT GIVEN OUR INFLATIONARY SITUATION, IT IS IMPERATIVE THAT THE VIETNAMESE MILITARY NOT PLACE FURTHER DRAINS ON THE LIMITED MANPOWER RESOURCES IN THIS COUNTRY. THESE DRAINS HAVE HAD A WEAKENING EFFECT ON THE ABILITY OF THE CIVIL GOVERNMENT TO PERFORM. WITH THE IMPROVEMENT IN OUR MILITARY POSITION DURING 1966, IT SEEMS DESIRABLE TO CONCENTRATE IN 1967 ON IMPROVING THE QUALITY OF THE VN ARMED FORCES RATHER THAN EXPANDING THEM IN SIZE.

B) WE HAVE ASSUMED A WAGE INCREASE BY THE GVN OF ONLY 10 PER CENT. CLEARLY THIS IS THE MINIMUM WAGE INCREASE THAT WOULD BE ACCEPTABLE.

C) WE HAVE HELD BOTH THE CIVIL AND THE MILITARY GVN BUDGETS TO BARE-BONES LEVELS.

D) WE HAVE ASSUMED THAT THE MILITARY WILL MAINTAIN THEIR PIASTER EXPENDITURES THROUGHOUT CALENDAR YEAR 1967 AT THE 42 BILLION PIASTER LEVEL. THIS IS A CRITICAL ASSUMPTION AND IS BASED ON MY UNDERSTANDING THAT SECRETARY MCNAMARA HAS ISSUED INSTRUCTIONS TO HOLD U.S. MILITARY PIASTER SPENDING TO WITHIN 36 BILLION PIASTERS DURING THIS FISCAL YEAR. ADMITTEDLY, THIS WILL MEAN A FURTHER STRETCHOUT OF CONSTRUCTION PROGRAMS, ADDITIONAL MEASURES TO REDUCE PERSONAL EXPENDITURES BY U.S. TROOPS, AND POSSIBLY THE NEED FOR ADDITIONAL U.S. SUPPORT TROOPS. IF THIS BUDGET LEVEL CANNOT BE HELD, IT WILL JEOPARDIZE OUR ENTIRE ANTI-INFLATIONARY PROGRAM HERE IN VIET-NAM. I AM MOST APPRECIATIVE OF THE UNDERSTANDING AND EXCELLENT COOPERATION WHICH SECRETARY MCNAMARA HAS GIVEN TO US ON THIS SUBJECT.

E) WE HAVE CUT THE USAID/GVN PROGRAMS BY ONE-THIRD, BRINGING THEM DOWN FROM THE 15 WHICH WAS REQUESTED TO 10 BILLION PIASTERS. I WAS MOST RELUCTANT TO MAKE A CUT OF SUCH PROPORTIONS IN THIS VITAL AREA, BUT FEEL THAT WE CANNOT MEET OUR STABILIZATION OBJECTIVES UNLESS BOTH THE CIVILIAN AND MILITARY PROGRAMS ARE CUT. CUTTING ONE WITHOUT THE OTHER NEITHER SERVES OUR INTERESTS NOR ALLOWS US TO MEET OUR OBJECTIVES. FURTHERMORE, IT SEEMS TO ME DESIRABLE ON THE CIVILIAN SIDE, TO CONCENTRATE ON IMPROVING THE QUALITY OF PROGRAMS AS WELL AS EXPANDING THEM. LODGE

In essence, what Ambassador Lodge seemed to be looking for was a solution which would balance the conflicting inexorables, especially those of battle and inflation. He ended up by straddling the fence. He stated that he believed that we should "bring as massive an American military force to bear in Vietnam that we can and that we should do so as quickly as we can." But he hedged by adding "so long as this can be done without a wildcat inflation and other lethal political effects." He seemed to think he had found a solution in Westmoreland's new fascination with the sanctuaries across the borders of South Vietnam. He hoped that with large numbers of troops employed in the less populated areas, it might be possible to have both the massive force quickly employed and a relatively small inflationary effect. However, he seems to have been misjudging what Westmoreland had in mind.

Nevertheless, his 42 billion piaster limit on U.S. military expenditures was to become one of the controlling factors in the decision on Program #4 strengths.

2. Westmoreland's Reclama

On 5 October, COMUSMACV sent a message to Washington to set forth his reclama to the Ambassador's proposed piaster expenditure limit. 44/

1. ....While MACV does not concur in the Ambassador's message, we are fully committed to maintaining restrictions on US spending in Vietnam. COMUSMACV's position concerning the military and economic situation in SVN is as follows:

A. The primary mission of US forces in RVN is to defeat the VC/NVA forces in SVN, and to assist GVN in extending governmental control throughout the land. If MACV must operate within a piaster ceiling of 42 billion for CY 67 and if our actual deployments approach the approved deployment level as identified in OSD's Southeast Asia Deployment Program No. 3 dated 1 Aug 66, it would mean that US troop deployments to RVN would have to stop about mid-December 1966. Such action would deprive us of at least one division and the required combat support and combat service support necessary to balance our forces as identified and approved in the CY 66 force requirements. A US military piaster expenditure ceiling of 47.4 billion is the minimum requirement needed by MACV in order to conduct sustained operations of the OSD FY 66 approved force level of 445,000, an average of 440,000 during CY 67.

B. While it is recognized that inflation is a serious problem, a reduction of US military piaster spending with a corresponding reduction of US forces or military efforts could seriously jeopardize our military progress.

103

C. Today, with the US/FW forces available, large scale sustained operations can be mounted within any geographical area of SVN. However, with the enemy's increasing buildup capability he has been able to increase his combat strength in SVN to 131,200, approximately 7 combat divisions. It is estimated that he will have a combat strength of 147,300 consisting of 181 Inf Bns and 63 Combat Spt Bns, or approximately 10 Combat Divisions, in country during the second quarter of CY 67. By maximizing his training capability in NVN, the input could be substantially increased. If the enemy adopts this course of action, further selected increases in US/FW strength in SVN may be required over requested 1967 force levels.

D. The CY 66 US/FW force increases will allow tactical commanders to step up their search and destroy and other offensive operations both in size and frequency. This increase is necessary to turn the tide of the enemy buildup. The estimated enemy attrition made possible by this force increase would hold the enemy buildup to approximately 147,300 combat strength as stated above. If the US/FW forces continue attrition of the enemy at the same increasing rate during the next 12 month period as accomplished during Jan-Jul 66, the enemy combat strength should start to decline during the second quarter CY 67. However, if the enemy accelerates buildup in SVN to his maximum capability, his strength probably will not start to decline until some time in CY 68. The enemy continues to show every inclination to continue his military efforts.

E. On the basis of the foregoing, it can be seen that a large scale forced deferral of troop increases at this time, while the enemy continues to build up, would be a most imprudent course of action that could jeopardize seriously....

* * * * *

2. Part C, Ref A discusses the dangers of inflation and refers to the RAND reports on Viet Cong prisoners. It is recognized that the political danger of inflation is a continuing threat to the GVN and that we must use all available resources to insure the economy is not faced with a "wildcat" rise in prices. However, we must not at this time impose a restriction that possibly would hamstring our military effort.

3. RAND reports are difficult to assess. The time lag in publication and the conclusions drawn from the studies will vary.

It is true that the majority of "hard core" captives and defectors
cited in the RAND reports no longer predict an inevitable VC
victory, many of this selected group now see the war as a stalemate with each side building up its respective force. Although
some of this group now see defeat, in the main the confidence of
the individual enemy soldier in a military victory has dwindled
due, in large measure, to the string of defeats he has suffered
at the hands of the US/GVN/Free World Forces. However, limitation of these US/GVN forces for economic reasons would curtail the
momentum of the military effort at this critical point and conceivably jeopardize the overall US effort in Vietnam.

4.   Para 10 & 11, Part C, Ref A discusses troop utilization
but does not depict clearly the military concept of operations in
Vietnam for CY 67. Our concept recognizes and is built around
two equally important, continuing and complementary requirements
which call for the same type of military resources and flexibility
in their application. On the one hand, we must maintain the
security of our bases and key population and food producing centers
and assist in expanding security of areas under Government control.
On the other hand we must seek out and destroy the enemy's main
forces and his bases to create the environment in which meaningful
Revolutionary Development can proceed. The priority of US/FW
military efforts will continue to be devoted to our main mission,
the destruction of enemy main forces and bases. The "entirely
new kind of work" referred to by the Ambassador is in reality a
continuation of our surveillance and rapid reaction tactics vis-
a-vis enemy forces occupying sanctuaries in adjacent territory. We
are according heightened emphasis to this effort, and may find it
necessary to ask for additional forces to insure its success.

Information copies of this message were sent to the Secretary of State,
Secretary of Defense, and the Joint Chiefs of Staff.

Also on 5 October, Dr. Alain Enthoven, Assistant Secretary of Defense
for Systems Analysis, in a memorandum for the Secretary of Defense, 45/
compared Lodge's proposed 42 billion piaster budget with several other
relevant figures. The first figure was 41 billion piasters, which would
allow Program 3 deployments based upon actual July and August piaster
spending rates, but which did not allow for any price increases during
CY 67. The next figure given was 44 billion piasters which allowed
for completion of Program 3 deployments and for prices to rise during
the period July 1966 to December 1967 by 7%. The third figure given was
43.6 billion piasters which would allow a rise in U.S. strength to a total
of 525,000 by December of 1967, but did not allow room for inflation. The
last figure given was 47.4 billion piasters, which would allow completion
of CINCPAC's deployment plan which envisioned an end '68 strength of
569,000, but which did not allow for any increase in prices. Assistant

105

Secretary Enthoven pointed out that differences in spending associated
with different deployments were small in CY 67 relative to the uncertainty about spending for a given deployment. However, he also added
that if Lodge's expenditure program were achieved, it was likely that
at best the rate of inflation would be reduced to about 20% per year.
At this rate, he estimated that even Program 3 would cost nearly 50
billion piasters.

3. The JCS: Issue Papers and World Wide Posture

        Meanwhile, the Joint Chiefs of Staff had completed their review
of CINCPAC's 18 June requirements for CY 66 and 67 and the issue papers
which the Secretary of Defense had given them on 5 August. On 24 September,
they forwarded their review of these requirements and their answers to the
issue papers. 46/ This document was reviewed by Dr. Enthoven's office
and on 29 September, he sent a memorandum to the Secretary of Defense. He
reported that deletions of requirements by CINCPAC and the JCS totaled
49,000 personnel of the 215,000 add-on requirements for US forces in
PACOM (excluding Hawaii). Of the deletions, 39,000 were included in the
issue papers. He added that his SEA Programs Division was in the process
of analyzing the detailed rationale for the remaining requested units and
that new deployment issue papers would be provided to the Secretary of
Defense for his approval on 3 October. 46a/ Apparently, the Secretary of
Defense approved them for on 6 October he forwarded another set of deployment issue papers to the Chairman of the Joint Chiefs of Staff, asking
that they review the issues and have their recommendations for him by
1 November when he planned to make his decision on the papers. The items
considered in the issue papers totaled some 54,000 troops out of CINCPAC's
total request of 569,000 for deployment to South Vietnam. The leading
items considered were the 15,000 troops (9,000 Army and 6,000 AF) which
were involved in IV Corps operations and 12,000 Artillery troops.

        By this time, Secretary McNamara had already decided to make a trip
to Saigon to see if he could get a better feel for the situation there.
However, before he departed, the Joint Chiefs of Staff forwarded to him
a paper analyzing the world-wide military posture of the United States in
light of the August CINCPAC requirements study for CY 1967. 47/

        Assuming that there would be no call-up of reserves, no change in
rotation policies, and that resources for the proposed deployments would
be obtained from the world-wide military structure, the impact of meeting
the CINCPAC 1967 requirements, as they saw it, would be tremendous. The
Army would suffer most, meeting the CINCPAC requirements (12 additional
maneuver battalions) on the average six to eight months late, and in the
process emasculating CONUS STRAF, leaving it but two airborne brigade
forces for 1967 and the first part of 1968. Other NATO reinforcing
division forces could not be ready from the Army until late 1968. USAREUR,
USARAL and PACOM reserve would all be at a reduced level because of
"qualitative personnel withdrawals." In total, the Army would have a
force deficiency of three and two-thirds active division forces if it
were to satisfy strategic reserve and sustaining base requirements.

Carrier pilots would remain the major Naval shortage. The Air Force, upon completion of the required deployments (in September of 1967) "would not have the capability to deploy rapidly any combat-ready tactical fighter forces." With one exception, all tactical and reconnaissance units in the United States were assigned and executing training tasks. To meet CINCPAC requirements would require drawing down from 21 TFS (486 aircraft) in Europe to 13 squadrons or 288 aircraft. Given all Air Force commitments and responsibilities to respond to NATO and provide other reinforcements a short-fall of some 22 TFS (445 aircraft), 5 TRS (90 aircraft) and 4 TCS (64 aircraft) would result.

In the "guts" portion of the memorandum detailed consideration was given to the extent which mobilization of the reserves could alleviate shortages. It noted these:

Army. Significant withdrawals of equipment have been made from the reserve components to support new activations. This has resulted in a degradation of the training capability and the mobilization potential of the reserve components. Therefore, full or partial mobilization of reserve units would have only limited effectiveness in accelerating Army deployments. However, mobilization of reserve units would permit a more rapid restoration, personnel-wise, of the STRAF. In addition, reserve unit mobilization and subsequent deployment of these units to Europe or Korea would accelerate restoration of Army forces in those areas. Selective mobilization of reservists possessing critical skills could greatly improve the quality of the training and sustaining base and the quality of deploying units which are now having to deploy with shortages of skills and experienced leaders. Selective mobilization would permit some acceleration of unit deployments.

Air Force. Mobilization could provide 20 deployable ANG tactical fighter squadrons (409 aircraft minimum) and 12 ANG tactical reconnaissance squadrons. While not nuclear capable and possessing less modern aircraft, the TFSs would partially provide for the 22 TFS shortfall anticipated. By using older equipment, shortfalls in TRSs would be reduced to zero, and the CONUS base posture improved. TCS shortfalls would be reduced through use of C-119 aircraft. Some personnel shortages would be alleviated.

* * * * *

In conclusion, the Services cannot fully respond to CINCPAC's CY 1966 (adjusted) and CY 1967 force requirements on the time schedule he has prescribed and under the conditions stated in paragraph 4, above. Providing the preponderance of his requirements, even on a delayed schedule, would further impair the US military posture and capability to maintain forward deployments to deter aggression world-wide. It would

TOP SECRET - Sensitive

further reduce the capability to reinforce NATO rapidly, to provide forces for other contingencies, and to maintain a sufficient rotation and training base. Mobilization of reserves, extension of terms of service, and extending over-seas tours would assist in alleviating shortfalls associated with satisfying CINCPAC's requirements. Certain critical problems cannot be fully resolved by mobilization because of equipment and skill shortages. Of particular note in the case of the Army, equipment withdrawals from the Reserve components have substantially weakened the Army's reserve structure. 48/

Interestingly enough, the kind of mobilization the JCS were talking about in JCSM-646-66 was a full-blown affair which added 688,500 reservists generally in units to the Army, Air Force, Navy and Marines by December 1966. Other than listing units, availability dates and programmed total strengths, the memorandum did not delve into specific applications of these reserve forces or how they would alleviate the manpower/unit/equip-ment crunch which the JCS described. 49/

D. McNamara Goes to Saigon -- Decision on Four

With all of this information in hand, Secretary McNamara departed for Saigon. While the records available do not indicate what went on in Saigon, the results were clearly spelled out in the Secretary of Defense's Memorandum for the President, submitted upon his return. 50/

1. A Memorandum for the President

1. Evaluation of the situation. In the report of my last trip to Vietnam almost a year ago, I stated that the odds were about even that, even with the then-recommended deployments, we would be faced in early 1967 with a military stand-off at a much higher level of conflict and with "pacification" still stalled. I am a little less pessimistic now in one respect. We have done somewhat better militarily than I anticipated. We have by and large blunted the communist military initiative -- any military victory in South Vietnam the Viet Cong may have had in mind 18 months ago has been thwarted by our emergency deployments and actions. And our program of bombing the North has exacted a price.

My concern continues, however, in other respects. This is because I
see no reasonable way to bring the war to an end soon. Enemy morale has not
broken -- he apparently has adjusted to our stopping his drive for military
victory and has adopted a strategy of keeping us busy and waiting us out
(a strategy of attriting our national will). He knows that we have not been,
and he believes we probably will not be, able to translate our military
successes into the "end products" -- broken enemy morale and political
achievements by the GVN.

The one thing demonstrably going for us in Vietnam over the past year
has been the large number of enemy killed-in-action resulting from the big
military operations. Allowing for possible exaggeration in reports, the
enemy must be taking losses -- deaths in and after battle -- at the rate of
more than 60,000 a year. The infiltration routes would seem to be one-way
trails to death for the North Vietnamese. Yet there is no sign of an impending break in enemy morale and it appears that he can more than replace
his losses by infiltration from North Vietnam and recruitment in South
Vietnam.

Pacification is a bad disappointment. We have good grounds to be pleased
by the recent elections, by Ky's 16 months in power, and by the faint signs
of development of national political institutions and of a legitimate civil
government. But none of this has translated itself into political achievements at Province level or below. Pacification has if anything gone backward.
As compared with two, or four, years ago, enemy full-time regional forces and
part-time guerrilla forces are larger; attacks, terrorism and sabotage have
increased in scope and intensity; more railroads are closed and highways cut;
the rice crop expected to come to market is smaller; we control little, if any,
more of the population; the VC political infrastructure thrives in most of the
country, continuing to give the enemy his enormous intelligence advantage; full
security exists nowhere (not even behind the US Marines' lines and in Saigon);
in the countryside, the enemy almost completely controls the night.

Nor has the ROLLING THUNDER program of bombing the North either significantly
affected infiltration or cracked the morale of Hanoi. There is agreement in the
intelligence community on these facts (see the attached Appendix).

In essence, we find ourselves -- from the point of view of the important
war (for the complicity of the people) -- no better, and if anything worse off.
This important war must be fought and won by the Vietnamese themselves. We have
known this from the beginning. But the discouraging truth is that, as was the
case in 1961 and 1963 and 1965, we have not found the formula, the catalyst,
for training and inspiring them into effective action.

2. Recommended actions. In such an unpromising state of affairs, what should we do? We must continue to press the enemy militarily; we must make demonstrable progress in pacification; at the same time, we must add a new ingredient forced on us by the facts. Specifically, we must improve our position by getting ourselves into a military posture that we credibly would maintain indefinitely -- a posture that makes trying to "wait us out" less attractive. I recommend a five-pronged course of action to achieve those ends.

a. Stabilize US force levels in Vietnam. It is my judgment that, barring a dramatic change in the war, we should limit the increase in US forces in SVN in 1967 to 70,000 men and we should level off at the total of 470,000 which such an increase would provide.a/ It is my view that this is enough to punish the enemy at the large-unit operations level and to keep the enemy's main forces from interrupting pacification. I believe also that even many more than 470,000 would not kill the enemy off in such numbers as to break their morale so long as they think they can wait us out. It is possible that such a 40 percent increase over our present level of 325,000 will break the enemy's morale in the short term; but if it does not, we must, I believe, be prepared for and have underway a long-term program premised on more than breaking the morale of main force units. A stabilized US force level would be part of such a long-term program. It would put us in a position where negotiations would be more likely to be productive, but if they were not we could pursue the all-important pacification task with proper attention and resources and without the spectre of apparently endless escalation of US deployments.

b. Install a barrier. A portion of the 470,000 troops -- perhaps 10,000 to 20,000 -- should be devoted to the construction and maintenance of an infiltration barrier. Such a barrier would lie near the 17th parallel -- would run from the sea, across the neck of South Vietnam (choking off the new infiltration routes through the DMZ) and across the trails in Laos. This interdiction system (at an approximate cost of $1 billion) would comprise to the east a ground barrier of fences, wire, sensors, artillery, aircraft and mobile troops; and to the west -- mainly in Laos -- an interdiction zone covered by air-laid mines and bombing attacks pin-pointed by air-laid acoustic sensors.

The barrier may not be fully effective at first, but I believe that it can be made effective in time and that even the threat of its becoming effective can substantially change to our advantage the character of the war. It would hinder enemy efforts, would permit more efficient use of the limited number of friendly troops, and would be persuasive evidence both that our sole aim is to protect the South from the North and that we intend to see the job through.

----

a/ Admiral Sharp has recommended a 12/31/67 strength of 570,000. However, I believe both he and General Westmoreland recognize that the danger of inflation will probably force an end 1967 deployment limit of about 470,000.

110

c. Stabilize the ROLLING THUNDER program against the North. Attack sorties in North Vietnam have risen from about 4,000 per month at the end of last year to 6,000 per month in the first quarter of this year and 12,000 per month at present. Most of our 50 percent increase of deployed attack-capable aircraft has been absorbed in the attacks on North Vietnam. In North Vietnam, almost 84,000 attack sorties have been flown (about 25 percent against fixed targets), 45 percent during the past seven months.

Despite these efforts, it now appears that the North Vietnamese-Laotian road network will remain adequate to meet the requirements of the Communist forces in South Vietnam -- this is so even if its capacity could be reduced by one-third and if combat activities were to be doubled. North Vietnam's serious need for trucks, spare parts and petroleum probably can, despite air attacks, be met by imports. The petroleum requirement for trucks involved in the infiltration movement, for example, has not been enough to present significant supply problems, and the effects of the attacks on the petroleum distribution system, while they have not yet been fully assessed, are not expected to cripple the flow of essential supplies. Furthermore, it is clear that, to bomb the North sufficiently to make a radical impact upon Hanoi's political, economic and social structure, would require an effort which we could make but which would not be stomached either by our own people or by world opinion; and it would involve a serious risk of drawing us into open war with China.

The North Vietnamese are paying a price. They have been forced to assign some 300,000 personnel to the lines of communication in order to maintain the critical flow of personnel and materiel to the South. Now that the lines of communication have been manned, however, it is doubtful that either a large increase or decrease in our interdiction sorties would substantially change the cost to the enemy of maintaining the roads, railroads, and waterways or affect whether they are operational. It follows that the marginal sorties -- probably the marginal 1,000 or even 5,000 sorties -- per month against the lines of communication no longer have a significant impact on the war. (See the attached excerpts from intelligence estimates.)

When this marginal inutility of added sorties against North Vietnam and Laos is compared with the crew and aircraft losses implicit in the activity (four men and aircraft and $20 million per 1,000 sorties), I recommend, as a minimum, against increasing the level of bombing of North Vietnam and against increasing the intensity of operations by changing the areas or kinds of targets struck. a/

----

a/ See footnote on page 82

Under these conditions, the bombing program would continue the pressure and would remain available as a bargaining counter to get talks started (or to trade off in talks). But, as in the case of a stabilized level of US ground forces, the stabilization of ROLLING THUNDER would remove the prospect of ever-escalating bombing as a factor complicating our political posture.and distracting from the main job of pacification in South Vietnam.

At the proper time, as discussed on pages 6-7 below, I believe we should consider terminating bombing in all of North Vietnam, or at least in the Northeast zones, for an indefinite period in connection with covert moves toward peace.

d. Pursue a vigorous pacification program. As mentioned above, the pacification (Revolutionary Development) program has been and is thoroughly stalled. The large-unit operations war, which we know best how to fight and where we have had our successes, is largely irrelevant to pacification as long as we do not lose it. By and large, the people in rural areas believe that the GVN when it comes will not stay but that the VC will; that cooperation with the GVN will be punished by the VC; that the GVN is really indifferent to the people's welfare; that the low-level GVN are tools of the local rich; and that the GVN is ridden with corruption.

Success in pacification depends on the interrelated functions of providing physical security, destroying the VC apparatus, motivating the people to cooperate and establishing responsive local government. An obviously necessary but not sufficient requirement for success of the Revolutionary Development cadre and police is vigorously conducted and adequately prolonged clearing operations by military troops, who will "stay" in the area, who behave themselves decently and who show some respect for the people.

This elemental requirement of pacification has been missing.

In almost no contested area designated for pacification in recent years have ARVN forces actually "cleared and stayed" to a point where cadre teams, if available, could have stayed overnight in hamlets and survived, let alone accomplish their mission. VC units of company and even battalion size remain in operation, and they are more than large enough to overrun anything the local security forces can put up.

Now that the threat of a Communist main-force military victory has been thwarted by our emergency efforts, we must allocate far more attention and a portion of the regular military forces (at least half of the ARVN and perhaps a portion of the US forces) to the task of providing an active and permanent security screen behind which the Revolutionary Development teams and police can operate and behind which the political struggle with the VC infrastructure can take place.

The US cannot do this pacification security job for the Vietnamese. All we can do is "massage the heart." For one reason, it is known that we do not intend to stay; if our efforts worked at all, it would merely postpone the eventual confrontation of the VC and GVN infrastructures. The GVN must do the job; and I am convinced that drastic reform is needed if the GVN is going to be able to do it.

The first essential reform is in the attitude of GVN officials. They are generally apathetic, and there is corruption high and low. Often appointments, promotions, and draft deferments must be bought; and kickbacks on salaries are common. Cadre at the bottom can be no better than the system above them.

The second needed reform is in the attitude and conduct of the ARVN. The image of the government cannot improve unless and until the ARVN improves markedly. They do not understand the importance (or respectability) of pacification nor the importance to pacification of proper, disciplined conduct. Promotions, assignments and awards are often not made on merit, but rather on the basis of having a diploma, friends or relatives, or because of bribery. The ARVN is weak in dedication, direction and discipline.

Not enough ARVN are devoted to area and population security, and when the ARVN does attempt to support pacification, their actions do not last long enough; their tactics are bad despite US prodding (no aggressive small-unit saturation patrolling, hamlet searches, quick-reaction contact, or offensive night ambushes); they do not make good use of intelligence; and their leadership and discipline are bad.

Furthermore, it is my conviction that a part of the problem undoubtedly lies in bad management on the American as well as the GVN side. Here split responsibility -- or "no responsibility" -- has resulted in too little hard pressure on the GVN to do its job and no really solid or realistic planning with respect to the whole effort. We must deal with this management problem now and deal with it effectively.

One solution would be to consolidate all US activities which are primarily part of the civilian pacification program and all persons engaged in such activities, providing a clear assignment of responsibility and a unified command under a civilian relieved of all other duties.a/ Under this approach, there would be a carefully delineated division of responsibility between the civilian-in-charge and an element of COMUSMACV under a senior officer, who would give the subject of planning for and providing hamlet security the highest priority in attention and resources. Success will depend on the men selected for the jobs on both sides (they must be among the highest rank and most competent administrators in the US Government), on complete cooperation among the US elements, and on the extent to which the South Vietnamese can be shocked out of their present pattern of behavior. The first work of this reorganized US pacification organization should be to produce within 60 days a realistic and detailed plan for the coming year.

From the political and public-relations viewpoint, this solution is preferable -- if it works. But we cannot tolerate continued failure. If it fails after a fair trial, the only alternative in my view is to place the entire pacification program -- civilian and military -- under General Westmoreland. This alternative would result in the establishment of a Deputy COMUSMACV for Pacification who would be in command of all pacification staffs in Saigon and of all pacification staffs and activities in the field; one person in each corps, province and district would be responsible for the US effort.

----

a/ If this task is assigned to Ambassador Porter, another individual must be sent immediately to Saigon to serve as Ambassador Lodge's deputy.

(It should be noted that progress in pacification, more than anything else, will persuade the enemy to negotiate or withdraw.)

e. <u>Press for negotiations</u>. I am not optimistic that Hanoi or the VC will respond to peace overtures now (explaining my recommendations above that we get into a level-off posture for the long pull). The ends sought by the two sides appear to be irreconcilable and the relative power balance is not in their view unfavorable to them. But three things can be done, I believe, to increase the prospects:

(1) Take steps to increase the credibility of our peace gestures in the minds of the enemy. There is considerable evidence both in private statements by the Communists and in the reports of competent Western officials who have talked with them that charges of US bad faith are not solely propagandistic, but reflect deeply held beliefs. Analyses of Communists' statements and actions indicate that they firmly believe that American leadership really does not want the fighting to stop, and that we are intent on winning a military victory in Vietnam and on maintaining our presence there through a puppet regime supported by US military bases.

As a way of projecting US bona fides, I believe that we should consider two possibilities with respect to our bombing program against the North, to be undertaken, if at all, at a time very carefully selected with a view to maximizing the chances of influencing the enemy and world opinion and to minimizing the chances that failure would strengthen the hand of the "hawks" at home: First, without fanfare, conditions, or avowal, whether the stand-down was permanent or temporary, stop bombing all of North Vietnam. It is generally thought that Hanoi will not agree to negotiations until they can claim that the bombing has stopped unconditionally. We should see what develops, retaining freedom to resume the bombing if nothing useful was forthcoming.

Alternatively, we could shift the weight-of-effort away from "Zones 6A and 6B" --- zones including Hanoi and Haiphong and areas north of those two cities to the Chinese border. This alternative has some attraction in that it provides the North Vietnamese a "face saver" if only problems of "face" are holding up Hanoi peace gestures; it would narrow the bombing down directly to the objectionable infiltration (supporting the logic of a stop-infiltration/full-pause deal); and it would reduce the international heat on the US. Here, too, bombing of the Northeast could be resumed at any time, or "spot" attacks could be made there from time to time to keep North Vietnam off balance and to require her to pay almost the full cost by maintaining her repair crews in place. The sorties diverted from Zones 6A and 6B could be concentrated on the infiltration routes in Zones 1 and 2 (the southern end of North Vietnam, including the Mu Gia Pass), in Laos and in South Vietnam.a/

-----

a/ Any limitation on the bombing of North Vietnam will cause serious psychological problems among the men who are risking their lives to help achieve our political objectives; among their commanders up to and including the JCS; and among those of our people who cannot understand why we should withhold punishment from the enemy. General Westmoreland, as do the JCS, strongly believes in the military value of the bombing program. Further, Westmoreland reports that the morale of his Air Force personnel may already be showing signs of erosion --- an erosion resulting from current operational restrictions.

To the same end of improving our credibility, we should seek ways -- through words and deeds -- to make believable our intention to withdraw our forces once the North Vietnamese aggression against the South stops. In particular, we should avoid any implication that we will stay in South Vietnam with bases or to guarantee any particular outcome to a solely South Vietnamese struggle.

(2) Try to split the VC off from Hanoi. The intelligence estimate is that evidence is overwhelming that the North Vietnamese dominate and control the National Front and the Viet Cong. Nevertheless, I think we should continue and enlarge efforts to contact the VC/NLF and to probe ways to split members or sections off the VC/NLF organization.

(3) Press contacts with North Vietnam, the Soviet Union and other parties who might contribute toward a settlement.

(4) Develop a realistic plan providing a role for the VC in negotiations, post-war life, and government of the nation. An amnesty offer and proposals for national reconciliation would be steps in the right direction and should be parts of the plan. It is important that this plan be one which will appear reasonable, if not at first to Hanoi and the VC, at least to world opinion.

3. The prognosis. The prognosis is bad that the war can be brought to a satisfactory conclusion within the next two years. The large-unit operations probably will not do it; negotiations probably will not do it. While we should continue to pursue both of these routes in trying for a solution in the short run, we should recognize that success from them is a mere possibility, not a probability.

The solution lies in girding, openly, for a longer war and in taking actions immediately which will in 12 to 18 months give clear evidence that the continuing costs and risks to the American people are acceptably limited, that the formula for success has been found, and that the end of the war is merely a matter of time. All of my recommendations will contribute to this strategy, but the one most difficult to implement is perhaps the most important one -- enlivening the pacification program. The odds are less than even for this task, if only because we have failed consistently since 1961 to make a dent in the problem. But, because the 1967 trend of pacification will, I believe, be the main talisman of ultimate US success or failure in Vietnam, extraordinary imagination and effort should go into changing the stripes of that problem.

President Thieu and Prime Minister Ky are thinking along similar lines. They told me that they do not expect the enemy to negotiate or to modify his program in less than two years. Rather, they expect the enemy to continue to expand and to increase his activity. They expressed agreement with us that the key to success is pacification and that so far pacification has failed. They agree that we need clarification of GVN and US roles and that the bulk

of the ARVN should be shifted to pacification. Ky will, between January and
July 1967, shift all ARVN infantry divisions to that role. And he is giving
Thang, a good Revolutionary Development director, added powers. Thieu and Ky
see this as part of a two-year (1967-68) schedule, in which offensive operations against enemy main force units are continued, carried on primarily by
the US and other Free World forces. At the end of the two-year period, they
believe the enemy may be willing to negotiate or to retreat from his current
course of action.

Note: Neither the Secretary of State nor the JCS have yet had an opportunity
      to express their views on this report. Mr. Katzenbach and I have dis-
      cussed many of its main conclusions and recommendations -- in general,
      but not in all particulars, it expresses his views as well as my own.

APPENDIX

Extracts from CIA/DIA Report "An Appraisal of the Bombing of North Vietnam
through 12 September 1966"

1. There is no evidence yet of any shortage of POL in North Vietnam and
stocks on hand, with recent imports, have been adequate to sustain necessary
operations.

2. Air strikes against all modes of transportation in North Vietnam increased
during the past month, but there is no evidence of serious transport problems
in the movement of supplies to or within North Vietnam.

3. There is no evidence yet that the air strikes have significantly weakened
popular morale.

4. Air strikes continue to depress economic growth and have been responsible
for the abandonment of some plans for economic development, but essential
economic activities continue.

Extracts from a March 16, 1966 CIA Report "An Analysis of the ROLLING THUNDER
Air Offensive against North Vietnam"

1. Although the movement of men and supplies in North Vietnam has been
hampered and made somewhat more costly [by our bombing], the Communists have
been able to increase the flow of supplies and manpower to South Vietnam.

2. Hanoi's determination [despite our bombing] to continue its policy of
supporting the insurgency in the South appears as firm as ever.

3. Air attacks almost certainly cannot bring about a meaningful reduction
in the current level at which essential supplies and men flow into South Vietnam.

Bomb Damage Assessment in the North by the Institute for Defense Analysis'
"Summer Study Group"

What surprised us [in our assessment of the effect of bombing North
Vietnam] was the extent of agreement among various intelligence agencies on
the effects of past operations and probable effects of continued and expanded
Rolling Thunder. The conclusions of our group, to which we all subscribe,
are therefore merely sharpened conclusions of numerous Intelligence summaries.
They are that Rolling Thunder does not limit the present logistic flow into
SVN because NVN is neither the source of supplies nor the choke-point on the
supply routes from China and USSR. Although an expansion of Rolling Thunder
by closing Haiphong harbor, eliminating electric power plants and totally
destroying railroads, will at least indirectly impose further privations on
the populace of NVN and make the logistic support of VC costlier to maintain,
such expansion will not really change the basic assessment. This follows
because NVN has demonstrated excellent ability to improvise transportation,
and because the primitive nature of their economy is such that Rolling Thunder
can affect directly only a small fraction of the population. There is very
little hope that the Ho Chi Minh Government will lose control of population
because of Rolling Thunder. The lessons of the Korean War are very relevant
in these respects. Moreover, foreign economic aid to NVN is large compared

to the damage we inflict, and growing. Probably the government of NVN has assurances that the USSR and/or China will assist the rebuilding of its economy after the war, and hence its concern about the damage being inflicted may be moderated by long-range favorable expectations. Specifically:

1. As of July 1966 the U.S. bombing of North Vietnam had had no measurable direct effect on Hanoi's ability to mount and support military operations in the South at the current level.

2. Since the initiation of the Rolling Thunder program the damage to facilities and equipment in North Vietnam has been more than offset by the increased flow of military and economic aid, largely from the USSR and Communist China.

3. The aspects of the basic situation that have enabled Hanoi to continue its support of military operations in the South and to neutralize the impact of U.S. bombing by passing the economic costs to other Communist countries are not likely to be altered by reducing the present geographic constraints, mining Haiphong and the principal harbors in North Vietnam, increasing the number of armed reconnaissance sorties and otherwise expanding the U.S. air offensive along the lines now contemplated in military recommendations and planning studies.

4. While conceptually it is reasonable to assume that some limit may be imposed on the scale of military activity that Hanoi can maintain in the South by continuing the Rolling Thunder program at the present, or some higher level of effort, there appears to be no basis for defining that limit in concrete terms, or for concluding that the present scale of VC/NVN activities in the field have approached that limit.

5. The indirect effects of the bombing on the will of the North Vietnamese to continue fighting and on their leaders' appraisal of the prospective gains and costs of maintaining the present policy have not shown themselves in any tangible way. Furthermore, we have not discovered any basis for concluding that the indirect punitive effects of bombing will prove decisive in these respects.

In this memorandum, McNamara reveals with striking clarity that many of the premises under which the war to that point had been fought (and manned) were shifting.

He agreed with COMUSMACV that the military situation has gone "somewhat better in 1966 than anticipated," but he found little cause for optimism in the longer run. In fact, he seemed almost disheartened as he noted that there was "no reasonable way to bring the war to an end soon." Finding an injured but undismayed opponent committed now to "waiting us out" while sapping our national will and seeing "pacification a basic disappointment...no better, and if anything worse off..." hardly was the kind of progress he hoped for.

His solution was to get ourselves into "a military posture that we credibly would maintain indefinitely -- a posture that makes trying to 'wait us out' less attractive." To do this, he proposed a five part program:

(1) First, he suggested that, barring a major change in the war, we should stabilize U.S. force levels in Vietnam at about 470,000. The new figure of 470,000 for U.S. force levels (only 25,000 above the latest figure of 445,000 for Program #3) apparently was arrived at during the sessions in Saigon. Before the meetings, Westmoreland had estimated that Program 3 would entail a piaster cost of 47.4 billion. The follow-up papers to the conference all continued to focus upon the piaster costs of various troop deployments with the intent to keep them under the 42 billion Lodge ceiling. The most probable explanation of the genesis of the 470,000 figure is that it represented the best guess at the time of the Saigon meeting of what strength could be supported within the 42 billion limit by making very strong efforts to reduce piaster costs per man.

(2) He recommended a barrier near the DMZ and "across the trails of Laos."

(3) He opposed expansion of the ROLLING THUNDER program, recommending instead a "stabilization" to prevent the unsettling escalations from complicating our political situation (and negotiating posture) and distracting from the main job of pacification.

(4) He said we should "pursue a vigorous pacification program" noting that "progress in pacification more than anything else, will persuade the enemy to negotiate or withdraw " 51/

(5) Finally, he proferred a three-sided attempt to get negotiations going by (a) shifting the pattern of our bombing (or perhaps even stopping it); (b) considering strategies designed to enhance the probability of a split between the VC and Hanoi; and (c) "developing a realistic plan providing a role for the VC in negotiations, postwar life, and the government of the nation."

119

The summation was a somber conclusion to a resounding new emphasis
in American strategic thought. He believed that there was no great
probability of success lurking on any of the routes he proposed, only
a "mere possibility." The solution in his eyes, was to gird openly for
a longer war.

> ...and in taking actions immediately which will in 12
> to 18 months give clear evidence that the continuing costs
> and risks to the American people are acceptably limited,
> that the formula for success has been found, and that the
> end of the war is merely a matter of time. 52/

The recommendations as a whole showed the influence of the studies
which had been done over the summer. The Jason studies on the anti-
infiltration barrier and the effects of U.S. bombing in the north were
apparently influential in the decisions to move ahead with the barrier
but to stabilize ROLLING THUNDER.

The increased emphasis on the pacification effort is apparently
a result of the feeling that, since it represented the heart of the problem in Vietnam, and the main force war was only contributory to it,
perhaps all that was needed in the main force war was to keep the enemy
off the back of the pacification effort in a strategic defensive, rather
than to destroy the enemy in a strategic offensive.

In a sense, the memorandum was a clear "no" to MACV, CINCPAC and
JCS proposals for expanded bombing and major ground force increases, but
it was a negative with a difference. It provided alternatives. From
this time on, the judgment of the military as to how the war should be
fought and what was needed would be subject to question. New estimates
of what was needed in Vietnam would have to be calculated in light of new
objectives and new criteria for success, as well as new assumptions about
"winning." The warning had rung and unless dramatic outcomes measured
in time and political advantage could be promised, additional force
increases in the upward direction promised to be sticky indeed.

2. The JCS Reclamas

The JCS reaction to the DPM was predictably rapid -- and violent.
The Chiefs expressed their agreement with McNamara's basic evaluation of
a long war, but disagreed on his guarded assessment of the military situation, which in their eyes had "improved substantially over the past year." 53/
They were especially concerned that the DPM did not take into account the
"adverse impact over time of continued bloody defeats on the morale of VC/
. NVA forces and the determination of their political and military leaders." 54/

However, they noted that the 470,000-man figure was "substantially
less" than earlier recommendations of COMUSMACV and CINCPAC, and they
wished to "reserve judgment" until they reviewed the revised programs
being prepared during the CINCPAC planning conference.

120

The disagreement was less veiled on the bombing:

> c....The Joint Chiefs of Staff do not concur in your
> recommendation that there should be no increase in level of
> bombing effort and no modification in areas and targets sub-
> ject to air attack. They believe our air campaign against
> NVN to be an integral and indispensable part of our over-all
> war effort. To be effective, 'the air campaign should be con-
> ducted with only those minimum constraints necessary to avoid
> indiscriminate killing of population.'

Nor did they find the new organizational arrangements for pacification especially appetizing:

> d....The Joint Chiefs of Staff informed you earlier that,
> to achieve early optimum effectiveness, the pacification pro-
> gram should be transferred to COMUSMACV. They adhere to that
> conclusion. However, if for political reasons a civilian-type
> organization should be considered mandatory by the President,
> they would interpose no objection. Nevertheless, they are not
> sanguine that an effective civilian-type organization can be
> erected, if at all, except at the expense of costly delays.
> As to the use of a substantial fraction of the ARVN for paci-
> fication purposes, the Joint Chiefs of Staff concur. However,
> they desire to flag that adoption of this concept will undoubt-
> edly elicit charges of a US takeover of combat operations at
> increased cost in American casualties.

Finally, they did not share the Secretary's views on how to induce
negotiations. They believed the bombing was one "trump card" in the
President's hand and should not be surrendered without an equivalent
quid pro quo, such as "an end to the NVN aggression in SVN." The essence
of disagreement here centered around what each party, Secretary of Defense
and JCS felt was adequate return for a "trump," the JCS believing that as
the military campaign wore on with "increasing success, the value of the
trump would become apparent." 55/

In this regard, the Chiefs seemed to sense that a significant turn
in our views about Vietnam had been taken in high policy circles of our
government. In final comment, they observed that the conflict had reached
a stage at which decisions taken over the next sixty days could determine
the outcome of the war, and therefore they wished to provide the President
with "their unequivocal views" on two salient aspects of the war situation:
the search for peace and military pressures on NVN.

> The frequent, broadly-based public offers made by the
> President to settle the war by peaceful means on a generous
> basis, which would take from NVN nothing it now has, have
> been admirable. Certainly, no one -- American or foreigner

121

-- except those who are determined not to be convinced, can doubt the sincerity, the generosity, the altruism of US actions and objectives. In the opinion of the Joint Chiefs of Staff the time has come when further overt actions and offers on our part are not only nonproductive, they are counterproductive. A logical case can be made that the American people, our Allies, and our enemies alike are increasingly uncertain as to our resolution to pursue the war to a successful conclusion.

They recommended a "sharp knock" on NVN military assets and war supporting facilities rather than the campaign of slowly increasing pressures which was adopted.

Whatever the political merits of the latter course, we deprived ourselves of the military effects of early weight of effort and shock, and gave to the enemy time to adjust to our slow quantitative and qualitative increase of pressure. This is not to say that it is now too late to derive military benefits from more effective and extensive use of our air and naval superiority.

Accordingly, they recommended:

(1) Approval of their ROLLING THUNDER 52 program, which is a step toward meeting the requirement for improved target systems. This program would decrease the Hanoi and Haiphong sanctuary areas, authorize attacks against the steel plant, the Hanoi rail yards, the thermal power plants, selected areas within Haiphong port and other ports, selected locks and dams controlling water LOCs, SAM support facilities within the residual Hanoi and Haiphong sanctuaries, and POL at Haiphong, Ha Gia (Phuc Yen) and Can Thon (Kep).

(2) Use of naval surface forces to interdict North Vietnamese coastal waterborne traffic and appropriate land LOCs and to attack other coastal military targets such as radar and AAA sites.

6. The Joint Chiefs of Staff request that their views as set forth above be provided to the President.

All of these developments persuaded the JCS that they needed a reply with powerful arguments for a program force level far above the 470,000 proposed by the Secretary.

The JCS hesitation in discussing the new 470,000 force level was rooted in an educated estimate of what was coming out of MACV-CINCPAC in the next two weeks. 56/

3. CINCPAC Planning Conference Results

On 20 October, the CINCPAC Planning Conference was done and the results forwarded to the JCS. 57/

There were few surprises. The concept had been changed to include a heavier emphasis on RD, set forth in a preamble to the concept contained in the 18 June submission. The estimate of Communist forces in South Vietnam was 83,000 combat, 46,000 combat support, with 35,000 guerrillas. Total strength was estimated at 144 infantry battalions, 60 of which were North Vietnamese. The enemy addition to his force was estimated at the monthly rate of 12,500 -- 9,500 NVA and 3,000 VC. A projection of enemy strength for the end of 1966 was 143,000 combat and combat support, while the projections for the end of 1967 was 190,000. The courses of action which seemed to be open to the enemy in October were:

1. To increase the level of operations to include the conduct of simultaneous widely separated operations, utilizing forces of up to division size.

2. To maintain the current level of operations which would include the conduct of simultaneous widely separated multi-battalion operations.

3. To threaten large-scale attacks in the DMZ in order to divert large numbers of forces into the hinterland, thus reducing forces available in populated areas to accomplish Revolutionary Development.

4. To decrease the level of operations to include reverting to guerrilla warfare.

CINCPAC's requirements and the services capabilities to provide them were listed as follows:

	Requirements Maneuver Bns, US	Capabilities Man.Bns.	Pers.
End CY 66	82	79	384,361
End CY 67	94	91	493,969
End CY 68	94	94	519,310
End CY 69	94	94	520,020
Plus Requirements with Availability Rates Unknown			555,741

Requirements for PACOM other than Vietnam would total 23 maneuver battalions and 271,666 personnel. The PACOM conference results clearly amplified what General Westmoreland had echoed over a month earlier as the manpower problem in Vietnam worsened. NVA infiltration in the DMZ area, the strategy of hitting the enemy in his sanctuaries and the additional manpower requirements of the pacification program punctuated the critical conclusion of the PACOM conference; they could not justify a reduction in requirements submitted. In the meantime, information which the Secretary of Defense had requested on alternative force structures possible under piaster ceilings of 42, 44, and 46 billion, had been forwarded to the JCS. 58/   The three packages did not cost out at the exact ceilings, because of the requirement for balanced forces, but the alternatives were as follows:

	CY 67 Piaster Cost (Billions)	Total Strength Man.Bns.	Total Strength Pers.	End '67 Strength Man.Bns.	End '67 Strength Pers.
MACV Requirement	46.21	94	555,741	94	493,969
Plan A	45.07	88	499,749	88	467,850
Plan B	44.54	84	481,705	84	457,803
Plan C	42.03	73	443,487	73	421,574

4. Manila

Before the formal JCS ratification of the CINCPAC-COMUSMACV requirements was forwarded, one other important contact between the major decision-makers on Program 4 occurred. This was at Manila in late October. What views were exchanged between the President and General Westmoreland remain a mystery, but the General twice sought out Mr. John McNaughton, Assistant Secretary of Defense, ISA, and laid out his thinking on force levels, ROLLING THUNDER, the barrier, and Revolutionary Development. 59/

The American commander was thinking about an end CY 67 strength of about 480,000, fleshed-out to 500,000 by the end of CY 68. Barring surprises, he would plan to hold it there. This was a substantial drop from his original request through CINCPAC, but apparently he had not yet resigned himself to McNamara's figure of 470,000. He believed that those levels were what "the U.S. /could/ sustain over time without mobilization and without calling up reserves and what the Vietnamese economy /could/ bear." He said the 480,000-500,000 man level would be enough "even if infiltration went on at a high level," but he waffled by adding he was not sure if he had enough troops to take on the Delta.

Westmoreland remained apprehensive about the absence of a sizeable
reserve located within quick reaction distance in the Pacific, asking
McNaughton to stress to the Secretary that he badly needed such a "Corps
Contingency Force." He reiterated his desire for a strategy devoted to
building "a balanced, powerful force that we can sustain indefinitely,"
a posture that would be of critical importance in communicating our
resolve to the North. 60/

On the bombing, Westmoreland favored reducing restrictions on targets
("more flexibility"), but he could not make a good case for the effects an
expanded RT program would have on his operations. McNaughton cited a CIA
study showing that even with enlarged strikes, the enemy could supply
several times the amount of material required to support a much increased
level of combat in the South. Pressed, Westmoreland observed that "I'm
not responsible for the bombing program. Admiral Sharp is. So I haven't
spent much time on it. But I asked a couple of my best officers to look
into it and they came up with the recommendations I gave you." 61/

The barrier idea appeared to be evolving as a substitute for some
ROLLING THUNDER activity -- and Westmoreland "shuddered" at this. Some
of his earlier resistance, founded on a belief that MACV resources in SVN
would be drawn down to man the barrier trace, seemed to have softened. In
a way, he seemed to sense that the NVA was providing the justification for
more U.S. troops in the area in much more eloquent fashion than he ever
could -- the threats in I CTZ, to Conthien and Khe Sanh, embryonic as
they were, would provide impulse for additional troops well beyond the
artificial program dates established.

Revolutionary Development figured heavily in his plans, but he predicted that it would be July 1967 before the new orientation of ARVN to
pacification would be in full effect. (He cited as a rough figure 75%
ARVN and 25% of US devoted to RD.)

Westmoreland did not outline the same picture of urgency as had the
JCS memoranda. (The fact he was really not set on some figures may suggest
that he (and his staff) were looking at "ballpark" figures and had not
really analyzed the new outputs they would produce.) Explaining why at
that time he soft-pedalled the threat developing in the border region
sanctuaries and I CTZ is difficult. He certainly had been concerned
earlier, even telling Lodge that the new enemy actions possibly made a
re-evaluation of basic strategy necessary. Possibly his formal warnings
(such as his 20 September message to Sharp) were exaggerated, or the
threat had diminished. Events were to prove neither was so. Probably
he missed an excellent opportunity to put his arguments for more troops
before the President, and then felt it best to fight the battle for more
troops "through channels," -- the CINCPAC-JCS funnel.

Nevertheless, his views surely had an important bearing on Mr.
McNamara's estimates in early November. The senior field commander was

saying he could get along with small force increases. Of course, he
added that such a force level would degrade his ability to meet time
deadlines ("it would be a longer war") but, as the 14 October DPM
clearly shows, the Secretary was thinking along different lines -- if
there was to be no quick, "successful" end to the war, why invest greater
resources and run greater political risks to get there -- still late.

The President returned from his highly publicized swing to Manila
and the Far East to find some press rumblings about the services exceeding
their budgeted FY 1967 strengths, and some speculation that the bombing
would increase; there had always been some change after such a trip. 62/
Richard Nixon had fired a final broadside in a belated attempt to heat up
the war issue for the election berating the President for making a trip
which "accomplished nothing" and which "resigned America and the free
Asian nations to a war which could last five years and cost more casualties
than Korea." 63/   These events notwithstanding, even though President
Johnson's administration was facing its first extensive national test
at the polls early in November, the Vietnam war was not a central public
issue. Basic uncertainty about how the electorate really felt about the
war, combined with the traditional wariness of old-line politicians in
bucking a "patriotic issue" had dampened some of the heat of the Vietnam
war as an issue. The only major race which focused on the war occurred
in Oregon, where Robert Duncan, an outspoken advocate of President Johnson's
VN policies, was defeated by what he described as "voter dissatisfaction with
the war." 64/

The war itself seemed to cooperate with the Administration's efforts
to low-key the issue. Our forces were doing well in Operation HASTINGS
near the Cambodian border where, in the words of one commander, we "had
blunted the spearhead of the enemy winter offensive." 65/

The superficial quiet of an off-year election was in no way reflected
by the President's private activity upon his return from Manila. It was
budget time and he was wrestling with a war budget, featuring a whopping
supplemental of $9.1 billion for Vietnam prior to the beginning of FY 68.
Working out of the Texas ranch, the President generated a constant stream
of travelers from official Washington as he sought information, counsel,
and exposure. Secretary McNamara and General Wheeler made two trips to
the Pedernales, visiting the President on Friday and Saturday, 4 and 5
November, and later on Friday, the 11th. 66/

The visits coincided with the decision branch-points in the Program 4
development, for they occurred in sequence with significant new inputs of
information and discussions, and in each case resulted in an important
decision or public announcement.

5. JCS Recommendations

On 4 November, the JCS forwarded to the Secretary of Defense the results of the October PACOM Planning Conference with their "refinements" added. The document, labeled JCSM 702-66, "Deployment of Forces to Meet CY Requirements," held few surprises. The memorandum addressed the crux of disagreement:

> ....As in past concepts, it goes beyond certain restraints that have been placed on US operating forces to date, such as those on the air campaign in North Vietnam, on cross border operations, on certain special operations, and on ground actions in the southern half of the demilitarized zone. Further, this concept should be carried out in its entirety, if achievement of US objectives is to be accomplished in the shortest time and at the least cost in men and materiel. The concept describes preparation for operations that have not as yet been authorized, such as mining ports, naval quarantine, spoiling attacks and raids against the enemy in Cambodia and Laos, and certain special operations. Such action will support intensified and accelerated revolutionary development and nation building programs. Since the force requirements are based on this concept in its entirety, continued restraints and the absence of authorization for recommended operations could generate significantly different requirements for forces and timing. 67/

In a sense, it embraced all of the right arguments (for "intensified and accelerated revolutionary development and programs" and "shortest time at the least cost," an overdetermined test) but unfortunately for all the wrong reasons. McNamara and Johnson were not politically and militarily enchanted with a costly major force increase at that time, nor with cross border and air operations which ran grave political risks. The specter of early mobilization, while briefly raised by the JCS, was temporarily erased by an ambiguous statement acknowledging that "capability to meet these requirements cannot be developed without significant modification to the criteria mentioned earlier: draw down latitude, rotation policy, no call-up of reserves, maintenance of CONUS training base. Nevertheless, the Joint Chiefs of Staff consider that, while the program is less than that desired, it will provide for the effective execution of the concept of operations set forth." 68/

Finally, the Chiefs expressed their views about the piaster ceiling which Lodge and members of the Mission Council had found so attractive.

> ....They consider that the requirement to reduce piaster expenditures in the interest of combating inflation in South Vietnam is important; however, this factor cannot be overriding in determining force levels because enemy actions could

require US force levels substantially above those recommended. They note especially that the equation and factors
used to price out piaster costs permit only rough approxi-
mations and have not been tested over a length of time.
They also note that the three force-level packages do not
cost out precisely at 42.0, 44.0, and 46.0 billion piasters,
respectively, since the operational requirement for balanced
forces prevented that degree of precision...." 69/

6. Decision on Program #4

With the Chiefs' views in hand the Secretary of Defense met
with the President on 4 November, and again at the ranch on Saturday,
the 5th. By late Saturday morning, the basic ground force deployment
decision had been made. Mr. McNamara announced in an open-air press
conference that increases in Vietnam would be forthcoming "but at a
substantially lower rate and that draft calls for the next four months
/would/ be significantly smaller." 70/ He also quoted a "new study"
based upon interrogations of NVA/VC captives and defectors which showed
that extensive allied air-ground operations impaired morale, exposed the
sanctuaries, reduced food supplies and brought the enemy death figure
to over 1,000 per week. He did not comment on how he thought the war
effort was going or what meaning he saw in the new report.

The elections were held on Tuesday, 8 November, with mixed results
for the Administration. It was difficult to tie specific results, or
even the general trend to the war issue. Even when there was some relationship, "basic dissatisfaction" was usually the explanation, a neutral
reply which failed to explain whether the respondents wanted to hasten
the end by escalation of our military efforts, by withdrawal, or what.
The fact that off-year elections are traditionally damaging to the party
in power further blurred the issue. In the end, 47 House seats and
8 Governorships had been gained by the Republicans and, in light of even
those "minor" gains, the 1968 Presidential race, potentially one debating
our war policies, promised to be a more interesting and heated campaign
than anyone had anticipated two years before.

E. Anti-Climaxes

    1. Program Four is Announced

McNamara and General Wheeler returned to the ranch on Friday,
the 10th, to participate in a joint news conference. In the meantime,
Dr. Enthoven had given the following memorandum to the Secretary of
Defense:

Enclosed for your signature is a memorandum to the
JCS replying to their November 4 memorandum submitting
recommended deployments to Southeast Asia for FY 67-68.
Their recommended program and my proposed alternative
(Program #4) are compared below with the CINCPAC P46
billion force. The major elements of the OSD and JCS
forces are compared in greater detail on the attached
table:

	Dec 66	Jun 67	Dec 67	Jun 68	Total
	(Thousands of Personnel in SVN)				
JCS Rec.	395	456	504	522	564
CINCPAC P.46 Bil.	392	448	476	484	508
Program #4	391	440	463	469	469

In general my proposal follows the CINCPAC 46 billion
piaster alternative force. The JCS recommended force ignores
piasters and the JCS do not endorse the P46 billion force.
My alternative adds five maneuver battalions (3 armored cavalry
and 2 infantry) compared to 6 maneuver battalions (3 armored
cavalry and 2 infantry and 2 airborne) in the CINCPAC P46
billion force. Both add 10 artillery battalions. The CINCPAC
force adds 5 tactical air squadrons, Program #4 cuts the current program by 1 squadron (the F-100 squadron to deploy in
March to replace the B-5 squadron to be converted to the VNAF).

My proposed force provides about 25,000 fewer Army support personnel with only 1 fewer maneuver battalion than in
the P46 billion force. The JCS will most likely claim that the
recommended force is not balanced. However, our forces are
operating effectively at present with an even leaner mix of
support personnel. Program #4 consists of about 6 1/3 Army
division equivalents. If the U.S. ARVN advisors and 2 separate
armored cavalry regiments are excluded, the division slice
is about 48,000. While U.S. forces are also providing some
support for 3rd country troops and to an extent to the ARVN,
this division slice appears adequate.

The JCS state their recommendation is exclusive of any
personnel needed by Task Force 728. In the absence of data
as to the TF 728 requirements, I cannot say that all of its
needs are met by my recommended force. However, the air
cavalry, armored cavalry, and related units were included
in my force primarily because of their usefulness for a
barrier operation. Furthermore, the inflationary situation

in SVN appears so critical in CY 1967 that I cannot recommend any additions to Program #4, at least until CY 1968.

A detailed troop list has been prepared to define precisely Program #4. As soon as it can be reproduced, it will be provided to you for transmission to the JCS. This should be by close of business tomorrow, November 10.

One can speculate that the two officials carried back detailed plans and costs associated with the earlier broad force decision made the preceding week-end.

It appears they were quite ready to talk about Vietnam. General Wheeler read a short prepared statement explaining that after his recent trip he was able to report to the President that "the war in my judgment continues in a very favorable fashion. General Westmoreland retains the initiative and in every operation to date has managed to defeat the enemy." Beyond this, questions about Vietnam were little more than rehash of the previous week's session. 72/

On 11 November, the Secretary of Defense informed the JCS formally that he had approved a new deployment program for MACV with an end strength of 470,000 by June of 1968.

I have reviewed your recommendations in JCSM-702-66, November 4, 1966, and the related military and economic effects of your recommended deployments. The attached table summarizes your plan and the forces which I am approving for planning purposes.

As you know, a reasonably stable economy in South Vietnam is essential to unite the population behind the Government of Vietnam -- indeed to avoid disintegration of the SVN society. Runaway inflation can undo what our military operations accomplish. For this reason, we have already taken actions to reduce military and contractor piaster spending towards the minimum level which can be accomplished without serious impact on military operations. Nevertheless, the price stability achieved last summer may be giving way to a new round of severe inflation. More must be done.

Ambassador Lodge has asked that U.S. military spending be held to P42 billion in CY 1967. The Ambassador proposed program of tightly constrained U.S. and GVN civilian and military spending will not bring complete stability to SVN; there would still be, at best, a 10 billion piaster inflationary gap. It would, however, probably hold price rises in CY 1967 to 10%-25% as opposed to 75%-90% in FY 1966. The

burden of inflation falls most heavily on just those
Vietnamese -- the ARVN and GVN civil servants --
upon whose efficient performance our success most
heavily depends. Unless we rigidly control inflation,
the Vietnamese Army desertion rate will increase further
and effectiveness will decline, thus at least partially
cancelling the effects of increased U.S. deployments.
Further, government employees will leave their jobs and
civil strife will occur, seriously hindering both the
military and the pacification efforts and possibly even
collapsing the GVN.

For these reasons we must fit our deployments to the
capacity of the Vietnamese economy to bear them without
undue inflation. As your memorandum indicates, the
program you recommend would cost over P46 billion in
CY 1967 at current prices. I believe implementation of
a program of this size would be self-defeating. The plan
I am approving at this time for budgetary planning appear
to me to be the maximum consistent with my reasonable
hope of economic stability. If contingencies arise during
the year, we can re-examine the plan accordingly. I plan
to provide sufficient combat-ready forces in the U.S. to
meet reasonable contingencies.

A troop list containing each unit in Program #4 is
attached. You may wish to suggest changes in the unit
mix, if there are units that have been deleted that have
a higher priority than those I have approved. I would
like to have these recommendations by December 1, 1966.
I also would like your proposals as to ways in which
approved units can be accelerated so as to provide maximum combat capability as early as possible in CY 1967.

SOUTHEAST ASIA DEPLOYMENT PROGRAM #4

PLAN SUMMARY 73/

	Jun 67 JCS Plan	Jun 67 OSD Plan	Dec 67 JCS Plan	Dec 67 OSD Plan	Jun 68 JCS Plan	Jun 68 OSD Plan
1. Personnel-SVN (000)						
Army	292.6	286.0	334.8	307.9	350.5	313.9
USMC	70.6	70.6	70.6	70.6	70.6	70.6
Air Force	60.6	55.3	63.3	55.4	65.3	55.4
Navy	32.1	27.6	35.3	29.4	35.8	29.4
	455.9	439.5	504.0	463.3	522.2	469.3
2. Maneuver Battalions-SVN						
Army	62	62	74	67	74	67
USMC	20	20	20	20	20	20
	82	82	94	87	94	87

He had disapproved the force recommendations of JCSM 702-66, but had
not commented on the "new" concept and objectives -- an omission which
left an excellent opening for the next round of force requirements
discussions. The 11 November memorandum explained the decision to hold
the force levels at 470,000 almost solely in terms of piaster costs and
the dangers of inflation.

2. Program Four is Explained

A fuller explanation of the reasoning behind the Program Four
decisions was given by the Secretary of Defense in his 17 November
Draft Memorandum for the President. 74/

* * * * *

I have reviewed the additional funding and forces required to support our planned deployments and operations in Southeast Asia. I
recommend a supplemental appropriation request totaling $12.4 billion
in Total Obligational Authority be submitted to Congress in January for
the following purposes:

	FY67 TOA ($ Billions)
I. Direct Support of SEA Operations	
a. Land forces	$5.4
b. Tactical air and B-52 forces	4.3
c. Naval forces	.3
d. Logistic support	1.0
II. Rotational Base and Strategic Reserve	
a. Land forces	.5
b. Air forces	.3
c. Naval forces	.03
d. Defense Agencies	.1
III. Non-Sea b/	.6
Total	$12.4 a/

a/ These costs are subject to revision in the budget review.
Construction costs are still under review and are excluded.
b/ Includes pay raise and home owners assistance.

Forces totaling 469,000 be approved, for planning and budgeting
purposes, for deployment to SVN by June 30, 1968.

Current U.S. military forces be augmented by 346,134 to total end
FY68 strength of 3,476,400 personnel to support these deployments to
Southeast Asia. Deployment, force augmentation, and financial summaries
follow. The December 1965 plan on which the FY67 Budget was based is shown
for comparison.

SUMMARY DEPLOYMENTS TO SEA

	1965 June	1966 Jun	1966 Dec	1967 Jun	1967 Dec	1968 June
Personnel - SVN (000)						
Dec Plan - Total	60	278	386	394	-	-
SecDef Rec - Army	27	160	244	286	308	314
Marines	18	54	69	71	71	71
Air Force	11	36	54	55	55	55
Navy	4	17	25	28	29	29
TOTAL	60	267	392	440	463	469
JCS Rec - Army			244	292	335	350
Marines			69	71	71	71
Air Force			57	61	63	65
Navy			25	32	35	36
TOTAL			395	456	504	522
Personnel - WESTPAC (000)						
Dec Plan	242	484	588	618	-	-
SecDef Rec	242	474	624	677	701	707
JCS Rec			634	703	756	774
Maneuver Bns						
Dec Plan	9	48	77	77	-	-
SecDef Rec	9	$51\frac{2}{3}$	79	82	87	87
JCS Rec			79	82	94	94
Artillery Bns						
Dec Plan	3	$33\frac{1}{3}$	47	47	-	-
SecDef Rec	3	$33\frac{2}{3}$	$47\frac{2}{3}$	$57\frac{2}{3}$	$61\frac{2}{3}$	$63\frac{2}{3}$
JCS Rec			$47\frac{2}{3}$	$57\frac{2}{3}$	$63\frac{2}{3}$	$69\frac{2}{3}$
Engineer Bns						
Dec Plan	$6\frac{1}{3}$	37	$47\frac{1}{3}$	$47\frac{1}{3}$	-	-
Sec Def Rec	$6\frac{1}{3}$	$30\frac{2}{3}$	44	56	56	56
JCS Rec			44	59	60	60
Fighter-Attack a/c (U.S)						
Dec Plan	599	801	894	929	-	-
SecDef Rec	599	849	1046	989	998	983
JCS Rec			1046	1061	1106	1127
Attack Sorties (000)						
Dec Plan	10	21	26	26	-	-
SecDef Rec	10	24	28	28	28	28
JCS Rec			28	30	32	34
Air Ordnance (000 Tons)						
Dec Plan	11	52	68	73	-	-
SecDef Rec	11	35	65	65	65	65
JCS Rec			70	89	93	96
Other Fixed Wing a/c						
Dec Plan	397	891	963	975	-	-
SecDef Rec	397	826	1134	1293	1376	1376
JCS Rec			1131	1385	1494	1521

I have not denied any funding request necessary to conduct the war and which can be effectively utilized during the current fiscal year. The FY67 supplemental and FY68 budgets have been designed to meet war needs through the FY68 funding leadtime. If the tempo of the conflict increases beyond the level now planned, additional funds will be required. The recommended Southeast Asia deployments and supporting supplemental budget requests are in accord with the views of the Joint Chiefs of Staff with the exceptions noted later.

To date, we have met virtually all of COMUSMACV's requirements for maneuver battalions at or near the time he requested them, without recall of the Reserves or withdrawals of units deployed to Europe or other key overseas areas. Moreover, we still have the capability to deploy additional active forces as well as a large ready force wherever they may be needed.

The decision to retain the organized reserve as a reserve led to a requirement to organize certain units that were not available in the CONUS active forces. With only a few exceptions, we have deployed them as required and on a schedule quite close to what we could have expected under a reserve mobilization. Many of the units that could not be provided as required (e.g., aviation units) were not available in the reserve structure either. The table below compares the current plan with the deployment schedule that the JCS last March estimated could be met if the reserve forces had been called to active duty.

	1966				1967	
	Mar	Jun	Sep	Dec	Mar	Jun
Strength in SVN (000)						
SecDef Rec	231	267	313	392	424	440
With Reserves a/	227	284	359	411	421	426
Maneuver Bns in SVN						
SecDef Rec	46	52	64	79	82	82
With Reserves a/	46	52	67	76	79	79

a/ Case I, CINCPAC Capabilities Conference, 12 February 1966.

U.S. forces in SEA have performed exceedingly well. In the summer of 1965 NVA forces threatened to destroy the SVN armed forces and achieve a military victory. The introduction of U.S. forces almost completely neutralized the VC/NVA large units. He has lost 114,000 troops in the last year, including invaluable cadre. The B-52 and tactical air effort has hurt enemy morale, produced casualties, and disrupted his operations and logistics operations. It is our success to date that permits the analysis in the next section of the incremental value of still more deployments.

The incremental annual cost of the conflict amounted to $9.4 billion in FY66 and is estimated at $19.7 billion for FY67. If in FY68 the forces and rates of operations stabilized at the levels shown in this paper, the cost will be about $24 billion, calculated as follows:

	($ Billions)
Military Personnel	$ 5.5
Operations and Maintenance	6.7
Ammunition Consumption	4.5
Aircraft & Helicopter Attrition	1.4
Other Procurement	4.3
Free World Force Support	1.5
Construction	.2
	$24.1

These data exclude economic aid to Vietnam and other SE Asia nations that might be attributed to the conflict. Economic aid for SVN currently is running at about $.7 billion per year.

I. MILITARY STRATEGY IN VIETNAM

The war in Vietnam has two highly interdependent parts: (1) the "regular" war against the main force VC/NVA battalions and regiments, and the interdiction of their men and supplies flowing down from North Vietnam, and (2) the "Pacification" or revolutionary development war to neutralize the local VC guerrillas and gain the permanent support of the SVN population.

The infiltrated men and supplies serve to bolster the regular units whose function is to support the local VC guerrillas and infrastructure by defeating the GVN forces in the area and generally exposing the GVN's inability to protect the rural populace. The local guerrillas and infrastructure maintain a constant VC presence in their area and support the offensive efforts of the regular units by providing intelligence, terrain guidance, supplies, and recruits. In addition, the guerrillas conduct many of the thousands of incidents of terror, harassment, and sabotage reported each month. The principal task of U.S. military forces in SVN must be to eliminate the offensive capability of the regular units in order to allow the GVN to counter the guerrilla forces and extend permanent control over areas from which regular units have been cleared.

We now face a choice of two approaches to the threat of the regular VC/NVA forces. The first approach would be to continue in 1967 to increase friendly forces as rapidly as possible, and without limit, and employ them primarily in large-scale "seek out and destroy" operations to destroy the main force VC/NVA units.

135

This approach appears to have some distinct disadvantages. First, we are finding very strongly diminishing marginal returns in the destruction of VC/NVA forces. If our estimates of enemy losses (killed, captured and defected) are correct, VC/NVA losses increased by only 115 per week - (less than 19%) during a period in which we increased friendly strength by 160,000 including 140,000 U.S. military personnel and 42 U.S. and Third Country maneuver battalions. At this rate, an additional 100,000 friendly personnel deployed would increase VC/NVA losses by some 70 per week. Second, expanding U.S. deployments have contributed to a very serious inflation in South Vietnam. Prices increased 75-90% in FY66. An extra 100,000 U.S. forces would add at least P9 billion to our piaster expenditures, doubling the 1967 inflationary gap in SVN. Third, the high and increasing cost of the war to the United States is likely to encourage the Communists to doubt our staying power and to try to "wait us out."

The second approach is to follow a similarly aggressive strategy of "seek out and destroy," but to build friendly forces only to that level required to neutralize the large enemy units and prevent them from interfering with the pacification program. It is essential to this approach that such a level be consistent with a stable economy in SVN, and consistent with a military posture that the United States credibly would maintain indefinitely, thus making a Communist attempt to "wait us out" less attractive.

I believe that this level is about 470,000 U.S. and 52,000 Free World personnel and less than half of the ARVN.* The remainder of the ARVN, plus a portion of the U.S. force, would give priority to improving the pacification effort. The enemy regular units would cease to perform what I believe to be their primary function of diverting our effort to give security to the population. This, plus the effects of a successful interdiction campaign to cut off their other support, would effectively neutralize them, possibly at the cost of far fewer casualties to both sides than the first approach would allow.

I believe it is time to adopt the second approach for three reasons: (1) if MACV estimates of enemy strength are correct, we have not been able to attrite the enemy forces fast enough to break their morale and more U.S. forces are unlikely to do so in the foreseeable future; (2) we cannot deploy more than about 470,000 personnel by the end of 1967 without a high

---

*Admiral Sharp has recommended a 12/31/67 U.S. strength of 570,000. However, I believe both he and General Westmoreland recognize that the danger of inflation will probably force a 6/30/68 deployment limit of about 470,000.

36

probability of generating a self-defeating runaway inflation in SVN and (3) an endless escalation of U.S. deployments is not likely to be acceptable in the U.S. or to induce the enemy to believe that the U.S. is prepared to stay as long as is required to produce a secure non-communist SVN. Obviously a greatly improved pacification campaign must be waged to take advantage of the protection offered by the major friendly forces. Alternatively, if enemy strength is greatly overstated and our "seek out and destroy" operations have been more effective than our strength and loss estimates would imply - a possibility discussed below - more than 470,000 U.S. personnel should not be required to neutralize the VC/NVA main force.

Attriting Enemy Forces. All of our estimates of enemy strength and variations in it contain very great uncertainties. Thus, any conclusions drawn from them must be considered to be highly tentative and conjectural. Nevertheless, the data suggest that we have no prospects of attriting the enemy force at a rate equal to or greater than his capability to infiltrate and recruit, and this will be true at either the 470,000 U.S. personnel level or 570,000. The table on the following page shows our estimates of the average enemy loss rate per month since April 1965. By 4th quarter 1965, estimated military losses (killed, captured, military defectors) reached 2215 per week. The weekly average for CY66 has remained about the same, although enemy losses increased to 2330 per week in the 3rd quarter and to 2930 in October.

Enemy losses from wounds are included above based on the U.S. Intelligence Board estimate that there are 1.5 enemy wounded for each one killed, with one-third of the wounded put out of action, resulting in a loss of .5 for each VC/NVA recorded killed, or 520 additional average losses per week. (MACV estimates .28 additional losses for each VC/NVA killed, or an average loss of 300 per week.) Also included are defectors not turning themselves into the GVN centers, based on the Board estimate that there is one unrecorded military deserter for each military defector, resulting in another 235 average losses per week.

The enemy loss rate was apparently not affected significantly by the greatly increased friendly activity during 1966, which included: 44% increase in battalion days of operation; 25% increase in battalion sized

137

VC/NVA LOSSES
(Weekly Average)

	1965			1966				Last 4
	2nd Qtr	3rd Qtr	4th Qtr	1st Qtr	2nd Qtr	3rd Qtr	Oct	Qtrs Plus Oc
Estimated Losses								
Killed a/	705	1165	1555	1505	1370	1805	1915	1585
Captured	100	145	135	130	145	170	545	175
Mil Defectors b/	345	435	525	580	430	355	470	470
Total Est Losses	1150	1745	2215	2215	1945	2330	2930	2230
Average Friendly Strengths (000)	672	759	871	930	982	1037	1113	967
Total Losses/1000 Friendly/Week	1.7	2.3	2.5	2.4	2.0	2.2	2.6	2.3

a/ 1.5 times recorded "body count."
b/ 2 times recorded military defectors.

operations contacting the enemy; and 28% increase in small unit actions
accompanied by a 12% increase in contacts. Moreover, armed helicopter
sorties doubled from 14,000 to 29,000 per month and attack sorties in SVN
rose from 12,800 to 14,000 per month.

The failure of enemy losses to increase during the first half of 1966
was primarily due to the January Vietnamese New Year lull, the political
turmoil during the Spring, the apparent decrease in ARVN efficiency, and an
increasing enemy reluctance to fight large battles.

Despite improvements during the past four months, it is impossible
to predict the point at which we can expect to attrite enemy forces at the
rate he introduces new ones. As the table above indicates, an average enemy
total loss rate of 2230 per week has prevailed for the past 13 months, compared to the calculated enemy personnel input rate of 2915 per week for the
same period. The input rate is that required to provide the average increase
of 685 per week reflected in the VC/NVA order of battle strength figures
estimated by MACV, it is not estimated independently. Assuming that the
weekly infiltration rate from NVN for the past 13 months averaged 1075 as
estimated (MACV indicates that the 1966 figure may be as high as 1638 per
week), VC recruitment (input minus infiltration) must have been about 1840
per week. This recruitment rate lies well within the current U.S. Intelligence Board estimate that the VC can recruit and train 1635 to 2335 men
per week, and can replace current losses solely from within South Vietnam
if necessary. But it lies far above the current MACV recruitment estimate
of 815 VC personnel per week.

138

As indicated in the VC/NVA losses table, enemy losses increased by 115 per week during a period in which friendly strength increased by 166,000; an increase of about 70 losses per 100,000 of friendly strength. There are far too many uncertain variables in the situation to permit a simple extrapolation of these results to the effect of introduction of the next 100,000, or a subsequent 100,000 troops. However, we have no evidence that more troops than the 470,000 I am recommending would substantially change the situation. For example, if it were assumed that new forces would produce enemy losses at a rate equal to the average of all forces deployed by the end of October 1966, each deployment of 100,000 additional friendly troops would produce only 230 more total enemy losses per week compared to the 2915 current enemy input rate. A U.S. force of 470,000 would result in enemy losses of 2450 per week; an extra 100,000 U.S. personnel would increase average weekly enemy losses to about 2680, still less than the 3500 per week that the enemy is supposed to be able to infiltrate/recruit. Moreover, it is possible that our attrition estimates substantially overstate actual VC/NVA losses. For example, the VC/NVA apparently lose only about one-sixth as many weapons as people, suggesting the possibility that many of the killed are unarmed porters or bystanders.

VC/NVA PERSONNEL INPUT
(Weekly Average)

	1965			1966				Last 4 Qtrs Plus Oct
	2nd Qtr	3rd Qtr	4th Qtr	1st Qtr	2nd Qtr	3rd Qtr	Oct.	
MACV Estimate of Strength (End of Qtr - 000) a/	231.5	238.3	250.3	265.6	277.4	282.0	277.0	
Net Change per wk. b/		520	920	1175	905	355	-1130.0	685
Estimated Losses		1745	2215	2215	1945	2330	2930	2230
Required Gross Personnel Input		2265	3135	3390	2850	2685	1800	2915
Less MACV Accepted NVA Infiltration		315	945	1760	1525	430	0 d/	1075
Calculated Residual VC Recruitment c/		1950	2190	1630	1325	2255	1800	1840

a/ Sources: MACV submission of August 15, 1966 and Table 101 OSD SEA Statistical Summary.

b/ Net quarterly gain divided by 13.

c/ No figures reported. Figures shown equal gross input minus NVA infiltration.

d/ MACV confirmation of infiltration figures normally lags several weeks behind actual entry of personnel.

In summary, despite the wide variations in estimates of infiltration, recruitment and losses, the data indicate that current enemy recruitment/infiltration rates and tactics have more than offset the increased friendly deployments, enabling the enemy to increase his forces in the past and in the foreseeable future. If we assume that the estimates of enemy strength are accurate, the ratio of total friendly to total enemy strength has only increased from 3.5 to 4.0 to 1 since the end of 1965. Under these circumstances, it does not appear that we have the favorable leverage required to achieve decisive attrition by introducing more forces. It may be possible to reduce enemy strength substantially through improved tactics or other means such as an effective amnesty/defection program or effective pacification to dry up VC sources of recruitment, but further large increases in U.S. forces do not appear to be the answer.

Enemy Offensive Capability. These estimates of enemy strength, losses and replacement rates raise some important questions. They assume that the enemy has all of the battalions carried in the MACV Enemy Order of Battle (OB), and that most of these battalions have retained their offensive capability. Neither assumption can be supported by available data.

In the last 7 months (February-August) for which data are available, friendly forces averaged 35 contacts per month with VC/NVA battalions. If each contact represented a different battalion, the contact rate would equal 20% of the average reported total enemy VC/NVA battalions; at best, we would contact each battalion one in 5 months. However, analyzing the August OB of 175 battalions, only 112 battalions had been positively identified as contacted during the 7 month period and 59 battalions were unrecorded as to last contact. (The remaining battalions were contacted prior to period.) Other battalions in addition to the 112 positively identified were undoubtedly active during the period. Nevertheless, it appears that the actual existence, or ability to operate, of some of the 59 units with no records of contact with friendly forces is open to question. Moreover, enemy activity rates reflected in the number of battalion contacts initiated by themselves or by us do not show increases that we might expect as the result of the 49 battalion increase reflected in the Order of Battle reports.

CONTACTS WITH VC/NVA BATTALIONS

	FEB	MAR	APR	MAY	JUN	JUL	AUG	AVG.
				1966				
VC/NVA Initiated Contacts	18	19	8	15	14	14	18	15
Total Contacts	46	43	20	22	35	39	34	35
Estimated Total Battalions in Force	126	145	152	157	174	175	175	158

Furthermore, the enemy is undertaking fewer large scale offensive operations in recent months and concentrating his small scale attacks, ambushes, and harassments against easier targets (troops in the field and isolated military posts). This indicates a possible regression to activities characteristic of earlier stages of guerrilla warfare, is inconsistent with large numbers of battalions and even divisions, and may reflect an increasing inability to conduct large scale operations without incurring unacceptably high casualties. The VC/NVA have not won a significant large scale military victory in several months. There is every reason to be on guard, as General Westmoreland is, but there is no reason to believe that we need to increase our planned deployment of large units to prevent such victories in the future.

The Interdiction Campaign. The VC force has reportedly increased by 20 battalions (from 74 to 94) since last December, NVA by 43 (from 43 to 86) during the same period. The NVA represented only 25,600 of 249,700 (10%) last December, increasing to 45,600 of 277,000 (16% in October. The weekly rate of accepted infiltration has been about 1115 in 1966 compared to 945 in 4th quarter 1965 and 510 for all of 1965. MACV has recently reported that infiltration may have been as high as 1630 per week in 1966. The NVA units, equipped almost exclusively with Chinese and Russian weapons, have a much greater requirement for infiltrated ammunition and supplies, thus increasing their dependence on the logistics network flowing from NVN to SVN.

Air Interdiction. The use of air power to interdict enemy infiltration and supply has been very great by any standard. Attack sorties in Laos and NVN have risen from 4750 per month at the end of last year to 9100 in 1st quarter of this year and to 10,600 and 12,900 in subsequent quarters. The interdiction campaign has absorbed most of the increase in deployed attack-capable aircraft in the past years.

A substantial air interdiction campaign is clearly necessary and worth-while. In addition to putting a ceiling on the size of the force that can be supported, it yields three significant military effects. First, it effectively harasses and delays truck movements down through the southern panhandles of NVN and Laos, though it has no effect on troops infiltrating on foot over trails that are virtually invisible from the air. Our experience shows that daytime armed reconnaissance above some minimum sortie rate makes it prohibitively expensive to the enemy to attempt daylight movement of vehicles, and so forces him to night movement. Second, destruction of bridges and cratering of roads forces the enemy to deploy repair crews, equipment, and porters to repair or bypass the damage. Third, attacks on vehicles, parks, and rest camps destroy some vehicles with their cargoes and inflict casualties. Moreover, our bombing campaign may produce a beneficial effect on U.S. and SVN morale by making NVN pay a price for its aggression and by showing that we are doing what we can to interdict the enemy. But at the scale we are now operating, I believe our bombing is yielding very small marginal returns, not worth the cost in pilot lives and aircraft.

* * * * *

141

II.   CONSOLIDATION AND EXTENSION OF GVN CONTROL

Pacification. Based on available reports of questionable validity, the table on the following page indicates the various degrees of GVN and VC/NVA population and hamlet control. In the 14 months between July 31, 1965 and September 30, 1966, the GVN reportedly gained control of an additional 1,500,000 people, raising its control of the total SVN population from 47% to 55% - the highest level to date. During the same period VC/NVA control of the total population decreased 6%, a loss of 800,000 people. GVN control of the rural population rose from 23% to 35%, while VC/NVA rural control fell from 35% to 28% during the same period.

It is highly likely that these figures are grossly optimistic. It should be noted that about 30% of the reported gains probably came from movement of refugees into cities and towns. Another report indicates that GVN increased its control of area only from 8% to 12% in 1966 through September. Since 1965 the VC/NVA have claimed control of 80% of the SVN territory and 75% of the population. At the end of September 1966, the GVN controlled about 25% of the vital roads in SVN. It controlled about 20% of the total roads, down from 35% in 1965 and 40% in 1964. The rest were marginal or closed and could be traveled only with adequate security precautions.

The pacification program has been stalled for years; it is stalled today. The situation in this regard is no better - possibly worse - than it was in 1965, 1963 and 1961. The large unit war, at which we are succeeding fairly well, is largely irrelevant to pacification as long as we keep the regular VC/NVA units from interfering and do not lose the major battles.

POPULATION AND HAMLET CONTROL a/

	July Pop	1965 %	Net Change Pop	Dec Pop	1965 %	Net Change Pop	Sep Pop	1966 %	Total Net Change Pop
Population Control (In Thousands)									
Total SVN Population									
GVN Control	6865	47	+859	7724	52	+627	8351	55	+1486
VC/NVA Control	3658	25	-301	3357	23	-470	2887	19	- 771
Rural Population b/									
GVN Control	2338	23	+756	3094	30	+554	3648	35	+1310
VC/NVA Control	3658	36	-301	3357	33	-470	2887	28	- 771
GVN Hamlet Control	3345		+558	3903		+287	4190		+845

a/ Source: MACV monthly Population and Area Control Report.

b/ Rural population equals total population minus the cities and towns under GVN control.

115

The most important problems are reflected in the belief of the rural Vietnamese that the GVN will not stay long when it comes into an area but the VC will; the VC will punish cooperation with the GVN; the GVN is indifferent to the people's welfare; the low-level GVN officials are tools of the local rich; and the GVN is excessively corrupt from top to bottom.

Success in changing these beliefs, and in pacification, depends on the interrelated functions of providing physical security, destroying the VC organization and presence, motivating the villager to cooperate, and establishing responsive local government.

Physical security must come first and is the essential prerequisite to a successful revolutionary development effort. The security must be permanent or it is meaningless to the villager, and it must be established by a well organized "clear and hold" operation continued long enough to really clear the area and conducted by competent military forces who have been trained to show respect for the villager and his problems. So far this prerequisite has been absent. In almost no area designated for pacification in recent years have ARVN forces actually "cleared and held" to a point where cadre teams could have stayed overnight in hamlets and survived, let alone accomplished their missions. VC units of company and even battalion size, too large for local defenses, have remained in operation.

Now that the threat of a Communist large-unit military victory has been eliminated, we must allocate far more attention and a significant portion of the regular military forces (at least half of the ARVN) to providing permanently secure areas in which Revolutionary Development (RD) teams, police, and civilian administrators can root out the VC infrastructure and establish the GVN presence. This has been our task all along. It is still our task. The war cannot come to a successful end until we have found a way to succeed in this task.

Assignment of ARVN to Revolutionary Development Role. The increasingly unsatisfactory performance of ARVN in combat operations is reflected in U.S. Army advisory reports and in ARVN and U.S. operational statistics. During the January-September period for which data are available, U.S. field advisors rated combat effectiveness as unsatisfactory or marginal in up to 32% of all ARVN combat battalions. Over 115,700 SVN military personnel (19%) deserted in 1965, and desertions in 1966 through October were at the annual rate of 130,000, 21% of the regular, regional, popular and CIDG forces. The poor ARVN performance also shows in the operational statistics. ARVN made contact in only 46% of its large-scale operations against a U.S. contact rate of 90%. Similar actions for small unit actions are not readily available.

143

ARVN & U.S. OPERATIONAL PERFORMANCES - CY1966 [a]
(Weekly Averages)

	1st Qtr	2nd Qtr	3rd Qtr	1966 Thru Sep
Maneuver Battalions (AVG)				
U.S.	44	51	62	52
ARVN	147	157	158	153
Large Operations				
Battalion Days per Bn				
U.S.	3.0	3.1	3.8	3.3
ARVN	2.9	2.2	1.8	2.3
% of Large Operations with Contact				
U.S.	79	94	97	90
ARVN	44	47	47	46

[a] Source: JCS (CM-1901-66).

ARVN effectiveness against the enemy has declined markedly during the January-September 1966 period. ARVN kills of VC/NVA dropped from a weekly average of 356 to 238, while the U.S. averages rose from 476 to 557 per week. VC/NVA killed per ARVN battalion per week averaged 1.8 compared to 8.6 for U.S. battalions. Conversely, the friendly killed rates were .6 per ARVN battalion and 1.7 per U.S. battalion per week. The enemy/friendly killed ratios for ARVN and U.S. were 3.2 and 5.4 to 1 respectively.

ARVN EFFECTIVENESS AGAINST VC/NVA [a] - CY1966
(Weekly Averages)

	1st Qtr	2nd Qtr	3rd Qtr	1966 Thru Sep
Results				
VC/NVA Killed by:				
U.S.	476 [b]	446	557	493
ARVN	356	244	238	279
VC/NVA Captured by:				
U.S.	45 [b]	52	54	50
All GVN Forces	67 [b]	79	105	84
Weapons Captured by:				
U.S.	105 [b]	119	110	111
ARVN	134	84	88	102

[a] Source: Secret NOFORN CINCVICID Message DTG 311950Z Oct 66. NMCC/MC Nr. 10163, Subject: Comparison of Ground Forces (U).
[b] January data unavailable.

144

In view of the ARVN's low efficiency in major combat operations and the increasing difficulties that SVN forces have had in recruiting and retaining the planned forces in an overtaxed economy, I believe that we should not increase the SVN forces (ARVN, Regional and Popular Forces) above the present strength of 158 battalions with 610,000 men. It is likely that GVN control can be extended most rapidly by using SVN forces mainly for revolutionary development, and using additional recruitable personnel for non-military and para-military revolutionary development duty. The ARVN must be retrained and assigned to RD duty, and General Westmoreland plans to do so. The performance of the ARVN and other SVN forces as an instrument for winning popular support for the GVN has been decidedly unsatisfactory. Apparently ARVN personnel have not appreciated the decisive importance of revolutionary development and popular support; the importance of these items will be heavily emphasized in the retraining programs.

The Problem of Inflation. To unite the population behind the Government -- indeed, to avoid disintegration of SVN society -- a sound economy is essential. Runaway inflation can undo what our military operations accomplish. For this reason, I have directed that a "piaster budget" be established for U.S. military funded activities. The intent of this program is to hold military and contracter piaster spending to the minimum level which can be accomplished without serious impact on military operations.

Ambassador Lodge has asked that U.S. military spending be held to P42 billion in CY 67. The Ambassador's proposed program of tightly constrained U.S. and GVN civilian and military spending will not bring complete stability to SVN; there will still be, at best, a P10 billion inflationary gap. It should, however, hold price rises in CY 67 to 10% to 25% as opposed to 75% to 90% in the current year. Unless we rigidly control inflation, the ARVN desertion rate will further increase and effectiveness will decline thus partially canceling the effects of increased U.S. deployments. Further, government employees will leave their jobs and civil strife will occur, possibly collapsing the GVN and, in any event, seriously hindering both the military and the pacification efforts.

The success of our efforts to hold U.S. military expenditures to P42 billion depends, among other things, on U.S. force levels. The impact of three differing deployment plans on piaster spending at constant prices is shown in the table below. The actual level of piaster spending associated with each deployment program is, of course, determined by what policies are pursued in saving piasters. The planning factors used in the table are based on little actual experience and may be either too high or too low to serve as a reliable basis for projection. They do, however, reflect first quarter FY 67 experience, MACV planning factors, and expected anti-inflationary programs.

145

U.S. TROOP DEPLOYMENTS AND DOD PIASTER SPENDING

	End Strength				Average Strength		
	CY66	CY67		CY68			
U.S. Deployments	Dec	Jun	Dec	Jun	FY67 a/	CY67	CY68
Current Program b/	392	434	434	434	368	424	434
SecDef Recommended	391	440	463	479	370	440	468
JCS Recommended	395	456	504	522	376	461	520
Piaster Spending c/							
Current Program					38	41	37
SecDef Recommended					38	43	39
JCS Recommended					39	46	47

a/ All FY 67 statistics based on actual figures for the first quarter and projections for final three.
b/ Program 3 through change 21. Assumes forces hold at June 1967 levels.
c/ Based on annual planning factors of P38,432($234) per man-year for personnel spending, P43,200($540) per man-year for O&M and, for construction:

	SecDef	JCS
FY 67	7,878	7,967
CY 67	6,702	8,343
CY 68	1,386	4,551

The table clearly illustrated that with the deployment of 463,000 troops the CY 67 goal of P42 billion is feasible. The planning factors used, however, entail a "pushing down" of O&M and personal spending from the MACV planning factors ($360 per man year for personal spending, $600 for O&M) in light of past performance and likely future savings;. application of the MACV planning factors result in P46 billion piaster spending. If these later planning factors hold, the P46 spending rate would increase the inflationary gap by 40% and would be a severe blow to the stabilization program. If inflation occurs and U.S. expenditures are maintained in constant dollar terms, piaster expenditures will increase and the problem will be worsened. If the CINCPAC construction program were approved, similar problems would result. It appears imperative to adopt a plan, such as the one exemplified in the table above, which will call for a strong effort to reduce spending below the levels embodied in the MACV planning factors.

In addition to U.S. military spending, stabilization of the SVN economy requires strict limitation of RVNAF spending. We must plan to support the RVNAF at no higher than the Ambassador's requested level of P50 billion during CY 67.

* * * * *

146

3. The Combined Campaign Plan is Published

Ten days earlier, on the 7th, COMUSMACV, in a formal ceremony had signed with General Vien, the Chairman of the RVNAF Joint General Staff, the Combined Campaign Plan 1967, which committed RVNAF to support pacification with the majority of its forces, and identified as priority for U.S. effort military operations in areas adjacent to the populated regions of Vietnam -- the concept advocated by Lodge and Komer throughout the summer. 75/

The concept for conducting operations was as follows:

a. Concept. The initiative achieved in the 1966 Campaign will be retained through a strategic and tactical offensive conducted in consonance with political, economic and sociological programs of GVN and US/FW agencies. RVNAF, U.S. and FWMA forces will be employed to accomplish the mission in accordance with the objectives established and tasks assigned for this campaign. RVNAF will have the primary mission of supporting Revolutionary Development activities, with priority in and around the National Priority Areas and other areas of critical significance, defending governmental centers, and protecting and controlling national resources, particularly rice and salt. U.S. forces will reinforce RVNAF; operate with other FWMAF; and as necessary, conduct unilateral operations. The primary mission of U.S. and FWMAF will be to destroy the VC/NVA main forces, base areas, and resources and/ or drive the enemy into the sparsely populated and food-scarce areas; secure their base areas and clear in the vicinity of these bases; and as directed assist in the protection and control of national resources.

Throughout this campaign increased emphasis will be given to identifying and eliminating the VC infrastructure and to small unit operations designed specifically to destroy the guerrilla force. These operations will be characterized by saturation patrolling, ambushes, and an increase in night operations by both ARVN and US/FWMAF.

River Assault Group forces will be used to the optimum in III and IV CTZ's in small unit operations against enemy river crossing points and tax collection points; in armed river patrol operations in the major rivers of the Delta; and in any other operations where their special capabilities may be profitably employed.

Surface LOC's will be used to the maximum, to include optimum use of River Assault Groups where appropriate, in

support of all operations with a corresponding decrease on
the dependence on airlift support. Riverine operations,
amphibious operations along the RVN coast, and rapid spoiling
attacks will be conducted against enemy units confirmed by
hard intelligence. Emphasis will be placed on all types of
reconnaissance, especially long range patrols, to acquire the
necessary hard intelligence.

The systematic neutralization of the enemy's base
areas will be pursued aggressively during this campaign.
By directing priority of effect to the neutralization of
those base areas which directly affect the National Priority
Areas, key population and economic centers, and vital communications arteries, the accomplishment of both objectives
for this campaign will be facilitated.

Although RVNAF is assigned the primary responsibility
of supporting Revolutionary Development and US/FWMAF are
assigned the primary mission of destroying the main VC/NVA
forces and bases, there will be no clear cut division of
responsibility. RVNAF General Reserve and ARVN Corps Reserve
units will conduct unilateral and participate in coordinated
and combined search and destroy operations. US/FWMAF will
continue to provide direct support and implicit aid to
Revolutionary Development activities.

The people are the greatest asset to the enemy and
control of the people is the enemy's goal. With them, the
enemy has most of the ingredients needed for success: food,
supplies, money, manpower, concealment and intelligence.
During this campaign every effort will be made to deny these
assets to the enemy. Map 1 reflects the National Priority
area for each corps tactical zone, and the area for priority
of military offensive operations. These priority areas
together cover a large majority of the population, food producing lands, and critical lines of communications within
SVN. The National Priority Areas are areas of major significance at the national level where critical civil and military
resources are figured on a priority basis for revolutionary
development. The purpose of designating the area for priority
of military offensive operations in conjunction with the
national priority areas is to focus the attention and effort
of RVNAF and US/FWMAF in those areas where operations will
destroy or drive the enemy into sparsely populated and food-
scarce areas; insure the protection of the population,
control of resources and provide unrestricted use of major
lines of communications, all of which will facilitate follow-
on Revolutionary Development. Spoiling attacks to frustrate
the VC strategy will continue to be conducted in other areas
as directed. 76/

148

Of particular interest in the Combined Campaign Plan is the emphasis given to Revolutionary Development. The concept for this was as follows:

    a. Strategic Concept.

       (1) The GVN strategic concept for defeating the VC/NVA forces and building a viable, free nation includes three separate but mutually supporting operations as follows:

          (a) A military offensive conducted by RVNAF and US/FWMAF to defeat the VC/NVA military forces.

          (b) Revolutionary development conducted by RVNAF and GVN civil elements, with the assistance of US/FWMAF and US/FW civil agencies, to establish and maintain security in populated areas and extend legal government control over these areas.

          (c) Nation building conducted by GVN civil elements, with the assistance of US/FW civil agencies, to complete the development of nationwide political, economic, and social institutions necessary for a viable, free, non-communist Republic of Vietnam.

       (2) The three operations will take place concurrently. In areas where there is adequate government control, nation building will be in progress. In other areas, RD will be underway, while in less secure areas, the military offensive will be prosecuted. Previously, the military offensive dominated national efforts; however, during 1967, RD will receive increasingly greater emphasis. With regard to the military offensive, priority of effort will be given to destroying the enemy forces in those areas where RD is expected to be carried out in the future. Offensive operations also will be conducted to prevent major VC/NVA main forces from interfering in RD and nation building programs that are in progress. _77_/

However, as the year wore on, attention was increasingly focused toward the border regions and the problems of halting enemy infiltration from sanctuaries outside South Vietnam. This is reflected in the operations just south of the DMZ in the I Corps, west of Pleiku, and Kontum in the II Corps, and the movement towards War Zone C in III Corps.

In I CTZ, by the end of October, the NVA 324B Division again was drawn back across the DMZ. Intelligence indicated that the 324B Division had been relieved by the NVA 341st and had withdrawn north of the DMZ. The 341st was in and just north of the DMZ near the eastern edge of the mountainous area. By the end of the year, the attention of the Marines in the I Corps Tactical Zone was fastened on the DMZ. 78/

In II CTZ, PAUL REVERE IV, which ran from 18 October through the end of the year, conducted by elements of the recently arrived 4th Infantry Division and the 25th Infantry Division with later reinforcement by two battalions of the 1st Cavalry Division, resulted in almost a thousand enemy killed. 79/

In III CTZ, in spite of the casualties which the enemy had sustained in EL PASO II, the 9th VC Division moved into well-concealed base areas where he absorbed replacements, retrained them on their equipment. In early November, the 9th VC Division moved into a new base area near the Michelin Plantation intending to use this base as a jumping off place for objectives in Tay Ninh. Instead, the enemy collided with the 196th Infantry Brigade, resulting in Operation ATTLEBORO. ATTLEBORO, begun on 14 September as a single battalion search and destroy operation, expanded as additional base areas were located and by 3 November, the operation had grown to include portions of the 1st Infantry Division, the 3rd Brigade of the 4th Infantry Division and 173rd Airborne Brigade. By the time ATTLEBORO was terminated in late November, the enemy had lost over 1,000 killed. The pattern in III Corps, with the exception of a couple of operations in Phuoc Tuy Province designed basically to clear the lines of communication from Saigon to Vung Tau, was a gradual shifting of emphasis northward from Long An Province to Hoa Ninh Province to Binh Duong and then north and west into Tay Ninh Province and War Zone C. 80/

By the end of the year, MACV estimated the total forces available to the enemy in Vietnam at 152 combat battalions, the total personnel strength of 280,600, of which 123,600 were combat or support troops, 112,000 were militia, and 39,000 were political cadre. MACV had accepted a figure of 48,400 infiltrators during the year. An additional 25,600 may have infiltrated on the basis of information evaluated as possibly true. This total of 74,000, accepted and possible, was based on information available to MACV as of 31 Dec 66. The infiltration rate for the first 6 months of 1966 was approximately 15 battalion equivalents. Although most of this infiltration took place through Laos, an increasing number had begun to infiltrate through the Demilitarized Zone as the year wore on. 81/

Program 4 was promulgated on 18 November 1966. 82/   At the time it was published events in Vietnam and decisions in Washington had essentially rendered the ground strategy concepts of AB 142 meaningless. Program 4 denied COMUSMACV the additional troops he proclaimed necessary for the tasks set forth in AB 142, while the troops he did have were engaged in War Zone C, in the highland border areas, and along the DMZ -- far from the populated regions of Vietnam, which constituted the National Priority areas of AB 142.

SOUTHEAST ASIA DEPLOYMENT PROGRAM #4 SUMMARY SCHEDULE
(To be used in Manpower and Logistical Planning and Financial Budgeting)

		1965				1966													1967													1968			
		Jan	Oct	Dec	Mar	Jun	Sep	Oct	Nov	Dec	Jan	Feb	Mar	Apr	May	Jun	Jul	Aug	Sep	Oct	Nov	Dec	Jan	Feb	Mar	Apr	May	Jun	Jul	Aug	Sep	Oct	Nov	Dec	Mar	Jun

MANEUVER BATTALIONS IN SVN:

US & VNAF FIGHTER AND ATTACK SORTIES

B-52 SORTIES

AIR OPERATIONS CONSUMPTION (Thousands of Tons)

USAF & VNAF FIGHTER AND ATTACK TACTICAL SQUADRONS

US FIGHTER AND ATTACK TACTICAL AIRCRAFT (INCL NAVY)

US & VNAF FIGHTER AND ATTACK AIRCRAFT LOSSES

ATTACK SORTIE LOSS RATES

HELICOPTER DEPLOYMENTS

HELICOPTER LOSSES (ARMY AND USMC)

TOTAL US HELICOPTERS

FORCES EXPOSED (Millions: Pl)

a/ Denotes preliminary data.
b/ Excludes approximately 100 tons per month accrued in overseas training.
c/ Figure is being verified for accuracy.
d/ Tentative pending detailed analysis.

Program 4
OASD/SA/SEA Programs Division
November 17, 1966

124

F. What Did It Mean?

Program 4 had important historical antecedents which provide the
basic texture of the decision-making on Program 5. The preceding
sections have outlined the major themes and historical developments
which projected into the succeeding program with telling effect. These
can be briefly summarized as follows:

(1) A precedent, albeit a seemingly fragile one, of essentially saying "no" to the COMUSMACV force requirements was established.
Actually, DoD and the President were beginning to question the concept
of operation for Vietnam which had led to programs, now becoming increasingly costly and depressingly barren of tangible results. The illusion
of quick victory "on the cheap" had fled, and hard reality intervened.
People in and out of government were beginning to seek alternatives to
our policies in Vietnam with increased interest, and Program 5 was to
increasingly reflect this basic mood surfacing in late 1966.

(2) The JCS had adopted a strategic concept based upon widely
expanded operations in the North, widened and intensified operations in
the South designed to seek out and destroy enemy forces, and committed
to assisting the GVN in building an "independent, viable, non-communist
society" -- a vestige of the unfortunate wording of NSAM 288. 83/   The
military heads had been denied the troops they said they required to
successfully accomplish the objectives developed under the concept, but
the concept itself had survived. This strategic thought was to provide
the conceptual baseline for Program 5.

(3) The basic troop requirement numbers, so important to
Program 5, were introduced during Program 4. In fact, the refined
figure the JCS proposed in JCSM 702-66 for mid-1968, 524,288, became
the eventual "approved" figure for Program 5. This number remained a
focal point throughout the planning period despite frequent important
changes in the strategic situation.

(4) Certain "oblique alternatives," those which were not
directly substitutable options appeared during this time -- all of them
designed to relieve pressure on U.S. resources, especially manpower.
Among these were the barrier plan (proposed by McNamara), new free
world military force sharing formulas (KANZUS), efforts to subtly hold
the RVNAF's "feet to the fire," and operations of various kinds in the
"sanctuaries."

(5) The Reserve mobilization line -- a political sound barrier
as it were, remained unbroken.

The JCS had made a two-pronged case for breaking it: One,
that we could not adequately meet CINCPAC's 1967 requirements and simultaneously fulfill our commitments to NATO and other threatened areas
without mobilization (and even then probably dangerously late); and

secondly, only such massive infusions of firepower in the North and manpower in the South as they proposed could possibly achieve our war
termination objectives "in the shortest time with the least cost" and
this could not be done unless we mobilized. Other arguments emerged
in discussions. There were those who feared the move because of the
inherent uncertainties about public reaction. To this the Chiefs
replied that mobilization had traditionally unified the country, and
it would also provide a strong indication of our national resolve --
an important message to relay to Hanoi, and one in which Westmoreland
as a field commander was also interested. Regardless, the issue loomed
as the ceiling figure in the majority of ground-force strategy deliberations -- it appeared that the level was periodically studied, possibly
negotiated, but always there -- the "Plimsoll line." 84/

(6) Public disenchantment with the war was growing, and this
was being manifested in diverse ways. On the "hawk" side powerful
political figures (and many lesser ones) were increasingly vocal in
their opposition to bombing restraints and restrictive force levels.
Senator Stennis was in the vanguard of this group. On the other side,
public and private figures alike were energetically working to create a
genuine political war issue and to generate palatable alternative policies
for the upcoming Presidential elections in 1968. Feeding a less focused
sense of public dissatisfaction was an increasing awareness of the opportunity costs of the war in terms of national resources -- men, money and
attention -- denied to domestic programs. As the defense slice of the
budget hovered near the eighty billion dollar mark, the public realized
it was "paying more and liking it less." There were strong inclinations
to "paying less" as long as the voter was resigned to liking it less.

The press was moving beyond the bounds of its traditional
adversary relationship vis-a-vis the Administration and assuming a leading
role in catalyzing the swell of public opposition and questioning about
the war. Acute even early on in the war, the press opposition intensified
and expanded as the divergence of official public pronouncements on the
war and what reporters and their sources saw on the ground increased.

(7) Failure is in the truest sense an orphan and as the sense
of futility and self-doubt about achieving our objectives in Vietnam
heightened, the architects of our military ground strategy found themselves increasingly isolated. The official base of support for the
MACV strategy narrowed as more alternatives to it were seriously examined
in Washington. This tended not only to aggravate a communications problem which had always hindered political-military planning, but it placed
COMUSMACV-CINCPAC on the defensive, creating an information and planning
bias (from those sources) toward protection, justification and continuation of present programs.

(8) Finally, we had a field commander facing a strategic
dilemma with no high prospect of satisfactory resolution. If it had

153

any hope of success, the Combined Campaign Plan for 1967 required both
a military "shield" to keep large enemy units from the populated areas
where pacification was proceeding, and a "shelter" under which pacified
areas could be respectably kept that way. The "shield" concept could be
implemented in a number of ways, statically or dynamically, (mobile vs.
position defense) geographically oriented or enemy force oriented, or by
different combinations of these at different times. General Westmoreland's
strategy based upon exploitation of our inherent superior mobility and
firepower was designed to simultaneously attrite the enemy and retain the
initiative by disrupting VC/NVA operations before they completely materialized. This led to seeking engagement with enemy main force units well
out into the border regions, where they literally could be held at distance
before jumping off in operations. Related to this was the notion that the
important thing was to fight -- to engage the enemy and create casualties.
It mattered little that you accepted combat in regions with certain
advantages for the enemy -- the prime objective was to engage and to kill
him.

Fighting the mobile defense kind of war provides an adequate but
not perfect shield. You can liken it to a vast semi-permeable membrane
which has significant leakage by small amounts, over time. Backing up this
kind of a "shield" is the "shelter" also manned by combat troops, geographically dispersed (actually occupying) in the areas where pacification
is going on. The combination of the two, shield and shelter, require
men and the balance is crucial, especially so if you have limited resources.
If your operating assumptions are those held by COMUSMACV in late 1966,
then what you have for the "shelter" is a function of the kind and sizes
of enemy forces you are fighting in the "shield" mission. If you are
fighting large units at many points simultaneously, you are forced to
strip "shelter" forces -- or to use ARVN (or request more U.S. forces).
As Program 4 closes we find MACV facing just those same large multiple
threats, stripping the "shelter" forces, and relying upon an inadequate
ARVN for the majority of pacification security. With sufficient forces,
U.S. and ARVN, the task was prodigious -- and precarious. To attempt to
"shield" without adequate forces to "shelter" was bound to be precarious.

154

FOOTNOTES

1. CINCPAC 3010, Ser: 000255, 18 Jun 66, Subj: Calendar Year 1966 Adjusted Requirements and Calendar Year 1967 Requirements.

2. National Intelligence Estimate 14.3-66, North Vietnamese Military Potential for Fighting in South Vietnam, 7 Jul 66.

3. JCSM 506-66, dated 5 Aug 66, Subj: CINCPAC CY 1966 Adjusted Force Requirements and CY 1967 Force Requirements.

4. SecDef Memo for Chairman of the JCS, dtd 5 Aug 66, Subj: CINCPAC CY 66 Adjusted Requirements and CY 67 Requirements.

4a. MACV 27578 dtd 10 Aug 66, Westmoreland to Admiral Sharp and General Wheeler, Subj: CY 66-67 Force Requirements, emphasis added.

5. Saigon 2564, dtd 3 Aug 66, from Lodge for the President.

6. Saigon 3129, dated 10 Aug 66.

7. Ibid.

8. Ibid.

9. CINCPAC 232333Z Aug 66 to COMUSMACV, Subj: Draft Military Strategy to Accomplish US Objectives for Vietnam.

10. Ibid.

11. Report of Inter-Agency "Roles and Missions" Study Group, U.S. Mission, Vietnam, 24 Aug 66.

12. MACV 29797 to CINCPAC, Subj: Concept of Military Operations in SVN (U), dated 26 Aug 66.

13. Ibid., p. 2.

14. Ibid.

15. Ibid., p. 6.

16. Saigon 4923, dated 31 Aug 66.

17. Ibid., p. 2.

18. Ibid., p. 3.

19. Ibid., Section two, page 2.

155

20. Command History, 1966, Hq USMACV, 19 Apr 67, pp. 21-22.

21. Ibid., pp. 366-369.

22. Ibid., p. 377.

23. MACV Command History, 1966, p. 376.

24. Ibid., p. 385.

25. Saigon 2934 from AmEmb Saigon to Sec/State, dtd 8 Aug 66.

26. Ibid.

27. Ibid.

28. MACV 27578, Subj: CY 66-67 Force Requirements dtd 10 Aug 66.

29. Saigon 3601 from AmEmb Saigon to SecState, dtd 16 Aug 66.

30. Air Supported Anti-Infiltration Barrier, Aug 66, Institute for Defense Analyses, JACN Division.

31. Ibid.

32. CINCPAC to JCS, DTG 071925Z Apr 66, Subj: Counter-Infiltration Barrier.

33. MACV 4287, 24 Sep 66.

34. MACV 4326, 2 Oct 66.

35. COMUSMACV 41191 to CINCPAC, Subj: Threat to I CTZ, dtd 13 Sep 66, emphasis added.

36. MACV 160519Z Sep 66 to CINCPAC, Subj: COMUSMACV Slam Concept

37. MACV 8212 from Westmoreland to Sharp, Subj: Containment of Enemy Forces in Sanctuary, DTG 201156Z Sep 66, emphasis added.

38. Saigon 3670 to SecState, Porter for Komer, dated 17 Aug 66.

39. Saigon 6100, Subj: Inflation Control in CY 1967 Programs, dtd 15 Sep 66.

40. State 53541, Subj: CY 67 Inflation Control, dtd 23 Sep 66.

41. Ibid.

42. CM-1774-66, Subj: Revised Piaster Limits on Military Spending in Vietnam, dtd 22 Sep 66.

156

43. Saigon 7332 to SecState, dtd 1 Oct 66.

44. MACV 44378, Subj: Piaster Budget, CY 1967, 5 Oct 66.

45. ASD(SA) Memo for SecDef, Subj: US Military Piaster Spending in
South Vietnam FY 67 and CY 67, dtd 5 Oct 66.

46. JCSM 613-66, Subj: CINCPAC CY 1966 Adjusted Force Requirements and
CY 1967 Force Requirements.

46a. Memo for SecDef, Subj: SEA Deployment Plan, dtd 29 Sep 66.

47. JCSM-646-66, Subj: World-Wide U.S. Military Posture (U), dtd 7 Oct
66. Its baseline for requirement analysis was JCSM 721-65, dtd 24 Sep 65,
Subj: "US Military Posture (U)," which provided a broad strategic
concept embracing the following objectives:

    a. In conjunction with allied forces, maintain forward deploy-
ments world-wide to deter communist aggression.

    b. A military capability to support NATO/Europe obligations with
active, readily deployable forces through the first month (M/D+30) in
the event or imminence of hostilities.

    c. A military capability to conduct other contingency operations
in which force commitments are of a minor nature but where timely
commitment of such forces may be crucial to the attainment of US
objectives.

    d. Support military operations in Southeast Asia.

    e. Maintain an adequate training and rotation base to support
the above.

48. Ibid.

49. Ibid. See: Tab F to Appendix A, "Summary of U.S. Army Forces (U)"
to JCSM 646-66, dated 7 October 1966.

50. SecDef memo for the President, Subj: Actions Recommended for Vietnam,
dated 14 Oct 66, emphasis added.

51. For a detailed analysis of this aspect, see Task Force Paper entitled
"Re-emphasis on Pacification."

52. Memorandum for the President, 14 Oct 66, op. cit.

53. JCSM-672-66, Subj: "Actions Recommended for Vietnam (U)," dtd
14 Oct 66.

54. Ibid.

151

55. Ibid.

56. In a sense, JCSM-672-66 appears to be a delaying device used to buy time for the COMUSMACV reclamas to the DPM. However, it concomitantly provided an excellent opening through which to drive home their views on the bombing and negotiations.

57. CINCPAC 3010, Ser 000438, Subj: Calendar Year 1966, and 1967 Force Requirements/Capabilities Programs (U), dtd 20 Oct 66.

58. CINCPAC Serial 000445, 23 Oct 66.

59. Memorandum for the Secretary of Defense from McNaughton, ASD(ISA), Subj: "McNaughton in Manila, October 23-25," dtd 26 Oct 66.

60. Ibid. For McNamara's views on the communications aspects of our force structure in SVN, see page 5, Memo for the President, 14 Oct 66.

61. Ibid., At another time Westmoreland reported that the President had asked him his views in front of Thieu and Ky and he had given them; that Rostow had asked him to put them into a memo which he was drafting. McNaughton observed that he had a sort of paired list of favorable targets -- ones related to air defense, ones to infiltration and ones to "bargaining," but none very explicitly analyzed.

62. The New York Times, 1 November 1966. The article said the Army had 76,451 men more than authorized, the Air Force 44,313, the Navy 12,029, and the Marines over 2,000. The conclusion was that with the increased forces (the Army had been told to go to 1,500,000 according to the piece) the country could support 500,000 troops in SVN in CY 1967 and to these increases 600,000 the following year. It did indicate that resistance from both civilian and military sources was growing in the Pentagon.

63. The New York Times, 4 November 1966.

64. The New York Times, 9 November 1966.

65. The New York Times, 6-12 Nov 66. The officer quoted in a front page story was M/G William DePuy, then CG, 1st Division.

66. The New York Times, 3-11 Nov 66.

67. Ibid.

68. Ibid. The ambiguity in the statement is interesting. The JCS acknowledge that the program as proposed was adequate (even in light of their earlier analysis of US worldwide posture deficiencies), but could not be developed without some yet unnamed "modifications" to the criteria. The door remained open to come back in for the reserves if need be.

158

69. Ibid.

70. The New York Times, 6 November 1966.

71. ASD(SA) Memo for the SecDef, Subj: Deployments to Southeast Asia, dtd 9 Nov 66.

72. The New York Times, 11 Nov 66. The subject of Vietnam was obscured at this conference by the Soviet ABM issue, for McNamara confirmed at this conference that the Soviets had an ABM system, and the US was studying the problem.

73. Memo for the Chairman of the JCS, Subj: Deployments to Southeast Asia (U), dtd 11 Nov 66.

74. Draft Memorandum for the President, Subject: Recommended FY 67 Southeast Asia Supplemental Appropriation (U), dtd 17 Nov 66.

75. See MACV 52414, Subj: "Military Planning and Progress in SVN," dated 8 December 1966. This message extends MACV 061300Z November 1966, same title. This plan, transparently an effort to get the GVN officially on the line for emphasis upon revolutionary development, in COMUSMACV's eyes incorporated two significant innovations:

    "...First, the plan requires RVNAF and MACV subordinate commands to prepare supporting plans to accomplish the objectives, tasks and goals stated in AB 142 and to support the achievement of goals stated in provincial revolutionary development (RD) plans. These plans are to be submitted for review by 15 December. Second, to maintain the viable nature of this plan, a requirement for quarterly reviews has been incorporated. These reviews will cover progress made, problems encountered, and recommendations for improvement. A combined RVNAF/MACV directive is being developed which establishes procedures for these reviews..." (See: MACV 341, 080245Z December 1966)

    The follow-up to this message, also an extension, is MACV 00989, 9 January 1967.

76. AB 142 Combined Campaign Plan, 1967, pp. B-1, B-2.

77. Ibid.

78. MACV Command History, 1966, pp. 368-369.

79. Ibid., pp. 378-379.

80. Ibid., pp. 386-387.

81. _Ibid._, p. 22.

82. Memo for Secretaries of the Military Departments, Chairman of the JCS, Assistant Secretaries of Defense, Subj: Southeast Asia Deployment Program #4, dtd 18 Nov 66.

83. JCSM 702-66, _op. cit._

84. An early plumbing of this line was an article in early 1965 by Hanson W. Baldwin, entitled: "We Must Choose -- (1) 'Bug Out'; (2) Negotiate; (3) Fight." He wrote:

> "How many United States soldiers would be needed is uncertain -- probably a minimum of three to six divisions (utilized chiefly in battalion or brigade sized units), possibly as many as 10 or 12 divisions. Including Air Force, Navy and supporting units perhaps 200,000 to 1,000,000 Americans would be fighting in Vietnam.

> "Obviously this would mean a Korea type conflict, a major war, no matter what euphemisms would be used. Nor could we wage it in the present 'business as usual' economy. We would require partial mobilization, vastly beefed up military production. Many weaknesses in our military structure would need strengthening. Even so, we could not anticipate quick success. The war would be long, nasty and wearing." (The New York Times, 21 February 1965, p. 63).

IV.C Evolution of the War (26 Vols.)
Direct Action: The Johnson Commitments, 1964-1968
(16 Vols.)
6. U.S. Ground Strategy and Force Deployments: 1965-1967
(3 Vols.)
b. Volume II: Program 5

IV.C Evolution of the War (26 Vols.)
Direct Action: The Johnson Commitments, 1964-1968
(16 Vols.)
6. U.S. Ground Strategy and Force Deployments: 1965-1967
(3 Vols.)
b. Volume II: Program 5

UNITED STATES - VIETNAM RELATIONS

1945 - 1967

VIETNAM TASK FORCE

OFFICE OF THE SECRETARY OF DEFENSE

SET #13

IV.C.6. (b)

U.S. GROUND STRATEGY
AND FORCE DEPLOYMENTS
1965--1967

VOLUME II

0295

TABLE OF CONTENTS
AND OUTLINE

VOLUME II
U.S. GROUND STRATEGY AND FORCE DEPLOYMENTS, 1965--1967

TABLE OF CONTENTS and OUTLINE

IV. PROGRAM 5

TOP SECRET - Sensitive

FIGURES

TOP SECRET - Sensitive

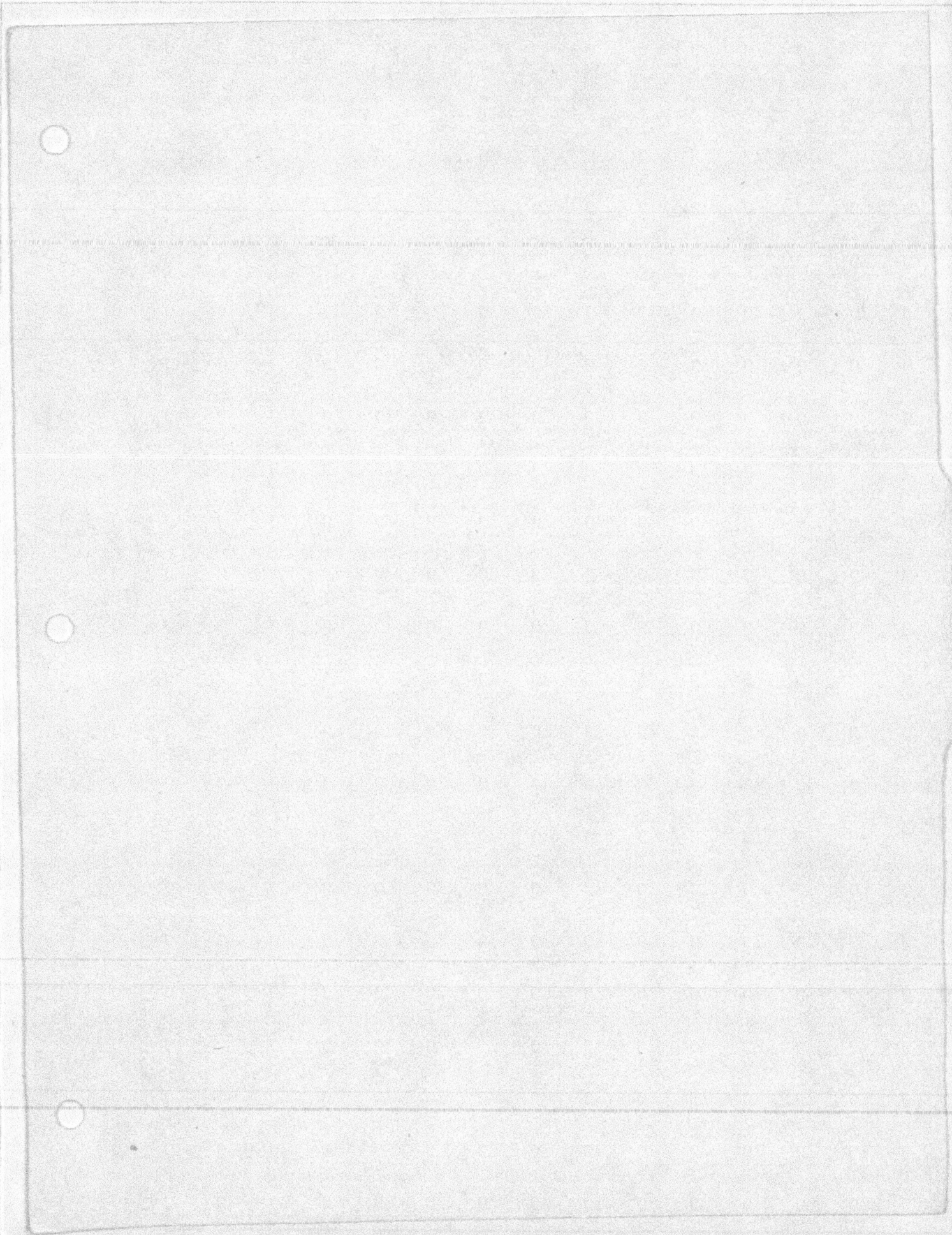

IV. PROGRAM 5

A. PRELUDE TO ACTION ON PROGRAM 5

1. Hedged Public Optimism Meets the New Year

The last month of 1966 was like all such months -- a time for official retrospection and tally. The mood was one of cautious optimism, buoyed by hopes that 1967 would prove to be the decisive year in Vietnam.

The indicators showed that great progress had been made -- quantitatively, anyway. The number of U.S. and FW maneuver battalions available for operations in South Vietnam had increased from 45 to 102. ARVN had added another 24 such units, bringing its total to 163, so altogether there were 265 battalions ready to commence operations in the new year. 1/ In short, the US-FW resources available for operations roughly doubled during the second year of the war, and they promised to be even higher during the third. 2/

Large ground operations were mounting in number and duration, and the trend promised to continue pointed sharply upward (see Figs. 1-8). This upswing in activity was attributed to the rapid infusion of U.S. battalions; indications were that such a high level of activity was not independent, but so strongly correlated with our presence that, if we willed, it could be "sustained indefinitely." 3/

More importantly, all of these gains seemed to be having a relevant impact on the enemy -- causing his battlefield fortunes to decline closer to the point where he would be forced to stop fighting or negotiate, or both. Even accepting the historical overstatement of enemy losses -- the bias is reasonably consistent -- and the trend in enemy losses to all causes was rising sharply. 4/   Kill ratios (enemy KIA vs. allied KIA) were up to 4.2 from 3.3 during the preceding six month period. RVNAF losses actually declined; but unfortunately US/FW KIA doubled -- a fact that the press was later to pick up and exploit in its criticism of the ARVN/GVN role in the war. (See Tables 4 and 5, Appendix B).

Observers believed that most of the enemy battalions, NVA and VC, were in place six months ahead of the U.S., and that only recently had the full consequences of our enlarged participation been reflected in enemy strength and OB figures. From July 1966, VC/NVA strength had appeared to decline slightly, although they had evidently been able to maintain their oft-cited target of 100,000 men in the field.

Irregular forces had apparently declined to about 180,000 (confirmed by a VC document captured on CEDAR FALLS) and their "solid" recruitment population base had shrunk. Another VC document contained an estimate that VC/NVA forces had lost about 1,000,000 people to GVN control during the last half of 1966. There was increasing evidence that NVA was furnishing large numbers of replacements for damaged VC units, even for local forces and some units in the Delta. The great uncertainty, surely, if you accepted the indicators and the analysis of what they meant, was the infiltration rate and how successful we assumed we would be in controlling it.

Just as crucial seemed to be the level of VC/NVA activity as the year closed. Systems Analysis estimated that incidents were down 19% ("incidents" being attacks, terror, harassment and sabotage). Battalion-sized and larger enemy attacks in late 1966 were down to less than half those of the preceding six months, while small attacks nearly trebled. The significance of some relationships holding here was lost on decision-makers until much later in the new year when we began to seriously question the search and destroy strategy in Vietnam. The assumption that major enemy unit activity was a function of the total size of our forces, i.e., the more we have the more extensively active we can be in search, finding and destroying large units, is just not a convincing one when you look at enemy activity (large units) vs. our build-up. Also, leading from this, no one had yet questioned another assumption implicit in the COMUS-MACV attrition strategy; we needed to ask: Who initiates the battles when they do occur?

Revolutionary development plans were moving ahead. By 9 January 1967, the provincial RD programs had been approved by General Thaing, Commissioner General of RD; some 1,091 hamlets with a total population of 1,272,950 people were to be the targets of extensive RD effort. However, inputs and plans do not constitute outputs or results and such flimsy evidence as this offered as proof of "progress" was surely transparent. Concurrently, however, the reaction of the enemy to pacification seemed to be confirmation that the program was making headway. Looking back to the 1964-1965 "pacification programs" the enemy hardly bothered to react to what he considered a minimal threat, and an unwanted diversion from his successful military campaign. Only in late 1966 did he begin to exert significant effort and begin attacking RD cadre teams. Many disagreed with this interpretation, but few could dispute the graphic evidence of basic RD weakness (security) the VC/NVA operations had revealed. RD cadre desertions increased markedly (33 to 84 per week from January to March 1967) and the program was grossly unable to meet its recruitment goals (approximately 10,000 short of the 41,000 CY 67 target). 5/

If military indicators were trending upward, the political indicators at the new year, both at home and abroad, were mixed. The Levy case had broken to the press and had become the temporary focus of anti-war group propaganda at the close of the year. U Thant had advanced his proposals for peace to the President who promised to give them "careful evaluation." 6/ Harrison Salisbury's dispatches from North Vietnam were generating an explosive debate about the bombing. Not only had he questioned the "surgical" precision claimed for the bombing of military targets in populated areas, but he questioned the basic purpose of the strategy itself. In his view, civilian casualties were being inflicted deliberately to break the morale of the populace, a course both immoral and doomed to failure. The counter-attack mounted by bombing advocates (and apologists) combined with the predictable quick denunciations and denials from official sources helped generate a significant public reaction. 7/

The Pentagon reaction to the Salisbury articles touched off a new round of editorial comment about the credibility gap. Polls at the start of the year reflected the public's growing cynicism about public statements. One Harris poll indicated that the public of January 1967 was just as likely to blame the United States for truce violations (despite public announcements to the contrary) as the enemy. Two years earlier this had not been so. 8/ Salisbury happened to be in North Vietnam when Hanoi was first bombed -- whether by accident or design is uncertain. Consequently, his dispatches carried added sting -- he was reporting on the less appealing aspects of a major escalation in the bombing campaign which would have attracted headlines on its own merits. His "in depth" of such an important benchmark added markedly to its public impact. 9/ So great was the cry that President Johnson felt impelled to express "deep regret" over civilian casualties on both sides.

Actual war news seemed good. Draft calls were down with the policy of "keeping /the/ induction rate at a reduced level for 1967." (McNamara press conference). Allies like Thailand were helping to ease our manpower and commitment problems, the Thais announced in January that they were dispatching 1,000 troops to South Vietnam. The U.S. 9th Infantry Division had commenced landing at Vang Tau, highlighting the continuing infusion of U.S. strength now reaching the 380,000-man mark. North Vietnam's MIG force had come up to engage our bombers over Hanoi on 7 January. The result was the foe's worst day of air war -- seven MIG's were downed. The United States made its first direct troop commitment to the Delta when Marines were landed at Thanh Phong Peninsula. This event generated a storm of criticism especially from Congressman Gerald Ford who attacked the Administration for expanding operations into the Delta without advising Congress. 10/

There was little to be hopeful about in regard to North Vietnam's resolution, it was not eroding. The Washington Star, in an exclusive, quoted Premier Phan Van Dong of the DRV as being convinced that American public opinion would eventually force the U.S. to leave South Vietnam. He confirmed the oft-expressed fears of U.S. officials who prophesied great danger of a wider and bloodier war if North Vietnam mis-read the peace marches and opposition to the war, interpreting it as lack of U.S. determination. 11/ Earlier, Salisbury had quoted the Premier when he discussed the bombing, saying "that once hostilities are brought to an end it would be possible to speak of other things." 12/ The North Vietnamese were evidently resigned to a long bitter war -- one they believed they could wait out better than we.

Declassified per Executive Order 13526, Section 3.3
NND Project Number: NND 63316. By: NWD Date: 2011

p>TOP SECRET - Sensitive</p>

p>To Walter Lippman, the New Year meant "there is hope only in a
negotiated compromise" (emphasis added), but to others optimism was
the keynote. Ambassador Lodge, in his New Year's statement, predicted
that "allied forces will make sensational military gains in 1967" and
"the war would end in an eventual fadeout once the allied pacification
effort made enough progress to convince Hanoi that the jig was up." 13/
The New York Daily News informed 15 million New Yorkers that the "U.S.
Expects to Crush Main Red Force in '67." 14/</p>

p>As if to balance the cacophony of war dialogue, a final dissonant
note was sounded during those first two weeks of the new year. The famous
"Goldberg Reply" to U Thant's note of 30 December had angered and dismayed
the Secretary General. At a news conference he discussed the U.S. reply
to his message which had basically implored the U.S. to discontinue the
bombing so some kind of talks could open. The U.S. rejection, outlining
its condition of "reciprocal acts" on the part of North Vietnam, he said
was "much regretted," for in his estimation it was based upon an unfortunate
misreading of history and the current situation as well as the result of
misguided assumptions about the "domino theory," which he rejected. The
strong opposition he voiced created important political "ripples" in the
United Nations, Washington, and abroad. A certain mood of frustration
and opposition which had already taken root was nourished and sustained
by the incident. 15/</p>

p>2. Official Optimism and a Spur to Action: The Komer Memo</p>

p>Seeds of optimism were not restricted to the public at large, but also
found sustenance in official circles -- primarily in the White House staff.
R. W. Komer, in what he titled a "Vietnam Prognosis for 1967-68," provided
a markedly optimistic view of the future and a firm conviction that the
military situation was manageable, if not well in hand. He was convinced
that COMUSMACV's "spoiling strategy" had thrown Hanoi's calculations badly
out of balance, and put us "well past the first turning point where we
stopped losing the war." 16/   In this he agreed with the McNamara 14 October DPM; both believed that we had stopped losing. He saw other major
turning points. He suspected that we had reached a point where we were
killing, defecting or otherwise attriting more VC/NVA strength than the
enemy could build up -- in the vernacular, the "cross-over" point. He
cited the favorable indicators, but he neither sounded completely convinced
nor conclusive.</p>

p>A critical psychological turning point may have been crossed, he
believed, because he detected that the bulk of SVN's population increasingly believed that we were winning the war. (He saw this as the chief
significance of the 80% voter turnout on 11 September.) He concluded
his introduction with:</p>

blockquote>"In sum--slow, painful, and incredibly expensive though
it may be--we're beginning to 'win' the war in Vietnam. This
is a far cry from saying, however, that we're going to win it
--in any meaningful sense,"</blockquote>

p>TOP SECRET - Sensitive</p>

He saw quite clearly the imponderables which made any prognosis a hazardous undertaking:

"A. <u>Will Hanoi materially increase its infiltration rate?</u> I gather this is feasible (though will the barrier make a major difference?).

"B. <u>Will the enemy escalate?</u> Aside from increasing infiltration, I see little more Hanoi itself could do. Or Moscow. Peking could intervene in Vietnam or widen the area of hostilities in SEA, but this seems quite unlikely.

"C. <u>Will the enemy revert to a guerrilla strategy?</u> This could be a serious complication before we get a major pacification effort underway. But the evidence suggests that the VC are still attempting to organize regiments and divisions. I'd also agree with Doug Pike's conclusion in his new book, 'Viet Cong' that such de-escalation would shatter VC morale.

"D. <u>Will Hanoi play the negotiating card, and how?</u> If I'm right about the trend line, Hanoi would find it wiser to negotiate. The only other options are escalation, growing attrition, or fading away. If Hanoi decides to talk sometime in 1967, a whole new calculus intervenes, involving questions of cease-fire, standstill, bombing pauses, etc. In this case we'll have to do a new prognosis.

"E. <u>Will the GVN fall apart politically?</u> While it was a risk worth taking, we've opened Pandora's box by promoting a political evolution to representative government. A series of coups or political crises in Cochin China or Annam could so undermine GVN cohesiveness as to cause a major setback of popular revulsion in the U.S. I expect plenty of political trouble, but would hazard that a crisis of such magnitude can be avoided in 1967 if we work hard at it.

"F. <u>Will our new pacification program work?</u> This too is a major imponderable. But we've nowhere to go but up. We're at long last planning a major new resource input plus the necessary focus on improving US management and redirecting ARVN assets. So to me the chief variable is how much progress we can make how soon. Will it be enough to make a significant difference in 1967 or even 1968?

"G. <u>Last but not least, will the US appear to settle down for a long pull if necessary?</u> This is hardest to predict, yet crucial from the standpoint of SVN and NVN reactions." 17/

Trends as he saw them would continue up (even sifting out the imponderables). The only explanation for under-achievement militarily, in pacification, and political development, would be "something unforeseeable" (not specified). We would be on the high-side of the curve, as he termed it, with the key issue one of "whether the U.S. appears prepared to stick it out as long as necessary or to be tiring of the war."

He closed by drawing the lessons imbedded in his analysis:

"...My prognosis of what is more likely than not to happen in Vietnam is reasonable only if we and the GVN mount a maximum effort in 1967-68 to make it so. The key is better orchestration and management of our Vietnam effort--both in Washington and Saigon. To me, the most important ingredient of such an outcome is less another 200,000 troops, or stepped-up bombing, or a $2 billion civil aid program--than it is more effective use of the assets we already have.

"A. The war will be 'won' (if we can use that term) in the South. Now that we are successfully countering NVA infiltration and the enemy's semi-conventional strategy, what needs to be added is increasing erosion of southern VC strength (it has probably already peaked out).

"B. Assuming the above is broadly valid, the key to success in the South is an effective pacification program, plus a stepped-up defection program and successful evolution toward a more dynamic, representative and thus more attractive GVN. These efforts will reinforce each other in convincing the Southern VC and Hanoi that they are losing.

"C. Our most important under-utilized asset is the RVNAF. Getting greater efficiency out of the 700,000 men we're already supporting and financing is the cheapest and soundest way to get results in pacification.

"D. By themselves, none of our Vietnam programs offer high confidence of a successful outcome (forcing the enemy either to fade away or to negotiate). Cumulatively, however, they can produce enough of a bandwagon psychology among the southerners to lead to such results by end-1967 or sometime in 1968. At any rate, do we have a better option?" 18/

Komer's primary misgivings related to the ability of GVN to exploit military successes and to convert them into meaningful steps forward in the nation-building program. Creating and sustaining viable political institutions in a revolutionary environment has never been easy, and

many agreed with Komer's apprehensions. A widely circulated National
Intelligence Estimate, published shortly thereafter, detailed the fragile
nature of political development in South Vietnam, characterizing it as
"a day-to-day, month-to-month phenomenon for some time to come, with
periodic upheavals and crises /that will/ threaten the entire process." 19/

Despite a cautiously optimistic approach to the prospects for a more
stable political situation, the same NIE identified serious potential
sources of instability in the small nation. It saw regionalism as a
factor whose influence might burgeon as political events quickened. The
military domination of the political life of the country remained an
explosive issue. Finally, United States presence and objectives remained
a major consideration in analyzing the future behavior of the political
actors in South Vietnam. Confidence in the American commitment and stead-
fastness in our objectives could remain as a counterweight to disruptive
SVN political effects and could at least tentatively submerge the politically debilitating civilian-military rivalries, the bickering and
jockeying for influence from within and without. 20/

3. Fishing for Ideas With a Dragnet: The Abortive NSAM on
    Strategic Guidelines for Vietnam

With the new year it was becoming increasingly clear that American
resolution, our massive presence and the determined pursuit of our objectives in South Vietnam would heavily influence political events there, but
the nature of our objectives, the political bases of our resolution and
the desirable magnitude of our presence were less than clear. In an effort
to crystallize our thinking in these areas and to provide some more carefully delineated guidance for operations, the President asked Walt Rostow
to float a draft NSAM embracing strategic guidelines for 1967 in Vietnam. 21/

The draft NSAM, too, in the Komer vein, was basically optimistic in
tone, opening with the observation that "skillful use of U.S. forces has
greatly improved our military position....it is imperative that we mount
and effectively orchestrate a concerted military, civil, and political
effort to achieve a satisfactory outcome as soon as possible." 22/   Accordingly, the draft laid out our strategic aims in 1967. They were to:

"A. Maximize the prospects for a satisfactory outcome in
Vietnam by December 1967 or, if this is not possible, put us
in the best position for the longer pull.

"B. Be equally suited to (a) forcing Hanoi to negotiate;
(b) weakening the VC/NVA to the point where Hanoi will opt to
fade away; or (c) at the minimum, making it patently clear to
all that the war is demonstrably being won.

"C. Complement our anti-main force campaign and bombing
offensive by greatly increased efforts to pacify the countryside and increase the attractive power of the GVN - all these
to the end of accelerating the erosion of southern VC strength
and creating a bandwagon psychology among the people of SVN.
This strategy is also well suited to exploiting any possibilities of a Hanoi/NLF split." 23/

To achieve these objectives, nine program areas each "requiring a
maximum continuing effort" were listed. These included pacification,
mounting a major national reconciliation program, pressing for emergence
of a popularly based GVN, continuing to strive for other objectives of
the Manila Program (local government, land reform, anti-corruption), and
keeping the lid on the economy. More relevant to our concerns were the
four directly concerned with the land war:

"B. Step up the Anti-Main Force Spoiling Offensive, as
made feasible by the increase in FW maneuver battalions.

1. Introduce modest US forces into certain key
Delta areas.

2. Stress offensive actions to clear VC base areas
and LOCs around Saigon.

3. Lay on a major re-examination of our intelligence
on VC/NVA strength.

"C. Make More Effective Programs to Limit Infiltration
and Impose a Cost on Hanoi for the Aggression.

1. Refine the bombing offensive with respect to both
efficiency of route harassment and quality of targets.

2. Press forward with barrier system.

3. Examine other ways to apply military pressure
on the North.

* * * * *

"H. Devise a Pre-Negotiating and Negotiating Strategy
Consistent with the Above.

1. Take such initiatives as will credibly enhance our
posture that we are always ready to talk and ever alert for new
avenues to negotiation.

2. Vigorously pursue serious negotiating leads.

"I. _Mount a Major Information Campaign_ to inform both
the US electorate and world opinion of the realities in Vietnam, finding ways of credibly to measure progress." 24/

The first two (B. and C.) would require force increases of varying
magnitudes, dependent upon whose estimates of enemy capability and U.S.
relative effectiveness you accept -- JCS or DoD's or Komer's. Programs
B. and C. patently endorse the offensive nature of our operations, but
leave their extent or intensity undefined. Interpretation of the third
item (H.) rests heavily upon what assumptions were held about negotiations; were they synonymous with military defeat and capitulation or
something less emotionally loaded, and less satisfying, like compromise.
Implicit in the last point (I.), concerning public information, is the
acceptance of a certain "reality" that we wanted to advertise, this
being also the mood that pervades the entire NSAM -- victory is near.

The principal interest in this paper, however, derives not from
disagreement as to technique and programs (nor even their basic configuration) but from the open discussion of basic objectives in South Vietnam
which it prompted. Formal Department of Defense comment on the draft
centered in two places: with McNaughton in ISA and in the JCS.

McNaughton's comments seem to reflect a growing concern with our
diminishing prospects of early success and a desire not to irreversibly
lock ourselves into either any fixed strategy or excessive ground commitments. These views were apparently shared with the Secretary of Defense.
In his draft reply to Rostow (through McNamara) McNaughton essentially
"loads the dice" against significant alteration of the strategic concept.
In the preamble paragraph he states that...

"...The national commitment of the United States in South
Vietnam (SVN), as stated in Manila, is that the South Vietnamese people shall not be conquered by aggressive force and
shall enjoy the inherent right to choose their own way of life
and their own form of government. The United States is committed to continue our military and all other efforts, as firmly
and as long as may be necessary, in close consultation with
our allies until the aggression is ended." 25/

In the draft, the Assistant Secretary was painstakingly developing
alternatives to continued widespread U.S. military involvement over time.
His additions (or line-ins) placed emphasis upon participation by other
Asian nations, development of a "rapid and effective" R/D effort, and
continued...

"...reorientation of the bulk of RVNAF toward and into a
steadily increasing role in R/D operations in coordination
with regional and local civil and military forces. The goal
is the establishment of security to permit revolutionary
development to take place." 26/

The reference to Manila was less than accidental. Paragraph 28 of the Joint Communique for the conference issued on the 25th of October 1966 stated:

> "The other participating governments reviewed and endorsed these as essential elements of peace and agreed they would act on this basis in close consultation among themselves in regard to settlement of the conflict. In particular, they declared that Allied forces are in the Republic of Vietnam because that country is the object of aggression and its government requested support in the resistance of its people to aggression. They shall be withdrawn, after close consultation, as the other side withdraws its forces to the North, and ceases infiltration, and as the level of violence thus subsides. Those forces will be withdrawn as soon as possible and not later than six months after the above conditions have been fulfilled."

McNaughton noted that President Johnson himself, in private session with the Heads of State, had negotiated the language of this paragraph. According to McNaughton's account, "the President was determined to get the language in, including the reference to 'six months' (opposed by State, supported by me)." 27/

He also qualified statements in the White House draft which seemingly disregarded considerations of feasibility, for instance, adding that such increments of the barrier system "as are determined to be militarily and politically useful and feasible only" should be completed at the early date specified and that expansion of the scope of offensive operations should be done only "as made feasible by the increase in FW forces." These seemingly minor alterations loom significant as indicators of a subtle shift in approach by both McNamara and McNaughton -- one which was more skeptical of the familiar projected claims of success and rapid solution to the South Vietnam problem.

JCS reaction to the draft was three-fold. They wanted to not only "refine" the bombing offensive, but to "adjust the air and naval offensive with respect to the extent and quality of targets." 28/ This was predictable, but the deeper disagreement about national objectives was more difficult to foretell. This cleavage appeared over two points in the draft.

The idea of developing any kind of contingency plan on how to handle VC/NLF in the approaching elections was abhorrent to the JCS. Just as distasteful was an enlargement of efforts to establish contacts with the VC/NLF. To them it was

> "...Inconsistent with the attainment of the US national objective. It is inconceivable that the VC, instilled with

ideals of communist domination for all of Vietnam, would
peacefully contribute to shaping the destiny of SVN in con-
formity with democratic principles and without any foreign
interference. To encourage contact with the VC would constitute a major shift in US policy in Southeast Asia which
would certainly appear to the communists as a sign of weakness and lack of firmness of purpose and undermine the
resolve of the GVN." 29/

Furthermore, the JCS detected an unacceptable fraternization with the
negotiating option which in their eyes might be justified by future
attainment of some degree of representative government and political
development. They stressed the "military role" in the GVN in both nation-
building and national security, arguing that regardless of the eventual
political outcomes and the success or failure of representative government, the extent of the present U.S. commitment had eliminated the option
of "abandoning" the country on the grounds that "the government is not
established by constitutional or legal processes and might be changed by
illegal methods." 30/

The crucial difference, however, arose over what the national objectives in South Vietnam should really be. In contrast to McNaughton's
view, the Chiefs believed that the

"...national objective of the United States in South
Vietnam (SVN) is an independent nation free of communist
subversion and able to determine its own government and
national aspirations." 31/

and that to achieve this required three interdependent undertakings:

"a. In the North - Take the war to the enemy by unremitting and selective application of US military power.

"b. In the South - Seek out and destroy communist forces
and infrastructure in concert with the GVN/FWMAF.

"c. Nation Building - Extend the secure areas of South
Vietnam by coordinated civil/military operations and assist
the GVN in building an independent, viable, noncommunist
society." 32/

The JCS were actually insisting upon the achievement of a non-
communist South Vietnam and their military aims accorded with that
view. They were holding to the basic strategic concept written in
JCSM 702-66, a month earlier, one which had elicited so little reaction
from either McNamara or his staff. 33/ No doubt the resistance of
the JCS was heavily influenced by the COMUSMACV-CINCPAC reaction to the

draft NSAM. The language of the Pacific commanders had been less cautious, and their message unmistakable -- we were militarily in South Vietnam to convincingly defeat the VC/NVA, that the war could be long and difficult, and the field commander should be granted the operational flexibility and resources he needed to do the job as he perceived it. To insure success, CINCPAC cabled, it was imperative that we get our guidance and objectives unequivocally and clearly laid down:

"A. The hard fact is that, even if there were no war in progress in Vietnam, many of the objectives listed in the civil and political fields could not be realized in the 1967 time frame. The draft paper does not assess the adequacy of resources to carry out the Program B. The objectives listed for accomplishment are so all inclusive that publication in a national policy paper, one likely to receive wide publicity, is to invite future criticism if many objectives are not realized.

"C. It could be interpreted that all aims and programs are to be pursued equally and simultaneously. It should be recognized that forces and other resources currently approved for South Vietnam do not provide the capabilities to accomplish all these programs in 1967.

"4. There is a danger that the detailed and specific guidance in the paper would reduce the flexibility required by the operational commander in utilizing assets available to him to best accomplish his mission. The situation in Vietnam is fluid and dynamic requiring that decisions in use of forces and other assets be made in accordance with the dictates of the situation. It is therefore recommended that NSAM be restricted to a clear, concise statement of national policy for Vietnam, accompanied by a broad statement of integrated military, civil and political objectives to be pursued in 1967 under that policy.

"5. The long range implications of the proposed actions for 1967 in Vietnam are of such magnitude that it is imperative that they be in consonance with our national objectives for South Vietnam. It is recommended that the NSAM stipulate in the preamble that 'actions taken to terminate hostilities shall be in accordance with our national objective to assist the government of Vietnam and its armed forces to defeat externally directed and supported communist subversion and aggression, and attain an independent non-communist society in South Vietnam functioning in a secure environment.'" 34/

We see that the problem of understanding and interpreting the country's objectives in South Vietnam was not limited to the JCS-Secretary of

Defense-President trio, it went to the major field commanders charged
with its execution as well. Events, as much conscious rational decisions, were to shape the outcome of the disagreement, but before the
gap was closed, and people began to understand (if not accept) the
dynamic and complex nature of our objectives in South Vietnam the
divergence between Washington policy and the ground direction of the
war was to assume important proportions.

4. The Strategic Concept Under Fire: Seeds of Doubt

State Department concern about the current strategic concept
paralleled the debate in DoD. A paper prepared in Under Secretary
Katzenbach's office historically analyzed the evolution (or more precisely non-evolution) of the strategic concept in Vietnam. It observed
that:

> "Basic precepts behind the counterinsurgency doctrine
> have survived in principle but have been little applied in
> practice. As program has succeeded program, not only have
> the principal deficiencies in implementation become increas-
> ingly clear, but it has also become evident that these
> deficiencies have been essentially the same ones from the
> outset. They may be summarized as follows:
>
>> 1. With rare exceptions arising from the
>> attributes of individual commanders, the Vietnamese
>> Army (ARVN) has never escaped from its conventional
>> warfare mold. Both in its military tactics and in
>> its relations with the people, it has all too often
>> acted counter to the basic principles of counterinsur-
>> gency rather than in support of them. The US military
>> leadership in Vietnam has, on balance, done little
>> to reorient ARVN toward counterinsurgency. In the
>> meantime, the paramilitary forces, locally recruited
>> and locally based and theoretically the backbone of
>> any counterinsurgency effort, have been repeatedly
>> ignored or misused.
>
>> 2. Despite elaborate planning and creation of
>> machinery to execute and sustain a combined political-
>> military pacification campaign, relatively few Viet-
>> namese leaders have clearly understood the goals of
>> pacification or articulated them effectively through
>> the supporting administrative apparatus. Some leaders
>> have viewed pacification largely in a military con-
>> text while others, however committed to the political
>> principles involved, have lacked either a pragmatic
>> appreciation of their impact on the peasant or a
>> willingness to approach pacification in revolutionary
>> terms.

3. As a result, the GVN, despite increasing US
assistance in men and materiel, has been relatively ineffectual in meeting the Communist military and subversive
threat at the rice-roots level. Pacification has thus far
failed to give the peasant sufficient confidence in the
GVN's ability to maintain security, the first prerequisite
in pacification, or, in longer run, to redress basic economic, political, and social inequities." 35/

The current strategic concept was viewed as a reaction to our basic
assumption that the military and political situation in South Vietnam in
the spring and early summer of 1965 was irretrievably lost unless the U.S.
committed substantial combat forces and unless Hanoi was forced to cease
its support of the Viet Cong. From this beginning emerged a current
strategy which...

"...divides the Vietnam conflict into two wars: (1) a
conventional war against the main Communist forces in the
northern provinces of South Vietnam and against their logistic
resources in North Vietnam and (2) an unconventional war or
counterinsurgency effort against Communist control of the
peasant in the southern provinces. The two wars are intended
to be mutually supporting and pursued simultaneously, with
relative equal priority.

"The conventional war is an effort to obtain quick military results by purely military means. It seeks to reduce or
terminate the infiltration of men and supplies into South
Vietnam by continuing air strikes over North Vietnam and Laos,
and to destroy regular North Vietnamese Army and Viet Cong
units and their logistic bases in the sparsely settled areas.
In this war, the primary role is played by US combat forces
deployed largely in the highlands area of Corps I and II
where the bulk of North Vietnamese forces are committed, and
where the enemy appears willing to engage in large formations.
Major battles can occur without the danger of large civilian
casualties. In support of their activities, the US forces
maintain direct control of their own logistic, communications,
and intelligence resources. In short, the highlands and the
defense perimeters around certain strategic installations in
effect constitute a US theater of operations.

"The unconventional war or counterinsurgency effort continues to give priority to political-military pacification of
the populated areas in the Mekong delta and coastal lowlands.
It is thus a continuation of the long-term effort to give the
population security and to win its support of the government
by measures responsive to popular needs. These war areas
remain under GVN control, despite the presence of thousands

of US civilian and military advisors. ARVN, relieved of
many of its combat and defense responsibilities elsewhere,
is theoretically able to commit more forces to pacification
as well as search-and-destroy missions, directed against the
Viet Cong mainforce. The paramilitary forces retain their
normal village-hamlet defense and pacification responsibilities." 36/

The author then turned to the problems in South Vietnam which he
saw as the direct or indirect result of our strategic emphasis:

"There is no clear delineation of the conventional and
unconventional wars either along territorial or population
lines. US combat forces have been increasingly committed
in search-and-destroy operations even outside the highlands
area, as far south as Long An and Hau Nghia provinces around
Saigon and as far east as the coastal regions of Binh Dinh
province. US marines around Danang, in attempting to secure
and expand their defense perimeter, have attempted to engage
in pacification operations, as have the Korean forces in
Corps II. On balance, however, US combat forces remain
essentially oriented toward conventional warfare, making
adjustments (which are at times ingenious) as needed for the
unusual physical settings in which their efforts take place.

"ARVN meanwhile is also fighting essentially conventional
war whether in sparsely settled areas or in populated ones
such as the Mekong delta. Its commitment to pacification is
negligible, and it continues to regard its mission essentially
in conventional military terms. Even in areas where ARVN is
engaged in pacification, the fairly low level of ARVN casualties
shows that its commanders still remain unwilling to commit their
troops in a manner best suited to finding the Viet Cong, and
for periods of time sufficient to establish a realistic base
of security from which pacification can begin. The principal
if not the only security force in most pacification areas continues to be the under-manned and inadequately trained paramilitary forces, which of all Vietnamese forces are now
suffering the greatest number of killed-in-action casualties
over the past year.

"The claims of top US and GVN military officials notwithstanding, the waging of a conventional war has overriding
priority, perhaps as much as 9 to 1, according to the personal
judgments of some US advisors. Saturation bombing by artillery
and airstrikes, for example, is an accepted tactic, and there
is probably no province where this tactic has not been widely
employed...." 37/

The new concept which appeared to be emerging, of recommitment of ARVN infantry divisions to pacification primarily in and around pacification areas did not, on the surface, appear to be anything but a long-term process, very sensitive to ARVN acceptance of the role. It failed the twin tests of being a panacea -- it would not be fast, it would not be cheap. There was little doubt that most ARVN division and corps commanders continued to regard pacification operations as dull, less prestigious, and generally not in keeping with the basic mission, past tradition and organization of ARVN. This should not have been startling to the American observer -- after all, U.S. units and commanders found pacification no more palatable, and they had nowhere near the same political or economic stakes in its consequences as their Vietnamese contemporaries.

The conclusions of the paper were not heartening. State believed that even assuming that all the attitudinal problems of ARVN could be overcome, many of its basic weaknesses would undermine its effectiveness in pacification -- just as it had in conventional combat. These included:

"a) poor leadership, preoccupation with political maneuvering at the senior officer level, the lack of experienced junior officers whose recruitment and promotion is based more on considerations having to do with economic and family status than with motivation or ability and whose assignments frequently reflect the use of influence to obtain headquarters or other safe and prestigious posts, and the lack also of competent and experienced NCOs;

"b) poor morale (reflected not only in a continuous rise in desertions dating from at least 1962 but also in a very high battlefield missing-in-action rate) resulting from low pay rates; inadequate dependent housing, concern over the welfare of families, infrequent rotation of units in isolated outposts, and inadequate medical care;

"c) poor relations with the population who, on the one hand, have had little reason for confidence in the ability of the military to afford them any lasting protection and, on the other, have all too frequently been victimized by them;

"d) low operational capabilities including poor coordination, tactical rigidity, overdependence on air and artillery support arising in part from inadequate firepower, overdependence on vehicular convoy, unwillingness to remain in the field at night or over adequately long periods, and lack of aggressiveness." 38/

Deployment of U.S. forces to the highly populated Mekong Delta would, in the writer's eyes, carry potentially adverse political repercussions. MACV was criticized for underestimating the impact on the grounds that they would be operating in remote and relatively unpopulated areas, the same justification used to generate State support for large operations in the border regions. But "remote" did not necessarily mean "remote," as the memorandum explained:

"...But even these areas, which do exist in the delta, are less remote and more populated than areas in the highlands where large US combat forces are currently committed. Moreover, the unpopulated stretches between populated areas are far smaller in size in the delta than in the highlands, and therefore there is greater danger that US forces operating in unpopulated areas could be drawn in the populated areas. Nor is it entirely certain that US forces will restrict their missions to search-and-destroy operations against Viet Cong mainforces. Indeed, it is to be expected that some US units will eventually participate in pacification, as in Danang for example, in order to protect the perimeters of US base facilities or encampments. As the size of the US force increases, it would be logical for MACV to attempt to expand these defense perimeters regardless of the proximity of populated areas. There is also the possibility that US commanders will be inclined to commit their units to pacification simply on the grounds that the Vietnamese are not doing the job efficiently.

"Finally, although it is generally accepted that a military stalemate has existed for sometime in the Mekong delta, it is by no means certain that the GVN's inability to shift the balance against Viet Cong forces in the area is the result of lack of manpower resources. The basic problem is the manner in which ARVN forces are deployed in the delta rather than in the number of ARVN forces committed there. The current ratio of ARVN to Viet Cong mainforces in Corps IV is already more than 2:1, better than in any other Corps area, and, if plans to reorient ARVN to pacification are implemented, the ratio of combat forces should theoretically improve in ARVN's favor since more ARVN units would be committed against the Viet Cong for greater periods of time." 39/

In effect, the presence of large numbers of active U.S. units would not only risk civilian disruption and casualties, but may tempt U.S. units to "moonlight" in pacification, possibly alienating, or at least relieving the ARVN primarily charged with the mission. It was in vogue in the United States at the time to number as one of the causes of ARVN combat ineffectiveness and lack of aggressiveness the rapid assumption by the United States of the major combat role, leading the Vietnamese to "let George do it." Katzenbach's staff seemed to sense the same danger in "too much" U.S. pacification.

The memorandum was directed toward a rethinking of strategic concepts --
in that it failed. It seemed to resolve the problem of achieving a unified
strategic concept by leaving the same undefined. As long as the crucial
force deployment and political settlement questions could be deferred, a
concept sufficiently ambiguous or undefined appeared to be the best one to
preserve harmony and encourage continued support. However, the memorandum
was useful to point up a basically faulty premise about ARVN effectiveness
in the pacification/security mission. If they were inadequate to assess
the pacification task, as Katzenbach's staff contended, then our strategy
and our manpower requirements could become quite different than was originally calculated as we pursued the elusive objective of "winning the war."
As he astutely pointed out, the cleavage between the mainforce and guerrilla
wars was more imagined than real, and we could not hope to win them seri-
ally -- they had to be controlled simultaneously or failing that, probably
not at all. All of the clues were there, it only remained for someone to
articulate the fear that so many decision-makers held -- massive U.S.
forces, engaged in every activity, provided the only reasonable probability
of "winning" in Vietnam.

The NSAM effort was abortive. 40/ The evident division in DoD over
the concept and objectives coupled with State's lukewarm response to producing any clear definition of aims/concepts convinced the White House
that the best way to retain flexibility in South Vietnam and at home was
to allow the ambiguity and uncertainty to continue.

1. It is of some interest that in early December COMUSMACV reported that for the previous five months ARVN had the following numbers of battalions with "minimally acceptable operational maneuver strength" (or 450 present for operations):

Month	Total Bns
May	33
June	35
July	31
August	33
September	52
October	78

See MACV 52414, op. cit.

2. OASD/SA, "An Assessment of the Course of the War in Vietnam," undated, but probably prepared in early December 1967.

3. Ibid.

4. The New York Times wrote that VC defections were up 82% to 20,242 in 1966 with 2,500 in each November and December.

5. All of the above discussion on military indicators is from OASD/SA "Assessment," op. cit., plus additional sources noted.

6. The New York Times, 31 December 1966.

7. One reaction from the "Hawk" side came from Chairman Mendel Rivers of the House Armed Services Committee, who called on the U.S. to "flatten Hanoi if necessary and let world opinion go fly a kite." Concern in the columns focused upon a fear that the Johnson Administration might heed the cry, because, in Rivers' own words "...they have not ignored others in the past." The New York Times, 30 December 1966.

8. The New York Times, 2 January 1967.

9. The New York Times, 2 January - 18 January 1967.

10. The New York Times, 11 January 1967. He observed: "The Administration is embarking on a major military operation in the Mekong Delta...as far as I know this was never told to the American people or to Congress in the last two years as a prospective operation."

11. The Washington Star, 10 January 1967.

12. The New York Times, 3 January 1967.

13. The New York Times, 9 January 1967.

14. The Daily News, 9 January 1967.

15. The New York Times, 11 January 1967.

16. R. W. Komer, Memorandum for the Secretary of Defense, Subject: "Vietnam Prognosis for 1967-68," dated 29 November 1966.

17. Ibid.

18. Ibid.

19. National Intelligence Estimate, Nr. 53-66, Subj: "Problems of Political Development in South Vietnam Over the Next Year or So," dated 15 December 1966.

20. Ibid.

21. Memorandum to Secretary of Defense and Acting Secretary of State from W. W. Rostow, no subject, dated 12 December 1966, with Draft NSAM, Subj: "Strategic Guidelines for 1967 in Vietnam," dated 10 December 1966, as an attachment.

22. Ibid.

23. Ibid.

24. Ibid.

25. Memorandum for the Secretary of Defense from John T. McNaughton, ASD(ISA), Subj: "Draft NSAM on Strategic Guidelines for 1967 in Vietnam," ISA 1-20383/67, dated 20 January 1967.

26. Ibid.

27. "Manila Summit Conference Joint Communique," October 24-25, 1966. Copy in the McNaughton papers with annotated comments by McNaughton. Files in VNS 2, L.

28. Emphasis added. JCSM 792-66, Subj: "Draft NSAM," dated 27 December 1966. Comment for this JCSM was obtained from CINCPAC and COMUSMACV. See JCS message 1363, 142018Z December 1966 and the reply CINCPAC to JCS, 200805Z December 1966.

TOP SECRET - Sensitive

29. JCSM 792-66, op. cit.

30. Ibid. A choice of wording directly attacking the "inherent right to choose" insertion made by ISA.

31. Ibid.

32. Ibid.

33. JCSM 702-66, op. cit., dated 4 November 1966. See Section I, C., pp. 32 for a discussion of the memorandum. The Joint Strategic Objectives Plan for FY 1969-1976 (JSOP 69-76), Appendix A to JCSM 798-66, dated 30 December 1966 prepared concurrently with JCSM 792-66 is vague on objectives, but repeats a view that military winning in SVN was vital to the collective security posture of the United States.

34. CINCPAC message 200805Z December 1966 to JCS.

35. "Strategic Concept for Vietnam: An Analysis," State Department, unsigned memorandum believed to have been prepared by Richard C. Holbrooke for Under Secretary Katzenbach, dated 12 December 1966.

36. Ibid.

37. Ibid.

38. Ibid. A December CIA report substantiated these views about the ARVN effectiveness and congenital weaknesses.

39. Ibid.

40. The ASD(ISA) draft of McNaughton's was approved and forwarded by Deputy Secretary of Defense Vance on 28 January 1967. See: Memorandum from Deputy Secretary of Defense for W. W. Rostow, Subject: "Draft NSAM on Strategic Guidelines for 1967 in Vietnam," dated 28 January 1967.

TOP SECRET - Sensitive

ON PROGRAM 5

B.   THE OPENING DIALOGUE ON PROGRAM 5

   1.   Reclamas to Program 4 - Fleshing Out

   The turn of the year policy debate over basic U.S. objectives
and strategic concepts was played out in the midst of a continuing
dialogue within DoD, one which focused upon the adequacy and composition of Program 4. An exchange of memoranda between the JCS and
SecDef in December 1966 and January 1967 fleshed out the profile of
the program to near the 470,000-man figure.

   The major reclama to Secretary McNamara's 18 November Program 4
decision was a sharply worded JCSM in which the Chiefs attacked the
premise (ostensibly supported by the Secretary of Defense) that the
restoration of economic stability in SVN was of overriding importance.
They not only took issue with the use of the piaster ceiling employed
to develop the force limit, but firmly regarded the ceiling of 470,000
men as inadequate and restrictive, a situation which might necessitate,
in their words, "subsequent adjustments," especially in view of the
I CTZ tactical situation. Additionally, they noted:

      "...projected opening of land lines of communication
   (LOCs) in II, III, and IV CTZs, important to military
   operations and the Revolutionary Development Program, will
   be curtailed. US operations in the IV CTZ will be impeded
   and the capability to conduct riverine operations in this
   area will be reduced to a critical degree. The over-all
   US military capability to support extension of control by
   the Government of Vietnam in SVN will be limited and flexibility will be curtailed....

      "....while the restoration of economic stability in
   SVN is most important, the achievement of such stability
   will depend primarily on the capabilities of military and
   paramilitary forces to defeat the enemy, to provide the secure
   environment required for political, economic, and social
   development, and, concurrently, to provide essential impetus
   to the Revolutionary Development Program. Further, the Joint
   Chiefs of Staff believe that, in comparison to the forces
   requested by them on 4 November 1966, the forces listed in
   Program 4 will reduce the military capability to achieve
   our national objectives and execute our military tasks in
   SVN. The rate at which Program 4 can undertake area control,
   open land LOCs, and provide essential security for Revolutionary Development and other associated programs will be

slower than was estimated with the forces previously
requested. The intensity and frequency of combat operations may therefore be restricted, resulting in a
slower rate of progress in SVN, some loss of momentum
in operations, and possibly a longer war at increasing
costs in casualties and materiel...." 1/

Despite such protestations and recounting of dire outcomes, the
recommendations of JCSM 739-66 primarily concerned no more than direct
substitution of units below the 470,000-man ceiling (with no increase
in piaster expenditures) and these were approved by the Secretary of
Defense a week later. 2/

While the actual numbers of troops and amounts of equipment involved
in the reclamas were minor, the underlying nature of the dispute over
Program 4, of which the small adjustments were barely sumptomatic, had
been more basic from its inception and both the press and Capitol Hill
were picking up the tempo of debate between the Chiefs and their civilian
superiors. General Wheeler was busy denying in a press conference that
the civilian chiefs prevented General Westmoreland from receiving the
troops he felt necessary. Simultaneously, Secretary Rusk was spending
a long four hours before the Senate Foreign Relations Committee, defending
the Administration's basic policies and those pursued by its Vietnam
commander. 3/

Two days later a poll of nineteen predominantly hawkish Senators
revealed two basic areas of consensus; they believed we should give our
military leaders more support (presumably troops) and we should hit
North Vietnam harder (notably in Haiphong). More political pressure
was generated on the troop issue by Senator Stennis' declaration that
General Westmoreland's requests for troops should be met, "even if it
should require mobilization or partial mobilization." Stennis publicly
estimated that we were 100,000 men shy of the total needed to contain
the Viet Cong militarily. A similar figure often appeared in classified
studies at the time. 4/

A public statement by Army Chief of Staff General Harold K. Johnson,
probably intended to be reassuring, only heightened the sense of cost in
manpower and national energy which the war might require. He said that
withdrawal of U.S. units may be possible in $1\frac{1}{2}$-$2\frac{1}{2}$ years because enemy
strength was being broken down into small units that could be contained
by smaller American units. 5/ Few people, as the commentators were
quick to observe, were enamored with the thought of any American units
in Vietnam in $2\frac{1}{2}$ years, whatever the size! As if to underline the costs
of an increasingly expanding war, Operation CEDAR FALLS in the Iron Triangle had produced a record number of U.S. deaths in a single week, 144,
along with 1,044 wounded and 6 missing. The prospect of suffering 1,194
casualties per week for the next indeterminate number of years was hardly
an appealing prospect, and a substantial number of the American people

TOP SECRET - Sensitive

seemed to believe that political restraints imposed upon our military leaders were the chief cause of so little concrete progress. This belief and the potential untapped political support it revealed, was to be a powerful lever in the hands of the JCS as they pressed for force increases during Program 5. 6/

Manpower, though, was becoming the crucial issue -- its political ramifications were enormous, and politicians were prone to best detect them. Senator Ted Kennedy delivered a major speech on the draft to the National Press Club, urging reform. On the same day, Senator Mike Mansfield reintroduced his resolution calling for a "substantial reduction" in the number of American troops in Europe. 7/ Men, money and political will were the crux issues of the domestic debate; by the end of January all three had highlighted the news. The troop issue outstanding between the JCS and McNamara had been wrung out in public, $73.1 billion had been asked for defense and on 23 January, The Arrogance of Power was published. 8/

2. Vietnam Strategy: Attention Rivets on the Borders and Sanctuaries

We have already described how MACV attention shifted to the borders and sanctuaries in late 1966. By January and February of the next year (1967), COMUSMACV and CINCPAC were riveted upon these crucial areas where major enemy units were being found and fought.

COMUSMACV assumed that a new phase of the struggle was beginning, one which demanded that we reexamine our military strategy. To take advantage of the existing opportunities which he detected, he decided to mount a "general offensive" designed to:

"A. Maintain the momentum of the offensive on a seven-day-a-week, around-the-clock basis.

"B. Decimate enemy forces, destroy his base areas and disrupt the VC infrastructure.

"C. Interdict enemy land and water lines of communication, denying him the opportunity to resupply and reinforce his units and bases in South Vietnam.

"D. Open, secure and use land and water lines of communication.

"E. Convince the enemy, through the vigor of our offensives and accompanying psychological operations, that he faces defeat.

"F. Support political and economic progress in SVN...." 9/

TOP SECRET - Sensitive

He envisioned a sustained series of offensives against enemy base areas and main forces thereby destroying the VC/NVA combat potential, and threatening his supply systems, which he described as "the Achilles Heel of the VC/NVA." Westmoreland provided a solution to the build-up problem at the end of the NVN-Laos funnel, but again no real solution for stopping the flow:

> "...The enemy is dependent on the buildup of weapons, equipment, food and medical supplies which are located in his base areas. Destruction of established enemy base areas denies him the opportunity to rest, retrain, recuperate and resupply easily. Thorough, meticulous search in areas in which our forces are operating is a key to the successful accomplishment of this important task. If we can neutralize the enemy base areas and prevent replenishment of the material captured or destroyed, we will have taken a long stride toward ultimate victory...." 10/

Westmoreland also stated what was to become a growing concern among Americans at all echelons:

> "...It is essential that the effectiveness of RVNAF be improved. Concurrently, the image of the military forces of South Vietnam in the eyes of the world and especially in the United States must reflect the contribution which has been and is being made to the overall effort in SVN. Much of the press reporting on this subject is unfair and indicates a lack of understanding of the RVNAF contribution. This, in turn, has a deleterious effect on RVNAF morale and effectiveness. RVNAF must be made to realize that there are military tasks as well as non-military tasks associated with RD. Every influence must be used to get RVNAF to cease conducting an intermittent war and instead to maintain continuous pressure on enemy forces. We must insure that maximum use is made of RVN forces in all our planned major offensives and that they are given tasks which are important and which will contribute to their continued growth potential. We then must insure that full credit is given to their accomplishments in each of these operations." 11/

COMUSMACV's "command guidance" from which this is quoted, must be taken in context; ringing proclamations like these are directed to the troops. They are the things command histories are made of, but they seldom provide an undistorted picture of tactical or strategic reality.

The 1967 MACV Campaign Plan had focused upon the areas outlined in the COMUSMACV message, but it contained less bandwagon psychology and more careful evaluation of enemy capabilities and strategy. The Campaign Plan had been broadly based upon Westmoreland's assessment

of the enemy's situation and his strategy, views which he repeated
in a year end cable to General Wheeler and Admiral Sharp. 12/

He wrote:

"...Forces currently available to the enemy in SVN
as identified in MACV order of battle are nine division
headquarters, 34 regimental headquarters, 152 combat
battalions, 34 combat support battalions, 196 separate
companies, and 70 separate platoons totaling some 128,600,
plus at least 112,800 militia and at least 39,175 political
cadre. The principal threats posed are in the DMZ area,
the Chu-Pong region, and the Tay-Ninh/Phuoc Long area of
northern III CTZ. Although enemy forces in these areas
have been punished in operations during 1966, they have
not been destroyed and are continuing efforts to reinforce,
resupply, and plan for resumption of operations in a
winter-spring campaign. Enemy capabilities throughout
SVN are summarized in the following paragraphs:

"A. Attack. The enemy can attack at any time
selected targets in I, II, and III CTZ in up to division
strength and in IV CTZ in up to regimental strength,
supported by local force and guerrillas. Simultaneously,
he can continue harassing attacks throughout SVN.

(1) In I CTZ, he can attack objectives in the
DMZ area (Quang Tri Province) with elements of the 324B
and 341st NVA divisions supported by one separate regiment.
Additionally, he can attack objectives in Quang Tin or
Quang Ngai Provinces with the 2d NVA division and two regi-
ments of the 3d NVA division. In Thua Tien and Quang Nam
Provinces he can attack in up to regimental strength.

(2) In II CTZ, he has the capability to attack in
Western Pleiku, Southern Kontum, or Northern Darlac Provinces
with elements of the 1st and 10th NVA divisions, in Northern
Binh Dinh Province with one regiment of the 3d NVA Division,
and in Phu Yen and Northern Khanh Hoa Provinces with elements
of the two regiments of the 5th NVA Division.

(3) In III CTZ, he can attack with the 9th VC
and possibly the 7th NVA Divisions in Tay Ninh, Binh Long,
Binh Duong, or Phuoc Long Provinces, and in Phuoc Tuy and
Southern Long Khanh Provinces with elements of the two
regiments of the 5th VC Division. He also can sabotage

GVN and FW shipping transiting the Rung Sat Special Zone
with a Sapper Battalion; harass installations and LOC's
in Gia Ding Province with elements of the 165A VC Regiment. He has the capability of continuing his terror
campaign in Saigon/Cholon.

  (4) In IV CTZ, he can attack in up to regimental strength in Chuong Thien and Dinh Tuong Provinces,
and in up to reinforced battalion strength throughout
the rest of the CTZ. Militia and guerrilla forces pre-
dominate, and emphasis is on harassing attacks and local
actions to consolidate and extend his control...." 13/

Westmoreland also expected what he labeled "political attack" and
"economic attack" to continue. These he described as efforts to...

  "...Destroy the effectiveness of hamlet, village,
district, provincial, and national governments by
elimination, intimidation, and subversion of GVN officials; discredit and erode GVN political authority at
all levels by conducting propaganda attacks against
elected and appointed GVN officials and against GVN
programs.

  "...Enemy to intensify efforts to impose an economic blockade against the GVN by denying the latter access
to its own resources; conduct overt and covert operations
throughout SVN against targets of vital economic significance to the maintenance and growth of the GVN economy;
stimulate inflation by diverting commodities destined for
SVN markets and by denying commodities from markets through
interdiction and harassment of LOC's; and undermine the
people's confidence in SVN currency by propaganda and
possible counterfeiting." 14/

COMUSMACV then addressed the crucial question of enemy reinforcement capability:

  "...The enemy has the demonstrated capability to
reinforce in SVN by infiltrating personnel and units
from NVN at a rate of about 8,400 men per month and by
in-country recruitment of about 3,500 per month in VC
Main and Local Forces. In the tactical sense, his dependence on foot movement normally precludes major reinforcement
on the battlefield beyond attack forces initially committed.
Defensively, he normally conducts holding actions to enable
extrication of the main body rather than reinforcing.

  (1) In I CTZ, he can reinforce his attack or
defense through the DMZ and from Laos within three to ten

days after commencing movement with three divisions,
three infantry regiments, and eight infantry battalions.
He can reinforce his attack or defense with one infantry
division from Binh Dinh Province in II CTZ and one infantry regiment from Kontum Province in II CTZ in twelve days
after commencing movement. Many of these units are presently
understrength.

(2) In II CTZ, he can reinforce his attack or
defense in Northern II CTZ within ten days by elements
of one infantry division from Southern I CTZ and in
Southern II CTZ within five to ten days after commending
movement by up to two regiments from III CTZ.

(3) In III CTZ, he can reinforce his attack or
defense in the Northern portion with three separate
battalions from II CTZ and with one regiment from IV CTZ
within three to ten days after commencing movement.

(4) Preponderance of militia and local forces
in IV Corps and the reliance upon encroachment through
local and harassing action makes large unit reinforcement
unlikely in IV CTZ...." 15/

COMUSMACV continued by divining the enemy's overall strategy:

"...The conclusion to be drawn from the enemy's
strength increase of some 42,000 during 1966 is that
despite known losses, he has been able to maintain a proportional counter buildup to the growth of US/FWMA forces.
Sources of this increase are in-country conscription and
foot infiltration down the trails from NVN through the
DMZ, but principally through Laos and the Cambodian extension. To understand what the enemy is doing and is likely
to do in the coming year, it is essential to understand
his objectives, strategy, and major tactics, all of which
derive from the principles of insurgency warfare (or
"Wars of National Liberation") which essentially are
political in nature and which have been described by
Mao Tse Tung, Vo Nguyen Giap, and others such as Chi
Guevara with clarity and conviction. To aid in conveying
this picture I have summarized in the succeeding sub-
paragraphs my estimate of his overall strategy and its
probable continued application.

"A. Objectives: The enemy's objectives in
SVN may be expressed under two dual headings: to
extend his control over the population of SVN and to

prevent the GVN from controlling that population; to reduce the will to resist of the RKF/FWMAF and their governments and correspondingly to strengthen his own posture and will.

"B. Strategy: The enemy's favored doctrine of "strategic mobility" has been the subject of debate in NVN. Politburo member Nguyen Chi Thanh has held that the proper application is to initiate mobile warfare with simultaneous attacks throughout SVN. Defense Minister Vo Nguyen Giap, whose view has prevailed as soon by our experience, favors a "defensive/offensive" version of strategic mobility consisting of these factors:

(1) Developing strong, multi-division forces in dispersed regions accessible to supplies and security.

(2) Enticing AF/FWMA forces into pre-pared positions where dug-in communist forces may inflict heavy casualties upon them.

(3) Conducting concurrent, intensified guerrilla and harassment pressure counter-wide to tie down our forces, destroy small units, attack morale, and extend his control.

"4. Evaluation:

"A. Present enemy dispositions, logistics, and level of combat indicate a continued adherence to the doctrine of strategic mobility implemented by Giap's "defense/offensive" major tactics. Our intelligence does not indicate a change in enemy strategy, tactics, or weapons now or in the coming year, although this possi-bility remains under continuous scrutiny. Specifically, we have no evidence of an intent to fragment his main-forces and revert exclusively to guerrilla-type operations.

"B. The enemy was hurt during 1966 in many areas, and his principal concentrations near sanctuaries at the DMZ, in the Chu Pong region, and in the Tay Ninh/ Binh Long areas have been contained by our preemptive operations as a result of which he has suffered heavy losses. He is avoiding major contact by fighting defen-sively when forced to do so, and attempting to rebuild

and reinforce for winter-spring campaign operations. It
would be premature to assume that an apparent decrease in
activity in December just prior to holiday stand-downs is
indicative of a change in trend. Further, it would be
erroneous to conclude that VC Main Force and NVA formations
are no longer dangerous, that their unit integrity has been
destroyed, or that their logistical capability has fallen
below that needed to sustain his war of conquest by attrition.

       "C. On level of battalion imbalance the enemy
has maintained throughout 1966 is about 1 day in 30. /sic/ This
level is consistent with his strategy of conserving his
forces while attriting US/FWMA forces, and is within his
capability to support logistically. If forced to a higher
level such as 1 day in 15, he will encounter difficulty.

       "D. It is probable that the enemy during the
coming year will attempt to infiltrate men and supplies
into SVN by sea, through Laos and Cambodia, and across
the DMZ to: Counter-balance the US/FWMAF build-up; maintain a credible threat posture, attrite friendly forces and
determination by inflicting casualties and prolonging the
conflict; maintain and promote expansion of the insurgency base
(intra-structure /sic/ and militia); and continue his protracted war to control the people of SVN." 16/

    The emphasis in the assessment is unmistakable -- the crucial
strategic areas would continue to be the highland border areas, the
DMZ-I CTZ area and the sanctuaries of Laos and Cambodia. The 1966
MACV Command History reveals that the enemy camp envisioned the highlands of MR5 as a "killing zone" where the mountainous and juggled terrain
favored VC/NVA operations; additionally the area was comfortably close
to buildup areas near the DMZ and the secure areas in Laos and Cambodia. 17/

    When General Westmoreland claimed to have "taken the initiative" he
usually appears to have referred to the manner in which FW forces (U.S.
in particular) had prohibited the shift by VC/NVA into what counterinsur-
gent scholars call the "final battle of annihilation phase." MACV evidence indicated that VC/NVA were prepared to do this as far back as 1965.
However, as an alternative (and this remained an important MACV operating
assumption), MACV believed that the enemy was attempting to build up
large forces in certain geographically distant areas -- again in accordance
with Giap's version of "strategic mobility." These areas were Quong Tri
Province in I CTZ and the highland border areas in II CTZ. It also
appeared that the opponent might create a holding force between the Delta
and highlands (in III CTZ) to pin down friendly units and prevent FWMAF
from reinforcing against the main threat in the highlands. 18/   An

American strategy intent upon retaining the initiative (or gaining it)
would logically concentrate upon enemy actions which promised to contest
it. Giap's creation of "killing grounds" and "holding forces" were the
kind of initiatives which COMUSMACV believed he had to disrupt ("spoil")
before they materialized as integral parts of a coordinated strategy.
This kind of thinking would lead U.S. forces to the border region battles,
the clearing of in-country redoubts and sanctuaries and to major unit
commitments in I CTZ in the North.

One Pacific commander during this time period, General Beach, put
his views on strategy and escalation in unequivocal terms. Determinedly,
he argued that we must "win" the war, and he outlined a plan which magni-
fied the issues central to the COMUSMACV strategy by its direct presentation
of the major ground strategy issues -- the sanctuaries, the infiltration
(and its relationship to the bombing), and the course which he believed
would best counter the enemy's strategy of tying down large numbers of
our forces away from the sensitive populated areas. 19/

The USARPAC commander also felt that operations in the base areas....

"...must be pursued on a sustained basis and must fully
penetrate, thoroughly cover, and sanitize these areas. Subsequently, these areas must be denied to the enemy's reentry
by leaving behind occupying forces. Concurrently, forces
should be deployed astride major routes the enemy habitually
uses between these bases and to his sanctuaries to interdict
his movements. If the enemy will stand and fight anywhere, he
will stand and fight for these bases if they are seriously
threatened. Moreover, serious inroads into the enemy supply
base in SVN would tend to force the local guerrilla out of
his lair to provide increased support to the main forces, thus
facilitating our efforts to find, fix and destroy him. Destruction of enemy in-country bases and tactical stockpiles
will have the most immediate adverse effect on enemy operations in SVN. COMUSMACV's campaign plan envisions such
operations. The suggestion of this headquarters relates
to ensuring that we penetrate the base areas completely and
then leave forces behind to prevent reoccupancy by the
enemy...." 20/

Beach accepted the "killing ground/holding" version of the enemy
strategic plan noting that:

"...The enemy is developing large forces in bases or
sanctuary north of the DMZ near I CTZ, and on Cambodia, in
the vicinity of Chu Pong Massif bordering II CTZ, and
opposite Tay Ninh/Binh Long Provinces in III CTZ. These
bases and forces, now politically beyond our reach, will

pose a constant and serious threat. The enemy will attempt
to tie down large numbers of our forces to preclude their
support of RD and conduct of offensive operations as well
as draw them into engagements staged in his favor. Our
forces must not meet the enemy where we cannot engage him
decisively. Rather, we should keep him under surveillance
and be prepared to concentrate rapidly to engage him at a
time and on ground of our choosing...." 21/

Infiltration also occupied his thoughts, but he was concerned lest
our efforts elsewhere become weakened by an undue emphasis on stemming
the flow.

"...I concur with your position to resist pressures to
devote a great share of our energies and resources to trying
to stem the flow of men and materiel into SVN from the North.
It is virtually impossible to stop or appreciably impede infiltration into SVN with ground forces now available or programmed
for the theater, especially in light of the contiguous sanctuaries the enemy now enjoys. Although it would be desirable
to stop or measurably impede infiltration, such action is not
imperative to our winning a military victory. Moreover, maintaining that long and difficult LOC saps a sizeable measure
of the enemy's effort and resources. It has, assuredly, exacted
its toll on the fighting capabilities of NVA units. Our air
and naval interdiction operations must be continued at the
present level and, if possible, they must be expanded. Although not in themselves capable of quelling infiltration,
their effects against the enemy and his movement of personnel
and equipment to the South are appreciable." 22/

While Beach's pessimism about stopping the infiltration jibes with
that of COMUSMACV and CINCPAC, his view of how it would affect the
chances of military victory were surely not. If killing VC/NVA was
to be the indicator of military success or "victory," could not an unim-
peded infiltration keep troops coming faster than they could be killed?
And furthermore, could not free (or freer) flow of supplies degrade your
kill capability/unit cost, e.g., your kill ratio could be adversely
affected by the improved status of his equipment and logistics which the
infiltration afforded. These negative aspects were not discussed, but
surely if Beach clearly believed that the infiltration was not crucial,
he would not have evinced less concern about the sanctuary routes and
the bombing. He closed with two observations:

"...Our country harbors a natural desire to ease the hardships in the Vietnam conflict. The military, however, must press to

go all out at all levels in SVN if we are to win. We are
faced with a full blown and difficult war and our government has committed a huge amount of combat power to this
conflict, yet we are still a long way away from achieving
our objectives. If we are to reach an acceptable military
decision in Vietnam, we must not permit our operational
tactics to reflect the reticence which currently character-
izes some bodies of public and official opinion. Our ground
forces must take the field on long term, sustained combat
operations. We must be prepared to accept heavier casualties
in our initial operations and not permit our hesitance to
take greater losses to inhibit our tactical aggressiveness.
If greater hardships are accepted now we will, in the long
run, achieve a military success sooner and at less overall
cost in lives and money....

"In summary, it is my opinion that the MACV campaign
plan for 1967 is adequate to meet the anticipated enemy
threat. However, within the plan's overall concept four
aspects of offensive action must be emphasized. First,
we must relentlessly attack and destroy enemy base areas
in SVN. Secondly, we must avoid pinning down sizeable forces
against his border-sanctuary areas. Rather, we should deal
with forays by his major forces into SVN at times and locations of our choosing. Thirdly, we must press forward with
an aggressive effort to destroy the guerrilla and his underground government in support of revolutionary development.
Finally, we must avoid devoting too great a measure of our
effort to anti-infiltration at the expense of more important
operations. We should continue and, if possible, expand
our air and naval interdiction of his infiltration system." 23/

3. Vietnam Strategy: On the Ground

On the ground, large unit operations increased during January to
341, but the number having "significant results" decreased for the third
consecutive month (from 24 to 19). Total enemy killed reached a new
monthly high of 5,954, contributing to a total loss figure of 10,440,
also a wartime high. 24/ Major military operations in January did
not yet clearly reflect the thinking Westmoreland had revealed in his
early January assessments and strategic prognosis; evidently MACV was
still in the planning stage preparing for the major operations of February
and March on the borders and in the sanctuaries. Furthermore, the magnitude of the threat in the DMZ-I CTZ that was to prompt the massive dislocation of troops to the North under TF OREGON in April was not yet
clear, and operations were moving slow motion.

Operation CEDAR FALLS in the Iron Triangle, which began on 8 January, was the most significant operation of the month and the largest operation of the war in terms of forces employed. The operation was aimed at clearing the Triangle, an area denied to the GVN for over 20 years. In the estimation of the MACV staff it gained outstanding results, capturing large numbers of weapons, ammunition and other war materials, plus nearly a half-million pages of enemy documents. 25/ MACV concluded that CEDAR FALLS had destroyed the Iron Triangle as a secure VC base area (although the operation which superseded CEDAR FALLS, JUNCTION CITY, was in basically the same area).

Operation THAYER II conducted by the 1st Cavalry Division in Binh Dinh Province reported killing over 500 enemy, the second consecutive month such a figure was reached in that province. FAIRFAX, an open-ended operation which was to continue in one form or another for months, aimed at destroying enemy forces and eliminating the VC infrastructure in Gia Dinh Province southeast of Saigon was "meeting significant results." Operation ADAMS in Phu Yen Province, a "search and destroy rice harvest security and road clearing operation" was specifically designed "to provide a shield behind which Revolutionary Development /was/ progressing." 26/ This was the precursor of the USMC Operation DESOTO in the Quang Ngai salt flats later that month. In preparation for DESOTO, ROK Marines conducted Operation SEINE in Quang Ngai, a ten-day search and destroy operation, which killed over 110 enemy in the period. The most significant RVNAF operations were conducted in the Capital Military District and in IV CTZ. 27/ Three areas were being closely watched for increased enemy activities, possibly large unit operations. In I CTZ the enemy troop build-up, resupply harassment, and reconnaissance increased in the DMZ area. Elements of the NVA 324th and 341st Divisions were confirmed as infiltrated south into Quang Tri Province. From every indication there would be future widespread enemy activity in that area. Enemy forces in II CTZ continued to evade friendly forces throughout the month, although the NVA NT 1 and NT 10 divisions located near the Kontum/Pleiku border were believed preparing to move, or actually moving, into those provinces. In III CTZ, despite the disruptive effects of CEDAR FALLS in the Iron Triangle, there were strong indications that elements of six VC/NVA divisions were preparing for future offensive operations in the Tay Ninh-Binh Long-Binh Tuong Province areas. 28/

January was characterized by the insertion of more ARVN battalions into the role of direct support of revolutionary development for 1967. In-country, there were 120 ARVN infantry battalions assigned to 10 divisional tactical areas and two special zones. Of these, 50 were to have been assigned missions of direct support of revolutionary development for 1967. Operational control of these RD battalions varied throughout the country and included command under the province chief, the regimental commander, special zone commander or the division commander. In

addition, three ranger, one marine and three airborne battalions were
to have been assigned a mission of direct support of RD. There were
eight U.S. battalions with an RD mission and other FWMAF contributed
three battalions. 29/ Some American observers, however, were less
than pleased with the ardor for RD which the Vietnamese were displaying.
One source in III CTZ observed that:

> "...The late 1966 enthusiasm which helped to launch
> 1967 RD progress has yet to work its way down to the dis-
> trict and village level where the impact must be realized.
>
> "The monthly meeting of the III CTZ RD council, sched-
> uled for 3 February, was postponed, probably due to prepar-
> ations for TET. The efficiency of the RD cadre teams
> continues in most areas to be marginal. Since the success
> of the entire 1967 hamlet program will be largely dependent
> upon the performance and accomplishments of these teams,
> their efficiency must be improved...." 30/

Such views undoubtedly contributed to the basic uneasiness about whether
ARVN could (or would) "cut the RD mustard," a fear voiced by Holbrooke
a month earlier.

Briefly, analyzing the pattern of operations (see "Major Operations
and Approximate Locations," next page) some sixty-two of the United States
maneuver battalions in Vietnam were engaged at some time on what MACV
termed "large operations." Realizing that the criterion for large operations of "100 or more enemy dead" is not necessarily the best for our
purposes, and that such actions were influenced by the monsoon patterns,
at least a rough picture of the operational center of gravity can be
developed. Of the sixty-two battalions so engaged, twenty-six were
participating on missions which had an RD component -- either protecting
the harvest, screening the local population, or keeping routes open so
the crops could reach market. Thus, the U.S. was devoting approximately
25-30% of its forces in January 1967 to RD effort country-wide, although
this simple statistic is misleading because some of the operations listed
were combination search and destroy/RD actions. No major ARVN combat
operations were specifically designed to support RD objectives, although
as we noted earlier, on a battalion level basis an increasing number of
Vietnamese units were being assigned such tasks. 31/

JANUARY LARGE OPERATIONS

ENEMY KILLED

SEINE	140	
THAYER II	549	(1529)
MAENG HO 8	158	
ADAMS	118	(282)
CEDAR FALLS	720	
TTB TAN BINH	118	
FAIRFAX	153	(246)
DECK HOUSE V	13	
DAN CHI 275B/S/D	181	

( ) DENOTES CUMULATIVE KIA
TOTALS FOR THE OPERATION.

MAJOR OPERATIONS
AND APPROXIMATE
LOCATIONS

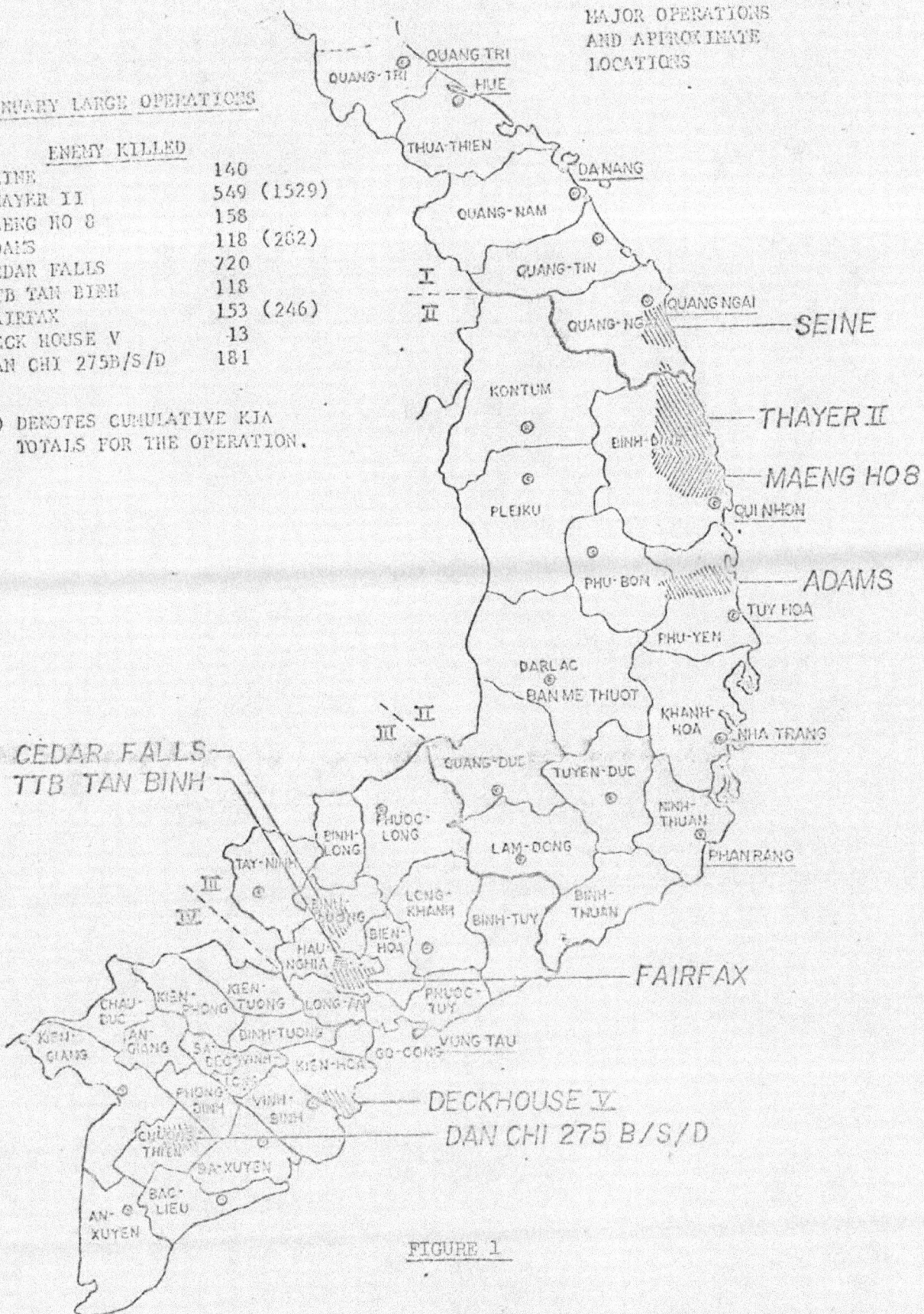

FIGURE 1

36

4. Sanctuaries Revisited: Renewed and Heightened Concern About Laos and Cambodia

As the ground war pursued the path just described, concern about the infiltration and the importance of the sanctuaries deepened. On 18 January CINCPAC had come into the JCS with a request to expand the bombing in NVN to twenty-five "remunerative targets" to counter infiltration. 32/ This request was followed on 25 January by a detailed cable addressing the broader range of anti-infiltration measures. After pleading for a more "balanced" program, the message turned to a major recommendation:

"...The enemy's capability to supply his forces in SVN has been degraded by our air interdiction campaign in SVN, Laos and NVN, and by our offensive ground operations in SVN. The confusion of his supply situation may account, in part, for his attempts to avoid significant contact with our forces. The enemy is dependent upon external sources for most of his weapons, ammunition, medical supplies and assorted technical equipment. The closing of Haiphong would disrupt the enemy's logistical capability to supply these items to SVN. Therefore, I recommend and will shortly submit a plan for closing the port of Haiphong, and other minor ports in NVN. Closing these ports would be the single most effective and economical method of drastically reducing the enemy's capability to carry on the war in SVN. The military advantages of this action would be manifold. It would still be necessary, however, to recognize the significance of infiltration throughout Cambodia. The more successful our operations in NVN and Laos become, the more communist pressure will be brought to bear on Cambodia to increase use of her ports and LOC's or infiltration of supplies into SVN.

"Measures to improve the counter infiltration aspects of our current programs are aimed at striking at the enemy's vulnerabilities and countering his strength. These include:

"A. Destroying his military and logistics bases.

B. Interdicting his LOC's.

C. Forcing the enemy into sustained combat operations.

D. Providing security for the SVN population to prevent impressment and to assist their economic, social, and political development."

Continuing, he reviewed various programs (MARKET TIME, GAME WARDEN, DANIEL BOONE, SEA DRAGON) and the detailed plans to broaden them, but once more the Pacific commander returned to the subject of the sanctuaries:

"The problem of sanctuaries has been mentioned several times. Those in NVN and Laos are limited sanctuaries since they are subject to air attacks, albeit, with certain restrictions. The sanctuary in Cambodia, however, is complete. It would appear appropriate to undertake actions at an early date aimed at persuading the Cambodian leadership to adopt a more neutral position. Pursuant to a request by DOD it is understood that a Joint State, Defense, and CIA committee is considering this problem. It is hoped that recommendations from this group will be forthcoming at an early date which will indicate positive measures which may be taken. The importance of Cambodia as sanctuary and as a source of supplies, particularly rice, cannot be overemphasized. Consequently, we must get on with a strong program to inhibit this use of Cambodia, preferably by non-belligerent political and diplomatic means. If we do not achieve the required degree of success by these means then we must be prepared in all respects to use the necessary degree of force to attain our objectives.

"In summary, the problem of countering infiltration of enemy forces into SVN is just one aspect of the total military problem in SEASIA. While infiltration cannot be absolutely stopped by direct military action, it can be made costly and its effectiveness blunted. The enemy's prodigious efforts to provide air defense and to repair damaged LOC's are strong evidence of the effectiveness of our air campaigns in NVN, Laos and SVN. Increasing interdiction of his supply system, especially by closing his ports, would be the most effective measure we could take against his capability to infiltrate. Additionally, shifting Rolling Thunder emphasis to attack selective target systems should have a significant impact upon his will to continue support to the insurgency in SVN. The more successful our operations become in NVN and Laos, the more use the enemy will seek to make of his supply sources and channels in Cambodia. To achieve our objectives in SEASIA our current strategy, a combination of carefully balanced military programs must be pursued in close coordination with political, economic, and sociological programs." 34/

The next day, attention shifted to a ground anti-infiltration program when General Westmoreland came in with his PRACTICE NINE Requirements Plan, the study of his manpower and logistics requirements to implement the barrier plan outlined a month earlier. The cover memorandum on the plan prepared by the JCS made a determined case against the proposed time frame (a target date of 1 November 1967 had been set), and argued for providing the additional forces from outside resources rather than relying upon assignment of in-country forces already programmed for use elsewhere in the 1967 Campaign Plan. 35/ In light of the anticipated manpower draw-down within South Vietnam, the plan was relatively austere.

COMUSMACV was protecting plans already approved and rolling; accordingly he considered his plan to be no more than "the optimum which /was/ reasonably attainable without an unacceptable impact upon the objectives of the 1967 Combined Campaign Plan." 36/

MACV envisioned a strong point and obstacle system constructed on the eastern portion of northern Quang Tri Province to impede infiltration and to detect invasions. The plan visualized that the system of strong points and obstacles would serve as a base for possible future expansion of the system into the western portion of Quang Tri Province to the Laotian border; this expansion being contingent upon time, forces, material and security conditions. COMUSMACV also indicated a preference for extension of the strong point/obstacle system into the Western Sector instead of reliance on air delivered munitions and sensors.

His force requirement provided the excitement. In his words:

> "To have an effective obstacle system across SVN,
> south of the DMZ, would require a minimum additional force
> of one division and one armored cavalry regiment." 37/

The concept of operations for employment of these forces contemplated two operational areas, an eastern sector and a western sector. Force availability and logistical limitations would permit operations initially only in the eastern section with the exception of one area in the Western portion, that near Khe Sanh. An Army brigade (or Marine RCT) and an ARVN regimental force would construct and man the strong point obstacle system, with artillery, air and NFG fires supporting along the entire trace. III MAF would be prepared to reinforce threatened areas and provide depth to the defense. Two Marine battalions (as a minimum) were earmarked for positioning in the Dong Ha and Khe Sanh areas "until relieved." This large additional troop requirement of nearly two division equivalents and the basic COMUSMACV concept in the plan was to quickly reappear in a CINCPAC message early in February, one which discussed the barrier and infiltration in broader terms. 38/

The JCS agreed with COMUSMACV citing objections which revolved around that they believed were two fundamental disadvantages:

"The increased anti-infiltration capability that would be established would be located in northeastern South Vietnam where North Vietnamese infiltration has been minimal.

"The diversion of resources required for execution of the plan would reduce the emphasis and impetus of essential on-going programs now approved for the conduct of thr war in South Vietnam." 39/

Furthermore, they observed that such diversion of resources and efforts might come at a crucial point...

"The Joint Chiefs of Staff consider that military actions now in progress in Southeast Asia, in support of the concepts and courses of action approved by them are demonstrating substantial successes toward national objectives and that if expanded and pressed with continued vigor, these successes will accelerate. The Joint Chiefs of Staff, less the Chairman, Joint Chiefs of Staff, conclude that any additional resources that might be provided can be used to a greater advantage in executing CINCPAC's concept of operations for Southeast Asia." 40/

There was no solid consensus among high officers on the barrier issue. In late February, General Wheeler wrote in reply to JCSM 97-67 that he believed, contrary to COMUSMACV and JCS conclusions, that the implementation of the PRACTICE NINE Plan might enhance rather than inhibit the flexibility available to COMUSMACV. He wrote:

"...although I support much of the paper (JCSM 97-67, PRACTICE NINE Requirements Plan), I disagree with the recommendation that the plan not be approved for execution.

"Although I recognize that the eastern portion of the DMZ does not now represent a major active infiltration corridor, it does possess a substantial potential for the rapid introduction of sizeable forces from the north; in fact, this portion of the border area provides the quickest and most trafficable routes from North Vietnam into South Vietnam. Thus, an obstacle system impeding enemy capability to exercise such an option seems to me to represent a prudent military action.

"Again, while I recognize that the obstacle system reflected in the COMUSMACV plan may require an undesirable diversion of in-country resources, it is not clear to me

that this will of necessity be so; it is also possible
that the level of activity in the vicinity of the DMZ
will require the commitment of comparable forces to that
area whether or not construction of the obstacle system
envisaged by COMUSMACV is undertaken. Furthermore, proceeding now with the actions required to provide additive
assets for support of the MACV plan does not, in my view,
rule out a subsequent decision to utilize these assets in
other ways should the turn of events so require. Thus,
it is my view that proceeding now with preparatory actions
to implement the COMUSMACV plan may enhance rather than
inhibit the flexibility available to COMUSMACV." 41/

In other words, the Chairman was displaying considerably more
prescience than his military colleagues. Either this or he was the
only one who really believed the MACV-CINCPAC reports of activity and
assessment of the threat in I CTZ. He anticipated that events might
outrun the requirement for decision on the barrier troop issue -- an
apprehension which materialized in rapid fashion.

The next day, the Central Intelligence Agency published a study
entitled "Significance of Cambodia to the Vietnamese War Effort" in
which it, too, disagreed with the assessment the military commanders
had been making. 42/ Although the availability of Cambodian territory
was granted to be of considerable psychological and military advantage
to the Communists, and the access to the Cambodian rice surplus had
evidently obviated any need to move substantial quantities of food
down the Laotian route system to feed Communist forces in the rice-
deficit Vietnamese highlands and Laotian panhandle, the study concluded:

"Denying the Communists the use of Cambodian territory and supplies would make life more difficult for them;
it would not constitute a decisive element in their ability
to conduct military operations in South Vietnam." 43/

The caveat added to this rather surprising conclusion noted that
probably during 1967 Communist use of Cambodia would increase primarily
due to:

"The logistic burdens imposed on the Communists by their
own military build-up and the increasing pressures imposed
by allied forces." 44/

If this were true, then, a very good argument could be made that as
of the moment denial of Cambodia "would not be decisive," but as the weight
of U.S. military pressure increased, and the Cambodian sanctuary and supply aspects increased in importance to the enemy, then it may become
decisive. The decisive nature of denial of Cambodia to the VC/NVA would
be a function of its increasing value to them.

5. Infiltration -- Remains the Key

Into February, infiltration held the focus of attention. Following up his 18 January request, on the first of February, CINCPAC requested authorization to conduct offensive mining against the North Vietnamese ports. 45/ He stated his case:

> "A drastic reduction of external support to the enemy would be a major influence in achieving our objectives in NVN. Despite fewer ship arrivals in 1966 compared to recent years the tonnage of imports has increased. This increase demonstrates the rising need for external support in NVN. While the nature of cargoes discharged cannot be stated with precision, there is little doubt that a major portion contains war supporting materials. Additionally, the ability of NVN to export products to other nations through its seaports contributes significantly to its capability to support hostilities in RVN. The closure of selected NVN ports would result in a severely strained economy and reduce Hanoi's capability to support military actions in SVN.

> "Closure of the port of Haiphong to ocean-going ships is of paramount importance and would be effective in compounding NVN logistic problems for the reasons indicated below:

>> "A. 85 percent of imports come through Haiphong. There is no satisfactory alternate port.

>> "B. Soviet cargo presently entering NVN through Haiphong would have to be re-routed through Communist China or off-loaded in time-consuming barge operations. Thus far the CHICOMs have not permitted the Soviets unlimited use of their rail systems.

>> "C. The ability of CHICOM/NVN rail systems to function as a substitute means to provide logistic support is marginal. A demand for increased rolling stock as well as new port facilities would be generated.

>> "Closure of NVN ports would be a sign of U.S. determination to prosecute the war successfully thus bringing increased pressure on Hanoi to terminate hostilities...." 46/

If Admiral Sharp received the "go" to conduct offensive mining against the NVN ports, initial efforts would be directed at Haiphong. He saw this action as...

"an effective means of depriving the enemy of imports
required to continue the war. If used in conjunction
with RT air strikes against the port system, Haiphong
can be virtually sealed as a source of war supplies." 47/

This CINCPAC bombing request message was followed on 6 February
by a comprehensive PRACTICE NINE cable, which reviewed the "barrier
plan" and discussed the previous MACV-CINCPAC planning. 48/   In it
CINCPAC reemphasized that unless the additional troops COMUSMACV had
requested were forthcoming the target date to reach the required levels
of effectiveness could not be met.

He summarized the operational and logistical considerations by
saying:

"The COMUSMACV plan responds to the requirement for
submission of an anti-infiltration plan in the northeastern area of Quang Tri Province, south of the DMZ.

"Within the constraints imposed, the concept is
feasible. The system of obstacles and strong points,
with forces assigned, would be capable of impeding
infiltration to a degree, and detecting any overt
invasion threat.

"The additive forces requested are essential to
implementation of this plan. Furthermore, the diversion
of in-country forces which would be required to support
the plan would have an adverse impact on other necessary
programs." 49/

Then the message took a surprising turn:

"The level of infiltration in the area the obstacle
system is to be installed does not justify diversion of
the effort required to construct and man such a system.
Moreover, there is no indication that present operations
are inadequate to cope with what has been an insignificant
infiltration problem in this particular area of SVN.

"Extension and expansion of the system of obstacles
westward from Dong Ha mountain to the Laotian border to
provide an effective anti-infiltration system is contingent upon additional forces, i.e., an infantry division
and an armored cavalry regiment.

"A rigid operational capability date of 1 November 67
should not obtain." 50/

Consistent with this, the summary stressed General Westmoreland's concern...

> "...over the inflexible time frame, the need for
> additional forces to construct and man the obstacle sys-
> tem, and the impact of using in-country or programmed
> forces. He has made clear that the U.S. brigade or
> regiment requested in the plan is but the first increment
> of a full division and armored cavalry regiment force
> required to man an effective obstacle system south of
> the DMZ. Finally, he emphasizes that the course of
> action set forth in the plan would not in itself stop
> infiltration. In view of the numerous disadvantages
> listed above, and in light of the need to maintain bal-
> ance in all anti-infiltration programs, CINCPAC recommends
> that the plan not be implemented within the time-frame
> envisioned." 51/

All of which seems to be saying that if the troops required (1 div-ision plus 1 regiment) were assigned to the barrier, it would probably reach the desired effectiveness, but since they most likely will not come from "outside" resources, and COMUSMACV does not desire to draw down other forces for them, the barrier would probably not be very effective or meet a real threat anyway.

On the ground in SEA observers were painstakingly searching the infiltration figures for indications of "reciprocal moves" on the part of the VC/NVA, or the "fade-out" various individuals had been predicting. The press was also speculating upon the political intent of North Vietnam, led there by MACV's year-end infiltration statistics. A MACV "backgrounder" in late 1966 had indicated a drastic falling off from earlier infiltration levels. Little had been done in the interim to correct (or update) these figures and speculation was rife in early February. Phil Goulding was frantically quizzing MACV for explanations. Military attaches were exper-iencing pressure from their ambassadors for interpretations and analysis. 52/ PACOM-MACV answered queries with a detailed discussion outlining the prob-lems of interpreting (or even developing) infiltration estimates; information which may be useful at this point to highlight the problems and pitfalls of "infiltration watching." CINCPAC wrote that it was:

> "Our position ... that the NVA must continue to infil-
> trate at significant levels to maintain maturing force
> structure. The VC cannot replace total communist losses
> as well as provide additional personnel to flesh out their
> joint (VC/NVA) planned force structure. It is true that
> figures may appear to suggest that infiltration dropped off
> sharply during last half 1966. Although statistical data
> indicates infiltration appears to have dropped during latter

half 1966, the figures for last five months of year are
not complete. Also, data after September 1966 represents only partial returns subject to considerable upward
revision. Recent intensive community-wide review of the
foregoing at CINCPAC resulted in an agreed data base with
Oct 65 through Dec 66 time frame. (Oct 65 selected as
historical start point attributable to initiation intensive
NVA build-up). The mean monthly infiltration during this
time frame has been about 6-7,000.

"An example of late data recently incorporated in
infiltration statistics follows: The 165 NVA regiment
began infiltrating into SVN in March 1966 but did not
complete infiltration until about July 66. Sufficient
information became available in January 1967 to permit
the acceptance of the 165 NVA regiment in the order of
battle. It had been unidentified and unknown earlier.
As the result, confirmed infiltration figures for July
1966 were revised upward in January 1967 by 1,950 to
reflect the 165th regiment's strength upon reorganization
in SVN. Review of statistical infiltration data also
shows that figures require 90 to 180 day time frame to
be developed. Concur, that the NVA may be approaching
their current planned force structure in SVN. In the
future, it will probably be even more difficult to generate short-term infiltration data. Infiltrators may enter
SVN more often in groups vice large units. Groups may
break up shortly after infiltration as replacements
compounding the problem for our intelligence gathering
agencies, and further complicating the statistical problem.

"This is an estimate and we feel more time is
required to gain substantiating information.

"We take particular exception with statement in the
reference that Hanoi may be willing to enter into negotiations to get bombing stopped.

"CINCPAC position is there are no repeat no indications
that indicate NVN has changed previously stated terms for
negotiation which is basis for USG resumption of bombing just
ordered. Negotiations embodying NVN terms would, in effect,
require the surrender of our stated objectives in SVN.

"In addition, there are no repeat no indications
available here that NVN has changed original intent to
vigorously prosecute the war notwithstanding allied bombing
which has caused NVN severe difficulty." 53/

In late February, as the debate over roles and missions (AB 142), progress in pacification, ARVN effectiveness, PRACTICE NINE Requirements, enemy intentions and infiltration reached a crescendo, it became clear that the deployment debate was centered upon one major uncertainty -- How many more U.S. troops would it require to achieve U.S. objectives in SVN, and more basically in the face of the infiltration trends past and present _could_ our massive infusions of U.S. forces turn the trick.

Operation CEDAR FALLS, deep into the Iron Triangle, redoubt had produced a windfall of enemy documents and plans, many of which bore directly upon enemy strategy and indirectly conditioned our expectations and confidence in our calculations. Some of them revealed a "new strategy developed after the entry of substantial US and Free World forces into South Vietnam." 54/ COMUSMACV, recounting the information obtained in the document, had stated that for the enemy:

> "...The main emphasis is on continued reinforcement
> from North Vietnam to defeat US and RVN forces in South
> Vietnam. This strategy reaffirms the concept of the necessity
> for a protracted war, but nonetheless stresses the need both
> to seize and to create opportunities for decisive tactical
> victories of high impact effect in a relatively short time.
> At the same time it stresses intensified guerrilla action and
> public disturbances, all featuring the customary coordination
> between military and political action. It appears that the
> principal objective area is the highlands, the secondary areas
> being Quang Tri and Thua Thien and the coastal provinces of
> the II Corps. It is understood, of course, that the Saigon
> area is the ultimate objective.

> "Analysis of the broad strategic guidance contained in
> the early 1966 document just mentioned, along with later
> prisoner interrogations suggests the conceptual framework
> of enemy planning. This would include attacks in the I Corps
> and II Corps coastal areas to cause our forces to be redeployed.
> If the enemy could then succeed in weakening our forces in the
> highlands by luring part of them into the coastal areas and
> then pinning them down, conditions might be achieved which he
> would consider favorable for a spectacular victory in the
> highlands employing main forces already located there and
> possibly reinforced by continued infiltration from North Viet-
> nam. Such an attempt probably would not be with the intent
> to hold ground permanently, but rather to create a psychologi-
> cal shock designed to affect US public opinion against continu-
> ation of the war, to bolster his own morale, and to improve his
> position for negotiation or further combat. To achieve this,
> his favored objective, as shown by documentary evidence, would
> be the entrapment and "annihilation" of a large US unit,

preferably a battalion of the 1st Air Cav Division; or
alternatively, employment of a sweep against Pleiku,
including destruction of installations, rapid withdrawal,
and the ambush of reaction forces.

"The present disposition of enemy forces can be
analyzed in relation to such a strategy. Despite several
major defeats and heavy casualties, the enemy still main-
tains three divisions near the demilitarized zone. Elements
of these forces have infiltrated again into Quang Tri and
Thua Thien provinces. They pose a constant threat to territory and installations in Quang Tri and Thua Thien Provinces
and have forced the prolonged deployment of four US Marine
battalions and four ARVN battalions to northern Quang Tri
Province, enemy initiative in Quang Tri and Thua Thien has
increased during the past several months and is expected to
increase further. The enemy has the capability of launching
large scale attacks across the DMZ at any time. This is
not meant to imply that massive multi-division attacks
necessarily will occur. More probably, by an increased
buildup and tempo of coordinated main force/guerrilla operations, the enemy may attempt to expand his forces southward
and gradually overwhelm the area below the DMZ. Whether by
attack or encroachment, such efforts would serve to force
the deployment of additional US and Vietnamese troops to the
area and thereby thin out those forces in support of Revolutionary Development. The enemy's deployment of a division
to Quang Ngai has served to increase his pressure in that
Province. His division formerly in Binh Dinh has been
mauled by the 1st Cavalry Division and either has dispersed
in Binh Dinh Province or has withdrawn to Quang Ngai. The
enemy division that was deployed to Phu Yen has been dispersed; however, one regiment has attempted to consolidate
itself in Khanh Hoa. The enemy's strategy in attempting to
pin down allied forces in the coastal areas in order to
divert attention from the highlands has been unsuccessful
thus far. However, his concentration of two divisions in
Cambodia west of Pleiku and Kontum Provinces has forced the
deployment of a minimum of four US battalions to the highlands to provide surveillance over the border areas. These
minimum forces had to be reinforced during the past year
from other areas, and further reinforcement probably will
be necessary during the coming month when these two North
Vietnamese Divisions ready themselves for offensive operations.
In the III Corps area the enemy has adopted a similar strategy.
He has deployed two divisions in the northwestern quadrant of
the III Corps Tactical Zone and has been developing a base
and assembling a division in the mountainous and jungle-
covered areas of Phouc Tuy Province.

"7. The enemy's implementation of his strategy is
characterized by:

A. Increasing his guerrilla forces and their
tempo of operations with emphasis on the sabotage of US
installations.

B. Expanding his local forces as manpower will
permit for the purpose of harassing RVN, FW and US installations and forces and disrupting Revolutionary Development.

C. Concentrating North Vietnamese Army and VC
main forces in numerous remote areas, thereby posing a
continual strategic threat intended to prevent concentration
of our forces in particular regions. These are areas from
which enemy forces can conduct training and supply operations
with minimum risk, and from which they may be deployed when
ready. These areas are:

(1) The DMZ.

(2) In Laos opposite Hua Thien Province.

(3) In Eastern Cambodia adjacent to the
Central Highlands.

(4) The jungle-covered areas of Northwestern
III Corps (and the adjacent areas in Cambodia) and of Phuoc
Tuy Province.

(5) The mountainous areas adjacent to the
fertile coastal plans of Central Vietnam in the Provinces
of Quang Ngai, Binh Dinh, Pu Yen and Khanh Hoa.

. . . .

"In summary, the enemy's strategy is a practical and
clever one designed to continue a protracted war, inflict
unacceptable casualties on our forces, establish a favorable political posture, minimize risks to main forces,
and maintain in the option of going on the military offensive of his covert troop deployment.

"Considering the desire of the world population to see
a peaceful solution to the conflict in Vietnam during the
coming months, it is likely that the enemy will attempt to
parlay this desire for peace and American impatience with
the war into major concessions prior to, or during, negotiations undertaken between opposing sides. This strategy

has been used effectively by the communists in the past, as the record of the Korean negotiations will reflect." 55/

To counter such a broad, coordinated strategy would require large numbers of troops -- even more than those listed under Program #4. To many observers the concept of "sheer mass" doing the job was appealing. Robert Komer returned from a mid-February trip to Vietnam no less optimistic than before. Ever the inveterate optimist he reported to the President that:

"After almost a year full-time in Vietnam, and six trips there, I felt able to learn a good deal more from my 11 days in-country, 13-23 February. I return more optimistic than ever before. The cumulative change since my first visit last April is dramatic, if not yet visibly demonstrable in all respects. Indeed, I'll reaffirm even more vigorously my prognosis of last November which would be achieved in 1967 on almost every front in Vietnam." 56/

He firmly believed that in time we would just overwhelm the VC in SVN:

"Wastefully, expensively, but nonetheless indisputably, we are winning the war in the South. Few of our programs -- civil or military -- are very efficient, but we are grinding the enemy down by sheer weight and mass. And the cumulative impact of all we have set in motion is beginning to tell. Pacification still lags the most, yet even it is moving forward." 57/

Finally, and contrary to all military reports, he saw some let-up in the pressures for additional resources:

"Indeed my broad feeling, with due allowance for over-simplication, is that our side now has in presently programmed levels all the men, money and other resources needed to achieve success...." 58/

The preceding statement curiously seems to contradict the tenor of the previous ones which plainly indicate the requirement for a massive influx of U.S. forces. Nevertheless, such optimism, even considering the source was surely to tell upon a President deeply engrossed in weighing alternatives in Vietnam and comparing their risks and benefits.

The most significant assessment of alternative strategies for Vietnam in late February was a short analysis prepared for the President's night reading by ISA and the JCS with an assist from Department of State. 59/ The assessment commenced with the presentation of three programs -- A, B and C -- each one analyzed in terms of its specific actions, the authority required and the policy changes required to implement them and the risk or political impact attendant to each. (See Table, p. 50.) The programs

MILITARY ACTION PROGRAMS FOR SOUTHEAST ASIA - SUMMARY

	ACTIONS	AUTHORITIES/POLICY CHANGES	RISKS/IMPACT
1.	ROLLING THUNDER - Electric Power System, Thai Nguyen Steel Plant, Haiphong Cement Plant, All Unoccupied Airfields; eliminate 10 NM Hanoi Prohibited Area.	No change in operation authorities except deletion of 10 NM radius around Hanoi where ordnance delivery is prohibited. This area then becomes part of 30 NM Restricted Area. No policy changes.	Risk to US forces consistent with normal ROLLING THUNDER operations in the heavily defended northeast area. Loss rates should not exceed acceptable limits commensurate with results to be achieved. Political risks are negligible.
2.	NAVAL SURFACE OPERATIONS - Expand offensive operations to include valid military targets ashore south of 19° N.	Forces now engaged in SEA DRAGON operations require authorization for offensive action against shore targets.	No military risk beyond normal combat. Political risk is low since US ships now fire against shore targets in self defense and against waterborne logistic craft beached and in rivers.
3.	SHINING BRASS - Within current operational limits delegate authorities now held at DOD/STATE level to CINCPAC in coordination with Embassy Vientiane.	Delegate existing authorities to CINCPAC in coordination with Embassy Vientiane. No policy changes.	No increase in military or political risk over that associated with current operations.
4.	LAOS OPERATIONS - Continue as at present plus Operation POP EYE to reduce trafficability along infiltration routes.	Authorization required to implement operational phase of weather modification process previously successfully tested and evaluated in same area.	Normal military operational risks. Risk of compromise is minimal.
5.	B-52 - Base part of operations at U-Tapao.	Requires country clearance for aircraft and personnel to enter Thailand.	No significant military risk. Political risk negligible; however, criticism is to be expected.
6.	LAND ARTILLERY - Fire from positions in SVN against valid military targets in and immediately north of DMZ.	No significant policy change; requires approval of targets only.	No significant military risk. Negligible political risk.
7.	DEPLOYMENTS - Accelerate Program #4 Deployments (including 3 Army Maneuver Battalions).	Requires 1 March 1967 decision to accelerate deployments. Requires corresponding end strength authorization.	Reduction of CONUS strategic reserve.
8.	ROLLING THUNDER - Elements of 3 ports, MIG airfields less those from which international civil transport operate, selected rail facilities, ammo dump, machine/tool plant, 7 locks; reduce Haiphong Restricted Area to 4 NM.	Requires significant policy change to attack MIG airfields.	Military risks are consistent with operations in heavily defended NE area. Loss rates acceptable in terms of expected results. Moderate political risk due to possibility endangering foreign ships, and increased civilian casualties.
9.	MINE INLAND WATERWAYS AND ESTUARIES SOUTH OF 20° N.	Operations can be authorized and conducted within framework of ROLLING THUNDER.	Negligible military risk. Insignificant political risk.
10.	NAVAL SURFACE OPERATIONS - Extend to 20° N.	Requires authorization for offensive action against shore targets.	Military risk/losses commensurate with ROLLING THUNDER operations in NVN. Political risk is acceptable.
11.	SHINING BRASS - Expand operational limits to 20 NM into Laos, increase helo operations, authorize larger forces, increase frequency of operations, decentralize control to CINCPAC in coordination with Embassy Vientiane.	Requires delegation of authority to CINCPAC/Embassy Vientiane. Policy change required to extend operational limits.	Will increase to minor degree risk of exposure of activity. Political risks increased only slightly over present levels.
12.	LAND ARTILLERY - Fire from positions in SVN against valid military targets in Laos.	Minor policy change required.	Negligible military risk. Political risk less than that associated with current air strikes and SHINING BRASS in Laos.
13.	DEPLOYMENTS - Deploy the 9th MAB (3 BLT, 2 TFS, 2 RFM) from Okinawa/Japan to the I CTZ in March 1967.	Requires by 1 March 1967 decision to accelerate deployments. Requires corresponding end strength authorization.	Moderate military risk associated with loss of PACOM amphibious reserve. Political risk less than moderate.
14.	ROLLING THUNDER - 4 ports, remaining MIG airfields, AD HQ, Ministry Defense HQ, dikes; eliminate prohibited/restricted areas.	Requires significant policy change, although operations can be conducted within framework of current ROLLING THUNDER program.	Military risk commensurate with objectives to be achieved. Higher losses initially, but lower thereafter as air defenses degraded. Political risk moderate or higher. Usual propaganda reaction expected on basis of "escalation."
15.	MINE MAJOR PORTS AND APPROACHES. Mine INLAND WATERWAYS and estuaries north of 20° N.	Major policy change required.	Military risk no greater than associated ROLLING THUNDER programs in port area. Political risk is acceptable - no direct military confrontation likely; no realignment of power blocs. Propaganda outcry severe. Possible increase in USSR/China cooperation to NVN.
16.	NAVAL SURFACE OPERATIONS - Expand north of 20° N.	Moderate policy change required.	Moderate military risk. Less than moderate political risk.
17.	SHINING BRASS - Battalion size exploitation forces - start guerrilla warfare.	Significant policy change required.	Moderate military risk associated with increased size/duration of operations. Political risk moderate, but acceptable. Deniability is lessened, but operations defensible on basis enemy conduct.
18.	DEPLOYMENTS - Deploy up to 4 US Divisions (3 Army, 1 USMC); and up to 9 TFS (5 AF, 4 USMC).	Requires decision by 1 March 1967 to call up reserves, extend tours and terms of service, repetitive tours, increase service strengths, and partial industrial mobilization.	Military risk significant in that strategic reserves degraded until end CY 67. Political/domestic risk in terms of increased draft, call up of reserves.

PROGRAM A →

PROGRAM B →

PROGRAM C →

themselves had been prepared by JCS at the request of Deputy Secretary
Vance and they actually incorporated the various separate proposals
made by the JCS over the past two months.

For instance, Program A included ROLLING THUNDER, naval surface
operations, SHINING BRASS, Laos operations, land artillery firing across
the DMZ and ground force deployments. The deployments recommended under
Program A consisted of merely accelerating Program 4 deployments and
possibly adding three Army maneuver battalions. The remainder of Program
A represented no more than minor expansions in operations, recommendations
for which the JCS had been on record since last fall. Program B featured
expanded ROLLING THUNDER operations to include attacking the North Vietnamese ports, mining the inland waterways and estuaries south of 20° North,
attacking the MIG airfields previously excepted, expansion of SHINING
BRASS operations into Laos and, significantly, the deployment of the 9th
Marine Amphibious Brigade from Okinawa/Japan to the I Corps Tactical Zone
in March 1967. Program C subsumed all of the recommendations of the two
preceding Programs A and B, but added an expansion of the mining quantitatively, to include all of approaches and inland waterways north of 20°,
authorized battalion-sized expedition forces in the SHINING BRASS area
and recommended deployments of up to four U.S. divisions (3 Army, 1 USMC)
and up to nine tactical fighter squadrons (5 Air Force, 4 USMC).

Major authorization would be required from the President to expand
the air attacks to the ports and MIG airfields as recommended in Program B,
but other than that, only minor policy changes were required to initiate
Programs A and B. In order to deploy the 9th MAB by 1 March 1967, a
decision had to be made concerning acceleration of deployments, some
corresponding end strength increases for Program 4 had to be authorized.
Program C, of course, was the major deployment proposal, one which
the JCS believed would require a decision by 1 March 1967 to call up
Reserves, to extend tours and terms of service, to authorize repetitive
tours, to increase service strengths, and effect partial industrial mobilization. None of the recommendations included in all of these programs
possessed more than "moderate military risk" in the eyes of the JCS.
Some, such as expansion of ROLLING THUNDER to the port targets, were rated
as possessing "moderate or higher" political risks. The major deployment
recommendation requiring Reserve mobilization carried "significant military risk in that strategic Reserves would be degraded until the end of
the Calendar Year" and "political domestic risk in terms of increased
draft and call-up of Reserves," but again the JCS played down the seriousness of such a move.

The documents available do not indicate what usage the President
made of this particular analysis. However, it remains interesting as an
historical event, being the first explicit presentation of new alternative
programs in the development of Program 5.

1. JCSM 739-66, "Deployments to Southeast Asia and Other PACOM Areas (U)," dated 2 December 1966. See Section I, above, for the discussion of deployment decisions prior to this memorandum.

2. See Memorandum for the Chairman of the Joint Chiefs of Staff from Secretary of Defense, Subj: "Deployments to SEA and Other PACOM Areas (U)," dated 9 December 1966. The JCS asked direct substitution of approximately 15,000 troops to provide "balanced forces." SecDef approved JCS recommendations for an additional A-1 squadron in Thailand, but advised that "...any additional requests to out-of-country areas should be fully justified as to their relation to the conflict in SEA." Another related issue, broached by Systems Analysis, was whether or not to announce to the Chiefs that the barrier plan about to be approved would be manned by MACV from forces within currently approved personnel strengths. If so, SA recommended that JCS should be requested to resubmit their recommendations on that basis. This was not done. See Memorandum from ASD(SA) for Secretary of Defense, Subj: "Deployments to SEA and Other PACOM Areas," dated 7 December 1966.

3. The New York Times, 16 January 1967.

4. The New York Times, 18 January 1967. See Section I for discussion of the 100,000-man figure in COMUSMACV-CINCPAC messages.

5. The New York Times, 22 January 1967.

6. The CIA Analysis of ROLLING THUNDER (CIA SC No. 04442/67, January 1967) had fallen into Senator Fulbright's hands and he was threatening to use it in his Vietnam hearings. Its conclusion, that the bombing was relatively ineffective given the political constraints, was confirmed by the McNamara testimony before the joint session of the House Armed Services Committee and Senate Sub-Committee on 23 January 1967.

7. A JCSM published a week later reveals that the JCS firmly believed "...that, in their judgment, there /was/ no military justification to reduce the strength of U.S. forces in Europe." (JCSM 46-67, Subj: "Redeployment of U.S. Forces Withdrawn from Europe (U)," dated 28 January 1967). One can speculate ad infinitum about Mansfield's motives and about with whom he was allied, but one can hardly deny that he, the Chiefs, the President and the Secretary of Defense were not acutely aware of just about at what point CONUS military manpower resources would be exhausted.

8. The New York Times, January 1967. There was an audible sigh of relief when the Salisbury dispatches ended on 18 January. However, five days later, Bill Boggs, of the Miami News, was filing reports from Hanoi which substantially corroborated Salisbury's stories about civilian casualties and the bombing.

9. COMUSMACV 02916 (Westmoreland Sends) to Deputy Commanding General, USARV, "Command Guidance (U)," dated 24 January 1967.

10. Ibid.

11. Ibid. The public relations aspect was real. Less than a month later, R. W. Apple, of the New York Times, was to write a major piece, cutting away the facade of "good" PR which had covered RVNAF performance to discuss the lack of effectiveness of such units as he found them.

12. COMUSMACV 00610 to CINCPAC for Admiral Sharp and General Wheeler from General Westmoreland, Subj: "Year-End Assessment of Enemy Situation and Enemy Strategy (U)," dated 2 January 1967.

13. Ibid. These figures roughly conform to corrected OB and strength estimates developed later in the year, when MACV reported 116,552 combat, 41,700 administrative service and 126,200 guerrilla troops for a total of 283,900 compared to 280,575 in this cable. See: MACV Monthly Order of Battle Summary, 31 October 1967.

14. Ibid.

15. Ibid. This infiltration figure of 8400 per month is slightly below the figure of 9100 contained in the MACV Command History 1966. At the end of 1966, MACV accepted a figure of 48,400 infiltrators during the year, plus an additional 25,600 "may have infiltrated into South Vietnam on the basis of information evaluated as possibly true." This total of 74,000 "possible" and "accepted" provided the base for MACV calculations at the time. See: USMACV Command History 1966, "Infiltration Into RVN," p. 22. A 7 November 1967 OSD STAT Summary gave an "accepted" figure of 55,300 infiltrators, or if you add the MACV "possible" figure about 9000 per month. See: "Southeast Asia Analysis Report," OASD(SA)SEA Programs Directorate, No. 8-0054 (Special Supplement). The recruitment figure conforms to a more sophisticated estimate on VC recruitment, one which concluded that the MACV estimate of 7000 VC recruited per month in 1966 was probably not valid for 1967. The key finding of the study was that the VC probable rate was near 3500 men per month. See: CICV Study ST 67-081, "VC In-Country Recruitment" dated 15 September 1967, and Ibid., SEA Analysis Report.

16. Ibid.

17. MACV Command History, op. cit., pp. 22-23.

18. Ibid.

19. CINCPAC to JCS, Exclusive for General Wheeler and General Westmoreland from Admiral Sharp, Subj: "Memo from General Beach
Reference USARPAC Views Relative to Probable Enemy Actions," dated
3 January 1967. This message refers to a verbal request from PACOM
for such views of major commanders and is a follow-up to a 24 December 1966 memorandum by General Beach devoted to the same subject.

20. Ibid.

21. Ibid.

22. Ibid. Emphasis added.

23. Ibid. The author never explained what he thought were "more important
operations," but one can gather from the preceding paragraphs that
he meant ground operations in the base areas and against main force
units.

24. USMACV "Monthly Evaluation" January 1967, p. 3.

25. Ibid.

26. Ibid.

27. Ibid. There were 136,591 small unit operations reported with 1,065
enemy contacts, 235 of these at night.

28. Ibid.

29. Ibid. The problem of operational control of RD battalions is one of
many "little" problems that complicated the greater problem of
COMUSMACV in allocating personnel between "shield" and "shelter" and
optimizing his strategic gains. In January, the Joint General Staff,
RVNAF, published a directive stating that ARVN units employed in support of RD may operate under the operational control of either division or sector as appropriate. The authority that exercised control
would designate a tactical area of responsibility (TAOR) to be approved
by the Corps Commander concerned. Units would not be withdrawn from
their assigned TAOR by division or sector without prior approval of
Corps. However, in an emergency (e.g., when the unit was needed to
assist a friendly force that came under attack suddenly), the unit
might be used outside the TAOR for a period not to exceed six hours,
provided other local military resources were already committed, and
a minimum security force remained in the TAOR while the unit was
away. See Ibid., p. 12-13.

30. Ibid., p. 24.

31. <u>Ibid</u>. This was derived from the lists of "Significant Engagements" and "Major Operations Map" on the monthly evaluation. Total activity of both GVN and US units for January was reported as:

	Operations (Bn or Larger/With Contact)	Battalion Days
GVN	292/152	2,165
US	38/35	1,400

32. CINCPAC 182210Z January 1967. Destruction and interdiction missions in the Laotian Panhandle had not been as productive in November and December 1966 as everyone had hoped, and as military calculations increasingly turned on infiltration figures, efforts were made in mid-January to seek improved measures. On 15 January 1967, General Westmoreland, LTG Momyer and their staffs met with Ambassadors Martin and Sullivan at Udorn. /See: COMUSMACV 01819 (Section I and II) for Admiral Sharp, info to General Wheeler from General Westmoreland, Subj: "Udorn Conference," dated 16 January 1967./ Little came of the conference except renewed efforts to cut reaction times and improve coordination. COMUSMACV's efforts to amend rules of engagement met State resistance, a harbinger of the resistance that was to meet future efforts to expand operations in Laos and Cambodia.

33. CINCPAC 252126Z January 1967 to JCS, "Modifications to Current Programs to Improve the Anti-Infiltration Aspect of Our Overall Strategy," 25 January 1967.

34. <u>Ibid</u>.

35. COMUSMACV "Practice Nine Requirements Plan," 26 January 1967, forwarded under CM 2134-67 (22 February 1967) and JCSM 97-67.

36. <u>Ibid</u>.

37. <u>Ibid</u>.

38. <u>Ibid</u>. See the discussion of CINCPAC 060820Z February 1967 in the following pages.

39. JCSM-97-67, Subj: "MACV PRACTICE NINE Requirements Plan," dated 22 February 1967.

40. <u>Ibid</u>.

41. CM-2134-67, "PRACTICE NINE Requirements Plan, dated 26 January 1967, (U)," dated 22 February 1967.

42. CIA SNIE 57-67, "Significance of Cambodia to the Vietnamese Communist War Effort," dated 26 January 1967.

43. Ibid.

44. Ibid.

45. CINCPAC 012005Z February 1967, to JCS, Subj: "Closing NVN Ports"

46. Ibid. CINCPAC 182210Z January 1967 requested authorization to hit 25 "selected lucrative targets in Haiphong" as a package. Essentially the same reasons were outlined in the January message. See Note 32, p. 28.

47. Ibid.

48. CINCPAC 060820Z February 1967 to JCS, Subj: "Barrier Plan." It may be helpful to trace the discussion and planning leading to this document. JCS 0619Z January 1967 initiated COMUSMACV-CINCPAC detailed planning to support the barrier concept, according to criteria and guidance contained in the DCPG Memorandum for the Secretary of Defense, Subj: "Plan for Increased Anti-Infiltration Capability for SEA," dated 22 December 1966. On 11 and 17 January CINCPAC directed COMUSMACV to submit an overall plan. (CINCPAC 112347Z January 1967 and 170051Z January 1967). COMUSMACV PRACTICE NINE Requirement Plans, 26 January 1967, was submitted in response to the CINCPAC order. The CINCPAC cable on 25 January seems an attempt to balance the barrier concept in light of COMUSMACV's requirements plan, and to present some anti-infiltration alternatives to PRACTICE NINE. The message being discussed tried to tie all of the proposals together.

49. CINCPAC 060820Z February 1967, Ibid.

50. Ibid. The general rejection of the concept implied in the opening paragraph probably refers to only the eastern sector, although it may be interpreted as a more sweeping denial.

51. Ibid.

52. See DEF 5563, 041758 February 1967, to COMUSMACV/CINCPAC, Subj: "Infiltration Statistics"; and CINCPAC 140433Z February 1967.

53. CINCPAC 140433Z February 1967 to USMILADREP SEATO.

54. COMUSMACV 06497 to JCS (CINCPAC info), Subj: "Assessment of the Military Situation," dated 23 February 1967.

55. Ibid.

56. R. W. Komer, Memorandum to the President, February 28, 1967.

57. Ibid.

58. _Ibid_.

59. Memorandum from the Deputy Secretary of Defense to the Honorable Nicholas deB. Katzenbach, Under Secretary of State, Subj: "Military Action Programs for Southeast Asia," dated 21 February 1967.

C. THE MACV REQUEST AND
THE SEARCH FOR OPTIONS

C.   THE MACV REQUEST AND THE SEARCH FOR OPTIONS

   1.   The Guam Conference, 20-21 March 1967

In late March, President Johnson, along with members of the White
House Staff, DoD and State met with President Thieu, Premier Ky, General
Westmoreland and other key military officials at Guam. The President was
determined to accelerate the rate of progress in the collective military
and nation-building task confronting the United States and South Vietnam
and he believed that a face-to-face meeting with Thieu and Ky could best
speed up the process and possibly relieve some of the heavy political
pressures on what he termed "the absolutely vital political base in the
country." 1/   The basic objectives of the Guam meeting in the Secretary
of State's words were to:

   "1. Stimulate good relations between them /Thieu and
Ky7 and our new team /Bunker and Locke7.

   2. Provide an opportunity to impress upon them the high
importance of expeditiously completing and bringing the constitutions into effect, and holding effective and honest elections.
Continued GVN unity and broadly based government are critical
to the maintenance of the U.S. political base.

   3. Help to dramatize post-war planning and the role of
David Lilienthal and his opposite number.

   4. Closely examine the current status of the land
reform program and determine what steps can be taken to accelerate the rate of progress in this field."

Noticeably missing from the list of objectives was any detailed discussion
or reevaluation of the military situation. In fact, the Agenda for the
conference included but two short sessions on the military effort. 2/
President Johnson had publicly announced that his purpose in calling the
Guam Conference was to introduce the newly appointed U.S. team of Bunker,
Locke and Komer to the leaders of the GVN. 3/   Just as the Agenda had
indicated it would, and as had been the case in the two previous occasions
of top US-GVN talks (Honolulu and Manila), the conference communique of
the two-day meeting emphasized political, economic and social concerns. 4/
The military picture was presumed to be so encouraging and improving that
it required no special attention. However, three general impressions about
the thrust of the military briefings emerge from the conference documents
and notes.

   First, is the basically optimistic view held by General Westmoreland.
He noted that we were pursuing a constant strategy aimed at destroying the
enemy's main forces, providing security for the populace so that pacification could proceed, improving the lot of the people, pressing the North

Vietnamese through the ROLLING THUNDER program and, finally, creating conditions favorable for settlement on U.S. terms. Westmoreland's main conclusions revolved around a new assessment that the enemy was weakening, that ROLLING THUNDER did help, and that the enemy's losses would soon exceed his gains. To buttress these views he quoted a number of "indicators": that intensity of allied operations was up versus those of last year; that the enemy's losses had doubled; that we were taking four times the number of prisoners we had; that the number of defectors had doubled; that the enemy was losing $2\frac{1}{2}$ times the weapons that he had in the past year; and that 18% more major roads in South Vietnam had been opened in the past three months. Enemy weakness was evident from the fact that 54 of his maneuver battalions were rated only 50% combat effective compared to ARVN's performance in having all but 7 of its 154 battalions combat effective. ARVN leadership was also cited as being "better." 5/

COMUSMACV's analysis of RVNAF effectiveness was based upon a MACV study completed early in 1967, one devoted to determining the shortfalls, weaknesses and limitations of that organization. The analysis indicated that the ARVN kill ratio had risen from 3.6 in 1965 to 3.7 in 1966 and that there was a noticeable decline (27%) in personnel missing in action. The MACV study had concluded "that it was apparent that both the Vietnamese Army and Vietnamese Air Force had made significant improvements during the year. 6/

A Systems Analysis study completed in DoD just prior to the Guam Conference concluded that U.S. and ARVN forces had surprisingly equal effectiveness per battalion day on search and destroy operations when the relative strengths of the battalions were taken into account. 7/ At a time when American decision-makers were casting about for any favorable reports on Vietnamese performance, these descriptions of ARVN progress were surely welcome. Unfortunately, they only contributed to the unrealistic military euphoria which pervaded the Guam discussions.

The second major impression one takes from reviewing the military briefings at Guam was that some increases in the Program 4 levels would be necessary, but these would not be major. The enemy strategy was reiterated; nothing found on CEDAR FALLS or other recent operations did anything but confirm the MACV year-end assessment of VC/NVA strategy. Recent American successes reinforced the belief that we had hit upon the key to winning -- despite continued large scale infiltration, Westmoreland and others on his staff believed we were again flirting with the illusive "crossover point" when enemy total strength would begin to decline, battle, disease and desertion losses would exceed gains. 8/ Yet, despite the indicators, infiltration remained an uncertainty, as did the continued good performance of ARVN. Without a relatively efficient RVNAF performance, pacification (especially as its roles and missions were allocated) was doomed to failure. The hope generated by the encouraging report on ARVN (from both MACV and OASD/SA) and the favorable outcomes of US current operations, seemed to confirm what most were led to believe: any forthcoming Program 4 requests would be small. 9/

The briefing papers prepared for the conference merely affirmed the prevalent belief when one concluded that:

"...There does not appear to be any great return to be realized from further force increases. The best alternatives are to increase the effectiveness of the force already employed. This may be done through improved tactics and intelligence as well as through greater firepower and mobility." 10/

The same paper listed some of the factors that it believed might lead to significant changes in Program #4. They were:

a) PRACTICE NINE - Should this concept be implemented significant troop increases may be necessary. The physical barrier on the east flank would require (according to MACV) about 7700 additional personnel - 1 brigade, support and 2 NMCBs. The remainder of the system would generate requirements for 2 or 3 more brigades (possibly ROK), an armored cavalry squadron and support - a total Practice 9 force of about 40,000.

b) Assuming the presently planned force levels and combat pace, some minor reductions in construction and support personnel should be possible in CY 1968. The magnitude and phasing cannot be determined at this time but might total 10-15,000 personnel, beginning mid CY 1968.

c) If the war against the hard-core VC/NVA units should drop off sharply next year, it may be possible to withdraw a major slice of U.S. combat and support units - perhaps as many as 100,000. This would encompass one or two divisions and support and five to ten tactical fighter squadrons. Such a step would reduce the overall cost of the war to the U.S.A. and hopefully stimulate the GVN to play a more responsible role. It would also lessen the economic dislocations caused by the massive U.S. presence, and ease the burden in the U.S. of supporting the effort in SEA. 11/

Interestingly only one of the three dealt with an increase while the others concentrated upon step-downs in U.S. strength. 12/ The barrier remained a high probability -- planning as we have seen (as well as some stationing) was proceeding; the other two were definitely low probability events. All of these considerations at Guam could only lead the decision-makers to conclude that although more troops would probably be requested, their numbers would be relatively small.

Finally, the third thrust of the military discussions at Guam could be detected in the military briefings which repeatedly stressed MACV's alarm about the enemy campaigns unfolding in I CTZ. He believed that the VC/NVA main force operations concentrated in the I CTZ area were part of their initial attempt to seize the tactical initiative. Westmoreland was more than ever impressed by the size and equipment of those enemy forces in the area; in his eyes they posed a serious threat to U.S. operations not only in I CTZ but all of SVN. The General also saw opportunity beckon, for here the decisive battles would be fought -- present and portended combat in I CTZ had become the schwerpunkt. 13/

The record of what additional views were exchanged between COMUSMACV and the Washington leaders remains unclear. One can speculate that Westmoreland surely indicated he might require more troops, but he probably did not use any but round numbers, if he used them at all. At one point in John McNaughton's notes the notation "100,000 more troops to VN?" is listed under "Dirties," or unpleasant subjects for consideration, but other than that no formal record of force level discussions remains. 14/

Guam 1967, was attacked in the press as a political jaunt that impressed few and exhausted many. Symbolic as it may have been, it hardly seemed worth a trip to the distant Pacific to introduce some new ambassadors and award some air crew medals in the rain. 15/ The rapid transit through time zones and wearing nature of the discussions generated little enthusiasm among the official entourage, a malaise reflected throughout the newspaper and official accounts of the trip. 16/ The mood of optimism about the ground war situation and the general low pressure aspect of the military side of the Guam Conference did little to prepare the decision-makers for the MACV-CINCPAC force requests which broke in late March.

2. The MACV Request: "Essential" Looks Like "Optimum"

On 18 March, General Westmoreland submitted his analysis of current MACV force requirements projected through FY 68. This request was to furnish the base line for all further force deployment calculations during the Program 5 period. In preface to his specific request, COMUSMACV reviewed his earlier CY 67 requirement which asked for 124 maneuver battalions with their necessary combat and combat service support, a total strength of 555,741. This figure was the maximum figure requested during the Program 4 deliberations. The approved Program 4 package included only 470,366 and was considerably below the MACV request, a fact which led to the series of reclamas described in Section II. Westmoreland related that MACV-CINCPAC had not strongly objected earlier to the 470,000 man ceiling because of adverse piaster impact and the realities of service capabilities, but, subsequent reassessment of the situation had indicated clearly to him that the Program 4 force, although enabling U.S. force to gain the initiative did not "permit sustained operations of the scope and intensity required to avoid an unreasonably protracted war." 17/

As the cable continued, the American commander in Vietnam briefly restated his earlier assessment of enemy trends: That the enemy had increased his force structure appreciably and was now confronting Free World Military Forces with large bodies of troops in and above the DMZ, in the Laotian and Cambodian sanctuaries and certain areas within SVN. In light of this new appraisal, he had established an early requirement for an additional 2-1/3 divisions which he proposed be accommodated by restructuring the original 555,741-man force package proposed during Program 4. This force was required "as soon as possible but not later than 1 July 1968." Part of the reasoning was that this in effect constituted no more than a 6-month "extension" of the CY 67 program and as such would permit shifting force programming from a Calendar Year to a Fiscal Year basis, a shift long needed in COMUSMACV's estimation to make force programming for Vietnam compatible with other programs and to provide essential lead time in the procurement of hardware. Westmoreland then looked further ahead, noting:

> "...It is entirely possible that additional forces, over
> and above the immediate requirement for 2-1/3 Divisions, will
> materialize. Present planning, which will undergo continued
> refinement, suggests an additional 2-1/3 division equivalents
> whose availability is seen as extending beyond FY 68." 18/

Then as if to take the edge off his request, COMUSMACV turned attention to two programs which were becoming increasingly attractive to American decision-makers. These were development of an improved RVNAF and an increase in the other Free World Military Forces committed to the war in Vietnam. He commented that despite the force ceiling on RVNAF currently in effect some selective increase in Vietnamese capabilities was required, such as creation of a suitable base for establishing a constabulary, an organization vital to the success of the Revolutionary Development program. Westmoreland stated that it was the position of his headquarters that provision for any and all Free World Military Forces was welcomed as "additive reinforcements," but they would be treated as additions only, thereby having no effect upon U.S. force computations.

The concept of operations under which the new forces he requested were to be employed varied little in its essential aspects from that outlined in MACV's February "Assessment of the Military Situation and Concept of Operations," 19/ which had reached Washington but a week earlier. However, the new cable integrated the new forces as part of the MACV operational forces. Westmoreland reviewed the period just past then turned to the future:

> "...our operations were primarily holding actions
> characterized by border surveillance, reconnaissance to
> locate enemy forces, and spoiling attacks to disrupt the
> enemy offensive. As a result of our buildup and successes,

we were able to plan and initiate a general offensive.
We now have gained the tactical initiative, and are conducting continuous small and occasional large-scale
offensive operations to decimate the enemy forces; to
destroy enemy base areas and disrupt his infrastructure;
to interdict his land and water LOC's and to convince him,
through the vigor of our offensive and accompanying psychological operations, that he faces inevitable defeat.

"Military success alone will not achieve the US objectives in Vietnam. Political, economic, and psychological
victory is equally important, and support of Revolutionary
Development program is mandatory. The basic precept for
the role of the military in support of Revolutionary Development is to provide a secure environment for the population
so that the civil aspects of RD can progress." 20/

He then detailed corps by corps the two troop request requirements
labeling them the "optimum force" (4-2/3 Divs) and the "minimum essential
force" (2-1/3 Divs):

"B. Force requirements FY 68

(1) The MACV objectives for 1967 were based on the
assumption that the CY 67 force requirements would be approved
and provided expeditiously within the capabilities of the
services. However, with the implementation of Program Four,
it was recognized that our accomplishments might fall short
of our objectives. With the additional forces cited above,
we would have had the capability to extend offensive operations into an exploitation phase designed to take advantage
of our successes.

(2) With requisite forces, we shall be able to
complete more quickly the destruction or neutralization of
the enemy main forces and bases and, by continued presence,
deny to him those areas in RVN long considered safe havens.
As the enemy main forces are destroyed or broken up, increasingly greater efforts can be devoted to rooting out and
destroying the VC guerrilla and communist infrastructure.
Moreover, increased assistance can be provided the RVNAF in
support of its effort to provide the required level of security for the expanding areas undergoing Revolutionary
Development.

(3) Optimum Force. The optimum force required
implement the concept of operations and to exploit success
is considered 4-2/3 divisions or the equivalent; 10 tactical

fighter squadrons with one additional base; and the full mobile riverine force. The order of magnitude estimate is 201,250 spaces in addition to the 1967 ceiling of 470,366 for a total of 671,616.

(A) In I Corps, the situation is the most critical with respect to existing and potential force ratios. As a minimum, a division plus a regiment is required for Quang Tri Province as a containment force. The latter has been justified previously in another plan. Employment of this force in the containment role would release the units now engaged there for expansion of the DaNang, Hue-Phu Bai and Chu Lai TAOR's as well as increase security and control along the corps northern coastal areas. One of the most critical areas in RVN today is Quang Ngai Province even if a major operation were conducted in this area during 1967, the relief would be no more than temporary. A force is needed in the province to maintain continuous pressure on the enemy to eliminate his forces and numerous base areas, and to remove his control over the large population and food reserves. The sustained employment of a division of 10 battalions is mandatory in Quang Ngai Province if desired results are to be realized. Employment of this force would provide security for the vital coastal areas, facilitate opening and securing Route 1 and the railroad and, perhaps equally important, relieve pressure on northern Binh Dinh Province.

(B) In II Corps, the task is two fold: destroy the enemy main and guerrilla forces in the coastal areas; and contain the infiltration of NVA forces from Cambodia and Laos. Continual expansion both north and south of the present capital coastal TARO's opening and securing Route 1 and the railroad, securing Route 20 from Dalat south to the III Corps boundary, destruction of enemy forces in Pleiku and Kontum Provinces, and containment of the enemy forces in the Cambodian and Laotian sanctuaries are all tasks to be accomplished given the large area in II Corps and the continuous enemy threat, an optimum force augmentation of four separate brigades is required to execute effectively an exploitation of our successes. An infantry brigade is needed in northern Binh Dinh Province to expand security along the coastal area and to facilitate operations in Quang Ngai Province to the north. A mechanized brigade in the western highlands will assist in offensive and containment operations in the Pleiku-Kontum area. An infantry brigade in the region of Ban Me Thout is needed to conduct operations against enemy forces and bases there and to add security to this portion

of II Corps now manned with limited ARVN forces, and
finally, a mechanized brigade is needed in Binh Thuan
Province to neutralize the enemy forces and bases in
the southern coastal area, and to open and secure highway 1 and the national railroad to the III Corps boundary.

(C) In III Corps, operations to destroy
VC/NVA main forces and bases in the northwestern & central
parts of the corps area and to intensify the campaign against
the enemy's infrastructure are being conducted. These
operations are to be completed by intensive efforts to open
and secure the principal land and water LOC's throughout the
Corps Zone. However, deployment of the US 9th Div to IV
Corps will create a gap in the forces available in III Corps
to operate against seen significant base areas in Phuoc Tuy,
Binh Tuy, and Long Khanh Provinces. These areas constitute
the home base of the still formidable 5th VC Division. This
unit must be destroyed, its bases neutralized and Route 1
and the national railroad opened and secured. Other critical
locales that will require considerable effort are War Zone
D and Phuoc Long area in which the VC 7th Division is
believed to be located. With the forces operating currently
in III Corps, substantial progress can be made, but to
exploit effectively our successes an addition of one division, preferably air mobile is required. By basing this
division in Bien Hoa Province just north of the RSSZ, it
would be in position to conduct operations against the 5th
Div, and War Zone D, as well as to reinforce the US 9th
Div in Delta operations as required.

(D) In IV Corps, with deployment of the US
9th Div to the Corps area and with increasing success of
ARVN operations there, the situation will be greatly improved.
Primary emphasis will be given to destroying VC main and
guerrilla units and their bases, to intensifying operations
to extend GVN control, to stopping the flow of food stuffs
and materials to the enemy through Cambodia, and to assisting
in the flow of goods to GVN outlets in Saigon. In addition
emphasis will be accorded the opening and securing of principal water and land LOC's which are the key to all operations
in the Delta. It is noteworthy on this score, that effectiveness of forces available is hampered severely by an
inadequate mobile riverine force. In IV Corps, the essential
requirement is to flesh out the mobile riverine force with
three APB's (Barracks Ships) one ARL (repair ship), and two
RAS (river assault squadrons).

(4) The Minimum Essential Force necessary to
exploit success of the current offensive and to retain

effective control of the expanding areas being cleaned
of enemy influence is 2-1/3 divisions with a total of 21
maneuver battalions. One division, with nine infantry
battalions -- each with 4 rifle companies -- and an ACR
of three squadrons are required. The other division of
nine maneuver battalions, each battalion organized with
four rifle companies is required in Quang Ngai Province.
Four tactical fighter squadrons, each generating 113
sorties per month per identified maneuver battalion, are
required. Two squadrons will be stationed at Phu Cat and
two at Tuy Hoa. One C-130 or equivalent type squadron
can provide adequate airlift and is justified on the basis
of current planning factors: This SQD would be based at
Cam Ranh Bay. A minimum essential logistic base can be
provided by selective augmentation of NSA Danang, and by
provision for lift capability equivalent to eight LST's
in addition to two LST's identified previously for the
containment force in Quang Tri Province. Two non-
divisional Army combat engineer battalions and four Army
construction battalions will be required to support
divisional engineering effort to augment two navy construction battalions that previously have been identified
with the containment force in Quang Tri Province.

(B) Effectiveness of the US 9th Division's
operations in IV Corps will be degraded unacceptably without
adequate mobility on the waterways. For this reason, addition of two river assault squadrons with their associated
support is deemed essential. The Mekong Delta Mobile
Riverine Force originally was tailored and justified as
a four RAS level. This requirement still is valid. The
primary media of transport in the Delta are air and water.
Air mobility is recognized as critical to success of operations in the area, but the size of offensive operations that
can be mounted is limited by the inherent physical limitations of airborne vehicles. Accordingly, any sizeable
offensive operation such as those visualized for the US
9th Division must utilize the 300km of waterways in the
Delta to exploit tactical mobility. Maintenance of LOC's
and population control in the areas secured by the division's operations, along with extension of the interdiction
effort, necessitates expansion of the game warden operation.
Fifty PBR's can provide this capability based on experience
factors accrued thus far. 21/

The piaster impact of this request to which much lip-service was
still being paid varied from 44 billion piasters for the 4-2/3 division
optimum force to 41.7 billion piasters for the minimum essential force.

The proposed increase added an estimated 1.1 billion piasters to the
1967 program for a total estimated cost of 46.7 billion estimated
additional costs for CY 68 under the projected programs would total
2.8 billion piasters, 1.2 billion coming during January through June
and the remaining 1.6 billion for July through December.

Westmoreland concluded the long request with an observation which
was to provide the basis for considerable dispute within the government.
He wrote:

> "...Whereas deployment of additional US forces in
> FY 68 will obviate the requirement for a major expansion
> of the RVNAF, selective increases are necessary to opti-
> mize combat effectiveness. Regular forces proposed for
> FY 68 total 328,322, an increase of 6,367 spaces of the FY
> 67 authorization. As US, Free World and RVNAF operations
> are expanded, additional areas will be made available for
> the conduct of Revolutionary Development operations. Based
> on experience gained thus far, an increase of 50,000 RF/PF
> spaces will be required to provide a planning figure of
> 350,000 spaces for this force. The increase will accom-
> modate necessary support of Revolutionary Development and
> concomitantly, will be compatible with requirements incident
> to implementation of the constabulary concept. 22/

His emphasis upon RF/PF spaces in lieu of expansion of the RVNAF which
could theoretically substitute for additional U.S. troops prompted many
who disagreed with the basic increases to ask why the US should meet
such expanded troop requirements when the Government of South Vietnam
would neither mobilize its manpower nor effectively employ it according
to US wishes. 23/

3. The JCS Take Up the March: The CINCPAC Force Requirements
Task Group and JCSM-218-67.

JCS reaction to the COMUSMACV message was predictably rapid. The
Chiefs realized that the general analysis provided in the original MACV
request would prove to be inadequate for the SecDef to either assess the
validity of the requirements or the sufficiency of the means of meeting
them. Consequently, they directed that detailed analyses be submitted to
them from MACV/CINCPAC on a time-phased basis commencing on 26 March. 24/
In a realistic reflection of the feasibility of the two proposals, the
JCS required that the minimum essential force be addressed in as much
detail as time permitted and that the optimum force be addressed in only
general terms. They asked that the analysis include not only an expansion
of the concept but: (1) a listing of the force requirements additive to
OSD Program 4; (2) the rationale to validate these increased requirements;
(3) the service capabilities to provide validated force requirements;

(4) the logistic implications and the discussion of any problem areas
which they (MACV) anticipated in meeting them. 25/

On 26 March COMUSMACV submitted to the CINCPAC Requirements Task
Group a detailed troop listing for the 2-1/3 division "minimum essential
force." Other than providing a detailed list of TO&E's and unit small
strengths, the document provides little of interest. It did stipulate
that the northern portion of the minimum essential force would be directed
toward an expanded infiltration interdiction mission and that the southern
portion of the force would pursue "presently prescribed operations." 26/

In a follow-up message to the Task Requirements Group on the 28th
of March COMUSMACV again commented on the restrictive aspects of Program 4. 27/
This in turn was picked up and amplified by CINCPAC in a message to the JCS
on the same day. 28/ CINCPAC pointed out that as of 9 March 1967 Program 4
was 38,241 spaces short of full implementation and that this figure included
spaces for five battalions or their equivalents which could not be considered
for trade-off purposes. All of these spaces, especially the battalion
equivalents, were significant elements when considered within the perspective of MACV's operational requirements and could not be deleted without
seriously impairing MACV capability to achieve its objectives. In light
of this shortfall in Program 4 CINCPAC requested that the JCS reconsider
its earlier proposal that a 4th rifle company be added to all U.S. Army
infantry battalions in Vietnam. The logic behind such a raise in program
ceiling which would increase materially the combat power and effectiveness
of the infantry without increasing unit overhead was irrefutable in
CINCPAC's eyes. CINCPAC proposed that the addition of the rifle companies,
a total of 8,821 men, be added to the Program 4 ceiling for a total of
479,231 of all services. The space requirements for the 2-1/3 division
minimum essential force reflected in the COMUSMACV request would then be
added on to the adjusted Program 4 total of 479,000. However, in the event
that any or all of the spaces reflected in that 479,000 were not approved
or that the package itself would be reduced, the Pacific Commander predicted
grave curtailment in MACV operations and a danger that the operational
objectives set for the force requirements initially would not be achieved.

By 28 March the JCS through the CINCPAC group had the detailed
justification and planning calculations for the COMUSMACV 67 force requirements in hand. MACV had added little that was new in the way of strategic
concept other than to reaffirm their intention to concentrate on certain
priority areas in each corps tactical zone. Priority areas themselves were
selected because they seemed best suited to achieve destruction or neutralization of enemy main forces and bases -- persistently prime MACV goals.
Despite this strong declaration of intent MACV hedged by noting that "the
enemy will be struck wherever he presents a lucrative target." 29/ Forces
would also be maintained by MACV outside the priority areas to contain the
enemy in his out of country sanctuaries. In this connection, the planners
anticipated that there would be large scale offensive operations continuously conducted during FY 68 to detect and destroy infiltration or invasion
forces in the IMZ-Highland Border regions.

Declassified per Executive Order 13526, Section 3.3
NND Project Number: NND 63316. By: NWD Date: 2011

TOP SECRET - Sensitive

If the forces outlined under the optimum force request were granted priority was to be accorded to the expansion of secure areas. The RVNAF would be given the primary responsibility of providing military support of Revolutionary Development activities and Revolutionary Development operations would be intensified throughout the country as the pacified areas were expanded. MACV explained that such increased demands on the RVNAF would establish a concomitant demand for additional U.S. force resources to fill the operational void resulting from the intensified Revolutionary Development orientation of the RVNAF. The long message also broke out the minimum essential and optimum package forces by service and by total troops as shown in the table below. 30/

	STRENGTH (2-1/3 Div Min essential Force)	STRENGTH (2-1/3 Div Addition for optimum force package)	STRENGTH (Total Optimum Force)
Army	69,359	100,527 *	169,886
Navy	5,739	8,023	13,762
Air Force	5,368	9,891	15,259
Marines	110	0	110
TOTAL	80,576	118,441	119,017

* Includes 5,547 spaces required to incorporate MACOV Study recommendations.

The total optimum force end strength was 678,248 arrived at by adding the approved Program 4 strength of 470,000 to the earlier MACV reclama of 8,821 (see page 68 this section) and the "optimum force" additive of 199,017. The justification for additional forces broken out by corps tactical zones were essentially the same as those presented in the original MACV request on 18 March. However, the later document prepared at PACOM Hqs on the 28th reflected the increased concern with the enemy threat developing in the I Corps tactical zone. Concerning this threat, COMUSMACV wrote:

"In I Corps tactical zone, the bulk of the population and the food producing regions are within 15 miles of the coast. In the northern part of the zone, multiple NVA Divisions possess the capability to move south of the DMZ. Additionally, there is constant enemy activity in much of the coastal area. The topography of I Corps lends itself to the establishment and maintenance of enemy base areas in the remote, sparsely populated regions. The enemy has operated for years virtually unmolested throughout most of Quang Ngai Province because friendly forces could not be diverted from other important tasks.

"There are several important tasks which must be performed in I Corps. Security of bases and key population

TOP SECRET - Sensitive

centers must be maintained. The area under GVN control must be extended by expanding existing TAOR's, and by opening and securing major LOC's, particularly Route 1. The enemy must be contained in his sanctuaries, and denied use of infiltration and invasion routes. Enemy main forces and bases must be sought out and destroyed. Surveillance and reconnaissance in force throughout the CTZ must complement the tasks discussed above.

"The deployment of a division and an armored cavalry regiment to Quang Tri Province, south of the DMZ, would make it possible for Marine Corps units now conducting containment operations to secure and expand tactical areas of responsibility (TAOR's).

"The RVNAF and US/FWMAF will intensify operations against organized enemy forces and base areas in and near the populated and food producing areas of the coastal plains thus denying them access to population and food resources.

"Clearing and securing operations will be pursued to facilitate the expansion of the secured areas, the ultimate goal being to connect the Hue-Phu Bai, Danang, and Chu Lai TAOR's. The following major LOC's will be opened and secured: Route 9, from Route 1 to Thon San Lam; and Route 1 and the railroad throughout the entire length of I CTZ, including the spur to the An Hoa industrial complex.

"One of the most critical areas in the RVN today is Quang Ngai Province. A division is required there to maintain continuous pressure on the enemy, to eliminate his forces and numerous base areas, and to remove his control over large population and food resources.

"Sustained employment of a division in Quang Ngai would obviate the necessity to use other forces to meet a critical requirement. The division would provide security for the coastal area, facilitate opening and securing Route 1 and the railroad, and relieve some of the pressure on northern Binh Dinh Province. Of particular significance is the support which would be provided to the RVNAF in securing the important Mo Duc Area with its dense population and three annual rice crops. Additionally, deployment of the division as discussed above would allow III MAF to expand its clearing and securing operations into the heavily populated Tam Ky area north of the Chu Lai TAOR. Long term security must be provided for

both of these areas so that Revolutionary Development
can progress.

"Failure to provide two and one-third divisions for
I CTZ would result in the diversion of existing forces
from other tasks to deny and defeat infiltration or invasion.
Security in support of Revolutionary Development could not
be increased to the desired degree in the coastal area, the
major LOC's could not be opened throughout the CTZ, and the
enemy would be able to continue operating virtually unmolested
throughout the key Quang Ngai Province.

"It is emphasized that the relationship of the two and
one-third division force requirement for I Corps to that
of Practice Nine is coincidental. This force is the minimum
essential required to support operations planned for FY 68
without reference to Practice Nine.

....." 31/

The next most dangerous situation appeared to be that in II Corps, a
diverse geographical area which included major population centers along the
coastal plains as well as sizeable population centers and military bases
on the western plateau, such as Binh Dinh, Anke, Kontum, and Pleiku. Here
the enemy, orienting himself on the population, presented a different problem which, in the words of General Westmoreland, required "a high degree of
mobility and flexibility in U.S./FWMAF/RVNAF." As he analysed the corps
tactical situation, Westmoreland reemphasized what he had already said
about containing the large enemy military forces at the boundaries of the
sanctuaries:

"Enemy forces in the Pleiku and Kontum areas must be
destroyed, and infiltration from Cambodia and Laos must be
contained. Forces in-country will continue to make progress
in areas of current deployment. Those programmed for deployment will augment this effort. However, there are gaps, as
discussed below, that must be filled before success can be
exploited and minimum essential security can be provided
within the II Corps area.

"Large enemy forces remaining in heavily populated
Binh Dinh Province must be destroyed. Security must be
established and maintained in the northern portion of the
province, particularly along the coastal area, so that
Revolutionary Development can progress, these security
forces also will facilitate the conduct of operations in
Quang Ngai Province.

"Inadequacy of forces in the border areas is a significant weakness in II Corps. Reinforcement of units in
the western highlands is needed to assist in the conduct
of offensive and containment operations. With the large
enemy forces located in border sanctuaries, II Corps is
faced constantly with the possible requirement to divert
critical resources from priority tasks to counter large
scale intrusion." 32/

The most pressing military objective in III Corps area was to expand
security radially from the Saigon-Cholon area. MACV planned to accomplish
this primarily by standard clearing and security operations featuring an
intensified campaign conducted to root out the VC infrastructure. In
conjunction with this, continuous pressure presumably in the form of
search and destroy operations would be applied to the enemy in War Zones
C and D, the Iron Triangle, and the base area clusters in the Phuoc Long
area. Denial of these areas to the enemy would provide a protective
shield behind which the Revolutionary Development programs could operate.
However, deployment of the U.S. 9th Division to the 4th Corps area would
create a gap in the forces available in III Corps and seriously degrade
the capability to provide this shield. The possible repositioning of the
assets existing within III Corps to either I CTZ in the north or the 9th
Division relocation just to the south just mentioned could also seriously
limit the offensive capabilities in the northern and central portion of
III Corps. Accordingly, COMUSMACV expressed an urgent requirement for an
additional division for III Corps. This unit would be positioned just
north of the Rung Sat operation zone and would assist in maintaining the
protective shield around Saigon-Cholon. Revolutionary Development operations would then be able to proceed unhindered and operations against the
VC 5th Division could be reinforced if required. 33/

Throughout the force requirement justifications, one is immediately
struck by the implicit ordering of the priorities for assignment of forces
and missions. It is quite clear that the "minimum essential force" which
COMUSMACV requested was intended to be employed against VC/NVA main force
units in a containment role in the border areas and a destruction-disruption
mode in I CTZ as well as the base areas within the country itself. Those
forces over and above the "minimum essential," so labelled the "optimum
force," were those intended to take up the slack in the RD "shield" role.
MACV, probably rightly, calculated that not even minimal gains such as
were forthcoming in the under-manned RD program would be possible unless
the VC/NVA main force operations could be stymied and kept from directly
assaulting the "shields."

Before the JCS could formally ratify the COMUSMACV-CINCPAC FY 68
force requirements, two other events transpired which had significant
influence on the development of ground force requirements. On 7 April,
as the situation in I CTZ deteriorated COMUSMACV posted a provisional
division named Task Force OREGON to Quang Ngai Province. This development caused a reappraisal of the 2-1/2 division minimum essential force

requirement submitted in the 28 March message. In effect, the requirement for a division in Quang Ngai Province which was identified in the
late March cable was being filled by Task Force OREGON. 34/ The provisional division was composed of the 3rd Brigade of the 25th Infantry
Division, 196th Light Infantry Brigade and the 1st Brigade of the 101st
Airborne Division. Permanent assignment of the airborne brigade to the
north had an especially adverse impact because it was the sole reserve
of the First Field Force. This shifting of forces created an undesirable
situation in that MACV would possibly be forced to assign a mechanized
battalion as the Field Force reserve. Accordingly, COMUSMACV cancelled
his urgent request for a cavalry unit in the north and asked to delay
further discussions on this subject until during his visit to Washington
in the next two weeks. 35/ Concurrent with the movement of Task Force
OREGON to the north COMUSMACV submitted via CINCPAC to the JCS a request to
deploy the 9th Marine Amphibious Brigade from Okinawa to South Vietnam.
JCSM 208-67, prepared by the Chiefs on the subject, proposed that two
special landing forces from the brigade be stationed off the Vietnamese
coast to be committed when required by COMUSMACV and the remainder of the
MAB placed on 15-day call in Okinawa. The proviso that unless these forces
were employed on a contingency basis they would revert to their normal
schedules by 1 September was inserted in the recommendation at CINCPAC's
request. He disagreed with the dismemberment of the PACOM strategic
reserve. This proposal was approved by the Secretary of Defense on 14 April
and the brigade removed to Vietnamese waters shortly thereafter. 36/

On 20 April, the JCS, in JCSM-218-67, formally reported to the
Secretary of Defense that MACV required additional forces to achieve
the objectives they considered the U.S. was pursuing in Vietnam. The
JCS announcement came as little surprise to the Secretary of Defense
since as early as 23 March he had seen the original message in which
COMUSMACV had outlined the minimum essential and optimum force requirements. 37/

JCSM-128-67 reaffirmed the basic objectives and strategic concepts
contained in JCSM 702-66 dated 4 November 1966. Briefly, these entailed
a national objective of attaining a stable and independent non-communist
government in South Vietnam and a four-fold military contribution toward
achieving the objectives of:

"(a) Making it as difficult and costly as possible for
the NVA to continue effective support of the VC and to cause
North Vietnam to cease direction of the VC insurgency.

"(b) To defeat the VC/NVA and force the withdrawal
of NVA forces.

"(c) Extend government dominion, direction and control.

"(d) To deter Chinese Communists from direct intervention in SEA.

The JCS listed three general areas of military effort that they felt
should be pursued in the war:

"(1) Operations against the Viet Cong/North Vietnamese
Army (VC/NVA) forces in SVN while concurrently assisting the
South Vietnamese Government in their nation-building efforts.

"(2) Operations to obstruct and reduce the flow of men
and materials from North Vietnam (NV) to SVN.

"(3) Operations to obstruct and reduce imports of war-
sustaining materials into NVN.

They continued by assessing the achievements of the US and allies in these
three areas:

"In the first area, the United States and its allies
have achieved considerable success in operations against
VC/NVA forces. However, sufficient friendly forces have not
been made available to bring that degree of pressure to bear
on the enemy throughout SVN which would be beyond his ability to accommodate and which would provide the secure environment essential to sustained progress in Revolutionary Development. The current reinforcement of I CTZ by diversion of forces
from II and III CTZs reduces the existing pressure in those
areas and inevitably will cause a loss of momentum that must
be restored at the earliest practicable date.

"In the second area, US efforts have achieved appreciable success. Greater success could be realized if an
expanded system of targets were made available.

"In the third area, relatively little effort has been
permitted. This failure to obstruct and reduce imports of
war-sustaining materials into NVN has affected unfavorably
the desired degree of success of operations in the other areas. 39/

The Joint Chiefs strongly recommended not only the approval of additional forces to provide an increased level of effort in SVN but that action
be taken to reduce and obstruct the enemy capability to import the material
support required to sustain the war effort. They argued that the cumulative
effect of all these operations, in South Vietnam, in North Vietnam and
against the enemy's strategic lines of communication would hasten the
successful conclusion of the war and would most likely reduce the overall
ultimate force requirements. Their rationale for the 1968 forces was summarized as follows:

"The FY 1968 force for SVN is primarily needed to
offset the enemy's increased posture in the vicinity of
the DMZ and to improve the environment for Revolutionary
Development in I and IV CTZs. To achieve the secure environment for lasting progress in SVN, additional military forces
must be provided in order to (1) destroy the enemy main
force, (2) locate and destroy district and provincial guerrilla forces, and (3) provide security for the population.
The increased effort required to offset VC/NVA main forces'
pressure is diminishing the military capability to provide
a secure environment to villages and hamlets. Diversion
of forces from within SVN and the employment of elements of
CINCPAC's reserve are temporary measures at the expense of
high-priority programs in other parts of SVN. Thus, if
sufficient units are to be available to provide both direct
and indirect support to Revolutionary Development throughout
SVN, added forces must be deployed.

"The three-TFS force for Thailand and the additional
Navy forces in the South China Sea and the Gulf of Tonkin
are required to bring increased pressures to bear on NVN." 40/

The service capabilities to meet the force requirements which the chiefs
recommended presented another problem. The JCS examined these capabilities
under two alternative cases:

"Case I - No Reserve callup or extension of terms of
service. Present tour and rotation policies would be maintained. By July 1968, only a one and one-third Army division
force, a part of the mobile riverine force, and no additional
Marine Corps forces could be in place in SVN. A second Army
division force to fill out the FY 1968 requirement probably
could not be provided until the first half of FY 1970. The
additional 8" gun cruiser, five additional destroyers, and
about half of the in-country naval forces could be provided in
FY 1968, but only by the undesirable expedient of extending
present periods of deployment. The three TFS in Thailand
and five in SVN requested by CINCPAC could be furnished in
FY 1968. Three TFS in SVN would be required to meet the need
for air support of the one and one-third divisions that could
be deployed in FY 1968.

"Case II -- Callup of Reserves and a twelve-month involuntary extension of terms of service. Present tour and
rotation policies would be maintained. A Reserve callup
and the collateral actions enumerated below would enable
the Services to provide the major combat forces required in

PACOM not later than end FY 1968. The forces would include one and one-third Army divisions, three US Air Force TFS, one Marine division/wing team which includes two TFS, the major portion of the mobile riverine force, naval patrol forces, and most of the required support forces for SVN; three US Air Force TFS in Thailand; one additional 8" gun cruiser and five additional destroyers." 41/

Prominently identified in each of these cases were issues revolving around requirements for calling up of the Reserves and extension of terms of service, end strength increases above current force levels, expansion of the CONUS sustaining base, additional funds in the FY 68 budget, drawdown of the war reserve and preposition stocks and partial mobilization of the industry. Fundamental to the development of the service plans was the effort to minimize the impact on the overall U.S. military posture but even the Chiefs concluded that:

"Considering our current worldwide commitments a Reserve callup for a minimum of 24 months and involuntary extension of terms of service for twelve months are the only feasible means of meeting the additional FY 1968 requirements in the stipulated time frame. The effect of a 24-month limitation on callup of Reserves is that the Armed Forces would expend their major reserve assets by end FY 1972 as a result of successive callup and commitment of Reserve units. This would be avoided if Reserve units were held for the duration of the emergency. Authority to do this and to extend terms of service involuntarily would require Congressional action." 42/

and consequently recommended that:

"a. The military strategy for the conduct of the war in Southeast Asia, as described in Appendix A, be approved in principle.

"b. The list of forces in Appendix C, Case II /2½ Divisions, approx. 71,000 Army and 5 TFSs/ less forces approved on 8 April 1967, be approved for deployment.

"c. Authority be obtained for a Reserve callup for a minimum of 24 months and involuntary extension of terms of service for twelve months in order to meet FY 1968 force requirements and to prepare for possible future requirements.

"d. To support the preceding recommended actions, authority be granted to provide for:

"(1) Access to equipment from sources in the following priority:

     "(a) CONUS depot assets and programmed
production deliveries not committed to higher priority
requirements.

     "(b) Operational project stocks.

     "(c) Contingency stocks.

     "(d) Reserve components not scheduled for callup.

     "(e) Pre-positioned equipment in Europe.

     "(f) Diversion of items for recently activated units.

     "(g) Drawdown from nondeploying active units in CONUS.

    "(2) Reopening of CONUS inactive installations, as
required." 43/

4. The Stimulation of Inter-Agency Reviews: A Proliferation of
Alternatives.

The Chiefs' recommendations, if carried out, promised to spawn significant political and economic repercussions and they stimulated a plethora
of inter-agency reviews and studies of the situation in Vietnam. The majority
of these in one way or another examined the wisdom of sending more forces
there. The first of these reviews originated in the State Department, in
the office of Undersecretary Nicholas deB. Katzenbach. In a memorandum, he
listed three jobs which he felt had to be done in Vietnam.

   "1. Assess the current situation in Viet-Nam and the
various political and military actions which could be taken
to bring this to a successful conclusion;

   "2. Review the possibilities for negotiation, including
an assessment of the ultimate U.S. position in relationship to
the DRV and NLF; and

   "3. Assess the military and political effects of intensification of the war in South Viet-Nam and in North Viet-Nam." 44/

He asked that the responsible agencies (Defense, White House, CIA,
State) prepare relevant study papers under the three tasks which he outlined. DOD was asked to define and analyze consequences of two likely
alternatives: the first, Course A, added a minimum of 200,000 men and
greatly intensified military actions outside the south especially against
the north. This option included two deployment phases. The first coin-
ciding to the minimum essential force which General Westmoreland and the
JCS had requested, that is 100,000 troops (2-1/3 divisions plus 4 tactical
air squadrons) to be deployed in FY 67 and a second phase of another 100,000

(2-1/3 divisions and 6 tactical air squadrons) to be deployed in FY 67.
Course A, as Katzenbach described it, also included "more later to fulfill the JCS alternate requirements." Course B confined troop increases
to "those that could be generated without calling up the reserves" --
perhaps 9 battalions or about 10,000 men in the next year. 45/

The first option, Course A, was to be analyzed across a matrix of
many factors such as cost, actions required, trends, call up of reserves,
extension of tours, enlargement of uniformed strength, effect on U.S.
force deployment, involvement in pacification, possible stimulation by
this course of great intensification of military actions outside South
Vietnam including invasion of North Vietnam, Laos and Cambodia. The
domestic reaction including possible polarization of opinion and stimulation of pressures for actions outside Vietnam, the manner in which to
approach the public and the Congress on this course, and finally the international reactions on the part of the North Vietnamese, Soviets, Chinese
and other nations were also to be examined. The Undersecretary also asked
for an analysis of the effect of Course A on the possibilities for a
settlement.

In addition to addressing the same considerations as under Course A
in Part B, the respondents were asked to analyze how our military strategy
under this meager troop level increase would differ from that of the larger
level, how the level of actions against North Vietnam and Cambodia would
look, the effect of such a small added increment on our flexibility, and
the effect on the VC/NVA. Finally, McNaughton representing DOD was requested
to analyze possible bombing strategies in the North as they related to both
courses of action.

Katzenbach suggested consideration of measures which could be taken
in the south to strengthen the GVN and develop the RVNAF as a substitute
for more U.S. troops, thereby placing primary emphasis on the war in the
South and perhaps allow us to cut back on the bombing in the North.
Katzenbach also felt that some consideration should be given to a study
of the present use of U.S. forces and whether they are being used in the
most efficient ways possible, in effect a reappraisal of ground force
strategy. He asked that such measures as the following be discussed:

(a) Expansion of RF/PF by 100,000 in FY 1968;

(b) Efforts to improve RVNAF leadership, including
insistence on dismissal of incompetent commanders, withholding of MAP from ineffective units, and some sort of US
rewards for competent commanders;

(c.) A Joint Command;

(d) A great expansion of the US advisory structure, especially with RF/PF;

(e) Increased training for ARVN;

(f) Increase RVNAF pay, housing, rations and other incentives; push for a better promotion policy;

(g) Improve RVNAF equipment." 46/

On the same day, 24 April, Robert Komer, upon his departure from Washington for Saigon submitted a memo to the President in which he presented his thoughts on future strategy in Vietnam. He began by lamenting the emergence of a tendency on the part of the United States to resort in our frustration to actions in Vietnam which we could control, e.g. bombing operations, U.S. ground force operations in lieu of what he termed "the much tougher, slower and less certain measures required to make the Vietnamese pull their weight." 47/ He recommended that we re-examine trade-offs for making the Vietnamese do their part because, in his estimation, measures which had been previously rejected looked a great deal more appealing now when matched against the potential alternatives of major troop increases or a widened bombing offensive. He concluded that the critical variable in the equation for success in Vietnam during the following 12-18 months was the conflict in the South. He saw the VC as the "weak sister" of the enemy team; in fact, he believed that the NVA strategy in I Corps was designed to take pressure off the VC in the south. Then he addressed ways to maximize the chances of a breakthrough in the South:

"Therefore, if we could maximize the pressures of all kinds on the VC--direct and indirect--political, economic, psychological and military--we might at the optimum force Hanoi to fade away, or at the minimum achieve such success as to make clear to all that the war was being won. Such a course would also reinforce the pressures for negotiation. But if we can't get a settlement in 12-18 months, at the least we should shoot for such concrete results in South Vietnam that it might permit us to start bringing a few troops home rather than sending ever more out.

"I confess here to a strong bias that we are already winning the war in the South. No one who compares the situation today to that of April 1966 (much less April 1965) can deny we're doing better. But many contend we've just stopped losing, not started winning. Much depends on one's confidence in our O/B estimates, which I for one flatly question--especially with regard to VC recruiting rates and losses in the South. Much also depends on how much weight one gives to political trends, changing popular

attitudes, etc. But I won't argue the case here--time
will tell who's right. In any case, we're not drawing
ahead clearly enough or fast enough to optimize our
confidence in achieving a 12-18 month turnaround." 48/

Finally, he questioned the rationale for the major force increases
COMUSMACV had asked:

"How Much Would We Achieve from a Major New US Force
Commitment? COMUSMACV is asking for 210,000 men no later than
June 1968 and roughly 100,000 as soon as possible (on top of
the 470,000 plus 60,000 ROK's, etc. already programmed). However, MACV's justification for these added forces needs further
review. To what extent are they based on inflated O/B estimates
of enemy strength? If enemy main force strength is now levelling
off because of high kill ratios, etc., would the added US forces
be used for pacification? General De Puy estimates that 50%
of US/ROK maneuver battalions are already supporting RD by
dealing with the "middle war", the VC main force provincial
battalions. How good are US forces at pacification-related
tasks, as compared to RVNAF? What are the trade-offs? A major
US force commitment to pacification also basically changes the
nature of our presence in Vietnam and might force us to stay
indefinitely in strength. Whether or not the added US forces
would become heavily involved in pacification, however, another
major US force increase raises so many other issues that we
must carefully examine whether this trip is necessary." 49/

To this Komer added a package of alternative measures designed to get the
GVN moving -- militarily, politically, economically -- all of which he felt
might reduce or obviate the need for a major U.S. force increase. This
program included:

"1. First is an all-out effort to get more for our
money out of RVNAF. We have trained and equipped over 650,000
(and for so little cost that it is a good investment in any case).
But can't we greatly increase the return?

(a) Insist on jacking up RVNAF leadership at all
levels. All observers agree that this is RVNAF's most critical
weakness. A massive attack on it could pay real short-run
dividends. Insist on dismissal of incompetent commanders.
Find US means for rewarding competent ones, such as withholding
MAP from ineffective units.

(b) Insist on a Joint Command. Putting at least
ARVN under Westy and his corps commanders might be the best
short-run way to get more response out of ARVN. If it would
ease the GVN problem, the contingents of the other five con-
tributors could be added. Whatever the problems entailed,
they seem small to me compared to sending another 200,000 men.

(c) Greatly Expand the US Advisory Structure,
Especially with RF/PF. Here's another quick way to get more
for our money. In some cases the troop to advisor ratio in
RF/PF is 1,000 to 1. Only 1,200 advisors (the strength of
one USMC maneuver battalion) might have many times the payoff.

(d) Expand RVNAF as a substitute for more US
forces. Westy wants 50,000 more RF/PF in FY 1968. Let's
consider 100,000 in a two-phase expansion.

(e) Increase RVNAF pay, housing, ration, and other
incentives. Bull through a better promotion policy. The
savings from cutting back on non-productive units and expenditures might finance much of the increase.

(f) Enrich RVNAF equipment. I'm told the rifles
and carbines are poor, that more radios for RF/PF would help
greatly, that new equipment would build up morale and effectiveness.

- - - - - - - - - - - - - -

A crash program along the above lines would be cheap at
the price, in fact so cheap that we probably ought to do most
of it anyway. Piaster and manpower constraints are manageable
in my view.

2. Expand civilian pacification programs along similar
lines:

(a) We're turning out RD teams about as fast as
feasible. So supplement them with "instant RD teams" on model
of civil/military team in Binh Dinh.

(b) Even 44 more US advisors for RD teams would make
a big supervisory difference. Ditto for 50 more US advisors for
the police.

(c) Give RD teams and police all the equipment they
need--from military stocks.

(d) Integrate the US advisory effort on pacification
to provide a new forward thrust.

(e) Press harder for removal of incompetent or corrupt province and district officials.

3. Revamp and put new steam behind a coordinated US/GVN intelligence collation and action effort targeted on the VC infrastructure at the critical provincial, district, and village levels. We are just not getting enough payoff yet from the massive intelligence we are increasingly collecting. Police/military coordination is sadly lacking both in collection and in swift reaction.

4. Press much harder on radical land reform initiatives designed to consolidate rural support behind the GVN.

5. Step up refugee programs deliberately aimed at depriving the VC of a recruiting base." 50/

His argument and one which he was about to have the opportunity to prove in Vietnam was simply that such a package of measures might offer just as much prospect of accelerating the favorable trends in SVN over the next 12-18 months as new U.S. military commitments. He closed by pointing out that the "Komer package" could be combined with other U.S. unilateral measures such as a minor force increase to the 500,000 level, accelerated emphasis on the barrier, and some increased bombing, but he cautioned that all of this was vitally dependent upon his underlying premise that we were already doing well enough in SVN "to see light at the end of the tunnel." But, despite his optimistic assumptions he believed that his package at least offered sufficient promise to deserve urgent review by the President. 51/

On 25 April, General Westmoreland returned to the U.S. ostensibly to address the Associated Press Annual Convention in New York, but actually to both undertake an intensive review of his strategy and force requirements for Vietnam in 1967 and to marshall public support for the war effort. John McNaughton, then ASD(ISA) reported portions of the conversation which occurred between the President, General Westmoreland, and General Wheeler on 27 April 1967. Westmoreland was quoted as saying that without the 2-1/3 additional divisions which he had requested "we will not be in danger of being defeated but it will be nip and tuck to oppose the reinforcements the enemy is capable of providing. In the final analysis we are fighting a war of attrition in Southeast Asia." 52/

Westmoreland predicted that the next step if we were to pursue our present strategy to fruition would probably be the second addition of 2-1/3 divisions or approximately another 100,000 men. Throughout the conversations he repeated his assessment that the war would not be lost but that progress would certainly be slowed down. To him this was "not an encouraging outlook but a realistic one." When asked about the influence of increased infiltration upon his operations the general replied that as he saw it "this war is action and counteraction. Anytime we take an action we expect a reaction." The President replied: "When we add divisions can't the enemy add divisions? If so, where does it all end?"

Westmoreland answered: "The VC and DRV strength in SVN now totals 285,000 men. It appears that last month we reached the crossover point in areas excluding the two northern provinces." (Emphasis added.) "Attritions will be greater than additions to the force....The enemy has 8 divisions in South Vietnam. He has the capability of deploying 12 divisions although he would have difficulty supporting all of these. He would be hard pressed to support more than 12 divisions. If we add 2-1/2 divisions, it is likely the enemy will react by adding troops." The President then asked "At what point does the enemy ask for volunteers?" Westmoreland's only reply was, "That is a good question." 53/

COMUSMACV briefly analyzed the strategy under the present program of 470,000 men for the President. He explained his concept of a "meat-grinder" where we would kill large numbers of the enemy but in the end do little better than hold our own, with the shortage of troops still restricting MACV to a fire brigade technique -- chasing after enemy main force units when and where it could find them. He then predicted that "unless the will of the enemy is broken or unless there was an unraveling of the VC infrastructure the war could go on for 5 years. If our forces were increased that period could be reduced although not necessarily in proportion to increases in strength, since factors other than increase in strength had to be considered. For instance, a non-professional force, such as that which would result from fulfilling the requirement for 100,000 additional men by calling reserves, would cause come degradation of normal leadership and effectiveness. Westmoreland concluded by estimating that with a force level of 565,000 men, the war could well go on for three years. With a second increment of 2-1/3 divisions leading to a total of 665,000 men, it could go on for two years." 54/

General Wheeler, who was present during the discussions, then inter-jected his concern about the possibility that U.S. may face military threats in other parts of the world simultaneous with an increase in strength in Vietnam. He commented that the JCS was then reviewing possible responses to threats in South Korea, Soviet pressure on Berlin, the appearance of "volunteers" sent to Vietnam from Soviet Union, North Korea and Red China and even overt intervention by Red China. Additionally, he listed three matters more closely related to Vietnam which were bothering the JCS. These were:

(a) DRV troop activity in Cambodia. US troops may be forced to move against these units in Cambodia.

(b) DRV troop activity in Laos. US troops may be forced to move against these units.

(c) Possible invasion of North Vietnam. We may wish to take offensive action against the DRV with ground troops. 55/

The bombing which had always attracted considerable JCS attention was
in Wheeler's estimation about to reach the point of target saturation --
when all worthwhile fixed targets except the ports had been struck. Once
this saturation level was reached the decision-makers would be impelled
to address the requirement to deny to the North Vietnamese use of the
ports. He summarized the JCS position saying that the JCS firmly believed
that the President must review the contingencies which they faced, the
troops required to meet them and additional punitive action against DRV.
Westmoreland parenthetically added that he was "frankly dismayed at even
the thought of stopping the bombing program."

There followed a short exchange devoted to Cambodia and Laos in
which Westmoreland described his impression of the role of Cambodia in the
DRV's grand design, one which incorporated the use of Cambodia as a supply
base, first for rice and later for ammunition. The American commander in
Vietnam also believed we should confront the DRV with South Vietnamese
forces in Laos. He reviewed his operational plan for Laos, entitled HIGH
PORT, which envisioned an elite South Vietnamese division conducting ground
operations in Laos against DRV bases and routes under cover of US artillery
and air support. He saw the eventual development of Laos as a major battlefield, a development which would take some of the military pressure off the
south. He also thought it would be wise to think in the same terms as
HIGH PORT for Cambodia; he revealed that he also possessed contingency plans
to move into Cambodia in the Chu Pong area, again using South Vietnamese
forces but this time accompanied by US advisors.

The President closed the meeting by asking: "What if we do not add
the 2-1/3 divisions?" General Wheeler replied first, observing that the
momentum would die; in some areas the enemy would recapture the initiative,
an important but hardly disastrous development, meaning that we wouldn't
lose the war but it would be a longer one. He added that...

> "Of the 2-1/3 divisions, I would add one division on the
> DMZ to relieve the Marines to work with ARVN on pacification;
> and I would put one division east of Saigon to relieve the 9th
> Division to deploy to the Delta to increase the effectiveness
> of the three good ARVN divisions now there; the brigade I would
> send to Quang Ngai to make there the progress in the next year
> that we have made in Binh Dinh in the past year." 56/

The President reacted by saying:

> "We should make certain we are getting value received
> from the South Vietnamese troops. Check the dischargees to
> determine whether we could make use of them by forming addi-
> tional units, by mating them with US troops, as is done in
> Korea, or in other ways." 57/

There is no record of General Westmoreland's reply, if any.

Little if anything new was revealed in the discussion but it serves
to indicate the President's concern with the opportunity costs associated
with the large force increase. The discussion also reveals the kind of
estimates about the duration of the war which were reaching the President.

Two other memoranda outlining alternatives to the Westmoreland
March request for additional troops were written by Mr. Richard Steadman
of ISA and Mr. William Bundy of State for Undersecretary Katzenbach. 58/
The Steadman memo was nothing more than a brief review of the original
MACV request and as such did not outline strategic alternatives. It was
to provide a basis for portions of the analysis in the DPM prepared by
McNaughton later in May. The Bundy memo, on the other hand, did analyze
possible changes in our military strategy. He analyzed several factors
which he believed seriously affected the direction of our military actions.
Among these were:

"Force Increases. In terms of contribution to our
strategy over the next nine months, I believe any increase
directly related to meeting the threat in the northern part
of SVN, and at the same time, not reducing our effort in
II and III Corps unacceptably, must be considered essential.
(I have just lunched with Paul Nitze, who gives an off-the-
cuff estimate that we may need a total increase of 50,000 to
meet this specification.)

"To the extent that any increase is related to needs in
the Delta, I would be most skeptical of the total advantage
of such action at least this year. The Delta does not lend
itself to the most effective application of our forces, and
the Viet Cong in the Delta are in key areas so deeply dug in
that in the end they will be routed out only by a major change
in the over-all situation, and particularly in the prestige
and effectiveness of the GVN. (For example, this is already
Colonel Wilson's conclusion with respect to key areas in
Long An.)

"In sum, we should leave IV Corps basically to the GVN,
trying to deny it as a source of food and men, but leaving
it to be truly pacified more slowly and later.

"Apart from the military merits, any force increase
that reaches the 'Plimsoll Line' -- calling up the Reserves --
involves a truly major debate in Congress. Under present
circumstances, I believe such a debate could only encourage
Hanoi, and might also lead to pressures to go beyond what is
wise in the North, specifically mining Haiphong. Unless

there are over-riding military reasons -- which I do not
myself see -- we should not get into such a debate this summer.

"Ground Action Against North Vietnam. I understand this
to be only a contingency thought in any event. I would be
totally against it, for the simple reason that I believe the
chances are 75-25 that it would bring the Chinese truly into
the war and, almost equally important, stabilize the internal
Chinese situation at least temporarily.

"Laos. Last Friday we went through General Starbird's
plans for more effective action against the Corridor in Laos.
I think these make sense, although they cannot be expected to
do more than make use of the Corridor somewhat more difficult.
(We should at once get away from linking these with the true
"Obstacle" planned in the eastern area of SVN next to the DMZ.
The two are entirely different, and the words "obstacle" or
"barrier" as related to Laos have very unfortunate political
implications in both Laos and Thailand.) The small ground
force teams Starbird needs in Laos can be handled, in Sullivan's
judgment.

"Beyond this point, Sullivan and I would both be strongly
opposed to any such idea as sending a GVN division into Laos.
It would almost certainly be ineffective, and the cry would
at once go up to send more. Sullivan believes, and I agree,
that Souvanna would object violently and feel that his whole
position had been seriously compromised." 59/

Bundy believed that Cambodia was becoming increasingly important
to the North Vietnamese war effort. Nevertheless, he doubted, at that
stage, if any significant change in our actions in Cambodia could really
affect the supply routes or be worth the broad political damage of
appearing to attack Cambodia.

Turning to the bombing in the north he commented:

"E. Additional Action in the North. Of the major targets still not hit, I would agree to the Hanoi power station,
but then let it go at that, subject only to occasional re-
strikes where absolutely required. In particular, on the airfields, I think we have gone far enough to hurt and not far
enough to drive the aircraft to Chinese fields, which I think
could be very dangerous.

"I would strongly oppose the mining of Haiphong at any time in the next nine months, unless the Soviets categorically use it to send in combat weapons. (It may well be that we should warn them quietly but firmly that we are watching their traffic into Haiphong very closely, and particularly from this standpoint.) Mining of Haiphong, at any time, is bound to risk a confrontation with the Soviets and to throw Hanoi into greater dependence on Communist China. These in themselves would be very dangerous and adverse to the whole nation of getting Hanoi to change its attitude. Moreover, I think they would somehow manage to get the stuff in through China no matter what we did to Haiphong." 60/

His concluding overall assessment of the situation was that Hanoi was waiting us out believing that the 1968 elections would cause us to change our position or even lose heart completely. He believed that our "herky-jerky" and impatient actions had greatly strengthened this belief in Hanoi. He felt that our major thrust must be now to persuade them that we were prepared to stick it out if necessary. 61/ He continued by turning to the political factors which he felt were really important:

"B. The Real Key Factors in the Situation. I believe we are making steady progress in the South, and that there are things we can do -- notably effort with ARVN -- to improve the present slow pace of pacification. Over-all progress in the South remains the key factor that could bring Hanoi to the right attitude and actions.

The really important element in the South over the next few months is political. There could be a tremendous gain if the elections are honest and widely participated in, and if the result is a balanced civilian/military government that commands real support in the South. Such a gain would do more than any marginal action, except for the essential job of countering the Communist thrust in I Corps.

At the same time, if the election process is thwarted by a military coup or if it is turned into a military steam-roller, the results could be sharply negative. We might even be forced to re-assess our basic policy. This is simply a measure of the vital importance of the political front for this year.

In addition, we must consider at all times the effect of the Chinese internal situation. We cannot affect whether convulsion resumes, but we should certainly avoid actions that might tend to reduce the possibility of convulsion. (This is argued strenuously by Edward Rice in Hong Kong 7581, received today.)

Argued in another way, I would now reckon that
the odds are considerably better than 50-50 that there will
be a renewal of convulsion in China in the next few months.
In December and January, I think this was the added factor
that caused Hanoi to give off a "tremor" and at least to
make a significant tactical change in its position. If convulsion now occurs again, it will offset whatever encouragement Hanoi may have received from the apparent recent promise
of additional Soviet aid and the easing of whatever transit
tensions may have existed between Moscow and Peking. In fact,
renewed convulsion in China could at some point become a really
major factor to Hanoi. This is a dubious effect on which we cannot and should not rely. But it serves to put into focus the
relative importance of any additional military actions, particularly in the North. And it is a very strong argument indeed
against any additional step-up in our bombing of the North,
or mining Haiphong.

"C. <u>Over-All Estimate</u>. If we go on as we are doing, if
the political process in the South comes off well, and if the
Chinese do not settle down, I myself would reckon that by the
end of 1967 there is at least a 50-50 chance that a favorable
tide will be running really strongly in the South, and that
Hanoi will be very discouraged. Whether they will move to
negotiate is of course a slightly different question, but we
could be visibly and strongly on the way.

"If China should go into a real convulsion, I would
raise these odds slightly, and think it clearly more likely
that Hanoi would choose a negotiating path to the conclusion." <u>62/</u>

Just as many others were doing, Bundy revealed an increasing sensitivity for the urgent development of a coherent negotiating strategy. On
this he wrote:

"While we need a thorough review of our whole objectives and negotiating position, I doubt very much if we
shall find any points on which we now wish to change our
public position or to take any new initiative viz-a-viz
Hanoi.

"Basically, in line with the idea of conveying an
impression of steady firmness to Hanoi, I think we should
avoid new initiatives except as we have to respond to some
significant third party such as U Thant or the Canadians.
I would certainly not go into the UN or the World Court.

"Behind this strategy lies the judgment that Hanoi is

in all probability dug in at least until after the Vietnamese elections. After that, we could take another look,
but I still doubt that any serious change will be indicated.
If it is, some approach like the Ne Win one seems to me by
far the most promising.

"A key question is of course how we handle the Soviets.
My own hunch is that Kosygin burned his fingers somewhat
in February, but that they have built their position in
Hanoi at least back to its former level. In the process,
they will have almost certainly undertaken some additional
aid. Knowing as they do all our peace moves, they may have
a strong feeling that we are in a hurry and perhaps susceptible to change. This would argue against pressing them hard
in the near future, as we did in early April in any event.

"On the other hand, we certainly could impress upon them
our belief that their own interest lies in getting the situation resolved, and that they should be exerting real influence
to this end. But this should be coupled with a calm firmness
in our own determination to go ahead and not to be thrown off
by anything additional they may be doing or threaten to do.
In the last analysis, they can judge whether they really have
any leverage and how to exert it.

"At any rate, the next major contacts with the Soviets --
Dobrynin's return and Brown's visit to Moscow in late May --
should in my judgment be played in this measured but essentially
low key unless they come up with something. Brown is not
himself inclined to try something new at the moment, and we
should do nothing to encourage him. (He has a full plate
anyway of other issues.) 63/

Bundy's basically optimistic estimate (50-50 was in the context
of the time optimistic) was partially supported by the reports of ground
action coming out of South Vietnam, although the increasing enemy threat
in I CTZ remained an ominous and somewhat puzzling development.

5. Developments in the Ground War: Strategy Takes Shape

Ground operations in the period February into early May followed
essentially the pattern predicted by COMUSMACV in his earlier assessments
and statements of strategy. The PRAIRIE series of operations conducted
by the Marines to counter infiltration through the DMZ had received permission during the month to employ artillery fire against military targets

north of the DMZ and the enemy had responded with heavy mortar attacks
on friendly positions throughout the PRAIRIE operations area. Operation
DE SOTO designed to clear and secure the Sa Huyen salt flats prior to the
April harvest had been termed "successful." Operation PERSHING in northern
Binh Dinh continued as part of an extensive allied effort to break the
enemy hold in the area.

The 1st Cavalry Division participated in OPERATION THAYER II, southwest of Bong Son in II Corps area. This clearing operation netted 228
enemy killed before it was terminated in mid-February. Across the Corps
Tactical Zone in Pleiku Province, OPERATION SAM HOUSTON operating on the
border between Pleiku and Kontum Provinces was countering increasing
enemy forces at the egress of their Highland border sanctuaries. In III
Corps the most significant operation was JUNCTION CITY, the largest operation of the war, initiated in 22 February with an airborne assault into
the long time enemy sanctuaries in northern Tay Ninh Province. Another
major offensive into War Zone C, OPERATION GADSTON began on 2 February but
achieved relatively insignificant results. FAIRFAX, on the outskirts of
Saigon, continued to screen that city and secondarily to conduct US-ARVN
buddy system operations concentrating on civic action during the day and
conducting extensive patrols and ambushes during the night. (See Figure
2, Monthly Evaluation (February 1967) map.)

In March the tempo of the war increased partially in reaction to
the burgeoning infiltration in I Corps Tactical Zone. South of the DMZ,
Marines continued to conduct counter infiltration operations with PRAIRIE
II and PRAIRIE III, operations characterized by bloody assaults designed
to retain control of key terrain features dominating infiltration corri-
dors leading down from the North. In the western highlands of II Corps,
U.S. forces in OPERATION SAM HOUSTON were experiencing frequent heavy
ground clashes with enemy units which sortied out of their sanctuaries
and attempted to operate in Pleiku and Southern Kontum Provinces. JUNCTION
CITY continuing in III Corps experienced heavier contact in War Zone C,
while FAIRFAX and other screening operations were regarded as successful
on the strength of a steady decline in enemy initiated incidents on the
outskirts of the city. ARVN divisions continued to operate in IV Corps but
there are no large operations reported. (See Figure 3, Monthly Evaluation
(March 1967) map.)

The first major operational dislocation of U.S. forces to the north
occurred in early April when TASK FORCE OREGON (a provisional division)
was created and moved north into Quang Ngai Province thereby releasing
Marine units for operations further north in the vicinity of the DMZ.
Some of the bitterest fighting of the war occurred in late April near
Khe Sanh in western Quang Tri Province, coming as a direct result of the
USMC strategy of fighting for control and holding of key terrain commanding
infiltration routes. The Marines were engaged in a series of sharp and

LAM SON 142
(112)

PRAIRIE II
(105)

INDEPENDENCE
(139)

STONE
(291)

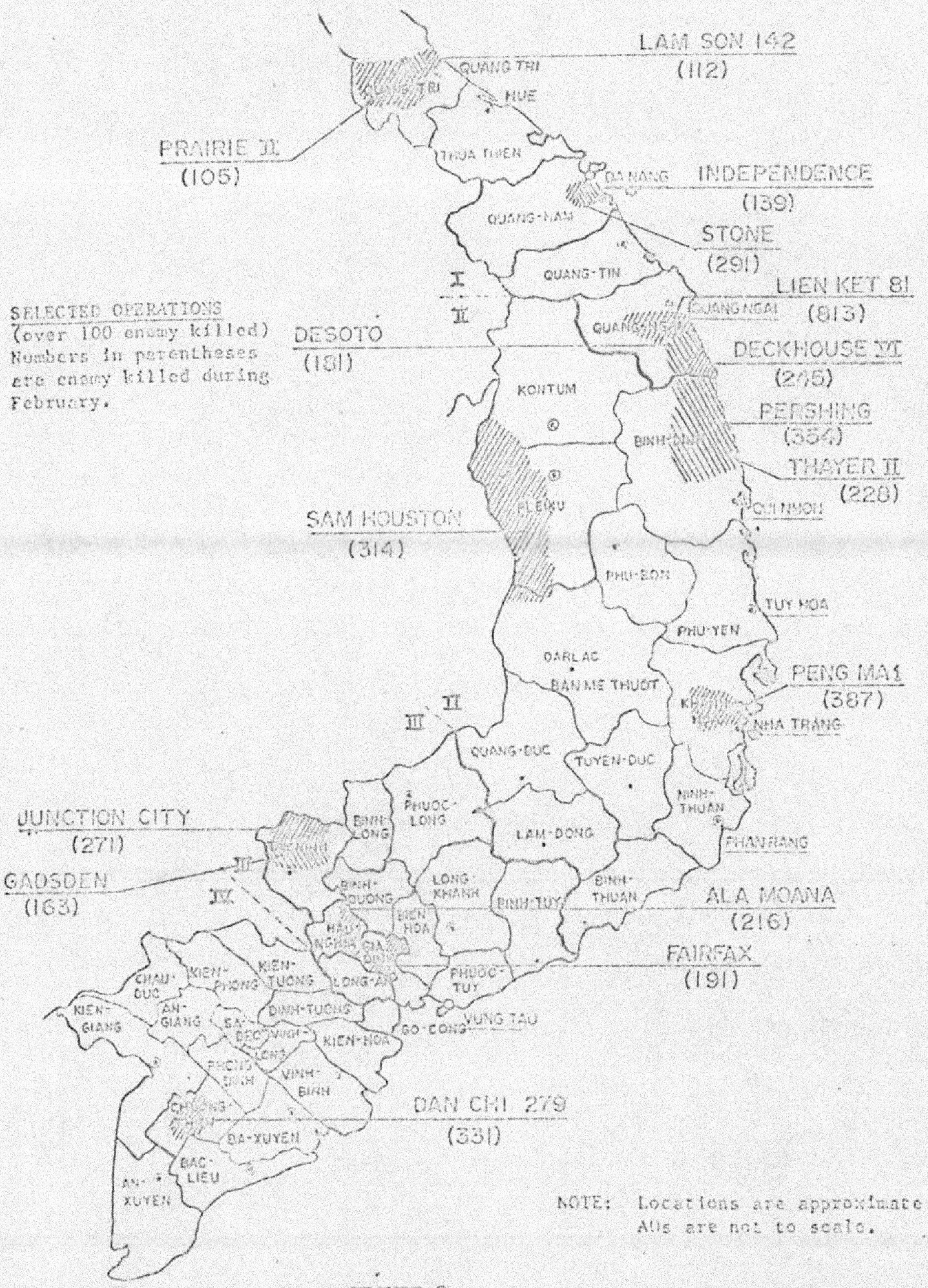

SELECTED OPERATIONS
(over 100 enemy killed)
Numbers in parentheses
are enemy killed during
February.

LIEN KET 81
(813)

DESOTO
(181)

DECKHOUSE VI
(265)

PERSHING
(354)

THAYER II
(228)

SAM HOUSTON
(314)

PENG MA1
(387)

JUNCTION CITY
(271)

GADSDEN
(163)

ALA MOANA
(216)

FAIRFAX
(191)

DAN CHI 279
(331)

NOTE: Locations are approximate
Alls are not to scale.

QUANG TRI, HUE, THUA THIEN, DA NANG, QUANG-NAM, QUANG-TIN, QUANG NGAI, QUANG, KONTUM, BINH-DINH, QUI NHON, PLEIKU, PHU-BON, TUY HOA, PHU-YEN, DARLAC, BAN ME THUOT, NHA TRANG, QUANG-DUC, TUYEN-DUC, NINH-THUAN, PHUOC-LONG, LAM-DONG, PHAN RANG, BINH-LONG, BINH-DUONG, LONG-KHANH, BINH-THUAN, BINH-TUY, HAU NGHIA, GIA DINH, BIEN HOA, CHAU-DUC, KIEN-PHONG, KIEN-TUONG, LONG-AN, PHUOC-TUY, KIEN-GIANG, AN-GIANG, SA DEC, DINH-TUONG, VINH-LONG, GO-CONG, VUNG TAU, KIEN-HOA, PHONG DINH, VINH-BINH, CHUONG, BA-XUYEN, AN-XUYEN, BAC-LIEU

I, II, III, IV

FIGURE 2

91

DEACON HILL
(334)

PRAIRIE II - III
(773)

LAMSON 25
(191)

QUANG TRI

TRI

HUE

THUA-THIEN

DA NANG

NEWCASTLE
(118)

QUANG-NAM

SELECTED OPERATIONS
(Over 100 Enemy Killed)
Numbers in parentheses
are enemy killed during
March.

PHI PHUNG 8
(125)

QUANG-TIN

I

II

QUANG NGAI

QUANG-NGAI

DESOTO
(133)

KONTUM

PERSHING
(615)

BINH-DINH

QUI NHON

SAM HOUSTON
(401)

PLEIKU

PHU-BON

ADAMS
(140)

TUY HOA

DARLAC

BAN ME THUOT

PHU-YEN

OH JAC KYO
(295)

KHANH-
HOA

NHA TRANG

CAI CACH
(243)

II

III

QUANG-DUC

TUYEN-DUC

NINH-
THUAN

JUNCTION CITY
(1672)

III

IV

PHUOC-
LONG

BINH-
LONG

LAM-DONG

PHAN RANG

BINH-
DUONG

LONG-
KHANH

BINH-TUY

BINH-
THUAN

HAU-
NGHIA GIA

SIEN-
HOA

LONG-A

PHUOC-
TUY

CHAU-
DUC

KIEN-
PHONG

KIEN-
TUONG

DINH-TUONG

LONG-A

FAIRFAX
(104)

AN-
GIANG

SA-
DEC

GO-CONG

VUNG TAU

KIEN-
GIANG

PHONG-
DINH

LONG

KIEN-HOA

ENTERPRISE
(318)

CHUONG-
THIEN

VINH-
BINH

BA-XUYEN

LONG PHI 999G
(142)

NOTE: Locations are
approximate, AO's
not to scale

BAC-
LIEU

AN-
XUYEN

DAN CHI 231/A/SD
(109)

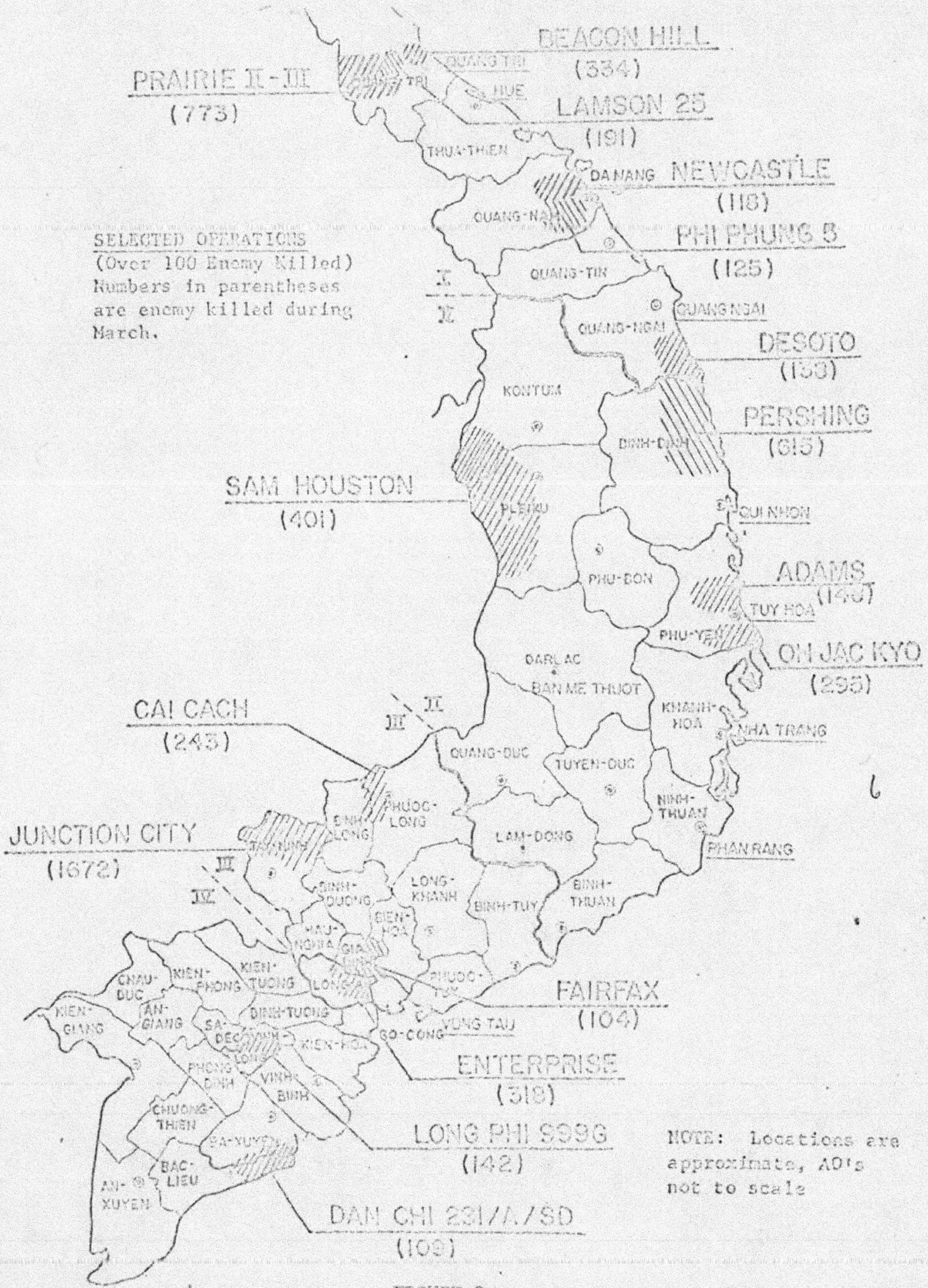

FIGURE 3

92

TOP SECRET - Sensitive

bloody hill battles reminiscent of those fought in the late stages of
the Korean War. The mounting pressure of the enemy forces in and adjacent
to the DMZ not only prompted creation of Task Force OREGON but hastened
additions of artillery and air support units in the area. In the Western
Highlands of II Corps, OPERATION SAM HOUSTON terminated to be followed
immediately by OPERATION FRANCES MARION. This new operation retained the
original mission of its predecessor border surveillance and protection of
installations in the Pleiku-Kontum area. JUNCTION CITY continued in III
Corps tactical zone, but there was a notable decline in activity in that
area, possibly partially attributable to the thinning out of U.S. units to
provide for the dispositions to I Corps Tactical Zone. Some 53 ARVN
infantry battalions, one Ranger battalion, and one regional force battalion
were reported performing missions in direct support of Revolutionary Development. Country-wide VC incidents directed at disruption of the RD effort
increased as the VC attempted to influence the hamlet elections conducted
during April. (See Figure 4, Monthly Evaluation (April 1967) map.)

In May attention focused on I Corps where heavy fighting continued.
Operation PRAIRIE IV conducted by the Marines in conjunction with smaller
operations BEAU CHARGER, HICKORY and LAM SON was directed toward blocking
the major enemy infiltration into northern Quang Tri. Indications were
that the enemy was building up in preparation for a probable coordinated
offensive and allied military activity was directed toward disrupting his
plans. Altogether 24 operations in I Corps tactical zone achieved "significant results," 14 of those operations resulting in over 100 enemy killed.
U.S. Marines and ARVN forces also entered the DMZ for the first time and
reported over 800 enemy killed. In Southeastern Quang Ngai Province,
OPERATION MALHEUR conducted by Task Force OREGON reported 369 enemy killed
by the month's end. In II Corps FRANCES MARION continued to experience
heavy fighting in the border regions as border infiltration attempts by
large NVA/VC units continued on the upswing. (See Figures 5, 6, 7 and 8 for
Corps Monthly Operational Maps, May 1967.)

6. The Domestic Debate Continues: Polarization at Home

Domestic views about the war were beginning to polarize in early
February. Edmund Reischauer, before the Senate Foreign Relations Committee,
expressed his dismay with the administration's persistent adherence to the
domino theory and its variations, one which he said was now "dropped in the
trash can of history wrapped in a Chinese rug." Student leaders in their
Washington Convention had denounced the draft system and urged the abolition
of selective service. In early February, 1,900 women marched upon the
Pentagon protesting the war policies and 5,000 American scientists, 17 of
them Nobel Prize winners, pleaded with the White House for a review of U.S.
policy on chemical and biological warfare in Vietnam. General Gavin was
urging before the Senate Foreign Relations Committee an immediate and unconditional halt of American bombing asking for what he termed "a strategy of
sanity." In early March, Robert Kennedy had delivered a strong speech in
the Senate calling for a halt to the bombing of North Vietnam, a proposal

KHE-SANH AREA
(554)

PRAIRIE III & IV
(112)

QUANG TRI
QUANG TRI
HUE
THUA-THIEN

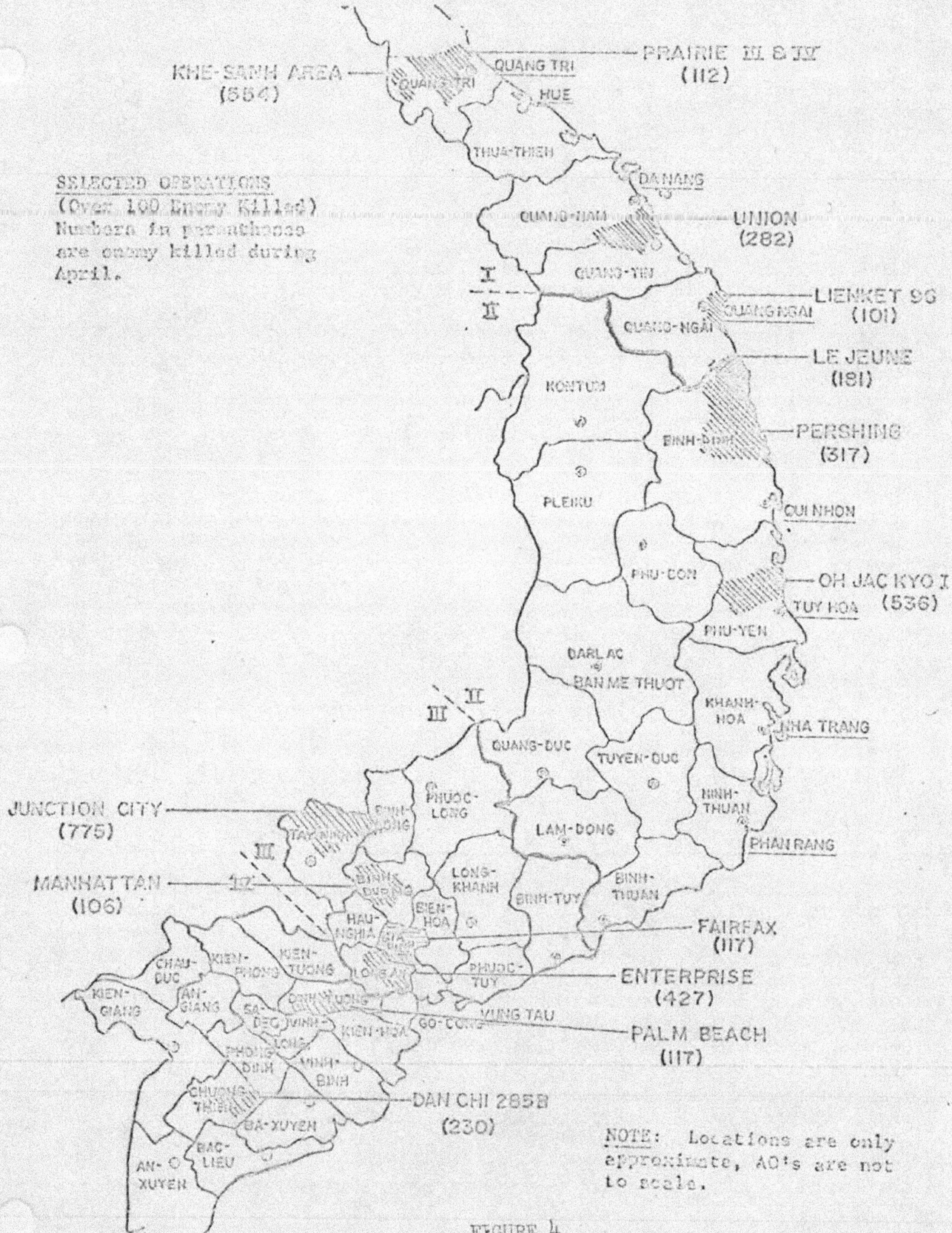

SELECTED OPERATIONS
(Over 100 Enemy Killed)
Numbers in parentheses
are enemy killed during
April.

DA NANG

QUANG-NAM

UNION
(282)

QUANG-TIN

I
II

LIENKET 96
(101)

QUANG NGAI

QUANG-NGAI

LE JEUNE
(181)

KONTUM

PERSHING
(317)

BINH-DINH

QUI NHON

PLEIKU

PHU-BON

OH JAC KYO I
(536)

TUY HOA

PHU-YEN

DARLAC
BAN ME THUOT

KHANH-HOA

NHA TRANG

III   II

QUANG-DUC

TUYEN-DUC

NINH-THUAN

JUNCTION CITY
(775)

PHUOC-LONG

LAM-DONG

PHAN RANG

BINH-LONG

TAY NINH

MANHATTAN
(106)

III

IV

BINH-DUONG

LONG-KHANH

BINH-TUY

BINH-THUAN

HAU-NGHIA

BIEN-HOA

FAIRFAX
(117)

CHAU-DUC

KIEN-PHONG

KIEN-TUONG

LONG-AN

PHUOC-TUY

ENTERPRISE
(427)

KIEN-GIANG

AN-GIANG

SA-DEC

VINH-LONG

DINH-TUONG

KIEN-HOA

GO-CONG

VUNG TAU

PALM BEACH
(117)

PHONG-DINH

VINH-LONG

MINH-BINH

CHUONG-THIEN

BA-XUYEN

DAN CHI 285B
(230)

NOTE: Locations are only
approximate. AO's are not
to scale.

AN-XUYEN

BAC-LIEU

FIGURE 4

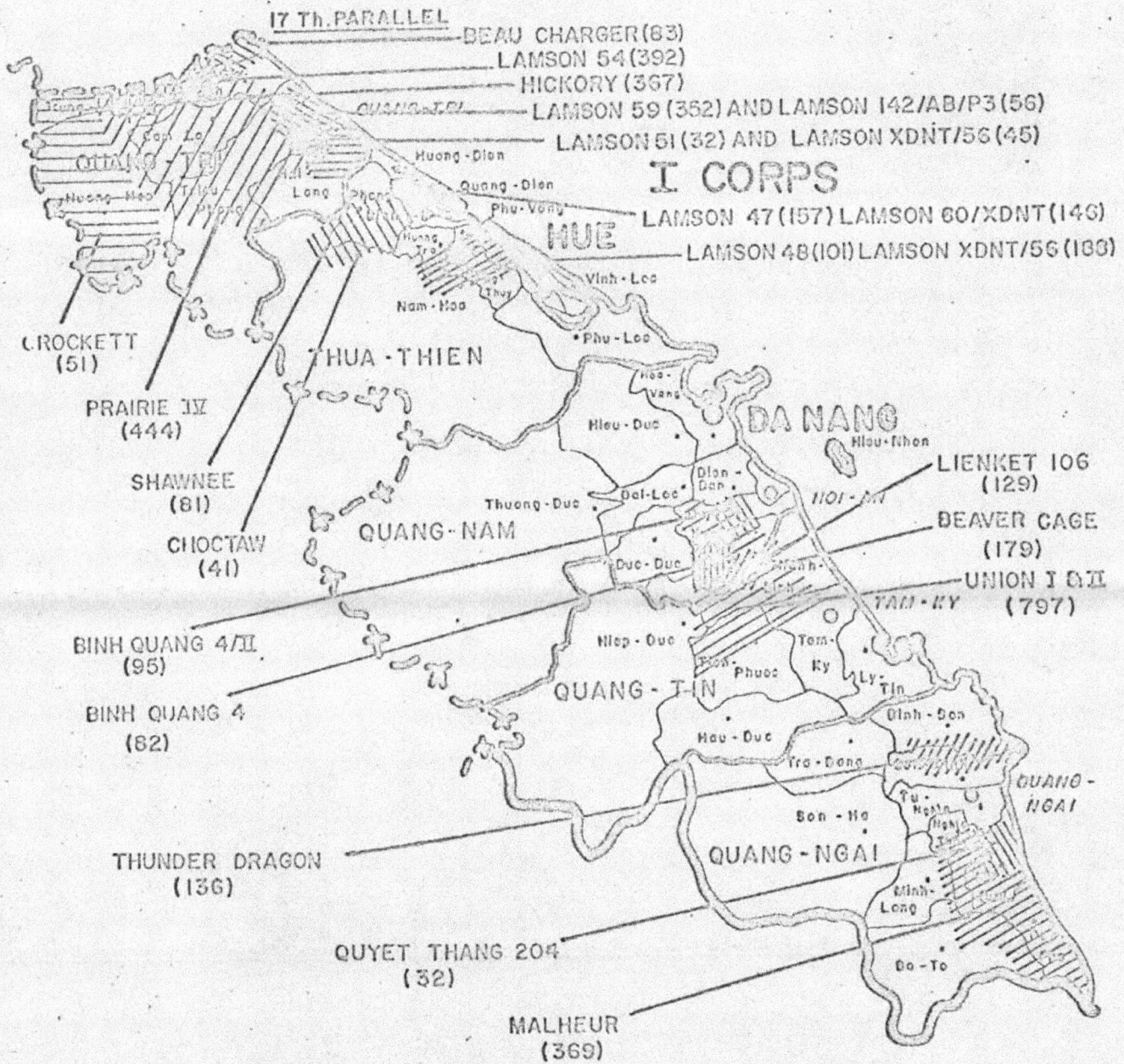

17 Th. PARALLEL
BEAU CHARGER (83)
LAMSON 54 (392)
HICKORY (367)
LAMSON 59 (352) AND LAMSON 142/AB/P3 (56)
LAMSON 51 (32) AND LAMSON XDNT/56 (45)

I CORPS

LAMSON 47 (157) LAMSON 60/XDNT (146)
LAMSON 48 (101) LAMSON XDNT/56 (188)

HUE

CROCKETT (51)

PRAIRIE IV (444)

SHAWNEE (81)

CHOCTAW (41)

THUA-THIEN

QUANG-NAM

DA NANG

LIENKET 106 (129)

BEAVER CAGE (179)

UNION I & II (797)

BINH QUANG 4/II (95)

BINH QUANG 4 (82)

QUANG-TIN

THUNDER DRAGON (136)

QUANG-NGAI

QUYET THANG 204 (32)

MALHEUR (369)

SELECTED OPERATIONS

NUMBERS IN PARENTHESES ARE
TOTAL ENEMY KIA DURING MAY

AD'S ARE APPROXIMATE ONLY

FIGURE 5

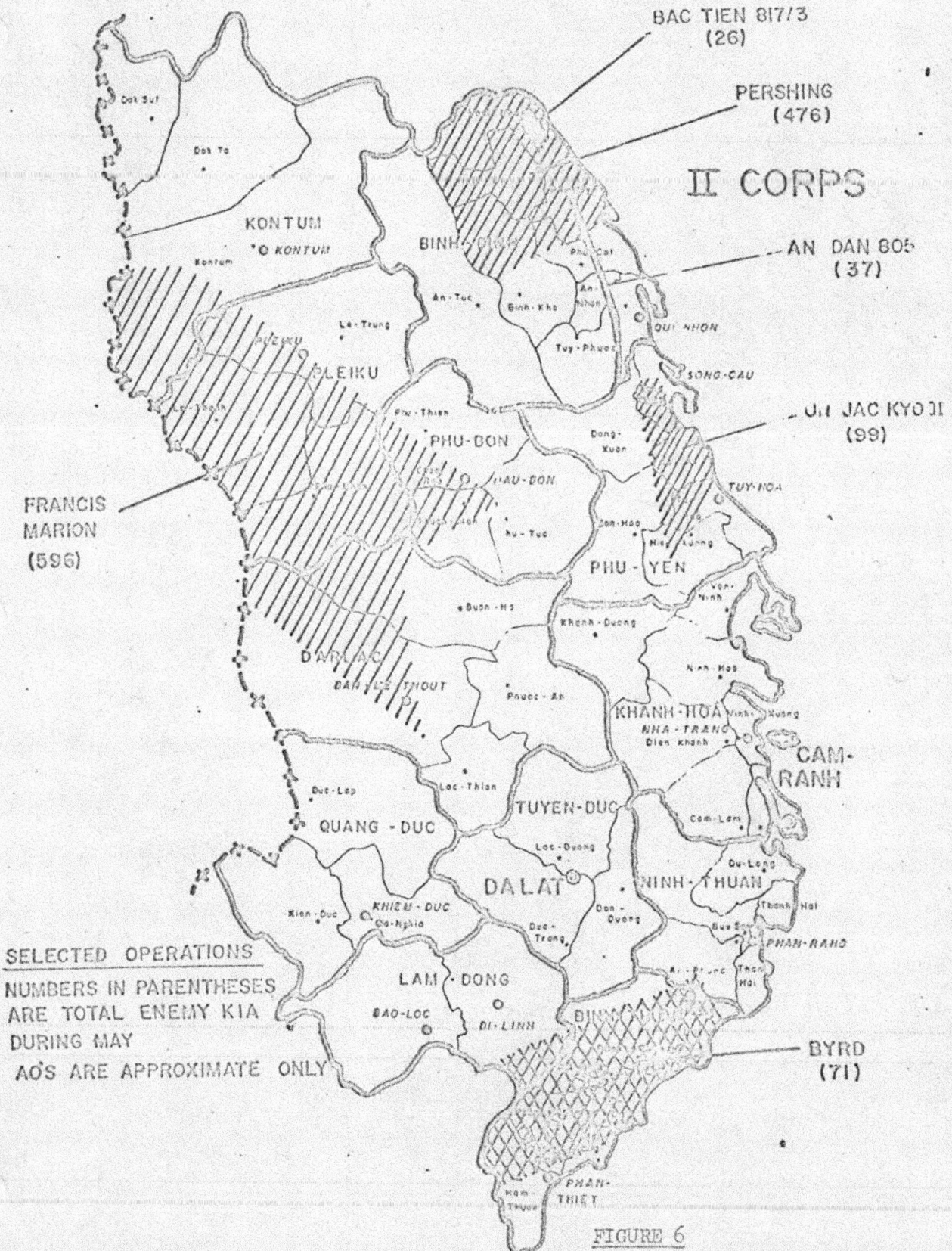

FIGURE 6

III CORPS

MANHATTAN (85)

KITTY HAWK (30)

FAIRFAX (96)

ENTERPRISE (124)

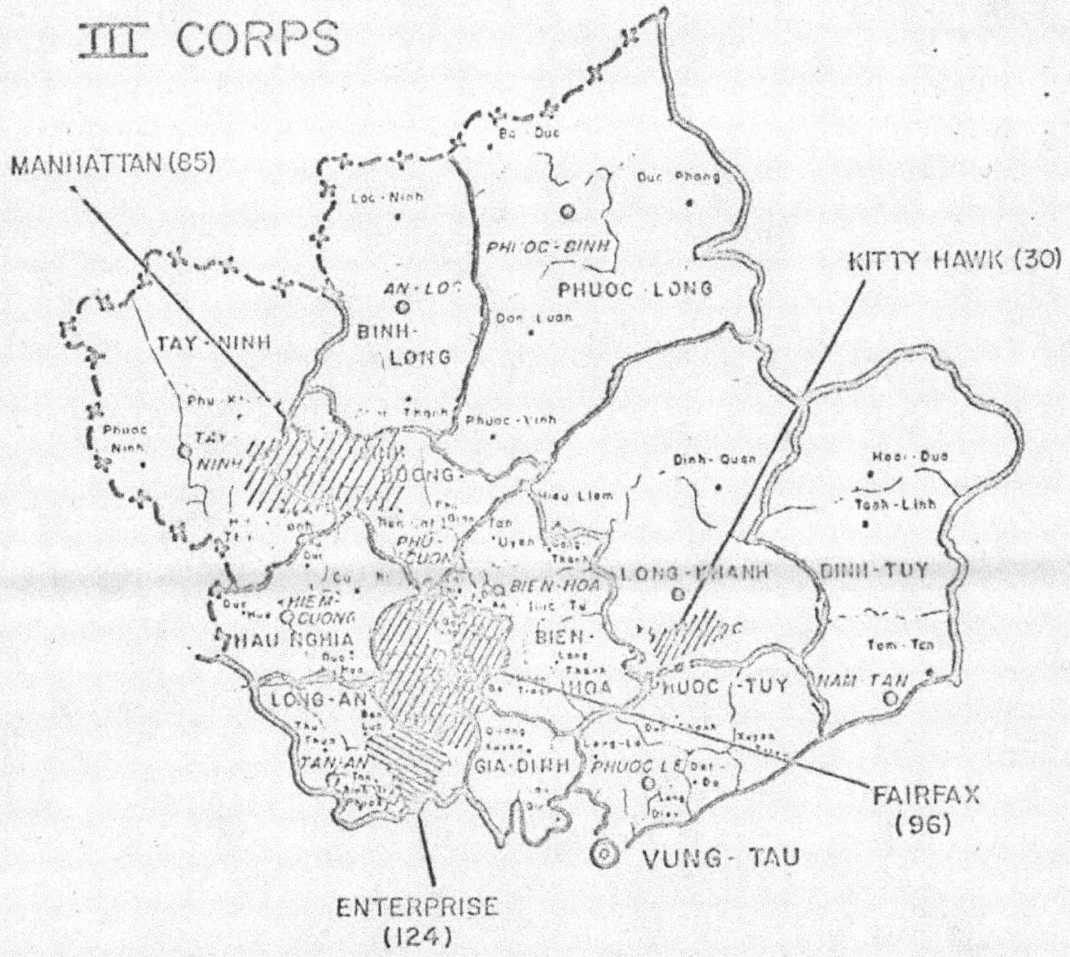

SELECTED OPERATIONS

NUMBERS IN PARENTHESES ARE
TOTAL ENEMY KIA DURING MAY
AO'S ARE APPROXIMATE ONLY

FIGURE 7

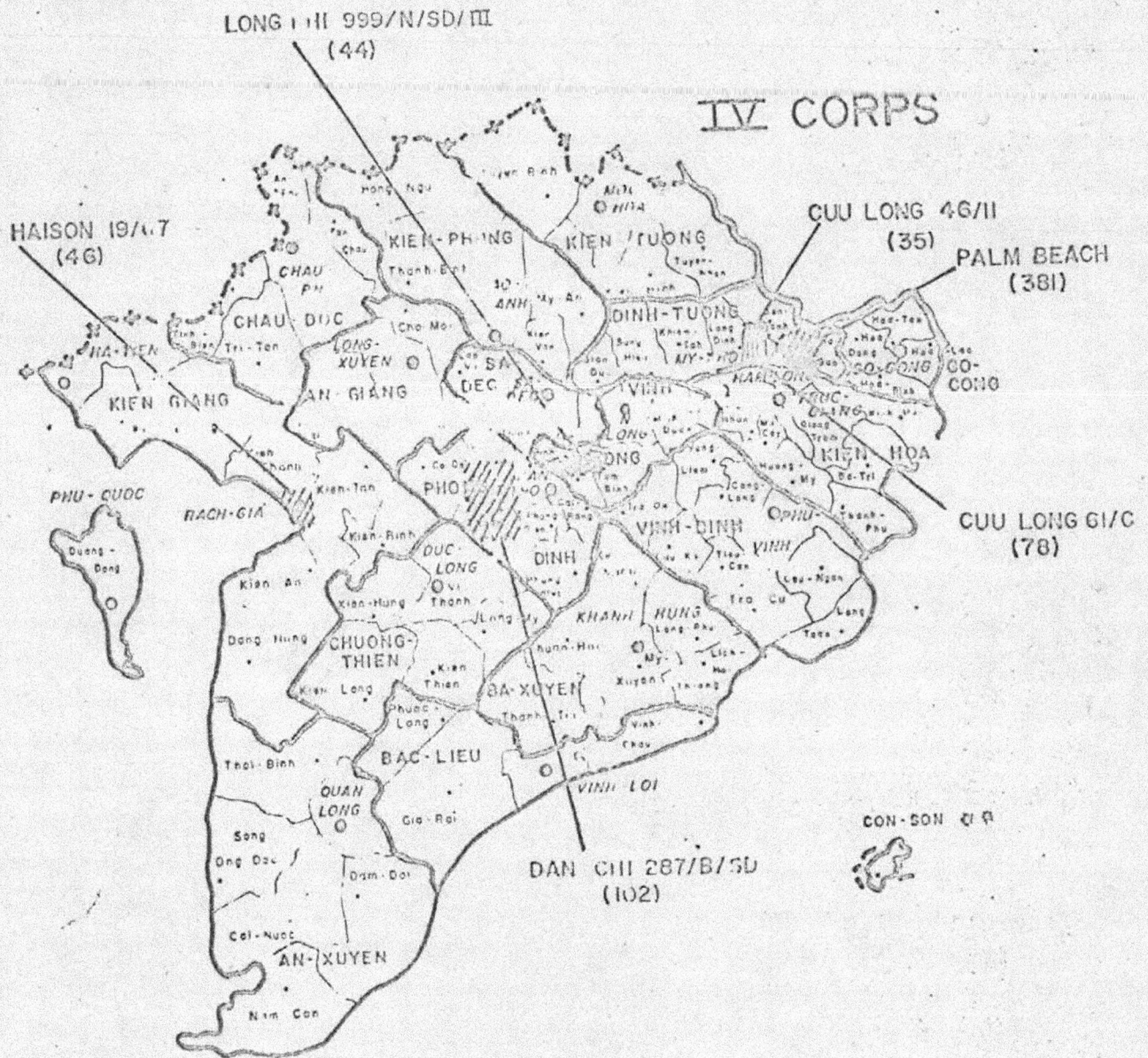

IV CORPS

LONG PHI 999/N/SD/III (44)

HAISON 19/G7 (46)

CUU LONG 46/11 (35)

PALM BEACH (381)

CUU LONG 61/C (78)

DAN CHI 287/B/SD (102)

SELECTED OPERATIONS

NUMBERS IN PARENTHESES ARE
TOTAL ENEMY KIA DURING MAY
AO'S ARE APPROXIMATE ONLY

FIGURE 8

TOP SECRET - Sensitive

which Secretary Rusk publicly buoyed by the preceding day's announcement of the Mansfield Resolution supporting the administration's policy in Vietnam.

Resistance to the war and its costs were beginning to be reflected in administration actions. In early February President Johnson asked for $6.2 billion in foreign aid for two years, the smallest appropriation in the 20-year history of the program noting that the opposition to a larger program stemmed from "a view of needs at home and the costs of the struggle in Vietnam." In early March the President announced that we were beginning to mine the rivers in the north, authorizing long-range artillery shelling across the DMZ and commencing naval bombardment of military targets in the DMZ in North Vietnam border areas. When questioned, he defended the new activities stating that he would "not describe them as a step up in the war" but only as boosts "desirable and essential in the face of immediate infiltration and build-up." 64/ There was increasing public emphasis from the White House on peace feelers to Hanoi and detent with the Soviet Government. The first exchange of letters between Kosygin and Johnson confirming the willingness of the Soviet Government to discuss means of limiting the arms race was publicly announced on 3 March. On 22 March the Johnson-Ho letters were released, an event which in the view of most commentators placed Johnson in a somewhat more tenable position vis-a-vis Vietnam war policy than he had previously enjoyed.

Despite intensive efforts to alleviate the problem of credibility, events continued to reveal that the administration was being less than frank with reporters. In early February the Pentagon acknowledged that it had lost 1800 aircraft in Vietnam as opposed to the 622 "combat planes" which it had quoted earlier. R. W. Appel wrote in the New York Times questioning COMUSMACV infiltration figures. A week later, in another article which received wide circulation, Appel reported that the pacification effort was greatly hindered by South Vietnamese Government foot-dragging, a conclusion which found considerable sympathy among the group already dissatisfied with South Vietnamese Government pacification performance.

The public and the press alike were becoming increasingly wary of the statistics coming out of Washington. Even the Chicago Tribune in early March surmised that either the figures coming out of MACV were wrong or those coming out of the Pentagon were misleading. The paper cited a recent joint press conference held by McNamara and Rusk in which they announced that communist military forces in Vietnam had suffered tremendous casualties in the past four months, quantitatively an increase of 40-50%, thus reducing their effectiveness significantly, but in the next sentence announcing that serious communist military activity in Vietnam had "increased substantially."

By mid-March editorial commentary was focusing on the theme that generally there would be more and wider war. American casualties announced on 10 March were higher than those for any other week of the war: 232 KIA, 1381 WIA, 4 MIA for a total of 1617. Four days later the U.S. conducted

99   TOP SECRET - Sensitive

the heaviest attacks of the 1967 air war on North Vietnam (128 missions
flown by approximately 450 aircraft). Not only was there a feeling that
the war would be longer and more intense, but the public was becoming
increasingly aware of its costs. In mid-March the House Appropriations
Committee approved a $12 billion supplemental appropriations bill and a week
later the Senate overwhelmingly approved a $20.8 billion military procure-
ment program. The ease with which the appropriations bills were being
passed was not truly indicative of the mood of Congress which was becoming
increasingly divided about the war. The Stennis Subcommittee (Preparedness)
was carrying the military's fight for more troops. In late March Stennis
charged that "American commanders in Vietnam are not getting all the troops
they want and the bombing of the north is overly restricted." 65/ The
Pentagon reply to this was that "there had been no reduction in any program
of troop deployments previously approved by the Department of Defense." 66/
Senator Symington was publicly urging wider air raids of North Vietnam to
include attack of the MIG airfields. By late March, Stennis' charges were
coming in drum-fire fashion focusing on charges that future troop deployments
to Vietnam would fall below approved levels; that urgent military appeals
for the bombing of more meaningful targets in North Vietnam were being
arbitrarily denied and that the Pentagon was responsible for a gross shortage
of ships in Vietnam. Prior to General Westmoreland's return to the U.S. in
late April, General Abrams had been named as his Deputy Commander and it
appears that indeed, despite Westmoreland's promises of victory, it would
be a long war. For early that week the infiltration/casualty figures for
the first quarter of 1967 were released, and they indicated that despite
huge Red losses of nearly 25,000 men in the first 12 weeks of that year,
nearly 4,000 more than that amount had infiltrated during the same period
and were now active in enemy units in the South. 67/

FOOTNOTES

1. State message 153550 to the American Embassy, Saigon from Rusk, dated March 12, 1967.

2. State message 158083 to AmEmb Saigon, Subject: "Guam Agenda," dated 17 March 1967.

3. See Task Force Paper IV.C.9., Evolution of the War - US-GVN Relations, 1963-1967, Part II. This shift of personnel represented the largest shake-up in US leadership in SVN since August 1965. Ambassador Bunker replaced Lodge; Locke took Porter's place; and Robert Komer took charge of Revolutionary Development under COMUSMACV.

4. Joint Communique, Guam Meetings, March 21, 1967.

5. Memorandum, Subject: Main Talking Points for the President in Trip Briefs for Conference on Guam, McNaughton III, 20-21 March 1967. This record of Westmoreland's comments, dated 20 March, was taken from a hand-written attachment to the cited memo, presumably written by McNaughton.

6. COMUSMACV 08435 to CINCPAC, Subject: Military Plans and Progress in SVN, dated 12 March 1967.

7. OSD/SA, Subject: "ARVN Effectiveness on Search and Destroy Type Operations," 16 March 1967.

8. Ibid.

9. OASD/SA, "ARVN Performance," Op. Cit.

10. OASD/SA, "Optimum U.S. Force Level in SVN," March 16, 1967 (Guam Briefing Book).

11. Ibid.

12. As early as the summer of 1966 detailed post-hostilities planning was begun in DOD, and the last item in the list just quoted reflects some of that thinking. See: OASD(ISA) "Post Hostilities Planning," dated 17 March 1967.

13. MACV Briefing Book, Guam Conference.

14. McNaughton Memorandum, 20 March 1967, op. cit.

15. New York Times, 23 March 1967.

16. New York Times, 20-26 March 1967.

17. COMUSMACV 09101 to CINCPAC, Subject: Force Requirements, dated 18 March 1967.

18. Ibid.

19. COMUSMACV to CINCPAC, "Assessment of the Military Situation and Concept of Operations," 1 March 1967.

20. COMUSMACV 09101, op. cit.

21. Ibid.

22. Ibid.

23. Vance Memo to COMUSMACV, late March 1967. Interview with LTC Vesser, then assigned to J32, MACV Headquarters, Saigon.

24. JCS msg 59881 to CINCPAC, Subject: PACOM Force Requirements, dated 24 March 1967.

25. Ibid. To meet this deadline CINCPAC followed its standard practice of convening a conference or, what in this case it labelled a "Force Requirements Task Group." This group met from 27 March to 3 April analyzing and synthesizing the MACV replies and preparing the final reply which was forwarded to the JCS between 26 and 28 March. See: CINCPAC 252120A Mar 67, Subject: Force Requirements.

26. COMUSMACV to CINCPAC, Subject: Force Requirements, 260650Z Mar 67.

27. COMUSMACV letter MACJ3, 28 Mar 67, and COMUSMACV 10248 to CINCPAC, Subject: Program 4 Force Requirements, 28 Mar 67.

28. CINCPAC message to JCS 280145Z Mar 67.

29. COMUSMACV 10311 to JCS, Subject: MACV FY 68 Force Requirements, dated 28 March 1967.

30. Ibid.

31. Ibid.

32. Ibid.

33. Ibid.

34. COMUSMACV Msg 115,570, to CINCPAC, 7 Apr 67, Subject: Force Requirements.

35. Ibid.

36. JCSM 208-67, Subj: Marine Corps Reinforcement of I Corps Tactical Zone, dated April 14, 1967.

37. SecDef Control No. X1935 and COMUSMACV 09101 attached, dated 23 Mar 67.

38. JCSM 218-67, Subject: Force Requirements - Southeast Asia, FY 1968, dated 20 April 1967, Encl A to JCS 2339/255-3.

39. Ibid.

40. Ibid.

41. Ibid.

42. Ibid.

43. Ibid.

44. Memorandum from Acting SecState Nicholas deB. Katzenbach to the Honorable John McNaughton, Subject: Vietnam, dated 24 April 1967.

45. Ibid.

46. Ibid. The other agencies assigned studies in this memo were the White House (primarily directed to study of pacification), State Department (primarily directed to study settlement), and the CIA (predicting the trends in the military pacification, political and economic situations).

47. Memo for the President from R. W. Komer, Subject: Thoughts on Future Strategy in Vietnam, dated 24 April 1967.

48. Ibid.

49. Ibid.

50. Ibid.

51. Ibid.

52. Unsigned, Notes on Discussions with the President, 27 April 1967 (McNaughton Papers).

53. Ibid.

54. Ibid. Emphasis added.

55. Ibid.

56. Ibid.

57. Ibid.

58. Memo from Mr. Richard Steadman for Asst SecDef (ISA) McNaughton,
    Subj: Additional Deployments to SVN, dated 2 May 67; Memo from
    Mr. Wm. Bundy for Undersecretary Katzenbach, Subj: Thoughts on
    Strategy in Vietnam dated 1 May 1967.

59. Ibid. Ambassador Sullivan's opposition to expanding operations in
    Laos was clearly laid out in a 1 May memorandum addressed to Katzenbach.
    In this memo he strongly opposed Westmoreland's HIGH PORT proposal as
    well as any expansion of the northern barrier which would either cut
    into Lao territory or if it operated as a hermetical seal to the north
    would force the North Vietnamese to make an end run through the Laotian
    corridor to the west of the barrier. He based his objections primarily
    on the serious political consequences which he believed might involve
    the withdrawal of Souvanna's collaboration on many other matters of
    importance to the U.S. He believed that for the limited operational
    advantages on the Ho Chi Minh Trail (none of which he believed would
    succeed anyway) that the U.S. would probably lose the entire Mekong
    Valley. Quoting President Kennedy, he described this as trading "an
    apple for an orchard." See: Memo from Ambassador Sullivan for Mr.
    William Bundy, Subject: Limitations on Military Action in Laos, dated
    1 May 1967.

60. Ibid.

61. Ibid.

62. Ibid.

63. Ibid.

64. The New York Times

65. The New York Times

66. Ibid.

67. The New York Times

D. RESISTANCE TO GROUND
FORCE INCREASES CRYSTALLIZES

D.   RESISTANCE TO THE GROUND FORCE INCREASES CRYSTALLIZES

1.   Systems Analysis -- Vanguard of the Reaction

The search for alternatives to the major force increases proposed
by the JCS was, as we have observed, intensive and widespread but the
most cogent critique of MACV's strategy developed in the Systems Analysis
Office headed by Assistant Secretary of Defense Alain Enthoven. Here a
concentrated attack was launched on the two most vulnerable aspects of
COMUSMACV's operations: the feasibility of the "war of attrition"
strategy pursued in the face of the uncertainty about NVN infiltration,
and "search and destroy tactics to support it." The reaction in Systems
Analysis to the 18 March troop request submitted by COMUSMACV was one
of surprise and incredulity. Everyone who had worked in the problem
area of ground force deployments believed that COMUSMACV had received
the message during the Program 4 discussions, that any troops were going
to be difficult to come by and those that were forthcoming had to be
completely and convincingly justified. 1/

Immediately upon receipt of the MACV requirements request Alain
Enthoven ordered that a detailed analysis of the request be made. The
initial cuts at the request made by his staff were simply in the form
of tables comparing the approved Program #4 and the new force levels
required. 2/   These were completed and to the Secretary of Defense
within a week after the initial MACV request reached the Pentagon.

The more detailed follow-up analysis prepared in Systems Analysis
initially concentrated upon the "unfortunate lack of analysis" in the
MACV/JCS request, one which failed to explain how the extra forces were
needed to avoid defeat. 3/   Despite this orientation toward the analytic
lacunae the germ of the basic, vital critique which was to emerge was
there. The preface of the draft lamented the lack of analysis and
evidence, seemingly proof in itself that the request should be denied,
but more fundamentally it continued:

> Despite considerable progress in the Vietnam conflict
> during the past year, an end to the conflict is not in
> sight and major unresolved problems remain. North Vietnam
> still believes it can win in the long run, in the name of
> nationalism if not communism. It has been fighting for
> over 25 years against the Japanese, French, and Americans
> and appears prepared to fight indefinitely. The reaction
> of COMUSMACV to this unsatisfactory situation is to request
> more U.S. forces, rather than to improve the effectiveness
> of the RVNAF, and U.S. and other Free World forces.

Hanoi is willing to wait. We have hurt them some,
and we can even hurt them some more, but not so badly as
to destroy their society or their hope for regaining in
the future the material things they sacrifice today.
Their policy will be to wait until dissent in the US
(coupled with world opinion) forces us to retire. Our
only hope is to establish an equally strong and patient
nationalism in South Vietnam.

We, too, must be willing to wait. We cannot establish a strong Southern nationalism in a few months or a
year. If we leave before that is one /sic/, we will have lost,
regardless of the military havoc we have caused in SEA.

Additional forces, added burdens on the US economy,
and calling of the reserves will only serve to increase
DRV's belief that the US will not remain in SVN for the
long pull. Additional forces make it appear that we are
trying for the "quick kill." Hanoi knows that we cannot
achieve it and that the American public will be bitter and
divided unless we do. We should be looking for ways to
ease the burden for the years ahead, rather than making
the war more costly. 4/

The diversion of resources from other national goals also had costs
which demanded accounting:

If we are to stay, we must have the backing of the
US electorate. As we divert resources from other
national goals, as US lives are lost, and as the electorate sees nothing but endless escalation for the future,
an increasing fraction will become discouraged. If this
keeps on in the future as it has in the past, we will
have to leave SEA before stability is achieved, losing
all that we have invested up to that point, and foregoing
the general stability of the world which was established
as a result of the Korean War. If we are not to lose everything, the trends will have to be changed: the increase
in unfavorable public opinion will have to be slowed; the
development of SVN society will have to be speeded. 5/

The memorandum recommended that only enough forces be provided to
meet minimum military goals:

Thus we must provide only enough US forces to meet
minimum military goals. These goals are: (1) to deter
a Chinese Communist invasion; (2) to prevent military
defeat in South Vietnam, and (3) to prevent excessive
terrorism. We have at least sufficient forces presently

deployed to meet these goals.

Additional forces will add additional cost, further degrading public opinion and preventing expansion of critical domestic programs. They would present the prospect of unending escalation, splitting the American public even more openly and seriously. 6/

These goals, of course, differed greatly from those outlined by the Joint Chiefs in JCSM 702-66 in November and JCSM 218-67 in April. The military aims in the Systems Analysis memo were passive in nature, and obviously based upon new assumptions about the likelihood of success, and therefore were directed toward much different terminal goals than those the JCS proposed.

The recommendations made by Systems Analysis were based upon two fundamental arguments: (1) That the additional forces were unlikely to increase VC/NVA losses beyond any level intolerable to the enemy; and (2) that the additional forces would not help the pacification task measurably. 7/ It argued:

Additional forces are very unlikely to increase VC/NVA losses beyond any level intolerable to the enemy. Assuming that the enemy has no control over his losses, the table below shows projected enemy losses. Only when the projection is based on recent peak losses does the rate of enemy losses exceed the rate at which MACV and USIB agree the enemy can go on replacing them indefinitely, and then only by 139 per week for the MACV "minimum essential" force, and 431 for the "optimum" force. Even at a decrease in enemy forces of 431 per week, over 10 years would be needed to eliminate the enemy.

ESTIMATED WEEKLY ENEMY LOSSES FOR DIFFERENT FORCE LEVELS

	Program IV force	MACV "minimum essential" force	MACV "optimal" force
Peak losses a/	3188	3404	3696
Avg. losses b/	2121	2265	22460

DIA USIB estimate of enemy capability to sustain losses indefinitely = 3265.

a/ Based on January-March 1967 enemy losses to all causes.
b/ Based on CY 66.

However, just as we can control our aircraft losses, there is clear evidence that the enemy has considerable control over his ground force losses. He is hurt most often when he chooses to assault U.S. forces (e.g., Junction City). On large operations, stealth is impossible. Consequently over 90% of the large firefights that develop in such operations are initiated by the enemy, and in over 80% of the cases there is a clear indication of a planned enemy attack. The enemy can probably hold his losses (all causes) to about 2000 per week regardless of our force levels or operations. Additional forces cannot defeat him so long as he has the will, some popular support and we lack timely intelligence.

Additional forces will not help the pacification task measurably. This cannot be accomplished with 480,000 or 560,000 U.S. military forces and probably not at all without (1) a far more effective Revolutionary Development (RD) program supported by Vietnamese forces and (2) a more stable and progressive GVN, both of which will require patience and emphasis on political-economic objectives rather than military ones. It is clear from the USMC experience in I CTZ that U.S. forces can deny VC control but cannot secure the population. There were fewer people in the "secured" category in I CTZ at the end of CY 66 than at the beginning.

Our experience in Operation FAIRFAX just west and south of Saigon further supports the conclusion that in spite of good intentions and good actions, the U.S. military cannot undertake pacification and expect to withdraw after a short period, leaving the area secure. In FAIRFAX, still being conducted, 3 U.S. battalions were "temporarily" deployed with 3 ARVN battalions to secure the area near Saigon. The U.S. battalions are still engaged $2\frac{1}{2}$ months longer than planned and will be for the foreseeable future. Fewer than 1 VC per U.S. battalion-equivalent per day has been killed, most of the VC infrastructure has temporarily moved out of the area but has not been captured, the U.S. has made many friends (but of unknown longevity), the ARVN made few friends and actually look worse than before, after comparison with the Americans, and the populace in general are reserving judgment until they know the VC have left permanently. Part of the reason for ARVN ineffectiveness is lack of supplies and support-items (e.g., barbed wire) which the U.S. troops had in ample supply. We would be much better off to provide the GVN with such supplies rather than deploy additional U.S. forces.

In brief, the additional forces are likely neither
to reduce the enemy force nor contribute significantly to
pacification. These goals can only be met by improving
the efficiency of the forces already deployed and, particularly, that of ARVN. But additional U.S. forces decrease
the incentive to MACV and the GVN to make the Vietnamese
shoulder a larger portion of the burden. The RVNAF appear
to have done well by all statistical measures in IV CTZ,
where they have been provided only logistical and combat
support by the U.S., and very badly in the other areas
where the U.S. has taken over the war while denying them
significant support. 8/

Finally, it returned to the "old" piaster issue which had proven
such a potent instrument of control earlier during the Program 4
deliberations:

Additional forces will also damage the SVN economy,
as we saw when Program 4 was approved. Inflation in
January-March 1967 was 20%. Even apart from the rice
situation, prices were up 7%, or 28% on an annual basis.
The inflation still hits hardest GVN civilian and military personnel, on whom we must rely to eventually pacify
the country.

MACV, of course, appears to be doing a good job of
holding down piaster spending. Program 4 forces now
appear to cost P41.0 billion in CY 67, after correcting
for an apparent reporting errors and MACV might be able
to hold to about P44 billion in CY 68 even with increased
forces. Nevertheless, the SVN economy is still far from
sound, and more forces compound the problem. 9/

It closed by carefully listing the following recommendations:

1. That additional forces for SEA not be approved
and the currently approved Program #4 ceiling be firmly
maintained.

2. MACV be directed to submit a plan by Aug 1,
1967 to enhance the effectiveness of the RVNAF forces.
In the long term the RVNAF must assume a greater role for
maintaining the security of SVN. The longer the task is
delayed, the more difficult it becomes. We have made the
Koreans into an effective fighting force, and we must do
the same for the RVNAF. They can do the job far better and
cheaper than we can, and they will remain after we leave.

3. MACV be directed to submit a plan by the same
date, to increase the effectiveness of approved US and
FWMAF forces. This should include consideration of changes
in tactical employment (e.g., greater use of long-range
patrols, fewer battalions in static defense, and more
efficient use of available helicopter resources).

4. Consideration be given by MACV, CINCPAC, and
the JCS and OSD of possible steps to reduce the cost of
our efforts in SEA. The conflict is almost certainly
going to be a long one. If we expect the American public
to support such an effort for an extended period of time
we must hold the costs to an acceptable level. 10/

The draft included two tables, one a summary of deployments to
Southeast Asia and the other a breakout of the additional MACV requirements request. These are shown in the tables on pages 111 and 112.

SUMMARY DEPLOYMENTS TO SEA

	Program #4			FY 1968 MACV Requirement b/	
	1967		1968	Minimum	Optimum
	June	Dec	June	Essential	
Personnel SVN (000)	441.0	473.2	482.6	558.9	676.4
US Maneuver Bns	82	90	90	108	130
Artillery Bns	$56\frac{2}{3}$	$59\frac{2}{3}$	$61\frac{2}{3}$	$75\frac{2}{3}$	$89\frac{2}{3}$
Engineer Bns	53	54	53	67	79
Fighter-Attack A/c (US)	999	1042	1002	1146	1182
InCountry Naval Vessels	381	424	430	589	589
Piaster Expenditures (6 months ending) a/	20.3	20.3	20.0	23.2	29.0

a/ OASD(SA) Estimate

b/ Level off cost for 6-month period. Includes CINCPAC estimated contract construction.

Additional MACV Requirements

	Minimum Essential a/	Optimum b/
Strength (000)	84.1 c/	201.6
Maneuver Bns	21	43 c/
Divisions	(2)	(3)
Brigades	(1)	(5)
Artillery Bns	15	28
Engineer Bns	14	26
Tactical Fighter	8	13
APB (Barracks Ships)	3	3
ARL (Repair Ship)	2	2
RAS (River Assault Sqds)	2	2
LST	9	10
PBR (River Patrol Boats)	50	50

a/ Required by 30 June 1968. Includes Practice Nine Forces (7822
personnel) approved on 8 Apr 67.

b/ Includes "Minimum Essential;" required ASAP, assumed to be 31 December
1968.

c/ JCS recommend 1 USMC and 1 USAR division if reserves are called,
adding 12,300 personnel.

NOTE: Includes organic as well as non-organic units.

Enthoven was given the final draft just discussed on the 28th.
He was not completely satisfied with the basic thrust of the paper --
to him it did not adequately emphasize the deeper political and psychological issues bound up in seemingly endless troop increases with little
or no promise of ultimate success. The Assistant Secretary sat down
and drafted an outline for a final memorandum he intended to take to
Mr. McNamara. In it he cogently laid out his opposition to further
increases and the reasons why. He believed that "adding 200,000
Americans" would not do anything significant, considering that:

    ...(a) VC/NVA losses don't go up in proportion to
our forces; they haven't in past 18 mos.

    (b) even if they did, additional 200,000 U.S.
forces wouldn't put VC/NVA losses above their ability to
sustain or their willingness to accept.

    (c) Our studies indicate VC/NVA control their
losses, within wide limits. They start most fights.
Their losses go up when they're attacking. 11/

The final point as to whether the VC/NVA could control their ground
force losses within wide limits was based upon a Systems Analysis study
of small unit engagements during 1966. 12/ In the study, SA concluded
that: 13/

OFFICE OF THE ASSISTANT SECRETARY OF DEFENSE
SECRETARY OF DEFENSE   WASHINGTON, D. C. 20301

4 MAY 1967

SYSTEMS ANALYSIS

MEMORANDUM FOR SECRETARY OF DEFENSE

SUBJECT: Force levels and enemy attrition (U)

Although MACV has admitted to you that the VC/NVA forces can refuse to
fight when they want to, this fact has played no role in MACV's analysis of
strategy and force requirements. (For example, in his October 1965 briefing, General DePuy said, "The more often we succeed at (search and destroy
operations) the less often will the VC stand and fight.") Because enemy
attrition plays such a central role in MACV's thinking, and because the
enemy's degree of control over the pace of the action determines how well
he can control his attrition, we have taken a hard look at the facts on
the enemy's tactical initiative. From reliable, detailed accounts of 56
platoon-sized and larger fire-fights in 1966 we have classified these
fights according to how they developed. The first four categories in the
table all represent cases in which the enemy willingly and knowingly stood
and fought in a pitched battle; these categories include 47 (84%) of the
56 battles. The first three categories, enemy ambushes and assaults on our
forces, have 66% of the cases; these three plus category 4a, comprising the
cases where the enemy has the advantage of surprise, have 78% of the cases.

The results are independently confirmed from two sources. First, the
ARCOV study, which analyzed a different set of battles in late 1965 and
early 1966, found that 46% of the fights begin as enemy ambushes and that
the enemy starts the fight in 88% of the cases; moreover, it found that
63% of the infantry targets encountered were personnel in trenches or
bunkers. Second, we have analyzed the After-Action Reports submitted to
MACV by the line commanders in the field; although generally vague and incomplete in their descriptions of what happened, they broadly confirm the
drift of the above numbers.

These results imply that the size of the force we deploy has little
effect on the rate of attrition of enemy forces. This conclusion should
scarcely surprise you in view of the trend of enemy losses in 1966 and in
view of the obvious sensitivity of month-to-month enemy losses to his
known strategic initiatives. What is surprising to me is that MACV has
ignored this type of information in discussing force levels. I recommend
that you inject this factor into the discussion.

GROUP 4
Downgraded at 3 year inte:
declassified after 12 ye.
DOD Dir. 5200.10

Alain Enthoven
Assistant Secretary of Defense

Enclosure

The table entitled: "Types of Enemy Engagements Described in Combat Narratives," (below) presents the study data in tabular form:

TYPE OF ENGAGEMENTS DESCRIBED IN COMBAT NARRATIVES

Category Description	Nr. of Engagements	Percent of Total	Percent Subtotals
1. Hot Landing Zone. Enemy attacks U.S. troops as they deploy onto the battlefield.	7	12.5	
2. Organized enemy attack against a U.S. static defense perimeter.	17	30.4	
3. VC/NVA ambush or encircle and surprise a moving U.S. unit, using what is evidently a preconceived battle plan.	13	23.3	
			66.2
4. A moving U.S. unit engages the enemy in a dug-in or fortified position:			
a. The main engagement comes as a virtual surprise to the American tactical commander because the enemy is well concealed and has been alerted either by observations of our unit or by our engaging apparent stragglers nearby.	7	12.5	
			78.7
b. The U.S. tactical commander has reasonably accurate knowledge of enemy positions and strength before committing his forces.	3	5.4	
			84.1
5. U.S. unit ambushes a moving enemy unit.	5	8.9	
6. Chance engagement, both sides surprised.	4	7.1	
TOTAL	56	100.1	

TOP SECRET - Sensitive

The United States could not adequately "pacify" either, in Enthoven's estimation, but it could provide an "umbrella" against VC/NVA main forces. He assumed our forces were adequate for that based on:

    (a) experience of past year (VC/NVA haven't won a battle; they've taken heavy losses trying)

    (b) look at force ratios, corps by corps and consider our firepower/mobility advantage on top of that. 14/

The finished memorandum as it emerged provided a powerful set of reasons for holding the ground force line: 15/

TOP SECRET - Sensitive

Draft #1
RMurray/hap
May 1, 1967

MEMORANDUM FOR SECRETARY OF DEFENSE

SUBJECT: Increase of SEA Forces

MACV has asked for a "minimum essential force" which would add
2-1/3 divisions, 8 tactical fighter squadrons, and 85,000 personnel
to Program 4. His "optimum force" would add 4-2/3 divisions, 13
tactical fighter squadrons, and 200,000 personnel, for a total of
about 670,000 in SVN.

MACV/JCS offer no analysis to show that these extra forces are
needed to avoid defeat, or even that they are likely to achieve any
specific goal. But I am concerned far less about this unfortunate
lack of analysis than I am by the whole strategy which such a massive
increase in combat forces must imply.

Though the North Vietnamese are indeed communists, we have come
up against something more than just Marxism. We are facing the
strongest political current in the world today: nationalism. That
is the force which welds the North Vietnamese together, just as it
does so many other peoples today.

Having seen both the Japanese and the French come and go, the
North Vietnamese are now fighting the United States. For their little
country to triumph finally over the greatest nation the world has ever
known would surely serve as the ultimate vindication of nationalism
as a policy. Enticed by this goal, and hardened by 25 years of more-or-
less continuous fighting, the North Vietnamese will, I fear, continue

to endure great hardship. We have hurt them with our bombing, and we can hurt them more. But we can't hurt them so badly as to destroy their society or, more to the point, their hope, not only for regaining the material things they sacrifice today, but the whole of South Vietnam.

But how can they hope to beat this great nation? As MACV himself said before the Congress, the enemy "believes our Achilles heel is our resolve." They believe that public opinion in the United States will eventually force our retirement. And they could be right.

As for our own goals, I see only one way of establishing stability in Vietnam. We must match the nationalism we see in the North with an equally strong and patient one in the South. No matter what military success we may achieve, if we leave before that is done, there can be no stability, and we will have lost everything we have invested in South Vietnam. Indeed, we will jeopardize much of the general stability in the world which we bought at the price of the Korean War.

Therefore, I see this war as a race between, on the one hand, the development of a viable South Vietnam and, on the other, a gradual loss in public support, or even tolerance, for the war. Hanoi is betting that we'll lose public support in the United States before we can build a nation in South Vietnam. We must do what we can to make sure that doesn't happen. We must work on both problems together: slow the loss in public support; and speed the development of South Vietnam. Our horse must cross the finish first.

With regard to public support, some people feel we simply have no business being in this war, while others are just against all wars. We can't do much about that. But there are other factors influencing

3

public support that we can control. Casualties are one. Diversion of the national wealth from badly needed domestic programs is another. But the biggest of all may well be escalation.

Since 1961, and particularly since 1965, the public has seen an apparently unending escalation of this war. This must have a strong psychological effect. There must be many who are more concerned about the unbroken upward movement of spending and casualty rates than they are about the current levels. Our escalation is designed to put pressure on the North Vietnamese. But they may be more resolved to withstand it than the United States electorate is. I believe that's the basis of Hanoi's strategy.

If MACV's additional forces are approved, our casualty rate may not rise, but our expenditure rate certainly will, and the ominous history of unending escalation will be maintained. That combination will reduce public support, and we will have even less time to develop a strong nation in the South.

With regard to developing that nation, more United States forces aren't going to solve the pacification problem. In spite of the Marines' ability to deny the Viet Cong control of an area, there were fewer people in the "Secured" category in I Corps at the end of 1966 than at the beginning. In Operation Fairfax, southwest of Saigon, the 3 U.S. battalions which were "temporarily" deployed with 3 ARVN battalions to secure the area were supposed to leave $2\frac{1}{2}$ months ago. But they are still there, and will be for the foreseeable future. The kill rate per U.S. battalion-equivalent has been less than one V.C. per day, and most of the V.C. infrastructure has evaded capture by

4

moving out. Though the U.S. forces have made many friends (of unknown loyalty), the ARVN has made few and, in comparison with the Americans, the ARVN has lost prestige in the eyes of the populace, who are still worried that the V.C. may return.

Part of the reason for the ineffectiveness of the ARVN is a lack of supplies and support items, such as barbed wire, which the U.S. forces have in abundance. While more U.S. forces would bring more barbed wire, that's doing it the hard way. The pacification program depends, instead, on better support for Vietnamese forces and a more energetic national Government. This program requires not only time and patience, but political and economic progress rather than military victories.

As we saw when Program 4 was approved, additional forces are a burden on the South Vietnamese economy. Inflation in the first 3 months of 1967 alone amounted to 20%. Even apart from the rice situation, prices rose 7%, or 28% on an annual basis. MACV is doing a good job in holding down piaster spending. It looks like the Program 4 forces will cost P41 billion in 1967, and MACV might be able to hold to P44 billion in 1968, even with increased forces. Nevertheless, the SVN economy is still far from sound, additional forces would mean slower progress, and the inflation would still hit hardest on the very civilian and military personnel on whom we must rely if pacification is ever to succeed.

Furthermore, if we continue to add forces and to Americanize the war, we will only erode whatever incentives the South Vietnamese people

5

may now have to help themselves in this fight. Similarly, it would be a further sign to the South Vietnamese leaders that we will carry any load, regardless of their actions. That will not help us build a strong nation.

If you agree that more U.S. forces would speed the "horse" that is carrying public opinion toward rejection of the war, while slowing the "horse" carrying the development of a strong nation in the South, the only justification left would be to achieve other military objectives, of which I can imagine four:

1) To deter a Communist Chinese invasion. I see no sign of a change in Communist Chinese intentions. Were they to invade, they would face a formidable force already in place, and more available if needed, particularly with mobilization. Furthermore, I feel that the very nationalism which drives the North Vietnamese also inhibits them from calling in the same Chinese who have subjugated them in the past.

2) To prevent a military defeat in South Vietnam. I do not think there is danger of any significant military defeat, given the forces we have in place now. I have attached an appendix to this memorandum which shows that we already enjoy favorable force ratios.

3) To prevent terrorism. Though there is terrorism in South Vietnam now, I doubt that additional U.S. combat forces would significantly reduce it. This is a job for police-type forces, not maneuver battalions.

4) To raise VC/NVA losses to a level they cannot sustain. Presumably, this would be something above the weekly loss rate of 3,265 which the DIA/USIB estimate they can swallow indefinitely.

On the most optimistic basis, 200,000 more Americans would raise their weekly losses to about 3,700, or about 400 a week more than they could stand. In theory, we'd then wipe them out in 10 years. But to bank on that, you have to assume that (1) enemy losses are just proportional to friendly strength, and (2) that the unusually favorable kill ratio of the first quarter of 1967 will continue. However, if the kill ratio should be no better than the 1966 average, their losses would be about 2,100 -- less than 2/3 of their sustaining capability.

But even that figure is misleading. Losses just aren't directly related to the size of our force. Between the first and fourth quarters of 1966, our forces increased 23%, but their losses increased only 13% -- little more than half as much.

Finally, the most important factor of all is that the enemy can control his losses within wide limits. The VC/NVA started the shooting in over 90% of the company-sized fire fights; over 80% began with a well-organized enemy attack. Since their losses rise (as in the first quarter of 1967) and fall (as they have done since) with their choice of whether or not to fight, they can probably hold their losses to about 2,000 a week regardless of our force levels. If, as I believe, their strategy is to wait us out, they will control their losses to a level low enough to be sustained indefinitely, but high enough to tempt us to increase our forces to the point of U.S. public rejection of the war.

In summary, I feel that adding more U.S. combat forces would be a step in the wrong direction. They are not needed for military security,

7

and they could not force higher losses on the North Vietnamese. But they might play right into the hands of Hanoi by burdening the United States and increasing internal opposition to the war, while delaying the birth of the strong nation in the South which is our only hope of real stability. Therefore, I recommend the following:

1) Maintain the Program 4 ceiling.

2) Tell the electorate that, barring the unexpected, we'll stick with the present forces which are all we need, not only to stop the VC/NVA militarily, but also to exact a high price from Hanoi. Tell them that our "escalation" will now turn toward the building of a nation which will be strong enough to bring a natural stability to Vietnam so that we can leave for good.

3) Tell MACV to start making good analyses of his operations and feeding them back into his planning so that we can get more out of not only the U.S. and allied forces, but the ARVN as well.

4) Find ways to reduce costs for the long haul ahead. For example, cut back on the costly but ineffective bombing north of Route Package 4.

I know it's much easier to write down these recommendations than it is to get agreement on carrying them out. But I think we're up against an enemy who just may have found a dangerously clever strategy for licking the United States. Unless we recognize and counter it now, that strategy may become all too popular in the future.

A.E.

Enclosure

Attached as an Appendix to the basic memorandum was also a detailed, corps by corps, analysis of COMUSMACV's minimum force requirement. Not only did this analysis question the calculations that had furnished the basis of the requirements but it criticized the unselective and unquantified goals: infiltration to be impeded, invasion deterred or defeated, TAORs expanded and joined, enemy driven to the hinterlands, base areas destroyed, LOC's secured, RD programs expanded, and GVN control extended.

The thrust of its conclusions was that emphasis should be placed not upon more forces, but upon employing the ones we already had in SVN more effectively.

In detail, it explicated the Systems Analysis view of how COMUSMACV's employment of forces by Corps could be improved: 16/

COMUSMACV's Minimum Force
Requirement - An Analysis

Ground Forces

MACV indicated on 18 March, and in Appendix B to JCSM 218-67, that
his minimum essential needs are 2-1/3 divisions for I CTZ. He now proposes
that 1-1/3 divisions go to I CTZ to supplement 2 brigades moved from III
CTZ, (a total of 2 divisions instead of 2-1/3) and 1 division goes to III
CTZ. The III CTZ thus gains one brigade on balance.

The 1-1/3 more divisions in I CTZ appears excessive for the mission.
The total threat to I CTZ is only 95,000 VC/NVA personnel, including
irregulars and political infrastructure. There are already more than
200,000 friendly forces there, not counting the 2 SLF battalions earmarked
for I CTZ support. Any invasion by the NVA divisions now near the DMZ
could easily be held with the forces now deployed and available to MACV.
Calculations indicate that the 2 Army brigades already sent to I CTZ plus
one more brigade (already in Program 4 for PRACTICE NINE) should be adequate to hold the DMZ and to extend the Marine tactical area of responsibility (TAOR) throughout the coastal plains area of I CTZ. Uncertainties
and other calculations may well produce different results, but informal
USMC staff review indicated our calculations were reasonable. In any
event, these calcualations are reproducible.

The MACV requirement is based on no known calculations. It is based
on unselective and unquantified goals: infiltration to be impeded,
invasion deterred or defeated, TAORs expanded and joined, enemy driven
to hinterlands, base areas destroyed, LOCs secured, RD programs expanded,
and GVN control extended.

The division for III CTZ is justified by MACV to replace the 9th
division, always designated for IV CTZ, not III CTZ. Nonetheless he could
have argued that at least 2/3rd of the division is required to replace the
2 brigades sent to I CTZ. There is no evidence that the programmed III CTZ
forces, without the 2 brigades but with the additional brigade equivalent
now programmed (1 more Australian bn, an airborne bn, and an armored
cavalry squadron) is inadequate; or that added forces could accomplish
more. The force ration would still be about 345,000 friendly to 74,000
enemy (4.7 to 1). In addition there is a mechanized battalion programmed
for IV CTZ that might well be used more effectively in II CTZ. Moreover,
the way III CTZ forces are employed, in multi-divisional operations of
the Junction City/Manhattan variety, should be analyzed with great care
before additional forces are even considered. Our analysis has shown that
present forces could be employed more effectively (and at less cost) if
greater emphasis were given small unit operations.

Furthermore, it is not clear that the entire 9th Division should be afloat, one brigade at the Dong Tam Base and one brigade at a base in III Corps (in addition to the separate mechanized battalion). These forces, working with the ARVN, should be adequate to counter the VC main force units and provide needed security for the RD effort. The threat in IV Corps is primarily from small units and guerrillas and should be encountered on that level, not with multi-brigade operations.

A greater return can probably be realized by giving the ARVN better support rather than increasing the size of the U.S. forces. The 2 ARVN divisions in IV Corps have less than half the artillery support of U.S. forces; five 105/155mm tubes and no heavy artillery tubes per ARVN battalion (in U.S. Army battalion equivalents) compared to ten 105/155mm tubes plus two and one half 175mm and 8" tubes per battalion for the U.S. Army forces. In addition, the amount of tactical air and armed helicopter support provided the ARVN forces country-wide is meager compared to that provided U.S. forces. During the 4th quarter of 1966 each U.S. battalion received about 500 hours per month of UH-1 support versus only 120 hours per battalion-equivalent for ARVN. In IV Corps the ARVN received 280 hours per battalion per month; in the other corps areas only 60 hours. There is no indication MACV has the same sense of urgency about increasing ARVN effectiveness as it has about increasing the number of U.S. forces.

This same document provided an alternative approach to calculating
the minimum essential force. It is quoted in its entirety below, for
it argues that given new objectives (those of preventing military disaster
and providing time for ARVN first to improve and then do its job) the
minimum essential force was 28 battalions smaller than that already
programmed in Program 4! 17/   (Again, assuming that the present enemy
threat remained constant.) The approach read:

ALTERNATIVE APPROACH TO CALCULATING THE MINIMUM ESSENTIAL FORCE

U.S. objectives in SVN require U.S. and FWMAF forces
sufficient to prevent military disaster and to provide time
for the ARVN first to improve and then to do its job. This
force is 28 battalions smaller than the Program 4 force for
the present enemy threat.

Before U.S. intervention, the VC decimated and demoral-
ized the ARVN reaction and reserve force by successful
ambushes and attacks. The 17 US/FW battalions deployed by
July 1965 ended the deteriorating trend. In both I CTZ and
II CTZ, VC control over the population peaked by July 1965,
and it declined even earlier in III and IV CTZ.

Since then, the enemy increased from 99 to 151 infantry-
type battalions at the end of December 1966. As of 31 December 1966 we had 98 infantry-type battalions, more than enough
to counter the enemy force considering the intelligence available. Of the 98 battalions 34 were engaged in TAOR patrol;
46 were engaged in operations that were initiated by hard
intelligence; and the 18 others were predictably unproductive.
The 46 battalions were obviously sufficient to counter the 151
VC/NVA infantry-type battalions, witness the total lack of
enemy success. This suggests that we need 1 battalion for
each 3 enemy infantry-type battalions, in addition to those
needed for static defense. The 18 battalions ineffectively
employed plus the 10 additional infantry-type battalions in
Program 4 that close after January 1, 1967 are enough to
counter 84 additional enemy bns. Thus we need deploy no
more forces until the enemy goes above 235 battalions,
which does not seem to be his present intent. (The enemy
peak was 155 infantry-type bns in July 1966, and was 147
at 31 March 1967).

127

US/FW Force Requirement

Enemy Force	Required Mobile US/FW Force	US/FW Force for TAOR Patrols	Total Required U.S. Force
151	46	34	80
235	74	34	108

The 3 to 1 ratio is supported by results in battle. Our forces routinely defeat enemy forces outnumbering them two or three to one. In no instance has a dug-in U.S. company been overrun, regardless of the size of the attacking enemy force, and nothing larger than a company has come close to annihilation when caught moving. Seven battalions of Marines defeated two NVA divisions in HASTINGS, and single battalions of 1st Air Cavalry defeated regimental-sized forces in pitched battles in the Ia Drang Valley in the Fall of 1965.

These factors need confirmation, in actual practice, by how well the forces are doing in the field and by progress in RD. VC/NVA military victories and large areas succumbing to VC require a reaction regardless of calculated force requirements. But there is no sign of anything like that in the foreseeable future. Moreover, a sharp improvement in our effectiveness should result from improvements in the flow of intelligence and in the tactical employment of our forces. Achieving such improvements should be the main objective at this time. 18/

So armed, on May Day Enthoven carried the finished memorandum to McNamara's office and proceeded to discuss its contents. However, probably not to his surprise, he found that McNamara was thinking along the same lines -- in fact, he had already set John McNaughton to preparing a Draft Presidential Memorandum setting forth the same basic political arguments that Systems Analysis was making. The "hard" data in the Enthoven memorandum was the kind of back-up McNamara understood and appreciated and it buttressed most of the beliefs he already held. He asked Enthoven for some detailed follow-up related to VC/NVA control of engagements and casualties. There is no record that the Assistant Secretary left the signed memorandum with the Secretary of Defense, but there seemed little requirement for that. The ideas and position in it had been escalated to the DPM level where such ideas would receive the highest level attention and consideration. 19/

2. A New Look At the "Plimsoll Line": Alternatives to Increases Restudied

Shortly after the first hard signs of resistance began to surface in May an SNIE analyzing Soviet attitudes and intentions toward the Vietnam war was published. It was an SNIE which in effect reinforced the fears which many held about increasing the intensity of the Vietnamese conflict. The SNIE concluded that at some point the USSR would create an atmosphere of heightened tension with the United States if, in fact, U.S. force increases and intensified bombing continued. In the words of the estimate:

> The Soviets might take certain actions designed to bolster North Vietnam and possibly to warn the United States such as the provision of limited numbers of volunteers or crews for defense equipment or possibly aircraft. They might also break off negotiations with the United States on various subjects and suspend certain agreements now in effect. The mining or the blockade of the North Vietnamese coast would be most likely to provoke these responses, since this would constitute a direct challenge to the Soviets and there would be little they could do on the scene. 20/

This document, coming as it did at such a crucial juncture in the deliberations over ground force strategy and deployments in Vietnam, had a significant impact upon the thinking of those charged with making the decision of "go" or "no go," and the document itself was quoted throughout some of the explicit development of alternatives which followed its publication in both Systems Analysis and in ISA.

As McNaughton worked on a series of drafts preparing the 19 May DPM which was to follow, a number of leads were being pursued throughout the government, all related in some way to relieving the pressures for more United States troops in Vietnam. One of these was a directed effort to obtain more allied troops especially from the nations on the periphery of South Vietnam or near Southeast Asia. On 4 May McNaughton asked that an analysis of South Vietnamese troop deployments in relation to population of the participating countries be prepared. This analysis, based upon population of the countries involved, concluded that for an increase of 100,000 U.S. troops the "allocable" share for various countries would range from 14.5 thousand for Korea to 53.4 thousand for Indonesia. For the details of this particular study see the following table: 21/

ATTACHMENT V
(5/4/67)

SVN TROOP DEPLOYMENTS IN RELATION TO POPULATION
(Population in Millions; Troops in Thousands)

	Population	Current or Approved Strength in SVN		Increase Required To	"Allocable" Share Per
		No.	Per Million of Population	Meet US Ratio	100,000 US Troops b/
US	200	470 a/	2.35	--	100.0
Korea	29.1	45.8	1.57	22.6	14.5
Australia	11.7	6.1	0.52	21.4	5.8
New Zealand	2.7	0.5	0.18	5.8	1.3
Philippines	33.5	2.1	0.06	76.6	16.7
Thailand	33.4	0.3	0.01	78.2	16.7
Indonesia	106.9	--	--	251.2	53.4
Rep of China	13.2	--	--	31.0	6.6
Malaysia	9.8	--	--	23.0	4.9
	440.3	524.8		509.7	219.9

a/ Excludes naval forces in South China Sea and US forces in Thailand.
b/ 100,000 troops represents 500 per 1,000,000 of US population. "Allocable" shares for other nations are calculated on this basis.

Somewhat along the same line, on 11 May, Walt W. Rostow prepared
a paper devoted to what he termed a "troop community chest operation
for Vietnam." Rostow had seen the ISA Annex which we just mentioned,
and commented that he felt that a project that Bill Leonhart had been
working on which related to Vietnamese force deployments to the level
of each contributor's armed forces might be more meaningful and realistic
plus having the very desirable characteristic of being more negotiable
because it would require no country to increase its total armed forces
in order to send troops to Vietnam. The table that he attached to the
paper showed that if each country dispatched the same percentage of its
total armed forces to Vietnam as the United States had done, about 14%,
that there would now be an additional 70,000 troops in that country.
Furthermore, if you asked each country to contribute an increment to
match an additional United States increase of 100,000, and if those
increments represented the same percentage of each country's total
armed forces, then the result would read something like this: Korea -
18,700; Australia - 2,000; New Zealand - 400; Thailand - 4,000; and
the Philippines - 1,300; for a total of 126,400 troops added. This
approach is interesting because later in July President Johnson was to
begin "arm twisting" a number of national Heads of State, and the force
totals developed here by Leonhart provided the base line from which he
negotiated. 22/

The other events of note, both directed at increasing the effectiveness of American forces already in Vietnam, occurred during early
May. The first was the issuance of NSAM 362, entitled "Responsibility
for U.S. Role in Pacification," in which Mr. R. W. Komer was appointed
the Deputy for Pacification (Revolutionary Development) with the personal
rank of Ambassador to operate under COMUSMACV. This, as we noted earlier,
was partially the outcome of President Johnson's desire to get the
pacification program back on the track. Komer as well as most of the
officials concerned with the decision, had known that this development
was coming since the time of the Guam Conference. In the NSAM the
President noted:

> Our purpose of unifying responsibility for Pacifica-
> tion (RD) under COMUSMACV is to permit logistic and admin-
> istrative economies through consolidation and cross-
> servicing. I expect sensible steps to be taken in this
> direction. Any inter-agency jurisdictional or other
> issues which may arise in country will be referred to the
> U.S. Ambassador....

> This new organizational arrangement represents an
> unprecedented melding of civil and military responsibil-
> ities to meet the overriding requirements of Viet Nam.

Declassified per Executive Order 13526, Section 3.3
NND Project Number: NND 63316. By: NWD Date: 2011

Therefore, I count on all concerned -- in Washington and
in Viet Nam -- to pull together in the national interest
to make this arrangement work. 23/

This NSAM, of course, represented the fruition of what had been a
long-standing recommendation to consolidate Revolutionary Development
under the individual who possessed primary responsibility and controlled
the resources, COMUSMACV. However, in the estimation of many, especially
those who evaluated its later effectiveness and tried to determine
whether or not any real good had been accomplished by the reorganization,
it represented yet one more instance of the American penchant for
organizational tinkering, one which usually relieved the people making
the organizational changes from really getting down and rooting out
the basic causes of the problem. 24/ The other interesting evaluation
concerned the question of what level of combat service support staffing
there should be in South Vietnam. In April, a number of studies were
made, all designed to try to determine whether the level of combat
service support was too high, about correct, or needed some revision in
the upward direction. 25/

Mr. Victor K. Heyman, Director of the SEA Programs Division in
the Office of the Assistant Secretary of Defense (Systems Analysis),
toured the Vietnam area in early May and visited the First Logistical
Command. He was concerned generally whether manning levels were adequate
to the task assigned by COMUSMACV, and, specifically, whether or not
the new peak level of 70,000 men to be reached during Program 4 was
excessive. In his trip report, he observed that the Army Program 4
strength of 322,000 included only 66,000 men in maneuver battalions.
Furthermore, if combat support, aviation companies, advisors, special
forces, division and brigade staffs, and construction battalions were
added, these increases would bring the "combat" total to only 165,000
men or 51% of the total Army force. He felt that the balance of 157,000
in other units appeared excessive and recommended to Secretary McNamara
that the JCS be asked to analyze it.

In particular, United States Army Vietnam, First Logistical Command was scheduled to total, as we noted, approximately 70,000 men at
the peak of Program 4. This was the equivalent of nearly 5 Army divisions
or 70 infantry battalions. Furthermore, the First Log Command did not
include aviation supplies/maintenance units or construction battalions
and the substantial combat service support staffing which was organic
to divisions and separate brigades. To these increments must be added
the 40,000 man equivalent furnished by contractors, local national
employment and support from the off-shore bases. Although comparing
the services could be misleading because of different doctrines and
organizations, a rough comparison revealed that the Army ratio was
about one man in First Log Command to support 3.6 men in other USARV

units compared to a Navy-Marine Support ratio in 1st Corps Tactical
Zone of 1:5.6 men. In view of the different tactical situations (the
I CTZ one was more intensive combat) Heyman was led to conclude that a
detailed review of Army support should be made -- since simply comparing
the ratios suggested that 45,000 men might be adequate for the 1st Log
Command or that the Command need not be increased until USARV strength
exceeded 462,000 men. In view of this analysis, Heyman recommended
that Program 4 should be cut to its essentials to "improve the tooth
to tail rate" and that until the review which he had recommended had
been completed the Secretary of Defense should defer approval for deployment of any First Log Command units through August 1967. 26/

The Secretary of Defense approved this recommendation to defer
further incremental increases to First Log Command and asked the Joint
Chiefs of Staff to prepare a detailed study justifying added increases
and analyzing in depth the Combat Service Support Staffing levels in
South Vietnam. 27/

3. The Quest for Capabilities: The Search for Limits

Great emphasis in May focused upon capabilities, with particular
attention being paid to just what capabilities the services had to provide troops and units (or equivalents) below the point where they would
be reduced to calling upon reserves or drawing down units already in
Europe. On May 5, Systems Analysis forwarded a brief study to the
Secretary of Defense which analyzed the additional MACV requirements
and compared them to the estimated capability of the services to provide
matching units. The study, which concluded that the services had only
the capability to provide 66,000 of the 186,000 troops requested under
the MACV "Optimum Plan" and only 19 maneuver battalions of the 42
included in that larger plan is presented in the table on the following
pages. 28/

Additional MACV Requirements
and Estimated Capabilities
December 31, 1968

	MACV Optimum	Estimated Capability
Land Forces		
Strength (000)	186	66
Divisions	3	2/3 b/
Brigades	5	4 a/
Maneuver Bns	(42)	(19) a/
Artillery Bns	28	28
Engineer Bns	20	0 c/
Aviation Cos.	22	0 c/
Signal Bns	5	3 d/
Naval Forces		
Strength - In-country only (000)	8.5	8.3
Riverine Assault Forces		
APB (Barracks Ships)	3	3
ARL (Repair Ship)	2	2
AN (Net Tender)	1	1
RAS (River Assault Sq)	2	2 e/
River Patrol Forces		
PBR (River Patrol Boats)	50	50
Landing Ships		
LST (Tank Landing Ship)	10	0 f/
Gunfire Ships		
CA (Cruiser--8")	1	1 g/
DD (Destroyer--5")	5	5 h/
Construction Battalions		
NMCB	5	5
Tactical Air Forces		
Strength (000)	6.5	6.5
Tactical Fighter	13	13 i/
Construction Squadron	1	1
Total Personnel (000)	201	81

OASD(SA)
5 May 1967

134

a/ Includes one Armored Cavalry Regiment of 3 squadrons, and 9th MAB from Okin.

b/ 6 bns of 101st Abn plus 1 airborne tank bn

c/ Trained personnel not available under current rotation policy

d/ Further analysis may show more available

e/ Using 70 LCM-6s from war reserve.

f/ Five LSTs now scheduled for transfer to MSTS (Korean manning) can be retained and added to SEVENTH Fleet. No real increase in SEA lift would result.

g/ To meet this requirement indefinitely two ships must be activated. Four 8"-gun cruisers now in fleet can meet requirement through Oct '68. Activation of BB as recommended by SecNav would provide needed ship through April 1969. Second ship must be activated for operations after 1969.

h/ Destroyer requirement can be met in various ways: 1) increase the number of LANTFLT destroyers rotated to PACFLT. This can be done without affecting SIXTH Fleet deployments but would require a further increase in LANTFLT operations tempo; 2) Reactivate mothballed DDs; or 3) Use Naval Reserve Training Fleet (Cat. A) DDs and replace them with reactivated Mothballed DDs.

i/ Includes 11 Air Force and 2 Marine squadrons. The 11 Air Force TFS can be provided two ways: 1) Deploy 5 CONUS F-4, 1 F-111, 1 F-100 and 3 A-1 squadrons. The A-1 squadrons would be formed using surplus Navy aircraft; 2) 3 F-4 squadrons from WESTPAC could be deployed in lieu of the A-1 squadrons but this would necessitate 2 or 3 of the remaining 4 WESTPAC squadrons being returned to CONUS to augment the training base.

This document reflected the Secretary of Defense's immediate concern with trying to find maneuver battalions and troops within existing
service capabilities and trying to avoid approaching the personnel
"sound barrier" and that of having to call up reserves or to partially
mobilize units. As a check on this analysis, on 8 May Secretary McNamara
distributed the estimate to the services and asked their comments. On
12 May, General Johnson of the Army replied that the Army could probably
exceed the estimated capability by about 6 maneuver battalions. He based
this new estimate upon the assumption that procurement of critical items
of equipment could be accelerated by mid-year 1967, that some withdrawal
of equipment from the Reserve Components and non-deploying STRAF units
would be authorized and that some new methods would be developed to
accelerate the Army's ability to sustain forces in short tour areas. He
did not elaborate upon this final assumption, one which was to prove
one of the Army's primary personnel problems, that of either extending
the length of short tours or changing basic policies about consecutive
tours to these areas.

The upshot of all of this concern about capabilities was a May 18
memorandum prepared for the Secretary of Defense by Alain Enthoven,
Assistant Secretary of Defense for Systems Analysis. In it, he analyzed
and synthesized the information presented on the additional deployment
capability of the services. Crucially it noted that the Army had the
capability of providing 84,000 more troops, some 24,000 greater than
the original estimate which had been given to McNamara earlier in the
month. It included 21 maneuver battalions instead of 16. But, again,
this estimate was based upon the assumptions that the deployment of
the 5th Mechanized Division, then NATO-committed, and the rest of the
101st Airborne Division would be approved for deployment to SEA; that
an as yet unidentified improved solution to the rotation base problem
could be found and that there would be more and faster procurement of
equipment, especially helicopters. End strength increases for the
Army at the end of FY 69 were estimated to be 177,000 compared with the
110 to 120,000 which had been previously calculated. The increase by
December 1967 was to be 77,000 and by June 1968, 118,000. The latter
figure was about 70% of the strength required by December of 1968. 30/

The significance of the 18 May memorandum seems to be that it
said: within rather narrow limits the figure of 60 - 65,000 is the
Army's capability to provide troops in the form of maneuver battalions
properly equipped, ready for deployment within the time frame - all
below the requirement to mobilize the reserves. It also indicated that
the Air Force, although strained and possibly drawing down units in
Europe and other STRAF directed missions could meet the deployment
schedules within both the "optimum" and the "minimum essential" range,
although it would be preferable in the view of Harold Brown to meet
only the minimum essential requirement and to leave the TFS's which

were already assigned to NATO on that station. The 60,000 figure
which we just mentioned was to reappear later, much later in fact,
when Secretary McNamara travelled to Saigon in late July to "negotiate"
the new force levels for Program 5.

    4. <u>Bombing in the North: Its Contribution to the Ground War
Reexamined</u>

      In early May attention also focused on how the bombing campaign
in the North could better contribute to successful military outcomes in
the South. Three important memos appeared during the first week in May,
all devoted to this problem. On 5 May, in a draft memorandum for the
President, John McNaughton proposed that all of the sorties allocated
to the ROLLING THUNDER program be concentrated on the lines of communication, or what he called the "funnel" through which men and supplies to
the south must flow between 17-20°, while reserving the options and the
intention to strike in the area north of this (or in the 20-23° area) as
necessary to keep the enemy's investment in defense and in repair crews
high throughout the country. In arguing for this course of action, he
noted that General Wheeler, when General Westmoreland was in Washington
in April, had said that the bombing campaign was reaching the point
where all of the worthwhile fixed targets, except the ports had been
struck. McNaughton did not believe that the ports should be struck nor
closed by mining, primarily because of the confrontation which he saw
this might cause with the Soviet Union. Examining the bombing alternatives, he observed that we <u>could</u> continue to conduct attacks north
of the 20° parallel, that is continue striking minor fixed targets while
conducting armed reconnaissance against movement on roads, railroads
and waterways. This course, though, was costly in American lives and
in his estimation involved serious dangers of escalation, either with
the Chinese or the Russians. The loss rate in Hanoi/Haiphong Route
Package 6 for example was more than six times the loss rate in the
southernmost route packages 1 and 2, and actions in the Hanoi/Haiphong
area involved serious risks of generating confrontations with the Soviet
Union and China, both because they involved destruction of MIGs on the
ground and counters with MIGs in the air and because they might be
construed as U.S. intention to crush the Hanoi regime. The military
gain of the expanded bombing appeared to be slight; in fact, McNaughton
could locate no evidence at the time to establish some convincing connection between operations in the north against targets north of the
20° parallel and enemy actions in the South. Furthermore, if the United
States believed that air attacks in the area would change Hanoi's will,
they might have been worthwhile, he added, and consequently reduce the
loss of American life in the south and the risk of the expansion of the
war in the North. However, McNaughton noted there was no evidence that
this would be the case, for there was considerable evidence that such

bombing would strengthen Hanoi's will. He quoted Consul General Rice
of Hong Kong when he said that there was very little chance that by
bombing we could reach the critical level of pain in North Vietnam
and that "below that level pain only increases the will to fight." 31/
Robert Thompson had also been quoted as saying, when he was here in
late April, that our bombing, particularly in the Red River Basin area
was "unifying North Vietnam." The old argument that bombing in the
northern area was necessary to maintain the morale of the South Vietnamese or American fighting men was discounted. Although General
Westmoreland had fully supported attacks against targets in the Hanoi/
Haiphong areas and had said during his visit here in late April that
he was "frankly dismayed at even the thought of stopping the bombing
program," his basic requirements had continued to be requests for
attacks on what he called the extended battle zone near the DMZ. 32/

McNaughton's closing paragraphs in this memorandum indicate that
he was not only interested in trying to develop a better fit between
bombing operations in the North and ground operations in the South, but
that he was also clearing the way for getting Hanoi to change its position on negotiations. He noted that to optimize the chances of a
favorable Hanoi reaction to an American restriction of the bombing the
scenario should be:

> ...to inform the Soviets quietly (on May 15) that
> within a few (5) days the policy would be implemented,
> stating no time limits and making no promise not to
> return to the Red River basin to attack targets which
> later acquired military importance, and then...to make
> an unhuckstered shift as predicted on May 20. We would
> expect Moscow to pass the May 15 information on to Hanoi,
> perhaps (but probably not) urging Hanoi to seize the
> opportunity to de-escalate the war by talks or otherwise.
> Hanoi, not having been asked a question by us and having
> no ultimatum-like time limit, might be in a better posture
> to react favorably than has been the case in the past.
> Nevertheless, no favorable response from Hanoi should be
> expected, and the change in policy is not based on any
> such expectation. 33/

This policy, he recommended, should then publicly be handled by
explaining (1) that, as always, we had said the war must be won in the
south; (2) that we had never believed that the bombing of the war would
produce a settlement by breaking Hanoi's will or by shutting off the
flow of supplies; (3) that the north must pay the price for its infiltration; and (4) that since the major military targets in the north
had been destroyed we were now concentrating on the narrow neck through
which supplies must flow, sincerely believing that concentrated effort
there as compared with dispersed effort throughout NVN would increase

the efficiency of our interdiction effort; and that (5) we retained
the option to return further north and restrike those targets if military considerations so required. 34/

A White House memorandum, prepared by Walt Rostow, on the same
subject, essentially repeated what McNaughton had said. To Rostow the
policy issues and contention were first revolving around choices
involving the North and these, in turn, broke out to either: (a) closing
the top of the funnel - under this strategy he meant that we could mine
the major harbors and perhaps bomb port facilities and even consider a
blockade; in addition, attacks would be made systematically against the
rail lines between Hanoi and mainland China. He exhibited little confidence that this would have a very important effect upon the North Vietnamese war effort especially in light of the tremendous costs which he
anticipated, especially the political costs vis-a-vis the Soviet Union
and the Chinese Communists. He concluded for this expanded course of
action that tension between the United States and the Soviet Union and
Communist China would surely increase but that if we were very determined we could impose additional burdens on Hanoi and its allies, that
we might cut their capacity below requirements, but that the outcome
was uncertain; (b) attacking what was inside the funnel. This was
essentially what the Air Force and Navy had been trying in the Hanoi/
Haiphong area for some weeks. Rostow disagreed with the contention that
the attacks on the Hanoi-Haiphong area had no bearing on the war in the
south, a significant difference from what McNaughton believed. In Rostow's
estimation the North Vietnamese had diverted massive amounts of resources,
energies and attention throughout the civil and military establishment of
North Vietnam. This gross dislocation, in turn, imposed general economic,
political and psychological difficulties on the north during a period
already complicated by a bad harvest and some food shortages. He did
not accept the CIA assessment that the bombings in the North in fact
hardened the will of the people, and in his judgment, up to that point
our bombing had been a painful additional cost that they had been willing
to bear to pursue their efforts in the south. Although he acknowledged
that there were uncertainties about the eventual political costs of
expanded or continued bombing in the Hanoi-Haiphong area, he played down
what was becoming an increasingly attractive line of argument -- that the
continuation of attacks at about the level that we had been conducting
in Hanoi-Haiphong area would lead to increased Soviet pressure on Berlin
or even some kind of general war with the Soviet Union. In fact, in
Rostow's words, "What the Soviets have been trying to signal is - keep
away from our ships, we may counter escalate to some degree; but we do
not want a nuclear confrontation over Vietnam." 35/

The next alternative (c) that Rostow discussed was the one which
McNaughton had recommended -- that of concentrating our bombing efforts
in Route Packages 1 and 2. The advantages of these he saw would plainly

cut our loss rate in pilots and planes, that we might somewhat improve
our harassment of infiltration into South Vietnam, and that we would
diminish the risk of counter-escalatory action by the Soviet Union and
Communist China, as compared with the first two courses he had listed.
He did not recommend that we pursue Course A since the returns "did not
on present evidence seem high enough to justify the risk of Soviet-
Chinese countermeasures and heightened world tensions." 36/   In this,
he felt that he was supported by the conclusions of the majority of the
intelligence community. With respect to the second option which he had
outlined, he felt:

> ...I believe we have achieved greater results in
> increasing the pressure on Hanoi and raising the cost of
> their continuing to conduct the aggression in the South
> than some of my most respected colleagues would agree.
> I do not believe we should lightly abandon what we have
> accomplished; and specifically, I believe we should mount
> the most economical and careful attack on the Hanoi power
> station our air tacticians can devise. Moreover, 1
> believe we should keep open the option of coming back
> to the Hanoi-Haiphong area, depending upon what we learn
> of their repair operations; and what Moscow's and Peiping's
> reactions are; and especially when we understand better
> what effects we have and have not achieved thus far.

> I believe the Soviet Union may well have taken cer-
> tain counter-steps addressed to the more effective pro-
> tection of the Hanoi-Haiphong area and may have decided --
> or could shortly decide -- to introduce into North Viet Nam
> some surface-to-surface missiles. 37/

Rostow favored the third option ((c) - bombing below the 20°) because,
in his words, he felt that we were "wasting a good many pilots in the
Hanoi-Haiphong area without commensurate results and that the major objectives of maintaining the B option, or the restrikes back into the Hanoi-
Haiphong could be achieved at a lower cost." 38/

He, too, addressed the problem of presenting this to the American
public, noting that "we shall have to devise a way of presenting our
total policy in Vietnam in a manner which is consistent with diminished
attacks in the Hanoi-Haiphong area; which is honest; and which is acceptable
to our own people. Surfacing the concept of the barrier may be critical to
that turnaround as will be other measures to righten infiltration and
improve RVNAF pacification and that provision of additional allied forces
to permit Westy to get on with our limited but real role in pacification,
notably with the defense of I Corps in the North and the hounding of
provincial main force units." 39/

These three memos reflect the basic trend of thought reference
the bombing campaigns in the north as they developed in early May.
Later in May, as we shall see, the Joint Chiefs of Staff came in with
their proposals to "shoulder out" foreign shipping and mining in the
harbors in the north and for more intensive interdiction both north of
and below the 20th parallel against North Vietnam. This basic dispute
led to the preparation of a draft Presidential memorandum at the end
of May devoted to an analysis of the bombing and which provided policy
recommendations on it for the President. 40/

FOOTNOTES

1. Interview with Mr. Philip Odeen, SEA Programs, OASD(SA), on 27-28 August 1968.

2. Draft, "Additional MACV Force Requirements," dtd 23 March 1967, with attached note for Secretary McNamara.

3. Draft memorandum for the Secretary of Defense, Subject: "SEA Force Requirements," VK Heyman, dtd 28 April 1967.

4. Ibid.

5. Ibid.

6. Ibid.

7. Ibid.

8. Ibid.

9. Ibid.

10. Ibid.

11. Draft memorandum for the Secretary of Defense, Subject: "SEA Force Requirements," Alain Enthoven, 28 April 1967.

12. Memorandum from Alain Enthoven, ASD(SA) for the Secretary of Defense, Subject: "Force Levels and Enemy Attrition" dtd 4 May 1967.

13. Ibid.

14. Ibid.

15. OASD(SA) Memorandum for the Secretary of Defense, "Increase of Southeast Asia Forces," dtd 1 May 1967.

16. "COMUSMACV's Minimum Force Requirement -- An Analysis," undated, but attached to 1 May 1967 Memorandum to SecDef.

17. Ibid.

18. Ibid.

19. This account was provided by Mr. Philip Odeen of Systems Analysis in an interview on 20 July 1968.

20. SNIE 11-11-67, Subject: Soviet Attitudes and Intentions Toward the Vietnam War, dated 4 May 1967.

21. "South Vietnamese Troop Deployments in Relation to Population," Attachment 5, dated 4 May 1967. This attachment was prepared to be included in the 19 May DPM. However, it was removed from the paper and never forwarded along with the finished DPM.

22. Ibid.; See Memorandum for the President from W. W. Rostow, Subject: "Vietnam Force Level Sharing," dated 10 May 1967. One of the problems which periodically reappeared and was discussed reference asking for greatly increased contributions of allied troops was what the command relationship should be in Vietnam. One of the proposals consistently forwarded was that of developing a "NATO-style" combined U.S. Republic of Vietnamese armed forces Free World Military Armed Forces Command under General Westmoreland. The judgment of all senior people in Saigon had been that the possible military advantages of such action would be outweighed by its adverse psychological impact; that it would cut across the picture of the Vietnamese winning their own war, and lay the United States open to hostile propaganda both within South Vietnam and around the world. This idea of a unified command although surfacing periodically as we have noted was never given serious consideration until much later when the United States at least floated the idea in an attempt to develop entrés to the eventual disengagement. (Memorandum, Subject: Position on U.S./Other Than Vietnamese Armed Forces Free World Military Armed Force Command Relationships, dated 19 May 1967 (in McNaughton papers).

23. NSAM 362, May 9, 1967, Subject: "Responsibility for U.S. Role in Pacification (Revolutionary Development).

24. Richard C. Holbrooke, Task Force Paper IV.C.11, "Reemphasis on Pacification," see pages 130-137.

25. Memorandum for the SecDef, Subject: Combat Service Support Staffing in South Vietnam, dated 23 May 1967.

26. Memo for SecDef, Subject: Combat Service Support Staffing in South Vietnam, dated 23 May 1967.

27. Memorandum for the Chairman, JCS, Subject: Combat Service Support Staffing in SVN, dated 23 May 1967, H-87175. An interesting and revealing incident occurred when Mr. Heyman visited the 1st Log Command. During the standard briefing, the Commanding General noted that he had "just about the right number of men to do the job now in South Vietnam." This prompted Heyman when he walked down the hallway to the Personnel Section of the 1st Log Command to inquire how many troops they actually had assigned. He was told 58,000. Upon his return he analyzed Program 4 to see that 70,000 had been approved for the program. This convinced him to recommend to McNamara that a hard look be taken at the 1st Log Command since it appeared in the view of the Commanding General that they were doing just fine with some 12,000 troops less than they had asked and had approved in Program 4. (Memorandum, Subject: SEA Trip Report, Victor K. Heyman, Director, SEA Programs Division, dated 11 May 1967.)

28. "Additional MACV Requirements and Estimated Capabilities," December 31, 1968, Prepared by OASD(SA), dated 5 May 1967.

29. Memorandum for the SecDef, from the Secretary of the Army, Subject: Army Capability to Deploy Additional Forces to Vietnam without Mobilization, dated 12 May 1967.

30. Memorandum for SecDef, Subject: Additional Requirement Capability, Alain Enthoven, 18 May 1967. Also see: Memo for the SecDef, from SA, Stanley R. Resor, Subject: Army Capability to Deploy Additional Forces to Vietnam without Mobilization, dated 12 May 1967; and Memo for the SecDef, Subject: MACV/CINCPAC FY 1968.

31. Ibid.

32. Draft Presidential Memorandum, John McNaughton, Subject: Proposed Bombing Program Against North Vietnam dated 5 May 1967.

33. Ibid.

34. Ibid.

35. Memorandum for Vance, et. al., from W. W. Rostow, Subject: U.S. Strategy in Vietnam, dated 6 May 1967.

36. Ibid.

37. Ibid.

38. Ibid.

Declassified per Executive Order 13526, Section 3.3
NND Project Number: NND 63316. By: NWD Date: 2011

TOP SECRET - Sensitive

39. <u>Ibid</u>. As the third leg of this intensive inter-agency review
of our bombing strategy, Wm. Bundy of State prepared an analysis
very similar to that presented by Rostow. He too believed that
our options were essentially those of concentrating on the supply
routes in Route Packages 1 and 2, restrikes north of the 20th
parallel, possible selective additional strikes on sensitive
targets in the North, and finally, a major expansion to extremely
sensitive targets north of the 20th parallel. His examination of
the options concluded that the final option, that is, of not
hitting additional sensitive targets, increasing our reaction in
our effort in Route Packages 1 and 2 were both preferable to the
political consequences of an expansion of the bombing north of
the 20th parallel. In this, he was generally in agreement with
McNaughton. He believed that basically overall progress in the
south was the key element in changing Hanoi's attitude and that
any bombing program below the major expansion option or any
cessation of bombing without certain reciprocity would be totally
negative in its effect on Hanoi. He relegated the bombing program
itself to basically a supplementary role in affecting Hanoi's
attitude. See memorandum from W. P. Bundy, Subject: Bombing
Strategy Options for the Rest of 1967, dated 8 May 1967 (McNaughton
papers).

40. See JCSM 286-67, Subject: Operations Against North Vietnam,
dated 20 May 1967; and JCSM 312-67, Subject: Air Operations
Against North Vietnam dated 2 June 1967.

TOP SECRET - Sensitive

E. DECISION

E.   DECISION

1.   The McNaughton Draft Presidential Memorandum

On 19 May, the memorandum on which McNaughton had been working
was floated. It was a comprehensive document drawing upon the arguments developed in the Office of Systems Analysis as well as recent
CIA studies and views both from the State Department and the White
House on the bombing. The preamble to the basic document noted that
it was written at a time when there appeared to be no attractive course
of action. McNaughton stated that he believed that Hanoi had decided
not to negotiate until the American electorate had been heard from in
November of 1968. His appraisal of the current situation dwelled on
the unpopular nature of the Vietnam war in the country. In his eyes
it was becoming:

> ....increasingly unpopular as it escalates -- causing
> more American casualties, more fear of its growing into a
> wider war, more privation of the domestic sector, and more
> distress at the amount of suffering being visited on the
> non-combatants in Vietnam, South and North. Most Americans
> do not know how we got where we are, and most, without
> knowing why, but taking advantage of hindsight, are con-
> vinced that somehow we should not have gotten this deeply
> in. All want the war ended and expect their President to
> end it. Successfully, or else.

> This state of mind in the US generates impatience in
> the political structure of the United States. It unfor-
> tunately also generates patience in Hanoi. (It is commonly
> supposed that Hanoi will not give anything away pending the
> trial of the US elections in November 1968.) 1/

There is sufficient evidence that McNaughton's feelings about the
war, and especially the increasing opposition to force increases in South
Vietnam, ran much deeper than even the cogent arguments he had been making
in the draft memorandum. In a memo for the Secretary of Defense written
on 6 May after McNaughton had examined an earlier 5 May "Rough Draft,"
he described his apprehensions about the ground force strategy which
he described as a "trap which had ensnared us," and which if unchecked
might lead us to almost an irreversible ground force escalation for
the next undetermined number of years. He wrote:

> I am afraid there is the fatal flaw in the strategy
> in the draft. It is that the strategy falls into the trap

that has ensnared us for the past three years. It actually gives the troops while only praying for their proper use and for constructive diplomatic action. Limiting the present decision to an 80,000 add-on does the very important business of postponing the issue of a Reserve call-up (and all of its horrible baggage), but postpone it is all that it does -- probably to a worse time, 1968. Providing the 80,000 troops is tantamount to acceding to the whole Westmoreland-Sharp request. This being the case, they will "accept" the 80,000. But six months from now, in will come messages like the "470,000-570,000" messages, saying that the requirement remains at 201,000 (or more). Since no pressure will have been put on anyone, the military war will have gone on as before and no diplomatic progress will have been made. It follows that the "philosophy" of the war should be fought out now so everyone will not be proceeding on their own major premises, and getting us in deeper and deeper; at the very least, the President should give General Westmoreland his limit (as President Truman did to General MacArthur). That is, if General Westmoreland is to get 550,000 men, he should be told "that will be all, and we mean it."

McNaughton was also very deeply concerned about the breadth and the intensity of public unrest and dissatisfaction with the war. To him the draft paper underplayed a bit the unpopularity of the conflict especially with young people, the underprivileged, the intelligentia, and the women. He examined those lining up on both sides of an increasingly polarized public and he did not especially like what he saw:

A feeling is widely and strongly held that "the Establishment" is out of its mind. The feeling is that we are trying to impose some US image on distant peoples we cannot understand (anymore than we can the younger generation here at home), and that we are carrying the thing to absurd lengths. Related to this feeling is the increased polarization that is taking place in the United States with seeds of the worst split in our people in more than a century. The King, Galbraith, etc., positions illustrate one near-pole; the Hebert and Rivers statements on May 5 about the need to disregard the First Amendment illustrates the other. In this connection, I fear that "natural selection" in this environment will lead the Administration itself to become more and more homogenized -- Mac Bundy, George Ball, Bill Moyers are gone. Who next?

Finally, he quarrelled with the way in which the paper had dealt
with the definition of "success." He felt that this definition was
the major problem, that the draft had not properly grappled with the
redefinition, since "winning" was what the strategy pursued by COMUS-
MACV tried to do. He suggested that as a matter of tactics maybe
the President should figure it out himself, a point which tied in
closely with an earlier one of his about getting the "philosophy of
the war" straightened out and thereby avoiding another diplomatic
default and military misuse of forces. 4/

McNaughton's review of the situation in South and North Vietnam
stressed that the big war in the south between the United States and
the North Vietnamese units seemed to be going well but that regretably
the "other war" against the VC was not going so well. In his words:

The "big war" in the South between the US and the North
Vietnamese military units (NVA) is going well. We staved
off military defeat in 1965; we gained the military initiative in 1966; snd since then we have been hurting the
enemy badly, spoiling some of his ability to strike. "In
the final analysis," General Westmoreland said, "we are
fighting a war of attrition." In that connection, the
enemy has been losing between 1500 and 2000 killed-in-action
a week, while we and the South Vietnamese have been losing
175 and 250 respectively. The VC/NVA 287,000-man order of
battle is leveling off, and General Westmoreland believes
that, as of March, we "reached the cross-over point" -- we
began attriting more men than Hanoi can recruit or infiltrate each month. The concentration of NVA forces across
the Demilitarized Zone (DMZ) and the enemy use of long-range
artillery are matters of concern. There are now four NVA
divisions in the DMZ area. The men infiltrate directly
across the western part of the plans to nibble at our forces,
seeking to inflict heavy casualties, perhaps to stage a
"spectacular" (perhaps against Quang Tri City or Hue), and/
or to try a major thrust into the Western Highlands. They
are forcing us to transfer some forces from elsewhere in
Vietnam to the I Corps area.

Throughout South Vietnam, supplies continue to flow
in ample quantities, with Cambodia becoming more and more
important as a supply base -- now of food and medicines,
perhaps ammunition later. The enemy retains the ability
to initiate both large- and small-scale attacks. Small-
scale attacks in the first quarter of 1967 are running at
double the 1966 average; larger-scale attacks are again on
the increase after falling off substantially in 1966. Acts
of terrorism and harassment have continued at about the
same rate.

The over-all troop strengths of friendly and VC/NVA
forces by Corps Area are shown in Attachments I and II.

All things considered, there is consensus that we
are no longer in danger of losing this war militarily.

Regrettably, the "other war" against the VC is still
not going well. Corruption is widespread. Real government control is confined to enclaves. There is rot in
the fabric. Our efforts to enliven the moribund political
infrastructure have been matched by VC efforts -- more now
through coercion than was formerly the case. So the VC
are hurting badly too. In the Delta, because of the
redeployment of some VC/NVA troops to the area north of
Saigon, the VC have lost their momentum and appear to be
conducting essentially a holding operation. On the
government side there, the tempo of operations has been
correspondingly low. The population remains apathetic,
and many local government officials seem to have working
arrangements with the VC which they are reluctant to dis-
turb.

The National Liberation Front (NLF) continues to
control large parts of South Vietnam, and there is little
evidence that the revolutionary development program is
gaining any momentum. The Army of South Vietnam (ARVN)
is tired, passive and accommodation-prone, and is moving
too slowly if at all into pacification work.

The enemy no doubt continues to believe that we will
not be able to translate our military success in the "big war"
into the desired "end products" -- namely, broken enemy morale
and political achievements by the Government of Vietnam (GVN).
At the same time, the VC must be concerned about decline in
morale among their ranks. Defections, which averaged 400
per week last year, have, until a slump near the end of
April, been running at more than 1000 a week; very few
defectors, however, are important people.

The transition to a government in Saigon responsive
to the South Vietnamese people is moving as well as can be
expected. A Constituent Assembly was elected last fall.
A constitution has been adopted. Local elections, involving
more than 50 per cent of the rural population and a 77-80
per cent turnout, have taken place despite the shadow cast
by VC assassinations and kidnappings. The Buddhists have
launched a new "peace" campaign with an immolation, but

their political power is less than it was before their
defeat in 1966. National elections are scheduled for
September 1. No one, unfortunately, has shown any
charismatic appeal. Ky and Thieu have promised not to
split over the presidency, but there is obviously a
serious struggle going on between them (Ky has announced
his candidacy, and Thieu, the weaker of the two, has
hinted that he may throw his weight behind a civilian).
So there is hope that there will be an orderly transition to stable constitutional rule.

Little has been done to remedy the economic and
social ills of the corruption from which VC popular support stems. Partly because of this inaction -- where
reform action would destroy the working consensus -- the
political situation at the top remains relatively stable.

The port is operating much better. Inflation
appears to be under control. But the flow of rice into
Saigon from the Delta, as good an indicator as any of
the state of affairs, continues to decrease: The flow
is 75 per cent of the 1966, and half of the 1965, rates;
national exports of rice ceased in 1964, and imports
continue to climb.

C. North Vietnam

Hanoi's attitude towards negotiations has never been
soft nor open-minded. Any concession on their part would
involve an enormous loss of face. Whether or not the Polish
and Burchett-Kosygin initiatives had much substance to them,
it is clear that Hanoi's attitude currently is hard and
rigid. They seem uninterested in a political settlement and
determined to match US military expansion of the conflict.
This change probably reflects these factors: (1) increased
assurances of help from the Soviets received during Pham
Van Dong's April trip to Moscow; (2) arrangements providing
for the unhindered passage of materiel from the Soviet Union
through China; and (3) a decision to wait for the results
of the US elections in 1968. Hanoi appears to have concluded
that she cannot secure her objectives at the conference table
and has reaffirmed her strategy of seeking to erode our ability to remain in the South. The Hanoi leadership has
apparently decided that it has no choice but to submit to
the increased bombing. There continues to be no sign that
the bombing has reduced Hanoi's will to resist or her ability
to ship the necessary supplies south. Hanoi shows no signs
of ending the large war and advising the VC to melt into the

jungles. The North Vietnamese believe they are right; they consider the Ky regime to be puppets; they believe the world is with them and that the American public will not have staying power against them. Thus, although they may have factions in the regime favoring different approaches, they believe that, in the long run, they are stronger than we are for the purpose. They probably do not want to make significant concessions, and could not do so without serious loss of face. 5/

He then analyzed two alternative military courses of action which he labeled "A" and "B". In Course A the full troop requirement request from COMUSMACV was to be honored, and subsequent military actions intensified not only in the south, but especially in the north. This program consisted of an addition of the minimum of 200,000 men; 100,000 in the 2-1/3 division "minimum essential" force in FY 68 and another 100,000 in FY 69, with possibly more later to fulfill the JCS ultimate requirement for Vietnam and associated worldwide contingencies. Course B proposed limiting the force increases to no more than 30,000 thereby stabilizing the ground conflict within the borders of South Vietnam and concommitantly concentrating the bombing on the infiltration routes south of the 20th parallel. He analyzed the two courses of action in the following terms.

COURSE A would be chosen with a view to bringing additional military pressure to bear on the enemy in the South while continuing to carry out our present missions not directly related to combating enemy main-force units. It would involve accepting the risk -- the virtual certainty -- that the action especially the Reserve call-up, would stimulate irresistible pressures in the United States for further escalation against North Vietnam, and for ground actions against "sanctuaries" in Cambodia and Laos.

Rationale

Proponents of the added deployments in the South believe that such deployments will hasten the end of the war. None of them believes that the added forces are needed to avoid defeat; few of them believe that the added forces are required to do the military job in due course; all of the proponents believe that they are needed if that job is to be done faster. The argument is that we avoided military defeat in 1965; that we gained the military initiative in 1966, since then hurting the enemy badly, spoiling much of his ability to strike, and thus diminishing the power he could project over the population; and that even more-vigorous military initiative against his main forces and base areas will hurt him more, spoil his efforts more, and diminish his projected power more than would be the case under presently approved force-deployment levels. This, the argument goes, will more readily create an environment in South Vietnam in which our pacification efforts can take root and thrive; at the same time -- because of our progress in the South and because of the large enemy losses -- it will more rapidly produce a state of mind in Hanoi conducive to ending the war on reasonable terms.

Estimates by the proponents vary as to how long the job will take without, and with, the additional forces. General Westmoreland has said that without the additions the war could go on five years. He has said that with 100,000 more men, the war could go on for three years and that with 200,000 more men it could go on for two. These estimates are after taking account of his view that the introduction of a non-professional force, such as that which would result from fulfilling the requirement by calling Reserves, would cause some degradation of morale, leadership and effectiveness.

Questions to be Answered

Addressing the force additions alone: We should expect no serious objections based on internal South Vietnamese reasons (the 44-billion piastre inflationary impact can probably be handled, and anti-Americanism is not likely to increase significantly); nor are dangerous reactions likely to come from the USSR, East Europe, or from the non-Communist nations of the world. The questions that must be answered are:

--(1) Will the move to call up 200,000 Reserves, to extend enlistments, and to enlarge the uniformed strength by 500,000 (300,000 beyond the Reserves), combined with the increased US larger initiative, polarize opinion to the extent that the "doves" in the US will get out of hand -- massive refusals to serve, or to fight, or to cooperate, or worse?

--(2) Can we achieve the same military effect by making more efficient use of presently approved US manpower (e.g., by removing them from the Delta, by stopping their being used for pacification work in I Corps, by transferring some combat and logistics jobs to Vietnamese or additional third-country personnel)?

--(3) Assuming no specific enemy counter-deployments, are the added US forces likely to make a meaningful military difference? (On the one hand, if we are now "past the cross-over point," cannot the military job be done without the added forces? On the other, if the enemy can conduct his terror "from the bushes," can the military job be done even with them?)

--(4) Will the effect of any US additions be neutralized, or stalemated, by specific enemy counter-deployments involving more forces from North Vietnam (and perhaps introduction of more Chinese in North Vietnam and Chinese and other "volunteers" into South Vietnam)?

--(5) Will the factors mentioned in (1) above generate such impatience in the United States that "hawk" pressures will be irresistible to expand the land war into Laos, Cambodia and North Vietnam and to take stronger air and naval actions against North Vietnam, with consequent risks of a much larger war involving China and Russia and of even more dove-hawk polarization at home and abroad?

The answer to Question 1 (regarding "dove" reaction), we believe, is a qualified no. Barring escalation of the "external" war discussed under Question 5, we believe that increased forces will not lead to massive civil disobedience. However, a request for Congressional authority to call Reserves would lead to divisive debate.

Question 2 (relating to more efficient use of US forces) is an important one, but its answer, even if most favorable, is not likely to free-up enough personnel to satisfy a 200,000-man request. It is true that one of the additional divisions could be eliminated if the US Army eschewed the Delta, and certain of the other ground-force requirements could be eliminated if the US Marines ceased grass-roots pacification activities. Additional fractions might be trimmed if the ARVN (whose uninspired performance is exasperating) were jacked up, if the Koreans provided more combat or usable logistics personnel, or if other third-country forces were forthcoming. Efforts along this line should be made, but the items that prove out will not go nearly as far as the 200,000 request.

Questions 3 and 4 (relating to the value of additional US forces and possible enemy action to offset them) are very difficult ones and can be treated together. In December 1965,

when the US had 175,000 men in Vietnam, I reported that
"the odds are even that, even with the recommended deployments, we will be faced in early 1967 with a military
standoff at a much higher level..." In October 1966, when
our deployments had reached 325,000, I pointed out that that
was substantially the case and that "I see no reasonable
way to bring the war to an end soon." That remains true
today. With respect to Question 3, this is because the
enemy has us "stalemated" and has the capability to tailor
his actions to his supplies and manpower and, by hit-and-
run terror, to make government and pacification very difficult
in large parts of the country almost without regard to the size
of US forces there; and, with respect to Question 4, because
the enemy can and almost certainly will maintain the military
"stalemate" by matching our added deployments as necessary.
(General Westmoreland has made the point that "this war is
action and counteraction; any time we take an action, we
can expect a reaction." He added," It is likely the enemy
will react by adding troops.") In any event, there is no
suggestion that the added deployments will end the war in
less than two years and no assurance that they will end it
in three, or five, years.

Question 5 (regarding irresistible pressures to expand
the war) is the toughest one.

The addition of the 200,000 men, involving as it does
a call-up of Reserves and an addition of 500,000 to the
military strength, would, as mentioned above, almost certainly
set off bitter Congressional debate and irresistible domestic
pressures for stronger action outside South Vietnam. Cries
would go up -- much louder than they already have -- to "take
the wraps off the men in the field." The actions would
include more intense bombing -- not only around-the-clock
bombing of targets already authorized, but also bombing of
strategic targets such as locks and dikes, and mining of
the harbors against Soviet and other ships. Associated actions
impelled by the situation would be major ground actions in
Laos, Cambodia, and probably in North Vietnam -- first as a
pincer operation north of the DMZ and then at a point such
as Vinh. The use of tactical nuclear and area-denial radi-
ological-bacteriological-chemical weapons would probably
be suggested at some point if the Chinese entered the war
in Vietnam or Korea or if US losses were running high while
conventional efforts were not producing desired results.

Bombing Purposes and Payoffs

Our bombing of North Vietnam was designed to serve three purposes:

--(1) To retaliate and to lift the morale of the people in the South who were being attacked by agents of the North.

--(2) To add to the pressure on Hanoi to end the war.

--(3) To reduce the flow and/or to increase the cost of infiltrating men and materiel from North to South.

We cannot ignore that a limitation on bombing will cause serious psychological problems among the men, officers and commanders, who will not be able to understand why we should withhold punishment from the enemy. General Westmoreland said that he is "frankly dismayed at even the thought of stopping the bombing program." But this reason for attacking North Vietnam must be scrutinized carefully. We should not bomb for punitive reasons if it serves no other purpose -- especially if analysis shows that the actions may be counterproductive. It costs American lives; it creates a backfire of revulsion and opposition by killing civilians; it creates serious risks; it may harden the enemy.

With respect to added pressure on the North, it is becoming apparent that Hanoi may already have "written off" all assets and lives that might be destroyed by US military actions short of occupation or annihilation. They can and will hold out at least so long as a prospect of winning the "war of attrition" in the South exists. And our best judgment is that a Hanoi prerequisite to negotiations is significant retrenchment (if not complete stoppage) of US military actions against them -- at the least, a cessation of bombing. In this connection, Consul-General Rice (Hong Kong 7581, 5/1/67) said that, in his opinion, we cannot by bombing reach the critical level of pain in North Vietnam and that, "below that level, pain only increases the will to fight." Sir Robert Thompson said to Mr. Vance on April 28 that our bombing, particularly in the Red River Delta, "is unifying North Vietnam."

With respect to interdiction of men and materiel,
it now appears that no combination of actions against
the North short of destruction of the regime or occupation of North Vietnamese territory will physically reduce
the flow of men and materiel below the relatively small
amount needed by enemy forces to continue the war in the
South. Our effort can and does have severe disruptive
effects, which Hanoi can and does compensate for by the
reallocation of manpower and other resources; and our effort
can and does have sporadic retarding effects, which Hanoi
can and does plan on and pre-stock against. Our efforts
physically to cut the flow meaningfully by actions in North
Vietnam therefore largely fail and, in failing, transmute
attempted interdiction into pain, or pressure on the North
(the factor discussed in the paragraph next above). The
lowest "ceiling on infiltration can probably be achieved
by concentration on the North Vietnamese "funnel" south of
20° and on the Trail in Laos.

But what if the above analyses are wrong? Why not
escalate the bombing and mine the harbors (and perhaps
occupy southern North Vietnam) -- on the gamble that it
would constrict the flow, meaningfully limiting enemy
action in the South, and that it would bend Hanoi? The
answer is that the costs and risks of the actions must be
considered.

The primary costs of course are US lives: The air
campaign against heavily defended areas costs us one pilot
in every 40 sorties. In addition, an important but hard-
to-measure cost is domestic and world opinion: There may
be a limit beyond which many Americans and much of the world
will not permit the United States to go. The picture of the
world's greatest superpower killing or seriously injuring
1000 non-combatants a week, while trying to pound a tiny
backward nation into submission on an issue whose merits
are hotly disputed, is not a pretty one. It could conceivably produce a costly distortion in the American national
consciousness and in the world image of the United States --
especially if the damage to North Vietnam is complete
enough to be "successful."

The most important risk, however, is the likely Soviet,
Chinese and North Vietnamese reaction to intensified US
air attacks, harbor-mining, and ground actions against North
Vietnam.

Likely Communist Reactions

At the present time, no actions -- except air strikes and artillery fire necessary to quiet hostile batteries across the border -- are allowed against Cambodian territory. In Laos, we average 5000 attack sorties a month against the infiltration routes and base areas, we fire artillery from South Vietnam against targets in Laos, and we will be providing 3-man leaders for each of 20 12-man US-Vietnamese Special Forces teams that operate to a depth of 20 kilometers into Laos. Against North Vietnam, we average 8,000 or more attack sorties a month against all worthwhile fixed and LOC targets; we use artillery against ground targets across the DMZ; we fire from naval vessels at targets ashore and afloat up to 19°, and we mine their inland waterways, estuaries and coastal waters up to 20°.

Intensified air attacks against the same types of targets, we would anticipate, would lead to no great change in the policies and reactions of the Communist powers beyond the furnishing of some new equipment and manpower.[*] China, for example, has not reacted to our striking MIG fields in North Vietnam, and we do not expect them to, although there are some signs of greater Chinese participation in North Vietnamese air defense.

Mining the harbors would be much more serious. It would place Moscow in a particularly galling dilemma as to how to preserve the Soviet position and prestige in such a

---

[*]The U.S. Intelligence Board on May 5 said that Hanoi may press Moscow for additional equipment and that there is a "good chance that under pressure the Soviets would provide such weapons as cruise missiles and tactical rockets" in addition to a limited number of volunteers or crews for aircraft or sophisticated equipment. Moscow, with respect to equipment, might provide better surface-to-air missiles, better anti-aircraft guns, the YAK-28 aircraft, anti-tank missiles and artillery, heavier artillery and mortars, coastal defense missiles with 25-50 mile ranges and 2200-pound warheads, KOMAR guided-missile coastal patrol boats with 20-mile surface-to-surface missiles, and some chemical munitions. She might consider sending medium jet bombers and fighter bombers to pose a threat to all of South Vietnam.

disadvantageous place. The Soviets might, but probably
would not, force a confrontation in Southeast Asia --
where even with minesweepers they would be at as great
a military disadvantage as we were when they blocked the
corridor to Berlin in 1961, but where their vital interest,
unlike ours in Berlin (and in Cuba), is not so clearly
at stake. Moscow in this case should be expected to send
volunteers, including pilots, to North Vietnam; to provide
some new and better weapons and equipment; to consider
some action in Korea, Turkey, Iran, the Middle East or,
most likely, Berlin, where the Soviets can control the
degree of crisis better; and to show across-the-board
hostility toward the US (interrupting any on-going conversations on ABMs, non-proliferation, etc). China could be
expected to seize upon the harbor-mining as the opportunity
to reduce Soviet political influence in Hanoi and to discredit the USSR if the Soviets took no military action to
open the ports. Peking might read the harbor-mining as
indicating that the US was going to apply military pressure until North Vietnam capitulated, and that this meant
an eventual invasion. If so, China might decide to intervene in the war with combat troops and air power, to which
we would eventually have to respond by bombing Chinese airfields and perhaps other targets as well. Hanoi would
tighten belts, refuse to talk, and persevere -- as it could
without too much difficulty. North Vietnam would of course
be fully dependent for supplies on China's will, and Soviet
influence in Hanoi would therefore be reduced. (Ambassador
Sullivan feels very strongly that it would be a serious
mistake, by our actions against the port, to tip Hanoi
away from Moscow and toward Peking.)

To US ground actions in North Vietnam, we would expect
China to respond by entering the war with both ground and
air forces. The Soviet Union could be expected in these
circumstances to take all actions listed above under the
lesser provocations and to generate a serious confrontation
with the United States at one or more places of her own
choosing.

Ground actions in Laos are similarly unwise. LeDuan,
Hanoi's third- or fourth-ranking leader, has stated the
truth when he said "the occupation of the Western Highlands
is a tough job but the attack on central and lower Laos is
a still tougher one. If a small force is used, the problem
remains insoluble. The US may face a series of difficulties

in the military, political and logistic fields if a
larger force goes into operation. In effect, an attack
on central and lower Laos would mean the opening of
another front nearer to North Vietnam, and then the
US troops would have to clash with the North Vietnamese
main force." In essence, a brigade will beget a division
and a division a corps, each calling down matching forces
from North Vietnam into territory to their liking and
suggesting to Hanoi that they take action in Northern
Laos to suck us further in. We would simply have a wider
war, with Souvanna back in Paris, world opinion against
us, and no solution either to the wider war or to the
one we already have in Vietnam.

Those are the likely costs and risks of COURSE A.
They are, we believe, both unacceptable and unnecessary.
Ground action in North Vietnam, because of its escalatory
potential, is clearly unwise despite the open invitation
and temptation posed by enemy troops operating freely
back and forth across the DMZ. Yet we believe that, short
of threatening and perhaps toppling the Hanoi regime
itself, pressure against the North will, if anything,
harden Hanoi's unwillingness to talk and her settlement
terms if she does. China, we believe, will oppose settlement throughout. We believe that there is a chance that
the Soviets, at the brink, will exert efforts to bring
about peace; but we believe also that intensified bombing
and harbor-mining, even if coupled with political pressure
from Moscow, will neither bring Hanoi to negotiate nor
affect North Vietnam's terms.

B. Analysis of Course B

As of March 18, 1967, the approved US Force Structure
(Program 4) for Southeast Asia provided for 87 maneuver
battalions, 42 air squadrons, and a total strength of
468,000 men. Based on current forecasts of enemy strength,
under COURSE B it should not be necessary to approve now
for deployment more than 9 of the 24 available maneuver
battalions and none of the air squadrons -- a total of
approximately 30,000 men including appropriate land and
sea support forces (see Attachment III).

This approach would be based, first, on General
Westmoreland's statement that "without /his requested7

forces, we will not be in danger of being defeated,...
but progress will be slowed down," and General
Wheeler's support of that view. General Wheeler
added, "We won't lose the war, but it will be a longer
one." It would be based, second, on the fact that no
one argues that the added forces will probably cause
the war to end in less than two years. COURSE B
implies a conviction that neither military defeat nor
military victory is in the cards, with or without the
large added deployments, and that the price of the
large added deployments and the strategy of COURSE A
will be to expand the war dangerously. COURSE B is
designed to improve the negotiating environment within
a limited deployment of US forces by combining continuous attacks against VC/NVA main force units with slow
improvements in pacification (which may follow the new
constitution, the national reconciliation proclamation,
our added efforts and the Vietnamese elections this
fall) and a restrained program of actions against the
North.

This alternative would give General Westmoreland
96 maneuver battalions -- an 85 per cent increase in
combat force over the 52 battalions that he had in
Vietnam in June of last year, and 22 per cent more
than the 79 we had there at the beginning of this
year. According to this report, we have already
passed the "cross-over point," where the enemy's
losses exceed his additions; we will soon have in
Vietnam 200,000 more US troops than there are in
enemy main force units. We should therefore, without
added deployments, be able to maintain the military
initiative, especially if US troops in less-essential
missions (such as in the Delta and in pacification

duty)* are considered strategic reserves.

The strategy of proponents of COURSE B is based on
their belief that we are in a military situation that
cannot be changed materially by expanding our military
effort, that the politico-pacification situation in
South Vietnam will improve but not fast, and that (in
view of all this) Hanoi will not capitulate soon. An
aspect of the strategy is a "cool" drive to settle the
war -- a deliberate process on three fronts: Large
unit, politico-pacification, and diplomatic. Its
approach on the large-unit front is to maintain the

---

*General Wheeler has explained where the first 2-1/3
divisions would go: "One on the DMZ to relieve the
Marines to work with ARVN on pacification; one east of
Saigon to relieve the 9th Division to deploy to the
Delta to increase the effectiveness of the three good
ARVN divisions now there; the brigade to Quang Ngai
to make there the progress in pacification in the next
year that we have made in Binh Dinh in the past year."
Thus the bulk of the first 100,000 men are for pacification and for the Delta. General Westmoreland said
regarding the Delta, "in the Fourth Corps, there is
no threat of strategic VC victories and there are
three good ARVN divisions there." The question arises
whether US combat troops should be devoted to pacification or to the Delta. Are these not matters for the
Vietnamese? The Delta may be a test case of the proposed strategy. It is normally stated that "in order
to win in Vietnam we must win in the Delta where the
people are." This obviously implies that Saigon's
writ must run throughout the Delta. But two facts
appear: (1) The Delta is a fairly active VC area, in
which a moderately high level of Stage II guerrilla
warfare tactics are pursued; and (2) the VC effort is
primarily indigenous (that is, the North Vietnamese
Main Force units play almost no role). If our "success"
objective is solely to check or offset North Vietnam's
forceful intervention in the South, we are in that
position already in the Delta! Must we go further and
do the job for the South Vietnamese? What kind of a
deal could the contending forces cut in the Delta?

initiative that "Program 4-plus" forces will permit,
to move on with pacification efforts and with the
national election in September, and to lay the groundwork by periodic peace probes, perhaps suggesting secret
talks associated with limitation of bombing and with a
view to finding a compromise involving, inter alia, a
role in the South for members of the VC.

This alternative would not involve US or Vietnamese
forces in any numbers in Laos or Cambodia, and definitely
not in North Vietnam. Since the US Reserves would still
be untapped, they would still be available for use later
in Asia, or elsewhere, if it became necessary.

Bombing Program

The bombing program that would be a part of this
strategy is, basically, a program of concentration of
effort on the infiltration routes near the south of
North Vietnam. The major infiltration-related targets
in the Red River basin having been destroyed, such interdiction is now best served by concentration of all effort
in the southern neck of North Vietnam. All of the sorties
would be flown in the area between 17° and 20°. This
shift, despite possible increases in anti-aircraft capability in the area, should reduce the pilot and aircraft
loss rates by more than 50 per cent. The shift will, if
anything, be of positive military value to General Westmoreland while taking some steam out of the popular effort
in the North.

The above shift of bombing strategy, now that almost
all major targets have been struck in the Red River basin,
can to military advantage be made at any time. It should
not be done for the sole purpose of getting Hanoi to
negotiate, although that might be a bonus effect. To
maximize the chances of getting that bonus effect, the
optimum scenario would probably be (1) to inform the
Soviets quietly that within a few days the shift would
take place, setting no time limits but making no promises
not to return to the Red River basin to attack targets
which later acquire military importance (any deal with
Hanoi is likely to be midwifed by Moscow); (2) to make
the shift as predicted, without fanfare; and (3) to
explain publicly, when the shift had become obvious,

that the northern targets had been destroyed, that that
had been militarily important, and that there would be
no need to return to the northern areas unless military
necessity dictated it. The shift should not be huckstered.
Moscow would almost certainly pass its information on to
Hanoi, and might urge Hanoi to seize the opportunity to
de-escalate the war by talks or otherwise. Hanoi, not
having been asked a question by us and having no ultimatum-like time limit, would be in a better posture to
answer favorably than has been the case in the past. The
military side of the shift is sound, however, whether or
not the diplomatic spill-over is successful. 6/

McNaughton concluded his case against force level increases by
proposing a time-phased "suggested strategy":

    (1) Now: Not to panic because of a belief that
Hanoi must be made to capitulate before the 1968 elections.
No one's proposal achieves that end.

    (2) Now: Press on energetically with the military,
pacification and political programs in the South, including
groundwork for successful elections in September. Drive
hard to increase the productivity of Vietnamese military
forces.

    (3) Now: Issue a NSAM nailing down US policy as
described herein. Thereafter, publicly, (a) emphasize consistently that the sole US objective in Vietnam has been
and is to permit the people of South Vietnam to determine
their own future, and (b) declare that we have already
either denied or offset the North Vietnamese intervention
and that after the September elections in Vietnam we will
have achieved success. The necessary steps having been
taken to deny the North the ability to take over South
Vietnam and an elected government sitting in Saigon, the
South will be in position, albeit imperfect, to start the
business of producing a full-spectrum government in South
Vietnam.

    (4) June: Concentrate the bombing of North Vietnam
on physical interdiction of men and materiel. This would
mean terminating, except where the interdiction objective
clearly dictates otherwise, all bombing north of 20° and
improving interdiction as much as possible in the infiltration "funnel" south of 20° by concentration of sorties

Declassified per Executive Order 13526, Section 3.3
NND Project Number: NND 63316. By: NWD Date: 2011

and by an all-out effort to improve detection devices, denial weapons, and interdiction tactics.

(5) <u>July</u>: Avoid the explosive Congressional debate and US Reserve call-up implicit in the Westmoreland troop request. Decide that, unless the military situation worsens dramatically, US deployments will be limited to Program 4-plus (which, according to General Westmoreland, will not put us in danger of being defeated, but will mean slow progress in the South). Associated with this decision are decisions not to use large numbers of US troops in the Delta and not to use large numbers of them in grass-roots pacification work.

(6) <u>September</u>: Move the newly elected Saigon government well beyond its National Reconciliation program to seek a political settlement with the non-Communist members of the NLF -- to explore a ceasefire and to reach an accommodation with the non-Communist South Vietnamese who are under the VC banner; to accept them as members of an opposition political party, and, if necessary, to accept their individual participation in the national government -- in sum, a settlement to transform the members of the VC from military opponents to political opponents.

(7) <u>October</u>: Explain the situation to the Canadians, Indians, British, UN and others, as well as nations now contributing forces, requesting them to contribute border forces to help make the inside-South Vietnam accommodation possible, and -- consistent with our desire neither to occupy nor to have bases in Vietnam -- offering to remove later an equivalent number of US forces. (This initiative is worth taking despite its slim chance of success.)*

His closing paragraph repeated his belief that it had to be made clear to political and military leaders alike that the troop limit as imposed by Course B which he recommended was firm and short of an imminent military defeat would not be breached. Westmoreland and the JCS had to be persuaded that the objective was not to attain "victory" but to make progress, albeit slow, without the risks attendant to Course A. He acknowledged that it would not be easy for the President to stick at 550,000 troops in South Vietnam or to limit the bombing program to targets south of the 20th parallel, but that it would be possible, and that in his estimation the benefits of such a course of action far outweighed the political risks which Course A included. 7/

Declassified per Executive Order 13526, Section 3.3
NND Project Number: NND 63316. By: NWD Date: 2011

From the standpoint of ground force strategy, what McNaughton was really, it appears, saying was that we should make a decision to basically set our objectives within a time frame geared to South Vietnamese Army and South Vietnamese government progress, and that in doing so our own troops in approximately the current strengths could be devoted to providing the shield while the government of South Vietnam provided the shelter and performed the vital pacification function. As he noted, associated in the decision was the very conscious determination not to use large numbers of U.S. troops in the delta and not to use large numbers of them in what he called "grass roots pacification work," the two justifications most frequently used to support requests for additional troops. The appraisal, as well as the alternative military courses of action and their analyses contained in this document provided the catalyst for the subsequent and final decisions on Program 5.

2. JCSM 286-67, Persistent Pressure Up the Ladder--"Shouldering Out" the Parts

On 20 May the Joint Chiefs of Staff submitted JCSM 286-67, entitled "Operations Against North Vietnam," a paper primarily concerned with the air campaign. It stated that the JCS were seriously concerned at the prospective introduction by the USSR into NVN of new weapons including improved antiaircraft and surface to air missiles, guided missile patrol boats, surface to surface missiles and a variety of artillery and direct fire weapons. They felt that such weapons would further improve the NVN air and coastal defense systems and provide offensive capabilities which would pose additional threats to our forces and installations in SEA. Since the Hanoi-Haiphong areas constituted the principal North Vietnam logistical base through which these arms passed the JCS recommended that this complex be neutralized. This was feasible by direct attack on the areas but such direct attack would entail increased danger of high civilian casualties. Preferable to direct attack the Chiefs recommended that the area be interdicted by cutting the land and sea lines of communications leading into it. However, for such an interdiction campaign to be effective, all the elements of the import system of North Vietnam had to be attacked concurrently on a sustained basis, or, in the Chiefs' estimation, the weight of the attack would be insufficient to reduce imports to a level which would seriously impair the overall North Vietnamese war supporting capability. Accordingly, they recommended first an attack of Haiphong, conducted first by surgically "shouldering out" foreign shipping and then mining the harbor and approaches. This concept of "shouldering out" which was to reappear many times in subsequent JCS communications was to be executed by a series of air attacks commencing on the periphery of the port area and gradually moving to the center of the complex. These attacks were designed to reduce the functional efficiency of the port and could be expected to force the foreign shipping out of the nearby estuaries for off-loading by lighterage. Once the foreign vessels cleared port, according to the JCS calculation the remaining elements of the port could be taken under attack and the harbor mined. While the Haiphong port was being attacked

TOP SECRET - Sensitive

an intensive interdiction campaign would commence against the roads and railroads from China. Concurrently, another series of attacks would be mounted against the eight major operational airfields. 8/ These recommendations met with predictably cool response and on 26 July 1967 the Deputy Secretary of Defense, in a memorandum to the Chairman of the JCS, stated that "a final decision on the proposals contained in the memorandum will be rendered in connection with the determination of overall future courses of action in Vietnam which should be completed in the near future." 9/

On the same date, 20 May, the Joint Chiefs of Staff submitted their World-wide Posture Paper. The most significant recommendation in it was a proposal that a selective call-up for the Reserves be made so that the U.S. could more effectively fulfill world-wide commitments. In it the Joint Chiefs of Staff stated that the nation must be able to (1) send large U.S. forces to any of the several trouble spots, such as Korea and Berlin; they also noted that we could not respond fast enough with sufficient forces to meet most of these contingencies. They also wrote that we must meet CINCPAC's FY 68 force requests, and to do so would require an addition of 2-1/3 division forces or the now familiar "minimum essential requirements" stated by General Westmoreland in his original 18 March request. The Chiefs also believed that we had to "regain the Southeast Asia initiative and exploit our military advantage." They stated that they believed present air restrictions crippled our war effort and that limitations should be reduced on targets as well as the rules of engagement, and that more forces, primarily air, evidently, should be sent. Moreover, they believed that we should reinforce as fast as possible, to prevent the enemy from adjusting to the increases in pressure, as he had been able to do thus far.

Of seven alternate U.S. force postures they reviewed, the JCS considered only two to be "adequate." The alternative they endorsed provided the following increases to the approved forces: 4-1/3 active army divisions; one navy attack carrier; two carrier air-wings; two battleships; two gun cruisers; as well as 570 UE Air Force tactical fighters, 72 UE Reconnaissance Aircraft and 80 UE C130's. They did not propose any new permanent additions to the United States Marine Corps. In their estimation the proposed force structure would be adequate to meet the FY 68 CINCPAC "minimum essential force requirements" for SEA without changing current rotation policies. It would also provide forces to reinforce NATO as well as respond to other major contingencies including MACV's tentative FY 1969 add-on requirement for 2-1/3 divisions and 90 tactical fighters. (This was, of course, the "optimum" force which the 18 March COMUSMACV request had contained.) The JCS proposed to extend terms of service, and to call up Reserves to provide this capability quicker. The Reserves they proposed to call would be two

166   TOP SECRET - Sensitive

Army and one Marine division forces, plus 15 Naval Reserve destroyers and two Naval construction battalions. In addition, an unspecified number of individual Reservists would be needed along with certain types of Reserve equipment and aircraft. The Reserves would be replaced by permanent units during FY 69-70. The Marine Reserve Division would be deployed to SVN to be replaced after a year by an Army Division, while the Marine Reserve Division would then revert to Reserve status. In the JCS estimate they stated that we could meet the FY 68 CINCPAC requirement by March 1968 if we called Reserves or by September 1969 if we did not. The Chiefs were particularly exercised at the prospect of very slow U.S. build-up over time which would continue to permit the VC/NVA to react. They commented that:

> The rate at which US power has been applied has permitted North Vietnamese and Viet Cong reinforcements and force posture improvements to keep pace with the graduated increases in US military actions. It is fundamental to the successful conduct of warfare that every reasonable measure be taken to widen the differential between the capabilities of the opposing forces. Target system limitations, rules of engagement, and force curtailments have combined to militate against widening the gap between the total Free World force capability, including South Vietnam, and the capability of the enemy to generate, deploy, and sustain his forces while improving the defense of his homeland.

> a. Successful prosecution of the war in Southeast Asia requires the maintenance of simultaneous pressure against all echelons of the enemy forces. In South Vietnam, this involves extensive ground, air, and naval operations against Viet Cong/North Vietnamese main forces and major base areas, while continuing revolutionary development and aggressive operations against Viet Cong provincial forces and guerrillas. In North Vietnam, the effectiveness of LOC interdiction cannot be greatly improved without significant reduction of the present restrictions on bombing and mining operations. Deep-water ports then can be closed or neutralized, and it will be worthwhile to intensify the interdiction effort against other LOCs in North Vietnam. Concomitantly, remaining high-value, war-supporting resources should be quickly, but methodically, destroyed. Attacks against population centers, per se, would continue to be avoided. (See Appendix B for requested changes in operating authorities and proposed expansion in air and naval operations against North Vietnam.) Limited ground action in North Vietnam might also become necessary to destroy forces threatening the northern provinces. 10/

As they continued, however, they fed a fear which was becoming predominent in the administration, that increases in forces might tempt COMUSMACV and our SEA commanders to expand operations into Cambodia and Laos, thereby complicating an already sensitive political situation:

     b. It may ultimately become necessary to conduct military operations into Cambodia to deny the Viet Cong/North Vietnamese Army forces the psychological, military, and logistical advantages of this sanctuary. Should the Viet Cong/North Vietnamese forces increase their use of the Laos Panhandle, it might become necessary to deploy additional forces to Thailand and expand operations further to protect South Vietnam. To counter large-scale CHICOM overt intervention in northern Laos, it would be necessary to establish a strategic defense. Invocation of the SEATO Treaty would be indicated. In the event the CHICOMs attack Thailand, use of nuclear weapons against LOCs and supply bases in southern China might be required. Similarly, should the CHICOMs intervene overtly with major combat forces in Vietnam, it might be necessary to establish a strategic defense in South Vietnam and use tactical nuclear weapons against bases and LOCs in South China. 11/

3. The Vance Options--Re-examination of Increases

On 24 May the JCS submitted to the Secretary of Defense their study entitled, "Alternative Courses of Action for Southeast Asia." This study was in response to a request made on 26 April by Deputy Secretary Vance asking the Joint Chiefs to study in detail the two alternative courses of action, outlined in the State paper prepared earlier by Acting Secretary of State Katzenbach. 12/ Strangely enough, between the time of the 26 April memorandum from Deputy Secretary Vance to the Director of the Joint Staff, Course A was altered, changing in the JCS paper from 200,000 personnel to approximately 250,000," roughly 125,000 in FY 68 and another 125,000 in FY 69. In the JCS study this was described as the "optimum force outlined in JCSM 218-67 and includes a 4-2/3 division force." Course B as it was outlined in the original Katzenbach memo confined troop increases to "those than can be generated without calling up reserves -- perhaps 9 battalions (10,000) men in the next year." 13/ This figure was altered in the JCS study so that Course B read: "add only forces that can be generated without calling up Reserves. This will amount to approximately 70,000 in FY 68 to include 1-1/3 Army division force equivalents with a limited capability in FY 69." 14/

Course A which would necessitate a Reserve call-up and a 12-month involuntary extension in terms of service effective 1 Jun 67 was estimated to cost $12.1 billion through FY 69, as compared to $7.7 billion

for Course B. The end strength increases for Course A and B were
602,900 and 276,000 men, respectively. Within South Vietnam the additional combat force in terms of battalion months available to COMUSMACV
for operations was markedly greater for A than under Course B. The
JCS calculated that Course A would add 111 battalion/months in FY 68 and
373 battalion/months in FY 69 for a total of 484. Course B, on the
other hand, could add but 39 in FY 68 and 144 in FY 69 for a grand total
of 183. This added combat power in Course A which was recommended for
deployment in JCSM 218-67 would, in the JCS estimation, improve chances
for "progress in the war to a greater extent than the Course B forces.
The primary advantage offered is that of flexibility. COMUSMACV would
have forces available with which to maintain his present momentum as
well as to expand combat and RD operations throughout the country." 15/

If Course A forces were deployed as they desired the JCS noted they
could be used to conduct operations in the DMZ, and into Laos or Cambodia
if such operations were desired. Otherwise they could be properly
employed in South Vietnam such as in the IV CTZ (the Delta). Course A
would, they predicted, contribute to a hastening of the war's conclusion.
The smaller Course B force would require the continued in-country deployment of additional forces to I Corps Tactical Zone to meet the "formidable enemy threat in that area." According to the Chiefs, this drawdown
of forces from other areas would inhibit the reaction capability of
U.S. forces in SVN that even with the increase proposed by Course B
the US/FW/RVNAF would not be able to sustain the momentum of present
offensive operations. The picture the memo painted of what would
happen under the smaller Course B force was bleak:

> (1) If the enemy maintains his current strength and
> force structure trends we cannot expect to attain objec-
> tives much beyond present goals, particularly the objective
> of expanding the areas under GVN control, unless forces
> are diverted from offensive operations. Thus we are con-
> fronted with an undesirable choice of a reduction of
> continued large-scale offensive operations in order to
> secure additional areas for expansion of RD activities or
> slowing the tempo of offensive operations in order to
> maintain security of areas cleared of the enemy.

> (2) Should the enemy successfully exploit a vulner-
> able point in our military posture we run the risk of having
> even a modest enemy success publicized as a regression. The
> present situation, with all forces in South Vietnam fully
> committed in their respective areas, would not be greatly
> improved. As a result COMUSMACV cannot influence effectively
> the course of one operation without disengaging from another. 16/

On the other hand, if Course A was pursued:

      e. The greatly intensified pressures against NVN
that could be applied by conducting the air and naval
operations described in Annex D are not dependent on
Course A or Course B force levels. These military actions
can be initiated at any time with existing forces. By
increasing pressure on the enemy's warmaking capability,
the cumulative effect would complement the effects of
added deployments in the south. On the other hand, continued restraint, further restrictions or cessation of
the air campaign would provide the enemy with an incentive
and allow him the means to sustain and increase his support of aggression in SVN relatively unmolested. 17/

On the bombing, the high military chiefs persisted in their recommendations contained in JCSM 218-67 asking for a more effective air/
naval campaign against North Vietnam, to include striking (closing)
principal North Vietnamese ports. The complete recommendations of
the study included:

      It is concluded that:

      a. The force levels of Course A for FY 68 should
be deployed as recommended in JCSM-218-67. They are
required in FY 68 to meet the threat posed in I CTZ, to
continue the pressures on the VC/NVA in SVN, and to sustain the progress of RD. Course B force levels would not
fulfill this requirement.

      b. Course A force levels would provide the capability
to deploy additional forces in FY 69 should such action be
indicated.

      c. Course A provides more flexibility in providing
the forces in the stipulated time frame for the immediate
need, a greater capability to accomplish the mission, and
a better posture for possible contingencies than does
Course B.

      d. As recommended in JCSM-218-67, a more effective
air/naval campaign against NVN to include the principal
NVN ports should be undertaken now with existing forces.

      e. Further restrictions or cessation of air action
against NVN would tend to prolong the war and could be
costly to friendly forces.

f. Significant measures to improve the RVNAF are being taken but only limited improvement can be expected within a reasonable time frame.

g. Efforts to obtain additional allied forces should continue; however, US requirements or capability should not be reduced until the commitments are firm.

h. Communist reactions to Courses A and B, and to the increased air and naval campaign would most likely fall short of forcing a confrontation with the Soviets or Chinese Communists but would involve attempted increased material assistance to NVN and increased propaganda against the United States. Free World support for the United States in each case would not differ materially from the present except where the attacks involved Cambodia.

i. US public reaction to Course A probably would be more favorable than to Course B over the long term.

j. A settlement of the conflict in shorter time at less cost should result from initiating Course A, together with a more effective air campaign.

k. Post-settlement conditions in SEAsia are likely to be better under Course A because of the greater level of US forces on the scene. 18/

A lay-out of the analysis of opposing courses of action as included in this document are presented in the following table: 19/

Part II

ANALYSIS OF OPPOSING COURSES OF ACTION

ASSUMPTIONS: For purposes of this portion of the analysis, the following level of military actions outside SVN are assumed: a. Expansion of the use of ARC LIGHT forces in Laos and southern NVN; b. Closing principal NVN ports c. Early destruction of remaining high value targets and intensified interdictions of supply movement into NVN by land/sea/air and from NVN to SVN.

FACTOR	COURSE A	COURSE B
1. Impact on progress of war.	Require forces, in FY 68, to control the enemy threat in the vicinity of the DMZ and simultaneously to maintain initiative and momentum in disrupting enemy main force unit operations, defeating enemy provincial forces and guerrilla forces at the margin of Revolutionary Development, and supporting an expanding area of RD effort. Provides in FY 69, forces for continuing momentum in further expanded area of RD, particularly in II until III CTZ, and a two RVN exploitation force to give COMUSMACV flexibility in destroying enemy main force units and major base areas and responding to their contingency situations.	Requires in-country re-deployment to meet threat to I CTZ thus inhibiting reaction capability in other areas. With only Course B forces, COMUSMACV may not be able to maintain momentum of present offensive operations and to attain objective of expanding area under SVN control. Course B will confront COMUSMACV with a choice between continued large scale offensive operations at expense of securing additional area for expansion of RD or slowing tempo of offensive operations to maintain security of areas cleared of enemy. Present situation wherein all forces in SVN are fully committed to their respective geographic area denies COMUSMACV the mean to influence the course of one operation without disengaging from another.
2. Effect on settlement.	While this course of action carries no pursuance of early settlement, psychologically, the nature of the actions taken should convince the enemy of US determination to pursue the war to a successful settlement, and militarily should result in rapid reduction of enemy controlled and organized effort in SVN. Net effect should force enemy to conference table or lead-in to final phase of war in which enemy will be defeated.	This incremental increase in effort in SVN, in conjunction with the increased pressures against NVN, under favorable circumstances, may permit progress towards settlement. It is more likely, however, that the enemy determination will not be undermined and that, by renewed effort, the enemy in the South will continue to be controlled and sustained at a sufficient level to unduly prolong the war.
3. Major policy decisions required.	(1) National decision for callup of Reserves and involuntary extension of terms of service. (2) Authorization for access to equipment from: CONUS depot assets and procurement production deliveries; operational project, contingency, and Reserve component stock; pre-mobilized equipment in Europe; and non-deploying units. (3) Authorization for reopening of CONUS inactive installations and expansion of facilities. (4) Timely provision of funds and authorization of end strength increases.	Except for decision in regard to callup of Reserves and extension of terms of service, decisions remain essentially the same but vary in magnitude. However, Course B entails a deliberate decision to pursue the conflict in SEAsia at a level less than that needed to progress steadily toward attainment of US objectives.
4. Probable reaction.		
a. Domestic.	In near term, expected to increase opposition and intensify polarization. In long term, expected to coalesce public opinion behind administrations apparent new determination and resolve to terminate war on acceptable terms, particularly if diplomatic efforts for negotiated settlement continue.	Course B provides little cause for a near term change to domestic reaction to the war in SVN but lack of marked results over the long term could result in further disenchantment with the war in SEAsia and increased pressures for the US to withdraw under less than acceptable terms.
b. NVN/Viet Cong.	NVN would defend the targets and seek additional aid, VC/NVA forces in South Vietnam would probably be directed to increase their harassment of the waterways in the South.	Same as Course A.
c. USSR/ChiCom.	Increased force levels should cause no significant direct Soviet or ChiCom military reaction. Propaganda, and increased material and technical support to NVN expected. Mining of ports and increased air actions expected provoke Soviet diplomatic reaction and deterioration in US Soviet relations. Increased and improved Soviet weapons.	Same as Course A.
d. International.	Some adverse reaction generated by callup of reserves and deployment of allied forces, required in certain quarters by realization US would be in better position to meet worldwide commitments. To major disruption of international attitudes so long as forces used as discussed Annex B. Increased cries of escalation and some loss of support due increased air/naval actions. Cambodian attack would generate world-wide pressures against US actions.	No appreciable reaction in international arena as result increased ground forces. Same as for Course A for increased air/naval actions and attacks on Cambodia.
5. Probable effects on SVN attitudes.	Favorable. Awareness of growing force on their side would be expected whet run leaders appetite for "total victory" and might make them reluctant to cooperate with US efforts to bring about a negotiated settlement short of defeating VC/NVA.	Same as Course A, with less impact on "total victory" appetite of SVN leaders.
6. Estimated costs (through FY 69) in addition to approved FY 68 DOD Budget. [1]	Army $ 8,650 million Navy 1,400 million Air Force 1,960 million Marine Corps 1,190 million Total $12,100 million	Army $ 5,800 Navy $ 1,345 Air Force 690 Marine Corps 0 Total 7,835
7. Approximate end strength increases above present force levels (through FY 69).	Army 465,000 (includes 150,000 Reserves mobilized) Navy 35,000 (all Reserves) Air Force 40,000 (includes 7,700 ANG mobilized) Marine Corps 54,200 (All Reserves) Total 632,900	Army 204,000 Navy 47,002 Air Force 25,000 Marine Corps 0 Total 276,000

[1] These gross estimates of costs include one time costs; such as equipping a division, reactivation BB, etc, and annual recurring costs such as pay, O&M, etc. For details see Annex A.

Part of the mystery as to why the numbers in the JCS analysis which we have just discussed differ from those stipulated by Secretary Vance in his request for an analysis of Courses A and B is explained by a 29 May 1967 memorandum for the Secretary of Defense from the Chairman of the Joint Chiefs. In it, General Wheeler identified certain factual corrections and annotations noted by the Joint Chiefs which should be entered so as to provide a "common basis of factual material." The corrections, General Wheeler noted, were factual only and did not address matters of policy, strategy, judgment, or opinion, as expressed in the Draft Presidential Memo of 19 May. He went on to comment that as the draft memorandum for the President indicated, COMUSMACV message 09101, 18 March 1967, included a "minimum essential force" for FY 68 and looking beyond, a probable requirement for an "optimum force" through FY 69. These forces totaled 4-2/3 division or force equivalents and 10 TFS -- 2-1/3 of these division force equivalents and 5 of the TFS to be deployed in FY 68 and the remainder thereafter. COMUSMACV estimated these forces at about 200,000. 20/ However, the Chairman continued, "the changed situation in South Vietnam including the formation and deployment of Task Force OREGON, the addition by CINCPAC of other PACOM requirements, and revised service estimates /had/ caused variation in the total numbers for FY 68 and beyond. While exact numbers of the larger forces /could not/ then be determined unless detailed troop lists are developed the following appeared at this time to reflect more accurately the probable personnel strengths, end strength increases and costs required to provide COMUSMACV a 4-2/3 DFE/PFS optimum force and the additional requirements through FY 69 that have been stated by CINCPAC.

Additional Forces for SEA ------------------ 250,000

Additional Service End Strengths ---------- 600,000

Estimated Additional Costs thru FY 69
over Approved FY 68---------- 12,000,000 " 21/

General Wheeler concluded that although the Joint Chiefs of Staff had not recommended the deployment of COMUSMACV's optimum force or even adoption of Course A as used in the Draft Presidential Memorandum, that the corrected figures which he quoted were more nearly representative of Course A than those of the DPM.

On 20 May, Secretary McNamara sent a short memorandum to the President replying to his request for comments on Senator Brooke's letter of 19 May, which proposed integration of the National Liberation Front into some kind of viable political role in South Vietnam's government or in its political life. Although these views coincided very closely to those submitted in the Draft Presidential Memorandum of the day earlier, McNamara commented that despite the fact that Brooke's proposals were almost identical to those which he had suggested he had not discussed any part of the paper or any of the ideas with Brooke.

On the last day of May, the Joint Chiefs of Staff replied to the 19 May Draft Presidential Memorandum prepared by McNaughton. It was a sharply worded and strong reply, expressing strong objections to the basic orientation of the paper as well as its specific recommendations and objectives. The Chiefs resented the implication of the DPM that Course A generally reflected their recommendations. They insisted that Course A as outlined in the DPM was an extrapolation of a number of proposals which were recommended separately but not in concert or ever interpreted as a single course of action as they were in the DPM. The JCS categorically denied that the combination force levels, deployments, and military actions of Course A accurately reflected the positions or recommendations of COMUSMACV, CINCPAC or the Joint Chiefs. They stated that the positions of the Joint Chiefs of Staff which would provide a better basis against which to compare other alternatives were already set forth in JCSM 218-67, JCSM 286-67 and JCSM 288-67.

There were five major areas of concern detailed in the JCSM: objectives, military strategy in operations, military strategy for air and naval war, the domestic attitude and predicted reactions in the international attitude and reaction. Reference objectives, the preferred course of action in the Draft Presidential Memorandum, Course B, was not considered by the military heads to be "consistent with NSAM 288 or with the explicit public statements of U.S. policy and objectives." In the eyes of the Joint Staff:

> The DPM would, in effect, limit US objectives to merely guaranteeing the South Vietnamese the right to determine their own future on the one hand and offsetting the effect of North Vietnam's application of force in South Vietnam on the other. The United States would remain committed to these two objectives only so long as the South Vietnamese continue to help themselves. It is also noted that the DPM contains no statement of military objectives to be achieved and that current US national, military, and political objectives are far more comprehensive and far-reaching. Thus:

>> a. The DPM fails to appreciate the full implications for the Free World of failure to achieve a successful resolution of the conflict in Southeast Asia.

>> b. Modification of present US objectives, as called for in the DPM, would undermine and no longer

provide a complete rationale for our presence in
South Vietnam or much of our effort over the past
two years.

c. The positions of the more than 35 nations
supporting the Government of Vietnam might be
rendered untenable by such drastic changes in US
policy. 22/

The strategy proposed in the Draft Presidential memorandum which
the Chiefs characterized as "making do" was not acceptable either:

Military Strategy and Operations (Other than Air/
Naval Operations in the North). The DPM favors Course B
with inadequate analysis of its implications for conduct
of the war in Vietnam. The strategy embodied in this
alternative - largely designed to "make do" with military
resources currently approved for Southeast Asia - would
not permit early termination of hostilities on terms
acceptable to the United States, supporting Free World
nations, and the Government of Vietnam. The force structure envisaged provides little capability for initiative
action and insufficient resources to maintain momentum
required for expeditious prosecution of the war. Further,
this approach would result in a significant downgrading
of the Revolutionary Development Program considered so
essential to the realization of our goals in Vietnam. It
would also result in the abandonment of the important delta
region on the basis of its being primarily a problem for the
Republic of Vietnam to solve without additional external
assistance. 23/

There was little more agreement expressed about the bombing, about
the domestic attitude or the international attitude:

Military Strategy for Air/Naval War in the North.
The DPM stresses a policy which would concentrate air
operations in the North Vietnamese "funnel" south of 20°.
The concept of a "funnel" is misleading, since in fact
the communists are supplying their forces in South Vietnam from all sides, through the demilitarized zone, Laos,
the coast, Cambodia, and the rivers in the Delta. According to the DPM, limiting the bombing to south of 20°
might result in increased negotiation opportunities with
Hanoi. The Joint Chiefs of Staff consider that such a
new self-imposed restraint resulting from this major change
in strategy would most likely have the opposite effect.
The relative immunity granted to the LOCs and distribution
system outside the Panhandle would permit: (a) a rapid

recovery from the damage sustained to date; (b) an
increase in movement capability; (c) a reduced requirement for total supplies in the pipeline; (d) a concentration of air defenses into the Panhandle; and (e) a
release of personnel and equipment for increased efforts
in infiltration of South Vietnam. Also, it would relieve
the Hanoi leadership from experiencing at first hand the
pressures of recent air operations which foreign observers
have reported. Any possible political advantages gained
by confining our interdiction campaign to the Panhandle
would be offset decisively by allowing North Vietnam to
continue an unobstructed importation of war materiel.
Further, it is believed that such a drastic reduction in
the scale of air operations against North Vietnam could
only result in the strengthening of the enemy's resolve
to continue the war. We doubt the reduction in scope of
air operations would also be considered by many as a
weakening of US determination and a North Vietnamese
victory in the air war over northern North Vietnam. The
combination of reduced military pressures against North
Vietnam with stringent limitations of our operations in
South Vietnam, as suggested in Course B, appears even more
questionable conceptually. It would most likely strengthen
the enemy's ultimate hope of victory and lead to a redoubling of his efforts. (See Part III, Appendix A, for
additional comments.)

Domestic Attitude and Predicted Reactions. The
DPM presents an assessment of US public attitude and
assumed reactions to several occurrences. Its orientation is toward the risks involved in Course A. The
difficulty of making accurate judgments in the area of
public response is acknowledged, and the Joint Chiefs of
Staff concede that their appraisal is subject to the same
degree of uncertainty that is inherent in the DPM. Nevertheless, they are unable to find due cause for the degree
of pessimism expressed in the DPM. The Joint Chiefs of
Staff firmly believe that the American people, when well
informed about the issues at stake, expect their Government to uphold its commitments. History illustrates that
they will, in turn, support their Government in its
necessary actions. The Joint Chiefs of Staff believe that
there is no significant sentiment for peace at any price.
They believe also that despite some predictable debate a
Reserve callup would be willingly accepted, and there would

be no "irresistible" drive from any quarter for unnecessary escalation of the conflict. (See Part IV, Appendix A,
for additional comments.)

International Attitude and Predicted Reaction. There
are several inconsistencies between the DPM and the published
intelligence estimates. For example, from these intelligence
estimates, there is no evidence that Hanoi is prepared to
shun negotiation, regardless of the pressure brought to
bear, until after the US elections. Also, it is estimated
that US prestige will not decline appreciably if prompt
military action is taken to bring the conflict to an early
close. In the long term, US prestige would probably rise.
The effect of signs of US irresolution on allies in Southeast
Asia and other friendly countries threatened by communist
insurgency could be most damaging to the credibility of US
commitments. The DPM contains the view that there is strong
likelihood of a confrontation between the United States and
the CHICOMs or the USSR, as a result of intensification of
air and naval operations against North Vietnam and/or a
major increase in US forces in South Vietnam. Intelligence
estimates do not support this contention. (See Part V,
Appendix A, for additional comments.) 24/

Summarizing, the Chiefs explained that the divergencies between
the DPM and the stated policies, objectives and concepts were individually important and in their eyes, reasons for concern. However, as they
viewed them collectively, an "alarming pattern" emerged which suggested
a major realignment of U.S. objectives and intentions in Southeast Asia.
The Joint Chiefs stated that they were not aware of any decision to
retract the policies and objectives which had been affirmed by responsible
officials many times in recent years (apparently stemming back to NSAM
288). In their view the DPM lacked adequate foundation for further consideration. Their conclusions were strong, namely that the DPM "did not
support current U.S. national policy objectives in Vietnam and should
not be considered further" and "there is no basis for change in their
views in the major issues in the DPM," and that "these views were
adequately stated in recent memorandums and reinforced herein." Implementation of Course B in the estimation of the joint body would serve
to prolong the conflict, reinforce Hanoi's belief in ultimate victory,
and probably add greatly to the ultimate cost in US lives and treasure.

The Joint Chiefs recommended that:

　　a.　The DPM NOT be forwarded to the President.

　　b.　The US national objective as expressed in NSAM
288 be maintained, and the national policy and objectives

for Vietnam as publicly stated by US officials be reaffirmed.

     c. The military objective, concept, and strategy
for the conduct of the war in Vietnam as stated in
JCSM-218-67 be approved by the Secretary of Defense. 25/

4. The Last Interagency Round of Alternatives

Certainly the Joint Chiefs of Staff had been correct in detecting
the basic policy realignment and the crystallization of opposition to
expansive increases in the war in South Vietnam or in the air war over
North Vietnam. If they had misread or underestimated anything it was
in the magnitude and the strength of this opposition as it began to
crystallize throughout different agencies of the government. As the
replies to the 19 May DPM from other agencies began to filter in there
was little doubt remaining that, in fact, the validity of the assumptions in the DPM were not those being called into question, but the
ones of JCSM 218-67 were under attack.

Before the other agency views on the DPM were received, however,
the JCS reported in again with their discussion of air operations
against North Vietnam. This was in response to a SecDef memo of 20 May
1967 in which McNamara requested the JCS to examine two alternative
bombing campaigns -- one concentrating the bombing of North Vietnam on
the lines of communication in the Panhandle Area of Route Packages 1,
2 and 3, with the concomitant termination of bombing in the remainder
of North Vietnam; and the other, to terminate the bombing of fixed
targets not directly associated with LOC's in Route Sectors 6A and 6B
and simultaneously expand the armed reconnaissance operations in those
sectors by authorizing strikes on all LOC's. Furthermore, the second
program was to be examined under two alternative assumptions, one in
which strikes against ports and port facilities were precluded, and
the other, in which every effort was made to deny importation from the
sea. (This final option was essentially that recommended in JCSM 288-67
dated 20 May.) To all of this, the JCS concluded that their original
recommendation on 20 May represented the most effective way to successfully prosecute the air and naval campaign against North Vietnam. The
Joint Chiefs' position was vigorously stated in their conclusion:

     The analysis provided in the Appendix supports the
conclusion that the recommendations submitted to you on
20 May 1967 represent the most effective way to prosecute
successfully the air and naval campaign against North Vietnam. Such a campaign would exert appropriate military
pressures on North Vietnamese internal resources while
substantially reducing the importation of the external
resources that support their war effort and could be
accomplished at risks and costs no greater than those

associated with the most desirable of the suggested alternatives, Alternative II (Ports Closed). Although the
Joint Chiefs of Staff recognize and appreciate the necessity for continuing review, they believe that the campaign
selected and recommended to you, together with expanded
efforts to increase the destruction and enemy consumption
of war materiels in South Vietnam would have a far-reaching
detrimental effect on the North Vietnamese capability to
support and direct the aggression against South Vietnam. 26/

Secretary McNaughton asked Mr. Martin Bailey to look this JCSM
over to determine if there were any areas of agreement between what
the JCS proposed on the bombing and what ISA at the time was proposing.
Particularly important was the key point on the unlikelihood of meaningful interdiction. Although the Chiefs did not specifically address this,
they did state that increased bombing as they had recommended in the
earlier JCSM on 20 May would bring about "a deterioration in the enemy's
total environment," leading to curtailment of his overall efforts and
increased difficulty in his support of the war in the South. The
Chiefs had objected to the first alternative that concentrated the bombing on the southern three route packages because they felt that it would
not appreciably reduce the flow of men and material to the south; that
it would permit the enemy increased freedom of action in the north by
allowing him to increase the density of his air defenses in the panhandle or Route Packages 1, 2 and 3, and finally, because they felt that
in the long term such a course of action would not appreciably reduce
U.S. losses. An undesirable side-effect, furthermore, was that such
cutting back might indicate to the DRV a weakening of the United States
resolve to the detriment of our basic goals and objectives in Vietnam.
Alternative 2 (ports open) was not felt desirable for all of the reasons
cited in the earlier JCSMs and, in addition, because it would not effectively degrade the enemy's war-making capability in any way. The "ports
closed" alternative was desirable, but, in a listing of priorities, the
JCS listed it behind the JCS course of action previously submitted in
JCSM 288-67, 20 May 1967, which proposed a wider, concerted attack against
all logistics facilities -- "the shouldering out" proposal. 27/

The issues then, as they were distilled and presented by the JCS,
involved first the notion that total pressure was what was required to
bring about some degradation of the North Vietnamese ability to support
the war in the south; that pilot losses would not be appreciably decreased,
and, finally, that shifting the bombing to the southern Route Packages
would be indicative of U.S. failure in North Vietnam. This JCSM was
carefully examined by McNaughton and his staff and the major arguments
as they were presented by the Joint Chiefs were incorporated in the
revised June 12th Draft Presidential Memorandum on the subject of
bombing options. 28/

The first detailed feedback from the circulation of the 19 May
McNaughton Draft Presidential Memorandum came from William P. Bundy
on 2 June when he wrote an incisive and highly perceptive memorandum
which argued that the "gut" point in Vietnam was not necessarily the
military effect of our bombing or the major force increases and all
the rest, but the effect that they had on the South Vietnamese. He
wrote:

> If we can get a reasonably solid GVN political struc-
> ture and GVN performance at all levels, favorable trends
> could become really marked over the next 18 months, the
> war will be won for practical purposes at some point, and
> the resulting peace will be secured. On the other hand,
> if we do not get these results from the GVN and the South
> Vietnamese people, no amount of US effort will achieve our
> basic objective in South Viet-Nam--a return to the essential
> provisions of the Geneva Accords of 1954 and a reasonably
> stable peace for many years based on these Accords....
>
> It follows that perhaps the most critical of all
> factors in assessing our whole strategy--bombing, major
> force increases, and all the rest--lies in the effect they
> have on the South Vietnamese. On the one hand, it is
> obvious that there must be a strong enough US role to
> maintain and increase GVN and popular confidence and
> physical security; although the point is not covered in
> the CIA papers, it surely is the fact that in early 1965
> virtually all South Vietnamese believed they were headed
> for defeat, whereas the general assumption today is strongly
> in the opposite direction, that with massive US help the
> country has a present chance to learn to run itself and
> a future expulsion of the North Vietnamese will take place
> although not perhaps for a long time. We have got to main-
> tain and fortify this underlying confidence and sense that
> it is worthwhile to get ahead and run the country properly.
>
> On the other hand, many observers are already reporting,
> and South Vietnamese performance appears to confirm, that
> the massive US intervention has in fact had a significant
> adverse effect in that South Vietnamese tend to think that
> Uncle Sam will do their job for them. This point was not
> included in the levy on CIA, and it may be that we need
> a judgment from the Agency, recognizing that it will be
> "broad brush" at best. The tentative judgment stated
> above need not be considered a shocking one; in our calcu-
> lations of two years ago, we anticipated the possibility.

But today, in facing decisions whether to make a
further major increase in the US performance and whether
to maintain at a high level that portion of the war that
is really wholly US--bombing--we must at least ask ourselves whether we are not at or beyond another kind of
"cross-over point", where we are putting in an undue proportion of US effort in relation to the essential fact
that in the last analysis the South Vietnamese have got
to do the job themselves. By "do the job themselves" we
mean concretely a much more effective South Vietnamese
role in security, pacification, and solid government while
the war is going on. But we mean also the progressive
development of a South Viet-Nam that can stand on its
own feet whenever North Viet-Nam calls it off, and can nail
down at that point what could otherwise be a temporary and
illusory "victory" which, if it unraveled, would make our
whole effort look ridiculous, undermine the gains in confidence that have been achieved in Southeast Asia and elsewhere, and have the most disastrous effects on our own
American resolve to bear burdens in Asia and indeed throughout the world. 29/

Turning to the specific question of the 200,000 man force increase
Bundy argued that the gains from such a major force increase were increasingly marginal while the effect on the South Vietnamese, a very much more
important factor and one which went to the heart of the conflict itself
and our ability to achieve a lasting peace, may not be so marginal:

Obviously, the assessment of the effect of our actions
on the South Vietnamese is an extremely difficult one. It
may be that the "cross-over point" was reached in late 1965,
when it became clear that we were conducting a massive intervention; perhaps any further change from additional forces,
on any scale, is at most one of slight degree. Certainly
we have all felt that our force increases up to their present
strength were absolutely required in order to bring about a
condition even more essential than maintaining South Vietnamese performance--the blunting and reversing of the North
Vietnamese effort that, in 1965, was about to take over the
country. But the question now presents itself in a new form,
when 200,000 more men do not make the difference between
victory and defeat, but at most the difference between victory in three years and victory in 5, on what is necessarily
a calculation assuming both South Vietnamese and North Vietnamese performance and morale as relative constants. And,
on the other side of the coin, we have reached a point where
the South Vietnamese have managed in part to pull themselves
together and must learn to do so more. Hence, the gains from

major force increases are now more marginal, while the effect on the South Vietnamese must be rated a very much more important factor and one which goes to the heart of the conflict itself and of our ability to achieve a lasting peace. 30/

On the basic objectives, Bundy disagreed with the Chiefs and expressed general agreement with what the McNaughton draft had stated. He believed that the minimum statement which we could make reference our objective in Vietnam was certainly "to see that the people of South Vietnam are permitted to determine their own future." But he felt it much too pat to say that "this commitment ceases if the country ceases to help itself," or even to observe that there are not further elements in our commitment. He believed additional commitments related not only to getting North Vietnamese forces off the backs of the South Vietnamese but to making sure that the political board, as he called it, in South Vietnam was not tilted to the advantage of the NLF. 31/

In his summary, he addressed this question of our commitment again, and then expanded upon what he called the hard core question, that is, what to do if "the country /Vietnam/ ceases to help itself." Using the teeter-totter analogy, he commented that our commitment must be to see that the people of South Vietnam were permitted to determine their own future and to see that the "political board" was level and not tilted in favor of elements that believed in force. He also believed that we should at least hold open the possibility that a future South Vietnamese government would need continuing military and security assistance and should be entitled to get it. He agreed with the Joint Chiefs analysis of the DOD draft and their contention that it displayed a negative turn to our strategy and to our commitment in Vietnam:

> In terms of our course of action, the major implication--as compared with the DOD draft--is that we will not take our forces out until the political board is level. The implication of the DOD draft is that we could afford to go home the moment the North Vietnamese regulars went home. This is not what we said at Manila, and the argument here is that we should not in any way modify the Manila position. Nor should we be any more hospitable than the South Vietnamese to coalitions with the NLF, and we should stoutly resist the imposition of such coalitions. 32/

On the second question, of what would happen if the Vietnamese could not help themselves or refused to help themselves Bundy argued for more time to take a closer look at the Vietnamese situation, especially the elections, before getting into a negative frame of mind about our Vietnamese military/political/economic commitment. In arguing this position he broadened the perspective embraced by the question and addressed the entire range of U.S. interests in Asia:

This is a tough question. What do we do if there is
a military coup this summer and the elections are aborted?
There would then be tremendous pressure at home and in
Europe to the effect that this negated what we were fighting
for, and that we should pull out.

But against such pressure we must reckon that the
stakes in Asia will remain. After all, the military rule,
even in peacetime, in Thailand, Indonesia, and Burma. Are
we to walk away from the South Vietnamese, as least as a
matter of principle, simply because they failed in what was
always conceded to be a courageous and extremely difficult
effort to become a true democracy during a guerrilla war.

We should not decide this lightly if the case arises,
and above all we should not get into a negative frame of
mind suggested by the DOD draft until we see what the situation actually looks like. As in Latin American cases, a
great deal would depend on how the military ruled, and
whether they made some pledge of returning to the Constitution and holding elections in the not-distant future. And
a great deal would depend on whether the military coup
appeared in any sense justified by extremist civilian
actions from any quarter. At any rate, let us not look
at this contingency--or any like it--in quite the negative
way that the DOD draft suggests. For the effects in Asia may
not be significantly reduced if we walk away from Viet-Nam
even under what we ourselves and many others saw as a gross
failure by the South Vietnamese to use the opportunity that
we had given them. 33/

If the ISA group proposing a stabilized ground strategy took heart
with the Bundy memorandum, it was positively elated when the reply came
from Under Secretary of State Nicholas deB Katzenbach. 34/

Katzenbach quote skillfully outlined the outstanding disagreements
included in the draft Presidential memorandum. First, Westmoreland and
McNamara disagreed on whether Course A, the infusion of 200,000 troops
would end the war sooner. Under Secretary Vance and the CIA disagreed
on the ability of North Vietnam to meet the force increases in the South
although, as Katzenbach later noted in his paper, the CIA figures were
somewhat outdated and the analysis was not "good." He listed a Wheeler-
Vance disagreement on the military effectiveness of cutting back bombing
to below the 20th parallel and on whether it would save U.S. casualties.
(The Wheeler label on this disagreement is not completely accurate since
JCSM 288-67 and the later JCSM 312-67, the bases for this disagreement,

were less the product of Wheeler, as the Chairman of the Joint Chiefs, than of the corporate body itself. As Chairman's Memoranda indicate, Wheeler had a much "softer" line on the military effectiveness of the bombing.) The CIA and Vance were seen as at odds because the CIA believed that the Chinese might not intervene if an invasion of North Vietnam did not seem to threaten Hanoi, while Vance stated that an invasion (of any kind) would cause Chinese intervention. Vance believed that the Chinese would decide to intervene if the ports were mined. CIA reports at the time did not mention this possibility. There was basic disagreement, as to whether or not we had achieved the "cross-over point" and more broadly how well the "big war" was going. One optimistic CIA analysis which Bundy quoted contradicted a later CIA statement expressing the view that the enemy's strategic position had improved over the past year. State's INR also disagreed with CIA on Hanoi's basic objectives, with CIA arguing that Hanoi was determined to wear us down or in the vernacular of the time "wait us out," while INR felt that Hanoi was really determined to seek more positive victories in the South. The INR also believed that the bombing was having a greater effect than did the CIA. CIA and Vance, of course, had been saying for some time that all of the worthwhile targets in North Vietnam except the ports had been struck, while as we have seen, the JCS disagreed with this assessment. There was some allusion to the dispute over whether or not inflationary pressures would be aggravated by the increase in U.S. forces under Course A. DOD said that these pressures were under control and could be handled if Course A were adopted, while the CIA felt otherwise. (Comment: This leads to the suspicion that the piaster limitation might not have been as critical as was originally believed and possibly was just an instrument of a sophisticated rationalization for limiting force increases in the earlier programs.) Katzenbach also cited a basic disagreement about just what message an increase of U.S. forces or a massive call-up of Reserves would communicate to Hanoi.

The general goals which the Undersecretary predicated in Vietnam and upon which he based the analysis which followed were: first, to withdraw U.S. forces from Vietnam; we would only do so with the high degree of confidence that three things were accomplished -- (1) that we would be behind a stable democratic government (democratic by Asian standards); (2) that we would confront the prospect of a reasonably stable peace in Southeast Asia for several years; and (3) that we will have demonstrated that we met our commitments to the government of Vietnam. To do these, we had to persuade the North Vietnamese to give up their aggression and we had to neutralize the internal Viet Cong threat while in the process being careful not to create an American satellite nor to generate widespread anti-American sentiment nor destroy the social fabric of South Vietnam, nor incur disproportionate losses in our relations with other countries or bring in so called "enemy" countries.

His overall prognosis for the war was not optimistic. He believed
that during the course of the next 18 months, the probability of achieving
our goals was quite low. In two or three years, it was possibly higher
depending again on what we did during the intervening period. He entered
a caveat, however, stating that because of our uncertain knowledge of
the motivation and intentions of both the Democratic Republic of Vietnam
and the VC in the South, that we may be closer to achieving our goals
than we thought. Moreover, the Soviet Union and Communist China would
influence the course of events in ways not easily predictable over the
next three years.

He assessed the battle in South Vietnam as "the key" and reviewed
the "big war" of attrition as one in which a flood of contradictory
indicators made it much more difficult to appraise. Enemy losses were
up 70% in the first quarter of 1967, but so were U.S. losses up 90%.
North Vietnamese/VC intentions were also doubtful but they appeared to
be set on an intensive grinding position-warfare campaign in the northern
provinces coordinated with offensive thrusts in the central coastal
provinces and the Western Highlands. All of these then possibly combined
with major actions against cities, provincial capitals in the III Corps
area. The overall object of such a strategy evidently being to inflict
maximum losses on the US/GVN in an effort to break our will. (Here he
noted that INR believed that the VC/NVA had a more positive approach and
were looking for real victories.

Pacification efforts came in for little praise. There was little
real progress reported and the short term prospects were not bright.
However, the long term prospects appeared better if ARVN could be more
effectively involved. However, it appeared that GVN and ARVN were going
to continue moving slowly, corruption was becoming more widespread and
the population was increasingly apathetic. Katzenbach said he could not
determine whether this was due to growing anti-Americanism or war-weariness
or what. He concluded that if we were winning the war, we were not winning it very quickly -- it had become a question of the will to persist
on either side rather than the attainment of an overwhelming military
victory.

With this assessment as background he then analyzed the two courses
of action. In his estimation, Course A, which added a 200,000 U.S. troop
increment and necessitated a call-up of Reserves possessed the following
advantages: It could hasten the end of the war by hurting the enemy
more. It could dispel Hanoi's notions about weakening U.S. resolve. It
could provide more U.S. troops to be used for main force sweeps and might
release U.S. units to help provide security for pacification. It might
persuade the Russians to counsel Hanoi to accept some kind of negotiations
rather than risk a much expanded war, possibly in North Vietnam. Katzenbach
listed a score of disadvantages for this course of action:

TOP SECRET - Sensitive

b. Disadvantages:

1. Introduction of these forces could lead to counter-moves by Hanoi, with result we have simply expanded the present war. (Need paper with better analysis of whether Hanoi could add troops.) Our position is one of meeting infiltration, not stimulating it. Even its proponents do not argue it could end the war in less than two years.

2. It might well be viewed by Hanoi as another sign of US impatience and unwillingness to persist. Hanoi might also see a call-up of reserves as a sign that we are running out of manpower.

3. Congressional and public debate on the reserve call-up would be divisive and give comfort to Hanoi.

4. It could mean a total eventual addition of 500,000 men; some limitation on our ability to act elsewhere in the world; and a cost of approximately $10 billion in FY '68.

5. It could lead to irresistible pressures for ground actions against sanctuaries in Cambodia and Laos, and increased actions against NVN. Problems involved in such moves -- NVN and even Chinese reactions. International disapproval. Problems with Souvanna.

6. Effect on US flexibility and, inevitably, US goals in Viet-Nam.

7. It could produce, to some extent, a growth in the South Vietnamese attitude of "let the US do it."

8. More troops probably mean growth of anti-Americanism. (Although we don't really know how strong it is now.)

9. Inflationary effects in South Viet-Nam.

10. Adverse international reaction to escalation and to what would appear to be significant US move towards a friendly occupation
of the country. 35/

Compared to this course the option of maintaining current force
levels possessed the twin advantages of avoiding all of those which we
just listed, plus it could improve the negotiating environment if some
progress were made without an expansion of forces. The disadvantages
of this course were also twofold: Hanoi could be encouraged by forces
levelling off and the possible bad effect on morale of U.S. and allied
forces.

To these original two options Katzenbach added what he called
two middle strategies. Each one of these would incur some of the
advantages and disadvantages of the two which we just listed above, but
to obvious lesser greater degrees. The first "middle" strategy was to
add 30,000 troops. This would not necessitate a Reserve call-up. The
second was to add enough U.S. forces to "operate effectively against
provincial main force units and to reinforce I Corps and the DMZ area." 36/
This he estimated would include a Reserve call-up.

The overall recommendation he made in this regard was, first, in
the South, to emphasize the war of attrition and to do this by adding
30,000 troops. The complete set of recommendations which followed read:

a. Add 30,000 more troops, in small increments,
over the next 18 months. This would show Hanoi
and our own forces that we are not levelling
off, and yet we would not appear impatient or
run into the risks and dangers which attend
force increases. Continue to try to get as
many more third country forces as possible.

b. Make a major effort to get the South Vietnamese
more fully involved and effective. A crucial
question. (Separate paper with recommendations --
advisers, joint command, threats, etc.) Tell the
GVN early in 1968 that we plan to start withdrawing troops at the end of 1968, or earlier if
possible, in view of progress in the "big war".
Pacification will be up to them.

c. Use the great bulk of US forces for search and
destroy rather than pacification--thus playing
for a break in morale. Emphasize combat units
rather than engineers. Leave all but the upper
Delta to the Vietnamese.

d. Use a small number of US troops with South
    Vietnamese forces in pacification, targetted
    primarily on enemy provincial main force units.
    Recognize that pacification is not the ultimate
    answer--we have neither the time nor the manpower.
    In any event, only the Vietnamese can make mean-
    ingful pacification progress. The GVN should
    therefore hold what it has and expand where possible.
    Any progress will (1) discourage the enemy and
    (2) deprive him of manpower.

e. We should stimulate a greater refugee flow through
    psychological inducements to further decrease the
    enemy's manpower base. Improve our ability to
    handle the flow and win the refugees' loyalty.

f. Devote more attention to attacking the enemy
    infrastructure. Consider giving MACV primary
    responsibility for US efforts in this regard.

g. Use all the political pressure we have to keep
    the GVN clean in its running of the elections.
    Press for some form of international observation.
    Play down the elections until they are held,
    then exploit them and their winner (probably Ky)
    in the international and domestic press.

h. After the elections, but prior to the Christmas-
    Tet period, press hard for the GVN to open
    negotiations with the NLF and for a meaningful
    National Reconciliation program.

2. In the North--the object is to cut the North off from
the South as much as possible, and to shake Hanoi from its
obdurate position. Concentrate on shaking enemy morale in
both the South and North by limiting Hanoi's ability to
support the forces in South Viet-Nam.

a. A barrier, if it will work.... or

b. Concentrate bombing on lines of communication
    throughout NVN, thus specifically concentrating
    on infiltration but not running into the problems
    we have had and will have with bombing oriented
    towards "strategic" targets in the Hanoi/Haiphong
    area. By continuing to bomb throughout NVN in
    this manner we would indicate neither a lessening
    of will nor undue impatience. 37/

This recommendation, essentially in line with that of McNaughton and his staff in ISA, was to provide powerful ammunition for the group pressing for a halt to the force increases and some stabilization of the bombing in North Vietnam.

On 8 June, McNaughton dealt once again with the dispute between the JCS and ISA over whether or not Course A as written into the DPM did or did not, in fact, reflect the recommendations of the JCS. Colonel Amos Wright of the Joint Staff had been queried by ISA as to why the JCS had objected to the wording in the DPM which asserted that Course A (or the addition of the 200,000 men) reflected JCS recommendations. The basis of the JCS objection, according to Colonel Wright, was first that the JCS had not yet actually recommended that COMUSMACV and CINCPAC be given the additional 100,000 men they requested for FY 69 and that the DPM discussed, in connection with Course A, various "extreme actions" especially ground actions that the JCS had not actually recommended.

ISA concluded, after this, that although the courses of action included under Course A had not actually been recommended as a complete package by the JCS. The DPM did not, or need not, say this. The Chiefs had discussed these courses of action as ones that "might be required" and had done so in close conjunction with increased force levels and escalated attacks on North Vietnam that they had recommended. Under these circumstances ISA felt justified to argue in the DPM that Course A should be rejected because it could quite probably lead to the "extreme" course of action flagged by the JCS even though the Chiefs had not actually recommended them. 38/

On 12 June, McNaughton submitted a draft memorandum for the President entitled "Alternative Military Actions Against North Vietnam" in which he incorporated the views of State, CIA and the JCS. He analyzed three major alternatives: Alternative A - the JCS proposal to expand the present program to include mining of the ports and attacks on roads and bridges closer to Hanoi and Haiphong; Alternative B - which would continue the present level of attacks but generally restricted to the neck of North Vietnam south of 20 degrees; and Alternative C - a refinement of the then currently approved program. In the memorandum, McNaughton (and later Vance) opposed the JCS program (Alternative A) on grounds that it would neither substantially reduce the flow of men and supplies to the South nor pressure Hanoi toward settlement; that it would be costly in American lives and in domestic and world opinion, and that it would run serious risks of enlarging the war into one with the Soviet Union or China, leaving the United States a few months from now more frustrated and with almost no choice but even further escalation. Refinement of the present program (Alternative C) was also opposed on grounds that it would involve most of the costs and some of the risks of Alternative A with less chance than Alternative A of interdicting supplies or moving Hanoi toward settlement. Finally, McNaughton recommended concentration of the bulk of the bombing efforts on infiltration routes south of the 20th parallel (Alternative B) because this course would, in his words "interdict supplies as effectively as the other alternatives, would cost the least in pilot's lives and would be consistent with effort to move toward negotiations." 39/

Implicit in the recommendations submitted by Vance and McNaughton on 12 June was the conviction that nothing short of toppling the Hanoi regime would pressure North Vietnam to settle so long as they believed they had a chance to win the "war of attrition" in the South. They judged that actions great enough to topple the Hanoi regime would put the United States into a war with the Soviet Union and/or China. Furthermore a shift to Alternative B could probably be timed and handled in such a way as to gain politically while not endangering the morale of our fighting men. In their recommendations, Vance and McNaughton were in agreement with Mr. Nitze, Mr. Brown and Mr. Helms in that none recommended Alternative A. Mr. Nitze, Secretary of the Navy at the time, joined with Vance and McNaughton in recommending B; Dr. Brown, Secretary of the Air Force preferred C; while the Director of the Central Intelligence Agency, Mr. Helms did not make a specific recommendation but stated that the CIA believed that none of the alternatives was capable of decreasing Hanoi's determination to persist in the war or of reducing the flow of goods sufficiently to effect the war in the South. 40/

The 12 June Draft Presidential Memorandum only momentarily diverted attention from the question of the ground force increases which it so skillfully skirted. However, it achieved one important purpose. It had crystallized opinion and also marshalled an impressive array of opposition against any significant expansion of the bombing for the time being, and reflected a surprising turn toward objectives much different than those originally stated in NSAM 288, anachronisms pursued in virtual isolation by the Chiefs.

Another argument against significant increases of forces in Southeast Asia came from the financial side of the Department of Defense. Balance of payment expenditures associated with the then current level of Southeast Asia hostilities was running about $1.35 billion per year above calendar year 1964 levels. If the effect of increased deployments were proportional, then a 25% increase in deployment would mean approximately $350 million dollars annual increase. However, as a later memorandum pointed out, the actual effect was not necessarily proportional. On the one hand there were two forces that would cause the increase to be greater than proportional, such as the increased demand leading to an increase in the prices of foreign products and, as demonstrated earlier in 1966, increased DOD expenditures had an effect on the domestic economy that tended to hurt the trade balance in that it caused inflation. On the other hand, and partially offsetting these two forces in the upward direction, there was some fraction of DOD gross IBP expenditures returned to the U.S. via increased exports to the benefitting nations. But this feedback was conservatively estimated at not more than 25%. Whatever the

effect might be, more or less than $350 million, it was agreed that
it would certainly be substantial and that this should be a major
consideration before recommending large force increases or larger
programs in Southeast Asia. 41/

Meanwhile, in the Department of Defense there was increasing
emphasis upon exploration of the increased use of South Vietnamese
civilians for U.S. troop support. This was partially in follow-up
to the directive from the SecDef to the JCS on 23 May of 1967 which asked
them to review their combat service support and headquarters staffing to
determine whether all units were required in light of the sharply
improved logistics posture and support provided from other sources. As
part of the overall program of improving the U.S. "tooth to tail" ratio,
the JCS were asked to determine which of the resulting "hard core logistical requirements" could be met by increased use of South Vietnamese
civilians for U.S. troop support. A preliminary review by Systems
Analysis had indicated a potential for saving approximately 20-25,000
troop spaces. 42/ These, in turn, could be reallocated to increase
combat force requirements recommended by the JCS or alternatively used to
reduce the U.S. burden in Vietnam. The deadline given the JCS for submitting their study was 1 August but as the press for decisions on
increased forces became greater McNamara went back to the JCS and asked
for both studies before his planned trip to South Vietnam at the end of
July. 43/ In detailed conversations over force increases with both
COMUSMACV and CINCPAC McNamara asked:

> Can we not make wider use of Vietnamese to reduce the
> number of U.S. military personnel performing support func-
> tions in SVN? This action would free U.S. men for combat
> duties and train Vietnamese in skills they will need to help
> build their nation. I believe it would be wise to expand
> the analysis I requested on May 23, 1967 (Combat Service
> Support Staffing in SVN) to include an analysis of each
> essential combat service support function to determine the
> extent it can be performed by SVN civilian personnel. The
> unit-by-unit, function-by-function review of support
> should be performed first; then, the essential require-
> ments should be evaluated to see which can be met by
> appropriately trained and supervised SVN civilians. The
> studies forwarded to me should separately show the line
> items and number of support personnel no longer required
> and the number for whom Vietnamese can be substituted.

> While organic U.S. military combat service support
> capability is obviously required in an active combat
> theater, the requirements in the permanent logistic enclaves,
> such as Saigon or DaNang, should be less than at forward
> locations, such an An Khe or Dong Ha. Further, some U.S.

military personnel are needed for such contingencies as
strikes, but the requirements should vary with the degree
of criticality of the functions involved. For example,
I understand that MACV's policy is to maintain at least
50% U.S. manning at each deep draft port. Why 50% and not
40% or 60%? Must this rule be followed for all types of
port personnel? USARV's use of Pacific Architects and
Engineers contract civilians for most of the repair and
utility work at 67 SVN locations suggests that neither
forward operations nor contingencies are adequate reasons
for using as many military personnel for support as we are
now.

I also doubt we have adequately explored the use of
"Type B" units which are a mix of military cadres and civilian
workers. A preliminary review indicates that there are
over 72,000 U.S. Army personnel in units which have alternative "Type B" TO&E's. Converting these units to "Type B"
would cut military personnel in support roles by over 25,000
men: this might provide another combat division. 44/

5. The McNamara Visit to Saigon

As the Pentagon feverishly prepared the background briefings for
Secretary McNamara's forthcoming trip to Vietnam an article discussing
the problem of mobilization and force levels in Vietnam broke in the
Washington Daily News. It touched a nerve around the Pentagon generating
a flurry of correspondence and studies. The article by Jim Lucas,
entitled "Partial Mobilization?" with dateline Saigon, observed that
the manpower squeeze was on in Vietnam. The United States had 472,000
men in Vietnam according to General William C. Westmoreland, who Lucas
quoted as having asked Washington for 200-250,000 more, bringing the
total to about 700,000. Lucas concluded on the basis of this remarkably
accurate estimate that such a total could not be achieved without some
sort of mobilization -- at least a partial Reserve call. He wrote that
it was equally obvious that the White House did not want any sort of
mobilization if it could be avoided before the elections upcoming next
year. Most Americans in Saigon, he noted, realized this, but they
weren't happy about it. He quoted a helicopter pilot as saying, "A lot
of us are going to die before then." The military officers that he had
interviewed were especially loathe to discuss manpower with anything
approaching candor. "I'll be damned if I'm going to tell Charlie how
much he has hurt us," one exploded. Lucas also questioned the credibility of military reports and estimates emanating from the White House.
He saw clear indications that some records were being camouflaged if not
falsified to hide the facts. Many commanders, among them a Marine air
group commander, said their reports on personnel and materiel were
being consistently upgraded in DaNang and Honolulu before going to
Washington. The article wound up on an equally sour note pointing out
the various personnel deficiencies by rank and by skills which existed

within both the Army and the Marine Corps in Vietnam. It noted that the Army was short of buck sergeants everywhere, rifle companies were extremely short of non-commissioned officers, Marine Corps squads and platoons were operating below acceptable manpower levels, and hundreds of Marine enlisted men with infantry training were being jerked out of other jobs and sent to combat units to replace men in battle. 45/

Lucas had come remarkably close to the truth and as a consequence the replies which were requested from the various service secretaries tended to focus upon the more detailed criticisms of manpower levels in different units in Vietnam, on military occupation specialty shortages, etc. None of the internally generated replies really grappled with the basic issue of whether or not the mobilization level was in fact dictating force levels and requirements in Vietnam.

The 3 July edition of the New York Times featured another article this time by Neil Sheehan, entitled "The Joint Chiefs Back Troop Rise Asked by Westmoreland" in which he noted that 70,000 additional men were needed to retain the U.S. initiative in the ground war. In this article, again very perceptive and accurate, a large amount of detailed information, supposedly classified, surfaced. The writer quoted the Joint Chiefs of Staff as having warned the Johnson Administration that if General William C. Westmoreland's minimum request for 70,000 more troops was not met the United States would run "a high risk of losing the initiative in the ground war in South Vietnam." 47/   Sheehan noted that the recommendation was submitted to Mr. McNamara on April 20 according to his sources and the administration had taken no action on it. This was, of course, JCSM 218-67. Sheehan believed the inaction on the COMUSMACV request was because the administration could not grant the increase without a partial mobilization of Reserves and significant rise in war costs--an estimate that was remarkably close to the truth. In the article Sheehan also revealed discussions about two alternatives, or what he called two levels of requirements, both of which he correctly identified as the "optimum" and the "minimum essential." He was a bit short of the level of the optimum quoting it as only 5 divisions or about 150,000 men. According to Sheehan's sources, Westmoreland had not supported his request for the "optimum" with the detailed arguments, apparently believing that he had little hope of obtaining it. But, the general had argued strongly for his minimum requirement of two more divisions with supporting units, about 70,000 men, warning that he needed these troops to retain the initiative in South Vietnam. On the 4th of July, Secretary McNamara sent a note to Mr. Phil Goulding, Public Affairs, asking him to follow up with Secretary of the Army Resor for replies to the charges made in the Sheehan article. On 5 July, Secretary Resor replied that in view of the low fill levels for officers in the Seventh Army, which reflected upon the overall Army readiness and which tended to substantiate some of the charges Sheehan had made about the problem of drawing down Army forces all over the world to supply Vietnam, he believed DOD should not attempt to answer Sheehan in the public press, and the matter rested there. 48/

To prepare the SecDef for his trip and to help him get at what were considered to be the "gut" questions to be asked on his field trips, especially reference pacification, Assistant Secretary of Defense Enthoven sent him a study entitled "Holbrooke/Burnham Study on Vietnam." Enthoven cited this study as a perfect example of why the U.S. involvement in Vietnam was so costly. In the Binh Chan district of Gia Dinh Province there were 6,000 U.S. and GVN troops that were tied down by the VC who really had more than a company stationed there. According to Enthoven and to the Holbrooke/Burnham Study, there was no prospect now that things would change or that anything resembling permanent pacification would take place. Holbrooke and Burnham attempted to tell why. According to them there had been a total failure in rooting out the VC infrastructure; that is, the VC officials and organizers, and unless such infrastructure was destroyed, US-GVN military and pacification forces soon degenerated into nothing more than an occupation Army. Holbrooke cited Operation FAIRFAX which began as a sweep of Binh Chan but bogged down rapidly into a static defense. He concluded that if U.S. forces were withdrawn after FAIRFAX, the VC would be in control of the area almost immediately. Enthoven was pleading for the Secretary of Defense to reorient his questioning as he toured the pacification and rural areas. He wanted the SecDef to specifically focus on the infrastructure questions. He recounted what he had seen as the typical briefing on pacification, the one which first covered the demoralization of the VC in area, the reduced number of incidents, but then skipped over the infrastructure question and went on to the pig program, the number of wells dug, hog cholera innoculations and so forth. Accordingly, he suggested that Mr. McNamara might pursue the following questions when talking to briefing officers on the field trip:

1. Is there an intelligence collection center in this district? Is there a U.S. adviser responsible for the center?

2. Who in this district has specific responsibility for rooting out the infrastructure? on the U.S. side? on the GVN side? What unit of command exists in intelligence gathering? in anti-infrastructure operations?

3. In this district what are the assets available for rooting out the infrastructure? Which are available full-time and which are available part-time? Are these assets sufficient given the population of the district, its area, etc?

TOP SECRET - Sensitive

4. In a step-by-step manner how do these assets
   function in rooting out the infrastructure?

5. What guidelines have you developed to measure
   success in rooting out the infrastructure? How
   can you tell how well you are doing?

Despite the prospect that these questions might prove very embarrassing to those giving the briefing, Enthoven felt that they were
extremely important and they must be answered or pacification might
not ever succeed. Of course, he did not include the crucial question,
this being whether or not U.S. forces should be or even could be
profitably engaged in pacification. The answer to that question, whatever it may be, could have a significant impact upon how U.S. decision-
makers viewed any future increases in U.S. forces justified by the
pacification requirement.

Probably the most important paper which the Secretary of Defense
took with him as he departed for Saigon on 5 July was a study prepared
by the Assistant Secretary of Defense for Systems Analysis, Alain
Enthoven, entitled "Current Estimate of Additional Deployment Capability."
In it, Systems Analysis had updated their original estimate of what the
Army could provide and was now convinced that approximately 3-2/3 division
equivalents could be provided to MACV by 31 December, 1968 without
changing tour policy, calling Reserves, or deploying NATO STRAF units.
Although development of this force would require drawing upon critical
skills and equipment from NATO STRAF, thus reducing their readiness, the
capability plan still satisfied the key requirement of not sheltering
the mobilization "pane" while still furnishing the 2-2/3 nominal division
force. The 2-2/3 force consisted of (1) the 198th Brigade, which had
already been approved for PRACTICE NINE; (2) the 9th Marine Amphibious
Brigade, partially approved and standing offshore, (3) the ARCOV Rifle
Company packets for use in making up the 33 additional rifle companies
(an earlier approval from the Secretary of the Army had been denied
because of the absence of trade-off slots for the 5,500 odd men in
this group); 50/ (4) the 101st Airborne Division minus one unit which
had already been deployed; (5) the 11th Infantry Brigade and a new
Infantry Division. Systems Analysis evaluated the augmentation of
33 additional companies as being worth one Division to which they
would add the 2-2/3 that were named units, thereby making up the 3-2/3
Division equivalents. The Table which accompanied this study is shown
below.

195   TOP SECRET - Sensitive

TOP SECRET - Sensitive

Additional MACV Requirements
and Estimated Capabilities
December 31, 1968 51/

Land Forces	Program 4 as of 3/18/67	MACV 3/18/67 Proposal	Estimated Capability	
Strength (000)	381	170	92	b/
Divisions	8-1/3 a/	4-2/3	2-2/3+1	c/
Maneuver Bns	(87)	(42)	(24+11)	d/
Artillery Bns	60-2/3	31	13	
Engineer Bns	48	14	14	e/
Helicopter Cos.	62	20	10	f/
Signal Bns	11	6	2	

a/ Excludes 1 Armored Cav Regt.
b/ Includes 6000 Army contract personnel.
c/ 2-2/3 nominal division equivalents plus 1 additional division
    equivalent representing the significance of ARCOV augmentations.
d/ 24 maneuver battalions plus the equivalent of 11 additional
    (approximate) because of ARCOV augmentations.
e/ Includes 6 battalion equivalents of contractor personnel.
f/ 17 companies by end Feb. 69.

The total basic units strength under this 3-2/3 division equivalent
was 51,249 troops, with a total force strength of 86,213. Although the
documents which are available are unclear on this point, it appears that
Secretary McNamara was prepared to authorize eventual deployment of all
of the 3-2/3 division equivalent force. Although, again, the documentation is incomplete it appears that he had been given the green light by
the President to negotiate anywhere below this level but not to exceed
it, that is, not to bump up against the crucial mobilization line.

Within the staffs preparing the briefings and the background papers
for the SecDef as he departed for Saigon there was a generally held
belief that this was the scenario which the Saigon visit would follow:
The Secretary would explore in detail the justifications for General
Westmoreland's minimum essential force after which he and the General
would bargain and negotiate the civilianization differences which could
be worked out. This "compromise" would be the ultimate force package --
Program V. There was little or any doubt among those working on the
exact force levels and composition of the different packages, that the
86,000 total which had been developed in the Systems Analysis memorandum would not be exceeded and probably that the final force program
package added would approximate closer to 50-65,000. 52/

TOP SECRET - Sensitive

The briefings given the Secretary in Saigon divulged very little different from the considerations and arguments presented ad nauseum in Washington. In fact they were devoted to nothing more than supporting the programs already submitted which were under consideration in Washington. But the discussions are useful to get a feel for what greeted McNamara in SEA and the tenor of thought of those operators on the ground in South Vietnam. Ambassador Bunker's remarks were guarded, attributed partly to the fact, as he noted, that he had been in Vietnam barely more than two months; Secretary McNamara and perhaps many others out from Washington had spent more total time in Vietnam than he had. Bunker proclaimed that there was general agreement as to what U.S. objectives were, but he wanted to recall them. They included:

1. A just durable and honorable peace through negotiations leading to a political settlement acceptable to the United States, the GVN, Hanoi and NLF/VC;

2. A chance for the Vietnamese people to choose freely the form of government under which they wish to live;

3. To help them build their own political institutions and develop a viable economy;

4. To make credible our obligations under the Charter of the UN and SEATO to resist aggression;

5. Eventually to develop regional organizations through which the Southeast Asian countries can carry on joint undertakings in economic development and mutual cooperation. 53/

He appraised our progress in the direction of achieving these objectives and noted that the difficulties that we were to face were still formidable. He disliked the term "the other war." To him, it was all one war having many aspects but all a part of the whole with each of them important and essential in achieving a successful conclusion. He thought the problem of Vietnamese capabilities and performance was partially a function of the fact that there was a relatively thin crust of managerial and organizational talent. This talent had to be located and the personnel possessing it trained as we went along. He counseled patience explaining that we could not expect the same degree of competence, efficiency or speed from the Vietnamese that we demanded of ourselves and that this tardiness on the part of the Vietnamese to react often became frustrating and required the exercising of great patience in the future. He did not sound like a man anticipating a quick solution to the problem -- especially a quick military solution. He felt that realism demanded that a number of programs receive top priority. He listed:

1. A vigorous, imaginative and flexible prosecution of the war within acceptable limits.

2. Through free and honest elections establishing a broadly based stable, functioning, constitutional government.

3. An expedited pacification program which will win the allegiance of the Vietnamese people including the Viet Cong, and which offers them the opportunity to become part of the social fabric of the country.

4. Reorientation of the mission of the Vietnamese Armed Forces and their revitalization with increased emphasis on improvement and quality.

5. The optimum use of available manpower.

6. Economic stability and development. 54/

He was basically optimistic about the progress of the military war:

In a series of splendidly executed offensive operations undertaken by General Westmoreland since late April in which a total of over 12,000 of the enemy have been killed in action, the enemy has been kept off balance and his time schedule has been disrupted. It seems apparent that the main effort of the enemy to achieve his summer campaign objectives has been postponed from May at least until July. General Westmoreland's strategy of anticipating enemy threats has paid off handsomely and is one which he intends to continue in view of what he foresees as an intensification of enemy attempts to achieve his summer campaign objectives.

An encouraging element of these recent operations has been evidence of increased effectiveness of the Vietnamese Armed Forces. In a number of heavy engagements throughout the country ARVN units have turned in highly creditable performances. They contributed materially to the success of the initial operations in the DMZ, killing 342 enemy with a loss of only 31 of their own forces. In a total of 14 other operations in the I Corps area during the past six weeks, ARVN units accounted for 1,400 enemy killed in action. In the II Corps area they also have given a good account of themselves and recently in the Delta

area of IV Corps conducted a highly successful operation.
I believe that where the ARVN is weakest, however, is in
their pacification role where motivation and performance
still leave much to be desired. Here, of course, the
Regional and Popular Forces are also important elements
and all are getting increased attention. While ARVN
morale and performance have been improving there is
evidence that that of the VC has been declining. It has
had increasing difficulties in recruiting and a growing
share of the enemy war effort is being assumed by Hanoi. 55/

But he too saw that the crux of the military problem was how to
choke off the North Vietnamese infiltration. To him doing this, which
he fully believed feasible, carried at least three primary advantages:

    a. It would drastically reduce the dimensions of
our problem in South Viet-Nam. Militarily we would be
dealing only with the Viet Cong whose problems of recruitment and supplies would be enormously multiplied lacking
the assistance and reinforcements of North Viet-Nam. I
believe the result would be that the Viet Cong would eventually wither on the vine.

    b. When the infiltration is choked off, it should
be possible to suspend bombings at least for a period and
thereby determine whether there is substance to the statement in many quarters that Hanoi would then come to negotiations; we should at least call their bluff.

    c. Tensions now existing between the U.S. and Viet-
Nam on the one side and Cambodia on the other should be,
over a period of time, relieved and our relations with
Cambodia improved, even though initially Sihanouk might
continue to allow the NVA/VC to use Cambodia as a haven
and a source of certain supplies. 56/

He realized full well that the means employed to achieve such an objective, of course, presented many difficult and delicate problems, both
military and political, but he expressed confidence "that with imagination and ingenuity, these can be met...."

    What is involved, of course, are operations within
Laos but I do not believe this fact should present
insuperable obstacles. The North Vietnamese Government
is a signatory to the 1962 Geneva Accords but its forces
have been in Laos both before and since the signing of
the Agreements. It is now using Laos as the main route

for infiltration into South Viet-Nam. Is it not logical
and reasonable, therefore, that South Vietnamese troops
should oppose and combat North Vietnamese offensive action
by whatever method can be devised in order to prevent the
invasion of their country? Guarantees, of course, would
have to be given to the Lao Government by the South Vietnamese, and I believe should be underwritten by us, that
Vietnamese troops were on Lao territory for defensive
purposes only and would be withdrawn immediately when peace
is secured. The operation, especially in its preparatory
stages, should be carried out with as much security and
secrecy as possible. I have made some recommendations as
to methods we might use to achieve these objectives. This
is a matter which I believe we should pursue with the utmost
concentration. 57/

These views, of course, accorded with those which the military had
been pressing for some time. COMUSMACV was fortunate in having such a
staunch ally in his battle for expanded operations into the sanctuaries
as well as the moral support for a more intensive war effort. Bunker
concluded his short introduction by outlining his current assessment
and summarized by saying that Hanoi's stance was one of determined
inflexibility until the situation developed more clearly in favor of
either the United States or the North Vietnamese. Under these conditions, he concluded that Hanoi might consider the next six-ten months
a crucial time of testing of wills. The period coincided with the
monsoon season, most favorable to the VC militarily and this, combined
with electoral pressures in South Vietnam followed by the pre-electoral
period in the United States with its mounting pressures for resolution
of the Vietnam conflict, seemed to indicate to Hanoi that a crucial
period of developments was emerging. Bunker estimated that Ho Chi Minh
held to the expectation that the United States could not significantly
curb infiltration or destroy the VC's military and political capability
in the next six to twelve months, and that by their domestic and international political pressures would dominate the course of events demanding
some sort of resolution of the war unfavorable to United States interests.

COMUSMACV, who followed the briefing by Ambassador Bunker, interpreted United States overall strategy as one of applying such pressure
on the enemy as would destroy his will to continue the aggression. In
COMUSMACV's words,

> ...we must convince the enemy that he cannot win,
> that time is not on his side. I believe that this strategy
> will succeed, provided we step up the pressure by rein-
> forcing our mounted successes. The grueling success of
> our air and sea offensive is being matched by the less
> dramatic success of our ground campaign. Although our

strategy in the South is necessarily defensive, our tactics are decidedly offensive. 58/

Of particular importance General Westmoreland felt was that the enemy had been refused strategic or significant tactical success:

It has been my objective to frustrate the enemy's plans, therefore I have given overriding attention to maneuvering troops to deny them battlefield successes and psychological opportunities.

During the past year, the enemy has --

a. Been forced by our naval operations to abandon plans to bring in large tonnages by sea.

b. Had to resort to use of the long rugged land supply route through Laos.

c. Been denied recruits in the numbers required from the populated areas along the coast, thereby forcing him to supply manpower form North Vietnam.

d. Been denied rice from the coastal provinces of I and II Corps in the quantities required, thereby forcing him to transport rice from North Vietnam or to buy rice from Cambodia. 59/

In summary, COMUSMACV believed that North Vietnam was paying a tremendous price with nothing to show in return. In his words: "The situation is not a stalemate; we are winning slowly but steadily and this pace can accelerate if we reinforce our successes. Therefore, I believe we should step up our operations in pacification in the south, increase the pressure in the north, and exercise new initiatives in Laos." 60/

The J2 estimate which followed COMUSMACV's overall assessment concluded that:

Overall, the enemy must be having personnel problems. His losses have been heavy, and his in-country recruiting efforts unsatisfactory. He is probably attempting to make good his losses by heavy infiltration, but we cannot conclusively prove this, nor do we know how successful he has been. We hear frequently of the so-called "Cross-over point" --- that is, when we put out of action more enemy per month than we estimate he brought into country and recruited for that month. This is a nebulous figure, composed as you have seen of several tenuous variables. We may have reached the "cross-over point" in March and May of this year, but we will not know for some months; 61/

and that the enemy could be expected to:

(1) present a constant threat in widely separated areas, (2) attrite US, FW and ARVN forces, and (3) gain military victories for propaganda purposes.

If our analysis is correct, his Main Forces have failed to carry out their part of the enemy's campaign plan. He has maintained his Main Force units as a threat-in-being, largely at the sacrifice of the other MF tasks. His immediate problem then, must be to improve his MF capabilities and operations.

From this analysis, what can we expect of the enemy in the future? First, we believe that direct participation and control of the war in the South by NVA will increase. The Northern Front, the DMZ Front, and B-3 Front have emerged as major NVA Control Headquarters. North Vietnamese leadership in III CTZ is increasing with the introduction of NVA units and political cadre. Senior Generals in COSVN are North Vietnamese. The B-3 Front and MR 5 are commanded by NVA generals. We have seen an increase in the number of personnel taken from MRIII in NVN whereas most of his personnel previously came from MR IV. This indicates an enemy willingness to draw down on his strategic reserves in the North to restore the situation in the South. Another indication of growing NVA control is the increased professionalism of his operations. His equipment is better, he uses heavier and more modern weapons, and his techniques (infantry - artillery coordination) more polished. It is obvious that the NVA effort has increased and will continue to increase as the VC effort falters.

Second, since we foresee increased NVA participation, we believe that the enemy is now, or will shortly, bring in significant numbers of NVA infiltrees or units. He must attempt to reinforce the units in the coastal areas. He must attempt to regain the initiative around the periphery of SVN. He must attempt to attrite us. To do this he will need more strength than we now see at hand.

To support this build-up the Laos corridor becomes
increasingly important to the enemy....You know of the
location of base areas in the Laos Panhandle which serve
as logistical, rest, and training bases and permit the
orderly movement of both men and material to SVN. There
has been heavy truck movement through the Laos Panhandle
which began in November and December and continued throughout the dry season. To improve his capability of supporting the war in SVN, he has constructed numerous bypasses at critical points along roads throughout the
Panhandle, extended Route 922 east into the Ashau Valley,
and improved and extended Route 96 south to Route 110 and
Base Area 609....Prior to the onset of the Monsoon Season,
Route 110 was a heavily used, main supply route leading
from Cambodia, through Laos into SVN.

Use of Cambodia will also be increased....The enemy has
established a Military Region 10 in SVN which extends into
Cambodia. He has stated that MR 10 is to become the biggest
base area of the war. He has formed a replacement and
refitting center reported to be 8,000 strong, in the Fishhook
Area for units badly mauled in SVN. An agent recently reported
a VC arsenal in the Parrot's Beak which produces assorted
mines, and repairs weapons. We do know that the Parrot's Beak
area is often used by the VC in moving men and supplies between
Tay Ninh Province and the Delta. 62/

Such an analysis held little prospect for the fading away which had
been predicted for this time of year in 1967. Furthermore, these trends
carried with them significant developments in terms of future enemy operations and these operations tended to shape the strategy which COMUSMACV
was planning to pursue for the remainder of the year. The J2 summarized
by noting, first, the advantages and disadvantages of the so-called
enemy "peripheral strategy," an exercise which emphasized that the Laos
and Cambodia sanctuaries were becoming increasingly important to the
enemy:

What does this mean in terms of future enemy operations?
From peripheral base areas in NVN, Laos, and Cambodia, he can
launch attacks designed to draw us into the border areas....
These operations can be mounted from terrain which is most
difficult for our intelligence effort to penetrate. When
forced to withdraw, the enemy will have sanctuaries into
which he can move to break contact, rest, refit and train.
This arrangement gives him flexibility in choice of operational objectives. For example, he can launch offensive
operations through the DMZ, he can attempt to seize the two

northern provinces; he can attempt a thrust through the
Central Highlands from Base Area 609 toward the coast, he
can threaten Pleiku and Darlac; he can launch an offensive
from MR 10 toward Phuc Tuy Province. Obviously, he can
combine several of these options. When he encroaches from
the sanctuaries in force, we must go to meet him. We cannot permit him to win territory, intimidate the people, and
move freely about the countryside and thus, gain the
psychological victory he wants.

This enemy "peripheral strategy" has disadvantages,
too. He will have to move supplies from secure areas in
Laos and Cambodia to those units located deep inside SVN,
where once he might have supported them with relative
ease by sea. Weather conditions impose restrictions upon
his land lines of communication, especially during the
wet season. POL and wheeled vehicle requirements are
increased as is his maintenance needs. Inside SVN, he
will be hard pressed to support large scale military operations along the coastal plains because of his long, insecure,
LOC's. Thus, he will find it difficult to make his main
force presence felt in the heavily populated areas. In
turn, this will reduce his access to manpower, taxes, rice
and other supplies normally procured from these populated
coastal areas.

SUMMARY

In summary, here are the significant elements of the
enemy situation as we see them:

1. His strategy of the war of attrition is unchanged,
and his determination to carry it out is evident.

2. He has been hurt, particularly in the coastal
areas of II Corps and around Saigon.

3. His Main Forces have not carried out their part
of the enemy's strategic plan.

4. His Main Force units require additional strength
to carry out their role.

5. The war is becoming more and more an NVA war, and
Laos and Cambodia are becoming increasingly important to him. 63/

The J3 briefing continually emphasized that a major redisposition
of U.S. forces had been required to take full advantage of the opportunities to engage the enemy. This was especially true in I, II and

III CTZ's, primarily in the DMZ area, in the Qui Nonh and in the border regions at the juncture of Kontum and Pleiku Provinces. After a brief discussion of the different force packages which had been requested by COMUSMACV/CINCPAC, the J3 went on to outline the major tasks to be accomplished. They were:

1) Contain enemy at borders

2) Locate and destroy VC/NVA

3) Neutralize enemy base areas

4) Maximum support to RD

5) Open and secure LOC

6) Interdict enemy LOC

7) Secure key installations

8) Emphasize Psy Ops 64/

J3 then presented a comparison of friendly and enemy maneuver battalions projected thru 30 June 1967. Then, he compared maneuver battalions, this time applying a weighted factor of 3 to each U.S. and Free World battalion and a factor of 1 for each RVNAF or VC/NVA battalion. These tables are shown on the following page. 65/

TOP SECRET - Sensitive

MANEUVER BATTALIONS

	U.S.	FW	RVNAF	TOTAL
31 Dec 66	79	23	153	255
30 Jun 67	85	23	154	262

837 RF Co's and 4028 PF Plt's

	U.S.	FW	RVNAF	TOTAL
30 Jun 68	111	24	154	289
Prog 4	(8)			
MEF	(18)			

MANEUVER BATTALION COMPARISON

	VC/NVA MNVR BNS	US/FW/GVN MNVR BNS	BN EQUIVALENT RATIOS*
End FY 66	161	220	2.2
End FY 67	162	262	3.1
End FY 68	162 (?)	289	3.5

* 1 US/FW Bn Equivalent to 3 VC/NVA Bn

206   TOP SECRET - Sensitive

Using these figures as a basis for comparison the J3 then
detailed what the enemy threats appeared to be especially in light
of increased or continued enemy infiltration. To meet these threats
he listed three roles in which our forces were deployed. One, containment or anti-invasion forces, countered the threat along the DMZ
and were needed for deployment opposite enemy sanctuaries in Laos and
Cambodia. Two, pacification and security forces required for support
of RD and security of base installations in LOC's; and three, offensive
forces required to defeat the enemy in the main force war and to invade
his in-country base areas. Under Course of Action A (Minimum Essential) -
21 battalions were required for containment; 168 for pacification and
security; and 100 for main force offensive, for a total of 289 by the
end of FY 67. These were, in the words of J-3 "within the time frame
under discussion a fixed overhead or a down payment on winning the war
which must be paid." 66/

Under Course of Action B (Optimum), the J3 estimated that containment forces would be increased to 27, this being based on the need to
counter the expected increased build-up of enemy forces along the DMZ,
in Laos and in Cambodia, all assumed possible because of restraints on
air interdiction plus the enemy's continued freedom of action in the
trans-border sanctuaries.

Of the 42 U.S. battalions then committed to pacification/security,
16 were in support of RD, 13 were in combined pacification/security
roles, and an additional 13 were assigned base and line of communication security missions. Of the 22 free world battalions, 21 were on
pacification and security roles and one on a security role only. Of
the 80 RVN armed force battalions 53 were assigned RD support roles and
an additional 27 were assigned security missions. Of the total number
of maneuver battalions available at the end of FY 67, 25 U.S., one Free
World and 71 ARVN battalions were considered available for offensive
operations. Then, using the battalion equivalents which he had quoted
earlier, the J3 analyzed what he had labelled Courses A and B:

> For a discussion of offensive capabilities under
> course of action A and B, let us turn to the second
> slide (UU). It summarizes the previous one and shows the
> aggregate number of US, Free World, and GVN battalions
> by the role to which committed. Note that the 97 batta-
> lions available for offensive operations at the end of
> FY 67 increases to 100 under course of action B. However,
> these numbers do not give the true picture. By applying
> the battalion equivalent ratio of 3 for a US or Free World
> battalion and 1 for an ARVN battalion, the offensive

capabilities at present are 149 ARVN bn equivalents.
Course of action A represents a 34% increase (200 bn
equivalents) over our present offensive capability.
Course of action B represents only a 4% increase (155)
over our present offensive capability. These offensive
forces are what remain after commitment of forces to
containment of the enemy threat and pacification and
security. (The end FY 67 column was the actual distribution of units as of 30 June 1967. However, during
any given week the forces in the containment and offensive
roles, and to a lesser degree, those performing pacifica-
tion/security missions will vary. It would be misleading
to say they represent precise estimates, rather the
numbers are representative of the basic distribution of
our forces to varying roles and illustrative of the type
of war we are fighting.) It is possible that additional
forces may be required for containment since the 27 battalions represent only an estimate of what will be
necessary. If so, we may be required to take units from
the pacification and security or offensive roles. Should
this be required, course of action A provides a greater
operational flexibility for offensive action or reinforcement of our containment forces. Under course of action B,
however, response to contingencies must be met at the
expense of forces committed to pacification and security
or offensive roles.

In summary, the reduced forces under course of
action B; the limitation of air operations north of 20°
latitude; and the restriction of ground action to South
Vietnam could reinforce Hanoi's determination to prolong
the conflict. In particular, the restriction of out-of-
country air and ground operations would increase the
enemy's capability to concentrate his defense, maintain
his LOC's and require us to divert additional ground forces
to the containment role. Under these circumstances, we
present the enemy increased options to prolonging the
war. Course of action B does not provide us with reasonable assurance that, given the present objectives, there
would be any prospects of an early settlement of the
conflict. This is not to imply we might not eventually
win the war of attrition but it would be a long drawn
out process and would postpone the time when US forces
could redeploy from South Vietnam. 67/

The sum total of the briefings did not vary from what McNamara
had heard so many times before: that there was an increasing NVA
presence in control of the war; that it was increasingly becoming a
main force battle; that the sanctuaries were becoming increasingly
important to the enemy both for the logistics and tactical advantages
they offered. It was clear that MACV's view of the war in these terms,
as increasingly a main force battle to be fought by American units,
had considerable influence upon the strategies that they pursued, as
well as their calculations of resources required to carry them out.
By the final day of his visit in Saigon no resolution of the ground
force requirements had really been arrived at. However, on the final
evening, Secretary McNamara and General Westmoreland, accompanied by
General Abrams sat down after dinner and worked out what seemed to be
an equitable provision of forces below the mobilization level. In
this, they took what was commonly accepted as available, approximately
the 3-2/3 divisions outlined by Enthoven, and subtracted those which
the COMUSMACV had stated were possibly available for civilianization
during the next year, some 14,400. Computed, this came to approximately
a 45,000 force increase, since part of the PRACTICE NINE barrier brigade
had already been included in the Program 5 total.

The events of the next week, July 8-13, indicated that COMUSMACV
was not completely prepared to support the 525,000 level which was agreed
upon, a level, incidentally, which coincided with the old program 4
optimum request submitted by COMUSMACV in the fall of the previous
year. General Dunn, who was General Westmoreland's force planner,
worked his staff throughout the night prior to the Secretary of Defense's
departure on the 9th. He prepared a rough troop list under the 525,000
limit which he hand carried back to the Joint Staff for refinement. 68/

6. The Compromise--Slightly More of the Same

At the point of Secretary McNamara's return to Washington, planning
on force structures travelled along two parallel tracks for the next week.
As General Dunn conferred with the JCS and the Joint Staff and they tried
to refine the force within the 525,000 level, Secretary McNamara initiated
a study in Systems Analysis to flesh out the 525,000, or as so often was
the case, to prepare the OSD position with which to compare and evaluate
the JCS recommendation which would come. According to Mr. McNamara's
instructions to Secretary Enthoven, the 525,000 package would include
19 battalions in addition to the 87 already included in Program 4 through
the previous March. The sources of the 19 battalions were to be as
follows: 3 PRACTICE NINE barrier brigade; 3 from the 9th MAB, 6 from
the deployment of the 101st Airborne Division; 3 from the 11th Infantry
Division (the Brigade in Hawaii), and 4 new battalions formed in lieu
of the 24 rifle companies proposed in the ARCOV recommendation. In
addition to these 19 battalions, 9 ARCOV rifle company equivalents,
equivalent to three more battalions in foxhole strength, would be

approved if they could be included in the 525,000 ceiling. (This
accounts for the original ARCOV total of 33 battalions dropping out
in the subsequent figures and planning for Program 5). The 525,000
also included five TFS, 3 Air Force and two Marine. Of these squadrons,
two Air Force would be scheduled to move. The other three would be
included in the plan but without a movement schedule, although as a
footnote, "their availability when needed" was recognized. Enthoven
proceeded by directing that Program 5 should be prepared for publication with a strength of 525,000 minus the strengths of the three air
squadrons now scheduled for deployment. 69/

Another subject which occupied much focus of attention in early
July when Program 5 approached final approval was how to go about
obtaining additional troops from our allies in South Vietnam.

A 13 July 1967 memorandum for Rusk, McNamara, Rostow and Katzenbach, Subject: Messages to Manila Nations and Possibilities for
Additional Troop Contributions, prepared by William P. Bundy following
a luncheon with the President indicates just how urgently everyone saw
the problem and how much they desired to obtain troops from these
sources. In accordance with the directives at the luncheon, Bundy had
put together a series of letters making the need for additional forces
more clear and blunt. Even though the letters were all put in terms
of early indication of prospects or exchanges of views rather than a
blunt request for additional forces, the message was unmistakeable. 70/
Australia and New Zealand were seen as being prepared to come in with
"more" but it was expected that their contribution would be modest in
relation to the need, perhaps 2,000 or 3,000 from the Australians and
a few hundred from the New Zealanders. The Philippines were characterized
as a "doubtful starter," at least in the immediate future. Anything over
2,000 from the Philippines by whatever route seemed highly unlikely. In
Korea, Park himself seemed to be willing, but he had already fended off
the Vice President's general approach completely and it was clear that
he intended to get his political situation straightened out before he
moved with any additional forces for the United States. At best Korea
appeared to be a prospect for action in late fall and with perhaps an
additional division coming by the end of the year. Thailand was considered a possibility with the thought that it might come through with
an additional 3 - 5,000 over the next six months, but it would, in
Bundy's words, "take very careful handling." In fact, earlier on
3 July the President had had a conversation with the King of Thailand
on just this very subject. The President had posed the problem raised
for the United States by the need to respond to General Westmoreland's
request for an additional 200,000 troops. He said that it would be
impossible for him, President Johnson, to get support for such additional forces unless the troop-contributing allies also put in more

troops on a proportional basis. Thanat pointed out that when the Thai
government asked for 2,500 volunteers in Vietnam, 50,000 had come forward, but the King pointed out the problem was not men willing to fight,
but training and weapons. The President said that we could help with
training and equipment. The problem was to get a distribution of the
200,000 which was fair and equitable. The President then asked Mr.
Rostow on the basis of population how might the extra 200,000 be distributed? Rostow had replied that it came out to something like 125,000
and 75,000, with Thailand required to put up about 20,000 as its share.
The King then cited three problems: the quality of recruits, to which
the President had said we also had to draw on and train men of lower IQ
and physical quality than we might wish; the training and equipment of
additional troops and the improved equipment of the forces left behind
in Thailand. The King elaborated at some length on the psychological
and political problems posed by the latter element, saying it was very
hard for the military to accept sending troops abroad well equipped when
they themselves were lacking in modern equipment. After discussing the
specific equipment, the President telephoned Secretary McNamara and
informed him of the King's response to which McNamara said that it would
not be worth our while to train and equip a few thousand more Thais for
Vietnam but if Thailand could furnish 10,000 he could guarantee their
training and equipment. 71/

On 20 July, the Joint Chiefs of Staff responded to the request
from the Secretary of Defense for the detailed troop list providing
the specified forces for COMUSMACV within the ceiling of 525,000. Significantly in this JCSM, the Joint Chiefs of Staff did not concur in
the inclusion of the elements of the 9th MAB and the non-deployed
tactical fighter squadrons in the Republic of Vietnam ceiling. They
argued that the 9th MAB was already included for PACOM under Program 4
and that it had never been included as part of the MACV force structure
and was not added in the RVN spaces in MACV's package 5 alternative
force structure. They wanted to maintain a string on it since the
brigade was ticketed for the PACOM Reserve and subject to employment in
other areas depending upon the criticality of the contingency. The
Chiefs wanted the 9th MAB when ashore in RVN to be carried as a temporary
augmentation as was being done under Program 4. Similarly, they wanted
the Tactical Fighter Squadrons to be maintained in a "ready to deploy
status" outside of RVN, included in the RVN ceiling only if and when
they deployed in-country. They also expressed doubt as to whether MACV
could recruit suitable civilian personnel in the competitive market on
a civilian direct-hire basis to replace 8,100 military spaces. They
believed "that the forces included in the attached troop list will
contribute significantly to the prosecution of the war, but are less
than those recommended by the Joint Chiefs of Staff in JCSM 218-67, dated
20 April 1967, Subject: Force Requirements -- Southeast Asia, FY 1968.
The views of the Joint Chiefs of Staff as set forth in JCSM 288-67 which
also provided an assessment of U.S. worldwide military posture are still

considered valid." 72/   This was, of course, reaffirming a force
requirement of 2-1/3 divisions "minimum essential" and the add-on
2-1/3 division for the "optimum" in FYs 68 and 69 respectively.

On 21 July, Systems Analysis prepared a comparison of the JCS
recommendations as contained in JCSM 416-67 and those proposed by
OSD. The OSD proposal was actually prepared in Systems Analysis
per McNamara's earlier 13 July directive. The major differences
between OSD & JCS occurred both over the MAB and the TFS battalion
which we just outlined and the civilianization issue with the JCS
recommendation requiring over 12,000 civilianization slots and the
OSD recommendation not quite half that number. A summary table of
the two recommendations appears below. 73/

JCS Recommendations

	Army	Navy	AF	MC	Total
Program #4	323,735 a/	30,039	56,148	74,550	484,472
FY 68 Added Forces	34,398 b/	7,772	3,380	7,523 c/	53,073
Civilianization	d/	d/	d/	d/	-12,545
Program #5	358,133 d/	37,811 d/	59,528 d/	82,073 d/	525,000

OSD Recommendations

	Army	Navy	AF	MC	Total
Program #4	323,735 a/	30,039	56,148	74,550	484,472
FY 68 Added Forces	33,297 b/	4,234	2,242	7,523 c/	47,296
Civilianization e/	-5,414	- 812	- 542	-	-6,768
Program #5	351,618	33,461	57,848	82,073	525,000

a/ Includes the 198th Brigade (3 Infantry battalions)
b/ Includes the 101 Div (-), 11th Brigade and 3 separate
    battalions (13 infantry battalions)
c/ Includes 9th MAB, currently authorized in SVN until
    1 Sept. (3 infantry battalions)
d/ Less Service portion of civilianization to be determined.
e/ OSD estimate of Service breakout of civilianization.
    Actual breakdown is undetermined.

There were several decisions which Enthoven in his memorandum to
McNamara recommended be deferred for the time being. These included
an Army intelligence augmentation and a MACV headquarters JTV, a Navy
request for two mobile construction battalions, two construction battalion
maintenance units and various staffs as well as an Air Force A-1 TFS
civil engineer squadron and UC 123 herbicide augmentation. JCSM 218-67
which recommended the original MACV "minimum essential force" included
certain out of country forces also, primarily three tactical fighter

squadrons in Thailand, five additional destroyers and two battleships and two cruisers for naval gunfire support. Although these forces were not specifically addressed in the latest JCSM 416-67, Enthoven recommended that they be addressed at that time. Accordingly, he recommended that the TFS recommended by the JCS be unfavorably considered since he felt it would not contribute significantly to our effort in Southeast Asia and that one battleship be authorized and that other than that the increments in JCSM 218-67 be disapproved. These recommendations were approved by Secretary McNamara in a memorandum for the Chairman of the Joint Chiefs, dated 10 August. In it, he wrote:

> I tentatively approve for planning the forces as recommended for SVN in the enclosure to JCSM 416-67 dated July 20, 1967 except for those units and augmentations listed in the enclosure, pending submission of adequate justification. The 9th MAB, the rotational APB, and tactical air squadrons ready for deployment will be included in the 525,000 SVN U.S. strength ceiling. Deployment authority for the two VMA/VMFA Marine squadrons will be considered separately.

The table below summarizes the approved force levels.

	Army	Navy	AF	MC	Total
Program #4	323,735	30,039	56,148	74,550	484,472
FY 68 Added Forces	33,297	4,234 a/	2,242	7,523	47,296
Civilianization	-5,414	- 812	- 542	-	-6,768
Program #5	351,618	33,461	57,848	82,073	525,000

a/ Includes transfer of 1 APB (199 personnel) from offshore to in-country.

I recognize that the FY 68 troop list has not been refined. In order to provide for timely budget actions, please submit for my detailed review your refined troop list, with detailed justification by September 15, 1967. Your submission should include a monthly schedule of civilianization/tradeoffs, identified by unit and Service, in order to insure that U.S. forces in SVN do not exceed 525,000. For planning purposes, Program #5 will reflect a total civilianization, trade-off schedule as follows:

	Jan 68	Feb	Mar	Apr	May	Jun	Total
Army	500	500	1000	1000	1000	1414	5414
Navy	100	100	100	100	200	212	812
AF	-	100	100	100	100	142	542

Any added requirements in your refined troop list including deferred units should be fully justified and accompanied by corresponding civilianization or trade-off spaces.

The additional out-of-country forces proposed in JCSM 218-67 are not approved except for the 5 additional destroyers for gunfire support. These destroyers are approved providing they can be made available from existing active fleet assets. In addition, I am considering the activation and deployment of 1 battleship in a separate action.

This was in the ratification of Program 5 which was to be formally published on 14 August. 74/

The final decision in mid-August came as no surprise to either the public or to the Secretaries or to anyone included in the distribution of the finished program for that matter, for in his tax budget message to Congress on 4 August President Johnson had disclosed plans to dispatch between 45 and 50,000 troops to Vietnam bringing the total to 525,000. A New York Times article noted that it was a "compromise between the 70,000 men sought by Westmoreland and the 15-30,000 men suggested by Secretary of Defense, Robert S. McNamara." That it was. However, the announcement was greeted in both the public press and in the public consciousness with a certain resignation which bordered on apathy. Clark Clifford and General Maxwell Taylor had already been dispatched to the Far East, ostensibly to visit allies and to explain the course of American policy in the war, but there was little secret that they were out scrounging troops and trying to induce commitments from some of the nations which had already contributed or those which were being reluctant to contribute more. Their return on 6 August only increased the public pressure for they reported "wide agreement among allies fighting in South Vietnam to increasing pressure on the enemy." A day later, Johnny Apple's article on "stalemate" broached the subject in the public press. In it, Apple outlined in consumate detail the infiltration figures showing that the United States was failing to "win" the big war because of the ability of the North Vietnamese to reinforce faster than we could kill them; he quoted the infiltration statistics both official and those which he had derived from his time in Vietnam from "unofficial sources," all quite accurate. He cited the constant need for reinforcements as a measure of our failure. The article which received wide circulation both in Vietnam and especially in the decision-making circles of the Pentagon merely confirmed what many had been saying officially and unofficially for some time -- that infiltration was a

crucial variable; that there was no indication that the North Vietnamese had lost stomach for the war; nor did the NVA lack the capability
to reinforce at a much higher level than we had anticipated.

As Program 5 broke almost as if programmed, General H. K. Johnson
announced in his visit to Saigon that there was "a smell of success
in every major area of the war." In a Senate Preparedness Subcommittee
report given by Senator Stennis he repeated their incessant demand
that we have a sharp intensification of the air war over North Vietnam
in an attempt to stem the infiltration. General Cao Van Bien, Chief of
Staff of the South Vietnamese Armed Forces said he was convinced, however, that bombing of North Vietnam would never adequately control
infiltration. That "we have to solve the problem of Laos and Cambodia
and the sanctuaries or the war might last 30 years."

The program which emerged and was ratified in this environment, of
public debate and concern, was essentially the result of the circular
path traced far back to the optimum request of Program 4. Its origins
and its limits can be traced to one primary factor -- that of mobilization.
When the President and the Secretary of Defense, as well as other
Congressional leaders and politically attuned decision makers in the
government began to search for the illusive point at which the costs of
Vietnam would become inordinate, they always settled upon the mobilization line, the point at which Reserves and large units would have to be
called up to support a war which was becoming increasingly distasteful
and intolerable to the American public. Domestic resource constraints
with all of their political and social repercussions, not strategic or
tactical military considerations in Vietnam, were to dictate American
war policy from that time on.

7. Follow-Ons

Hardly had the ink dried on approval of Program 5 deployments, when
pressures began to build for the acceleration of these deployments to
Vietnam. On 6 September 1967, the Acting Chairman informed the Joint
Chiefs of Staff that he had been queried as to what could be done to
speed up or accelerate Program 5 deployments. Although ostensibly the
reason for accelerated deployments was to meet the threat in the DMZ
and I CTZ, the Acting Chairman indicated he had been specifically asked
to look at:

  a. What could be done prior to Christmas.

  b. What could be done prior to March 12, the date of the
New Hampshire primary election.

The Chiefs were to look into the subject on an urgent basis and to
provide their views to the Acting Chairman by 9 September 1967. 75/

A Director's Memorandum to the Acting Chairman, in response to this inquiry, was forwarded on 9 September. This Memorandum indicated that the refined Program 5 troop list then being developed by the Joint Staff indicated that a total of 62,132 Program 5 forces had not been ordered deployed as of that date. Of these, approximately 9% were scheduled to be deployed in Calendar Year 67, 35% to be deployed 1 January to 1 March 1968, and the remainder scheduled to be deployed after 1 March. Most of the forces scheduled to deploy in FY 1969 were controlled by long lead time equipment and were not subject to acceleration into the January-February 1968 time frame. A hurried analysis, however, indicated that about 1,700 Navy personnel, scheduled to deploy after 1 March, might be accelerated to January-February 1968 deployments. Since neither the Air Force nor the Marines had an appreciable number scheduled to deploy after 1 March 1968, the fruitful area for further exploration quickly turned to the Army capability for accelerating deployment. The bulk of the Army combatant units was scheduled to deploy in February-March 1968. These included the 101st Airborne Division (-), and the 11th Light Infantry Brigade in February 1968, and 4 separate infantry battalions in March 1968.

The Army indicated that 1 brigade task force plus the division head-quarters, approximately 4,500 personnel, of the 101st Airborne Division (-), could, in fact, be accelerated to arrive in-country by 15 December 1967, and the remainder of the division (-), approximately 5,500 personnel, could be accelerated to arrive in-country on 31 January 1968, under the following conditions:

    a. Movement by air would be required and would cost $15M more than movement by surface;

    b. Non-divisional support units which were planned to accompany the division could not be accelerated; therefore the support must be provided by in-country resources.

    c. Additional unit training in-country of approximately four weeks would be required before the units would be fully combat ready.

The 11th Light Infantry Brigade could be accelerated for arrival in-country by 31 January 1968, if it were to be deployed by air.

The Director's memorandum listed several possible actions to be explored with the Services which might speed up Program 5 deployments. Among these were:

    1. Delay commencement of civilianization program until after 1 March 1968. Thereafter use personnel released by civilianization for fill of skeleton units or for in-country activation of new units.

    TOP SECRET - Sensitive

2. Deploy unit without equipment to join like unit in South Vietnam for double shifting on the available equipment. This pertains primarily to service support type units.

3. Withdraw deployable elements from existing combat/ mission ready units in CONUS and Europe for deployment to South Vietnam. Replace these units by others presently being readied for South Vietnam.

4. Draw down personnel and equipment from existing units in CONUS (including reserve equipment) and Europe as required to expedite readiness of units for deployment.

5. Substitute ready units located in CONUS and Europe for early deployment to South Vietnam for those units which cannot be readied by 1 March 1968.

6. Deploy units to South Vietnam in substandard readiness condition in personnel, training and/or equipage. Raise the unit to satisfactory state of combat/mission readiness in South Vietnam prior to commitment to combat or combat service support role.

7. Deploy units to bases in PACOM (Hawaii, Guam, Okinawa, Philippines, Japan and Korea) in substandard readiness condition in personnel, training and/or equipage. Raise unit to satisfactory state of combat/mission readiness at these bases and then move them into South Vietnam.

8. Establish training facilities at PACOM bases and in Vietnam or use existing ARVN facilities there to complete training of units deployed under conditions defined in 6 and 7 above.

9. Services expedite funding and equipment and material procurement so units can be equipped ahead of present Program 5 schedule.

10. Surge air and surface transportation means in cases where transportation is pacing factor to early deployments.

11. Provide inducements to reserves with desired skills to volunteer for active service.

12. Accelerate and compress training schedules. 76/

The Acting Chairman (General Johnson) apparently took the Director, Joint Staff Memorandum to the White House on 12 September. The nature of the discussion is not known. However, upon his return from the White House, General Johnson indicated that the President desired the Joint Staff to indicate recommended actions, within present policy limitations, which would increase pressure on North Vietnam. 77/ Nothing was said concerning accelerated deployments, and the Joint Staff did not further consider this subject.

However, on 16 September 1968, in a memorandum to the Secretary of Defense, the Secretary of the Army indicated that the Army had re-analyzed its capability to deploy the 101st Airborne Division (-) to Vietnam and had determined that a brigade task force and a headquarters and control element of the division (approximately 4,500 personnel) could be deployed by air to close in Vietnam before Christmas. The remainder of the division (-) could either deploy by surface to close in Vietnam before February or could deploy by air in mid to late January 1968 to close before TET (31 January 1968). 78/

On 22 September, the Secretary of Defense approved the plan to deploy the brigade task force and headquarters element by air in December 1967, but indicated that a decision on the accelerated deployment of the remainder of the division would be made at a later date. 79/

In the meantime, on 15 September, the Joint Chiefs of Staff approved and forwarded to the Secretary of Defense the refined troop list for the "tentatively approved FY 1968 additive forces for South Vietnam and a civilianization schedule to remain within the specific military personnel strength ceiling of 525,000." Civilianization, the 525,000 ceiling, plus Program 4 trade-offs, permitted an additive force structure of 50,978 for FY 1968, which was allocated as follows: Army 39,365; Navy 7,483; Marine Corps 969; and Air Force 3,161.

The Joint Chiefs of Staff pointed out again, however, that even with the high civilianization goal, many requirements still could not be accommodated.

For example, a Marine Corps requirement for 6,124 spaces plus integral Navy personnel to permit III MAF to be manned at full strength is not included in the troop list. This requirement is based on modification of existing T/Os and augmentations caused by the nature of operations being conducted in I CTZ, the introduction of newer and more sophisticated equipment, and the expanding functions and responsibilities being assigned to III MAF. The Marine Corps has indicated that approximately 3,500 of these additional Marines could be provided by December 1967. Also, both the Army and Air Force identified additional priority requirements that could not be incorporated within ceiling; approximately

Declassified per Executive Order 13526, Section 3.3
NND Project Number: NND 63316. By: NWD Date: 2011

3,000 spaces for the Army and 1,000 for the Air Force. These
requirements, and others, now outside the ceiling, will be
the subject for future recommendations.

Inclusion of elements of the 9th Marine Amphibious
Brigade, which CINCPAC plans to operate ashore in South
Vietnam only on a temporary basis, of nondeploying tactical
fighter squadrons, and of the 1,164 spaces for the augmented
hospital facilities for civilian war casualties, as directed
by references, has further reduced the force level recommended
by the Joint Chiefs of Staff in JCSM-218-67, dated 20 April
1967, subject: "Force Requirements - Southeast Asia FY 1968 (U),"
and prevented inclusion of high priority units and personnel,
some of which are now available for deployment. 80/

The major differences in the refined troop list were the addition
of 3 light helicopter companies, 2 C-140 jet aircraft for the Ambassador
and visiting dignitaries, a Radio Research Aviation Company, and a
Marine fixed-wing reconnaissance squadron. Additionally, the helicopter
requirements included ambulance detachments and helicopters in the
supporting aviation headquarters for the 101st Airborne Division and
the Americal Division. Other lower priority units were deleted.

The Secretary of Defense, on 5 October, approved for deployment
those forces listed in JCSM 505-67, and indicated that subsequent
requests for additional high priority units should be accompanied by
appropriate trade-offs to insure forces remained within the total
personnel authorization of 525,000. 81/

On 28 September, General Westmoreland forwarded to CINCPAC and the
JCS his plan for reorienting in-country forces for the northeast monsoon
season. This reassessment of planned operations and force deployments
was necessitated, COMUSMACV indicated, in view of the accelerated deployment of the 101st Airborne Division and the heavy enemy pressure in
I CTZ. COMUSMACV indicated that his overall fall-winter objectives were
to:

A. Relieve the 1st Cav Div in Binh Dinh and commit it to
    successive country-wide offensive operations...

B. Reinforce I CTZ to the extent practicable without unduly
    retarding other progress.

C. Move additional elements of the 9th Inf Div to the Delta.

D. Reinforce III CTZ so that we can attack during favorable
    weather...and force the enemy into a vulnerable posture
    away from populated areas. 82/

The prospective early arrival of the 101st Airborne Division, General Westmoreland indicated,

> ...will now allow for initiation of planned operations in III CTZ while diverting the 1st Cav Div to I CTZ as required by the intensified enemy situation there. To insure adequate combat ready forces for III CTZ operations, I now plan to delay the movement of additional 9th Div elements to the delta; however, a Vietnamese Marine battalion will deploy to IV CTZ to reinforce our mobile Riverine operations planned for that area.

> 3. (TS) These moves are carefully planned to preclude any regression in the vital coastal areas of II CTZ; to insure that the ultimate posture of forces required to meet objectives for next year is not changed significantly; to do that is necessary to relieve and reverse the situation near the DMZ; and to conduct large scale operations in selected areas when weather is favorable. By this reoriented effort I desire to preempt the enemy strategy of attempting to tie down forces and denude the pacification shield. 83/

General Westmoreland indicated that higher authority could provide him the following additional assistance to help accomplish his strategy:

> A. Accelerate the deployment of the 101st Div to close all major elements of the Div prior to 20 December 1967. This will facilitate early combat readiness of this force and allow its employment in late January...

> B. Continue the retention of the elements of 9th MAB now in-country. My evaluation now of the situation in I CTZ indicates a continuing requirement for this force through the spring of 1968.

> C. Accelerate deployment of 11th Separate Infantry BDE to arrive in-country during December 1967. Early arrival would permit early release of the 173d ABN Bde which would be employed in II CTZ. A consideration in all accelerated deployments is the possibility of an extended holiday moritorium resulting in an agreement of status quo on force deployments. 84/

In a memorandum for the President on 4 October 1967, the Secretary of Defense indicated the actions taken to date on COMUSMACV's recommendations, to include:

(1) Recommendation: Accelerate the deployment of the 101st
    Division to close all major elements of the Division
    prior to 20 December 1967.

    Action: Deployment of a brigade task force (3 battalions)
    of the 101st Airborne Division had already been accelerated
    from February 1968 to December 1967. The Army now believes
    that deployment of the remaining brigade can be accelerated
    from February 1968 to January 1968.

(2) Recommendation: Retain the elements of the 9th Marine
    Amphibious Brigade now in-country.

    Action: The current deployment plan authorizes this action.

(3) Recommendation: Accelerate deployment of the 11th Separate
    Infantry Brigade from February 1968 to December 1967.

    Action: The Secretary of the Army believes this date can
    be met. 85/

The Army, meanwhile, continued to assess the possibility of accelerating deployment of its Program 5 combat units.

On 16 October 1967, in a memorandum to the Secretary of Defense, the Secretary of the Army indicated that the remainder of the 101st AB Division could be deployed by air to close in Vietnam by 20 December 1967. This accelerated deployment would require the completion of four weeks of training in-country prior to commitment to combat. Additional transportation costs to the Army would be $10 M, and support of the element in South Vietnam over the CONUS cost for the same period would be approximately $5.3 M. The acceleration, however, would not provide General Westmoreland an operational element earlier than now programmed, but would ensure the Division's early closure in South Vietnam in the event of an extended moratorium on deployment at Christmas. 86/ In response to this memorandum, the Secretary of Defense asked: "Why spend $15M without an earlier operational capability"? 87/ On 20 October the Secretary of the Army indicated that, contrary to his earlier assertion, the Division would be available for operations in South Vietnam five weeks earlier than the Program 5 availability date.

> The Program 5 availability date, using surface transportation and allowing for one month's in-country orientation, is 1 March 1968. Using air movement and conducting the normal one-month orientation concurrent with completion of training will provide an availability date of 22 January 1968. 88/

On 21 October, the Secretary of Defense approved the Army recommendation to deploy by air the remainder of the 101st Airborne Division (-) in December 1967. 89/

On 31 October, in a memorandum to the Secretary of Defense, the Secretary of the Army replied to General Westmoreland's request for the deployment of the 11th Infantry Brigade to arrive in Vietnam before Christmas. He stated that the Army Staff had determined that the Brigade could be deployed on or about December 10, by surface transportation from Hawaii to close in South Vietnam by 24 December. It would be necessary for the Brigade to have the same kind of in-country training on arrival in South Vietnam as the 101st Airborne Division (-). The only additional costs involved would be the slightly increased operating costs from having the unit in South Vietnam one month earlier and being combat ready in January rather than in February. 90/

On 6 November, Secretary of Defense approved the Army request for the early deployment of the 11th Light Infantry Brigade by surface transportation to South Vietnam in December 1967, and directed that necessary in-country training should be conducted in a low risk area. 91/

In the meantime, on 17 October 1967, the Joint Chiefs of Staff forwarded to the President through the Secretary of Defense their reply to the questions raised by the President at the White House luncheon on 12 September concerning what military actions consistent with present policy guidelines would serve to increase pressure on North Vietnam, thereby accelerating the rate of progress toward achievement of the U.S. objective in South Vietnam. 92/

The Chiefs considered that North Vietnam was paying heavily for its aggression and had lost the initiative in the South. They further considered that many factors indicated a military trend favorably to Free World Forces in Vietnam. However, they again concluded that if acceleration in the pace of progress was to be achieved, an appropriate increase in military pressure was required.

The Chiefs then reiterated the policy guidelines established for the conduct of military operations in SEA to achieve U.S. objectives, among which were:

a. We seek to avoid widening the war into a conflict with Communist China or the USSR.

b. We have no present intention of invading NVN.

c. We do not seek the overthrow of the Government of NVN.

d. We are guided by the principles set forth in the Geneva Accords of 1954 and 1962. 93/

In a rather resigned tone, the Joint Chiefs indicated that they considered the rate of progress to have been and to continue to be slow largely because U.S. military power has been constrained in a manner which had reduced significantly its impact and effectiveness. Limitations have been imposed on military operations in four ways, they indicated:

a. The attacks on the enemy military targets have been on such a prolonged, graduated basis that they enemy has adjusted psychologically, economically, and militarily, e.g., inured themselves to the difficulties and hardships accompanying the war, dispersed their logistic support system, and developed alternate transport routes and a significant air defense system.

b. Areas of sanctuary, containing important military targets, have been afforded the enemy.

c. Covert operations in Cambodia and Laos have been restricted.

d. Major importation of supplies into NVN by sea has been permitted.

The Chiefs indicated that they considered that U.S. objectives in SEA could be achieved within this policy framework providing the level of assistance the enemy received from his communist allies was not significantly increased and there was no diminution of U.S. efforts.

However, the Chiefs concluded pessimistically that progress would continue to be slow so long as present limitations on military operations continued in effect and, further, at the present pace, termination of NVN's military effort was not expected to occur in the near future.

The Joint Chiefs then listed a series of actions which could be taken in the near future to increase pressures on NVN and accelerate progress toward the achievement of U.S. objectives (see table, p. 224) and recommended they be authorized to direct these actions.

The Joint Chiefs of Staff recognize that expansion of US efforts entails some additional risk. They believe that as a result of this expansion the likelihood of overt introduction of Soviet/Bloc/CPR combat forces into the war would be remote. Failure to take additional action to shorten the Southeast Asia conflict also entails risks as new and more efficient weapons are provided to NVN by the Soviet Union and as USSR/CPR support of the enemy increases. 94/

Information indicates that the President reviewed this paper and stated that it was not what was desired, that it recommended actions which had previously been denied and would not now be approved.

TOP SECRET – Sensitive

APPENDIX

TOP SECRET – Sensitive

However, Administration actions to find a way to accelerate progress in South Vietnam continued. On 7 November 1967, the Chairman of the Joint Chiefs of Staff indicated, in a memorandum to the Director, Joint Staff, that he had been urged again to take all feasible measures to deploy Program 5 forces at the earliest possible date. He directed that the Joint Staff explore what further foreshortening of the deployment dates could be accomplished. 95/

On 8 November, at the White House luncheon meeting, the Secretary of State recommended that the Department of State and the Department of Defense prepare a joint policy document which would govern political and military operations in Southeast Asia for the next four months. Secretary Rusk's proposal was expressed in broad terms. He considered that parameters should be established for political, military, and economic operations over the upcoming four months' period in order to preclude the need for weekly examinations of many small and short-range operations. This proposal was agreed to by the principals at the meeting, and the Chairman directed the Joint Staff to prepare as a matter of priority the recommendations of the JCS for military operations in SEA over the cited time period. He directed that the recommendations of the Joint Chiefs of Staff cover the following as a minimum:

    a. Air operations against North Vietnam --

    Fixed targets important to our air effort against North Vietnam; authorization for re-strike of important targets; allocation of air effort between North Vietnam and South Vietnam.

    b. Ground operations --

    Large ground operations in South Vietnam to include operations in the Delta region; ground operations in Laos; ground operations in Cambodia; and possible ground operations against North Vietnam.

    c. Bombing Pauses --

    In addressing this subject the Joint Staff should take note of American Embassy Saigon to State cable #10563. Ambassador Bunker reported that Vice President Ky believes that bombing pauses of 24 hours each for Christmas and New Years and 48 hours at TET should be announced in the near future by the allied forces. 96/

In reply to the Chairman's request to explore foreshortening of deployment dates, the Director, Joint Staff on 21 November furnished the following resume:

                                TOP SECRET - Sensitive

Army - Based on a comprehensive capability study recently
completed, Army concludes it is not in a position to make
further accelerations without jeopardizing capability to
deploy remaining units in Program 5 in an orderly manner.

Navy - The bulk of the 3000 Navy forces scheduled to deploy
after 1 March 1968, are linked to ship/waterborne craft
conversion or construction. They are susceptible to little
acceleration and cannot be accelerated into the JAN/FEB 68
time frame.

Air Force - Excluding the TFS maintained in CONUS ready for
deployment, the Air Force has only 760 personnel scheduled
to deploy after 1 March 1968. These include a CE Squadron
(scheduled for civilianization had funds been available) and
6 UC-123 herbicide aircraft. The CE Squadron must be
activated and equipped and the aircraft must be spray equipped.

Marine Corps - Contingent upon Department of Defense approval
(which is expected in the near future) of a PCR for additional
end strength increase to deploy and sustain 800 CAC personnel,
the Marine Corps will have only 164 Program 5 spaces remaining
for deployment after 1 March 1968. The 164 personnel are
associated with an observation squadron for which pilots and
aircraft are not available. 97/

On 27 November 1967, the Joint Chiefs of Staff provided the Secretary
of Defense their views on planned and recommended military operations to
be conducted in Southeast Asia over the next four months. They concluded,
rather pessimistically again, that:

> There are no new programs which can be undertaken under
> current policy guidelines which would result in a rapid or
> significantly more visible increase in the rate of progress
> in the near term. 98/

The Chiefs recommended against a stand-down in military operations
for any of the forthcoming holidays, as progress during the next four
months would be dependent upon the maintenance of pressure upon the
enemy.

> Any action which serves to reduce the pressure will be
> detrimental to the achievement of our objectives. 99/

While progress toward U.S. military objectives was expected to be
sustained during the period under consideration, the Joint Chiefs held
that additional gains could be realized through the modification and
expansion of certain current policies. Thus, they recommended that current
policies for the conduct of the war in SEA during the next four months be
modified and expanded to permit a fuller utilization of our military
resources.

On 22 December 1967, the ASD/ISA, in a memorandum to the Chairman, Joint Chiefs of Staff, forwarded the joint comments of the Secretary of Defense and the Secretary of State on the JCS recommendations. Their comments were:

a. recommend against aerial mining or bombing of North Vietnamese deep water ports. Possible military gains are far outweighed by risk of confrontation with Soviets or Chinese.

b. recommend that strike authorization for high density population centers of government and domestic commerce continue to be controlled at the highest level of Government which is most closely in touch with the political significance of air attacks in these areas.

c. every recommendation for authorization of a new target should be considered on its own merits. The military significance of the target is, of course, a dominant factor in the evaluation of a target recommendation, but our policy is to minimize civilization casualties and this consideration must be weighed in every determination. Recommend no change in this policy.

d. recommend authorization for use of CS in rescues in Laos. Effectiveness of such use can be evaluated against possible adverse public reaction to use of agents combined with firepower if conducted in NVN and given propaganda play by NVN.

FOOTNOTES

1. Draft Memorandum for the President, Subject: Future Actions in
    Vietnam, 19 May 1967. A series of drafts revealed that McNaughton
    had been working on the basic memorandum since late April or early
    May. The drafts as they took shape began to incorporate not only
    the views of the CIA which we mentioned, especially those related
    to the effects of the bombing in the north and the so-called ratchet
    effect, where actions in the bombing in the north were having little
    effect on the outcomes in the south, the views of the State Depart-
    ment, such as those incorporated in the Bundy memo on the bombing,
    and even those of the White House, primarily ones prepared at
    Walt Rostow's direction. Throughout the period, the same basic
    six arguments continued to be developed and expanded until they
    appear in the finished document on 19 May. See Memorandum dated
    16 May 1967, Subject: Arguments Opposing Further U.S. Forces for
    South Vietnam (McNaughton papers -- draft prepared for 19 May DPM);
    and McNaughton papers - hand written draft, subject: Issues to
    Add to Paper, dated 5 May 67.

2. Memorandum for the SecDef from ASD(ISA) McNaughton, Subject:
    "My Comments on the 5 May 'First Rough Draft'," dtd 6 May 67.

3. Ibid.

4. Ibid.

5. Draft Memorandum for the President, Subject: Future Actions in
    Vietnam, dtd 19 May 67.

6. Ibid.

7. Ibid.

8. JCSM 286-67, Subject: Operations Against North Vietnam, dated
    20 May 67.

9. Memorandum from the Deputy SecDef to Chairman, JCS, Subject:
    Operations Against North Vietnam, dated 26 July 1967. JCSM 286-67
    was forwarded to the President on 20 May with a note from Secretary
    McNamara stating that he would forward to the President his
    comments on the document after more extensive analysis of the
    proposals.

10. JCSM 288-67, Subject: U.S. Worldwide Military Posture, 20 May 67.

11. Ibid. The appendix to this JCSM indicated changes or additions to ROLLING THUNDER which were also interesting. Among these were to delete the 10 n.m. radius Hanoi as prohibited areas; to reduce the 30 n.m. restricted area around Hanoi to 10; to reduce the 10 n.m. radius of Haiphong restrictive to 4. And also to authorize armed reconnaissance throughout North Vietnam and adjacent coastal waters against North Vietnamese military targets except in populated areas in the ChiCom buffer zone and restricted area.

12. CM-2278-67, Memorandum for the Director, Joint Staff, Subject: Alternative Force Postures, dated 26 April 1967. Also, See: Memorandum from Acting Secretary Nicholas deB Katzenbach to Mr. McNaughton re: Vietnam, 24 Apr 67.

13. Ibid.

14. Ibid.

15. Ibid.

16. CM-2377-67, "Alternative Courses of Action," 24 May 67.

17. Ibid.

18. Ibid.

19. Ibid.

20. COMUSMACV message 280940E March 1967 and JCS IN 93855.

21. CM-2381-67, Subject: Future Actions in Vietnam, dtd 29 May 67.

22. JCSM-307-67, 1 Jun 67, Draft Memorandum for the President on Future Actions in Vietnam.

23. Ibid.

24. Ibid.

25. Ibid.

26. JCSM-312-67, 2 Jun 67, Air Operations Against NVN.

27. Ibid.

28. Draft Memorandum for the President, Subject: Alternative Military Actions Against North Vietnam, 12 June 1967.

29. Note, Wm. P. Bundy to Mr. McNaughton, et al, June 2, 1967, Comments on DOD First Rough Draft of 19 May, dtd 30 May 67.

30. Ibid.

31. Ibid.

32. Ibid.

33. Ibid.

34. Memorandum for Under Secretary of Defense Vance from Under Secretary of State Katzenbach, title: Preliminary Comments on DOD Draft of 19 May, dated 8 Jun 67.

35. Under Secretary Katzenbach, Memo for Mr. Vance, "Preliminary Comments on DOD Draft of 19 May," dtd June 8, 1967.

36. Ibid.

37. Ibid.

38. Memorandum for Mr. McNaughton from "SRV," Subject: "DPM on Vietnam, and Chairman's Memo 2381-67 of 29 May," dated 8 Jun 67.

39. Draft Memo for the President from ASD(ISA), Subject: Alternative Military Actions Against North Vietnam dtd 12 Jun 67, with summary DPM attached.

40. Ibid. Secretary Brown's recommendation was partially based upon detailed analyses which his staff had been preparing on the subject of anti-infiltration bombing in the North and in all route packages of the Air Force target complex. In a study which he forwarded to the SecDef on June 9th, Mr. Brown commented on the quantitative analyses which had been made of the effectiveness of the bombing:

> One can use the same cost and casualty estimates to make the subjective judgment in a different set of units. The above cost figures for troops and for the air campaign out-of-country in dollars can be expressed by saying that the out-of-country air campaign has paid for itself in dollars if it has saved us from having to send 35,800 more ground troops into South Vietnam in order to achieve the same situation in SVN that we have now. Or, it has paid for itself in lives if it has saved us from having to send 19,000 more ground troops.
>
> Alternatively, one can compare air and ground

campaign casualty costs by saying that if for
every 123 attack sorties in Route Packages IV
through VI, or for every 557 sorties in Route
Packages I through III, or for every 881 attack
sorties in Laos we have reduced allied deaths in
the South by one, they are worth their human cost.

In terms of dollar costs, if every 1000
attack sorties per calendar year in out-of-
country operations reduce the requirements for
US ground troops by about 300, they pay their
way. If the proportionality of friendly force
increments to enemy force increments is a correct concept, this means that, to pay their way,
every 1000 out-of-country sorties per year must
account for 37 of the infiltrators who could have
come in but didn't.

(Memo for SecDef, June 9, 1967, from Dr. Harold Brown,
Secretary of the Air Force re Possible Courses of Action in
SEA.)

41. Memo for SecDef from ASD Robert N. Anthony, Subject: Effect
of Increased Southeast Asia Deployment on Balance of Payments,
dated 9 June 1967. Anthony's office used the round figure
of $50,000 per year, per deployed man in SVN. This was the
same figure which the SecDef and the Under SecDef used in
their rough calculations of cost increases for recommended
deployments. (SecDef Control No. X-4239, 11 Jul 1967.)

42. Memorandum for SecDef from ASD(SA), "Increased Use of Civilians
for U.S. Troop Support (C)," 13 June 1967.

43. Memo for CJCS from SecDef, Subject: "Increased Use of Civilians
for U.S. Troop Support (C)," 13 Jun 67.

44. Ibid. See also, Memo for SecDef from ASD(SA) Alain Enthoven,
Subject: Increased Use of SVN Civilians for U.S. Troop
Support (C), dated 10 Jun 67.

45. The Washington Daily News, 23 June 1967, Jim Lucas, "Partial
Mobilization."

46. Memo for the Secys of the Army, Navy and Air Force from Deputy
Secretary Vance, dated 23 June 1967; Memo for the SecDef from
the Secy of the Navy, Subject: Jim Lucas Article, Partial
Mobilization, dated 26 June 1967; Memo for the DepSecDef from
Secy of the Army, Subject: Lucas Article, dated 28 June 1967;
Memo for the DepSecDef from the Secy of the Navy, Subject:
Lucas Article, dated 29 June 1967.

47. Neil Sheehan, "Joint Chiefs Back Troop Rise Asked by Westmoreland," 3 July 1967, The New York Times.

48. Ibid. Memo for SecDef from Stanley R. Resor, SecArmy, 5 July 1967.

49. Memo for SecDef from AsstSecDef Enthoven, Subj: Holbrooke/Burnham Study on Binh Chanh, dtd 4 Jul 67.

50. Discussion concerning adding an additional rifle company to 33 battalions already deployed had persisted since early May when Secretary McNamara questioned the Secretary of the Army about the seventy battalions in Program 4 and discovered that approximately 30 had moved with only three companies. If this was so, he asked should not a fourth be added? (SecDef Control No. X-2637, Memorandum for the Secretary of the Army from the Secretary of Defense, dtd 2 May 67.)

 Secretary of the Army, Stanley R. Resor, replied that according to the Army there remained 33 airborne infantry or air-mobile infantry battalions in or approved for deployment to the Republic of Vietnam for which a fourth rifle company had not been approved. He subsequently recommended that a fourth company be added to these 33 battalions. To provide and sustain this increase in capability he projected that an increase of 7,903 spaces in the Army trained military strength would be required. Of this, 5,577 were required for the companies themselves and 3,326 were for the sustaining base. After detailed deliberation, however, McNamara disapproved the request stating that although he was "inclined to approve the deployment of these companies it would not be possible to find space trade-offs for the 5,577 personnel involved." (Memo for SecDef, Subj: Program 4 Strength Increases, dated 20 May 67, ASD(SA) 6-1733; Memo for SA from SecDef, Subj: Rifle Companies for South Vietnam, dated 15 Jun 67.)

51. Encl to Memo for SecDef from ASD(SA) Enthoven, Subj: Current Estimate of Additional Deployment Capability, 5 Jul 67.

52. Ibid. Interview with Mr. Philip Odeen, Southeast Asia Programs Division, OASD(SA), 20 Jul 1968.

53. Saigon Briefing Notes, 7-8 July, Prepared by OASD(SA), 18 Jul 67.

54. Ibid.

55. Ibid. (Bunker's source here, of course, was MACV.)

56. Ibid.

57. Ibid.

58. Ibid.; COMUSMACV's Overall Assessment.

59. Ibid.

60. Ibid.

61. Ibid.; "J2 Assessment."

62. Ibid.

63. Ibid.

64. Ibid.; "J3 Briefing."

65. Ibid.

66. Ibid.

67. Ibid.

68. Interview with Mr. Philip Odeen, 20 Jul 68, and Memo for Record, Subject: Fallout from SecDef Trip to South Vietnam, dated July 13, 1967, signed by Alain Enthoven.

69. See also Memo for Record, Brehm, Subject: SEA Deployments, dtd July 14, 1967, which outlines the decisions made in Saigon and directs work priorities and assignments for OASD(SA).

70. Memo for SecDef from Mr. Richard C. Steadman, DASD, Subj: Additional Third Country Forces for Vietnam, dtd 13 Jul 67, with memo for Secys Rusk, McNamara and Mr. Walt Rostow and Under Secretary Katzenbach, Subj: Messages to Manila Nations dtd 13 Jul 67 attached.

71. Ibid.

72. JCSM 416-67, Subject: U.S. Force Deployments - Vietnam, dtd 20 Jul 67.

73. OASD/SA/POdeen, Memo for SecDef, 21 Jul 67, Subj: FY 68 Force Requirements for SVN (Program #5).

74. Memo for CJCS from SecDef, Subj: FY 68 Force Requirements for South Vietnam (Program #5) dtd 10 Aug 67; and Memo for Secys of Mil Depts, CJCS, ASD from the ASD(SA), Subject: SEA Deployment Program #5, 14 Aug 67.

75. Note to Control Division, DJS, 6 Sept 1967, Subject: Examination of Speed-up in Program 5 Deployments.

76. DJSM 1118-67, 9 Sept 1967, Subject: Examination of Speed-up in Program 5 Deployments.

77. CM 2640-67, 12 Sept 1967.

78. Secretary of the Army Memo for Secretary of Defense, 16 Sept 1967, Subject: Deployment Schedule for 101st Airborne Division (-)

79. Secretary of Defense Memo for Secretary of the Army, 22 Sept 1967, Subject: Deployment of 101st Airborne Division (-) (U)

80. JCSM-505-67, 15 September 1967, Subject: US Force Deployments in Vietnam (U).

81. Secretary of Defense Memo for Secretaries of the Military Departments and CJCS, 5 October 1967, Subject: FY 68 US Force Deployments, Vietnam (U)

82. COMUSMACV Msg 31998, 281500Z Sept 67, Subject: Reorientation of In-Country Forces.

83. Ibid., p2

84. Ibid., pp 3-4

85. Secretary of Defense Memorandum for the President, 4 October 1967.

86. Secretary of the Army Memo for Secretary of Defense, 16 Oct 1967, Subject: Deployment of 101st Airborne Division (-).

87. Secretary of Defense Note for Record, 17 October 1967.

88. Secretary of the Army Memo for Secretary of Defense, 20 Oct 1967, Subject: Early Deployment of the 101st Airborne Division (-).

89. Secretary of Defense Memo for Secretary of the Army, 21 October 1967, Subject: Deployment of the 101st Airborne Division (-), (U).

90. Secretary of the Army Memorandum for Secretary of Defense, 31 Oct 1967, Subject: Deployment of the 11th Infantry Brigade.

91. Secretary of Defense Memorandum for Secretary of the Army, 6 November 1967, Subject: Deployment of the 11th Infantry Brigade.

92. JCSM 555-67, 17 October 1967, Subject: Increased Pressure on North Vietnam, (U).

93. Ibid.

94. Ibid.

95. CM-2743-67, 7 November 1967, Subject: Program 5.

96. CM 2752-67, 10 November 1967, Subject: Policies for the Conduct
     of Operations in SEA over the next four months.

97. DJSM-1409-67, 21 November 1967, Subject: Program 5 Accelerated
     Deployments (U).

98. JCSM-663-67, 27 November 1967, Subject: Policies for the Conduct
     of Operations in Southeast Asia over the Next Four Months (U).

99. Ibid.

IV.C Evolution of the War (26 Vols.)
Direct Action: The Johnson Commitments, 1964-1968
(16 Vols.)
6. U.S. Ground Strategy and Force Deployments: 1965-1967
(3 Vols.)
c. Volume III: Program 6

TOP SECRET - SENSITIVE

UNITED STATES - VIETNAM RELATIONS

1945 - 1967

VIETNAM TASK FORCE

OFFICE OF THE SECRETARY OF DEFENSE

SET #13

TOP SECRET - SENSITIVE

Sec Def Cont Nr. ___

IV.C.6.(c)

U.S. GROUND STRATEGY
AND FORCE DEPLOYMENTS
1965--1967

VOLUME III

TABLE OF CONTENTS
AND OUTLINE

VOLUME III
U.S. GROUND STRATEGY AND FORCE DEPLOYMENTS, 1965--1967

TABLE OF CONTENTS and OUTLINE

V.   PROGRAM 6

V. PROGRAM NO. 6

V.   PROGRAM 6

1. Emergency Augmentation

Thus, the year ended with the combat elements of Program 5 either
closing in Vietnam or on their way to Vietnam on an accelerated schedule.
The Joint Chiefs of Staff, however, could only promise that, even with
these deployments, the rate of progress in Vietnam would continue to be
slow in light of the continuing restrictions imposed on the conduct of
military operations.

In his year-end assessment of the military situation, however,
COMUSMACV had a somewhat more optimistic outlook. He indicated that
the Program 5 deployments had "provided us with an increased force
structure and logistics base for offensive operations". The past year,
he indicated, had been marked by steady free world progress, a noticeable deterioration of the enemy's combat effectiveness, and his loss of
control over large areas and population.

> "During 1967, the enemy lost control of large sectors of
> the population. He faces significant problems in the areas
> of indigenous recruiting, morale, health and resources control.
> Voids in VC ranks are being filled by regular NVA. Sea infiltra-
> tion through the Market Time area has diminished to near-insignifica-
> tion proportions. Interdiction of the enemy's logistics train
> in Laos and NVN by our indispensable air efforts has imposed
> significant difficulties on him. In many areas the enemy has
> been driven away from the population centers; in others he has
> been compelled to disperse and evade contact, thus nullifying
> much of his potential. The year ended with the enemy increasingly
> resorting to desperation tactics in attempting to achieve military/
> psychological victory; and he has experienced only failure in
> these attempts. Enemy bases, with sparse exception, are no
> longer safe havens and he has necessarily become increasingly
> reliant on Cambodian and Laotian sanctuaries..."

> "The friendly picture gives rise to optimism for increased
> successes in 1968. In 1967, our logistics base and force
> structure permitted us to assume a fully offensive posture...
> A greatly improved intelligence system frequently enabled us
> to concentrate our superior military assets in preempting enemy
> military initiatives leading us to decisive accomplishments in
> conventional engagements. Materiel and tactical innovations
> have been further developed and employed: Long range recon-
> naissance patrols, aerial reconnaissance sensors, new O-2A
> observation aircraft, Rome plows, 47 (Spooky) gunships, air-
> mobile operations and the Mobile Riverine Force (MRF), to name

a few. The MRF has been significantly successful in depriving
the enemy of freedom and initiative in the population and
resources rich Delta areas. The helicopter has established
itself as perhaps the single most important tool in our
arsenal -- and we will welcome more. To air support in both
RVN and NVN (Army, Navy, Marine and Air Force) goes much of
the credit for our accomplishments." 1/

The enemy's TET offensive, which began with the attack on the U.S.
Embassy in Saigon on 31 January 1968, although it had been predicted, 2/
took the U.S. command and the U.S. public by surprise, and its strength,
length, and intensity prolonged this shock. As the attacks continued,
the Secretary of Defense, on 9 February, requested the Joint Chiefs of
Staff to furnish plans which would provide for emergency reinforcement
of COMUSMACV.

After extensive backchannel communication with General Westmoreland,
the JCS forwarded these plans on 12 February. 3/ The Joint Chiefs'
assessment of the current Vietnam situation differed markedly from
COMUSMACV's year-end assessment submitted only 17 days earlier:

"a. The VC/NVA forces have launched large-scale offensive
operations throughout South Vietnam.

"b. As of 11 February 1968, Headquarters, MACV, reports that
attacks have taken place on 34 provincial towns, 64 district
towns, and all of the autonomous cities.

"c. The enemy has expressed his intention to continue offensive
operations and to destroy the Government of Vietnam and its Armed
Forces.

"d. The first phase of his offensive has failed in that he
does not have adequate control over any population center to
install his Revolutionary Committees which he hoped to form
into a coalition with the NLF.

"e. He has lost between 30 and 40 thousand killed and captured,
and we have seized over seven thousand weapons.

"f. Reports indicate that he has committed the bulk of his
VC main force and local force elements down to platoon level
throughout the country, with the exception of six to eight
battalions in the general area of Saigon.

"g. Thus far, he has committed only 20 to 25 percent of his
North Vietnamese forces. These were employed as gap fillers
where VC strength was apparently not adequate to carry out his
initial thrust on the cities and towns. Since November, he has

increased his NVA battalions by about 25. The bulk of
these and the bulk of the uncommitted NVA forces are in the
I Corps area.

"h. It is not clear whether the enemy will be able to
recycle his attacks in a second phase. He has indicated his
intention to do so during the period from 10 to 15 February.

"i. South Vietnamese forces have suffered nearly two
thousand killed, over seven thousand wounded, and an unknown
number of absences. MACV suspects the desertion rate may be
high. The average present for duty strength of RVN infantry
battalions is 50 percent and Ranger Battalions, 43 percent.
Five of nine airborne battalions are judged by MACV to be
combat ineffective at this time."

Based on this assessment, COMUSMACV voiced to the Joint Chiefs three
major concerns:
"a. The ability of the weakened RVNAF to cope with additional
sustained enemy offensive operations.

"b. Logistic support north of Danang, because of weather
and sea conditions in the Northern I Corps area, enemy interdiction of Route 1, and the probability of intensified combat
in that area.

"c. The forces available to him are not adequate at the
moment to permit him to pursue his own campaign plans and to
resume offensive operations against a weakened enemy, considering the competing requirements of reacting to enemy initiatives,
assisting in defending Government centers, and reinforcing weakened
RVNAF units when necessary."

The three plans for emergency reinforcement examined by the Joint
Chiefs of Staff were:

"a. Plan One, which is based upon prompt deployment of the
82nd Airborne Division and 6/9 Marine division/wing team, callup
of some 120,000 Army and Marine Corps Reserves, and appropriate
legislative action to permit extension of terms of service of
active duty personnel and the recall of individual Reservists.

"b. Plan Two, which would deploy as many Marine Corps
battalions as are now available in CONUS, less one battalion
in the Caribbean, the battalion in the Mediterranean, and the
Guantanamo Defense Force. This plan would not be based upon
a callup of Reservists or legislative action.

"c.   Plan Three, which would deploy the 82nd Airborne
Division but would leave Marine Corps battalions in CONUS.
This plan would likewise envisage no Reserve callup and no
legislative action."

Under Plan One, elements of one brigade of the 82nd Airborne
Division could commence movement within 24 hours and the division itself
36-48 hours later. 6/9ths of a Marine Corps Division/wing team could be
ready for deployment to Vietnam in one week without utilizing Vietnam
replacement drafts. Dependent upon the availability of aircraft and
the degree of drawdown on the current level of Southeast Asia airlift
support, the deployment could be completed within three to four weeks.

Under Plan Two, elements of two CONUS Marine Divisions, consisting
of 12 battalions could be air transported to Vietnam, although two weeks
preparation would be required. This deployment, however, would deplete
Marine Corps assets except for three battalions -- one afloat in the
Mediterranean, one afloat in the Caribbean, and one ashore at Guantanamo
Bay, Cuba.

Under Plan Three, as under Plan One, elements of one brigade of the
82nd Airborne Division could commence movement in 24 hours, the division
itself 36-48 hours later.

All of these plans, however, would require drawdowns on previously
protected CONUS stocks during procurement lead-time for new production
and would further aggravate the shortage of long procurement lead time
items currently short, such as helicopters, tracked combat vehicles,
and ammunition.

An examination was also made of the feasibility of an increased
acceleration in the deployment of the four infantry battalions scheduled
to deploy in March-April under Program 5. It was concluded that these
units could not be deployed earlier "except under the most critical
circumstances."

In examining the capacity to meet the possibility of widespread
civil disorder in the United States, the Joint Chiefs of Staff concluded
that, whether or not deployments under any of the plans were directed,
it appeared that sufficient forces would still be available for civil
disorder control.

However, the Joint Chiefs of Staff cautioned that the residual CONUS-
based active combat-ready ground forces that would result from the extension of each of the plans examined would be:

"a.   Plan One - 6/9 Marine Division/Wing Team.

b.   Plan Two - One Airborne Division.

4

c. Plan Three - One and 3/9 Marine Division/Wing Team."

Moreover, these forces were at various levels of readiness and a high
percentage of their personnel were Vietnam returnees or close to the
end of the obligated active service. The capability of these uncommitted general purpose forces was further constrained, the Joint Chiefs
pointed out, by shortages of critical skilled specialists and shortages
in mission essential items of equipment and materiel. Thus, the Joint
Chiefs emphasized, our posture of readily available combat forces was
seriously strained. Any decision to deploy emergency augmentation
forces should be accompanied by the recall of at least an equivalent
number, or more prudently, additional Reserve component forces and
an extension of terms of service for active duty personnel. Indeed,
the Chiefs, warned,

"It is not clear at this time whether the enemy will be able
to mount and sustain a second series of major attacks throughout
the country. It is equally unclear as to how well the Vietnamese
Armed Forces would be able to stand up against such a series of
attacks if they were to occur. In the face of these uncertainties,
a more precise assessment of USMACV's additional force requirements,
if any, must await further developments. The Joint Chiefs of
Staff do not exclude the possibility that additional developments could make further deployments necessary."

Based on this assessment of the situation, the Joint Chiefs of
Staff concluded and recommended that:

"a. A decision to deploy reinforcements to Vietnam be
deferred at this time.

"b. Measures be taken now to prepare the 82nd Airborne
Division and 6/9 Marine Division/Wing team for possible deployment to Vietnam.

"c. As a matter of prudence, call certain additional
Reserve units to active duty now. Deployment of emergency
reinforcements to Vietnam should not be made without concomitant
callup of Reserves sufficient at least to replace those deployed
and provide for the increased sustaining base requirements of all
Services. In addition, bring selected Reserve force units to
full strength and an increased state of combat readiness.

"d. Legislation be sought now to (1) provide authority to
call individual Reservists to active duty; (2) extend past
30 June 1968 the existing authority to call Reserve units to
active duty; and (3) extend terms of service for active duty
personnel.

TOP SECRET - Sensitive

TOP SECRET - Sensitive

"e. Procurement and other supply actions be taken now to overcome shortages existing in certain critical items of materiel and equipment such as munitions, helicopters, and other combat aircraft."

Thus, for perhaps the first time in the history of American involvement in Vietnam, the Joint Chiefs of Staff recommended against deploying the additional forces requested by the field commander, in the absence of other steps to reconstitute the strategic reserve. At long last, the resources were beginning to be drawn too thin, the assets became unavailable, the support base too small.

Notwithstanding the recommendation of the Joint Chiefs of Staff, the Secretary of Defense almost immediately approved the deployment of one brigade of the 82nd Airborne Division and one Marine regimental landing team to South Vietnam. A total strength of almost 10,500 was assumed and publicly announced. These deployments were directed by the JCS on 13 February. Airlift of the brigade from the 82nd Airborne Division, at a strength of approximately four thousand, was to begin on 14 February and the brigade was to close in-country not later than 26 February 1968. 4/ After coordination with CINCSTRIKE and USCONARC, the strength of this unit was fixed at 3,702. 5/

The Marine Corps Regiment was to close in SVN not later than 26 February also. The Regiment (reinforced) less one battalion, was to be deployed by air from California at a strength of about 3,600. One battalion (reinforced) which was then embarked, was to be deployed by surface at a strength of about 1,600. 6/

In view of the wide variation of strength associated with a Marine Corps Regiment (reinforced), CINCPAC was directed to advise all concerned of the identity, composition and strength of the force selected for deployment. 7/ CINCPAC nominated the 27th Marine Regiment, which included 5247 Marine and 327 Navy personnel. Additionally, he included the deployment of a logistic support element of 389 personnel from Okinawa to reduce the impact on the already heavily committed logistic units in I CTZ. In addition, CINCPAC took the precautionary step of identifying, for follow-on deployment, a sea-tail of reinforcing units totalling 1,400 personnel. This element, scheduled to follow in April 1968, would provide the regiment the necessary self-sustaining combat power in the event early replacement was not provided. 8/ Thus, the total number of troops deployed or alerted for the follow-on sea-tail numbered 11,065. 9/

The Joint Chiefs of Staff reacted almost immediately to the national decision to deploy these forces without a concomitant reserve callup. On 13 February 1968 they forwarded to the Secretary of Defense their recommendations for actions which should be taken relative to callup of reserves, obtaining legislation and instituting procurement actions to provide support for these forces and to sustain their deployment. 10/

6   TOP SECRET - Sensitive

A minimum callup of Reserve units to replace deploying forces and to sustain and support them was justified, the Joint Chiefs stated, by the following situation:

"a. <u>Army</u>. The 82nd Airborne Division represents the only readily deployable Army division in the CONUS-based active strategic reserve. The impending reduction of this division by one-third to meet approved deployments establishes an immediate requirement for its prompt reconstitution which is possible only by the callup of Reserve units. In order to replace the forces deployed from the strategic reserve, to provide support units to meet anticipation requirements in I CTZ and to provide a wider rotation base of requisite ranks and skills, it will be necessary for the Army to call up two infantry brigade forces of the Reserve components. This callup will total approximately 32,000 personnel. These two brigades should attain a combat-ready and deployable status in 12 weeks following callup.

"b. <u>Marine Corps</u>.

"(1) The Marine Corps cannot sustain additional deployments to Southeast Asia under current personnel policies. Thus, the force authorized for deployment must be replaced with a comparable Reserve unit as soon as possible. The Reserve force required for this purpose will consist of one Marine regiment, reinforcing combat support and combat service support units, and one composite Marine Air Group with one VMA, one VMF, and two medium helicopter squadrons (HMM).

"(2) The Reserve force will consist of approximately 12,000 personnel. It will provide the capability to deploy a balanced, self-sustaining air/ground combat force in relief of the lightly structured 27th Marines (Rein) and permit return of the 27th Marine Regiment (Rein) to the training/rotation base in CONUS/Hawaii. This exchange would commence as soon as the Reserve unit becomes combat-ready (approximately 60 days after callup) and must be completed not later than 120 days after deployment of RLT-27.

"(3) It is envisioned that the Reserve forces will be redeployed to CONUS without replacement after 13 months in South Vietnam. However, if this does not occur, it will be best to deploy a relief brigade from the 4th Marine Division/wing team. Alternately, an adequate rotation base in CONUS to sustain the continued deployment can be created but to do so requires extensions of terms of service and other personnel policy changes.

"(4) In addition, it must be recognized that the anticipated proportionate increase in personnel losses will require an increase in the end strength of the active forces to sustain these losses.

"c. <u>Navy</u>. Support of the newly authorized deployments will require the callup of two Navy mobile construction battalions (NMCB) totalling 1,700 personnel and 600 individual medical/dental/chaplain Reservists. These callups will provide for bringing recalled Marine units up to strength, sustaining the Navy personnel organic to the deployed RLT, and adding medical staffing required by the increased level of activity in Southeast Asia to forward hospital facilities including Guam.

"d. <u>Air Force</u>. The Air Force plans to support this approved deployment operation without recall of individuals or units. Reserve airlift augmentation needed to supplement the deployment airlift can be accomplished by Reservists on a voluntary basis."

In addition, the Joint Chiefs indicated that it would be both prudent and advisable to reach a readiness level that could be responsive to further COMUSMACV force requirements, if the remainder of the 82nd Airborne Division and one more RLT were required. COMUSMACV had already indicated the potential need for these units at an early date. To reach such a readiness level, the Joint Chiefs indicated that the following Reserve forces would have to be activated:

"a. <u>Army</u>. Should the additional deployments be made, it would be necessary for the Army to recall (in addition to the two brigade forces previously discussed) one infantry division force and one infantry brigade force of the Army Reserve components, totalling 58,000 men. These forces will be needed to reconstitute the strategic reserve and to broaden the source of critical ranks and skills to be applied against the increased rotation base requirements. The Reserve units should be recalled at this time to bring them closer to a combat-ready status prior to the probable deployment of the balance of the 82nd Airborne Division. The Reserve division force should attain a combat-capable status in 15 weeks after recall and the brigade force should require 12 weeks.

"b. <u>Marine Corps</u>.

(1) The most desirable Reserve callup consists of the entire 4th Marine Expeditionary Force (MEF), plus other units and selected individual Reserves. This totals about 51,000. Mobilization and subsequent deployment of the Reserve forces should be accomplished incrementally. This callup permits the early and orderly replacement of the 5th Marine Division (-) in South Vietnam and the subsequent redeployment of the 5th Marine Division (-) to CONUS, or, alternatively, the 4th Division/Wing Team can meet the additional requirements....

"c. <u>Navy</u>. Support of these additional deployments would require the callup of an additional three NMCB (total of five) totalling 4,150 personnel and an additional 400 (for a total of 1,000) medical/dental/chaplain Reservists. These callups

would provide for 14 NMCB in RVN for direct construction support
and an adequate rotation base to maintain these deployments.
The additional medical/dental/chaplain personnel will provide
for bringing recalled Marine units up to strength, sustaining
the Navy personnel in the additional deploying RLT, and adding
some medical staffing to forward hospital facilities. Recall
of an additional 2,800 personnel would be required to augment
the logistic operations in Vietnam. The increased requirement
for naval gunfire support for the larger deployments would
necessitate the activation of two heavy cruisers to fill CINCPAC's
requirements for additional shore bombardment capability to
maintain two large calibre gun ships on station in the SEA
DRAGON area and off RVN. Additionally, 15 destroyers should
be activated from the mothball fleet to replace 15 Naval Reserve
Training destroyers to be called to active duty. This would
fill CINCPAC's requirement for an additional five destroyers
on station off Vietnam and provide the rotation base to support
them. The recall of 6,000 Naval Reserve personnel would provide
the additional manpower and skills base to man these reactivated
ships.

"d. Air Force. The deployment of the remainder of the 82nd
Airborne Division to Southeast Asia will require the support of
three tactical fighter squadrons, a tactical reconnaissance
squadron, necessary elements of the Tactical Air Control System,
one PRIME BEEF unit, and one security squadron. In order to
provide support of the deployment and the broadening of the
training and rotation base and to retain a minimum acceptable
number of combat-ready deployable squadrons in the CONUS, these
Air Force organizations will have to be replaced by activation
of the following Air Reserve Forces: eight tactical fighter
squadrons, five tactical reconnaissance squadrons, one Tactical
Control Group, two military airlift groups, and one tactical
airlift wing, totalling 22,497 spaces. Activation of these Air
National Guard/Reserve units include organizations not currently
manned under COMBAT BEEF standards (100 percent)."

The Joint Chiefs reiterated their recommendation that legislation
be sought to: "(1) provide authority to call selected individual
Reservists to active duty; (2) extend beyond 30 June 1968 the existing
authority to call Reserve units to active duty; and (3) extend terms
of service for active duty personnel." The provisions of such legislation would, the Joint Chiefs indicated, impact on the Services in the
following manner:

"a. Army.

(1) Extension of terms of Service. Provides an immediate
impact on readiness worldwide in that critical skill specialists
in short supply are retained on active duty. It is estimated that

between 30,000 and 40,000 additional trained personnel will be retained in the Army for each month of extension. For example, during the first six-month period of extension of terms of service, the Army would gain in excess of 500 helicopter pilots, of which there is a critical shortage. Other critical skill shortages would be similarly affected.

"(2) Selective callup of individual Reservists. The Army Immediate Ready Reserve contains 490,000 personnel, of which more than 90 percent are in grades of E-4 and E-5. A selective callup of individual Reservists, coupled with an extension of terms of service, will alleviate virtually all of the Army's current critical skill shortages.

"b. Marine Corps.

(1) Involuntary extension of enlistments of all enlisted personnel would produce an average of 5,766 enlisted men per month through June. Within this gain, an average of 1,728 experienced NCOs per month would be gained.

"(2) Selective recall of individual Reservists would be necessary in order to bring mobilized units up, to provide the essential rank and skills not contained in the organized Reserve. Within the Marine Corps Reserve, but outside of the organized units, there is an invaluable pool of key personnel: noncommissioned officers, officers (particularly pilots), and Marines possessing long lead time "hard skill" Military Occupational Specialties.

"c. Navy. In the deploying ships of the Navy, there is a shortfall of 32,500 in officers and the top six enlisted pay grades.

(1) Involuntary extension of Reserve Officers and selected recall of Reserves would fulfill officer manning requirements in one to three months.

"(2) Cancellation of early releases and selective involuntary extensions, recall of Fleet Reserves, deferral of transfers to Fleet Reserve, and recall of Ready Reserves would achieve 100 percent enlisted requirements by rate/rating in one to three months.

"d. Air Force. If extension of terms of service were granted the Air Force could, on a selective basis, hold approximately 20,000 skilled personnel out of a possible 70,000 that would be discharged over a six-month period. Retaining these critical skills would sustain the force at an acceptable level. Should additional forces be deployed to meet possible future MACV requirements, legislation would be necessary in order that active units can be replaced by activation of corresponding Air National Guard units after 30 June 1968."

Based on all the foregoing, the Joint Chiefs of Staff recommended that:

"a. The following Reserve component units be called to active duty immediately:

(1) Two infantry brigade forces.

(2) One Marine regiment, plus the support forces indicated in paragraph 3b(1).

(3) Two NMCBs.

"b. The following Reserve component units be brought to a high state of readiness for probable call to active duty on short notice:

(1) One infantry division force and one infantry brigade force, in addition to the two brigade forces indicated above.

(2) The remainder of the 4th Marine Expeditionary Force.

(3) Three NMCBs, in addition to the two indicated above. Also, de-mothball work and long lead time procurement should begin on two heavy cruisers and 15 destroyers. Fifteen Naval Reserve Training destroyers should be placed on active duty and commence immediate installation of modern communications/electronics equipment.

"(4) Eight TPS, five TPS, one TACS, five ARS, one PRIME BEEF unit, and one security squadron.

"c. Measures be taken immediately to obtain the legislation to (1) provide authority to call selected individual Reservists to active duty; (2) extend beyond 30 June 1968 the existing authority to call Reserve units to active duty; and (3) extend terms of service for active duty personnel.

"d. A supplemental appropriation be requested to cover the unprogrammed cost of the approved and probable future deployments."

In addition, the Joint Chiefs of Staff indicated that an updated assessment of U.S. military posture worldwide pertaining to additional problems for U.S. military capabilities, to include specific recommendations for required improvement, would be reported in the near future.

This request was overtaken, as we shall see, by subsequent requirements submitted by COMUSMACV.

2. The Troop Request

Although the new Secretary of Defense, Clark Clifford, was formally sworn into office by the President on 1 March, his work had begun many days before.

In order to ascertain the situation in SVN and to determine subsequent MACV force requirements, General Earle Wheeler, Chairman of the Joint Chiefs of Staff, had been sent by the President to Saigon on 23 February. His report was presented to the President on 27 February 1968.11/ On the basis of this report, and the recommendations it contained, the President ordered the initiation of a complete and searching reassessment of the entire U.S. strategy and commitment in South Vietnam. The Secretary of Defense-designate, Mr. Clifford, was directed to conduct this review, aided by other members of the Cabinet.

In his report, General Wheeler summarized the situation in Vietnam as follows:

- The enemy failed to achieve his initial objective but is continuing his effort. Although many of his units were badly hurt, the judgment is that he has the will and the capability to continue.

- Enemy losses have been heavy; he has failed to achieve his prime objectives of mass uprisings and capture of a large number of the capital cities and towns. Morale in enemy units which were badly mauled or where the men were oversold the idea of a decisive victory at TET probably has suffered severely. However, with replacements, his indoctrination system would seem capable of maintaining morale at a generally adequate level. His determination appears to be unshaken.

- The enemy is operating with relative freedom in the countryside, probably recruiting heavily and no doubt infiltrating NVA units and personnel. His recovery is likely to be rapid; his supplies are adequate; and he is trying to maintain the momentum of his winter-spring offensive.

- The structure of the GVN held up but its effectiveness has suffered.

- The RVNAF held up against the initial assault with
gratifying, and in a way, surprising strength and fortitude.
However, ARVN is now in a defensive posture around towns
and cities and there is concern about how well they will
bear up under sustained pressure.

- The initial attack nearly succeeded in a dozen places,
and defeat in those places was only averted by the timely
reaction of US forces. In short, it was a very near thing.

- There is no doubt that the RD Program has suffered
a severe set back.

- RVNAF was not badly hurt physically -- they should
recover strength and equipment rather quickly (equipment
in 2 - 3 months -- strength in 3 - 6 months). Their problems are more psychological than physical.

- US forces have lost none of their pre-TET capability.

- MACV has three principal problems. First, logistic
support north of Danang is marginal owing to weather, enemy
interdiction and harassment and the massive deployment of
US forces into the DMZ/Hue area. Opening Route 1 will
alleviate this problem but takes a substantial troop commitment. Second, the defensive posture of ARVN is permitting
the VC to make rapid inroads in the formerly pacified countryside. ARVN, in its own words, is in a dilemma as it cannot
afford another enemy thrust into the cities and towns and yet
if it remains in a defensive posture against this contingency,
the countryside goes by default. MACV is forced to devote
much of its troop strength to this problem. Third, MACV
has been forced to deploy 50% of all US maneuver battalions
into I Corps, to meet the threat there, while enemy syn-
chronizes an attack against Khe Sanh/Hue-Quang Tri with an
offensive in the Highlands and around Saigon while keeping the
pressure on throughout the remainder of the country, MACV
will be hard pressed to meet adequately all threats. Under
these circumstances, we must be prepared to accept some
reverses. 12/

As to the future, General Wheeler saw the enemy pursuing a strategy of
a reinforced offensive in order to enlarge his control throughout the
countryside and keep pressure on the government and the allies. The enemy
is likely, the Chairman indicated:

To maintain strong threats in the DMZ area, at Khe Sanh,
in the highlands, and at Saigon, and to attack in force when
conditions seem favorable. He is likely to try to gain

control of the country's northern provinces. He will continue efforts to encircle cities and province capitals to
isolate and disrupt normal activities, and infiltrate them
to create chaos. He will seek maximum attrition of RVNAF
elements. Against US forces, he will emphasize attacks by
fire on airfields and installations, using assaults and
ambushes selectively. His central objective continues to
be the destruction of the Government of SVN and its armed
forces. As a minimum he hopes to seize sufficient territory
and gain control of enough people to support establishment
of the groups and committees he proposes for participation
in an NLF dominated government. 13/

General Wheeler stated that MACV believed the central thrust of U.S.
strategy must be to defeat the enemy offensive. If this were done well,
the situation overall would be greatly improved over the pre-TET condition.

While accepting the fact that its first priority must be the security
of the GVN in Saigon and in provincial capitals, MACV described its objectives as:

    --First, to counter the enemy offensive and to destroy
or eject the NVA invasion force in the north.

    -- Second, to restore security in the cities and towns.

    -- Third, to restore security in the heavily popu-
lated areas of the countryside.

    -- Fourth, to regain the initiative through offensive
operations. 14/

In discussing how General Westmoreland would accomplish these objectives, General Wheeler indicated the following tasks:

    (1) Security of Cities and Government. MACV recog-
nizes that US forces will be required to reinforce and
support RVNAF in the security of cities, towns and government structure. At this time, 10 US battalions are operating
in the environs of Saigon. It is clear that this task will
absorb a substantial portion of US forces.

    (2) Security in the Countryside. To a large extent
the VC now control the countryside. Most of the 54 battalions formerly providing security for pacification are
now defending district or province towns. MACV estimates
that US forces will be required in a number of places to
assist and encourage the Vietnamese Army to leave the cities
and towns and reenter the country. This is especially true
in the Delta.

TOP SECRET - Sensitive

(3) Defense of the borders, the DMZ and the northern provinces. MACV considers that it must meet the enemy threat in I Corps Tactical Zone and has already deployed there slightly over 50% of all US maneuver battalions. US forces have been thinned out in the highlands, notwithstanding an expected enemy offensive in the early future.

(4) Offensive Operations. Coupling the increased requirement for the defense of the cities and subsequent reentry into the rural areas, and the heavy requirement for defense of the I Corps Zone, MACV does not have adequate forces at this time to resume the offensive in the remainder of the country, nor does it have adequate reserves against the contingency of simultaneous large-scale enemy offensive action throughout the country. 15/

The conclusion was obvious:

Forces currently assigned to MACV, plus the residual Program Five forces yet to be delivered, are inadequate in numbers and balance to carry out the strategy and to accomplish the tasks described above in the proper priority.

However, it was the extent and magnitude of General Wheeler's request that stimulated the initiation of a thorough review of the direction of U.S. policy in SVN. To contend with, and defeat, the new enemy threat, MACV indicated a total requirement of 206,756 spaces over the 525,000 ceiling imposed by Program Five, or a new proposed ceiling of 731,756. All of these forces, which included three Division equivalents, 15 tactical fighter squadrons, and augmentation for current Navy programs, were to be deployed into country by the end of CY 68. These additional forces were to be delivered in three packages as follows:

(1) Immediate Increment, Priority One: To be deployed by 1 May 68. Major elements include one brigade of the 5th Mechanized Division with a mix of one infantry, one armored and one mechanized battalion; the Fifth Marine Division (less RLT-26); one armored cavalry regiment; eight tactical fighter squadrons; and a groupment of Navy units to augment on going programs.

(2) Immediate Increment, Priority Two: To be deployed as soon as possible but prior to 1 Sep 68. Major elements include the remainder of the 5th Mechanized Division, and four tactical fighter squadrons. It is desirable that the ROK Light Division be deployed within this time frame.

(3) Follow-On Increment: To be deployed by the end of CY 68. Major elements include one infantry division, three tactical fighter squadrons, and units to further augment Navy Programs. 16/

15

TOP SECRET - Sensitive

TOP SECRET - Sensitive

        A fork in the road had been reached. Now the alternatives stood
out in stark reality. To accept and meet General Wheeler's request for
troops would mean a total U.S. military commitment to SVN -- an Americanization of the war, a callup of reserve forces, vastly increased expenditures.
To deny the request for troops, or to attempt to again cut it to a size which
could be sustained by the thinly stretched active forces, would just as surely
signify that an upper limit to the U.S. military commitment in SVN had been
reached.

    3. "A to Z" Reassessment

        These thoughts were very much on Secretary Clifford's mind during
his first meeting on 29 February with the people who were to conduct the
reassessment of U.S. strategy. Present, in addition to Clifford, were McNamara,
General Taylor, Nitze, Fowler, Katzenbach, Rostow, Helms, Bundy, Warnke, and
Habib. 17/   Mr. Clifford outlined the task as he had received it from the
President. He indicated to the group that he felt that the real problem to
be addressed was not whether we should send 200,000 additional troops to Vietnam. The real questions were: Should we follow the present course in SVN;
could it ever prove successful even if vastly more than 200,000 troops were
sent? The answers to these questions, the formulation of alternative courses
open to the U.S., was to be the initial focus of the review. To that end,
general assignments were made concerning papers to be written. These papers
were to be prepared for discussion among the Group on Saturday, March 2.
The general division of labor and outline of subjects assigned was indicated
by Mr. Bundy in a memorandum the subsequent day, as follows:

        1. What alternative courses of action are available to
    the US?

            Assignment: Defense - General Taylor - State (Secretary)

        2. What alternative courses are open to the enemy?

            Assignment - Defense and CIA

        3. Analysis of implications of Westmoreland's request for
    additional troops.

            Series of papers on the following.

            Military implications - JCS

            Political implications - State

                (Political implications in their broadest
                 domestic and international sense to include
                 internal Vietnamese problem).

            Budgetary results - Defense

Economic implications - Treasury

Congressional implications - Defense

Implications for public opinion - domestic and
    international - State.

4. Negotiation Alternatives

Assignment - State 18/

In addition, Secretary Clifford indicated that certain military options
were to be examined in this review. These options were:

Option I: Add approximately 196,000 troops to the present
           total authorized force level, i.e. Program 5
           (525,000) plus the six additional battalions
           already deployed (10,500). Restrictions cur-
           rently imposed on air and ground operations in
           Cambodia, Laos, and North Vietnam are relaxed
           to permit destruction of the ports, mining of
           the waterways, attack of complete target systems
           in NVN and offensive operations against VC/NVA
           Army forces in Laos and Cambodia.

Option IA: No change from Option I except that current
           restrictions on ground and air operations in
           Cambodia, Laos, and NVN are maintained.

Option II: No change to total authorized force level
           (525,000 plus 10,500 augmentation) except to
           deploy 3 fighter squadrons authorized within
           the ceiling but not deployed.

Option III: Add 50,000 troops above those currently authorized.

Option IV: Add 100,000 troops above those currently authorized. 19/

The main work in preparing a paper for Secretary Clifford to present
to the President was to be done in the Defense Department by a group of
staff action officers working intensively under the direction of Mr. Leslie
Gelb. These staff officers worked as a drafting committee while a group
consisting of Mr. Warnke, Mr. Enthoven, Mr. Halperin and Mr. Steadman
acted as a policy review board. Of the work done outside the Pentagon,
only the papers on negotiations and SVN domestic policies prepared by
Mr. Bundy and Mr. Habib at State and General Taylor's paper on alternative
strategies went to the White House. The other materials contributed by
CIA, State, Treasury, and the Joint Staff were fed into the deliberative
process at the Pentagon but were not included as such in the final product.
Thus, the dominant voice in the consideration of alternatives as the reassessment progressed was that of the OSD.

These agency views were, however, read and assessed by the working group and, although they were not furnished to the President, they were part of the background of the deliberative process. It would be misleading, therefore, to say that they were not considered or had no influence on the decisions taken. In any case, they provided some sense of the ideas and alternatives being considered and debated during these few frantic days of late February - early March, 1968.

The CIA furnished three papers which were considered in the reassessment. The first, dated 26 February 1968, was prepared for the Director of Central Intelligence prior to the formation of the Task Group. Entitled "The Outlook in Vietnam," this paper stated the following conclusion:

We believe that the Communists will sustain a high level of military activity for at least the next two or three months. It is difficult to forecast the situation which will then obtain, given the number of unknowable factors which will figure. Our best estimate is as follows:

a. The least likely outcome of the present phase is that the Communist side will expend its resources to such an extent as to be incapable thereafter of preventing steady advances by the US/GVN.

b. Also unlikely, though considerably less so, is that the GVN/ARVN will be so critically weakened that it can play no further significant part in the military and political prosecution of the struggle.

c. More likely than either of the above is that the present push will be generally contained, but with severe losses to both the GVN and Communist forces, and that a period will set in during which neither will be capable of registering decisive gains. 20/

The second CIA paper, dated 29 February, was entitled "Communist Alternatives in Vietnam." Two main military alternatives were identified, as follows:

a. maintain widespread military pressure in Vietnam at least for the next several months;

b. increase the level of military pressures by one or more of the following measures:

(1) committing all of their reserves from NVN, tantamount to an all-out invasion, to gain decisive results as quickly as possible;

(2) committing two or three additional divisions;

TOP SECRET - Sensitive

(3) seeking one major battle which promised significant political gains.

(4) expanding current efforts in Laos. 21/

Based on this analysis, Communist intentions were assessed as follows:

The Communists probably intend to maintain widespread military pressures in Vietnam for at least the next several months. A special effort will be made to harass urban areas and keep them under threat. They will probably calculate that the US/GVN will be forced to defend the towns and the countryside will be left more vulnerable to Communist domination. At some time, new Communist attacks will probably be launched to seize and hold certain cities and towns. Where conditions appear favorable they will engage US forces, seeking some significant local success which would have a major political return. The total result of their campaign, they hope, will be to so strain the resources of the US and the GVN/ARVN, that the Saigon government will lose control of much of the country and the US will have little choice but to settle the war on Communist terms. 22/

The third CIA paper, submitted on 1 March 1968, attempted to answer specific questions posed by the Secretary of Defense in his initial meeting with his senior working group on 29 February. Pertinent questions and the CIA assessment are listed below:

Q. What is the likely course of events in South Vietnam over the next 10 months, assuming no change in U.S. policy or force levels?

A. In the assumed circumstances a total military victory by the Allies or the Communists is highly unlikely in the next 10 months. It is manifestly impossible for the Communists to drive U.S. forces out of the country. It is equally out of the question for US/GVN forces to clear South Vietnam of Communist forces. It is possible, however, that the overall situation in this period will take a decisive turn.

We think it unlikely that this turn could be in the US/GVN favor....We see no evidence yet that the GVN/ARVN will be inspired to seize the initiative, go over to the attack, exploit the Communist vulnerabilities, and quickly regain the rural areas. We doubt they have the will and capability to make the effort.

Far more likely is an erosion of the ARVN's morale and effectiveness. We do not believe that the GVN will collapse, or that the ARVN will totally disintegrate. But

19   TOP SECRET - Sensitive

there is a fairly good chance that Communist presssures
will result in a serious weakening of the GVN/ARVN apparatus
and an end to its effective functioning in parts of the
country. In these circumstances, virtually the entire
burden of the war would fall on US forces.

* * *

In sum, there is a high risk that both the ARVN
and GVN will be seriously weakened in the next months,
and perhaps decisively so. Our best estimate is that
in the assumed circumstances the overall situation 10
months hence will be no better than a standoff.

Q. What is the likely Communist reaction to a change
in US strategy toward greater control over population
centers, with or without increased forces?

A. In general the Communists would view this move
as a success for their strategy. Their tactical response
in such circumstances would depend mainly on the nature
of US enclaves. If these were fairly large and embraced
much of the outlying countryside, the Communists would
believe them to be porous enough to infiltrate and harass,
much as they are doing now. If the defensive perimeters
were fairly solid, however, the Communists would not try
to overrun them in frontal assaults. Instead, they
would concentrate for a time on consolidating the countryside and isolating the various defended enclaves, in
particular interdicting supply lines and forcing the US
to undertake expensive supply movements from out of
country. A Communist-controlled regime with a "coalition"
facade would be set up in "liberated" areas and attempts
at terrorist activity inside the enclaves would be undertaken. Hanoi would hope that a combination of military and
political pressure, together with the dim prospect for
achievement of the original US aims in the Vietnam struggle,
would eventually persuade the US to extricate itself through
negotiations.

Q. What is the likely NVA/VC strategy over the next
10 months if US forces are increased by 50,000, by 100,000,
or by 200,000?

A. We would expect the Communists to continue the war.
They still have resources available in North Vietnam and
within South Vietnam to increase their troop strength. Their

strong logistical effort and their ability to organize and
exploit the people under their control in the South enable them
to counter US increases by smaller increases of their own.
Over a ten-month period the Communists would probably be able
to introduce sufficient new units into the South to offset
the US maneuver battalion increments of the various force
levels given above. 23/

These CIA assessments, then, painted very bleak alternatives for
U.S. policymakers. If U.S. policy and force levels did not change, there
was a high risk that ARVN and the GVN would be seriously weakened, perhaps
decisively so. The US would assume the major burden of the war, and the
situation would be no better than a standoff. If U.S. forces were increased
by as much as 100,000, the Communists would probably be able to introduce
sufficient new units in the South to offset this increase. If the U.S.
changed its strategy toward greater control over population centers, with
or without increased forces, the Communists would adjust their strategy
so as to preclude the achievement of U.S. aims.

In his various papers for the Working Group, Assistant Secretary of
State William Bundy attempted a deliberate approach. He furnished one
paper which outlined alternative courses of action which he considered
deserved serious consideration. 24/ Another paper outlined a checklist
"to serve as a rough guide to the papers that need preparation under a
systematic code." 25/

The alternative courses listed by Mr. Bundy were:

    a. Accept the Wheeler/Westmoreland recommendation aimed
at sending roughly 100,000 men by 1 May and another 100,000
men by the end of 1968.

    b. Change our military strategy, reducing the areas and
places we seek to control and concentrating far more heavily
on the protection of populated areas.

    c. Adopt option b above in the south, but extend our
bombing and other military actions against the North to try
to strangle the war there and put greater pressure on Hanoi
in this area.

    d. Accept immediately those elements of the Wheeler/
Westmoreland proposals that could hope to affect the situation favorably over the next four months or so, but do not
go beyond that in terms of force plans and related actions.

    e. "Cut and shave" the Wheeler/Westmoreland proposals
and their action implications, but carry on basically in
accordance with present strategy.

    f. "All-out option." Announce that we were prepared
to hold in Vietnam no matter what developed." 26/

TOP SECRET - Sensitive

The Department of State also prepared papers on the following
subjects:

      a. Introductory Paper on Key Elements in the Situation 27/

      b. Probable Soviet, Chinese, Western European Reactions 28/

      c. Ambassador Thompson's Cable on Soviet Reactions to
Possible U.S. Government Courses of Action 29/

      d. European and Other Non-Asian Reactions to Major Force
Increases 30/

      e. Asian Reaction to a Major U.S. Force Increase 31/

      f. Options on our Negotiating Posture 32/

These papers were presented to the Clifford Group at the meeting on
3 March 1968. However, as will be seen, they were quickly overtaken by
the rapidly moving situation and, with the exception of the paper on negotiating options, did not figure in the final memorandum which was forwarded
to the President on 4 March.

General Maxwell Taylor's paper on alternative courses of action is
of greater interest in that it was furnished both to the Clifford Working
Group and to the White House directly through General Taylor's capacity
as Military Advisor to the President. Although it is not known what weight
was given to this paper, it was received by the President even prior to the
Memorandum from the Clifford Group, and thereby could have gained some
special weight in the deliberations of the President.

After a brief listing of the U.S. objectives in SVN, General Taylor
concluded that, since there was no serious consideration being given at the
moment to adding to or subtracting from our present objective, the discussion
should be limited to considerations of alternative strategies and programs
to attain that objective. 33/

General Taylor concluded that, basically, our government had only two
choices:

      a. We can tell General Westmoreland that he must make do
with his present forces in Viet-Nam and ask him to report to
us what he is capable of accomplishing therewith. This would
be an invitation to him to cut back sharply upon the military
objectives he has defined in his latest Combined Campaign
Plan (1968). Alternatively, while making this decision to
provide no further forces, we could give new strategic
guidance to General Westmoreland which would assist him in
establishing the priorities for his efforts necessary to
bring his mission within capabilities of the forces allotted
him.

b. The other broad alternative is to increase his present
forces by some amount varying from less than his figure of
205,000 and ranging up to the full amount. Also in this case,
we might well consider giving him revised strategic guidance
in the light of what we have learned from the Tet offensive
and its sequel.

General Taylor thus indicated that in the reassessment of our strategy,
the government would be required to answer the following questions:

(1) Do we decide at this time to send any additional
reinforcements to General Westmoreland?

(2) If the answer is affirmative, should we agree to
send all or part of the 205,000 requested by General
Westmoreland?

(3) Whether the response is affirmative or negative, should
we send General Westmoreland new strategic guidance, hoping to
limit further demands on U.S. military manpower?

(4) What Strategic Reserve should be retained in the U.S.
in the foregoing situations?

General Taylor then listed some of the political considerations of the
military course of action decided upon. He listed the following political
actions as worth considering in connection with any decision on reinforcement:

(1) A renewed offer of negotiation, possibly with a private
communication that we would suspend the bombing for a fixed period
without making the time limitation public if we were assured that
productive negotiations would start before the end of the period.

(2) A public announcement that we would adjust the bombing
of the North to the level of intensity of enemy ground action
in the South.

(3) As a prelude to sharply increased bombing levels, possibly
to include the closing of Haiphong, a statement of our intentions
made necessary by the enemy offensive against the cities and
across the frontiers.

(4) Announcement of the withdrawal of the San Antonio
formula in view of the heightened level of aggression conducted
by North Viet-Nam.

(5) Keep silent.

In choosing among these alternatives, General Taylor argued that the present military situation in South Vietnam argued strongly against a new negotiation effort or any thought of reducing the bombing of the North. He further argued that, in any case, we would appear well-advised to withdraw from the San Antonio formula.

Thus, he concluded, there seemed to be at least three program packages worth serious consideration. They were:

Package A

a. No increase of General Westmoreland's forces in South Viet-Nam.

b. New strategic guidance.

c. Build-up of Strategic Reserve.

d. No negotiation initiative.

e. Withdrawal of San Antonio formula.

f. Pressure on GVN to do better.

Package B

a. Partial acceptance of General Westmoreland's recommendation.

b. New strategic guidance.

c. Build-up of Strategic Reserve.

d. No negotiation initiative.

e. Withdrawal of San Antonio formula.

f. Pressure on GVN to do better.

Package C

a. Approval of General Westmoreland's full request.

b. New strategic guidance.

c. Build-up of Strategic Reserve.

d. No negotiation initiative.

e. Withdrawal of San Antonio formula and announcement of intention to close Haiphong.

f. Pressure on GVN to do better.

g. Major effort to rally the homefront.

The working group within ISA had access to all of these documents. In addition, and at the request of the working group, other papers were prepared within the Department of Defense by the Assistant Secretary (Systems Analysis) and the Assistant Secretary (Public Affairs).

Initially, Systems Analysis undertook a capability study in order to determine if the MACV requirement could indeed be met. They concluded that, with the exception of Army aviation units, the MACV manpower request could be filled essentially as desired. This could even be done, the analysis concluded, without changing the one-year tour policy, without drawing down on Europe, and without widespread second tours with less than 24 months in CONUS. This assumed a reserve recall, added funds, and the required strength increases.

Our maximum capability would be to provide 6 maneuver battalions in May, 9 more in June, 9 in July and as many as 6 more in August -- faster than the MACV request. These units would have the necessary artillery, transportation and engineer support. Added tactical air units could deploy on a matching schedule.

The only significant shortfall would be in Army Aviation. Even with a reserve recall, present deployment schedules cannot be significantly accelerated. Production limitations are such that at least one year would be required to increase the output of UH-1/AF-1 helicopters. Thus, it would be mid-1969 before any added aviation units could deploy and mid-1971 before the total MACV requirement could be met. 34/

This SA paper also considered several other deployment options, as follows: cut 50,000 from present authorization; no increase in current authorization; increase by 50,000; increase by 100,000; increase by 200,000. The units required under all these options, it was concluded, could deploy to Vietnam in a matter of months. The 50,000 man package could arrive in May and June; the 100,000 man package by August; and the full 200,000 (with minor exceptions) by December. The principal exceptions under all options would continue to be Army aviation units. A summary of the various options considered is shown below:

Optional Deployments

	A Cut 50,000	B Current Plan	C Add 50,000	D Add 100,000	E Add 200,000
Total U.S. personnel	485,000	535,000	585,000	635,000	631,000
U.S. Maneuver Bns	103	112	118	124	133
Artillery Bns	68	72	77	83	92
Tac Air Sqds	44	45	51	56	60
Annual Cost	$23 Bil.	$25 Bil.	$28 Bil.	$30 Bil.	$35 Bil.
Reserve Recall	--	--	65,000	200,000	250,000 35/

Other papers prepared by Systems Analysis during this period were furnished to the ISA working group upon their request. Indeed, the subject matter and thrust of these papers indicated fairly early the bias of the people preparing them as well as the direction in which the reassessment of U.S. strategy was moving, at least within the working group in ISA.

Papers were also furnished concerning pacification, costs and probable results of alternative U.S. strategies in South Vietnam, the status of RVNAF, problems of inflation, and data for analysis of strategies. The main thrust of most of these papers was that "more of the same" in South Vietnam would not achieve decisive results and, indeed, would not be satisfactory. The paper on pacification indicated that:

> Hamlet Evaluation System (HES) reports for CY 1967 indicate that pacification progressed slowly during the first half of 1967, and lost ground in the second half. Most (60%) of the 1967 gain results from accounting type changes to the HES system, not from pacification progress; hamlet additions and deletions, and revised population estimates accounted for half of the January-June increase and all of the June-December increase. In the area that really counts--VC-D-E hamlets rising to A-B-C ratings--we actually suffered a net loss of 10,100 people between June and December 1967. 36/

Based on General Wheeler's statement in his report to the President, that "to a large extent the VC now control the countryside," the paper concluded that "the enemy's current offensive appears to have killed the program once and for all." 37/

In analyzing the status of RVNAF, the Systems Analysis paper concluded:

> Highest priority must be given to getting RVNAF moving. In the short run re-equipping the Vietnamese and helping them regain their combat power insures that we can prevent unnecessary loss should the enemy attack the cities or put pressure there while hitting Khe Sanh. Further, present US force commitments mean that only a recuperated RVNAF will permit release of US units for other missions and accomplish any objectives in pacification. Finally, restoration of security in the cities in conjunction with the National Police is a major new mission for RVNAF which requires forces.

> What can we do? There are many indications that the manpower situation is worse than reported. Every effort must be made to determine how many deserters there are and to approach them. Rounding up trained manpower delinquent in returning from Tet will help. US advisors can pressure the JGS to upgrade selected RF/PF into ARVN in addition to measures already initiated by RVNAF.

COMUSMACV must identify weak RVNAF units. III Corps
need special study and preparation of revised contingency
plans. Priority on remanning, re-equipping and retraining
must be given to the RVNAF elite units (VNMC) which constitute the general reserve. COMUSMACV must plan for the
use of this reserve and earmarked US units to defect VC
attack of weak RVNAF units during the interim period.

RVNAF modernization should take precedence over equipping all US forces except those deploying to the combat
zone. The remaining 82,000 M16 rifles must be delivered
ASAP. It is also in the US interest to equip the RF/PF
with M16s before equipping the US training base, which is
already programmed.

Lastly, COMUSMACV must make decisions about what
missions RVNAF need not accomplish now. RVNAF is stretched
too thin given its past and expected missions. It alone
cannot protect the cities and hold the countryside where
it is still deployed. Decision is needed to permit the
build-up of weak units and better integrated use of US
and RVNAF against whatever enemy scenario develops. 38/

The paper entitled "Alternate Strategies" painted a bleak picture of
American failure in Vietnam:

We lost our offensive stance because we never achieved
the momentum essential for military victory. Search and
Destroy operations can't build this kind of momentum and
the RVNAF was not pushed hard enough. We became mesmerized
by statistics of known doubtful validity, choosing to place
our faith only in the ones that showed progress. We judged
the enemy's intentions rather than his capabilities because
we trusted captured documents too much. We were not alert
to the perils of time lag and spoofing. In short, our setbacks were due to wishful thinking compounded by a massive
intelligence collection and/or evaluation failure.

Indeed, in examining U.S. objectives in SVN, the picture of failure was
manifest:

Since the original commitment of large US forces in 1965,
our stated objectives have been to:

(1) Make it as difficult and costly as possible for
NVN to continue effective support of the VC and cause NVN to
cease its direction of the VC insurgency.

(While we have raised the price to NVN of aggression and

27   TOP SECRET - Sensitive

support of the VC, it shows no lack of capability or will
to match each new US escalation. Our strategy of "attrition"
has not worked. Adding 206,000 more US men to a force of
525,000, gaining only 27 additional maneuver battalions and
270 tactical fighters at an added cost to the US of $10 bil-
lion per year raises the question of who is making it costly
from whom.)

(2) Extend GVN dominion, direction and control over
SVN.

(This objective can only be achieved by the GVN through
its political and economic processes and with the indispensable
support of an effective RVNAF. The TET offensive demonstrated
not only that the US had not provided an effective shield, it
also demonstrated that the GVN and RVNAF had not made real
progress in pacification -- the essential first step along the
road of extending GVN dominion, direction and control.)

(3) Defeat the VC and NVA forces in SVN and force
their withdrawal. (The TET offensive proved we were further
from this goal than we thought. How much further remains
to be seen.)

(4) Deter the Chinese Communists from direct intervention in SEA. (This we have done successfully so far;
however, greatly increased U.S. forces may become counter-
productive.)

We know that despite a massive influx of 500,000 US troops,
1.2 million tons of bombs a year, 400,000 attack sorties per year,
200,000 enemy KIA in three years, 20,000 US KIA, etc., our control
of the countryside and the defense of the urban areas is now
essentially at pre-August 1965 levels. We have achieved stalemate at a high commitment. A new strategy must be sought. 39/

Several alternative strategies were briefly discussed and all but one
were quickly dismissed as being unlikely to bring success:

(1) No change but increase the resources.

This strategy alternative is implicit in the recommendations of MACV and CJCS....In brief, the MACV and CJCS recommendations are for additional forces to regain this ground lost since
January, 1968. Nothing is said as to whether still more US
forces will be required to finish the job. Another payment on
an open-ended commitment is requested.

(2) Widen the War.

Adoption of this alternative would require more forces than are now being considered and it runs further risks of involving China and the USSR. The course of events already set in motion could lead to adoption of this alternative; increasing US forces in SVN would undoubtedly increase the possibilities of it. And the option is open for North Korea or other aggressive countries to test our will elsewhere.

(3) Opt Out of the War.

The price of quitting now would include the undermining of our other commitments world-wide, bitter dissension at home, and a probable resurgence of active Chinese-USSR territorial aggrandizements.

Before TET we could have done this with less risk than now.

(4) Resuscitate GVN and RVNAF.

This option is to return to the concept of a GVN war with US assistance instead of the present situation of a US war with dubious GVN assistance.

Adoption of this alternative requires:

(a) A solid commitment to a US force ceiling. This commitment must be communicated to the highest levels of GVN/RVNAF and our own military leaders.

(b) A skillful conditioning of US and world opinion to the limited US commitment to the South Vietnamese war and to our right of withdrawal if GVN/RVNAF determination or performance wavers.

(c) A statement that the US objective in SVN is to develop the GVN capability to defeat the VC and NVA forces in SVN and force their withdrawal. 40/

The remaining Systems Analysis paper cited statistics to show that, in the past, the North Vietnamese had been able to match the U.S. buildup in SVN with their own buildup. Also statistics were used to project the cost to the U.S. in casualties resulting from various deployment options and various strategies on the ground. These projections showed that a shift to a population control strategy which was unchallenged by the enemy would stabilize casualty rates, as some units would be underemployed. 41/

The paper prepared by the Assistant Secretary of Defense (Public Affairs) was entitled "Possible Public Reaction to Various Alternatives." Five alternative options were examined:

    1. Increased mobilization and deployment. This includes sending General Westmoreland 50,000 to 200,000 more troops and the additional moves this would require at home -- calling reserves, extending enlistments, extra expenditures, bigger tax bill, etc.

    2. Increased mobilization/deployment plus expanded bombing of North Vietnam.

    3. Increased mobilization/deployment plus a bombing pause.

    4. Denial of the Westmoreland requests and continuation of the war "as is" -- as it was being fought prior to the Tet offensive and Khe Sanh.

    5. Denial of the Westmoreland requests and a change in war-fighting policy with greater concentration on defending populated areas and less on search-and-destroy in unpopulated areas. This would include an announced program to begin troop withdrawal at a fixed date. 42/

The Assistant Secretary, Mr. Goulding, emphasized that all options were being examined from a public reaction standpoint only. He also emphasized that no action would unite the country. The question to be attacked was which option will most coalesce supporters and most isolate the opposition.

In analyzing the various options above, Mr. Goulding divided the public into hawks, doves, and middle-of-the-roaders. Under Option 1, he argued, increased mobilization and deployment moves, without other new actions:

    ...will make the doves unhappy because we become more and more enmeshed in the war. They will make the hawks unhappy because we still will be withholding our military strength, particularly in the North. And the middle-of-the-roaders who basically support the President out of conviction or patriotism will be unhappy because they will see the ante going up in so many ways and still will not be given a victory date, a progress report they can believe or an argument they can accept that all of this is in the national interest. (Further, they will read in the dissent columns and editorials that 18 months from now, when the North Vietnamese have added 30,000 more troops, we will be right back where we started.)

Thus, public reaction to this option would be extremely negative, and would become increasingly so as the deployment numbers, the financial costs, and the life-disrupting actions increase.

The next two options, Mr. Goulding indicated, should be considered together since, from a public affairs standpoint, the decision to deploy additional troops of any significant number must be accompanied by some "new" move. The two options discussed were deployment plus expanded bombing of the North, and increased mobilization plus a bombing pause.

The first course, Goulding concluded, would elicit more support in the country than does the present course.

> This course would clearly bring aboard more hawks and
> further isolate the doves. It would also make the war much
> easier to accept by the middle-of-the-roaders. It would
> help unite the country. Some fence sitters, however, would
> be added to those who already view the war as an unforgiveable
> sin. I think the campus and "liberal" reaction would sur-
> pass anything we have seen.

The other option envisioned continuing to fight as we are in the south, strengthening General Westmoreland with part or all of his request, and coupling these moves with a visible "peace" campaign based upon a cessation of the bombing in the North. This course, Goulding concluded:

> ...would alienate those who take the hardest line.
> We would be adding much to our cost, both by the extra
> deployment and the military price paid for the pause,
> without receiving any immediate or concrete results. If
> the Communists took advantage of the bombing halt, the
> hawks and many of the military would react strongly....
> The doves, of course, would enthusiastically endorse the
> pause and would immediately begin pleading and praying
> that it be continued long enough to explore every possible
> and conceivable corridor....Additionally, the doves would
> deplore the extra deployments. They would complain that
> the pause was not unlimited or unconditional. They would
> argue that the deployments plus the failure to be "uncon-
> ditional" detracted from the effort. This two-pronged
> approach -- strengthen but seek negotiation -- would give
> new confidence to the middle-of-the-roaders. They would
> applaud the government for doing "something" different,
> for seeking a way out of the quagmire. They would be
> more patient than the hawks to give the pause a chance,
> and less disturbed than the doves at the mobilization.
> For them, it could be a way out -- and even a "could be"
> is better than the frustration they now feel....The deploy/
> pause option would be more favorably received by the nation
> than the deploy/escalate North, since it would, in the public
> mind, offer more hope of an eventual solution to the war.

The fourth option, denial of the Westmoreland request and continue the war "as is," would please no one, according to Mr. Goulding. The hawks (and the military) would protest vehemently. They would be less satisfied, and the doves would be no more satisfied by this failure to take new initiatives toward peace. However, Mr. Goulding concluded, since fewer people would be affected by this course than by Option One, and therefore it would be preferable to that Option.

The advantages of Option Five - denial of General Westmoreland's requests and a change in strategy in South Vietnam -- from a public affairs standpoint were overwhelming, the paper concluded.

> ....The pain of additional deployments, Reserve callups, increased draft calls, increased casualties, extended tours would be eliminated. The hazards of bombing escalation would be eliminated. The dangers of a bombing pause would be eliminated. The frustration of more-and-more-and-more into the endless pit would be eliminated. What the people want most of all is some sign that we are making progress, that there is, somewhere, an end. While this does not necessarily show progress, it does show change. It does show the search for new approaches....It would prevent the middle-of-the-roaders from joining the doves. While the doves want a pause, I would think they would prefer this to deployment-mobilization plus pause. While the hawks want to escalate in the North, most of them (not all) also want an end to increased ground strength in the South. I believe that we would be successful in getting members of Congress to make speeches in support of this.

In summary, then, and strictly from a public reaction standpoint, Mr. Goulding noted the options as follows:

Acceptable: Only #5 -- Denial of requests and a change in policy in the South.

Most acceptable of the others: #3 -- Deploy and pause.

Next most acceptable: #2 -- Deploy and expand Air War North.

Next most acceptable: #4 -- Deny Westmoreland and continue as is.

Most objectionable: #1 -- Deploy and continue as is, north and south. 43/

4. Drafting a Memorandum

There is, of course, no way of knowing how much consideration
and weight were given to each of these papers by the small group of action
officers in the Pentagon who were, in the last analysis, charged with
digesting all of these factors, considerations, and views and actually
drafting the reassessment of U.S. strategy required by the President of
his new Secretary of Defense. The predilections of these drafters, perhaps were hinted at by the subject matter of the backup papers prepared at
their specific request and summarized above.

By 29 February, this group had produced an initial draft of a memorandum for the President which examined the situation in SVN "in light of U.S.
political objectives and General Westmoreland's request for additional
troops, as stated in General Wheeler's report." 44/

This draft was slightly revised by senior officers in ISA and apparently
was discussed within the Defense Establishment on 1 March. 45/

This paper began with an assessment of the current situation in South
Viet Nam and a discussion of the prospects over the next 10 months. Quoting
General Wheeler's report, the draft memorandum indicated that the most important VC goal in the winter-spring offensive was the takeover of the countryside. In many parts of the country, it was stated, they may have already
succeeded in achieving this goal.

The 'main event' thus is still to come, not in a one-night
offensive but in a week-by-week expulsion of GVN presence and
influence from the rural areas, showing up on the pacification
maps as a 'red tide' flowing up to the edges of the province
and district towns, and over some of them. 46/

Although ARVN held up well under initial assaults, the ISA memorandum
concluded that they would not soon move out of their defensive posture
around the cities and towns. They would, in the future, challenge the VC
offensively much less than before.

In the new, more dangerous environment,to come about in
the countryside, and as currently led, motivated, and influenced at the top, ARVN is even less likely than before to
buckle down to the crucial offensive job of chasing district
companies and (with U.S. help) provincial battalions. In that
environment, informers will clam up, or be killed; the VC will
get more information and cooperation, the GVN less; officials
and police will be much less willing to act on information or
VC suspects and activities. 47/

The memorandum was even more pessimistic concerning the future direction
and abilities of the South Vietnamese Government, and read more into the TET
offensive than had been noted there by other observers.

It is unlikely that the GVN will rise to the challenge.
It will not move toward a Government of National Union.
Current arrests of oppositionists further isolate and discredit it, and possibly foreshadow the emasculation of the
Assembly and the undoing of all promising political developments of the past year. Furthermore, it is possible that
the recent offensive was facilitated by a newly friendly
or apathetic urban environment, and a broad low-level
cooperative organization that had not existed on the same
scale before. If, in fact, the attacks reflect new VC
opportunities and capability in the cities, then the impact
of the attacks themselves, the overall military response,
and the ineffective GVN political response may still further
improve the VC cause in the cities, as well as in the countryside. Even if the political makeup of the GVN should change
for the better, it may well be that VC penetration in the
cities has now gone or will soon go too far for real non-
communist political mobilization to develop. 48/

Based upon this bleak assessment of the future of the Government and
Army of South Vietnam, the IDA draft memorandum undertook to examine
alternative military strategies. Two such strategies were to be compared,
the current one and an alternative which emphasized population security.
(Actually, only one was analyzed in detail.) The two strategies were to be
compared at current force levels and with added increments of 50,000,
150,000 and 200,000.

In analyzing our current strategy, the memorandum undertook a review
of how our strategy in Vietnam evolved. At the time U.S. forces were first
committed in South Vietnam in early 1965, the draft Presidential memorandum
indicated, the political situation was a desperate one. There was imminent
danger of a North Vietnamese-controlled seizure of power in SVN and the
imposition of a communist regime by force. Thus, the immediate objective
of the U.S. was a military one--to arrest this trend and to deny to the
NVA/VC the seizure of political control by force.

Once U.S. forces were committed in increasingly large numbers, however,
the military and political situation began to improve significantly. By
the end of 1966, our initial military objective had been achieved--no longer
was it possible for NVN to impose its will upon SVN by force. By this time,
however, our military objectives had been expanded at the expense of our
political objectives.

In the absence of political directives limiting the goals to be
attained by U.S. military force, our objectives became:

    a. To make it as difficult and costly as possible for
NVN to continue effective support of the VC and to cause NVN
to cease direction of the insurgency.

b. To defeat the VC and NVA forces in SVN and force the withdrawal of NVN forces....

c. To extend GVN control over all of SVN.

Indeed, in asking for increased forces, General Wheeler and General Westmoreland described their current tasks as follows:

a. Security of Cities and Government.

b. Security in the Countryside.

c. Defense of the Borders, the DMZ, and the Northern Province.

d. Offensive Operations. 49/

The question to be answered, then, suggested the memorandum, was what we could hope to accomplish with these increased force levels in pursuit of our current strategy. The answer was not encouraging.

With current force levels we cannot continue to pursue all of the objectives listed by General Wheeler. Can we do so with increased forces?

MACV does not clearly specify how he would use the additional forces he requests, except to indicate that they would provide him with a theater reserve and an offensive capability. Even with the 200,000 additional troops requested by MACV, we will not be in a position to drive the enemy from SVN or to destroy his forces. MACV's description of his key problems makes clear that the additional forces would be used to open Route 1, north of Danang; support ARVN units, particularly in the Delta; and to maintain a reserve against enemy offensives. With lesser increases of 50,000 or 100,000, MACV would be in an even less favorable position to go on the offensive. Moreover, even before the TET offensive the enemy was initiating about two-thirds of the clashes and could, in response to our buildup, adopt a casualty limiting posture.

The more likely enemy response, however, is that with which he has responded to previous increases in our force levels, viz., a matching increase on his part. Hanoi has maintained a constant ratio of one maneuver battalion to 1.5 U.S. maneuver battalions from his reserve in NVN of from 45-70 maneuver battalions (comprising 40,000-60,000 men in 5-8 divisions).

Even if the enemy stands and fights as he did before TET, the results can only be disappointing in terms of attriting his capability.

Over the past year the United States has been killing between 70 and 100 VC/NVA per month per U.S. combat battalion in theater. The return per combat battalion deployed has been falling off, but even assuming that additional deployments will double the number of combat battalions, and assuming that the kill-ratios will remain constant, we could expect enemy deaths, at best, on the order of magnitude of 20,000 per month, but the infiltration system from North Viet Nam alone could supply 13,000-16,000 per month, regardless of our bombing pattern, leaving the remainder -- 4,000 -- to be recruited in South Viet Nam -- a demonstrably manageable undertaking for the VC.

The current strategy thus can promise no early end to the conflict, nor any success in attriting the enemy or eroding Hanoi's will to fight. Moreover, it would entail substantial costs in South Viet Nam, in the United States, and in the rest of the world. 50/

These substantial costs, the paper indicated, would indeed preclude the attainment of U.S. objectives. In South Vietnam,

...the presence of more than 700,000 U.S. military can mean nothing but the total Americanization of the war. There is no sign that ARVN effectiveness will increase, and there will be no pressure from the U.S. or the GVN for ARVN to shape up if the U.S. appears willing to increase its force levels as necessary to maintain a stalemate in the country.

The effect on the GVN would be even more unfortunate. The Saigon leadership shows no signs of a willingness--let alone an ability--to attract the necessary loyalty or support of the people. It is true that the GVN did not totally collapse during TET, but there is not yet anything like an urgent sense of national unity and purpose. A large influx of additional U.S. forces will intensify the belief of the ruling elite that the U.S. will continue to fight its war while it engages in backroom politics and permits widespread corruption. The proposed actions will also generate increased inflation, thereby reducing the effectiveness of the GVN and making corruption harder to control. Reform of the GVN will come only when and if they come to believe that our continued presence in South Viet Nam depends on what the GVN does. Certainly, a U.S. commitment to a substantial troop increase before the GVN commits itself to reform and action can only be counterproductive. Whatever

our success on the battlefield, our chances of leaving behind
an effective functioning national government when we at last
withdraw will be sharply diminished.

In the United States, the effects would be equally unfortunate.

We will have to mobilize reserves, increase our budget
by billions, and see U.S. casualties climb to 1,300-1,400
per month. Our balance of payments will be worsened considerably, and we will need a larger tax increase--justified
as a war tax, or wage and price controls....

It will be difficult to convince critics that we are not
simply destroying South Viet Nam in order to "save" it and
that we genuinely want peace talks. This growing disaffection
accompanied, as it certainly will be, by increased defiance
of the draft and growing unrest in the cities because of the
belief that we are neglecting domestic problems, runs great
risks of provoking a domestic crisis of unprecedented proportions. 51/

Thus, if our current strategy, even with increased troops, could not
promise an early end to the conflict, what alternatives were available
to the United States? No U.S. ground strategy and no level of U.S. forces,
alone, could by themselves accomplish our objective in South Viet Nam,
the draft memorandum stated.

We can obtain our objective only if the GVN begins to
take the steps necessary to gain the confidence of the people
and to provide effective leadership for the diverse groups
in the population. ARVN must also be turned into an effective
fighting force. If we fail in these objectives, a military
victory over the NVN/VC main forces, followed by a U.S. withdrawal, would only pave the way for an NLF takeover.

Our military presence in South Viet Nam should be designed
to buy the time during which ARVN and the GVN can develop effective capability. In order to do this, we must deny the enemy
access to the populated areas of the country and prevent him
from achieving his objectives of controlling the population and
destroying the GVN.

The memorandum concluded that MACV should be told that his mission
was to provide security to populated areas and to deny the enemy access to
the population; that he should not attempt to attrite the enemy or to
drive him out of the country. MACV should be asked to recommend an appropriate strategy and to determine his force requirements to carry out this
objective with the minimum possible casualties.

However, in the next section of the Presidential draft memorandum, the Working Group relieved MACV of this responsibility by sketching one possible strategy (obviously the preferred one) which should be able to be pursued "without substantially increasing our level of forces in South Viet Nam, thus avoiding the adverse domestic and foreign consequences sketched above." 52/

The strategy outlined in the memorandum was designed to attain the initiative along the "demographic frontier." It consisted of the following:

Those forces currently in or near the heavily populated areas along the coast should remain in place. Those forces currently bordering on the demographic frontier* should continue to operate from those positions, not on long search-and-destroy missions, but in support of the frontier. Eight to 10 battalions from the DMZ areas would be redeployed and become strategic research in I Corps; six battalions from the interior of II Corps would be redeployed to Dien Binh province as a strategic reserve for defense of provincial capitals in the highlands. As security is restored in the previously neglected populated areas of coastal Viet Nam, additional U.S. battalions would move forward to the demographic frontier....

Based just beyond the populated areas, the forces on the demographic frontiers would conduct spoiling raids, long-range reconnaissance patrols and, when appropriate targets are located, search-and-destroy operations into the enemy's zone of movement in the unpopulated areas between the demographic and the political frontiers. They would be available as a quick reaction force to support RVNAF when it was attacked within the populated areas. Where RVNAF patrolling in the populated areas is inadequate, U.S. forces would be in a position to assist. 53/

The advantages of the "demographic strategy of population security" were listed as follows:

1. It would become possible to keep the VC/NVA off balance in their present zone of movement. This area is now largely available to them for maneuver and massing, no more than a day's march from any of the major cities north of Saigon.

2. It would lengthen enemy LOC's from their sanctuaries in Laos and Cambodia. Base areas and LOC's within SVN would be the subject of attack and disruption, without extending the war to neighboring countries.

_____
* This frontier runs along the eastern foothills of the Annamite chain, from Quang-Tri Province to Phan Thiet in Binh Thuan, cuts across SVN along the northern edge of the Delta from Phuc Tuy to the Cambodian Border in Tay Ninh. Garrisons would be established as at Bong Son and An Khe.

3. RVNAF, knowing the availability of support from U.S. reaction forces, would perform more aggressively.

4. This would permit the patrolling and securing of populated areas to be accomplished primarily by Vietnamese forces.

5. U.S. forces would keep active in what is now the enemy's zone of movement, no longer presenting static positions against which the enemy can mass and attack. This, plus his increased logistical problems, would reduce U.S. casualties while increasing his. In effect, we would force him to come to us, fight on terrain of our choosing.

6. The increased patrolling of the populated areas by RVNAF combined with U.S. actions in the zone of movement would make it harder for the enemy to mass against and attack targets within the populated areas. This would reduce civilian casualties and refugee generation.

7. Garrisoning U.S. forces closer to RVNAF would facilitate joint operations at the maneuver level (battalion, company), again increasing RVNAF aggressiveness.

8. With RVNAF thus supported by U.S. forces, it can be expected to remain in uniform and engage in operations as long as it is paid and fed. 54/

No disadvantages of this strategy were noted or listed in the memorandum.

Details of this strategy, by Corps area, were examined in an appendix. In I Corps, our present precarious position could be relieved.

Were MACV to be provided guidance to forego position defense in areas remote from population centers and concentrate upon mobile offensive operations in and contiguous to the coastal plain, one division equivalent - eight to 10 U.S. maneuver battalions - could eventually be relieved from operations in, or related to defense of Khe Sanh. Undoubtedly, however, these eight to 10 battalions would be required to restore tactical flexibility to and insure logistical sufficiency for the forces presently disposed in the Quang-Tri-Hue-Danang area. MACV presently is planning operations in the Aeschau /sic/ Valley after April 1968; the new guidance would preclude these.

Guidance to MACV in II Corps

"...should counsel continued economy of force and should specifically exclude determined defense of all but province

capitals in the highlands. Permission to withdraw from
Special Forces camps (e.g., Dak To), and other exposed
positions remote from the coastal plain should be included.
Under this guidance, six U.S. battalions could be withdrawn from border defense operations in the highlands for
use as a mobile reserve or for operations on the coastal plain.

In III Corps, no redeployment from present positions, with U.S.
forces concentrated in the immediate environs of Saigon were envisaged.

The guidance to MACV should be to concentrate on offensive
operations in and around the densely populated portions of
III CTZ. MACV should maintain a mobile strike force for
defense of remote province capitals, but he should otherwise
forego long range or regional search-and-destroy operations.
Withdrawals from Special Forces camps should be authorized.

Fourth Corps - the Mekong Delta region - is the only region of SVN in
which the burden of the war was still borne, chiefly by RVNAF. U.S.
strategy should avoid Americanizing the conflict there. Instead, our
efforts should be aimed at catalyzing increased RVNAF efforts there.

Guidance provided to MACV should be geared to galvanizing
RVNAF by a strategy of:

1. Defending province capitals, major towns, principal
communication centers, and commercially important routes.

2. Extending GVN control into the countryside, consistent with RVNAF capability to defend RD teams and other
public administration there.

3. Stimulating RVNAF operations by providing U.S. forces
on an occasional basis for combined operations against
particularly promising targets, or in conjunction with key
defensive operations. U.S. forces in the Delta for this
effort should draw on the existing Dong Tam and Saigon bases.

4. Providing limited assistance to RVNAF with sophisticated engineer equipment and reconnaissance apparatus where
such would improve their ability to perform the missions
sketched above.

5. Bringing serious pressure to bear on RVN leaders in
Saigon and within IV CTZ to mount active, sustained, offensive
operations consistent with the foregoing missions. Consideration should be given to:

Providing additional RVNAF battalions to IV CTZ on
a temporary basis from III CTZ--conceptually, battalions or
regiments from the 5th or 18th ARVN Divisions would be deployed
to IV CTZ, minus dependents, for periods of one month or more
of active operations. 55/

In another appendix, the memorandum analyzed the effects of this
strategy on those interior provinces outside the "demographic frontier."
It would be desirable to maintain all interior Province capitals, the
appendix concluded, because "the political consequences of withdrawal from
whole Provinces would be to recreate the atmosphere of 1954 or 1965, and
while the situation may be that grim, we should at least strive to make
it appear otherwise."56/

The Province capitals would be garrisoned with ARVN units of the 22nd
and 23rd Divisions and, initially, some American units. These units would
have as their mission the holding of the Province town for a minimum of
four days, giving time for the arrival of a relief strike force.

Having secured the Province capitals, however, this strategy envisaged
evacuating other installations in the interior Provinces,

> ...such as the frontier series running from Bu Dop to
> Dak To and the interior but vulnerable points as Vo Dat
> and Vinh Thanh. Although these points are not held by
> allied main force units, they do tie down other assets,
> such as Special Forces, CIDG, PF, and RF. Furthermore,
> their combined existence represents a potential strain for
> the limited reaction ability currently available since we
> must respond, as we did at Dak To, when the enemy massed
> for an attack. If a presence is required in some of these areas,
> it should be in the form of a mobile striking unit, and not a
> garrison.

Based upon this "analysis" of our current strategy and a strategy of
protecting the demographic frontier, the draft memorandum recommended the
following actions to the President:

> 1. Approve a NSAM, stating that our political objective
> is a peace which will leave the people of South Viet Nam
> free to fashion their own political institutions....The NSAM
> should state that the primary role of U.S. military forces is
> to provide security in the populated areas of South Viet Nam
> rather than to destroy the VC/NVA or drive them out of the
> country. We should plan on maintaining the posture necessary
> to accomplish this objective for a considerable period.
>
> 2. Approve the immediate dispatch of an additional
> 10,500 military personnel to South Viet Nam.
>
> 3. Approve an accelerated and expanded program of
> increased fire power and mobility for ARVN and other ele-
> ments of the GVN Armed Forces.
>
> 4. Send General Taylor to Saigon to explain the NSAM
> to MACV and the GVN, and to request General Westmoreland to
> develop a strategy and force requirements to implement the
> military objectives stated in the NSAM.

5. Dispatch one or two high-level civilians to Saigon
with General Taylor to warn the GVN that it must broaden
their base of political support, end its internal bickering,
purge corrupt officers and officials, and move to develop
efficient administration and effective forces. They should
also begin a discussion of negotiations while informing the
GVN of the increased support to be provided for ARVN.

6. Deliver a Presidential address to the American public,
explaining our new strategy in light of the enemy's new
tactics. 57/

In short, then, this initial reassessment of our strategy in SVN
indicated to the President that no ground strategy and no level of additional U.S. forces alone could achieve an early end to the war. That
could be done only if the GVN took the steps necessary to provide effective military and political leadership to its population. In order to
speed up this process, the U.S. should limit its objectives in SVN and
adopt a strategy of population security. This would give the GVN time to
organize and develop democratic institutions, and would give RVNAF time to
grow in effectiveness while our forces provided a protective screen for
the populated areas at minimum cost in resources and casualties.

This paper was discussed within the military community at a meeting
in the Secretary of Defense's office on 1 March. General Wheeler, the
Chairman of the Joint Chiefs of Staff, was appalled at the apparent repudiation of American military policy in South Viet Nam contained in the ISA
Draft Memorandum. He detected two "fatal flaws" in the population security
strategy.

1. The proposed strategy would mean increased fighting in or close
to population centers and, hence, would result in increased civilian casualties.

2. By adopting a posture of static defense, we would allow the enemy
an increased capability of massing near population centers, especially north
of Saigon.

In addition, General Wheeler was equally appalled at the statement in
the ISA Draft Presidential Memorandum to the effect that "MACV does not
clearly specify how he would use the additional forces he requests, except
to indicate that they would provide him with a theater reserve and an
offensive capability." MACV had indeed clearly and specifically indicated
to CINCPAC on 27 February, concurrent with General Wheeler's original memorandum to the President, the locations and missions of the requested add-on
units. These had been transmitted through the Joint Staff to each of the
Services, who indeed were engaged in studying and staffing these proposals. 58/
Apparently, this information had not specifically been furnished to the
Office of the Secretary of Defense.

The debate within the Defense Establishment continued into the following day. In a memorandum for the Secretary of Defense, dated 2 March,
Assistant Secretary of Defense Warnke gave his answer to General Wheeler's
"two fatal flaws" of the population control strategy.

    1. <u>Increasing Fighting in the Cities</u>. General Wheeler
is concerned that the proposed strategy will mean increased
fighting in or close to population centers and, hence, will
result in increased civilian casualties. This argument over-
looks, I believe, the fact that the enemy demonstrated during
the TET offensive his willingness and ability to attack
populated centers regardless of our strategy. He is demonstrating that capability again right now in the Quang Tri-Hue
area and may soon do so in the Delta. If the enemy continues
to choose to fight in the cities, we will have no choice
but to engage him in those areas at the cost of civilian
casualties. The proposed strategy may actually reduce civilian
casualties if we can succeed in attacking enemy concentrations
before he can attack the cities. Moreover, in attacking the
cities, the enemy will face American as well as ARVN forces
engaged in offensive patrolling operations around the cities.
This should result in fewer casualties than have come from the
liberation of cities in the post-TET period. By freeing
forces now engaged along the DMZ and in lightly populated highlands for active offensive operations near population centers,
we should make the enemy effort against cities less effective.

    2. <u>Enemy Ability to Mass Near Population Centers</u>. General
Wheeler's concern that under the proposed strategy the enemy
will be more capable of massing near population centers north
of Saigon is difficult to understand. In fact, prior to TET,
because we were operating primarily along the coast, along the
DMZ, and in the highlands, we were permitting the enemy to
mass along the demographic frontier as he did prior to the TET
offensive. In fact, one of the advantages of the new strategy
is that we will be able to keep the enemy off-balance in this
area. General Wheeler may believe we advocate a posture of
static defense. This is not true. In the strategy sketched in
the paper, one of the primary missions of U.S. forces would be
to operate in this area, remain highly mobile and carry out
attacks against suspected enemy base camps. 59/

      TOP SECRET - Sensitive

General Wheeler fought back with arguments contained in two documents. The first was a backchannel message from COMUSMACV, dated 2 March, which answered specific questions concerning the planned use of additional forces. These questions had been asked by General Wheeler in a backchannel message the previous day. The first question concerned the military "and other" objectives additional forces were designed to advance. General Westmoreland was ambitious, indeed, and stated that these objectives were to:

(1) Defeat and evict from SVN the new NVA units now present in Western Quang Tri and Central Thua Trien provinces, to include the Ashau Valley and base areas 131 and 114.

(2) Maintain positive governmental and military control over Quang Tri and Thua Thien provinces, particularly the populous areas of the coastal lowlands and the DMZ area. Be prepared to block or interdict the infiltration/invasion routes from NVN through Laos.

(3) Destroy VC/NVA main force units and base areas in the remainder of I Corps and in the northeastern coastal and northwestern Laos border areas of II Corps.

(4) Reduce the "calculated risk" currently entailed in our economy of force posture in II and III Corps by providing the added flexibility and "punch" of an armored cavalry regiment.

(5) Conduct aggressive and continuing offensive campaigns throughout the coastal areas of II Corps and into traditional enemy base areas and sanctuaries in III Corps along the Cambodian border; especially in war zones "C" and "D". Restore the offensive combat and pacification momentum lost in III Corps as a result of the enemy's TET offensive and the requirement to transfer the 101st Airborne Division (-) to I Corps to stem the NVA incursion into Quang Tri.

(6) Be prepared for contingency operations if required.

The second question asked by General Wheeler was:

Question B: What specific dangers are their dispatch to SVN designed to avoid, and what specific goals would the increment of force aim to achieve -

In the next 6 months?

Over the next year?

44

In his answer, General Westmoreland was equally optimistic

...additive forces would serve to forestall the danger of local defeats due to the tactical degeneration or temporary disorganization of some ARVN units in the event of another general enemy offensive coupled with a massive invasion across the DMZ. The need to be prepared to support or reinforce ARVN units that are surprised by the nature and intensity of VC/NVA attacks became manifest during the enemy's TET drive and must be recognized in US troop requirement and deployment plans for the foreseeable future. By providing a two division mobile "swing force" which could be positioned and employed as required, the need to draw down on forces directly engaged in territorial security tasks probably would be reduced. Thus the danger of losing popular confidence in and support for GVN/US capabilities, policies and aspirations as a result of temporary military or psychological setbacks would also be diminished.

(2) Provision of the immediately required additional forces also would make it possible to apply continuous pressure to some degree in all corps areas and thus reduce the danger of allowing the enemy the opportunity to solicit support from the population and to reorganize, refit and recoup so that he could soon field rejuvenated units, despite heavy losses suffered during the TET offensive. This is particularly important in view of the enemy capability to move additional divisions south through the panhandle or DMZ without any clear intelligence indicators of such action. (This matter is of particular concern to me) these forces will also make it possible to retain that degree of flexibility and rapid responsiveness necessary to cope with an apparent new enemy tactic of searching for thin spots in our force structure or deployment in order to launch his concentrated mass attacks.

(3) In the next six months the presence of the armored cavalry regiment in II or III Corps would reduce the degree of calculated risk inherent in the economy of force posture in those areas, provide added territorial security and further the goal of providing added combat flexibility. Addition of another Marine regiment and its division headquarters in I Corps would thicken troop density in critical I CTZ, add to combat flexibility and improve command and control capabilities in that critical area.

(4) Over the next year the increment of force would make it possible to:

A. Move progressively from north to south with a continuing series of hard hitting offensive campaigns to invade base areas, interdict and disrupt infiltration routes, and eliminate or evict VC/NVA forces from SVN.

B. At the same time, the highly mobile exploitation force (two divisions) would be available to counter enemy aggression or to exploit opportunities for tactical success anywhere in SVN without reducing the minimal essential force necessary to guarantee maintenance of security in those areas where successful military campaigns have already been waged.

C. Addition of the new division in III Corps during this time frame would re-establish the capability for conducting constant operations in and around war zones "C" and "D" and make possible the constant use of a division size force in the IV CTZ which capability was removed with transfer of the 101st Airborne Division (-) to I Corps. In addition, combat operations conducted by this division would provide added security for LOC and the vital seat of government and economic center of Saigon.

D. With the total additive combat forces requested it will be possible to deal with the invader from the north, and to face with a greater degree of confidence the potential tank, rocket and tactical air threat as well as the ever present possibility that he may reinforce with additional elements of his home army. 60/

The second document available to General Wheeler was an analysis of the military implications in South Vietnam of the deployment of various increments of U.S. forces. This analysis was done by the Short Range Branch, Plans and Policy Directorate, Joint Staff. It was an informal staff document which had not been addressed by the Joint Chiefs of Staff or any of the military services separately. 61/ The five options addressed were those indicated by the Secretary of Defense in his meeting of 29 February (see pages 7-8). This paper documented the large enemy buildup in South Vietnam:

1. The enemy, since November, has increased his forces in South Viet Nam by at least 41 maneuver battalions, some armored elements, a large number of rockets, and additional artillery. There are indications he is preparing for the use of limited air support, including logistical air drops and bombing missions.

The Joint Staff paper took exception to COMUSMACV's stated first priority of insuring "the security of the GVN in Saigon and in the provincial capitals."

The basic strategy which must be followed by MACV in any circumstances is to defeat the current enemy offensive both in Northern I Corps Tactical Zone where it is the most formidable, in the Highlands where it is highly dangerous, and throughout South Vietnam in defense of the government and the cities and towns....Allied forces are not conducting offensive operations of any great magnitude or frequency and therefore they are not wresting control of the countryside from the enemy....

If the enemy offensive can be broken with sustained heavy casualties, then, and only then, will the cities be secure and the countryside reentered. Even with the largest force contemplated (Option 1) it will not be possible to perform adequately all of the tasks unless the current enemy offensive is decisively defeated. This, therefore, is the first and most important task upon which all else depends....

If the forces now in Vietnam or the forces under any of the options prove to be inadequate to break the enemy offensive, or if, conversely, the enemy sustained offensive breaks the Vietnamese armed forces (even short of destroying the GVN), then our objectives in South Vietnam and the tasks associated with them will be unobtainable. Specifically, we would be unable to regain the initiative, that is, we would not be able to conduct offensive operations at the scope and pace required either to prevent further enemy buildup or to reenter the countryside. This would force US and allied forces into a defensive posture around the major population centers....

Therefore, immediate action to break the enemy's current offensive is not only the first but the decisive requirement.

In specifically addressing each of the options, the Joint Staff reached the following conclusions:

OPTIONS	CONCLUSIONS (To Defeat the VC/NVA in SVN)
I	
Add approximately 196,000 to the present MACV Program 5 authorized level (525,000) plus 6 additional bns already deployed (10,500). Relaxation of restrictions on operations in Cambodia/Laos/NVN. TOTAL - 133 maneuver bns	This Option would: a. Assuming no additional deployments, break enemy offensive and permit early and sustained operations against the enemy. b. Permit simultaneous operations against enemy main force, base areas, and border sanctuaries. c. Permit resumption of program to develop effectiveness of RVNAF. d. Permit greater employment of air assets in conducting an expanded air campaign against NVN, Laos, Cambodia.
I-A	Essentially the same as Option I except:
Same additive forces as Option I. No relaxation of restrictions on operations.	a. The rate of conducting operations would be reduced by higher military risk. b. The enemy would enjoy sanctuary across the Cambodian/Laotian/NVN borders. c. The rebuilding of the RVNAF would be at a slower pace.
II	
No change to present MACV Program 5 authorized level (525,000) plus 6 additional bns already deployed (10,500). TOTAL - 112 maneuver bns	US objectives in SVN cannot be achieved as allied forces must remain in defensive posture. At present levels, allied forces can expect increasingly grave threats to their security with high casualty rates.
III	
Add 50,000 US troops to the approximately 535,000 in Option II. TOTAL - 118 maneuver bns	This option could probably secure the cities but would be insufficient to counter the current enemy offensive or to restore security in the countryside.
IV	
Add 100,000 to the approximately 535,000 in Option II. TOTAL - 124 maneuver bns	The results of this Option are essentially the same as Option I, except: a. The rate of progress would be slower. b. The enemy would retain the initiative in the border areas.

The paper, then, concluded that the larger forces of Option I and IA would "greatly reduce risks to Free World forces in SVN and will accomplish U.S. objectives more rapidly than the forces of the other options," and recommended that immediate action be taken to provide the forces of Option I.

Read another way, however, the Joint Staff analysis could be taken to indicate that the United States could successfully pursue a strategy of "population security" by adopting Option III, adding 50,000 troops to the current level in SVN.

At the 2 March meeting of the senior members of the Secretary of Defense's Working Group conducting the reassessment, no consensus was reached on a new U.S. strategy. Apparently, Mr. Warnke and Mr. Goulding were given the task of drafting a new memorandum for the President which would be less controversial than the initial ISA document.

The draft memorandum for the President, dated 3 March 1968, which was prepared by these two individuals, differed markedly in tone from the initial memorandum presented to the Clifford Group on 2 March. Gone was any discussion of grand strategy. This memorandum recommended simply:

    1. Meeting General Westmoreland's request by deploying as close to May 1 as practical 20,000 additional troops (approximately 1/2 of which would be combat).

    2. Approval of a Reserve call-up and an increased end strength adequate to meet the balance of the request and to restore a strategic reserve in the United States, adequate for possible contingencies.

    3. Reservation of the decision to deploy the balance of General Westmoreland's new request. While we would be in a position to make these additional deployments, the future decision to do so would be contingent upon:

        a. Continuous reexamination of the desirability of further deployments on a week-by-week basis as the situation develops;

        b. Improved political performance by the GVN and increased contribution in effective military action by the ARVN;

        c. The results of a study in depth, to be initiated immediately, of a possible new strategic guidance for the conduct of US military operations in South Vietnam.

Two appendices to this paper addressed the basis for these recommendations and the context in which additional troop commitments to Vietnam should be examined.

In explaining the basis for the recommendation to deploy 20,000 troops, the memorandum indicated that the first increment of forces requested by General Westmoreland should be provided as an emergency measure to meet the prospect of continued abnormal levels of enemy activity. "This would, by May 1st, furnish him with an additional 20,000 troops, 10,500 of whom would be for combat purposes. Because of the possibility that the North Vietnamese leaders may decide to launch a larger scale invasion by main force units, we should put ourselves in a position to provide the other 185,000 ground, sea, and air forces involved in General Westmoreland's request." 63/

Additional forces, however, should not be dispatched until the situation in Vietnam developed.

A continuing and intensive review should focus not only on future enemy activity but also on the demonstrated ability of the GVN and the ARVN to pull themselves together, to get back into business, and to demonstrate significant improvements both in their ability to win popular support and their willingness to fight aggressively for their own security. Unless these qualities are evidenced, there can be no real hope for the accomplishment of our political aims.

Finally, we believe that the striking change in the enemy's tactics, the willingness to commit at least two additional divisions to the fighting in the South over the past few weeks, the obvious and not wholly anticipated strength of the Viet Cong infrastructure, there can be no prospect of a quick military solution to the aggression in South Vietnam. Under these circumstances, we should give intensive study to the development of a new strategic guidance to General Westmoreland. This guidance should make clear the fact that he cannot be expected either to destroy the enemy forces or to rout them completely from South Vietnam. The kind of American commitment that would be required to achieve these military objectives cannot even be estimated. There is no reason to believe that it could be done by an additional 200,000 American troops or double or triple that quantity....

The exact nature of the strategic guidance which should be adopted cannot now be predicted. It should be the subject of a detailed inter-agency study over the next several weeks. During the progress of the study, discussions of the appropriate strategic guidance and its nature and implications for the extent of our military commitment in South Vietnam should be undertaken with both General Westmoreland and Ambassador Bunker. 64/

In placing these additional troop commitments in a larger context, an additional appendix concluded:

No matter what the result in South Vietnam itself, we will have failed in our purposes if:

    a. The war in Vietnam spreads to the point where it is a major conflict leading to direct military confrontation with the USSR and/or China;

    b. The war in Vietnam spreads to the point where we are so committed in resources that our other world-wide commitments -- especially NATO -- are no longer credible;

    c. The attitudes of the American people towards "more Vietnams" are such that our other commitments are brought into question as a matter of US will;

    d. Other countries no longer wish the US commitment for fear of the consequences to themselves as a battlefield between the East and the West.

Under these circumstances, we recommend that under the leadership of the State Department, with the assistance of the Office of the Secretary of Defense, the JCS, and the Treasury, a review of our Vietnamese policy in the context of our global politico-military strategy be undertaken with a due date of May 15. 65/

Thus, the net result of this period of frantic preparation, consultation, writing, and reassessing was similar to all previous requests for reinforcement in Vietnam. The litany was familiar: "We will furnish what we can presently furnish without disrupting the normal political and economic life of the nation, while we study the situation as it develops." No startling reassessment of strategy was indicated, although for the first time it was recognized that such a reassessment was needed, that a limit to U.S. involvement in SVN had to be determined, and that any number of U.S. troops could not achieve our objectives without significant improvement in the ability of the GVN to win popular support and to fight aggressively for their own security.

5. Recommendation to the President

This draft memorandum was discussed again within the Defense Department on 3 March, and several changes were made. The 4 March draft memorandum for the President was apparently approved by the Secretary of Defense and forwarded to the President. The paper which was forwarded to the President bore a great resemblance to the 3 March draft, although the Systems Analysis influence on the 4 March paper was evidenced by its greater detail, especially concerning actions to be required of the GVN.

The memorandum recapitulated General Westmoreland's request for personnel and indicated that General Wheeler believed that we should meet this request, and should act to increase and improve our strategic reserve in the United States. To achieve both these goals, the paper stated, staff examination indicated that the following actions would be required:

   a.   A call-up of reserve units and individuals totaling approximately 262,000 (194,000 in units, 68,000 as individuals).

   b.   Increased draft calls.

   c.   Extension of terms of service. These actions would produce a total increase in end strength in the Armed Forces of approximately 511,000 by June 30, 1969. (The staff examination referred to above included spaces to add 31,500 troops in South Korea and a US naval proposal to add two cruisers and fifteen destroyers to the naval forces in Southeast Asia. If these proposals are disapproved in their entirety, the figures above will be decreased to approximately 242,000 and 454,000 respectively.

The Secretary of Defense then recommended:

   1.   An immediate decision to deploy to Vietnam an estimated total of 22,000 additional personnel (approximately 60% of which would be combat). An immediate decision to deploy the three tactical fighter squadrons deferred from Program 5 (about 1,000 men). This would be over and above the four battalions (about 3700 men) already planned for deployment in April which in themselves would bring us slightly above the 525,000 authorized level....

   2.   Either through Ambassador Bunker or through an early visit by Secretary Clifford, a highly forceful approach to the GVN (Thieu and Ky) to get certain key commitments for improvement, tied to our own increased effort and to increased US support for the ARVN....

   3.   Early approval of a Reserve call-up and an increased end strength adequate to meet the balance of the Westmoreland request and to restore a strategic reserve in the United States, adequate for possible contingencies world-wide....

   4.   Reservation of the decision to meet the Westmoreland request in full. While we would be putting ourselves in a position to make these additional deployments, the future decision to do so would be contingent upon:

a. Reexamination on a week-by-week basis of the desirability of further deployments as the situation develops;

b. Improved political performance by the GVN and increased contribution in effective military action by the ARVN;

c. The results of a study in depth, to be initiated immediately, of possible new political and strategic guidance for the conduct of US operations in South Vietnam, and of our Vietnamese policy in the context of our world-wide politico-military strategy....

5. No new peace initiative on Vietnam. Re-statement of our terms for peace and certain limited diplomatic actions to dramatize Laos and to focus attention on the total threat to Southeast Asia....

6. A general decision on bombing policy, not excluding future change, but adequate to form a basis for discussion with the Congress on this key aspect. Here your advisers are divided:

a. General Wheeler and others would advocate a substantial extension of targets and authority in and near Hanoi and Haiphong, mining of Haiphong, and naval gunfire up to a Chinese Buffer Zone;

b. Others would advocate a seasonal step-up through the spring, but without these added elements. 66/

In proposing this course of action, the Secretary of Defense indicated that he recognized that there were many negative factors and certain difficulties. Nevertheless, he indicated the belief that this course of action, at least in its essential outline, was urgently required to meet the immediate situation in Vietnam, as well as wider possible contingencies there and elsewhere.

Eight tabs to the draft memorandum elaborated upon the reasoning which led to the recommendations contained therein. TAB A reviewed the justification for immediately sending additional forces to Vietnam. The situation in SVN was analyzed as follows:

Hanoi has made a basic change in its strategy and scale of operations. Perhaps because they thought they were losing as the war and pacification were going, Hanoi is pressing hard for decisive results over the next few months. They are committing a high proportion of their assets, although it appears likely that they would retain both the capability and will to keep up the pressure next year if this effort does not succeed. There is hope that, if this year's effort could be thwarted, Hanoi and Viet Cong morale would be sufficiently affected to open up possibilities of peace, but this cannot be assessed as likely.

Within South Vietnam, there are key variables that could move the situation sharply, one way or the other, in the coming months. Specifically:

a. The degree to which Hanoi and the VC are able to keep pressing, and how effectively they are countered in the military sphere.

b. The degree to which the VC are able to extend their control in the countryside and recoup their losses -- or whether conversely the South Vietnamese can take the initiative and either neutralize such recoupment or set in motion a new favorable trend.

c. The degree to which the GVN improves its performance and galvanizes potentially greater popular support than it can now have.

Thus, there was created an urgent need, both practical and psychological, to send such forces as could be effective within the next four or five months.

The following additional forces of about 22,000 men could be deployed by June 15 in accordance with the schedule set forth below:

```
Six Tactical Fighter Squadrons      - 3,000 men
              2 Squadrons by  - 1 April
              3 Squadrons by  - 1 May
              1 Squadron by   - 1 June

4th Marine Expeditionary Force (minus) - 18,100 men
                        by  - 15 June

Naval Mobile Construction Battalion    -   700 men
                        by  - 1 May
```

In addition, it was reiterated that an urgent effort was required to improve and modernize the equipment of the SVN Armed Forces.

Tab B elaborated on what should be done to increase the effectiveness of Vietnamese efforts in conjunction with the U.S. troop increase. Two possible GVN reactions were foreseen to the deployment of additional U.S. forces. The reaffirmation of the U.S. commitment would be welcomed, would add to the feeling of confidence, and might stiffen the GVN's will at a time "when the tasks it faces are rather monumental." On the other hand, there was always the danger that the Vietnamese would be tempted to relax behind the refuge of American power, and the sense of anxiety and urgency which had resulted from the TET offensive could suffer. The memorandum indicated, however, that the GVN had the capacity to take those civil and military actions which would materially improve the political and security climate of South Vietnam, as well as the image of the GVN in the United States. This involved, the memorandum indicated, a readiness for the U.S. to make specific demands upon the GVN in order to get it to take a wide range of decisions and actions. Among those things considered essential and feasible, the following actions were listed:

1. Mobilization - The Vietnamese Armed Forces should be increased to the maximum. As a first step, present plans to increase Vietnamese forces by 65,000 men should be amended to provide for an additional 30,000 men under arms by the end of 1968. The draft of 18 and 19 year olds should proceed as presently scheduled. This should be consistent with the ability to train and supply the forces, but avoid undercutting the need for key civilians in other governmental functions by diversion of skilled personnel.

2. The Thieu-Ky Relationship and Unity of Leadership - The failure of Thieu and Ky to cooperate fully and apply their individual talents to the needs of the situation has continued to plague the effective management of the Vietnamese effort. In turn this has had ramifications down the line in both the military and civilian chain of command. It has also complicated the chances of rallying the various elements in the society, as the rivalry translates itself into interference with attempts at forming a national anti-communist front.

Thieu and Ky and their followers, as well as other elements in the society not associated directly with them, must be brought to realize that we are no longer prepared to put up with anything but the maximum effort on their part. A clear and precise role for Ky should be defined. Thieu and Ky must bring their followers into line. The government should be prepared to engage the services of people with administrative and executive talent who are now not participating in the common task. Our expectations in this regard have to be made crystal clear to each and every Vietnamese leader in and out of Government. Without this fundamental change in the attitude and dedication of the leadership, the necessary reforms and the necessary inspiration of the Vietnamese people will not be forthcoming quickly or sufficiently.

3. Getting the Government Back into the Countryside - We must win the race to the countryside, go on the offensive, re-establish security in the rural areas, and restore the government's presence in the villages. The ARVN and other security forces must deploy aggressively, the RD cadre must return to their tasks, and governmental services reach out from the province capitals.

In the final analysis rural security, the sine qua non
of popular identification with the GVN, must be provided by
the Vietnamese themselves. The two keys here are (1) the
calibre and role of the 44 province chiefs (and their supporting staffs) and (2) a properly offensive sense of mission
on the part of ARVN units - and their commanders - assigned
to rural security support missions. In every area (village,
district, province, DTZ and corps) the RVNAF unit commanders
responsible for security in that area must be graded (i.e.
promoted, commended or sacked) primarily on their ability
to find, fix and eradicate the VC Force indigenous to that
area. They must also be graded (with commensurate effect
on their careers) with respect to the behavior of their
troops vis-a-vis the populace in that area.

4. Drive on the Viet Cong Infrastructure - In our concern over the behavior of our allies, we must not neglect our
enemies and the present opportunity to compound and exacerbate
communist problems. Operation Phoenix which is targetted
against the Viet Cong must be pursued more vigorously in closer
liaison with the US. Vietnamese armed forces should be devoted
to anti-infrastructure activities on a priority basis. The
Tet offensive surfaced a good deal of the infrastructure and
the opportunity to damage it has never been better. This
would force the VC on the defensive and head off the establishment of local VC administrative organizations and VC
attempts to set up provisional governmental committees.

5. US-ARVN Command Relationships - While we accept the
Mission's reluctance to create a joint command, we believe
that alternative arrangements which give the US a greater
role in ARVN employment are necessary. This can be done at
the Corps level and below. It would involve US participation
in the planning and control of ARVN operations. It might
even call for the prior approval by US advisors of ARVN
operational plans -- this now exists in certain cases
depending upon individual advisor relationships. We
should request MACV to study the matter and come up with
a specific plan to meet the requirement.

6. Government Reform and Anti-Corruption Campaign -
The beginning steps at administrative reform which President
Thieu has announced must be accelerated. This should be
directly associated with a new deal on corruption, which must
be dealt with by relief of a specified list of corrupt officials now and the promise of severe action in the future.
A capable Inspectorate should be established. Incompetent
ARVN officers must be removed, beginning with a specific
list that should be made available by MACV. Incompetent
province chiefs who have plagued our efforts in the past
must be removed. The removal of incompetent commanders

and officials is now more feasible in the light of performance during the Tet offensive. We should not hesitate to make our desires known and back them up by refusing to provide support for the incompetent. For key commanders, we should require the right of prior approval on a secret and discreet basis. The precise tools of leverage to be applied in this regard should be left to the US Mission, but could include withholding advice and assistance at local levels in extreme cases.

7. The Prime Minister - We should solicit Ambassador Bunker's views on the desirability of replacing the Prime Minister. If he is to be replaced we should agree on his successor beforehand, in consultation with Thieu and Ky.

8. The United Front - A nationalist spirit of cooperation and unity came to the fore in the immediate wake of the Tet offensive. It is being manifested incompletely in attempts to organize groups in support of the national task. Despite the personal misgivings of old antagonists there has been some success. This is now threatened by personal rivalries, and most significantly by differences between Thieu and Ky. We need to find a formula for joint efforts. Ambassador Bunker suggests that the optimum result would be a "super front" of the anti-communist groups. Although not directly tied to the government, such a front could serve to rally the people broadly and emotionally against the Viet Cong. To succeed it must be backed by the leadership of the government - both Thieu and Ky - but not appear to compete with the National Assembly. It should encompass all elements in the society, but not be the vehicle for any one power group.

9. Economic Measures - There will be increased inflation in Vietnam this year, and additional US troops will make it more severe. Steps need to be taken now to counter the threat of inflation, if we are not to be faced with a severe crisis next fall and winter. The GVN needs to move on tax increases, and U.S. and GVN expenditures for non-essential programs in Vietnam should be restrained. On the other hand, wage increases for civil and military personnel in the GVN are needed if inflation is not to weaken their will and support.

Additionally, we must demand of the GVN some measure of action on their part to compensate for the effect of additional US troops on the US balance of payments. This can be done by having the GVN provide to the US at no cost the additional piaster costs incurred by our troop increase. We should also insist that GVN reserves be reduced to $250 million from the present maximum reserve level of $300 million and that a significant portion of the reserve be invested in medium and long term US securities. The details of these

economic measures cannot be discussed in this paper, but
a comprehensive economic package should be prepared and
presented to the GVN - to include what the US is prepared
to do in the way of increased financing of commercial imports.

10. Resource Allocation - Non-essential use of resources
should be eliminated. Present government programs to
eliminate new luxury construction must be tightened and continued. Bars and night clubs should remain closed. Austerity
should be fostered. 68/

The Appendix recommended that a high-level mission, probably headed
by the Secretary of Defense, should go to Saigon to emphasize to the GVN
that we consider improved GVN performance essential; that any further U.S.
support must be matched by GVN actions; and that the above recommendations
would be used as a checklist for judging Vietnamese performance. In addition, this Appendix emphasized that we should do what was necessary to
improve the capability of RVNAF. Although no details were given, the statement was made that: "On the basis of current planning estimates, this
would involve additional expenditure of about $475 million over a period
of 18 months."

Tab C of the Memorandum for the President consisted of a brief justification for increasing the strategic reserve. The basic argument was that
we would then be prepared to provide the additional ground, sea, and air
forces involved in General Westmoreland's request if the military situation
required. In addition, the paper indicated:

If these additional forces are not deployed to Vietnam,
our action in thus reconstituting the strategic reserve would
nevertheless be fully warranted. Our strategic reserve has
been appreciably depleted because of Vietnam demands. At
present, the active division forces in the Continental United
States, Hawaii and Okinawa, and including the Marine units
in the Caribbean and Mediterranean, consist of 4-2/3 Army
divisions and 1-1/3 Marine divisions. This compares with
the 9 Army divisions and 3 Marine divisions in our strategic
reserve on 30 June 1965. A call-up of 245,000, with no
deployments to South Vietnam in excess of the 20-30,000
now recommended, would yield a strategic reserve of 7 Army
divisions and 2 Marine divisions. The unsettled situations
in many parts of the world make this build-up a prudent
action entirely apart from possible Vietnam contingencies. 69/

Relegated to Tab D of the Memorandum for the President was what had
begun as the major task of the Working Group--the necessity for in-depth
study of Vietnam policy and strategic guidance.

General Westmoreland's request, this Appendix pointed out, does not
purport to provide any really satisfactory answer to the problem in Vietnam.

There can be no assurance that this very substantial additional deployment would leave us a year from today in any more favorable military position. All that can be said is that the additional troops would enable us to kill more of the enemy and would provide more security if the enemy does not offset them by lesser reinforcements of his own. There is no indication that they would bring about a quick solution in Vietnam and, in the absence of better performance by the GVN and the ARVN, the increased destruction and increased Americanization of the war could, in fact, be counter-productive. 70/

There were many other reasons for conducting a study of our Vietnamese policy in the context of the U.S. worldwide political/military strategy. No matter what the result in Vietnam itself, we will have failed in our purpose, the memorandum stated, if:

   a. The war in Vietnam spreads to the point where it is a major conflict leading to direct military confrontation with the USSR and/or China;

   b. The war in Vietnam spreads to the point where we are so committed in resources that our other world-wide commitments -- especially NATO -- are no longer credible;

   c. The attitudes of the American people towards "more Vietnams" are such that our other commitments are brought into question as a matter of US will;

   d. Other countries no longer wish the US commitment for fear of the consequences to themselves as a battlefield between the East and the West. 71/

In addition, any intensive review should focus on the ability of the GVN and the ARVN to demonstrate significant improvement, both in their ability to win popular support and their willingness to fight aggressively for their own security.

Finally, the memorandum stated:

   ...the striking change in the enemy's tactics, his willingness to commit at least two additional divisions to the fighting in the South over the past few weeks and the obvious and not wholly anticipated strength of the Viet Cong infrastructure, shows that there can be no prospect of a quick military solution to the aggression in South Vietnam. Under these circumstances, we should give intensive study to the development of new strategic guidance to General Westmoreland. This study may show that he should not be expected either to destroy the enemy forces or to rout them completely from South Vietnam. The kind of American commitment that might be required to achieve these military

objectives cannot even be estimated. There is no reason
to believe that it could be done by an additional 200,000
American troops or double or triple that quantity....

The exact nature of the strategic guidance which should
be adopted cannot now be predicted. It should be the subject
of a detailed interagency study over the next several weeks.
During the progress of the study, discussions of the appropriate strategic guidance and its nature and implications
for the extent of our military commitment in South Vietnam
should be undertaken with both General Westmoreland and
Ambassador Bunker. 72/

Thus, the "A to Z reassessment" of U.S. strategy requested by the
President was relegated by the Working Group to a future date.

Tab E remained intact from the original 29 February draft memorandum.
Prepared by the State Department, it discussed negotiating options and
possible diplomatic actions in connection with a buildup of U.S. forces.
Concerning our negotiating posture, three broad options were listed:

    1. Stand pat on the San Antonio formula and on our basic
position toward the terms of a negotiated settlement -- the
Geneva Accords plus free choice in the South, rejecting a
coalition or any special position for the NLF.

    2. Take some new initiative, either privately or publicly,
that might involve a change in our position on the San Antonio
formula and/or a change in our position on the elements of a
settlement.

    3. No change in our position for the present, but pitching
our course of action toward a strong move for negotiations when
and if we have countered Hanoi's offensive -- i.e., in a matter
of four months or so perhaps. 73/

The crucial question, the paper indicated, was really to examine
what we could conceivably do by way of a new initiative under Option 2.
After examining the situation, however, the conclusion was reached that:

    ...any change in our position on the terms of a peaceful
settlement would be extremely unwise at the present time. We
may well wish to work on opening up channels to the NLF, but
this must be done in the utmost secrecy and in full consultation with the GVN. We do not know what the possibilities
may be in this direction, but any public stress on this avenue
would feed the fires of a VC propaganda line that has already
had significant disturbing effect in South Vietnam.

As to our conditions for stopping the bombing and
entering into talks, we continue to believe that the San
Antonio formula is "rock bottom." The South Vietnamese
are in fact talking about much stiffer conditions, such
as stopping the infiltration entirely. Any move by us to
modify the San Antonio formula downward would be extremely
disturbing in South Vietnam, and would have no significant
offsetting gains in US public opinion or in key third countries....

This being said, we believe that it would strengthen our
over-all posture, and involve no significant risks in Vietnam,
if we were to reiterate our basic position on our terms of
settlement in South Vietnam. A systematic restatement of our
position on the Geneva Accords and free choice in the South
could be a vital part of selling our whole course of action
to the public, to Congress, and the world. Although we have
stated all the elements at different times, we have not pulled
them together for a long time and we could get a considerable
impression of freshness, even novelty, and certainly reasonable-
ness by identifying more precisely the elements of the Geneva
Accords; our position on free choice, and perhaps adding
something on external guarantees, which have always been a
generalized part of our position and that of the South Vietnamese. 74/

Further diplomatic actions, the Appendix indicated, would be designed
to dramatize the Communist threats to Laos, Thailand, and Cambodia. Among
the actions suggested were the following:

First, that the restatement of our position on South Vietnam include substantial emphasis on restoration of the Laos
Accords of 1962 and on the preservation of the neutrality and
territorial integrity of Cambodia under the 1954 Accords.

Indeed, we could go still further and take the occasion
to talk in terms of an over-all settlement for Southeast Asia
that would specifically provide that each nation was free to
assume whatever neutral or other international posture it
wished to take. We could explicitly state that we were prepared to accept a Southeast Asia that was "neutral" in the
sense of not adhering to any power bloc or forming a part
of any alliance directed at others.

We could say a favorable word about regional arrangements in Southeast Asia consistent with the concept, and
could indicate our willingness to join with other outside
nations to consider what kind of general assurances of support could be given to such a Southeast Asia....

Second, there are strong diplomatic steps that could be

61   TOP SECRET - Sensitive

taken to dramatize the situation in Laos. We could encourage
Souvanna to take the case to the UN where Laos and Souvanna
have strong appeal. Concurrently, but we believe less effective in practice, Souvanna could press the British and Soviets
to take action or even to reconvene the Geneva Conference of 1962.

Third, we could attempt similar action for Cambodia. This
might be through the Australians, to get Sihanouk to take his
case also to the UN. Even if he made some accusations against
us in the process, he would be likely at the present time to
highlight his internal Chinese-backed threat, and the net result
could be useful.

A further possibility would be to seek to enlist India more
deeply in the Cambodian situation. This is worth trying, but
the Indians are a weak reed for action or for effective diplomatic dramatization.

Fourth, we could consider getting the Thai to dramatize
their situation more than they have done. This takes careful
thought, since they do not wish to alarm their own people. 75/

Other possibilities discussed were the enlisting and engaging of other
Asian nations in the search for peace in Vietnam and the Soviet Union in an
effort to find peace in Southeast Asia.

In Tab F appeared a discussion of military action against North Vietnam. This tab contained two contrary views concerning the bombing campaign
against NVN, and is discussed in detail in another Task Force paper. This
is the first place that any written discussion of the bombing campaign
against the North appears in any of the papers of the Working Group. It is
interesting to note, in the light of subsequent developments, that neither
the Chairman of the Joint Chiefs of Staff nor the Secretary of Defense made
mention of a partial or complete bombing suspension of the North at this
time. They differed only on the extent to which the bombing campaign
against North Viet Nam should be intensified. 76/

Tabs G and H, the final Tabs, considered the public affairs problems
in dealing with increased U.S. troop commitments to SVN and to the calling
up of reserve forces. In dealing with public opinion and with Congress,
these Appendices concluded that from a public affairs viewpoint:

Beyond the basic points of establishing that the war is in
the national interest, that there is a plan to end it satisfactorily and that we can identify the resources needed to
carry out that plan, we must prove:

1. That General Westmoreland needs the additional troops
being sent him.

2. That he does not need further additional troops at this time.

3. That the Strategic Reserve does need reconstitution at this time.

4. That the possible need of General Westmoreland for possible future reinforcement is sufficiently important to merit the callup.

5. That there is not a bottomless pit.

6. That the nation still has the resources for the ghetto fight. 77/

Thus, the memorandum forwarded to the President by the Secretary of Defense in response to the Presidential request for an "A to Z reassessment" of our Vietnam policy again represented a compromise. In this case, it was a compromise brought about by differences between the Assistant Secretary of Defense for International Security Affairs and his staff, and the Chairman of the Joint Chiefs of Staff and his officers. Initially, ISA had prepared a draft Presidential memorandum which had indeed reassessed U.S. strategy in SVN, found it faulty, and recommended a new strategy of protecting the "demographic frontier" with basically the U.S. forces presently in-country. The Chairman of the Joint Chiefs of Staff found "fatal flaws " in this strategy, could not accept the implied criticism of past strategy in the ISA proposal, did not think that the Defense Department civilians should be involved in issuing specific guidance to the military field commander, and supported this field commander in his request for the forces required to allow him to "regain the initiative." The compromise reached, of course, was that a decision on new strategic guidance should be deferred pending a complete political/military reassessment of the U.S. strategy and objectives in Vietnam in the context of our worldwide commitments.

The recommendation for additional forces was also a compromise and was based, as had past decisions of this nature, on what could be done by the forces in-being without disrupting the nation. However, there were additional reasons adduced for not meeting all of COMUSMACV's requirements for forces. The situation in SVN was not clear. The ability of the Government and of the Army of South Vietnam to survive and to improve were in serious question. The ability of the U.S. to attain its objectives in SVN by military force of whatever size was not clear. Weighing heavily upon the minds of the senior officials who prepared and approved the 4 March memorandum to the President was, indeed, what difference in the war, what progress toward victory such a buildup as requested by MACV would make. These leaders were, finally, prepared to go a long way down the road in meeting COMUSMACV's request. They recommended to the President that the first increment of this request be met. They also recommended a partial mobilization so as to be prepared to meet additional requirements if and when it was demonstrated that these forces were necessary and would make a strategic difference.

More importantly, however, these officials finally came to the realization
that no military strategy could be successful unless a South Vietnamese
political and military entity was capable of winning the support of its
people. Thus, for the first time, U.S. efforts were to be made contingent
upon specific reform measures undertaken by the GVN, and U.S. leverage was
to be used to elicit these reforms. South Vietnam was to be put on notice
that the limit of U.S. patience and commitment had been approached.

Concerning negotiations and the bombing of the North, the Memorandum
for the President was conventional. No changes in our negotiating position
were recommended and no really new diplomatic initiatives were suggested.
Concerning the bombing of the North, the only issue indicated concerned
the degree of intensification. There was no mention made of a partial reduction or cessation.

Thus, faced with a fork in the road of our Vietnam policy, the Working
Group failed to seize the opportunity to change directions. Indeed, they
seemed to recommend that we continue rather haltingly down the same road,
meanwhile consulting the map more frequently and in greater detail to insure
that we were still on the right road.

6. The Climate of Opinion

This memorandum was presented to the President on Monday evening,
4 March, and at his request, the recommendations were passed to General
Westmoreland for his comments. These comments were received by the Chairman
of the Joint Chiefs of Staff and passed to the Secretary of Defense on
8 March 1968. General Westmoreland welcomed the additional airpower which
"would greatly enhance the tactical air support available to ground units."
The chairman indicated, however, that there had been no change in General
Westmoreland's requirements as originally proposed and, indeed, additional
combat service-support forces had been requested.

General Westmoreland states that although immediate
authorization for deployment of 22,000 additional personnel
would provide much needed combat and combat support forces,
the combat service support forces now in Vietnam are insufficient to support our present force structure. This is especially critical in view of the recent deployment of the 3rd
Brigade of the 82d Airborne Division and RLT 27 to the I Corps
tactical zone without the appropriate slice of combat support.
He emphasizes the absolute requirement to provide the support
forces identified with the increased deployments prior to or
at the same time the tactical forces are deployed. In this
regard, General Westmoreland has this date forwarded his
specific strength recommendations for the immediate essential
combat service support forces to provide adequate support for
combat units in I CTZ, including the 3rd Brigade of the 82d
Airborne Division, RLT 27 and Army units which have been
redeployed to Northern I Corps tactical zone. This request

has not yet been validated by CINCPAC, but is currently under consideration here by the Joint Staff in anticipation of early action by Admiral Sharp's headquarters.

Finally, General Westmoreland recognizes that the forces which were contained in the Committee's recommendations were apparently based upon the capabilities of the Services to produce troops for deployment. He states that there has been no change in his appraisal of the situation since my visit to Vietnam and thus there has been no change in his requirements as originally proposed. 78/

From the 4th of March until the final Presidential decision was announced to the country, the written record becomes sparse. The debate within the Administration was argued and carried forward on a personal basis by the officials involved, primarily, the Secretary of Defense and the Secretary of State.

The decision, however, had been placed squarely on the shoulders of the President. The recommendations of the 4 March memorandum had left him a profound political/military dilemma. The memorandum had recommended "a little bit more of the same" to stabilize the military situation, plus a level of mobilization in order to be prepared to meet any further deterioriation in the ground situation. Any new strategic guidance, any new direction in policy, however, were to be left to a subsequent study.

But many political events in the first few weeks of March 1968 gave strong indications that the country was becoming increasingly divided over and disenchanted with the current Vietnam strategy, and would no longer settle for "more of the same" with no indication of an eventual end to the conflict. That the President was aware of these external political pressures and that they influenced his decision is evident.

Focus to this political debate and sense of dissatisfaction was given by a startlingly accurate account, published in The New York Times on 10 March, of General Westmoreland's request and of the strategic reassessment which was being conducted within the executive branch of the government. It also indicated the growing doubt and unease in the nation concerning this policy review.

Written by Neil Sheehan and Hedrick Smith, the article stated:

General William C. Westmoreland has asked for 206,000 more American troops for Vietnam, but the request has touched off a divisive internal debate within high levels of the Johnson Administration.

A number of sub-Cabinet civilian officials in the Defense Department, supported by some senior officials in the State Department, have argued against General Westmoreland's plea

for a 40 per cent increase in his forces 'to regain the
initiative' from the enemy.

....Many of the civilian officials are arguing that
there should be no increase beyond the movement of troops
now under way....

The contention of these high ranking officials is that
an American increase will bring a matching increase by
North Vietnam, thereby raising the level of violence without giving the allies the upper hand.

Senior Pentagon civilians have put forward a written
counter-proposal to President Johnson, calling for a
shift in American strategy to a concept of close-in
defense of populated areas with more limited offensive
thrusts than at present. Much of the military hierarchy
is reported to oppose this approach....

The President has not yet decided on the question of
substantial increases in American forces in Vietnam....

Nonetheless, the scope and depth of the internal debate
within the Government reflect the wrenching uncertainty
and doubt in this capital about every facet of the war left
by the enemy's dramatic wave of attacks at Tet, the Asian
New Year holiday, six weeks ago. More than ever this has
left a sense of weariness and irritation over the war.

Officials themselves comment in private about widespread and deep changes in attitudes, a sense that a water-
shed has been reached and that its meaning is just now
beginning to be understood....

But at every level of Government there is a sense that
the conflict, if expanded further, can no longer be called
'a limited war.' Officials acknowledge that any further
American involvement carries serious implications for the
civilian life of the nation--not only the call-up of military reserves and enactment of a tax increase but problems
with the budget, the economy and the balance of payments.

In Congress, uneasy and divided, as the Senate debate
on Thursday showed, there is a rising demand that Capitol Hill
be consulted before any critical new step is taken. Even
supporters of Administration policy, such as Senator Richard
B. Russell, Democrat of Georgia, who is chairman of the
Senate Armed Services Committee, are openly critical of
American combat strategy. Mr. Russell has suggested that the

United States has lost the battlefield initiative not only through
the enemy's bold tactics but by what he calls its own defensive,
gradualist psychology....

General Westmoreland's request for another 206,000 troops,
beyond the present authorized 525,000-man level to be reached by
next fall, was brought from Saigon last month by Gen. Earle G.
Wheeler, chairman of the Joint Chiefs of Staff....

General Wheeler presented the request to President Johnson at
the White House on Feb. 28, when he delivered a report on his three-
day survey of the war situation in South Vietnam. The request was
also forwarded to the President by the Joint Chiefs as a body
'with our approval'....

Military leaders also contend that only a massive infusion of
troops will restore the allied initiative. They say it would also
permit the allied forces to resume the pacification of the countryside and the war of attrition against the Vietcong that they contend
was being successfully waged before the Tet offensive.

The main lines of the case against General Westmoreland's
request are contained in a position paper prepared over the last
weekend by senior civilian officials in the Defense Department,
including assistant secretaries. Most of these officials were
brought into the Government by former Secretary of Defense Robert S.
McNamara.

The argument goes like this:

Since the United States military build-up began in 1965, Hanoi
has gradually increased its forces in South Vietnam and maintained
a reasonable ratio to the fighting strength of the American Forces.
There is every reason to believe, these officials contend, that
Hanoi is able and willing to continue to do so if more American
troops are sent to Vietnam within the next year.

The reinforcements that General Westmoreland wants would thus
not restore the initiative. They would simply raise the level of
violence. The United States would spend billions more on the war
effort and would suffer appreciably higher casualties.

North Vietnam would likewise endure substantially greater losses.
But the experience of the Tet offensive shows, according to this
line of reasoning, that American Military commanders have gravely
underestimated the capacity of the enemy to absorb such punishment
and to be still able to launch bold offensive operations.

'So there would just be a lot more killing,' one analyst said.

The White House is also reported to have received an analysis from the Central Intelligence Agency that support this view of North Vietnam's manpower resources and its will to resist.

'Essentially,' said one official, 'we are fighting Vietnam's birth rate.'

The Defense Department's paper was verbally endorsed by Deputy Secretary of Defense Paul T. Nitze and forwarded by him to Clark M. Clifford, the new Defense Secretary, for transmittal to the President on Monday.

Mr. Clifford was impressed with the caliber of the analysis, informants said, but it is not known whether he endorsed the document personally.

The thrust of the argument in the Pentagon paper is reported to have gained the sympathetic support of a number of senior State Department officials, including Under Secretary Nicholas deB. Katzenbach, William P. Bundy, Assistant Secretary for East Asian and Pacific Affairs, and others close to Vietnam policy.

'I can tell you that all of us in this building are against a troop increase,' one State Department official said. However, Secretary Rusk's position on the matter was unknown.

The defense position paper concludes by proposing a change in American strategy in South Vietnam. This would entail withdrawing from exposed positions like Khesanh in the sparsely populated frontier regions and concentrating on a mobile defense of the cities and populated areas nearer the sea.

But some military officials contend this is not a realistic option.

'Each town will become a Khesanh,' they assert, and civilian casualties will soar.

Although most civilian officials declined to use the term 'enclave' to describe their proposed strategy, some conceded that it does amount to a modification of the theory advanced by Lieut. Gen. James M. Gavin, retired. He has for months urged that the allies pull back to defensive positions around cities and other important enclaves along the coast.

The Pentagon document suggests that on the political side the United States encouraged the Saigon regime to broaden itself by including non-Communist opposition elements such as the followers of the militant Buddhist leader Tri Quang. A broader base would help the regime establish a better relationship with its population and make its army more effective, the paper asserts.

In their discussion of the American predicament in Vietnam, some civilian officials go significantly further and suggest that the Administration should concede that 'you cannot completely defeat the enemy.' The United States, they say, should instead 'buy time' with its present forces while the non-Communist South Vietnamese can strengthen themselves to the point where they 'believe in their ability to survive against the Communists after some sort of internal compromise.'

Officials are vague about the ingredients of this compromise, but they acknowledge that it would probably involve negotiations between the Vietcong and the non-Communists in the South.

Although it clearly entails abandonment of the military solution that is implicit in current Administration policy, they argue that such a compromise would not violate any public American commitment to South Vietnam.

While avoiding any decision so far, President Johnson has gained time by putting pressure on General Westmoreland to obtain maximum use of the troops he now has. The President has instructed the general to justify in detail his request for reinforcements.

Mr. Johnson has also set in motion extensive staff studies of the full political, economic and military ramifications of giving General Westmoreland more troops. Included among these may be an examination of the possibility of acquiring additional forces from Washington's allies in South Vietnam—Australia, South Korea, Thailand and the Philippines.

The thrust of the President's concern, however, has been with the consequences of troop increases. There is no indication at this time that Mr. Johnson and his closest advisers, Mr. Rusk, Mr. Clifford and Mr. Rostow are seriously interested in extending the war to Cambodia and Laos or in changing to a strategy of close-in defense of populated areas.

They reject a political compromise with the Vietcong at this point. Some senior civilian officials, in fact, believe Mr. Johnson is 'still intensely committed to a military solution.'

These officials consider General Westmoreland's request for an additional 206,000 men 'unrealistic,' however, and do not believe the President will grant it. 79/

Even prior to this article, there had been a great deal of speculation in the press concerning the need for additional troops in SVN, and the general conclusion seemed to be that some additions would be required. Members of Congress had already demanded that Congress be consulted before any decision was made to increase troop strength in Vietnam significantly. A number of prominent senators had interrupted debate on civil rights on 7 March to make this demand because of "disturbing information that a Presidential Decision was imminent." 80/

The Sheehan article appeared one day before Secretary of State Dean Rusk appeared to testify before the Senate Foreign Relations Committee. His 2-day grilling indicated a considerable growth in open dissent within the Committee concerning U.S. policy in South Vietnam. Rusk even came under criticism from one of the few Administration supporters on the Committee, Senator Karl E. Mundt (R-SD), who warned him, "You are as aware as we are that the shift of opinion in this country is in the wrong direction" - meaning away from support of U.S. policy in Vietnam. "Something more convincing," said Mundt, "has to come from the Administration as to what this is all about 'to match' the sacrifices we are making." Rusk sidestepped all attempts by Senators Fulbright, Gore, and other questioners to pin him down on a possible increase in troops or other element of future Vietnam strategy. It would "not be right for me to speculate about numbers of possibilities," said Rusk, "while the President is consulting his advisors." 81/

Later, on 12 March, both friends and foes of the President's policy in Vietnam served notice that the present course must be reassessed before more troops were sent to Vietnam.

"Senator Fulbright (D-Ark), Foreign Relations Committee chairman, warned against an escalation that could lead to 'all-out war,' and insisted during a televised hearing with Dean Rusk, Secretary of State, that Congress be consulted before crucial new decisions are made."

But Senator Russell (D-Ga), Armed Services Committee chairman, took a different tack, contending that air and sea power should be used to the fullest extent before ground-force levels are increased.

"If we are not willing to take this calculated risk," Russell told a Veterans of Foreign Wars dinner, "we should not still be increasing the half-million men in Vietnam who are exposed to danger daily from weapons that might have been kept from the hands of our enemies." 82/

These comments from two powerful committee chairmen demonstrated the cross-currents of opinion swirling around the President as he contemplated General Westmoreland's request and the recommendations of his advisors.

Adding fuel to this controversy was the unexpected triumph in the New Hampshire Presidential Primary on 12 March of the Democratic "peace" candidate, Senator Eugene McCarthy. This triumph was widely heralded as a repudiation by the voters of the present Administration and its Vietnam policies, and it encouraged another critic of these policies, Senator Robert Kennedy, to announce on 16 March his intention to seek the Democratic Presidential nomination.

7. The President Ponders

At a meeting at the White House on 13 March, the President decided to deploy 30,000 troops to South Vietnam in addition to the 10,500 emergency augmentation already made. This would substantially meet General Westmoreland's initial package request. Army forces would replace those Marine Corps forces requested, as the Marine Corps could not sustain the requested deployments. Also an additional Army brigade (7,363 personnel) would be deployed to replace Marine RLT 27, and its associated support. RLT 27 sould begin to return to CONUS on 15 July. The forces to be deployed were as follows:

			Deployment Date
A.	US ARMY		
	Inf Bde (3 Inf Bns)	4,500	15-30 June
	Mech Bde (1 Inf Bn, 1 Inf Bn (Mech), 1 Tk Bn)	5,041	12 July
	Avn Co, Sep Bde	238	15 July
	Armd Cav Sqdn	1,030	15-30 June
	MP Bn	955	15-30 June
	Cbt Svc Spt	3,316	15-30 June
	Cbt and Cbt Svc Spt	9,120	15-30 June
	SUB-TOTAL	24,200	15-30 June
B.	7th AF		
	4 TFS	2,164	5 April
	FAC/TACP	191	1 June
	Airlift	741	1 June
	Support	929	1 June
	SUB-TOTAL	4,025	
C.	USN		
	NSA Da Nang Support	1,775	1 June
	SUB-TOTAL	1,775	
D.	TOTAL MACV	30,000	

There would be two reserve callups to meet and sustain these deployments, one in March and one in May. The callup in March would support
the 30,000 deployment. The one in May would reconstitute the strategic
reserve at seven active divisions. Other ground rules decided upon were:
(1) those Reservists to be called in May would not now be notified; (2)
there would be no extensions of terms of service for personnel presently
on active duty; (3) no individuals would be recalled, only units. 83/

This decision was formalized by the Deputy Secretary of Defense in a
memorandum to the Chairman of the Joint Chiefs of Staff on 14 March 1968.
Mr. Nitze asked the chairman to inform General Westmoreland of these proposals, and to ask him whether he considered the substitutions satisfactory. 84/

On 14 March, the Secretary of the Army forwarded to the Secretary of
Defense his recommendations concerning these Program Six deployments, and
the Reserve callup necessary to sustain them and to reconstitute the
strategic reserve. Secretary Resor pointed out, however, that an additional 13,500 men would have to be added to the figure of 30,000 to be
deployed. "If the 3d Brigade of the 82nd Airborne is to be left in-country
permanently and if the Army is to replace the RLT with an infantry brigade
on a permanent basis then units with TOAE strength of 13,500 must be
included in the March 15 call-up and deployed....In addition, the MACV
ceiling will have to be increased from 565,000 to 578,500, unless MACV can
provide trade-off spaces for all or part of this add-on." 85/

The strength of units to be called up in March would be 45,000, as
follows:

    a. Units to provide for the additional deployments - 31,563.

    b. Units to provide the sustaining troops for 82d Airborne
and RLT 27 replacement - 13,437.

The May 15 callup would comprise the following:

1 division plus 1 ISI	32,000
1 brigade	4,000
Post, camp and station comple-ment to open 1 additional station	5,000
Total	41,000

This would reconstitute the STRAF at the following levels:

Division	6
ISI	6
SSI	1-1/3 86/

In addition, the Secretary indicated that the Chief of Staff of the Army recommended:

> ...that one division, its ISI and the station comple-
> ment, a total of 37,000 TOE strength, be alerted 15 March
> and called up 15 April instead of 15 May in order to provide
> an earlier capability to react to the unpredicted, a stronger
> STRAF in light of growing uncertainties in Southeast and
> Northeast Asia and to assure an earlier improvement of the
> sustaining base to support the increased deployments and to
> avoid drawdown on Europe. 87/

The approval of an additional 13,500 deployment to support the emergency augmentation was apparently approved very quickly.

In a memorandum for the record on 16 March, the latest tentative plan for Vietnam Deployments and reserve call-ups were listed as follows by the Assistant Secretary of Defense (Systems Analysis):

1. Deployment

Program #5	525,000
Emergency Augmentation	10,500
Support for 10,500	13,500
Additional Deployment	30,000
Total	579,000

2. The March reserve call, to be announced around 20 March will be:

Support deployment	36,621
Support personnel for the 10,500	13,437
Total	50,058

The March call will waive the 30 days notice, so troops will report around March 27.

3. Around a week or 10 days later, "after a study" there will be a second call of 48,393....These reservists will be given 30 days, therefore reporting around 1 May. 88/

Still, the President was troubled. In public he continued to indicate firmness and resoluteness, but press leaks and continued public criticism continued to compound his problem. On March 17, the New York Times, again amazingly accurate, forecast that the President would approve dispatch of an additional 35,000 to 50,000 men to Vietnam over the next six months. 89/ On March 18, nearly one-third of the House of Representatives, a total of 139 members, - 98 Republicans and 41 Democrats - joined in sponsoring a resolution calling for an immediate Congressional review of the United States policy in Southeast Asia. 90/

On that same day, 18 March, Mr. Johnson answered these critics, as he charged in a speech before the National Farmers' Union Convention in Minneapolis, that Hanoi is seeking "to win in Washington what it cannot win in Hue or Khe Sanh. Your President welcomes suggestions from commissions, from congressmen, from private individuals or groups," he continued, "or anyone who has a plan or program which can stand inspection and open a hope of reaching our goal of peace in the world." 91/

At this time, the President sought the advice of a group of his friends and confidants outside of government. These men came to Washington on 18 March at the request of the President to receive briefings on the latest developments in the war and to advise the President on the hard decision he faced. Present were: former Undersecretary of State George Ball; Arthur Dean, a Republican New York lawyer who was a Korean War negotiator during the Eisenhower Administration; Dean Acheson, former President Truman's Secretary of State; Gen. Matthew B. Ridgeway, the retired commander of United Nations troops in Korea; Gen. Maxwell Taylor, former Chairman of the Joint Chiefs of Staff; Cyrus Vance, former Deputy Defense Secretary and a key troubleshooter for the Johnson Administration; McGeorge Bundy, Ford Foundation President who had been special assistant for National Security Affairs to Mr. Johnson and former President Kennedy; former Treasury Secretary C. Douglas Dillon and Gen. Omar Bradley.

The only published account of this consultation, which is considered reliable, was written by Stuart H. Loory and appeared in the Los Angeles Times late in May. According to this report, the group met over dinner with Secretary of State Dean Rusk; Defense Secretary Clark M. Clifford; Ambassador W. Averell Harriman; Walt W. Rostow, the President's special assistant for National security affairs; General Earle G. Wheeler, Chairman of the Joint Chiefs of Staff; Richard Helms, Director of the Central Intelligence Agency; Paul Nitze, Deputy Defense Secretary; Nicholas Katzenbach, Under Secretary of State; and William P. Bundy, Assistant Secretary of State for East Asian and Pacific Affairs.

The outsiders questioned the government officials carefully on the war, the pacification program and the condition of the South Vietnamese government after the Tet offensive. They included in their deliberations the effect of the war on the United States.

After dinner the government officials left and the group received three briefings.

Philip C. Habib, a deputy to William Bundy and now a member of the American negotiating team in Paris, delivered an unusually frank briefing on the conditions in Vietnam after the Tet offensive. He covered such matters as corruption in South Vietnam and the growing refugee problem.

Habib, according to reliable sources, told the group that the Saigon government was generally weaker than had been realized as a result of the Tet offensive. He related the situation, some said, with greater frankness than the group had previously heard.

In addition to Habib, Maj. Gen. William E. DePuy, special assistant to the Joint Chiefs for counterinsurgency and special activities, briefed the group on the military situation, and George Carver, a CIA analyst, gave his agency's estimates of conditions in the war zone.

The briefings by DePuy and Carver reflected what many understood as a dispute over enemy strength between the Defense Department and the CIA which has been previously reported. Discrepancies in the figures resulted from the fact that DePuy's estimates of enemy strength covered only identifiable military units, while Carver's included all known military, paramilitary and parttime enemy strength available.

The morning of March 19, the advisory group assembled in the White House to discuss what they had heard the previous evening and arrived at their verdict. It was a striking turnabout in attitude for all but Ball.

After their meeting, the group met the President for lunch. It was a social affair. No business was transacted. The meal finished, the advisers delivered their verdict to the President.

Their deliberations produced this verdict for the chief executive:

Continued escalation of the war--intensified bombing of North Vietnam and increased American troop strength in the South--would do no good. Forget about seeking a battlefield solution to the problem and instead intensify efforts to seek a political solution at the negotiating table.

He was reportedly greatly surprised at their conclusions. When he asked them where they had obtained the facts on which the conclusions were based, the group told him of the briefings by Habib, DePuy and Carver.

Mr. Johnson knew that the three men had also briefed his governmental advisers, but he had not received the same picture of the war as Rostow presented the reports to him.

As a result of the discrepancy, the President ordered his own direct briefings. At least Habib and DePuy--and almost certainly Carver--had evening sessions with the President.

75

Habib was reportedly as frank with the President as he had been with the advisory group. The President asked tough questions. 'Habib stuck to his guns,' one source reported.

Whatever impact this group's recommendations and the direct briefings he received had on the President was not immediately apparent in any decision which affected the deployment of forces. Even as the President announced, on 22 March, that General William C. Westmoreland would be recalled from Vietnam to become the Army Chief of Staff, 93/ the Defense Department continued to plan for the deployment of 43,500 additional troops. In a memorandum to the Secretary of Defense on 23 March 1968, the Assistant Secretary (Systems Analysis) forwarded his Program #6 Summary Table based on 579,000 men in South Vietnam, 54,000 over the approved Program #5 ceiling. This 54,000 was made up of the 10,500 emergency reinforcement package, the 13,500 support forces for it, and the 30,000 additional package. The Assistant Secretary added, that upon notification of approval and desire to announce the new plan, the tables would be published. 94/

However, these particular tables were not to be published. The President sought further advice as he wrestled with the problem which had plagued his Administration. On March 26, General Creighton Abrams, Deputy COMUSMACV, arrived suddenly and without prior announcement, and was closeted with the President and his senior officials. These conferences were conducted in the utmost secrecy amid press speculation that Abrams would be named to succeed General Westmoreland. Further press speculation was that the conferences dealt primarily with expansion and modernization of the South Vietnamese armed forces and that this tended to buttress earlier predictions that any increase in American forces in South Vietnam would be modest. 95/

8. The President Decides

Apparently the Presidential decision on deployment of additional U.S. forces to Vietnam was made on 28 March and concurred in by General Abrams. In an undated memorandum (probably written on 27 or 28 March) for the Chief of Staff, U.S. Army, the Deputy Chief of Staff for Military Operations, Lt General Lemley, indicated that the Joint Staff had informed him of:

....tentative decisions arising from the recent conference between the President, the Chairman, and General Abrams, as well as telecons between the Chairman and General Westmoreland. It is believed that a Presidential decision may be made by Friday (29 March) morning.

New ceiling in RVN: 549,500
a. Program 5: 525,000.
b. Emergency deployment of 82d Abn, 27th RLT: 11,000.*
c. Support and sustain emergency deployment: 13,500.*
d. Total: 549,500.

*Includes estimated 1,444 Air Force and Navy.

1st Bde, 5th Inf Div (Mech) will replace 27th RLT.
Reserve call-up of approximately 62,000.
a. Army   53,957
      (13,301 - Support of 3/82d Abn Div & 1/5th Inf Div)
      (40,656 - Reconstitute STRAF)
b. Navy   1,453
c. Air Force   6,590

d. Total   62,000 96/

A Joint Staff paper entitled "MACV Troop List of Program 6 Add-on," dated 28 March, summarized service capability to satisfy "MACV's 28 March 1968 request for U.S. forces" as follows:

Two Brigade Increment (Combat Forces)

		STRENGTH	CONUS AVAIL DATE*
USARV	- Inf Bde, Sep	4,639	In-Country as 3d Bde/82d Div
	- Mech Bde, Sep	4,882	Jul 68
	- Armored Cav Sqdn	1,049	Aug 68
7th AF	- 2 TFS (F-100) (469 ea)	994	Jun/Jul 68
Total Brigade Increment		11,564	

Support Increment (Combat Support and Combat Service Support Forces)

		STRENGTH	CONUS AVAIL DATE*
USARV	- 2 FA Bn (155mm)	1,132	Aug/Sep 68
	- Engr Bn (Cbt)	812	Aug 68
	- Other Support Units	169	Jun/Jul 68
		2,752	Aug 68
		2,219	Sep 68
		1,411	Oct 68
		900	Unknown/May 69
NAVFORV -		1,775	Jun 68
7th AF -		895	Jun/Jul 68
		707	Unknown
III MAF -		496	Apr/Sep 68
Total Support Increment		13,268	

TOTAL DEPLOYMENT   24,832   (Excess over 24,500 can be taken from existing credit/debit account)

* CONUS availability date based on decision to call up reserve elements. 97/

9. <u>The Decision is Announced</u>

On Sunday, 31 March, it was announced that the President would address the nation that evening concerning the war in Vietnam. The night before, Saturday, 30 March, a cable was dispatched to the U.S. Ambassadors in Australia, New Zealand, Thailand, Laos, the Philippines, and South Korea. This cable, slugged "Literally Eyes Only for Ambassador or Charge", instructed the addressees to see their respective heads of government and inform them of the following major elements of the President's planned policy announcement on Sunday night: 98/

a. Major stress on importance of GVN and ARVN increased effectiveness, with our equipment and other support as first priority in our own actions.

b. 13,500 support forces to be called up at once in order to round out the 10,500 combat units sent in February.

c. Replenishment of strategic reserve by calling up 48,500 additional reserves, stating that these would be designed to strategic reserve.

d. Related tax increases and budget cuts already largely needed for non-Vietnam reasons.

3. In addition, after similar consultation and concurrence, President proposes to announce that bombing will be restricted to targets most directly engaged in the battle-field area and that this meant that there would be no bombing north of 20th parallel. Announcement would leave open how Hanoi might respond, and would be open-ended as to time. However, it would indicate that Hanoi's response could be helpful in determining whether we were justified in assumption that Hanoi would not take advantage if we stopping (sic) bombing altogether. Thus, it would to this extent foreshadow possibility of full bombing stoppage at a later point.

This cable offered the Ambassadors some additional rationale for this new policy for their discretionary use in conversations with their respective heads of government. This rationale represents the only available statement by the Administration of some of its underlying reasons and purposes for and expectations from this policy decision.

a. You should call attention to force increases that would be announced at the same time and would make clear our continued resolve. Also our top priority to re-equipping ARVN forces.

b. You should make clear that Hanoi is most likely to denounce the project and thus free our hand after a short period. Nonetheless, we might wish to continue the limitation even after a formal denunciation, in order to reinforce its sincerity and put the monkey firmly on Hanoi's back for whatever follows. Of course, any major military change could compel full-scale resumption at any time.

c. With or without denunciation, Hanoi might well feel limited in conducting any major offensives at least in the northern areas. If they did so, this could ease the pressure where it is most potentially serious. If they did not, then this would give us a clear field for whatever actions were then required.

d. In view of weather limitations, bombing north of the 20th parallel will in any event be limited at least for the next four weeks or so -- which we tentatively envisage as a maximum testing period in any event. Hence, we are not giving up anything really serious in this time frame. Moreover, air power now used north of 20th can probably be used in Laos (where no policy change planned) and in SVN.

e. Insofar as our announcement foreshadows any possibility of a complete bombing stoppage, in the event Hanoi really exercises reciprocal restraints, we regard this as unlikely. But in any case, the period of demonstrated restraint would probably have to continue for a period of several weeks, and we would have time to appraise the situation and to consult carefully with them before we undertook any such action.

Thus, in reassuring our allies of our "continued resolve", the cable clearly indicated that not very much was expected of this change in policy. It could possibly reinforce our sincerity and "put the monkey on Hanoi's back for whatever follows." It was not expected that Hanoi would react positively although they might "feel limited in conducting any major offensives at least in the northern areas", admittedly a highly dubious likelihood.

What, then, was the purpose of this change in policy? If it was not expected that Hanoi would respond positively, or that any other major military benefits would accrue, what then was expected? The answer to these questions, of course, could only be speculation at the time, although many of the answers were to be contained in the President's speech on 31 March.

10. I Shall Not Seek, and I Will Not Accept...

    The President's speech to the nation on 31 March began with a summary of his efforts to achieve peace in Vietnam over the years. 99/

    Good evening, my fellow Americans.

    Tonight I want to speak to you of peace in Vietnam and Southeast Asia.

    No other question so preoccupies our people. No other dream so absorbs the 250 million human beings who live in that part of the world. No other goal motivates American policy in Southeast Asia.

    For years, representatives of our government and others have travelled the world -- seeking to find a basis for peace talks.

    Since last September, they have carried the offer that I made public at San Antonio.

    That offer was this:

    That the United States would stop its bombardment of North Vietnam when that would lead promptly to productive discussions -- and that we would assume that North Vietnam would not take military advantage of our restraint.

    Hanoi denounced this offer, both privately and publicly. Even while the search for peace was going on, North Vietnam rushed their preparations for a savage assault on the people, the government, and the allies of South Vietnam.

This attack during the TET holidays, the President indicated, failed to achieve its principal objectives:

    It did not collapse the elected government of South Vietnam or shatter its army -- as the Communists had hoped.

    It did not produce a 'general uprising' among the people of the cities as they had predicted.

    The Communists were unable to maintain control of any of the more than 30 cities that they attacked. And they took very heavy casualties.

But they did compel the South Vietnamese and their allies to move certain forces from the countryside, into the cities.

They caused widespread disruption and suffering. Their attacks, and the battles that followed, made refugees of half a million human beings.

The Communists may renew their attack any day.

They are, it appears, trying to make 1968 the year of decision in South Vietnam -- the year that brings, if not final victory or defeat, at least a turning point in the struggle.

This much is clear:

If they do mount another round of heavy attacks, they will not succeed in destroying the fighting power of South Vietnam and its allies.

But tragically, this is also clear: many men -- on both sides of the struggle -- will be lost. A nation that has already suffered 20 years of warfare will suffer once again. Armies on both sides will take new casualties. And the war will go on.

There is no need for this to be so.

In dramatically announcing the partial suspension of the bombing of North Vietnam as a new initiative designed to lead to peace talks, President Johnson did not voice any of the doubts of the State Department cable of the previous night that this initiative was not expected to be fruitful. Indeed, the central theme of this portion of the speech was that our unilateral action was designed to lead to early talks. The President even designated the United States representatives for such talks.

There is no need to delay the talks that could bring an end to this long and this bloody war.

Tonight, I renew the offer I made last August -- to stop the bombardment of North Vietnam. We ask that talks begin promptly, that they be serious talks on the substance of peace. We assume that during those talks Hanoi will not take advantage of our restraint.

We are prepared to move immediately toward peace through negotiations.

So, tonight, in the hope that this action will lead to early talks, I am taking the first step to de-escalate the conflict. We are reducing -- substantially reducing -- the present level of hostilities.

And we are doing so unilaterally, and at once.

Tonight, I have ordered our aircraft and our naval vessels to make no attacks on North Vietnam, except in the area north of the DeMilitarized Zone where the continuing enemy build-up directly threatens allied forward positions and where the movements of their troops and supplies are clearly related to that threat.

The area in which we are stopping our attacks includes almost 90 percent of North Vietnam's population, and most of its territory. Thus there will be no attacks around the principal populated areas, or in the food-producing areas of North Vietnam.

Even this very limited bombing of the North could come to an early end -- if our restraint is matched by restraint in Hanoi. But I cannot in good conscience stop all bombing so long as to do so would immediately and directly endanger the lives of our men and our allies. Whether a complete bombing halt becomes possible in the future will be determined by events.

Our purpose in this action is to bring about a reduction in the level of violence that now exists.

It is to save the lives of brave men -- and to save the lives of innocent women and children. It is to permit the contending forces to move closer to a political settlement.

And tonight, I call upon the United Kingdom and I call upon the Soviet Union -- as co-chairmen of the Geneva Conferences, and as permanent members of the United Nations Security Council -- to do all they can to move from the unilateral act of de-escalation that I have just announced toward genuine peace in Southeast Asia.

Now, as in the past, the United States is ready to send its representatives to any forum, at any time, to discuss the means of bringing this ugly war to an end.

I am designating one of our most distinguished Americans, Ambassador Averell Harriman, as my personal representative for such talks. In addition, I have asked Ambassador Llewellyn Thompson, who returned from Moscow for consultation, to be available to join Ambassador Harriman at Geneva or any other suitable place -- just as soon as Hanoi agrees to a conference.

I call upon President Ho Chi Minh to respond positively, and favorably, to this new step toward peace.

If peace did not come through negotiations, however, the President indicated that our common resolve was unshakable and our common strength invincible. As evidence of this, he listed the achievements of the South Vietnamese nation.

Tonight, we and the other allied nations are contributing 600,000 fighting men to assist 700,000 South Vietnamese troops in defending their little country.

Our presence there has always rested on this basic belief: the main burden of preserving their freedom must be carried out by them -- by the South Vietnamese themselves.

We and our allies can only help to provide a shield -- behind which the people of South Vietnam can survive and can grow and develop. On their efforts -- on their determinations and resourcefulness -- the outcome will ultimately depend.

That small, beleaguered nation has suffered terrible punishment for more than twenty years.

I pay tribute once again tonight to the great courage and endurance of its people. South Vietnam supports armed forces tonight of almost 700,000 men -- and I call your attention to the fact that that is the equivalent of more than 10 million in our own population. Its people maintain their firm determination to be free of domination by the North.

There has been substantial progress, I think, in building a durable government during these last three years. The South Vietnam of 1965 could not have survived the enemy's Tet offensive of 1968. The elected government of South Vietnam survived that attack -- and is rapidly repairing the devastation that it wrought.

The South Vietnamese know that further efforts are going to be required:

-- to expand their own armed forces,

-- to move back into the countryside as quickly as possible,

-- to increase their taxes,

-- to select the very best men that they have for civilian and military responsibility,

-- to achieve a new unity within their constitutional government,

-- and to include in the national effort all of those groups who wish to preserve South Vietnam's control over its own destiny.

Last week President Thieu ordered the mobilization of 135,000 additional South Vietnamese. He plans to reach -- as soon as possible -- a total military strength of more than 800,000 men.

To achieve this, the government of South Vietnam started the drafting of 19-year-olds on March 1st. On May 1st, the Government will begin the drafting of 18-year-olds.

Last month, 10,000 men volunteered for military service -- that was two and a half times the number of volunteers during the same month last year. Since the middle of January, more than 48,000 South Vietnamese have joined the armed forces -- and nearly half of them volunteered to do so.

All men in the South Vietnamese armed forces have had their tours of duty extended for the duration of the war, and reserves are now being called up for immediate active duty.

President Thieu told his people last week:

"We must make greater efforts and accept more sacrifices because, as I have said many times, this is our country. The existence of our nation is at stake, and this is mainly a Vietnamese responsibility."

He warned his people that a major national effort is required to root out corruption and incompetence at all levels of government.

We applaud this evidence of determination on the part
of South Vietnam. Our first priority will be to support
their effort.

We shall accelerate the re-equipment of South Vietnam's
armed forces -- in order to meet the enemy's increased firepower. This will enable them progressively to undertake
a larger share of combat operations against the Communists
invaders.

The token increase in U.S. troop deployments to South Vietnam which
presaged for the first time a limit to our commitment and pointed to a
change in ground strategy, an issue which had caused such great speculation in the press and controversy in Congress and within the Administration,
received short mention in the speech. It seemed almost a footnote to the
dramatic statements which had preceded it.

On many occasions I have told the American people that
we would send to Vietnam those forces that are required to
accomplish our mission there. So, with that as our guide,
we have previously authorized a force level of approximately
525,000.

Some weeks ago -- to help meet the enemy's new offensive
-- we sent to Vietnam about 11,000 additional Marine and
airborne troops. They were deployed by air in 48 hours, on
an emergency basis. But the artillery, tank, aircraft, and
other units that were needed to work with and support these
infantry troops in combat could not accompany them on that
short notice.

In order that these forces may reach maximum combat
effectiveness, the Joint Chiefs of Staff have recommended to
me that we should prepared to send -- during the next five
months -- support troops totalling approximately 13,500 men.

A portion of these men will be made available from our
active forces. The balance will come from Reserve Component
units which will be called up for service.

The next portion of the President's speech detailed the cost of
the Vietnam War and made a plea for Congressional action to reduce the
deficit by passing the surtax which had been requested almost a year
before.

In summary, the President reiterated the U.S. objectives in South
Vietnam, and gave his appraisal of what the U.S. in pursuit of those
objectives, hoped to accomplish in Southeast Asia.

I cannot promise that the initiative that I have announced tonight will be completely successful in achieving peace any more than the 30 others that we have undertaken and agreed to in recent years.

But it is our fervent hope that North Vietnam, after years of fighting that has left the issue unresolved, will now cease its efforts to achieve a military victory and will join with us in moving toward the peace table.

And there may come a time when South Vietnam -- on both sides -- are able to work out a way to settle their own differences by free political choice rather than by war.

As Hanoi considers its course, it should be in no doubt of our intentions. It must not miscalculate the pressures within our democracy in this election year.

We have no intention of widening this war.

But the United States will never accept a fake solution to this long and arduous struggle and call it peace.

No one can foretell the precise terms of an eventual settlement.

Our objective in South Vietnam has never been the annihilation of the enemy. It has been to bring about a recognition in Hanoi that its objective -- taking over the South by force -- could not be achieved.

We think that peace can be based on the Geneva Accords of 1954 -- under political conditions that permit the South Vietnamese -- all the South Vietnamese -- to chart their course free of any outside domination or interference, from us or from anyone else.

So tonight I reaffirm the pledge that we made at Manila -- that we are prepared to withdraw our forces from South Vietnam as the other side withdraws its forces to the North, stops the infiltration, and the level of violence thus subsides.

Our goal of peace and self-determination in Vietnam is directly related to the future of all of Southeast Asia --

where much has happened to inspire confidence during the past
10 years. We have done all that we knew how to do to contribute and to help build that confidence....

Over time, a wider, framework of peace and security in
Southeast Asia may become possible. The new cooperation of
the nations in the area could be a foundation-stone. Certainly friendship with the nations of such a Southeast Asia
is what the United States seeks -- and that is all that the
United States seeks.

One day, my fellow citizens, there will be peace in Southeast Asia.

It will come because the people of Southeast Asia want
it -- those whose armies are at war tonight, and those who,
though threatened, have thus far been spared.

Peace will come because Asians were willing to work for
it -- and to sacrifice for it -- and to die by the thousands
for it.

But let it never be forgotten: peace will come also
because America sent her sons to help secure it.

It has not been easy -- far from it. During the past
four and a half years, it has been my fate and my responsibility to be commander-in-chief. I have lived -- daily and
nightly -- with the cost of this war. I know the pain that
it has inflicted. I know perhaps better than anyone the
misgivings that it has aroused.

Throughout this entire, long period, I have been sustained by a single principle:

-- that what we are doing now, in Vietnam, is vital
not only to the security of Southeast Asia, but it is
vital to the security of every American.

Surely we have treaties which we must respect.
Surely we have commitments that we are going to keep.
Resolutions of the Congress testify to the need to
resist aggression in the world and in Southeast Asia.

But the heart of our involvement in South Vietnam --
under three Presidents, three separate Administrations --
has always been America's own security.

And the larger purpose of our involvement has always
been to help the nations of Southeast Asia become independent and stand alone, self-sustaining as members of a
great world communitsy.

-- At peace with themselves, and at peace with all
others.

With such an Asia, our country -- and the world --
will be far more secure than it is tonight.

I believe that a peaceful Asia is far nearer to
reality, because of what America has done in Vietnam.
I believe that the men who endure the dangers of battle
-- fighting there for us tonight -- are helping the
entire world avoid far greater conflicts, far wider wars,
far more destruction, than this one.

I pray that it will not be rejected by the leaders
of North Vietnam. I pray that they will accept it as a
means by which the sacrifices of their own people may be
ended. And I ask your help and your support, my fellow
citizens, for this effort to reach across the battlefield
toward an early peace.

Finally, the President addressed himself in a highly personal manner
to the issue that had seemed uppermost in his mind throughout the preceding
month of deliberation, reassessment and reappraisal of our Vietnam policy --
the issue of domestic unity.

Yet, I believe that we must always be mindful of this one
thing, whatever the trials and the tests ahead. The ultimate
strength of our country and our cause will lie not in powerful
weapons or infinite resources or boundless wealth, but will
lie in the unity of our people.

This, I believe very deeply.

Throughout my entire public career I have followed the
personal philosophy that I am a free man, an American, a public
servant and a member of my Party, in that order always and only.

For 37 years in the service of our nation, first as a
Congressman, as a Senator and as Vice President and now as
your President, I have put the unity of the people first.
I have put it ahead of any devisive partisanship.

And in these times as in times before, it is true that a house divided against itself by the spirit of faction, of party, of region, of religion, of race, is a house that cannot stand.

There is division in the American house now. There is devisiveness among us all tonight. And holding the trust that is mine, as President of all the people, I cannot disregard the peril to the progress of the American people and the hope and the prospect of peace for all peoples.

So, I would ask all Americans, whatever their personal interests or concern, to guard against devisiveness and all its ugly consequences.

Fifty-two months and ten days ago, in a moment of tragedy and trauma, the duties of this office fell upon me. I asked then for your help and God's, that we might continue America on its course, binding up our wounds, healing our history, moving forward in new unity, to clear the American agenda and to keep the American commitment for all of our people.

United we have kept that commitment. United we have enlarged that commitment.

Through all time to come, I think America will be a stronger nation, a more just society, and a land of greater opportunity and fulfillment because of what we have all done together in these years of unparalleled achievement.

Our reward will come in the life of freedom, peace, and hope that our children will enjoy through ages ahead.

What we won when all of our people united just must not now be lost in suspicion, distrust, selfishness, and politics among any of our people.

Having eloquently stated the need for unity in a nation divided, the President then made the dramatic announcement which shocked and electrified the nation and the world, an announcement intended to restore unity to the divided nation:

Believing this as I do, I have concluded that I should not permit the Presidency to become involved in the partisan divisions that are developing in this political year.

With America's sons in the fields far away, with America's future under challenge right here at home, with our hopes

and the world's hopes for peace in the balance every day,
I do not believe that I should devote an hour or a day
of my time to any personal partisan causes or to any duties
other than the awesome duties of this office -- the Presidency of your country.

Accordingly, I shall not seek, and I will not accept, the
nomination of my Party for another term as your President.

But let men everywhere know, however, that a strong, a
confident, and a vigilant America stands ready tonight to
seek an honorable peace -- and stand ready tonight to defend
an honored cause -- whatever the price, whatever the burden,
whatever the sacrifices that duty may require.

Thank you for listening.

Good night and God bless all of you.

11. Epilogue

On April 4, 1968, the Deputy Secretary of Defense, in a memorandum
for the Secretaries of the Military Departments and the Chairman of the
Joint Chiefs of Staff established Southeast Asia Deployment Program #6.
This program added 24,500 personnel to the approved Program #5, and placed
a new ceiling of 549,500 on U.S. forces in South Vietnam. 100/ None of
the some 200,000 troops requested by General Westmoreland on 27 February
were to be deployed.

Late in the afternoon of April 3, 1968, the White House released the
following statement by President Johnson:

Today the Government of North Vietnam made a statement
which included the following paragraph, and I quote:

"However, for its part, the Government of the Democratic Republic of Vietnam declares its readiness to
appoint its representatives to contact the United States
representative with a view to determining with the
American side the unconditional cessation of the United
States bombing raids and all other acts of war against
the Democratic Republic of Vietnam so that talks may
start."

Last Sunday night I expressed the position of the
United States with respect to peace in Vietnam and Southeast Asia as follows:

"Now, as in the past, the United States is ready to
send its representatives to any forum, at any time, to
discuss the means of bringing this war to an end."

Accordingly, we will establish contact with the representatives of North Vietnam. Consultations with the Government of South Vietnam and our other allies are now taking place. 101/

The first step on what would undoubtedly be a long and tortuous road to peace apparently had been taken. In one dramatic action, President Johnson had for a time removed the issue of Vietnam from domestic political contention. In an unexpectedly prompt and responsive reply to his initiative, Hanoi had moved the struggle for South Vietnam into a new path.

As has been indicated, little had been expected to result from the partial bombing halt and the limitation upon U.S. troop commitments to South Vietnam. Why, then, were these steps taken?

In March of 1968, the President and his principal advisers were again confronted with a dilemma which they had faced before, but which they had postponed resolving. Although seldom specifically stated, the choice had always been either to increase U.S. forces in South Vietnam as necessary to achieve military victory or to limit the U.S. commitment in order to prevent the defeat of our South Vietnamese allies while they put their political-military house in order. In the past, the choice had not been so clear-cut. Progress toward military victory had been promised with small increases in force levels which did not require large reserve call-ups or economic dislocations. Military victory would then assure a viable South Vietnamese political body capable of protecting and gaining the support of its people.

In March of 1968, the choice had become clear-cut. The price for military victory had increased vastly, and there was no assurance that it would not grow again in the future. There were also strong indications that large and growing elements of the American public had begun to believe the cost had already reached unacceptable levels and would strongly protest a large increase in that cost.

The political reality which faced President Johnson was that "more of the same" in South Vietnam, with an increased commitment of American lives and money and its consequent impact on the country, accompanied by no guarantee of military victory in the near future, had become unacceptable to these elements of the American public. The optimistic military reports of progress in the war no longer rang true after the shock of the TET offensive.

Thus, the President's decision to seek a new strategy and a new road to peace was based upon two major considerations:

(1) The convictions of his principal civilian advisers, particularly Secretary of Defense Clifford, that the troops requested by General Westmoreland would not make a military victory any more likely; and

(2) A deeply-felt conviction of the need to restore unity to the American nation.

For a policy from which so little was expected, a great deal was initiated. The North Vietnamese and the Americans sat down at the conference table in Paris to begin to travel the long road to peace; the issue of Vietnam largely was removed from American political discord; a limit to the commitment of U.S. forces was established; and the South Vietnamese were put on notice that, with our help, they would be expected to do more in their own defense.

The "A to Z" reassessment of U.S. strategy in South Vietnam in the wake of the TET offensive did not result in the announcement of a new ground strategy for South Vietnam. But in placing General Westmoreland's request for forces squarely in the context of the achievement of U.S. political-military objectives in South Vietnam, the limited political nature of those objectives was for the first time affirmed. A new ground strategy, based on these limited objectives and upon the ceiling on U.S. troops became a corollary for the new U.S. commander.

American forces initially were deployed to Vietnam in order to prevent the South Vietnamese from losing the war, to insure that aggression from the north would not succeed. Having deployed enough troops to insure that NVN aggression would not succeed, it had been almost a reflex action to start planning on how much it would take to "win" the war. Lip service was given to the need for developing South Vietnamese political institutions, but no one at high levels seemed to question the assumption that U.S. political objectives in South Vietnam could be attained through military victory.

However, it was quickly apparent that there was an embarrassing lack of knowledge as to how much it would take to win the war. This stemmed from uncertainty in two areas: (1) how much effort the North Vietnamese were willing to expend in terms of men and materiel; and (2) how effective the South Vietnamese armed forces would be in establishing security in the countryside. As the war progressed, it appeared that our estimates of the former were too low and of the latter too high. However, committed to a military victory and having little information as to what was needed militarily, the civilian decision makers seemed willing to accept the field commander's estimate of what was needed. Steady progress was promised and was apparently being accomplished, although the commitment of forces steadily increased.

The TET offensive showed that this progress in many ways had been illusory. The possibility of military victory had seemingly become remote and the cost had become too high both in political and economic terms. Only then were our ultimate objectives brought out and re-examined. Only then was it realized that a clear-cut military victory was probably not possible or necessary, and that the road to peace would be at least as

dependent upon South Vietnamese political development as it would be on
American arms. This realization, then, made it possible to limit the
American military commitment to South Vietnam to achieve the objectives
for which this force had originally been deployed. American forces would
remain in South Vietnam to prevent defeat of the Government by Communist
forces and to provide a shield behind which that Government could rally,
become effective, and win the support of its people.

FOOTNOTES

1. COMUSMACV 61742, 260755 Jan 68, Subject: "Annual Assessment."

2. "U.S. Aides Predict All Out Red Drive as Prelude to Talks," by George R. Packard, Philadelphia Bulletin, 11 Jan 68, p. 1.

3. JCSM 91-68, 12 Feb 68, Subject: "Emergency Reinforcement of COMUSMACV."

4. JCS Msg 9926, 130218Z Feb 68, Subject: "Deployment of Brigade Task Force of 82nd Airborne Division to SVN (S)."

5. Ibid.

6. JCS Msg 9929, 130341Z Feb 68, Subject: "Deployment of Marine Corps Regiment (Reinforced) to SVN (S)."

7. Ibid.

8. CINCPAC Msg to JCS/CINCUSARPAC, 190129Z Feb 68, Subject: "Deployment of Marine Regiment (U)" JCS in 12316.

9. DJSM 259-68, Memorandum for the Secretary of Defense, Subject: "Marine Deployments to Vietnam (U)," dated 6 Mar 68.

10. JCSM 96-68, 13 Feb 68, Subject: "Emergency Reinforcement of COMUSMACV(C)."

11. Report of Chairman, JCS on Situation in Vietnam and MACV Force Requirements, 27 Feb 1968 (TS).

12. Ibid., pp. 1-2.

13. Ibid., p. 12.

14. Ibid., pp. 12-13.

15. Ibid., p. 13.

16. Ibid., p. 14.

17. Handwritten notes by Morton Halperin from conversation with Paul Warnke, 29 Feb 1968 (TS-EYES ONLY).

18. Memorandum from William Bundy to General Taylor and Mr. Warnke, 29 Feb 1968 (TS-NODIS).

TOP SECRET - Sensitive

19. Halperin notes, op. cit.

20. Office of National Estimates, Central Intelligence Agency, Memorandum for the Director, Subject: The Outlook in Vietnam, dated 26 Feb 1968 (S).

21. Central Intelligence Agency, Memorandum, Subject: Communist Alternatives in Vietnam, dated 29 Feb 1968 (S)

22. Ibid., p. 1

23. Central Intelligence Agency, Memorandum, Subject: Questions Concerning the Situation in Vietnam, dated 1 March 1968 (S).

24. W. P. Bundy, Draft Memorandum for the Group, Subject: Alternative Courses of Action, dated 29 Feb 1968 (TS).

25. Department of State, Memorandum for the Group, Subject: Checklist of Factors Affecting Alternative Courses of Action, dated 29 Feb 1968, initialed by Nicholas deB. Katzenbach (TS-NODIS).

26. W. P. Bundy, Draft Memorandum for the Group, op. cit., 29 Feb 68.

27. W. P. Bundy, Draft Memorandum for the Group, Subject: Introductory Paper on Key Elements in the Situation, dated 29 Feb 1968 (TS).

28. Department of State, "Possible Soviet Responses to Various US Actions in Indochina -- Vietnam, Laos and Cambodia;" "Probable Chinese Responses to Certain US Courses of Action in Indochina--Vietnam, Laos and Cambodia;" "Probable Western European Reaction to Various US Courses of Action in Indochina -- Vietnam, Laos, Cambodia," undated papers (TS).

29. Cable, MOSCOW 2983, 011515Z March 1968, TS-LITERALLY EYES ONLY for Under Secretary from Ambassador.

30. W. P. Bundy, Draft Memorandum, Subject: European and Other Non-Asian Reactions to a Major US Force Increase, dated 1 Mar 1968 (TS).

31. W. P. Bundy, Draft Memorandum, Subject: Asian Reaction to a Major U.S. Force Increase, dated 1 Mar 68 (TS).

32. W. P. Bundy, First Draft, Subject: Options on Our Negotiating Posture, dated 29 Feb 68 (TS).

TOP SECRET - Sensitive

33. Undated Memorandum, Subject: Viet-Nam Alternatives, signed M.D.T., General Taylor took, as the U.S. objective, the statement of Pres. Johnson in his speech at Johns Hopkins University in April 1965: "Our objective is the independence of South Viet-Nam and its freedom from attack. We want nothing for ourselves, only that the people of South Viet-Nam be allowed to guide their country in their own way."

34. OASD/SA, Draft Memorandum, Subject: Deployments - A Discussion of Alternatives, undated (S).

35. Ibid.

36. OASD/SA, Draft Memorandum, Subject: Pacification Slowdown, undated (C)

37. Ibid., p. 2

38. OASD/SA, Draft Memorandum, Subject: The Status of RVNAF, undated (TS).

39. OASD/SA, Draft Memorandum, Subject: Alternative Strategies, dated 29 Feb 1968, pp. 1-2 (TS).

40. Ibid., pp. 2-4.

41. OASD/SA, Draft Memorandum, Subject: Data for Analysis of Strategies, undated (TS).

42. Phil G. Goulding, Draft Memorandum, Subject: Possible Public Reaction to Various Alternatives, undated (TS).

43. Ibid., p. 5

44. Memorandum for the President, Subject: Alternative Strategies in SVN, 1st Draft, 29 Feb 1968 (TS-SENS)

45. Ibid., 3rd Draft, 1 Mar 1968 (TS-SENS)

46. Ibid., p. 3

47. Ibid., pp 5-6.

48. Ibid., pp. 6-7.

49. Ibid., pp. 8-10.

50. Ibid., Annex II, Alternative Courses of Military Action, pp. 8-10.

51. Ibid., pp. 12-13.

52. Ibid., Annex II, Population Security, p. 15.

53. Ibid., p. 16.

54. Ibid., pp. 16-17.

55. Ibid., Appendix, Strategy by Corps Tactical Zone, pp. A-3 - A-8.

56. Ibid., Appendix, Effects of Strategy on Interior Provinces, pp. A-1 - A-3.

57. Ibid., p. 2.

58. Brig. Gen. Harris W. Hollis, Director of Operations, ODCSOPS, DA; Memorandum for LTG Lemley, Subject: CINCPAC Force Requirements, dated 27 Feb 1968 (S); Lt Col Spiller, ODCSOPS, DA, Supplemental Information, Subject: MACV Requirements and Major Ground Forces Deployment by Option, 1 Mar 1968 (S).

59. Assistant Secretary of Defense, ISA, Memorandum for the Secretary of Defense, Subject: General Wheeler's View of the Two Fatal Flaws in the Population Control Strategy, dated 2 Mar. 1968 (TS-SENS).

60. MAC 02951, 020947Z, from General Westmoreland to General Wheeler, (TS-LIMDIS,EYES ONLY).

61. Organization of the Joint Chiefs of Staff, Plans and Policy Directorate, Short Range Branch, J-5, Subject: Analysis of COMUSMACV Force Requirements and Alternatives, dated 1 Mar 1968 (TS-SENS).

62. Memorandum for the President, 3 Mar Draft (Goulding -Warnke) (TS-SENS).

63. Ibid., p. 8.

64. Ibid., pp. 8-10.

65. Ibid., pp. 5-6.

66. Draft Memorandum for the President, 4 Mar 1968 (TS-SENS), pp. 1-2.

67. Ibid., Tab A, The Justification for Immediate Additional Forces in South Vietnam, pp. 1-2.

68. Ibid., Tab B, Increasing the Effectiveness of Vietnamese Efforts in Conjunction with a U.S. Troop Increase, pp. 1-7.

69. Ibid., Tab C, Justification for Increasing the Strategic Reserve, pp. 1-2.

70. Ibid., Tab D, Necessity for In-Depth Study of Vietnam Policy and Strategic Guidance, p. 1.

71. Ibid., pp. 1-2.

72. Ibid., pp. 2-3.

73. Ibid., Tab E, Negotiating Posture Options, and Possible Diplomatic Actions, p. 1.

74. Ibid., pp. 4-6.

75. Ibid., pp. 8-10.

76. Ibid., Tab F, Military Action Against North Vietnam.

77. Ibid., Tab G, Difficulties and Negative Factors in the Course of Action; Tab H, Problems We Can Anticipate in U.S. Public Opinion, p. 4.

78. CM-3098-68, Memorandum for the Secretary of Defense, Subject: COMUSMACV Force Requirements, dated 8 Mar 68 (TS-SENS).

79. Neil Sheehan and Hedrick Smith, "Westmoreland Requests 206,000 More Men, Stirring Debate in Administration, New York Times, 10 Mar 1968, pp. 1,11.

80. Joseph R.L. Sterne, "War Critics Denounce Any Troop Rises," Baltimore Sun, March 8, 1968, p. 1; John W. Finney, "Criticism of War Widens in Senate on Build-Up Issue," New York Times, 8 Mar 68, p. 1.

81. Joseph R.L. Sterne, "For Different Aims, Russell, Fulbright Ask Viet Restudy," Baltimore Sun, 13 March 1968, p. 1.

82. Ibid.

83. Handwritten notes by Alain Enthoven from meeting with Secretary Clifford, Mr. Warnke, Mr. Resor, General Wheeler, 13 Mar. 1968. (S)

84. Deputy Secretary of Defense, Memorandum for Chairman of the Joint Chiefs of Staff, Subject: Southeast Asia Deployments, dated 14 Mar 1968. (TS)

85. Secretary of the Army, Memorandum for the Secretary of Defense, 14 Mar 1968 (S).

86. Ibid.

87. Chief of Staff, USA, Memorandum for the Secretary of the Army, Subject: Call-Up of Reserves and Program 6 Deployment, dated 14 Mar 1968.

88. Alain Enthoven, Memorandum for the Record, 16 Mar 1968.

89. Robert H. Phelps, "More U.S. Troops Going to Vietnam," New York Times, 17 Mar. 1968, p. 1.

90. John W. Finney, "Third of House Wants Review of War Policy," New York Times, 19 Mar. 1968, p. 32.

91. Muriel Dubbin, "War Foes Censured by Johnson," Baltimore Sun, 19 Mar. 1968, p. 1.

92. Stuart H. Loory,

93. Charles W. Corddry, "Westmoreland Attains No. 1 Goal," Baltimore Sun, 23 Mar. 1968, pp. 1, 25.

94. Assistant Secretary of Defense (Systems Analysis), Memorandum for Secretary of Defense, Subject: Program #6 Summary Table (Tentative) (U), dated 23 Mar. 1968, (TS).

95. Murray Mardes, "General Abrams, LBJ Confer on Vietnam," Washington Post, 27 Mar. 1968, p. 1; Neil Sheehan, "Gen. Abrams in Capitol, Sees President and Aides," New York Times, March 27, 1968, p. 2.

96. Office of the Deputy Chief of Staff for Military Operations, Memorandum for Chief of Staff, U.S. Army, Subject: MACV Requirements, undated, (S).

97. Joint Staff, Pacific Division, J-3, Subject: MACV Troop List, Program 6 Add-On, dated 28 March 1968. Corrected 5 April 1968.

98. Department of State Message 139431, 30 March 1968 (TS-NODIS LITERALLY EYES ONLY, FOR AMBASSADOR OR CHARGE).

99. Remarks of the President to the Nation, March 31, 1968.

100. Deputy Secretary of Defense, Memorandum for Secretaries of the
      Military Departments, Chairman of the Joint Chiefs of Staff,
      Assistant Secretaries of Defense, Subject: Southeast Asia
      Deployment Program #6(U), dated 4 April 1968(S).

101. White House Press Release, 3 April 1968.

IV.C Evolution of the War (26 Vols.)
Direct Action: The Johnson Commitments, 1964-1968
(16 Vols.)
7. Air War in the North: 1965 – 1968 (2 Vols.)
a. Volume I

IV.C Evolution of the War (26 Vols.)
Direct Action: The Johnson Commitments, 1964-1968
(16 Vols.)
7. Air War in the North: 1965 – 1968 (2 Vols.)
a. Volume I

UNITED STATES - VIETNAM RELATIONS
1945 - 1967

VIETNAM TASK FORCE

OFFICE OF THE SECRETARY OF DEFENSE

SET #13

TOP SECRET - Sensitive

IV. C. 7.(a)

Volume I

THE AIR WAR IN NORTH VIETNAM

Sec Def Cont Nr. X-_____

TOP SECRET - Sensitive

ROLLING THUNDER DIGEST

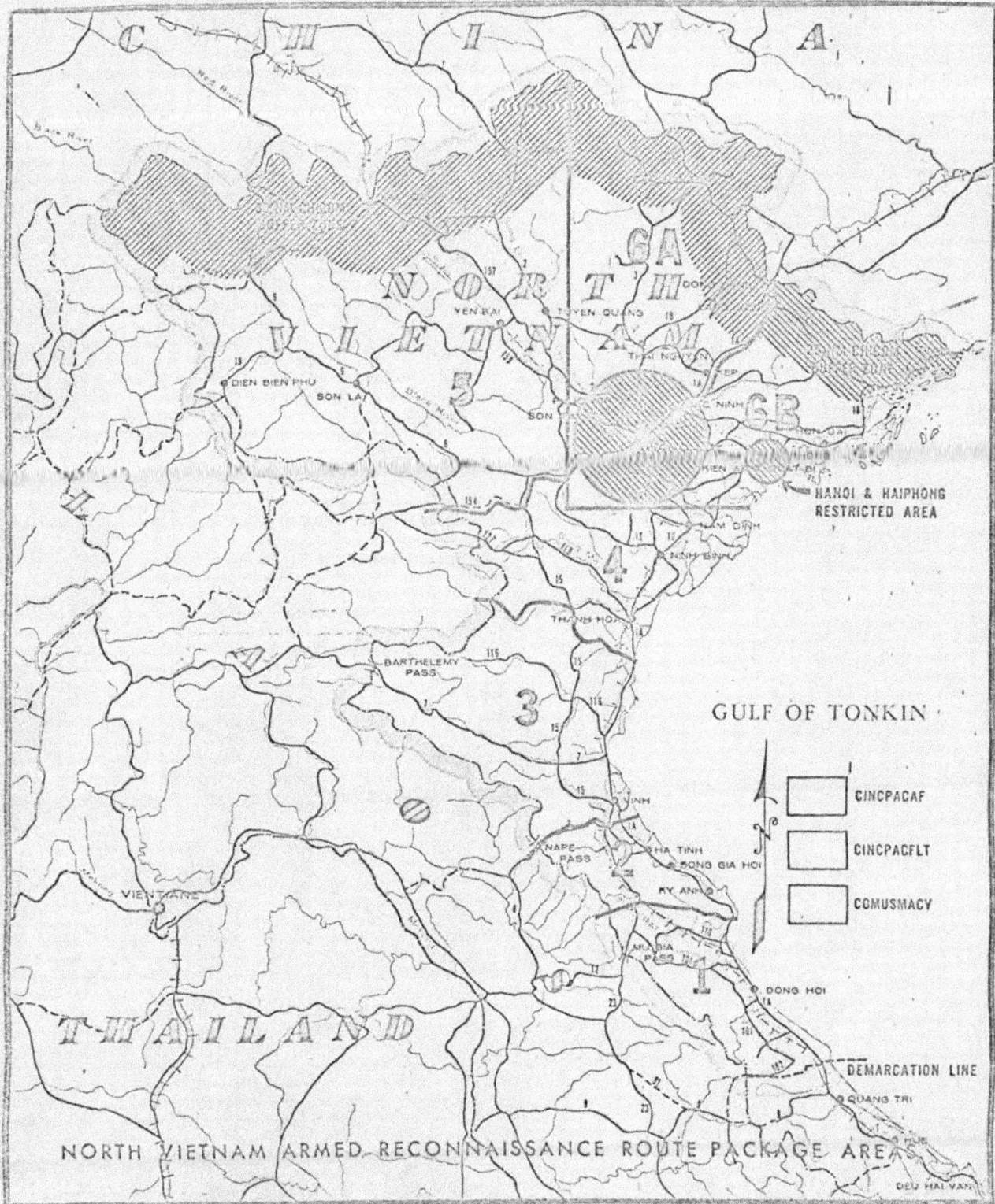

NORTH VIETNAM ARMED RECONNAISSANCE ROUTE PACKAGE AREAS

4

CHRONOLOGY

1 Jul 65	Under SecState George Ball memo to the President	Ball argues for "cutting our losses" in Vietnam and negotiating an end to the war. A massive US intervention would likely require complete achievement of our objectives or humiliation, both at terrible costs.
	Rusk memo to the President	US had to defend South Vietnam from aggression even with US troops to validate the reliability of the US commitment.
	McNamara DPM (revised 20 Jul)	The gravity of the military situation required raising 3rd country troops in SVN from 16 to 44 battalions and intensifying the air war through the mining of Haiphong and other ports, destruction of rail and road bridges from China, and destruction of MIG airfields and SAM sites.
2 Jul 65	JCSM 515-65	The JCS advocate virtually the same air war program as the DPM adding only attacks on "war-making" supplies and facilities. Sorties should increase from 2,000 to 5,000.
13 Jul 65	McNaughton draft memo	Negotiations are unlikely, but even 200,000-400,000 men may only give us a 50-50 chance of a win by 1968; infiltration routes should be hit hard to put a "ceiling" on infiltration.
14-21 Jul 65	McNamara trip to Vietnam	After a week in Vietnam, McNamara returned with a softened version of the DPM.

5

20 Jul 65	McNamara memo to the President	Backing away from his 1 July views, McNamara recommended mining the harbors only as a "severe reprisal." Sorties should be raised to 4,000. Political improvement a must in SVN; low-key diplomacy to lay the groundwork for a settlement.
30 Jul 65	McNamara memo for the President	Future bombing policy should emphasize the threat, minimize DRV loss of face, optimize interdiction over political costs, be coordinated with other pressures on the DRV, and avoid undue risks of escalation.
4-6 Aug 65	McNamara before Senate Armed Services and Appropriation Comte and HASC.	McNamara justifies the Administration's bombing restraint, pointing to the risk of escalation in attacks on POL, airfields or Hanoi-Haiphong areas.
2 Sep 65	JCSM-670-65	The JCS recommend air strikes against "lucrative" NVN targets -- POL, power plants, etc.
15 Sep 65	McNamara memo to CJCS	JCSM 670 is rejected as a dangerous escalatory step.
12 Oct 65	Amb. Thompson memo to McNamara	Thompson, discussing the possibility of a pause, notes need to tell Hanoi we'd resume if the effort failed.
3 Nov 65	McNamara memo to the President	McNamara urges the approval of the bombing "pause" he had first suggested in his 20 Jul memo to test NVN's intentions.
9 Nov 65	State Dept. memo to the President	A State memo to the President, written by U. Alexis Johnson with Rusk's endorsement, opposes a pause at a time when Hanoi has given no sign of willingness to talk. It would waste an important card and give them a chance to blackmail us about resumption.

6

10 Nov 65	JCSM-810-65	The Chiefs propose a systematic air attack on the NVN POL storage and distribution network.
17 Nov 65	DIA memo to McNamara	General Carroll (Dir. DIA) gives an appraisal of the bombing with few bright spots.
28-29 Nov 65	McNamara-Wheeler trip to Vietnam	McNamara and General Wheeler make a hurried trip to Vietnam to consider force increases.
30 Nov 65	McNamara report to the President	Among other parts of the report, McNamara urges a pause in the bombing to prepare the American public for future escalations and to give Hanoi a last chance to save face.
1 Dec 65	W. Bundy draft memo to the President	Bundy summarizes the pros and cons with respect to a pause and concludes against it.
3 Dec 65	McNaughton memo	McNaughton favors a "hard-line" pause with resumption unless the DRV stopped infiltration and direction of the war, withdrew infiltrators, made the VC stop attacks and stopped interfering with the GVN's exercise of its functions.
6 Dec 65	State Dept. memo to the President	Rusk having apparently been convinced, this new draft by Bundy and Johnson recommends a pause.
8 Dec 65	McNamara memo to the President	McNamara states that he is giving consideration to the JCS proposal for attacking the NVN POL system.
24 Dec 65	State msg 1786 to Lodge	The bombing pause begins. It lasts for 37 days until the 31st of January.

7

26 Dec 65	CINCPAC msg 262159Z Dec 65	CINCPAC, dissenting from the pause from the outset, argues for the resumption of the bombing promptly.
27 Dec 65	MACV msg 45265	Westmoreland argues that "immediate resumption is essential."
28 Dec 65	Helms memo to DepSecDef Vance	Estimates that neither the Soviets nor Chinese will actively intervene in the war if the POL system is attacked.
12 Jan 66	CINCPAC msg 120205Z Jan 66	Admiral Sharp urges that the bombing be resumed at substantially higher levels immediately.
15 Jan 66	Bundy "Scenario for Possible Resumption"	Bundy urges that the resumption be at a low level building up again gradually before major new targets like POL are struck.
18 Jan 66	JCSM-41-66	"...offensive air operations against NVN should be resumed now with a sharp blow and thereafter maintained with uninterrupted, increasing pressure." Specifically, the Chiefs called for immediate mining of the ports.
	McNaughton draft, "Some Observations about Bombing..."	Purposes of the bombing are (1) to interdict infiltration; (2) to bring about negotiation; (3) to provide a bargaining counter; and (4) to sustain GVN morale.
24 Jan 66	McNamara memo to the President	McNamara, drawing on the language of McNaughton's earlier memo, recommends resumption with sorties to rise gradually to 4,000 per month and stabilize. Promises are all cautious.

8

Date	Event	Description
25 Jan 66	Ball memo to the President	Ball warns that resumption will pose a grave danger of starting a war with China. He points to the self-generating pressure of the bombing for escalation, shows its ineffectiveness and warns of specific potential targets such as mining the harbors.
31 Jan 66	Bombing resumes	After 37 days the bombing is resumed but with no spectacular targets.
4 Feb 66	SNIE 10-1-66	This special estimate states that increasing the scope and intensity of bombing, including attacks on POL, would not prevent DRV support of higher levels of operations in 1966.
19 Feb 66	JCSM 113-66	The Chiefs urge a sharp escalation of the air war with maximum shock effect.
1 Mar 66	JCSM 130-66	Focusing their recommendations on POL, the Chiefs call it "highest priority action not yet approved." It would have a direct effect in cutting infiltration.
10 Mar 66	JCSM 153-66	Again attacks on POL are urged.
late Mar 66	McNamara memo to the President	This memo to the President contained McNamara's bombing recommendations for April which included hitting 7 of 9 JCS recommended POL storage sites.
28 Mar 66	White House Tuesday Lunch	McNamara's POL recommendation is deferred by the President because of political turmoil in SVN.

5

9 Apr 66	White House Review	A general policy review at the White House includes most of the second-level members of the Administration. Meetings and paper drafting continued until the political crisis in SVN abated in mid-April.
14 Apr 66	JCSM 238-66	The JCS forwarded a voluminous study of the bombing that recommends a much expanded campaign to hit the Haiphong POL, mine the harbors, hit the airfields.
16 Apr 66	Policy debate continues	The high-level policy review continues. Bundy, McNaughton, Carver & Unger draft position papers on the alternatives if the GVN collapses.
26 Apr 66	JCS msg 9326	CINCPAC is informed that RT50 will not include the POL.
27 Apr 66	Taylor memo to the President	General Taylor in a major memo to the President discusses the problem of negotiations describing the bombing and other US military actions as "blue chips" to be bargained away at the negotiation table not given away as a precondition beforehand.
4 May 66	W. Bundy memo to Rusk	Bundy, commenting on Taylor's "blue chip" memo takes a harder position on what we should get for a bombing halt -- i.e. both an end of infiltration and a cessation of VC/NVA military activity in the South.
6 May 66	W. W. Rostow memo to Rusk and McNamara	Rostow urges the attack on POL based on the results such attacks produced against Germany in W.W. II.

10

10 May 66	CINCPAC msg 100730Z May 66	Admiral Sharp again urges the authorization of POL attacks.
22 May 66	MACV msg 17603	General Westmoreland supports CINCPAC's request for strikes on the POL system.
3 Jun 66	UK PM Wilson opposes POL State Dept msg 48 to Oslo.	The President, having decided sometime at the end of May to approve the POL attacks, informs UK PM Wilson. Wilson urges the President to reconsider.
7 Jun 66	Brussels msg 87	Rusk, travelling in Europe, urges the President to defer the POL decision because of the forthcoming visit of Canadian Ambassador Ronning to Hanoi and the possibility of some peace feeler.
8 Jun 66	CIA SC No. 08440/66	"It is estimated that the neutralization of the bulk petroleum storage facilities in NVN will not in itself preclude Hanoi's continued support of essential war activities."
14 Jun 66	CINCPAC msg 140659Z Jun 66	Having been informed of high level consideration of the POL strikes by McNamara, CINCPAC assures they will cause under 50 civilian casualties.
14-18 Jun 66	Ronning Mission	Canadian Ambassador Ronning goes to Hanoi and confers with top DRV leaders. He returns with no message or indication of DRV interest in talks.
22 Jun 66	JCS msg 5003	CINCPAC is ordered to strike the POL at first light on 24 June.
24 Jun 66	POL deferred	Bad weather forces rescheduling of the strikes for 25 June.
25 Jun 66	JCS msg 5311	The POL execute order is rescinded because of a press leak.

28 Jun 66	JCS msg 5414	The POL order is reinstated for 29 June.
29 Jun 66	POL attacks	At long last the POL facilities are struck with initially highly positive damage reports.
8 Jul 66	ROLLING THUNDER Conference in Honolulu	After having been briefed by CINCPAC on the effects of the POL strikes to date, McNamara informs Admiral Sharp that the President wants first priority given to strangulation of the NVN POL system.
	CINCPAC msg 080730Z Jul 66	RT 51 specifies a program for intensive attacks on POL as 1st priority.
24 Jul 66	CINCPAC msg 242069Z Jul 66	As a part of a comprehensive attack on POL storage, Sharp recommends attacks on Kep and Phuc Yen airfields.
1 Aug 66	DIA Special Intelligence	70% of NVN's large bulk POL storage capacity has been destroyed along with 7% of its dispersed storage.
4 Aug 66	SNIE 13-66	NVN was using the POL attacks as a lever to extract more aid from the Chinese and the Soviets.
13-14 Aug 66	Westmoreland sees LBJ	General Westmoreland spends two days at the ranch conferring with the President on the progress of the war and new troop requirements
20 Aug 66	CINCPAC msg 202226Z Aug 66	CINCPAC emphatically opposes any standdown, pause or reduction in the air war.
29 Aug 66	JASON studies	IDA's JASON Division submits four reports on the war done by a special study group of top scientists who stress the ineffectiveness of the bombing, including POL, and recommend the construction of an anti-infiltration barrier across northern South Vietnam and Laos.

12

3 Sep 66	McNamara memo to CJCS	McNamara requests the views of the Chiefs on the proposed barrier.
4 Sep 66	CINCPAC msg 042059Z Sep 66	RT is redirected from a primary POL emphasis to "attrition of men, supplies, equipment...."
8 Sep 66	CM-1732-66	General Wheeler agrees to the creation of a special project for the barrier under General Starbird, but expresses concern that funding of the program not be at the expense of other activities.
12 Sep 66	Joint CIA/DIA Assessment of POL Bombing	The intelligence community turns in an overwhelmingly negative appraisal of the effect of POL attacks. No POL shortages are evident, and in general the bombing has not created insurmountable transportation difficulties, economic dislocations, or weakening of popular morale.
13 Sep 66	CINCPAC msg 130705Z Sep 66	CINCPAC ridicules the idea of a barrier.
15 Sep 66	McNamara memo to Lt Gen Starbird	Starbird is designated as the head of a Joint Task Force for the barrier.
7 Oct 66	JCSM 646-66	In a report on the US worldwide force posture the Chiefs express grave concern at the thinness with which manpower is stretched. They recommend mobilization of the reserves.
10-13 Oct 66	McNamara trip to Vietnam	McNamara, Katzenbach, Wheeler, Komer, McNaughton and others spend three days in Vietnam on a Presidential fact-finder.

Declassified per Executive Order 13526, Section 3.3
NND Project Number: NND 63316. By: NWD Date: 2011

13

14 Oct 66	McNamara memo to the President	With Katzenbach's concurrence, McNamara recommended only 40,000 more troops and the stabiliza-tion of the air war. Noting the inability of the bombing to interdict infiltration, he recommended the barrier to the President. To improve the negotiating climate he proposed either a bombing pause or shifting it away from the northern cities.
	JCSM 672-66	The Chiefs disagree with vir-tually every McNamara recommenda-tion. In addition they urge an escalatory "sharp knock" against NVN.
15 Oct 66	George Carver memo for Dir., CIA	Carver concurs in McNamara's assessment of the bombing and agrees with its stabilization at about 12,000 sorties per month but urges the closing of Haiphong port.
23-25 Oct 66	Manila Conference	The President meets with the heads of government of all the troop contributing nations and agreed positions on the war and the framework of its settlement are worked out. In a private conference, Westmoreland opposes any curtailment of the bombing and urges its expansion. He seemed to have reluctantly accepted the barrier concept.
4 Nov 66	JCSM 702-66	The Chiefs in forwarding the CINCPAC force proposals add a rationale of their own for the bombing: to "make it as diffi-cult and costly as possible" for NVN to continue the war, thereby giving it an incentive to end it.
8 Nov 66	Off-Year Election	In an off-year election, the peace candidates in both parties are all resoundingly defeated.

14

11 Nov 66	McNamara memo to CJCS	The President approved only the modest McNamara force increases and ordered a stabilization of the air war.
17 Nov 66	McNamara DPM on Supplemental Appropriations	McNamara describes for the President the failure of the bombing to reduce infiltration below the essential minimum to sustain current levels of combat in SVN. He argues for the barrier as an alternative.
22 Nov 66	JCSM-727-66	The Chiefs once again oppose holiday standdowns for Christmas, New Year's and Tet citing the massive advantage of them taken by the DRV during the 37-day pause.
13-14 Dec 66	Hanoi attacks hit civilian areas	A series of air attacks on targets in Hanoi in early Dec. culminated in heavy strikes on Dec. 13-14. In the immediate aftermath, the DRV and other communist countries claimed extensive damage in civilian areas. The attacks came at a time when contacts with the DRV through the Poles apparently had appeared promising.
23 Dec 66	10-mile Hanoi prohibited area established	In response to the worldwide criticism for the attacks on civilian areas, a 10-n.m. prohibited area around Hanoi was established with a similar zone for Haiphong. Henceforth attacks within it could only be by specific Presidential authorization.
24 Dec 66	48-hour truce	A 48-hour truce and bombing pause is observed.
31 Dec 66	New Year's truce	A second 48-hour truce is observed. Heavy communist resupply efforts are observed during the standdown.

15

2 Jan 67	MACV msg 00163	Westmoreland opposes the Tet truce based on VC violations of the two truces just completed.
4 Jan 67	CINCPAC msg 040403Z Jan 67	CINCPAC endorses Westmoreland's opposition to the Tet truce.
4 Jan 67	JCSM-6-67	The Chiefs note the heavy DRV resupply during the two truces and oppose the proposed 96-hour Tet truce.
18 Jan 67	JCSM-25-67	The Chiefs renew their opposition to the Tet truce.
	CINCPAC msg 182210Z Jan 67	Admiral Sharp recommends six priority targets for RT in 1967: (1) electric power, (2) the industrial plant, (3) the transportation system in depth, (4) military complexes, (5) POL, (6) Haiphong and the other ports.
25 Jan 67	CINCPAC msg 252126Z Jan 67	Sharp again urges the attack of Haiphong and an intensified overall campaign.
28 Jan 67	RT 53	No new target categories are approved.
1 Feb 67	CINCPAC msg 012005Z Feb 67	Keeping up his barrage of cables, Sharp urges the closing of the NVN ports by aerial mining.
2 Feb 67	Marks (Dir., USIA) memo to Rusk	Marks proposes extending the Tet truce for 12 to 24 hours in an effort to get negotiations started.
	JCSM 59-67	The Chiefs propose the mining of selected inland waterways and selected coastal areas to inhibit internal sea transportation in NVN.
3 Feb 67	McNaughton "Scenario"	A handwritten "Scenario" for the pause by McNaughton which notes McNamara's approval calls for extension of the Tet truce to 7 days to get negotiations started

16

8 Feb 67	President's letter to Ho Chi Minh	The President invites Ho to indicate what reciprocity he might expect from a bombing halt. The letter is transmitted in Moscow Feb. 8.
8-14 Feb 67	Tet truce	While this truce was in effect frantic efforts were undertaken by UK PM Wilson and Premier Kosygin in London to get peace talks started. In the end these failed because the enormous DRV resupply effort forces the President to resume the bombing after having first extended the pause.
15 Feb 67	Ho Chi Minh letter to President	Replying to the President's letter, Ho rejects the US conditions and reiterates that unconditional cessation of the bombing must precede any talks.
19 Feb 67	Moscow msg 3568	Amb. Thompson indicates the Soviets would react extremely adversely to the mining of Haiphong.
21 Feb 67	Vance memo to Katzenbach	Vance sends Katzenbach a package of proposals for the President's night reading. Eight categories of new targets are analyzed; none can seriously undercut the flow of supplies South.
21 Feb 67	W. Bundy memo	Bundy notes that mining of the waterways and coastal areas of the DRV panhandle could be approved without the mining of Haiphong.
	Maxwell Taylor memo to the President	Taylor again considers the question of ceasefire, political settlement and sequencing of agreements. No direct bearing on the situation.

22 Feb 67	Mining waterways approved	The President approved the aerial mining of the water-ways and the attack on the Thai Nguyen Iron and Steel works.
27 Feb 67	1st aerial mining	The first aerial mining of the waterways begins.
10 Mar 67	Thai Nguyen plant struck	The Thai Nguyen Iron and Steel complex is hit for the first time.
	Bundy gives Thieu assurances	Bundy in Saigon sees Thieu with Lodge and assures him the President believes that more pressure must be applied in the North before Ho will change his position.
20-21 Mar 67	Guam Conference	The President leads a full delegation to a conference with Thieu and Ky. Questions of constitutional progress and war progress in the South dominate the discussions. During the conference Ho releases the exchange of letters during Tet. A decision to base B-52s in Thailand is also taken.
8 Apr 67	RT 55	RT 55 includes the Kep airfield, Hanoi power transformer and other industrial sites.
20 Apr 67	JCSM 218-67	The Chiefs endorse Westmoreland's request for 100,000 more troops and 3 more tactical fighter squadrons to keep up the pressure on the North.
	Haiphong power plants struck	After numerous weather aborts, the two Haiphong power plants are struck for the 1st time.
24 Apr 67	Airfields attacked	Two MIG fields come under first-time attack shortly after their authorization.

18

24 Apr 67	R. W. Komer memo	Komer leaves behind some views on the war as he leaves for Vietnam. Negotiations are now unlikely, but bombing won't make Hanoi give in, hence the "critical variable is in the South."
	Moscow msg 4566	Amb. Thompson reports the bad effect of the recent Haiphong attacks on Soviet attitudes.
27 Apr 67	Westmoreland sees the President	Back in the US to speak to LBJ about his troop request and address Congress, Westy tells Johnson, "I am frankly dismayed at even the thought of stopping the bombing...."
1 May 67	W. Bundy memo to Katzenbach	As a part of the policy review in progress since 24 April, Bundy writes a strategy paper opposing more bombing (among other things) because of the likely adverse international effects.
4 May 67	SNIE 11-11-67	Soviets will likely increase aid to the DRV but not help get the conflict to the negotiating table.
	McGeorge Bundy letter to the President	Bundy argues for a ceiling on the US effort in Vietnam and no further escalation of the air war, particularly the mining of Haiphong harbor.
5 May 67	CM-3218-67	General Wheeler takes sharp exception to Bundy's views. Haiphong is the single most valuable and vulnerable NVN target yet unstruck. Also explains the rationale for the attack on the NVN power grid.

19

5 May 67	McNaughton DPM	As a part of the policy review, McNaughton drafts a proposal for cutting the bombing back to 20°. The action was to enhance military effectiveness not improve negotiation prospects, which were dim.
6 May 67	W. W. Rostow memo	After considering three options: closing Haiphong, heavier attacks in the Hanoi-Haiphong area and restriction of bombing to the panhandle only, Rostow recommended concentrating on the panhandle while holding open the option to up the ante farther north if we desired later.
8 May 67	W. Bundy memo	Bundy considers five different bombing packages and finally favors levelling off at current levels with no new targets and more concentration on the panhandle.
12 May 67	CIA Memo Nos. 0642/67 and 0643/67	The bombing has not eroded NVN morale, materially degraded NVN ability to support the war, nor significantly eroded the industrial-military base.
16 May 67	Hanoi power plant authorized	As the debate continues, the President approves the Hanoi power plant.
19 May 67	Hanoi power plant bombed	The power plant, 1 mile from the center of Hanoi, is hit for the first time.
	McNamara DPM (given to the President)	McNamara considered two courses: approval of the military recommendations for escalation in both North and South; de-escalation in the North (20°) and only 30,000 troops in the South. In spite of unfavorable negotiations climate, the second course is recommended because costs and risks of the 1st course were too great.

TOP SECRET - Sensitive

20 May 67	JCSM 286-67	The Chiefs rebut the DPM and call for expansion of the air war "...to include attacks on all airfields, all port complexes, all land and sea lines of communication in the Hanoi-Haiphong area, and mining of coastal harbors and coastal waters."
20 May 67	McNamara memo	McNamara asks CJCS, Dir. CIA, SecNav, and SecAF to analyze (a) cutting back bombing to 20°; and (b) intensifying attacks on LOCs in route packages 6A and 6B but terminating them against industrial targets.
03 May 67	CIA memo 0649/67	CIA opposes the mining of the harbors as too provocative for the Soviets.
26 May 67	CIA memo	With the recent attacks on NVN's power grid 87% of national capacity had been destroyed.
1 Jun 67	JCSM 307-67	The Chiefs take strong exception to the DPM noting its inconsistency with NSAM 288 and the jeopardy into which it would place national objectives in SEA because of the radical and conceptually unsound military methods it proposed, including any curtailment of the bombing.
	Helms letter to McNamara	Responding to McNamara's May 20 request for analysis of two bombing options, Helms states neither will cut down the flow of men and supplies enough "to decrease Hanoi's determination to persist in the war."
2 Jun 67	W. Bundy memo	Bundy, like the Chiefs, rejected the reformulation of objectives in the May 19 DPM. He leaves aside the question of the courses of action to be followed.

TOP SECRET - Sensitive

21

2 Jun 67	JCSM-312-67	The Chiefs, replying to McNamara's May 20 request, again reject all suggestions for a cutback in the bombing.
	SecNav memo to McNamara	The Secretary of the Navy concluded, in reply to the May 20 request, that the cutback to the panhandle would be marginally more productive than the current campaign.
3 Jun 67	SecAF memo to McNamara	Harold Brown favored the expanded campaign against LOCs in northern NVN in his reply to McNamara's May 20 request.
8 Jun 67	Katzenbach memo to McNamara	Katzenbach favors concentrating the bombing against LOCs throughout the country and abandoning attacks on "strategic" targets.
11 Jun 67	Kep Airfield struck	The Kep airfield comes under attack for the 1st time and ten MIGs are destroyed.
12 Jun 67	McNamara DPM	Three bombing programs are offered: (a) intensified attack on Hanoi-Haiphong logistical base; (b) emphasis south of 20°; (c) extension of the current program. McNamara, Vance & SecNav favor B; JCS favor A; SecAF favors C.
15 Jun 67	INR memo to Rusk	Hanoi was possibly reconsidering the desirability of negotiations.
17 Jun 67	Saigon msg 28293	Bunker doubts the effectiveness of bombing at interdiction and therefore urges the rapid completion of the barrier.
21 Jun 67	CINCPAC msg 210430Z Jun 67	Sharp argues that results of the bombing in recent months demonstrate its effectiveness and are a powerful argument for its expansion.

22

23-25 Jun 67	Glassboro Conference	President Johnson meets Soviet Premier Kosygin at Glassboro, N.J. No breakthrough on the war.
3 Jul 67	SecAF memo to McNamara	In a lengthy analytical memo Brown argues for option C, a general expansion of the bombing.
5 Jul 67	JCSM 382-67	The Chiefs reject a Canadian proposal to exchange a bombing halt for re-demilitarization of the DMZ.
7-11 Jul 67	McNamara trip to Vietnam	During McNamara's five day trip, CINCPAC argues against any further limitation of the bombing.
18 Jul 67	JCS msg 1859	RT 57 will be only a limited extension of previous targets. No cutback is planned.
9 Aug 67	Addendum to RT 57	Sixteen JCS fixed targets are added to RT 57 including six within the 10-mile Hanoi zone.
9-25 Aug 67	Stennis Hearings	The Senate Preparedness Sub-committee hears two weeks of testimony on the air war from Wheeler, Sharp, McConnell and finally McNamara. The committee's report condemns the Administration's failure to follow military advice.
11-12 Aug 67	Hanoi struck	Several of the newly authorized Hanoi targets, including the Paul Doumer Bridge are struck.
19 Aug 67	Attacks on Hanoi suspended	CINCPAC is ordered to suspend attacks on Hanoi's 10-mile zone from 24 Aug to 4 Sep.
20 Aug 67	Largest attack of the war	209 sorties are flown, the highest number in the war to date.

TOP SECRET - Sensitive

21 Aug 67	US aircraft lost over China	Two US planes are shot down over China after having strayed off course.
1 Sep 67	President's press conference	The President denies any policy rift within the Administration on the bombing.
7 Sep 67	Hanoi prohibition extended	The prohibition of attack in the 10-mile Hanoi zone is extended indefinitely.
10 Sep 67	Campha port struck	For the first time the port of Campha is struck including its docks.
20 Sep 67	CINCPAC msg 202352Z Sep 67	CINCPAC recommends hitting the MIGs at Phuc Yen air field and air defense controls at Bac Mai.
21 Sep 67	CINCPAC msg 210028Z Sep 67	Sharp urges lifting the 10-mile prohibition around Hanoi.
22 Sep 67	CM-2660-67	General Johnson (Acting CJCS) agrees with CINCPAC: hit Phuc Yen and Bac Mai and lift the 10-mile restriction.
29 Sep 67	San Antonio Formula	The President offers a new basis for stopping the bombing in a San Antonio speech: assurance of productive discussions and that no advantage will be taken of the cessation.
6 Oct 67	CM-2679-67	Specific authority to hit the Hanoi power plant is requested.
8 Oct 67	CINCPAC msg 080762Z Oct 67	Sharp again requests authority to strike Phuc Yen.
17 Oct 67	JCSM 555-67	Reviewing the objectives and limitations of the bombing policy for the President, the Chiefs recommended ten new measures against NVN including mining the ports and removal of all current restrictions on the bombing.

24

20 Oct 67	San Antonio Formula rejected	In an interview with a western communist journalist, NVN's Foreign Minister rejects the San Antonio formula.
21 Oct 67	Pentagon anti-war demonstration	A massive demonstration in Washington against the war ends with a 50,000-man march on the Pentagon.
23 Oct 67	JCSM 567-67	The Chiefs oppose any holiday standdowns or pauses at year's end.
23 Oct 67	JCS msg 9674	Phuc Yen authorized for attack.
25 Oct 67	Phuc Yen struck	Phuc Yen is hit for the 1st time.
27 Oct 67	CM-2707-67	Wheeler proposes reducing the Hanoi-Haiphong prohibited areas to 3 and 1.5 n.m. respectively.
9 Nov 67	Reduction of Hanoi-Haiphong zones refused.	The White House lunch rejects the proposal to reduce the Hanoi-Haiphong prohibited zones.
16 Nov 67	Haiphong bombed	Haiphong's #2 shipyard is hit for the 1st time.
17 Nov 67	Bac Mai hit	Bac Mai airfield near the center of Hanoi is struck for the 1st time.
22 Nov 67	SEACABIN Study	A joint ISA/JS study of the likely DRV reaction to a bombing halt lays stress on the risks to the US.
27 Nov 67	JCSM-663-67	The Chiefs present a plan for the next four months that calls for mining the harbors and lifting all restrictions on Hanoi-Haiphong, except in a 3 and 1.5 n.m. zone respectively. In all, 24 new targets are recommended.

25

28 Nov 67	McNamara's resignation	McNamara's resignation leaks to the press.
14-15 Dec 67	Hanoi RR Bridge struck	The Paul Doumer island highway bridge in Hanoi is struck again.
16 Dec 67	Rusk-McNamara agreement on new targets	The two secretaries reach agreement on ten of the 24 new targets proposed by the Chiefs in late Nov.
	IDA JASON Study	IDA's JASON Division again produces a study of the bombing that emphatically rejects it as a tool of policy.
	JCSM 698-67	Noting that the SEACABIN study did not necessarily reflect JCS views, the Chiefs advise against any bombing halt.
22 Dec 67	Pope asks bombing halt	The Pope calls on both sides to show restraint and on the US to halt the bombing in an effort to start negotiations. The President visits him the next day to reject the idea.
24 Dec 67	Christmas truce	A 24-hour Christmas truce is observed.
31 Dec 67	New Year's truce	Another 24-hour truce.
1 Jan 67	CINCPAC msg 010156Z Jan 68	CINCPAC's year end wrapup asserts RT was successful because of materiel destroyed, and manpower diverted to military tasks.
2 Jan 68	COMUSMACV msg 02891	Westmoreland describes the bombing as "indispensable" in cutting the flow of supplies and sustaining his men's morale.
3 Jan 68	JCS msg 6402	Bombing is completely prohibited again within 5 n.m. of Hanoi and Haiphong, apparently related to a diplomatic effort.

26

16 Jan 68	White House meeting	Two new targets are authorized but the 5 n.m. zones are reaffirmed.
25 Jan 68	Clifford testimony	Clark Clifford in his confirmation hearings states that "no advantage" means normal resupply may continue.
29 Jan 68	Tet truce begins	The Tet truce begins but is broken almost immediately by communist attacks.
31 Jan 68	Tet offensive	The VC/NVA attack all major towns and cities, invade the US Embassy and the Presidential Palace. Hue is occupied and held well into Feb.
3 Feb 68	JCSM 78-68	Citing the Tet offensive, the Chiefs ask for reduction of the restricted zones to 3 and 1.5 n.m.
5 Feb 68	Warnke memo to McNamara	Warnke opposes the reduction of the sanctuary because of the danger of civilian casualties. Reduction not approved.
10 Feb 68	Haiphong struck	After a month of restriction, Haiphong is again struck.
23-25 Feb 68	Wheeler visits Vietnam	Gen. Wheeler at the President's direction goes to Vietnam and confers with Westmoreland on required reinforcements.
27 Feb 68	Wheeler Report	Wheeler endorses Westmoreland's request for 200,000 more men.
	CIA memo	Hanoi unlikely to seek negotiations but rather will press the military campaign.
28 Feb 68	Clifford Group	The President asks Clifford to conduct a high-level "A to Z" review of US policy in Vietnam. The Group meets at the Pentagon and work begins. It continues until a DPM is finally agreed on Mar. 4.

27

29 Feb 68	W. Bundy memo to Warnke, et. al.	Bundy considers several alternative courses including mining the harbors and all-out bombing. Without indicating a preference he indicates no unacceptably adverse Soviet or Chinese reaction to any course except invasion.
29 Feb 68	Taylor memo to the President	Taylor proposes three possible packages of responses to Tet and Westmoreland's request. All three called for removal of the San Antonio formula and no new negotiating initiative.
1 Mar 68	Moscow msg 2983	Thompson gives his assessment of Soviet reactions to various US actions. "...any serious escalation except in South Vietnam would trigger strong Soviet response...."
3 Mar 68	DPM	The 3 Mar. draft memo rejects any bombing escalation, particularly mining the harbors or reducing the Hanoi-Haiphong restriction circles. It also rejects Westmoreland's troop requests.
	Clifford Group meeting	The Clifford Group rejects the DPM's "demographic frontier" tactical concept for SVN and is divided about the bombing. Wheeler is adamant for an escalation.
4 Mar 68	DPM	A new draft is completed and Clifford sends it to the President. It proposes no new peace initiative and includes both the JCS proposal for escalation of the bombing, and the ISA position that it should be stabilized. In transmitting the DPM, Clifford apparently also suggested to the President the idea of halting the bombing north of 20°, an idea discussed in the Clifford Group.

TOP SECRET - Sensitive

4 Mar 68	SecAF memo to Nitze	Brown presents three alternative air war escalations that might produce better results.
5 Mar 68	Rusk "Draft Statement"	A note to Wheeler for information from Clifford transmits a "draft statement" by Rusk announcing a bombing halt north of 20°. An attached rationale does not foresee negotiations resulting but indicates the time is opportune because of forthcoming bad weather over much of NVN.
11 Mar 68	New Hampshire Primary	President Johnson only narrowly defeats Eugene McCarthy in a great moral victory for anti-Administration doves.
16 Mar 68	Kennedy announces	Robert Kennedy, spurred by the New Hampshire results, announces for the Presidency.
	ISA DPM	An ISA draft memo that never gets SecDef signature proposes the concentration of the bombing south of 20° on the infiltration routes, with only enough sorties northward to prevent relocation of DRV air defenses to the south.
18-19 Mar 68	"Senior Informal Advisory Group"	Nine prestigious former Presidential advisors gather at the White House for briefings on the Vietnam situation. After hearing a report from State, DoD and CIA, they recommended against further escalation in favor of greater efforts to get peace talks started.
22 Mar 68	Westmoreland reassigned	The President announced that Westmoreland would return to become CofS Army in the summer.

TOP SECRET - Sensitive

29

25-26 Mar 68	Abrams confers with the President	General Abrams, DepCOMUSMACV, returns unexpectedly to Washington and confers with the President. He is presumably told of his new assignment to replace Westmoreland and of the President's decision for a partial bombing halt.
30 Mar 68	State msg 139431	US Ambassadors to the allied countries are informed of the forthcoming announcement of a partial bombing halt. The likelihood of a DRV response is discounted.
31 Mar 68	The President withdraws	The President announces the partial bombing halt on nation-wide TV and ends his speech with the surprise announcement of his own withdrawal as a candidate for re-election.

TABLE OF CONTENTS
AND INDEX

31

VOLUME I

THE AIR WAR IN NORTH VIETNAM

TABLE OF CONTENTS AND OUTLINE

I. JULY 1965 TO THE YEAR-
END BOMBING PAUSE

THE AIR WAR IN NORTH VIETNAM

I.   JULY 1965 TO THE YEAR-END BOMBING PAUSE

A.   Introduction -- Where We Stood At Mid-Summer

By the summer of 1965, a U.S. campaign of sustained, almost daily air strikes against NVN was well underway, with token GVN participation. Most of the important bombing policy issues had been settled, and the general outlines of the campaign had become clear. Military proposals to seek a quick and decisive solution to the Vietnam War through bombing NVN -- proposals which called for an intensive campaign to apply maximum practicable military pressure in a short time -- had been entertained and rejected. Instead, what was undertaken was a graduated program, nicknamed ROLLING THUNDER, definitely ascending in tempo and posing a potential threat of heavy bombing pressure, but starting low and stretching out over a prolonged period.

U.S. decision-makers apparently accepted the military view that a limited, gradual program would exert less pressure upon NVN than a program of heavy bombing from the outset, and they apparently granted that less pressure was less likely to get NVN to scale down or call off the insurgency, or enter into reasonable negotiations. They felt, however, that all-out bombing would pose far greater risks of widening the war, would transmit a signal strength out of all proportion to the limited objectives and intentions of the U.S. in Southeast Asia, would carry unacceptable political penalties, and would perhaps foreclose the promise of achieving U.S. goals at a relatively low level of violence.

The decision-makers accordingly elected to proceed with the bombing in a slow, steady, deliberate manner, beginning with a few infiltration-associated targets in southern NVN and gradually moving northward with progressively more severe attacks on a wider variety of targets. The pattern adopted was designed to preserve the options to proceed or not, escalate or not, or quicken the pace or not, depending on NVN's reactions. The carrot of stopping the bombing was deemed as important as the stick of continuing it, and bombing pauses were provided for. It was hoped that this track of major military escalation of the war could be accompanied by a parallel diplomatic track to bring the war to an end, and that both tracks could be coordinated.

By the summer of 1965, bombing NVN had also been relegated to a secondary role in U.S. military strategy for dealing with the war. Earlier expectations that bombing and other pressures on NVN would

constitute the primary means for the U.S. to turn the tide of the war
had been overtaken by the President's decision to send in substantial
U.S. ground forces for combat in SVN. With this decision the main
hope had shifted from inflicting pain in the North to proving, in the
South, that NVN could not win a military victory there. ROLLING
THUNDER was counted as useful and necessary, but in the prevailing
view it was a supplement and not a substitute for efforts within SVN.
From the first, strike requirements in SVN had first call on U.S. air
assets in Southeast Asia.

Nonetheless, ROLLING THUNDER was a comparatively risky and
politically sensitive component of U.S. strategy, and national authorities kept it under strict and careful policy control. The strikes
were carried out only by fighter-bombers, in low-altitude precision-
bombing modes, and populated areas were scrupulously avoided. Final
target determinations were made in Washington, with due attention to
the nature of the target, its geographical location, the weight of
attack, the risk of collateral damage, and the like. Armed reconnaissance was authorized against targets of opportunity not individually
picked in Washington, but Washington did define the types of targets
which could be hit, set a sortie ceiling on the number of such missions,
and prescribed the areas within which they could be flown.

National authorities also closely regulated the rate of
escalation by discouraging the preparation of extended campaign plans
which might permit any great latitude in the field. They accepted
bombing proposals only in weekly target packages. Each target package,
moreover, had to pass through a chain of approvals which included senior
levels of OSD, the Department of State, and the White House, up to and
including the principals themselves.

Within this framework of action the ROLLING THUNDER program
had been permitted to grow in intensity. By mid-1965 the number of
strikes against targets in the JCS master list of major targets had
increased from one or two per week to ten or twelve per week. The geographic coverage of the strikes had been extended in stages, first across
the 19th parallel, from there to the 20th, and then up to 20°30' North.
The assortment of targets had been widened, from military barracks,
ammunition depots, and radar sites at first, to bridges, airfields,
naval bases, radio facilities, railroad yards, oil storage sites, and
even power plants. The targets authorized for strike by armed reconnaissance aircraft were also expanded from vehicles, locomotives, and
railroad cars to ferries, lighters, barges, road repair equipment, and
.bivouac and maintenance areas; and aircraft on these missions were
authorized to interdict LOCs by cratering, restriking, and seeding
chokepoints as necessary. The number of attack sorties -- strike and
flak suppression -- had risen to more than 500 per week, and the total
sorties flown to about 900 per week, four or five times what they had
been at the outset.

35

        This early ROLLING THUNDER program had already scored some
immediate political and psychological gains. Prior to the bombing,
U.S. authorities were coping with what Presidential Assistant McGeorge
Bundy called a "widespread belief" that the U.S. lacked the will and
determination to do what was necessary in Southeast Asia. The initiation of ROLLING THUNDER, followed by a series of military actions
which in effect made the U.S. a full co-belligerent in the war, did
much to correct that belief. The South Vietnamese were given an
important boost in morale, both by the show of greater U.S. support
and by the inauguration of joint retaliation against their enemy in
the North. Thailand and other countries in Southeast Asia, which had
been watching SVN slide rapidly downhill while the U.S. seemed to be
debating what to do, no doubt received the same kind of lift as well.

        The bombing had also served several unilateral U.S. inter-
ests. It gave a clear signal to NVN -- and indirectly to China --
that the U.S. did not intend to suffer the takeover of SVN without a
fight. It served notice that if pressed the U.S. would not necessarily
recognize privileged sanctuaries. And it provided the U.S. with a
new bargaining chip, something which it could offer to give up in
return for a reduction or cessation of NVN's effort in the South.

        Despite such gains, the overall effect of initiating
ROLLING THUNDER was somewhat disappointing. The hopes in some quarters that merely posing a credible threat of substantial damage to
come might be sufficient "pressure" to bring Hanoi around had been
frustrated. U.S. negotiation overtures had been rejected, and Hanoi's
position had if anything hardened. Infiltration South had continued
and intensified. The signs indicated that Hanoi was determined to
ride out the bombing, at least at the levels sustained up to mid-1965,
while continuing to prosecute the war vigorously in the South. It was
evident that the U.S. faced a long-haul effort of uncertain duration.

        Although the real target of the early ROLLING THUNDER
program was the will of NVN to continue the aggression in the South,
the public rationale for the bombing had been expressed in terms of
NVN's capability to continue that aggression. The public was told
that NVN was being bombed because it was infiltrating men and supplies
into SVN; the targets of the bombing were directly or indirectly related
to that infiltration; and the purpose of attacking them was to reduce
the flow and/or to increase the costs of that infiltration. Such a
rationale was consistent with the overall position which morally justified U.S. intervention in the war in terms of NVN's own intervention;
and it specifically put the bombing in a politically acceptable military
idiom of interdiction.

36

This public rationale for the bombing had increasingly become the most acceptable internal rationale as well, as decision-makers sought to prevent runaway escalation and to hold down the bombing in what they thought should be a secondary role in the war. As a venture in "strategic persuasion" the bombing had not worked. The most obvious reason was that it was too light, gave too subdued and uncertain a signal, and exerted too little pain. Hardly any of the targets most valued by Hanoi -- the "lucrative" targets of the JCS master list -- had been hit. If the main purpose of ROLLING THUNDER was to impose strong pressure on Hanoi's will, the "lucrative" targets in the Hanoi/Haiphong area, not those in the barren southern Panhandle, were the ones to go after, and to hit hard. Aerial bombardment could then perform in its proven strategic role, and even if the risks of such a course were greater it was precisely because the potential payoff was greater.

If, however, the emphasis could be shifted toward interdiction, it would be easier to confine targets to those of direct military relevance to the VC/NVA campaign in the South, and it would be easier to contain the pressures to escalate the bombing rapidly into the northern heart of NVN's population and industry. A continuing emphasis on the Panhandle LOCs could be defended more easily, if the main purpose was to actually handicap NVN's efforts to support and strengthen VC/NVA forces in the South, and it was less likely to generate adverse political repercussions.

The interdiction rationale had come to the fore by mid-1965, both within the government and before the public. There were still internal and external pressures to proceed faster and farther, of course, because interdiction effects had not been impressive either. Official spokesmen conceded that complete interdiction was impossible: the flow of men and supplies from the North, however vital to the enemy effort in the South, was quite small and could hardly be cut off by bombing alone. They explained that the bombing had "disrupted" the flow, "slowed" it down, and made it "more difficult" and "costly." They showed dramatic aerial photos of bridges destroyed, and implied that the enemy was being forced "off the rails onto the highways and off the highways onto their feet." They could not, however, point to any specific evidence that bombing the North had as yet had any impact on the war in the South. Almost inevitably, therefore, even within the interdiction rationale, the conclusion was that the bombing had been too restrained. It was argued that the predictably gradual pace had allowed NVN to easily adjust to, circumvent, or otherwise overcome the effects of the disruptions and other difficulties caused by the bombing, and that only an expanded bombing program could produce significant material results.

37

TOP SECRET - Sensitive

Thus, the outlook in mid-1965 was for some further escalation of the bombing, with a certain amount of tension between pressures to speed it up and counter-pressures to keep it in check. With the debate increasingly forced into the interdiction context, the prospect was for gradual rather than sudden escalation, and strong resistance to going all the way if necessary to break Hanoi's will could be predicted. There was still a gap between those who thought of the bombing as a primarily political instrument and those who sought genuine military objectives, and this would continue to confuse the debate about how fast and far to go, but the main lines of the debate were set.

Still unresolved in mid-1965 was the problem of the diplomatic track. Could the U.S. continue to escalate the bombing, maintaining a credible threat of further action, while at the same time seeking to negotiate? Could the U.S. orchestrate communications with Hanoi with an intensifying bombing campaign? As of mid-1965 this was an open question.

B.   The July Escalation Debate

The full U.S. entry into the Vietnam War in the spring of 1965 -- with the launching of air strikes against NVN, the release of U.S. jet aircraft for close support of ARVN troops in SVN, and the deployment to SVN of major U.S. ground forces for combat -- did not bring an immediate turnabout in the security situation in SVN. The VC/NVA may have been surprised and stunned at first by the U.S. actions, but by the summer of 1965 they had again seized the initiative they held in late 1964 and early 1965 and were again mounting large-scale attacks, hurting ARVN forces badly. In mid-July Assistant Secretary McNaughton described the situation in ominous terms:

The situation is worse than a year ago (when it was worse than a year before that)....A hard VC push is on....The US air strikes against the North and US combat-troop deployments have erased any South Vietnamese fears that the US will forsake them; but the government is able to provide security to fewer and fewer people in less and less territory, fewer roads and railroads are usable, the economy is deteriorating, and the government in Saigon continues to turn over. Pacification even in the Hop Tac area is making no progress. The government-to-VC ratio overall is now only 3-to-1, and in combat battalions only 1-to-1; government desertions are at a high rate, and the Vietnamese force build-up is stalled; the VC reportedly are trying to double their combat strength. There are no signs that the VC have been throttled by US/GVN interdiction efforts; indeed, there is evidence of further PAVN build-up in the I and II Corps areas. The DRV/VC

5

TOP SECRET - Sensitive

38

seem to believe that SVN is near collapse and show no
signs of being interested in settling for less than a
complete take-over. 1/

Faced with this gloomy situation, the leading question on
the U.S. agenda for Vietnam was a further major escalation of troop
commitments, together with a call-up of reserves, extension of military tours, and a general expansion of the armed forces.

The question of intensifying the air war against the North
was a subsidiary issue, but it was related to the troop question in
several ways. The military view, as reflected in JCS proposals and
proposals from the field, was that the war should be intensified on
all fronts, in the North no less than in the South. There was political merit in this view as well, since it was difficult to publicly
justify sending in masses of troops to slug it out on the ground
without at least trying to see whether stronger pressures against
NVN would help. On the other hand, there was continued high-level
interest in preventing a crisis atmosphere from developing, and in
avoiding any over-reaction by NVN and its allies, so that a simultaneous escalation in both the North and the South needed to be
handled with care. The bombing of the North, coupled with the deployment of substantial forces should not look like an effort to soften
up NVN for an invasion.

During the last days of June with U.S. air operations
against North Vietnam well into their fifth month, with U.S. forces
in South Vietnam embarking for the first time upon major ground
combat operations, and with the President near a decision that would
increase American troop strength in Vietnam from 70,000 to over
200,000, Under-Secretary of State George Ball sent to his colleagues
among the small group of Vietnam "principals" in Washington a memorandum warning that the United States was poised on the brink of a military
and political disaster. 2/ Neither through expanded bombing of the
North nor through a substantial increase in U.S. forces in the South
would the United States be likely to achieve its objectives, Ball
argued. Instead of escalation, he urged, "we should undertake either
to extricate ourselves or to reduce our defense perimeters in South
Viet-Nam to accord with the capabilities of a limited US deployment."

"This is our last clear chance to make this decision," the
Under-Secretary asserted. And in a separate memorandum to the President,
he explained why:

The decision you face now, therefore, is crucial.
Once large numbers of US troops are committed to direct
combat they will begin to take heavy casualties in a

34

war they are ill-equipped to fight in a non-cooperative
if not downright hostile countryside.

Once we suffer large casualties we will have started
a well-nigh irreversible process. Our involvement will be
so great that we cannot -- without national humiliation --
stop short of achieving our complete objectives. Of the
two possibilities I think humiliation would be more likely
than the achievement of our objectives -- even after we
have paid terrible costs. 3/

"Humiliation" was much on the minds of those involved in
the making of American policy for Vietnam during the spring and summer of 1965. The word, or phrases meaning the same thing, appears
in countless memoranda. No one put it as starkly as Assistant Secretary of Defense John McNaughton, who in late March assigned relative
weights to various American objectives in Vietnam. In McNaughton's
view the principal U.S. aim was "to avoid a humiliating US defeat (to
our reputation as a guarantor)." To this he assigned the weight of
70%. Second, but far less important at only 20% was "to keep SVN
(and then adjacent) territory from Chinese hands." And a minor third,
at but 10%, was "to permit the people of SVN to enjoy a better, freer
way of life." 4/

Where Ball differed from all the others was in his willingness to incur "humiliation" that was certain -- but also limited and
short-term -- by withdrawing American forces in order to avoid the
uncertain but not unlikely prospect of a military defeat at a higher
level of involvement. Thus he entitled his memorandum "Cutting Our
Losses in South Viet-Nam." In it and in his companion memorandum to
the President ("A Compromise Solution for South Viet-Nam") he went on
to outline a program, first, of placing a ceiling on U.S. deployments
at present authorized levels (72,000 men) and sharply restricting their
combat roles, and, second, of beginning negotiations with Hanoi for a
cessation of hostilities and the formation in Saigon of a "government
of National Union" that would include representatives of the National
Liberation Front. Ball's argument was based upon his sense of relative
priorities. As he told his colleagues:

The position taken in this memorandum does not
suggest that the United States should abdicate leadership in the cold war. But any prudent military commander carefully selects the terrain on which to stand
and fight, and no great captain has ever been blamed for
a successful tactical withdrawal.

From our point of view, the terrain in South Viet-
Nam could not be worse. Jungles and rice paddies are
not designed for modern arms and, from a military point

of view, this is clearly what General de Gaulle described
to me as a "rotten country."

Politically, South Viet-Nam is a lost cause. The
country is bled white from twenty years of war and the
people are sick of it. The Viet Cong -- as is shown by
the Rand Corporation Motivation and Morale Study -- are
deeply committed.

Hanoi has a Government and a purpose and a discipline.
The "government" in Saigon is a travesty. In a very real
sense, South Viet-Nam is a country with an army and no
government.

In my view, a deep commitment of United States forces
in a land war in South Viet-Nam would be a catastrophic
error. If ever there was an occasion for a tactical withdrawal, this is it. 5/

Ball's argument was perhaps most antithetic to one being put
forward at the same time by Secretary of State Rusk. In a memorandum
he wrote on 1 July, Rusk stated bluntly: "The central objective of
the United States in South Viet-Nam must be to insure that North Viet-
Nam not succeed in taking over or determining the future of South
Viet-Nam by force. We must accomplish this objective without a general
war if possible." 6/ Here was a statement that the American commitment to the Vietnam war was, in effect, absolute, even to the point
of risking general war. The Secretary went on to explain why he felt
that an absolute commitment was necessary:

The integrity of the U.S. commitment is the principal
pillar of peace throughout the world. If that commitment
becomes unreliable, the communist world would draw conclusions
that would lead to our ruin and almost certainly to a catastrophic war. So long as the South Vietnamese are prepared to
fight for themselves, we cannot abandon them without disaster
to peace and to our interests throughout the world.

In short, if "the U.S. commitment" were once seen to be unreliable, the risk of the outbreak of general war would vastly increase.
Therefore, prudence would dictate risking general war, if necessary,
in order to demonstrate that the United States would meet its commitments. In either case, some risk would be involved, but in the latter
case the risk would be lower. The task of the statesman is to choose
among unpalatable alternatives. For the Under-Secretary of State,
this meant an early withdrawal from Vietnam. For the Secretary, it
meant an open-ended commitment.

411

Ball was, of course, alone among the Vietnam principals in arguing for de-escalation and political "compromise." At the same time that he and Rusk wrote these papers, Assistant Secretary of State William Bundy and Secretary of Defense McNamara also went on record with recommendations for the conduct of the war. Bundy's paper, "A 'Middle Way' Course of Action in South Vietnam," argued for a delay in further U.S. troop commitments and in escalation of the bombing campaign against North Vietnam, but a delay only in order to allow the American public time to digest the fact that the United States was engaged in a land war on the Asian mainland, and for U.S. commanders to make certain that their men were, in fact, capable of fighting effectively in conditions of counter-insurgency warfare without either arousing the hostility of the local population or causing the Vietnamese government and army simply to ease up and allow the Americans to "take over" their war. 7/

For McNamara, however, the military situation in South Vietnam was too serious to allow the luxury of delay. In a memorandum to the President drafted on 1 July and then revised on 20 July, immediately following his return from a week-long visit to Vietnam, he recommended an immediate decision to increase the U.S.-Third Country presence from the current 16 maneuver battalions (15 U.S., one Australian) to 44 (34 U.S., nine Korean, one Australian), and a change in the mission of these forces from one of providing support and reinforcement for the ARVN to one which soon became known as "search and destroy" -- as McNamara put it, they were "by aggressive exploitation of superior military forces...to gain and hold the initiative...pressing the fight against VC/DRV main force units in South Vietnam to run them to ground and destroy them." 8/

At the same time, McNamara argued for a substantial intensification of the air war. The 1 July version of his memorandum recommended a total quarantine of the movement of war supplies into North Vietnam, by sea, rail, and road, through the mining of Haiphong and all other harbors and the destruction of rail and road bridges leading from China to Hanoi; the Secretary also urged the destruction of fighter airfields and SAM sites "as necessary" to accomplish these objectives. 9/

On 2 July the JCS, supporting the views in the DPM, reiterated a recommendation for immediate implementation of an intensified bombing program against NVN, to accompany the additional deployments which were under consideration. 10/ The recommendation was for a sharp escalation of the bombing, with the emphasis on interdiction of supplies into as well as out of NVN. Like the DPM, it called for interdicting the movement of "war supplies" into NVN by mining the major ports and cutting the rail and highway bridges on the LOCs from China to Hanoi; mounting intensive armed reconnaissance against all LOCs and LOC facilities

9

42

within NVN; destroying the "war-making" supplies and facilities of NVN, especially POL; and destroying airfields and SAM sites as necessary to accomplish the other tasks. The JCS estimated that an increase from the then 2000 to about 5000 attack sorties per month would be required to carry out the program.

The elements of greater risk in the JCS proposals were obvious. The recommendation to mine ports and to strike airfields and SAM sites had already been rejected as having special Soviet or Chinese escalatory implications, and even air strikes against LOCs from China were considered dangerous. U.S. intelligence agencies believed that if such strikes occurred the Chinese might deliberately engage U.S. aircraft over NVN from bases in China. CIA thought the chances were "about even" that this would occur; DIA and the Service intelligence agencies thought the chances of this would increase but considered it still unlikely; and State thought the chances "better than even." 11/

Apart from this element of greater risk, however, intelligence agencies held out some hope that an intensified bombing program like that proposed by the JCS (less mining the ports, which they were not asked to consider) would badly hurt the NVN economy, damage NVN's ability to support the effort in SVN, and even lead Hanoi to consider negotiations. An SNIE of 23 July estimated that the extension of air attacks only to military targets in the Hanoi/Haiphong area was not likely to "significantly injure the Viet Cong ability to persevere" or to "persuade the Hanoi government that the price of persisting was unacceptably high." Sustained interdiction of the LOCs from China, in addition, would make the delivery of Soviet and Chinese aid more difficult and costly and would have a serious impact on the NVN economy, but it would still not have a "critical impact" on "the Communist determination to persevere" and would not seriously impair Viet Cong capabilities in SVN, "at least for the short term." However:

If, in addition, POL targets in the Hanoi-Haiphong area were destroyed by air attacks, the DRV's capability to provide transportation for the general economy would be severely reduced. It would also complicate their military logistics. If additional PAVN forces were employed in South Vietnam on a scale sufficient to counter increased US troop strength /which the SNIE said was "almost certain" to happen/ this would substantially increase the amount of supplies needed in the South. The Viet Cong also depend on supplies from the North to maintain their present level of large-scale operations. The accumulated strains of a prolonged curtailment of supplies received from North Vietnam would obviously have an impact on the Communist effort in the South. They would certainly inhibit and

43

might even prevent an increase in large-scale Viet
Cong military activity, though they would probably not
force any significant reduction in Viet Cong terrorist
tactics of harassment and sabotage. These strains,
particularly if they produced a serious check in the
development of Viet Cong capabilities for large-scale
(multi-battalion) operations might lead the Viet Cong
to consider negotiations. 11a/

There were certain reservations with respect to the above
estimate. The State and Army intelligence representatives on USIB
registered a dissent, stating that even under heavier attack the LOC
capacities in NVN and Laos were sufficient to support the war in SVN
at the scale envisaged in the estimate. They also pointed out that
it was impossible to do irreparable damage to the LOCs, that the Communists had demonstrated considerable logistic resourcefulness and
considerable ability to move large amounts of war material long dis-
tances over difficult terrain by primitive means, and that in addition
it was difficult to detect, let alone stop, sea infiltration. On
balance, however, the SNIE came close to predicting that intensified
interdiction attacks would have a beneficial effect on the war in the
South.

Facing a decision with these kinds of implications, the
President wanted more information and asked McNamara to go on another
fact-gathering trip to Vietnam before submitting his final recommendations on a course of action. In anticipation of the trip, McNaughton
prepared a memo summarizing his assessment of the problem. McNaughton
wrote that "meaningful negotiations" were unlikely until the situation
began to look gloomier for the VC, and that even with 200,000-400,000
U.S. troops in SVN the chances of a "win" by 1968 (i.e., in the next
$2\frac{1}{2}$ years) were only 50-50. But he recommended that the infiltration
routes be hit hard, "at least to put a 'ceiling' on what can be infiltrated;" and he recommended that the limit on targets be "just short"
of population targets, the China border, and special targets like SAM
sites which might trigger Soviet or Chinese reactions. 12/

McNamara left for Vietnam on July 14 and returned a week
later with a revised version of his July 1st DPM ready to be sent to
the President as a final recommendation. The impact of the visit was
to soften considerably the position he had apparently earlier taken.
His 20 July memorandum backed off from the 1 July recommendations --
perhaps, although it is impossible to tell from the available materials --
because of intimations that such drastic escalation would be unacceptable
to the President. Instead of mining North Vietnam's harbors as a quarantine measure, the Secretary recommended it as a possible "severe reprisal
should the VC or DRV commit a particularly damaging or horrendous act"
such as "interdiction of the Saigon river." But he recommended a gradual

increase in the number of strike sorties against North Vietnam from the existing 2,500 per month to 4,000 "or more," still "avoiding striking population and industrial targets not closely related to the DRV's supply of war material to the VC."

The urgency which infused McNamara's recommendations stemmed from his estimate that "the situation in South Vietnam is worse than a year ago (when it was worse than a year before that)." The VC had launched a drive "to dismember the nation and maul the army"; since 1 June the GVN had been forced to abandon six district capitals and had only retaken one. Transport and communications lines throughout the country were being cut, isolating the towns and cities and causing sharp deterioration of the already shaky domestic economy. Air Marshal Ky presided over a government of generals which had little prospect of being able to unite or energize the country. In such a situation, U.S. air and ground actions thus far had put to rest Vietnamese fears that they might be abandoned, but they had not decisively affected the course of the war. Therefore, McNamara recommended escalation. His specific recommendations, he noted, were concurred in by General Wheeler and Ambassador-designate Lodge, who accompanied him on his trip to Vietnam, and by Ambassador Taylor, Ambassador Johnson, Admiral Sharp, and General Westmoreland, with whom he conferred there. The rationale for his decisions was supplied by the CIA, whose assessment he quoted with approval in concluding the 1 July version of his memorandum. It stated:

> Over the longer term we doubt if the Communists are likely to change their basic strategy in Vietnam (i.e., aggressive and steadily mounting insurgency) unless and until two conditions prevail: (1) they are forced to accept a situation in the war in the South which offers them no prospect of an early victory and no grounds for hope that they can simply outlast the US and (2) North Vietnam itself is under continuing and increasingly damaging punitive attack. So long as the Communists think they scent the possibility of an early victory (which is probably now the case), we believe that they will persevere and accept extremely severe damage to the North. Conversely, if North Vietnam itself is not hurting, Hanoi's doctrinaire leaders will probably be ready to carry on the Southern struggle almost indefinitely. If, however, both of the conditions outlined above should be brought to pass, we believe Hanoi probably would, at least for a period of time, alter its basic strategy and course of action in South Vietnam.

McNamara's memorandum of 20 July did not include this quotation, although many of these points were made elsewhere in the paper. Instead, it concluded with an optimistic forecast:

45

> The overall evaluation is that the course of action
> recommended in this memorandum -- if the military and
> political moves are properly integrated and executed with
> continuing vigor and visible determination -- stands a
> good chance of achieving an acceptable outcome within a
> reasonable time in Vietnam.

Never again while he was Secretary of Defense would McNamara make so
optimistic a statement about Vietnam -- except in public.

This concluding paragraph of McNamara's memorandum spoke of
political, as well as military, "vigor" and "determination." Earlier
in the paper, under the heading "Expanded political moves," he had
elaborated on this point, writing:

> Together with the above military moves, we should
> take political initiatives in order to lay a groundwork
> for a favorable political settlement by clarifying our
> objectives and establishing channels of communications.
> At the same time as we are taking steps to turn the tide
> in South Vietnam, we would make quiet moves through diplo-
> matic channels (a) to open a dialogue with Moscow and
> Hanoi, and perhaps the VC, looking first toward disabusing
> them of any misconceptions as to our goals and second toward
> laying the groundwork for a settlement when the time is ripe;
> (b) to keep the Soviet Union from deepening its military in
> the world until the time when settlement can be achieved;
> and (c) to cement support for US policy by the US public,
> allies and friends, and to keep international opposition
> at a manageable level. Our efforts may be unproductive
> until the tide begins to turn, but nevertheless they should
> be made.

Here was scarcely a program for drastic political action.
McNamara's essentially procedural (as opposed to substantive) recommendations amounted to little more than saying that the United States
should provide channels for the enemy's discrete and relatively face-
saving surrender when he decided that the game had grown too costly.
This was, in fact, what official Washington (again with the exception
of Ball) meant' in mid-1965 when it spoke of a "political settlement."
(As McNamara noted in a footnote, even this went too far for Ambassador-
designate Lodge, whose view was that "'any further initiative by us
now /before we are strong/ would simply harden the Communist resolve not
to stop fighting.'" In this view Ambassadors Taylor and Johnson concurred, except that they would maintain "discreet contacts with the
Soviets.") 13/

46

McNamara's concluding paragraph spoke of "an acceptable outcome." Previously in his paper he had listed "nine fundamental elements" of a _favorable_ outcome. These were:

(a) VC stop attacks and drastically reduce incidents of terror and sabotage.

(b) DRV reduces infiltration to a trickle, with some reasonably reliable method of our obtaining confirmation of this fact.

(c) US/GVN stop bombing of North Vietnam.

(d) GVN stays independent (hopefully pro-US, but possibly genuinely neutral).

(e) GVN exercises governmental functions over substantially all of South Vietnam.

(f) Communists remain quiescent in Laos and Thailand.

(g) DRV withdraws PAVN forces and other North Vietnamese infiltrators (not regroupees) from South Vietnam.

(h) VC/NLF transform from a military to a purely political organization.

(i) US combat forces (not advisors or AID) withdraw.

These "fundamental elements," McNamara said, could evolve with or without express agreement and, indeed, except for what might be negotiated incidental to a cease-fire they were more likely to evolve without an explicit agreement than with one. So far as the difference between a "favorable" and an "acceptable" outcome was concerned, he continued, there was no need for the present to address the question of whether the United States should "ultimately settle for something less than the nine fundamentals," because the force deployments recommended in the memorandum would be prerequisite to the achievement of _any_ acceptable settlement; "a decision can be made later, when bargaining becomes a reality, whether to compromise in any particular."

In summary, then, McNamara's program consisted of first substantially increasing the pressure on the enemy by every means short of those, such as the bombing of population centers in the North, that would run sizeable risks of precipitating Soviet or Chinese direct intervention in the war, and then seeking a _de facto_ political settlement essentially on US/GVN terms.

47

The July 20 memo to the President was followed up by two others on specific aspects of the problem before the end of July. On July 28, he replied to a series of eighteen points made by Senator Mansfield with respect to the Vietnam war. In so doing, Secretary McNamara informed the President of his doubts that even a "greatly expanded program" could be expected to produce significant NVN interest in a negotiated settlement "until they have been disappointed in their hopes for a quick military success in the South." Meanwhile he favored "strikes at infiltration routes" to impose a ceiling on what NVN could pour into SVN, "thereby putting a ceiling on the size of war that the enemy can wage there." He warned that a greatly increased program would create even more serious risks of "confrontations" with the Soviet Union and China. 14/

McNamara stated that the current bombing program was on the way to accomplishing its purposes and should be continued. The future program, he said, should:

a. Emphasize the threat. It should be structured to capitalize on fear of future attacks. At any time, 'pressure' on the DRV depends not upon the current level of bombing but rather upon the credible threat of future destruction which can be avoided by agreeing to negotiate or agreeing to some settlement in negotiations.

b. Minimize the loss of DRV 'face.' The program should be designed to make it politically easy for the DRV to enter negotiations and to make concessions during negotiations. It may be politically easier for North Vietnam to accept negotiations and/or to make concessions at a time when bombing of their territory is not currently taking place.

c. Optimize interdiction vs. political costs. Interdiction should be carried out so as to maximize effectiveness and to minimize the political repercussions from the methods used. Physically, it makes no difference whether a rifle is interdicted on its way into North Vietnam, on its way out of North Vietnam, in Laos or in South Vietnam. But different amounts of effort and different political prices may be paid depending on how and where it is done. The critical variables in this regard are (1) the type of targets struck, (e.g., port facilities involving civilian casualties vs. isolated bridges), (2) types of aircraft (e.g., B-52s vs. F-105s), (3) kinds of weapons (e.g., napalm vs. ordinary bombs), (4) location of target (e.g., in Hanoi vs. Laotian border area), and (5) the accompanying declaratory policy (e.g., unlimited vs. a defined interdiction zone).

d. Coordinate with other influences on the DRV. So
long as full victory in the South appears likely, the effect
of the bombing program in promoting negotiations or a settlement will probably be small. The bombing program now and
later should be designed for its influence on the DRV at
that unknown time when the DRV becomes more optimistic about
what they can achieve in a settlement acceptable to us than
about what they can achieve by continuation of the war.

e. Avoid undue risks and costs. The program should
avoid bombing which runs a high risk of escalation into war
with the Soviets or China and which is likely to appall allies
and friends. 15/

C. Incremental Escalation

Secretary McNamara's 5 principles prevailed. The bombing
continued to expand and intensify, but there was no abrupt switch in
bombing policy and no sudden escalation. The high-value targets in
the Hanoi/Haiphong area were kept off limits, so as not to "kill the
hostage." Interdiction remained the chief criterion for target selection, and caution continued to be exercised with respect to sensitive
targets. The idea of a possible bombing pause, longer than the last,
was kept alive. 16/ The Secretary refused to approve an overall JCS
concept for fighting the Vietnam War which included much heavier
ROLLING THUNDER strikes against key military and economic targets
coordinated with a blockade and mining attack on NVN ports, 17/ and
he also continued to veto JCS proposals for dramatic attacks on major
POL depots, power plants, airfields, and other "lucrative" targets. 18/

The expansion of ROLLING THUNDER during the rest of 1965
followed the previous pattern of step-by-step progression. The approval
cycle shifted from one-week to two-week target packages. New fixed
targets from the JCS list of major targets, which grew from 94 to 236
by the end of the year, continued to be selected in Washington. The
number of these new targets was kept down to a few per week, most of
them LOC-related. Few strikes were authorized in the vital northeast
quadrant, north of 21° N. and east of 106° E., which contained the
Hanoi/Haiphong urban complexes, the major port facilities, and the
main LOCs to China. In addition, de facto sanctuaries were maintained
in the areas within 30 nautical miles from the center of Hanoi, 10 from
the center of Haiphong, 30 from the Chinese border in the northwest (to
106° E.), and 25 from the Chinese border in the northeast. 19/

The scope of armed reconnaissance missions was also enlarged
but kept within limits. The boundary for such missions was shifted to
the north and west of Hanoi up to the Chinese buffer zone, but it was
kept back from the northeast quadrant, where only individually approved

49

fixed target strikes were authorized. The operational latitude for armed reconnaissance missions was also widened. They were authorized to strike small pre-briefed fixed military targets not on the JCS list (e.g., minor troop staging areas, warehouses, or depots) in the course of executing their LOC attacks, and to restrike previously authorized JCS targets in order to make and keep them inoperable. An armed reconnaissance sortie ceiling continued in effect. It was lifted to 600 per week by October, but then held there until the end of the year. 20/

By the end of 1965 total ROLLING THUNDER attack sorties had levelled off to about 750 per week and total sorties to a little over 1500 per week. All told, some 55,000 sorties had been flown during the year, nearly half of them on attack (strike and flak suppression) missions, and three-fourths of them as armed reconnaissance rather than JCS-directed fixed target strikes. Altogether, ROLLING THUNDER represented only 30 percent of the U.S. air effort in Southeast Asia during the year, in keeping with the rough priorities set by decision-makers at the outset. 21/

Although bombing NVN had done much to generate, as Secretary McNamara put it, "a new school of criticism among liberals and 'peace' groups," whose activities were reflected in a wave of teach-ins and other demonstrations during 1965, 22/   the bombing also drew abundant criticism from more hawkish elements because of its limited nature. As a result, the Secretary and other officials were frequently obliged to defend the bombing restrictions before Congress and the press.

Most of the hawkish criticism of the bombing stemmed from basic disagreement with an air campaign centered upon a tactical inter-diction rationale rather than a punitive rationale more in keeping with strategic uses of air power, a campaign in which the apparent target was the infiltration system rather than the economy as a whole, and in which, as one CIA report put it,

> ...almost 80 percent of North Vietnam's limited modern industrial economy, 75 percent of the nation's population, and the most lucrative military supply and LOC targets have been effectively insulated from air attack. 23/

This kind of criticism of the bombing concentrated on the most conspic-uous aspect of the program, the strikes against fixed targets, and it faulted the program for failing to focus on the kinds of targets which strategic bombing had made familiar in World War II -- power plants, oil depots, harbor facilities, and factories.

Such "strategic" targets had not been entirely exempted from attack, of course, but they had been exempted from attack where they counted most, in the sanctuary areas. This occasioned some embarrassment in the Administration because any attack on such targets seemed inconsistent with a purely interdiction rationale, while failure to attack the most important of them did not satisfy a strategic bombing rationale. Secretary McNamara was pressed hard on these points when he appeared before the Congressional armed services and appropriations committees in August 1965 with a major supplemental budget request for the Vietnam War. Senator Cannon asked:

> I know that our policy was to not attack power stations and certain oil depots and so on earlier. But within the past two weeks we have noticed that you have attacked at least one or more power stations. I am wondering if your policy has actually changed now in regard to the targets. In other words, are we stepping up the desirability of certain targets?

Secretary McNamara replied:

> I would say we are holding primarily to these targets I have outlined. This week's program, for example, includes primarily, I would say, 95 percent of the sorties against fixed targets are against supply depots, ammo depots, barracks...but only one or two percent of the sorties directed against /one power plant/.

> I don't want to mislead you. We are not bombing in the Hanoi...or the Haiphong area. There is a very good reason for that. In Haiphong there is a substantial petroleum dump /for example/. First, there is question whether destruction of that dump would influence the level of supply into South Vietnam. Secondly, General Westmoreland believes that an attack on that would lead to an attack on the petroleum dumps outside of Saigon that contain eighty percent of the petroleum storage for SVN. Thirdly, there is the real possibility that an attack on the Haiphong petroleum would substantially increase the risk of Chinese participation....for all those reasons it seems unwise at this time...to attack that petroleum dump....

In defending the policy of not attacking the powerplants and POL sites concentrated in the Hanoi/Haiphong area, the Secretary did not stress the interdiction purposes of the bombing but rather the risks of widening the war. He explained that an attack on the powerplants and POL sites would require also attacking Phuc Yen airfield and the surrounding SAM sites:

51

I had better not describe how we would handle it
but it would be one whale of a big attack....this might
well trigger, in the view of some, would trigger Chinese
intervention on the ground....This is what we wish to
avoid. 24/

Before the House Committee on Armed Services two days later,
Secretary McNamara stressed both the irrelevance of targets like the
POL facilities at Haiphong to infiltration into the South and the risks
of Chinese intervention:

At present our bombing program against the North is
directed primarily against the military targets that are
associated with the infiltration of men and equipment into
the South, ammo depots, supply depots, barracks areas, the
particular lines of communication over which these move
into the South. For that reason, we have not struck in
the Hanoi area because the targets are not as directly
related to the infiltration of men and equipment as those
outside the area....As to the Haiphong POL....if we
strike that there will be greater pressure on Communist
China to undertake military action in support of the
North Vietnamese....We want to avoid that if we possibly
can. 25/

On other occasions the Secretary put such stress on the limited
interdiction purposes of the bombing that it seemed to virtually rule out
altogether industrial and other "strategic" targets:

...we are seeking by our bombing in North Vietnam
to reduce and make more costly the movement of men and
supplies from North Vietnam into South Vietnam for the
support of the Viet Cong operations in South Vietnam.
That's our primary military objective, and that requires
that we bomb the lines of communication primarily and
secondarily, the ammunition and supply depots....The great
bulk of our bombing...is directed against traffic moving on
roads and railroads, and the other portion...is directed
against specific targets associated with the lines of communication, primarily supply depots and...bridges....We
think our bombing policy is quite properly associated with
the effort to stop the insurgency in South Vietnam. We've
said time after time: It is not our objective to destroy
the Government of North Vietnam. We're not seeking to
widen the war. We do have a limited objective, and that's
why our targeting is limited as it is.

52

When asked whether the U.S. refrained from bombing NVN's more vital
installations because it would escalate the war, the Secretary added:

> Well, I'm saying that the other installations you're
> speaking of are not directly related to insurgency in the
> South, and that's what we're fighting. And that our tar-
> geting should be associated with that insurgency....our
> objective is to show them they can't win in the South.
> Until we do show that to them it's unlikely the insurgency
> in the South will stop. 26/

The Secretary's arguments had difficult sledding, however.
As 1965 ended, the bombing restrictions were still under attack. The
U.S. was heavily engaged in the ground war in the South, and a limited
bombing campaign in the North did not make much sense to those who
wanted to win it. The hawks were very much alive, and there was mounting
pressure to put more lightning and thunder into the air war. At that
point, in not very propitious circumstances, the Administration halted
the bombing entirely, and for 37 days, from 24 December 1965 to 31 January 1966, pursued a vigorous diplomatic offensive to get negotiations
started to end the war.

D.   The "Pause" -- 24 December 1965 to 31 January 1966

   1. The Pre-Pause Debate

          An important element of the program developed by McNamara
and his Assistant Secretary for International Security Affairs, John
McNaughton in July 1965 was a pause in the bombing of North Vietnam.
There had been a five-day pause in May, from the 13th through the 18th,
apparently inspired by the President himself in an effort to see if the
North Vietnamese government -- which had previously indicated that any
progress towards a settlement would be impossible so long as its territory was being bombed -- would respond with de-escalatory measures of
its own. Yet the President also saw a pause as a means of clearing the
way for an increase in the tempo of the air war in the absence of a
satisfactory response from Hanoi. The May pause had been hastily
arranged -- almost, so the record makes it seem, as if on the spur of
the moment -- and advance knowledge of it was so closely held, not only
within the international community but also within the U.S. government,
that no adequate diplomatic preparation could be made. Its most serious shortcoming as an effective instrument of policy, however, lay in
its very brief duration. To have expected a meaningful response in so
short a time, given the complexity of the political relationships not
only within the North Vietnamese government and party, but also between
Hanoi and the NLF in the South, and between Hanoi and its separate (and
quarrelling) supporters within the Communist world, was to expect the
impossible. 27/   Therefore, in his 20 July memorandum to the President,

52

Secretary McNamara wrote: "After the 44 US/third-country battalions
have been deployed and after some strong action has been taken in the
program of bombing the North (e.g., after the key railroad bridges
north of Hanoi have been dropped), we could, as part of a diplomatic
initiative, consider introducing a 6-8 week pause in the program of
bombing the North."

The pause which eventually occurred -- for 37 days, from
December 1965 until 31 January 1966 -- was somewhat shorter than the
six-to-eight weeks McNamara suggested, but it was clearly long enough
to allow the North Vietnamese fully to assess the options before them.
They were not very attractive options, at least in the way they were
seen in Washington. McNamara summarized them in a memorandum to the
President on 30 November:

It is my belief that there should be a three- or
four-week pause /note that McNamara himself no longer
held to the six-to-eight week duration/ in the program
of bombing the North before we either greatly increase
our troop deployments to Vietnam or intensify our strikes
against the North. The reasons for this belief are,
first, that we must lay a foundation in the mind of the
American public and in world opinion for such an enlarged
phase of the war and, second, we should give North Vietnam a face-saving chance to stop the aggression. 28/

In other words, Hanoi should be given the implicit
(although, naturally, not explicitly stated) choice of either giving
up "its side of the war," as Secretary Rusk often put it, or facing
a greater level of punishment from the United States. In an earlier
memorandum, dated 3 November, and given to the President on the 7th,
McNamara had remarked that "a serious effort would be made to avoid
advertising /a pause/ as an ultimatum to the DRV," 29/ yet Hanoi
could scarcely have seen it as anything else. John McNaughton had perfectly encapsulated the Washington establishment's view of a bombing
pause the previous July, when he had noted in pencil in the margin of
a draft memorandum the words "RT /i.e., ROLLING THUNDER/ (incl. Pause),
ratchet." 30/ The image of a ratchet, such as the device which raises
the net on a tennis court, backing off tension between each phase of
increasing it, was precisely what McNaughton and McNamara, William
Bundy and Alexis Johnson at State, and the Joint Chiefs of Staff, had
in mind when they thought of a pause. The only danger was, as McNamara
put it in his memorandum of 3 November, "being trapped in a status-
quo cease-fire or in negotiations which, though unaccompanied by real
concessions by the VC, made it politically costly for us to terminate
the Pause."

54

McNamara and McNaughton were optimistic that, by skillful diplomacy, this pitfall could be avoided. Rusk, Bundy and Johnson,
who had to perform the required diplomatic task, and the Chiefs, who
were professionally distrustful of the diplomatic art and of the ability
of the political decision-makers in Washington to resist the pressures
from the "peace movement" in the United States, were not so sure. The
Chiefs (echoing General Westmoreland and Admiral Sharp) were also opposed
to any measures which would, even momentarily, reduce the pressure on
North Vietnam. The arguments for and against a pause were summarized
in a State Department memorandum to the President on 9 November:

The purposes of -- and Secretary McNamara's arguments
for -- such a pause are four:

(a) It would offer Hanoi and the Viet Cong a chance
to move toward a solution if they should be so inclined,
removing the psychological barrier of continued bombing
and permitting the Soviets and others to bring moderating
arguments to bear;

(b) It would demonstrate to domestic and international critics that we had indeed made every effort for
a peaceful settlement before proceeding to intensified
actions, notably the latter stages of the extrapolated
Rolling Thunder program;

(c) It would probably tend to reduce the dangers of
escalation after we had resumed the bombing, at least insofar as the Soviets were concerned;

(d) It would set the stage for another pause, perhaps in late 1966, which might produce a settlement.

Against these propositions, there are the following
considerations arguing against a pause:

(a) In the absence of any indication from Hanoi as
to what reciprocal action it might take, we could well
find ourselves in the position of having played this very
important card without receiving anything substantial in
return. There are no indications that Hanoi is yet in a
mood to agree to a settlement acceptable to us. The chance
is, therefore, very slight that a pause at this time could
lead to an acceptable settlement.

(b) A unilateral pause at this time would offer an
excellent opportunity for Hanoi to interpose obstacles to
our resumption of bombing and to demoralize South Vietnam

55

by indefinitely dangling before us (and the world) the
prospect of negotiations with no intent of reaching an
acceptable settlement. It might also tempt the Soviet
Union to make threats that would render very difficult a
decision to resume bombing.

(c) In Saigon, obtaining South Vietnamese acquiescence to a pause would be difficult. It could adversely
affect the Government's solidity. Any major falling out
between the Government and the United States or any over-
turn in the Government's political structure could set us
back very severly (sic).

(d) An additional factor is that undertaking the
second course of action following a pause /i.e., "extrapolation"of ROLLING THUNDER/ would give this course a much
more dramatic character, both internationally and domestically, and would, in particular, present the Soviets with
those difficult choices that we have heretofore been successful in avoiding.

After this summary of the competing arguments, the State paper --
speaking for Secretary Rusk -- came down against a bombing pause.
The paper continued:

On balance, the arguments against the pause are convincing to the Secretary of State, who recommends that it
not be undertaken at the present time. The Secretary of
State believes that a pause should be undertaken only when
and if the chances were significantly greater than they
now appear that Hanoi would respond by reciprocal actions
leading in the direction of a peaceful settlement. He
further believes that, from the standpoint of international
and domestic opinion, a pause might become an overriding
requirement only if we were about to reach the advanced
stages of an extrapolated Rolling Thunder program involving
extensive air operations in the Hanoi/Haiphong area. Since
the Secretary of State believes that such advanced stages
are not in themselves desirable until the tide in the South
is more favorable, he does not feel that, even accepting
the point of view of the Secretary of Defense, there is
now any international requirement to consider a "Pause." 31/

Basic to Rusk's position, as John McNaughton pointed out
in a memorandum to Secretary McNamara the same day, was the assumption
that a bombing pause was a "card" which could be "played" only once.
In fact, McNaughton wrote, "it is more reasonable to think that it
could be played any number of times, with the arguments against it,

56

but not those for it, becoming less valid each time." 32/   It was
this argument of McNaughton's which lay behind the Defense position
that one of the chief reasons for a pause was that even if it were to
produce no response from Hanoi, it might set the stage for another
pause, perhaps late in 1966, which might be "productive."

The available materials do not reveal the President's
response to these arguments, but it is clear from the continuing flow
of papers that he delayed positively committing himself either for or
against a pause until very shortly before the actual pause began. Most
of these papers retraced old ground, repeating the arguments which we
have already examined. A State memorandum by William Bundy on 1 December, however, added some new ones. 33/   In summary, they were:

FOR a bombing pause (in addition to those we have already
seen):

--Soviet Ambassador Dobrynin had "recently urged a 'pause'
   on McGeorge Bundy and had pretty clearly indicated the
   Soviets would make a real effort if we undertook one;
   however, he was equally plain in stating that he could
   give no assurance of any clear result."

--"American casualties are mounting and further involvement appears likely. A pause can demonstrate that the
   President has taken every possible means to find a peaceful solution and obtain domestic support for the further
   actions that we will have to take."

--"There are already signs of dissension between Moscow,
   Peking, Hanoi and the Viet Cong. The pause is certain
   to stimulate further dissension on the other side and
   add to the strains in the Communist camp as they argue
   about how to deal with it." Moreover, it would decrease
   the ability of Hanoi or Peking to bring pressure on
   Moscow to escalate Soviet support.

--"Judging by experience during the last war, the resumption of bombing after a pause would be even more painful
   to the population of North Vietnam than a fairly steady
   rate of bombing."

--"The resumption of bombing after a pause, combined with
   increased United States deployments in the South, would
   remove any doubts the other side may have about U.S.
   determination to stay the course and finish the job."

AGAINST a bombing pause, fewer new arguments were
adduced. Those which we have seen, however, were restated with
greater force. Thus it was noted that while Hanoi had said it
could never "negotiate" so long as the bombing continued, it had
given no sign whatsoever that even with a complete cessation (this,
the paper pointed out, and not a "pause," was what the DRV really
insisted upon) it would be led to "meaningful" negotiations or to
de-escalatory actions. It might, for example, offer to enter into
negotiations on condition that the bombing not be resumed and/or
that the NLF be seated at the conference on a basis of full equality
with the GVN. Both of these conditions would be clearly unacceptable to the U.S., which would run the danger of having to resume
bombing in the face of what major sectors of domestic and international
opinion would regard as a "reasonable" Hanoi offer: "In other words,
instead of improving our present peace-seeking posture, we could actually end up by damaging it severely." And in doing so, the U.S. would
"lose the one card that we have which offers any hope of a settlement
that does more than reflect the balance of forces on the ground in
the South." (Here, it may be noted, was the ultimate claim that
could be made for the bombing program in the face of criticism that
it had failed to achieve its objective of interdicting the flow of
men and materials to the South.)

To these arguments, essentially restatements of ones
we have previously seen, were added:

--"There is a danger that, in spite of any steps we may
take to offset it, Hanoi may misread a pause at this
time as indicating that we are giving way to international pressures to stop the bombing of North Vietnam
and that our resolve with respect to South Vietnam is
thus weakening." This danger had recently increased,
the paper noted, because of peace demonstrations in the
United States and the first heavy American casualties
in South Vietnam.

--Just as a pause would make it more difficult to cope
with the domestic "doves," so it would the "hawks"
as well: "Pressure from the Rivers/Nixon sector to
hit Hanoi and Haiphong hard might also increase very
sharply...."

--"If a 'pause' were in fact to lead to negotiations
(with or without resumed bombing), we would then have
continuing serious problems in maintaining South Vietnamese stability. We must also recognize that, although
we ourselves have some fairly good initial ideas of the
positions we would take, we have not been able to go over
the ground with the GVN or to get beyond general propositions on some of which we and they might well disagree."

58

These statements amounted, then, to the contention
that just as the United States could not afford to initiate a bombing
pause that might fail to produce negotiations and a de-escalation,
neither could it afford to initiate one that succeeded.

Bundy's memorandum of 1 December contained no recommendations. It was a draft, sent out for comment to Under-Secretary
Ball, Ambassadors Thompson and Johnson, John McNaughton, and McGeorge
Bundy. Presumably, although there is no indication of it, copies also
went to Secretaries Rusk and McNamara. By 6 December, William Bundy
and Alexis Johnson were able to prepare another version, repeating
the same arguments in briefer compass, and this time making an agreed
recommendation. It stated: "After balancing these opposing considerations, we unanimously recommend that you /i.e., the President/ approve
a pause as soon as possible this month. The decision would, of course,
be subject to consultation and joint action with the GVN." 34/   Thus,
at some point between 9 November and 6 December (the available documents
do not reveal when), Secretary Rusk evidently dropped his objection to
a pause.

Getting the agreement of the Ky government to a pause
was no easy task. Ambassador Lodge reported that he himself opposed
the notion of a pause because of the unsettling effects it would have
on the South Vietnam political situation. Only by making very firm
commitments for large increases in American force levels during the
coming year, Lodge warned, could Washington obtain even Saigon's grudging
acquiescence in a pause. This is not the place to describe the process
by which the GVN's consent was obtained; it is sufficient to note that
nowhere in Saigon, neither within the government nor within the American
Embassy and Military Assistance Command, was the prospect of any relaxation of pressure on the North -- for any reason -- greeted with any
enthusiasm.

2.   Resumption -- When and At What Level?

Implicit in the very notion of "pause," of course, is
the eventual resumption of the activity being discontinued. Among the
principals in Washington concerned with Vietnam, consideration of the
circumstances and conditions in which the bombing of North Vietnam would
be resumed went hand-in-hand with consideration of its interruption.
Relatively early in this process, in his Presidential memorandum of
3 November, Secretary McNamara distinguished between what he termed a
"hard-line" and a "soft-line" pause. "Under a 'hard-line' Pause," he
wrote, "we would be firmly resolved to resume bombing unless the Communists were clearly moving toward meeting our declared terms....Under
a 'soft-line' Pause, we would be willing to feel our way with respect
to termination of the Pause, with less insistence on concrete concessions by the Communists." 35/

26   TOP SECRET - Sensitive

59

McNamara himself came down on the side of a "hard-line" pause -- a "soft-line" pause would make sense, he noted, only if the U.S. sought a "compromise" outcome. The words "hard-line" and "soft-line" became terms of art, employed by all of the principals in their papers dealing with the question of a pause. Throughout this discussion, it was taken for granted that bombing would be resumed. The only point at issue was how. On 3 December, John McNaughton wrote an "eyes only" memorandum (whose eyes was not specified, but presumably they included those of the Secretary of Defense) entitled, "Hard-Line Pause Packaged to Minimize Political Cost of Resuming Bombing." He specified four conditions, all of which would have to be met by the enemy in order to forestall the resumption of bombing:

"a. The DRV stops infiltration and direction of the war.

b. The DRV moves convincingly toward withdrawal of infiltrators.

c. The VC stop attacks, terror and sabotage.

d. The VC stop significant interference with the GVN's exercise of governmental functions over substantially all of South Vietnam." 36/

Clearly it was unlikely that the enemy would even begin to meet any of these conditions, but Hanoi, at least (if not the NLF), might move towards some sort of negotiations. In that event, the resumption of bombing when "peace moves" were afoot would incur a heavy political price for the United States. In order to maintain the political freedom to resume bombing without substantial costs, the U.S. government would have to make clear from the outset that it intended only a pause, certainly not a permanent cessation of the bombing, and that its continuation would depend upon definite actions by the enemy. Yet there was a problem, as McNaughton saw it, as to which definite actions to specify. He recognized that the United States could not easily list the conditions he had put forward earlier in his memorandum. McNaughton expressed his dilemma in the following terms:

Inconsistent objectives. A Pause has two objectives-- (a) To influence the DRV to back out of the war and (b) to create a public impression of US willingness "to try everything" before further increases in military action. To maximize the chance that the DRV would decide to back out would require presenting them with an explicit proposal, in a form where some clearly defined conduct on their part would assure them of no more bombings. The truth of the matter, however, is that the hard-line objective is, in effect, capitulation

by a Communist force which is far from beaten, has unlimited (if unattractive) reserves available in China,
and is confident that it is fighting for a just principle.
To spell out such "capitulation" in explicit terms is
more likely to subject us to ridicule than to produce a
favorable public reaction. It follows that the hard-line
objectives should be blurred somewhat in order to maximize
favorable public reaction, even though such blurring would
reduce the chances of DRV acceptance of the terms.

If McNaughton was reluctant to spell out U.S. "hard-line"
objectives, he was nevertheless anxious not to allow a situation to
develop where the enemy could make its mere participation in negotiations a sufficient quid pro quo for a continuation of the pause. Regarding negotiations, McNaughton suggested, the American position should be:
"We are willing to negotiate no matter what military actions are going
on." Moreover, when bombing was resumed, the ending of the pause should
be tied to Hanoi's failure to take de-escalatory actions. "People might
criticize our Pause for not having been generous," McNaughton wrote, "but
they will be unlikely to attack the US for having failed to live up to the
deal we offered with the Pause." 37/

McNaughton recommended that the first strikes after a
resumption should be "identified as militarily required interdiction,"
in order to minimize political criticism. "Later strikes could then be
escalated to other kinds of targets and to present or higher levels."
(At the time McNaughton wrote, the pause had not yet gone into effect.)
Similar advice came from William Bundy, writing on 15 January during the
pause:

Resumed bombing should not begin with a dramatic
strike that was even at the margin of past practice (such
as the power plant in December). For a period of two-
three weeks at least, while the world is digesting and
assessing the pause, we should do as little as possible
to lend fuel to the charge -- which will doubtless be
the main theme of Communist propaganda -- that the pause
was intended all along merely as a prelude to more drastic action.

Moreover, from a military standpoint alone, the
most immediate need would surely be to deal with the
communications lines and barracks areas south of the
20th parallel. A week or two of this would perhaps
make sense from both military and political stand-
points. After that we could move against the northeast
rail and road lines again, but the very act of gradual-
ness should reduce any chance that the Chicoms /the

61

Chinese Communists_7 will react to some new or dramatic
way when we do so. Extensions of past practice, such
as Haiphong POL /petroleum, oil, and lubricants_7, should
be a third stage. 38/

McNaughton and Bundy were in essential agreement: the
bombing should be resumed; it should be resumed on a low key at first;
but after a decent interval it should be escalated at least to the
extent of striking at the Haiphong POL storage facilities, and perhaps
other high-priority targets as well. In their own eyes the two Assistant
Secretaries were cautious, prudent men. Their recommendations were in
marked contrast to those of the Joint Chiefs of Staff, who (as this paper
shows in greater detail later) pressed throughout the autumn and winter
of 1965-66 for permission to expand the bombing virtually into a program
of strategic bombing aimed at all industrial and economic resources as
well as at all interdiction targets. The Chiefs did so, it may be added,
despite the steady stream of memoranda from the intelligence community
consistently expressing skepticism that bombing of any conceivable sort
(that is, any except bombing aimed primarily at the destruction of North
Vietnam's population) could either persuade Hanoi to negotiate a settlement on US/GVN terms or effectively limit Hanoi's ability to infiltrate
men and supplies into the South.

These arguments of the Chiefs were essentially an extension and amplification of arguments for large-scale resumption received
from the field throughout the pause. Apparently, neither Lodge, Westmoreland, nor Sharp received advance intimation that the suspension might
continue not for a few days, as in the preceding May, but for several weeks.
When notified that full-scale ground operations could recommence, following
the Christmas cease-fire, as soon as there was "confirmed evidence of
significant renewed Viet Cong violence," they were simply told that air
operations against North Vietnam would not immediately resume. They were
assured, however,

We will stand ready to order immediate renewal of
ROLLING THUNDER...at any time based on your reports and
recommendations. 39/

None of the three hesitated long relaying such recommendations. "Although I am not aware of all the considerations leading to the
continuation of the standdown in ROLLING THUNDER," General Westmoreland
cabled on December 27, "I consider that their immediate resumption is
essential." He continued,

"...our only hope of a major impact on the ability of
the DRV to support the war in Vietnam is continuous air
attack over the entire length of their LOC's from the
Chinese border to South Vietnam....Notwithstanding the
heavy pressure on their transportation system in the

62

past 9 months, they have demonstrated an ability to
deploy forces into South Vietnam at a greater rate than
we are deploying U.S. forces....Considering the course
of the war in South Vietnam and the capability which has
been built up here by the PAVN/VC forces -- the full
impact of which we have not yet felt -- the curtailment
of operations in North Vietnam is unsound from a military
standpoint. Indeed, we should no/w_/ step up our effort
to higher levels. 40/

Ambassador Lodge seconded this recommendation, and Admiral Sharp filed
his own pleas not only that ROLLING THUNDER be resumed "at once" but
that his previous recommendations for enlarging it be adopted. The aim
should be to "drastically reduce the flow of military supplies reaching
the DRV and hence the VC," he argued, adding "the armed forces of the
United States should not be required to fight this war with one arm tied
behind their backs." 41/

One reason for ignorance in Saigon and Honolulu of the
bombing suspension's possible continuation was that the President had
apparently never fully committed himself to the timetable proposed by
McNamara. Replying to Lodge on December 28, Rusk cabled a summary of the
President's thinking. As of that moment, said the Secretary of State,
the President contemplated extending the pause only "for several more
days, possibly into middle of next week," i.e., until January 5 or 6.
His aim in stretching out the pause was only in small part to seek negotiations.

We do not, quite frankly, anticipate that Hanoi will
respond in any significant way.... There is only the slimmest
of chances that suspension of bombing will be occasion for
basic change of objective by other side but communist propaganda on this subject should be tested and exposed.

The key reasons for extending the pause, Lodge was told, were diplomatic
and domestic. Some hope existed of using the interval to "drive /a_/
rift between Communist powers and between Hanoi and NLF." Even more
hopeful were indications that the government's act of self-abnegation
would draw support at home. The latest Harris poll, Lodge was informed,
showed 73% favoring a new effort for a cease-fire, 59% in favor of a
bombing pause, and 61% in favor of stepping up bombing if the pause produced no result.

The prospect of large-scale reinforcement in men and
defense budget increases of some twenty billions for the
next eighteen month period requires solid preparation of
the American public. A crucial element will be clear
demonstration that we have explored fully every alternative but that aggressor has left us no choice. 42/

63

This message went to Lodge as "EYES ONLY" for himself
and Ambassador Porter. To what extent its contents were shared with
General Westmoreland or other military or naval personnel, available
documents do not indicate. In any case, the Embassy in Saigon had
received from the very highest authority the same kind of intimation
that opponents of the pause had been given in Washington. If the
period of inaction would prepare American and world opinion for more
severe measures, it followed that the next stage would see such measures
put into effect.

As the pause continued beyond the deadline mentioned to
Lodge, military planners in Saigon, Honolulu, and Washington worked
at defining what these severe measures ought to be. On January 12,
Admiral Sharp sent the Joint Chiefs a long cable, summarizing the
conclusions of intensive planning by his staff and that of COMUSMACV.

> We began R/olling7 T/hunder7 with very limited
> objectives, at a time when PAVN infiltration was of less
> significance than it is now,

CINCPAC commented,

> ....When RT began, there was considerable hope of
> causing Hanoi to cease aggression through an increasing
> pressure brought to bear through carefully timed destruc-
> tion of selected resources, accompanied by threat of
> greater losses...But...the nature of the war has changed
> since the air campaign began. RT has not forced Hanoi
> to the decision which we sought. There is now every indi-
> cation that Ho Chi Minh intends to continue support of the
> VC until he is denied the capability to do so....We must
> do all that we can to make it as difficult and costly as
> possible for Hanoi to continue direction and support of
> aggression. In good conscience, we should not long delay
> resumption of a RT program designed to meet the changed
> nature of the war.

Specifically, Admiral Sharp recommended:

1. "....interdiction of land LOC's from China and closing
   of the ports..../the7 northeast quadrant....must be
   opened up for armed recce with authority to attack
   LOC targets as necessary."

2. "Destruction of resources within NVN should begin
   with POL. Every known POL facility and distribution
   activity should be destroyed and harassed until the
   war is concluded. Denial of electric power facilities
   should begin at an early date and continue until all

64

plants are out of action....All large military
facilities should be destroyed in Northern NVN....

3. We should mount an intensified armed reconnsaissance
program without sortie restriction, to harass, disrupt and attrit/e 7 the dispersed and hidden military
facilities and activities south of 20 deg/rees7....

These three tasks well done will bring the enemy to
the conference table or cause the insurgency to wither
from lack of support. The alternative appears to be a
long and costly counterinsurgency -- costly in U.S. and
GVN lives and material resources. 43/

Writing the Secretary of Defense on January 18, the
Joint Chiefs offered an equally bold definition of a post-pause
bombing campaign. The Chiefs argued that the piecemeal nature of
previous attacks had permitted the DRV to adapt itself to the bomb-
-ing, replenish and disperse its stocks, diversify its transportation
system and improve its defenses. Complaining about the geographic
and numerical restrictions on the bombing, the Chiefs recommended
that "offensive air operations against NVN should be resumed now with
a sharp blow and thereafter maintained with uninterrupted, increasing
pressure. 44/ The Chiefs further argued that,

These operations should be conducted in such a
manner and be of sufficient magnitude to: deny the
DRV large-scale external assistance; destroy those
resources already in NVN which contribute most to the
support of aggression; destroy or deny use of military
facilities; and harass, disrupt and impede the movement
of men and materials into SVN. 45/

The shutting off of external assistance would require,

...closing of the ports as well as sustained interdiction of land LOCs from China....Military considerations would dictate that mining be conducted now; however,
the Joint Chiefs...appreciate the sensitivity of such a
measure and recognize that precise timing must take into
account political factors. 46/

In addition to endorsing the full-scale attacks on POL,
electric power plants, large military facilities in northern NVN, and
LOC centers and choke points with intensified armed reconnaissance,

65

unhampered by the existing restrictions on sortie number, that CINCPAC
has recommended, the Chiefs urged the reduction of the size of the
sanctuaries around Hanoi, Haiphong and the China border. More importantly, the Chiefs requested authorization to eliminate the airfields
if required and permission for operational commanders "to deal with the
SAM threat, as required to prevent interference with planned air operations." 47/

The Chiefs acknowledged the likely adverse response to
this sharp escalation in the international community, but urged the
necessity of the proposed actions. In dealing with the anxieties about
Chinese communist entry into the war, they neatly turned the usual argument that China would enter the war in response to escalatory provocation
on its head by arguing that a greater likelihood was Chinese entry through
miscalculation.

> The Joint Chiefs...believe that continued US restraint
> may serve to increase rather than decrease the likelihood
> of such intervention /Chinese/ by encouraging gradual
> responses on the part of the Chinese Communists. This is
> in addition to the probable interpretation of such restraint
> as US vacillation by both the Communist and Free World
> leadership. 48/

The Chiefs spelled out their specific proposals in their concluding recommendations:

> a. The authorized area for offensive air operations
> be expanded to include all of NVN less the area encompassed
> by a ten-mile radius around Hanoi/Phuc Yen Airfield, a
> four-mile radius around Haiphong, and a twenty-mile China
> buffer zone. Exceptions to permit selected strikes within
> these restricted areas, in accordance with the air campaign
> described herein, will be conducted only as authorized by
> the Joint Chiefs....

> b. Numerical sortie limitations on armed reconnais-
> sance in NVN be removed.

> c. No tactical restrictions or limitations be imposed
> upon the execution of the specific air strikes.

> d. The Joint Chiefs...be authorized to direct CINCPAC
> to conduct the air campaign against the DRV as described
> herein. 49/

On the same day as the Chiefs' Memorandum, and perhaps in
reaction to it, John McNaughton set down what he termed "Some Observations about Bombing North Vietnam." 50/ It is not clear to whom the

33

66

paper was addressed, or who saw it. But it comprises perhaps the most effective political case that could have been made for the bombing program in early 1966, by a writer who was intimately involved with every detail of the program and who was fully aware of all its limitations. As such its most important sections are worth extensive quotation here. They were the following:

      3. Purposes of the program of bombing the North. The purposes of the bombing are mainly:

          a. To interdict infiltration.

          b. To bring about negotiations (by indirect third-party pressure flowing from fear of escalation and by direct pressure on Hanoi).

          c. To provide a bargaining counter in negotiations (or in a tacit "minuet").

          d. To sustain GVN and US morale.

Short of drastic action against the North Vietnamese population (and query even then), the program probably cannot be expected directly or indirectly to persuade Hanoi to come to the table or to settle either (1) while Le Duan and other militants are in ascendance in the politburo or (2) while the North thinks it can win in the South. The only questions are two: (3) Can the program be expected to reduce (not just increase the cost of) DRV aid to the South below what it would otherwise be -- and hopefully to put a ceiling on it -- so that we can achieve a military victory or, short of that, so that their failure in the South will cause them to lose confidence in victory there? (Our World War II experience indicates that only at that time can the squeeze on the North be expected to be a bargaining counter). And (4) is the political situation (vis a vis the "hard-liners" at home, in the GVN and elsewhere) such that the bombing must be carried on for morale reasons? (The negative morale effect of now stopping bombing North Vietnam could be substantial, but it need not be considered unless the interdiction reason fails.)

      4. Analysis of past interdiction efforts. The program so far has not successfully interdicted infiltration of men and materiel into South Vietnam (although it may have caused the North to concentrate its logistic resources on the trail, to the advantage of our efforts in support of Souvanna). Despite our armed reconnaissance efforts and strikes on railroads, bridges, storage centers, training bases and other key

links in their lines of communications, it is estimated
that they are capable of generating in the North and
infiltrating to the South 4500 men a month and between
50 and 300 (an average of 200) tons a day depending on
the season. The insufficiency of the interdiction effort
is obvious when one realizes that the 110 battalions of
PAVN (27) and VC (83) forces in Vietnam need only 20 or
so tons a day from North Vietnam to sustain "1964" levels
of activity and only approximately 80 tons a day to sustain
"light combat" (1/5th of the force in contact once every
7 days using 1/3d of their basic load). The expansion of
enemy forces is expected to involve the infiltration of
9 new PAVN and the generation of 7 new VC combat battalions
a month, resulting (after attrition) in a leveled-off force
of 155 battalions at end-1966. The requirements from the
North at that time -- assuming that the enemy refuses, as it
can, to permit the level of combat to exceed "light" --
should approximate 140 tons a day, less than half the dry-
season infiltration capability and less than three-quarters
the average infiltration capability.

5. The effective interdiction program. The flow
of propaganda and military communications cannot be
physically interdicted. But it is possible that the flow
of men and materiel to the crucial areas of South Vietnam
can be. The interdiction can be en route into North Vietnam
from the outside world, inside North Vietnam, en route from
the North by sea or through Laos or Cambodia to South Vietnam, and inside South Vietnam. It can be by destruction or
by slow down. The effectiveness can be prolonged by exhausting the North's repair capability, and can be enhanced
by complicating their communications and control machinery.
The ingredients of an effective interdiction program in
North Vietnam must be these:

      a. Intensive around-the-clock armed recon-
         naissance throughout NVN.

      b. Destruction of the LOC targets heretofore tar
         targeted.

      c. Destruction of POL.

      d. Destruction of thermal power plants.

      e. Closing of the ports.

....It has been estimated (without convincing back-up) that an
intensive program could reduce Hanoi's capability to supply

forces in the South to 50 tons a day -- too little for
flexibility and for frequent offensive actions, perhaps
too little to defend themselves against aggressive US/GVN
forces, and too little to permit Hanoi to continue to
deploy forces with confidence that they could be supplied.

6. Possible further efforts against the North.
Not included in the above interdiction program are these
actions against the North:

       f. Destruction of industrial targets.

       g. Destruction of locks and dams.

       h. Attacks on population targets (per se).

The judgment is that, because North Vietnam's economy and
organization is predominantly rural and not highly inter-
dependent, attacks on industrial targets are not likely to
contribute either to interdiction or to persuasion of the
regime. Strikes at population targets (per se) are likely
not only to create a counterproductive wave of revulsion
abroad and at home, but greatly to increase the risk of
enlarging the war with China and the Soviet Union. Destruction of locks and dams, however -- if handled right -- might
(perhaps after the next Pause) offer promise. It should be
studied. Such destruction does not kill or drown people.
By shallow-flooding the rice, it leads after time to widespread starvation (more than a million?) unless food is
provided -- which we could offer to do "at the conference
table."

7. Nature of resumed program against the North. The
new ROLLING THUNDER program could be:

       a. None, on grounds that net contribution to
           success is negative.

       b. Resume where we left off, with a "flat-line"
           extrapolation.

       c. Resume where we left off, but with slow
           continued escalation.

       d. Resume where we left off, but with fast
           escalation.

69

On the judgment that it will not "flash" the Soviet Union
or China -- we should follow Course d (fast escalation).
Failure to resume would serve none of our purposes and
make us appear irresolute. A "flat line" program would
reduce infiltration (but not below PAVN/VC needs) and
would placate GVN and domestic pressures. But this is
not good enough. A fast (as compared with a slow) escalation serves a double purpose -- (1) it promises quickly
to interdict effectively, i.e., to cut the DRV level of
infiltration to a point below the VC/PAVN requirements,
and (2) it promises to move events fast enough so that
the Chinese "take-over" of North Vietnam resulting from
our program will be a visible phenomenon, one which the
DRV may choose to reject. There is some indication that
China is "smothering North Vietnam with a loving embrace."
North Vietnam probably does not like this but, since it is
being done by "salami slices" in reaction to our "salami-
slice" bombing program, North Vietnam is not inspired to
do anything about it. This condition, if no other, argues
for escalating the war against North Vietnam more rapidly --
so that the issue of Chinese encroachment will have to be
faced by Hanoi in bigger bites, and so that the DRV may
elect for a settlement rather than for greater Chinese
infringement of North Vietnam's independence. The objections to the "fast" escalation are (1) that it runs serious
risks of "flashing" the Chinese and Soviets and (2) that
it gets the bombing program against the North "out of phase"
with progress in the South. With respect to the first objection, there are disagreements as to the likelihood of such
a "flash"; as for the second one, there is no reason why the
two programs should be "in phase" if, as is the case, the
main objective is to interdict infiltration, not to "persuade
the unpersuadable."

....

9. <u>Criticisms of the program</u>. There are a number of
criticisms of the program of bombing North Vietnam:

a. <u>Cost in men and materiel</u>. The program of
bombing the North through 1965 cost 100(?) airmen (killed
and missing or prisoner) and 178 US or South Vietnamese
aircraft (costing about $250 (?) million) in addition to
the ammunition and other operating costs. The losses and
costs in 1966 are expected to be 200(?) airmen and 300(?)
aircraft.

b. <u>Damage to peaceful image of the US</u>. A price
paid for because of our program of bombing the North
has been damage to our image as a country which eschews
armed attacks on other nations. The hue and cry corre-
lates with the kind of weapons (e.g., bombs vs. napalm),
the kind of targets (e.g., bridges vs. people), the location of targets (e.g., south vs. north), and not least the
extent to which the critic feels threatened by Asian communism (e.g., Thailand vs. the UK). Furthermore, for a
given level of bombing, the hue and cry is less now than
it was earlier, perhaps to some extent helped by Communist
intransigence toward discussions. The objection to our
"warlike" image and the approval of our fulfilling our
commitments competes in the minds of many nations (and
individuals) in the world, producing a schizophrenia....

c. <u>Impact on US-Soviet detente</u>. The bombing
program -- because it appears to reject the policy of
"peaceful co-existence," because it involves an attack
on a "fellow socialist country," because the Soviet
people have vivid horrible memories of air bombing, because it challenges the USSR as she competes with China
for leadership of the Communist world, and because US
and Soviet arms are now striking each other in North
Vietnam -- has seriously strained the US-Soviet detente,
making constructive arms-control and other cooperative
programs more difficult....At the same time, the bombing
program offers the Soviet Union an opportunity to play a
role in bringing peace to Vietnam, by gaining credit for
persuading us to terminate the program. There is a chance
that the scenario could spin out this way; if so, the
effect of the entire experience on the US-Soviet detente
could be a net plus.

d. <u>Impact on Chicom role in DRV</u>. So long as the
program continues, the role of China in North Vietnam
will increase. Increased Chinese aid will be required
to protect against and to repair destruction. Also, the
strikes against North Vietnamese "sovereign territories,"
by involving their "honor" more than would otherwise be the
case, increases the risk that the DRV would accept a substantially increased Chinese role, however unattractive
that may be, in order to avoid a "national defeat" (failure
of the war of liberation in the South).

e. <u>Risk of escalation</u>. The bombing program --
especially as strikes move toward Hanoi and toward China
and as encounters with Soviet/Chinese SAMs/MIGs/vessels-
at-sea occur -- increases the risk of escalation into a

71

broader war. The most risky actions are mining of the
ports, bombing of cities (or possibly dams), and landings
in North Vietnam.

10. <u>Requirements of a program designed to "persuade"</u>
<u>(not interdict)</u>. A bombing program focused on the objective
of "persuasion" would have these characteristics:

a. <u>Emphasize the threat</u>. The program should be
structured to capitalize on fear of the future. At a given
time, "pressure" on the DRV depends not upon the <u>current</u>
level of bombing but rather upon the credible threat of
<u>future</u> destruction (or other painful consequence, such as an
unwanted increased Chinese role) which can be avoided by
agreeing to negotiate or agreeing to some settlement in
negotiations. Further, it is likely that North Vietnam would
be more influenced by a threatened <u>resumption</u> of a given level
of destruction -- the "hot-cold" treatment -- than by a threat
to <u>maintain</u> the same level of destruction; getting "irregu-
larity" into our pattern is important.

b. <u>Minimize the loss of DRV "face."</u> The program
should be designed to make it politically easy for the DRV
to enter negotiations and to make concessions during negotiations. It is politically easier for North Vietnam to accept
negotiations and/or to make concessions at a time when bombing
of their territory is not currently taking place. Thus we
shall have to contemplate a succession of Pauses.

. . . .

e. <u>Maintain a "military" cover</u>. To avoid the
allegation that we are practicing "pure blackmail," the
targets should be military targets and the declaratory policy
should not be that our objective is to squeeze the DRV to
the talking table, but should be that our objective is only
to destroy military targets.

Thus, for purposes of the objective or promoting a settlement, three guidelines emerge: (1) Do not practice "strategic"
bombing; (2) do not abandon the program; and (3) carry out
strikes only as frequently as is required to keep alive fear
of the future. Because DRV "face" plays a role and because
we can never tell at what time in the future the DRV might
be willing to talk settlement, a program with fairly long
gaps between truly painful strikes at "military" targets
would be optimum; it would balance the need to maintain the
threat with the need to be in an extended pause when the
DRV mood changed. Unfortunately, so long as full VC victory

72

in the South appears likely, the effect of the bombing
program in promoting negotiations or a settlement will
probably be small. Thus, because of the present balance
in the South, the date of such a favorable DRV change of
mood is not likely to be in the near future....

11. _Elements of a compromise program._ There is a
conflict between the objective of "persuading Hanoi,"
which would dictate a program of painful surgical strikes
separated by fairly long gaps, and the objective of interdiction, which would benefit from continuous heavy bombings.
No program can be designed which optimizes the chances of
achieving both objectives at the same time. The kind of
program which should be carried out in the future therefore
depends on the relative importance and relative likelihood
of success of the objectives at any given time. In this
connection, the following questions are critical:

a. _How likely is it that the Communists will
start talking?_ The more likely this is, the more emphasis
should be put on the "pressure/bargaining counter" program
(para 10 above). The judgment is that the Communists are
not likely to be interested in talking at least for the
next few months.

b. _How important to the military campaign is
infiltration and how efficiently can we frustrate the
flow?_ The more important that preventable infiltration
is, the more emphasis should be put on the interdiction
program (para 5 above). Unfortunately, the data are not
clear on these points....

12. _Reconciliation._ The actions which these considerations seem now to imply are these, bearing in mind
that our principal objective is to promote an acceptable
outcome:

a. _Spare non-interdiction targets._ Do not
bomb any non-interdiction targets in North Vietnam, since
such strikes are not consistent with either of the two
objectives. Such painful non-interdiction raids should
be carried out only occasionally, pursuant to the rationale
explained in para 10 above.

b. _Interdict._ Continue an interdiction program
in the immediate future, as described in para 5 above, since
the Communists are not likely to be willing to talk very
soon and since it is possible that the interdiction program
will be critical in keeping the Communist effort in South
Vietnam within manageable proportions.

73

c. Study politically cheaper methods. Conduct a
study to see whether most of the benefits of the interdiction campaign can be achieved by a Laos-SVN barrier or
by a bombing program which is limited to the Laos-SVN
border areas of North Vietnam, to Laos and/or to South
Vietnam (and, if so, transition the interdiction program
in that direction). The objective here is to find a way
to maintain a ceiling on potential communist military
activity in the South with the least political cost and
with the least interference with North Vietnam willingness
to negotiate.

McNaughton prepared a second memorandum complementing and
partially modifying the one on bombing. It concerned the context for
the decision. Opening with a paragraph which warned, "We...have in
Vietnam the ingredients of an enormous miscalculation," it sketched the
dark outlines of the Vietnamese scene:

...the ARVN is tired, passive and accommodation-
prone....The PAVN/VC are effectively matching our deployments....The bombing of the North...may or may not be
able effectively to interdict infiltration (partly
because the PAVN/VC can simply refuse to do battle if
supplies are short)....Pacification is stalled despite
efforts and hopes. The GVN political infrastructure
is moribund and weaker than the VC infrastructure among
most of the rural population....South Vietnam is near
the edge of serious inflation and economic chaos. 51/

The situation might alter for the better, McNaughton conceded. "Attrition -- save Chinese intervention -- may push the DRV
'against the stops' by the end of 1966." Recent RAND motivation and
morale studies showed VC spirit flagging and their grip on the peasantry
growing looser. "The Ky government is coming along, not delivering its
promised 'revolution' but making progress slowly and gaining experience
and stature each week." Though McNaughton termed it "doubtful that
a meaningful ceiling can be put on infiltration," he said "there is
no doubt that the cost of infiltration can...be made very high and
that the flow of supplies can be reduced substantially below what it
would otherwise be." Possibly bombing, combined with other pressures,
could bring the DRV to consider terms after "a period of months, not
of days or even weeks."

The central point of McNaughton's memorandum, following
from its opening warning, was that the United States, too, should consider
coming to terms. He wrote:

74

c. The present US objective in Vietnam is to avoid humiliation. The reasons why we went into Vietnam to the present depth arc varied; but they are now largely academic. Why we have not withdrawn from Vietnam is, by all odds, one reason: (1) To preserve our reputation as a guarantor, and thus to preserve our effectiveness in the rest of the world. We have not hung on (2) to save a friend, or (3) to deny the Communists the added acres and heads (because the dominoes don't fall for that reason in this case), or even (4) to prove that "wars of national liberation" won't work (except as our reputation is involved). At each decision point we have gambled; at each point, to avoid the damage to our effectiveness of defaulting on our commitment, we have upped the ante. We have not defaulted, and the ante (and commitment) is now very high. It is important that we behave so as to protect our reputation. At the same time, since it is our reputation that is at stake, it is important that we not construe our obligation to be more than do the countries whose opinions of us are our reputation.

d. We are in an escalating military stalemate. There is an honest difference of judgment as to the success of the present military efforts in the South. There is no question that the US deployments thwarted the VC hope to achieve a quick victory in 1965. But there is a serious question whether we are now defeating the VC/PAVN main forces and whether planned US deployments will more than hold our position in the country. Population and area control has not changed significantly in the past year; and the best judgment is that, even with the Phase IIA deployments, we will probably be faced in early 1967 with a continued stalemate at a higher level of forces and casualties.

2. US commitment to SVN. Some will say that we have defaulted if we end up, at any point in the relevant future, with anything less than a Western-oriented, non-Communist, independent government, exercising effective sovereignty over all of South Vietnam. This is not so. As stated above, the US end is solely to preserve our reputation as a guarantor. It follows that the "softest" credible formulation of the US commitment is the following:

a. DRV does not take over South Vietnam by force. This does not necessarily rule out:

b. A coalition government including Communists.

c. A free decision by the South to succumb to the VC or to the North.

d. A neutral (or even anti-US) government in SVN.

e. A live-and-let-live "reversion to 1959." Furthermore, we must recognize that even if we fail in achieving this "soft" formulation, we could over time come out with minimum damage:

f. If the reason was GVN gross wrongheadedness or apathy.

g. If victorious North Vietnam "went Titoist."

h. If the Communist take-over was fuzzy and very slow.

Current decisions, McNaughton argued, should reflect awareness that the U.S. commitment could be fulfilled with something considerably short of victory. "It takes time to make hard decisions," he wrote, "It took us almost a year to take the decision to bomb North Vietnam; it took us weeks to decide on a pause; it could take us months (and could involve lopping some white as well as brown heads) to get us in position to go for a compromise. We should not expect the enemy's molasses to pour any faster than ours. And we should 'tip the pitchers' now if we want them to 'pour' a year from now."

But the strategy following from this analysis more or less corresponded over the short term to that recommended by the Saigon mission and the military commands: More effort for pacification, more push behind the Ky government, more battalions for MACV, and intensive interdiction bombing roughly as proposed by CINCPAC. The one change introduced in this memorandum, prepared only one day after the other, concerned North Vietnamese ports. Now McNaughton advised that the ports not be closed. Why he did so is not apparent. The intelligence community had concurred a month earlier that such action would create "a particularly unwelcome dilemma" for the USSR, but would provoke nothing more than vigorous protest. 52/ Perhaps, however, someone had given McNaughton a warning sometime on January 18 or 19 that graver consequences could be involved. In any case, McNaughton introduced this one modification.

The argument which coupled McNaughton's political analysis with his strategic recommendations appeared at the end of the second memorandum:

The dilemma. We are in a dilemma. It is that the situation may be "polar." That is, it may be that while going for victory we have the strength for compromise, but if we go for compromise we have the strength only for defeat -- this because a revealed lowering of sights from victory to compromise (a) will unhinge the GVN and (b) will give the DRV the "smell of blood." The situation therefore requires a thoroughly loyal and disciplined US team in Washington and Saigon and great care in what is said and done. It also requires a willingness to escalate the war if the enemy miscalculates, misinterpreting our willingness to compromise as implying we are on the run. The risk is that it may be that the "coin must come up heads or tails, not on edge." 53/

Much of McNaughton's cautious language about the lack of success -- past or predicted -- of the interdiction efforts appeared six days later, 24 January, in a memorandum from McNamara for the President. 54/ The memorandum recommended (and its tone makes clear that approval was taken for granted) an increase in the number of attack sorties against North Vietnam from a level of roughly 3,000 per month -- the rate for the last half of 1965 -- to a level of at least 4,000 per month to be reached gradually and then maintained throughout 1966. The sortie rate against targets in Laos, which had risen from 511 per month in June 1965 to 3,047 in December, would rise to a steady 4,500, and those against targets in South Vietnam, having risen from 7,234 in June to 13,114 in December, would drop back to 12,000 in June 1966, but then climb to 15,000 in December. By any standards, this was a large bombing program, yet McNamara could promise the President only that "the increased program probably will not put a tight ceiling on the enemy's activities in South Vietnam," but might cause him to hurt at the margins, with perhaps enough pressure to "condition /him/ toward negotiations and an acceptable /to the US/GVN, that is/ end to the war -- and will maintain the morale of our South Vietnamese allies."

Most of McNamara's memorandum dealt with the planned expansion of American ground forces, however. Here it indicated that the President had decided in favor of recommendations the Secretary had brought back from his trip to Vietnam on 28 and 29 November, and had incorporated in memoranda for the President on 30 November and 7 December. 55/ These were to increase the number of US combat battalions from 34 at the end of 1965 to 74 a year later, instead of to 62 as previously planned, with comparable increases for the Korean and Australian contingents (from nine battalions to 21, and from one to two, respectively). Such an increase in US combat strength would raise total US personnel in Vietnam from 220,000 to over 400,000. At the same time, McNamara noted in his memorandum of 7 December, the Department of Defense would come before the Congress in January to ask for a

supplemental appropriation of $11 billion of new obligational authority
to cover increased Vietnam costs.

The Secretary recommended these measures, he said, because
of "dramatic recent changes in the situation...on the military side."
Infiltration from the North, mainly on greatly improved routes through
Laos, had increased from three battalion equivalents per month in late
1964 to a recent high of a dozen per month. With his augmented forces,
the enemy was showing an increased willingness to stand and fight in
large scale engagements, such as the Ia Drang River campaign in November.
To meet this growing challenge the previously planned US force levels
would be insufficient. Identical descriptions of the increased enemy
capability appeared in both McNamara's 30 November and 7 December memoranda.
In the former, but not the latter, the following paragraph also appeared:

> We have but two options, it seems to me. One is to go
> now for a compromise solution (something substantially less
> than the "favorable outcome" I described in my memorandum of
> November 3), and hold further deployments to a minimum. The
> other is to stick with our stated objectives and with the war,
> and provide what it takes in men and materiel. If it is
> decided not to move now toward a compromise, I recommend that
> the United States both send a substantial number of addi-
> tional troops and very gradually intensify the bombing of
> North Vietnam. Ambassador Lodge, General Wheeler, Admiral
> Sharp and General Westmoreland concur in this two-pronged
> course of action, although General Wheeler and Admiral Sharp
> would intensify the bombing of the North more quickly.

McNamara did not commit himself -- in any of these papers,
at least -- on the question of whether or not the President should now
opt instead for a "compromise" outcome. The President, of course,
decided against it. He did so, it should be noted, in the face of a
"prognosis" from McNamara that was scarcely optimistic. There were
changes in this prognosis as it went through the Secretary's successive
Presidential memoranda on 30 November, 7 December and 24 January. The
first of these stated simply:

> We should be aware that deployments of the kind I
> have recommended will not guarantee success. US killed-
> in-action can be expected to reach 1000 a month, and the
> odds are even that we will be faced in early 1967 with a
> "no decision" at an even higher level. My overall evalu-
> ation, nevertheless, is that the best chance of achieving
> our stated objectives lies in a pause followed, if it fails,
> by the deployments mentioned above.

In the latter two memoranda, McNamara elaborated on this prognosis, and
made it even less optimistic. The versions of 7 December and 24 January

were similar, but there were important differences. They are set
forward here with deletions from the 7 December version in brackets,
and additions in the 24 January version underlined:

[Deployments of the kind we have recommended will
not guarantee success.] Our intelligence estimate is
that the present Communist policy is to continue to
prosecute the war vigorously in the South. They continue
to believe that the war will be a long one, that time is
their ally, and that their own staying power is superior
to ours. They recognize that the US reinforcements of 1965
signify a determination to avoid defeat, and that more US
troops can be expected. Even though the Communists will
continue to suffer heavily from GVN and US ground and air
action, we expect them, upon learning of any US intentions
to augment its forces, to boost their own commitment and
to test US capabilities and will to persevere at a higher
level of conflict and casualties (US killed-in-action with
the recommended deployments can be expected to reach 1000
a month).

If the US were willing to commit enough forces --
perhaps 600,000 men or more -- we could probably ultimately
prevent the DRV/VC from sustaining the conflict at a
significant level. When this point was reached, however,
the question of Chinese intervention would become critical.
(We are generally agreed that the Chinese Communists will
intervene with combat forces to prevent destruction of the
Communist regime in North Vietnam; it is less clear that they
would intervene to prevent a DRV/VC defeat in the South.) 56/
The intelligence estimate is that the chances are a little
better than even that, at this stage, Hanoi and Peiping
would choose to reduce their effort in the South and try to
salvage their resources for another day. [; but there is an
almost equal chance that they would enlarge the war and bring
in large numbers of Chinese forces (they have made certain
preparations which could point in this direction).]

It follows, therefore, that the odds are about even
that, even with the recommended deployments, we will be
faced in early 1967 with a military stand-off at a much
higher level, with pacification [still stalled, and with
any prospect of military success marred by the chances of
an active Chinese intervention] hardly underway and with
the requirement for the deployment of still more US forces. 57/

On 25 January 1966, before the bombing had yet been resumed, George Ball sent to the President a long memorandum on the matter. Its first page warned:

> I recognize the difficulty and complexity of the problem and I do not wish to add to your burdens. But before a final decision is made on this critical issue, I feel an obligation to amplify and document my strong conviction: <u>that sustained bombing of North Viet-Nam will more than likely lead us into war with Red China --</u> <u>probably in six to nine months.</u> And it may well involve at least a limited war with the Soviet Union. 58/

There were, Ball said, "forces at work <u>on both sides of the conflict</u> that will operate in combination to bring about this result."

The Under-Secretary dealt with the U.S. side of the conflict first. The bombing, he wrote, would inevitably escalate; the passage of time, he contended, had demonstrated <u>"that a sustained bombing program</u> <u>acquires a life and dynamism of its own."</u> For this there were several reasons. First was that the U.S. <u>"philosophy of bombing requires gradual</u> <u>escalation."</u> Ball explained:

> Admittedly, we have never had a generally agreed rationale for bombing North Viet-Nam. But the inarticulate major premise has always been that bombing will somehow, some day, and in some manner, create pressure on Hanoi to stop the war. This is accepted as an article of faith, not only by the military who have planning and operational responsibilities but by most civilian advocates of bombing in the Administration.

> Yet it is also widely accepted that for bombing to have this desired political effect, we must gradually extend our attack to increasingly vital targets. In this way -- it is contended -- we will constantly threaten Hanoi that if it continues its aggression it will face mounting costs -- with the destruction of its economic life at the end of the road.

On an attached chart, Ball demonstrated that in the eleven months of bombing target selection had gradually spread northward to a point where it was nearing the Chinese border and closing in on the Hanoi-Haiphong area, "steadily constricting the geographical scope of immunity."

80

Just as the geographical extent of the bombing would inexorably increase, Ball argued, so would the value of the targets struck. "Unless we achieve dramatic successes in the South -- which no one expects /Ball wrote/ -- we will be led by frustration to hit increasingly more sensitive targets." He listed four categories of likely operations: (1) the mining of Haiphong harbor, and the destruction of (2) North Vietnam's POL supplies, (3) its system of power stations, and (4) its airfields. Each of these targets had already been recommended to the President by one of his principal military or civilian advisors in Washington or Saigon, Ball noted, and each had "a special significance for the major Communist capitals." The mining of Haiphong harbor would "impose a major decision" on the Soviet Union. "Could it again submit to a blockade, as at the time of the Cuban missile crisis," Ball asked, "or should it retaliate by sending increased aid or even volunteers to North Viet-Nam or by squeezing the United States at some other vital point, such as Berlin?" Would Hanoi feel compelled to launch some kind of attack on crowded Saigon harbor or on U.S. fleet units -- perhaps using surface-to-surface missiles provided by the Soviet Union? Similarly, the bombing of North Vietnam's POL supplies might bring in response an attack on the exposed POL in Saigon harbor. Then there were the airfields. Ball wrote:

> The bombing of the airfields would very likely lead the DRV to request the use of Chinese air bases north of the border for the basing of North Vietnamese planes, or even to request the intervention of Chinese air. This would pose the most agonizing dilemma for us. Consistent with our decision to bomb the North, we could hardly permit the creation of a sanctuary from which our own planes could be harassed. Yet there is general agreement that for us to bomb China would very likely lead to a direct war with Peiping and would -- in principle at least -- trigger the Sino-Soviet Defense Pact, which has been in force for fifteen years.

The same process of action-reaction, Ball noted, would also apply to surface-to-air missile sites (SAMs) within North Vietnam. The wider the bombing the greater the number of SAM sites -- manned substantially by Soviet and Chinese technicians -- the North Vietnamese would install. "As more SAMs are installed, we will be compelled to take them out in order to safeguard our aircraft. This will mean killing more Russians and Chinese and putting greater pressure on those two nations for increased effort." Ball summarized this process in general terms: "Each extension of our bombing to more sensitive areas will increase the risk to our aircraft and compel a further extension of bombing to protect the expanded bombing activities we have staked out."

81

These risks would be run, Ball observed, for the sake
of a bombing program that would nevertheless be ineffective in producing the political results being asked of it. Ten days before sending
his memorandum to the President, Ball had asked the CIA's Office of
National Estimates to prepare an estimate of likely reactions to various
extensions of the bombing, and also an assessment of the effects they
would be likely to have on North Vietnam's military effort in the south. 59/
He cited the estimate's conclusions in his Presidential memorandum. None
of the types of attacks he had specified -- on Haiphong harbor, on the
POL, or on power stations -- "would in itself, have a critical impact on
the combat activity of the Communist forces in South Viet-Nam." This
was, of course, scarcely a new conclusion. In various formulations it
had figured in intelligence estimates for the preceding six months. From
it Ball was led to the premises which motivated him to write his vigorously dissenting paper: "if the war is to be won -- it must be won in
the South," and "the bombing of the North cannot win the war, only enlarge
it."

Ball's paper was at its most general (and perhaps least
persuasive) in its discussion of "enlargement" of the war. He started
from a historical example -- the catastrophic misreading of Chinese
intentions by the United States during the Korean war -- and a logical
premise:

Quite clearly there is a threshold which we cannot
pass over without precipitating a major Chinese involvement. We do not know -- even within wide margins of error --
where that threshold is. Unhappily we will not find out
until after the catastrophe.

In positing his own notions of possible thresholds, Ball could only reiterate points he had already made: that forcing the North Vietnamese air
force to use Chinese bases, by bombing their own airfields, would be likely
to escalate into armed conflict between the U.S. and China, and that the
destruction of North Vietnam's industry would call in increased Chinese
assistance to a point "sooner or later, we will almost certainly collide
with Chinese interests in such a way as to bring about a Chinese involvement."

There were, strikingly enough, no recommendations in Ball's
memorandum. Given his assumption that "sustained bombing" would acquire
"a life of its own," and invariably escalate, the only consistent recommendation would have been that the U.S. should not resume bombing the
North, but should instead confine the war to the South. There were no
compromise positions. To a President who placed the avoidance of war
with China (not to mention with the U.S.S.R.) very high on his list of
objectives, and yet who felt -- for military and political reasons --
that he was unable not to resume bombing North Vietnam, but that, once

49

82

resumed, the bombing must be carefully controlled, Ball offered disturbing analysis but little in the way of helpful practical advice.

The week including the Tet holidays (January 23-29) saw some final debate at the White House on the question of whether to resume at all in which Ball's memo surely figured. The outcome was a Presidential decision that ROLLING THUNDER should recommence on January 31. The President declined for the time being, however, to approve any extension of air operations, despite the strong recommendations of the military and the milder proposals of the Secretary of Defense for such action.

E.   Accomplishments by Year's-End

After 10 months of ROLLING THUNDER, months longer than U.S. officials had hoped it would require to bring NVN to terms, it was clear that NVN had neither called off the insurgency in the South nor been obliged to slow it down. Still, decision-makers did not consider bombing the North a failure. While willing to entertain the idea of a temporary pause to focus the spotlight on the diplomatic track they were pursuing, they were far from ready to give up the bombing out of hand. Why not? What did they think the bombing was accomplishing, and what did they think these accomplishments were worth? What did they hope to achieve by continuing it?

As already noted, certain political gains from the bombing were evident from the start. Morale in SVN was lifted, and a certain degree of stability had emerged in the GVN. NVN and other countries were shown that the U.S. was willing to back up strong words with hard deeds. These were transient gains, however. After the bombing of the North was begun, other U.S. actions -- unleashing U.S. jet aircraft for air strikes in the South, and sending U.S. ground troops into battle there -- had as great or even greater claim as manifestations of U.S. will and determination. Similarly, breaking through the sanctuary barrier had been accomplished, and once the message was clear to all concerned it did not require daily and hourly reinforcement. The acquisition of an important bargaining chip was a gain of uncertain value as yet, since it might have to be weighed against the role of the bombing as an obstacle to getting negotiations underway in the first place. As one high-level group stated in the fall of 1965:

> ...it would be difficult for any government, but
> especially an oriental one, to agree to negotiate while
> under sustained bombing attacks. 60/

If this particular chip had to be given up in order to establish what the group called "the political and psychological framework for initiating negotiations," the gain in leverage might be small.

Public opinion about the bombing was mixed. On the hawk side, as Secretary McNamara summed it up for the President:

> Some critics, who advocated bombing, were silenced; others are now as vocal or more vocal because the program has been too limited for their taste. 61/

People who believed that the U.S. was justified in intervening in the war and who identified Hanoi as the real enemy naturally tended to approve of the bombing. People who questioned the depth of U.S. involvement in Southeast Asia and who feared that the U.S. was on a collision course with China seemed to be more appalled by the bombing than by any other aspect of the war. The peace fringe attacked it as utterly reckless and immoral. Abroad, in many countries, the U.S. was portrayed as a bully and NVN as a victim. Even U.S. allies who had no illusions about Hanoi's complicity in the South were unhappy with the bombing. As McNamara viewed it:

> The price paid for improving our image as a guarantor has been damage to our image as a country which eschews armed attacks on other nations....The objection to our 'warlike' image and the approval of our fulfilling our commitments competes in the minds of many nations (and individuals) in the world, producing a schizophrenia. Within such allied countries as UK and Japan, popular antagonism to the bombings per se, fear of escalation, and belief that the bombings are the main obstacle to negotiation, have created political problems for the governments in support of US policy. 62/

Bombing NVN, the Secretary added, had also complicated US-Soviet relations, mostly for the worse though conceivably -- barely so -- for the better:

> The bombing program -- because it appears to reject the policy of 'peaceful coexistence,' because the Soviet people have vivid horrible memories of air bombing, because it challenges the USSR as she competes with China for leadership of the Communist world, and because US and Soviet arms are now striking each other in North Vietnam -- has strained the US-Soviet detente, making constructive arms control and other cooperative programs difficult. How serious this effect will be and whether the detente can be revived depend on how far we

84

carry our military actions against the North and how
long the campaign continues. At the same time, the
bombing program offers the Soviet Union an opportunity
to play a role in bringing peace to Vietnam, by gaining
credit for persuading us to terminate the program.
There is a chance that the scenario could spin out this
way: if so, the effect of the entire experience on the
US-Soviet detente could be a net plus. 63/

In addition, the Secretary continued, more countries than before
were "more interested in taking steps to bring the war to an end." The
net effect of this, however, was generally to increase the international
pressures on the U.S. to seek an accommodation, not Hanoi, so that it
was hardly an unmixed blessing.

Immediate gains and losses in the domestic and international political arenas were less important, however, than the overall influence of
the bombing on the course of the war itself. Short-term political
penalties were not hard to bear, at home or abroad, if the bombing could
materially improve the prospects for a favorable outcome. This did not
necessarily mean that the bombing had to contribute to a military victory.
ROLLING THUNDER was begun at a time when the war was being lost and even
the minimum task of preventing an outright defeat was far from assured.
Almost any military contribution from the bombing could be viewed as a
boon.

It was not easy to assess the contribution of ROLLING THUNDER to
the war as a whole. Decision-makers like Secretary McNamara received
regular monthly reports of measurable physical damage inflicted by the
strikes, together with a verbal description of less readily quantifiable economic, military and political effects within NVN, but it was
difficult to assess the significance of the results as reported or to
relate them to the progress of the war in the South. Reports of this
kind left it largely to the judgment or the imagination to decide what
the bombing was contributing to the achievement of overall U.S. objectives.

CIA and DIA, in a joint monthly "Appraisal of the Bombing of North
Vietnam" which had been requested by the SecDef in August, attempted
to keep a running tabulation of the theoretical cost of repairing or
reconstructing damaged or destroyed facilities and equipment in NVN.
According to this, the first year of ROLLING THUNDER inflicted $63 million
worth of measurable damage, $36 million to "economic" targets like
bridges and transport equipment, and $27 million to "military" targets
like barracks and ammunition depots. 64/ In addition to this measurable
damage, the bombing was reported to have "disrupted" the production and
distribution of goods; created "severe" problems and "reduced capacity"
in all forms of transportation; created more "severe problems" in managing the economy; reduced production; caused "shortages" and "hardships";

85

forced the diversion of "skilled manpower and scarce resources" from productive uses to the restoration of damaged facilities and/or their dispersal and relocation; and so on.

In terms of specific target categories, the appraisals reported results like the following:

Power plants. 6 small plants struck, only 2 of them in the main power grid. Loss resulted in local power shortages and reduction in power available for irrigation but did not reduce the power supply for the Hanoi/Haiphong area.

POL storage. 4 installations destroyed, about 17 percent of NVN's total bulk storage capacity. Economic effect not significant, since neither industry nor agriculture is large user and makeshift storage and distribution procedures will do.

Manufacturing. 2 facilities hit, 1 explosive plant and 1 textile plant, the latter by mistake. Loss of explosives plant of little consequence since China furnished virtually all the explosives required. Damage to textile plant not extensive.

Bridges. 30 highway and 6 railroad bridges on JCS list destroyed or damaged, plus several hundred lesser bridges hit on armed reconnaissance missions. NVN has generally not made a major reconstruction effort, usually putting fords, ferries, and pontoon bridges into service instead. Damage has neither stopped nor curtailed movement of military supplies.

Railroad yards. 3 hit, containing about 10 percent of NVN's total railroad cargo-handling capacity. Has not significantly hampered the operations of the major portions of the rail network.

Ports. 2 small maritime ports hit, at Vinh and Thanh Hoa in the south, with only 5 percent of the country's maritime cargo-handling capacity. Impact on economy minor.

Locks. Of 91 known locks and dams in NVN, only 8 targeted as significant to inland waterways, flood control, or irrigation. Only 1 hit, heavily damaged.

Transport equipment. Destroyed or damaged 12 locomotives, 819 freight cars, 805 trucks, 109 ferries, 750

85

forced the diversion of "skilled manpower and scarce resources" from
productive uses to the restoration of damaged facilities and/or their
dispersal and relocation; and so on.

In terms of specific target categories, the appraisals reported
results like the following:

Power plants. 6 small plants struck, only 2 of them
in the main power grid. Loss resulted in local power
shortages and reduction in power available for irrigation but did not reduce the power supply for the
Hanoi/Haiphong area.

POL storage. 4 installations destroyed, about 17 percent of NVN's total bulk storage capacity. Economic
effect not significant, since neither industry nor
agriculture is large user and makeshift storage and
distribution procedures will do.

Manufacturing. 2 facilities hit, 1 explosive plant
and 1 textile plant, the latter by mistake. Loss of
explosives plant of little consequence since China
furnished virtually all the explosives required. Damage
to textile plant not extensive.

Bridges. 30 highway and 6 railroad bridges on JCS list
destroyed or damaged, plus several hundred lesser bridges
hit on armed reconnaissance missions. NVN has generally
not made a major reconstruction effort, usually putting
fords, ferries, and pontoon bridges into service instead.
Damage has neither stopped nor curtailed movement of
military supplies.

Railroad yards. 3 hit, containing about 10 percent of
NVN's total railroad cargo-handling capacity. Has not
significantly hampered the operations of the major
portions of the rail network.

Ports. 2 small maritime ports hit, at Vinh and Thanh Hoa
in the south, with only 5 percent of the country's maritime cargo-handling capacity. Impact on economy minor.

Locks. Of 91 known locks and dams in NVN, only 8 targeted
as significant to inland waterways, flood control, or
irrigation. Only 1 hit, heavily damaged.

Transport equipment. Destroyed or damaged 12 locomotives, 819 freight cars, 805 trucks, 109 ferries, 750

86

barges, and 354 other water craft. No evidence of seri-
our problems due to shortages of equipment. 65/

What did all of this amount to? The direct losses, in the language
of one of the monthly appraisals,

> ...still remain small compared to total economic
> activity, because the country is predominantly agricul-
> tural and the major industrial facilities have not been
> attacked. 66/

The "cumulative strains" resulting from the bombing had "reduced industrial performance," but "the primarily rural nature of the area permits
continued functioning of the subsistence economy." The "economic deterioration so far has not affected the capabilities of North Vietnam's
armed forces, which place little direct reliance on the domestic economy
for material." The bombing had "still" not reduced NVN capabilities
to defend itself from attack and to support existing NVA/VC forces in
Laos and SVN, but it had "limited" "freedom of movement" in the southern
provinces, and it had "substantially curtailed" NVA capabilities to
mount "a major offensive action" in Southeast Asia. Altogether, however, "the air strikes do not appear to have altered Hanoi's determination to continue supporting the war in South Vietnam." 67/

An evaluation which had to be couched in such inexact and impressionistic language was of little help in coming to grips with the most
important questions about the bombing: (1) How much "pressure" was
being applied to NVN to scale down or give up the insurgency, and how
well was it working? (2) In what ways and to what degree was the bombing
affecting NVN's capacity to wage war in the South? Whether the bombing
program was viewed primarily as a strategic-punitive campaign against
Hanoi's will or a tactical-interdiction campaign against NVN's military
capabilities in the South -- or, as some would have it, both -- these
were the questions to address, not the quantity of the damage and the
quality of the dislocations.

In dealing with the above questions, it had to be recognized that
NVN was an extremely poor target for air attack. The theory of either
strategic or interdiction bombing assumed highly developed industrial
nations producing large quantities of military goods to sustain mass
armies engaged in intensive warfare. NVN, as U.S. intelligence agencies
knew, was an agricultural country with a rudimentary transportation
system and little industry of any kind. Nearly all of the people were
rice farmers who worked the land with water buffaloes and hand tools,
and whose well-being at a subsistence level was almost entirely dependent
on what they grew or made themselves. What intelligence agencies liked
to call the "modern industrial sector" of the economy was tiny even by
Asian standards, producing only about 12 percent of a GNP of $1.6 billion

87

in 1965. There were only a handful of "major industrial facilities."
When NVN was first targeted the JCS found only 8 industrial installations worth listing on a par with airfields, military supply dumps,
barracks complexes, port facilities, bridges, and oil tanks. Even by
the end of 1965, after the JCS had lowered the standards and more than
doubled the number of important targets, the list included only 24
industrial installations, 18 of them power plants which were as important for such humble uses as lighting streets and pumping water as for
operating any real factories. 68/

Apart from one explosives plant (which had already been demolished),
NVN's limited industry made little contribution to its military capabilities. NVN forces, in intelligence terminology, placed "little direct
reliance on the domestic economy for material." NVN in fact produced
only limited quantities of simple military items, such as mortars,
grenades, mines, small arms, and bullets, and those were produced in
small workshops rather than large arsenals. The great bulk of its
military equipment, and all of the heavier and more sophisticated items,
had to be imported. This was no particular problem, since both the
USSR and China were apparently more than glad to help.

The NVN transportation system was austere and superficially looked
very vulnerable to air attack, but it was inherently flexible and its
capacity greatly exceeded the demands placed upon it. The rail system,
with single-track lines radiating from Hanoi, provided the main link-up
to China and, via the port of Haiphong, to the rest of the world; it
was more important for relatively long-haul international shipments than
for domestic freight. The latter was carried mostly over crude roads
and simple waterways, on which the most common vehicles were oxcarts
and sampans, not trucks or steamers. The system was quite primitive,
but immensely durable.

Supporting the war in the South was hardly a great strain on NVN's
economy. The NVA/VC forces there did not constitute a large army. They
did not fight as conventional divisions or field armies, with tanks and
airplanes and heavy artillery; they did not need to be supplied by huge
convoys of trucks, trains, or ships. They fought and moved on foot,
supplying themselves locally, in the main, and simply avoiding combat
when supplies were low. What they received from NVN was undoubtedly
critical to their military operations, but it amounted to only a few
tons per day for the entire force -- an amount that could be carried by
a handful of trucks or sampans, or several hundred coolies. This small
amount did not have to be carried conspicuously over exposed routes,
and it was extremely difficult to interdict, by bombing or any other
means.

In sum, then, NVN did not seem to be a very rewarding target for
air attack. Its industry was limited, meaningful targets were few, and

they did not appear critical to either the viability of the economy,
the defense of the nation, or the prosecution of the war in the South.
The idea that destroying, or threatening to destroy, NVN's industry
would pressure Hanoi into calling it quits seems, in retrospect, a
colossal misjudgment. The idea was based, however, on a plausible
assumption about the rationality of NVN's leaders, which the U.S. intelligence community as a whole seemed to share. 69/ This was that the
value of what little industrial plant NVN possessed was disproportionately
great. That plant was purchased by an extremely poor nation at the
price of considerable sacrifice over many years. Even though it did
not amount to much, it no doubt symbolized the regime's hopes and desires
for national status, power, and wealth, and was probably a source of
considerable pride. It did not seem unreasonable to believe that NVN
leaders would not wish to risk the destruction of such assets, especially
when that risk seemed (to us) easily avoidable by cutting down the
insurgency and deferring the takeover of SVN until another day and perhaps in another manner -- which Ho Chi Minh had apparently decided to
do once before, in 1954. After all, an ample supply of oriental patience
is precisely what an old oriental revolutionary like Ho Chi Minh was
supposed to have.

For 1965, at least, these assumptions about Hanoi's leaders were
not borne out. The regime's public stance remained one of strong defiance, determined to endure the worst and still see the U.S. defeated.
The leadership directed a shift of strategy in the South, from an attempt
at a decisive military victory to a strategy of protracted conflict
designed to wear out the opposition and prepare the ground for an eventual
political settlement, but this decision was undoubtedly forced upon it
by U.S. intervention in the South. There was no sign that bombing the
North, either alone or in combination with other U.S. actions, had brought
about any greater readiness to settle except on their terms.

In the North, the regime battened down and prepared to ride out
the storm. With Soviet and Chinese help, it greatly strengthened its
air defenses, multiplying the number of AAA guns and radars, expanding
the number of jet fighter airfields and the jet fighter force, and introducing an extensive SAM system. Economic development plans were laid
aside. Imports were increased to offset production losses. Bombed
facilities were in most cases simply abandoned. The large and vulnerable
barracks and storage depots were replaced by dispersed and concealed ones.
Several hundred thousand workers were mobilized to keep the transportation
system operating. Miles of by-pass roads were built around choke-points
to make the system redundant. Knocked-out bridges were replaced by fords,
ferries, or alternate structures, and methods were adopted to protect
them from attack. Traffic shifted to night time, poor weather, and
camouflage. Shuttling and transhipment practices were instituted. Construction material, equipment, and workers were prepositioned along key

routes in order to effect quick repairs. Imports of railroad cars
and trucks were increased to offset equipment losses.

In short, NVN leaders mounted a major effort to withstand the
bombing pressure. They had to change their plans and go on a war
footing. They had to take drastic measures to shelter the population
and cope with the bomb damage. They had to force the people to work
harder and find new ways to keep the economy operating. They had to
greatly increase imports and their dependence on the USSR and China.
There were undoubtedly many difficulties and hardships involved. Yet,
NVN had survived. Its economy had continued to function. The regime
had not collapsed, and it had not given in. And it still sent men
and supplies into SVN.

1. Draft memorandum, "Analysis and Options for South Vietnam,"
   7/13/65, TOP SECRET, filed with compilation of data assembled
   by Secretary McNamara for his 14-21 July 1965 trip to Vietnam.

2. Memorandum for Rusk, McNamara, McG. Bundy, W. Bundy, McNaughton,
   Unger, "Cutting Our Losses in South Viet-Nam," TOP SECRET. Ball
   distributed this paper in two parts, a summary on 28 June 1965
   and the paper itself on the 29th.

3. Memorandum for the President, "A Compromise Solution for South
   Viet-Nam," 1 July 1965, TOP SECRET. (Underlining in original.)

4. Draft, "Plan of Action for South Vietnam," 24 March 1965, TOP SECRET.

5. From Ball's summary, 28 June 1965, of his memorandum of the 29th,
   cited above, n. 2.

6. Memorandum, "Viet-Nam," 1 July 1965, TOP SECRET. (Emphasis added.)
   Rusk's name is typed as drafter at the foot of the memorandum.

7. Bundy's memorandum, 1 July 1965 (TOP SECRET), summarized points
   Bundy made in a longer paper, "Holding on in South Vietnam,"
   30 June 1965 (TOP SECRET).

8. Memorandum for the President, "Recommendations of additional deployments to Vietnam," 20 July 1965, TOP SECRET.

9. Memorandum for the President, "Program of expanded military and
   political moves with respect to Vietnam," first draft 26 June 1965,
   revised 1 July, TOP SECRET. The copy used here is the typed draft
   of 26 June with extensive pencilled revisions in McNamara's own
   hand and his signature.

10. JCSM 515-65, 2 July 1965, "Deployments to South Vietnam," TS;
    Fact Sheet, "Military Pressures Against NVN," in Cable File 34,
    SecDef Saigon Trip, 14-21 July 1965.

11. SNIE 10-9-65, 23 July 1965, "Communist and Free World Reactions
    to a Possible US Course of Action," TOP SECRET.

11a. Ibid.

12. Draft Memorandum, "Analysis and Options for South Vietnam," 7/13/65, TS.

13. Footnote on p. 4 of McNamara's memorandum of 20 July 1965, cited
    above, n. 8.

14. Memorandum for the President, 28 July 1965, UNCLASSIFIED, commenting on 18 points made by Senator Mansfield to the President on the Vietnam situation.

15. Memorandum for the President, "Evaluation of the Program of Bombing North Vietnam," 30 July 1965, TOP SECRET.

16. Even as early as 7 July the SecDef apparently planned to take up the idea of a 6-8 week bombing pause with Ambassador Taylor and General Westmoreland. See OSD 5319 to Saigon, 07/2352 Z July 1965, TS, NODIS.

17. JCSM 652-65, 27 Aug 1965, "Concept for Vietnam," TS; Memorandum for the SecDef from ASD/ISA, I-3614/65, "Concept for Vietnam," 9/8/65, TS; and Memorandum for the CJCS from the SecDef, "Concept for Vietnam," 9/11/65, TS.

18. JCUM 670-65, 9/2/65, JCSM 686-65, 9/11/65; SecDef Memorandum for CJCS, "Air Strikes on North Vietnam," 9/15/65, TS. JCS recommendations along these lines continued to be submitted throughout 1965. See JCSM 810-65, 11/10/65, and JCSM 811-65, 11/11/65, both TS.

19. The Hanoi and Haiphong circles and the Chinese buffer zones developed into sanctuaries during 1965 from a decision in August to exclude them from an authorization to strike SAM sites at will, provided photography had shown them to be occupied. See JCSM 238-66, 14 April 1966, "ROLLING THUNDER Study Group Report -- Air Operations Against North Vietnam," Annex B to Appendix A to Section II, "Chronology," TS.

20. JCSM 238-66, 14 April 1966, op. cit., contains a chronological account of ROLLING THUNDER missions to March 1966. See also CINCPAC Command History, 1965, Vol. II, pp. 324-389, TS.

21. The statistics are taken from CIA SC No. 04442/67, Jan. 1967, "The ROLLING THUNDER Program."

22. Memorandum for the President, 30 July 1965, op. cit.

23. CIA SC No. 0828/66, "The Role of Air Strikes in Attaining Objectives in North Vietnam."

24. Testimony before Senate committees on Armed Services and Appropriations, 4 August 1965, SECRET.

25. Testimony, House Committee on Armed Services, 6 August 1965, SECRET.

26. SecDef Background briefing for the press, 21 October 1965, OUO.

27. The circumstances and the diplomacy of the May pause are treated in detail in another paper in this project.

28. Memorandum for the President, 30 November 1965, TOP SECRET. This paper, written immediately following a visit to Vietnam by McNamara and General Wheeler on 28 and 29 November, was intended as a supplement to the Secretary's memorandum of 3 November, cited below.

29. Memorandum for the President, "Courses of Action in Vietnam," 3 November 1965, TOP SECRET. This paper is headed "1st Rough Draft," but a note in McNamara's handwriting states: "A copy of this was sent to the Pres. by courier thru Mac's office on 11/7 & discussed with him by me, George, & Mac on 11/7. RMcN."

30. McNaughton draft, "Analysis and Options for South Vietnam," 13 July 1965, TOP SECRET.

31. Memorandum, "Courses of Action in Viet-Nam," 9 November 1965, TOP SECRET. A pencilled note by McNaughton on the copy used here indicates that Ambassador U. Alexis Johnson was the author of the paper.

32. Memorandum for Secretary McNamara, "State's Memo to the President (Courses of Action in Viet-Nam)," 9 November 1965, TOP SECRET - EYES ONLY.

33. Draft Memorandum for the President, "A Pause," 1 December 1965, TOP SECRET. A cover note indicates that this is an up-dating of a paper originally circulated on 16 November.

34. Memorandum, "Possible Political Actions, Specifically a 'Pause'," TOP SECRET. A pencilled note indicates the paper was by Johnson and Bundy, on 6 December 1965.

35. McNamara's memorandum of 3 November 1965, op. cit.

36. McNamara's memorandum, 3 December 1965, TOP SECRET - EYES ONLY.

37. Ibid.

38. Bundy draft, "Scenario for Possible Resumption of Bombing," 15 January 1966, SECRET.

39. State 1786 to Lodge, MACV, and CINCPAC, 24 Dec 1965, CF 44.

40. MACV 45265, 27 Dec 65, Ibid.

41. CINCPAC 262159Z Dec 1965, CF 44; CINCPAC 271955Z Dec 1965, Ibid.

42. State 1805 to Lodge and Porter, 28 Dec 1965, _Ibid_. (This cable is misfiled under 23 Dec 1965.)

43. CINCPAC 120205Z Jan 1966, _Ibid_.

44. JCSM 41-66, 18 Jan 1966.

45. _Ibid_.

46. _Ibid_. (emphasis added)

47. _Ibid_.

48. _Ibid_.

49. _Ibid_.

50. McNaughton 2nd Draft, "Some Observations about Bombing North Vietnam," 18 January 1966, (TS-SENSITIVE) in McNaughton Book II, Tab DD.

51. McNaughton 3rd Draft, "Some Paragraphs on Vietnam," 19 Jan 1966 (TS-Sensitive), in McNaughton Book, Tab BB.

52. SNIE 10-12-65, 10 Dec 1965, p. 9 (TS).

53. McNaughton Draft "Some Paragraphs...," _op_. _cit_.

54. Memorandum for the President, "The Military Outlook in South Vietnam," 24 January 1966, TOP SECRET.

55. These were: Memorandum for the President (no title), 30 November 1965, TOP SECRET, and Memorandum for the President, "Military and Political Actions Recommended for South Vietnam," 7 December 1965, TOP SECRET.

56. In the 7 December version, this parenthetical sentence was a footnote.

57. The following footnote, expressing the reservations of the Joint Chiefs of Staff, was appended to the 24 January 1966 version of McNamara's memorandum:

"The Joint Chiefs of Staff believe 'that the evaluation set forth in paragraph 7 is on the pessimistic side in view of the constant and heavy military pressure which our forces in Southeast Asia will be capable of apploying. While admittedly the following factors are to a degree imponderables, they believe that greater weight should be given to the following:

"a. The cumulative effect of our air campaign against the

94

DRV on morale and DRV capabilities to provide and move men and material from the DRV to South Vietnam.

"b. The effects of constant attack and harassment on the ground and from the air upon the growth of Viet Cong forces and on the morale and combat effectiveness of Viet Cong/PAVN forces.

"c. The effect of destruction of Viet Cong base areas on the capabilities of VC/PAVN forces to sustain combat operations over an extended period of time.

"d. The constancy of will of the Hanoi leaders to continue a struggle which they realize they cannot win in the face of progressively greater destruction of their country."

58. Memorandum for the President, "The Resumption of Bombing Poses Grave Danger of Precipitating a War with China," 25 January 1966, SECRET-NODIS. Ball noted in a covering letter that he sent copies only to the President and to Secretaries Rusk and McNamara.

59. Letter, Ball to Raborn, 16 January 1966, SECRET.

60. Memorandum for the SecDef from Ambassador-at-Large Llewellyn E. Thompson, 12 October 1965, SECRET, forwarding a study of ROLLING THUNDER options. The study, Thompson wrote, "was largely prepared in State and was reviewed by General Taylor, Mr. McNaughton, Mr. William Bundy, Mr. Unger, and myself."

61. Memorandum for the President, 30 July 1965, op. cit.

62. Ibid.

63. Ibid. Although this was written at the end of July, the basic situation continued essentially as Secretary McNamara described it and there is no reason to believe his comments would have been different at the end of the year.

64. CIA/DIA, "An Appraisal of the Effects of the First Year of Bombing in North Vietnam," SC No. 08437/66, 1 June 1966. A 1967 CIA publication, "The Rolling Thunder Program -- Present and Potential Target Systems," SC No. 04442/67, January 1967, upped the value of military damage in 1965 to $33.6 million and the total to $69.8 million.

65. CIA/DIA, "An Appraisal of the Effects of the First Year of Bombing in North Vietnam," op. cit.

66. Memorandum for the SecDef from Gen. J. F. Carroll, DIA, "An Appraisal of the Bombing of North Vietnam," 17 November 1965.

67. Ibid.

68. JCSM 16-66, 10 Jan 1966 (TS).

69. CIA/DIA, "An Appraisal...," op. cit.

II. THE POL DEBATE -- NOVEMBER 1965 - JUNE 1966

    A. Background

        When the 37-day bombing pause was terminated at the end of
January 1966, the principal issue before decision-makers was not whether
to intensify the bombing but whether the intensification should be
gradual as before or be sharply accelerated.

        Some kind of escalation if the bombing pause failed, i.e.,
if the North Vietnamese did not give "concrete evidence of a willingness
to come to terms," was foreshadowed by the October paper from State
recommending the pause:

        We would have to convey our intent to reinstitute
        the bombing if the North Vietnamese refused to negoti-
        ate or if their willingness to negotiate is not accom-
        panied by a manifest reduction of VC aggression in the
        South. If it is necessary to reinstitute bombing, we
        should be prepared to consider increasing the pressure,
        e.g. through striking industrial targets, to make clear
        our continuing, firm resolve. 1/

According to this thinking, failure of the pause would indicate that
the bombing had not exerted enough pressure; greater effort was needed
to convince Hanoi that the U.S. intended not only to continue the bombing
but to do so on an increasing scale. Moreover, the pause had improved
the political atmosphere for escalation. U.S. willingness to negotiate
and NVN's unreasonableness had been amply and dramatically displayed
for all the world to see. If the U.S. now decided to intensify the
bombing, the decision could at least be presented as one that was made
reluctantly after trying to find a more peaceful alternative.

        The debate over the form of escalation in early 1966 was a
continuation of the debate over bombing policy which had surfaced again
in the fall of 1965, and which had mixed into the debate over the long
pause. Regardless of any pause, it was clear by November that even the
gradual rate of escalation of 1965 was approaching a point at which any
further increase would be possible only by attacking the sensitive targets
in the Hanoi/Haiphong sanctuaries and the China buffer zone. As of the
end of October, 126 of the 240 existing JCS targets had been struck; and
of the remaining 114, two thirds (75) were in the off-limits areas, and
29 of the other 39 remaining were in the touchy northeast quadrant. 2/
As the debate gathered momentum in the winter of 1965 without a clear
decision to begin attacking "the hostage," the bombing actually levelled
off. During November and December only 8 more JCS targets were struck
and armed reconnaissance missions were held to a sortie ceiling of 1200
per two-week period. 3/

TOP SECRET - Sensitive

97

Apart from general cautiousness about the next obvious escalatory step, one of the reasons for the Administration's hesitancy was apparently the fear that the timing might not be right. As the bombing drew closer to Hanoi and Haiphong, some officials felt forcing the pace might oblige NVN to confront the issue of negotiations versus greater Chinese and/or Soviet involvement prematurely, i.e. before NVN was sufficiently convinced that it could not outlast the U.S. and win in the South. The theory was that so long as Hanoi was hopeful there was a greater risk that it would opt for escalation rather than a compromise settlement. As the October paper from State put it:

> We may be able to recognize the optimum time for exerting further pressure by increasing the level of our bombing, but an increase in our bombing of the North at the present time may bring matters to a head too soon. 4/

In addition, of course, there was good reason to hold off any escalation until a substantial bombing pause was undertaken, both to test Hanoi's intentions and to disarm critics on the dovish side who felt that the Administration had not gone far enough to meet Hanoi halfway.

1. JCS Recommendations

Dissatisfied with the measured pace of the bombing program from the start, they again began advocating a sharp intensification of the bombing in early November. Diplomatic and political considerations were secondary. Their position was that ROLLING THUNDER had succeeded in making it "substantially" more costly and difficult for NVN to support the insurgents in Laos and SVN, and had "substantially" degraded NVN's capability to conduct a conventional invasion of the South, but they agreed that the campaign had not materially reduced NVN's other military capabilities, damaged its economy, deterred it from supporting the war in the South, or brought it closer to the conference table. It was not because of any difficulty in applying pressure on Hanoi by bombing or in interdicting support South that the program had not been more successful, however; it was because numerous "self-imposed restraints" had limited the potential effectiveness of the program:

> ...we shall continue to achieve only limited success in air operations in DRV/Laos if required to operate within the constraints presently imposed. The establishment and observance of de facto sanctuaries within the DRV, coupled with a denial of operations against the most important military and war supporting targets, precludes attainment of the objectives of the air campaign....Thus far, the DRV has been able and willing to absorb damage and destruction at the slow rate. Now required is an immediate and sharply accelerated

98

program which will leave no doubt that the US intends to win
and achieve a level of destruction which they will not be
able to overcome. Following such a sudden attack, a follow-on
program of increasing pressures is necessary, but at a rate of
increase significantly higher than the present rate. 5/

The JCS accordingly recommended an immediate acceleration
in the scale, scope, and intensity of the bombing, beginning with heavy
strikes against POL targets and power plants in the Hanoi/Haiphong area
and continuing with aerial mining of NVN ports and air strikes against
the remaining "military and war-supporting" targets. Specifically, the
JCS proposed an immediate sharp blow against the remaining 9 of the
original 13 major POL tank farms, most of them in the Hanoi/Haiphong
area, and against 5 key power plants, 2 in Hanoi and others at Uong Bi,
Thai Nguyen, and Hon Gai, in order to "materially reduce enemy military
capabilities." These strikes would be followed by an accelerated program
of fixed target and armed reconnaissance strikes to cut down NVN's
ability to direct and support the war in the South. The follow-on program
would attack first the major airfields in the Hanoi/Haiphong area; then
the rail, road, and waterway LOCs throughout NVN, including the major LOC
targets in the Hanoi/Haiphong area, "at a rate of destruction that would
exceed the recuperability rate"; then the ports at Haiphong, Hon Gai,
and Cam Pha; and finally military installations and other targets of
military significance, such as the Ministry of Defense, the Radio Transmitter
Station, and the Machine Tool Plant in Hanoi; the Ammunition Depot at
Haiphong; and the Iron-Steel Combine and Army Supply Depot at Thai Nugyen.
SAM installations and other antiaircraft defenses would be attacked in
order to keep friendly losses down. According to the proposal, most
of the significant fixed targets in NVN would be destroyed within three
or four months. Thereafter, the effort would concentrate on keeping the
targets inoperative and maintaining the pressure on LOCs. 6/

The JCS proposal to escalate all aspects of the bombing
was largely oriented toward greatly increasing the pressure on Hanoi's
will. On the same day, however, in a separate memorandum, the JCS made
a strong pitch for an immediate attack on the NVN POL system as an interdiction measure:

> Attack of this system would be more damaging to the
> DRV capability to move war-supporting resources within
> country and along the infiltration routes to SVN than an
> attack against any other single target system. 7/

It is not surprising that the JCS singled out the POL target
system for special attention. NVN had no oil fields or refineries, and
had to import all of its petroleum products, in refined form. During 1965,
it imported about 170,000 metric tons, valued at about $4.8 million. Nearly
all of it came from the Black Sea area of the USSR and arrived by sea at

Haiphong, the only port capable of conveniently receiving and handling bulk POL brought in by large tankers. From large tank farms at Haiphong with a capacity of about one-fourth of the annual imports, the POL was transported by road, rail, and water to other large storage sites at Hanoi and elsewhere in the country. Ninety-seven percent of the NVN POL storage capacity was concentrated in 13 sites, 4 of which had already been hit. The other 9 were still off limits. They were, of course, highly vulnerable to air attack. 8/

In making the recommendation, the JCS emphasized the interdiction effects. They pointed out that the strikes would not hurt the industrial base or the civilian economy very much. They would directly affect the military establishment, which consumed some 60 percent of all POL, and the "government transportation system," which consumed nearly all the rest. Supplying the armed forces in NVN as well as in Laos and SVN depended heavily on POL-powered vehicles, and this dependence had if anything increased as a result of air attacks on the railroads:

The flow of supplies to all communist military forces, both in and through the country to SVN and Laos, would be greatly impeded since POL-fueled carriers are the principal vehicles for this transport. Further, the interdiction of rail lines and destruction of railroad rolling stock has resulted in the need to move increased tonnages by alternate means, primarily trucks and motor driven water craft. Thus, the most effective way to compound the current interdiction of DRV LOCs, and to offset the introduction and use of substitute modes and routes, is to reduce drastically the available supply of POL. 9/

The JCS also suggested that POL in NVN was becoming increasingly important to the effort in the South. There were now 5 confirmed and 2 suspected NVA regiments in SVN, increasing the load on the supply lines through Laos, and the roads there were being improved, indicating that NVN planned to rely more heavily on trucks to handle the load. Significantly, the importation of trucks was increasing, and despite losses inflicted by ROLLING THUNDER strikes, the size of the truck fleet was growing.

The JCS recommended hitting the most important target, Haiphong POL storage, first, followed closely by attack on the remaining 8 targets. The weight of effort required was 336 strike and 80 flak suppression aircraft, with not more than 10 losses predicted. All POL targets could be destroyed with only light damage to surrounding areas and few civilian casualties (less than 50).

100

According to the JCS, the destruction of the Haiphong target "would drastically reduce the capability to receive and distribute the major portions of DRV bulk POL imports." Destruction of the others would "force reliance upon dispersed POL storages and improvised distribution methods." Recovery would be difficult and time-consuming. As stated in an annex to the JCSM:

> Recuperability of the DRV POL system from the effects of an attack is very poor. Loss of the receiving and and distribution point at Haiphong would present many problems. It would probably require several months for the DRV, with foreign assistance, to establish an alternate method for importing bulk POL, in the quantities required. An alternative to bulk importation would be the packaging of POL at some point for shipment into NVN and subsequent handling and distribution by cumbersome and costly methods over interdicted LOCs. Loss of bulk storage facilities would necessitate the use of small drums and dispersed storage areas and further compound the POL distribution problem. 10/

Any further delay in carrying out the strikes, on the other hand, "will permit further strengthening of DRV active defenses of the POL, as well as the improvement of countermeasures, such as dispersed and underground storages." On the latter point, the appendix to the JCSM added detailed intelligence information that boded ill for any procrastination:

> Current evidence shows that the DRV has in progress an extensive program of installing groups of small POL tanks in somewhat isolated locations and throughout the Hanoi area. Photographs reveal groups of tanks ranging in number of 16 to 120 tanks per group. The facilities are generally set into shallow excavations and are then earth-covered leaving only the vents and filling apparatus exposed. This construction was observed at several places in the Hanoi area in August and appeared to be an around-the-clock activity.... In addition, considerable drum storage has been identified. 11/

It appeared that NVN had already begun a crash program to drastically reduce the vulnerability of its POL storage and handling system. As in other instances, NVN expected further escalation of the bombing, and was preparing for it.

101

2. The Intelligence Community Demurs

There was no immediate action on the November 1965 JCS recommendations, but they were taken under study. Secretary McNamara asked for intelligence evaluations, and on 27 November and 3 December, respectively, he received special reports from the Board of National Estimates on (a) U.S. air attacks on NVN petroleum storage facilities, and (b) a generally stepped-up effort involving doubling or tripling U.S. troop commitments, bombing military and industrial targets in the Hanoi/Haiphong area, and mining NVN harbors. 12/

The Board reported that strikes against POL targets in the Hanoi/Haiphong area would represent "a conspicuous change in the ground rules" which the U.S. had hitherto observed, but would not appreciably change the course of the war:

the Communists would unquestionably regard the proposed US attacks as opening a new stage in the war, and as a signal of US intention to escalate the scale of conflict....We do not believe, however, that the attacks in themselves would lead to a major change of policy on the Communist side, either toward negotiations or toward enlarging the war.... 13/

The strikes would cause strains and embarrassment but would not have a major military or economic impact:

Hanoi would not be greatly surprised by the attacks. Indeed...it has already taken steps to reduce their impact. It has developed some underground storage facilities, and some capacity for dispersed storage in drums....We believe that the DRV is prepared to accept for some time at least the strains and difficulties which loss of the major POL facilities would mean for its military and economic activity. It is unlikely that this loss would cripple the Communist military operations in the South, though it would certainly embarrass them. 14/

NVN might possibly ask the Chinese to intervene with fighter aircraft to help defend the targets but would probably not ask for ground troops. The Chinese would probably decline to intervene in the air and would not volunteer ground forces, though they would urge NVN to continue the war. The Soviets would be "concerned" at the prospect of a further escalation of the bombing:

The Soviets would find their difficulties and frustrations increased....They are committed to provide defense for North Vietnam, and...their inability to do so effectively

102

would be dramatized....We believe that they would not change
their basic policy of avoiding overt involvement in combat
while giving extensive military equipment and economic
assistance to NVN. But their relations with the US would
almost certainly deteriorate, for it is the bombing of
North Vietnam which is, for Moscow, the most nearly intolerable aspect of /the War-7 15/

In its estimate of the likely reactions to the wider
course of substantially expanding the U.S. effort in the South, together
with the bombing and aerial mining of the North, the Board similarly
offered little hope that the escalation would produce any marked improvement in the situation. They characterized NVN's will to resist in the
North and to persevere in the South as virtually unshakeable in the short
run and extremely tough even in the long run:

Present Communist policy is to continue to prosecute
the war vigorously in the South. The Communists recognize
that the US reinforcements of 1965 signify a determination
to avoid defeat. They expect more US troops and probably
anticipate that targets in the Hanoi-Haiphong area will come
under air attack. Nevertheless, they remain unwilling to
damp down the conflict or move toward negotiation. They
expect a long war, but they continue to believe that time
is their ally and that their own staying power is superior. 16/

Heavier air attacks by themselves would not budge them:

The DRV would not decide to quit; PAVN infiltration
southward would continue. Damage from the strikes would
make it considerably more difficult to support the war in
the South, but these difficulties would neither be immediate nor insurmountable. 17/

Aerial mining would create serious problems, but NVN would keep supplies
moving by resorting to shallow-draft coastal shipping and intensive
efforts to keep the rail lines open. As for the South, NVN would accept
the challenge:

Rather than conclude in advance that the tide of battle
would turn permanently against them, the Communists would
choose to boost their own commitment and to test US capabilities and will to persevere at a higher level of conflict
and casualties. Thus the DRV reaction would probably be a
larger program of PAVN infiltration. 18/

The Board's picture of Hanoi was one of almost unbelievably
strong commitment and dogged determination, by contrast with previous
estimates. Thus, if the U.S. committed enough forces in the South to

103

prevent NVA/VC forces from sustaining the conflict at a significant level -- and the Board would not estimate how many U.S. forces were "enough" --

> ...they might believe it necessary to make a more fundamental choice between resorting to political tactics or enlarging the war. /But/ We believe that it would take a prolonged period of military discouragement to convince the DRV and the VC, persuaded as they are of their inherent advantages, that they had reached such a pass. 19/

Even if it found itself in such straits, however, the chances were close to 50-50 that NVN would bring in Chinese forces rather than quit:

> If this point were reached....Prudence would seem to dictate that Hanoi...should choose...to reduce the effort in the South, perhaps negotiate, and salvage their resources for another day. We think that the chances are a little better than even that this is what they would do. But their ideological and emotional commitment, and the high political stakes involved, persuade us that there is an almost equal chance that they would do the opposite, that is, enlarge the war and bring in large numbers of Chinese forces. 20/

The two CIA intelligence estimates of the probable consequences of the proposed escalatory measures were apparently closely held, but the available documentary evidence does not reveal how influential they may have been. Secretary McNamara's response to the JCS was merely that he was considering their recommendations "carefully" in connection with "decisions that must be taken on other related aspects of the conflict in Vietnam." 21/ He was apparently not satisfied with the estimate of reactions to the POL strikes, however, which was largely confined to an estimate of political reactions, and asked CIA for another estimate, this time related to two options: (a) attack on the storage and handling facilities at Haiphong, and (b) attack on the facilities at Haiphong together with the other bulk storage sites.

The new estimate was submitted by Richard Helms, then Acting Director of CIA, on 28 December (with the comment that it had been drafted without reference to any pause in the bombing "such as is now the subject of various speculative press articles." 22/ The estimate spelled out with greater force than before what "strains" the POL strikes might create in the North and how they might "embarrass" NVA/VC military operations in the South, and its tone was much more favorable to carrying out the strikes.

The estimate made little distinction between the two options. Haiphong was by far the most important and most sensitive of the targets and the closest to a major city; the attacks on the others were

70

104

of secondary importance. Neither option was likely to bring about a change in NVN policy, either toward negotiations or toward sharply enlarging the war, but either option would substantially increase NVN's economic difficulties in the North and logistics problems in the South.

First, the estimate said, NVN would have to resort to much less efficient methods of receiving, storing and handling POL:

Destruction of the storage tanks and bulk unloading equipment at Haiphong would substantially increase the Communists' logistic problems and force them to improvise alternate POL import and distribution channels. These could include, subject to the hazards of interdiction, the use of rail or highway tankers and the transport of POL in drums by road, rail, or coastal shipping. The DRV is already increasing its use of drums because this facilitates dispersal and concealment. However, handling POL this way also requires greater expenditures of time and effort, and very large numbers of drums. Resort to these methods would necessitate transhipping through Chinese ports or transport directly across China by rail, which would in turn not only involve physical delays and difficulties but also increase the DRV's political problems in arranging for the the passage of Soviet supplies through China. 23/

This in turn would interfere with the production and distribution of goods in NVN:

The economy would suffer appreciably from the resultant disruption of transportation. This...would somewhat curtail the output of the DRV's modest industrial establishment and complicate the problems of internal distribution. 24/

And make it more difficult to support the war in the South (although it would not force a reduction in such support):

The loss of stored POL and the dislocation of the distribution system would add appreciably to the DRV's difficulties in supplying the Communist forces in the South. However, we have estimated that the Communist effort in South Vietnam, at present levels of combat, does not depend on imports of POL into the South and requires only relatively small tonnages of other supplies (say 12 tons per day, on an annual basis). Accordingly, we believe that adequate quantities of supplies would continue to move by one means or another to the Communist forces in South Vietnam, though the supplies would not move as fast and it would hence require more to keep the pipeline filled.... 25/

105

But was not likely to break Hanoi's will:

> Although there presumably is a point at which one more
> turn of the screw would crack the enemy resistance to
> negotiations, past experience indicates that we are unlikely
> to have clear evidence when that point has been reached....
> Though granting that each increase of pressure on the DRV
> bears with it the possibility that it may be decisive, we
> do not believe the bombing of the Haiphong facility is likely
> to have such an effect. 26/

With the exception of State's INR, other intelligence
agencies appeared to look with favor upon escalating the bombing. In
a SNIE issued on 10 December, they agreed that intensified air attacks,
beginning with POL facilities and key power plants and extending to
other targets in the Hanoi/Haiphong area and mining the harbors, would
not bring about any basic change in NVN policy but would in time hamper
NVN's operations and set a lid on the war in the South:

> We believe that Hanoi's leaders would not decide to
> quit and that PAVN infiltration southward would continue.
> Though damage from the strikes would make it considerably
> more difficult to support the war in South Vietnam, these
> difficulties would not be immediate. Over the long run,
> the sustained damage inflicted upon North Vietnam might
> impose significant limitations on the numbers of PAVN and
> VC main force units which could be actively supported in
> South Vietnam from North Vietnam. 27/

Mining the ports, despite the dilemma created for the Soviets, would
probably succeed in blocking all deep-water shipping:

> The difficulty of clearing such mine fields and the
> ease of resowing would virtually rule out efforts to reopen
> the ports. The Soviets would protest vigorously and might
> try for some kind of action in the UN. We do not believe,
> however, that the Soviets would risk their ships in mined
> Vietnamese harbors. Peking and Hanoi would try to compensate
> by keeping supplies moving in shallow-draft coastal shipping
> and overland. 28/

DIA, NSA, and the 3 Service intelligence agencies even
recorded a judgment that the intensified air strikes, combined with the
projected build-up of U.S. ground forces in SVN to about 350,000 troops
by the fall of 1966, might ultimately result in a change of heart in
Hanoi. In a footnote to the SNIE they said they believed:

106

...that as time goes on and as the impact of sustained bombing in NVN merges with the adverse effects of the other courses of action as they begin to unfold, the DRV would become clearly aware of the extent of US determination and thus might reconsider its position and seek a means to achieve a cessation of the hostilities. 29/

INR dissented. Its Director, Thomas L. Hughes, wrote that the escalation would evoke stronger reactions than indicated in the SNIE, "because it would be widely assumed that we were initiating an effort to destroy the DRV's modest industrial establishment":

The distinction between such operations and all-out war would appear increasingly tenuous. As these attacks expanded, Hanoi would be less and less likely to soften its opposition to negotiations and at some point it would come to feel that it had little left to lose by continuing the fighting.... 30/

B. The Issue Focuses

1. POL and the Pause

Meanwhile, the flow of JCS papers urging POL strikes as the next step continued. Secretary McNamara sent the Chairman, General Wheeler, the 27 November CIA estimate which had suggested that the strikes would not have great impact on the war (they would only "embarrass" operations in the South). General Wheeler commented that the loss of POL storage would do much more:

It would, in fact, have a substantial impact not only on their military operations but also would significantly impede their efforts to support the anticipated build-up of VC/PAVN forces in South Vietnam during the coming months. 31/

General Wheeler also forwarded a Joint Staff-DIA study of the POL target system, with the comment that destruction of the system would force NVN to curtail all but the most vital POL-powered activities and resort to "more extensive use of porters, animal transport, and non-powered water craft." The net result would be to considerably reduce NVN's capability to move large units or quantities of equipment, an important consideration in view of the fact that motorable segments of the Ho Chi Minh trail were being extended. 32/

The Joint Staff-DIA study 33/ showed that NVN's bulk POL storage capacity was greatly in excess of what NVN required to sustain current consumption levels -- 179,000 metric tons available as compared

107

with 32,000 metric tons needed -- indicating that the strikes would
have to be very damaging in order to cause NVN any major difficulties.
The study also hinted that an adequate substitute system could be
improvised, with lighterage from ocean tankers and dispersed storage,
but it nonetheless concluded that the strikes would result in "a reduction of essential transport capabilities for military logistic and
infiltration support opeations," i.e., as a result of a deprivation of
necessary POL. 34/

     As already noted, during the 37-day Pause, the JCS con-
tinued to recommend not only the resumption of the bombing but resumption
with a dramatic sharp blow on major targets, including POL, followed by
uninterrupted, increasing "pressure" bombing. They wished, in short,
to turn the limited bombing program into a major strategic assault on NVN.
In mid-January 1966 they sent Secretary McNamara a memo reiterating old
arguments that the current ROLLING THUNDER program would not cause NVN
to stop supporting the war in the South, and that the piecemeal nature
of the attacks left NVN free to replenish and disperse its supplies and
contend with interdictions. The way to achieve U.S. objectives, the JCS
said, was to implement the bombing program they had recommended long ago,
in JCSM 982-64 of 23 November 1964, which called for the rapid destruction
of the entire NVN target system. In order to get the program started, the
JCS recommended extending armed reconnaissance to all areas of NVN except
the sanctuaries, which they would shrink (to a 10-mile radius around
Hanoi and Phuc Yen airfield, a 4-mile radius around Haiphong, and a strip
20 miles along the Chinese border); lifting the sortie ceiling on armed
reconnaissance; and removing "tactical restrictions" on the execution of
specific strikes. The strikes would be heavy enough to deny NVN external
assistance, destroy in-country resources contributing to the war, destroy
in-country resources contributing to the war, destroy all military facilities, and harass, disrupt, and impede movement into SVN. 35/

     The idea of resuming the bombing with a large and dramatic
bang did not appeal much to decision-makers. Apart from the old problem
of triggering an unwanted Chinese reaction, the Administration was interested in giving the lie to NVN and Chinese claims that the Pause was a
cynical prelude to escalation. Although it was possible that resuming
merely where the bombing left off (following as it would an extended pause
and a display of great eagerness for peace) might signal too much irresolution and uncertainty, there was good reason to put off any escalatory
acts for a while. As Assistant Secretary of State William Bundy wrote:

     For a period of two-three weeks at least, while the
world is digesting and assessing the Pause, we should do as
little as possible to lend fuel to the charge -- which will
doubtless be the main theme of Communist propaganda -- that
the Pause was intended all along merely as a prelude to more
drastic action. 36/

108

Bundy in fact suggested resuming at a lesser level, opening with strikes below the 20th parallel, and only after a few weeks again moving north-ward. McNaughton wrote:

> No consideration argues for a 'noisy' resumption....
> The program at first should be at the level and against
> the kinds of targets involved prior to the Pause (only
> two weeks later should the program begin...to escalate). 37/

He also suggested that criticism would be less if the first strikes were clearly identified with the effort to stop the southward flow of men and supplies, which had been greatly increased during the Pause.

The decisions went against ending the Pause with a bang. When the bombing was resumed on 31 January (Saigon time) it was limited "until further notice" to armed reconnaissance. No new major targets were authorized. The former sanctuary restrictions and the sortie ceilings were maintained. 38/

It was also decided to postpone any serious escalation for the time being. Secretary McNamara informed the JCS that their proposals for rapid escalation were being considered, and on 24 January he sent the President a memorandum on the overall Vietnam program which side-stepped the issue. For 1966, the memorandum said, the bombing program against NVN should include 4000 attack sorties per month "at a minimum." It should consist of day and night armed reconnaissance against rail and road targets and POL storage sites. The present sanctuaries should be preserved. There should be more intense bombing of targets in Laos, along the Bassac and Mekong Rivers running into SVN from Cambodia, and better surveillance of the sea approaches. 39/

The use of interdiction rather than pressure terms in the Presidential memorandum, and the emphasis on bombing infiltration routes into SVN, rather than the flow of supplies into or within NVN, indicates that the Secretary was still interested in keeping the objectives of the bombing limited and any escalation in check. The memorandum said that the bombing had already achieved the objective of raising the cost of infiltration, and was reducing the amount of enemy supplies reaching the South. In NVN it had also diverted manpower to air defense and repair work, interfered with mobility, and forced the decentralization of many activities. It could further reduce the flow of supplies to NVA/VC forces in the South, and limit their "flexibility" to defend themselves adequately or undertake frequent offensive action, but it was doubtful that even heavier bombing would put a "tight ceiling" on the NVN effort in the South. 40/

Despite the application of the brake on ROLLING THUNDER operations, the debate over escalation wore on. Further proposals were made and further studies and reviews were requested. DIA was asked to conduct a special analysis of the NVN POL system. The study said that the exceptionally high ratio of storage capacity to consumption allowed the system to "absorb a high degree of degradation," and noted that the dispersed sites in the system were "relatively invulnerable," but concluded nonetheless that (a) the loss of storage at Haiphong would be "critical to the entire bulk distribution system" and would require either a "modification" in the handling of marine imports or a switch to importation by rail or truck through China, and (b) the loss of the other facilities would produce local POL shortages and transportation bottlenecks until substitutes and alternatives could be devised. 41/

2. The February Debate

In February a SNIE was published, estimating how NVN's physical capabilities (not its will) to support the war in the South would be affected by increasing the scope and intensity of ROLLING THUNDER. The enlarged program which the estimate considered included attacks to destroy all known POL facilities, destroy all large military facilities except airfields and SAM sites (unless they seriously interfered with our operations), interdict the land LOCs from China, (a) with or (b) without closing the ports, put and keep electric power plants out of action, and restrict the use of LOCs throughout NVN but especially south of Hanoi. 42/

The SNIE concluded that although the increased bombing might set a limit somewhere on the expansion of NVA/VC forces and their operations in SVN, it would not prevent their support at substantially higher levels than in 1965. The destruction of electric power facilities would practically "paralyze" NVN's industry, but

> ...because so little of what is sent south is produced in the DRV, an industrial shutdown would not very seriously reduce the regime's capability to support the insurgency. 43/

Destruction of POL storage facilities would force NVN to almost complete dependence on current imports, but NVN could manage. Destruction of military facilities would mean the loss of some stockpiled munitions, "although most such storage is now well dispersed and concealed." Closing the ports and interdicting the LOCs from China would reduce the level of imports--leaving the ports open would not--but NVN could continue to bring in enough supplies that were critical to the survival of the regime and essential military tasks, including the "small quantities" necessary for transshipment to SVN.

110

Importation of POL would be a key problem, but would
be surmountable in a comparatively short time, probably a
few weeks, since quantities involved would not be large,
even if increased somewhat over previous levels. Soviet
POL could be unloaded from tankers at Chan-chiang in South
China, moved thence by rail to the DRV border and from there
to the Hanoi area by truck. It could also move from the USSR
by rail directly across China, or down the coast from Chan-
chiang in shallow-draft shipping. 44/

Restricting the LOCs south of the Hanoi region would create logistical
problems for NVN military forces in Military Region IV south of the 20th
parallel, but would not stop the relatively small amounts of material
forwarded to SVN.

The cumulative effect of the proposed bombing program
would make life difficult for NVN, therefore, but it would not force it
to curtail the war in the South:

The combined impact of destroying in-country stockpiles, restricting import capabilities, and attacking the
southward LOCs would greatly complicate the DRV war effort.
The cumulative drain on material resources and human energy
would be severe. The postulated bombing and interdiction
campaign would harass, disrupt, and impede the movement
of men and material into South Vietnam and impose great
overall difficulty on the DRV. However, we believe that,
with a determined effort, the DRV could still move substantially greater amounts than in 1965. 45/

The bombing program would not prevent NVN from further expanding NVA/VC
forces in the South at the projected reinforcement rate of 4500 men per
month and from further providing them with heavier weapons, but it might
set some limit on their size and their operations:

...an attempt by the Communists to increase their
strength...to intensify hostilities...or...to meet
expanded US/GVN offensive operations...will use up
supplies at a higher rate.../This/ might raise supply
requirements to a level beyond the practical ceiling
imposed on their logistic capabilities by the bombing
campaign....There are, however, too many uncertainties
to permit estimating at just what level the limit on
expansion would be. 46/

///

Also in February, Secretary McNamara asked the JCS to develop an optimum air interdiction program "to reduce to the maximum extent the support in men and materiel being provided by North Vietnam to the Viet Cong and PAVN forces in South Vietnam." 47/ The study, forwarded to the Secretary on 14 April, managed to frame an interdiction program which embraced virtually everything the JCS had been recommending. It pointed out that less than half of the JCS targets, "the most critical to North Vietnam's support of the insurgency, military capabilities, and industrial output," had been hit, "due to self-imposed restraints":

> These restraints have caused a piecemealing of air operations which has allowed the enemy a latitude of freedom to select and use methods that significantly increase his combat effectiveness. It has permitted him to receive war supporting materiel from external sources through routes of ingress which for the most part have been immune from attack and then to disperse and store this materiel in politically assured sanctuaries. From these sanctuaries the enemy then infiltrates this materiel to SVN/Laos....Throughout the entire movement, maximum use is made of villages and towns as sanctuaries. These and the Hanoi, Haiphong, and China border buffer areas cloak and protect his forces and materiel, provide him a military training and staging area free from attack, and permit him to mass his air defense weapons.

> ....The less than optimum air campaign, and the relatively unmolested receipt of supplies from Russia, China, satellite countries, and certain elements of the Free World have undoubtedly contributed to Hanoi's belief in ultimate victory. Therefore, it is essential that an intensified air campaign be promptly initiated against specific target systems critical to North Vietnam's capability for continued aggression and support of insurgency. 48/

The study went on to outline an intensified bombing campaign to cause NVN to stop supporting the insurgency in the South

> by making it difficult and costly for North Vietnam to continue effective support of the NVN/VC forces in South Vietnam and to impose progressively increasing penalties on NVN for continuing to support insurgency in Southeast Asia. 49/

Its language left no doubt that while the strikes were intended "to restrict NVN capability to support and conduct armed aggression in

SEAsia," the ultimate purpose was to apply pressure against Hanoi's will:

> The strategy of this plan requires initial application of air attacks over a widespread area against the NVN military base structure and war supporting resources. The intensity of air operations and the number of targets to be attacked gradually increase. Under such pressure of attack, NVN must further disperse or face destruction in depth of its military base and resources. The dispersal will increase the stresses on command, control, and logistic support and should cause some concern in the Military Command of the wisdom of further aggression....The combined effects of reducing and restricting external assistance to NVN, the progressive attacks against NVN military and war supporting resources, the interdiction of infiltration routes in NVN and Laos, and the destruction of NVN/VC forces and bases in SVN and Laos should cause a reappraisal in Hanoi as to NVN's military capability to continue aggression. 50/

The plan, which was merely "noted" and not red-striped by the JCS, called for the "controlled and phased intensification of air strikes" and a "modest adjustment" in the sanctuaries (to 10 miles around Hanoi, 4 around Haiphong, and 20 from the Chinese border, as previously recommended by the JCS). A first phase extended armed reconnaissance to the northeast, and struck 11 more JCS-listed bridges, the Thai Nguyen railroad yards and shops, 14 headquarters/barracks, 4 ammunition and 2 supply depots, 5 POL storage areas, 1 airfield, 2 naval bases, and 1 radar site, all outside the (reduced) sanctuaries. The second phase attacked 12 "military and war supporting installations" within the Hanoi and Haiphong sanctuaries: 2 bridges, 3 POL storage areas, 2 railroad shops and yards, 3 supply depots, 1 machine tool plant, and 1 airfield. The third phase attacked the 43 remaining JCS targets, including 6 bridges, 7 ports and naval bases, 6 industrial plants, 7 locks, 10 power plants, the NVN ministries of national and air defense, and assorted railroad, supply, radio, and transformer stations.

The plan also provided for three special attack options for execution during any of the phases "as a counter to enemy moves or when strong political and military action is desired." The options were: attack on the POL center at Haiphong; aerial mining of the channel approaches to Haiphong, Hon Gai, and Cam Pha, the three principal maritime ports; and strikes against the major jet airfields at Hanoi, Haiphong, and Phuc Yen. 51/

113

The JCS were apparently not in complete sympathy with the gradual phasing of stronger attacks over several months, as proposed in the study. In their formal memoranda to the SecDef they continued to restate their mid-January recommendations for the sharp blows with maximum shock effect as "the soundest program from a military standpoint" which offered "the greatest return for the air effort expended." 52/ Apparently sensing that this was more than the traffic would bear, however, they began to push for early strikes against POL as "one of the highest priority actions not yet approved." They pointed out that NVN was busily expanding and improving its LOCs, and its "offensive and defensive" air capabilities; it was expediting its import of trucks. POL was becoming increasingly significant to NVN's war effort, and its destruction would have an "immediate effect on the military movement of war supporting materials." 53/

3. The CIA Recommends Escalation

While the JCS kept up its barrage of recommendations during March, CIA broke into the debate with an apparently very influential report on the past accomplishments and future prospects of the bombing. The report virtually wrote off the bombing results to date as insignificant, in terms of either interdiction or pressure; blamed "the highly restrictive ground rules" under which the program operated; and took the bold step, for an intelligence document, of explicitly recommending a preferred bombing program of greater intensity, redirected largely against "the will of the regime as a target system." 54/

The report held that the economic and military damage sustained by NVN had been moderate and the cost had been passed along to the USSR and China. The major effect of the bombing had been to disrupt normal activity, particularly in transportation and distribution, but with considerable external help the regime had been singularly successful in overcoming any serious problems. It had been able to strengthen its defenses, keep its economy going, and increase the flow of men and supplies South. Most of the direct damage so far had been to facilities which NVN did not need to sustain the military effort, and which the regime merely did without. It had been able to maintain the overall performance of the transportation system at the levels of 1964 or better. It had increased the capacity of the LOCs to the South and made them less vulnerable to air attack by increasing the number of routes and bypasses. Despite the bombing, truck movement through Laos, with larger vehicles and heavier loads, had doubled.

The program had not been able to accomplish more because it had been handicapped by severe operational restrictions:

> Self-imposed restrictions have limited both the choice
> of targets and the areas to be bombed. Consequently, almost
> 80 percent of North Vietnam's limited modern, industrial

114

economy, 75 percent of the nation's population and the
most lucrative military supply and LOC targets have been
effectively insulated from air attack. Moreover, the
authorizations for each of the ROLLING THUNDER programs
often have imposed additional restrictions, such as limiting
the number of strikes against approved fixed targets. The
policy decision to avoid suburban casualties to the extent
possible has proved to be a major constraint.

    The overall effect of those area and operational
restrictions has been to grant a large measure of
immunity to the military, political, and economic assets
used in Hanoi's support of the war in the South and to
insure an ample flow of military supplies from North
Vietnam's allies. Among North Vietnam's target systems,
not one has been attacked either intensively or extensively
enough to provide a critical reduction in national capacity.
No target system can be reduced to its critical point under
existing rules. 55/

Moreover, the bombing had been too light, fragmented, and slowly paced:

    The ROLLING THUNDER program has spread bomb tonnage
over a great variety of military and economic targets
systems, but the unattacked targets of any one system have
consistently left more than adequate capacity to meet all
essential requirements. Furthermore, the attacks on major
targets have often been phased over such long periods of
time that adequate readjustment to meet the disruption could
be accomplished. 56/

    What was required was a basic reorientation of the
program:

    Fundamental changes must be made if the effective-
ness of the campaign is to be raised significantly.
First, the constraints upon the air attack must be
reduced. Secondly, target selection must be placed on
a more rational basis militarily. 57/

    Putting the program on a "more rational" military basis
apparently involved abandoning interdiction as a primary goal. The
report held out little promise that any acceptable bombing program
could physically interfere with the flow of supplies to the South.
The NVN economy, it stated, was not "an indigenous economic base heavily
committed to the support of military operations in the South," but rather

81

115

a "logistic funnel" through which supplies from the USSR and China flowed. As such, it was a hard target, easy to maintain in operation and quite large for the load. This was particularly the case in the lower half of the "funnel", where the bombing had been concentrated:

> ...the rudimentary nature of the logistic targets
> in the southern part of North Vietnam, the small volume
> of traffic moving over them in relation to route capaci-
> ties, the relative ease and speed with which they are
> repaired, the extremely high frequency with which they
> would have to be restruck -- once every three days --
> all combine to make the logistic network in this region
> a relatively unattractive target system, except as a
> supplement to a larger program. A significant lesson from
> the ROLLING THUNDER program to date is that the goals of
> sustained interdictions of the rudimentary road and trail
> networks in southern North Vietnam and Laos will be
> extremely difficult and probably impossible to obtain in
> 1966, given the conventional ordnance and strike capabili-
> ties likely to exist. 58/

The upper half of the "funnel" was a much more lucrative target -- not, however, because attacking it would choke the volume of supplies flowing into the South, but because it would inflict more pain on the regime in the North.

The flow of military logistics supplies from the USSR and China cannot be cut off, but the movement could be made considerably more expensive and unreliable if authoriza- tion is granted to attack intensively the rail connections to Communist China and if the three major ports are effectively mined. About 2/3 of North Vietnam's imports are carried by sea transport and the remainder move principally over the rail connections from Communist China. Mining the entrances to the three major ports would effectively transfer all imports to rail transport, including the flow of imports needed to maintain economic activity. The rail connections to Com- munist China would then become a more lucrative target and the disruptive effect of interdiction would then be more immediately felt. Sustained interdiction would then force Hanoi to allocate considerable amounts of manpower and materials to maintain the line. 59/

Bombing the supplies and supply facilities at the top of the "funnel" was therefore a "preferred LOC target system." It was not advanced as an interdiction measure, however, but as a means of increasing the penalty to Hanoi (and its allies), in terms of economic,

82

116

social, and political consequences, of supporting the war in the South, and thus presumably to reduce the desire to continue it. Other targets which might be attacked in order to similarly influence the will of the regime were: 26 military barracks and/or supply facilities on the JCS list, the neutralization of which would "impede the flow of military supplies and disrupt the military training programs of NVN"; 8 major POL storage facilities, which had a "direct bearing" on the regime's ability to support the war in the South, but which had to be hit almost simultaneously in order to reduce NVN to the critical point in meeting essential requirements; the Haiphong cement plant, the loss of which would "create a major impediment to reconstruction and repair programs" until cement could be imported; 3 major and 11 minor industrial plants which, though they made "no direct or significant contribution to the war effort" and "only a limited contribution" to the economy, were "highly prized and nominally lucrative" targets; or, as an alternative method of knocking out industrial production, the main electric power facilities. 60/

As for other potential targets in NVN -- the command and control system, agriculture, and manpower --

Attacks on these targets are not recommended at this time. In each case the effects are debatable and are likely to provoke hostile reactions in world capitals. 61/

The March CIA report, with its obvious bid to turn ROLLING THUNDER into a punitive bombing campaign and its nearly obvious promise of real payoff, strengthened JCS proposals to intensify the bombing. In particular, however, the report gave a substantial boost to the proposal to hit the POL targets. The POL system appeared to be the one target system in NVN to which, what the report called, "the principle of concentration" might be applied; that is, in which enough of the system could be brought under simultaneous attack to cut through any cushion of excess capacity, and in which a concentrated attack might be able to overwhelm the other side's ability to reconstruct, repair, or disperse its capacity. 62/

The POL targets had other qualities to commend them as the next escalatory step in ROLLING THUNDER. They really were pressure targets, but they could be plausibly sold as interdiction targets. The main ones were in the Hanoi/Haiphong sanctuaries, so that over and above any economic or military impact, strikes against them would signal that the last sanctuaries were going and the industrial and other targets there were now at risk. They fit the image of "war-supporting" facilities which strategic bombing doctrine and ample military precedent had decreed to be fair game in bringing a war machine to a standstill. They had, in fact, been struck before in other parts of NVN without any unusual political repercussions. They were situated in the arbitrarily-defined urban/industrial centers, but somewhat set apart from the densest civilian housing areas, and thus might not entail as many civilian casualties

.83

as other targets in those areas.

Moreover, even if the impact of POL strikes would be
within NVN itself -- because NVN supplied no POL at all to NVA/VC forces
in the South and used next to none in transporting other goods there --
POL was at least relevant as an interdiction target. It did power trucks
and boats which were involved in carrying men and supplies South. If
any truck in the NVN fleet was an acceptable interdiction target, wherever
it was and whatever its cargo, why not any POL?

4. McNamara Endorses POL, The President Defers It

Resumption of ROLLING THUNDER, as initiation of the pause,
did not, of course, constitute a final decision on escalation. The views
of CINCPAC and the JCS remained unaltered, and Secretary McNamara stood
committed, unless he reversed himself, to enlarging the area and intensity
of interdiction bombing and to destroying North Vietnamese POL. Neither
in OSD nor the White House had anyone opposed these measures on other than
prudential grounds -- the risk of alienating allies or provoking Chinese
or Russian intervention or uncertainty that results would justify either
the risks or the costs. Everyone seemed agreed that, were it not for these
factors, intensified bombing of the North would help to accomplish American
objectives. Nevertheless, the position of the decision-makers can best be
characterized as hesitant.

The services naturally undertook to tip the balance toward
the rapid and extensive escalation they had all along advocated. To
McNamara's memorandum to the President, the JCS had attached a dissent.
They felt that the Secretary underrated the "cumulative effect of our
air campaign against the DRV on morale and DRV capabilities" and overestimated the "constancy of will of the Hanoi leaders to continue a
struggle which they realize they cannot win in the face of progressively
greater destruction of their country." 63/

When McNamara reported to the Chairman the President's ruling
on ROLLING THUNDER, he apparently spoke of the difficulty of making out a
convincing case that air operations against North Vietnam could seriously
affect PAVN/VC operations in the South. In any event, following a conversation with the Secretary, General Wheeler ordered formation of a special
study group to devise a bombing effort "redirected for optimum military
effect." He explained, "the primary objective should be to reduce to the
maximum extent the support in men and materiel being provided by North
Viet-Nam to the Viet Cong and PAVN forces in South Viet-Nam." 64/ Headed
by a Brigadier General from SAC, composed of five Air Force, three Navy,
two Army, and one Marine Corps officers, and making extensive use of
CINCPAC assistance, this study group went to work in early February, with
an assignment to produce at least an interim report by 1 March and a final
report no later than 1 August. 65/

118

Meanwhile, routine continued, with CINCPAC recommending programs thirteen days prior to the beginning of a month and the JCS acting on these recommendations two days later. 66/ In consequence, McNamara received from the Chiefs on 19 February the same advice that had been given during the pause. 67/ He and the President responded much as before, though now permitting armed reconnaissance within the geographical limits fixed just before the pause and authorizing a significant increase -- to above 5,000 -- in numbers of sorties. 68/

On 1 March, when this slightly enlarged campaign opened, the Chiefs filed a memorandum stressing the special importance of an early attack on North Vietnamese POL. 69/ They had singled out POL somewhat earlier, writing McNamara in November, 1965, that attack on this target "would be more damaging to the DRV capability to move war-supporting resources within country and along infiltration routes to SVN than an attack against any other single target system." While causing relatively little damage to the civilian economy, it would, they reasoned force a sharp reduction in truck and other road traffic carrying men and supplies southward. They held also that the attack should be made soon, before North Vietnam succeeded in improving air defenses and in dispersing POL storage. 70/

McNamara had rejected this recommendation, not only because of the planned pause, but also because CIA sources questioned some of the Chiefs' reasoning and stressed counterarguments which they tended to minimize. Assessing the probable results of not only taking out North Vietnamese POL, but also mining harbors and bombing military and industrial targets in the northeast quadrant, the Board of National Estimates said, "Damage from the strikes would make it considerably more difficult to support the war in the South, but these difficulties would neither be immediate nor insurmountable." 71/ With regard to the POL system alone, the Board observed "It is unlikely that this loss would cripple the Communist military operations in the South, though it would certainly embarrass them." Pointing out that the bulk of storage facilities stood near Haiphong and Hanoi, the Board went on to say that "the Communists would unquestionably regard the proposed U.S. attacks as opening a new stage in the war, and as a signal of U.S. intention to escalate the scale of conflict." 72/ This appraisal did not encourage adoption of the JCS recommendation.

The Chiefs continued nevertheless to press for a favorable decision. Before and during the pause, they presented fresh memoranda to McNamara. 73/ A more detailed CIA study, obtained just after Christmas, provided somewhat more backing for their view. It conceded that the Communists were dispersing POL facilities and that an early attack on those at Hanoi and Haiphong "would add appreciably to the DRV's difficulties in supplying the Communist forces in the South." Nevertheless, it forecast that "adequate quantities of supplies would continue to move by one means or another to the Communist forces in South Vietnam." 74/

85

119

In mid-January, the DIA prepared an estimate considerably more favorable to the scheme. 75/ But in early February appeared a SNIE estimating effects on "DRV physical capabilities to support the insurgency in the South" of the various measures, including attacks on POL, previously recommended by CINCPAC and the JCS. Its conclusion, subscribed to by all intelligence services except that of the Air Force, was that, even with a campaign extended to port facilities, power plants, and land LOC's from China, "with a determined effort, the DRV could still move substantially greater amounts than in 1965." 76/

In renewing their recommendation on 1 March, and again on 10 March, the JCS once more disputed such assessments. In an appendix to their long March 1 memorandum to the Secretary, the Chiefs outlined a concept of operations upon which they proposed to base future deployments. With respect to the air war, they urged that it be expanded to include POL and the aerial mining of ports and attacks on Hanoi and Haiphong. Their rationale was as follows:

> To cause...NVN to cease its control, direction, and support of the communist insurgency in SVN and Laos, air strikes are conducted against military and war-sustaining targets in all areas, including the Hanoi/Haiphong complex and areas to the north and northeast. Armed reconnaissance within NVN and its coastal waters is conducted to interdict LOCs, harass, destroy and disrupt military operations and the movement of men and materials from NVN into Laos and SVN. Aerial mining of ports and interdiction of inland waterways and coastal waters, harbors and water LOCs are conducted to reduce the flow of war resources. Air reconnaissance and special air operations are conducted in support of the overall effort." 77/

Ten days later the Chiefs again requested attacks on the POL together with authorization to mine the approaches to Haiphong. This time they noted that Ambassador Lodge and Admiral Sharp had each recently endorsed such measures (no documents so indicating are available to the writer). Supporting their request they cited recent intelligence reports of North Vietnamese orders for expedited delivery of additional trucks. With the arrival of more trucks, POL would become even more critical to the North Vietnamese logistical effort. Once POL reserves were initially destroyed, however, the mining of Haiphong harbor would be the next immediate priority to prevent resupply by North Vietnam's allies. 78/ The Chiefs argued that the elimination as a package of these high value targets would significantly damage the DRV's war-sustaining capability.

This time, moreover, the Chiefs possessed support in the intelligence community. A study by CIA addressed the question which had been deliberately omitted from the terms of reference for the 4 February

86

120

SNIE, i.e., what effect bombing might produce on the will of the North Vietnamese regime. Judging from a summary with some extracts, preserved in Task Force files, it made a strong case for almost unlimited bombing such as CINCPAC and the JCS had steadily advocated. It accepted previous judgments that "the goals of sustained interdictions of the rudimentary road and trail networks in southern North Vietnam and Laos will be extremely difficult and probably impossible to obtain in 1966, given the conventional ordnance and strike capabilities likely to exist." Though arguing that more payoff could result from regarding North Vietnam as a "logistic funnel" and attempting to stop what went into it rather than what came out, it conceded that the "flow of military logistics supplies from the USSR and China cannot be cut off." But the report contended that such measures as mining harbors, maintaining steady pressure on LOC's with China, and destroying militarily insignificant but "highly prized" industrial plants would not only reduce North Vietnam's capacity to support the insurgency in the South but would influence her leaders' willingness to continue doing so. "Fundamental changes must be made if the effectiveness of the campaign is to be raised significantly," said the report, "First, the constraints upon the air attack must be reduced. Secondly, target selection must be placed on a more rational basis militarily." One point stressed was the importance of taking out all remaining POL storage facilities simultaneously and at an early date. 79/

With memoranda from the JCS now reinforced by this CIA report, Secretary McNamara had to reconsider the POL issue. Conferring with Wheeler on 23 March, he put several specific questions, among them whether destruction of POL storage facilities would produce significant results if not coupled with mining of North Vietnamese ports, what exact targets were to be hit, and with how many sorties. 80/ Responding with the requested details, the Chiefs said that they attached the highest importance to the operation, even if enemy harbors remained open. They strongly recommended, in addition, attacks on adjoining industrial targets and LOC's, in order to enhance the effect of destroying POL facilities. 81/

In a memorandum for the President on bombing operations for April, McNamara endorsed most of these JCS recommendations. He proposed authorizing attacks on seven of the nine POL storage facilities in the Hanoi-Haiphong area. Of the two he omitted, one lay near the center of Hanoi. In addition, McNamara recommended attacks on the Haiphong cement plant and on roads, bridges, and railroads connecting Haiphong and Hanoi and leading from the two cities to the Chinese border, and asked that the military commanders be permitted to run up to 900 sorties into the northeast quadrant, at their discretion.

For this marked stepping-up of the air war, McNamara put on paper a much more forceful presentation than that in his January memorandum. Using as a point of departure the general estimate that bombing could neither interdict supply of the South nor halt flow from China and Russia into the North, he argued that:

121

....The movement can be made considerably more
expansive and unreliable (a) by taking action to overload the roads and railroads (e.g., by destroying the
domestic source of cement), (b) by attacking the key
roads, railroads and bridge between Hanoi on the one hand
and Haiphong and China on the other, and (c) by pinching
the supply of POL, which is critical to ground movement
and air operations.

Amplifying one of these recommendations, McNamara commented that destruction of the plant, which produced 50% of North Vietnam's cement, would
make bridge and road rebuilding difficult. As for POL, he observed that
the facilities targeted represented 70-80% of those in the country.
Though the North Vietnamese possessed reserves and had probably already
built up some in the South, their transportation system depended on a
continuous supply. They were known to have recently doubled their orders
for imported Soviet POL. Eventually, though not necessarily in the short
run, he said, they were bound to suffer a shortage.

While McNamara conceded that he did not expect the proposed
program to yield quick results in South Vietnam, he predicted that it
would ultimately have some effect. Addressing some political issues that
had influenced the previous hesitancy, he asserted that the South would
probably do nothing more than adopt "a somewhat harsher diplomatic and
propaganda line" and that the Chinese "would not react to these attacks
by active entry -- by ground or air," unless the United States took
further steps, the decisions on which "at each point would be largely
within our own control." And offsetting such risks stood the possibility
of favorable political effects. McNamara ventured no promises. He said,
"We would not expect Hanoi to change its basic policy until and unless it
concluded that its chances of winning the fight in the South had become
so slim that they could no longer justify the damage being inflicted upon
the North." Nevertheless, he commented that destruction of POL facilities
"should cause concern in Hanoi about their ability to support troops in
South Vietnam" and concluded his memorandum by writing:

In the longer term, the recommended bombing program....
can be expected to create a substantial added burden on North
Vietnam's manpower supply for defense and logistics tasks and
to engender popular alienation from the regions should shortages
become widespread. While we do not predict that the regime's
control would be appreciably weakened, there might eventually
be an aggravation of any differences which may exist within the
regime as /to/ the policies to be followed.

Reading this memorandum, one might conclude that the
Secretary, after passing through a season of uncertainty, had finally

.88

made up his mind -- that he now felt the right action to be sharp
escalation such as CINCPAC, the JCS, and McNaughton had advocated during
the pause. But even now, despite the comparatively vigorous language of
the memorandum, one cannot be sure that McNamara expected or wanted the
President to approve his recommendations.

The memorandum was probably brought up at the White House
Tuesday luncheon on 28 March. Just sixteen days earlier, in response to
Marshal Ky's removal of General Nguyen Chanh Thi from Command of the
I Corps Area, Buddhist monks had initiated anti-Ky demonstrations in DaNang
and Hue. Soon, with other groups joining in, dissidents dominated the
northern and central part of the country. Many not only attacked the Ky
regime but denounced the American presence in Vietnam and called for negotiation with the NLF. Controlling the Hue radio and having easy access to
foreign newsmen, these dissidents won wide publicity in the United States.
As a result, Americans previously counted as supporters of administration
policy began to ask why the United States should expend its resources on
people who apparently did not want or appreciate help. Such questioning
was heard from both Democrats and Republicans in Congress. Quite probably,
the political situation in Vietnam and its repercussions in America stood
uppermost in the President's mind. Equally probably, McNamara recognized
this fact. If so, it should not have surprised him to find the President
taking much the same position as that which they had both taken, and
recorded in NSAM 288 in March, 1964, when the Khanh government trembled --
that it was imprudent to mount new offensives "from an extremely weak base
which might at any moment collapse and leave the posture of political
confrontation worsened rather than improved." 83/

In any event, the principal outcome of White House meetings
at the end of March was a string of urgent cables from Rusk to Lodge,
suggesting steps which might be urged on the Ky government and saying,
among other things,

....We are deeply distressed by the seeming unwillingness or inability of the South Vietnamese to put aside their
lesser quarrels in the interest of meeting the threat from
the Viet Cong. Unless that succeeds, they will have no
country to quarrel about....We face the fact that we ourselves cannot succeed except in support of the South Vietnamese. Unless they are able to mobilize reasonable solidarity,
the prospects are very grim." 84/

As for McNamara's proposals, the President approved only giving commanders
discretion to launch 900 sorties into the northeast quadrant during April
and permission to strike roads, railroads, and bridges outside or just on
the fringe of the prohibited circles around Hanoi and Haiphong. He did
not consent to measures involving more visible escalation of the air war.

McNamara returned to the Pentagon to inform the Chiefs that, while
these operations had not been vetoed, they were not yet authorized. 85/

    The President had authorized the extension of armed
reconnaissance into the northeast quadrant and strikes on 4 of the 5
bridges recommended by McNamara but deferred any decision on the crucial
portion, the strikes against the 5th bridge, the cement plant, the radar,
and above all the 7 POL targets. The JCS execution message for ROLLING
THUNDER 50, which was sent out on 1 April, directed implementation of what
had been approved. In addition, it ordered CINCPAC to "plan for and be
prepared to execute when directed attacks during April" against the 5th
bridge, the cement plant, the radar, and the 7 POL sites. 86/ A pencilled notation by Secretary McNamara with reference to these targets also
mentions April: "Defer...until specifically authorized but develop specific
plans to carry out in April." 87/

C. April and May -- Delay and Deliberation

1. Reasons to Wait

    Although the President's reasons for postponing the POL
decision are not known, and although the initial postponement seemed
short, a matter of weeks, it is evident from the indirect evidence available that the proposal to strike the POL targets ran into stiffening
opposition within the Administration, presumably at State but perhaps in
other quarters as well. Before the question was settled it had assumed
the proportions of a strategic issue, fraught with military danger and
political risk, requiring thorough examination and careful appraisal,
difficult to come to grips with and hotly contended. The question remained
on the agenda of senior officials for close to three months, repeatedly
brought up for discussion and repeatedly set aside inconclusively. Before
it was resolved a crisis atmosphere was generated, requiring the continuing
personal attention of all the principals.

    There can be little doubt that the POL proposal instigated
a major policy dispute. The explanation seems to be two-fold. One,
those who saw the bombing program, whatever its merits, as seriously
risking war with China or the USSR, decided to seize the occasion as
perhaps the last occasion to establish a firebreak against expanding the
bombing to the "flash points." Two, those who saw the bombing program
as incurring severe political penalties saw this as the last position
up to which those penalties were acceptable and beyond which they were
not. Both points no doubt merged into a single position. Both turned
the POL question into an argument over breaching the Hanoi/Haiphong
sanctuaries in any major way.

124

McNamara's Memorandum for the President, which had treated the POL strikes as a logical extension of the previous interdiction program into an area in which it might be more remunerative, did not address these questions of sanctuaries. No other single document has been located in the available files which does. Pieced together and deduced from the fragmentary evidence, however, it appears that the view that POL strikes ran too great a risk of counter-escalation involved several propositions. One was that the strikes might trigger a tit-for-tat reprisal (presumably by the VC) against the vulnerable POL stores near Saigon. The Secretary of Defense had himself made this point as early as mid-1965 in holding off Congressional and other proponents of Hanoi/Haiphong area POL strikes, citing the endorsement of General Westmoreland. 88/ The JCS had recognized the possibility in their November 1965 paper on POL strikes, although they considered it "of relatively small potential consequence, minor in comparison to the value of destruction of the DRV POL system." 89/ General Wheeler had also gone out of his way to allude to it. 90/ Under Secretary of State Ball, in a January 1966 memorandum, saw the possibility of an enemy reprisal in SVN as only the first act of a measure-countermeasure scenario which could go spiralling out of control: a VC reprisal against POL in SVN would put unbearable pressure on the U.S. to counter-retaliate against the North in some dangerous manner, which in turn would force the other side to react to that, and so on. 91/

More important than the fear of a VC reprisal, one assumes, was the belief that the POL sites were the first of the "vital" targets, high-value per se but also generally co-located with and fronting for NVN's other high-value targets. NVN, with its "vital" targets attacked and its economic life at stake, would at a minimum defend itself strenuously (again, provoking us to attack its airfields in our defense, which in turn might set off an escalatory sequence); or, at the other extreme, NVN might throw caution to the winds and call on its allies to intervene. This might be only a limited intervention at first, e.g. use of Chinese fighters from Chinese bases to protect NVN targets, but even this could go escalating upward into a full-scale collision with China. On the other hand, the strikes at the "vital" targets might be the Southeast Asian equivalent of the march to the Yalu, convince the other side that the U.S. was embarked on a course intolerable to its own interests, such as the obliteration of the NVN regime, and cause it to intervene directly. 92/

These arguments were not new, of course; they were arguments which could be, and no doubt were, used against any bombing at all. They gained force, however, as the bombing became more intense and the more the bombing was thought to really hurt Hanoi. (It was an irony of the original concept of the air war North that the more pressure it really applied and hence the more successful it was, the more difficult it was to prosecute.)

91

125

The belief that POL strikes would overload the negative side of the scale on political grounds had to do with the possibility that, since the targets were situated in relatively populated "urban" areas (even though outside of the center cities), the strikes would be construed as no less than the beginning of an attack on civilian targets and/or population centers. This possibility, too, could widen the war if it were taken by NVN and its allies as indicating a U.S. decision to commence "all-out" bombing aimed at an "unlimited" objective. But even if it did not widen the war, it could cause a storm of protest world-wide and turn even our friends against us. The world had been told repeatedly that the U.S. sought a peaceful settlement, not a total military victory; that the U.S. objectives were limited to safeguarding SVN; that bombing NVN was confined to legitimate military targets related to the aggression against SVN; and that great care was taken to avoid civilian casualties. Any or all of this could be called into question by the POL strikes, according to the argument, and the U.S. could be portrayed as embarking on a course of ruthless brutality against a poor defenseless population.

The argument about the escalatory implications of the proposed POL strikes was difficult to deal with. Official intelligence estimates were available which said, on balance, that Chinese or Soviet intervention in the war was unlikely, but no estimate could say that such intervention was positively out of the question, and of course intelligence estimates could misjudge the threshold of intervention, it was said, as they had in Korea. 93/

The argument about the political repercussions made some headway, however. Progress became possible because of the development of military plans to execute the strikes with "surgical" precision, thus minimizing the risk of civilian casualties, and because of the development of a "scenario" for the strikes in which military, diplomatic, and public affairs factors were coordinated in an effort to contain adverse reactions. There slowly unfolded a remarkable exercise in "crisis management."

2. The April Policy Review

Though McNamara's memorandum, and the President's indication that he might later approve POL, brought the Administration somewhat nearer to a decision for escalation, there was as yet no new consensus on how the air war against the North might be tailored to serve American objectives or, indeed, on what those objectives were or ought to be. The study group in the Joint Staff, completing its work early in April, offered a straightforward answer: "The overall objective is to cause NVN to cease supporting, directing, and controlling the insurgencies in South Vietnam and Laos." With his understanding, they could recommend a three phase

126

campaign leading to destruction of between 90 and 100% of all POL
storage, bridges, airfields, rail facilities, power plants, communications, port structures, and industry in North Vietnam. Whether the
Chiefs reasoned similarly is not apparent from the papers available.
Although they came out with comparable recommendations, they merely
"noted" this study. 94/

    Certainly, in spite of McNamara's memorandum recommending
escalation, no clear view prevailed within OSD or among civilians
elsewhere in the government occupied with Vietnam policy. Among the
papers left behind by McNaughton are some fragments relating to an attempt
early in April, 1966, to rethink the question of what the United States
sought in Vietnam. These fragments suggest an evolution between winter,
1965-66, and spring, 1966, from hesitancy to perplexity.

    The political situation in South Vietnam became increas-
ingly explosive. On March 31, 10,000 Buddhists had demonstrated in
Saigon against the government and the demonstrations had spread to other
cities in the next several days. On April 5, Premier Ky flew to Danang
to quell the rebellion and threatened to use troops if necessary. 95/
In this context, a meeting was convened at the White House on Friday,
9 April. Vance and McNaughton represented Defense; Ball, Bundy, and
Leonard Unger the State Department; and George Carver the CIA. Walt Rostow,
who had just replaced McGeorge Bundy, took part. So did Robert Komer
and Bill Moyers. 96/

    In preparation for this meeting, McNaughton, Ball, Unger,
and Carver undertook to prepare memoranda outlining the broad alternatives
open. Carver would make the case for continuing as is, Unger and McNaughton
for continuing but pressing for a compromise settlement -- Unger to take
an optimistic and McNaughton a pessimistic view and Ball to argue for
disengagement. Then four options were labelled respectively, A, B-O, B-P,
and C.

    Carver, advocating Option A, wrote:

OPTION A

I. Description of the Course of Action

    1. Option A involves essentially persevering in our
present policies and programs, adhering to the objectives of

        a. Preventing a North Vietnamese takeover of
South Vietnam by insurrectionary warfare, thus

            (1) Checking Communist expansion in
Southeast Asia

(2) Demonstrating U.S. ability to provide support which will enable indigenous non-Communist elements to cope with "wars of national liberation" and, hence,

(3) Demonstrating the sterile futility of the militant and aggressive expansionist policy advocated by the present rulers of Communist China.

b. Aiding the development of a non-Communist political structure within South Vietnam capable of extending its writ over most of the country and acquiring sufficient internal strength and self-generated momentum to be able to survive without the support of U.S. combat forces whenever North Vietnam ceases its present campaign of intensive military pressure.

To adopt this option, Carver reasoned, required, on the political side, work with all non-Communist Vietnamese factions "to insure that the transition to civilian rule is as orderly as possible and effected with a minimum disruption of current programs." The United States would have to make plain in Saigon that continued support was "contingent upon some modicum of responsible political behavior" and would have to "initiate the Vietnamese in the techniques of developing political institutions such as constitutions and parties." An "intensive endeavor at provincial and district levels" would have to complement efforts in the capital.

On the military side, Carver judged the demands of Option A to be as follows:

a. Current U.S. force deployments in Vietnam will have to be maintained and additional deployments already authorized should be made.

b. Efforts to hamper Communist use of Laos as a corridor for infiltrating troops and supplies into South Vietnam should be continued and in some respects intensified. There should be further employment of B-52's against selected choke points vulnerable to this type of attack. Additional programs should be developed to make our interdiction attacks more effective.

c. The aerial pressure campaign on North Vietnam should be sustained for both military and psychological purposes. Attacks should not be mounted against population centers such as Hanoi or Haiphong, but major POL storage depots should be destroyed and, probably, Haiphong harbor should be mined.

128

    d. Within South Vietnam we must recognize that the
period of political transition now in train -- even if it
evolves in the most favorable fashion possible -- will produce some diminution in the effectiveness of central authority
and some disruption in current programs. At best, we will be
in for a situation like that of late 1963. It is essential
that the Communists be prevented from making major military
gains during this time of transition or scoring military
successes which would generate an aura of invincibility or
seriously damage the morale of our South Vietnamese allies.
Therefore, it is essential that during this period, Communist
forces be constantly harried, kept off balance, and not permitted to press their advantage. The bulk of this task will
have to be borne by U.S. and allied forces during the immediate future and these forces must be aggressively and offensively
employed.

    Option B-O, as developed by Unger, assumed a "policy
decision that we will undertake to find a way to bring to an end by
negotiation the military contest in South Viet-Nam." (This paper, dated
"4/14/66," was prepared after the April 9 meeting but was filed with the
other papers of that date.) It was the optimistic version of this option
because Unger assumed the possibility of reaching a settlement "on terms
which preserve South Vietnam intact and in a condition which offers at
least a 60-40 chance of its successfully resisting Communist attempts
at political takeover."

    In pursuit of this option the United States would persuade
the GVN to negotiate with the NLF, offering amnesty and a coalition
government, though not one giving the NLF control of the military, the
police, or the treasury. The United States would withdraw troops "in
return for the withdrawal of North Vietnamese military forces and political
cadre." Perhaps, agreements between South Vietnam and North Vietnam would
provide for economic intercourse and mutual recognition.

    It would not be easy to persuade the GVN, Unger conceded.
Doing so might require not only words but withholding of funds or withdrawal of some American forces. And once the GVN appreciated that the
United States was in earnest, there would be danger of its collapse. Even
if these problems were surmounted, there would remain the difficulty of
pressing the negotiations to conclusion. "There is no assurance," Unger
wrote, "that a negotiated settlement can pass successfully between the
upper millstone of excessively dangerous concessions to the VC/NLF and
the nether millstone of terms insufficiently attractive to make the
VC/NLF consider it worthwhile to negotiate."

129

Militarily, Unger reasoned, Option B-0 would call for continuation of current efforts, perhaps with a modest increase in ground forces but with no step-up in the air war. Total refusal to talk on the part of the Communists would, however, Unger wrote,

> ...leave us with a question of what kind of stick we have to substitute for the proferred carrot and this might bring us up against the judgment of whether intensification and extension of our bombing in North Viet-Nam, coupled with whatever greater military efforts could be made in the South would bring the Communists to the table.

McNaughton's papers do not contain his original memorandum setting forth the pessimistic version of Option B. One can, however, infer its outlines from various other pieces in the McNaughton collection.

The difference between McNaughton and Unger presumably did not concern the objective -- negotiating out. It lay in McNaughton's expressing less confidence in an outcome not involving Communist control of South Vietnam. On the first Monday in April, he had talked with Michael Deutch, freshly back from Saigon. His notes read:

1. Place (VN) in unholy mess.

2. We control next to no territory.

3. Fears economic collapse.

4. People would not vote for 'our ride.'

5. Wants to carry out economic warfare in VC.

6. This is incorruptible and popular. Chieu /sic/ is best successor for Ky. '

7. Militarily will be same place year from now.

8. Pacification won't get off ground for a year.

If McNaughton himself accepted anything like this estimate, he would have been pessimistic indeed about prospects for the GVN's survival. Even if he did not take quite so gloomy a view, he probably felt, as he had intimated in one of his January memoranda, that the United States should prepare to accept something less than the conditions which Unger sketched. What practical consequences followed from this difference in view, one can only guess.

130

Option C, as stated by Ball, rested on the assumption that "the South Vietnamese people will not be able to put together a government capable of maintaining an adequate civil and military effort or -- if anything resembling actual independence is ever achieved -- running the country." On this premise, he concluded, much as in earlier memoranda, "we should concentrate our attention on cutting our losses." Specifically, he recommended official declarations that United States support depended on a representative government which desired American aid and which demonstrated its ability to create "the necessary unity of action to assure the effective prosecution of the war and the peace." Seizing upon the next political crisis in South Vietnam, the United States should, said Ball, "halt the deployment of additional forces, reduce the level of air attacks on the North, and maintain ground activity at the minimum level required to prevent the substantial improvement of the Viet Cong position."

Ball described two alternative outcomes from Option C. One was that the South Vietnamese might unify and "face reality," the other, far more likely in Ball's estimation, was that South Vietnam would fragment still further, "leading to a situation in which a settlement would be reached that contemplated our departure." He closed:

> Let us face the fact that there are no really attrac-
> tive options open to us. To continue to fight the war with
> the present murky political base is, in my judgment, both
> dangerous and futile. It can lead only to increasing com-
> mitments, heavier losses, and mounting risks of dangerous
> escalation.

In McNaughton's files are pencil notes which may relate either to his own missing memorandum or to a conversation that took place among some of the officials concerned. Despite its cryptic nature, it is worth reproducing in its entirety, in part because it gives a clue to thoughts passing at this time through McNamara's mind:

Do we press VNese or do they move themselves $\sqrt{?}$

What the point of probes if (w$\sqrt{\text{oul}}$d be counterproductive otherwise)

Ball

    1. No more US forces unless better govt

131

2. Reemph/asis/ of cond/itions/

   (a) Rep govt ask/ed/

   (b) Performance

3. Fashion govt unified and stable govt. Give time. Protect selves.

   Defend selves.

4. Effect

   (a) Nationalist

   (b) VC deal by GVN

If squeeze GVN first, and go to /Ball's position/ later, have contaminated Course C. Better to claim we want to win and they rush out to settle.

Timing critical. 10 days ago. Not today. Will have new chance when advisors decide how election set up. Unless elections rigged, Buddhists to streets.

Need Pres. statements re (a) cond/itio/ns and (b) optimism VNese moving that way.

W/oul/dn't the SVNese just comply and knuckle down and not do any better /?/ How do we move them toward compromise /?/ Maybe second time, we do throw in the towel and they make deal.

Lodge more likely to go for Ball ultimatum than B.

Anti-US govt likely to follow. How handle actual departure /?/ Do we want to precipitate anti-US /?/

Must we condition US and world public for 6 mos before 'ultimatum.'

Pres. to press, ans. qn. giving bases of our help.

BUT, why not get better deal for SVN by RSM approach? Give them choice now between (1) chaos 6 mos from now (via Ball) and VC govt. and (2) chance at compromise now with even chance of something better.

Who can deal -- Don, Thi?

. 98

132

If we followed RSM approach, ruin our image (pushing for deal) and cause demoralization. Tri Quang may even say we selling out.

We chilled bids earlier.

Could there be an independent Delta? Already accommodation.

As McNaughton's notes reveal, the group that met at the White House on April 9 was preoccupied with the immediate political crisis in South Vietnam. Early that morning, Walt Rostow had addressed a memo to Secretaries Rusk and McNamara suggesting a course of action for "breaking Tri Quang's momentum." 97/ His proposal -- which was the form the subsequent solution took -- called for giving substantial tactical concessions to the Buddhists on the issue of the Constituent Assembly in order to bring the regime-threatening demonstrations to an end. At the White House meeting later that day several participants were called on to prepare papers on the crisis.

Leonard Unger of the State Department drafted a paper outlining five possible outcomes of the crisis, the last two of which were a secession of neutralist northern provinces and/or a complete collapse of Saigon political machinery with the VC moving into the vacuum. 98/ His paper was probally considered at a meeting on Monday, April 12, as suggested by McNaughton's handwritten notes. 99/ At the same meeting, a long memorandum prepared by George Carver of CIA in response to a request at the Friday meeting, and entitled "Consequences of Buddhist Political Victory in South Vietnam," was also considered. 100/ Carver argued that while a Buddhist government would have been difficult for us to deal with it would not have been impossible and, given the evident political strength of the Buddhists, might even work to our long range advantage. The three American options in such a contingency were: (1) trying to throw out the new government; (2) attempting to work with it; or (3) withdrawing from South Vietnam. Clearly, he argued, the second was the best in view of our commitments.

That same day, Maxwell Taylor sent the President a detailed memo with recommendations for dealing with the Buddhist uprising. In essence he recommended that the U.S. take a tough line in support of Ky and against the Buddhists. In his words,

...we must prevent Tri Quang from overthrowing the Directorate (with or without Ky who personally is expendable) and support a conservative, feasible schedule for a transition to constitutional government. In execution of such a program, the GVN (Ky, for the present) should be encouraged to use the necessary force to restore and maintain order, short of attempting to reimpose government rule by bayonets on

133

Danang-Hue which, for the time being, should be merely
contained and isolated. 101/

These recommendations, however, had been overtaken by events. The GVN
had already found a formula for restoring order and appeasing the Buddhists.
In a three day "National Political Congress" in Saigon from April 12-14,
the GVN adopted a program promising to move rapidly toward constitutional
government which placated the main Buddhist demands. 102/ For a few
weeks the demonstrations ceased and South Vietnam returned to relative
political quiet. While not unusual as policy problems go, this political
crisis in South Vietnam intervened temporarily to divert official attention
from the broader issues of the war and indirectly contributed to the
deferral of any decision to authorize attacks on the POL in North Vietnam.
Other issues and problems would continue to defer the POL decision, both
directly and indirectly, for another two months.

With some semblance of calm restored momentarily to South
Vietnamese politics, the second-level Washington policy officials could
turn their attention once again to the broader issues of U.S. policy
direction. On April 14, Walt Rostow sent McNaughton a memo entitled
"Headings for Decision and Action: Vietnam, April 14, 1966," (implying
topics for discussion at a meeting later that day?). Item one on Rostow's
agenda was a proposed high-level U.S. statement endorsing the recent evolution of events in South Vietnam and stipulating that continued U.S. assistance and support would be contingent on South Vietnamese demonstration
of unity, movement toward constitutional government, effective prosecution
of the war, and maintenance of order. His second topic was the bombing of
the North, and subheading "b" re-opened the POL debate with the simple
question, "Is this the time for oil?" 103/ Other issues which he listed
for consideration included: accelerating the campaign against main force
units, economic stabilization, revolutionary construction, Vietnamese
politics (including constitution-making), and negotiations between the
GVN and the VC (if only for political warfare purposes).

On the same day, the JCS forwarded to the Secretary the
previously mentioned "ROLLING THUNDER Study Group Report: Air Operations
Against NVN" with a cover memo noting that its recommendations for a
stepped up bombing campaign were "in consonance with the general concept
recommended in JCSM-41-66...." 104/ The voluminous study itself recommended a general expansion of the bombing with provision for three special
attack options, one against the Haiphong POL center; the second for the
aerial mining of the sea approaches to Haiphong, Hon Gai, and Cam Pha; and
the third for strikes at the major airfields of Hanoi, Haiphong, and Phuc
Yen. 105/ In offering these options, the report stated that, "Military
considerations would require that two of the special attack options, POL
and mining, be conducted now. However, appreciation of the sensitivity of
such attacks is recognized and the precise time of execution must take
into account political factors." 106/ Somewhat optimistically, the report

134

estimated that the POL strike would involve only 13 civilian casualties, and the mining would cause none. 107/ While there is no specific record of the Secretary's reaction to this full-blown presentation of the arguments for expanded bombing, he had sent a curt memo to the Chiefs the previous day in reply to their JCSM 189-66 of March 26, in which they had again urged attacking the POL. Tersely reflecting the President's failure to adopt their (and his) recommendation, he stated, "I have received JCSM-189-66. Your recommendations were considered in connection with the decision on ROLLING THUNDER 50." 108/

As the second-echelon policy group returned to its consideration of the four options for U.S. policy (previously known as A, B-O, B-P, and C), the weight of recent political instability shifted its focus somewhat. When the group met again on Friday, April 16, at least three papers were offered for deliberation. William Bundy's draft was titled, "Basic Choices in Viet-Nam"; George Carver of CIA contributed "How We Should Move"; and a third paper called "Politics in Vietnam: A 'Worst' Outcome" was probably written by John McNaughton.

Bundy began with a sober appraisal of the situation:

The political crisis in South Viet-Nam has avoided outright disaster up to this point, but the temporary equilibrium appears to be uneasy and the crisis has meant at the very least a serious setback of the essential non-military programs. 109/

But the closeness with which political disaster had been averted in the South in the preceding week, "forces us to look hard at our basic position and policy in South Viet-Nam. We must now recognize that three contingencies of the utmost gravity are in some degree, more likely than our previous planning had recognized...."110/ The three contingencies Bundy had in mind were: (1) a state of total political chaos and paralysis resulting from an uprising by the Buddhists countered by the Catholics, Army, etc.; (2) the emergence of a neutralist government with wide support that would seek an end to the war on almost any basis and ask for a U.S. withdrawal; and (3) a continuation of the present GVN but in an enfeebled condition unable to effectively prosecute the war, especially the vital non-military aspects of it. Bundy's estimate was that the third contingency was the most likely at that moment, and that even the most optimistic scenario for political and constitutional evolution could not foresee a change within the succeeding three to four months. Nevertheless, he outlined the four possible U.S. lines of action much as they had been presented before:

Option A: To continue roughly along present lines, but to hope that the setback is temporary.

135

Option B: To continue roughly along present lines, but
to move more actively to stimulate a negotiated solution,
specifically through contact between the Saigon government
and elements in the Viet Cong and Liberation Front. This
option /lined out in McNaughton/ could be approached on an
"optimistic" /underlined in McNaughton/ or "lesser risk"
/lined out in McNaughton with "harder" penciled in above and
question marks in the margin/ basis, or on a "pessimistic"
/McNaughton underline/ or "greater-risk" /lined out in
McNaughton with "softer" pencilled in/ basis. The opening
moves might be the same in both options, but more drastic
indications of the U.S. position would /"be involved" penned
in by McNaughton/ in the "pessimistic" approach /, which
shades into option C below." penned by McNaughton/.

Option C: To decide now that the chances of bringing about an
independent (and non-Communist) /parenthesis added by McNaughton/
South Viet-Nam have shrunk to the point where, on an over-all
basis, the US effort is no longer warranted /lined out by
McNaughton and replaced in pencil with "should be directed at a
minimum-cost disengagement." Stet pencilled in the margin./
This would mean setting the stage rapidly /circled by McNaughton/
for US disengagement and withdrawal irrespective of whether any
kind of negotiation would work or not." /question marks in the
margin./ 111/

        Bundy did not identify in the paper his preferred option.
The tone of his paper, however, suggested a worried preference for "A".
In a concluding section he listed a number of "broader factors" which
"cut, as they always have, in deeply contradictory directions." 112/   The
first was the level of support for the Vietnam policy within the U.S.
While it was adequate for the moment, continued GVN weakness and political
unrest could seriously undermine it. With an eye on the 1968 Presidential
elections, Bundy prophetically summed up the problem:

        As we look a year or two ahead, with a military program
        that would require major further budget costs--with all their
        implications for taxes and domestic programs--and with steady
        or probably rising casualties, the war could well become an
        albatross around the Administration's neck, at least equal to
        what Korea was for President Truman in 1952. 113/

Moreover, if the prevailing malaise about the war among our non-SEATO
allies degenerated into open criticism, a far wider range of world issues
on which their cooperation was required might be seriously affected. With
respect to the Soviet Union, no movement on disarmament or other matters
of detente could be expected while the war continued. But since no

136

significant change in Chinese or North Vietnamese attitudes had been
expected in any circumstances, continuing the war under more adverse
conditions in South Vietnam would hardly worsen them. Bundy ended his
paper with an analysis of the impact of a U.S. failure in South Vietnam
on the rest of non-communist Asia, even if the failure resulted from a
political collapse in Saigon.

> 5. Vis-a-vis the threatened nations of Asia, we must
> ask ourselves whether failure in Viet-Nam because of clearly
> visible political difficulties not under our control would be
> any less serious than failure by our own choice /lined out in
> McNaughton7 without this factor. The question comes down, as
> it always has, to whether there is any tenable line of defense
> in Southeast Asia if Viet-Nam falls. Here we must recognize
> that the anti-Communist regime in Indonesia has been a tremen-
> dous "break" for us, both for in /McNaughton7 removing the
> possibility of a Communist pincer movement, which appeared
> irresistible almost certain /McNaughton7 a year ago, and
> in /McNaughton7 opening up the possibility that over a period
> of some years Indonesia may become a constructive force. But
> for the next year or two any chance of holding the rest of
> Southeast Asia hinges on the same factors assessed a year
> ago, whether Thailand and Laos in the first instance and
> Malaysia, Singapore, and Burma close behind, would--in the
> face of a US failure for any reason in Viet-Nam--have any
> significant remaining will to resist the Chinese Communist
> pressures that would probably then be applied. Taking the
> case of Thailand as the next key point, it must be our present
> conclusion that--even if sophisticated leaders understood the
> Vietnamese /McNaughton7 political weaknesses and our inability
> to control them--to the mass of the Thai people the failure
> would remain a US failure and a proof that Communism from the
> north was the decisive force in the area. Faced with this
> reaction, we must still conclude that Thailand simply could
> not be held in these circumstances, and that the rest of South-
> east Asia would probably follow in due course. In other words,
> the strategic stakes in Southeast Asia are fundamentally
> unchanged by the possible political nature of the causes for
> failure in Viet-Nam. The same is almost certainly true of the
> shockwaves that would arise against other free nations--Korea,
> Taiwan, Japan, and the Philippines--in the wider area of East
> Asia. Perhaps these shockwaves can be countered, but they
> would not /McNaughton7 be mitigated by the fact that the failure
> arose from internal political /sic7 causes rather than any US
> major error or omission." 114/

137

Once again, the domino theory, albeit in a refined
case by case presentation, was offered by this key member of the
Administration as a fundamental argument for the continuing U.S.
involvement in Vietnam. Bundy rejected even the subtle argument,
offered by some longtime Asian experts, that the uniqueness of the
Vietnamese case, particularly its extraordinary lack of political
structure, invalidated any generalization of our experience there to
the rest of Asia. Thus, he argued the American commitment was both
open-ended and irreversible.

George Carver of CIA argued quite a different point
of view. His paper began, "The nature and basis of the U.S. commitment in Vietnam is widely misunderstood within the United States,
throughout the world, and in Vietnam itself." 115/ Placing himself
squarely in opposition to the kind of analysis presented by Bundy,
Carver argued that we had allowed control over our policy to slip from
our grasp into the "sometimes irresponsible and occasionally unidentifi-
able hands of South Vietnamese over whom we have no effective control.
This is an intolerable position for a great power. 116/ By inferring
that our commitment was irreversible and open-ended, Carver maintained
we permitted the Vietnamese to exercise leverage over us rather than
vice versa. To correct this mistaken view of our commitment and get
our own priorities straight, Carver proposed a reformulation of objectives:

Whatever course of policy on Vietnam we eventually
decide to adopt, it is essential that we first clarify the
nature of our commitment in that country and present it in
a manner which gives us maximum leverage over our Vietnamese
allies and maximum freedom of unilateral action. What we
need to do, in effect, is return to the original 1954
Eisenhower position and make it abundantly clear that our
continued presence in Vietnam in support of the South Vietnamese struggle against the aggressive incursions of their
northern compatriots is contingent on the fulfillment of
both of two necessary conditions:

(a) A continued desire by the South Vietnamese
for our assistance and physical presence.

(b) Some measure of responsible political
behavior on the part of the South Vietnamese themselves
including, but not limited to, their establishment of a
reasonably effective government with which we can work. 117/

Carver was careful to state, however, that two to three
months would be required to prepare the ground for this kind of clarification so as not to have it appear we were reversing directions on Vietnam

138

or presenting the GVN with an ultimatum. Effectively carried out, such
a clarification would broaden the range of available options for the U.S.
and place us in a much better position to effect desired changes. The
mechanics of his proposal called for a Presidential speech in the near
future along the lines suggested earlier that week by Walt Rostow. The
President should express satisfaction at the evolution of political events
in South Vietnam toward constitutional government and indicate "that our
capacity to assist South Vietnam is dependent on a continued desire for
our assistance and on the demonstration of unity and responsibility in
the widening circle of those who will now engage in politics in South
Vietnam." 118/   Other speeches by the Vice President and members of
Congress in the succeeding weeks might stress the contingency of our
commitment, and press stories conveying the new message could be stimulated. Finally, three or four months in the future, the President would
complete this process by making our position and commitment crystal clear,
possibly in response to a planted press conference question. This public
effort would be supplemented by private diplomatic communication of the
new message to South Vietnamese leaders by the Embassy.

        Carver argued that putting the U.S. in a position to
condition its commitment would considerably enhance U.S. flexibility in
an uncertain policy environment.

        Once the U.S. position is clear we can then see whether
        our word to the Vietnamese stimulates better and more respon-
        sible political behavior. If it does, we will have improved
        Option A's chances for success. If it does not, or if South
        Vietnam descends into chaos and anarchy, we will have laid
        the groundwork essential to the successful adoption of Option C
        with minimal political cost. 119/

Questions which remained to be answered included: (1) whether to continue
with scheduled troop deployments; (2) whether to give the GVN a specific
list of actions on which we expected action and then rate their performance,
or rely on a more general evaluation; (3) whether the U.S. should continue
to probe the DRV/NLF on the possibility of negotiations; (4) whether to
encourage the GVN to make negotiation overtures to the VC.

        The third paper, Politics in Vietnam: A "Worst" Outcome,
(presumably by McNaughton) dealt with the unsavory possibility of a fall
of the current government and its replacement by a "neutralist" successor
that sought negotiations, a ceasefire, and a coalition with the VC. After
considering a variety of possible, although equally unpromising, courses
of action, the paper argued that in such a case the U.S. would have "little
choice but to get out of Vietnam....Governing objectives should be:
minimizing the inevitable loss of face and protecting U.S. forces, allied
forces, and those South Vietnamese who appeal to us for political refuge." 120/
An intriguing tab to the same paper considered the impact on the U.S. position in the Pacific and East Asia in the event of a withdrawal from Vietnam.

139

Unlike the Bundy paper this analysis eschewed pure domino theorizing
for a careful country by country examination. The overall evaluation
was that, "Except for its psychological impact, withdrawal from Vietnam
would not affect the present line of containment from its Korean anchor
down the Japan-Ryukyus-Taiwan-Philippine Island chain." 121/   Four
possible alternate defense lines in Southeast Asia were considered: (1)
the Thai border; (2) the Isthmus of Kra on the Malay peninsula; (3) the
"Water Line" from the Strait of Malacca to the North of Borneo; and (4) an
"Interrupted Line" across the gap between the Philippines and Australia.
Like other analyses of the strategic problem in Southeast Asia, this
paper rejected any in-depth defense of Thailand as militarily untenable.
The best alternatives were either the Isthmus of Kra or the Strait of
Malacca; alternative four was to be considered only as a fall back position. The paper stands as a terse and effective refutation of the full-
blown domino theory, offering as it does cool-headed alternatives that
should have evoked more clear thinking than they apparently did about
the irrevocability of our commitment to South Vietnam.

What the exact outcome of the deliberations on these
papers was is not clear from the available documents. Nor is there any
clear indication of the influence the documents or the ideas contained
in them might have had on the Principals or the President. Judgments
on this score must be by inference. A scenario drafted by Leonard Unger
and included by McNaughton with Carver's paper suggests that some consensus was reached within the group reflecting mostly the ideas contained
in Carver's draft. Its second point stated:

On U.S. scene and internationally we will develop in
public statements and otherwise the dual theme that the U.S.
has gone into South Viet-Nam to help on the assumption that
(a) the Government is representative of the people who do want
our help (b) the Government is sufficiently competent to hold
the country together, to maintain the necessary programs and
use our help. President will elaborate this at opportune
moment in constructive tone but with monetary overtones if
there is any political turmoil or if Government unwilling to
do what we consider essential in such fields as countering
inflation, allocating manpower to essential tasks and the like. 122/

In fact, however, while we did attempt to steer the South Vietnamese
toward constitutional government on a democratic model, when the President
spoke out in succeeding weeks it was to reiterate the firmness of our
commitment and the quality of our patience, not to condition them. At a
Medal of Honor ceremony at the White House on April 21, he said:

There are times when Viet-Nam must seem to many a
thousand contradictions, and the pursuit of freedom there
an almost unrealizable dream.

140

But there are also times--and for me this is one of
them--when the mist of confusion lifts and the basic
principles emerge:

--that South Viet-Nam, however young and frail, has
the right to develop as a nation, free from the interference
of any other power, no matter how mighty or strong;

--that the normal processes of political action,
if given time and patience and freedom to work, will some-
day, some way create in South Viet-Nam a society that is
responsive to the people and consistent with their traditions.... 123/

The third point in the Unger scenario was to encourage
the GVN to establish contacts with the VC in order to promote defections
and/or to explore the possibilities of "negotiated arrangements." This
emphasis on contacts between the GVN and the VC may well have reflected
the flurry of highly public international activity to bring about negotiations between the U.S. and the DRV that was taking place at that time
(considered in more detail below). In any event, this entire effort at
option-generation came to an inconclusive end around April 20.

The last paper to circulate was a much revised redraft
of Course B that reflected the aforementioned ideas about GVN/VC contacts.
It was, moreover, a recapitulation of ideas circulating in the spring
of 1966 at the second-level of the government. That they were considerably
out of touch with reality would shortly be revealed by the renewed I Corps-
Buddhist political problem in May. The paper began with a paragraph discussing the "Essential element" of the course of action -- i.e. "...our
decision now to press the GVN to expand and exploit its contacts with
the VC/NLF." 124/ The point of these contacts was to determine what
basis, if any, might exist for bringing the insurgency to an end.

The proposed approach to the GVN was to be made with three
considerations in mind. The first was the dual theme that U.S. assistance
in South Vietnam depended on a representative and effective GVN and the
genuine desire of the people for our help. Continued political turmoil
in South Vietnam would force us to state this policy with increasing
sharpness. The second consideration was the U.S. military effort.
McNaughton specifically bifurcated this section in his revision to include
two alternatives, as follows:

(b) Continuation of the military program including U.S.
deployments and air sorties.

(1) Alternative A. Forces increased by the end of

the year to 385,000 men and to attacks on the key military
targets outside heavily populated areas in all of North
Vietnam except the strip near China.

(2) Alternative B. Forces increased in modest
amounts by the end of the year to about 300,000 (with
the possibility of halting even the deployments implicit
in that figure in case of signal failure by the GVN to
perform) and air attacks in the northeast quadrant of
North Vietnam kept to present levels in terms of intensity
and type of target. 125/

The third consideration was a continuation of U.S. support for GVN revolutionary development and inflation control.

Two alternative GVN tactics for establishing contact with
the NLF were offered. The first alternative would be an overt, highly
publicized GVN appeal to the VC/NLF to meet with representatives of the
GVN to work out arrangements for peace. Alternative two foresaw the
initiation of the first contacts through covert channels with public
negotiations to follow if the covert talks revealed a basis for agreement.
All of this would produce, the paper argued, one of the following outcomes:

(a) If things were going passably for our side but
the VC/NLF showed no readiness to settle on terms providing
reasonable assurances for the continuation of a non-Communist
regime in SVN, we might agree to plod on with present programs
(with or without intensified military activity) until the VC/
NLF showed more give.

(b) If things were going badly for our side we might
feel obliged to insist on the GVN's coming to the best
terms it could get with the VC/NLF, with our continuing military and other support conditioned on the GVN moving along
those lines.

(c) If things were going well for our side, the VC/NLF
might accede to terms which entailed no serious risks for
a continuing non-Communist orientation of the GVN in the
short term. It would probably have to be assumed that this
would represent no more than a tactical retreat of the VC/NLF. 126/

3. Exogeneous Factors

No precise reason can be adduced for the termination of
this interdepartmental effort to refine options for American action. In
a general way, as the preceding paper shows, the effort had lost some

touch with the situation; the GVN was far too fragile a structure at
that point (and about to be challenged again in May by I Corps Commander General Thi and his Buddhist allies) to seriously contemplate
contacts or negotiations with the VC. In Washington, the President
and his key advisors Rusk and McNamara were preoccupied with a host of
additional immediate concerns as well. The President had a newly appointed
Special Assistant, Robert Komer, who had recently returned from a trip
to Vietnam urging greater attention to the non-military, nation-building
aspects of the struggle. In addition, the President was increasingly
aware of the importance of the war, its costs, and its public relations
to the upcoming Congressional elections. McNamara and the JCS were
struggling to reach agreement on force deployment schedules and requirements; and Rusk was managing the public U.S. response to a major international effort to bring about U.S. negotiations with Hanoi. These concerns, as we shall see, served to continue the deferral of any implementation of strikes against North Vietnamese POL reserves.

On April 19, about the time the option drafting exercise
was ending, Robert Komer addressed a lengthy memo to the President
(plus the Principals and their assistants) reporting on his trip to
Vietnam to review the non-military aspects of the war. Presidential
concern with what was to be called "pacification" had been piqued during
the Honolulu Conference in February. Upon his return to Washington,
President Johnson named Komer to become Special Assistant within the
White House to oversee the Washington coordination of the program. To
emphasize the importance attached to this domain, Komer's appointment
was announced in a National Security Action Memorandum on March 28. 127/
As a "new boy" to the Vietnam problem, Komer betook himself to Saigon
in mid-April to have a first-hand look. His eleven page report represents more a catalogue of the well-known problems than any very startling
suggestion for their resolution. 128/   Nevertheless, it did provide the
President with a detailed review of the specific difficulties in the RD
effort, an effort that the President repeatedly stressed in his public
remarks in this period. 129/

At Defense, problems of deployment phasing for Vietnam occupied a good portion of McNamara's time during the spring of 1966. On
March 1, the JCS had forwarded a recommendation for meeting planned
deployments that envisaged extending tours of service for selected
specialties and calling up some reserve units. 130/   Whatever McNamara's
own views on calling the reserves, the President was clearly unprepared
to contemplate such seemingly drastic measures at that juncture. Like
attacks on North Vietnamese POL, a reserve callup would have been seen
as a complete rejection of the international efforts to get negotiations
started and as a decisive escalation of the war. Moreover, to consider
such an action at a time when South Vietnam was in the throes of a protracted political crisis would have run counter to the views of even
some of the strongest supporters of the war. So, on March 10, the Secretary asked the Chiefs to redo their proposal in order to meet the stipulated
deployment schedule, stating that it was imperative that, "...all necessary

143

actions...be taken to meet these deployment dates without callup of
reserves or extension of terms of service." 131/   The JCS replied on
April 4 that it would be impossible to meet the deployment deadlines
because of shortages of critical skills. They proposed a stretch-out
of the deployments as the only remedy if reserve callups and extension
of duty tours were ruled out. 132/   Not satisfied, the Secretary asked
the Chiefs to explain in detail why they could not meet the requirements within the given time schedule. 133/   The Chiefs replied on
April 28 with a listing of the personnel problems that were the source
of their difficulty, but promised to take "extraordinary measures" in
an effort to conform as closely as possible to the desired closure
schedule. 134/   The total troop figure for Vietnam for end CY 66 on
which agreement was then reached was some 276,000 men. This constituted
Program 2-AR.

These modifications and adjustments to the troop deployment schedules, of course, had implications for the supporting forces
as well. The Chiefs also addressed a series of memos to the Secretary
on required modifications in the deployment plans for tactical aircraft
to support ground forces, and for increases in air munitions requirements. 135/
These force expansions generated a requirement for additional airfields. 136/
When these matters are added to the problems created for McNamara and his
staff by the French decision that spring to request the withdrawal of all
NATO forces from French soil, it is not hard to understand why escalating
the war was momentarily set aside.

Another possible explanation for delaying the POL strikes
can be added to those already discussed. The spring of 1966 saw one of
the most determined and most public efforts by the international community
to bring the U.S. and North Vietnam to the negotiating table. While at
no time during this peace initiative was there any evidence, public or
private, of give in either sides' uncompromising position and hence real
possibility of talks, the widespread publicity of the effort meant that
the Administration was constrained from any military actions that might
be construed as "worsening the atmosphere" or rebuking the peace efforts.
Air strikes against DRV POL reserves would obviously have fallen into this
category.

In February, after the resumption of the bombing, Nkrumah
and Nasser unsuccessfully attempted to get negotiations started, the former
touring several capitals including Moscow to further the effort. DeGaulle
replied to a letter from Ho Chi Minh with an offer to play a role in settling the dispute, but no response was forthcoming. Prime Minister Wilson
met with Premier Kosygin in Moscow from Feb. 22-24 and urged reconvening
the Geneva Conference; the Soviets countered by saying the U.S. and DRV
must arrange a conference since the conflict was theirs. Early in March,
Hanoi reportedly rejected a suggestion by Indian President Radharrishnon
for an Asian-African force to replace American troops in South Vietnam.

144

Later that month Canadian Ambassador Chester Ronning went to Hanoi
to test for areas in which negotiations might be possible. He returned
with little hope, other than a vague belief the ICC could eventually
play a role.

Early in April, UN Secretary General U Thant advocated
Security Council involvement in Vietnam if Communist China and North
Vietnam agreed, and he reiterated his three point proposal for getting
the parties together (cessation of bombing; scaling down of all military activity; and willingness of both sides to meet). No response was
forthcoming from the DRV, but later that month during meetings of the
"Third National Assembly" Ho and Premier Pham Van Dong reiterated the
unyielding North Vietnamese position that the U.S. must accept the four
points as the basis for solving the war before negotiations could start.
On April 29, Canadian Prime Minister Pearson proposed a ceasefire and
a gradual withdrawal of troops as steps toward peace. The ceasefire was
seen as the first part of peace negotiations without prior conditions.
Phased withdrawals would begin as the negotiations proceeded. The U.S.
endorsed the Pearson proposal which was probably enough at that stage
to insure its rejection by Hanoi. On the same day, Danish PM Krag urged
the US to accept a transitional coalition government as a realistic step
toward peace.

In May, Netherlands Foreign Minister Luns proposed a mutual
reduction in the hostilities as a step toward a ceasefire and to prevent
any further escalation. Neither side made any direct response. On May
22, Guinea and Algeria called for an end to the bombing and a strict
respect for the Geneva Agreements as the basis of peace in Vietnam. In
a major speech on May 25, U Thant called for a reduction of hostilities,
but rejected the notion that the UN had prime responsibility for finding
a settlement. Early in June press attention was focused on apparent
Romanian efforts to bring Hanoi to the negotiating table. Romanian
intermediaries made soundings in Hanoi and Peking but turned up no new
sentiment for talks. In mid-June Canadian Ambassador Ronning made a
second trip to Hanoi but found no signs of give in the DRV portion (detailed
discussion below). Near the end of June a French official, Jean Sainteny,
reported from Hanoi and Peking through Agence France-Presse that the DRV
had left him with the impression that negotiations might be possible if
the U.S. committed itself in advance to a timetable for the withdrawal of
forces from South Vietnam. With pressure again mounting for additional U.S.
measures against the North and the failure of the Ronning mission, the
State Department closed out this international effort on June 23 (the day
after the original POL execute order), stating that neither oral reports
nor public statements indicated any change in the basic elements of
Hanoi's position. On June 27, Secretary Rusk told the SEATO Conference
in Camberra, "I see no prospect of peace at the present moment." 137/
The bombing of the POL storage areas in Hanoi and Haiphong began on
June 29.

Declassified per Executive Order 13526, Section 3.3
NND Project Number: NND 63316. By: NWD Date: 2011

143

TOP SECRET - Sensitive

The seriousness with which these international efforts were being treated within the U.S. Government is reflected in two memos from the period of late April and early May. On April 27, Maxwell Taylor, in his capacity as military advisor to the President, sent a memo to the President entitled, "Assessment and Uses of Negotiation Blue Chips." The heart of his analysis was that bombing was a "blue chip" like cease-fire, withdrawal of forces, amnesty for VC/NVA, etc., to be given away at the negotiation table for something concrete in return, not abandoned beforehand merely to get negotiations started. The path to negotiations would be filled with pitfalls, he argued,

> Any day, Hanoi may indicate a willingness to negotiate provided we stop permanently our bombing attacks against the north. In this case, our Government would be under great pressure at home and abroad to accept this precondition whereas to do so would seriously prejudice the success of subsequent negotiations. 138/

To avoid this dilemma, Taylor urged the President to clearly indicate to our friends as well as the enemy that we were not prepared to end the bombing except in negotiated exchange for a reciprocal concession from the North Vietnamese. His analysis proceeded like this:

> To avoid such pitfalls, we need to consider what we will want from the Communist side and what they will want from us in the course of negotiating a cease-fire or a final settlement. What are our negotiating assets, what is their value, and how should they be employed? As I see them, the following are the blue chips in our pile representing what Hanoi would or could like from us and what we might consider giving under certain conditions.
>
> a. Cessation of bombing in North Viet-Nam.
>
> b. Cessation of military operations against Viet Cong units.
>
> c. Cessation of increase of U.S. forces in South Viet-Nam.
>
> d. Withdrawal of U.S. forces from South Viet-Nam.
>
> e. Amnesty and civic rights for Viet Cong.
>
> f. Economic aid to North Viet-Nam.
>
> The Viet Cong/Hanoi have a similar stack of chips representing actions we would like from them.
>
> a. Cessation of Viet Cong incidents in South Viet-Nam.
>
> b. Cessation of guerrilla military operations.

112   TOP SECRET - Sensitive

146

> c. Cessation of further infiltration of men and supplies from North Viet-Nam to South Viet-Nam.
>
> d. Withdrawal of infiltrated North Vietnamese Army units and cadres.
>
> e. Dissolution or repatriation of Viet Cong. 139/

Continuing his argument, Taylor outlined his views about which "blue chips" we should trade in negotiations for concessions from the DRV.

> If these are the chips, how should we play ours to get theirs at minimum cost? Our big chips are a and d, the cessation of bombing and the withdrawal of U.S. forces; their big ones are c and e, the stopping of infiltration and dissolution of the Viet Cong. We might consider trading even, our a and d for their c and e except for the fact that all will require a certain amount of verification and inspection except our bombing which is an overt, visible fact. Even if Hanoi would accept inspection, infiltration is so elusive that I would doubt the feasibility of an effective detection system. Troop withdrawals, on the other hand, are comparatively easy to check. Hence, I would be inclined to accept as an absolute minimum a cessation of Viet Cong incidents and military operations (Hanoi a and b) which are readily verifiable in exchange for the stopping of our bombing and of offensive military operations against Viet Cong units (our a and b). If Viet Cong performance under the agreement were less than perfect, we can resume our activities on a scale related to the volume of enemy action. This is not a particularly good deal since we give up one of our big chips, bombing, and get neither of Hanoi's two big ones. However, it would achieve a cease-fire under conditions which are subject to verification and, on the whole, acceptable. We would not have surrendered the right to use our weapons in protection of the civil population outside of Viet Cong-controlled territory. 140/

Summing up, Taylor argued against an unconditional bombing halt in these words:

> Such a tabulation of negotiating blue chips and their purchasing power emphasized the folly of giving up any one in advance as a precondition for negotiations. Thus, if we gave up bombing in order to start discussions, we would not have the coins necessary to pay for all the concessions required for a satisfactory terminal settlement. My estimate of assets and values may be challenged, but I feel that it is important for us to go through some such exercise and make up our collective minds as to the value of our holdings and how

113

to play them. We need such an analysis to guide our own
thoughts and actions and possibly for communication to some
of the third parties who, from time to time, try to get
negotiations started. Some day we may be embarrassed if some
country like India should express the view to Hanoi that the
Americans would probably stop their bombing to get discussions
started and then have Hanoi pick up the proposal as a formal
offer. To prepare our own people as well as to guide our
friends, we need to make public explanation of some of the
points discussed above. 141/

In conclusion he sounded a sharp warning about allowing ourselves to
become embroiled in a repetition of our Korean negotiating experience,
where casualties increased during the actual bargaining phase itself.
It is hard to assess how much influence this memo had on the President's
and the Administration's attitudes toward negotiations, but in hind-
sight it is clear that thinking of this kind prevailed within the U.S.
Government until the early spring of 1968.

Taylor's memo attracted attention both at State and Defense
at least down to the Assistant Secretary level. William Bundy at State
sent a memo to Secretary Rusk the following week commenting on Taylor's
ideas with his own assessment of the bargaining value and timing of a
permanent cessation of the bombing. Since they represent views on the
bombing which were to prevail for nearly two years, Bundy's memo is reproduced in substantial portions below. Recapitulating Taylor's analysis
and his own position, Bundy began,

Essentially, the issue has always been whether we would
trade a cessation of bombing in the North for some degree of
reduction or elimination of Viet Cong and new North Vietnamese activity in the South, or a cessation of infiltration
from the North, or a combination of both. 142/

Worried that Taylor's willingness to trade a cessation of US/GVN bombing
and offensive operations for a cessation of VC/NVA activity might be
prejudicial to the GVN, Bundy outlined his own concept of what would be
a reciprocal concession from the DRV:

...I have myself been more inclined to an asking price,
at least, that would include both a declared cessation of
infiltration and a sharp reduction in VC/NVA military operations in the South. Even though we could not truly verify
the cessation of infiltration, the present volume and routes
are such that we could readily ascertain whether there was
any significant movement, using our own air. Moreover, DRV

action concerning infiltration would be a tremendous
psychological blow to the VC and would constitute an
admission which they have always declined really to make.

Whichever form of trade might be pursued if the issue
even arose -- as it conceivably might through such nibbles
as the present Ronning effort -- I fully agree with General
Taylor that we should do all we can to avoid the pitfalls
of ceasing bombing in return simply for a willingness to talk. 143/

Concerned that the current spate of international peace moves might entice
the Administration in another bombing pause, Bundy reminded the Secretary
that,

...during our long pause in January, we pretty much
agreed among ourselves that as a practical matter, if Hanoi
started to play negotiating games that even seemed to be
serious, we would have great difficulty in resuming bombing
for some time. This was and is a built-in weakness of the
"pause" approach. It does not apply to informal talks with
the DRV, directly or indirectly, on the conditions under
which we would stop bombing, nor does it apply to possible
third country suggestions. As to the latter, I myself believe
that our past record sufficiently stresses that we could stop
the bombing only if the other side did something in response.
Thus, I would not at this moment favor any additional public
statement by us, which might simply highlight the issue and
bring about the very pressures we seek to avoid. 144/

Hence, he concluded,

As you can see, these reactions are tentative as to the
form of the trade, but quite firm that there must in fact be
a trade and that we should not consider another "pause" under
existing circumstances. If we agree merely to these points,
I think we will have made some progress. 145/

Bombing was thus seen from within the Administration as a counter to be
traded during negotiations, a perception not shared by large segments of
the international community where bombing was always regarded as an
impediment to any such negotiations. Hanoi, however, had always clearly
seen the bombing as the focal point in the test of wills with the U.S.

While Secretary Rusk was fending off this international
pressure for an end to the bombing and de-escalation of the war as a
means to peace, the President was having increasing trouble with war-
dissenters within his own party. The US had scarcely resumed the bombing

149

of the North after the extended December-January pause when Senator
Fulbright opened hearings by his Senate Foreign Relations Committee
into the Vietnam war. Witnesses who took varying degrees of exception
to U.S. policy as they testified in early February included former
Ambassador George Kennan and retired General James Gavin. Secretary
Rusk appeared on February 18 and defended U.S. involvement as a fulfillment of our SEATO obligations. In a stormy confrontation with Fulbright
the Secretary repeatedly reminded the Senator of his support for the
1964 Tonkin Gulf Resolution. The next day, Senator Robert Kennedy stated
that the NLF should be included in any postwar South Vietnamese government. Three days later, he clarified his position by saying that he had
meant the NLF should not be "automatically excluded" from power in an
interim government pending elections. Speaking no doubt for the President and the Administration, the Vice President pointedly rejected
Kennedy's suggestion on February 21. On the other side of the political
spectrum, Senator Russell, otherwise a hawk on the war, reacted in April
to the continuing political turmoil in South Vietnam by suggesting a
poll be taken in all large Vietnamese cities to determine whether our
assistance was still desired by the Vietnamese. If the answer was no,
he asserted, the U.S. should pull out of Vietnam.

The President was also regularly reminded by the press of
the possible implications for the November Congressional elections of a
continuing large effort in South Vietnam that did not produce results.
Editorial writers were often even more pointed. On May 17, James Reston
wrote:

> President Johnson has been confronted for some time
> with a moral question in Vietnam, but he keeps evading it.
> The question is this: What justifies more and more killing
> in Vietnam when the President's own conditions for an effec-
> tive war effort -- a government that can govern and fight in
> Saigon -- are not met?
>
> By his own definition, this struggle cannot succeed
> without a regime that commands the respect of the South
> Vietnamese people and a Vietnamese army that can pacify the
> country. Yet though the fighting qualities of the South
> Vietnamese are now being demonstrated more and more against
> one another, the President's orders are sending more and more
> Americans into the battle to replace the Vietnamese who are
> fighting among themselves. 146/

Public reaction to the simmering political crisis in South Vietnam was
reflected in declining popular approval of the President's performance.
In March, 68% of those polled had approved the President's conduct in
office, but by May, his support had declined sharply to only 54%. 147/

150

Some indication of the concern being generated by these adverse
U.S. political effects of the governmental crisis in South Vietnam is
offered by the fact that State, on May 21, sent the Embassy in Saigon
the results of a Gallup Poll on whether the U.S. should continue its
support for the war. These were the questions and the distribution of
the responses:

> 1. Suppose South Vietnamese start fighting on big scale
> among themselves. Do you think we should continue help them,
> or should we withdraw our troops? (A) Continue to help 28
> percent; (b) Withdraw 54 percent; (C) No opinion 18 percent.

> 2. If GVN decides stop fighting (discontinue war), what
> should US do -- continue war by itself, or should we withdraw?
> (A) Continue 16 percent; (B) Withdraw 72 percent; (C) No
> opinion 12 percent. Comparison August 1965 is 19, 63 and 18
> percent.

> 3. Do you think South Vietnamese will be able to estab-
> lish stable government or not? (A) Yes 32 percent; (B) No
> 48 percent; (C) No opinion 20 percent. Comparison January
> 1965 is 25, 42 and 33 percent. 148/

Lodge, struggling with fast moving political events in Hue and DaNang,
replied to these poll results on May 23 in a harsh and unsympathetic tone,

> We are in Viet-Nam because it cannot ward off external
> aggression by itself, and is, therefore, in trouble. If it
> were not in trouble, we would not have to be here. The time
> for us to leave is when the trouble is over -- not when it is
> changing its character. It makes no sense for us here to help
> them against military violence and to leave them in the lurch
> to be defeated by criminal violence operating under political,
> economic and social guise.

> It is obviously true that the Vietnamese are not today
> ready for self-government, and that the French actively tried
> to unfit them for self-government. One of the implications
> of the phrase 'internal squabbling' is this unfitness. But
> if we are going to adopt the policy of turning every country
> that is unfit for self-government over to the communists, there
> won't be much of the world left. 149/

Lodge rejected the implications of these opinion polls in the strongest
possible terms, reaffirming his belief in the correctness of the U.S.
course,

> The idea that we are here simply because the Vietnamese
> want us to be here -- which is another implication of the

phrase 'internal squabbling' -; that we have no national
interest in being here ourselves; and that if some of
them don't want us to stay, we ought to get out is to
me fallacious. In fact, I doubt whether we would have
the moral right to make the commitment we have made here
solely as a matter of charity towards the Vietnamese and
without the existence of a strong United States interest.
For one thing, the U.S. interest in avoiding World War
III is very direct and strong. Some day we may have to
decide how much it is worth to us to deny Viet-Nam to Hanoi
and Peking -- regardless of what the Vietnamese may think. 150/

Apparently unable to get the matter off his mind, Lodge brought it up
again in his weekly NODIS to the President on May 25,

    I have been mulling over the state of American opin-
    ion as I observed it when I was at home. I have also been
    reading the recent Gallup polls. As I commented in my
    EMBTEL 4880, I am quite certain that the number of those
    who want us to leave Viet-Nam because of current 'internal
    squabbling' does not reflect deep conviction but a super-
    ficial impulse based on inadequate information.

    In fact, I think one television fireside chat by you
    personally -- with all your intelligence and compassion --
    could tip that figure over in one evening. I am thinking of
    a speech, the general tenor of which would be; 'we are
    involved in a vital struggle of great difficulty and
    complexity on which much depends. I need your help.'

    I am sure you would get much help from the very
    people in the Gallup poll who said we ought to leave
    Viet-Nam -- as soon as they understood what you want them
    to support. 151/

Lodge's reassurances, however, while welcome bipartisan political support
from a critical member of the team, could not mitigate the legitimate
Presidential concerns about the domestic base for an uncertain policy.
Thus, assailed on many sides, the President attempted to steer what he
must have regarded as a middle course.

    The President's unwillingness to proceed with the bombing
of the POL storage facilities in North Vietnam continued in May in spite
of the near consensus among his top advisors on its desirability. As
already noted, the JCS recommendation that POL be included in Program 50
of the ROLLING THUNDER strikes for the month of May had been disapproved.152/
An effort was made to have the strikes included in the ROLLING THUNDER

152

series for the month of May, which ordinarily would have been ROLLING THUNDER 51, but the decision was to extend ROLLING THUNDER 50 until further notice, holding the POL question in abeyance. 153/ On May 3, McNaughton sent Walt Rostow a belated list of questions, "to put into the 'ask-Lodge' hopper." The first set of proposed queries had to do with the bombing program and included specific questions about attacking POL. Whether Rostow did, in fact, query Lodge on the matter is not clear from the available cables, but in any case, Rostow took up the matter of the POL attacks himself in an important memorandum to Rusk and McNamara on May 6. Rostow developed his argument for striking the petroleum reserves on the basis of U.S. experience in the World War II attacks on German oil supplies and storage facilities. His reasoning was as follows:

> From the moment that serious and systematic oil attacks started, front line single engine fighter strength and tank mobility were affected. The reason was this: it proved much more difficult, in the face of general oil shortage, to allocate from less important to more important uses than the simple arithmetic of the problem would suggest. Oil moves in various logistical channels from central sources. When the central sources began to dry up the effects proved fairly prompt and widespread. What look like reserves statistically are rather inflexible commitments to logistical pipelines. 154/

The same results might be expected from heavy and sustained attacks on the North Vietnamese oil reserves,

> With an understanding that simple analogies are dangerous, I nevertheless feel it is quite possible the military effects of a systematic and sustained bombing of POL in North Vietnam may be more prompt and direct than conventional intelligence analysis would suggest.

> I would underline, however, the adjectives 'systematic and sustained.' If we take this step we must cut clean through the POL system--- and hold the cut -- if we are looking for decisive results. 155/

> On May 9, recalling that the VC had recently attacked three South Vietnamese textile factories, Westmoreland suggested that to deter further assaults against South Vietnamese industry, the U.S. should strike a North Vietnamese industrial target with considerable military significance such as the Thai Nguyen iron and steel plant. 156/ Concurring with the basic intent of the proposal, CINCPAC recommended that the target be the North Vietnamese POL system instead. "Initiation of strikes against NVN POL system and subsequent completed destruction, would be more meaningful and further deny NVN essential war making resources. 157/

153

Lending further support to these military and civilian recommendations was a study completed on May 4 by the Air Staff which suggested that civilian casualties and collateral damage could be minimized in POL strikes if only the most experienced pilots, with thorough briefing were used; if the raids were executed only under favorable visual flight conditions with maximum use of sophisticated navigational aids; and if weapons and tactics were selected for their pinpoint accuracy rather than area coverage. 158/ On May 22, COMUSMACV sent CINCPAC yet another recommendation for retaliatory air strikes against North Vietnamese industrial and military targets. He called for plans that would permit the U.S. to respond to any VC terror attacks by an air strike against a similar target in the North. In particular, the Hanoi and Haiphong oil storage sites were recommended as reprisal targets for VC attacks against U.S. or South Vietnamese POL. 159/

Intervening again in mid-May, however, was yet another round of the continuing South Vietnamese political crisis. It is not clear whether or not a decision on the strikes against Hanoi/Haiphong POL was deferred by the President for this reason, but it is plausible to think that it was a factor. In brief, the Buddhists in Hue and DaNang, with the active support and later leadership of General Thi, the I Corps commander, defied the central government. Thi refused to return to Saigon when ordered and only when Ky flew to DaNang and intervened with troops and police to recapture control of the two cities was GVN authority restored to the area. The crisis temporarily put the constitutional processes off the track and diverted high level American attention from other issues. 160/ The effect of this dispute on public support for the U.S. involvement in the war has already been discussed. Concern with bringing an end to this internal strife in South Vietnam and with pushing a reluctant GVN steadily along the road to constitutional and democratic government preoccupied the highest levels of the U.S. Government throughout May. These concerns momentarily contributed to forcing the military aspects of the war into the background for harried U.S. leaders whose time is always insufficient to the range of problems to be dealt with.

D.   The Decision to Strike

The POL decision was rapidly coming to a head. On May 31, a slight relaxation of the restrictions against attacking POL was made when six minor storage areas in relatively unpopulated areas were approved for attack. 161/ Apparently sometime in late May, possibly at the time of the approval of the six minor targets, the President decided that attacks on the entire North Vietnamese POL network could not be delayed much longer. In any case, sometime near the end of the month he informed British Prime Minister Wilson of his intentions. When Wilson protested, McNamara arranged a special briefing by an American officer for Wilson and Foreign Minister Michael Stewart on June 2. The following day, Wilson

154

cabled his appreciation to the President for his courtesy, but expressed
his own feeling of obligation to urge the President not to make these
new raids. Thus, he stated:

> I was most grateful to you for asking Bob McNamara to
> arrange the very full briefing about the two oil targets near
> Hanoi and Haiphong that Col. Rogers gave me yesterday....

> I know you will not feel that I am either unsympathetic
> or uncomprehending of the dilemma that this problem presents
> for you. In particular, I wholly understand the deep concern
> you must feel at the need to do anything possible to reduce
> the losses of young Americans in and over Vietnam; and Col.
> Rogers made it clear to us what care has been taken to plan
> this operation so as to keep civilian casualties to the
> minimum.

> However,...I am bound to say that, as seen from here,
> the possible military benefits that may result from this
> bombing do not appear to outweigh the political disadvantages
> that would seem the inevitable consequence. If you and the
> South Vietnamese Government were conducting a declared war
> on the conventional pattern...this operation would clearly
> be necessary and right. But since you have made it abundantly
> clear -- and you know how much we have welcomed and supported
> this -- that your purpose is to achieve a negotiated settlement,
> and that you are not striving for total military victory in
> the field, I remain convinced that the bombing of these targets,
> without producing decisive military advantage, may only increase
> the difficulty of reaching an eventual settlement....

> The last thing I wish is to add to your difficulties, but,
> as I warned you in my previous message, if this action is taken
> we shall have to dissociate ourselves from it, and in doing so
> I should have to say that you had given me advance warning and
> that I had made my position clear to you....

> Nevertheless I want to repeat...that our reservations
> about this operation will not affect our continuing support
> for your policy over Vietnam, as you and your people have
> made it clear from your [April 1965] Baltimore speech onwards.
> But, while this will remain the Government's position, I know
> that the effect on public opinion in this country -- and I
> believe throughout Western Europe -- is likely to be such as
> to reinforce the existing disquiet and criticism that we have
> to deal with. 162/

155

The failure of the special effort to obtain Wilson's support
must have been disappointing, but it did not stop the onward flow of
events. Available information leaves unclear exactly how firmly the
President had decided to act and gives no specific indication of the
intended date for the strikes. A package of staff papers prepared by
McNaughton suggests that the original date was to have been June 10.
A scenario contained in the package proposes a list of actions for the
period 8-30 June and begins with strike-day minus 2. The suggested
scenario was as follows:

> S-/Strike/ day minus 2: Inform UK, Australia, Japan
> S-day minus 1: Notify Canada, New Zealand, Thailand, Laos,
>   Philippines (Marcos only), GRC (Chiang only), Korea
> S-hour minus 1: Inform GVN
> S-hour: Strike Hanoi, Haiphong
> S-hour plus 2: Announce simultaneously in Washington and
>   Saigon
> S-hour plus 3-5: SecDef press backgrounder (depends on
>   strike timing and completeness of post-strike reports) 163/

The package also included a draft JCS execute message, a draft State
cable to the field on notifying third countries, a draft public announcement, a talking paper for a McNamara press conference, a list of anticipated
press questions, and maps and photographs of the targets.

The circle of those privy to this tentative Presidential decision
probably did not include more than a half dozen of the key Washington
advisers. Certainly the military commanders in the field had not been
informed. On June 5, Westmoreland urged that strikes be made against POL
at the "earliest possible" moment, noting that ongoing North Vietnamese
dispersal efforts would make later attacks less effective. 164/ Admiral
Sharp took the occasion to reiterate to Washington that the strikes,
besides underscoring the US resolve to support SVN and increase the pressure against NVN, would make it difficult for Hanoi to disperse POL,
complicate off-loading from tankers, necessitate new methods of transshipment, "temporarily" halt the flow to dispersed areas, and have a
"direct effect" on the movement of trucks and watercarft -- perhaps (if
imports were inadequate) limiting truck use. Sharp called the POL targets
the most lucrative available in terms of impairing NVN's military logistics capabilities. 165/ Two days later, in reporting the results of a
review of the armed recce program, CINCPAC again urged that POL be
attacked. He particularly noted the importance of,

> ...the effort being made by the NVN to disperse, camou-
> flage and package things into ever smaller increments. This
> is particularly true of POL....This again emphasizes the
> importance of souce /sic/ targets such as ports and major
> POL installations.

156

It is hoped that June will see a modification to
the RT /ROLLING THUNDER/ rules with authorization to
syrike /sic/ key POL targets, selected targets in the
Hon Gai and Cam Pha complexes /sic/, and relaxation of
the restrictions against coastal armed recce in the NE.
In addition, reduction in the size of the Hanoi/Haiphong
restricted areas would be helpful.... 166/

The CIA, however, remained skeptical of these expectations for strikes
against POL. On June 8, they produced a special assessment of the likely
effects of such an attack, probably in response to a request from the
Principals for a last minute evaluation. The report emphasized that
"neutralization" of POL would not in itself stop North Vietnamese support
of the war, although it would have an adverse general effect on the
economy.

It is estimated that the neutralization of the bulk
petroleum storage facilities in NVN will not in itself
preclude Hanoi's continued support of essential war activities. The immediate impact in NVN will be felt in the need
to convert to an alternative system of supply and distribution. The conversion program will be costly and create
additional burdens for the regime. It is estimated, however, that the infiltration of men and supplies into SVN
can be sustained. The impact on normal economic activity,
however, would be more severe. New strains on an already
burdened economic control structure and managerial talent
would cause reductions in economic activity, compound
existing distribution problems, and further strain manpower resources. The attacks on petroleum storage facilities in conjunction with continued attacks on transportation
targets and armed reconnaissance against lines of communications will increase the burden and costs of supporting the
war. 167/

The sequence of events in the POL scenario drawn up by McNaughton
was interrupted on June 7 by yet another international diplomatic effort
to get negotiations started, or at least to test Hanoi's attitudes toward
such a possibility. Canadian Ambassador Chester Ronning had been planning
a second visit to Hanoi for June 14-18 with State Department approval.
Thus, when Rusk, who was travelling in Europe, learned on June 7 of the
possibility of strikes before Ronning's trip, he urgently cabled the
President to defer them.

...Regarding special operation in Vietnam we have had
under consideration, I sincerely hope that timing can be
postponed until my return. A major question in my mind is
Ronning mission to Hanoi occurring June 14 through 18. This

157

is not merely political question involving a mission with
which we have fully concurred. It also involves importance of our knowing whether there is any change in the
thus far harsh and unyielding attitude of Hanoi. 168/

Much on his mind in making the request, as he revealed in a separate
cable to McNamara the following day, was the likelihood of "...general
international revulsion...." toward an act that might sabotage Ronning's
efforts.

> ...I am deeply disturbed by general international
> revulsion, and perhaps a great deal at home, if it becomes
> known that we took an action which sabotaged the Ronning
> mission to which we had given our agreement. I recognize
> the agony of this problem for all concerned. We could
> make arrangements to get an immediate report from Ronning.
> If has a negative report, as we expect, that provides a
> firmer base for the action we contemplate and would make
> a difference to people like Wilson and Pearson. If, on
> the other hand, he learns that there is any serious break-
> through toward peace, the President would surely want to
> know of that before an action which would knock such a
> possibility off the tracks. I strongly recommend, there-
> fore, against ninth or tenth. I regret this because of my
> maximum desire to support you and your colleagues in your
> tough job. 169/

The President responded to the Secretary's request and suspended action
until Ronning returned. When Ronning did return, William Bundy flew to
Ottawa and met with him on June 21. Bundy reported that he was "markedly
more sober and subdued" and had found no opening or flexibility in the
North Vietnamese position. 170/

> While these diplomatic efforts were underway, McNamara had
> informed CINCPAC of the high level consideration for the POL strikes, but
> stated:

> Final decision for or against will be influenced by
> extent they can be carried out without significant civilian
> casualties. What preliminary steps to minimize would you
> recommend and if taken what number of casualties do you
> believe would result? 171/

CINCPAC replied eagerly listing the conditions and safeguards for the
attack that the Air Staff study had suggested in early May. He would
execute only under favorable weather conditions, with good visibility
and no cloud cover, in order to assure positive identification of the
targets and improved strike accuracy; select the best axis of attack to

avoid populated areas; select weapons with optimum ballistic characteristics for precision; make maximum use of ECM support in order to hamper
SA-2 and AAA radars and reduce "pilot distraction" during the strikes;
and employ the most experienced pilots, thoroughly briefed. He added
that NVN had an excellent alert system, which would provide ample time
for people to take cover. In all, he expected "under 50" civilian
casualties. 172/ (This was the Joint Staff estimate, too, but CIA in
its 8 June report estimated that civilian casualties might run to 200-300.)

McNamara cabled his approval of the measures suggested and indicated that they would be included in the execute message. He stressed
that the President's final decision would be greatly influenced by the
ability to minimize civilian casualties and inquired about restrictions
against flak and SAM suppression that might endanger populated areas. 173/
On June 16, CINCPAC offered further assurances that all possible measures
would be taken to avoid striking civilians and that flak and SAM suppression
would be under the rightest of restrictions. 174/

The stage was thus set, and when the feedback from the Ronning
mission revealed no change in Hanoi's position, events moved quickly.

On 22 June the execution message was released. 175/ It authorized strikes on the 7 POL targets plus the Kep radar, beginning with
attacks on the Hanoi and Haiphong sites, effective first light on 24 June
Saigon time.

The execution message is a remarkable document, attesting in
detail to the political sensitivity of the strikes and for some reason
ending in a "never on Sunday" injunction. The gist of the message was
as follows:

> Strikes to commence with initial attacks against
> Haiphong and Hanoi POL on same day if operationally
> feasible. Make maximum effort to attain operational
> surprise. Do not conduct initiating attacks under mar-
> ginal weather conditions but reschedule when weather
> assures success. Follow-on attacks authorized as opera-
> tional and weather factors dictate.

> At Haiphong, avoid damage to merchant shipping. No
> attacks authorized on craft unless US aircraft are first
> fired on and then only if clearly North Vietnamese. Piers
> servicing target will not be attacked if tanker is berthed
> off end of pier.

> Decision made after SecDef and CJCS were assured every
> feasible step would be taken to minimize civilian casual-
> ties would be small. If you do not believe you can accom-
> plish objective while destroying targets and protecting

159

crews, do not initiate program. Take the following
measures: maximum use of most experienced ROLLING
THUNDER personnel, detailed briefing of pilots stressing
need to avoid civilians, execute only when weather permits visual identification of targets and improved strike
accuracy, select best axis of attack to avoid populated
areas, maximum use of ECM to hamper SAM and AAA fire
control, in order to limit pilot distraction and improve
accuracy, maximum use of weapons of high precision
delivery consistent with mission objectives, and limit
SAM and AAA suppression to sites located outside populated areas.

Take special precautions to insure security. If
weather or operational considerations delay initiation
of strikes, do not initiate on Sunday, 26 June. 176/

The emphasis on striking Hanoi and Haiphong POL targets on the
same day and trying to achieve operational surprise reflected an acute
concern that these targets were in well-defended areas and U.S. losses
might be high. The concern about merchant shipping, especially tankers
which might be in the act of off-loading into the storage tanks, reflected
anxiety over sparking an international incident, especially one with the
USSR.

With the execute message out, high-level interest turned to the
weather in the Hanoi/Haiphong area. The NMCC began to send Secretary
McNamara written forecasts every few hours. These indicated that the
weather was not promising. Twice the strikes were scheduled but had to
be postponed. Then, on 24 June, Philip Geyelin of the Wall Street Journal
got hold of a story that the President had decided to bomb the POL at
Haiphong, and the essential details appeared in a Dow Jones news wire that
evening. This was an extremely serious leak, because of the high risk of
U.S. losses if NVN defenses were fully prepared. The next day an order
was issued cancelling the strikes. 177/

The weather watch continued, however, under special security
precautions. The weather reports, plus other messages relating to the
strikes, continued, handled as Top Secret Special Category (SpeCat)
Exclusive for the SecDef, CJCS, and CINCPAC. (It is not known whether
the diplomatic scenario which involved informing some countries about
the strikes ahead of time was responsible for the press leak; in any case,
the classification and handling of these messages kept them out of State
Department channels.) The continued activity suggests that the cancellation of the strikes on the 25th may have been only a cover for security
purposes.

TOP SECRET - Sensitive

160

On the 28th Admiral Sharp cabled General Wheeler that his forces were ready and the weather was favorable for the strikes; he requested authority to initiate them on the 29th. 178/ General Wheeler responded with a message rescinding the previous cancellation, reinstating the original execution order, and approving the recommendation to execute on the 29th. The message informed Admiral Sharp that preliminary and planning messages should continue as SpeCat Exclusive for himself and the SecDef. 179/

The strikes were launched on 29 June, reportedly with great success. The large Hanoi tank farm was apparently completely knocked out; the Haiphong facility looked about 80 percent destroyed. One U.S. aircraft was lost to ground fire. Four MIGs were encountered and one was probably shot down. The Deputy Commander of the 7th Air Force in Saigon called the operation "the most significant, the most important strike of the War."

161

FOOTNOTES

1. Memorandum for the SecDef from Ambassador-at-Large Llewellyn E. Thompson, 12 October 1965, op. cit.

2. JCSS Armed Reconnaissance Study Group Report, "An Analysis of the Armed Reconnaissance Program in North Vietnam," 15 November 1965, Appendix 1 to Annex C.

3. JCSM 238-66, ROLLING THUNDER Study Group Report, "Air Operations Against North Vietnam," 14 April 1966, Tab B to Annex C to Appendix A to Section II, and Appendix B to Section II.

4. Memorandum for the SecDef from Ambassador-at-Large Llewellyn E. Thompson, 12 October 1965, op. cit.

5. JCSM 811-65, 10 November 1965, "Future Operations and Force Deployments with Respect to the War in Vietnam."

6. Memorandum for the DepSecDef from McNaughton, 9 November 1965, summarizing the JCS position.

7. JCSM 810-65, "Air Operations Against the North Vietnam POL System," 10 November 1965.

8. "Attack on the North Vietnam Petroleum Storage System -- A Study," prepared by J-3 in collaboration with DIA, 23 April 1965, revised 22 December 1965.

9. JCSM 810-65, 10 November 1965, op. cit.

10. Ibid., Appendix, Annex D.

11. Ibid.

12. Memorandum for the Director, CIA, from Sherman Kent, for the Board of National Estimates, "Probable Reactions of the DRV, Communist China, and the USSR to US Air Attacks on Petroleum Storage Facilities in North Vietnam," 27 November 1965; and Memorandum for the SecDef from Admiral W. F. Raborn, 3 December 1965, forwarding Memorandum for the Director, CIA, from Sherman Kent, for the Board of National Estimates, "Reactions to a US Course of Action in Vietnam," 2 December 1965.

13. Memorandum for Director, CIA from Sherman Kent, 27 November 1965, op. cit.

14. Ibid.

15. Ibid.

Declassified per Executive Order 13526, Section 3.3
NND Project Number: NND 63316. By: NWD Date: 2011

162

16. Memorandum for the Director, CIA, from Sherman Kent, 2 December 1965, op. cit.

17. Ibid.

18. Ibid.

19. Ibid.

20. Ibid.

21. Memorandum for the CJCS from the SecDef, 8 December 1965, "Military Operations in North and South Vietnam."

22. Memorandum for the DepSecDef from the Acting Director, CIA, 28 December 1965, "Probable Reactions to US Bombing Attacks on POL Targets in North Vietnam."

23. Ibid.

24. Ibid.

25. Ibid.

26. Ibid.

27. SNIE 10-2-65, 10 December 1965, "Probable Communist Reactions to a US Course of Action."

28. Ibid.

29. Ibid.

30. Ibid.

31. CM-1006-65, Memorandum for the SecDef, "Probable Reactions of the DRV, Communist China, and the USSR to US Air Attacks on the Petroleum Storage Facilities in North Vietnam," 2 December 1965.

32. CM 1071-65, Memorandum for ASD/ISA, 28 December 1965.

33. "Attack on the North Vietnam Petroleum Storage System--A Study" prepared by J-3 in collabroation with DIA, 23 April 1965, revised 22 December 1965.

34. Ibid.

35. JCSM 41-66, 18 January 1966.

129   TOP SECRET - Sensitive

163

36. Draft, W. P. Bundy, 1/15/66, "Scenario for Possible Resumption of Bombing."

37. Draft, McNaughton, 1/18/66, "Some Observations About Bombing North Vietnam."

38. JCS 2830, 292126Z January 1966, directed the resumption. This was the beginning of ROLLING THUNDER 48.

39. Memorandum for the President, "The Military Outlook in South Vietnam," 24 January 1966.

40. Ibid.

41. DIA Special Report AP-1-630-1-15-66, "Relationship Between Petroleum Storage and Distribution System and Petroleum Consumption in North Vietnam," January 1966.

42. SNIE 10-1-66, "Possible Effects of a Proposed US Course of Action on DRV Capability to Support the Insurgency in South Vietnam," 4 February 1966.

43. Ibid.

44. Ibid.

45. Ibid.

46. Ibid.

47. CM-1147-66, 1 February 1966, "Interdiction Operations Against the DRV."

48. JCSM 238-66, 14 April 1966, "ROLLING THUNDER Study Group Report," op. cit., Section I, Basic Report.

49. Ibid.

50. Ibid.

51. Ibid.

52. JCSM 113-66, 19 February 1966.

53. JCSM 130-66, 1 March 1966; JCSM 153-66, 10 March 1966.

54. CIA SC No. 0828/66, "The Role of Air Strikes in Attaining Objectives in North Vietnam," March 1966.

55. Ibid.

164

56. Ibid.

57. Ibid.

58. Ibid.

59. Ibid.

60. Ibid.

61. Ibid.

62. Ibid.

63. Memo, SecDef to President, 24 Jan 1966, op. cit.

64. CM 1147-66: Memo, Chairman to Director, Joint Staff, 1 Feb 1966, JCS Study Group Report, Sect. I, App A, Annex B; JCSM 238-66: Memo, Director, Joint Staff to SecDef, 14 Apr 1966, states that the Study Group was formed "In furtherance of your conversation with the Chairman...."

65. JCS Study Group Report, Sect. I, App A, Annex B, and App B.

66. Ibid., Sect. II, App A, Annex D, pp. 12-13.

67. JCSM 113-66 (19 Feb 1966).

68. JCS Study Group Report, Sec. II, App A, Annex B, p. 13.

69. JCSM 130-66 (1 Mar 1966).

70. JCSM 810-65 (10 Nov 1965).

71. Memo, Sherman Kent to Director, CIA, 2 Dec 1965.

72. Memo, Sherman Kent to Director, CIA, 27 Nov 1965.

73. Ibid.

74. Memo, Acting Director, CIA, to DepSecDef, 28 Dec 1965.

75. DIA Special Report AP-1-630, 15 Jan 1966.

76. SNIE 10-1-66 (4 Feb 1966).

165

77. JCSM-130-66, 1 March 1966, Appendix A, p. A-3 (TS), emphasis added.

78. JCSM-153-66, 10 March 1966 (TS).

79. CIA SC No. 0828/66, "The Role of Air Strikes in Attaining Objectives in North Vietnam," March 1966.

80. JCSM 189-66, 26 Mar 1966.

81. Ibid.

82. Memo, SecDef to President (no date, but late March 1966), Subject: April Program of Air Strikes Against North Vietnam and Laos" (In McNaughton Book II, Tab V.)

83. NSAM No. 288, 17 Mar 1964.

84. State 2884 to Lodge, 30 Mar 1966, CF 49.

85. Notes on Memo, SecDef to President, "April Program...," copy in McNaughton Book VII, Tab L.)

86. JCS 7480, 010112Z April 1966.

87. Memorandum for the President, "April Program...," op. cit.

88. Testimony before the Senate Committees on Armed Services and Appropriations, 4 August 1965, SECRET.

89. JCSM 810-65, 10 November 1965, op. cit.

90. CM-1006-65, 2 December 1965, op. cit.

91. Memorandum for the President from Under SecState Ball, 25 January 1966.

92. Ibid.

93. Ibid.

94. JCS Study Group Report, Section III, Appendix A, pp. 2-3; JCSM 238-66, 14 April 1966.

95. Background Information Relating to Southeast Asia and Viet-Nam, op. cit., p. 28.

TOP SECRET - Sensitive

166

96. The papers and notes presented at this meeting for consideration and described in detail below are all contained in McNaughton Book II, Tab W (S-Sensitive).

97. W. W. Rostow Memorandum for Secretary Rusk and Secretary McNamara, April 9, 1966 -- 7:00 a.m., Subject: Breaking Tri Quang's Momentum (S), in McNaughton Book II, Tab S.

98. Leonard Unger, State, Far East, Planning for Viet-Nam Contingencies, April 11, 1966 (TS), in McNaughton Book II, Tab R.

99. McNaughton's handwritten notes dated "4/12/66" suggest such a meeting; they begin withha list of names (of participants?) and contain a numbered summary of probable discussion points. (McNaughton, Book II, Tab R.)

100. George A. Carver, CIA, Memorandum for the Honorable John T. McNaughton (copies to Rostow, Bundy, Moyers, Unger, Ball, Vance, Komer), 12 April 1966, with attached Memorandum entitled "Consequences of a Buddhist Political Victory in South Vietnam," 11 April 1966, (S-SENSITIVE); McNaughton Book II, Tab Q.

101. Maxwell D. Taylor, Memorandum for the President, Subject: "Current Situation in South Vietnam," April 12, 1966 (S); in McNaughton Book II, Tab P.

102. U.S. Senate, Committee on Foreign Relations, Background Information Relating to Southeast Asia and Vietnam (4th Revised edition), (Washington; GPO, March 1968), p. 28; for a good review of events at the time see Embassy Saigon msg. 4033, 16 April 1966 (S-LIMDIS).

103. W. W. Rostow, Headings for Decision and Action: Vietnam, April 14, 1966, April 14, 1966 (S), copy for Mr. McNaughton; in McNaughton Book II, Tab O.

104. JCSM-238-66, op. cit.

105. JCS ROLLING THUNDER Study Group Report: Air Operations Against NVN, 6 April 1966 (TS), Section III, Annexes D, E, and F.

106. Ibid., Section III, Appendix B, p. 6.

107. Ibid.

108. Robert S. McNamara Memorandum for the Chairman, Joint Chiefs of Staff, Subject: Air Operations Against North Vietnam, April 13, 1966.

167

109. DRAFT, FE: WPBundy;mk, 4/16/66, Basic Choices in Viet-Nam (S); in McNaughton Book II, Tab N.

110. Ibid.

111. Ibid.

112. Ibid.

113. Ibid.

114. Ibid., emphasis added.

115. How We Should Move, unsigned, undated paper (TS-SENSITIVE, "By Carver, 4/16/66" pencilled in by McNaughton) in McNaughton Book II, Tab Mc.

116. Ibid.

117. Ibid., emphasis added.

118. Ibid.

119. Ibid.

120. Politics in Vietnam: A "Worst" Outcome, 16 April 1966, unsigned paper in McNaughton Book II, Tab M (S).

121. Ibid., Tab A.

122. Scenario, FE: LUnger;hjh, 4/16 in McNaughton Book II, Tab Mc.

123. Weekly Compilation of Presidential Documents, vol. 2, no. 16, Monday, April 25, 1966, p. 555, emphasis added.

124. Course B, Unger 4/19/66; McNaughton revision 4/20/66; Unger re-revision 4/21/66 (S-SENSITIVE) in McNaughton Book II, Tab J.

125. Ibid.

126. Ibid.

127. NSAM 343, March 28, 1966 (S).

128. R. W. Komer Memorandum for Secretaries Rusk and McNamara, and Administrators Bell, Marks and Raborn, April 19, 1966 (S); with attached Memorandum for the President, April 19, 1966 (S).

168.

129. See, for instance, his Statementoon Vietnam during a News Conference at the White House, June 18, 1966, in <u>Weekly Compilation of Presidential Documents</u>, Monday, June 27, 1966, pp. 805-7.

130. JCSM-130-66, 1 March 1966 (TS).

131. Robert S. McNamara Memorandum to the Chairman, Joint Chiefs of Staff, Subject: "Deployments to Southeast Asia," 10 March 1966 (TS).

132. JCSM-218-66, 4 April 1966 (TS).

133. Robert S. McNamara Memorandum for the Chairman, Joint Chiefs of Staff, Subject: "Deployment Program for South Vietnam," 12 April 1966 (TS).

134. JCSM-274-66, 28 April 1966 (TS).

135. See JCSM-215-66, 2 April 1966 (TS); JCSM-233-66, 15 April 1966 (TS); and JCSM-375-66, 4 June 1966 (TS) on Tac Air requirements; and JCSM-317-66, 10 May 1966 (TS) on air munitions requirements.

136. JCSM-264-66, 27 April 1966 (TS).

137. The <u>New York Times</u>, 28 June 1966.

138. Maxwell D. Taylor Memorandum for the President, Subject: "Assessment and Use of Negotiation Blue Chips," April 27, 1966 (S); in McNaughton Book II, Tab H.

139. <u>Ibid</u>.

140. <u>Ibid</u>.

141. <u>Ibid</u>.

142. William P. Bundy Memorandum to the Secretary /of State_7, Subject: "General Taylor's Memorandum of April 27 on Negotiation Blue Chips," May 4, 1966 (S-NODIS); in McNaughton Book II, Tab K.

143. <u>Ibid</u>.

144. <u>Ibid</u>.

145. <u>Ibid</u>.

146. James Reston, "Washington: The Evaded Moral Question in Vietnam," <u>New York Times</u>, May 18, 1966.

147. Tabular presentation of Presidential popularity showing Truman, Eisenhower, Kennedy, and Johnson in SecDef Cable File 52, Tab F.

148. State Department message 3553, May 21, 1966 (C).

149. Embassy Saigon message 4880, May 23, 1966 (C-LIMDIS).

150. Ibid.

151. Embassy Saigon message 4952 for the President from Lodge, May 25, 1966, 7:20 a.m. (S-NODIS).

152. Robert S. McNamara Memorandum for the Chairman, JCS, April 13, 1966, op. cit.

153. JCS 9326, 261842Z April 1966.

154. W. W. Rostow Memorandum for the Secretary of State /and/ the Secretary of Defense, May 6, 1966 (TS-SENSITIVE).

155. Ibid.

156. COMUSMACV message to CINCPAC 091226Z May 1966 (S).

157. CINCPAC message to JCS 100730Z May 1966 (S); emphasis in original.

158. Memorandum apparently prepared in the Air Staff, "Safeguards for Success," May 4, 1966.

159. COMUSMACV message for CINCPAC 17603, 221145Z May 1966 (S).

160. For a complete review of these political events and the U.S. reactions and involvement in them, see Task Force Vol. IV. C., "Evolution of the War: US-GVN Relations: 1963-1967, part II" (TS-SENSITIVE).

161. History of Restrictions on Attack on NVN POL System, briefing paper prepared by the JCS, 10 August 1967 for Secretary of Defense Backup Book for appearance before Preparedness Subcommittee of the Senate Armed Services Committee, 25 Aug 1967, Section IV, Tab A(S).

162. State Department msg. 48 to OSLO (ToSec), 3 Jun 66, For Secretary and Ambassador Bruce, transmitting "for your eyes only" msg. received by President from P. M. Wilson (S-NODIS).

163. I-35728/66 (no date), Memorandum for the SecDef from ASD/ISA.

164. COMUSMACV msg 051201Z June 1966, personal for CINCPAC (TS).

165. CINCPAC to JCS, 060705Z June 1966.

166. CINCPAC msg. to JCS 080757Z June 1966 (TS).

167. CIA SC No. 08440/66, "The Effect of Destruction of NVN Petroleum Storage Facilities on the War in SVN," 8 June 1966.

168. Brussels msg 79 to State, Literally Eyes Only for the President from the Secretary, 7 June 1966 (TS-NODIS).

169. Brussels msg. 87 to State, Eyes Only for Secretary McNamara from the Secretary, 8 June 1966 (TS-NODIS).

170. State Department Memorandum of Conversation, "Visit of Ambassador Ronning to Hanoi, June 14-17, 1966," 21 June 1966.

171. OSD msg. to CINCPAC 3339-66, 132146Z June 1966, SECDEF to CINCPAC Eyes Only.

172. CINCPAC msg to SecDef, 140659Z June 1966, Exclusive.

173. OSD msg 3395-66, 152000Z June 1966, SecDef to CINCPAC, Eyes Only.

174. CINCPAC msg to SecDef, 160920Z June 1966, Exclusive.

175. JCS 5003 to CINCPAC, 222055Z June 1966. This execute message was drafted as an amendment to JCS 9326 of 26 April, which had extended ROLLING THUNDER 50 until further notice. The amendment simply made provision for an A, or Alpha, element to ROLLING THUNDER 50 consisting of these particular JCS fixed targets. The operation thus came to be identified as ROLLING THUNDER 50-A.

176. Ibid.

177. JCS msg 5311, to CINCPAC, 251859Z June 1966; New York Times, 1 July 1966.

178. CINCPAC msg 281015Z June 1966, SpeCat Exclusive to SecDef and CJCS.

179. JCS msg 5414 to CINCPAC, 281340Z, SpeCat Exclusive.

III. McNAMARA'S DISEN-
CHANTMENT -- JUL-DEC.1966

172.

III. McNAMARA'S DISENCHANTMENT -- JULY-DECEMBER 1966

The attack on North Vietnam's POL system was the last major escalation of the air war recommended by Secretary McNamara. Its eventual failure to produce a significant decrease in infiltration or cripple North Vietnamese logistical support of the war in the South, when added to the cumulative failure of the rest of ROLLING THUNDER, appears to have tipped the balance in his mind against any further escalation of air attacks on the DRV. As we shall see, a major factor in this reversal of position was the report and recommendation submitted at the end of the summer by an important study group of America's top scientists. Another consideration weighing in his mind must have been the growing antagonism, both domestic and international, to the bombing, which was identified as the principle impediment to the opening of negotiations. But disillusionment with the bombing alone might not have been enough to produce a recommendation for change had an alternative method of impeding infiltration not been proposed at the same time. Thus, in October when McNamara recommended a stabilization of the air war at prevailing levels, he was also able to recommend the imposition of a multi-system anti-infiltration barrier across the DMZ and the Laos panhandle. The story of this momentous policy shift is the most important element in the evolution of the air war in the summer and fall of 1966.

A. Results of the POL Attacks

1. Initial Success

Official Washington reacted with mild jubilation to the reported success of the POL strikes and took satisfaction in the relatively mild reaction of the international community to the escalation. Secretary McNamara described the execution of the raids as "a superb professional job," and sent a message of personal congratulation to the field commanders involved in the planning and execution of the attacks shortly after the results were in. 1/

In a press conference the next day, the Secretary justified the strikes "to counter a mounting reliance by NVN on the use of trucks and powered junks to facilitate the infiltration of men and equipment from North Vietnam to South Vietnam." He explained that truck movement in the first half of 1966 had doubled, and that daily supply tonnage and troop infiltration on the Ho Chi Minh trail were up 150 and 120 percent, respectively, over 1965. The enemy had built new roads and its truck inventory by the end of the year was expected to be double that of January 1965, an increase which would require 50-70 percent more POL. 2/

173

The Department of State issued instructions to embassies abroad to explain the strikes to foreign governments in counter-infiltration terms. The guidance was to the effect that since the Pause, the bombing of NVN had been carefully restricted to actual routes of infiltration and supply; there had been no response whatever from Hanoi suggesting any willingness to engage in discussions or move in any way toward peace; on the contrary, during the Pause and since, NVN had continued to increase the infiltration of regular NVN forces South, and to develop and enlarge supply routes; it was relying more heavily on trucking and had sharply increased the importation and use of POL. The U.S. could no longer afford to overlook this threat. Major POL storage sites in the vicinity of Hanoi and Haiphong were military targets that needed to be attacked.

The targets, the guidance continued, were located away from the centers of both cities. Strike forces had been instructed to observe every precaution to confine the strikes to military targets and there had been no change in the policy of not carrying out attacks against civilian targets or population centers. There was no intention of widening the war. The U.S. still desired to meet Hanoi for discussions without conditions or take any other steps which might lead toward peace. 3/

The strikes made spectacular headlines everywhere. Hanoi charged that U.S. planes had indiscriminately bombed and strafed residential and economic areas in the outskirts of Hanoi and Haiphong, and called this "a new and extremely serious step." The USSR called it a step toward further escalation. The UK, France, and several other European countries expressed official disapproval. India expressed "deep regret and sorrow," and Japan was understanding but warned that there was a limit to its support of the bombing of NVN. Nevertheless, according to the State Department's scoreboard, some 26 Free World nations indicated either full approval or "understanding" of the strikes, and 12 indicated disapproval. Press reaction to the attacks was short-lived, however, and within a week or so they were accepted as just another facet of the war. 4/

Meanwhile in the U.S., following a familiar pattern of the Vietnam war, in which escalations of the air war served as preludes to additional increments of combat troops, Secretary McNamara informed the Joint Chiefs of Staff, the Service Secretaries and the Assistant Secretaries of Defense on July 2 that the latest revision of the troop deployment schedule had been approved as Program #3. 5/ The troop increases were not major as program changes have gone in the Vietnam war, an increase in authorized year-end strength from 383,500 approved in April to 391,000 and an increase of the final troop ceiling from 425,100 to 431,000. 6/ But McNamara had personally rewritten the draft memo submitted to him by Systems Analysis inserting as its title, "Program #3." His handwritten

changes also included a closing sentence which read, "Requests for
changes in the Program may be submitted by the Service Secretaries
or JCS whenever these appear appropriate." 7/   This language clearly
reflected the following instruction that McNamara had received from
the President on June 28:

> As you know, we have been moving our men to Viet Nam
> on a schedule determined by General Westmoreland's require-
> ments.
>
> As I have stated orally several times this year, I should
> like this schedule to be accelerated as much as possible so
> that General Westmoreland can feel assured that he has all
> the men he needs as soon as possible.
>
> Would you meet with the Joint Chiefs and give me at
> your early convenience an indication of what acceleration
> is possible for the balance of this year. 8/

While the Chiefs were unable to promise any further speed-up in the
deployment schedule, the Secretary assured the President on July 15
that all possible steps were being taken. 9/   But as in the air war,
so also in the question of troop deployments a turning point was
being reached. By the fall of 1966 when Program #4 was under consideration, the President would no longer be instructing McNamara to honor
all of General Westmoreland's troop requests as fully and rapidly as
possible.

2. ROLLING THUNDER 51

In the air campaign strikes continued on the other major
POL storage sites, and were soon accepted as a routine part of the
bombing program. On 8 July, at a Honolulu conference, Secretary McNamara
was given a complete briefing on the POL program. He informed CINCPAC
that the President wished that first priority in the air war be given to
the complete "strangulation" of NVN's POL system, and he must not feel
that there were sortie limitations for this purpose. (He also stressed
the need for increased interdiction of the railroad lines to China.) 10/
As a result, ROLLING THUNDER program No. 51, which went into effect the
next day, specified a "strangulation" program of armed reconnaissance
against the POL system, including dispersed sites. The ceiling for
attack sorties on NVN and Laos was raised from 8100 to 10,100 per month. 11/

McNamara left CINCPAC with instructions to develop a comprehensive plan to accomplish the maximum feasible POL destruction while
maintaining a balanced effort against other priority targets. On July 24,
CINCPAC forwarded his concept for the operation to Washington. 12/   In
addition to the fixed and dispersed sites already under attack, he recommended strikes against the storage facilities at Phuc Yen and Kep airfields;

175

against the DRV's importation facilities (i.e., foreign ships in Haiphong harbor, destruction of harbor dredges, destruction of doc s, etc.); and the expansion of the reconnaissance effort to provide more and better information on the overall POL system. Also recommended was a step-up in attacks on rolling stock of all kinds carrying POL, and strikes on the Xom Trung Hoa lock and dam. In spite of this recommendation and a follow-up on August 8, ROLLING THUNDER 51 was only authorized to strike previously approved targets plus some new bridges and a bypass as outlined in the July 8 execute order. 13/

While CINCPAC and his subordinates were making every effort to hamstring the DRV logistical operation through the POL attacks, the Secretary of Defense was keeping tabs on results through specially commissioned reports from DIA. These continued through July and into August. By July 20, DIA reported that 59.9% of North Vietnam's original POL capacity had been destroyed. 14/ By the end of July, DIA reported that 70% of NVN's large bulk (JCS-targeted) POL storage capacity had been destroyed, together with 7% of the capacity of known dispersed sites. The residual POL storage capacity was down from some 185,000 metric tons to about 75,000 tons, about 2/3 still in relatively vulnerable large storage centers -- two of them, those at the airfields, still off limits -- and 1/3 in smaller dispersed sites. 15/ This still provided, however, a fat cushion over NVN's requirements. What became clearer and clearer as the summer wore on was that while we had destroyed a major portion of North Vietnam's storage capacity, she retained enough dispersed capacity, supplemented by continuing imports (increasingly in easily dispersable drums, not bulk), to meet her on-going requirements. The greater invulnerability of dispersed POL meant an ever mounting U.S. cost in munitions, fuel, aircraft losses, and men. By August we were reaching the point at which these costs were prohibitive. It was simply impractical and infeasible to attempt any further constriction of North Vietnam's POL storage capacity.

As the POL campaign continued, the lucrative POL targets disappeared and the effort was confined more and more to the small scattered sites. Finally, on September 4, CINCPAC (probably acting by direction although no instructions appear in the available documents) directed a shift in the primary emphasis of ROLLING THUNDER strikes. Henceforth they were to be aimed at, "...attrition of men, supplies, equipment and...POL...." 16/ Stressing the new set of priorities CINCPAC instructed, "POL will also receive emphasis on a selective basis." 17/ By mid-October, even PACAF reported that the campaign had reached the point of diminishing returns. 18/

176

3. POL - Strategic Failure

It was clear in retrospect that the POL strikes had been
a failure. Apart from the possibility of inconveniences, interruptions,
and local shortages of a temporary nature, there was no evidence that
NVN had at any time been pinched for POL. NVN's dependence on the
unloading facilities at Haiphong and large storage sites in the rest of
the country had been greatly overestimated. Bulk imports via ocean-
going tanker continued at Haiphong despite the great damage to POL docks
and storage there. Tankers merely stood offshore and unloaded into
barges and other shallow-draft boats, usually at night, and the POL
was transported to hundreds of concealed locations along internal waterways. More POL was also brought in already drummed, convenient for dispersed
storage and handling and virtually immune from interdiction. 19/

The difficulties of switching to a much less vulnerable
but perfectly workable storage and distribution system, not an unbearable
strain when the volume to be handled was not really very great, had also
been overestimated. Typically, also, NVN's adaptability and resourcefulness had been greatly underestimated. As early as the summer of 1965,
about six months after the initiation of ROLLING THUNDER, NVN had begun
to import more POL, build additional small, dispersed, underground tank
storage sites, and store more POL in drums along LOCs and at consumption
points. It had anticipated the strikes and taken out insurance against
them; by the time the strikes came, long after the decision had been
telegraphed by open speculation in the public media, NVN was in good
position to ride them out. Thus, by the end of 1966, after six months
of POL attacks, it was estimated that NVN still had about 26,000 metric
tons storage capacity in the large sites, about 30-40,000 tons capacity
in medium-sized dispersed sites, and about 28,000 tons capacity in smaller
tank and drum sites. 20/

One of the unanticipated results of the POL strikes, which
further offset their effectiveness, was the skillful way in which Ho Chi
Minh used them in his negotiations with the Soviets and Chinese to extract
larger commitments of economic, military and financial assistance from
them. Thus, on July 17 he made a major appeal to the Chinese based on
the American POL escalation. 21/   Since North Vietnam is essentially a
logistical funnel for supplies originating in the USSR and China, this
increase in their support as a direct result of the POL strikes must
also be discounted against whatever effect they may have had on hampering
North Vietnam's transportation.

The real and immediate failure of the POL strikes was
reflected, however, in the undiminished flow of men and supplies down
the Ho Chi Minh trail to the war in the South. In early July, the

intelligence community had indicated that POL could become a factor in constricting the truck traffic to the South. The statement was, however, qualified,

> The POL requirement for trucks involved in the infiltration movement has not been large enough to present significant supply problems. But local shortages have occurred from time to time and may become significant as a result of attacks on the POL distribution system. 22/

By the end of the month, however, the CIA at least was more pessimistic:

> Hanoi appears to believe that its transportation system will be able to withstand increased air attacks and still maintain an adequate flow of men and supplies to the South.

> ...Recent strikes against North Vietnam's POL storage facilities have destroyed over 50 percent of the nation's petroleum storage capacity. However, it is estimated that substantial stocks still survive and that the DRV can continue to import sufficient fuel to keep at least essential military and economic traffic moving. 23/

DIA continued to focus its assessments on the narrower effectiveness of the strikes in destruction of some percentage of North Vietnamese POL storage capacity without directly relating this to needs and import potential. 24/ By September, the two intelligence agencies were in general agreement as to the failure of the POL strikes. In an evaluation of the entire bombing effort they stated, "There is no evidence yet of any shortage of POL in North Vietnam and stocks on hand, with recent imports, have been adequate to sustain necessary operations." 25/ The report went even further and stated that there was no evidence of insurmountable transport difficulties from the bombing, no significant economic dislocation and no weakening of popular morale.

> Powerful reinforcement about the ineffectiveness of the strikes came at the end of August when a special summer study group of top American scientists submitted a series of reports through the JASON Division of the Institute for Defense Analyses (treated comprehensively below). One of their papers dealt in considerable detail with the entire bombing program, generally concluding that bombing had failed in all its specified goals. With respect to the recent petroleum attacks to disrupt North Vietnamese transportation, the scientists offered the following summary conclusions:

> In view of the nature of the North Vietnamese POL system, the relatively small quantities of POL it requires, and the options available for overcoming the effects of U.S. air strikes thus far, it seems doubtful that any critical denial

178

of essential POL has resulted, apart from temporary and
local shortages. It also seems doubtful that any such denial
need result if China and/or the USSR are willing to pay
greater costs in delivering it.

Maintaining the flow of POL to consumers within North
Vietnam will be more difficult, costly, and hazardous,
depending primarily on the effectiveness of the U.S. armed
reconnaissance effort against the transportation system.
Temporary interruptions and shortages have probably been
and can no doubt continue to be inflicted, but it does not
seem likely that North Vietnam will have to curtail its
higher priority POL-powered activities as a result.

Since less than 5 percent of North Vietnamese POL
requirements are utilized in supporting truck operations
in Laos, it seems unlikely that infiltration South will
have to be curtailed because of POL shortages; and since
North Vietnamese and VC forces in South Vietnam do not
require POL supplied from the North, their POL-powered
activities need not suffer, either. 26/

Coming as they did from a highly prestigious and respected group of
policy-supporting but independent-thinking scientists and scholars, and
coming at the end of a long and frustrating summer in the air war, these
views must have exercised a powerful influence on McNamara's thinking.
His prompt adoption of the "infiltration barrier" concept they recommended
as an alternative to the bombing (see below) gives evidence of the overall
weight these reports carried.

McNamara, for his part, made no effort to conceal his dissatisfaction and disappointment at the failure of the POL attacks. He
pointed out to the Air Force and the Navy the glaring discrepancy between
the optimistic estimates of results their pre-strike POL studies had
postulated and the actual failure of the raids to significantly decrease
infiltration. 27/ The Secretary was already in the process of rethinking
the role of the entire air campaign in the U.S. effort in Southeast Asia.
He was painfully aware of its inability to pinch off the infiltration to
the South and had seen no evidence of its ability to break Hanoi's will,
demoralize its population, or bring it to the negotiation table. The full
articulation of his disillusionment would not come until the following
January, however, when he appeared before a joint session of the Senate
Armed Services and Appropriations Committees to argue against any further
extension of the bombing. To illustrate the ineffectualness of bombing
he cited our experience with the POL strikes:

There is no question but what petroleum in the North is an essential material for the movement, under present circumstances, of men and equipment to their borders. But neither is there any doubt that with, in effect, an unrestricted bombing campaign against petroleum, we were not able to dry up the supply.

The bombing of the POL system was carried out with as much skill, effort, and attention as we could devote to it, starting on June 29, and we haven't been able to dry up those supplies....

We in effect took out the Haiphong docks for unloading of POL and we have had very little effect on the importation level at the present time. I would think it is about as high today as it would have been if we had never struck the Haiphong docks. And I think the same thing would be true if we took out the cargo docks in Haiphong for dry cargo....

I don't believe that the bombing up to the present has significantly reduced, nor any bombing that I could contemplate in the future would significantly reduce, actual flow of men and materiel to the South. 28/

Thus disenthralled with air power's ability to turn the tide of the war in our favor, McNamara would increasingly in the months ahead recommend against any further escalation of the bombing and turn his attention to alternative methods of shutting off the infiltration and bringing the war to an end.

B. Alternatives -- The Barrier Concept

1. Genesis

The fact that bombing had failed to achieve its objectives did not mean that all those purposes were to be abandoned. For an option-oriented policy adviser like McNamara the task was to find alternative ways of accomplishing the job. The idea of constructing an anti-infiltration barrier across the DMZ and the Laotian panhandle was first proposed in January 1966 by Roger Fisher of Harvard Law School in one of his periodic memos to McNaughton. 29/ The purpose of Fisher's proposal was to provide the Administration with an alternative strategic concept for arresting infiltration, thereby permitting a cessation of the bombing (a supporting sub-thesis of his memo was the failure of the bombing to break Hanoi's will). He had in mind a primarily air-seeded line of barbed wire, mines

and chemicals since the terrain in question would make actual on-the-
ground physical construction of a barrier difficult and would probably
evoke fierce military opposition. In his memo, Fisher dealt at length
with the pros and cons of such a proposal including a lengthy argument
for its political advantages.

The memo must have struck a responsive cord in McNaughton
because six weeks later he sent McNamara an only slightly revised
version of the Fisher draft. 30/   McNaughton's changes added little to
the Fisher ideas; they served merely to tone down some of his assertions
and hedge the conclusions. The central argument for the barrier concept
proceeded from a negative analysis of the effects of the bombing,

B. Present Military Situation in North Vietnam

1. Physical consequences of bombing

a. The DRV has suffered some physical hardship and
pain, raising the cost to it of supporting the VC.

b. Best intelligence judgment is that:

(1) Bombing may or may not - by destruction
or delay - have resulted in net reduction in the flow of men or
supplies to the forces in the South;

(2) Bombing has failed to reduce the limit on
the capacity of the DRV to aid the VC to a point below VC needs;

(3) Future bombing of North Vietnam cannot be
expected physically to limit the military support given the VC
by the DRV to a point below VC needs.

2. Influence consequences of bombing

a. There is no evidence that bombings have made
it more likely the DRV will decide to back out of the war.

b. Nor is there evidence that bombings have
resulted in an increased DRV resolve to continue the war to
an eventual victory. /Fisher's draft had read "There is some
evidence that bombings...."7

C. The Future of a Bombing Strategy

Although bombings of North Vietnam improve GVN morale
and provide a counter in eventual negotiations (should they
take place) there is no evidence that they meaningfully reduce

146

181

either the capacity or the will for the DRV to support the
VC. The DRV knows that we cannot force them to stop by bombing
and that we cannot, without an unacceptable risk of a major war
with China or Russia or both, force them to stop by conquering
them or "blotting them out." Knowing that if they are not
influenced we cannot stop them, the DRV will remain difficult
to influence. With continuing DRV support, victory in the
South may remain forever beyond our reach.

Having made the case against the bombing, the memo then spelled out the
case for an anti-infiltration barrier:

    II.   SUBSTANCE OF THE BARRIER PROPOSAL

        A. That the US and GVN adopt the concept of physically
cutting off DRV support to the VC by an on-the-ground barrier
across the Ho Chi Minh Trail in the general vicinity of the 17th
Parallel and Route 9. To the extent necessary the barrier would
run from the sea across Vietnam and Laos to the Mekong, a straight-
line distance of about 160 miles.

        B. That in Laos an "interdiction and verification zone,"
perhaps 10 miles wide, be established and legitimated by such
measures as leasing, international approval, compensation, etc.

        C. That a major military and engineering effort be
directed toward constructing a physical barrier of minefields,
barbed wire, walls, ditches and military strong points flanked
by a defoliated strip on each side.

        D. That such bombing in Laos and North Vietnam as
takes place be narrowly identified with interdiction and with
the construction of the barrier by

        1. Being within the 10-mile-wide interdiction
zone in Laos, or

        2. Being in support of the construction of the
barrier, or

        3. Being interdiction bombing pending the completion
of the barrier.

        E. That, of course, intensive interdiction continues at
sea and from Cambodia.

(It might be stated that all bombings of North Vietnam will stop
as soon as there is no infiltration and no opposition to the construction of the verification barrier.) 32/

        TOP SECRET - Sensitive

Among the McNaughton additions to the Fisher draft were
several suggested action memos including one to the Chiefs asking for
military comment on the proposal. Available documents do not reveal
whether McNamara sent the memo nor indicate what his own reaction to
the proposal was. He did, however, contact the Chiefs in some way
for their reaction to the proposal because on March 24 the Chiefs sent a
message to CINCPAC requesting field comment on the barrier concept. 33/
After having in turn queried his subordinates, CINCPAC replied on April 7
that construction and defense of such a barrier would require 7-8 U.S.
divisions and might take up to three and one half to four years to become
fully operational. 34/   It would require a substantial diversion of
available combat and construction resources and would place a heavy strain
on the logistics support system in Southeast Asia, all in a static defense
effort which would deny us the military advantages of flexibility in
employment of forces. Not surprisingly, after this exaggerated catalog
of problems, CINCPAC recommended against such a barrier as an inefficient
use of resources with small likelihood of achieving U.S. objectives in
Vietnam. These not unexpected objections notwithstanding, the Army (presumably at McNamara's direction) had begun an R&D program in March to
design, develop, test and deliver within six to nine months for operational evaluation a set of anti-personnel route and trail interdiction
devices. 35/

At approximately the same time an apparently unrelated offer
was made by four distinguished scientific advisors to the Government to
form a summer working group to study technical aspects of the war in
Vietnam. It is possible that the idea for such a study really originated
in the Pentagon, although the earliest documents indicate that the four
scholars (Dr. George Kistiakowsky - Harvard; Dr. Karl Kaysen - Harvard;
Dr. Jerome Wiesner - MIT; and Dr. Jerrold Zacharias - MIT) made the
first initiative with Adam Yarmolinsky, then working for McNaughton. 36/
In any case, McNamara liked the idea and sent Zacharias a letter on April 16
formally requesting that he and the others arrange the summer study on
"technical possibilities in relation to our military operations in
Vietnam." 37/   On April 26 he advised John McNaughton, who was to oversee
the project, that the scientists' group should examine the feasibility of
"A 'fence' across the infiltration trails, warning systems, reconnaissance
(especially night) methods, night vision devices, defoliation techniques,
and area-denial weapons." 38/   In this way the barrier concept was officially brought to the attention of the study group.

During the remainder of the spring, while McNamara and the
other Principals were preoccupied with the POL decision, the summer study
group was organized and the administrative mechanics worked out for providing

its members with briefings and classified material. The contract, it was determined, would be let to the Institute for Defense Analyses (IDA) for the study to be done through its JASON Division (ad hoc high-level studies using primarily non-IDA scholars). The group of 47 scientists (eventually to grow to 67 with the addition of 20 IDA personnel), representing the cream of the scholarly community in technical fields, finally met in Wellesley on June 13 for ten days of briefings by high-level officials from the Pentagon, CIA, State and the White House on all facets of the war. Thereafter they broke into four sub-groups to study different aspects of the problem from a technical (not a political) point of view. Their work proceeded through July and August and coincided with McNamara's disillusionment over the results of the POL strikes.

2. The JASON Summer Study Reports

At the end of August the Jason Summer Study, as it had come to be known, submitted four reports: (1) The Effects of US Bombing in North Vietnam; (2) VC/NVA Logistics and Manpower; (3) An Air Supported Anti-Infiltration Barrier; and (4) Summary of Results, Conclusions and Recommendations. The documents were regarded as particularly sensitive and were extremely closely held with General Wheeler and Mr. Rostow receiving the only copies outside OSD. The reason is easy to understand. The Jason Summer Study reached the conclusion that the bombing of North Vietnam was ineffective and therefore recommended that the barrier concept be implemented as an alternative means of checking infiltration.

Several factors combined to give these conclusions and recommendations a powerful and perhaps decisive influence in McNamara's mind at the beginning of September 1966. First, they were recommendations from a group of America's most distinguished scientists, men who had helped the Government produce many of its most advanced technical weapons systems since the Second World War, and men who were not identified with the vocal academic criticism of the Administration's Vietnam policy. Secondly, the reports arrived at a time when McNamara, having witnessed the failure of the POL attacks to produce decisive results, was harboring doubts of his own about the effectiveness of the bombing, and at a time when alternative approaches were welcome. Third, the Study Group did not mince words or fudge its conclusions, but stated them bluntly and forcefully. For all these reasons, then, the reports are significant. Moreover, as we shall see, they apparently had a dramatic impact on the Secretary of Defense and provided much of the direction for future policy. For these reasons, then, the reports are significant. Moreover, as we shall see, they .apparently had a dramatic impact on the Secretary of Defense and provided much of the direction for future policy. For these reasons important sections of them are reproduced at some length below.

184

The report evaluating the results of the U.S. air campaign against North Vietnam began with a forceful statement of conclusions:

SUMMARY AND CONCLUSIONS

1. As of July 1966 the U.S. bombing of North Vietnam (NVN) had had no measurable direct effect on Hanoi's ability to mount and support military operations in the South at the current level.

Although the political constraints seem clearly to have reduced the effectiveness of the bombing program, its limited effect on Hanoi's ability to provide such support cannot be explained solely on that basis. The countermeasures introduced by Hanoi effectively reduced the impact of U.S. bombing. More fundamentally, however, North Vietnam has basically a subsistence agricultural economy that presents a difficult and unrewarding target system for air attack.

The economy supports operations in the South mainly by functioning as a logistic funnel and by providing a source of manpower. The industrial sector produces little of military value. Most of the essential military supplies that the VC/NVN forces in the South require from external sources are provided by the USSR and Communist China. Furthermore, the volume of such supplies is so low that only a small fraction of the capacity of North Vietnam's rather flexible transportation network is required to maintain the flow. The economy's relatively under-employed labor force also appears to provide an ample manpower reserve for internal military and economic needs including repair and reconstruction and for continued support of military operations in the South.

2. Since the initiation of the ROLLING THUNDER program the damage to facilities and equipment in North Vietnam has been more than offset by the increased flow of military and economic aid, largely from the USSR and Communist China.

The measurable costs of the damage sustained by North Vietnam are estimated by intelligence analysts to have reached approximately $86 million by 15 July 1966. In 1965 alone, the value of the military and economic aid that Hanoi received from the USSR and Communist China is estimated to have been on the order of $250-400 million, of which about $100-150 million was economic, and they have continued to provide aid, evidently at an increasing rate, during the current year. Most of it has been from the USSR, which had virtually cut off aid during the 1962-64 period. There can be little doubt, therefore, that

185

Hanoi's Communist backers have assumed the economic costs
to a degree that has significantly cushioned the impact
of U.S. bombing.

3.   The aspects of the basic situation that have
enabled Hanoi to continue its support of military operations in the South and to neutralize the impact of U.S.
bombing by passing the economic costs to other Communist
countries are not likely to be altered by reducing the
present geographic constraints, mining Haiphong and the
principal harbors in North Vietnam, increasing the number
of armed reconnaissance sorties and otherwise expanding the
U.S. air offensive along the lines now contemplated in
military recommendations and planning studies.

An expansion of the bombing program along such lines
would make it more difficult and costly for Hanoi to
move essential military supplies through North Vietnam to the
VC/NVN forces in the South. The low volume of supplies
required, the demonstrated effectiveness of the countermeasures already undertaken by Hanoi, the alternative options
that the NVN transportation network provides and the level
of aid the USSR and China seem prepared to provide, however, make it quite unlikely that Hanoi's capability to
function as a logistic funnel would be seriously impaired.
Our past experience also indicates that an intensified air
campaign in NVN probably would not prevent Hanoi from infiltrating men into the South at the present or a higher rate,
if it chooses. Furthermore, there would appear to be no
basis for assuming that the damage that could be inflicted by
an intensified air offensive would impose such demands on
the North Vietnamese labor force that Hanoi would be unable
to continue and expand its recruitment and training of military forces for the insurgency in the South.

4.   While conceptually it is reasonable to assume that
some limit may be imposed on the scale of military activity
that Hanoi can maintain in the South by continuing the
ROLLING THUNDER program at the present, or some higher level
of effort, there appears to be no basis for defining that
limit in concrete terms or, for concluding that the present
scale of VC/NVN activities in the field have approached that
limit.

The available evidence clearly indicates that Hanoi has
been infiltrating military forces and supplies into South
Vietnam at an accelerated rate during the current year.
Intelligence estimates have concluded that North Vietnam is
capable of substantially increasing its support.

186

5. The indirect effects of the bombing on the will of the North Vietnamese to continue fighting and on their leaders' appraisal of the prospective gains and costs of maintaining the present policy have not shown themselves in any tangible way. Furthermore, we have not discovered any basis for concluding that the indirect punitive effects of bombing will prove decisive in these respects.

It may be argued on a speculative basis that continued or increased bombing must eventually effect Hanoi's will to continue, particularly as a component of the total U.S. military pressures being exerted throughout Southeast Asia. However, it is not a conclusion that necessarily follows from the available evidence; given the character of North Vietnam's economy and society, the present and prospective low levels of casualties and the amount of aid available to Hanoi. It would appear to be equally logical to assume that the major influences on Hanoi's will to continue are most likely to be the course of the war in the South and the degree to which the USSR and China support the policy of continuing the war and that the punitive impact of U.S. bombing may have but a marginal effect in this broader context. 39/

In the body of the report these summary formulations were elaborated in more detail. For instance, in assessing the military and economic effect of the bombing on North Vietnam's capacity to sustain the war, the report stated:

The economic and military damage sustained by Hanoi in the first year of the bombing was moderate and the cost could be (and was) passed along to Moscow and Peiping.

The major effect of the attack on North Vietnam was to force Hanoi to cope with disruption to normal activity, particularly in transportation and distribution. The bombing hurt most in its disruption of the roads and rail nets and in the very considerable repair effort which became necessary. The regime, however, was singularly successful in overcoming the effects of the U.S. interdiction effort.

Much of the damage was to installations that the North Vietnamese did not need to sustain the military effort. The regime made no attempt to restore storage facilities and little to repair damage to power stations, evidently because of the existence of adequate excess capacity and

because the facilities were not of vital importance. For
somewhat similar reasons, it made no major effort to restore
military facilities, but merely abandoned barracks and dispersed materiel usually stored in depots.

The major essential restoration consisted of measures
to keep traffic moving, to keep the railroad yards operating, to maintain communications, and to replace transport
equipment and equipment for radar and SAM sites. 40/

A little further on the report examined the political effects of the
bombing on Hanoi's will to continue the war, the morale of the population, and the support of its allies.

The bombing through 1965 apparently had not had a major
effect in shaping Hanoi's decision on whether or not to
continue the war in Vietnam. The regime probably continued
to base such decisions mainly on the course of the fighting
in the South and appeared willing to suffer even stepped-up
bombing so long as prospects of winning the South appeared
to be reasonably good.

Evidence regarding the effect of the bombing on the
morale of the North Vietnamese people suggests that the
results were mixed. The bombing clearly strengthened
popular support of the regime by engendering patriotic
and nationalistic enthusiasm to resist the attacks. On the
other hand, those more directly involved in the bombing
underwent personal harships and anxieties caused by the
raids. Because the air strikes were directed away from
urban areas, morale was probably damaged less by the direct
bombing than by its indirect effects, such as evacuation
of the urban population and the splitting of families.

Hanoi's political relations with its allies were in
some respects strengthened by the bombing. The attacks had
the effect of encouraging greater material and political
support from the Soviet Union than might otherwise have
been the case. While the Soviet aid complicated Hanoi's
relationship with Peking, it reduced North Vietnam's
dependence on China and thereby gave Hanoi more room for
maneuver on its own behalf. 41/

This report's concluding chapter was entitled
"Observations" and contained some of the most lucid and
penetrating analysis of air war produced to that date, or
this! It began by reviewing the original objectives the
bombing was initiated to achieve:

TOP SECRET - Sensitive

188

> ...reducing the ability of North Vietnam to support the Communist insurgencies in South Vietnam and Laos, and...increasing progressively the pressure on NVN to the point where the regime would decide that it was too costly to continue directing and supporting the insurgency in the South. 42/

After rehearsing the now familiar military failure of the bombing to halt the infiltration, the report crisply and succinctly outlined the bombing's failure to achieve the critical second objective --the psychological one:

> ...initial plans and assessments for the ROLLING THUNDER program clearly tended to overestimate the persuasive and disruptive effects of the U.S. air strikes and, correspondingly, to underestimate the tenacity and recuperative capabilities of the North Vietnamese. This tendency, in turn, appears to reflect a general failure to appreciate the fact, well-documented in the historical and social scientific literature, that a direct, frontal attack on a society tends to strengthen the social fabric of the nation, to increase popular support of the existing government, to improve the determination of both the leadership and the populace to fight back, to induce a variety of protective measures that reduce the society's vulnerability to future attack, and to develop an increased capacity for quick repair and restoration of essential functions. The great variety of physical and social counter-measures that North Vietnam has taken in response to the bombing is now well documented in current intelligence reports, but the potential effectiveness of these counter-measures was not stressed in the early planning or intelligence studies. 43/

Perhaps the most trenchant analysis of all, however, was reserved for last as the report attacked the fundamental weakness of the air war strategy -- our inability to relate operations to objectives:

> In general, current official thought about U.S. objectives in bombing NVN implicitly assumes two sets of causal relationships:

> 1. That by increasing the damage and destruction of resources in NVN, the U.S. is exerting pressure to cause the DRV to stop their support of the military operations in SVN and Laos; and

2. That the combined effect of the total military effort
against NVN -- including the U.S. air strikes in NVN and
Laos, and the land, sea, and air operations in SVN -- will
ultimately cause the DRV to perceive that its probable losses
accruing from the war have become greater than its possible
gains and, on the basis of this net evaluation, the regime
will stop its support of the war in the South.

These two sets of interrelationships are assumed in
military planning, but it is not clear that they are systematically addressed in current intelligence estimates and
assessments. Instead, the tendency is to encapsulate the
bombing of NVN as one set of operations and the war in the
South as another set of operations, and to evaluate each
separately; and to tabulate and describe data on the physical,
economic, and military effects of the bombing, but not to
address specifically the relationship between such effects and
the data relating to the ability and will of the DRV to continue
its support of the war in the South.

The fragmented nature of current analyses and the lack of
an adequate methodology for assessing the net effects of a
given set of military operations leaves a major gap between the
quantifiable data on bomb damage effects, on the one hand, and
policy judgments about the feasibility of achieving a given set
of objectives, on the other. Bridging this gap still requires
the exercise of broad political-military judgments that cannot
be supported or rejected on the basis of systematic intelligence indicators. It must be concluded, therefore, that there
is currently no adequate basis for predicting the levels of
U.S. military effort that would be required to achieve the
stated objectives -- indeed, there is no firm basis for determining if there is any feasible level of effort that would
achieve these objectives. 44/

The critical impact of this study on the Secretary's thinking is revealed
by the fact that many of its conclusions and much of its analysis would
find its way into McNamara's October trip report to the President.

Having submitted a stinging condemnation of the bombing,
the Study Group was under some obligation to offer constructive alternatives and this they did, siezing, not surprisingly, on the very idea
McNamara had suggested -- the anti-infiltration barrier. The product
of their summer's work was a reasonably detailed proposal for a multi-
system barrier across the DMZ and the Laotian panhandle that would make
extensive use of recently innovated mines and sensors. The central
portion of their recommendation follows:

190

The barrier would have two somewhat different parts,
one designed against foot traffic and one against vehicles.
The preferred location for the anti-foot-traffic barrier is
in the region along the southern edge of the DMZ to the
Laotian border and then north of Tchepone to the vicinity
of Muong Sen, extending about 100 by 20 kilometers. This
area is virtually unpopulated, and the terrain is quite
rugged, containing mostly V-shaped valleys in which the
opportunity for alternate trails appears lower than it is
elsewhere in the system. The location of choice for the
anti-vehicle part of the system is the area, about 100 by 40
kilometers, now covered by Operation Cricket. In this area
the road network tends to be more constricted than elsewhere, and there appears to be a smaller area available for
new roads. An alternative location for the anti-personnel
system is north of the DMZ to the Laotian border and then
north along the crest of the mountains dividing Laos from
North Vietnam. It is less desirable economically and militarily because of its greater length, greater distance
from U.S. bases, and greater proximity to potential North
Vietnamese counter-efforts.

The air-supported barrier would, if necessary, be
supplemented by a manned "fence" connecting the eastern
end of the barrier to the sea.

The construction of the air-supported barrier could be
initiated using currently available or nearly available
components, with some necessary modifications, and could
perhaps be installed by a year or so from go-ahead. However, we anticipate that the North Vietnamese would learn
to cope with a barrier built this way after some period of
time which we cannot estimate, but which we fear may be
short. Weapons and sensors which can make a much more
effective barrier, only some of which are now under development, are not likely to be available in less than 18 months
to 2 years. Even these, it must be expected, will eventually be overcome by the North Vietnamese, so that further
improvements in weaponry will be necessary. Thus we
envisage a dynamic "battle of the barrier," in which the
barrier is repeatedly improved and strengthened by the
introduction of new components, and which will hopefully
permit us to keep the North Vietnamese off balance by
continually posing new problems for them.

This barrier is in concept not very different from
what has already been suggested elsewhere; the new aspects
are: the very large scale of area denial, especially mine

fields kilometers deep rather than the conventional
100-200 meters; the very large numbers and persistent
employment of weapons, sensors, and aircraft sorties
in the barrier area; and the emphasis on rapid and
carefully planned incorporation of more effective
weapons and sensors into the system.

The system that could be available in a year or so
would, in our conception, contain /sic/ the following
components:

-- Gravel mines (both self-sterilizing for harassment and non-sterilizing for area denial).

-- Possibly, "button bomblets" developed by Picatinny
Arsenal, to augment the range of the sensors against
foot traffic.*

-- SADEYE/BLU-26B clusters,** for attacks on area-
type targets of uncertain locations.

-- Acoustic detectors, based on improvements of
the "Acoustic Sonobuoys" currently under test
by the Navy.

-- P-2V patrol aircraft, equipped for acoustic
sensor monitoring, Gravel dispensing, vectoring
strike aircraft, and infrared detection of
campfires in bivouac areas.

-- Gravel Dispensing Aircraft (A-1's, or possibly
C-123's)

-- Strike Aircraft

-- Photo-reconnaissance Aircraft

-- Photo Interpreters

--(Possibly) ground teams to plant mines and sensors,
gather information, and selectively harass traffic
on foot trails.

---

* These are small mines (aspirin-size) presently designed to give
a loud report but not to injure when stepped on by a shod foot.
They would be sown in great density along well-used trails, on
the assumption that they would be much harder to sweep than
Gravel. Their purpose would be to make noise indicating pedestrian traffic at a range of approximately 200 feet from the
acoustic sensors.

** CBU-24 in Air Force nomenclature.

TOP SECRET - Sensitive

192

The anti-troop infiltration system (which would also
function against supply porters) would operate as follows.
There would be a constantly renewed mine field of non-
sterilizing Gravel (and possibly button bomblets), distributed in patterns covering interconnected valleys and
slopes (suitable for alternate trails) over the entire
barrier region. The actual mined area would encompass
the equivalent of a strip about 100 by 5 kilometers.
There would also be a pattern of acoustic detectors to
listen for mine explosions indicating an attempted penetration. The mine field is intended to deny opening of
alternate routes for troop infiltrators and should be
emplaced first. On the trails and bivouacs currently used,
from which mines may--we tentatively assume--be cleared
without great difficulty, a more dense pattern of sensors
would be designed to locate groups of infiltrators. Air
strikes using Gravel and SADEYES would then be called
against these targets. The sensor patterns would be
monitored 24 hours a day by patrol aircraft. The struck
areas would be reseeded with new mines.

The anti-vehicle system would consist of acoustic
detectors distributed every mile or so along all truckable roads in the interdicted area, monitored 24 hours
a day by patrol aircraft, with vectored strike aircraft
using SADEYE to respond to signals that trucks or truck
convoys are moving. The patrol aircraft would distribute
self-sterilizing Gravel over parts of the road net at
dusk. The self-sterilization feature is needed so that
road-watching and mine-planting teams could be used in
this area. Photo-reconnaissance aircraft would cover the
entire area each few days to look for the development
of new truckable roads, to see if the transport of supplies
is being switched to porters, and to identify any other
change in the infiltration system. It may also be desirable to use ground teams to plant larger anti-truck mines
along the roads, as an interim measure pending the development of effective air-dropped anti-vehicle mines.

The cost of such a system (both parts) has been
estimated to be about $800 million per year, of which by
far the major fraction is spent for Gravel and SADEYES.
The key requirements would be (all numbers are approximate because of assumptions which had to be made regarding
degradation of system components in field use, and regarding
the magnitude of infiltration): 20 million Gravel mines
per month; possibly 25 million button bomblets per month;

10,000 SADEYE-BLU-26B clusters* per month; 1600 acoustic
sensors per month (assuming presently employed batteries with
2-week life), plus 68 appropriately equipped P-2V patrol
aircraft; a fleet of about 50 A-1's or 20 C-123's for Gravel
dispensing (1400 A-1 sorties or 600 C-123 sorties per month);
500 strike sorties per month (F-4C equivalent); and sufficient
photo-reconnaissance sorties, depending on the aircraft, to
cover 2500 square miles each week, with an appropriate team of
photo interpreters. Even to make this system work, there
would be required experimentation and further development
for foliage penetration, moisture resistance, and proper dispersion of Gravel; development of a better acoustic sensor
than currently exists (especially in an attempt to eliminate
the need for button bomblets); aircraft modifications; possible
modifications in BLU-26B fuzing; and refinement of strike-
navigation tactics.

For the future, rapid development of new mines (such as
tripwire, smaller and more effectively camouflaged Gravel,
and various other kinds of mines), as well as still better
sensor/information processing systems will be essential. 45/

Thus, not only had this distinguished array of American
technologists endorsed the barrier idea McNamara had asked them to consider, they had provided the Secretary with an attractive, well-thought-
out and highly detailed proposal as a real alternative to further
escalation of the ineffective air war against North Vietnam. But, true
to their scientific orientations, the study group members could not conclude their work without examining the kinds of counter-measures the North
Vietnamese might take to circumvent the barrier. Thus, they reasoned:

Assuming that surprise is not thrown away, countermeasures will of course still be found, but they may take some
time to bring into operation. The most effective countermeasures we can anticipate are mine sweeping; provision of
shelter against SADEYE strikes and Gravel dispersion;
spoofing of sensors to deceive the system or decoy aircraft
into ambushes, and in general a considerable step-up of North
Vietnamese anti-aircraft capability along the road net.
Counter-countermeasures must be an integral part of the
system development.

---

* These quantities depend on an average number of strikes consistent
with the assumption of 7000 troops/month and 180 tons/day of supplies
by truck on the infiltration routes. This assumption was based on
likely upper limits at the time the barrier is installed. If the
assumption of initial infiltration is too high, or if we assume that
the barrier will be successful, the number of weapons and sorties
will be reduced accordingly.

Apart from the tactical countermeasures against the barrier itself, one has to consider strategic alternatives available to the North Vietnamese in case the barrier is successful. Among these are: a move into the Mekong Plain; infiltration from the sea either directly to SVN or through Cambodia; and movement down the Mekong from Thakhek (held by the Pathet Lao-North Vietnamese) into Cambodia.

Finally, it will be difficult for us to find out how effective the barrier is in the absence of clearly visible North Vietnamese responses, such as end runs through the Mekong plain. Because of supplies already stored in the pipeline, and because of the general shakiness of our quantitative estimates of either supply or troop infiltration, it is likely to be some time before the effect of even a wholly successful barrier becomes noticeable. A greatly stepped-up intelligence effort is called for, including continued road-watch activity in the areas of the motorable roads, and patrol and reconnaissance activity south of the anti-personnel barrier. 46/

This, then, was the new option introduced into the Vietnam discussions in Washington at the beginning of September.

Their work completed, the Jason Group met with McNamara and McNaughton in Washington on August 30 and presented their conclusions and recommendations. McNamara was apparently strongly and favorably impressed with the work of the Summer Study because he and McNaughton flew to Massachusetts on September 6 to meet with members of the Study again for more detailed discussions. Even before going to Massachusetts, however, McNamara had asked General Wheeler to bring the proposal up with the Chiefs and to request field comment. 47/ After having asked CINCPAC for an evaluation, Wheeler sent McNamara the preliminary reactions of the Chiefs. 48/ They agreed with the Secretary's suggestion to establish a project manager (General Starbird) in DDR&E, but expressed concern that, "the very substantial funds required for the barrier system would be obtained from current Service resources thereby affecting adversely important current programs."

CINCPAC's evaluation of the barrier proposal on September 13 was little more than a rehash of the overdrawn arguments against such a system advanced in April. The sharpness of the language of his summary arguments, however, is extreme even for Admiral Sharp. In no uncertain terms he stated:

The combat forces required before, during and after construction of the barrier; the initial and follow-on logistic support; the engineer construction effort and time required; and the existing logistic posture in Southeast Asia with respect to ports and land LOCs make construction of such a barrier impracticable.

....Military operations against North Vietnam and operations in South Vietnam are of transcendent importance. Operations elsewhere are complementary supporting undertakings. Priority and emphasis should be accorded in consideration of the forces and resources available to implement the strategy dictated by our objectives. 49/

To some extent, the vehemence of CINCPAC's reaction must have stemmed from the fact that he and General Westmoreland had just completed a paper exercise in which they had struggled to articulate a strategic concept for the conduct of the war to achieve U.S. objectives as they understood them. This effort had been linked to the consideration of CY 1967 force requirements for the war, the definition of which required some strategic concept to serve as a guide. With respect to the war in the North, CINCPAC's final "Military Strategy to Accomplish United States Objectives for Vietnam," stated:

In the North - Take the war to the enemy by unremitting but selective application of United States air and naval power. Military installations and those industrial facilities that generate support for the aggression will be attacked. Movement within, into and out of North Vietnam will be impeded. The enemy will be denied the great psychological and material advantage of conducting an aggression from a sanctuary. This relentless application of force is designed progressively to curtail North Vietnam's warmaking capacity. It seeks to force upon him major replenishment, repair and construction efforts. North Vietnamese support and direction of the Pathet Lao and the insurgency in Thailand will be impaired. The movement of men and material through Laos and over all land and water lines of communications into South Vietnam will be disrupted. Hanoi's capability to support military operations in South Vietnam and to direct those operations will be progressively reduced. 50/

With this formulation of intent for the air war, it is not surprising that the barrier proposal should have been anathema to CINCPAC.

McNamara, however, proceeded to implement the barrier proposal in spite of CINCPAC's condemnation and the Chiefs' cool reaction. On September 15 he appointed Lt. General Alfred Starbird to head Joint Task Force 728 within DDR&E as manager for the project. 51/   The Joint Task Force was eventually given the cover name Defense Communications Planning Group to protect the sensitivity of the project. Plans for implementing the barrier were pushed ahead speedily. Early in October, just prior to the Secretary's trip, General Starbird made a visit to Vietnam to study the problem on the ground and begin to set the administrative wheels in motion. In spite of the fact that McNamara was

196

vigorously pushing the project forward, there is no indication that
he had officially raised the matter with the President, although it
is hard to imagine that some discussion of the Jason Summer Study recommendations had not taken place between them. In any case, as McNamara
prepared to go to Vietnam again to assess the situation in light of new
requests for troop increases, he made arrangements to have General Starbird
remain for the first day of his visit and placed the anti-<u>infiltration</u>
barrier first on the agenda of discussions. 52/

3. A Visit to Vietnam and a Memorandum for the President

McNamara's trip to Vietnam in October 1966 served a variety
of purposes. It came at a time when CINCPAC was involved in a force
planning exercise to determine desired (required in his view) force levels
for fighting the war through 1967. This was related to DOD's fall DPM
process in which the Pentagon reviews its programs and prepares its budget
recommendations for the coming fiscal year. This in turn engenders a
detailed look at requirements in all areas for the five years to come. As
a part of this process, just three days before the Secretary's departure,
the Joint Chiefs of Staff had sent him an important memo reviewing force
posture the world over and recommending a call-up of the reserves to meet
anticipated 1967 requirements. 53/ This recommendation as a part of the
overall examination of force requirements needed his personal assessment
on the spot in Vietnam. Other important reasons for a trip were, no
doubt, the ones to which we have referred in detail: McNamara's dissatisfaction with the results of the POL attacks; and the reports of the Jason
Summer Study. Furthermore, the off-year Congressional elections were
only a month away and the President had committed himself to go to Manila
for a heads of state meeting later in October. For both these events
the President probably felt the need of McNamara's fresh impressions
and recommendations.

Whatever the combination of reasons, McNamara left Washington
on October 10 and spent four days in Vietnam. Accompanying the Secretary
on the trip were Under Secretary of State Katzenbach, General Wheeler,
Mr. Komer, John McNaughton, John Foster, Director of DDR&E, and Henry
Kissinger. In the course of the visit McNamara worked his way through
a detailed seventeen item agenda of briefings, visited several sections
of the country plus the Fleet, and met with the leaders of the GVN. 54/

His findings in those three days in South Vietnam must have
confirmed his disquiet about the lack of progress of the war and the
ineffectualness of U.S. actions to date, for when he returned to Washington
he sent the President a gloomy report with recommendations for leveling
off the U.S. effort and seeking a solution through diplomatic channels. 55/
McNamara recommended an increase in the total authorized final troop
strength in Vietnam of only about 40,000 over Program #3, for an end
strength of 470,000. This was a direct rejection of CINCPAC's request
for a 12/31/67 strength of 570,000 and marked a significant turning point

in McNamara's attitude toward the force buildup. 56/ The issue would continue to be debated until the President's decision shortly after the election in November to approve the McNamara recommended total of 469,300 troops under Program #4.

With respect to the air war he stated that the bombing had neither significantly reduced infiltration nor diminished Hanoi's will to continue the fight, and he noted the concurrence of the intelligence community in these conclusions. Pulling back from his previous positions, he now recommended that the President level off the bombing at current levels and seek other means of achieving our objectives. The section of the memo on bombing follows:

Stabilize the ROLLING THUNDER program against the North. Attack sorties in North Vietnam have risen from about 4,000 per month at the end of last year to 6,000 per month in the first quarter of this year and 12,000 per month at present. Most of our 50 percent increase of deployed attack-capable air craft has been absorbed in the attacks on North Vietnam. In North Vietnam, almost 84,000 attack sorties have been flown (about 25 percent against fixed targets), 45 percent during the past seven months.

Despite these efforts, it now appears that the North Vietnamese-Laotian road network will remain adequate to meet the requirements of the Communist forces in South Vietnam -- this is so even if its capacity could be reduced by one-third and if combat activities were to be doubled. North Vietnam's serious need for trucks, spare parts and petroleum probably can, despite air attacks, be met by imports. The petroleum requirement for trucks involved in the infiltration movement, for example, has not been enough to present significant supply problems, and the effects of the attacks on the petroleum distribution system, while they have not yet been fully assessed, are not expected to cripple the flow of essential supplies. Furthermore, it is clear that, to bomb the North sufficiently to make a radical impact upon Hanoi's political, economic and social structure, would require an effort which we could make but which would not be stomached either by our own people or by world opinion; and it would involve a serious risk of drawing us into open war with China.

The North Vietnamese are paying a price. They have been forced to assign some 300,000 personnel to the lines of communication in order to maintain the critical flow of personnel and materiel to the South. Now that the lines of communication have been manned, however, it is doubtful that either a

large increase or decrease in our interdiction sorties would
substantially change the cost to the enemy of maintaining
the roads, railroads, and waterways or affect whether they
are operational. It follows that the marginal sorties --
probably the marginal 1,000 or even 5,000 sorties -- per
month against the lines of communication no longer have a
significant impact on the war.

When this marginal inutility of added sorties against
North Vietnam and Laos is compared with the crew and aircraft losses implicit in the activity (four men and aircraft
and $20 million per 1,000 sorties), I recommend, as a minimum,
against increasing the level of bombing of North Vietnam and
against increasing the intensity of operations by changing
the areas or kinds of targets struck.

Under these conditions, the bombing program would continue
the pressure and would remain available as a bargaining counter
to get talks started (or to trade off in talks). But, as in
the case of a stabilized level of US ground forces, the
stabilization of ROLLING THUNDER would remove the prospect of
ever-escalating bombing as a factor complicating our political
posture and distracting from the main job of pacification in
South Vietnam.

At the proper time, as discussed on pages 6-7 below,
I believe we should consider terminating bombing in all of
North Vietnam, or at least in the Northeast zones, for an
indefinite period in connection with covert moves toward
peace. 57/

As an alternative to further escalation of the bombing, McNamara recommended the barrier across the DMZ and Laos:

Install a barrier. A portion of the 470,000 troops --
perhaps 10,000 to 20,000 -- should be devoted to the construction and maintenance of an infiltration barrier. Such a
barrier would lie near the 17th parallel -- would run from
the sea, across the neck of South Vietnam (choking off the
new infiltration routes through the DMZ) and across the trails
in Laos. This interdiction system (at an approximate cost
of $1 billion) would comprise to the east a ground barrier
of fences, wire, sensors, artillery, aircraft and mobile troops;
and to the west -- mainly in Laos -- an interdiction zone
covered by air-laid mines and bombing attacks pin-pointed
by air-laid acoustic sensors.

199

The barrier may not be fully effective at first, but I believe that it can be made effective in time and that even the threat of its becoming effective can substantially change to our advantage the character of the war. It would hinder enemy efforts, would permit more efficient use of the limited number of friendly troops, and would be persuasive evidence both that our sole aim is to protect the South from the North and that we intend to see the job through. 58/

The purpose of these two actions would be to lay the groundwork for a stronger U.S. effort to get negotiations started. With the war seemingly stalemated, this appeared to be the only "out" to the Secretary that offered some prospect of bringing the conflict to an end in any near future. In analyzing North Vietnamese unwillingness to date to respond to peace overtures, McNamara noted their acute sensitivity to the air attacks on their homeland (recalling the arguments of the Jason Summer Study) and the hostile suspicion of U.S. motives. To improve the climate for talks, he argued, the U.S. should make some gesture to indicate our good faith. Foremost of these was a cessation or a limitation of the bombing.

As a way of projecting /sic/ U.S. bona fides, I believe that we should consider two possibilities with respect to our bombing program against the North, to be undertaken, if at all, at a time very carefully selected with a view to maximizing the chances of influencing the enemy and world opinion and to minimizing the chances that failure would strengthen the hand of the "hawks" at home: First, without fanfare, conditions, or avowal, whether the stand-down was permanent or temporary, stop bombing all of North Vietnam. It is generally thought that Hanoi will not agree to negotiations until they can claim that the bombing has stopped unconditionally. We should see what develops, retaining freedom to resume the bombing if nothing useful was forthcoming.

Alternatively, we could shift the weight-of-effort away from "Zones 6A and 6B" -- zones including Hanoi and Haiphong and areas north of those two cities to the Chinese border. This alternative has some attraction in that it provides the North Vietnamese a "face saver" if only problems of "face" are holding up Hanoi peace gestures; it would narrow the bombing down directly to the objectionable infiltration (supporting the logic of a stop-infiltration/full-pause deal); and it would reduce the international heat on the US. Here, too, bombing of the Northeast could be resumed at any time, or "spot" attacks could be made there from time to time to keep North Vietnam off balance and to require

200

her to pay almost the full cost by maintaining her repair
crews in place. The sorties diverted from Zones 6A and 6B
could be concentrated on the infiltration routes in Zones 1
and 2 (the southern end of North Vietnam, including the
Mu Gia Pass), in Laos and in South Vietnam. a/

a/ Any limitation on the bombing of North Vietnam will cause
serious psychological problems among the men who are risking
their lives to help achieve our political objectives; among
their commanders up to and including the JCS; and among those
of our people who cannot understand why we should withhold
punishment from the enemy. General Westmoreland, as do the
JCS, strongly believes in the military value of the bombing
program. Further, Westmoreland reports that the morale of
his Air Force personnel may already be showing signs of
erosion -- an erosion resulting from current operational
restrictions. 59/

The Secretary's footnote was judicious. The Chiefs did
indeed oppose any curtailment of the bombing as a means to get negotiations started. They fired off a dissenting memo to the Secretary the
same day as his memo and requested that it be passed to the President.
With respect to the bombing program per se they stated:

The Joint Chiefs of Staff do not concur in your recommendation that there should be no increase in level of
bombing effort and no modification in areas and targets subject
to air attack. They believe our air campaign against NVN to be
an integral and indispensable part of our over all war effort.
To be effective, the air campaign should be conducted with
only those minimum constraints necessary to avoid indiscriminate killing of population. 60/

As to the Secretary's proposal for a bombing halt:

The Joint Chiefs of Staff do not concur with your proposal that, as a carrot to induce negotiations, we should
suspend or reduce our bombing campaign against NVN. Our
experiences with pauses in bombing and resumption have not
been happy ones. Additionally, the Joint Chiefs of Staff
believe that the likelihood of the war being settled by
negotiation is small, and that, far from inducing negotiations, another bombing pause will be regarded by North
Vietnamese leaders, and our Allies, as renewed evidence
of lack of US determination to press the war to a successful

conclusion. The bombing campaign is one of the two trump cards in the hands of the President (the other being the presence of US troops in SVN). It should not be given up without an end to the NVN aggression in SVN. 61/

The Chiefs did more than just dissent from a McNamara recommendation, however. They closed their memo with a lengthy counter-proposal with significant political overtones clearly intended for the President's eyes. In their own words this is what they said:

The Joint Chiefs of Staff believe that the war has reached a stage at which decisions taken over the next sixty days can determine the outcome of the war and, consequently, can affect the over-all security interests of the United States for years to come. Therefore, they wish to provide to you and to the President their unequivocal views on two salient aspects of the war situation: the search for peace and military pressures on NVN.

a. The frequent, broadly-based public offers made by the President to settle the war by peaceful means on a generous basis, which would take from NVN nothing it now has, have been admirable. Certainly, no one - American or foreigner - except those who are determined not to be convinced, can doubt the sincerity, the generosity, the altruism of US actions and objectives. In the opinion of the Joint Chiefs of Staff the time has come when further overt actions and offers on our part are not only non-productive, they are counterproductive. A logical case /sic/ can be made that the American people, our Allies, and our enemies alike are increasingly uncertain as to our resolution to pursue the war to a successful conclusion. The Joint Chiefs of Staff advocate the following:

(1) A statement by the President during the Manila Conference of his unswerving determination to carry on the war until NVN aggression against SVN shall cease;

(2) Continued covert exploration of all avenues leading to a peaceful settlement of the war; and

(3) Continued alertness to detect and react appropriately to withdrawal of North Vietnamese troops from SVN and cessation of support to the VC.

b. In JCSM-955-64, dated 14 November 1964, and in JCSM-962-64, dated 23 November 1964, the Joint Chiefs of Staff provided their views as to the military pressures which should be

202

brought to bear on NVN. In summary, they recommended a
"sharp knock" on NVN military assets and war-supporting
facilities rather than the campaign of slowly increasing
pressure which was adopted. Whatever the political merits
of the latter course, we deprived ourselves of the military effects of early weight of effort and shock, and gave
to the enemy time to adjust to our slow quantitative and
qualitative increase of pressure. This is not to say that it
is now too late to derive military benefits from more
effective and extensive use of our air and naval superiority.
The Joint Chiefs of Staff recommend:

(1) Approval of their ROLLING THUNDER 52
program, which is a step toward meeting the requirement
for improved target systems. This program would decrease
the Hanoi and Haiphong sanctuary areas, authorize attacks
against the steel plant, the Hanoi rail yards, the thermal
power plants, selected areas within Haiphong port and other
ports, selected locks and dams controlling water LOCs, SAM
support facilities within the residual Hanoi and Haiphong
sanctuaries, and POL at Haiphong, Ha Gia (Phuc Yen) and
Can Thon (Kep).

(2) Use of naval surface forces to interdict
North Vietnamese coastal waterborne traffic and appropriate
land LOCs and to attack other coastal military targets such
as radar and AAA sites.

5. The Joint Chiefs of Staff request that their views
as set forth above be provided to the President.

For the Joint Chiefs of Staff

(Sgd) EARLE G. WHEELER 62/

Such a memo from the Chiefs represents more than a dissent or an alternative recommendation; it constitutes a statement for the record to
guarantee that in the historical accounts the Chiefs will appear having
discharged their duty. It always comes as a form of political notification, not merely a military recommendation.

The available documents do not show what the reaction at
the State Department was (apart from Mr. Katzenbach's apparent endorsement), nor do they indicate the views of the White House staff under
W. W. Rostow. McNaughton's files do contain a commentary on the McNamara
recommendations prepared by George Carver of CIA for the Director,
Richard Helms. Carver agreed with the basic McNamara analysis of the
results of the air war but did not think they constituted a conclusive
statement about possible results from an escalation. Carver wrote,

We concur in Secretary McNamra's analysis of the
effects of the ROLLING THUNDER program, its potential
for reducing the flow of essential supplies, and his
judgment on the marginal inutility of added sorties against
lines of communication. We endorse his argument on
stabilizing the level of sorties. We do not agree, however, with the implied judgment that changes in the bombing
program could not be effective. We continue to judge that
a bombing program directed both against closing the port
of Haiphong and continuously cutting the rail lines to
China could have a significant impact. 63/

Carver also opposed any halt or de-escalation of the bombing to start
negotiations, arguing that we could either pursue negotiations or try
to build up the GVN but we could not do both. His preference was to build
in the South. Hence, a bombing halt or pause was not required. As to
a reduction, he argued that,

Shifting the air effort from the northeast quadrant
to the infiltration areas in Laos and southern North Vietnam
would be quite unproductive. Such a course of action would
not induce Hanoi to negotiate (since it would still involve
bombing in the north) and would probably have little effect
in changing present international attitudes. Furthermore,
a concentration of sorties against the low-yield and elusive
targets along the infiltration routes in the southern end of
North Vietnam and in Laos would not appreciably diminish North
Vietnam's ability to maintain the supply of its forces in
South Vietnam. 64/

As for the anti-infiltration barrier, neither the Chiefs
nor Carver had a great deal of comment. The Chiefs reiterated their
reservations with respect to resource diversion but endorsed the barrier
concept in principle. Carver somewhat pessimistically observed that,

In order to achieve the objectives set for the barrier
in our view it must be extended well westward into Laos.
Air interdiction of the routes in Laos unsupplemented by
ground action will not effectively check infiltration. 65/

To no one's surprise, therefore, McNamara proceeded with the barrier
project in all haste, presumably with the President's blessing.

C. The Year End View

1. Presidential Decisions

The President apparently did not react immediately to the
McNamara recommendations, although he must have approved them in general.
He was at the time preparing for the Manila Conference to take place
October 23-25 and major decisions before would have been badly timed.
Thus, formal decisions on the McNamara recommendations, particularly
the troop level question would wait until he had returned and the elections were over. At Manila, the President worked hard to get the South
Vietnamese to make a greater commitment to the war and pressed them for
specific reforms. He also worked hard to get a generalized formulation
of allied objectives in the war and saw his efforts succeed in the agreed
communique. Its most important feature was an appeal to the North Vietnamese for peace based on a commitment to withdraw forces within six
months after the end of the war. It contained, however, no direct reference to the air war.

While in Manila, the President and his advisors also conferred with General Westmoreland. As McNaughton subsequently reported
to McNamara (who did not attend), Westmoreland opposed any curtailment
of the air war in the North, calling it "our only trump card." 66/
Unlike the Jason Study Group, Westmoreland felt the strikes had definite
military value in slowing the southward movement of supplies, diverting
DRV manpower and creating great costs to the North. Rather than stabilize
or de-escalate, Westmoreland advocated lifting the restrictions on the
program. Citing the high level of aircraft attrition on low priority
targets, he warned, "you are asking for a very bad political reaction." 67/
He recommended that strikes be carried out against the MIG airfields, the
missile assembly area, the truck maintenance facility, the Haiphong port
facilities, the twelve thermal power plants, and the steel plant. When
McNaughton pressed him on the question of whether the elimination of
these targets would have much payoff in reduced logistical support for the
Southern war, Westmoreland backed off stating, "I'm not responsible for
the bombing program. Admiral Sharp is. So I haven't spent much time on it.
But I asked a couple of my best officers to look into it, and they came
up with the recommendations I gave you." In any event, he opposed any
pause in the bombing, contending that the DRV would just use it to
strengthen its air defenses and repair air fields. McNaughton reported
that Westmoreland had repeated these views to the President in the presence
of Ky and Thieu at Johnson's request; moreover, he planned to forward
them to the President in a memo /not available/ at the request of Walt
Rostow.

As to the barrier, McNaughton reported that, "Westy seems
to be fighting the barrier less (although he obviously fears that it
is designed mainly to justify stopping RT /ROLLING THUNDER/, at which

205

he 'shudders'...." 69/   Apart from that his concerns about the barrier
were minor (although he did propose a NIKE battalion for use in a
surface to surface role in support of the barrier).

On his way home from Manila, the President made the now
famous dramatic visit to U.S. troops at Cam Ranh Bay. Once home, however, he deferred any major decisions on the war until after the elections.
Several "peace" candidates were aggressively challenging Administration
supporters in the off-year Congressional contests and the President wished
to do nothing that might boost their chances. As it turned out, they were
overwhelmingly defeated in the November 8 balloting.

Meanwhile, at the Pentagon the dispute over the level of
effort for the air war continued. Even before Manila, the Chiefs had
attempted to head off McNamara's recommendation for stabilizing the
bombing with a request for a 25 percent increase in B-52 sorties per
month. 70/   The Secretary, for his part, was showing considerable concern over the high attrition rates of ROLLING THUNDER aircraft. Among
other things he questioned the utility of committing pilots to repeated
risks when the operational return from many of the missions was so small
and the expectations for achieving significant destruction so minimal. 71/

The force level arguments had continued during the President's
trip too. On October 20, CINCPAC forwarded his revised Force Planning Program
containing the results of the October 5-14 Honolulu Planning Conference to
the JCS. 72/   In effect, it constituted a reclama to the Secretary's
October 14 recommendations. CINCPAC requested U.S. ground forces totalling
493,969 by end CY 1967; 519,310 by end CY 1968; and 520,020 by end CY 1969.
But the total by end CY 1969 would really be 555,262 reflecting an additional 35,721 troops whose availability was described in the planning
document as "unknown." 73/

With respect to the air war, CINCPAC stated a requirement
for an additional ten tactical fighter squadrons (TFS) and an additional
aircraft carrier to support both an intensification of the air war in the
North and the additional maneuver battalions requested for the war in the
South. These new squadrons were needed to raise sortie levels in the North
above 12,000/month in CY 1967. Of these ten TFS, the Air Force indicated
that three were unavailable and the Secretary of Defense had previously
deferred deployment of five. Nonetheless, the requirement was reiterated. 74/
They were needed to implement the strategic concept of the air mission in
SEA that CINCPAC had articulated on September 5 and that was included
again here as justification. 75/   Moreover, the objective of attacking
the ports and water LOCs was reiterated as well. 76/

On November 4, the JCS sent the Secretary these CINCPAC
force planning recommendations with their own slight upward revision of
the troop figures to an eventual end strength of 558,432. 77/   In the
body of the memo they endorse the CINCPAC air war recommendations in

206

principle but indicated that 3 TFS and the carrier would not be available. They supplemented CINCPAC's rationale with a statement of their own on the matter in appendix A. The two objectives of the air war were to "make it as difficult and costly as possible" for NVN to support the war in the South and to motivate the DRV to "cease controlling and directing the insurgency in South Vietnam." 78/ Their evaluation of the effectiveness of the bombing in achieving these objectives was that:

> Air operations in NVN have disrupted enemy efforts to support his forces and have assisted in preventing the successful mounting of any major offensives. The NVN air campaign takes the war home to NVN by complicating the daily life, causing multiple and increasing management and logistic problems, and preventing the enemy from conducting an aggression from the comfort of a sanctuary. 79/

Failures to date were attributed to the constraints imposed on the bombing by the political authorities, and the Chiefs again urged that these be lifted and the target base be widened to apply increasing pressure to the DRV.

These were the standard old arguments. But on October 6, the Secretary had addressed them a memo with an attached set of 28 "issue papers" drafted in Systems Analysis. One of these took sharp issue with any increase in the air war on purely force effectiveness grounds. The Chiefs attempted to rebut all 28 issue papers in one of the attachments to the November 4 memo. The original Systems Analysis "issue paper" on air war effectiveness had argued that additional deployments of air squadrons should not be made because: (1) the bulk of the proposed new sorties for North Vietnam were in Route Package I (see Map) and could be attacked much more economically by naval gunfire; (2) although interdiction had forced the enemy to make greater repair efforts and thereby had diverted some resources, had forced more reliance on night operations, and had inflicted substantial casualties to vehicular traffic, none of these had created or were likely to create insuperable problems for the DRV; and (3) CINCPAC's increased sortie requirements would generate 230 aircraft losses in CY 1967 and cost $1.1 billion while only doing negligible damage to the DRV. 80/ The similarity of much of this analysis to the conclusions of the Jason Summer Study is striking.

The Chiefs rejected all three of the Systems Analysis arguments. Naval gunfire, in their view, should be regarded as a necessary supplement for the bombing, not as a substitute since it lacked flexibility and responsiveness. As to the question of comparative costs in the air war, the Chiefs reasoned as follows:

The necessity for this type of air campaign is created
by constraints imposed, for other than military reasons,
upon the conduct of the war in NVN. These constraints
result in maximizing exposure of larger numbers of aircraft
for longer periods against increasingly well defended targets
of limited comparative values. /sic/ The measure of the
effectiveness of the interdiction effort is the infiltration
and its consequence which would be taking place if the air
campaign were not being conducted. The cost to the enemy
is not solely to be measured in terms of loss of trucks but
in terms of lost capability to pursue his military objectives
in SVN. Similarly, the cost to the US must consider that
damage which the enemy would be capable of inflicting by
infiltrating men and supplies now inhibited by the interdiction effort; this includes increased casualties in RVN
for which a dollar cost is not applicable. 81/

Sensing that the thrust of the OSD analysis was to make a case for the
barrier at the expense of the bombing, the Chiefs at last came down hard
against any diversion of resources to barrier construction. In no uncertain terms they stated:

The Joint Chiefs of Staff agree that improved interdiction strategy is needed, but such improvement would not
necessarily include the barrier operation. As mentioned above
and as recommended previously, an effective air campaign
against NVN should include closing the ports, destruction of
high value military targets, attack of their air defense
systems and airfields and the other fixed targets on the
target list that have not been struck. These improvements
have thus far been denied.

Preliminary information developed by Task Force 728 indicates that the forces and cost for the barrier will be substantial. The concept and equipment for the barrier have
not been subjected to a cost analysis study. Its effectiveness
is open to serious question and its cost could well exceed
the figure of $1.1 billion given for projected aircraft losses
in this issue paper. 82/

As already indicated, these issues were all decided upon
by the President immediately after the election. On November 11, McNamara
sent the Chiefs a memo with the authorized levels for Program #4. CINCPAC's
proposed increases in sortie levels were rejected and the McNamara recommendation of October 14 for their stabilization was adopted. 83/ As a
reason for rejecting expansion of the air war, the Secretary simply stated
that such would not be possible since no additional tactical fighter
squadrons had been approved. The one upward adjustment of the air war

208

that was authorized was the increase of B-52 sorties from 600 to 800 in February 1967 as proposed by CINCPAC and the JCS. 84/

2. Stabilization of the Air War

With the President's decision not to increase squadrons or sorties for the air campaign in 1967 added to McNamara's strong recommendation on stabilizing the level of the bombing, activity for the remainder of 1966 was kept at about the current level. Among the continuing constraints that was just beginning to alleviate itself was an insufficiency of certain air munitions to sustain higher levels of air combat. 85/ The real constraints, however, as CINCPAC and the JCS correctly stated were political.

The principle supporters of halting the expansion of the air war, as we have already seen, were the Secretary of Defense and his civilian advisors. The arguments they had used during the debate over Program #4 and its associated air program were reiterated and somewhat enlarged later in November in the backup justification for the FY 1967 Southeast Asia Supplemental Appropriation. Singled out for particular criticism was the ineffective air effort to interdict infiltration. The draft Memorandum for the President began by making the best case possible, on the basis of results, for the bombing, and then proceeded to demonstrate that those accomplishments were simply far below what was required to really interdict. The section of the memo in question follows:

A substantial air interdiction campaign is clearly necessary and worthwhile. In addition to putting a ceiling on the size of the force that can be supported, it yields three significant military effects. First, it effectively harasses and delays truck movements down through the southern panhandles of NVN and Laos, though it has no effect on troops infiltrating on foot over trails that are virtually invisible from the air. Our experience shows that daytime armed reconnaissance above some minimum sortie rate makes it prohibitively expensive to the enemy to attempt daylight movement of vehicles, and so forces him to night movement. Second, destruction of bridges and cratering of roads forces the enemy to deploy repair crews, equipment, and porters to repair or bypass the damage. Third, attacks on vehicles, parks, and rest camps destroy some vehicles with their cargoes and inflict casualties. Moreover, our bombing campaign may produce a beneficial effect on U.S. and SVN morale by making NVN pay a price for its enemy. But at the scale we are now operating, I believe our bombing is yielding very small marginal returns, not worth the cost in pilot lives and aircraft.

209

The first effect, that of forcing the enemy into a
system of night movement, occurs at a lower frequency of
armed reconnaissance sorties than the level of the past
several months. The enemy was already moving at night
in 1965, before the sortie rate had reached half the
current level; further sorties have no further effect on
the enemy's overall operating system. The second effect,
that of forcing the enemy to deploy repair crews, equipment, and porters, is also largely brought about by a
comparatively low interdiction effort. Our interdiction
campaign in 1965 and early this year forced NVN to assign
roughly 300,000 additional personnel to LOCs; there is no
indication that recent sortie increases have caused further
increases in the number of these personnel. Once the
enemy system can repair road cuts and damaged bridges in
a few hours, as it has demonstrated it can, additional
sorties may work this system harder but are unlikely to
cause a significant increase in its costs. Only the third
effect, the destruction of vehicles and their cargoes, continues to increase in about the same proportion as the number
of armed reconnaissance sorties, but without noticeable
impact on VC/NVA operations. The overall capability of
the NVN transport system to move supplies within NVN
apparently improved in September in spite of 12,200 attack
sorties. 86/

In a summary paragraph, the draft memo made the entire case against the
bombing:

The increased damage to targets is not noticeable results. No serious shortage of POL in North Vietnam
is evident, and stocks on hand, with recent imports, have
been adequate to sustain necessary operations. No serious
transport problem in the movement of supplies to or within
North Vietnam is evident; most transportation routes appear
to be open, and there has recently been a major logistical
build-up in the area of the DMZ. The raids have disrupted
the civil populace and caused isolated food shortages, but
have not significantly weakened popular morale. Air strikes
continue to depress economic growth and have been responsible
for abandonment of some plans for economic development, but
essential economic activities continue. The increasing
amounts of physical damage sustained by North Vietnamese are
in large measure compensated by aid received from other
Communist countries. Thus, in spite of an interdiction
campaign costing at least $250 million per month at current
levels, no significant impact on the war in South Vietnam
is evident. The monetary value of damage to NVN since the

start of bombing in February 1965 is estimated at about
$140 million through October 10, 1966. 87/

As an alternative method of arresting the infiltration the
memo proposed the now familiar barrier, preparatory work on which was
proceeding rapidly. No new arguments for it were offered, and its
unproven qualities were acknowledged. But it seemed to offer at that
point a better possibility of significantly curtailing infiltration
than an escalation of the ineffective air war. Its costs were estimated,
however, at an astounding $1 billion per year.

While these considerations were dominant at the Pentagon,
the air war in the North continued. The only exceptions to the even
pattern of air strikes at the end of 1966 were strikes authorized in
early December within the 30-mile Hanoi sanctuary against the Yen Vien
rail classification yard and the Van Dien vehicle depot. 88/ The former
was attacked on December 4 and again on the 13th and 14th with extensive
damage to buildings but little destruction of rolling stock. The Van
Dien vehicle depot was struck six times between December 2 and 14 with
some two thirds of its 184 buildings being either destroyed or damaged. 89/
Hanoi's reaction was prompt and vociferous. The DRV accused the U.S. of
blatantly attacking civilian structures and of having caused substantial
civilian casualties. On December 13, the Soviet Press Agency TASS picked
up the theme claiming that U.S. planes had attacked residential areas in
Hanoi. This brought a prompt State Department denial, but on December 15
further attacks on the two targets were suspended. Three days later
there were new charges. This time the Communist Chinese claimed the U.S.
had bombed their embassy in Hanoi. On December 17 the Rumanians made a
similar allegation. The net result of all this public stir was another
round of world opinion pressure on Washington. 90/ In this atmosphere,
on December 23, attacks against all targets within 10 n.m. of Hanoi were
prohibited without specific Presidential authorization.

The most important result of these attacks, however, was to
undercut what appeared to be a peace feeler from Hanoi. In late November,
the DRV had put out a feeler through the Poles for conversations in
Warsaw. The effort was given the code name Marigold, but when the attacks
were launched inadvertently against Hanoi in December, the attempt to
start talks ran into difficulty. A belated U.S. attempt to mollify
North Vietnam's bruised ego failed and formal talks did not materialize.
Some significant exchanges between Hanoi and Washington on their respective terms apparently did take place, however. 91/

The controversy over civilian casualties from the bombing
continued through the end of the year and into January 1967. Harrison
Salisbury, a respected senior editor of the New York Times, went to
Hanoi at Christmas and dispatched a long series of articles that attracted
much world-wide attention. He corroborated DRV allegations of civilian
casualties and damage to residential areas including attacks on Nam Dinh,

211

North Vietnam's third city, and other towns and cities throughout the country. 92/ The matter reached a level of concern such that the President felt compelled to make a statement to the press on December 31 to the effect that the bombing was directed against legitimate military targets and that every effort was being made to avoid civilian casualties. 93/

At no time in the fall of 1966 is there any evidence that a second major "pause" like that of the previous year was planned for the holiday period to pursue a diplomatic initiative on negotiations. But as the holidays drew near a brief military standdown was expected. The Chiefs went on record in November opposing any suspension of military operations, North or South, at Christmas, New Year's or the Lunar New Year the coming February. 94/ The failure of the initiative through Poland in early December left the U.S. with no good diplomatic reason for lengthening the holiday suspensions into a pause, so the President ordered only 48-hour halts in the fighting for Christmas and New Year's. The Pope had made an appeal on December 8 for both sides to extend the holiday truces into an armistice and begin negotiations, but this had fallen on deaf ears in both capitals. 95/ As window-dressing, the U.S. had asked UN Secretary General U Thant to take whatever steps were necessary to get talks started. He replied in a press conference on the last day of the year that the first step toward negotiations must be an "unconditional" U.S. bombing halt. 96/ This evoked little enthusiasm and some annoyance in the Johnson Administration.

Thus, 1966 drew to a close on a sour note for the President. He had just two months before resisted pressure from the military for a major escalation of the war in the North and adopted the restrained approach of the Secretary of Defense, only to have a few inadvertent raids within the Hanoi periphery mushroom into a significant loss of world opinion support. He was in the uncomfortable position of being able to please neither his hawkish nor his dovish critics with his care-fully modulated middle course.

3. 1966 Summary

ROLLING THUNDER was a much heavier bombing program in 1966 than in 1965. There were 148,000 total sorties flown in 1966 as compared with 55,000 in 1965, and 128,000 tons of bombs were dropped as compared with 33,000 in the 10 months of bombing the year before. The number of JCS fixed targets struck, which stood at 158 at the end of 1965, increased to 185, or 27 more, leaving only 57 unstruck out of a list of 242. 97/ Armed reconnaissance, which was still kept out of the northeast quadrant at the end of 1965, was extended during 1966 throughout NVN except for the Hanoi/Haiphong sanctuaries and the China buffer zone, and beginning with ROLLING THUNDER 51 on 6 July was even permitted to penetrate a short way into the Hanoi circle along small selected route segments. Strikes had

TOP SECRET - Sensitive

212

even been carried out against a few "lucrative" POL targets deep within the circles.

The program had also become more expensive. 318 ROLLING THUNDER aircraft were lost during 1966, as compared with 171 in 1965 (though the loss rate dropped from .66% of attack sorties in 1965 to .39% in 1966). CIA estimated that the direct operational cost of the program (i.e., production costs of aircraft lost, plus direct sortie overhead costs -- not including air base or CVA maintenance or logistical support -- plus ordnance costs) came to $1,247 million in 1966 as compared with $460 million in 1965. 98/

Economic damage to NVN went up from $36 million in 1965 to $94 million in 1966, and military damage from $34 million to $36 million. As CIA computed it, however, it cost the U.S. $9.6 to inflict $1 worth of damage in 1966, as compared with $6.6 in 1965. 99/

Estimated civilian and military casualties in NVN also went up, from 13,000 to 23-24,000 (about 80% civilians), but the numbers remained small relative to the 18 million popula ion. 100/

The program in 1966 had accomplished little more than in 1965, however. In January 1967, an anlaysis by CIA concluded that the attacks had not eliminated any important sector of the NVN economy or the military establishment. They had not succeeded in cutting route capacities south of Hanoi to the point where the flow of supplies required in SVN was significantly impeded. The POL attacks had eliminated 76% of JCS-targeted storage capacity, but not until after NVN had implemented a system of dispersed storage, and the POL flow had been maintained at adequate levels. 32% of NVN's power-generating capacity had been put out of action, but the remaining capacity was adequate to supply most industrial consumers. Hundreds of bridges were knocked down, but virtually all of them had been quickly repaired, replaced, or bypassed, and traffic continued. Several thousand freight cars, trucks, barges, and other vehicles were also destroyed or damaged, but inventories were maintained through imports and there was no evidence of a serious transport problem due to equipment shortages. The railroad and highway networks were considerably expanded and improved during the year. 101/

The main losses to the economy, according to the CIA analysis, had been indirect -- due to a reduction in agricultural output and the fish catch, a cut in foreign exchange earnings because of a decline in exports, disruptions of production because of dispersal and other passive defense measures, and the diversion of effort to repair essential transportation facilities. On the military side, damage had disrupted normal military practices, caused the abandonment of many facilities, and forced the widespread dispersal of equipment, but overall military capabilities had continued at a high level. 102/

213

The summary CIA assessment was that ROLLING THUNDER had not helped either to reduce the flow of supplies South or to shake the will of the North:

> The evidence available does not suggest that ROLLING THUNDER to date has contributed materially to the achievement of the two primary objectives of air attack -- reduction of the flow of supplies to VC/NVA forces in the South or weakening the will of North Vietnam to continue the insurgency. ROLLING THUNDER no doubt has lessened the capacity of the transport routes to the South -- put a lower 'cap' on the force levels which North Vietnam can support in the South -- but the 'cap' is well above present logistic supply levels. 103/

The bombing had not succeeded in materially lowering morale among the people, despite some "war weariness." The leaders continued to repeat in private as well as public that they were willing to withstand even heavier bombing rather than accept a settlement on less than their terms. As to the future:

> There may be some degree of escalation which would force the regime to reexamine its position, but we believe that as far as pressure from air attack is concerned the regime would be prepared to continue the insurgency indefinitely in the face of the current level and type of bombing program. 104/

A key factor in sustaining the will of the regime, according to the CIA analysis, was the "massive" economic and military aid provided by the USSR, China, and Eastern Europe. Economic aid to NVN from these countries, which ran about $100 million a year on the average prior to the bombing, increased to $150 million in 1965 and $275 million in 1966. Military aid was $270 million in 1965 and $455 million in 1966. Such aid provided NVN with the "muscle" to strengthen the insurgency in the South and to maintain its air defense and other military forces; and it provided the services and goods with which to overcome NVN's economic difficulties. So long as the aid continued, CIA said, NVN would be able and willing to persevere "indefinitely" in the face of the current ROLLING THUNDER program. 105/

The military view of why ROLLING THUNDER had failed in its objectives in 1966 was most forcefully given by Admiral Sharp, USCINCPAC, in a briefing for General Wheeler at Honolulu on January 12, 1967. Admiral Sharp described three tasks of the air campaign in achieving its objective of inducing Hanoi to "cease supporting, controlling, and directing" the insurgency in the South: "(1) reduce or deny external assistance; (2) increase pressures by destroying in depth those resources that contributed most to support the aggression; and (3) harass, disrupt and impede movement of men and materials to South Vietnam." 106/ CINCPAC

214

had developed and presented to the Secretary of Defense an integrated plan to perform these tasks, but much of it had never been approved. Therein lay the cause of whatever failure could be attributed to the bombing in Admiral Sharp's view.

The rest of the briefing was a long complaint about the lack of authorization to attack the Haiphong harbor in order to deny external assistance, and the insignificant number of total sorties devoted to JCS numbered targets (1% of some 81,000 sorties). Nevertheless, CINCPAC was convinced the concept of operations he had proposed could bring the DRV to give up the war if "self-generated US constraints" were lifted in 1967. <u>107</u>/

Thus, as 1966 drew to a close, the lines were drawn for a long fifteen month internal Administration struggle over whether to stop the bombing and start negotiations. McNamara and his civilian advisers had been disillusioned in 1966 with the results of the bombing and held no sanguine hopes for the ability of air power, massively applied, to produce anything but the same inconclusive results at far higher levels of overall hostility and with significant risk of Chinese and/or Soviet intervention. The military, particularly CINCPAC, were ever more adamant that only civilian imposed restraints on targets had prevented the bombing from bringing the DRV to its knees and its senses about its aggression in the South. The principle remained sound, they argued; a removal of limitations would produce dramatic results. And so, 1967 would be the year in which many of the previous restrictions were progressively lifted and the vaunting boosters of air power would be once again proven wrong. It would be the year in which we relearned the negative lessons of previous wars on the ineffectiveness of strategic bombing.

FOOTNOTES

1. DEF 5517, 291238Z, to CINCPAC, COMUSMACV, CINCPACFLT, and CINCPACAF.

2. USAF Historical Division Liaison Office, "USAF Plans and Operations: The Air Campaign Against North Vietnam, 1966."

3. State Circular 2568, 291300Z June 1966.

4. "Current Foreign Relations," 6 July 1966.

5. Robert S. McNamara Memorandum for Secretaries of the Military Departments, Chairman of the Joint Chiefs of Staff, Assistant Secretaries of Defense, Subject: "Southeast Asia Deployment Plan," 2 July 1966 (S).

6. Alain Enthoven, ASD/SA, Memorandum for the Secretary of Defense, Subject: "Southeast Asia Deployment Plan," 30 June 1966 (TS), transmitting the recommended changes and a draft memo to the JCS, Services and ASDs.

7. McNamara's handwritten and signed changes to the draft memo submitted by Alain Enthoven, ASD/SA, ibid.

8. President Lyndon B. Johnson Memorandum for the Secretary of Defense, Tuesday, June 28, 1966, 5:05 p.m. (S).

9. David L. McDonald, Acting CJCS, Memorandum for the Secretary of Defense, JCSM-450-66, 8 July 1966 (TS); and Robert S. McNamara Memorandum for the President, Subject: "Schedule of Deployments to South Vietnam," 15 July 1966 (TS). For a full treatment of the troop deployment issue see Task Force paper IV.C.6, "U.S. Ground Strategy and Force Deployment, 1965-1967," (TS-Sensitive).

10. USAF Historical Division Liaison Office, "USAF Plans and Operations: The Air Campaign Against North Vietnam, 1966," op. cit.

11. CINCPAC msg. 080730Z July 1966 (TS).

12. CINCPAC msg. to JCS 242069Z July 1966 (TS).

13. CINCPAC msg. to JCS 081937Z August 1966 (TS); and CINCPAC msg. 080730Z July 1966, op. cit.

14. DIA Special Intelligence Summary, "NVN POL Status Report," 20 July 1966 (TS)

15. DIA Special Intelligence Summary, "NVN POL Status Report," 1 August 1966.

16. CINCPAC msg to CINCPACAF 042059Z September 1966 (TS-LIMDIS).

17. Ibid.

18. USAF Historical Division Liaison Office, "USAF Plans and Operations: The Air Campaign Against North Vietnam, 1966."

19. CIA SC No. 04442/67, January 1967, "The Rolling Thunder Program, Present and Potential Target Systems," Appendix A.

20. Ibid.

21. SNIE 13-66, "Current Chinese Communist Intentions in the Vietnam Situation," 4 August 1966 (S).

22. NIE 14.3-66, 7 July 1966, "North Vietnamese Potential for Fighting in South Vietnam," (TS), p. 12.

23. CIA Intelligence Memorandum No. 1684/66, "North Vietnamese Intentions and Attitudes Toward the War," 25 July 1966 (S), pp. 3-4.

24. See the daily DIA Special Intelligence Summaries, "NVN POL Status Report" for July and August 1966.

25. Joint CIA/DIA Report, "An Appraisal of the Bombing of North Vietnam through 12 September 1966," (TS).

26. Institute for Defense Analysis Study, IDA TS/HQ66-49, "The Effects of US Bombing on North Vietnam's Ability to Support Military Operations in South Vietnam and Laos: Retrospect and Prospect," 29 August 1966 (TS), p. 58, emphasis added.

27. USAF Historical Division Liaison Office, "USAF Plans and Operations: The Air Campaign Against North Vietnam, 1966."

28. Quoted in the Washington Post, 15 February 1967.

29. Roger Fisher, Memorandum, A Barrier Strategy, Draft/1-30-66, in McNaughton Book II, Tab AA (S-Eyes Only).

30. Unsigned "Memorandum for the Secretary of Defense, Subject: 'A Barrier Strategy'," dated in pencil in McNaughton's hand 1/30/66 with additional pencil note, "copy given to RSM 3/22/66" (S-Eyes Only).

31. Ibid.

217

TOP SECRET - Sensitive

32. Ibid.

33. JCS msg. 2339/222 to CINCPAC 24 Mar 1966 (TS); and JCS msg. 252305Z Mar 1966 to CINCPAC (TS).

34. CINCPAC msg. to JCS 071925Z April 1966 (TS).

35. Program is referred to in DA msg. to COMUSMACV 774060, 161456Z July 1966 (S).

36. Adam Yarmolinsky (Principle Deputy ISA) Memorandum for the Secretary of Defense, 30 March 1966.

37. Robert S. McNamara letter to Jerrold Zacharias, 16 April 1966, copies to Kistiakowsky, Kaysen and Wiesner.

38. Robert S. McNamara Memorandum for the Assistant Secretary of Defense, International Security Affairs, 26 April 1966 (S).

39. Institute for Defense Analyses Report, IDA TS/HQ66-49, "The Effects of US Bombing on North Vietnam's Ability to Support Military Operations in South Vietnam and Laos: Retrospect and Prospect," 29 August 1966 (TS), pp. v-viii.

40. Ibid., pp. 10-11.

41. Ibid., pp. 12-13.

42. Ibid., pp. 37-38.

43. Ibid., p. 39.

44. Ibid., pp. 45-46.

45. Institute for Defense Analyses, JASON Division, Study S-255 (TS), August 1966, "Air-Supported Anti-Infiltration Barrier," pp. 2-6.

46. Ibid., p. 7.

47. Robert S. McNamara Memorandum for the Chairman, Joint Chiefs of Staff, Subject: "Proposal for Barrier Systems," 3 September 1966 (S).

48. JCS msg. 1975 to CINCPAC, 072155Z September 1966 (TS); JCS msg. 2160 to CINCPAC, 082307Z September 1966 (S); and CM-1732-66, 8 September 1966 (S).

49. CINCPAC msg. to JCS 130705Z September 1966 (TS).

50. CINCPAC msg. to field commands, 052050 September 1966 (TS).

TOP SECRET - Sensitive

51. Robert S. McNamara Memorandum for Lieutenant General Alfred D. Starbird, 15 September 1966 (S).

52. Defense msg. 4244, from SecDef to AmEmbassy Saigon, 021801Z October 1966 (S).

53. JCSM-646-66, 7 October 1966 (TS).

54. SecDef's Saigon Trip, October 1966, CF-54, Tab C.

55. Robert S. McNamara Memorandum for the President, Subject: "Actions Recommended for Vietnam," 14 October 1966 (TS). A note at the end of the memo states, "Mr. Katzenbach and I have discussed many of its (the memo's) main conclusions and recommendations -- in general, but not in particulars, it expresses his views as well as my own."

56. See Task Force paper IV.C.8 for a detailed examination of the background and decision on Program #4.

57. Ibid.

58. Ibid.

59. Ibid.

60. JCSM-672-66, 14 October 1966 (TS).

61. Ibid.

62. Ibid.

63. George A. Carver, Jr., Memorandum for the Director, CIA, Subject: "Comments on Secretary McNamara's Trip Report," 15 October 1966 (TS). A pencil note in the margin in McNamara's hand says, "prepared by Dick at my request."

64. Ibid.

65. Ibid.

66. John T. McNaughton, ASD/ISA, Memorandum for Secretary McNamara, Subject: "McNaughton in Manila, October 23-25, 1966," 26 October 1966 (S-Eyes Only); with a copy of the Manila Communique annotated in McNaughton's hand attached.

67. Ibid., quoted in the McNaughton memo.

68. Ibid., quoted in the McNaughton memo.

69. Ibid.

70. JCSM-667-66, 15 October 1966 (TS); requests an increase in B-52 sorties from 600 to 800 per month beginning in February 1967. The Chiefs also noted they had a proposal for forward basing the B-52s under study and would forward a recommendation later.

71. Memo to Mr. Vance, 18 October 1966, signed "ACG" (Col Abbot C. Greenleaf, military assistant to the Deputy Secretary) with a summary of McNamara's views of an attached JCS study of attrition factors.

72. CINCPAC letter to JCS 3010, Ser: 000438, 20 October 1966, Subject: "Calendar Year 1966 and 1967 Force Requirements/Capabilities Programs," in three volumes (TS).

73. Ibid., Vol. II, p. 1.

74. Ibid., Vol. I, p. C-2.

75. See above, p.

76. CINCPAC letter 3010, op. cit., p. B-7.

77. JCSM-702-66, 4 November 1966 (TS) with appendices A-C, p. B-1.

78. Ibid., p. A-1.

79. Ibid.

80. Robert S. McNamara Memorandum for the Chairman, Joint Chiefs of Staff, Subject: "CINCPAC Additional CY 1966 and CY 1967 Force Requirements," 6 October 1966 (TS), with appendix.

81. JCSM-702-66, op. cit., Annex C, p. 68.

82. Ibid., p. 70.

83. Robert S. McNamara Memorandum for the Chairman of the Joint Chiefs of Staff, Subject: "Deployments to Southeast Asia," 11 November 1966 (TS).

84. For a complete treatment of the issues and background to the Program #4 decision on ground forces see Task Force paper IV.C. 8 (TS-Sensitive).

85. Chairman's Memoranda to the Secretary of Defense, CM-1770-66, 22 September 1966 (TS); CM-1794-66, 29 September 1966; and 2014-66, 22 December 1966 (S).

86. Draft Memorandum for the President (For Comment), Subject: "Recommended FY67 Southeast Asia Supplemental Appropriation," 17 Nov. 1966 (TS), pp. 13-14, in McNaughton Book VII, Tab Q.

220

87. Ibid.

88. Authorized in RT-52, November 12, 1966.

89. Information on both targets is in CINCPAC Command History - 1966, Vol. II, pp. 504-505 (TS).

90. Ibid., and New York Times, Dec. 13, 14, 16, 17, 1966.

91. Kraslow and Toory, The Secret Search for Peace in Vietnam, (Random House, NY, 1968), p.

92. See the New York Times, December 25, 1966 - January 30, 1967.

93. New York Times, Jan. 1, 1967.

94. JCSM-727-66, 22 November 1966 (S).

95. New York Times, December 9, 1966.

96. New York Times, January 1, 1967.

97. CIA SC No. 04442/67, "The Rolling Thunder Program -- Present and Potential Target Systems," January 1967.

98. Ibid.

99. Ibid.

100. Ibid.

101. Ibid.

102. Ibid.

103. Ibid.

104. Ibid.

105. Ibid.

106. CINCPAC Command History - 1966, op. cit., vol. II, p. 511.

107. Ibid., pp. 511-514.

IV.C Evolution of the War (26 Vols.)
Direct Action: The Johnson Commitments, 1964-1968
(16 Vols.)
7. Air War in the North: 1965 – 1968 (2 Vols.)
b. Volume II

TOP SECRET - SENSITIVE

UNITED STATES - VIETNAM RELATIONS
1945 - 1967

VIETNAM TASK FORCE

OFFICE OF THE SECRETARY OF DEFENSE

TOP SECRET - SENSITIVE

SET #13

0295

TOP SECRET - Sensitive

IV. C. 7. (b)

Volume II

THE AIR WAR IN NORTH VIETNAM

0295

VOLUME II

THE AIR WAR IN NORTH VIETNAM

TABLE OF CONTENTS and OUTLINE

Page

TOP SECRET - Sensitive

TOP SECRET - Sensitive

IV. THE ATTEMPT TO DE-
ESCALATE – JAN - JUL 1967

IV. THE ATTEMPT TO DE-ESCALATE -- JANUARY-JULY 1967

        During the first seven months of 1967 a running battle was fought
within the Johnson Administration between the advocates of a greatly
expanded air campaign against North Vietnam, one that might genuinely
be called "strategic," and the disillusioned doves who urged relaxation,
if not complete suspension, of the bombing in the interests of greater
effectiveness and the possibilities for peace. The "hawks" of course were
primarily the military, but in war-time their power and influence with an
incumbent Administration is disproportionate. McNamara, supported quantitatively by John McNaughton in ISA, led the attempt to de-escalate the
bombing. Treading the uncertain middle ground at different times in the
debate were William Bundy at State, Air Force Secretary Harold Brown and,
most importantly, the President himself. Buffetted from right and left
he determinedly tried to pursue the temperate course, escalating gradually
in the late spring but levelling off again in the summer. To do so was
far from easy because such a course really pleased no one (and, it should
be added, did not offer much prospect for a breakthrough one way or the
other). It was an unhappy, contentious time in which the decibel level
of the debate went up markedly but the difficult decision was not taken --
it was avoided.

    A. The Year Begins with No Change

        1. Escalation Proposals

            The year 1967 began with the military commands still
grumbling about the Christmas and New Year's truces ordered from Washington. Both had been grossly violated by multiple VC incidents, and both
had been the occasions of major VC/NVA resupply efforts. The restrictions
placed on U.S. forces were felt by the field commands to be at the expense
of American life. U.S. military authorities would argue long and hard
against a truce for the TET Lunar New Year holiday, but in the end they
would loose.

            Early in 1967, CINCPAC reopened his campaign to win
Washington approval for air strikes against a wider list of targets in
North Vietnam. On January 14 CINCPAC sent the JCS a restatement of the
objectives for ROLLING THUNDER he had developed in 1966, noting his belief
that they remained valid for 1967. 1/   Four days later he forwarded a
long detailed list of proposed new targets for attack. What he proposed
was a comprehensive destruction of North Vietnam's military and industrial
base in Route Package 6 (Hanoi-Haiphong). 2/   This called for the destruction of 7 power plants (all except the one in the very center of Hanoi,
and the 2 in Haiphong included in a special Haiphong package); 10 "war
supporting industries" (with the Thai Nguyen iron and steel plant at the
head of the list); 20 transportation support facilities; 44 military
complexes; 26 POL targets; and 28 targets in Haiphong and the other
ports (including docks, shipyards, POL, power plants, etc.). CINCPAC

optimistically contended that this voluminous target system could be attacked with no increase in sorties and with an actual decline in aircraft lost to hostile fire.

The proposal was evidently received in Washington with something less than enthusiasm. The Chiefs did not send such a recommendation to the Secretary and there is no evidence that the matter was given serious high level attention at that time. On January 25 in a cable on anti-infiltration (i.e. the much-maligned barrier), CINCPAC again raised the question. He was careful to note (as he had previously in a private cable to Wheeler and Westmoreland on January 3) 3/ that, "...no single measure can stop infiltration." 4/ But he argued that the extraordinary measures the enemy had taken to strengthen his air defenses and generate a world opinion against the bombing were evidence of how much the air strikes were hurting him.

These arguments were reinforced by the January CIA analysis which also made something of a case for a heavier bombing campaign. It considered a number of alternative target systems -- modern industry, shipping, the Red River levees, and other targets -- and two interdiction campaigns, one "unlimited" and the other restricted to the southern NVN panhandle and Laos, and concluded that the unlimited campaign was the most promising. 5/

On the modern industry target list, CIA included 20 facilities, 7 of them electric power plants. Knocking out these facilities, it said, would eliminate the fruits of several hundred million dollars capital investment, cut off the source of one-fourth of the GNP and most foreign exchange earnings, disrupt other sectors of the economy which used their products, add to the burden of aid required from NVN's allies, and temporarily displace the urban labor force. The loss would be a serious blow to NVN's hopes for economic progress and status, negating a decade of intense effort devoted to the construction of modern industry. This would exert additional pressure on the regime, but would not by itself, CIA believed, be intense enough to bring Hanoi to the negotiating table. Outside aid could no doubt make up the deficit in goods to sustain the economy and the national defense of the North as well as to continue the war in the South. 6/

Aerial mining, provided it was extended to coastal and inland waters as well as the harbors, and especially if accompanied by intensive armed reconnaissance against all LOCs to China, would be very serious. NVN would almost certainly have to reduce some import programs, not sufficiently perhaps to degrade the flow of essential military supplies or prevent continued support of the war in SVN, but enough to hurt the economy. 7/

Bombing the levee system which kept the Red River under control, if timed correctly, could cause large crop losses and force NVN to import large amounts of rice. Depending on the success of interdiction efforts, such imports might overload the transport system. The levees themselves could be repaired in a matter of weeks, however, and any military effects of bombing them would be limited and short-lived. 8/

An "unlimited" campaign against transportation and remaining targets, in addition to attacking industry and mining the harbors and waterways, would greatly increase the costs and difficulties in maintaining the flow of the most essential military and civilian goods within NVN. If the attack on transportation were able to cut the capacity of the railroads by 1/3 on a sustained basis and roads by 1/4, the remaining available route capacity would not be sufficient to satisfy NVN's minimum daily needs:

If an unlimited interdiction program were highly successful, the regime would encounter increasing difficulty and cost in maintaining the flow of some of their most essential military and economic goods. In the long term the uncertainties and difficulties resulting from the cumulative effect of the air campaigns would probably cause Hanoi to undertake a basic reassessment of the probable course of the war and the extent of the regime's commitment to it. 9/

By contrast, according to the CIA analysis, restricting the bombing to the Panhandle of NVN and Laos would tend to strengthen Hanoi's will. The main effect would be to force NVN to increase the repair labor force in southern NVN and Laos by about 30 percent, which could easily be drawn from other areas no longer being bombed. The flow of men and supplies would continue. NVN would regard the change in the bombing pattern as a clear victory, evidence that international and domestic pressures on the U.S. were having an effect. It would be encouraged to believe that the U.S. was tiring of the war and being forced to retreat. 10/

Other considerations, however, were dominant in Washington at the highest levels. In mid-January another effort to communicate positions with the DRV had been made and there was an understandable desire to defer escalatory decisions until it had been determined whether some possibility for negotiations existed. 11/ Moreover, the TET holiday at the beginning of February, for which a truce had been announced, made late January an inpropitious time to expand the bombing. Thus, on January 28, ROLLING THUNDER program #53 authorized little more than a continuation of strikes within the parameters of previous authorizations. 12/

2. The TET Pause -- 8-14 February

As noted in the previous section of this paper, the Chiefs had recorded their opposition to any truce or military standdown for the holidays in late November. 13/ On January 2, General Westmoreland had strongly recommended against a truce for TET because of the losses to friendly forces during the Christmas and New Year's truces just concluded. 14/

CINCPAC endorsed his opposition to any further truce as did the JCS on January 4. 15/ The Chiefs pointed out that the history of U.S. experience with such holiday suspensions of operations was that the VC/NVA had increasingly exploited them to resupply, prepare for attacks, redeploy forces and commit violations. Perhaps of most concern was the opportunity such standdowns provided the enemy to mount major unharassed logistical resupply operations. Thus, they concluded:

> Against this background of persistent exploitation of the standdown periods by the enemy, the Joint Chiefs of Staff view the forthcoming standdown for TET with grave concern. To grant the enemy a respite during a four-day standdown at TET will slow our campaign, allow him time to reconstitute and replenish his forces, and cost us greater casualties in the long run. 16/

This unanimous military opposition was falling on deaf ears. The President and his advisors had already committed the U.S. to a four-day truce and such a belated change of course would have clearly rebounded to the public opinion benefit of the North Vietnamese (who had already, on January 1, announced their intention to observe a 7-day TET truce). Thus, on January 14, Ambassador Lodge was instructed to get the GVN's concurrence to maintain just the 96-hour standdown, but to tell them that the Allies should be prepared to extend the pause if fruitful contacts developed during it. 17/ Lodge replied the following day that the proposal was agreeable to the GVN and to the Allied Chiefs of Mission in Saigon. 18/

Acknowledging the political considerations which required a pause, the Chiefs on January 18 proposed the announcement of a set of conditions to the standdown: (1) that SEA DRAGON countersea infiltration operations continue up to 19°; (2) that CINCPAC be authorized to resume air attacks against major land resupply efforts south of 19°; (3) that operations be resumed in the DMZ area to counter any major resupply or infiltration; and (4) that warning be given that violations or VC/NVA efforts to gain tactical advantage in SVN during the truce, would prompt direct military counteractions. 19/ The reaction at State to these new JCS conditions was vigorous. On January 21, Bundy sent Katzenbach a memo urging him to oppose anything that would compromise our suspension of operations against North Vietnam.

> ...I strongly recommend against approving JCS proposals for broader military authority to respond to North Viet-Namese resupply activities in North Viet-Nam....In my view, resupply activities in North Viet-Nam cannot be considered a sufficiently immediate and direct threat to our forces to justify the great political and psychological disadvantages of U.S. air and naval strikes against North Viet-Namese territory during a truce period. 20/

No information is available on McNamara's reaction to the proposed JCS
truce limitations, but on the basis of his general position on the
bombing at that time he can be presumed to have opposed them. In any
case, they were not adopted. The execute order for the suspension of
hostilities authorized CINCPAC strikes only in the case of an immediate
and direct threat to U.S. forces, and stipulated that, "In the event
reconnaissance disclosed major military resupply activity in North Vietnam
south of 19 degrees north latitude, report immediately to the JCS." 21/
Decisions on how and when to respond to such resupply efforts would be made
in Washington not Honolulu. This, then, was the issue whose merits would
be the focus of debate at the end of the pause when furious diplomatic
efforts to get talks started would generate pressure for an extension.

Even before the holiday arrived pressure to extend the
pause had begun to mount. On February 2, Leonard Marks, Director of
USIA proposed to Rusk that the truce be extended, "in 12 or 24 hour
periods contingent upon DRV and VC continued observance of the truce
conditions." 22/ The latter included in his definition, "...suspension
of all infiltration and movement toward infiltration...." 23/ At the
Pentagon, at least within civilian circles, there was sentiment for
extending the pause too. In the materials that John McNaughton left
behind is a handwritten scenario for the pause with his pencilled changes.
The authorship is uncertain since the handwriting is neither McNaughton's
nor McNamara's (nor apparently that of any of the other key Pentagon
advisors), but a note in the margin indicates it had been seen and approved
by the Secretary. Therefore it is reproduced below. Underlined words
or phrases are McNaughton's modifications.

SCENARIO

1. President tell DRV before Tet, "We are stopping
bombing at start of Tet and at the end of Tet we will not
resume."

2. During Tet and in days thereafter:
   a. Observe DRV/VC conduct for 'signs'
   b. Try to get talks started.

3. Meantime, avoid changes in 'noise level' in other
areas of conduct -- e.g., no large US troop deployments for
couple weeks, no dramatic changes in rules of engagement in
South, etc.

4. As for public handling:
   a. At end of 4 days of Tet merely extend to 7 days.
   b. At end of 7 days just keep pausing, making make no
      expansion.
   c. Later say "We are seeing what happens."
   d. Even later, say (if true) infiltration down, etc.

5. If we must resume RT, have reasons justifications·
and start in Route packages 1 & 2, working werk North as
excuses appear (and excuses will appear).

6. If talks start and DRV &-they demands ceasefire in
South or cessation of US troop additions, consider exact deal
then.

7. Accelerate readiness of Project 728. /anti-infiltration
barrier/

8. Avoid allowing our terms to harden just because things
appear to be going better.

(Vance: How handle case if resupply keeps up during Pause?) 24/

In a puzzling marginal note, McNaughton recorded McNamara's reaction to
the scenario: "SecDef (2/3/67: 'Agreed we will do this if answer
to note is unproductive' (?). Something like this even if productive.
JTM." 25/ It is not clear what the Secretary may have had in mind in
his reference to a "note." The U.S. had exchanged notes with the DRV
through the respective embassies in Moscow in late January and he may
have meant this contact. Another possibility is that he was thinking of
the letter from the President to Ho that must have been in draft at that
time (it was to have been delivered in Moscow on February 7 but actual
delivery was not until the 8th). In either case, McNamara must have
foreseen this scenario for unilateral extension of the pause based on
DRV actions on the ground as an alternative if they formally rejected
our demands for reciprocity.

Whatever the explanation, the President's letter to Ho
reiterated the demand for reciprocity:

I am prepared to order a cessation of bombing against
your country and the stopping of further augmentation of
U.S. forces in South Vietnam as soon as I am assured that
infiltration into South Vietnam by land and by sea has stopped. 26/

The President did, however, tie his proposal to the Tet pause and voiced
the hope that an answer would be received before the end of Tet that would
permit the suspension to continue and peace talks to begin.

Pressures on the President to continue the pause also came
from his domestic critics and from the international community. On the
very day the pause began, the Pope sent a message to both sides in the
conflict expressing his hope that the suspension of hostilities could be
extended and open the way to peace. The President's reply was courteous

6

but firm:

> We are prepared to talk at any time and place, in
> any forum, and with the object of bringing peace to
> Vietnam; however, I know you would not expect us to
> reduce military action unless the other side is willing
> to do likewise. 27/

Meanwhile the possibility that a definitive suspension of
the bombing might produce negotiations became increasingly likely.
Premier Kosygin had arrived in London to confer with Prime Minister
Wilson on February 6, two days before the truce started. They immediately began a frantic weeklong effort to bring the two sides together.
Multiple interpretations of position were passed through the intermediaries in London, but in the end, the massive DRV resupply effort
forced the U.S. to resume the bombing without having received a final
indication from the DRV as to their willingness to show restraint. But
this was not before the bombing halt had been extended from 4 to 6 days,
and not before the Soviets had informed the DRV of the deadline for an
answer.

The factor which took on such importance and eventually
forced the President's hand was the unprecedented North Vietnamese
resupply activity during the bombing suspension. As already noted, the
military had opposed the halt for just this reason and the Christmas
and New Year's halts had given warning of what might be expected. By
the time the truce had been in effect 24 hours, continuing surveillance had
already revealed the massive North Vietnamese effort to move supplies into
its southern panhandle. Washington sounded the alarm. On February 9
Rusk held a press conference and warned about the high rate of supply
activity. The same day Bundy called Saigon and London with details of
the rate of logistical movement and with instructions for dealing with
the press. To London he stated:

> Ambassador Bruce...should bring this story to the
> attention of highest British levels urgently, pointing out
> its relevance both to the problems we face in continuing
> the Tet bombing suspension and to the wider problem involved
> in any proposal that we cease bombing in exchange for mere
> talks. In so doing, you should not repeat not suggest that
> we are not still wide open to the idea of continuing the
> Tet bombing suspension through the 7-day period or at least
> until Kosygin departs London. You should emphasize, how-
> ever, that we are seriously concerned about these develop-
> ments and that final decision on such additional two- or
> three-day suspension does involve serious factors in light
> of this information. 28/

On February 10 DIA sent the Secretary a summary of the resupply situation in the first 48-hours of the truce. If the pattern of the first 48 hours continued, the DRV would move some 34,000 tons of materiel southward, the equivalent of 340 division-days of supply. 29/

Thus the pressure on the President to resume mounted. On February 12 when the truce ended, the bombing was not resumed, but no announcement of the fact was made. The DRV were again invited to indicate what reciprocity the U.S. could expect. But no answer was forthcoming. Finally after more hours of anxious waiting by Kosygin and Wilson for a DRV reply, the Soviet Premier left London for home on February 13. The same day, the New York Times carried the latest Harris poll which showed that 67% of the American people supported the bombing. Within hours, the bombing of the North was resumed. The President, in speaking to the press, stressed the unparalleled magnitude of the North Vietnamese logistical effort during the pause as the reason he could no longer maintain the bombing halt. 30/ On February 15, Ho sent the President a stiff letter rejecting U.S. demands for reciprocity and restating the DRV's position that the U.S. must unconditionally halt the bombing before any other issues could be considered. 31/ Thus, the book closed on another effort to bring the conflict to the negotiating table.

B. More Targets

1. The Post-TET Debate

The failure of the Tet diplomatic initiatives once again brought attention back to measures which might put more pressure on the DRV. CINCPAC's January targetting proposals were reactivated for consideration in the week following the resumption of bombing. In early February, before the pause, CINCPAC had added to his requests for additional bombing targets a request for authority to close North Vietnam's ports through aerial mining. Arguing that, "A drastic reduction of external support to the enemy would be a major influence in achieving our objectives...," he suggested that this could be accomplished by denying use of the ports. Three means of closing the ports were considered: (1) naval blockade; (2) air strikes against port facilities; and (3) aerial mining of the approaches. The first was rejected because of the undesirable political ramifications of confrontations with Soviet and third country shipping. But air strikes and mining were recommended as complementary ways of denying use of the ports. Closure of Haiphong alone, it was estimated, would have a dramatic effect because it handled some 95% of North Vietnamese shipping. 32/ In a related development, the JCS, on February 2, gave their endorsement to mining certain inland waterways including the Kien Giang River and its seaward approaches. 33/

In the week following the Tet pause the range of possible escalatory actions came under full review. The President apparently requested a listing of options for his consideration, because on February 21, Cyrus Vance, the Deputy Secretary of Defense, forwarded a package of proposals to Under Secretary Katzenbach at State for comment. Vance's letter stated, "The President wants the paper for his night reading tonight." 34/ The paper Vance transmitted gives every indication of having been written by McNaughton, although that cannot be verified. In any case, it began with the following outline "shopping list" of possible actions with three alternative JCS packages indicated:

TOP SECRET - Sensitive

21 Feb 67

OUTLINE

JCS Program A	B	C		Page
			1. Military actions against North Vietnam and in Laos	
			A. Present program	1
			B. Options for increased military programs	2
			1. Destroy modern industry	3
X	X	X	- Thermal power (7-plant grid)	
X	X	X	- Steel and cement	
	X	X	- Machine tool plant	
			- Other	
		X	2. Destroy dikes and levees	6
			3. Mine ports and coastal waters	7
	X	X	- Mine estuaries south of 20°	
		X	- Mine major ports and approaches, and estuaries north of 20°	
			4. Unrestricted LOC attacks	10
X	X	X	- Eliminate 10-mile Hanoi prohibited area	
	X	X	- Reduce Haiphong restricted area to 4 miles	
		X	- Eliminate prohibited/restricted areas except Chicom zone	
	X	X	- Elements of 3 ports (Haiphong, Cam Pha and Hon Gai)	
		X	- 4 ports (Haiphong, Cam Pha, Hon Gai and Hanoi Port)	
	X	X	- Selected rail facilities	
	X	X	- Mine inland waterways south of 20°	
		X	- Mine inland waterways north of 20°	
	X	X	- 7 locks	
			5. Expand naval surface operations	12
X	X	X	- Fire at targets ashore and afloat south of 19°	
	X	X	- Expand to 20°	
		X	- Expand north of 20° to Chicom buffer zone	
			6. Destroy MIG airfields	14
X	X	X	- All unoccupied airfields	
	X	X	- 4 not used for international civil transportation	
		X	- 2 remaining airfields (Phuc Yen and Gia Lam)	
			7. SHINING BRASS ground operations in Laos	15
X	X	X	- Delegate State/DOD authority to CINCPAC/Vientiane	
	X	X	- Expand operational limits to 20 km into Laos, increase helo operations, authorize larger forces, increase frequency of operation	
		X	- Battalion-size forces; start guerrilla warfare	
X	X	X	8. Cause interdicting rains in or near Laos	16
			9. Miscellaneous	
X	X	X	- Base part of B-52 operations at U-Tapao, Thailand	
X	X	X	- Fire artillery from SVN against DMZ and north of DMZ	
	X	X	- Fire artillery from SVN against targets in Laos	
	X	X	- Ammunition dump 4 miles SW of Haiphong	
		X	- Air defense HQ and Ministry of Defense HQ in Hanoi	
			II. Actions in South Vietnam	
			A. Expand US forces and/or their role	17
			- Continue current force build-up	
			- Accelerate current build-up (deploying 3 Army bns in 6/67)	
X	X	X	- Deploy Marine brigade from Okinawa/Japan in 3/67	
	X	X	- Deploy up to 4 divisions and up to 9 air squadrons	
		X	B. Improve pacification	18

10   TOP SECRET - Sensitive

TOP SECRET - Sensitive

The discussion section of the paper dealt with each of the eight specific option areas noting our capability in each instance to inflict heavy damage or complete destruction to the facilities in question. The important conclusion in each instance was that elimination of the targets, individually or collectively, could not sufficiently reduce the flow of men and materiel to the South to undercut the Communist forces fighting the war. The inescapable fact which forced this conclusion was that North Vietnam's import potential far exceeded its requirements and could sustain considerable contraction without impairing the war effort. The point was dramatically made in the following table:

When Option 4 is taken together with Options 1-3, the import and need figures appear as follows:

NORTH VIETNAM'S POTENTIAL FOR OBTAINING
IMPORTS BEFORE AND AFTER U.S. ATTACK
(tons per day)

	Potential Now	Potential After Attack
By sea	6,500	650
By Red River from China	1,500	150
By road from China	3,200	2,400
By rail from China	6,000	4,000
TOTAL	17,200	7,200

Without major hardship, the need for imports is as follows (tons per day):

Normal imports	4,200
If imports replace destroyed industrial production	1,400
If imports replace rice destroyed by leveee breaks	600-2,500
TOTAL	6,200-8,100 35/

With respect to crippling Hanoi's will to continue the war, the paper stated:

Unless things were going very badly for them there /in the South/, it is likely that the North Vietnamese would decide to continue the war despite their concern over the increasing destruction of their country, the effect of this on their people, and their increasing apprehension that the US would invade the North. 36/

11   TOP SECRET - Sensitive

The expected reaction of the Soviet Union and China to these escalatory
options varied, but none was judged as unacceptable except in the case
of mining the harbors. Here the Soviet Union would be faced with a
difficult problem. The paper judged the likely Soviet reaction this
way:

> ....To the USSR, the mining of the ports would be
> particularly challenging. Last year they moved some
> 530,000 tons of goods to North Vietnam by sea. If the
> ports remained closed, almost all of their deliveries --
> military and civilian -- would be at the sufferance of
> Peiping, with whom they are having increasing difficulties.
> They would be severely embarrassed by their inability to
> prevent or counter the US move. It is an open question
> whether they would be willing to take the risks involved
> in committing their own ships and aircraft to an effort
> to reopen the ports.
>
> In these circumstances, the Soviets would at least
> send a token number of "volunteers" to North Vietnam if
> Hanoi asked for them, and would provide Hanoi with new
> forms of military assistance -- e.g., floating mines and
> probably cruise missiles (land-based or on Komar boats),
> which could appear as a direct response to the US mining
> and which would endanger our ships in the area.
>
> The Soviets would be likely to strike back at the US
> in their bilateral relations, severely reducing what remains
> of normal contacts on other issues. They would focus their
> propaganda and diplomatic campaign to get US allies in
> Europe to repudiate the US action. They would probably
> also make other tension-promoting gestures, such as
> pressure in Berlin. The situation could of course become
> explosive if the mining operations resulted in serious
> damage to a Soviet ship. 37/

This confirmed Ambassador Thompson's judgment of a few days before,

> Mining of Haiphong Harbor would provoke a strong
> reaction here and Soviets would certainly relate it to
> their relations with China....They would consider that
> we are quite willing to make North Vietnam entirely
> dependent upon CHINCOMs with all which that would imply. 38/

Thus, while considering a long list of possible escalations, it did not
offer forceful arguments for any of them. The copy preserved in McNaughton's
materials contains a final section entitled "Ways to Advance a Settlement."
A pencil note, however, indicates that this section was not sent to State
and presumably not to the President either.

　　　　　　　　　TOP SECRET - Sensitive

At State, Bundy drafted some comments on the OSD paper which generally supported its analysis. With respect to the proposals for mining North Vietnamese waters, however, it made a significant distinction:

> ...we would be inclined to separate the mining of ports used by Soviet shipping from the mining of coastal waters where (we believe) most of the shipping, if not all, is North Vietnamese. Mining of the waterways would have a more limited effect on Hanoi will and capacity, but would also be much less disturbing to the Soviets and much less likely to throw Hanoi into the arms of China, or to induce the Soviets to cooperate more fully with the Chinese. 39/

The distinction is important because the President the next day did in fact approve the limited mining of internal waterways but deferred any decision on mining the ports. Beyond this, Bundy sought to reinforce the undesirability of striking the sensitive dyke and levee system and to emphasize that the Chinese buffer zone was a more important sanctuary (from the point of view of likely Soviet and/or Chinese reactions) than the Hanoi-Haiphong perimeters. 40/

Several other memos of the same period appear in the files, but it is unlikely they had any influence on the new targets the President was considering. Roger Fisher had sent McNaughton another of his periodic notes on "future Strategy." After rehearsing the failures of the bombing program he suggested that "...all northern bombing be restricted to a narrower and narrower belt across the southern part of North Vietnam until it merges into air support for an on-the-ground interdiction barrier." 41/ By thus concentrating and intensifying our interdiction efforts he hoped we might finally be able to choke off the flow of men and goods to the South.

A memo from the President's special military advisor, General Maxwell Taylor, on February 20 considered some of the difficulties of negotiations, in particular the sequence in which we should seek to arrange a ceasefire and a political settlement. He argued that it was in the U.S. interest to adopt a "fight and talk" strategy, in which the political issues were settled first and the cease-fire arranged afterwards, hopefully conducting the actual negotiations in secret while we continued to vigorously press the VC/NVA in combat. 42/ The President passed the memo on to the Secretaries of State and Defense and the Chairman of the JCS for their comment but since the question of negotiations was for the moment academic it probably had no bearing on the next bombing decisions. 43/

2. A "Little" Escalation

The President approved only a limited number of the measures presented to him, by and large those that would incur little risk of counter-escalation. He authorized naval gunfire up to the 20th parallel against targets ashore and afloat, artillery fire across the DMZ, a slight expansion of operation in Laos, the mining of rivers and estuaries south of 20°, and new bombing targets for ROLLING THUNDER 54. The latter included the remaining thermal power plants except Hanoi and Haiphong, and a reiteration of authority to strike the Thai Nguyen Steel Plant and the Haiphong Cement Plant (initially given in RT 53 but targets not struck). 44/ The President was neither ready nor willing, however, to consider the mining of the ports nor, for the moment, the removal of the Hanoi sanctuary. A decision on basing B-52s in Thailand was also deferred for the time being.

CINCPAC promptly took steps to bring the newly authorized targets under attack. On February 24 U.S. artillery units along the DMZ began shelling north of the buffer with long-range 175mm. cannon. The same day the Secretary told a news conference that more targets in the North might be added to the strike list, thereby preparing the public for the modest escalation approved by the President two days before. On February 27 U.S. planes began the aerial mining of the rivers and coastal estuaries of North Vietnam below the 20th parallel. The mines were equipped with de-activation devices to neutralize them at the end of three months. Weather conditions, however, continued to hamper operations over North Vietnam and to defer sorties from several of the authorized targets that required visual identification weather conditions before strike approval could be given. The Thai Nguyen Iron and Steel complex, for example, was not struck until March 10. The slow squeeze was once more the order of the day with the emphasis on progressively destroying North Vietnam's embryonic industrial capability.

But the President intended that the pressure on the North be slowly increased to demonstrate the firmness of our resolve. Thus William Bundy in Saigon in early March told Thieu on behalf of the President that:

> GVN should have no doubt that President adhered to
> basic position he had stated at Manila, that pressure must
> continue to be applied before Hanoi could be expected to
> change its attitude, while at the same time we remained
> completely alert for any indication of change in Hanoi's
> position. If was now clear from December and January events
> that Hanoi was negative for the time being, so that we were
> proceeding with continued and somewhat increased pressures
> including additional measures against the North.

The President perceived the strikes as necessary in the psychological test of wills between the two sides to punish the North, in spite of the near-consensus opinion of his advisers that no level of damage or destruction that we were willing to inflict was likely to destroy Hanoi's

determination to continue the struggle. In a March 1st letter to
Senator Jackson (who had publicly called for more bombing on February 27)
he pointed to the DRV's violation of the two Geneva Agreements of 1954
and 1962 as the reason for the bombing, its specific purposes being:

> ...first...to back our fighting men and our fighting
> allies by demonstrating that the aggressor could not illegally
> bring hostile arms and men to bear against them from the
> security of a sanctuary.

> Second...to impose on North Viet-Nam a cost for violating
> its international agreements.

> Third...to limit or raise the cost of bringing men and
> supplies to bear against the South. 46/

The formulation of objectives for the bombing was almost identical two
weeks later when he spoke to the Tennessee State Legislature:

> --To back our fighting men by denying the enemy a
>   sanctuary;
> --To exact a penalty against North Vietnam for her
>   flagrant violations of the Geneva Accords of 1954
>   and 1962;
> --To limit the flow, or to substantially increase the
>   cost of infiltration of men and materiel from North
>   Vietnam. 47/

In both instances the President put the psychological role of the bombing
ahead of its interdiction functions. There was little evidence to suggest, however, that Hanoi was feeling these pressures in the way in which
Mr. Johnson intended them.

3. The Guam Conference and More Salami Slices

Sometime early in March the President decided to arrange
a high level conference to introduce his new team for Vietnam (Ambassadors
Bunker and Komer, General Abrams, et al.) to the men they were to replace
and to provide them comprehensive briefings on the problems they would
face. Later it was decided to invite Thieu and Ky to the conference as
well. The conference was scheduled for March 20-21 on Guam and the
President led a large high-level delegation from Washington. Two important
events occurred just before the group gathered and in large degree provided the backdrop if not the entire subject matter of their deliberations.
First, the South Vietnamese Constituent Assembly completed its work on
a draft constitution on March 18 and Thieu and Ky proudly brought the
document with them to present to the President for his endorsement. 48/
Not surprisingly the great portion of the conference was given over to
discussions about the forthcoming electoral process envisaged in the new
constitution through which legitimate government would once again be

restored to South Vietnam. The second significant development also occurred on the 18th when General Westmoreland sent CINCPAC a long cable requesting additional forces. 49/ His request amounted to little more than a restatement of the force requirements that had been rejected in November 1966 when Program #4 was approved. The proposal must have hung over the conference and been discussed during it by the Principles even though no time had been available before their departure for a detailed analysis.

The bombing program and the progress of the anti-infiltration barrier were also items on the Guam agenda but did not occupy much time since other questions were more pressing. Some handwritten "press suggestions" which McNaughton prepared for McNamara reflect the prevalent Guam concern with the war in the South. McNaughton's first point (originally numbered #4 but renumbered 1 in red pen) was, "Constant Strategy: A. Destroy Main Forces B. Provide Security C. Improve lot of people D. Press NVN (RT) E. Settle." 50/ As if to emphasize the preoccupation with the war in the South, the Joint Communique made no mention of the air war. But, if ROLLING THUNDER was only fourth priority in our "Constant Strategy," the Guam Conference nevertheless produced approval for two significant new targets -- the Haiphong thermal power plants. They were added to the authorized targets of RT 54 on March 22. A related action also announced on March 22 after discussion and Presidential approval at Guam was the decision to assign B-52s conducting ARC LIGHT strikes in North and South Vietnam to bases in Thailand as the JCS had long been recommending. Slowly the air war was inching its way up the escalatory ladder.

During the Guam Conference one of the more unusual, unexpected and inexplicable developments of the entire Vietnam war occurred. Hanoi, for reasons still unclear, decided to make public the exchange of letters between President Johnson and Ho during the Tet truce. The North Vietnamese Foreign Ministry released the texts of the two letters to the press on March 21 while the President, his advisers and the South Vietnamese leadership were all closeted in Guam reviewing the progress of the war. Hanoi must have calculated that it would embarrass the President, make the South Vietnamese suspicious of U.S. intentions, and enhance their own peaceful image. By admitting past contacts with the U.S., however, the DRV assumed some of the direct responsibility for the failure of peace efforts. Moreover, the President's letter was conciliatory and forthcoming whereas Ho's was cold and uncompromising. In any case, the disclosure did the President no real harm with public opinion, a miscalculation which must have disappointed Hanoi greatly. After their return to Washington McNaughton sent McNamara a memo with some State Department observations on other aspects of the disclosure:

Bill Bundy's experts read this into Ho Chi Minh's
release of the Johnson-Ho exchange of letters: (a) Ho
thereby "played the world harp," thereby "losing" in the
Anglo-Saxon world; (b) to Ho's Hanoi public, he "told off
the Americans," showing the hard line but simultaneously
reiterating the Burchette line (which China did not like);
(c) in the process of quoting the President's letter, Ho
leaked the fact of previous exchanges, thereby admitting
past contacts and preparing the public for future ones;
and (d) Ho ignored the NLF. 51/

The most immediate and obvious effect of the disclosure, however, was
to throw cold water on any hopes for an early break in the Washington-
Hanoi deadlock.

Shortly after the President's return from the Pacific he
received a memo from the Chairman of the JCS, General Wheeler, describing
the current status of targets authorized under ROLLING THUNDER 54. While
most of the targets authorized had been struck, including the Thai Nguyen
Iron and Steel plant and its associated thermal power facility, bad weather
was preventing the kind of sustained campaign against the approved industrial
targets that the JCS would have liked. 52/ The Thai Nguyen complex, for
instance, had been scheduled for attack 51 times by March 21, but only 4 of
these could be carried out, the rest being cancelled because of adverse
weather. Piecemeal additions to the authorized target list continued
through the month of April. On April 8, ROLLING THUNDER program 55 was
approved, adding the Kep airfield; the Hanoi power transformer near the
center of town; and the Haiphong cement plant, POL storage, and ammunition
dump to the target list along with more bridges, railroad yards and vehicle
parts elsewhere in the country. 53/ The restrictions on the Hanoi and
Haiphong perimeters were relaxed to permit the destruction of these new
targets.

In spite of the approval of these new "high-value" industrial
targets that the JCS and CINCPAC had lusted after for so long, the Chairman
in his monthly progress report to the President in April could report little
progress. Unusually bad weather conditions had forced the cancellation
of large numbers of sorties and most of the targets had been struck
insufficiently or not at all.

In addition to broadening the NVN target base, increased
pressure must be attained by achieving greater effectiveness
in destruction of targets, maintaining continuous harassment
during periods of darkness and marginal attack weather, and
generating surge strike capabilities during periods of visual
attack conditions. In view of the increased hostility of NVN
air environment, achievement of around-the-clock strike
capability is imperative to effect maximum possible degradation of the NVN air defense system which, in turn, will

increase over-all attack effectiveness. As radar bombing/
pathfinder capabilities are expanded and techniques per-
fected, the opportunity to employ additional strike
forces effectively in sustained operations will improve
significantly. 55/

These problems did not deter them from recommending the approval of three
additional tactical fighter squadrons (to be based at Nam Phong, Thailand)
for the war in the North. 56/ The concept of operations under which
these and other CINCPAC assigned aircraft were to operate was little more
than a restatement of the goals set down the previous fall. The purpose
was, "To make it as difficult and costly as possible for NVN to continue
effective support of the VC and to cause NVN to cease direction of the
VC insurgency." 57/ As usual, however, there was no effort to relate
requested forces to the achievement of the desired goals, which were to
stand throughout the war as wishes not objectives against which one
effectively programmed forces.

On the same day the JCS endorsed Westy's force proposals
CINCPAC's planes finally broke through the cloud cover and attacked the
two thermal power generating facilities in Haiphong. The raids made
world headlines. Two days later the specific go-ahead was given from
Washington for strikes on the MIG airfields and on April 24th they too
came under attack. At this point, with the JCS endorsement of Westmoreland's
troop requests, a major debate over future Vietnam policy, in all its
aspects, began within the Johnson Administration. It would continue
through the month of May and into June, not finally being resolved until
after McNamara's trip to Vietnam in July and the Presidential decisions
on Program #5. But even while this major policy review was gearing up,
the impetus for the salami-slice escalation of our assault on North Vietnam's industrial base produced yet another ROLLING THUNDER program. RT 56,
whose principle new target was the thermal power plant located only 1 mile
north of the center of Hanoi, became operational May 2. On May 5, at
McNamara's request, General Wheeler sent the President a memo outlining
the rationale behind the attack on the entire North Vietnamese power grid.
In his words,

As you know, the objective of our air attacks on the
thermal electric power system in North Vietnam was not...to
turn the lights off in major population centers, but were [sic]
designed to deprive the enemy of a basic power source needed
to operate certain war supporting facilities and industries.
You will recall that nine thermal power plants were tied
together, principally through the Hanoi Transformer Station,
in an electric power grid in the industrial and population
complex in northeastern North Vietnam....These nine thermal
power plants provided electric power needed to operate a
cement plant, a steel plant, a chemical plant, a fertilizer
plant, a machine tool plant, an explosives plant, a textile
plant; the ports of Haiphong and Hon Gai, major military
installations such as airfields, etc. The power grid

referred to above tied in the nine individual thermal
electric power plants and permitted the North Vietnamese
to switch kilowattage as required among the several consumers. All of the factories and facilities listed above
contribute in one way or another and in varying degrees
to the war effort in North Vietnam. For example, the
steel plant fabricated POL tanks to supplement or replace
fixed POL storage, metal pontoons for the construction
of floating bridges, metal barges to augment infiltration
capacity, etc.; the cement plant produced some 600,000
metric tons of cement annually which has been used in the
rehabilitation of lines of communication. 58/

Wheeler went on to describe the "specific military benefits" derived
from the attacks on the two Haiphong power plants,

The two power plants in Haiphong had a total capacity
of 17,000 kilowatts, some 9 per cent of the pre-strike
national electric power capacity. Between them they
supplied power for the cement plant, a chemical plant,
Kien An airfield, Cat Bi airfield, the naval base and
repair facilities, the Haiphong shipyard repair facilities and the electric power to operate the equipment in
the port itself. In addition, the electric power generated
by these two plants could be diverted through the electric
grid, mentioned above, to other metropolitan and industrial
areas through the Hanoi transformer station. All of the
aforementioned industrial, repair, airbase, and port facilities contribute to the North Vietnamese war effort and, in
their totality, this support is substantial. 59/

Striking the newly approved Hanoi power plant would derive the following
additional military advantages, Wheeler argued:

The Hanoi Thermal Power Plant has a 32,500 kilowatt
capacity comprising 17 per cent of the pre-strike electric
power production. Major facilities which would be affected
by its destruction are the Hanoi Port Facility, the Hanoi
Supply Depot, a machine tool plant, a rubber plant, a lead
battery plant, the Van Dien Vehicle Repair Depot, an international telecommunications site, an international radio transmitter receiver site, the Bac Mai airfield, and the national
military defense command center. All of these facilities
contribute substantially to the North Vietnamese war effort.
In addition, it should be noted a 35-kilovolt direct transmission
line runs from the Hanoi Thermal Power Plant to Haiphong and
Nam Dinh. We believe that, since the two Haiphong Thermal

TOP SECRET - Sensitive

Power Plants were damaged, the Hanoi Thermal Power Plant
has been supplying 3,000 kilowatts of power to Haiphong
over this direct transmission line; this quantity is sufficient to meet about 10 per cent of Haiphong's electric
power requirements. 59a/

Exactly how reassuring this line of argument was to the
President is impossible to say. In any case, the long-awaited attack
on the Hanoi power facility was finally given the operational go-ahead
on May 16, and on May 19 the strike took place. When it did the cries
of civilian casualties were again heard long and loud from Hanoi. But
the Hanoi power plant was the last major target of the U.S. "spring
offensive" against North Vietnam's nascent industrial sector. The CIA
on May 26 produced a highly favorable report on the effectiveness of
the campaign against the DRV's electric power capacity. In summary it
stated:

Air strikes through 25 May 1967 against 14 of the 20
JCS-targeted electric power facilities in North Vietnam
have put out of operation about 165,000 kilowatts (kw) of
power generating capacity or 87 percent of the national
total. North Vietnam is now left with less than 24,000 kw
of central power generating capacity.

Both Hanoi and Haiphong are now without a central
power supply and must rely on diesel-generating equipment
as a power source. The reported reserve power system in
Hanoi consisting of five underground diesel stations has
an estimated power generating capacity of only 5,000 kw, or
less than ten percent of Hanoi's normal needs. 60/

The last phases of this attack on the North's electric power generating
system in May 1967 were being carried out against a backdrop of very high
level deliberations in Washington on the future course of U.S. strategy
in the war. They both influenced and were in turn influenced by the
course of that debate, which is the subject of the next section of this
paper. The fact that this major assault on the modern sector of the
North Vietnamese economy while highly successful in pure target-destruction
terms, had failed to alter Hanoi's determined pursuit of the war would
bear heavily on the consideration by the Principles of new directions for
American policy.

C.   The Question Again -- Escalate or Negotiate?

   1.   Two Courses - Escalate or Level Off

As already discussed, the JCS had transmitted to the
Secretary of Defense on April 20 their endorsement of General Westmoreland's March troop requests (100,000 immediately and 200,000 eventually).
In so doing the military had once again confronted the Johnson Administration with a difficult decision on whether to escalate or level-off
the U.S. effort. What they proposed was the mobilization of the Reserves,
a major new troop commitment in the South, an extension of the war into
the VC/NVA sanctuaries (Laos, Cambodia, and possibly North Vietnam),
the mining of North Vietnamese ports and a solid commitment in manpower
and resources to a military victory. 61/   The recommendation not unsur-
prisingly touched off a searching reappriasal of the course of U.S.
strategy in the war.

Under Secretary Katzenbach opened the review on May 24 in
a memo to John McNaughton in which he outlined the problem and assigned
the preparation of various policy papers to Defense, CIA, State and
the White House. As Katzenbach saw it,

Fundamentally, there are three jobs which have to be done:

1. Assess the current situation in Viet-Nam and the
various political and military actions which could be taken
to bring this to a successful conclusion;

2. Review the possibilities for negotiation, including
an assessment of the ultimate U.S. position in relationship
to the DRV and NLF; and

3. Assess the military and political effects of intensification of the war in South Vietnam and in North Viet-Nam. 62/

Katzenbach's memo asked Defense to consider two alternative courses of
action: course A, the kind of escalation the military proposed including
the 200,000 new troops; and course B, the leveling-off of the U.S. troop
commitment with an addition of no more than 10,000 new men. Bombing
strategies in the North to correlate with each course were also to be
considered. Significantly, a territorially limited bombing halt was
suggested as a possibility for the first time.

Consider with Course B, for example, a cessation, after
the current targets have been struck, of bombing North Vietnamese areas north of 20° (or, if it looked sufficiently
important to maximize an attractive settlement opportunity,
cessation of bombing in all of North Viet-Nam.) 63/

The White House was assigned a paper on the prospects and possibilities in the pacification program. State was to prepare a paper on U.S. settlement terms and conditions, and the CIA was to produce its usual estimate of the current situation.

With respect to the air war, the CIA had already to some extent anticipated the alternatives in a limited distribution memo in mid-April. 64/ Their judgment was that Hanoi was taking a harder line since the publication of the Johnson-Ho letters in March and would continue the armed struggle vigorously in the next phase waiting for a better negotiating opportunity. Three bombing programs were considered by the CIA. The first was an intensified program against military, industrial and LOC targets. Their estimate was that while such a course would create serious problems for the DRV the minimum essential flow of supplies into the North and on to the South would continue. No great change in Chinese or Soviet policies was anticipated from such a course of action. By adding the mining of the ports to this intensified air campaign, Hanoi's ability to support the war would be directly threatened. This would confront the Soviet Union with difficult choices, although the CIA expected that in the end the Soviets would avoid a direct confrontation with the U.S. and would simply step up their support through China. Mining of the ports would put China in "...a commanding political position, since it would have control over the only remaining supply lines to North Vietnam."65/ If the mining were construed by Hanoi and/or Peking as the prelude to an invasion of the North, Chinese combat troops could be expected to move into North Vietnam to safeguard China's strategic southern frontier. As to the Hanoi leadership, the CIA analysis did not foresee their capitulating on their goals in the South even in the face of the closing of their ports. A third possibility, attacking the airfields, was expected to produce no major Soviet response and at most only the transfer of some North Vietnamese fighters to Chinese bases and the possible entry of Chinese planes into the air war.

With a full-scale debate of future strategy in the offing, Robert Komer decided to leave behind his own views on the best course for U.S. policy before he went to Saigon to become head of CORDS. Questioning whether stepped up bombing or more troops were likely to produce the desired results, Komer identified what he felt were the "Critical Variables Which Will Determine Success in Vietnam." 66/ He outlined them as follows:

A. It is Unlikely that Hanoi will Negotiate. We can't count on a negotiated compromise. Perhaps the NLF would prove more flexible, but it seems increasingly under the thumb of Hanoi.

B. More Bombing or Mining Would Raise the Pain Level but Probably Wouldn't Force Hanoi to Cry Uncle. I'm no expert on this, but can't see it as decisive. Could it

prevent Hanoi from maintaining substantial infiltration
if it chose? Moreover, some facets of it contain dangerous risks.

      C. <u>Thus the Critical Variable is in the South!</u> The
greatest opportunity for decisive gains in the next 12-18
months lies in accelerating the erosion of the VC in
South Vietnam, and in building a viable alternative with
attractive power. Let's assume that the NVA could replace
its losses. <u>I doubt that the VC could</u>. They are now the
"weak sisters" of the enemy team. The evidence is not
conclusive, but certainly points in this direction.
Indeed, the NVA strategy in I Corps seems designed to take
pressure off the VC in the South. 67/

This was the first time that Komer, whose preoccupation was pacification,
had seriously questioned the utility of more bombing. Apparently the
McNamara analysis was reaching even the more determined members of the
White House staff.

      A different view of the bombing was presented to the
President, however, by General Westmoreland on April 27. He had returned
from Vietnam to argue in favor of his troop requests and for a considerable expansion of the war, as well as to appear before Congress and in
public to strengthen support for the President's war policy. In his
conversation with the President on the 27th he stated, "I am frankly dismayed at even the thought of stopping the bombing program." 68/ General
Wheeler in the same conversation, however, went even farther, taking the
initiative to urge the closing of the ports as the next logical step
against the DRV. But in addition he suggested that U.S. troops be
authorized to extend the war into the Laotian and Cambodian sanctuaries
and that we consider the "possible invasion of North Vietnam. We may
wish to take offensive action against the DRV with ground troops." 69/
The President remained skeptical to say the least. When Westmoreland
spoke to Congress the following day he mentioned the bombing only in
passing as a reprisal for VC terror and depradation in the South.

      Meanwhile, the Principles continued their deliberations.
They met on May 1 although there is no record of what transpired in
their discussions. The only available paper for the meeting is one that
Bill Bundy wrote for Secretary Katzenbach. Bundy's paper offered a fairly
optimistic view of the overall prospects for the coming six months:

      <u>Over-All Estimate</u>. If we go on as we are doing, if
the political process in the South comes off well, and if
the Chinese do not settle down, I myself would reckon
that by the end of 1967 there is at least a 50-50 chance
that a favorable tide will be running really strongly in
the South, and that Hanoi will be very discouraged.

Whether they will move to negotiate is of course a slightly
different question, but we could be visibly and strongly
on the way.

If China should go into a real convulsion, I would
raise these odds slightly, and think it clearly more likely
that Hanoi would choose a negotiating path to the conclusion. 70/

Much of Bundy's sanguine optimism was based on the convulsions going on
in China. He estimated that the odds for another significant Chinese
internal upheaval were at least 50-50, and that this would offset
Hanoi's recent promise of additional aid from the Soviets. He argued
that it should be the principle factor in the consideration of any additional step-up in the bombing, or the mining of Haiphong harbor. Specifically, he gave the following objections to more bombing:

Additional Action in the North. Of the major targets
still not hit, I would agree to the Hanoi power station,
but then let it go at that, subject only to occasional
re-strikes where absolutely required. In particular, on
the airfields, I think we have gone far enough to hurt and
not far enough to drive the aircraft to Chinese fields, which
I think could be very dangerous.

I would strongly oppose the mining of Haiphong at any
time in the next nine months, unless the Soviets categorically use it to send in combat weapons. (It may well be
that we should warn them quietly but firmly that we are
watching their traffic into Haiphong very closely, and
particularly from this standpoint.) Mining of Haiphong, at
any time, is bound to risk a confrontation with the Soviets
and to throw Hanoi into greater dependence on Communist
China. These in themselves would be very dangerous and
adverse to the whole notion of getting Hanoi to change its
attitude. Moreover, I think they would somehow manage to
get the stuff in through China no matter what we did to
Haiphong. 71/

In addition to these considerations, however, Bundy was worried about
the international implications of more bombing:

International Factors. My negative feeling on serious
additional bombing of the North and mining of Haiphong is
based essentially on the belief that these actions will
not change Hanoi's position, or affect Hanoi's capabilities
in ways that counter-balance the risks and adverse reaction
in China and with the Soviets alone.

Nonetheless, I cannot leave out the wider international factors, and particularly the British and
Japanese as bellwethers. Both the latter have accepted
our recent bombings with much less outcry than I,
frankly, would have anticipated. But if we keep it
up at this pace, or step up the pace, I doubt if the
British front will hold. Certainly we will be in a very
bad Donnybrook next fall in the UN.

Whatever the wider implications of negative reactions
on a major scale, the main point is that they would
undoubtedly stiffen Hanoi, and this is always the gut
question. 72/

With respect to negotiations, Bundy was guarded. He did
not expect any serious moves by the other side until after the elections
in South Vietnam in September. Thus, he argued against any new U.S.
initiatives and in favor of conveying an impression of "steady firmness" on our part. It was precisely this impression that had been
lacking from our behavior since the previous winter and that we should
now seek to restore. This was the main point of his overall assessment
of the situation, as the following summary paragraph demonstrates:

A Steady, Firm Course. Since roughly the first of
December, I think we have given a very jerky and impatient
impression to Hanoi. This is related more to the timing
and suddenness of our bombing and negotiating actions than
to the substance of what we have done. I think that Hanoi
in any event believes that the 1968 elections could cause
us to change our position or even lose heart completely.
Our actions since early December may well have encouraged and
greatly strengthened this belief that we wish to get the
war over by 1968 at all costs. Our major thrust must be
now to persuade them that we are prepared to stick it if
necessary. This means a steady and considered program of
action for the next nine months. 73/

An SNIE a few days later confirmed Bundy's views about
the unlikelihood of positive Soviet efforts to bring the conflict to
the negotiating table. It also affirmed that the Soviets would no doubt
continue and increase their assistance to North Vietnam and that the
Chinese would probably not impede the flow of materiel across its
territory. 74/

Powerful and unexpected support for William Bundy's general
viewpoint came at about this time from his brother, the former Presidential adviser to Kennedy and Johnson, McGeorge Bundy. In an unsolicited letter

TOP SECRET - Sensitive

to the President he outlined his current views as to further escalation
of the air war (in the initiation of which he had had a large hand in
1965) and further troop increments for the ground war in the South:

> Since the Communist turndown of our latest offers in
> February, there has been an intensification of bombing in
> the North, and press reports suggest that there will be
> further pressure for more attacks on targets heretofore
> immune. There is also obvious pressure from the military
> for further reinforcements in the South, although General West-
> moreland has been a model of discipline in his public pro-
> nouncements. One may guess, therefore, that the President
> will soon be confronted with requests for 100,000-200,000
> more troops and for authority to close the harbor in Haiphong.
> Such recommendations are inevitable, in the framework of
> strictly military analysis. It is the thesis of this paper
> that in the main they should be rejected, and that as a
> matter of high national policy there should be a publicly
> stated ceiling to the level of American participation in
> Vietnam, as long as there is no further marked escalation on
> the enemy side.
>
> There are two major reasons for this recommendation:
> the situation in Vietnam and the situation in the United
> States. As to Vietnam, it seems very doubtful that further
> intensifications of bombing in the North or major increases
> in U.S. troops in the South are really a good way of bringing
> the war to a satisfactory conclusion. As to the United
> States, it seems clear that uncertainty about the future
> size of the war is now having destructive effects on the
> national will. 75/

Unlike the vocal critics of the Administration, Mac Bundy was not opposed
to the bombing per se, merely to any further extension of it since he
felt such action would be counter-productive. Because his views carry
such weight, his arguments against extending the bombing are reproduced
below in full:

> On the ineffectiveness of the bombing as a means to
> end the war, I think the evidence is plain -- though I would
> defer to expert estimators. Ho Chi Minh and his colleagues
> simply are not going to change their policy on the basis of
> losses from the air in North Vietnam. No intelligence
> estimate that I have seen in the last two years has ever
> claimed that the bombing would have this effect. The
> President never claimed that it would. The notion that
> this was its purpose has been limited to one school of
> thought and has never been the official Government position,
> whatever critics may assert.

I am very far indeed from suggesting that it would make
sense now to stop the bombing of the North altogether. The
argument for that course seems to me wholly unpersuasive at
the present. To stop the bombing today would be to give the
Communists something for nothing, and in a very short time
all the doves in this country and around the world would be
asking for some further unilateral concessions. (Doves and
hawks are alike in their insatiable appetites; we can't
really keep the hawks happy by small increases in effort --
they come right back for more.)

The real justification for the bombing, from the start,
has been double -- its value for Southern morale at a moment
of great danger, and its relation to Northern infiltration.
The first reason has disappeared but the second remains
entirely legitimate. Tactical bombing of communications and
of troop concentrations -- and of airfields as necessary --
seems to me sensible and practical. It is strategic bombing
that seems both unproductive and unwise. It is true, of
course, that all careful bombing does some damage to the
enemy. But the net effect of this damage upon the military
capability of a primitive country is almost sure to be
slight. (The lights have not stayed off in Haiphong, and
even if they had, electric lights are in no sense essential
to the Communist war effort.) And against this distinctly
marginal impact we have to weigh the fact that strategic
bombing does tend to divide the U.S., to distract us all
from the real struggle in the South, and to accentuate the
unease and distemper which surround the war in Vietnam, both
at home and abroad. It is true that careful polls show
majority support for the bombing, but I believe this support
rests upon an erroneous belief in its effectiveness as a
means to end the war. Moreover, I think those against
extension of the bombing are more passionate on balance than
those who favor it. Finally, there is certainly a point at
which such bombing does increase the risk of conflict with
China or the Soviet Union, and I am sure there is no majority
for that. In particular, I think it clear that the case
against going after Haiphong Harbor is so strong that a
majority would back the Government in rejecting that course.

So I think that with careful explanation there would be
more approval than disapproval of an announced policy restricting
the bombing closely to activities that support the war in the
South. General Westmoreland's speech to the Congress made
this tie-in, but attacks on power plants really do not fit the
picture very well. We are attacking them, I fear, mainly
because we have "run out" of other targets. Is it a very good
reason? Can anyone demonstrate that such targets have been
very rewarding? Remembering the claims made for attacks on
oil supplies, should we not be very skeptical of new promises? 76/

In a similar fashion Bundy developed his arguments against a major
increase in U.S. troop strength in the South and urged the President
not to take any new diplomatic initiatives for the present. But the
appeal of Bundy's analysis for the President must surely have been its
finale in which Bundy, acutely aware of the President's political
sensitivities, cast his arguments in the context of the forthcoming
1968 Presidential elections. Here is how he presented the case:

> There is one further argument against major escalation
> in 1967 and 1968 which is worth stating separately, because
> on the surface it seems cynically political. It is that
> Hanoi is going to do everything it possibly can to keep its
> position intact until after our 1968 elections. Given their
> history, they are <u>bound</u> to hold out for a possible U.S. shift
> in 1969 -- that's what they did against the French, and they
> got most of what they wanted when Mendes took power. Having
> held on so long this time, and having nothing much left to
> lose -- compared to the chance of victory -- they are bound to
> keep on fighting. Since only atomic bombs could really knock
> them out (an invasion of North Vietnam would not do it in
> two years, and is of course ruled out on other grounds), they
> have it in their power to "prove" that military escalation
> does not bring peace -- at least over the next two years.
> They will surely do just that. However much they may be
> hurting, they are not going to do us any favors before
> November 1968. (And since this was drafted, they have been
> publicly advised by Walter Lippmann to wait for the Republicans --
> as if they needed the advice and as if it was his place to give
> it!)

> It follows that escalation will not bring visible victory
> over Hanoi before the election. Therefore the election will
> have to be fought by the Administration on other grounds.
> I think those other grounds are clear and important, and that
> they will be obscured if our policy is thought to be one of
> increasing -- and ineffective -- military pressure.

> If we assume that the war will still be going on in
> November 1968, and that Hanoi will not give us the pleasure
> of consenting to negotiations sometime before then what we
> must plan to offer as a defense of Administration policy is
> not victory over Hanoi, but growing success -- and self-
> reliance -- in the South. This we can do, with luck, and on
> this side of the parallel the Vietnamese authorities should be
> prepared to help us out (though of course the VC will do their
> damnedest against us.) Large parts of Westy's speech (if not
> quite all of it) were wholly consistent with this line of argu-
> ment. 77/

His summation must have been even more gratifying for the beleaguered
President. It was both a paean to the President's achievements in
Vietnam and an appeal to the prejudices that had sustained his policy
from the beginning:

>   ...if we can avoid escalation-that-does-not-seem-
> to-work, we can focus attention on the great and central
> achievement of these last two years: on the defeat we
> have prevented. The fact that South Vietnam has not been
> lost and is not going to be lost is a fact of truly massive
> importance in the history of Asia, the Pacific, and the U.S.
> An articulate minority of "Eastern intellectuals" (like Bill
> Fulbright) may not believe in what they call the domino
> theory, but most Americans (along with nearly all Asians)
> know better. Under this Administration the United States
> has already saved the hope of freedom for hundreds of
> millions -- in this sense, the largest part of the job is
> done. This critically important achievement is obscured
> by seeming to act as if we have to do much more lest we
> fail. 78/

Whatever his own reactions, the President was anxious to
have the reactions of others to Bundy's reasoning. He asked McNamara
to pass the main portion of the memo to the Chiefs for their comment
without identifying its author. Chairman Wheeler promptly replied.
His memo to the President on May 5 rejected the Bundy analysis in a
detailed listing of the military benefits of attacking the DRV power
grid and in a criticism of Bundy's list of bombing objectives for
failing to include punitive pressure as a prime motive. With respect
to Bundy's recommendation against interdicting Haiphong Harbor, the
General was terse and pointed:

>   As a matter of cold fact, the Haiphong port is the
> single most vulnerable and important point in the lines of
> communications system of North Vietnam. During the first
> quarter of 1967 general cargo deliveries through Haiphong
> have set new records. In March 142,700 metric tons of cargo
> passed through the port; during the month of April there
> was a slight decline to 132,000 metric tons. ·Nevertheless,
> it is noteworthy that in April 31,900 metric tons of bulk
> foodstuffs passed through the port bringing the total of
> foodstuffs delivered in the first four months of 1967 to
> 100,680 metric tons as compared to 77,100 metric tons of
> food received during all of calendar 1966. These tonnages
> underscore the importance of the port of Haiphong to the
> war effort of North Vietnam and support my statement that
> Haiphong is the most important point in the entire North
> Vietnamese lines of communications system. Unless and
> until we find some means of obstructing and reducing the
> flow of war supporting material through Haiphong, the North

Vietnamese will continue to be able to support their war effort both in North Vietnam and in South Vietnam. 79/

But the lines were already clearly being drawn in this internal struggle over escalation and for the first time all the civilians (both insiders and significant outsiders) were opposed to the military proposals in whole or part. At this early stage, however, the outcome was far from clear. On the same day the Chairman criticized the Bundy paper, Roger Fisher, McNaughton's longtime advisor from Harvard, at the suggestion of Walt Rostow and Doug Cater, sent the President a proposal re-orienting the U.S. effort both militarily and diplomatically. The flavor of his ideas, all of which had already appeared in notes to McNaughton, can be derived from a listing of the headings under which they were argued without going into his detailed arguments. His analysis fell under the following six general rubrics:

1. Pursue an on-the-ground interdiction strategy (barrier);

2. Concentrate air attacks in the southern portion of North Vietnam;

3. Offer Hanoi some realistic "yes-able" propositions;

4. Make the carrot more believable;

5. Give the NLF a decidable question;

6. Give local Viet Cong leaders a chance to opt out of the war. 80/

The arguments to the President for applying the brakes to our involvement in this seemingly endless, winless struggle were, thus, being made from all sides, except the military who remained adamant for escalation.

2. The May DPM Exercise

The available documents do not reveal what happened to the option exercise that Katzenbach had launched on April 24. But at this point in the debate over future direction for U.S. policy in Southeast Asia, attention shifted to a draft memorandum for the President written by John McNaughton for McNamara's eventual signature. (A W. Bundy memo on May 30 suggests the Katzenbach exercise was overtaken by Defense's DPM effort.) The DPM at the Pentagon is more than a statement of the Secretary's views, however, it is an important bureaucratic device for achieving consensus (or at least for getting people's opinions recorded on paper). McNaughton began his DPM by stating that the question before the house was:

whether to continue the program of air attacks in the
Hanoi-Haiphong area or for an indefinite period to
concentrate all attacks on the lines of communication in
the lower half of North Vietnam (south of 20°). 81/

Short of attacking the ports, which was rejected as
risking confrontation with the USSR, the Memorandum said, there were
few important targets left. The alternative of striking minor fixed
targets and continuing armed reconnaissance against the transportation
system north of 20° was relatively costly, risky, and unprofitable:

We have the alternative open to us of continuing to
conduct attacks between 20-23° -- that is, striking minor
fixed targets (like battery, fertilizer, and rubber plants
and barracks) while conducting armed reconnaissance against
movement on roads, railroads and waterways. This course,
however, is costly in American lives and involves serious
dangers of escalation. The loss rate in Hanoi-Haiphong
Route Package 6 / the northeast quadrant/, for example, is
more than six times the loss rate in the southernmost
Route Packages 1 and 2; and actions in the Hanoi-Haiphong
area involve serious risks of generating confrontations with
the Soviet Union and China, both because they involve
destruction of MIGs on the ground and encounters with the
MIGs in the air and because they may be construed as a US
intention to crush the Hanoi regime.

The military gain from destruction of additional military targets north of 20° will be slight. If we believed
that air attacks in that area would change Hanoi's will, they
might be worth the added loss of American life and the risks
of expansion of the war. However, there is no evidence that
this will be the case, while there is considerable evidence
that such bombing will strengthen Hanoi's will. In this
connection, Consul-General Rice /of Hong Kong/...said what
we believe to be the case -- that we cannot by bombing reach
the critical level of pain in North Vietnam and that, "below
that level, pain only increases the will to fight." Sir
Robert Thompson, who was a key officer in the British
success in Malaya, said...that our bombing, particularly
in the Red River basin, "is unifying North Vietnam." 82/

Nor, the Memorandum continued, was bombing in northernmost NVN essential
for the morale of SVN and US troops. General Westmoreland fully supported
strikes in the Hanoi/Haiphong area and had even said, as noted before,
that he was "frankly dismayed at even the thought of stopping the bombing
program," but his basic requirement was for continuation of bombing in
the "extended battle zone" near the DMZ.

The Memorandum went on to recommend what Roger Fisher had been suggesting, namely concentrating strikes in the lower half of NVN, without, however, turning the upper half into a completely forbidden sanctuary:

> We therefore recommend that all of the sorties allocated to the ROLLING THUNDER program be concentrated on the lines of communications -- the "funnel" through which men and supplies to the South must flow -- between $17\text{-}20^\circ$ reserving the option and intention to strike (in the $20\text{-}30^\circ$ area) as necessary to keep the enemy's investment in defense and in repair crews high throughout the country. 83/

The proposed change in policy was not aimed at getting NVN to change its behavior or to negotiate, and no favorable response from Hanoi should be expected:

> But to optimize the chances of a favorable Hanoi reaction, the scenario should be (a) to inform the Soviets quietly (on May 15) that within a few (5) days the policy would be implemented, stating no time limits and making no promises not to return to the Red River basin to attack targets which later acquired military importance, and then (b) to make an unhuckstered shift as predicted on May 20. We would expect Moscow to pass the May 15 information on to Hanoi, perhaps (but probably not) urging Hanoi to seize the opportunity to de-escalate the war by talks or otherwise. Hanoi, not having been asked a question by us and having no ultimatum-like time limit, might be in a better posture to react favorably than has been the case in the past. 84/

The Memorandum recommended that the de-escalation be explained as improving the military effectiveness of the bombing, in accordance with the interdiction rationale:

> Publicly, when the shift had become obvious (May 21 or 22), we should explain (a) that as we have always said, the war must be won in the South, (b) that we have never said bombing of the North would produce a settlement by breaking Hanoi's will or by shutting off the flow of supplies, (c) that the North must pay a price for its infiltration, (d) that the major northern military targets have been destroyed, and (e) that now we are concentrating on the narrow neck through which supplies must flow, believing that the concentrated effort there, as compared with a dispersed effort throughout North Vietnam, under present circumstances will increase the efficiency of our interdiction effort, and (f) that we may have to return to targets further north if military considerations require it. 85/

This McNaughton DPM on bombing was prepared as an adjunct to a larger DPM on the overall strategy of the war and new ground force deployments. Together they were the focus of a frantic weekend of work in anticipation of a White House meeting on Monday, May 8. That meeting would not, however, produce any positive decisions and the entire drafting exercise would continue until the following week when McNamara finally transmitted a draft memorandum to the President. Among those in the capital that weekend to advise the President was McGeorge Bundy with whom McNamara conferred on Sunday. 86/

Walt Rostow at the White House circulated a discussion paper on Saturday, May 6, entitled "U.S. Strategy in Viet Nam." Rostow's paper began by reviewing what the U.S. was attempting to do in the war: frustrate a communist takeover "by defeating their main force units; attacking the guerilla infrastructure; and building a South Vietnamese governmental and security structure...." 87/ The purpose of the air war in the North was defined as "To hasten the decision in Hanoi to abandon the aggression...," for which we specifically sought:

(i) to limit and harass infiltration; and

(ii) to impose on the North sufficient military and civil cost to make them decide to get out of the war earlier rather than later. 88/

Sensitive to the criticisms of the bombing, Rostow tried to dispose of certain of their arguments:

We have never held the view that bombing could stop infiltration. We have never held the view that bombing of the Hanoi-Haiphong area alone would lead them to abandon the effort in the South. We have never held the view that bombing Hanoi-Haiphong would directly cut back infiltration. We have held the view that the degree of military and civilian cost felt in the North and the diversion of resources to deal with our bombing could contribute marginally--and perhaps significantly--to the timing of a decision to end the war. But it was no substitute for making progress in the South. 89/

Rostow argued that while there were policy decisions to be made about the war in the South, particularly with respect to new force levels, there existed no real disagreement with the Administration as to our general strategy on the ground. Where contention did exist was in the matter of the air war. Here there were three broad strategies that could be pursued. Rostow offered a lengthy analysis of the three options which is included here in its entirety since to summarize it would sacrifice much of its pungency.

A. Closing the top of the funnel

Under this strategy we would mine the major harbors and, perhaps, bomb port facilities and even consider blockade. In addition, we would attack systematically the rail lines between Hanoi and mainland China. At the moment the total import capacity into North Viet Nam is about 17,200 tons per day. Even with expanded import requirement due to the food shortage, imports are, in fact, coming in at about 5700 tons per day. It is possible with a concerted and determined effort that we could cut back import capacity somewhat below the level of requirements; but this is not sure. On the other hand, it would require a difficult and sustained effort by North Viet Nam and its allies to prevent a reduction in total imports below requirements if we did all these things.

The costs would be these:

--The Soviet Union would have to permit a radical increase in Hanoi's dependence upon Communist China, or introduce minesweepers, etc., to keep its supplies coming into Hanoi by sea;

--The Chinese Communists would probably introduce many more engineering and anti-aircraft forces along the roads and rail lines between Hanoi and China in order to keep the supplies moving;

--To maintain its prestige, in case it could not or would not open up Hanoi-Haiphong in the face of mines, the Soviet Union might contemplate creating a Berlin crisis. With respect to a Berlin crisis, they would have to weigh the possible split between the U.S. and its Western European allies under this pressure against damage to the atmosphere of detente in Europe which is working in favor of the French Communist Party and providing the Soviet Union with generally enlarged influence in Western Europe.

I myself do not believe that the Soviet Union would go to war with us over Viet Nam unless we sought to occupy North Viet Nam; and, even then, a military response from Moscow would not be certain.

With respect to Communist China, it always has the option of invading Laos and Thailand; but this would not be a rational response to naval and air operations designed to strangle Hanoi. A war throughout Southeast Asia would not help Hanoi; although I do believe Communist China would fight us if we invaded the northern part of North Viet Nam.

One can always take the view that, given the turmoil inside Communist China, an irrational act by Peiping is possible. And such irrationality cannot be ruled out.

I conclude that if we try to close the top of the funnel, tension between ourselves and the Soviet Union and Communist China would increase; if we were very determined, we could impose additional burdens on Hanoi and its allies; we might cut capacity below requirements; and the outcome is less likely to be a general war than more likely.

B. Attacking what is inside the funnel

This is what we have been doing in the Hanoi-Haiphong area for some weeks. I do not agree with the view that the attacks on Hanoi-Haiphong have no bearing on the war in the South. They divert massive amounts of resources, energies, and attention to keeping the civil and military establishment going. They impose general economic, political, and psychological difficulties on the North which have been complicated this year by a bad harvest and food shortages. I do not believe that they "harden the will of the North." In my judgment, up to this point, our bombing of the North has been a painful additional cost they have thus far been willing to bear to pursue their efforts in the South.

On the other hand:

--There is no direct, immediate connection between bombing the Hanoi-Haiphong area and the battle in the South;

--If we complete the attack on electric power by taking out the Hanoi station -- which constitutes about 80% of the electric power supply of the country now operating -- we will have hit most of the targets whose destruction imposes serious military-civil costs on the North.

-- With respect to risk, it is unclear whether Soviet warnings about our bombing Hanoi-Haiphong represent decisions already taken or decisions which might be taken if we persist in banging away in that area.

It is my judgment that the Soviet reaction will continue to be addressed to the problem imposed on Hanoi by us; that is, they might introduce Soviet pilots as they did in the Korean War; they might bring ground-to-ground missiles into North Viet Nam with the object of attacking our vessels at sea and our airfields in the Danang area.

I do not believe that the continuation of attacks at about the level we have been conducting them in the Hanoi-Haiphong area will lead to pressure on Berlin or a general war with the Soviet Union. In fact, carefully read, what the Soviets have been trying to signal is: Keep away from our ships; we may counter-escalate to some degree; but we do not want a nuclear confrontation over Viet Nam.

C. Concentration in Route Packages 1 and 2

The advantages of concentrating virtually all our attacks in this area are three:

--We would cut our loss rate in pilots and planes;

--We would somewhat improve our harassment of infiltration of South Viet Nam;

--We would diminish the risks of counter-escalatory action by the Soviet Union and Communist China, as compared with courses A and B.

With this analysis of the pros and cons of the various options, Rostow turned to recommendations. He rejected course A as incurring too many risks with too little return. Picking up McNaughton's recommendation for concentrating the air war in the North Vietnamese panhandle, Rostow urged that it be supplemented with an open option to return to the northern "funnel" if developments warranted it. Here is how he formulated his conclusions:

With respect to Course B I believe we have achieved greater results in increasing the pressure on Hanoi and raising the cost of their continuing to conduct the aggression in the South than some of my most respected colleagues would agree. I do not believe we should lightly abandon what we have accomplished; and specifically, I believe we should mount the most economical and careful attack on the Hanoi power station our air tacticians can devise. Moreover, I believe we should keep open the option of coming back to the Hanoi-Haiphong area, dpending upon what we learn of their repair operations; and what Moscow's and Peiping's reactions are; especially when we understand better what effects we have and have not achieved thus far.

I believe the Soviet Union may well have taken certain counter-steps addressed to the more effective protection of

the Hanoi-Haiphong area and may have decided -- or could
shortly decide -- to introduce into North Viet Nam some
surface-to-surface missiles.

With respect to option C, I believe we should, while
keeping open the B option, concentrate our attacks to
the maximum in Route Packages 1 and 2; and, in conducting
Hanoi-Haiphong attacks, we should do so only when the targets
make sense. I do not expect dramatic results from increasing
the weight of attack in Route Packages 1 and 2; but I believe
we are wasting a good many pilots in the Hanoi-Haiphong area
without commensurate results. The major objectives of
maintaining the B option can be achieved at lower cost. 90/

Although he had endorsed a strike on the Hanoi power plant, he rejected
any attack on the air fields in a terse, one sentence final paragraph,
"Air field attacks are only appropriate to the kind of sustained operations
in the Hanoi-Haiphong area associated with option A."

Two important members of the Administration, McNaughton
and Rostow, had thus weighed in for confining the bombing to the panhandle
under some formula or other. On Monday, May 8, presumably before the
policy meeting, William Bundy circulated a draft memo of his own which
pulled the problem apart and assembled the pieces in a very different
way. Like the others, Bundy's draft started from the assumption that
bombing decisions would be related to other decisions on the war for
which a consensus appeared to exist: pressing ahead with pacification;
continued political progress in the South; and continued pressure on the
North. To Bundy's way of thinking there were four broad target categories
that could be combined into various bombing options:

1. "Concentration on supply routes." This would comprise attacks on supply routes in the southern "bottleneck"
areas of North Vietnam, from the 20th parallel south.

2. "Re-strikes." This would comprise attacks on targets
already hit, including unless otherwise stated sensitive targets
north of the 20th parallel and in and around Hanoi/Haiphong, which
were hit in the last three weeks.

3. "Additional sensitive targets." North of the 20th
parallel, there are additional sensitive targets that have
been on our recent lists, including Rolling Thunder 56.
Some are of lesser importance, some are clearly "extremely
sensitive" (category 4 below), but at least three -- the
Hanoi power station, the Red River bridge, and the Phuc Yen
airfield -- could be said to round out the April program.
These three are the essential targets included in this
category 3.

4. "Extremely sensitive targets." This would comprise targets that are exceptionally sensitive, in terms of Chinese and/or Soviet reaction, as well as domestic and international factors. For example, this list would include mining of Haiphong, /'bombing of critical port facilities in Haiphong,' - pencilled in/ and bombing of dikes and dams not directly related to supply route waterways and/or involving heavy flooding to crops. 92/

Bundy suggested that by looking at the targetting problem in this way a series of options could be generated that were more sensitive to considerations of time-phasing. He offered five such options:

Option A would be to move up steadily to hit all the target categories, including the extremely sensitive targets.

Option B would be to step up the level a little further and stay at that higher level through consistent and fairly frequent re-strikes. Specifically, this would involve hitting the additional sensitive targets and then keeping all sensitive targets open to re-strike, although with individual authorization.

Option C would be to raise the level slightly in the near future by hitting the additional sensitive targets, but then to cut back essentially to concentration on supply routes. Re-strikes north of the 20th parallel would be very limited under this option once the additional sensitive targets had been hit, and would be limited to re-strikes necessary to eliminate targets directly important to infiltration and, as necessary, to keep Hanoi's air defense system in place.

Option D would be not to hit the additional sensitive targets, and to define a fairly level program that would concentrate heavily on the supply routes but would include a significant number of re-strikes north of the 20th parallel. Since these re-strikes would still be substantially less bunched than in April, the net effect would be to scale down the bombing slightly from present levels, and to hold it there.

Option E would be to cut back at once to concentration on supply routes. Re-strikes north of the 20th parallel would be limited to those defined under Option C. 93/

To crystallize more clearly in his readers' minds what the options implied in intensity compared with the current effort he employed a numerical analogy:

> To put a rough numerical index on these options, one might start by saying that our general level in the past year has been Force 4, with occasional temporary increases to Force 5 (POL and the December Hanoi strikes). On such a rough numerical scale, our April program has put us at Force 6 at present. Option A would raise this to 8 or 9 and keep it there, Option F would raise it to 7 and keep it there, Option C would raise it to 7 and then drop it to 3, Option D would lower it to 5 and keep it there, and Option E would lower it to 3 and keep it there. 94/

Bundy's analysis of the merits of the five options began with the estimate that the likelihood of Chinese intervention in the war was slight except in the case of option A, a probability he considered a major argument against it. He did not expect any of the courses of produce a direct Soviet intervention, but warned against the possibility of Soviet pressures elsewhere if option A were selected. He underscored a report from Ambassador Thompson that the Soviets had been greatly concerned by the April bombing program and were currently closeted in deliberations on general policy direction. Bombing of any major new targets in the immediate future would have an adverse effect on the Soviet leadership and was discouraged by Bundy. Option A was singled out for further condemnation based on the views of some China experts who argued that an intensive bombing program might be just what Mao needed to restore internal order in China and resolidify his control.

With respect to the effect of the bombing on North Vietnam, Bundy cited the evidence that strikes against the sensitive military targets were having only temporary and marginal positive benefits, and they were extremely costly in planes and pilots lost. By restricting the bombing to South of the 20th parallel as McNaughton had suggested, the military payoff might just be greater and the psychological strengthening of North Vietnamese will and morale less. The main factor in Hanoi attitudes, however, was the war in the South and neither a bombing halt nor an intensive escalation would have a decisive impact on it one way or the other. In Bundy's estimation Hanoi had dug in for at least another six months, and possibly until after the US elections in 1968. In the face of this the U.S. should try to project an image of steady, even commitment without radical shifts. This approach seemed to Bundy best suited to maximizing U.S. public support as well, since none of the courses would really satisfy either the convinced "doves" or the unflinching "hawks." The bombing had long since ceased to have much effect on South

Vietnamese morale, and international opinion would react strongly to any serious escalation. Closing out his analysis, Bundy argued for a decision soon, possibly before the upcoming one-day truce on Buddha's birthday, May 23, when the new program might be presented.

On the basis of this analysis of the pros and cons, Bundy concluded that options A and B had been clearly eliminated. Of the three remaining courses he urged the adoption of D, thus aligning himself generally with McNaughton and Rostow. The specific reasons he adduced for his recommendation were the following:

Option D Elaborated and Argued

The first element in Option D is that it would not carry the April program to its logical conclusion by hitting the Hanoi power station, the Red River bridge, and the Phuc Yen airfield, even once.

The argument against these targets is in part based on reactions already discussed. Although we do not believe that they would have any significant chance of bringing the Chinese into the war, they might have a hardening effect on immediate Soviet decisions, and could significantly aggravate criticism in the UK and elsewhere.

The argument relates above all to the precise nature and location of these targets. The Hanoi power station is only a half mile from the Russian and Chinese Embassies, and still closer to major residential areas. The Red River bridge is the very area of Hanoi that got us into the greatest outcry in December. In both cases, the slightest mistake could produce really major and evident civilian casualties and tremendously aggravate the general reactions we have already assessed.

As to the Phuc Yen airfield, we believe there is a significant chance that this attack would cause Hanoi to assume we were going to make their jet operational airfields progressively untenable. This could significantly and in itself increase the chances of their moving planes to China and all the interacting possibilities that then arise. We believe we have gone far enough to hurt them and worry them. Is it wise to go this further step?

The second element in this strategy is that it would level off where we are, but with specific provision for periodic re-strikes against the targets we have already hit. This has clear pros and cons.

> Pros. Continued re-strikes would maintain the
> concrete results already attained--the lights would
> stay out in Haiphong for the most part.

> Continued re-strikes would tend to keep the "hawks"
> under control. Indeed, without them, it would almost
> certainly be asked why we had ever hit the targets in
> the first place. This might conceivably happen without
> re-strikes, but would be at least doubtful.

> Most basically, Hanoi and Moscow would be kept at
> least a little on edge. As we have noted earlier, fear
> of ultimate expansion of the war is an element that tends
> to impel the Soviets to maximize and use their leverage
> on Hanoi toward a peaceful settlement. 95/

This significant convergence of opinion on bombing strategy
in the next phase among key Presidential advisers could not have gone
unnoticed in the May 8 meeting, but there being no record of what transpired, the consensus can only be inferred from the fact that the 19 May
DPM did incorporate a bombing recommendation along these lines. Intervening before then to reinforce the views of the civilian Principles
were several CIA intelligence memos. Together they constituted another
repudiation of the utility of the bombing. The summary CIA view of the
effect of the bombing on North Vietnamese thinking was that:

> Twenty-seven months of US bombing of North Vietnam
> have had remarkably little effect on Hanoi's over-all
> strategy in prosecuting the war, on its confident view
> of long-term Communist prospects, and on its political
> tactics regarding negotiations. The growing pressure of
> US air operations has not shaken the North Vietnamese
> leaders' conviction that they can withstand the bombing
> and outlast the US and South Vietnam in a protracted war
> of attrition. Nor has it caused them to waver in their
> belief that the outcome of this test of will and endurance
> will be determined primarily by the course of the conflict
> on the ground in the South, not by the air war in the North. 96/

As to the state of popular morale after two years of U.S. bombing, the
CIA concluded that:

> Morale in the DRV among the rank and file populace,
> defined in terms of discipline, confidence, and willing-
> ness to endure hardship, appears to have undergone only
> a small decline since the bombing of North Vietnam began.

* * * * *

With only a few exceptions, recent reports suggest a continued willingness on the part of the populace to abide by Hanoi's policy on the war. Evidence of determination to persist in support of the war effort continues to be as plentiful in these reports as in the past. The current popular mood might best be characterized, in fact, as one of resolute stoicism with a considerable reservoir of endurance still untapped. 97/

Even the extensive physical damage the bombing had done to North Vietnam could not be regarded as meaningfully reducing Hanoi's capacity to sustain the war:

Through the end of April 1967 the US air campaign against North Vietnam--Rolling Thunder--had significantly eroded the capacities of North Vietnam's limited industrial and military base. These losses, however, have not meaningfully degraded North Vietnam's material ability to continue the war in South Vietnam. 98/

Certain target systems had suffered more than others, particularly transportation and electric power, but throughput capacity for materiel had not been significantly decreased. One of the fundamental reasons was the remarkable ability the North Vietnamese had demonstrated to recuperate quickly from the strikes:

North Vietnam's ability to recuperate from the air attacks has been of a high order. The major exception has been the electric power industry.

* * * * *

The recuperability problem is not significant for the other target systems. The destroyed petroleum storage system has been replaced by an effective system of dispersed storage and distribution. The damaged military targets systems--particularly barracks and storage depots--have simply been abandoned, and supplies and troops dispersed throughout the country. The inventories of transport and military equipment have been replaced by large infusions of military and economic aid from the USSR and Communist China. Damage to bridges and lines of communications is frequently repaired within a matter of days, if not hours, or the effects are countered by an elaborate system of multiple bypasses or pre-positioned spans. 99/

3. The May 19 DPM

By the 19th of May the opinions of McNamara and his key
aides with respect to the bombing and Westy's troop requests had
crystalized sufficiently that another Draft Presidential Memorandum
was written. It was entitled, "Future Actions in Vietnam," and was
a comprehensive treatment of all aspects of the war -- military, political,
and diplomatic. It opened with an appraisal of the situation covering both
North and South Vietnam, the U.S. domestic scene and international opinion.
The estimate of the situation in North Vietnam hewed very close to the
opinions of the intelligence community already referred to. Here is how
the analysis proceeded:

C. North Vietnam

Hanoi's attitude towards negotiations has never been
soft nor open-minded. Any concession on their part would
involve an enormous loss of face. Whether or not the Polish
and Burchett-Kosygin initiatives had much substance to them,
it is clear that Hanoi's attitude currently is hard and rigid.
They seem uninterested in a political settlement and determined to match US military expansion of the conflict. This
change probably reflects these factors: (1) increased assurances of help from the Soviets received during Pham Van Dong's
April trip to Moscow; (2) arrangements providing for the
unhindered passage of materiel from the Soviet Union through
China; and (3) a decision to wait for the results of the
US elections in 1968. Hanoi appears to have concluded that
she cannot secure her objectives at the conference table
and has reaffirmed her strategy of seeking to erode our
ability to remain in the South. The Hanoi leadership has
apparently decided that it has no choice but to submit to
the increased bombing. There continues to be no sign that
the bombing has reduced Hanoi's will to resist or her ability
to ship the necessary supplies south. Hanoi shows no signs
of ending the large war and advising the VC to melt into the
jungles. The North Vietnamese believe they are right; they
consider the Ky regime to be puppets; they believe the world
is with them and that the American public will not have
staying power against them. Thus, although they may have
factions in the regime favoring different approaches, they
believe that, in the long run, they are stronger than we are
for the purpose. They probably do not want to make significant
concessions, and could not do so without serious loss of face. 100/

When added to the continuing difficulties in bringing the
war in the South under control, the unchecked erosion of U.S. public support for the war, and the smoldering international disquiet about the need

and purpose of such U.S. intervention, it is not hard to understand the
DPM's statement that, "This memorandum is written at a time when there
appears to be no attractive course of action." 101/ Nevertheless,
'alternatives' was precisely what the DPM had been written to suggest.
These were introduced with a recapitulation of where we stood militarily
and what the Chiefs were recommending. With respect to the war in the
North, the DPM stated:

> Against North Vietnam, an expansion of the bombing
> program (ROLLING THUNDER 56) was approved mid-April. Before
> it was approved, General Wheeler said, "The bombing campaign
> is reaching the point where we will have struck all worth-
> while fixed targets except the ports. At this time we will
> have to address the requirement to deny the DRV the use of
> the ports." With its approval, excluding the port areas,
> no major military targets remain to be struck in the North.
> All that remains are minor targets, restrikes of certain
> major targets, and armed reconnaissance of the lines of com-
> munication (LOCs) -- and, under new principles, mining the
> harbors, bombing dikes and locks, and invading North Vietnam
> with land armies. These new military moves against North
> Vietnam, together with land movements into Laos and Cambodia,
> are now under consideration by the Joint Chiefs of Staff. 102/

> The broad alternative courses of action it considered were
two:

> COURSE A. Grant the request and intensify military
> actions outside the South -- especially against the North.
> Add a minimum of 200,000 men -- 100,000 (2-1/3 division plus
> 5 tactical air squadrons) would be deployed in FY 1968, another
> 100,000 (2-1/3 divisions and 8 tactical air squadrons) in FY
> 1969, and possibly more later to fulfill the JCS ultimate
> requirement for Vietnam and associated world-wide contingencies.
> Accompanying these force increases (as spelled out below) would
> be greatly intensified military actions outside South Vietnam --
> including in Laos and Cambodia but especially against the North.

> COURSE B. Limit force increases to no more than 30,000;
> avoid extending the ground conflict beyond the borders of
> South Vietnam; and concentrate the bombing on the infiltration
> routes south of 20°. Unless the military situation worsens
> dramatically, add no more than 9 battalions of the approved
> program of 87 battalions. This course would result in a level
> of no more than 500,000 men (instead of the currently planned
> 470,000) on December 31, 1968. (See Attachment IV for details.)
> A part of this course would be a termination of bombing in
> the Red River basin unless military necessity required it,
> and a concentration of all sorties in North Vietnam on the

infiltration routes in the neck of North Vietnam, between
17° and 20°. 103/

For the purposes of this paper, it is not necessary to
develop the entire DPM argumentation of the pros and cons of the respective courses of action. It will suffice to include the sections dealing
with the air war elements of the two options. (It should be noted,
however, that the air and ground programs were treated as an integrated
package in each option.) This then was the way the DPM developed the
analysis of the war segment of course of action A:

Bombing Purposes and Payoffs

Our bombing of North Vietnam was designed to serve
three purposes:

--(1) To retaliate and to lift the morale of the people
in the South who were being attacked by agents of the North.

--(2) To add to the pressure on Hanoi to end the war.

--(3) To reduce the flow and/or to increase the cost
of infiltrating men and materiel from North to South.

We cannot ignore that a limitation on bombing will
cause serious psychological problems among the men,
officers and commanders, who will not be able to understand why we should withhold punishment from the enemy.
General Westmoreland said that he is "frankly dismayed
at even the thought of stopping the bombing program."
But this reason for attacking North Vietnam must be
scrutinized carefully. We should not bomb for punitive
reasons if it serves no other purpose -- especially if
analysis shows that the actions may be counterproductive.
It costs American lives; it creates a backfire of
revulsion and opposition by killing civilians; it creates
serious risks; it may harden the enemy.

With respect to added pressure on the North, it is
becoming apparent that Hanoi may already have "written
off" all assets and lives that might be destroyed by
US military actions short of occupation of annihilation.
They can and will hold out at least so long as a prospect
of winning the "war of attrition" in the South exists.
And our best judgment is that a Hanoi prerequisite to
negotiations is significant retrenchment (if not complete

stoppage of US military actions against them -- at the least, a cessation of bombing. In this connection, Consul-General Rice (Hong Kong 7581, 5/1/67) said that, in his opinion, we cannot by bombing reach the critical level of pain in North Vietnam and that, "below that level, pain only increases the will to fight." Sir Robert Thompson said to Mr. Vance on April 28 that our bombing, particularly in the Red River Delta, "is unifying North Vietnam."

With respect to interdiction of men and materiel, it now appears that no combination of actions against the North short of destruction of the regime or occupation of North Vietnamese territory will physically reduce the flow of men and materiel below the relatively small amount needed by enemy forces to continue the war in the South. Our effort can and does have severe disruptive effects, which Hanoi can and does plan on and pre-stock against. Our efforts physically to cut the flow meaningfully by actions in North Vietnam therefore largely fail and, in failing, transmute attempted interdiction into pain, or pressure on the North (the factor discussed in the paragraph next above). The lowest "ceiling" on infiltration can probably be achieved by concentration on the North Vietnamese "funnel" south of 20° and on the Trail in Laos.

But what if the above analyses are wrong? Why not escalate the bombing and mine the harbors (and perhaps occupy southern North Vietnam) -- on the gamble that it would constrict the flow, meaningfully limiting enemy action in the South, and that it would bend Hanoi? The answer is that the costs and risks of the actions must be considered.

The primary costs of course are US lives: The air campaign against heavily defended areas costs us one pilot in every 40 sorties. In addition, an important but hard-to-measure cost is domestic and world opinion: There may be a limit beyond which many Americans and much of the world will not permit the United States to go. The picture of the world's greatest superpower killing or seriously injuring 1000 non-combatants a week, while trying to pound a tiny backward nation into submission on an issue whose merits are hotly disputed, is not a pretty one. It could conceivably produce a costly distortion in the American national consciousness and in the world image of the United States -- especially if the damage to North Vietnam is complete enough to be "successful."

The most important risk, however, is the likely Soviet, Chinese and North Vietnamese reaction to intensified US air attacks, harbor-mining, and ground actions against North Vietnam.

Likely Communist Reactions

At the present time, no actions -- except air strikes and artillery fire necessary to quiet hostile batteries across the border -- are allowed against Cambodian territory. In Laos, we average 5000 attack sorties a month against the infiltration routes and base areas, we fire artillery from South Vietnam against targets in Laos, and we will be providing 3-man leadership for each of 20 12-man US-Vietnamese Special Forces teams that operate to a depth of 20 kilometers into Laos. Against North Vietnam, we average 8,000 or more attack sorties a month against all worthwhile fixed and LOC targets; we use artillery against ground targets across the DMZ; we fire from naval vessels at targets ashore and afloat up to 19°; and we mine their inland waterways, estuaries...up to 20°.

Intensified air attacks against the same types of targets, we would anticipate, would lead to no great change in the policies and reactions of the Communist powers beyond the furnishing of some new equipment and manpower.* China, for example, has not reacted to our striking MIG fields in North Vietnam, and we do not expect them to, although there are some signs of greater Chinese participation in North Vietnamese air defense.

Mining the harbors would be much more serious. It would place Moscow in a particularly galling dilemma as to how to preserve the Soviet position and prestige in such a disadvantageous place. The Soviets might, but probably would not, force a confrontation in Southeast Asia -- where even with minesweepers they would be at as great a military disadvantage as we were when they blocked the corridor to Berlin in 1961, but where their vital interest, unlike ours in Berlin (and in Cuba), is not so clearly at stake. Moscow in this case should be expected to send volunteers, including pilots, to North Vietnam; to provide some new and better weapons and equipment;

---

* The U.S. Intelligence Board on May 5 said that Hanoi may press Moscow for additional equipment and that there is a "good chance that under pressure the Soviets would provide such weapons as cruise missiles and tactical rockets" in addition to a limited number of volunteers or crews for aircraft or sophisticated equipment. Moscow, with respect to equipment, might provide better surface-to-air missiles, better anti-aircraft guns, the YAK-28 aircraft, anti-tank missiles and artillery, heavier artillery and mortars, coastal defense missiles with 25-50 mile ranges and 2200-pound warheads, KOMAR guided-missile coastal patrol boats with 20-mile surface-to-surface missiles, and some chemical munitions. She might consider sending medium jet bombers and fighter bombers to pose a threat to all of South Vietnam.

to consider some action in Korea, Turkey, Iran, the Middle
East or, most likely, Berlin, where the Soviets can control
the degree of crisis better; and to show across-the-board
hostility toward the US (interrupting any on-going conversations on ABMs, non-proliferation, etc.). China could be
expected to seize upon the harbor-mining as the opportunity
to reduce Soviet political influence in Hanoi and to discredit the USSR if the Soviets took no military action to
open the ports. Peking might read the harbor-mining as
indicating that the US was going to apply military pressure
until North Vietnam capitulated, and that this meant an
eventual invasion. If so, China might decide to intervene
in the war with combat troops and air power, to which we
would eventually have to respond by bombing Chinese airfields and perhaps other targets as well. Hanoi would
tighten belts, refuse to talk, and persevere -- as it could
without too much difficulty. North Vietnam would of course
be fully dependent for supplies on China's will, and Soviet
influence in Hanoi would therefore be reduced. (Ambassador
Sullivan feels very strongly that it would be a serious mistake, by our actions against the port, to tip Hanoi away
from Moscow and toward Peking.)

To US ground actions in North Vietnam, we would expect
China to respond by entering the war with both ground and
air forces. The Soviet Union could be expected in these
circumstances to take all actions listed above under the lesser
provocations and to generate a serious confrontation with
the United States at one or more places of her own choosing. 104/

The arguments against Course A were summed up in a final paragraph:

Those are the likely costs and risks of COURSE A. They
are, we believe, both unacceptable and unnecessary. Ground
action in North Vietnam, because of its escalatory potential,
is clearly unwise despite the open invitation and temptation
posed by enemy troops operating freely back and forth across
the DMZ. Yet we believe that, short of threatening and perhaps toppling the Hanoi regime itself, pressure against the
North will, if anything, harden Hanoi's unwillingness to talk
and her settlement terms if she does. China, we believe, will
oppose settlement throughout. We believe that there is a
chance that the Soviets, at the brink, will exert efforts to
bring about peace; but we believe also that intensified
bombing and harbor-mining, even if coupled with political
pressure from Moscow, will neither bring Hanoi to negotiate
nor affect North Vietnam's terms. 105/

With Course A rejected, the DPM turned to consideration
of the levelling-off proposals of Course B. The analysis of the de-
escalated bombing program of this option proceeded in this manner:

The bombing program that would be a part of this
strategy is, basically, a program of concentration of
effort on the infiltration routes near the south of
North Vietnam. The major infiltration-related targets
in the Red River basin having been destroyed, such interdiction is now best served by concentration of all effort
in the southern neck of North Vietnam. All of the sorties
would be flown in the area between 17° and 20°. This shift,
despite possible increases in anti-aircraft capability in the
area, should reduce the pilot and aircraft loss rates by more
than 50 per cent. The shift will, if anything, be of positive military value to General Westmoreland while taking
some steam out of the popular effort in the North.

The above shift of bombing strategy, now that almost
all major targets have been struck in the Red River basin,
can to military advantage be made at any time. It should
not be done for the sole purpose of getting Hanoi to negotiate, although that might be a bonus effect. To maximize
the chances of getting that bonus effect, the optimum scenario
would probably be (1) to inform the Soviets quietly that
within a few days the shift would take place, stating no
time limits but making no promises not to return to the
Red River basin to attack targets which later acquire military importance (any deal with Hanoi is likely to be midwifed by Moscow); (2) to make the shift as predicted, without
fanfare; and (3) to explain publicly, when the shift had
become obvious, that the northern targets had been destroyed,
that that had been militarily important, and that there would
be no need to return to the northern areas unless military
necessity dictated it. The shift should not be huckstered.
Moscow would almost certainly pass its information on to
Hanoi, and might urge Hanoi to seize the opportunity to
de-escalate the war by talks or otherwise. Hanoi, not having
been asked a question by us and having no ultimatum-like
time limit, would be in a better posture to answer favorably
than has been the case in the past. The military side of
the shift is sound, however, whether or not the diplomatic
spill-over is successful. 106/

In a section dealing with diplomatic and political considerations, the DPM outlined the political view of the significance
of the struggle as seen by the US and by Hanoi. It then developed
a conception of larger US interests in Asia around the necessity of
containing China. This larger interest required settling the Vietnam

war into perspective as only one of three fronts that required U.S. attention (the other two being Japan-Korea and India-Pakistan). In the overall view, the DPM argued, long-run trends in Asia appeared favorable to our interests:

> The fact is that the trends in Asia today are running mostly for, not against, our interests (witness Indonesia and the Chinese confusion); there is no reason to be pessimistic about our ability over the next decade or two to fashion alliances and combinations (involving especially Japan and India) sufficient to keep China from encroaching too far. To the extent that our original intervention and our existing actions in Vietnam were motivated by the perceived need to draw the line against Chinese expansionism in Asia, our objective has already been attained, and COURSE B will suffice to consolidate it! 107/

With this perspective in mind the DPM went on to reconsider and restate U.S. objectives in the Vietnam contest under the heading "Commitment and Hopes Distinguished":

> The time has come for us to eliminate the ambiguities from our minimum objectives -- our commitments -- in Vietnam. Specifically, two principles must be articulated, and policies and actions brought in line with them: (1) Our commitment is only to see that the people of South Vietnam are permitted to determine their own future. (2) This commitment ceases if the country ceases to help itself.

> It follows that no matter how much we might hope for some things, our commitment is not:

>> -- to expel from South Vietnam regroupees, who are South Vietnamese (though we do not like them),

>> -- to ensure that a particular person or group remains in power, nor that the power runs to every corner of the land (though we prefer certain types and we hope their writ will run throughout South Vietnam),

>> -- to guarantee that the self-chosen government is non-Communist (though we believe and strongly hope it will be), and

>> -- to insist that the independent South Vietnam remain separate from North Vietnam (though in the short-run, we would prefer it that way).

(Nor do we have an obligation to pour in effort out
of proportion to the effort contributed by the people of
South Vietnam or in the face of coups, corruption, apathy
or other indications of Saigon failure to cooperate effectively with us.)

We are committed to stopping or off setting the effect
of North Vietnam's application of force in the South, which
denies the people of the South the ability to determine
their own future. Even here, however, the line is hard to
draw. Propaganda and political advice by Hanoi (or by
Washington) is presumably not barred; nor is economic aid
or economic advisors. Less clear is the rule to apply to
military advisors and war materiel supplied to the contesting
factions.

The importance of nailing down and understanding the
implications of our limited objectives cannot be overemphasized. It relates intimately to strategy against the
North, to troop requirements and missions in the South,
to handling of the Saigon government, to settlement terms,
and to US domestic and international opinion as to the
justification and the success of our efforts on behalf of
Vietnam. 108/

This articulation of American purposes and commitments in
Vietnam pointedly rejected the high blown formulations of U.S. objectives
in NSAM 288 ("an independent non-communist South Vietnam," "defeat the
Viet Cong," etc.), and came forcefully to grips with the old dilemma of
the U.S. involvement dating from the Kennedy era: only limited means
to achieve excessive ends. Indeed, in the following section of specific
recommendations, the DPM urged the President to, "Issue a NSAM nailing
down US policy as described herein." 109/ The emphasis in this scaled-
down set of goals, clearly reflecting the frustrations of failure, was
South Vietnamese self-determination. The DPM even went so far as to
suggest that, "the South will be in position /sic/, albeit imperfect,
to start the business of producing a full-spectrum government in South
Vietnam." 110/ What this amounted to was a recommendation that we
accept a compromise outcome. Let there be no mistake these were radical
positions for a senior U.S. policy official within the Johnson Administration to take. They would bring the bitter condemnation of the Chiefs
and were scarcely designed to flatter the President on the success of his
efforts to date. That they represented a more realistic mating of U.S.
strategic objectives and capabilities is another matter.

The scenario for the unfolding of the recommendations in
the DPM went like this:

(4) June: Concentrate the bombing of North Vietnam on physical interdiction of men and materiel. This would mean terminating, except where the interdiction objective clearly dictates otherwise, all bombing north of 20° and improving interdiction as much as possible in the infiltration "funnel" south of 20° by concentration of sorties and by an all-out effort to improve detection devices, denial weapons, and interdiction tactics.

(5) July: Avoid the explosive Congressional debate and US Reserve call-up implicit in the Westmoreland troop request. Decide that, unless the military situation worsens dramatically, US deployments will be limited to Program 4-plus (which, according to General Westmoreland, will not put us in danger of being defeated, but will mean slow progress in the South). Associated with this decision are decisions not to use large numbers of US troops in the Delta and not to use large numbers of them in grass-roots pacification work.

(6) September: Move the newly elected Saigon government well beyond its National Reconciliation program to seek a political settlement with the non-Communist members of the NLF--- to explore a ceasefire and to reach an accommodation with the non-Communist South Vietnamese who are under the VC banner; to accept them as members of an opposition political party, and, if necessary, to accept their individual participation in the national government -- in sum, a settlement to transform the members of the VC from military opponents to political opponents.

(7) October: Explain the situation to the Canadians, Indians, British, UN and others, as well as nations now contributing forces, requesting them to contribute border forces to help make the inside-South Vietnam accommodation possible, and -- consistent with our desire neither to occupy nor to have bases in Vietnam -- offering to remove later an equivalent number of U.S. forces. (This initiative is worth taking despite its slim chance of success.) 111/

Having made the case for de-escalation and compromise, the DPM ended on a note of candor with a clear statement of its disadvantages and problems:

The difficulties with this approach are neither few nor small: There will be those who disagree with the circumscription of the US commitment (indeed, at one time or another, one US voice or another has told the Vietnamese, third countries, the US Congress, and the public of "goals" or "objectives"

that go beyond the above bare-bones statement of our
"commitment"); some will insist that pressure, enough
pressure, on the North can pay off or that we will have
yielded a blue chip without exacting a price in exchange
for our concentrating on interdiction; many will argue
that denial of the larger number of troops will prolong
the war, risk losing it and increase the casualties of
the Americans who are there; some will insist that this
course reveals weakness to which Moscow will react with
relief, contempt and reduced willingness to help, and to
which Hanoi will react by increased demands and truculence;
others will point to the difficulty of carrying the
Koreans, Filipinos, Australians and New Zealanders with us;
and there will be those who point out the possibility that
the changed US tone may cause a "rush for the exists" in
Thailand, in Laos and especially inside South Vietnam,
perhaps threatening cohesion of the government, morale of
the army, and loss of support among the people. Not least
will be the alleged impact on the reputation of the United
States and of its President. Nevertheless, the difficulties
of this strategy are fewer and smaller than the difficulties
of any other approach. 112/

McNamara showed the draft to the President the same day it
was completed, but there is no record of his reaction. 113/ It is worth
noting, however, that May 19 was the day that U.S. planes struck the
Hanoi power plant just one-mile north of the center of Hanoi. That the
President did not promptly endorse the McNamara recommendations as he
had on occasions in the past is not surprising. This time he faced a
situation where the Chiefs were in ardent opposition to anything other
than a significant escalation of the war with a callup of reserves. This
put them in direct opposition to McNamara and his aides and created a
genuine policy dilemma for the President who had to consider the necessity
of keeping the military "on-board" in any new direction for the U.S. effort
in Southeast Asia.

4. JCS, CIA and State Reactions

In the two weeks after McNamara's DPM, the Washington paper-
mill must have broken all previous production records. The JCS in particular literally bombarded the Secretary with memoranda, many of which had
voluminous annexes. Their direct comments on the DPM did not come until
ten days after it was transmitted to the President. Before then, however,
aware of the McNamara proposals, they forwarded a number of studies each
of which was the occasion to advance their own arguments for escalation.

On May 20, the Chiefs sent the Secretary two memos, one
urging expansion of operations against North Vietnam (which they requested

he pass on to the President) and the other on worldwide force posture. 114/
In the former they argued that the objectives of causing NVN to pay an
increasing price for support of the war in the South and interdicting such
support had only been partially achieved, because the "incremental and
restrained" application of air power had enabled NVN to "anticipate US
actions and accomodate to the slow increase in pressure." They noted
that NVN had greatly increased its imports in 1966 and that record tonnages were continuing in 1967, and said they were concerned about the
possible introduction of new weapons which could improve NVN's air and
coastal defenses and pose an offensive threat to friendly forces and
installations in SVN. They called for an immediate expansion of the
bombing

> ...to include attacks on all airfields, all port
> complexes, all land and sea lines of communication in
> the Hanoi-Haiphong area, and mining of coastal harbors
> and coastal waters. 115/

The intensified bombing should be initiated during the favorable May-
September weather season, before the onset of poor flying conditions over
NVN. The bombing should include "target systems whose destruction would
have the most far-reaching effect on NVN's capability to fight," such as
electric power plants, ports, airfields, additional barracks and supply
depots, and transportation facilities. The 30-mile circle around Hanoi
should be shrunk to 10 miles and the 10-mile circle around Haiphong should
be reduced to 4. Armed reconnaissance should be authorized throughout
NVN and adjacent coastal waters except in populated areas, the China buffer
zone, and the Hanoi/Haiphong circles. Inland waterways should be mined
all the way up to the China buffer zone. 116/

On May 24 General Wheeler provided his views on two alternative courses of action in response to a request from Vance: (1) add 250,000
troops in SVN and intensify the bombing against NVN, and (2) hold the troop
increase to 70,000 more and hold the bombing below 20° unless required by
military necessity -- or, "if necessary to provide an opportunity for a
negotiated settlement," stop it altogether. In his memorandum to the
SecDef, to which a lengthy Joint Staff study of the alternatives was attached,
General Wheeler said that a partial or complete cessation of strikes against
NVN would allow NVN to recoup its losses, expand its stockpiles, and continue to support the war from a sanctuary. This would be costly to
friendly forces and prolong the war. It could be interpreted as a NVN
victory -- an "aerial Dien Bien Phu." 117/

The Chairman recommended instead the adoption of the JCS
program for the conduct of the war, which included air strikes to reduce
external aid to NVN, destroy its in-country resources, and disrupt movement into the South. The strikes would be designed to "isolate the

Hanoi-Haiphong logistic base" by interdicting the LOCs and concurrently
attacking the "remaining reservoir of war-supporing resources" and the
flow of men and materials to the South. The import of war-sustaining
material would be obstructed and reduced, movement on rails, roads, and
inland waterways would be degraded, "air terminals" would be disrupted,
storage areas and stockpiles would be destroyed, and movement South
would be curtailed. The campaign would impair NVN's ability to control,
direct, and support the insurgency in the South. NVN would be under
increasing pressure to seek a political rather than a military solution
to the war. 118/

     At the end of May the Chiefs sent the Secretary their
response to the DPM. The Chairman sent McNamara a memo with a line-in,
line-out factual correction of the DPM that did not comment on policy.
Its most significant change was to raise the total troop figure in option
A (Westy's 4-2/3 Division request) from 200,000 to 250,000. 119/ On
the 1st of June the Secretary received the Chiefs collective views on
the substantive policy recommendations of the DPM. As might have been
expected, they were the stiffest kind of condemnation of the proposals.
The JCS complained that the DPM passed off option A and its supporting
arguments as the views of the military when in fact they were a distortion
of those views,

     Course A is an extrapolation of a number of proposals
which were recommended separately but not in combination or
as interpreted in the DPM. The combination force levels,
deployments, and military actions of Course A do not accurately
reflect the positions or recommendations of COMUSMACV, CINCPAC,
or the Joint Chiefs of Staff. The positions of the Joint
Chiefs of Staff, which provide a better basis against which to
compare other alternatives, are set forth in JCSM-218-67,
JCSM 286-67, and JCSM-288-67. 120/

While they may have been annoyed at what they felt was a misrepresentation
of their views on the best course of action for the U.S., the Chiefs were
outraged by the compromising of U.S. objectives in the DPM:

     Objectives. The preferred course of action addressed
in the DPM (Course B) is not consistent with NSAM 288 or
with the explicit public statements of US policy and objectives enumerated in Part I, Appendix A, and in Appendix B.
The DPM would, in effect, limit US objectives to merely
guaranteeing the South Vietnamese the right to determine
their own future on the one hand and offsetting the effect
of North Vietnam's application of force in South Vietnam
on the other. The United States would remain committed
to these two objectives only so long as the South Vietnamese

continue to help themselves. It is also noted that the
DPM contains no statement of military objectives to
be achieved and that current US national, military,
and political objectives are far more comprehensive and
far-reaching. Thus:

a. The DPM fails to appreciate the full implications for the Free World of failure to achieve a successful resolution of the conflict in Southeast Asia.

b. Modification of present US objectives, as
called for in the DPM, would undermine and no longer
provide a complete rationale for our presence in South
Vietnam or much of our effort over the past two years.

c. The positions of the more than 35 nations supporting the Government of Vietnam might be rendered
untenable by such drastic changes in US policy. 121/

The strategy the DPM had proposed under option B was
completely anathema to their view of how the war should be conducted.
After having condemned the ground forces and strategy of the DPM as
a recipe for a protracted and indecisive conflict, the Chiefs turned
their guns on the recommended constriction of the air war to the DRV
panhandle:

Military Strategy for Air/Naval War in the North.
The DPM stresses a policy which would concentrate air
operations in the North Vietnamese "funnel" south of 20°.
The concept of a "funnel" is misleading, since in fact
the communists are supplying their forces in South Vietnam from all sides, through the demilitarized zone, Laos,
the coast, Cambodia, and the rivers in the Delta. According
to the DPM, limiting the bombing to south of 20° might
result in increased negotiation opportunities with Hanoi.
The Joint Chiefs of Staff consider that such a new self-
imposed restraint resulting from this major change in
strategy would most likely have the opposite effect.
The relative immunity granted to the LOCs and distribution
system outside the Panhandle would permit: (a) a rapid
recovery from the damage sustained to date; (b) an increase
in movement capability; (c) a reduced requirement for total
supplies in the pipeline; (d) a concentration of air defenses
into the Panhandle; and (e) a release of personnel and equipment for increased efforts in infiltration of South Vietnam.
Also, it would relieve the Hanoi leadership from experiencing
at first hand the pressures of recent air operations which
foreign observers have reported. Any possible political
advantages gained by confining our interdiction campaign to
the Panhandle would be offset decisively by allowing North

Vietnam to continue an unobstructed importation of war
material. Further, it is believed that such a drastic
reduction in the scale of air operations against North
Vietnam could only result in the strengthening of the
enemy's resolve to continue the war. No doubt the reduction in scope of air operations would also be considered
by many as a weakening of US determination and a North
Vietnamese victory in the air war over northern North
Vietnam. The combination of reduced military pressures
against North Vietnam with stringent limitations of our
operations in South Vietnam, as suggested in Course B,
appears even more questionable conceptually. It would
most likely strengthen the enemy's ultimate hope of
victory and lead to a redoubling of his efforts. 122/

Completing their rejection of the DPM's analysis, the
Chiefs argued that properly explained a mobilization of the reserves and
a full U.S. commitment to winning the war would be supported by the
American public and would bolster not harm U.S. prestige abroad. The
Chiefs did not think the likelihood of a Chinese intervention in response
to their proposed actions was high and they completely discounted a
Soviet entry into the hostilities in any active role. Summing up their
alarm at the complete turnabout in U.S. policy suggested by the DPM, the
Chiefs stated:

Most of the foregoing divergencies between the DPM
and the stated policies, objectives, and concepts are
individually important and are reason for concern. However, when viewed collectively, an alarming pattern
emerges which suggests a major realignment of US objectives and intentions in Southeast Asia without regard
for the long-term consequences. The Joint Chiefs of Staff
are not aware of any decision to retract the policies and
objectives which have been affirmed by responsible officials
many times in recent years. Thus, the DPM lacks adeqaute
foundation for further consideration. 123/

With the expectation that the implementation of course B would result
in a prolongation of the war, a reinforcing of Hanoi's belief in ultimate
victory, and greatly increased costs for the U.S. in lives and treasure,
the Chiefs recommended that:

a. The DPM NOT be forwarded to the President.

b. The US national objective as expressed in NSAM 288
be maintained, and the national policy and objectives for
Vietnam as publicly stated by US officials be reaffirmed.

    c. The military objective, concept, and strategy for
the conduct of the war in Vietnam as stated in JCSM-218-67
be approved by the Secretary of Defense.

They were evidently unaware that the President had already seen the DPM
ten days before. 124/

    At about this time, the latter part of May, CIA also pro-
duced an estimate of the consequences of several different U.S. actions,
including de-escalating the bombing. The actions considered were
essentially those of the DPM: increase U.S. troop levels in SVN by
another 200,000; intensify the bombing against military, industrial,
and transportation targets; intensify the bombing plus interdict the
harbors; or level off rather than increase troop commitments; and
reduce rather than intensify the bombing. 125/

    The tone of this estimate was not quite as favorable to
further bombing or quite as unfavorable to de-escalation as the January
CIA analysis had been. The estimate said that NVN was counting upon
winning in the South, and was willing to absorb considerable damage in
the North so long as the prospects were good there. More intensive
bombing was therefore not likely to be the decisive element in breaking
Hanoi's will and was not likely to force Hanoi to change its attitude
toward negotiations:

    Short of a major invasion or nuclear attack, there is
    probably no level of air or naval actions against North
    Vietnam which Hanoi has determined in advance would be so
    intolerable that the war had to be stopped. 126/

The pressure would be greater if, in addition, NVN's ports were closed.
If, as was most likely, the USSR did not accept the challenge and NVN
was forced to rely primarily on rail transport across China, and if,
as a consequence, the situation in NVN gradually deteriorated, it was
"conceivable" that NVN would choose to negotiate or otherwise terminate
the war; but even this was unlikely unless the war in the South was also
deteriorating seriously. 127/

    As for reducing the bombing by restricting it to southern
NVN, it would depend upon the circumstances:

    In some circumstances North Vietnam would attribute
    this to the pressure of international opinion and domestic
    criticism, and it would confirm the view that the US would
    not persist. This view might be dispelled if the US made
    it clear that the bombing was being redirected to raise
    the cost of moving men and supplies into the South; and
    even more if the US indicated it intended to increase US
    forces in the South and take other action to block or
    reduce infiltration from North Vietnam. 128/

        TOP SECRET - Sensitive

William Bundy at State drafted comments on the DPM on
May 30 and circulated them at State and Defense. In his rambling
and sometimes contradictory memo, Bundy dealt mainly with the nature
and scope of the U.S. commitment -- as expressed in the DPM and as he
saw it. He avoided any detailed analysis of the two military options
and focused his attention on the strategic reasons for American involvement; the objectives we were after; and the terms under which we could
consider closing down the operation. His memo began with his contention
that:

> The gut point can almost be summed up in a pair of
> sentences. If we can get a reasonably solid GVN political
> structure and GVN performance at all levels, favorable
> trends could become really marked over the next 18 months,
> the war will be won for practical purposes at some point, and
> the resulting peace will be secured. On the other hand, if
> we do not get these results from the GVN and the South Viet-
> namese people, no amount of US effort will achieve our basic
> objective in South Viet-Nam--a return to the essential
> provisions of the Geneva Accords of 1954 and a reasonably
> stable peace for many years based on these Accords.

It is this view of the central importance of the South that dominates
the remainder of Bundy's memo. But his own thinking was far from clear
about how the U.S. should react to a South Vietnamese failure for at the
end of it he wrote:

> None of the above decides one other question clearly
> implicit in the DOD draft. What happens if "the country
> ceases to help itself." If this happens in the literal
> sense, if South Viet-Nam performs so badly that it simply
> is not going to be able to govern itself or to resist the
> slightest internal pressure, then we would agree that we
> can do nothing to prevent this. But the real underlying
> question is to what extent we tolerate imperfection, even
> gross imperfection, by the South Vietnamese while they are
> still under the present grinding pressure from Hanoi and the
> NLF.

> This is a tough question. What do we do if there is a
> military coup this summer and the elections are aborted?
> There would then be tremendous pressure at home and in
> Europe to the effect that this negated what we were fighting
> for, and that we should pull out.

> But against such pressure we must reckon that the stakes
> in Asia will remain. After all, the military rule, even in

peacetime, in Thailand, Indonesia, and Burma. Are we
to walk away from the South Vietnamese, at least as a
matter of principle, simply because they failed in what was
always conceded to be a courageous and extremely difficult
effort to become a true democracy during a guerrilla war? 130/

Bundy took pointed issue with the DPM's reformulation of
U.S. objectives. Starting with the DPM's discussion of U.S. larger
interests in Asia, Bundy argued that:

In Asian eyes, the struggle is a test case, and indeed
much more black-and-white than even we ourselves see it.
The Asian view bears little resemblance to the breast-
beating in Europe or at home. Asians would quite literally
be appalled -- and this includes India -- if we were to
pull out from Viet-Nam or if we were to settle for an
illusory peace that produced Hanoi control over all Viet-
Nam in short order.

In short, our effort in Viet-Nam in the past two years
has not only prevented the catastrophe that would otherwise have unfolded but has laid a foundation for a progress
that now appears truly possible and of the greatest historical significance. 131/

Having disposed of what he saw as a misinterpretation of
Asian sentiment and U.S. interests there, Bundy now turned to the DPM's
attempt to minimize the U.S. commitment in Vietnam. He opposed the DPM
language because in his view it dealt too heavily with our military commitment to get NVA off the South Vietnamese back, and not enough with
the equally important commitment, to assure that "the political board
in South Vietnam is not tilted to the advantage of the NLF." 132/   Bundy's
conception of the U.S. commitment was twofold:

--To prevent any imposed political role for the NLF
in South Vietnamese political life, and specifically the
coalition demanded by point 3 of Hanoi's Four Points, or
indeed any NLF part in government or political life that
is not safe and acceptable voluntarily to the South Vietnamese Government and people.

--To insist in our negotiating position that "regroupees,"
that is, people originally native to South Viet-Nam who went
North in 1954 and returned from 1959 onward, should be expelled
as a matter of principle in the settlement. Alternatively,
such people could remain in South Viet-Nam if, but only if,
the South Vietnamese Government itself was prepared to receive
them back under a reconciliation concept, which would provide in essence that they must be prepared to accept peaceful

political activity under the Constitution (as the reconciliation appeal now does). This latter appears to be the
position of the South Vietnamese Government, which--as
Tran Van Do has just stated in Geneva--argues that those
sympathetic to the Northern system of government should go
North, while those prepared to accept the Southern system
of government may stay in the South. Legally, the first
alternative is sound, in that Southerners who went North
in 1954 became for all legal and practical purposes Northern
citizens and demonstrated their allegiance. But if the
South Vietnamese prefer the second alternative, it is in
fact exactly comparable to the regroupment provisions of
the 1954 Accords, and can legally be sustained. But in
either case the point is that the South Vietnamese are not
obliged to accept as citizens people whose total pattern
of conduct shows that they would seek to overthrow the
structure of government by force and violence. 133/

The remainder of Bundy's comments were addressed to
importance of this last point. The U.S. could not consider withdrawing
its forces until not only the North Vietnamese troops but also the regroupees had returned to the North. Nowhere in his comments does he specifically touch on the merits of the two military options, but his arguments
all seem to support the tougher of the two choices (his earlier support
of restricting the bombing thus seems paradoxical). He was, it is clear,
less concerned with immediate specific decisions on a military phase of
the war than with the long term consequences of this major readjustment
of American sights in Southeast Asia.

The only other reaction on the DPM from the State Department was a belated memo from Katzenbach to Vance on June 8. Katzenbach's
criticisms were more focused on specific language and conclusions than
Bundy's. In general they did not reject the analysis of the DPM, however. With respect to the bombing, Katzenbach observed that, "...we
ought to consider concentrating on infiltration routes throughout North
Viet-Nam and leaving 'strategic' targets, particularly those in urban
areas alone." 134/   This departed slightly from the Bundy-Rostow-
McNaughton thesis of confining the bombing to the panhandle infiltration
network. As to the DPM's effort to circumscribe U.S. objectives in the
war, Katzenbach achieved a new low in understatement, "I agree with the
arguments for limited objectives. But these are not easy to define." 135/
In short, if the intent of the DOD draft had been to precipitate an
Administration-wide debate on the fundamental issues of the U.S. involvement, it had certainly achieved its purpose.

5. The McNamara Bombing Options

Long before McNamara received these views from the Chiefs, CIA and State, however, he had requested comments from several quarters on two possible bombing programs. Perhaps reflecting a cool Presidential reaction to the DPM proposals, Secretary McNamara, on May 20, asked the JCS, the CIA, and the two military services involved in the ROLLING THUNDER program, the Air Force and the Navy, to study the question. He referred to the "controversy" surrounding the program, said that several alternatives had been suggested, and asked for an analysis of the two most promising ones:

> (1) Concentrate on LOCs in the Panhandle area, Route Packages 1, 2, and 3, and terminate bombing in the rest of North Vietnam unless there is reconstruction of important fixed targets destroyed by prior raids or unless new military actions appear; or

> (2) Terminate bombing against fixed targets not directly associated with LOCs in Route Packages 6a and 6b /the northeast quadrant/ and simultaneously expand armed reconnaissance in Route Packages 6a and 6b by authorizing strikes against all LOCs except within 8 miles of the centers of Hanoi and Haiphong. This would undoubtedly require continuous strikes against MIG aircraft on all airfields. 136/

Under alternative (2) above, the Secretary provided two alternate assumptions: (a) that strikes against the ports and port facilities were precluded, and (b) that every effort was made to deny importation from the sea. 137/

The Secretary asked each addressee to analyze the two main alternatives plus any others they considered worth discussing. He asked, for each of the alternatives, the effect it would have on reducing the flow of men and material to SVN, on losses of pilots and aircraft, and on the risk of "increased military pressure" from the USSR or China. He also asked that the studies be carried out independently, and requested reports by 1 June. 138/

The CIA reply, a "Dear Bob" memo from Helms, arrived as requested on June 1st. In his cover memo Helms stated that the goal of interdicting supplies to the South was essentially beyond reach:

> In general, we do not believe that any of the programs presented in your memorandum is capable of reducing the flow of military and other essential goods sufficiently to affect the war in the South or to decrease Hanoi's deter- mination to persist in the war. 139/

Based on the results of ROLLING THUNDER to date and on
the nature of the logistic target system, CIA said, concentrating the
bombing in southern NVN would undoubtedly increase the costs of maintaining the LOCs and degrade their capacity "somewhat further," but
could not be expected to reduce the flow of men and materiel below
present levels. This was because of the excess capacity of the road
network and NVN's impressive ability to maintain and improve it. It
cited the example of the traffic from NVN through Mu Gia pass into
Laos. During the 1965-1966 dry season, truck traffic on the route
averaged 28 trucks or about 85 tons of supplies a day, a level of traffic
which used it to less than 20 percent of its then theoretical capacity
of 450 tons a day, and, since the route had been improved, less than
10 percent of its present capacity of 740 tons a day. The rest of the
road network had also been expanded in spite of the bombing. Some 340
miles of alternative routes were built in southern NVN during 1966 and
more than 400 miles of new roads were constructed in Laos. Even if the
bombing could reduce road capacities by 50 percent, the capacity remaining
would still be at least five times greater than required to move supplies
at the current rate. In summary:

> ...the excess capacity on the road networks in Route
> Packages I, II, and III provides such a deep cushion that
> it is almost certain that no interdiction program can
> neutralize the logistics target system to the extent neces-
> sary to reduce the flow of men and supplies to South Vietnam
> below their present levels. 140/

As to concentrating the bombing north instead of south of
20°, neither the open or the closed port variants "could obstruct or
reduce North Vietnam's import of military or war-supporting materials
sufficiently to degrade its ability to carry on the war." NVN now had
the capacity to import about 14,000 tons of goods a day over its main
rail, road, and inland water routes; and it currently imported about
5,300 tons a day. An optimum interdiction program against all means
of land and water transportation could "at most" reduce transport capacity
to about 3,900 tons a day, or about 25 percent below present levels.
However, if NVN eliminated all but essential military and economic goods,
it would need only about 3000 tons a day, a volume of traffic which could
still be handled comfortably. 141/

The CIA also went into some detail on Soviet and Chinese
responses to bombing north versus south of 20°. The Chinese would
attribute any cutback to a lack of will in the face of rising domestic
and international criticism and would continue to egg NVN on. The Soviets
would construe it in this light, also, but would be relieved that the
U.S. had broken the cycle of escalation, and if the U.S. accompanied the
cutback with political initiatives toward negotiations might even press
Hanoi to respond. As to Hanoi,

　　　　　TOP SECRET - Sensitive

Whether or not Hanoi responded to these initiatives would depend on its view of the military outlook in the South, and on whether it believed that a
move toward negotiation would bring success nearer. 142/

Bombing north of 20° without closing the ports would not
bring on new or different Chinese or Soviet responses except for the
attacks on airfields. These might lead to greater Chinese involvement,
especially if NVN transferred air defense operations to bases in China.
If the ports were closed, however, there would be a direct challenge
to the USSR. While it was unlikely that the USSR (or China, for that
matter) would undertake new military actions, it would make every effort
to continue supplying NVN and would attempt to put maximum political
pressures on the U.S. China's leverage with Hanoi would grow, and
China would urge Hanoi to continue the war more vigorously than ever. 143/

The formal JCS response to the SecDef's questions on
bombing north versus south of the 20th parallel, quite apart from troop
levels, was submitted on 2 June. It was predictably cool toward
restricting the bombing to southern NVN, a good deal warmer toward
continuing the bombing in northern NVN, and warmest by far toward
proceeding from there to close the ports. 144/

The JCS opposed any cutback on bombing north of the 20th
parallel on grounds that it would decrease the effectiveness of interdiction and make things easier for NVN. It would reduce the distance
over which the flow of men and supplies was subject to attack. It would
provide NVN free and rapid access down to Thanh Hoa, decreasing transport
time, rolling stock requirements, pipeline assets, and man-hours for
moving supplies South. It would release resources currently required
north of 20°. It would enable NVN to accelerate the import of weapons
and munitions, strengthen the Panhandle defenses, and increase U.S. attrition. The U.S. action would be interpreted as yielding to pressure and
weakening resolve; NVN would be sure to claim victory and press for greater
concessions as a price for any settlement. 145/

The JCS also argued that terminating strikes against non-
LOC targets in the north and switching to expanded armed reconnaissance
there would have the disadvantage of not maintaining the level of damage
achieved with respect to fixed installations and industry, but would have
the advantages of adding to NVN's difficulties -- from interruptions of
the LOCs, having to resort to inferior means of transport, shifting its
management and labor resources, and the like. However, leaving the ports
open would permit NVN to absorb the damage and adjust to the campaign.
With the ports open, NVN could continue to handle imports even if the
LOC strikes were successful. With the ports closed, on the other hand,
sustained attack on the roads and railroads would become militarily

profitable, and the concurrent and sustained interdiction of imports would become possible. 146/

A cryptic pencil note on copy 4 of this JCSM initialled by McNaughton indicated, "all incorporated in my 6/3/67 draft," and listed "Main issues" as "(1) Total pressure (2) pilot losses (3) U.S. 'failure'." 147/ It is hard to know exactly what this could mean since the JCS position was certainly not being adopted by the Secretary. Moreover, there is no record of a 3 June draft. We will discuss a later draft below, but it does not endorse the JCS position.

The Secretary of the Navy responded to Secretary McNamara's questions with an attempt to construct models of the alternative north and south of 20° target systems and war game attacks against them. It concluded that an interdiction effort in southern NVN concentrated on specified areas where traffic was already constricted by the terrain would be more effective than the current program, "but by an uncertain increment over an undefinable base." U.S. losses would be lower initially, but would rise in time because NVN could be expected to redeploy anti-aircraft defenses south. The manpower strain on NVN would not be as at present, however, with the cessation of attacks on the high-value targets in the northern part of the country. 148/

The Navy analysis also concluded that a greater interdiction effort north of 20°, without closing the ports, could not be carried out with available resources "in a manner producing results better than the present effort." The program would create greater demand for repair and bypass construction, but it was not clear that it would have a major effect on NVN's capability to import goods and ship them to SVN. This alternative would be the most expensive in U.S. aircraft and aircrews and would provide the least return in reducing NVN supplies to SVN. 149/

Closing the ports in addition to stepping up the armed reconnaissance effort in northern NVN would have a substantial effect on imports at first but in time NVN could switch to other LOCs. The cost would be mainly in efficiency. Reducing imports below NVN's minimum requirements was probably beyond the current capability of the bombing campaign. 150/

The Air Force response to Secretary McNamara was given on 3 June. Cutting back the bombing to below the 20th parallel would permit NVN to increase the input of men and supplies at the top of the "funnel" with the same or less effort than it was now expending, and would result in a greater inflow into SVN. U.S. losses might go down temporarily, but NVN would shift its anti-aircraft resources southward, and losses would rise again. The cutback would reduce the risk of Chinese or Soviet involvement and might conceivably even start a process

of mutual de-escalation, but it was more likely to be taken as a
sign of U.S. weakness and encourage Hanoi to take a still stronger
stand. 151/

> Expanded armed reconnaissance in northern NVN, especially
if coupled with denying or inhibiting importation through Haiphong,

>> ...would have a substantial effect on NVN economy
>> and logistic net and would...force enough additional
>> diversion of resources to reduce NVN infiltration and
>> support. 152/

However, closure of Haiphong -- which might not shut off all access from
the sea -- would carry unacceptable risks of wider war, an allout attack
on the railroads and roads from China was preferable, and would still
complicate NVN's logistic problems. Still more preferable, on balance,
was maintaining the present level of operations:

> Because closure of Haiphong is probably not acceptable,
> what would otherwise be a reasonable price in terms of air-
> craft loss for greatly reducing the inflow along the northern
> roads and railroads becomes an unreasonable loss in the
> presence of a possible increase of sea import....This option
> is not, without Haiphong port denial, an optimum use of air-
> power. It is a war of attrition, forced by the risk of a
> wider war or other actions by the Soviets if we do try to
> close Haiphong. In that sense, it is analogous to the
> ground war in the South....153/

On June 9, Secretary of the Air Force Brown sent McNamara a supplemental
memo in which he tried to make a case for interdiction bombing based on
a statistical demonstration that it was the most important factor in
explaining the difference between uninterdicted infiltration capability
and actual infiltration. 154/

> Thus, the responses to the SecDef's questions on bombing
north versus south of the 20th parallel divided about evenly, with the
JCS and the Air Force strongly opposed to a cutback to 20° and backing
the more escalatory route, and the Navy and CIA concluding that interdiction either north or south was a difficult if not impossible goal but
that a cutback would cost little.

6. The June 12th DPM

> The Defense Department having fully explored the various air
war options, attention within the Administration again focused on preparing
a memorandum to the President, this time on strategy against North Vietnam
alone. But other events and problems were intervening to consume the

time and energies of the Principles in early June. On June 5, the
four-day Arab-Israeli War erupted to dominate all other problems during
that week. The intensive diplomatic activity at the UN by the U.S.
would heavily engage the President's attention and eventually lead to
the Summit meeting with Soviet Premier Kosygin in Glassboro, N.J. later
in the month. In the actual war in Vietnam, the one-day truce on
Buddha's birthday, May 23rd, had produced such gross enemy violations
that some intensification of the conflict ensued afterwards. Nevertheless in late May, Admiral Sharp was informed of the reimposition
of the 10-mile prohibited zone around Hanoi. His response was predictable:

> We have repeatedly sought to obtain authority for a
> systematic air campaign directed against carefully selected
> targets whose destruction and constant disruption would
> steadily increase the pressure on Hanoi. It seems unfor-
> tunate that just when the pressure is increasing by virtue
> of such an air campaign, and the weather is optimum over
> northern NVN, we must back off. 155/

On June 11, however, the Kep airfield was struck for the first time
with ten MIGs reportedly destroyed or damaged. Prior to that, on
June 2, an unfortunate case of bad aiming had resulted in a Soviet ship,
the Turkestan, being struck by cannon fire from a U.S. plane trying to
silence a North Vietnamese AAA battery. The Soviets lodged a vigorous
protest with the U.S., but we initially denied the allegation only to
acknowledge the accident later (on June 20 to be exact just three days
before the Glassboro meeting and presumably to improve its atmosphere).

In Washington, in addition to the time consuming Middle
East crisis, Administration officials were still far from consensus on
the question of whether to add another major increment to U.S. ground
forces in South Vietnam and to call up the reserves to reconstitute
depleted forces at home and elsewhere. Indeed, as we shall see, it
appears that the troop question went unresolved longer than the air
strategy problem. The issues must have been discussed in a general
review of the Vietnam question at a meeting at State on June 8 in
Katzenbach's office, but no record of the discussion was preserved. A
two-page outline of positions entitled "Disagreements" and preserved
in McNaughton's files does, however, give a very good idea of where
the principle Presidential advisers stood on the major issues at that
point:

DISAGREEMENTS

1. Westmoreland-McNamara on whether Course A would
end the war sooner.

2. Vance-CIA on the ability of NVN to meet force increases in the South.

3. Wheeler-Vance on the military effectiveness of cutting back bombing to below the 20th Parallel, and on whether it would save US casualties.

4. CIA believes that the Chinese might not intervene if an invasion of NVN did not seem to threaten the Hanoi regime. Vance states an invasion would cause Chinese intervention. Vance believes that the Chinese could decide to intervene if the ports were mined; CIA does not mention this possibility.

5. CIA and the Mission disagree with Vance on whether we have achieved the cross-over point and, more broadly, on how well the "big war" is going. One CIA analysis, contradicted in a latter /sic/ CIA statement, expresses the view that the enemy's strategic position has improved over the past year.

6. CIA-INR on whether Hanoi seeks to wear us down (CIA) or seeks more positive victories in the South (INR).

7. INR believes that the bombing has had a greater effect than does CIA.

8. Vance and CIA say we have struck all worthwhile targets in NVN except the ports. Wheeler disagrees.

9. CIA cites inflationary pressures and the further pressure that would be caused by Course A. Vance says that these pressures are under control and could be handled if Course A were adopted.

10. Rostow believes that a call-up of reserves would show Hanoi that we mean business and have more troops coming-- Vance believes that a reserve call-up would lead to divisive debate which would encourage Hanoi. Would not the call-up indicate that we had manpower problems?

11. Bundy-Vance disagreements on the degree to which we have contained China, whether our commitment ends if the SVNamese don't help themselves, the NLF role in political life, regroupees, and our and Hanoi's rights to lend support to friendly forces in SVN after a settlement. 156/

Another indication of what may have transpired in the
June 8 meeting is an unsigned outline for a policy paper (probably
done in Bundy's office) in McNaughton's files. This ambitious document suggests that U.S. goals in the conflict include leaving behind
a stable, democratic government; leaving behind conditions of stable
peace in Asia; persuading the DRV to give up its aggression; and
neutralizing the internal security threat in the South. All this to
be done without creating an American satellite, generating anti-
American sentiment, destroying the social fabric in the South or
alienating other countries. 157/   Strategies considered to achieve
the objectives included the Westmoreland plan for 200,000 men with a
reserve callup (10 disadvantages listed against it); limiting the
increase to 30,000 men but without a reserve callup; "enough US forces
to operate effectively against provincial main force units and to
reinforce I Corps and the DMZ area," with a reserve callup; and no
change from current force levels. Options against North Vietnam
included: (A) expanded air attacks on military, industrial and LOC
targets including mining the harbors; (B) stopping the bombing north
of the 20th parallel except for restrikes; (C) invasion; and (D) the
barrier. The section ends cryptically, "Our over-all strategy must
consist of a combination of these." 158/   The last paragraph of the
outline deals with the intended strategy against the North:

> ...the object is to cut the North off from the South
> as much as possible, and to shake Hanoi from its obdurate
> position. Concentrate on shaking enemy morale in both the
> South and North by limiting Hanoi's ability to support the
> forces in South Viet-Nam.
>
> a. A barrier, if it will work, or
>
> b. Concentrate bombing on lines of communication
> throughout NVN, thus specifically concentrating on infil-
> tration but not running into the problem we have had and
> will have with bombing oriented towards 'strategic' targets
> in the Hanoi/Haiphong area. By continuing to bomb through-
> out NVN in this manner we would indicate neither a lessening
> of will nor undue impatience. 159/

The broad outlines of the eventual decision on bombing that would emerge
from this prolonged debate are contained in this cryptic outline in
early June.

At Defense, McNaughton began once again to pull together
a DPM for McNamara, this time devoted exclusively to the air war. A
June 12 version preserved in McNaughton's files appears to be the final

Declassified per Executive Order 13526, Section 3.3
NND Project Number: NND 63316. By: NWD Date: 2011

form it took, although whether it was shown to the President is not clear. McNaughton's draft rejected the more fulsome expressions of the U.S. objective advanced by the Chiefs and Bundy in favor of following a more closely defined set of goals:

> The limited over-all US objective, in terms of the narrow US commitment and not of wider US preferences, is to take action (so long as they continue to help themselves) to see that the people of South Vietnam are permitted to determine their own future. Our commitment is to stop (or generously to offset when we cannot stop) North Vietnamese military intervention in the South, so that "the board will not be tilted" against Saigon in an internal South Vietnamese contest for control...The sub-objectives, at which our bombing campaign in the North has always been aimed, are these:

> --(1) To retaliate and to lift the morale of the people in the South, including Americans, who are being attacked by agents of the North;

> --(2) To add to the pressure on Hanoi to end the war;

> --(3) To reduce the flow and/or to increase the cost of infiltrating men and materiel from North to South. 160/

In light of these objectives, three alternative air war programs were examined in the memo. They were:

> ALTERNATIVE A. Intensified attack on the Hanoi-Haiphong logistical base. Under this Alternative, we would continue attacks on enemy installations and industry and would conduct an intensified, concurrent and sustained effort against all elements of land, sea and air lines of communication in North Vietnam -- especially those entering and departing the Hanoi-Haiphong areas. Foreign shipping would be "shouldered out" of Haiphong by a series of air attacks that close in on the center of the port complex. The harbor and approaches would be mined, forcing foreign shipping out into the nearby estuaries for offloading by lighterage. Intensive and systematic armed reconnaissance would be carried out against the roads and railroads from China (especially the northeast railroad), against coastal shipping and coastal transshipment locations, and against all other land lines of communications. The eight major operational airfields would be systematically attacked, and the deep-water ports of Cam Pha and Hon Gai would be struck or mined as required. ALTERNATIVE A could be pursued full-force between now and September (thereafter the onset of unfavorable weather conditions would seriously impair operations).

ALTERNATIVE B. Emphasis on the infiltration routes south of the 20th Parallel. Under this alternative, the dominant emphasis would be, not on preventing material from flowing into North Vietnam (and thus not on "economic pressure on the regime), but on preventing military men and materiel from flowing out of the North into the South. We would terminate bombing in the Red River basin except for occasional sorties (perhaps 3%) -- those necessary to keep enemy air defenses and damage-repair crews positioned there and to keep important fixed targets knocked out. The same total number of sorties envisioned under ALTERNATIVE A--together with naval gunfire at targets ashore and afloat and mining of inland waterways, estuaries and coastal waters -- would be concentrated in the neck of North Vietnam, between 17° and 20°, through which all land infiltration must pass and in which the "extended battle zone" north of the DMZ lies. The effort would be intensive and sustained, designed especially to saturate choke points and to complement similar new intensive interdiction efforts in adjacent areas in Laos and near the 17th Parallel inside South Vietnam.

ALTERNATIVE C. Extension of the current program. This alternative would be essentially a refinement of the currently approved program and therefore a compromise between ALTERNATIVE A and ALTERNATIVE b. Under it, while avoiding attacks within the 10-mile prohibited zone around Hanoi and strikes at or mining of the ports, we would conduct a heavy effort against all other land, sea, and air lines of communication. Important fixed targets would be kept knocked out; intensive, sustained and systematic armed reconnaissance would be carried out against the roads and railroads and coastal shipping throughout the country; and the eight major airfields would be systematically attacked. The total number of sorties would be the same as under the other two alternatives. 161/

The positions of the various members of the Defense establishment with respect to the three alternatives were:

Mr. Vance and I recommend ALTERNATIVE B.

The Joint Chiefs of Staff recommend ALTERNATIVE A.

The Secretary of the Navy recommends ALTERNATIVE B.

The Secretary of the Air Force recommends ALTERNATIVE C modified to add some targets (especially LOC targets) to the present list and to eliminate others.

The Director of the CIA does not make a recommendation.
The CIA judgment is that none of the alternatives is capable
of decreasing Hanoi's determination to persist in the war
or of reducing the flow of goods sufficiently to affect the
war in the South. 162/

The arguments for and against the three alternatives were
developed at considerable length in the memo. The summary gave the following rationale for the McNamara-Vance position:

In the memorandum, Mr. Vance and I:

--Oppose the JCS program (ALTERNATIVE A) on grounds
that it would neither substantially reduce the flow of men
and supplies to the South nor pressure Hanoi toward settlement, that it would be costly in American lives and in
domestic and world opinion, and that it would run serious
risks of enlarging the war into one with the Soviet Union
and China, leaving us a few months from now more frustrated
and with almost no choice but even further escalation.

--Oppose mere refinement of the present program
(ALTERNATIVE C) on grounds that it would involve most of
the costs and some of the risks of ALTERNATIVE A with less
chance that ALTERNATIVE A of either interdicting supplies
or moving Hanoi toward settlement.

--Recommend concentration of the bulk of our efforts
on infiltration routes south of 20° (ALTERNATIVE B) because
this course would interdict supplies as effectively as the
other alternatives, would cost the least in pilots' lives,
and would be consistent with effort to move toward negotiations. 163/

These views were stated in somewhat expanded form in in the concluding
paragraphs of the DPM:

I am convinced that, within the limits to which we can
go with prudence, "strategic" bombing of North Vietnam will
at best be unproductive. I am convinced that mining the
ports would not only be unproductive but very costly in
domestic and world support and very dangerous -- running
high risks of enlarging the war as the program is carried
out, frustrated and with no choice but to escalate further.
At the same time, I am doubtful that bombing the infiltration routes north or south of 20° will put a meaningful

ceiling on men or materiel entering South Vietnam. Nevertheless, I recommend ALTERNATIVE B (which emphasizes
bombing the area between 17° and 20°) because (1) it holds
highest promise of serving a military purpose, (2) it
will cost the least in pilots' lives, and (3) it is consistent with efforts to move toward negotiations.

Implicit in the recommendation is a conviction that
nothing short of toppling the Hanoi regime will pressure
North Vietnam to settle so long as they believe they have
a chance to sin the "war of attrition" in the South, a
judgment that actions sufficient to topple the Hanoi
regime will put us into war with the Soviet Union and
China, and a belief that a shift to ALTERNATIVE B can be
timed and handled in such a way as to gain politically
while not endangering the morale of our fighting men. 164/

There is no evidence as to whether the President saw this
memo or not. If he did, any decision on bombing was probably deferred
to be made in conjunction with the decision on ground forces. Moreover, the middle of June was heavily taken up with the question of
whether or not to meet Kosygin, and once that was decided with preparing for the confrontation. Therefore, no decision on bombing was
forthcoming during June. What is significant is the coalescence of
civilian opinion against the JCS recommended escalation.

7. The RT 57 Decision -- No Escalation

There is some evidence that in spite of the burden of
other problems, some attention was also being devoted to the possibility
of negotiations and U.S. positions in the event they should occur. 165/
Bundy had had an extensive interview with the recently defected Chargé of
the Hungarian Embassy in Washington who had confirmed that at no time
during any of the past peace efforts with the DRV had there been any
North Vietnamese softening of its position. 166/ This view of the current situation was challenged, however, by INR in a report at mid-month.
They noted that, "Several recent indicators suggest that Hanoi may
again be actively reviewing the issue of negotiations. Some of the
indicators show possible flexibility; others show continuing hardness." 167/
In retrospect these were hardly more than straws in the wind. In early
July they would become more immediate, however, with a Canadian proposal
for redemilitarization of the DMZ and a bombing halt (see below). The
June review of the situation no doubt was done with a view to determining
what possibilities might exist if the President met with Kosygin as he
eventually did.

TOP SECRET - Sensitive

On June 17, Ambassador Bunker added his voice to the chorus already doubting the effectiveness of the bombing in interdicting the flow of North Vietnamese support for the war. In his first major pronouncement on the subject he told Rusk in an "eyes only" cable:

Aerial bombardment has been helpful in greatly increasing the difficulties of infiltration by the NVN forces and in keeping them supplied. It has also destroyed or damaged a large amount of the NVN infrastructure. Aerial bombardment, however, though extremely important, has neither interdicted infiltration nor broken the will of the NVN and it is doubtful that it can accomplish either. 168/

Continuing his analysis, he stated:

It seems apparent therefore that the crux of the military problem is to choke off NVN infiltration.

*   *   *   *   *

When the infiltration is choked off, it should be possible to suspend bombings at least for a period and thereby determine whether there is substance to the statement in many quarters that Hanoi would then come to negotiations. If the bombings were stopped it would at least call their bluff. 169/

In the remainder of this cable he advanced the arguments for an anti-infiltration barrier even in view of the political problems it would create. Disillusioned, like so many others, with the bombing, he pinned his hopes on this untried military alternative to "choke off the infiltration."

A few days later, CINCPAC, undoubtedly aware of the air war debate in Washington and the direction in which it was tending, sent a long cable to the Chiefs evaluating the results of recent months in the ROLLING THUNDER program, results which argued for intensification of the bombing he felt. Reviewing the history of the bombing since February, he noted the curtailment of sorties during the early spring because of bad weather but stated that, "Starting in late April and over a period of five weeks, the air campaign in the NE quadrant increased the level of damage in that area and the consequent stress on the Hanoi government more than during the entire previous ROLLING THUNDER program." 170/   In an apparent attempt to head off the arguments for limiting the bombing to below the 20th parallel, Admiral Sharp pointed out that the significant achievements in the NE quadrant in the previous two months had not been at the expense of sorties in the panhandle and, perhaps more importantly,

had experienced a declining aircraft loss rate compared with the
previous year. The numbers of trucks, railroad cars, boats, etc.,
destroyed were offered as evidence of the effectiveness of bombing
in interdicting the flow of supplies. No mention is made of the
undiminished rate of that flow. The mining of the rivers south of
20° is also judged a success, although no evidence is offered to support the statement. After fulminating about the reimposition of the
10-mile restriction around Hanoi, CINCPAC notes the significant
achievements of the last months -- all in terms of increased DRV defensive activity (MIG, SAM, AAA, etc.). In a peroration worthy of Billy
Mitchell, CINCPAC summed up the achievements of the recent past and made
the case for intensification:

> ...we believe that our targeting systems concept, our
> stepped up combat air effort over the Northeast and the
> continued high sortie rate applied against enemy infiltra-
> tion is paying off. With the exception of RT 55 and RT 56,
> air power for the first time began to realize the sort of
> effectiveness of which it is capable. This effectiveness
> can be maximized if we can be authorized to strike the many
> important targets remaining.

> We are at an important point in this conflict. We
> have achieved a position, albeit late in the game, from
> which a precisely executed and incisive air campaign
> against all the target systems will aggregate significant
> interrelated effects against the combined military, politi-
> cal, economic, and psychological posture of North Vietnam.
> In our judgment the enemy is now hurting and the operations
> to which we attribute this impact should be continued with
> widest latitude in planning and execution in the months of
> remaining good weather. 171/

CINCPAC's arguments, however, were largely falling on deaf
ears. The debate had resolved itself as between options B and C. On
July 3, the energetic Secretary of the Air Force, Harold Brown, sent
McNamara another long detailed memo supporting his preference for
alternative C. Convinced that the bombing did have some utility in
northern North Vietnam, Brown had sent supplementary memos to his 3 June
basic reply on 9 and 16 June. His July memo compared the objectives of
the two alternatives and noted that the only difference was that alternative C would somewhat impede the import of supplies into North Vietnam
and would allot 20% of the available sorties north of 20° compared with
3% under alternative B. 172/ The principle arguments for maintaing the
northern attack were: (1) the fact that a substantial erosion of interdiction effectiveness would occur if it was curtailed; (2) the political
irreversibility of de-escalation (and the current lack of diplomatic

reason for such an initiative); and (3) the declining loss rates of
aircraft and pilots in Route Packages 4-6. The appeal of Brown's
analysis, however, for McNamara must have clearly been its reliance on
statistical data -- hard facts. This is now Brown argued that ending
the northern sorties would reduce interdiction effectiveness:

> ...the increase in weight of effort south of 20° from
> transferring 1500 sorties out of the area north of 20° is
> only about 21% (or about 13% increase of the total effort
> south of 20° and in Laos). Even if there is no law of
> diminishing returns south of 20°, for that overall increase
> to compensate the decrease in effect north of 20° would
> require that the former be presently five times as effective
> as the latter. I believe there would be diminishing returns
> south of 20°, because there are no targets south of 20°
> which are now not struck for lack of availability of sorties.
> North of 20° the question is a different one. The damage
> to LOCs can be increased by increasing the weight of effort
> (and this has been done in the past few months). What we
> have not been able to measure well is the incremental effort
> this forces on the North Vietnamese, or the extent to which
> they could and would use it to increase infiltration if
> they did not have to expend it on keeping supplies flowing
> to the 20° line.

> It can be argued that because the flow into SVN is a
> larger fraction of what passes through Route Packages I-III
> than it is of what passes through Route Packages IV-VI, an
> amount of materiel destroyed in the former area has more
> effect than the same amount destroyed in the latter. This
> is true, but to argue that sorties in the northern region
> are therefore less important overlooks the fact that this
> very gradient is established largely by the attrition
> throughout the LOC. In analogous transport or diffusion
> problems of this sort in the physical world (e.g., the
> diffusion of heat) it is demonstrable that interferences
> close to the source have a greater effect, not a lesser
> effect, than the same interferences close to the output.
> If the attacks on the LOCs north of 20° stopped, the flow
> of goods past 20° could easily be raised by far more than
> 20% and the 20% increase of attack south of 20° would
> nowhere near compensate for this.

> One interesting observation about the NE LOC is that
> the enemy has expended a significant percentage of his
> total imports in executing military defensive operations
> for the NVN heartland. From 1 January 1967 through 19 June
> 1967, he has launched 1062 SAM missiles in Route Package VI.
> A record total of 556 surface-to-air missiles were fired at

US aircraft during the period 1 May through 31 May. This one
month expenditure equates to 2600 metric tons in missile hardware (consumables used in delivering missiles to launch pad
not considered). MIG jet fuel consumption for a one-month
period is estimated to be approximately 7,500 metric tons
(resources expended to accomplish delivery not included).
AAA munitions-firing equates to approximately 18,000 metric
tons per month. Based on the CIA estimate of 5300 metric
tons per day import rate, it is notable that the enemy is
willing to use up to 15% of his total imports (by weight)
in air defense. Most of this tonnage is used in defense of
the industrial/economic structure in Route Packages V and VI.
Even though 83% of all US attack sorties are flown in Route
Packages I-IV, the enemy has not expended an equivalent
amount of air defense consumables to protect this area. It
can be assumed he would, which should add to the probability
of increased losses to AAA/SA-2 south of 20°, if we greatly
reduce attacks north of 20°. 173/

Brown's political point was familiar but had not been stated
quite so precisely in this particular debate. Bombing was regarded by
Brown as an indivisible blue chip to be exchanged in toto for some
reciprocity by the North Vietnamese, a condition that did not seem likely
in the present circumstances. Once stopped, the bombing would be extremely
difficult to resume even if the DRV stepped up its infiltration and its
half of the war generally. Moreover, the timing for such a halt was bad
with the South Vietnamese elections only two months away.

With respect to the loss rates in the various parts of the
country, Brown noted that losses in Route Packages IVA & B had declined
dramatically over the preceding year, even though the DRV was expending
far more resources to combat the sorties. If bombing were suspended
north of 20° we could expect the DRV to redeploy much of its anti-aircraft
resources into the panhandle thereby raising the currently low loss rates
there. Since bombing effectiveness in the northern area was marginally
more productive, the return pure aircraft loss overall would decline by
such a geographical limitation of the air war. 174/

It is not clear what impact this line of analysis had on
McNamara, but since he had previously gone on record in favor of alternative B, and no other new evidence or argumentation appears before the
final decision in mid-July to adopt alternative C, it seems very likely
that Brown's thinking swayed his oral recommendations to the President.
Reinforcing Brown's analysis was the internal U.S. Government rejection

of a Canadian proposal to exchange a bombing halt for a redemilitarization
of the DMZ. The Chiefs adamantly opposed the idea as a totally inequitable
trade-off. We would sacrifice a valuable negotiating blue chip without
commensurate gain (such as a cessation of DRV infiltration). 175/   With
no other promising prospects for a diplomatic break-through, there was
little reason on that score to suspend even a part of the bombing at that
time.

The only other event that might have influenced the Secretary's thinking was his trip to Vietnam July 7-12. With a decision on
the additional ground forces to be sent to Vietnam narrowing down, the
President sent McNamara to Saigon to review the matter with General
Westmoreland and reach agreement on a figure well below the 200,000
Westy had requested in March. As it turned out, the total new troops
in Program #5 were about 25,000. In the briefings the Secretary received
in Saigon, the Ambassador spoke briefly about the need for an effective
interdiction system which he hoped we would find in the barrier. He
reiterated most of the points he had made to Rusk by wire in June. 176/
CINCPAC's briefing on the air war began with the now standard self-
justifications based on denied requests for escalation. The body of
his presentation did contain some interesting new information, however.
For instance, Admiral Sharp confirmed that the increased effort in the NE
quadrant had not been at the expense of sorties elsewhere in North Vietnam
or Laos. The decline in U.S. losses in the Red River valley was attributable in part to the declining effectiveness of North Vietnam's MIG, SA-2,
and AAA defenses. This in turn was explained by better U.S. tactics, and,
most importantly, new weapons and equipment like the WALLEYE guided bomb,
the CBU-24 cluster bomb, the MK-36 Destructor and a much improved ECM
capability. The rest of his presentation was given over to complaints
about the unauthorized targets still on the JCS list and to the familiar
muddled arguments for not stopping the northern bombing because it was
pressuring Ho to behave as we wanted and because in some mysterious
fashion it was interdicting infiltration, actual statistics in the South
to the contrary notwithstanding. 177/

After 7th Air Force commander, General Momyer, had given
a glowing detailed account of the success of the new tactics and weapons
(a 4-fold increase in effectiveness against the NE RR in the previous
year), and the 7th Fleet had described its air operations, CINCPAC summed
up his arguments against any further limitations on the bombing. His
closing point, on which he based recommendations, was that both sides
were fighting both offensive and defensive wars. The DRV had the offensive
initiative in the South but we were on the defensive. However,

The opposite holds for the air war in the north. Here
we hold the initiative. We are conducting a strategic
offensive, forcing the enemy into a defensive posture. He
is forced to react at places and times of our choosing. If

we eliminate the only offensive element of our strategy,
I do not see how we can expect to win. My recommendations
are listed below. You will recognize that they are essentially the same actions proposed by the Joint Chiefs of Staff.

RECOMMENDATIONS:

1. Close the Haiphong Harbor to deep water shipping
by bombing and/or mining.

2. Destroy six basic target systems (electricity,
maritime ports, airfields, transportation, military complexes,
war supporing industry).

3. Conduct integrated attacks against entire target
base, including interdiction in NVN and Laos.

NECESSARY CHANGES AND ADDITIONS TO RT OPERATING RULES

1. Delete Hanoi 10 NM prohibited area.

2. Reduce Hanoi restricted areasto 10 NM.

3. Reduce Haiphong restricted area to 4 NM.

4. Move the northern boundary of the special coastal
armed recce area to include Haiphong area.

5. Authorize armed recce throughout NVN and coastal
waters, (except populated areas, buffer zone, restricted
areas).

6. Mine inland waterways to Chicom buffer zone as
MK-36 destructors become available.

7. Extend Sea Dragon to Chicom buffer zone as forces
become available.

8. Implement now to exploit good weather. 178/

McNamara's time in Vietnam, however, was mostly preoccupied
with settling on the exact figure for troop increases. When he returned
to Washington, he promptly met with the President and with his approval
authorized the Program #5 deployments. He presumably also discussed with
the President a decision on the next phase of the air campaign. There is
no evidence of what he might have recommended at that stage. The decision
was one that would have been made at the White House, so in any case the
responsibility for it could be only partially his. Examination of the
available documents does not reveal just how or when the decision on the

Secretary of Defense proposal was made, but it is clear what the decision was. It was to adopt alternative C--i.e., push onward with the bombing program essentially as it had been, continuing the bit-by-bit expansion of armed reconnaissance and striking a few new fixed targets in each ROLLING THUNDER series, but still holding back from closing the ports and such sensitive targets as the MIG airfields.

The next ROLLING THUNDER series, No. 57, was authorized on 20 July. Sixteen fixed targets were selected, including one air-field, one rail yard, two bridges, and 12 barracks and supply areas, all within the Hanoi and Haiphong circles but not within the forbidden 10-mile inner circle around the center of Hanoi against which Admiral Sharp had sailed. Armed reconnaissance was expanded along 23 road, rail, and waterway segments between the 30-mile and the 10-mile circles around Hanoi. 179/

For the moment at least neither the hawks nor the doves had won their case. The President had decided merely to extend ROLLING THUNDER within the general outlines already established. In effect, the RT 57 was a decision to postpone the issue, insuring that the partisans would continue their fight. As for the President, he would not move decisively until the next year when outside events were heavily forcing his hand and a new Secretary of Defense had entered the debate.

FOOTNOTES

1. CINCPAC msgs. to JCS 142140Z January 1967 (TS).

2. CINCPAC msg. to JCS 182210Z January 1967 (TS-LIMDIS).

3. CINCPAC msg. to JCS and COMUSMACV, Exclusive for General Wheeler and General Westmoreland from Admiral Sharp, 030520Z January 1967 (S-EXDIS-SPECAT).

4. CINCPAC msg. to JCS 252126Z January 1967 (TS-LIMDIS).

5. CIA SC #04442/67, op. cit.

6. Ibid.

7. Ibid.

8. Ibid.

9. Ibid.

10. Ibid.

11. See Task Force paper IV.C.3 for a detailed study of this particular effort.

12. Robert S. McNamara letter to the Honorable Richard B. Russell, United States Senate, 30 January 1967 with attached chronology of ROLLING THUNDER (TS).

13. JCSM-727-66, 22 November 1966, op. cit.

14. COMUSMACV msg. to CINCPAC 00163, 021430 January 1967.

15. CINCPAC msg. to JCS 040403Z January 1967 and JCSM-6-67, 4 January 1967.

16. JCSM-6-67, ibid.

17. State msg. to AmEmbassy, Saigon 118861, 14 January 1966.

18. Embassy Saigon msg. 15822, 17 January 1967.

19. JCSM-25-67, 18 January 1967 (TS).

20. William Bundy Memorandum to Under Secretary Katzenbach, no date ("drafted 21 Jan 67" pencilled in)(TS) with Katzenbach's initialed approval at the bottom.

21. JCS msg. to CINCPAC, and CINCSAC 4708, JCS send, 27 January 1967 (TS).

22. Ibid.

23. Leonard H. Marks, Director USIA, Memorandum for Dean Rusk, Subject:
     Regaining Initiative on Tet Truce, 2 February 1967 (S).

24. "SCENARIO" unsigned, undated, handwritten paper in McNaughton Book
     III, Tab RR.

25. Ibid.

26. "Vietnam, Search for Peace," Department of State, 1967.

27. White House Press Release, February 8, 1967.

28. State msg. 134409, Saigon for Ambassador, London for Ambassador
     and Cooper, February 9, 1967, 7:27 p.m. (TS-NODIS).

29. DIA Intelligence Supplement, "North Vietnamese Resupply Activity
     during Tet Stand-Down," 10 February 1967 (S).

30. New York Times, February 15, 1967.

31. "Vietnam, Search for Peace," op. cit.

32. CINCPAC msg. to JCS 012005Z February 1967 (TS-LIMDIS)

33. JCSM-59-67, 2 February 1967 (TS).

34. Cyrus Vance, Deputy Secretary of Defense, letter to Nicholas deB.
     Katzenbach, Under Secretary of State, 21 February 1967 (TS); with
     a paper on escalation options attached.

35. Ibid., p. 10.

36. Ibid., p. 11.

37. Ibid., pp. 7-8.

38. Embassy Moscow msg. 3568, 19 February 1967 (TS-NODIS).

39. "Comment on DoD Analysis - Courses of Action," W.P. Bundy, 2/21/67 (TS).

40. Ibid.

41. Roger Fisher, "Future Strategy Against North Vietnam," February 21,
     1967 in McNaughton Book III, Tab QQ.

42. Maxwell D. Taylor Memorandum for the President, Subject: "Possible Forms of Negotiation with Hanoi," 20 February 1967 (TS).

43. W. W. Rostow Memorandum for Secretary of State; Secretary of Defense; Chairman, Joint Chiefs of Staff, February 21, 1967 (TS).

44. Targets listed in CM-2194-67, Memorandum for the President from Earle G. Wheeler, Chairman, Joint Chiefs of Staff, 22 March 1967 (TS).

45. Embassy Saigon msg. 20060, 10 March 1967 (S-EXDIS).

46. Lyndon B. Johnson letter to Senator Henry M. Jackson, March 1, 1967, Department of State, Bureau of Public Affairs, Public Information Series, released March 2, 1967.

47. "Remarks of the President at a Joint Session of the Tennessee State Legislature, March 15, 1967," White House Press release, March 15, 1967.

48. Embassy Saigon msg. 20668, 18 March 1967 (C-LIMDIS).

49. COMUSMACV msg. to CINCPAC 09101, 18 March 1967 (TS).

50. "My 'press suggestions' for SecDef in Guam, 3/21/67," in McNaughton Book III, Tab GG.

51. John T. McNaughton, ASD/ISA, Memorandum for the Secretary of Defense, "Two Items on Vietnam," 27 March 1967 (C).

52. CM-2194-67, Chairman of the Joint Chiefs of Staff, General Earle G. Wheeler, Memorandum for the President, Subject: "ROLLING THUNDER 54 Status Report," 23 March 1967 (TS).

53. CINCPAC msg. to CINCPACFLT 080408Z April 1967 (TS).

54. CM-2249-67, Chairman of the Joint Chiefs of Staff, General Earle G. Wheeler, Memorandum for the President, 19 April 1967 (TS).

55. JCSM-218-67, 20 April 1967, Appendix B, "Rationale for Additional Forces," p. 11 (TS-Sensitive).

56. Ibid.

57. Ibid., Appendix A, "Concept of Operations for Southeast Asia with Respect to Vietnam," p. 1.

58. CM-2318-67, Chairman of the Joint Chiefs of Staff, General Earle G. Wheeler, Memorandum to the President, Subject: "The Target System in North Vietnam," 5 May 1967 (TS).

59.   Ibid.

59a. Ibid.

60.   CIA Intelligence Memorandum No. 0651/67, "The Status of North
      Vietnam's Electric Power Industry as of 25 May 1967," 26 May 1967 (S).

61.   For a complete treatment of the issues and debate on the Program #5
      ground force deployments see Task Force paper IV.C.6, "U.S. Ground
      Strategy and Force Deployments: 1965-1967" (TS-Sensitive).

62.   Nicholas deB. Katzenbach, Acting Secretary, Memorandum to Honorable
      John McNaughton, Re: Vietnam, April 24, 1967 (TS-EYES ONLY).

63.   Ibid.

64.   Sherman Kent, Director National Estimates, Memorandum for the
      Honorable Robert S. McNamara, 13 April 1967 with CIA, Office of
      National Estimates, Memorandum TS 186015, Subject: "Communist
      Policy and the Next Phase in Vietnam," 12 April 1967 (TS) attached.

65.   Ibid., p. 18.

66.   R. W. Komer Memorandum, Subject: "Thoughts on Future Strategy in
      Vietnam," 24 April 1967 (S-EYES ONLY).

67.   Ibid.

68.   "Notes on Discussions with the President," 27 April 1967 (TS), no
      indication of who took the notes.

69.   Ibid.

70.   Memorandum to the Under Secretary, Subject: "Thoughts on Strategy
      in Vietnam," May 1, 1967 (TS); the paper is not signed or is
      authorship otherwise indicated except by the following final note:
      "I am sending you copies of this, and retaining one in a totally
      private file. This memorandum has been seen and discussed with
      no one except the typist. Copies 1 through 6 - The Under Secretary,
      Copy 7 - Bundy file."

71.   Ibid.

72.   Ibid.

73.   Ibid.

74.   SNIE-11-11-67, "Soviet Attitudes and Intentions Toward the Vietnam
      War," 4 May 1967 (S).

75. McGeorge Bundy letter to President Lyndon B. Johnson, no date ("rec'd 5-4-67, 12n" in pencil) with attached "Memorandum on Vietnam Policy."

76. Ibid.

77. Ibid.

78. Ibid.

79. CM-2318-67, 5 May 1967, op. cit.

80. Roger Fisher letter to President Johnson, May 5, 1967.

81. Draft Memorandum for the President, 5 May 1967, "Proposed Bombing Program Against North Vietnam," (TS).

82. Ibid.

83. Ibid.

84. Ibid.

85. Ibid.

86. Referred to in McGeorge Bundy Memorandum to Secretary McNamara, May 11, 1967.

87. W. W. Rostow Memorandum for Secretaries Rusk, Vance, Katzenbach, McNaughton and Bundy, and CIA Director Helms, Subject: "U.S. Strategy in Viet Nam," May 6, 1967 (TS-EYES ONLY ADDRESSEE).

88. Ibid.

89. Ibid.

90. Ibid.

91. Ibid.

92. WPBundy Memorandum, "Bombing Strategy Options for the Rest of 1967," (revised draft), May 8, 1967 (TS).

·93. Ibid.

94. Ibid.

95. Ibid.

96. CIA, "The Effect of the Bombing on North Vietnamese Thinking,"
May 1967 (S).

97. CIA Intelligence Memorandum No. 0642/67, "The Current State of
Morale in North Vietnam," 12 May 1967 (S).

98. CIA Intelligence Memorandum No. 0643/67, "Bomb Damage Inflicted
on North Vietnam Through April 1967," 12 May 1967 (S).

99. <u>Ibid</u>.

100. Draft Memorandum for the President, Subject: "Future Actions in
Vietnam," 19 May 1967"(first rough draft; data and estimates have
<u>not</u> been checked.)" (TS-SENSITIVE).

101. <u>Ibid</u>.

102. <u>Ibid</u>.

103. <u>Ibid</u>.

104. <u>Ibid</u>.

105. <u>Ibid</u>.

106. <u>Ibid</u>.

107. <u>Ibid</u>.

108. <u>Ibid</u>.

109. <u>Ibid</u>.

110. <u>Ibid</u>., emphasis in original.

111. <u>Ibid</u>.

112. <u>Ibid</u>.

113. Robert S. McNamara Memorandum for the President, 20 May 1967, commenting on Sen. Brooke's proposals for negotiations between the
GVN and the VC and for a reconciliation program. McNamara notes
that, "Brook's proposals are almost identical to those which I
suggested in the Draft Memorandum submitted to you yesterday." (TS).

114. JCSM 286-67, 20 May 1967; JCSM 288-67, 20 May 1967 (TS-SENSITIVE).

115. Robert S. McNamara Memorandum for the President, 20 May 1967 transmitting JCSM-286-67 (TS).

116. Ibid.

117. CM-2377-67, Memorandum for the SecDef, "Alternative Courses of Action," 24 May 1967.

118. Ibid.

119. CM-2381-67, 29 May 1967 (TS-SENSITIVE).

120. JCSM-307-67, 1 June 1967 (TS-SENSITIVE).

121. Ibid.

122. Ibid.

123. Ibid.

124. Ibid.

125. CIA SC No. 0646/67, 23 May 1967, "Reactions to Various US Courses of Action."

126. Ibid.

127. Ibid.

128. Ibid.

129. W. P. Bundy Memorandum, "Comments on DOD First Draft of 19 May," May 30, 1967 (TS); forwarded to Katzenbach, W. Rostow, Vance, Helms, and McNaughton on June 2, 1967.

130. Ibid.

131. Ibid.

132. Ibid.

133. Ibid.

134. Nicholas deB. Katzenbach Memorandum for Cyrus R. Vance, Subject: "Preliminary Comments on the DOD Draft of May 19, June 8, 1967 (S-EYES ONLY).

135. Ibid.

136. Memorandum for the CJCS, DCI, SecNav, and SecAF, 20 May 1967.

137. Ibid.

138. Ibid.

139. Letter from Richard Helms, Director of CIA to SecDef, 1 June 1967, forwarding Memorandum, "Evaluation of Alternative Programs for Bombing North Vietnam," TS-196752/67 (TS).

140. Ibid.

141. Ibid.

142. Ibid.

143. Ibid.

144. JCSM 312-67, Memorandum for the SecDef, 2 June 1967 (TS).

145. Ibid.

146. Ibid.

147. Ibid.

148. Memorandum for the SecDef from the SecNav, "Alternative Bombing Programs in North Vietnam," 2 June 1967 (TS)

149. Ibid.

150. Ibid.

151. Memorandum for the SecDef, "Possible Courses of Action in Southeast Asia," 3 June 1967 (TS).

152. Ibid.

153. Ibid.

154. Harold Brown, Secretary of the Air Force, Memorandum for the Secretary of Defense, June 9, 1967 (TS).

155. CINCPAC msg. to JCS 290506Z May 1967 (TS).

156. Unsigned outline, dated "6/8/67" in pencil and preserved in McNaughton Book XIII, Tab B (S-EYES ONLY).

157. Untitled, unsigned outline in McNaughton Book XIII, Tab B dated 6/8/67 in pen (TS-EYES ONLY, "This paper to be read by McNaughton ONLY.").

158. Ibid.

159. Ibid.

160. Draft Memorandum for the President, Subject: "Alternative
     Military Actions against North Vietnam," 6/12/67 (TS-SENSITIVE).

161. Ibid.

162. Ibid.

163. Ibid.

164. Ibid.

165. See W.P.Bundy note for Vance, et. al., 12 June 1967 (S-EYES ONLY).

166. W. P. Bundy Memorandum for the Secretary (of State), Subject:
     "First Full Interview with Radvanyi," June 1, 1967 (TS-SENSITIVE).

167. State Department INR Memorandum to the Secretary, Subject: "Prospects
     for Vietnam Negotiations in Next Three Months," June 15, 1967 (TS-NODIS).

168. Embassy Saigon msg. 28293, Eyes Only for the Secretary from Bunker,
     17 June 1967 (TS-NODIS).

169. Ibid.

170. CINCPAC msg. to JCS 210430Z June 1967 (TS-LIMDIS).

171. Ibid.

172. Secretary of the Air Force, Harold Brown, Memorandum for the
     Secretary of Defense, July 3, 1967 (TS).

173. Ibid.

174. Ibid.

175. JCSM-382-67, 5 July 1967 (TS).

176. "Briefings Given the Secretary of Defense, Saigon, South Vietnam,
     July 7 and 8, 1967," abridged version prepared by OASD/SA,
     July 22, 1967 (TS), pp. 2-5, 12-16.

177. Ibid., pp. 129-134.

178. Ibid., p. 246.

179. JCS Fact Sheet, "ROLLING THUNDER 57," 10 August 1967.

V. THE LONG ROAD TO DE-
ESCALATION – AUG - DEC 1967

V.   THE LONG ROAD TO DE-ESCALATION -- AUGUST-DECEMBER 1967

After the decision on ROLLING THUNDER 57, the debate on the air
war against North Vietnam, particularly the public debate, entered a
last long phase of increasing acrimony on both sides. As he had been
throughout the war, President Johnson was once again caught in the
crossfire of his critics of the right and the left. The open-season
on Presidential war policy began in August with the high intensity
Senate Preparedness Subcommittee hearings where Senator Stennis and
his colleagues fired the first shots. In September, the embattled
President tried again for peace, capping his secret efforts with a
new public offer to Hanoi in a speech in San Antonio. The attempt
was unavailing and, under pressure from the military and the hawkish
elements of public and Congressional opinion, the President authorized
a selected intensification of the air war. The doves were not long
in responding. In October they staged a massive demonstration and
march on the Pentagon to oppose the war, there confronting specially
alerted troops in battle gear. A month later, Senator McCarthy announced
himself as a peace candidate for the Presidency to oppose Lyndon Johnson
within his own party. By Christmas, however, the issue had subsided a
bit. Ambassador Bunker and General Westmoreland had both returned home
and spoken in public to defend the Administration's conduct of the war,
and reports from the field showed a cautious optimism. The stage was
thus set for the dramatic Viet Cong Tet offensive in January of the
new year, an assault that would have a traumatic impact on official
Washington and set in motion a re-evaluation of the whole American policy.

   A. Senator Stennis Forces an Escalation

      1. The Addendum to ROLLING THUNDER

            Sometime after his return from Vietnam in late July,
Secretary McNamara was informed by Senator Stennis that the Preparedness Subcommittee of the Senate Armed Services Committee intended to
conduct extensive hearings in August into the conduct of the air war
against North Vietnam. In addition to their intention to call the
Secretary, they also indicated that they would hear from all the top
military leaders involved in the ROLLING THUNDER program including
USCINCPAC, Admiral Sharp. The subcommittee had unquestionably set
out to defeat Mr. McNamara. Its members, Senators Stennis, Symington,
Jackson, Cannon, Byrd, Smith, Thurmond, and Miller, were known for
their hard-line views and military sympathies. They were defenders
of "airpower" and had often aligned themselves with the "professional
military experts" against what they considered "unskilled civilian
amateurs." They viewed the restraints on bombing as irrational, the
shackling of a major instrument which could help win victory. With

Vietnam blown up into a major war, with more than half a million U.S. troops and a cost of more than $2 billion a month, and with no clear end in sight, their patience with a restrained bombing program was beginning to wear thin. But more was involved than a disagreement over the conduct of the war. Some passionately held convictions had been belittled, and some members of the subcommittee were on the warpath. As the subcommittee subsequently wrote in the introduction to its report, explaining the reasons for the inquiry:

> Earlier this year many statements appeared in the press which were calculated to belittle the effectiveness of the air campaign over North Vietnam. Many of these statements alleged, or at least implied, that all military targets of significance had been destroyed, that the air campaign had been conducted as effectively as possible, and that continuation of the air campaign was pointless and useless--possibly even prolonging the war itself. At the same time reports were being circulated that serious consideration was being given in high places to a cessation of the air campaign over North Vietnam, or a substantial curtailment of it. Many of these reports were attributed to unnamed high Government officials.
>
> In view of the importance of the air campaign, on June 28, 1967, the subcommittee announced it would conduct an extensive inquiry into the conduct and effectiveness of the bombing campaign over North Vietnam. 1/

In July the President had decided against both an escalatory and a de-escalatory option in favor of continuing the prevailing level and intensity of bombing. However, the prospect of having his bombing policy submitted to the harsh scrutiny of the Stennis committee, taking testimony from such unhappy military men as Admiral Sharp, must have forced a recalculation on the President. It is surely no coincidence that on August 9, the very day the Stennis hearings opened, an addendum to ROLLING THUNDER 57 was issued authorizing an additional sixteen fixed targets and an expansion of armed reconnaissance. Significantly, six of the targets were within the sacred 10-mile Hanoi inner circle. They included the thermal power plant, 3 rail yards, and 2 bridges. Nine targets were located on the northeast rail line in the China buffer zone; the closest one 8 miles from the border, and consisted of 4 bridges and 5 rail yards/sidings; the tenth was a naval base, also within the China buffer zone. Armed reconnaissance was authorized along 8 road, rail, and waterway segments between the 10-mile and a 4-mile circle around Haiphong, and attacks were permitted against railroad rolling stock within the China buffer zone up to within 8 miles of the border. 2/ But the power of Congress was not to be denied. Where the military alone had tried unsuccessfully for so long to erode the Hanoi/Haiphong sanctuaries, the pressure implicit in the impending hearings, where military men would be asked to speak their minds to a friendly audience, was enough to succeed -- at least for the moment.

Attacks against the newly authorized targets began
promptly and continued through the two-week period of the Stennis
hearings. On August 11 the Paul Doumer Rail and Highway Bridge, the
principle river crossing in the direction of Haiphong located very
near the center of Hanoi, was struck for the first time and two of
its spans were dropped. Other important Hanoi targets were also struck
on the 11th and 12th. The intensity of the strikes continued to mount,
and on August 20, 209 sorties were launched, the highest number to date
in the war. During that day and the succeeding two, heavy attacks continued against the Hanoi targets and within the China buffer zone. On
the 21st in connection with these attacks a long feared danger of the
northern air war became reality. Two U.S. planes strayed over the Chinese
border and were shot down by Chinese MIGs. On August 19, at McNamara's
direction, the JCS instructed CINCPAC to suspend operations within the
ten mile Hanoi perimeter from August 24 to September 4. 3/ The Stennis
hearings were ending and a particularly delicate set of contacts with
North Vietnam were under way in Paris (see below). The suspension was
designed both to avoid provocation and to manifest restraint.

2. The Stennis Hearings

Meanwhile in Washington, the Stennis hearings opened on
August 9 with Admiral U. S. Grant Sharp, USCINCPAC, as the first witness.
In the following two weeks the subcommittee heard testimony from the entire
senior echelon of U.S. military leaders involved in the air war, including
the Joint Chiefs, CINCPAC, CINCPACFLT, CINCPACAF, and the commander and
former deputy commander of the 7th Air Force in Saigon. The final witness
on August 25 was Secretary McNamara who found himself pitted against the
military men who had preceded him by the hostile members of the subcommittee as he sought to deflate the claims for U.S. air power. The
hearings, released by the subcommittee only days after the testimony
was completed, and given extensive treatment by the media, exposed to
public view the serious divergence of views between McNamara and the
country's professional military leaders. The subcommittee's summary
report, which sided with the military and sharply criticized McNamara's
reasoning, forced the Administration into an awkward position. 4/   Ultimately, the President felt compelled to overrule McNamara's logic in his
own version of the matter. Once again the President was caught unhappily
in the middle satisfying neither his critics of the right nor the left.

The subcommittee heard first from the military leaders
involved in the air war. It was told that the air war in the North
was an important and indispensable part of the U.S. strategy for fighting
the war in the South. It was told that the bombing had inflicted extensive destruction and disruption on NVN, holding down the infiltration of
men and supplies, restricting the level of forces that could be sustained
in the South and reducing the ability of those forces to mount major

sustained combat operations, thus resulting in fewer U.S. casualties.
It was told that without the bombing, NVN could have doubled its forces
in the South, requiring as many as 800,000 additional U.S. troops at a
cost of $75 billion more just to hold our own. It was told that without
the bombing NVN could have freed 500,000 people who were at work maintaining and repairing the LOCs in the North for additional support of
the insurgency in the South. It was told that a cessation of the bombing
now would be "a disaster," resulting in increased U.S. losses and an
indefinite extension of the war.

The subcommittee was also told that the bombing had been
much less effective than it might have been -- and could still be --
if civilian leaders heeded military advice and lifted the overly restrictive controls which had been imposed on the campaign. The slow tempo of
the bombing; its concentration for so long well south of the vital Hanoi/
Haiphong areas, leaving the important targets untouched; the existence of
sanctuaries; the failure to close or neutralize the port of Haiphong--
these and other limitations prevented the bombing from achieving greater
results. The "doctrine of gradualism" and the long delays in approving
targets of real significance, moreover, gave NVN time to build up formidable air defenses, contributing to U.S. aircraft and pilot losses, and
enabled NVN to prepare for the anticipated destruction of its facilities
(such as POL) by building up reserve stocks and dispersing them.

When Secretary McNamara appeared before the subcommittee
on August 25, he took issue with most of these views. He defended the
bombing campaign as one which was carefully tailored to our limited
purposes in Southeast Asia and which was therefore aimed at selected
targets of strictly military significance, primarily the routes of
infiltration. As he restated the objectives which the bombing was intended
to serve:

Our primary objective was to reduce the flow and/or to
increase the cost of the continued infiltration of men and
supplies from North to South Vietnam.

It was also anticipated that these air operations would
raise the morale of the South Vietnamese people who, at the
time the bombing started, were under severe military pressure.

Finally, we hoped to make clear to the North Vietnamese
leadership that so long as they continued their aggression
against the South they would have to pay a price in the North.

The bombing of North Vietnam has always been considered
a supplement to and not a substitute for an effective counterinsurgency land and air campaign in South Vietnam.

These were our objectives when our bombing program
was initiated in February 1965. They remain our objectives
today. 5/

Weighed against these objectives, the bombing campaign
had been successful:

It was initiated at a time when the South Vietnamese
were in fear of a military defeat. There can be no question
that the bombing raised and sustained the morale of the
South Vietnamese at that time. It should be equally clear
to the North Vietnamese that they have paid and will
continue to pay a high price for their continued aggression.
We have also made the infiltration of men and supplies from
North Vietnam to South Vietnam increasingly difficult and
costly. 6/

With respect to infiltration, the Secretary said, military leaders had never anticipated that complete interdiction was
possible. He cited the nature of combat in SVN, without "established
battle lines" and continuous large-scale fighting, which did not
require a steady stream of logistical support and which reduced the
amount needed. Intelligence estimated that VC/NVA forces in SVN
required only 15 tons a day brought in from outside, "but even if the
quantity were five times that amount it could be transported by only
a few trucks." By comparison with that amount, the capacity of the
transportation network was very large:

North Vietnam's ability to continue its aggression
against the South thus depends upon imports of war-supporting
material and their transhipment to the South. Unfortunately
for the chances of effective interdiction, this simple
agricultural economy has a highly diversified transportation
system consisting of rails and roads and waterways. The
North Vietnamese use barges and sampans, trucks and foot
power, and even bicycles capable of carrying 500-pound
loads to move goods over this network. The capacity of
this system is very large -- the volume of traffic it is
now required to carry, in relation to its capacity, is very
small....Under these highly unfavorable circumstances, I
think that our military forces have done a superb job in
making continued infiltration more difficult and expensive. 7/

The Secretary defended the targeting decisions which had
been made in carrying out the program, and the "target-by-target analysis"
which balanced the military importance of the target against the cost
in U.S. lives and the risks of expanding the war. He argued that the
target selection had not inhibited the use of airpower against targets
of military significance. The target list in current use by the JCS

contained 427 targets, of which only 359 had been recommended by the Chiefs. Of the latter, strikes had been authorized against 302, or 85 percent. Of the 57 recommended by the JCS but not yet authorized, 7 were recognized by the JCS themselves as of little value to NVN's war effort, 9 were petroleum facilities holding less than 6 percent of NVN's remaining storage capacity, 25 were lesser targets in populated, heavily defended areas, 4 were more signficant targets in such areas, 3 were ports, 4 were airfields, and 5 were in the China buffer zone. Some of these targets did not warrant the loss of American lives; others did not justify the risk of direct confrontation with the Chinese or the Soviets; still others would be considered for authorization as they were found to be of military importance as compared with the potential costs and risks. 8/

The Secretary argued that those who criticized the limited nature of the bombing campaign actually sought to reorient it toward different -- and unrealizable objectives:

Those who criticize our present bombing policy do so, in my opinion, because they believe that air attack against the North can be utilized to achieve quite different objectives. These critics appear to argue that our airpower can win the war in the South either by breaking the will of the North or by cutting off the war-supporting supplies needed in the south. In essence, this approach would seek to use the air attack against the North not as a supplement to, but as a substitute for the arduous ground war that we and our allies are waging in the South. 9/

First, as to breaking the will of the North, neither the nature of NVN's economy nor the psychology of its people or its leaders suggested that this could be accomplished by a more intensive bombing campaign. For one thing, it was difficult to apply pressure against the regime through bombing the economy:

...the economy of North Vietnam is agrarian and simple. Its people are accustomed to few of the modern comforts and conveniences that most of us in the Western World take for granted. They are not dependent on the continued functioning of great cities for their welfare. They can be fed at something approaching the standard to which they are accustomed without reliance on truck or rail transportation or on food processing facilities. Our air attack has rendered inoperative about 85 percent of the country's electric generating capacity, but it is important to note that the Pepco plant in Alexandria, Va., generates five times the power produced by all of

North Vietnam's power plants before the bombing. It
appears that sufficient electricity for war-related
activities and for essential services can be provided
by the some 2,000 diesel-driven generating sets which
are in operation. 10/

Second, the people were inured to hardship and by all the evidence
supported the government:

> ...the people of North Vietnam are accustomed to
> discipline and are no strangers to deprivation and
> death. Available information indicates that, despite
> some war weariness, they remain willing to endure hard-
> ship and they continue to respond to the political
> direction of the Hanoi regime. There is little reason
> to believe that any level of conventional air or naval
> action short of sustained and systematic bombing of
> the population centers will deprive the North Vietnamese
> of their willingness to continue to support their
> government's efforts. 11/

Third, NVN's leaders were hard to crack, at least so long as their cause
in the South was hopeful:

> There is nothing in the past reaction of the North
> Vietnamese leaders that would provide any confidence that
> they can be bombed to the negotiating table. Their regard
> for the comfort and even the lives of the people they
> control does not seem to be sufficiently high to lead them
> to bargain for settlement in order to stop a heightened
> level of attack.

> The course of the conflict on the ground in the south,
> rather than the scale of air attack in the north appears
> to be the determining factor in North Vietnam's willingness
> to continue. 12/

> The second alternative aim might be to stop the flow of
supplies to the South, either through an expanded campaign against the
supply routes within NVN or by closing sea and land importation routes
to NVN, or both. But it was doubtful whether heavier bombing of the
LOCs could choke off the required flow:

> ...the capacity of the lines of communication and of
> the outside sources of supply so far exceeds the minimal
> flow necessary to support the present level of North

Vietnamese military effort in South Vietnam that the
enemy operations in the south cannot, on the basis of
any reports I have seen, be stopped by air bombardment--
short, that is, of the virtual annihilation of North
Vietnam and its people. 13/

Nor could bombing the ports and mining the harbors stop the infiltration
of supplies into SVN. The total tonnage required in SVN (15 tons a
day) could be quintupled and would still be dwarfed by NVN's actual
imports of about 5800 tons a day and its even greater import capacity
of about 14,000 tons a day. Even if Haiphong and the other ports were
closed -- "and on the unrealistic assumption that closing the ports would
eliminate seaborne imports" -- NVN could still import over 8400 tons a
day by rail, road, and waterway. Even if the latter amount could be
further cut by 50 percent through air attacks, NVN could still maintain
70 percent of its current imports, only a fraction of which -- 550 tons per
day -- need be taken up with military equipment. In fact, however,
eliminating Haiphong and the other ports would not eliminate seaborne
imports. The POL experience had shown that NVN could revert to lightering
and over-the-beach operations for unloading ocean freighters, and it
could also make greater use of the LOCs from China, and still manage
quite well.

Accordingly, the Secretary urged that the limited objectives and the restrained nature of the bombing campaign be maintained as
is:

A selective, carefully targeted bombing campaign, such
as we are presently conducting, can be directed toward
reasonable and realizable goals. This discriminating use
of air power can and does render the infiltration of men and
supplies more difficult and more costly. At the same time,
it demonstrates to both South and North Vietnam our resolve
to see that aggression does not succeed. A less discriminating
bombing campaign against North Vietnam would, in my opinion,
do no more. We have no reason to believe that it would break
the will of the North Vietnamese people or sway the purpose
of their leaders. If it does not lead to such a change of
mind, bombing the North at any level of intensity would not
meet our objective. We would still have to prove by ground
operations in the South that Hanoi's aggression could not
succeed. Nor would a decision to close /the ports7, by
whatever means, prevent the movement in and through North
Vietnam of the essentials to continue their present level
of military activity in South Vietnam.

On the other side of the equation, our report to a less
selective campaign of air attack against the North would

involve risks which at present I regard as too high to
accept for this dubious prospect of successful results. 14/

The Secretary spent the day on the witness stand, answering
questions, rebutting charges, and debating the issues. His use of facts
and figures and reasoned arguments was one of his masterful performances,
but in the end he was not persuasive. The subcommittee issued a report
on 31 August which castigated the Administration's conduct of the bombing
campaign, deferred to the authority of the professional military judgments
it had heard, accepted virtually all the military criticisms of the program,
and advocated a switch-over to escalating "pressure" concepts.

The Secretary had emphasized the inability of the bombing
to accomplish much more, given the nature of U.S. objectives and of the
difficult challenged presented by the overall military situation. The
subcommittee disagreed:

> That the air campaign has not achieved its objectives
> to a greater extent cannot be attributed to inability or
> impotence of airpower. It attests, rather, to the frag-
> mentation of our air might by overly restrictive controls,
> limitations, and the doctrine of 'gradualism' placed on
> our aviation forces which prevented them from waging the
> air campaign in the manner and according to the timetable
> which was best calculated to achieve maximum results. 15/

The Secretary had said there was no evidence of any kind to indicate
that an accelerated campaign would have reduced casualties in the South;
the subcommittee reported that the overwhelming weight of the testimony
by military experts was to the contrary. The Secretary had minimized
the importance of the 57 recommended targets which had not yet been
approved, and implied that few if any important military targets remained
unstruck; CINCPAC and the Chiefs said the 57 included many "lucrative"
targets. The Secretary had discounted the value of closing Haiphong;
all of the military witnesses said that this was feasible and necessary
and would have a substantial impact on the war in the South. In all
of these matters the subcommittee did not believe that the Secretary's
position was valid and felt that the military view was sounder and should
prevail:

> In our hearings we found a sharp difference of opinion
> between the civilian authority and the top-level military
> witnesses who appeared before the subcommittee over how
> and when our airpower should be employed against North Viet-
> nam. In that difference we believe we also found the roots
> of the persistent deterioration of public confidence in
> our airpower, because the plain facts as they unfolded in
> the testimony demonstrated clearly that civilian authority
> consistently overruled the unanimous recommendations of

of military commanders and the Joint Chiefs of Staff for
a systematic, timely, and hard-hitting integrated air
campaign against the vital North Vietnam targets. Instead,
and for policy reasons, we have employed military aviation
in a carefully controlled, restricted, and graduated build-
up of bombing pressure which discounted the professional
judgment of our best military experts and substituted
civilian judgment in the details of target selection and
the timing of strikes. We shackled the true potential
of airpower and permitted the buildup of what has become
the world's most formidable antiaircraft defenses....

It is not our intention to point a finger or to second
guess those who determined this policy. But, the cold fact
is that this policy has not done the job and it has been
contrary to the best military judgment. What is needed
now is the hard decision to do whatever is necessary,
take the risks that have to be taken, and apply the force
that is required to see the job through....

As between these diametrically opposed views /of the
SecDef and the military experts/ and in view of the unsatisfactory progress of the war, logic and prudence requires
that the decision be with the unanimous weight of professional
military judgment....

It is high time, we believe, to allow the military
voice to be heard in connection with the tactical details
of military operations. 16/

3. The Fallout

This bombing controversy simmered on for the next few
months and when a major secret peace attempt associated with the
San Antonio formula failed, the President authorized most of the 57
unstruck targets the JCS had recommended and which the Stennis report
had criticized the Administration for failing to hit. In addition,
the Chairman of the JCS was thereafter asked to attend the Tuesday
policy luncheon at the White House as a regular participant.

The Stennis hearings also created considerable confusion
and controversy within the Pentagon over the target classification and
recommendation system. The Senators had been at pains to try to establish whether targets recommended by the military were being authorized
and struck or conversely to what extent the military was being ignored.

In trying to respond to the question McNamara discovered a great deal
of fluidity in the number of targets on JCS lists over time, and in
the priority or status assigned to them. He therefore set out to
reconcile the discrepancies. The effort unearthed a highly complex
system of classification that began with the military commands in the
Pacific and extended through the Joint Staff to his own office. Part
of the problem lay with the changing damage assessments and another
part with differing categories at different echelons. To untangle
the process, reconcile past discrepancies and establish a common basis
for classification and recommendation, McNamara, Warnke, the ISA staff
and the Joint Staff spent long hours in September and October in highly
detailed target by target analysis and evaluation. After much wrangling
they did achieve agreement on a procedure and set of rules that made it
possible for everyone to work with the same data and understanding of
the target system. The procedure they set up and the one that operated
through the fall and winter until the March 31 partial suspension was
described in a memo from Warnke to incoming Secretary Clark Clifford on
March 5, 1968:

> Twice a month the Joint Staff has been revising the
> Rolling Thunder Target List for the bombing of North Vietnam.
> The revisions are forwarded to my office and reconciled
> with the prior list. This reconciliation summary is then
> forwarded to your office....
>
> Every Tuesday and Friday the Joint Staff has been
> sending me a current list of the authorized targets on the
> target list which have not been struck or restruck since
> returning to a recommended status. After our review, this
> list also is sent to your office....
>
> In the normal course of events, new recommendations by
> the Chairman of the Joint Chiefs of Staff for targets lying
> within the 10 and 4 mile prohibited circles around Hanoi and
> Haiphong, respectively, or in the Chinese Buffer Zone have
> been submitted both to the Secretary of Defense's office
> and to my office in ISA. ISA would then ensure that the
> State Department had sufficient information to make its
> recommendation on the new proposal. ISA also submitted
> its evaluation of the proposal to your office. On occasions
> the Chairman would hand-carry the new bombing proposals
> directly to the Secretary of Defense for his approval.
> Under those circumstances, the Secretary, if he were not
> thoroughly familiar with the substance of the proposal,
> would call ISA for an evaluation. State Department and
> White House approval also were required before the Chairman's
> office could authorize the new strikes. 17/

The Stennis report also raised a furor by exposing the policy rift within the Administration. In an attempt to dampen its effect the President called an unscheduled news conference on September 1 to deny differences among his advisors and to generally overrule his Secretary of Defense on the bombing. More stinging for McNamara, however, than this oral repudiation must have been the subsequent escalatory decisions against his advice. On September 10, for instance, North Vietnam's third port at Cam Pha, a target he had specifically counseled against in his testimony was struck for the first time. McNamara's year-end resignation seems in retrospect the only logical course for someone who found himself so far out of line with the direction of Administration policy.

B.   The San Antonio Formula

1.   Peace Feelers

In the midst of all this pressure on the President to raise the ante in the bombing, a countervailing opportunity for contact with the DRV on terms for peace developed in Paris. In mid-August a channel to the North Vietnamese through U.S. and French academics apparently opened up in Paris. Eager as always to test whether Hanoi had softened its position, the U.S. picked up the opportunity. As already noted, on 19 August a cessation of the attacks in the 10-mile Hanoi perimeter was ordered for a ten day period beginning on August 24. Sometime thereafter, what was regarded as a conciliatory proposal, embodying the language of the subsequent San Antonio speech, was apparently transmitted to the North Vietnamese. The unfortunate coincidence of heavy bombing attacks on Hanoi on August 21-23, just prior to the transmission of the message, coupled with the fact that the Hanoi suspension was to be of limited duration must have left the DRV leadership with the strong impression they were being squeezed by Johnsonian pressure tactics and presented with an ultimatum. Apparently, no reply from Hanoi had arrived by the 1st of September because the Hanoi suspension was extended for 72-hours, and then on 7 September the suspension was impatiently extended again pending a reply from North Vietnam. When the reply finally came, it was an emphatic rejection of the U.S. proposal. The U.S. sought to clarify its position and elicit some positive reaction from the Hanoi leadership but to no avail. The contacts in Paris apparently continued throughout September since the bombing restraint around Hanoi was not relaxed, but Hanoi maintained its charge that the circumstances in which the message was communicated placed it in the context of an ultimatum. 18/

2.   The President's Speech and Hanoi's Reaction

With Hanoi complaining that the raids deflected from Hanoi were merely being retargeted against Haiphong, Cam Pha and other parts of the North and that the U.S. was escalating not de-escalating the air war, the President decided to make a dramatic public attempt to overcome the communications barrier between the two capitals. In San Antonio, on September 29, the President delivered a long impassioned plea for reason in Hanoi. The central function of the speech was to repeat publicly the language of the negotiations proposal that had been transmitted in August. The President led up to it in melodramatic fashion:

> "'Why not negotiate now?' so many ask me. The answer is that we and our South Vietnamese allies are wholly prepared to negotiate tonight.

> "I am ready to talk with Ho Chi Minh, and other chiefs of state concerned, tomorrow.

> "I am ready to have Secretary Rusk meet with their Foreign Minister tomorrow.

> "I am ready to send a trusted representative of America to any spot on this earth to talk in public or private with a spokesman of Hanoi." 19/

Then he stated the U.S. terms for a bombing halt in their mildest form to date:

> As we have told Hanoi time and time and time again, the heart of the matter is this: The United States is willing to stop all aerial and naval bombardment of North Vietnam when this will lead promptly to productive discussions. We, of course, assume that while discussions proceed, North Vietnam would not take advantage of this bombing cessation or limitation. 20/

After the speech, the contacts in Paris presumably continued in an effort to illicit a positive response from Hanoi, but, in spite of the continued restraint around Hanoi, none was apparently forthcoming. The North Vietnamese objections to the proposal had shifted it seems from the circumstances of its delivery to the substance of the proposal itself. Instead of their earlier complaints about pressures and ultimata, they now resisted the "conditions" of the San Antonio formula -- i.e. the U.S. desire for advance assurance that "no advantage" would be taken if the bombing were halted. Continued U.S. probing for a response apparently reinforced the impression of "conditions." In any case, on October 3, the San Antonio formulation was emphatically rejected in the North Vietnamese party newspaper, Nham Dan, as a "faked desire for peace" and "sheer deception." This was apparently confirmed through the Paris channel in mid-October. In his press conference on October 12, Secretary Rusk as much as said so when, after quoting the President's offer, he stated:

A rejection, or a refusal even to discuss such a formula for peace, requires that we face some sober conclusions.
It would mean that Hanoi has not abandoned its effort to
seize South Vietnam by force. It would give reality and
credibility to captured documents which describe a 'fight
and negotiate' strategy by Vietcong and the North Vietnamese
forces. It would reflect a view in Hanoi that they can
gamble upon the character of the American people and of
our allies in the Pacific. 22/

Final confirmation that the attempt to find a common ground on which to
begin negotiations had failed came in an article by the Communist
journalist Wilfred Burchette on October 20. Reporting from Hanoi the
views of Pham Van Dong, Burchette stated that, "There is no possibility
of any talks or even contacts between Hanoi and the U.S. government
unless the bombardment and other acts of war against North Vietnam are
definitively halted." 23/   But the American Administration had already
taken a series of escalatory decisions under pressure from the military
and the Stennis committee.

3. More Targets

The September-long restriction against striking targets
within the ten mile Hanoi perimeter was imposed on the military command
with no explanation of its purpose since apparently every effort was
being made to maintain the security of the contacts in Paris. Thus, not
surprisingly, CINCPAC complained about the limitation and regularly
sought to have it lifted throughout the month. On September 11, General
McConnell forwarded a request to the Secretary for a restrike of the
Hanoi thermal power plant. 24/   On September 21, CINCPAC again reiterated
his urgent request that the Hanoi ban be lifted. 25/   The day before he
had also requested authority to strike the Phuc Yen air field. 26/   In
sending his endorsement of these requests to McNamara, the acting Chairman,
General Johnson, noted that there were fifteen lucrative targets within
the prohibited Hanoi area including critical rail and highway bridges and
the Hanoi power plant, the latter reportedly back to 50% of capability. 27/
McNamara replied tersely and simply, in his own hand, "The Hanoi restriction remains in effect so this strike has not been approved." 28/   The
requested authorization to hit Phuc Yen air field was not a strike within
the Hanoi ten mile zone but was militarily important because Phuc Yen
was the largest remaining unstruck MIG field and a center of much of
North Vietnam's air defense control. On September 26, it was approved
for strike, but before one could be launched the authorization was rescinded on September 29, no doubt because of concern about upsetting the
delicate Paris contacts. 29/

To these continuing pressures on the President from the JCS
to remove the Hanoi restrictions were added at the end of September an

additional request from General Westmoreland bearing on the effort
against North Vietnam. The enemy buildup in the DMZ area had become
serious and to counter it an increasing number of B-52 strikes were
being employed. Eventually this confrontation at the DMZ would involve
the heavy artillery exchanges of the fall of 1967 and culminate in
the protracted seige of Khe Sanh. For the moment, however, Westmoreland
was seeking as a part of his DMZ reinforcement an augmentation in the
monthly B-52 sortie authorization. His request was outlined by the Chiefs
in a memo to Mr. Nitze on September 28. They indicated a capability to
raise the sorties to 900 per month immediately and were studying the
problem of raising them to 1200 as requested by Westy. The use of
2,000 lb. bombs was feasible and the Chiefs recommended it depending on
their availability. 30/   McNamara gave his OK to the increase in a memo
to the President on October 4, but indicated that the increase to 1200
per month could not be achieved before January or February 1968. 31/

Undaunted by repeated rebuffs, the Chiefs, under the
temporary leadership of Army Chief of Staff, General Harold K. Johnson
(General Wheeler had been stricken by a mild heart attack in early
September and was away from his desk for a little over a month), continued to press for lifting the Hanoi restrictions and for permission
to attack Phuc Yen. On October 4 they gave McNamara a package of papers
on the current target list complete with draft execute messages lifting
the Hanoi ban and authorizing Phuc Yen, both of which they recommended. 32/
Two days later a specific request to hit the Hanoi power plant was forwarded, noting the DIA estimate that the power plant was back to 75% of its
original capacity. 33/   On October 7, CINCPAC sent the JCS a monthly summary of the ROLLING THUNDER program in September and used the opportunity
once again to complain about the detrimental effects of maintaining the
Hanoi restriction. Adverse weather because of the northeast Monsoon had
severely curtailed the number of sorties flown to 8,540 compared with
11,634 in August. This had permitted a considerable amount of damage-
recovery in North Vietnam. The maintenance of the Hanoi sanctuary only
compounded the problem for the U.S. "This combination of circumstances
provides the enemy the opportunity to repair rail lines, reconstruct
downed bridges, and accommodate to much of the initial efforts to maintain pressure against the vital LOC network." 34/   In Admiral Sharp's
view, countering these recovery efforts was of the first priority.

The following day he sent the Chiefs another message specifically requesting that the rescinded approval for strikes against Phuc Yen
airfield be reinstated. Increased MIG activity against our jets over North
Vietnam was cited as requiring the destruction of this last remaining major
airfield. The crux of his argument, however, was the necessity of such
a strike to the maintenance of pilot morale — a rationale entirely exempt
from statistical analysis in OSD. He stated the case as follows:

The morale of our air crews understandably rose when briefed to strike Phuc Yen airfield and its MIG's -- A target which has continually jeopardized their well-being. The unexplained revocation of that authority coupled with the increasing numbers and aggressiveness of MIG-21 attacks cannot help but impact adversely on air crew morale. Air crews flying combat missions through the intense NVN defenses, air to air and ground to air, have demonstrated repeatedly their courage and determination to press home their attack against vital targets. Every effort should be made to reduce the hazard to them, particularly from a threat in which the enemy is afforded a sanctuary and can attack at his own choosing. 35/

With the failure of the peace initiative in Paris, these escalatory pressures could no longer be resisted. As it became evident that peace talks were not in the offing, the President approved six new targets on October 6 (including 5 in or near Haiphong). Secretary Rusk in his October 12 news conference strongly questioned the seriousness of North Vietnamese intent for peace and finally on October 20 the Paris contacts were closed in failure. The Tuesday lunch on October 24 would thus have to make important new bombing decisions. The day before, Warnke outlined current JCS recommendations for Secretary McNamara, including Phuc Yen. 36/ The White House meeting the following day duly approved Phuc Yen along with a restrike of the Hanoi power transformer and the temporary lifting of the Hanoi restrictions. 37/ On October 25, the MIGs at Phuc Yen were attacked for the first time and Hanoi was struck again after the long suspension.

The Tuesday luncheon at which the Phuc Yen decision was made was a regular decision-making forum for the air war and one that came to public attention as a result of the Stennis hearings. Indicative of the public interest in these gatherings is the following impressionistic account by CBS newsman Dan Rather of how they were conducted:

First Line Report, 6:55 a.m.
WTOP Radio, October 17, 1967

Dan Rather: This is Target Tuesday. Today President Johnson decides whether North Vietnam will continue to be bombed. If it is, how much and where. These decisions are made at which Washington insiders call, for short, the Tuesday lunch. This is the way it goes.

At about 1:00 in the afternoon Defense Secretary McNamara, Secretary of State Rusk, and Presidential Assistant Walter Rostow gather in the White House second floor sitting room. They compare notes briefly over Scotch or Fresca. President

Johnson walks in with Press Secretary George Christian.
McNamara, Rusk, Rostow, Christian, and the President--
they are the Tuesday lunch regulars. The principal cast .
for Target Tuesday.

Sometimes others join. Chairman of the Military Joint
Chiefs, General Earle Wheeler, for example. He's been coming
more often recently, ever since the Senate Subcommittee on
Preparedness Committee griped about no military man being
present many times when final bombing decisions were made.
Central Intelligence Director Richard Helms seldom comes.
Vice President Humphrey almost never.

Decision making at the top is an intimate affair.
Mr. Johnson prefers it that way. He knows men talk more
freely in a small group.

After a bit of chatter over drinks in the sitting room,
the President signals the move to the dining room. It is
semi-oval, with a huge chandelier, a mural around the wall-
brightly colored scenes of Cornwallis surrendering his sword
at Yorktown. The President sits at the head, of course. Sits
in a high back stiletto swivel chair. Rusk is at his right,
McNamara on his left, Rostow is at the other end. Christian and
the extras, if any, in between. Lunch begins, so does the
serious conversation. There is an occasional pause, punctuated by the whirl of Mr. Johnson's battery-powered pepper
grinder. He likes pepper and he likes the gadget.

Around the table the President's attention goes, sampling
recommendations, arguments, thoughts. It is now the time for
a bombing pause. How about just a bombing reduction? Laos,
Haiphong, Hanoi, everything around population centers, confined
bombing to that tiny part of North Vietnam bordering the
Demilitarized Zone. McNamara long has favored this. He
thinks it worth a try. Rusk has been going for some indica-
tion--the slightest hint will do--that a bombing pause or
reduction will lead to meaningful negotiations. Rostow,
least known of the Tuesday lunch regulars, also is a hard-
liner. He more than Rusk is a pour-it-on man. Christian
doesn't say much. He is there to give an opinion when asked
about press and public reaction. The military representative,
when there is one, usually speaks more than Christian, but
less than McNamara, Rusk, and Rostow.

McNamara is the man with the target list. He gives his
recommendations. If bomb we must, these are the targets he
suggests. His recommendations are based on, but by no means
completely agree with those of the military Joint Chiefs.

Their recommendations, in turn, are based on those of
field commanders. Field commanders are under instructions not to recommend certain targets in certain areas--
Haiphong docks, the air defense command center in Hanoi,
and so forth. There is much controversy and some bitterness
about these off-limit targets. There have been fewer and
fewer of them since July. Some new ones went off the list
just last week.

The luncheon meeting continues over coffee until 3:00,
3:30, sometimes even 4:00. When it is over, the President goes
for a nap. The bombing decisions have been made for another
week.

In thinking about Target Tuesday and the White House
luncheon where so many decisions are on the menu, you may
want to consider the words of 19th Century writer F. W. Borum:
"We make our decisions, and then our decisions turn around
and make us."

Even before the Phuc Yen decision was taken, the Chiefs had
sent McNamara for transmittal to the President a major memo outlining
their overall recommendations for the air war as requested by the President on September 12. The President had asked to see a set of proposals
for putting more pressure on Hanoi. On October 17 that was exactly what
he got and the list was not short. The Chiefs outlined their understanding
of the objectives of the war, the constraints within which the national
authorities wished it to be fought, the artificial limitations that
were impeding the achievement of our objectives and a recommended list
of ten new measures against North Vietnam. Since the memo stands as
one of the last major military arguments for the long-sought wider war
against North Vietnam before the trauma of Tet 1968 and the subsequent
U.S. de-escalation, and because of its crisp, terse articulation of the
JCS point of view, it is included here in its entirety.

OFFICE OF THE
SECRETARY OF DEFENSE

THE JOINT CHIEFS OF STAFF
WASHINGTON, D. C. 20301

JCSM-555-67
17 October 1967

MEMORANDUM FOR THE SECRETARY OF DEFENSE

Subject: Increased Pressures on North Vietnam (U)

1. (U) Reference is made to:

a. NSAM 288, dated 17 March 1964, subject: "Implementation of South Vietnam Program (U)."

b. JCSM-982-64, dated 23 November 1964, subject: "Courses of Action in Southeast Asia (U)."

c. JCSM-811-65, dated 10 November 1965, subject: "Future Operations and Force Deployments with Respect to the War in Vietnam (U)."

2. (U) The purpose of this memorandum is to identify those military actions consistent with present policy guidelines which would serve to increase pressures on North Vietnam (NVN), thereby accelerating the rate of progress toward achievement of the US objective in South Vietnam.

3. (TS) The Joint Chiefs of Staff consider that NVN is paying heavily for its aggression and has lost the initiative in the South. They further consider that many factors--though not uniform nor necessarily controlling--indicate a military trend favorable to Free World Forces in Vietnam. South Vietnam, in the face of great difficulty, is making slow progress on all fronts--military, political, and economic. However, pace of progress indicates that, if acceleration is to be achieved, an appropriate increase in military pressure is required.

GROUP - 1
Excluded from automatic
downgrading and
declassification

4. (S) Military operations in Southeast Asia have been conducted within a framework of policy guidelines established to achieve US objectives without expanding the conflict. Principal among these policy guidelines are:

a. We seek to avoid widening the war into a conflict with Communist China or the USSR.

b. We have no present intention of invading NVN.

c. We do not seek the overthrow of the Government of NVN.

d. We are guided by the principles set forth in the Geneva Accords of 1954 and 1962.

5. (TS) Although some progress is being made within this framework, the Joint Chiefs of Staff consider that the rate of progress has been and continues to be slow, largely because US military power has been restrained in a manner which has reduced significantly its impact and effectiveness. Limitations have been imposed on military operations in four ways:

a. The attacks on the enemy military targets have been on such a prolonged, graduated basis that the enemy has adjusted psychologically, economically, and militarily; e.g., inured themselves to the difficulties and hardships accompanying the war, dispersed their logistic support system, and developed alternate transport routes and a significant air defense system.

b. Areas of sanctuary, containing important military targets, have been afforded the enemy.

c. Covert operations in Cambodia and Laos have been restricted.

d. Major importation of supplies into NVN by sea has been permitted.

6. (TS) The Joint Chiefs of Staff consider that US objectives in Southeast Asia can be achieved within the policy framework set forth in paragraph 4, above, providing the level of assistance the enemy receives from his communist allies is not significantly increased and there is no diminution of US efforts. However, progress will continue to be slow so long as present limitations on military operations continue in effect. Further, at our present pace, termination of NVN's military effort is not expected

to occur in the near future. Set forth in the Appendix are those actions which can be taken in the near future within the present framework of policy guidelines to increase pressures on NVN and accelerate progress toward the achievement of US objectives. They require a relaxation or removal of certain limitations on operations. The Joint Chiefs of Staff recognize that expansion of US efforts entails some additional risk. They believe that as a result of this expansion the likelihood of overt introduction of Soviet Bloc/CPR combat forces into the war would be remote. Failure to take additional action to shorten the Southeast Asia conflict also entails risks as new and more efficient weapons are provided to NVN by the Soviet Union and as USSR/CPR support of the enemy increases.

7. (U) The Joint Chiefs of Staff recommend that they be authorized to direct the actions in the Appendix.

8. (S) This memorandum is intended to respond to the questions raised by the President at the White House luncheon on 12 September 1967; therefore, the Joint Chiefs of Staff request that this memorandum be submitted to the President.

For the Joint Chiefs of Staff:

EARLE G. WHEELER
Chairman
Joint Chiefs of Staff

Attachment

TOP SECRET - Sensitive

SUMMARY OF ACTIONS WHICH MIGHT ____ ____ IN ____ ____ ON THE ____

ACTIONS	SPECIFIC ACTIONS	ADVANTAGES	RISKS/DISADVANTAGES

TOP SECRET - Sensitive

Ten days after this joint memo from the Chiefs, General
Wheeler sent the Secretary a proposal of his own for the expansion of
the air war under a new ROLLING THUNDER program, number 58. 38/ Its
most important proposal was the reduction of Hanoi Haiphong restricted
circles down to 3 and 1.5 n.m. respectively. With other specific
targets requested for authorization (of which the most important was
Gia Lam airfield), this new proposal would have opened up an additional 15 valid targets for attack on the authority of the field commander. On the basis of an ISA recommendation, the reduction of the
restricted zones around the two cities was rejected on November 9, but
some of the additional individual targets were added to the authorized
list. Consistent with these little escalatory measures was McNamara's
decision on November 6 to authorize the deployment to Southeast Asia of
a squadron of the first six F-111A aircraft to enter the Air Force active
inventory. 40/ Like so many other decisions with respect to this ill-
fated aircraft, this one would come to an unhappy end too. One of the
specific objectives of the Chairman's proposal for constricting the prohibited areas had been to attempt the isolation of Haiphong on the ground,
thereby effectively cutting off seaborne imports from their destinations
in the rest of North Vietnam and to the war in the South. An independent
CIA analysis of the air war at about this same time, however, had stated:

> Even a more intense interdiction campaign in the North
> would fail to reduce the flow of supplies sufficiently to
> restrict military operations. Prospects are dim that an air
> interdiction campaign against LOC's leading out of Haiphong
> alone could cut off the flow of seaborne imports and isolate
> Haiphong. 41/

In late November the Chiefs sent the Secretary still another
and far more detailed memo describing their plans for the conduct of all
aspects of the war for the ensuing four months. In it they spelled out
requests for expanding the air war against 24 new targets. They desired
authorization once again to mine the harbors of Haiphong, Hon Gai, and
Cam Pha noting that bad weather in the coming months would force curtailment of much normal strike activity in the Red River delta. The harbor
mining was offered as the most effective means of shutting off supplies
to the North. The CIA analysis previously referred to had, however, also
rejected such mining proposals as unlikely to succeed in their objective
of cutting off imports to support the war, although they would raise the
costs to the DRV.

> Political considerations aside, the combined interdic-
> tion of land and water routes, including the mining of the
> water approaches to the major ports and the bombing of ports
> and transshipment facilities, would be the most effective

type of interdiction campaign. This program would increase
the hardships imposed on North Vietnam and raise further
the costs of the support of the war in the South. It would,
however, not be able to cut off the flow of essential supplies and, by itself, would not be the determining factor
in shaping Hanoi's outlook toward the war. 42/

        In addition to mining the harbors, the Chiefs requested
that the comprehensive prohibition of attacks in the Hanoi/Haiphong
areas be removed with the expected increase in civilian casualties to
be accepted as militarily justified and necessary. They suggested as an
alternative a 3 n.m. "restricted" area for the very center of Hanoi and
a similar zone of 1.5 n.m. for Haiphong. They also requested the expansion
of SEADRAGON naval activity north of 21.30° all the way to the Chinese
border, and authorization of all the remaining targets on the JCS ROLLING
THUNDER list. 43/   In spite of all these requests for expansion of the
war (as well as several others for expanding the ground war in South Vietnam and operations in Laos and Cambodia), the Chiefs avoided the kind
of vaunted claims for success from such new steps that had characterized
past recommendations. This time they cautiously noted, "...there are no
new programs which can be undertaken under current policy guidelines
which would result in a rapid or significantly more visible increase in
the rate of progress in the near term." 44/

        The Chiefs 24-target proposal was considered at the Tuesday
lunch on December 5, but no action was taken. A memo from Warnke to
McNamara gives a clue as to why, "I have been informed that Secretary
Rusk will not be prepared to consider the individual merits of the 24
unauthorized targets proposed and discussed in the JCS Four Months Plan." 45/
On December 16, McNamara and Rusk did reach agreement on ten new targets
from the 24 target list including seven within the 10-mile Hanoi radius
and two within the 4-mile Haiphong perimeter. 46/   Disapproved were five
Haiphong port targets and the mining proposal.

        None of the increased war activity over North Vietnam
which these decisions authorized, however, would be able to prevent the
enemy's massive offensive the following January. The fact that the
President had acceded to the wishes of the military and the political
pressures from Congress on this vital issue at this point when all the
evidence available to McNamara suggested the continuing ineffectiveness
of the bombing must have been an important if not determining factor in
the Secretary's decision in November to retire. For the moment, however,
the escalation continued.

        As always, the President moved cautiously in allowing some
military expansion of the air war in the fall of 1967. By the end of
October, 6 of the 7 MIG-capable airfields which Secretary McNamara had

taken a strong stand against in the Stennis hearings had been hit, and only 5 of the August list of 57 recommended targets (which had meanwhile grown to 70 as new recommendations were made) remained unstruck. Thus, except for the port of Haiphong and a few others, virtually all of the economic and military targets in NVN that could be considered even remotely significant had been hit. Except for simply keeping it up, almost everything bombing could do to pressure NVN had been done.

In early December Defense spokesmen announced that the U.S. bombing in North and South Vietnam together had just topped the total of 1,544,463 tons dropped by U.S. forces in the entire European Theater during World War II. Of the 1,630,500 tons dropped, some 864,000 tons were dropped on NVN, already more than the 635,000 tons dropped during the Korean War or the 503,000 tons dropped in the Pacific Theater during World War II. 47/

4. The Decibel Level Goes Up

The purely military problems of the war aside, the President was also experiencing great difficulty in maintaining public support for this conduct of the war in the fall of 1967.

With the apparent failure of the San Antonio formula to start negotiations, the acrimony and shrillness of the public debate over the war reached new levels. The "hawks" had had their day during the Stennis hearings and the slow squeeze escalation that followed the failure of the Paris contacts. Among the "doves" the new escalation was greeted by new and more forceful outcries from the critics of the war. On October 12, the very day that Rusk was castigating the North Vietnamese in his press conference for their stubbornness, thirty dovish Congressmen sent the President an open letter complaining about the inconsistency of the recent bombing targets and Secretary McNamara's testimony during the Stennis hearings:

> The bombing of targets close to the Chinese border, and of the port cities of Cam Pha and Haiphong conflicts with the carefully reasoned and factual analysis presented prior to those steps by Secretary of Defense Robert S. McNamara on August 25, 1967. We refer particularly to the Secretary's contention that 'our resort to a less selective campaign of air attack against the North would involve risks which at present I regard as too high to accept for this dubious prospect of successful risks.' 48/

On the basis of McNamara's recommendations, the Congressmen urged the President to stop the bombing and start negotiations.

While this public identification of the inconsistency of
the positions taken by various members of the Administration was
embarrassing, a more serious problem was the massive anti-war demonstration organized in Washington on October 21. The leaders of the "New
Left" assembled some 50,000 anti-war protestors in the Capitol on this
October Saturday and staged a massive march on the Pentagon. While the
"politics of confrontation" may be distasteful to the majority of
Americans, the sight of thousands of peaceful demonstrators being confronted by troops in battle gear cannot have been reassuring to the
country as a whole nor to the President in particular. And as if to
add insult to injury, an impudent and dovish Senator McCarthy announced
in November that he would be a candidate for the Democratic nomination
for President. He stated his intention of running in all the primaries
and of taking the Vietnam war to the American people in a direct challenge
to an incumbent President and the leader of his own party.

To counter these assaults on his war policy from the left,
the President dramatically called home Ambassador Bunker and General
Westmoreland (the latter to discuss troop levels and requests as well)
in November and sent them out to publicly defend the conduct of the war
and the progress that had been achieved. Bunker spoke to the Overseas
Press Club in New York on November 17 and stressed the progress that the
South Vietnamese were making in their efforts to achieve democratic self-
government and to assume a larger burden of the war. General Westmoreland
addressed the National Press Club in Washington on November 21 and outlined his own four-phase plan for the defeat of the Viet Cong and their
North Vietnamese sponsors. He too dwelled on the progress achieved to
date and the increasing effectiveness of the South Vietnamese forces.
Neither discussed the air war in the North in any serious way, however, and
that was the issue that was clearly troubling the American public the most.

C. New Studies

1. SEACABIN

In the early winter of 1967-68 several new studies of the
bombing were completed within the Government and by contract researchers
all of which had some bearing on the deliberations of February and March
1968 when the next major reassessment took place. The first of these
was entitled SEACABIN, short for "Study of the Political-Military Implications in Southeast Asia of the Cessation of Aerial Bombardment and the
Initiation of Negotiations." It was a study done by the Joint Staff and
ISA to specifically address the question of what could be expected from
a cessation of the bombing and the beginning of negotiations, a possibility
that seemed imminent at the time of the President's San Antonio speech
in September. As it turned out, the time was not ripe. The study, however, was an important effort by the Defense Department to anticipate
such a contingency.

Summarizing its findings and conclusions, the SEACABIN report began with a general assessment of the role of the bombing in the war:

Role of Bombardment. There are major difficulties and uncertainties in a precise assessment of the bombing program on NVN. These include inadequate data on logistic flow patterns, limited information on imports into NVN, season effects of weather, and the limitations of reconnaissance. But it is clear that the air and naval campaigns against NVN are making it difficult and costly for the DRV to continue effective support of the VC. Our operations have inflicted heavy damage on equipment and facilities, inhibited resupply, compounded distribution problems, and limited the DRV's capability to undertake sustained large-scale military operations in SVN. The economic situation in NVN is becoming increasingly difficult for the enemy. However, as a result of extensive diversion of manpower and receipt of large-scale military and economic assistance from communist countries, the DRV has retained the capability to support military operations in SVN at current levels. A cessation of the bombing program would make it possible for the DRV to regenerate its military and economic posture and substantially increase the flow of personnel and supplies from NVN to SVN. 49/

Implications of a bombing halt were dealt with in terms of advantages to the DRV and risks to the U.S. In the former category, the SEACABIN Study Group concluded as follows:

D. IMPLICATIONS OF A CESSATION OF BOMBARDMENT

6. For DRV: Potential Gains

a. Potential DRV Responses. Following a cessation of bombardment in return for its acceptance of the President's offer, the DRV could choose among one of three potential alternative courses of action: (1) to pursue an immediate-pay-off, short-term strategy of advantage; (2) to enter discussions with no intention of settling, while pursuing either its present strategy, or a revised political/military strategy of gaining a long-term advantage in SVN; and (3) to negotiate meaningfully within the United States. Under all courses, the immediate action of the DRV would be to reconstitute its LOC, stockpile near its borders, and begin general reapirs of its war damage.

b. DRV Reaction Time and US Detection of
    Changes

(1) Under conditions of bombing, NVN
units and infiltration groups have taken from only a few
days up to eight months to infiltrate to a CTZ. US
detection and identification may take up to six months,
or longer, and confirmation even longer. Following
cessation, infiltration rates would be brought closer
to minimum time.

(2) Given its present capability to
expand its training base by almost 100%, the DRV could
achieve a significant increase in present pipeline level
of infiltration in about 3 months following decision to
expand its training base.

(3) The DRV could regenerate major
segments of its economic infrastructure in 6 months,
its LOC in NVN in 30-60 days, its logistic system in
12 months. Port congestion would be alleviated. Materiel
transit time would be significantly reduced.

c. Capabilities Over Time

10-15 days:

-- reinforce NVA forces at DMZ with
up to 5 division equivalents. Allied/enemy battalion
ratios in I CTZ could shift from 1.7/1 to 0.9/1

--increase artillery bombardment from
beyond DMZ, and reinforce AAA and SAM units.

30-60 days:

--Restore to operational use major
ports and LOC within NVN, to include RR, highway, and
combination RR/highway bridges; airfields; and over half
of the vehicle repair facilities.

--Accomplish a restructuring (depots,
shelters, alternate routes) of the logistic system within
NVN to increase the flexibility of the LOC in Laos.

2-6 months:

--Achieve undetected a new position of
military advantage in SVN, through increased infiltration,
with at least two divisions in place in SVN, and three
others in transit.

--Transfer to military service,
from NVN LOC maintenance and construction, managerial
and supervisory personnel to alleviate the apparent
shortage of leaders.

    d. DRV Constraints. These considerations
probably would continue to constrain DRV's choices among
options at cessation:

    (1) Strategy of protracted war. The
DRV would probably continue to put at risk in SVN only
those minimum forces it considers necessary to prosecute
its strategy of protracted war.

    (2) Fear of US invasion.

    (3) Desire to preserve appearance of
VC primacy in SVN.

    (4) Limitations on ability to trans-
fer trained personnel and leadership to SVN because of
possibility of US resumption of attacks on NVN.

    (5) DRV may be miscalculating the
progress of the war in SVN. 50/

Obviously these potential advantages to the DRV involved reciprocal risk
for the U.S. in curtailing the bombing. As the SEACABIN group saw them
they were the following:

    7. For US: Potential Risk

    a. To Operations in SVN. The most far-
reaching risk is an increase in enemy combat strength that
may well go undetected by the US/RVN/FWMAF. Additionally,
the US position could be disadvantaged by:

    (1) Movements of heavy artillery and AAA.

    (2) Loss of US supporting fire at DMZ.

    (3) Increased threat from DMZ and border
area.

    (4) Impairment of pacification program.

    (5) Lowering of morale of US/RVN/FWMAF.

(6) Resulting pressures to cease bombing in Laos.

(7) Vulnerability of barrier system.

b. Possible Offset: Present bombardment forces could be reallocated to SVN and Laos missions.

c. Critical Times to Offset Risks. US should enter cessation resolved to limit the time for DRV response generally as follows:

--Discussions should begin within 30-60 days of cessation.

--Discussions should be productive within four months of cessation; i.e., actions are being taken or are agreed to be taken to reduce the threats posed by the NVN to the achievement of US/GVN military objectives in SVN. 51/

The international reaction to a bombing halt was expected to be entirely positive, hence not a problem for analysis. The study postulated that the DRV would seek to prolong the bombing halt but try to maintain a level of military activity below the provocative that would maintain its strengths in the war while trying to erode the U.S. position through protracted negotiations. In approaching a bombing halt, the U.S. could escalate before it, de-escalate before it, or maintain the current intensity of combat. The latter course was recommended as the best method of demonstrating continued U.S. resolution in anticipation of a dramatic act of restraint. With respect to the negotiations themselves, the SEACABIN Group cautioned against the U.S. being trapped in the kind of protracted negotiations we experienced in Korea while the enemy took military advantage of the bombing suspension. To guard against this, unilateral verification was essential through continued aerial surveillance. To round out their recommendations, the SEACABIN Group looked at the reasons and methods of resuming bombing if required.

H. THE RESUMPTION OF BOMBARDMENT

18. Resumption - When. The conditions under which the bombardment of NVN should be resumed cannot be determined in advance with assurance. However, the US/RVN should

probably resume bombardment whenever one or more of the
following situations are perceived:

> a. The security of US/RVN/FWMAF in
northern I CTZ is threatened by enemy reinforcements.

> b. No discussions are in prospect 30-60
days after cessation.

> c. Discussions or negotiations are not pro-
ductive of militarily significant DRV/NLF concessions
within four months.

> d. The DRV has infiltrated significant
new forces into SVN -- the raising of the NVA force level
in SVN by a division equivalent or more (over 10%) is
judged to be sufficient provocation.

> e. An enemy attack of battalion size or
larger is initiated while a cease-fire is in effect.

> 19. Resumption - How. Actual resumption of
bombardment of NVN should be preceded by a program of
actions which:

> a. Demonstrate (to those who are able to make
an objective judgment) that the DRV is taking advantage of
the cessation in a way which is exposing US/RVN/FWMAF and
the people of SVN to substantially increased dangers.

> b. To the maximum practicable extent,
demonstrate or encourage the conclusion that the DRV
is, in fact, the aggressor in SVN.

> c. After the maximum political advantage
has been derived from the above actions and in the
absence of an acceptable response from NVN, resume aerial
and naval bombardment of NVN without restrictions on any
militarily significant targets. Attacks should be
planned to achieve maximum impact and with due regard
to the advantages of surprise. 52/

The ISA/Joint Staff analysis closed with an appraisal of
the overall value of a bombing halt in the context of negotiations with
the DRV. Summing up, they said,

> 21. On balance, that DRV response to the US offer
which carries with it the greatest risk to the United

States militarily is an ambiguous response in which the
DRV would appear to engage in productive talks in order
to gain time to concurrently regenerate support facilities
in NVN and gradually build up personnel strength and support
bases in Laos, Cambodia and SVN, without overt and visible
provocation. Once discussions were initiated and extended
for 2-6 months, the DRV would expect world pressure to exercise a heavy restraint on resumption of bombardment -- in fact,
to prevent it in the absence of a demonstrable provocation
of considerable consequence.

22. US intelligence evaluations of the impact of
bombardment on NVN are sufficiently uncertain as to cast
doubt on any judgment that aerial and naval bombardment
is or is not establishing some upper limit on the DRV's
ability to support the war in SVN. The effect on NVN itself
is equally uncertain. If NVN is being seriously hurt by
bombardment, the price for cessation should be high. However, if NVN can continue indefinitely to accommodate to
bombardment, negotiation leverage from cessation -- or a
credible threat of resumption -- is likely to be substantially
less. A penalty to the United States of underevaluating the
impact of bombardment of NVN would be an unnecessarily weak
negotiating stance. 53/

In their final paragraphs, the Study Group turned to the question of DRV
good faith. The President's statement that bombing could halt and
negotiations begin if we had assurances that the DRV would "not take
advantage" of our restraint obliged us to look at which we would regard
as a violation of that principle.

27. It has not been possible to detect and measure
increased infiltration into SVN until 4-6 months have
elapsed. If discussions following a cessation of bombardment are protracted, the enemy could take advantage of the
opportunity for increased infiltration with confidence that
detection would be so slow and uncertain that insufficient
provocation could be demonstrated to justify termination of
talks or resumption of bombardment. The following are minimum acceptable actions which operationally define "not take
advantage."

a. Stop artillery fire from and over the DMZ
into SVN prior to or immediately upon cessation.

b. Agree that for the DRV to increase over the
current level the flow of personnel and materiel south of

19° N latitude would be to take advantage of cessation
and that it will refrain from doing so.

      c. Accept "open skies" over NVN upon cessation.

      d. Withdraw from the DMZ within a specified time,
say two weeks, after cessation.

    28. Cessation of bombing of NVN for any protracted
period while continuing the war in SVN would be difficult
to reconcile with any increase in US casualties.

    29. If the DRV/NLF act in good faith, formal negoti-
ations toward a cessation of hostilities should begin within
two months after a cessation of bombardment. Preliminary
discussions lasting any longer than two months will require
a resumption of bombardment or the application of other
pressures as appropriate. 54/

    As a document, the SEACABIN study was important because
it represented a first major effort to pull together a positive DOD
position on the question of a bombing halt. The analysis and recommendations were compromises to be sure, but they were formulations that
gave the Administration room for maneuver in approaching the problem of
negotiations. Probably most importantly they established a basis of
cooperation and collaboration between the Joint Staff and ISA on this
issue that would be useful during the crisis of the following March when
a new direction was being sought for the whole U.S. effort in Vietnam.

    In mid-December, the Chiefs themselves sent the Secretary
a memo noting that the SEACABIN study was the product of staff work and
did not necessarily reflect the views of the JCS. The Chiefs stressed
again their belief in the effectiveness of the bombing in punishing
North Vietnamese aggression, and recorded their opposition to a halt in
the bombing as a means of starting negotiations. North Vietnamese
performance on the battlefield and diplomatically clearly indicated
their unwillingness to enter negotiations except as a means of handi-
capping American power. Such a bombing halt would also endanger the
lives of U.S. troops. Thus, while the study had been a useful exercise,
the Secretary was advised against any endorsement of a cessation of
bombing. 55/

2. The JASON Study

    While DOD was internally examining bombing suspension
scenarios, IDA's JASON division had called together many of the people
who had participated in the 1966 Summer Study for another look at the
effectiveness of the bombing and at various alternatives that might get

better results. Their report was submitted in mid-December 1967 and
was probably the most categorical rejection of bombing as a tool of our
policy in Southeast Asia to be made before or since by an official or
semi-official group. The study was done for McNamara and closely held
after completion. It was completed after his decision to leave the
Pentagon, but it was a powerful confirmation of the positions on the
bombing that he had taken in the internal councils of the government
over the preceding year.

The study evaluated the bombing in terms of its achievement
of the objectives that Secretary McNamara had defined for it:

Secretary McNamara on August 25, 1967 restated the
objectives of the bombing campaign in North Vietnam. These
objectives are:

1. To reduce the flow and/or to increase the cost of
the continued infiltration of men and supplies from North
to South Vietnam.

2. To raise the morale of the South Vietnamese people
who, at the time the bombing started, were under severe
military pressure.

3. To make clear to the North Vietnamese political
leadership that so long as they continued their aggression
against the South, they would have to pay a price in the
North. 56/

Taking up the first of these stated objectives, the JASON
study reached an emphatically negative conclusion about the results from
ROLLING THUNDER:

As of October 1967, the U.S. bombing of North Vietnam
has had no measurable effect on Hanoi's ability to mount
and support military operations in the South. North Vietnam
supports operations in the South mainly by functioning as
a logistic funnel and providing a source of manpower, from
an economy in which manpower has been widely under-utilized.
Most of the essential military supplies that the VC/NVA forces
in the South require from external sources are provided
by the USSR, Eastern Europe, and Communist China. Furthermore, the volume of such supplies is so low that only a
small fraction of the capacity of North Vietnam's flexible
transportation network is required to maintain that flow.

In the face of Rolling Thunder strikes on NVN, the
bombing of infiltration routes in Laos, the U.S. naval
operations along the Vietnamese coast, and the tactical

bombing of South Vietnam, North Vietnam infiltrated over 86,000 men in 1966. At the same time, it has also built up the strength of its armed forces at home, and acquired sufficient confidence in its supply and logistic organization to equip VC/NVA forces in South Vietnam with a modern family of imported 7.62mm weapons which require externally supplied ammunition. Moreover, NVN has the potential to continue building the size of its armed forces, to increase the yearly total of infiltration of individual soldiers and combat units, and to equip and supply even larger forces in South Vietnam for substantially higher rates of combat than those which currently prevail.

Since the beginning of the Rolling Thunder air strikes on NVN, the flow of men and materiel from NVN to SVN has greatly increased, and present evidence provides no basis for concluding that the damage inflicted on North Vietnam by the bombing program has had any significant effect on this flow. In short, the flow of men and materiel from North Vietnam to the South appears to reflect Hanoi's intentions rather than capabilities even in the face of the bombing.

NVN's ability to increase the rate of infiltration of men and materiel into SVN is not currently limited by its supply of military manpower, by its LOC capabilities, by the availability of transport carriers, or by its access to materiels and supplies. The VC/NVA are effectively limited by constraints of the situation in the South -- including the capacity of the VC infrastructure and distribution system to support additional materiel and troops -- but even given these constraints could support a larger force in the South. The inference which we have drawn from these findings is that NVN determines and achieves the approximate force levels that they believe are needed to sustain a war of attrition for an extended period of time.

Despite heavy attacks on NVN's logistic system, manufacturing capabilities, and supply stores, its ability to sustain the war in the South has increased rather than decreased during the Rolling Thunder strikes. It has become increasingly less vulnerable to aerial interdiction aimed at reducing the flow of men and materiel from the North to the South because it has made its transportation system more redundant, reduced the size and increased the number of depots and eliminated choke points.

The bombing of North Vietnam has inflicted heavy costs not so much to North Vietnam's military capability or its infiltration system as to the North Vietnamese economy as a whole. Measurable physical damage now exceeds $370 million and the regime has had to divert 300,000 to 600,000 people (many on a part-time basis) from agricultural and other tasks to counter the bombing and cope with its effects. The former cost has been more than met by aid from other Communist countries. The latter cost may not be real, since the extra manpower needs have largely been met from what was a considerable amount of slack in NVN's under-employed agricultural labor force. Manpower resources are apparently still adequate to operate the agricultural economy at a tolerable level and to continue simultaneously to support the war in SVN and maintain forces for the defense of the North at current or increased levels.

Virtually all of the military and economic targets in North Vietnam that can be considered even remotely signifi-cant have been struck, except for a few targets in Hanoi and Haiphong. Almost all modern industrial output has been halted and the regime has gone over to decentralized, dis-persed, and/or protected modes of producing and handling essential goods, protecting the people, and supporting the war in the South. NVN has shown that it can find alterna-tives to conventional bridges and they continue to operate trains in the face of air strikes.

NVN has transmitted many of the material costs imposed by the bombing back to its allies. Since the bombing began, NVN's allies have provided almost $600 million in economic aid and another $1 billion in military aid -- more than four times what NVN has lost in bombing damage. If economic criteria were the only consideration, NVN would show a sub-stantial net gain from the bombing, primarily in military equipment.

Because of this aid, and the effectiveness of its counter-measures, NVN's economy continues to function. NVN's adjust-ments to the physical damage, disruption, and other difficul-ties brought on by the bombing have been sufficiently effective to maintain living standards, meet transportation require-ments, and improve its military capabilities. NVN is now a stronger military power than before the bombing and its remaining economy is more able to withstand bombing. The USSR could furnish NVN with much more sophisticated weapon systems; these could further increase the military strength of NVN and lead to larger U.S. losses.57/

These conclusions were supported copiously in a separate volume of the study devoted specifically to such analysis. The second objective of the bombing, to raise South Vietnamese morale, had been substantially achieved. There had been an appreciable improvement in South Vietnamese morale immediately after the bombing began and subsequent buoyancy always accompanied major new escalations of the air war. But the effect was always transient, fading as a particular pattern of attack became a part of the routine of the war. There was no indication that bombing could ever constitute a permanent support for South Vietnamese morale if the situation in the South itself was adverse.

The third function of the bombing, as described by McNamara, was psychological -- to win the test of wills with Hanoi by showing U.S. determination and intimidating DRV leaders about the future. The failure of the bombing in this area, according to the JASON study, had been as signal as in purely military terms.

The bombing campaign against NVN has not discernably weakened the determination of the North Vietnamese leaders to continue to direct and support the insurgency in the South. Shortages of food and clothing, travel restrictions, separations of families, lack of adequate medical and educational facilities, and heavy work loads have tended to affect adversely civilian morale. However, there are few if any reliable reports on a breakdown of the commitment of the people to support the war. Unlike the situation in the South, there are no reports of marked increases of absenteeism, draft dodging, black market operations or prostitution. There is no evidence that possible war weariness among the people has shaken the leadership's belief that they can continue to endure the bombing and outlast the U.S. and SVN in a protracted war of attrition.

Long term plans for the economic development have not been abandoned but only set aside for the duration of the war. The regime continues to send thousands of young men and women abroad for higher education and technical training; we consider this evidence of the regime's confidence of the eventual outcome of the war.

The expectation that bombing would erode the determination of Hanoi and its people clearly overestimated the persuasive and disruptive effects of the bombing and, correspondingly, underestimated the tenacity and recuperative capabilities of the North Vietnamese. That the bombing has not achieved anticipated goals reflects a general failure to appreciate the fact, well-documented in the historical

and social scientific literature, that a direct, frontal
attack on a society tends to strengthen the social fabric
of the nation, to increase popular support of the existing
government, to improve the determination of both the
leadership and the populace to fight back, to induce a
variety of protective measures that reduce the society's
vulnerability to future attack and to develop an increased
capacity for quick repairs and restoration of essential
functions. The great variety of physical and social
countermeasures that North Vietnam has taken in response
to the bombing is now well documented but the potential
effectiveness of these countermeasures has not been adequately considered in previous planning or assessment
studies. 58/

The JASON study took a detailed look at alternative means
of applying our air power in an effort to determine if some other combination of targets and tactics would achieve better results. Nine different
strategies were examined including mining the ports, attacking the dikes
and various combinations of attack emphasis on the LOC systems. This was
the emphatic conclusion: "We are unable to devise a bombing campaign in
the North to reduce the flow of infiltrating personnel into SVN." 59/
All that could really be said was that some more optimum employment of
U.S. air resources could be devised in terms of target damage and LOC
disruption. None could reduce the flow even close to the essential minimum for sustaining the war in the South.

After having requested that some portions of the study be
reworked to eliminate errors of logic, Mr. Warnke forwarded the final
version to Secretary McNamara on January 3, 1968 with the information
copies to Secretary Rusk, the Joint Chiefs and CINCPAC. In his memo he
noted the similarity of the conclusions on bombing effectiveness to those
reached not long before in the study by the CIA (see above). Specifically,
Mr. Warnke noted that, "Together with SEA CABIN, the study supports the
proposition that a bombing pause -- even for a significant period of time --
would not add appreciably to the strength of our adversary in South Vietnam."
Thus was laid the analytical groundwork for the President's decision to
partially curtail the bombing in March. 61/

3. Systems Analysis Study on Economic Effects

An unrelated but complementary study of the economic effects
of the bombing on North Vietnam was completed by Systems Analysis right
after the New Year and sent to the Secretary. It too came down hard on
the unproductiveness of the air war, even to the point of suggesting that
it might be counter-productive in pure economic terms. Enthoven's cover
memo to McNamara stated,

...the bombing has not been very successful in imposing economic losses on the North. Losses in domestic production have been more than replaced by imports and the availability of manpower, particularly because of the natural growth in the labor force, has been adequate to meet wartime needs. It is likely that North Vietnam will continue to be able to meet extra manpower and economic requirements caused by the bombing short of attacks on population centers or the cities. 62/

The paper itself examined two aspects of the problem: the impact of the bombing on GNP and on labor supply/utilization. The most telling part of the analysis was the demonstration that imports had more than offset the cost of the war to the North in simple GNP terms as the following passage shows:

II. Effects on North Vietnam's Gross National Product

Prior to 1965, the growth rate of the North Vietnamese economy averaged 6% per year. It is estimated that this rate continued (and even increased slightly) during 1965 and 1966, the first two years of the bombing (Table 1). In 1967, however, domestically-produced GNP declined sharply to only $1,688 million -- a level roughly comparable to the prewar years of 1963 and 1964. The cumulative loss in GNP caused by the bombing in the last three years is estimated to be $294 million (Table 2).

To offset these losses, North Vietnam has had an increased flow of foreign economic aid. Prior to the bombing, economic aid to North Vietnam averaged $95 million annually. Since the bombing began, the flow of economic aid has increased to $340 million per year (Table 1). The cumulative increase in economic aid in the 1965-1967 period over the 1953-1964 average has been an estimated $490 million.

Thus, over the entire period of the bombing, the value of economic resources gained through foreign aid has been greater than that lost because of the bombing (Table 3). The cumulative foreign aid increase has been $490 million; losses have totaled $294 million.

In addition to the loss of current production, North Vietnam has lost an estimated $164 million in capital assets destroyed by the bombing. These capital assets include much of North Vietnam's industrial base - its manufacturing plants, power plants, and bridges.

It is not certain that Russia and China will
replace North Vietnam's destroyed capital assets through
aid programs, thus absorbing part of the bombing cost
themselves. However, they could do so in a short period
of time at relatively small cost; if economic aid remained
at its wartime yearly rate of $340 million and half were
used to replace capital stock, North Vietnam's losses
could be replaced in a year. If the capital stock is
replaced, the economic cost to North Vietnam of the
bombing will be the cumulative loss of output from the
time the bombing began until the capital stock is fully
replaced. Even this probably overstates the cost, however. Even if the pre-bombing capital stock were only
replaced, it would be more modern and productive than it
otherwise would have been.

While the aggregate supply of goods in North
Vietnam has remained constant, standards of living may
have declined. The composition of North Vietnam's total
supply has shifted away from final consumer goods toward
intermediate products related to the war effort, i.e.,
construction and transportation.

Food supplies, vital to the health and efficiency of North Vietnam, have been maintained with only
a slight decline. As shown in Table 4, the estimated
North Vietnamese daily intake of calories has fallen
from 1,910 in 1963 to 1,880 in 1967. Even considering
that imported wheat and potatoes are not traditional
table fare in North Vietnam, the North Vietnamese are
not badly off by past North Vietnamese standards or
the standards of other Asian countries.

The output of industrial and handicraft output
declined 35% in 1967 (Table 1). Economic aid has
probably not replaced all of this decline. With lower
war priority, the supply of non-food consumer goods
such as textiles and durables has probably declined more
than the food supply.

Despite lower standards of living, the ability
of North Vietnamese government to sustain its population
at a level high enough to prevent mass dissatisfaction is
evident. 63/

The analysis of the manpower question in the Systems
Analysis paper revealed that there was as yet no real squeeze for
the North Vietnamese because of population growth. In a word, the

bombing was unable to beat the birth rate. This is how Systems'
Analysis assessed the problem:

III. Effects on Total North Vietnamese Manpower Supply

In addition to the economic effects, the air
war has drawn North Vietnamese labor into bomb damage
repair, replacement of combat casualties, construction,
transportation, and air defense. Over the last three
years, these needs have absorbed almost 750,000 able-
bodied North Vietnamese (Table 5).

But, again there are offsetting factors. First,
over 90% of the increase in manpower has been provided
by population growth (Table 5). Since the start of the
bombing, 720,000 able-bodied people have been added to the
North Vietnamese labor force.

Second, the bombing has increased not only the
demand for labor but also the supply. The destruction of
much of North Vietnam's modern industry has released an
estimated 33,000 workers from their jobs. Similarly, the
evacuation of the cities has made an estimated 48,000
women available for work on roads and bridges in the
countryside. Both of these groups of people were available for work on war-related activity with little or no
extra sacrifice of production; if they weren't repairing
bomb damage, they wouldn't be doing anything productive.

Third, North Vietnam has been supplied with manpower as a form of foreign aid. An estimated 40,000 Chinese
are thought to be employed in maintaining North Vietnam's
road and rail network.

Finally, additional workers could be obtained
in North Vietnam from low productivity employment. In
less developed countries, agriculture typically employs
more people than are really needed to work the land, even
with relatively primitive production methods. Also, further
mobilization may be possible through greater use of women
in the labor force. The available statistics are not precise
enough to identify the magnitude of this potential labor
pool, but the estimates given in Table 6 show that even after
two years of war the total North Vietnamese labor force is
only 54% of its population - scarcely higher than it was in
1965.

In sum, the total incremental need for war-related manpower of roughly 750,000 people appears to have been offset (Table 5) with no particular strain on the population.
Future manpower needs may outstrip North Vietnamese population growth, but the North Vietnamese government can import
more manpower (though there may be limits to how many Chinese
they want to bring into the country), use women and/or
underemployed workers, and draw workers from productive
employment, replacing their output with imports. Given these
options, it appears that the North Vietnamese government is
not likely to be hampered by aggregate manpower shortages. 64/

D.   The Year Closes on a Note of Optimism

The negative analyses of the air war, however, did not reflect
the official view of the Administration, and certainly not the view of
the military at any level in the command structure at year's end. The
latter had, for instance, again vigorously opposed any holiday truce
arrangements, and especially the suspension of the air war against North
Vietnam's logistical system. 65/   On this they had been duly overruled,
the holiday pauses having become the standard SOP to domestic and international war protesters. The 1967 pauses produced, as expected, no major
breakthrough towards peace between the belligerents through any of their
illusive diplomatic points of contact.

Averell Harriman had stopped in Bucharest in late November to
test whether the Romanians had any new information from Hanoi. Despite
their intensive effort and even stronger desire to bring the two sides
together (primarily through a bombing halt), the Romanians apparently
could only reformulate the previously held positions of the Hanoi leadership without any substantive change. Harriman, therefore, patiently
explained again the full meaning and intent of the President's San Antonio
offer and urged its communication to Hanoi.

What was absent of course for both sides was any fundamental
reassessment that could move either or both to modify their positions
on negotiations. The DRV was at the time in the midst of the massive
preparations for the Tet offensive in January while the U.S. remained
bouyed by the favorable reports from the field on seeming military progress
in the last months of 1967. The missing ingredient for peace moves at that
time was motivation on both sides. Each had reason to wait. When, just
before Christmas, Pope Paul called on the U.S. to halt the bombing and
the DRV to demonstrate restraint as a step towards peace he received a
personal visit from President Johnson the following day (on return from a
Presidential trip to Australia). The President courteously but firmly
explained the U.S. policy to the Pope, "mutual restraint" was necessary
before peace talks could begin.

Contributing to the firmness of the U.S. position were the optimistic reports from the field on military progress in the war. Both statistically and qualitatively, improvement was noted throughout the last quarter of the year and a mood of cautious hope pervaded the dispatches. Typical of these was Admiral Sharp's year end wrap-up cable. Having primary command responsibility for the air war, CINCPAC devoted a major portion of his message to the ROLLING THUNDER program in 1967, presenting as he did not only his view of accomplishments in the calendar year but also a rebuttal to critics of the concept and conduct of the air war.

Admiral Sharp outlined three objectives which the air campaign was seeking to achieve: disruption of the flow of external assistance into North Vietnam, curtailment of the flow of supplies from North Vietnam into Laos and South Vietnam, and destruction "in depth" of North Vietnamese resources that contributed to the support of the war. 66/ Acknowledging that the flow of fraternal communist aid into the North had grown every year of the war, CINCPAC noted the stepped up effort in 1967 to neutralize this assistance by logistically isolating its primary port of entry -- Haiphong. The net results, he felt, had been encouraging:

> The overall effect of our effort to reduce external assistance has resulted not only in destruction and damage to the transportation systems and goods being transported thereon but has created additional management, distribution and manpower problems. In addition, the attacks have created a bottleneck at Haiphong where inability effectively to move goods inland from the port has resulted in congestion on the docks and a slowdown in offloading ships as they arrive. By October, road and rail interdictions had reduced the transportation clearance capacity at Haiphong to about 2700 short tons per day. An average of 4400 short tons per day had arrived in Haiphong during the year. 67/

The assault against the continuing traffic of men and materiel through North Vietnam toward Laos and South Vietnam, however, had produced only marginal results. Success here was measured in the totals of destroyed transport, not the constriction of the flow of personnel and goods.

> Although men and material needed for the level of combat now prevailing in South Vietnam continue to flow despite our attacks on LOCs, we have made it very costly to the enemy in terms of material, manpower, management, and distribution. From 1 January through 15 December 1967, 122,960 attack sorties were flown in Rolling Thunder

route packages I through V and in Laos, SEA Dragon offensive operations involved 1,384 ship-days on station and contributed materially in reducing enemy seaborne infiltration in southern NVN and in the vicinity of the DMZ. Attacks against the NVN transport system during the past 12 months resulted in destruction of carriers cargo carried, and personnel casualties. Air attacks throughout North Vietnam and Laos destroyed or damaged 5,261 motor vehicles, 2,475 railroad rolling stock, and 11,425 watercraft from 1 January through 20 December 1967. SEA DRAGON accounted for another 1,473 WBLC destroyed or damaged from 1 January - 30 November. There were destroyed rail-lines, bridges, ferries, railroad yards and shops, storage areas, and truck parks. Some 3,685 land targets were struck by Sea Dragon forces, including the destruction or damage of 303 coastal defense and radar sites. Through external assistance, the enemy has been able to replace or rehabilitate many of the items damage or destroyed, and transport inventories are roughly at the same level they were at the beginning of the year. Nevertheless, construction problems have caused interruptions in the flow of men and supplies, caused a great loss of work-hours, and restricted movement particularly during daylight hours. 68/

The admission that transport inventories were the same at year's end as when it began must have been a painful one indeed for CINCPAC in view of the enormous cost of the air campaign against the transport system in money, aircraft, and lives. As a consolation for this signal failure, CINCPAC pointed to the extensive diversion of civilian manpower to war related activities as a result of the bombing.

A primary effect of our efforts to impede movement of the enemy has been to force Hanoi to engage from 500,000 to 600,000 civilians in full-time and part-time war-related activities, in particular for air defense and repair of the LOCs. This diversion of manpower from other pursuits, particularly from the agricultural sector, has caused a drawdown on manpower. The estimated lower food production yields, coupled with an increase in food imports in 1967 (some six times that of 1966), indicate that agriculture is having great difficulty in adjusting to this hanged composition of the work force. The cost and difficulties of the war to Hanoi have sharply increased, and only through the willingness of other communist countries to provide maximum replacement of goods and material has NVN managed to sustain its war effort. 69/

To these manpower diversions CINCPAC added the cost to North
Vietnam in 1967 of the destruction of vital resources -- the third of
his air war objectives:

C. Destroying vital resources:

Air attacks were authorized and executed by target
systems for the first time in 1967, although the attacks
were limited to specific targets within each system. A
total of 9,740 sorties was flown against targets on the
ROLLING THUNDER target list from 1 January - 15 December
1967. The campaign against the power system resulted in
reduction of power generating capability to approximately
15 percent of original capacity. Successful strikes against
the Thai Nguyen iron and steel plant and the Haiphong cement
plant resulted in practically total destruction of these
two installations. NVN adjustments to these losses have
had to be made by relying on additional imports from China,
the USSR or the Eastern European countries. The requirement for additional imports reduces available shipping space
for war supporting supplies and adds to the congestion at
the ports. Interruptions in raw material supplies and the
requirement to turn to less efficient means of power and distribution has degraded overall production.

Economic losses to North Vietnam amounted to more
than $130 million dollars in 1967, representing over one-half
of the total economic losses since the war began. 70/

This defense of the importance and contribution of the air
campaign to the overall effort in Vietnam was seconded by General Westmoreland later in January when he sent his year-end summary of progress
to Washington. In discussing the efforts of his men on the ground in the
South he described the bombing of the North as "indispensable" in cutting
the flow of support and maintaining the morale of his forces. 71/   It
is worth noting that COMUSMACV's optimistic assessment was dispatched
just 4 days before the enemy launched his devastating Tet offensive,
proving thereby a formidable capability to marshall men and materiel for
massive attacks at times and places of his choosing, the bombing notwithstanding.

Less than a week later, Secretary McNamara appeared before
Congress for the presentation of his last annual "posture" statement.
These regular January testimonies had become an important forum in which
the Secretary reviewed the events of the preceding year, presented the
budget for the coming year and outlined the programs for the Defense
establishment for the next five years. In all cases he had begun with
a broad brush review of the international situation and in recent years

devoted a major portion of the review to the Vietnam problem. In his valedictory on February 1, 1968 (just after the beginning of Tet) he offered a far more sober appraisal of the effectiveness of the bombing than the military commanders in the field. In it he drew on much of the analysis provided to him the previous fall by the JASON and SEACABIN studies and his own systems analysts. His estimate of the bombing is perhaps the closest to being realistic ever given by the Administration and was a wise and tempered judgment to offer in the face of the enemy's impressive Tet attacks.

The air campaign against North Vietnam has included attacks on industrial facilities, fixed military targets, and the transportation system.

Attacks against major industrial facilities through 1967 have destroyed or put out of operation a large portion of the rather limited modern industrial base. About 70 percent of the North's electric generating capacity is currently out of operation, and the bulk of its fixed petroleum storage capacity has been destroyed. However, (imported diesel generators are probably producing sufficient electricity for essential services and, by dispersing their petroleum supplies, the North Vietnamese have been able to meet their minimum petroleum needs. Most, if not all, of the industrial output lost has been replaced by imports from the Soviet Union and China.

Military and economic assistance from other Communist countries, chiefly the Soviet Union, has been steadily increasing. In 1965, North-Vietnam received in aid a total of $420 million ($270 million military and $150 million economic); in 1966, $730 million ($455 million military and $275 million economic); and preliminary estimates indicate that total aid for 1967 may have reached $1 billion ($660 million military and $340 million economic). Soviet military aid since 1965 has been concentrated on air defense materiel -- SAM's, AAA guns and ammo, radars, and fighter aircraft.

Soviet economic assistance has included trucks, railroad equipment, barges, machinery, petroleum, fertilizer, and food. China has provided help in the construction of light industry, maintenance of the transportation system and improvements in the communications and irrigation systems, plus some 30,000 to 50,000 support troops for use in North Vietnam for repair and AAA defense.

Damage inflicted by our air attacks on fixed military targets has led to the abandonment of barracks and supply

and ammunition depots and has caused a dispersal of supplies
and equipment. However, North Vietnam's air defense system
continues to function effectively despite increased attacks
on airfields, SAM sites, and AAA positions. The supply of
SAM missiles and antiaircraft ammunition appears adequate,
notwithstanding our heavy attacks, and we see no indication
of any permanent drop in their expenditure rates.

Our intensified air campaign against the transportation
system seriously disrupted normal operations and has increased
the cost and difficulties of maintaining traffic flows.
Losses of transportation equipment have increased, but inventories have been maintained by imports from Communist countries.
The heavy damage inflicted on key railroad and highway bridges
in the Hanoi-Haiphong areas during 1967 has been largely offset by the construction of numerous bypasses and the more
extensive use of inland waterways.

While our overall loss rate over North Vietnam has been
decreasing steadily, from 3.4 aircraft per 1,000 sorties
in 1965 to 2.1 in 1966 and to 1.9 in 1967, losses over the
Hanoi-Haiphong areas have been relatively high.

The systematic air campaign against fixed economic and
military target systems leaves few strategically important
targets unstruck. Other than manpower, North Vietnam provides few direct resources to the war effort, which is sustained primarily by the large imports from the Communist
countries. The agrarian nature of the economy precludes
an economic collapse as a result of the bombing. Moreover
while we can make it more costly in time and manpower, it
is difficult to conceive of any interdiction campaign that
would pinch off the flow of military supplies to the south
as long as combat requirements remain at anything like the
current low levels. 72/

FOOTNOTES

1. U.S. Congress, Senate Committee on Armed Services, "Air War Against North Vietnam," Summary Report and Hearings, August 1967.

2. JCS Fact Sheet, "ROLLING THUNDER 57," 10 August 1967.

3. Referred to in CM-2660-67, Gen. H. K. Johnson (Acting CJCS) Memorandum for the Secretary of Defense, 22 September 1967 (TS).

4. Ibid.

5. Ibid.

6. Ibid.

7. Ibid.

8. Ibid.

9. Ibid.

10. Ibid.

11. Ibid.

12. Ibid.

13. Ibid.

14. Ibid.

15. Ibid.

16. Ibid.

17. ASD(ISA) Memorandum for the Secretary of Defense, 5 March 1968, Subject: Rolling Thunder Target List and Procedures.

18. See David Kraslow and Stuart H. Loory, The Secret Search for Peace in Vietnam, (Random House, N.Y., 1968), pp. 218-227.

19. Background Information Relating to Southeast Asia and Vietnam, op. cit., pp. 235-236.

20. Ibid., emphasis added.

21. David Kraslow and Stuart H. Loory, The Secret Search for Peace in Vietnam, (Random House Inc. N.Y., 1968), p. 227.

22. Background Information..., op. cit., p. 239.

23. New York Times, October 20, 1967.

24. Handwritten memo to "Secretary McNamara, Recommend your approval of attached message authorizing restrike against JCS target #81. McConnell", 11 September 1967, with attached briefing papers.

25. CINCPAC msg. 210028Z September 1967 (TS).

26. CINCPAC msg. 202352Z September 1967 (TS).

27. CM-2660-67, 22 September 1967 (TS).

28. Handwritten memo from "R McN" to General McConnell, 22 September 1967.

29. JCSmmsg. to CINCPAC 7307, 262109Z September 1967 and Telecon 293/67, 290505Z September 1967 NOTAL (TS).

30. CM 2668-67, 28 September 1967 (TS).

31. Robert S. McNamara Memorandum for the President, October 4, 1967 (TS).

32. CM-2676-67, 4 October 1967 (TS).

33. CM-2679-67, 6 October 1967 (TS).

34. CINCPAC msg. 072055Z October 1967 (TS).

35. CINCPAC msg. to JCS 080726Z October 1967 (TS-LIMDIS).

36. ASD/ISA Paul C. Warnke Memorandum for the Secretary of Defense, Subject: "NVN Bombing (Comments on Valid Targets on 10/12 List Not Yet Recommended)," 23 October 1967 (TS-SENSITIVE).

37. JCS msg. to CINCPAC 9674, 232212Z October 1967 (TS-LIMDIS).

38. CM-2707-68, 27 October 1968, Subject: "ROLLING THUNDER 58" (TS).

39. ASD/ISA Paul C. Warnke Memorandum for the Secretary of Defense, Subject: "New NVN Bombing Proposal - ROLLING THUNDER 58," 31 October 1967 (TS-SENSITIVE).

40. Robert S. McNamara Memorandum for the Chairman, Joint Chiefs of Staff, November 6, 1967 (TS).

41. Quote from an unnamed CIA analysis in a Memorandum for Mr. Warnke by Charles W. Havens, Special Assistant to the ASD/ISA, without date but filed with materials for early November 1967 (TS).

TOP SECRET - Sensitive

42. Ibid.

43. JCSM-663-67, "Policies for the Conduct of Operations in Southeast Asia over the Next Four Months," 27 November 1967 (TS-SENSITIVE), with Appendix and Annexes.

44. Ibid.

45. ASD/ISA Paul C. Warnke Memorandum for the Secretary of Defense, Subject: "NVN Bombing Proposal," 5 December 1967 (TS-SENSITIVE).

46. "Summary SecState and SecDef Position on 24 New Target Recommendations," 16 December 1967 (TS-SENSITIVE).

47. Washington Post, 3 December 1967.

48. Letter to President Lyndon B. Johnson from 30 Congressmen, 12 October 1967.

49. Study of the Political-Military Implications in Southeast Asia of the Cessation of Aerial Bombardment and the Initiation of Negotiations (SEACABIN), SEACABIN Study Group, OJCS 22 November 1967 (TS-SENSITIVE), pp. 4-5.

50. Ibid., pp. 4-6.

51. Ibid., pp. 7-8.

52. Ibid., pp. 13-14.

53. Ibid., p. 15.

54. Ibid., p. 17.

55. JCSM 698-67, 16 December 1967 (TS).

56. IDA, JASON Division, "The Bombing of North Vietnam," Vol. I, "Summary," IDA Log No. TS/HQ 67-127, Dec. 16, 1967 (TS), p. 1.

57. Ibid., pp. 3-7, emphasis in original.

58. Ibid., pp. 7-8, emphasis in original.

59. Ibid., p. 10, emphasis in original.

60. ASD/ISA Paul C. Warnke Memorandum for the Secretary of Defense, Subject: "Study of Alternative Bombing Strategies," 3 January 1968 (TS-SENSITIVE).

61. Ibid.

62. Alain Enthoven Memorandum for the Secretary of Defense, Subject:
"The Economic Effects of Bombing North Vietnam," January 2, 1968,
(TS), with enclosure.

63. OASD(SA) Economics & Mobility Forces paper, "The Bombing - Its
Economic Costs and Benefits to North Vietnam," Jan. 2, 1968, (TS)
attached to Alain Enthoven Memorandum, op. cit.

64. Ibid.

65. JCSM-567-67, 23 October 1967 (TS).

66. CINCPAC msg. to JCS 010156Z January 1968 (TS-LIMDIS).

67. Ibid.

68. Ibid.

69. Ibid.

70. Ibid.

71. COMUSMACV msg. to CINCPAC 02891, 260755Z January 1968 (S).

72. Background Information..., op. cit., pp. 268-269.

JANUARY - MARCH 1968

VI. THE CORNER IS TURNED -- JANUARY-MARCH 1968

The Johnson Administration began 1968 in a mood of cautious hope
about the course of the war. Within a month those hopes had been
completely dashed. In late January and early February, the Viet Cong
and their North Vietnamese supporters launched the massive Tet assault
on the cities and towns of South Vietnam and put the Johnson Administration
and the American public through a profound political catharsis on the
wisdom and purpose of the U.S. involvement in Vietnam and the soundness
of our policies for the conduct of the war. The crisis engendered the
most soul-searching debate within the Administration about what course to
take next in the whole history of the war. In the emotion laden atmosphere of those dark days, there were cries for large-scale escalation on
the one side and for significant retrenchment on the other. In the end
an equally difficult decision -- to stabilize the effort in the South
and de-escalate in the North -- was made. One of the inescapable conclusions of the Tet experience that helped to shape that decision was
that as an interdiction measure against the infiltration of men and
supplies, the bombing had been a near total failure. Moreover, it had
not succeeded in breaking Hanoi's will to continue the fight. The only
other major justification for continuing the bombing was its punitive
value, and that began to pale in comparison with the potential (newly
perceived by many) of its suspension for producing negotiations with the
DRV, or failing that a large propaganda windfall for the U.S. negotiating
position. The President's dramatic decision at the end of March capped a
long month of debate. Adding force to the President's announcement of
the partial bombing halt was his own personal decision not to seek re-
election.

A. The Crisis Begins

1. Public Diplomacy Gropes On

Following Ambassador Harriman's visit to Bucharest in
November 1967 the next move in the dialogue of the deaf between Hanoi
and Washington was a slightly new formulation of the North Vietnamese
position by Foreign Minister Trinh on December 29. Speaking at a
reception at the Mongolian Embassy he stated:

After the United States has ended the bombing and all
other acts of war, /North Vietnam/ will hold talks with
the United States on questions concerned.

By shifting his tense from the "could" of his 28 January 1967 statement
to "will", Trinh had moved his position just slightly closer to that of
the U.S. This statement was, no doubt, a part of a secret diplomatic
dialogue, possibly through the Rumanians, that must have continued into
the new year. The State Department readily acknowledged that Trinh's

statement was a "new formulation," but quickly pointed out that it had been prefaced by a reaffirmation of the four points and did not deal with the specifics of when, where and how negotiations would take place. 2/

Rusk's efforts to downplay the significance of the Trinh statement notwithstanding, it can be assumed that some U.S. response was sent to Hanoi. Reinforcing this impression is the fact that on January 3 bombing was again completely prohibited within 5 n.m. of both Hanoi and Haiphong for an indefinite period. 3/ (Some confusion may arise as to the various constraints that were placed on the bombing near the two major cities at different times and for different radii. "Prohibited" meant that no strikes had been or would be authorized; "restricted" meant that the area was generally off limits but that individual targets, on a case by case basis, might be approved by "highest authority" for a single attack. The 30 n.m. restricted zone around Hanoi and its 10 n.m. counterpart around Haiphong had existed since the beginning of the bombing in 1965. The prohibited zones were established in December 1966. In 1967 they had been 10 n.m. for Hanoi and 4 n.m. for Haiphong.) on January 16 when the White House Luncheon group met they authorized only two targets that McNamara and Rusk had not already agreed to in December and they specifically reaffirmed the prohibition around the two cities. 4/

The following day, the President, in his annual State of the Union address, softened somewhat the U.S. position in what may have been intended as a message to Hanoi. He called for "serious" negotiations rather than the "productive" talks he had asked for in the San Antonio speech. Unfortunately, he also stated that the North Vietnamese "must not take advantage of our restraint as they have in the past." 5/ Newsmen mistakenly took this for a hardening of the U.S. position by the President, an error Dean Rusk tried to dispel the following day. But, as on many occasions in the past, if this was intended as a signal to Hanoi it must have been a confusing one. Once again the problem of multiple audiences scrambled the communication. Not surprisingly then, on January 21, Nham Dan, the official North Vietnamese newspaper condemned the San Antonio formula as the "habitual trick" of the President who was attempting to impose "very insolent conditions" on Hanoi. The U.S. had no right to ask reciprocity for a cessation of the bombing since it was the aggressor. 6/

His intent having been misconstrued, the President used the next most convenient opportunity to convey his message -- the confirmation hearings of the Senate Armed Services Committee on the appointment of his close friend and advisor, Clark Clifford, to be Secretary of Defense. In the course of his testimony, Clifford replied to questions by Senator Strom Thurmond about the timing and conditions the Administration intended for a bombing halt. Here is the essential portion of that testimony:

SENATOR THURMOND:....This morning you testified about the large quantities of goods that were brought in during the cessation of bombing, and in view of your experience and your knowledge, and the statements you made this morning, I presume that you would not favor cessation of bombing where American lives would be jeopardized?

MR. CLIFFORD: I would not favor the cessation of bombing under present circumstances. I would express the fervent hope that we could stop the bombing if we had some kind of reciprocal word from North Vietnam that they wanted to sit down and, in good faith, negotiate.

I would say only that as I go into this task, the deepest desire that I have is to bring hostilities in Vietnam to a conclusion under those circumstances that permit us to have a dignified and honorable result that in turn will obtain for the South Vietnamese that goal which we have made such sacrifices to attain.

SENATOR THURMOND: When you spoke of negotiating, in which case you would be willing to have a cessation of bombing, I presume you would contemplate that they would stop their military activities, too, in return for a cessation of bombing.

MR. CLIFFORD: No, that is not what I said.

I do not expect them to stop their military activities. I would expect to follow the language of the President when he said that if they would agree to start negotiations promptly and not take advantage of the pause in the bombing.

SENATOR THURMOND: What do you mean by taking advantage if they continue their military activities?

MR. CLIFFORD: Their military activity will continue in South Vietnam, I assume, until there is a cease fire agreed upon. I assume that they will continue to transport the normal amount of goods, munitions, and men, to South Vietnam. I assume that we will continue to maintain our forces and support our forces during that period. So what I am suggesting, in the language of the President is, that he would insist that they not take advantage of the suspension of the bombing. 7/

Several days later, the Clifford testimony was confirmed by the State Department as the position of the U.S. Government. This, then, was the final public position taken by the Administration prior to the launching of the Tet offensive by the enemy on January 30. While it amounted to a further softening, it was still considerably short of the unconditional cessation the North Vietnamese were demanding. In the aftermath of the Tet attack, both sides would scale down their demands in the interests of opening a direct dialogue.

2. The Tet Offensive

As planned, the Allies began a 36-hour truce in honor of the Tet holidays on January 29. The order was shortly cancelled, however, because of fierce enemy attacks in the northern provinces. Then, suddenly on January 31, the Viet Cong and NVA forces launched massive assaults on virtually every major city and provincial capital, and most of the military installations in South Vietnam. In Saigon, attackers penetrated the new American Embassy and the Palace grounds before they were driven back. Whole sections of the city were under Viet Cong control temporarily. In Hue an attacking force captured virtually the entire city including the venerable Citadel, seat of the ancient capital of Vietnam and cultural center of the country. Everywhere the fighting was intense and the casualties, civilian as well as military, were staggering. Coming on the heels of optimistic reports from the field commands, this offensive caught official Washington off guard and stunned both the Administration and the American public. The Viet Cong blatantly announced their aim as the overthrow of the Saigon regime. But the Allied forces fought well and the main thrust of the attacks on Saigon, Danang, and elsewhere were blunted with the enemy suffering enormous casualties. Only in Hue did the communists succeed in capturing the city temporarily. There the fighting continued as the most costly of the war for nearly a month before the Viet Cong were finally rooted out of their strongholds.

The lesson of the Tet offensive concerning the bombing should have been unmistakably clear for its proponents and critics alike. Bombing to interdict the flow of men and supplies to the South had been a signal failure. The resources necessary to initiate an offensive of Tet proportions and sustain the casualties and munitions expenditures it entailed had all flowed south in spite of the heavy bombing in North Vietnam, Laos and South Vietnam. It was now clear that bombing alone could not prevent the communists from amassing the materiel, and infiltrating the manpower necessary to conduct massive operations if they chose. Moreover, Tet demonstrated that the will to undergo the required sacrifices and hardships was more than ample.

The initial military reaction in Washington appears to have been addressed to the air war. On February 3, the Chiefs sent the

Secretary a memo renewing their earlier proposal for reducing the
restricted zone around Hanoi and Haiphong to 3 and 1.5 n.m. respectively, with field authority granted to make strikes as required outside. The memo opened with a reference to the Tet offensive: "Through
his buildup at Khe Sanh and actions throughout South Vietnam during
the past week, the enemy has shown a major capability for waging war
in the South." 8/ In view of the evident ineffectiveness of the bombing
in preventing the offensive, the succeeding sentence in the memo, providing the justification for the request, can only appear as a non sequitur:
"The air campaign against NVN should be conducted to achieve maximum effect
in reducing this enemy capability." 9/

The arguments against such authorization were formulated by
ISA. Mr. Warnke observed that:

In addition to the lines of communication that would be
opened for attack by shrinking the control areas around Hanoi
and Haiphong only a couple of fixed targets not previously
authorized would be released for strike. These targets do
not appear to have large civilian casualties or other political liabilities associated with them. A description of
these targets is attached. (Tab B) The major effects thus
would be (1) to open to armed recce attack the primary and
secondary LOCs between the present "regular" 10 and 4 mile
circles and the proposed 3 and 1-1/2 mile circles, and, if
the Joint Staff interpretation is accepted, (2) to release
for strike the previously authorized targets within the
"special" 5 mile circles. 10/

Other considerations also argued in favor of deferring action on this
proposal for the moment:

I recommend that, if this proposal is accepted, the
new circles be treated as containing areas where no strikes
are to be made without new individual authorization. In
any event, I believe the present restrictions should be
continued pending the return of the 3 American PWs who have
been designated by Hanoi for release. Our information is
that these men will be picked up by 2 American pacifists
who are leaving from Vientiane, Laos, for Hanoi on the
next available flight. The next scheduled ICC flight to
Hanoi is on 9 February. 11/

The issue was probably raised at the White House Luncheon on February 6,
but the JCS proposal was not approved. Strikes against targets in
Haiphong apparently were authorized, however, since the first such raids
in over a month took place on February 10. These, however, were only
the most immediate reactions to the trauma of Tet 1968.. To be sure, as

time went on, the air war would be shoved aside somewhat by considerations of force augmentation in the south -- the principle concern after the massive Viet Cong attack. Bombing as an issue would more and more be considered in relation to the possibility of negotiations and the improvement of the U.S. diplomatic position. The failure of the bombing to interdict infiltration and break Hanoi's will meant that it could be militarily justified for the future only as a punitive measure. Nevertheless, many in the Pentagon would continue to advocate its expansion. As events moved forward this punitive value would gradually seem less and less important to the President compared with the potential of a bombing suspension (even partial) for producing serious peace negotiations and/or appeasing public opinion. For the moment, however, the Tet assault appeared only as a massive repudiation of U.S. peace overtures, hardly something to warrant a reduction in our side of the conflict.

On Sunday, February 4, Secretaries Rusk and McNamara appeared jointly on a special one-hour program of "Meet the Press" to answer questions primarily about the Tet offensive. When asked about the meaning of these new attacks for the diplomatic effort and the role of the bombing, Rusk replied as follows:

MR. SPIVAK. Secretary Rusk, may I ask you a question?

SECRETARY RUSK. Yes.

MR. SPIVAK. The President the other day asked this question, he said, what would the North Vietnamese be doing if we stopped the bombing and let them alone? Now there is some confusion about what we want them to do. What is it we want them to do today if we stop the bombing?

SECRETARY RUSK. Well, many, many months ago the President said almost anything as a step toward peace. Now I think it is important to understand the political significance of the events of the last 3 or 4 days in South Vietnam. President Johnson said some weeks ago that we are exploring the difference between the statement of their Foreign Minister about entering into discussions and his own San Antonio formula.

Now we have been in the process of exploring the problems that arise when you put those two statements side by side. Hanoi knows that. They know that these explorations are going on because they were a party to them. Secondly, we have exercised some restraint in our bombing in North Vietnam during this period of exploration, particularly in the immediate vicinity of Hanoi and Haiphong. Again, Hanoi knows this. They also knew that the Tet cease-fire period was coming up.

MR. SPIVAK. Have we stopped the bombing there?

SECRETARY RUSK. No, we have not had a pause in
the traditionally accepted sense but we have limited
the bombing at certain points in order to make it somewhat easier to carry forward these explorations so that
particularly difficult incidents would not interrupt
them. We have not gone into a pause as that word is
generally understood.

But they've also known that the Tet cease-fire was
coming up. And they've known from earlier years that
we've been interested in converting something like a Tet
cease-fire into a more productive dialogue, into some
opportunity to move toward peace.

Now in the face of all these elements they participated in laying on this major offensive. Now I think it
would be foolish not to draw a political conclusion from
this that they are not seriously interested at the present
time in talking about peaceful settlement. Or in exploring the problems connected with the San Antonio formula.
I remind those who don't recall that formula that it was
that we would stop the bombing when it would lead promptly
to productive discussions. And we assumed that they
would not take advantage of this cessation of bombing
while such discussions were going on.

Now it's hard to imagine a more reasonable proposal
by any nation involved in an armed conflict than that. And
I think we have to assume that these recent offensives in
the south are an answer, are an answer, in addition to
their public denunciation of the San Antonio formula.

MR. ABEL. Are you saying, Mr. Secretary, that we
interpret this offensive as their rejection of the diplomatic
overtures that have been made?

SECRETARY RUSK. Well, they have rejected the San
Antonio formula publicly, simply on the political level.
And I think it would be foolish for us not to take into
account what they're doing on the ground when we try to
analyze what their political position is. You remember
the old saying that what you do speaks so loud I can't
hear what you say. Now we can't be indifferent to these
actions on the ground and think that these have no consequences from a political point of view. So they know
where we live. Everything that we've said, our 14 points,
28 proposals to which we've said yes and to which they've

said no, the San Antonio formula, all these things remain
there on the table for anyone who is interested in moving
toward peace. They're all there. But they know where
we live and we'd be glad to hear from them sometime at their
convenience when they decide that they want to move toward
peace.

MR. ABEL. I'm assuming, sir, that the San Antonio
formula stands as our longer term position here.

SECRETARY RUSK. That is correct. 12/

These views of the Secretary of State were reinforced on
February 8 when the North Vietnamese, obviously in the flush of their
psychological victory, again broadcast a repudiation of the San Antonio
formula. Meanwhile, they had been engaged in secret contacts with the
U.S. through the Italian Foreign Office in Rome. On February 14, the
Italians disclosed that two representatives from Hanoi had visited Rome
on February 4 to meet Foreign Minister Fanfani "for talks about the
Vietnam conflict and about possible hypotheses of a start of negotiations
to settle it." 13/   Washington was fully informed, yet Rusk announced
on the same day that all U.S. attempts to launch peace talks "have resulted
in rejection" by Hanoi and that there was no indication she would restrain
herself in exchange for a bombing halt. To this the President, at an
unscheduled news conference two days later, added that Hanoi was no more
ready to negotiate at that time than it had been three years previously. 14/
These reciprocating recriminations in the two capitals were the logical
outcome of such dramatic events as the Tet offensive. They would, however,
soon give way to cooler evaluations of the situation, presumably on both
sides.

The primary focus of the U.S. reaction to the Tet offensive
was not diplomatic, however. It was another reexamination of force
requirements for avoiding defeat or disaster in the South. On February 9,
McNamara asked the Chiefs to provide him with their views on what forces
General Westmoreland would require for emergency augmentation and where
they should come from. The Chiefs replied on February 12 to the startling
effect that while the needs in South Vietnam were pressing, indeed perhaps urgent, any further reduction in the strategic reserve in the U.S.
would seriously compromise the U.S. force posture worldwide and could not
be afforded. They reluctantly recommended deferring the requests of
General Westmoreland for an emergency augmentation. 15/   Rather, they
proposed a callup of reserves to meet both the requirements of Vietnam
augmentation in the intermediate future and to bring drawn-down forces in
the strategic reserve up to strength. The tactic the Chiefs were using
was clear: by refusing to scrape the bottom of the barrel any further
for Vietnam they hoped to force the President to "bite the bullet" on
the callup of the reserves -- a step they had long thought essential,
and that they were determined would not now be avoided. Their views notwithstanding, the Secretary the next day ordered an emergency force of

10,500 to Vietnam immediately to reconstitute COMUSMACV's strategic reserve and put out the fire. 16/

With the decision to dispatch, among others, the remainder of the 82d Airborne Division as emergency augmentation and its public announcement, the policy process slowed down appreciably for the following ten days. The troops were loaded aboard the aircraft for the flight to Vietnam on February 14 and the President flew to Ft. Bragg to personally say farewell to them. The experience proved for him to be one of the most profoundly moving and troubling of the entire Vietnam war. The men, many of whom had only recently returned from Vietnam, were grim. They were not young men going off to adventure but seasoned veterans returning to an ugly conflict from which they knew some would not return. The film clips of the President shaking hands with the solemn but determined paratroopers on the ramps of their aircraft revealed a deeply troubled leader. He was confronting the men he was asking to make the sacrifice and they displayed no enthusiasm. It may well be that the dramatic decisions of the succeeding month and a half that reversed the direction of American policy in the war had their genesis in those troubled handshakes.

B. The "A to Z" Review

1. The Reassessment Begins

For roughly ten days, things were quiet in Washington. In Vietnam, the battle for the recapture of the Citadel in Hue raged on until the 24th of February before the last North Vietnamese defenders were overrun. As conditions in South Vietnam sorted themselves out and some semblance of normality returned to the command organizations, MACV began a comprehensive reassessment of his requirements. Aware that this review was going on and that it would result in requests for further troop augmentation, the President sent General Wheeler, the Chairman of the JCS to Saigon on February 23 to consult with General Westmoreland and report back on the new situation and its implication for further forces. Wheeler returned from Vietnam on the 25th and filed his report on the 27th. The substance of his and General Westmoreland's recommendations had preceded him to Washington, however, and greatly troubled the President. The military were requesting a major reinforcement of more than 3 divisions and supporting forces totalling in excess of 200,000 men, and were asking for a callup of some 280,000 reservists to fill these requirements and flesh out the strategic reserve and training base at home. 17/ The issue was thus squarely joined. To accept the military recommendations would entail not only a full-scale callup of reserves, but also putting the country economically on a semi-war footing, all at a time of great domestic dissent, dissatisfaction, and disillusionment about both the purposes and the conduct of the war. The President was understandably reluctant to take such action, the more so in an election year.

The assessments of North Vietnamese intention, moreover, were not reassuring. The CIA, evaluating a captured document, circulated a report on the same day as General Wheeler's report that stated:

> Hanoi's confident assessment of the strength of its position clearly is central to its strategic thinking. Just as it provided the rationale for the Communists' 'winter-spring campaign,' it probably will also govern the North Vietnamese response to the present tactical situation. If Hanoi believes it is operating from a position of strength, as this analysis suggests, it can be expected to press its military offensive--even at the cost of serious setbacks. Given their view of the strategic balance, it seems doubtful that the Communists would be inclined to settle for limited military gains intended merely to improve their bargaining position in negotiations. 18/

The alternatives for the President, therefore, did not seem very attractive. With such a major decision to make he asked his incoming Secretary of Defense, Clark Clifford, to convene a senior group of advisors from State, Defense, CIA, and the White House and to conduct a complete review of our involvement, re-evaluating both the range of aims and the spectrum of means to achieve them. The review was soon tagged the "A to Z Policy Review" or the "Clifford Group Review." 19/

2. The Clifford Group

The first meeting of the Clifford Group was convened in the Secretary's office at the Pentagon on Wednesday, February 28. Present were McNamara, General Taylor, Nitze, Fowler, Katzenbach, Walt Rostow, Helms, Warnke, and Phil Habib from Bundy's office. 20/ In the meeting, Clifford outlined the task as he had received it from the President and a general discussion ensued from which assignments were made on the preparation of studies and papers. The focus of the entire effort was the deployment requests from MACV. The general subjects assigned were recapitulated the following day by Bundy:

OUTLINE FOR SUBJECTS AND DIVISION OF LABOR ON VIET NAM STAFF STUDY

Subjects to be Considered

1. What alternative courses of action are available to the US?

   Assignment: Defense - General Taylor - State - (Secretary)

2. What alternative courses are open to the enemy?

   Assignment: Defense and CIA

3. Analysis of implications of Westmoreland's request for additional troops.

   Series of papers on the following.

       Military implications - JCS

       Political implications - State

          (Political implications in their broadest domestic and international sense to include internal Vietnamese problem).

       Budgetary results - Defense

       Economic implications - Treasury

       Congressional implications - Defense

       Implications for public opinion - domestic and international - State.

4. Negotiation Alternatives

   Assignment: State 21/

The papers were to be considered at a meeting to be held at Defense on Saturday, March 2 at 10:00 A.M. In fact, the meeting was later deferred until Sunday afternoon and the whole effort of the Task Force shifted to the drafting of a single Memorandum for the President with a recommended course of action and supporting papers. The work became so intensive that it was carried out in teams within ISA, one operating as a drafting committee and another (Mr. Warnke - ASD/ISA, Dr. Enthoven - ASD/SA, Dr. Halperin - DASD/ISA/PP, Mr. Steadman - DASD/EA & PR) as a kind of policy review board. Of the work done outside the Pentagon only the paper on negotiations prepared by Bundy at State and General Taylor's paper went to the White House. The other materials contributed by the CIA and State were fed into the deliberative process going on at the Pentagon but did not figure directly in the final memo. It would be misleading, however, not to note that the drafting group working within ISA included staff members from both the State Department and the White House, so that the final memo did represent an interagency effort. Nevertheless, the dominant voice in the consideration of alternatives as the working group progressed through three different drafts before the Sunday meeting was that of OSD. To provide some sense of the ideas being debated with respect to the air war and negotiations, relevant sections of a number of papers written during

those frantic days of late February-early March are included below,
even though most of them never reached the President.

The CIA, responding to the requirements of the Clifford
Group for an assessment of the current communist position and the
alternatives open to them, sent several memos to the drafting committee
before the Sunday meeting. On February 29, they argued that the VC/NVA
could be expected to continue the harassment of the urban areas for the
next several months in the hope of exacting a sufficient price from the
U.S. and the GVN to force us to settle the war on their terms. But, no
serious negotiation initiative was anticipated until the conclusion of
the military phase:

4. Political Options. Until the military campaign has
run its course and the results are fairly clear, it is unlikely that Hanoi will be seriously disposed to consider
negotiations with the U.S. A negotiating ploy is possible,
however, at almost any point in the present military campaign.
It would be intentionally designed to be difficult for the
US to reject. The purpose, however, would not be a serious
intent to settle the war, but rather to cause new anxieties
in Saigon, which might cause a crisis and lead to the collapse
of the Thieu-Ky government.

5. As of now Hanoi probably foresees two alternative
sets of circumstances in which a serious move to negotiate
a settlement might be entertained:

a. Obviously, if the military campaign is producing significant successes and the GVN is in serious
disarray at some point Hanoi would probably give the
US the opportunity to end the war. This might take the
form of offering a general cease-fire followed by negotiations on terms which would amount to registering a
complete Communist political success.

b. If, on the other hand, the military campaign
does not go well and the results are inconclusive, then
Hanoi would probably change its military strategy to continue the struggle on a reduced level. 22/

To this assessment was added a somewhat more detailed
estimate the following day addressed to several specific questions.
Expanding on their memo of the previous day in response to a question
about whether the North Vietnamese had abandoned the "protracted conflict"
concept, the Agency concluded:

In our view the intensity of the Tet offensive and the exertions being made to sustain pressures confirms that Hanoi is now engaged in a major effort to achieve early and decisive results. Yet the Communists probably have no rigid timetable. They apparently have high hopes of achieving their objectives this year, but they will preserve considerable tactical flexibility. 23/

Again in more detail, they responded to a question about negotiations, a bombing suspension and terms of settlement:

What is the Communist attitude toward negotiations: in particular how would Hanoi deal with an unconditional cessation of US bombing of NVN and what would be its terms for a settlement?

8. The Communists probably still expect the war to end eventually in some form of negotiations. Since they hope the present military effort will be decisive in destroying the GVN and ARVN, they are not likely to give any serious consideration to negotiations until this campaign has progressed far enough for its results to be fairly clear.

9. If, however, the US ceased the bombing of North Vietnam in the near future, Hanoi would probably respond more or less as indicated in its most recent statements. It would begin talks fairly soon, would accept a fairly wide ranging exploration of issues, but would not moderate its terms for a final settlement or stop fighting in the South.

10. In any talks, Communist terms would involve the establishment of a new "coalition" government, which would in fact if not in appearance be under the domination of the Communists. Secondly, they would insist on a guaranteed withdrawal of US forces within some precisely defined period. Their attitude toward other issues would be dictated by the degree of progress in achieving these two primary objectives, and the military-political situation then obtaining in South Vietnam.

11. Cessation of bombing and opening of negotiations without significant Communist concessions would be deeply disturbing to the Saigon government. There would be a real risk that the Thieu-Ky regime would collapse, and this would in fact be part of Hanoi's calculation in accepting negotiations. 24/

On March 2, the CIA made one additional input to the
deliberations, this time on the question of Soviet and Chinese aid
to North Vietnam. The intelligence offered was based on the report
of a high-level defector and concluded with a disturbing estimate of
how the Soviets would react to the closing of Haiphong harbor. In
summary this is what the CIA expected in the way of international communist aid to Hanoi:

International Communist Aid to North Vietnam

Summary

The USSR continues to provide the overwhelming share
of the increasing amounts of military aid being provided
to North Vietnam and is willing to sustain this commitment
at present or even higher levels. A recent high-level
defector indicates that aid deliveries will increase even
further in 1968. He also makes it clear that there is
no quantitative limit to the types of the assistance that
the USSR would provide with the possible exception of
offensive weapons that would result in a confrontation
with the U.S. He also reports that the USSR cannot afford
to provide aid if it wishes to maintain its position in
the socialist camp.

This source does not believe that the recent increase
in aid deliveries reflects an awareness on the part of
European Communist power that the Tet offensive was imminent.

The defector confirms intelligence estimates that the
USSR has not been able to use its aid programs as a means
of influencing North Vietnam's conduct of the war. In
his opinion the Chinese are a more influential power.

Finally, the defector reports that the USSR will use
force to maintain access to the port of Haiphong. The
evidence offered to support this statement conflicts
sharply with the present judgment of the intelligence community and is undergoing extremely close scrutiny. 25/

Bundy's office at State furnished a copious set of papers
dealing with many aspects of the situation that are covered in greater
detail in Task Force Paper IV.C.6. For our purposes I will consider
only some of the judgments offered about Soviet, Chinese and other
reactions to various courses of action against North Vietnam. The basic
alternatives which were the basis of the appraisals of likely foreign
reaction were drafted by Bundy and approved by Katzenbach as follows:

Option A

This would basically consist of accepting the Wheeler-Westmoreland recommendation aimed at sending roughly 100,000 men by 1 May, and another 100,000 men by the end of 1968.

This course of action is assumed to mean no basic change in strategy with respect to areas and places we attempt to hold. At the same time, the option could include some shift in the distribution of our increased forces, in the direction of city and countryside security and to some extent away from "search and destroy" operations away from populated areas.

The option basically would involve full presentation to the Congress of the total Wheeler/Westmoreland package, with all its implications for the reserves, tax increases, and related actions.

At the same time, there are sub-options with respect to the negotiating posture we adopt if we present such a total package. These sub-options appear to be as follows:

Option A-1: Standing pat on the San Antonio formula and on our basic position of what would be acceptable in a negotiated settlement.

Option A-2: Accompanying our presenting the announcement with a new "peace offensive" modifying the San Antonio formula or our position on a negotiated settlement, or both.

Option A-3: Making no present change in our negotiating posture, but making a strong noise that our objective is to create a situation from which we can in fact move into negotiations within the next 4 - 8 months if the situation can be righted.

Option B

The essence of this option would be a change in our military strategy, involving a reduction in the areas and places we sought to control. It might involve withdrawal from the western areas of I Corps and from the highland areas, for example. The objective would be to concentrate our forces, at whatever level, far more heavily on the protection of populated areas. Again, there are sub-options, roughly as follows: .

Option B-1: Such a change in strategy, with no increase or minimal increase in forces.

Option B-2: Such a change in strategy accompanied by a substantial increase in forces, although possibly less than the totals indicated in the Wheeler-Westmoreland proposals.

Option C:

This might be called the "air power" or "greater emphasis on the North" option. It would appear to fit most readily with an Option B course of action in the South, but would mean that we would extend our bombing and other military actions against the North to try to strangle the war there and put greater pressure on Hanoi in this area. 26/

Three other options were also offered but carried no specific proposals for the air war or the negotiations track.

These generalized options took on more specific form when Bundy examined possible Soviet and Chinese reactions. Among the possible U.S. actions against North Vietnam, he evaluated mining the harbors, all-out bombing of the North, and invasion. These were the Soviet responses he anticipated:

3. Mining or Blockade of DRV Ports. This is a prospect the Soviets have dreaded. Mining, in particular, is a tough problem for them because it would not readily permit them to play on our own worries about escalation. They could attempt to sweep the mines which we would then presumably resow. They could somehow help the DRV in attacking US aircraft and ships engaged in the mining operation, even if this was occurring outside territorial waters, but such operations, apart from risking firefights with the US, do not seem very promising. Blockade, on the other hand, confronts the Soviets with the choice of trying to run it. They might decide to try it in the hope that we would stand aside. They would almost certainly authorize their ship captains to resist US inspection, capture or orders to turn around. What happens next again gets us into the essentially unknowable. In any case, however, it is unlikely that the Soviets would attempt naval or DRV-based air escorts for their ships. Naval escort would of course require the dispatch of vessels from Soviet home ports. On balance, but not very confidently, I would conclude that in the end the Soviets would turn their ships around, a highly repulsive possibility for

Moscow. Presumably, in such an event, they would seek to
increase shipments via China, if China lets them. (Purely
in terms of the military impact on the DRV, it should be
understood that the bulk of Soviet military hardware goes
to the DRV by rail and a blockade would therefore not in
and of itself impede the flow of Soviet arms).

4. <u>All-out US Bombing of the DRV</u>. This one poses
tougher problems for the Soviets and hence for any assessment of what they would do. Moscow has in the past shown
some sensitivity to the consequences of such a US course.
If the US program resulted in substantial damage to the
DRV air defense system (SAMs, MIGs, AAA, radars, etc.) the
Soviets will seek to replenish it as rapidly as possible
via China and, assuming the Chinese will let them, i.e.
permit trains to pass and planes to overfly and land en route.
Soviet personnel can be expected to participate in the DRV
air defense in an advisory capacity and in ground operations
and the Soviets will presumably keep quiet about any casualties they might suffer in the process. It is likely, however,
that this kind of Soviet involvement would increase up to
and including, in the extreme, the overt dispatch, upon
DRV request, of volunteers. (Moscow has long said it would
do so and it is difficult to see how it could avoid delivering
on its promise.) Such volunteers might actually fly DRV
aircraft if enough DRV pilots had meanwhile been lost.
Needless to say, once this stage is reached assessments
become less confident, if only because the US Administration
itself will have to consider just how far it wants to go in
engaging the Soviets in an air battle in Vietnam. The
Soviets for their part are not well situated to conduct a
major air defense battle in Vietnam and there is the further
question whether the Chinese would be prepared to grant
them bases for staging equipment and personnel or for
sanctuary. (On past form this seems unlikely, but this
might change if the US air offensive produced decisive
effects on the DRV's capacity to continue the war, in itself
a dubious result.)

5. <u>Invasion of the Southern DRV</u>. In this case, the
Soviets would continue and, if needed, step up their hardware assistance to the DRV. If the fighting remained confined to the Southern part of the DRV and did not threaten
the viability of the DRV regime, there would probably not
be additional Soviet action, though conceivably some Soviet
personnel might show up in advisory capacities, especially

if new and sophisticated Soviet equipment were being
supplied. If the invasion became a general assault on
the DRV, an overt DRV call for volunteers might ensue
and be acted on. At this point of course the Chinese
would enter into the picture too and we are in a complex
new contingency. In general, it is hard to visualize
large numbers of Chinese and Soviet forces (transported
through China) fighting side by side against us in Vietnam and I would assume that what we would have would be
largely a US landwar against the DRV-China.

    6. Matters would become even stickier if the US
offensive led to repeated damage to Soviet ships in DRV
ports. (There are roughly eleven Soviet ships in these
ports on any one day). The Soviets might arm their
vessels and authorize them to fire at US planes. Once
again, when this point has been reached we are in a
new contingency, although the basic fact holds that
the Soviets are not well situated, geographically
and logistically, for effective military counter-action
in the DRV itself. 27/

    China's expected reactions to these three possible courses
of action were quite different in view of the lower level of its economic
and military support, the existence of ample land LOCs to China, etc.
Here is how Bundy foresaw Chinese responses:

3. _Mining and/or Blockading of Haiphong_

    China would probably not regard the loss of Haiphong
port facilities as critically dangerous to the war effort
since it could continue to supply North Vietnam by rail
and road and by small ships and lighters. In addition,
Peking might seek to replace Haiphong as a deep sea
port, by expanding operations (Chanchiang, Ft. Bayard),
which is already serving as an unloading point for
goods destined for shipment by rail to North Vietnam.
China would be all means make sure that the flow of
both Soviet and Chinese material for North Vietnam--
by land and by sea--continued uninterrupted and might
welcome the additional influence it would gain as the
remaining main link in North Vietnam's life line. It
also would probably put at North Vietnam's disposal as
many shallow draft vessels as it could possibly spare,
and assist Hanoi in developing alternate maritime off-
loading facilities and inland waterway routes. At the
same time, the Chinese would probably be ready to
assist in improving North Vietnamese coastal defenses,
and might provide additional patrol boats, possibly
including guided missile vessels.

4. All-Out Conventional Bombing of North Vietnam,
   Including Hanoi and Haiphong

China would probably be prepared to provide as
much logistical support and labor as the North Vietnamese
might need to keep society functioning in North Vietnam and to help Hanoi maintain the war effort in the
South. Peking would probably be ready to increase its
anti-aircraft artillery contingent in the South, (possibly
sending SAM batteries), and would probably supply the
North Vietnamese air force with MIG-19's from its own
inventory. Chinese airspace and airfields would be
made available, as and when necessary, as a refuge for
North Vietnamese aircraft. There is a strong possibility
that Chinese pilots in MIG's with North Vietnamese
markings would engage US bombers over North Vietnam.
However, we would anticipate overt Chinese intervention
only if the scope of the bombing seemed intended to
destroy North Vietnam as a viable Communist state.

5. US Invasion of North Vietnam

Chinese reaction would depend on the scale of US
moves, on North Vietnamese intentions and on Peking's
view of US objectives. If it became evident that we
were not aiming for a rapid takeover of North Vietnam
but intended chiefly to hold some territory in southern
areas to inhibit Hanoi's actions in South Vietnam and to
force it to quit fighting, we would expect China to
attempt to deter us from further northward movement and
to play on our fears of a Sino-US conflict, but not to
intervene massively in the war. Thus, if requested by
Hanoi, Peking would probably be willing to station infantry
north of Hanoi to attach some ground forces to North Vietnamese units further south, and to contribute to any
"volunteer" contingent that North Vietnam might organize.
At home, China would probably complement these deterrents
by various moves ostensibly putting the country on a
war footing.

If the North Vietnamese, under threat of a full-
scale invasion, decided to agree to a negotiated settlement, the Chinese would probably go along. On the other
hand, if the Chinese believed that the US was intent on
destroying the North Vietnamese regime (either because
Hanoi insisted on holding out to the end, or because Peking
chronically expects the worst from the US), they would
probably fear for their own security and intervene on a
massive scale. 28/

Probably more influential than these State Department
Views on international communist reactions was a cable from Ambassador
Thompson in Moscow offering his personal assessment of the Soviet mood
and what we might expect from various US decisions. The cable was
addressed to Under Secretary Katzenbach, but there is little doubt it
made its way to the White House in view of Thompson's prestige and the
importance of his post. For these reasons it is included here in its
entirety.

DEPARTMENT OF STATE   TELEGRAM

TOP SECRET

PP RUEMC
DE RUEHCR 2933FD 0611525
ZNY TTTTT
P 011515Z MAR 68
FM AMEMBASSY MOSCOW
TO SECSTATE WASHDC PRIORITY 7620
STATE GRNC
BT
T O P S E C R E T MOSCOW 2983

CONTROL: 2390

RECD: MARCH 1, 1968

2:11 P.M.

NODIS

LITERALLY EYES ONLY FOR UNDER SECRETARY FROM AMBASSADOR

REF: STATE 122443

1. BEFORE ADDRESSING SPECIFIC ACTION ALTERNATIVES I SUBMIT FOLLOWING
GENERAL OBSERVATIONS APPLICABLE TO ALL. MUCH WOULD DEPEND UPON
GENERAL SETTING IN WHICH GIVEN ACTION TOOK PLACE. IF ANY OF THEM
COME-OUT OF THE BLUE OR IN SITUATION WHICH APPEARED TO REFLECT U.S.
DECISION TO ACHIEVE CLEAR MILITARY VICTORY, SOVIET REACTION WOULD
BE FAR STRONGER THAN IF IT APPEARED TO BE EFFORT TO OFFSET MILITARY
REVERSES. IMPORTANT ALSO WOULD BE CURRENT WEIGHT OF OPINION IN

PAGE 2 RUEHCR 2983FD T O P S E C R E T
POLITBURO BETWEEN HAWKS AND DOVES OF WHICH WE KNOW LITTLE. HOWEVER,
SOVIET FRUSTRATIONS AT BUDAPEST CONFERENCE, PROBABLE EFFECT ON
SOVIET LEADERSHIP OF THEIR OWN PROPAGANDA WHICH HAS BEEN INCREASING
IN STRIDENCY RECENTLY AND WHICH HAS TENDED TO STRENGTHEN SOVIET
COMMITMENT NOT ONLY TO NVN BUT ALSO TO NLF, AND EFFECT ON LEADERSHIP
OF OTHER PROBLEMS SUCH AS MIDDLE EAST AND KOREA, ALL, IT SEEMS TO
ME, HAVE OPERATED TO MAKE SOVIET REACTIONS MORE LIKELY TO BE VIGOROUS
THAN WAS THE CASE A YEAR AGO.

2. IT SHOULD ALSO BE NOTED THAT SOVIET REACTIONS WOULD NOT
NECESSARILY BE CONFINED TO VIETNAM. THEY COULD INCREASE TENSION
IN GERMANY, PARTICULARLY IN BERLIN, IN KOREA AND MIDDLE EAST.
THEY COULD REVERT TO ALL-OUT COLD WAR AND IN ANY EVENT WOULD STEP
UP DIPLOMATIC AND PROPAGANDA ACTIVITY.

3. IN ALL OF ALTERNATIVES MENTIONED I WOULD EXPECT INCREASED

PAGE 3 RUEHCR 2983FD T O P S E C R E T
SOVIET MILITARY AID WHICH IN SOME CASES MIGHT GO AS FAR AS USE OF

-2- MOSCOW 2983, MARCH 1, 1968

VOLUNTEERS IF NORTH VIETNAM WOULD ACCEPT THEM, ALTHOUGH MOST LIKELY
IN ANTIAIRCRAFT AND OTHER DEFENSIVE ROLES. IN SOME CASES THEY
MIGHT ASK FOR USE CHINESE AIRFIELDS. I SHOULD THINK SUPPLY OF
MEDIUM RANGE ROCKETS OR OTHER SOPHISTICATED EQUIPMENT A REAL
POSSIBILITY.

4. FOLLOWING ARE COMMENTS ON SPECIFIC CASES ALTHOUGH I MUST ADMIT
MY CRYSTAL BALL IS VERY CLOUDY:
A. MINING OF HAIPHONG HARBOR WOULD CERTAINLY PROVOKE STRONG SOVIET
REACTION. AS A MIMUM I WOULD EXPECT THEM TO PROVIDE MINESWEEPERS,
POSSIBLY WITH SOVIET NAVAL CREWS. BECAUSE OF INCREASED DEPENDENCE
OF NVN ON CHINA FOR SUPPLIES AS A RESULT SUCH ACTION, SOVIETS WOULD
READ INTO THIS WIDER IMPLICATIONS RELATED TO THE SINO-SOVIET QUARREL.
B. INTENSIFIED BOMBING OF HANOI HAIPHONG AREA MIGHT CAUSE SOVIETS
TO ARM THEIR MERCHANT SHIPS OR POSSIBLY EVEN ESCORT THEM IF ONE
WERE SUNK. IF HEAVY CIVILIAN CASUALTIES RESULTED THEY MIGHT PERSUADE
NVN TO AGREE TO BRING MATTER TO THE UN AND WOULD AT LEAST ORGANIZE
WORLDWIDE PROPAGANDA CAMPAIGN AND POSSIBLY PUSH FOR INTERNATIONAL
BOYCOTT.

PAGE 4 RUEHCR 2983FD T O P S E C R E T
C. AN INCHON-TYPE LANDING WOULD PROBABLY CAUSE EXTREMELY GRAVE
REACTION. NATURE SOVIET ACTION WOULD BE AFFECTED BY WHAT CHINESE
COMMUNISTS DID. SOVIETS WOULD NOT WISH TO BE IN POSITION OF
DOING LESS. THEY WOULD PROBABLY CONSIDER LANDING AS PRELUDE TO
FULL SCALE INVASION AND DESTRUCTION NVN GOVERNMENT REGARDLESS OF
HOW WE DESCRIBED THE OPERATION.
D. I DOUBT THAT OUR ACTIVITY IN NORTHERN PORTION OF DMZ WOULD BE
REGARDED AS VERY SERIOUS BUT RAIDS BEYOND THAT WOULD CAUSE STRONGER
REACTION DEPENDING SOMEWHAT UPON HOW IT WAS REPORTED IN WORLD PRESS.
THEY WOULD BE CONCERNED THAT WE MIGHT BE LAUNCHING TRIAL BALLOON
AND THAT THEIR FAILURE TO REACT STRONGLY MIGHT INVITE ACTUAL INVASION.
E. I AM INCLINED TO BELIEVE THEY WOULD TAKE US/GVN GROUND ACTION
IN LAOS LESS SERIOUSLY THAN SIMILAR ACTION IN CAMBODIA, PARTICULARLY
IF THIS FOLLOWED FURTHER SUCCESSFUL PATEREY LAO VNV OFFENSIVES.
F. I THINK THERE WOULD BE VERY LITTLE SOVIET REACTION TO INCREASED
U.S. DEPLOYMENTS IN SVN ALTHOUGH THERE WOULD PROBABLY BE SOME
INCREASE IN QUANTITY AND QUALITY OF MILITARY EQUIPMENT SUPPLIED BY
SOVIETS. THE SAME WOULD BE TRUE OF REQUEST FOR MASSIVE BUDGET
INCREASE.

-3- MOSCOW 2983, MARCH 1, 1968

PAGE 5 RUEHCR 2983FD T O P S E C R E T

5. IN SUM, ANY SERIOUS ESCALATION EXCEPT IN SOUTH VIETNAM WOULD
TRIGGER STRONG SOVIET RESPONSE ALTHOUGH I BELIEVE THEY WILL ENDEAVOR
TO AVOID DIRECT CONFRONTATION WITH US IN THAT AREA. A PRIOR BOMBING
PAUSE WOULD MITGATE THEIR REACTION TO ALTERNATIVES DISCUSSED EVEN
THOUGH WE MIGHT HAVE TO RESUME AFTER SHORT PERIOD BECAUSE OF INCREAS-
ED INFILTRATION OR CLEARLY UNACCEPTABLE DEMANDS PUT FORWARD BY NVN
AT START OF NEGOTIATIONS. ANYTHING WE CAN DO THAT WOULD DIMINISH
PICTURE SOVIETS HAVE BUILT UP IN THEIR OWN MINDS OF U.S. PUSUIT OF
WORLDWIDE OFFENSIVE POLICY, AS FOR EXAMPLE PROGRESS TOWARD MIDDLE
EAST SETTLEMENT, WOULD PROBABLY MAKE THEM MORE TOLERANT OF OUR
ACTIONS IN VIETNAM.

GP-1. THOMPSON
BT

General Maxwell Taylor, like Bundy, sought to place the
alternatives available to the U.S. into some sort of framework and to
package the specific actions and responses to the situation the U.S.
might take so as to create several viable options for consideration
by the group. The memo he drafted on alternatives was more important
finally than the one done by Bundy since Taylor sent a copy of it
directly to the President in his capacity as Special Military Advisor,
as well as giving it to the Clifford Group. With his background as a
military man, past Chairman of the JCS, and former Ambassador to Saigon
Taylor's views carry special weight in any deliberation. His memo was
sent to the White House even before the DPM the Clifford Group was
working on and is therefore included in part here. Taylor wisely
began by reconsidering the objectives of the U.S. involvement in Vietnam,
both past and potential. They were, as he saw it, four:

Alternative Objectives of U.S. Policy in South Viet-Nam

2. The overall policy alternatives open to the U.S.
have always been and continue to be four in number. The
first is the continued pursuit of our present objective
which has been defined in slightly different terms but always
in essentially the same sense by our political leaders. For
the purpose of this paper, I am taking the statement of
President Johnson in his speech at Johns Hopkins University
in April, 1965: "Our objective is the independence of
South Viet-Nam and its freedom from attack. We want nothing
for ourselves, only that the people of South Viet-Nam be
allowed to guide their own country in their own way."

3. We have sometimes confused the situation by suggesting that this is not really our objective, that we
have other things in mind such as the defeat of the "War
of Liberation" technique, the containment of Red China,
and a further application of the Truman Doctrine to the
resistance of aggression. However, it is entirely possible
to have one or more of these collateral objectives at the
same time since they will be side effects of the attainment
of the basic objective cited above.

4. Of the other three possible objectives, one is
above and two are below the norm established by the present
one. We can increase our present objective to total
military victory, unconditional surrender, and the destruction of the Communist Government in North Viet-Nam.
Alternatively, we can lower our objective to a compromise
resulting in something less than an independent Viet-Nam
free from attack or we can drop back further and content
ourselves with punishing the aggressor to the point that
we can withdraw, feeling that the "War of Liberation"
technique has at least been somewhat discredited as a
cheap method of Communist expansion.

5. We should consider changing the objective
which we have been pursuing consistently since 1954
only for the most cogent reasons. There is clearly
nothing to recommend trying to do more than what we are
now doing at such great cost. To undertake to do less
is to accept needlessly a serious defeat for which we
would pay dearly in terms of our world-wide position of
leadership, of the political stability of Southeast Asia,
and of the credibility of our pledges to friends and
allies.

6. In summary, our alternatives are to stay with
our present objective (stick it out), to raise our
objective (all out), to scale down our objective (pull
back), or to abandon our objective (pull out). Since
there is no serious consideration being given at the
moment to adding to or subtracting from the present
objective, the discussion in this paper is limited to
considerations of alternative strategies and programs
to attain the present objective. 29/

With this review of the possible objectives and his own
statement of preference, Taylor turned to the possible responses to
General Westmoreland's troop request and the ramifications of each.
Here he devoted himself more to trying to develop the multiplicity
of considerations that needed to be weighed in each instance than to
passionate advocacy of one or another course. At the end of his
memo he considered the political implications of various options
with special attention to the problem of negotiations with Hanoi --
a subject with which he had long been preoccupied. He concluded
by packaging the various military, political and diplomatic courses of
action into three alternative programs. Here is how he reasoned:

b. As the purpose of our military operations is
to bring security to South Viet-Nam behind which the GVN
can restore order and normalcy of life and, at the same
time, to convince Hanoi of the impossibility of realizing
its goal of a Communist-controlled government imposed
upon South Viet-Nam, we have to consider the political
effect of our military actions both on Saigon and on
Hanoi. With regard to Saigon, a refusal to reinforce
at this time will bring discouragement and renewed suspicion of U.S. intentions; in Hanoi, an opposite effect.
On the other hand, a large reinforcement may lessen the
sense of urgency animating the Vietnamese Government and
result in a decrease of effort; in Hanoi, it may cause them
to undertake further escalation.

<u>c</u>. Our decision on reinforcement inevitably will raise the question of how to relate this action to possible negotiations. Anything we say or do with regard to negotiations causes the sharpest scrutiny of our motives on the part of our Vietnamese allies and we should be very careful at this time that we do not give them added grounds for suspicion. If it appears desirable for us to make a new negotiation overture in connection with reinforcement, it will need careful preliminary discussion with the GVN authorities.

<u>d</u>. The following political actions are worth considering in connection with our decision on reinforcement:

(1) A renewed offer of negotiation, possibly with a private communication that we would suspend the bombing for a fixed period without making the time limitation public if we were assured that productive negotiations would start before the end of the period.

(2) A public announcement that we would adjust the bombing of the North to the level of intensity of enemy ground action in the South.

(3) As a prelude to sharply increased bombing levels, possibly to include the closing of Haiphong, a statement of our intentions made necessary by the enemy offensive against the cities and across the frontiers.

(4) Announcement of the withdrawal of the San Antonio formula in view of the heightened level of aggression conducted by North Viet-Nam.

(5) Keep silent.

The foregoing is merely a tabulation of possible political actions to consider in chossing the military alternative. In the end, military and political actions should be blended together into an integrated package.

<u>e</u>. The choice among these political alternatives will depend largely on our decision with regard to reinforcements for General Westmoreland. However, the present military situation in South Viet-Nam argues strongly against a new negotiation effort (<u>d</u>. (1)) and any thought of reducing the bombing of the North. If we decide to meet General Westmoreland's request, we could underline the significance of our action by <u>d</u>. (3). In any case, we would appear well-advised to withdraw from the San Antonio formula (<u>d</u>. (4)).

13. From the foregoing considerations, there appear
to be at least three program packages worth serious consideration. They follow:

Package A

a. No increase of General Westmoreland's forces
in South Viet-Nam.

b. New strategic guidance.

c. Build-up of Strategic Reserve.

d. No negotiation initiative.

e. Withdrawal of San Antonio formula.

f. Pressure on GVN to do better.

Package B

a. Partial acceptance of General Westmoreland's
recommendation.

b. New strategic guidance.

c. Build-up of Strategic Reserve.

d. No negotiation initiative.

e. Withdrawal of San Antonio formula.

f. Pressure on GVN to do better.

Package C

a. Approval of General Westmoreland's full
request.

b. New strategic guidance.

c. Build-up of Strategic Reserve.

d. No negotiation initiative.

e. Withdrawal of San Antonio formula and announcement of intention to close Haiphong.

f. Pressure on GVN to do better.

g. Major effort to rally the homefront.

M. D. T. 30/

While these papers were all being written outside the
Pentagon, the Clifford working roup under the direction of Assistant
Secretary Warnke had worked feverishly on several succeeding drafts of
a Memorandum for the President including various combinations of tabs
and supporting material. The intent of the group was to produce a memo
that made a specific recommendation on a course of action rather than
presenting a number of alternatives with their pros and cons. The process
required the reconciling of widely divergent views or the exclusion of
those that were incompatible with the thrust of the recommendation. With
respect to the war in the South the memo in its late-stage form on March 3
proposed a sweeping change in U.S. ground strategy based on a decision not
to substantially increase U.S. forces as General Westmoreland and the
Chiefs desired. In essence, the draft memo recommended the adoption of
a strategy of population protection along a "demographic frontier" in
South Vietnam and the abandonment of General Westmoreland's hitherto
sacrosanct large unit "search and destroy" operations. The portion of
the paper devoted to the air war recommended no escalation above current
levels. It specifically turned back proposals for reducing the Hanoi-
Haiphong restricted perimeters, closing Haiphong harbor, and bombing
population centers as all likely to be unproductive or worse. The section
in question argued as follows:

SIGNIFICANCE OF BOMBING CAMPAIGN IN NORTH TO OUR OBJECTIVES IN VIETNAM

The bombing of North Vietnam was undertaken to limit
and/or make more difficult the infiltration of men and
supplies in the South, to show them they would have to
pay a price for their continued aggression and to raise
the morale in South Vietnam. The last two purposes
obviously have been achieved.

It has become abundantly clear that no level of
bombing can prevent the North Vietnamese from supplying
the necessary forces and materiel necessary to maintain
their military operations in the South. The recent Tet
offensive has shown that the bombing cannot even prevent
a significant increase in these military operations, at
least on an intermittent basis.

The shrinking of the circles around Hanoi and
Haiphong will add to North Vietnam's costs and difficulty

in supplying the NVA/VC forces. It will not destroy their
capability to support their present level of military
activity. Greater concentration on the infiltration routes
in Laos and in the area immediately North of the DMZ might
prove effective from the standpoint of interdiction.

Strikes within 10 miles of the center of Hanoi and
within four miles of the center of Haiphong have required
initial approval from the Joint Chiefs of Staff, the Secretaries of State and Defense, and, finally, the President.
This requirement has enabled the highest level of government to maintain some control over the attacks against
targets located in the populous and most politically
sensitive areas of North Vietnam. Other than the Haiphong
Port, no single target within these areas has any appreciable significance for North Vietnam's ability to supply
men and material to the South. If these areas of control
were reduced to circles having a radii of 3 miles from the
center of Hanoi and 1-1/2 miles of the center of Haiphong,
some minor fixed targets not previously authorized would be
released for strike. More significant is the fact that the
lines of communication lying within the area previously
requiring Washington approval would be open for attack by
shrinking the control areas around Hanoi and Haiphong. The
question would simply be whether it is worth the increase in
airplane and pilot losses to attack these lines of communication in the most heavily defended part of North Vietnam
where our airplane loss ratio is highest.

The remaining issue on interdiction of supplies has to
do with the closing of the Port of Haiphong. Although this
is the route by which some 80% of North Vietnamese imports
come into the country, it is not the point of entry for most
of the military supplies and ammunition. These materials
predominantly enter via the rail routes from China.

Moreover, if the Port of Haiphong were to be closed
effectively, the supplies that now enter Haiphong could,
albeit with considerable difficulty, arrive either over
the land routes or by lighterage, which has been so successful in the continued POL supply. Under these circumstances, the closing of Haiphong Port would not prevent
the continued supply of sufficient materials to maintain
North Vietnamese military operations in the South.

Accordingly, the only purpose of intensification of the
bombing campaign in the North and the addition of further
targets would be to endeavor to break the will of the North
Vietnamese leaders. CIA forecasts indicate little if any
chance that this would result even from a protracted bombing
campaign directed at population centers.

A change in our bombing policy to include deliberate
strikes on population centers and attacks on the agricultural
population through the destruction of dikes would further
alienate domestic and foreign sentiment and might well lose
us the support of those European countries which now support
our effort in Vietnam. It could cost us Australian and
New Zealand participation in the fighting.

Although the North Vietnamese do not mark the camps
where American prisoners are kept or reveal their locations,
we know from intelligence sources that most of these facilities are located in or near Hanoi. Our intelligence also
indicates that many more than the approximately 200 pilots
officially classified by us as prisoners of war may, in
fact, be held by North Vietnam in these camps. On the
basis of the debriefing of the three pilots recently
released by Hanoi, we were able to identify over 40 additional American prisoners despite the fact that they
were kept in relative isolation. Heavy and indiscriminate
attacks in the Hanoi area would jeopardize the lives of
these prisoners and alarm their wives and parents into
vocal opposition. Reprisals could be taken against them
and the idea of war crimes trials would find considerable
acceptance in countries outside the Communist bloc.

Finally, the steady and accelerating bombing of the
North has not brought North Vietnam closer to any real
move toward peace. Apprehensions about bombing attacks
that would destroy Hanoi and Haiphong may at some time
help move them toward productive negotiations. Actual
destruction of these areas would eliminate a threat
that could influence them to seek a political settlement
on terms acceptable to us. 31/

The Clifford Group principals convened on the afternoon of Sunday, March 3, to consider this draft memo. Mr. Warnke read the memo, completed only shortly before the meeting, to the assembled group. The ensuing discussion apparently produced a consensus that abandoning the initiative completely as the draft memo seemed to imply could leave allied forces and the South Vietnamese cities themselves more, not less, vulnerable. With respect to the bombing, opinion was sharply divided. General Wheeler advocated the reduction of the restricted zones around Hanoi and Haiphong and an expansion of naval activity against North Vietnam. The Chiefs had apparently abandoned for the moment efforts to secure authority for mining the approaches to the ports, although this alternative was considered in the State drafts. ISA on the other hand sharply opposed any expansion of the air war but particularly in Route Packages 6A and 6B which a recent Systems Analysis study had shown to be especially unproductive as an anti-infiltration measure. 32/ As for negotiations, all were agreed that not much could be expected in the near future from Hanoi and that there was no reason to modify the current U.S. position. The conclusion of the long meeting was to request Warnke's working group to write an entirely new draft memo for the President that: (a) dealt only with the troop numbers issue, recommending only a modest increase; (b) called for more emphasis on the RVNAF contribution to the war effort; (c) called for a study of possible new strategic guidance; (d) recommended against any new initiative on negotiations; and (e) acknowledged the split in opinion about bombing policy by including papers from both sides. Thus, after five days of exhausting work, the working group started over again and produced a completely fresh draft for the following day.

3. The March 4 DPM

The new DPM was completed on Monday and circulated for comment but later transmitted to the President without change by Secretary Clifford. In its final form this DPM represented the recommendations of the Clifford Group. The main proposals of the memo were those mentioned above. The specific language of the cover memo with respect to bombing and negotiations was the following:

5. No new peace initiative on Vietnam. Re-statement of our terms for peace and certain limited diplomatic actions to dramatize Laos and to focus attention on the total threat to Southeast Asia. Details in Tab E.

6. A general decision on bombing policy, not excluding future change, but adequate to form a basis for discussion with the Congress on this key aspect. Here your advisers are divided:

171

a. General Wheeler and others would advocate a
substantial extension of targets and authority in and
near Hanoi and Haiphong, mining of Haiphong, and naval
gunfire up to a Chinese Buffer Zone;

b. Others would advocate a seasonal step-up
through the spring, but without these added elements. 33/

The two detailed tabs to the memo of special interest to
this study were "E" and "F" dealing with negotiations and bombing respectively. The negotiations paper was written by Bundy and was a lengthy
argument for doing nothing we had not already done. Its central message
was contained in a few paragraphs near the middle of the paper:

As to our conditions for stopping the bombing and
entering into talks, we continue to believe that the San
Antonio formula is "rock bottom." The South Vietnamese
are in fact talking about much stiffer conditions, such
as stopping the infiltration entirely. Any move by us
to modify the San Antonio formula downward would be extremely
disturbing in South Vietnam, and would have no significant
offsetting gains in US public opinion or in key third
countries. On the contrary, we should continue to take the
line that the San Antonio formula laid out conditions under
which there was a reasonable prospect that talks would get
somewhere and be conducted in good faith. Hanoi's major
offensive has injected a new factor, in which we are bound
to conclude that there is no such prospect for the present.

Moreover, we should at the appropriate time --
probably not in a major statement, but rather in response
to a question -- make the point that "normal" infiltration
of men and equipment from the North cannot mean the much
increased levels that have prevailed since October. We
do not need to define exactly what we would mean by
"normal" but we should make clear that we do not mean the
levels since San Antonio was set out.

Apart from this point on our public posture, we should
be prepared -- in the unlikely event that Hanoi makes an
affirmative noise on the "no advantage" assumption -- go
go back at them through some channel and make this same
point quite explicit.

In short, our public posture and our private actions
should be designed to:

a. Maintain San Antonio and our general public
willingness for negotiations.

b. Add this new and justified interpretation
of San Antonio so that in fact we would not be put on
the spot over the next 2-4 months.

c. Keep sufficient flexibility so that, if the
situation should improve, we could move during the summer
if we then judged it wise. 54/

This position represented the widely held belief at the time that the
question of negotiations, in spite of continuing contacts through third
parties, was no less moribund than it had been at any time in the
previous year. The San Antonio formula was regarded as eminently
reasonable and DRV failure to respond to it was interpreted as evidence
of their general disinterest in negotiations at the time. In that
context, and in the wake of the ferocious attacks in South Vietnam, new
initiatives could only be construed by Hanoi as evidence of allied
weakness. Hence, no new offers were recommended.

As already noted, the Clifford Group was split on the
issue of bombing policy, therefore, two papers on the subject were
included. The first had been written by the Joint Staff and was submitted by General Wheeler. It advocated reduction of the Hanoi/Haiphong
perimeters, the extension of naval operations and authority to use
sea-based surface-to-air missiles against North Vietnamese MIGs. The
cover memo for this tab noted that: "In addition General Wheeler would
favor action to close the Port of Haiphong through mining or otherwise.
Since this matter has been repeatedly presented to the President,
General Wheeler has not added a specific paper on this proposal." 35/
The General had apparently gotten the word that closing the ports just
wasn't an action the President was going to consider, even in this
"comprehensive" review. The JCS bombing paper began with a discussion
of the history of the air war and offered some explanations for its
seeming failure to date:

1. The air campaign against North Vietnam is now
entering the fourth year of operations. Only during the
latter part of the past favorable weather season of April
through October 1967, however, has a significant weight
of effort been applied against the major target systems.
During this period, even though hampered by continuous and
temporarily imposed constraints, the air campaign made a
marked impact on the capability of North Vietnam to prosecute the war. Unfortunately, this impact was rapidly
overcome. The constraints on operations and the change
in the monsoon weather provided North Vietnam with numerous
opportunities to recuperate from the effects of the air
strikes. Facilities were rebuilt and reconstituted and
dispersal of the massive material aid from communist
countries continued.

2. There is a distinct difference between the North
Vietnam that existed in early 1965 and the North Vietnam
of today. The difference is a direct result of the material
aid received from external sources and the ability to
accommodate to limited and sporadic air strikes. The Hanoi
regime throughout the air campaign has not shown a change
in national will, but outwardly displays a determination to
continue the war. The viability of the North Vietnam military posture results from the availability of adequate
assets received from communist countries which permits
defense of the homeland and support of insurgency in the
South. 36/

To make the air campaign effective in its objectives in the months ahead,
the Chiefs recommended modification of the existing regulations. The
campaign they had in mind and the changes in present policy required for
it were as follows:

4. A coordinated and sustained air campaign could
hamper severely the North Vietnam war effort and the
continued support of aggression throughout Southeast
Asia. An integrated interdiction campaign should be
undertaken against the road, rail and waterway lines
of communication with the objective of isolating the
logistics base of Hanoi and Haiphong from each other and
from the rest of North Vietnam. To achieve this objective,
the following tasks must be performed employing a properly
balanced weight of effort:

a. Destroy war supporting facilities as well as
those producing items vital to the economy.

b. Attack enemy defenses in order to protect
our strike forces, destroy enemy gun crews and weapons,
and force the expenditure of munitions.

c. Conduct air attacks throughout as large an
area and as continuously as possible in order to destroy
lines of communication targets and associated facilities,
dispersed material and supplies and to exert maximum
suppression of normal activities because of the threat.

d. Attack and destroy railroad rolling stock,
vehicles and waterborne logistics craft throughout as
large an area as possible, permitting minimum sanctuaries.

5. Targeting criteria for the effective accomplishment of a systematic air campaign would continue to
preclude the attack of population as a target, but accept

174

greater risks of civilian casualties in order to achieve the stated objective. The initial changes in operating authorities necessary to the initiation of an effective air campaign are:

     a. Delete the 30/10NM Hanoi Restricted/Prohibited Area and establish a 3NM Hanoi Control Area (Map, TAB   ).

     b. Delete the 10/4NM Haiphong Restricted/Prohibited Area and establish a 1.5NM Haiphong Control Area (Map, TAB   ).

     c. Delete the Special Northeast Coastal Armed Reconnaissance Area. 37/

     As explanations of how the removal of these restrictions would achieve the desired results, the Chiefs gave the following arguments:

     6. The present Restricted Areas around Hanoi and Haiphong have existed since 1965. The Prohibited Areas were created in December 1966. Numerous strikes, however, have been permitted in these areas over the past two and one-half years, e.g., dispersed POL, SAM and AAA sites, SAM support facilities, armed reconnaissance of selected LOC and attacks of LOC associated targets, and attack of approved fixed targets. The major political requirements for having established control areas in the vicinity of Hanoi and Haiphong are to provide a measure of control of the intensity of effort applied in consonance with the national policy of graduated pressures and to assist in keeping civilian casualties to a minimum consistent with the importance of the target. These requirements can still be satisfied in the control areas are reduced to 3NM and 1.5NM around Hanoi and Haiphong, respectively. These new control areas will contain the population centers, but permit operational commanders the necessary flexibility to attack secondary, as well as primary, lines of communication to preclude NVN from accommodating to the interdiction of major routes. A reduction of the control areas would expose approximately 140 additional miles of primary road, rail and waterway lines of communication to armed reconnaissance, as well as hundreds of miles of secondary lines of communication, dependent upon NVN reactions and usage. Additional military targets would automatically become authorized for air strikes under armed reconnaissance operating authorities. This would broaden the target base, spread the defenses, and thus add to the cumulative effects of the interdiction program as well as reducing risk of

aircraft loss. At the present time, the air defense
threat throughout all of the northeast area of NVN is
formidable. It is not envisioned that aircraft will
conduct classifical low level armed reconnaissance up
and down the newly exposed lines of communication until
the air defense threat is fairly well neutralized.
Attacks of LOC or LOC associated targets and moving
targets in these areas will continue to be conducted
for the time being using dive bombing, or "fixed target"
tactics as is currently employed throughout the heavily
defended northeast. Consequently, the risk to aircraft
and crews will not be increased. In fact these new
operating areas should assist in decreasing the risks.
New targets within the control areas will continue to
be approved in Washington.

7. There have been repeated and reliable intelligence
reports that indicate civilians not engaged in essential
war supporting activities have been evacuated from the
cities of Hanoi and Haiphong. Photographic intelligence,
particularly of Haiphong, clearly shows that materials of
war are stockpiled in all open storage areas and along
the streets throughout almost one-half of the city.
Rather than an area for urban living, the city has become
an armed camp and a large logistics storage base. Consequently, air strikes in and around these cities endanger
personnel primarily engaged directly or indirectly in
support of the war effort.

8. The special coastal armed reconnaissance area
in the Northeast has limited attacks on NVN craft to those
within 3 NM of the NVN coast or coastal islands. This
constraint has provided another sanctuary to assist NVN
in accommodating to the interdiction effort. To preclude
endangering foreign shipping the requirement is imposed
on strike forces to ensure positive identification prior
to attack. Identification can be accomplished beyond
an arbitrary 3 NM line as well as within it, and deny
the enemy a privileged area. 38/

To complement the expanded strike program lifting these restrictions
envisaged, the Chiefs asked for the expansion of the SEA DRAGON naval
activities against coastal water traffic from 20° to the Chinese border,
thereby opening up the possibility of attacks against some of the
traffic moving supplies in and near the ports. Furthermore they desired
permission to use sea-based SAMs, particularly the 100-mile range TALOS,
against MIGs north of 20°. In concluding their discussion of the need
for these new authorizations, the Chiefs were careful to hedge about

what results might be expected immediately. It was pointed out that
adverse weather would continue to inhibit operations for several months
and partially offset the new measures.

13. Authorization to conduct a campaign against North
Vietnam employing air and naval forces under the proposed
operating authorities should have a significant impact on
the ability of NVN to continue to prosecute insurgency.
It is not anticipated that this impact will be immediately
apparent. Unfavorable weather, while partially offset by
the expanded use of naval forces, will preclude air strike
forces from applying the desired pressures at the most
advantageous time and place. The cumulative effects of
the air strikes and naval bombardment will gradually
increase to significant proportions as erosion of the
distribution system progresses. In addition to the material effects against NVN's capability to wage war, approval
of the proposed operating authorities and execution of the
campaign envisioned will signal to NVN and the remainder
of the world the continued US resolve and determination to
achieve our objectives in Southeast Asia. 39/

The ISA memo on bombing policy, drafted in Warnke's own
office, tersely and emphatically rejected all of these JCS recommendations
for expanding the air war, including mining the harbor approaches. The
case against further extension of the bombing was made as follows:

The Campaign Against North Vietnam: A Different View

Bombing Policy

It is clear from the TET offensive that the air attack
on the North and the interdiction campaign in Laos have not
been successful in putting a low enough ceiling on infiltration of men and materials from the North to the South to
prevent such a level of enemy action. We do not see the
possibility of a campaign which could do more than make
the enemy task more difficult. Bombing in Route Packages 6A
and 6B is therefore primarily a political tool.

The J.C.S. recommend a substantial reduction in previous
political control over the attacks in the Haiphong and
Hanoi areas. Except for General Wheeler, we do not recommend such a reduction.

It is not until May that more than four good bombing
days per month can be anticipated. The question arises as

to how best to use those opportunities. We believe the
political value of the attacks should be optimized. We
believe the political value of the attacks should be
optimized. The effective destruction of clearly important
military and economic targets without excessive population damage would seem indicated. Excessive losses in
relation to results would have an adverse political effect.
The air fields (perhaps including Gia Lam) would meet
the criteria. The Hanoi power plant would probably meet
the criteria. There are few other targets of sufficient
importance, not already authorized, to do so.

In particular, this view opposes the proposal to
define only 3-mile and 1-1/2-mile "closed areas" around
Hanoi and Haiphong respectively. Individual targets
within Hanoi and Haiphong and between the 10- and 3-mile
circles for Hanoi and the 4 and 1-1/2 mile-circles for
Haiphong, should be considered on a case-by-case basis
in accordance with the above criteria. However, blanket
authority for operations up to the 3-mile and 1-1/2-mile
circles, respectively, appears to take in only small
targets hving no appreciable military significance; on
the other hand, experience has indicated that systematic
operations particularly against road and rail routes
simply and slightly to the repair burdens, while at the
same time involving substantial civilian casualties in
the many suburban civilian areas located along these routes.

In addition, a picture of systematic and daily bombing
this close to Hanoi and Haiphong seems to us to run significant risks of major adverse reactions in key third
nations. There is certainly some kind of "flash point"
in the ability of the British Government to maintain its
support for our position, and we believe this "flash
point" might well be crossed by the proposed operations,
in contrast to operations against specified targets of
the type that have been carried out in the Hanoi and
Haiphong areas in the past.

Mining of Haiphong

We believe it to be agreed that substantial amounts
of military-related supplies move through the Port of
Haiphong at present. Nevertheless, it is also agreed
that this flow of supplies could be made up through far
greater use of the road and rail lines running through
China, and through lightering and other emergency techniques

at Haiphong and other ports. In other words, even from a
military standpoint the effect of closing the Port of
Haiphong would be to impose an impediment only for a period
of time, and to add to difficulties which Hanoi has shown
in the past it can overcome. Politically, moreover, closing
the Port of Haiphong continues to raise a serious question
of Soviet reaction. Ambassador Thompson, Governor Harriman,
and others believe that the Soviets would be compelled to
react in some manner -- at a minimum through the use of
minesweepers and possibly through protective naval action
of some sort. Again, we continue to believe that there
is some kind of "flash point" both in terms of these likely
actions and their implications for our relation with the
Soviets in other matters, and for such more remote -- but
not inconceivable -- possibilities as Soviet compensating
pressure elsewhere, for example against Berlin. Even a
small risk of a significant confrontation with the Soviets
must be given major weight against the limited military
gains anticipated from this action.

Finally, by throwing the burden of supply onto the
rail and road lines through China, the mining of Haiphong
would tend to increase Chinese leverage in Hanoi and would
force the Soviets and the Chinese to work out cooperative
arrangements for their new and enlarged transit. We do
not believe this would truly drive the Soviets and Chinese
together, but it would force them to take a wider range of
common positions that would certainly not be favorable to
our basic interests.

Expanded Naval Operations (SEA DRAGON)

These operations, expanded north along the coast to
Haiphong and to other port areas, would include provision
for avoiding ocean-going ships, while hitting coast-wise
shipping assumed to be North Vietnamese.

We believe this distinction will not be easy to apply
without error, and that therefore the course of action
involves substantial risks of serious complications with
Chinese and other shipping. In view of the extensive
measures already authorized further south, we doubt if
the gains to be achieved would warrant these risks.

Surface-to-Air Missiles

As in the past, we believe this action would involve
substantial risk of triggering some new form of North

Vietnamese military action against the ships involved.
Moreover, another factor is whether we can be fully
certain of target identification. The balance on this
one is extremely close, but we continue to question
whether expected gains would counter-balance the risks. 40/

It is interesting that the entire discussion of bombing on
both sides in the DPM is devoted to various kinds of escalation. The proposal that was eventually to be adopted, namely cutting back the bombing
to the panhandle only, was not even mentioned, nor does it appear in any
of the other drafts or papers related to the Clifford Group's work. The
fact may be misleading, however, since it apparently was one of the
principle ideas being discussed and considered in the forums at various
levels. It is hard to second-guess the motivation of a Secretary of
Defense, but, since it is widely believed that Clifford personally advocated
this idea to the President, he may well have decided that fully countering
the JCS recommendations for escalation was sufficient for the formal DPM.
To have raised the idea of constricting the bombing below the 19th or 20th
parallel in the memo to the President would have generalized the knowledge
of such a suggestion and invited its sharp, full and formal criticism by
the JCS and other opponents of a bombing halt. Whatever Clifford's reasons,
the memo did not contain the proposal that was to be the main focus of the
continuing debates in March and would eventually be endorsed by the President.

C.   The President Weighs the Decision

1.   More Meetings and More Alternatives

The idea of a partial bombing halt was not new within the
Administration. It had been discussed in some form or other as a possible
alternative at various times for more than a year. (In the DPM of May 20,
1967, McNamara had formally proposed the idea to the President.) It was
brought up anew early in the Clifford Group deliberations and, while not
adopted in the final report, became the main alternative under consideration in the continuing meetings of the various groups that had been formed
for the Clifford exercise. As indicated previously, Secretary Clifford
reportedly suggested personally to the President the idea of cutting back
the bombing to the North Vietnamese panhandle. The first appearance of
the idea in the documents in March is in a note from Clifford to Wheeler
on the 5th transmitting for the latter's exclusive "information" a proposed "statement" drafted by Secretary Rusk. The statement, which was
given only the status of a "suggestion" and therefore needed to be closely
held, announced the suspension of the bombing of North Vietnam except in
the "area associated with the battle zone." It was presumably intended
for Presidential delivery. Attached to the draft statement, which shows
Rusk himself as the draftee, was a list of explanatory reasons and conditions for its adoption. Rusk noted that bad weather in northern North

Vietnam in the next few months would severely hamper operations around
Hanoi and Haiphong in any event and the proposal did not, therefore,
constitute a serious degradation of our military position. It was to
be understood that in the event of any major enemy initiative in the south,
either against Khe Sanh or the cities, the bombing would be resumed.
Further, Rusk did not want a major diplomatic effort mounted to start peace
talks. He preferred to let the action speak for itself and await Hanoi's
reaction. Finally, he noted that the area still open to bombing would include
everything up to and including Vinh (just below 19°) and there would be no
limitations on attacks in that zone. 41/ Clifford's views of the proposal
and its explanation do not appear in his note. It can be inferred, however,
that he endorsed the idea. In any case, by the middle of March the question
of a partial bombing halt became the dominant air war alternative under
consideration in meetings at State and Defense. It is possible that the
President had already indicated to Clifford and Rusk enough approval of the
idea to have focused the further deliberative efforts of his key advisors
on it.

On March 8, Bundy sent a TS-NODIS memo to CIA Director Helms
requesting a CIA evaluation of four different bombing options and troop
deployment packages, none of which, however, included even a partial bombing
halt. Indicating that he had consulted with Secretary Rusk and Walt Rostow
before making his request, he noted the CIA papers already discussed in this
study but expressed a need for one overall summary paper. The options he
wanted evaluated were:

A. An early announcement of reinforcements on the order
of 25,000 men, coupled with reserve calls and other measures
adequate to make another 75,000 men available for deployment
by the end of the year if required and later decided. The
bombing would be stepped up as the weather improved, and would
include some new targets, but would not include the mining of
Haiphong or major urban attacks in Hanoi and Haiphong.

B. A similar announcement of immediate reinforcement
action, coupled with greater actions than in A to raise our
total force strength, making possible additional reinforcements of roughly 175,000 men before the end of 1968. Bombing
program as in A.

C. Option A plus mining of Haiphong and/or significantly
intensified bombing of urban targets in Hanoi and Haiphong areas.

D. Option B plus an intensified bombing program and/or
mining of Haiphong. 42/

In addition to an assessment of likely DRV reactions, he wanted to know
what could be expected from the Chinese and the Soviets under each option.
He also noted that, "At this stage, none of us knows what the timing of

the decision-making will be. I think this again argued for a CIA-only paper at the outset, to be completed perhaps by next Wednesday night /March 13/." 43/

A more complicated draft memo to CIA asking for a review of various bombing alternatives was prepared at about the same time in ISA, but apparently not sent. It contained twelve highly specific different bombing alternatives, including three different bombing reduction or halt options: (1) a concentration of bombing in Route Packages 1, 2 and 3 with only 5% in the extreme north; (2) a complete halt over North Vietnam; and (3) a complete halt over both North Vietnam and Laos. 44/ No particular attention was focused on a partial halt, again indicating that knowledge of the proposal was being restricted to the immediate circle of Presidential advisors. Presumably the CIA did prepare a memo in response to Bundy's request, but it does not appear in the available material.

Meanwhile, a separate set of escalatory options had been proposed to Mr. Nitze by Air Force Secretary Brown on March 4 in response to the latter's February 28 request. 45/ Brown's view was that apart from the various ground strategy alternatives, there were also a number of ways the air war, both north and south, could be expanded to meet the changed situation after Tet. The three alternatives he suggested were:

1. First, actions against North Vietnam could be intensified by bombing of remaining important targets, and/or neutralization of the port of Haiphong by bombing and mining.

2. Second, air actions could be intensified in the adjoining panhandle areas of Laos/NVN.

3. Third, a change to the basic strategy in SVN is examined, in which increased air actions in SVN are substituted for increased ground forces. 46/

Brown appraised the relative advantages of the various proposed campaigns in this way:

Intensification of air actions against NVN would be aimed at forcing the enemy to the conference table or choking off imports to NVN to an extent which would make their level of effort in SVN insupportable. The second and third campaigns, individually or together, are more limited in aim. It appears likely that, given adequate sortie capability, the greatest adverse effect on the enemy would result from a plan which simultaneously employed all three campaigns. 47/

Under program #1, Brown envisaged the elimination of virtually all the constraints under which the bombing then operated and an aggressive attack on North Vietnamese resources, import capability and population centers along the lines of proposals from CINCPAC:

The present restrictions on bombing NVN would be lifted so as to permit bombing of military targets without the present scrupulous concern for collateral civilian damage and casualties. The following targets systems would be emphasized:

1. Military control points, military headquarters, storage facilities, government control centers, and such population centers as are known to harbor dispersed materiel and vehicles.

2. The Ports of Haiphong, Hon Gai and Cam Pha, by a combination of mining and bombing. This would be designed to force over-the-beach delivery of seaborne imports which would require shipping to remain off the coast in unsheltered waters, thereby restricting operations to periods of relative calm seas.

3. Over-the-beach deliveries by bombing and possibly mining.

4. Intensified bombing attacks on the northeast and northwest rail lines and other road LOCs contiguous to the NVN-Chicom border. 48/

The objective to be achieved by this expanded campaign was described in the succeeding paragraph:

The aims of this alternative campaign would be to erode the will of the population by exposing a wider area of NVN to casualties and destruction; to reduce maritime imports by closing the major ports, and by attacking the resulting over-the-beach deliveries; to bring about a saturation of remaining import arteries, thereby creating greater target densities; and to disrupt the movement of supplies into SVN by attacking military control points and storage facilities wherever located. The hopeful assumption is that North Vietnam would then be forced to decide on a priority of imports—war-making goods vs. life-supporting goods—and that it would choose the latter. This in turn would attenuate its ability to supply forces in SVN and would thus slow down the tempo of the fighting there. In time, these cumulative pressures would be expected to bring NVN to negotiation of a compromise settlement, or to abandonment of the fight in SVN. 49/

The Soviet and Chinese reactions to these measures were expected to be
confined to increased aid, some "volunteers" and an overall worsening
of relations with the U.S. All these were regarded as manageable if not
desirable. But in evaluating the likely results of such a bombing
program, Brown was forced to admit that:

> Barring that effect, I would judge that Campaign #1
> can, in military terms, limit SVN actions by NVN near
> their pre-Tet level, and below the level of February 1968.
> This campaign cannot be demonstrated quantitatively to be
> likely to reduce NVN capability in SVN substantially below the
> 1967 level, but in view of possible disruption of North Viet-
> namese distribution capability around Hanoi and Haiphong, such
> an effect could take place. The campaign would take place
> beginning in March, and should conceivably have its maximum
> effect by October. During the following season of poor
> weather, the North Vietnamese transportation system would begin
> to be reconstituted.

> The other possible impact is on the North Vietnamese will
> to continue the war. Clearly their society would be under
> even greater stress than it is now. But so long as they have
> the promise of continued Soviet and Chinese material support,
> and substantial prospect of stalemate or better in SVN, the
> North Vietnamese government is likely to be willing to undergo
> these hardships. Its control over the populace will remain
> good enough so that the latter will have no choice but to do
> so. 50/

The other two programs were regarded as having even less
potential for inhibiting communist activity in the south. Program #2
involved simply a greatly intensified program of strikes in the panhandle
areas of North Vietnam and Laos, while Program #3 proposed the substantial
relocation of South Vietnamese population into secure zones and the designation of the remaining cleared areas as "free strike" regions for intensified air attack. Brown's three alternatives apparently did not get wide
attention, however, and were never considered as major proposals within
the inner circle of Presidential advisors. Nevertheless, the fact that
they were supported by over fifty pages of detailed analysis done by the
Air Staff is a reflection of the importance everyone attached to the reassessment going on within the Administration.

Of the other major advisors, Katzenbach had participated
to a limited degree in the Clifford Group work and reportedly was opposed
to the subsequent proposal for a partial suspension because he felt that
a bombing halt was a trump card that could be used only once and should
not be wasted when the prospects for a positive North Vietnamese response
on negotiations seemed so poor.. He reportedly hoped to convince the

President to call a complete halt to the air war later in the spring
when prospects for peace looked better and when the threat to Khe
Sanh had been eliminated. 51/ Walt Rostow, the President's personal
advisor on national security matters, apparently resisted all suggestions for a restriction of the bombing, preferring to keep the
pressure on the North Vietnamese for a response to the San Antonio
formula. These various opinions represented the principal advice
the President was receiving from his staff within the Administration.
Other advice from outside, both invited and uninvited, also played a
part in the final decision.

2. The New Hampshire Primary

In the days immediately following the early March deliberations, the President, toiling over the most difficult decision of his
career, was faced with another problem of great magnitude -- how to
handle the public reaction to Tet and the dwindling public support for
his war policies. From this point of view probably the most difficult
week of the Johnson Presidency began on March 10 when the New York
Times broke the story of General Westmoreland's 206,000 man troop request
in banner headlines. 52/ The story was a collaborative effort by
four reporters of national reputation and had the kind of detail to give
it the ring of authenticity to the reading public. In fact, it was very
close to the truth in its account of the proposal from MACV and the
debate going on within the Administration. The story was promptly
picked up by other newspapers and by day's end had reached from one end
of the country to the other. The President was reportedly furious at
this leak which amounted to a flagrant and dangerous compromise of
security. Later in the month an investigation was conducted to cut down
on the possibility of such leaks in the future.

The following day, March 11, Secretary Rusk went before
Fulbright's Senate Foreign Relations Committee for the first time in
two years for nationally televised hearings on U.S. war policy. In
sessions that lasted late that Monday and continued on Tuesday, the
Secretary was subjected to sharp questioning by virtually every member.
While he confirmed the fact of an "A to Z" policy review within the
Administration, he found himself repeatedly forced to answer questions
obliquely or not at all to avoid compromising the President. These
trying two days of testimony by Secretary Rusk was completed only hours
before the results from the New Hampshire primary began to come in.
To the shock and consternation of official Washington, the President
had defeated his upstart challenger, Eugene McCarthy, who had based
his campaign on a halt in the bombing and an end to the war, by only
the slenderest of margins. (In fact, when the write-in vote was finally
tabulated later that week, McCarthy had actually obtained a slight
plurality over the President in the popular vote.) The reaction across

the country was electric. It was clear that Lyndon Johnson, the master
politician, had been successfully challenged, not by an attractive and
appealing alternative vote-getter, but by a candidate who had been able
to mobilize and focus all the discontent and disillusionment about the
war. National politics in the election year 1968 would not be the same
thereafter.

Critics of the President's policies in Vietnam in both parties were
buoyed by the New Hampshire results. But for Senator Robert Kennedy
they posed a particularly acute dilemma. With the President's vulnerability on Vietnam now demonstrated, should Kennedy, his premier political
opponent on this and other issues, now throw his hat in the ring? After
four days of huddling with his advisers, and first informing both the
President and Senator McCarthy, Kennedy announced his candidacy on March 16.
For President Johnson, the threat was now real. McCarthy, even in the
flush of a New Hampshire victory, could not reasonably expect to unseat
the incumbent President. But Kennedy was another matter. The President
now faced the prospect of a long and divisive battle for renomination
within his own party against a very strong contender, with the albatross
of an unpopular war hanging around his neck.

For the moment at least, the President appeared determined.
On March 17, he spoke to the National Farmers' Union and said that the
trials of American responsibility in Vietnam would demand a period of
domestic "austerity" and a "total national effort." 53/ Further leaks,
however, were undercutting his efforts to picture the Administration as
firm and resolute about doing whatever was necessary. On March 17, the
New York Times had again run a story on the debate within the Administration. This time the story stated that the 206,000 figure would not be
approved but that something between 35,000 and 50,000 more troops would
be sent to Vietnam, necessitating some selective call-up of reserves. 54/
Again the reporters were disturbingly accurate in their coverage. Criticism of the President continued to mount. Spurred by the New Hampshire
indications of massive public disaffection with the President's policy,
139 members of the House of Representatives co-authored a resolution
calling for a complete reappraisal of U.S. Vietnam policy including a
Congressional review.

3. ISA Attempts to Force a Decision

The President's reluctance to make a decision about Vietnam
and the dramatic external political developments in the U.S. kept the
members of the Administration busy in a continuing round of new draft
proposals and further meetings on various aspects of the proposals the
President was considering. Within ISA at the Pentagon, attention focused
on ways to get some movement on the negotiations in the absence of any

decisions on forces or bombing. On March 11, Policy Planning produced
a lengthy draft memo to Clifford outlining the history of Hanoi's
positions on "talks","negotiations", "settlement", and "no advantage"
provision of the San Antonio formula. Its conclusion was that Hanoi
had indicated "acceptance of the operative portion of the San Antonio
formula," if we really wished to acknowledge it. 55/ Policy Planning
suggested testing this by asking them to repeat recent private assurances
about not attacking Khe Sanh, the cities, across the DMZ, etc. In an
effort to move the Administration to a more forthcoming interpretation
of the San Antonio formula, this memo proposed discussions with GVN to
define what constituted North Vietnamese acceptance.

The memo which Warnke signed the next day went to both
Clifford and Nitze and began with the statement: "I believe that we
should begin to take steps now which will make possible the opening of
negotiations with Hanoi within the next few months. I believe that
such negotiations are much much in our interest...." 56/ His arguments
were: With respect to the San Antonio formula, he pointed to a number
of Hanoi statements accepting the "prompt and productive" U.S. stipula-
tion for the negotiations, and offered his opinion that Hanoi had also
hinted understanding and acquiescence in the "no advantage" provision.
Warnke argued that further U.S. probing for assurances about "no advantage"
would only reinforce Hanoi's impression that this was really a condition.
If this occurred, he argued, Hanoi "may continue to denounce the San
Antonio formula in public. This will make it difficult for us to halt
the bombing if we decide that it is in our interest to do so." 57/ On
the basis of these conclusions, Warnke recommended discussions with the
GVN to explain our view of the desirability of negotiations and urged
the completion of an inter-agency study preparing a U.S. position for
the negotiations. He summed up his recommendation as follows:

> After holding discussions with the GVN and completing
> the interagency study, we should halt the bombing and enter
> into negotiations, making "no advantage" and mutual de-
> escalation the first and immediate order of business at
> the negotiations.

> If you approve this course of action, we will work
> with State on a detailed scenario for you to discuss with
> Mr. Rusk and the President. 58

Attached to Warnke's memo were separate supporting tabs outlining
Hanoi's public and private responses to the San Antonio formula and
arguing that Hanoi's conception of an acceptable negotiated settlement,
as revealed in its statements, embodied a good deal of flexibility.

On the same day, Warnke signed a memo to the Director of
CIA requesting a study of seven alternative bombing campaigns for the
future. For unknown reasons, the memo was apparently never sent. 59/
The options for examination in this memo were all taken from the
earlier draft memo with twelve options. Options 1-3 were all reduction
or half options, but the wording of them suggests again that ISA was not
aware of the high level attention being focused on a complete bombing
halt north of 20°.

Neither Clifford's nor Nitze's reaction to Warnke's memo
is available in the files, but two days later the Policy Planning Staff
drafted a memorandum to the President for Clifford's signature which
recommended a leveling off of our effort in the war -- i.e., no new
troops and a reconcentration of the bombing to the panhandle area.
The memo went through several drafts and is probably typical of efforts
going on simultaneously in other agencies. In its final form it urged
the retargetting of air strikes from the top of the funnel in North
Vietnam to the panhandle with only enough sorties northward to prevent
the DRV from relocating air defenses to the south. 60/ A more detailed
discussion of the bombing alternatives was appended to the memo and
included consideration of four alternative programs. The first two
were (1) a continuation of the current bombing program; and (2) an
increase in the bombing including the reduction of the restricted zones
and the mining of Haiphong. These two were analyzed jointly as follows:

> The bombing of North Vietnam was undertaken to limit and/or
> make more difficult the infiltration of men and supplies in the
> South, to show Hanoi that it would have a price for its continued
> aggression, and to raise morale in South Vietnam. The last two
> purposes obviously have been achieved.
>
> It has become abundantly clear that no level of bombing can
> prevent the North Vietnamese from supplying the forces and
> materiel necessary to maintain their military operations in
> the South at current levels. The recent Tet offensive has
> shown that the bombing cannot even prevent a significant increase
> in these military operations, at least on an intermittent basis.
> Moreover, the air war has not been very successful when measured
> by its impact on North Vietnam's economy. In spite of the large
> diversion of men and materiels necessitated by the bombing,
> communist foreign aid and domestic reallocation of manpower have
> sharply reduced the destruction effect of our air strikes." 61/

The other two alternatives considered were a partial and a complete
cessation of the bombing. Here is how ISA presented them:

3.   A revision of the bombing effort in North Vietnam so
that a maximum effort is exerted against the LOC's in Route
Packages 1, 2, and 3 with bombing north of the 20th parallel
limited to a level designed to cover only the most significant
military targets and prevent the redistribution southward of
air defenses, e.g. 5% of the attack sorties.

This reprogramming of our bombing efforts would devote
primary emphasis on the infiltration routes south of the
20th parallel in the panhandle area of North Vietnam just to
the north of the DMZ. It includes all of the areas now within
Route Packages 1, 2 and 3. This program recognizes that our
bombing emphasis should be designed to prevent military men
and materiel from moving out of North Vietnam and into the
South, rather than attempting to prevent materiel from
entering North Vietnam. Occasional attack sorties north
of this area would be employed to keep enemy air defenses
and damage repair crews from relocating and to permit attack
aginst the most important fixed targets. The effort against
this part of North Vietnam through which all land infiltration
passes would be intensive and sustained. Yet it provides
Hanoi with a clear message that for political reasons we are
willing to adjust our military tactics to accommodate a constructive move toward peace. A distinct benefit of this decision
would be the lower plane loss rates which are realized in the
southern areas of North Vietnam. (In 1967 the joint loss rate
per thousand sorties in Route Packages 1, 2 and 3 was 1.36,
while it was 5.73 in the more heavily defended Route Package 6
in which Hanoi and Haiphong are located.)

4.   A complete cessation of all bombing in North Vietnam.

It would be politically untenable to initiate a complete
cessation of the bombing of North Vietnam at a time when our
forces in the northern provinces of South Vietnam are seriously
threatened by large forces of North Vietnamese regulars, unless
we were confident that these attacks would cease. Nevertheless,
we must recognize that our intelligence analysts have advised
that in spite of our significant bombing effort over the last
2-1/2 years, Hanoi retains the capability and the will to support
the present or an increased level of hostilities in South Vietnam.
On the other hand, they inform us that:

"If, however, the U.S. ceased the bombing of North
Vietnam in the near future, Hanoi would probably respond

more or less as indicated in its most recent statements.
It would begin talks fairly soon, would accept a fairly
wide ranging exploration of issues, but would not moderate
its terms for a final settlement or stop fighting in the
South."

As discussed elsewhere in this memorandum, a cessation of the
bombing by us in North Vietnam is the required first step if a
political solution to the conflict is to be found. We may want
to seek some assurance from Hanoi that it would not attack from
across the DMZ if we halt the bombing. Alternatively, we could
stop all bombing except that directly related to ground operations and indicate that our attacks are in the nature of
returning fire and will be halted when the enemy halts its
attacks in the area. 62/

These views of Clifford's staff never went to the White House, but
are indicative of the direction and tone of the debates in the policy
meetings within the Administration. Another aspect of the policy environment in March 1968 was ISA's isolation in arguing that Hanoi was moving
toward acceptance of the San Antonio formula and a negotiated settlement.
As we shall see, when the decision to halt the bombing north of 20° was
finally made, it was not in the expectation that North Vietnam would
come to the negotiating table.

4. The "Senior Informal Advisory Group"

At this juncture in mid-March, with the President vacillating
as to a course of action, probably the most important influence on his
thinking and ultimate decision was exercised by a small group of prominent
men outside the Government, known in official Washington as the "Senior
Informal Advisory Group." All had at one time or another over the last
twenty years served as Presidential advisers. They gathered in Washington
at the request of the President on March 18 to be briefed on the latest
developments in the war and to offer Mr. Johnson the benefit of their
experience in making a tough decision. Stuart Loory of the Los Angeles
Times in an article in May reported what has been generally considered
to be a reliable account of what took place during and after their visit
to Washington and what advice they gave the President. The story as
Loory reported it is included here in its entirety.

Hawks' Shift Precipitated Bombing Halt

Eight prominent hawks and a dove -- all from outside the
government -- gathered in the White House for a night and day
last March to judge the progress of the Vietnam war for
President Johnson.

Their deliberations produced this verdict for the chief executive:

Continued escalation of the war -- intensified bombing of North Vietnam and increased American troop strength in the South -- would do no good. Forget about seeking a battlefield solution to the problem and instead intensify efforts to seek a political solution at the negotiating table.

The manner in which Mr. Johnson sought the advice of the nine men before arriving at the conclusion to de-escalate the war announced in his now famous March 31 speech, has been pieced together from conversations with reliable sources who asked to remain anonymous.

The nine men, Republicans and Democrats with extensive experience in formulating foreign policy, were among those frequently consulted by Mr. Johnson from time to time during the war. At each consultation prior to March they had been overwhelmingly in favor of prosecuting the war vigorously with more men and material, with intensified bombing of North Vietnam, with increased efforts to create a viable government in the South.

As recently as last December they had expressed this view to the President. The only dissenter among them -- one who had been a dissenter from the beginning -- was former Undersecretary of State George Ball.

March 18th Meeting

The men who have come to be known to a small circle in the government as the President's "senior informal advisory group" convened in the White House early on the evening of March 18th.

Present in addition to Ball were: Arthur Dean, a Republican New York lawyer who was a Korean War negotiator during the Eisenhower administration; Dean Acheson, former President Truman's Secretary of State; Gen. Matthew B. Ridgeway, the retired commander of United Nations troops in Korea; Gen. Maxwell Taylor, former Chairman of the Joint Chiefs of Staff; Cyrus Vance, former Deputy Defense Secretary and a key troubleshooter for the Johnson Administration; McGeorge Bundy, Ford Foundation President who had been special assistant for National security affairs to Mr. Johnson and former President Kennedy; former Treasury Secretary C. Douglas Dillon and Gen. Omar Bradley, a leading supporter of the President's war policies.

First the group met over dinner with Secretary of State
Dean Rusk; Defense Secretary Clark M. Clifford; Ambassador
W. Averell Harriman; Walt W. Rostow, the President's special
assistant for National security affairs; Gen. Earle G. Wheeler,
Chairman of the Joint Chiefs of Staff; Richard Helms, Director
of the Central Intelligence Agency; Paul Nitze, Deputy Defense
Secretary; Nicholas Katzenbach, Under Secretary of State; and
William P. Bundy, Assistant Secretary of State for East Asian
and Pacific Affairs.

The outsiders questioned the government officials carefully
on the war, the pacification program and the condition of the
South Vietnamese government after the Tet offensive. They
included in their deliberations the effect of the war on the
United States.

Three Briefings

After dinner the government officials left and the group
received three briefings.

Philip C. Habib, a deputy to William Bundy and now a
member of the American negotiating team in Paris, delivered
an unusually frank briefing on the conditions in Vietnam after
the Tet offensive. He covered such matters as corruption in
South Vietnam and the growing refugee problem.

Habib, according to reliable sources, told the group that
the Saigon government was generally weaker than had been
realized as a result of the Tet offensive. He related the
situation, some said, with greater frankness than the group
had previously heard.

In addition to Habib, Maj. Gen. William E. DePuy, special
assistant to the Joint Chiefs for counterinsurgency and special
activities, briefed the group on the military situation, and
George Carver, a CIA analyst, gave his agency's estimates of
conditions in the war zone.

The briefings by DePuy and Carver reflected what many
understood as a dispute over enemy strength between the
Defense Department and the CIA which has been previously
reported. Discrepancies in the figures resulted from the
fact that DePuy's estimates of enemy strength covered only
identifiable military units, while Carver's included all known
military, paramilitary and parttime enemy strength available.

Striking Turnabout

The morning of March 19, the advisory group assembled in
the White House to discuss what they had heard the previous
evening and arrived at their verdict. It was a striking
turnabout in attitude for all but Ball.

After their meeting, the group met the President for
lunch. It was a social affair. No business was transacted.
The meal finished, the advisers delivered their verdict to
the President.

He was reportedly greatly surprised at their conclusions.
When he asked them where they had obtained the facts on which
the conclusions were based, the group told him of the briefings
by Habib, DePuy and Carver.

Mr. Johnson knew that the three men had also briefed his
governmental advisers, but he had not received the same
picture of the war as Rostow presented the reports to him.

As a result of the discrepancy, the President ordered
his own direct briefings. At least Habib and DePuy -- and
almost certainly Carver -- had evening sessions with the
President.

Habib was reportedly as frank with the President as he
had been with the advisory group. The President asked tough
questions. "Habib stuck to his guns," one source reported.

On top of all this, Clifford, since he had become Defense
Secretary, came to the same conclusions Robert S. McNamara
had reached -- that the bombing of North Vietnam was not
achieving its objectives.

The impact of this group's recommendation coupled with the new
briefings the President received about conditions and prospects in the
war zone were major factors in cementing the decision not to expand
the war but to attempt a de-escalation. The Joint Chiefs for their
part were still seeking authorization to strike targets with the Hanoi
and Haiphong restricted areas and further escalation of the bombing.
On March 19, a Tuesday, they proposed hitting one target in Hanoi and
one in Haiphong that had previously been rejected by both Rusk and
McNamara plus the Hanoi docks near large population concentrations. 63/
These were probably considered at the noon luncheon at the White House,
but they were apparently not approved as no attacks occurred. The
military leaders, even at this late hour when the disposition of the
administration against any further escalation seemed clear, still pressed
for new targets and new authority.

D.   March 31 -- "I Shall Not Seek...Another Term as Your President.

1.   The Decision.

No exact date on which the President made the decision to curtail the bombing can be identified with certainty. It is reasonably clear that the decisions on the ground war were made on or before March 22. On that date, the President announced that General William Westmoreland would be replaced as COMUSMACV during the coming summer. He was to return to Washington to become Chief of Staff of the Army. The decision was clearly related to the force deployment decisions explicitly taken and the new strategy they implied. Three days after this announcement, that had been greeted in the press as a harbinger, General Creighton Abrams, Deputy COMUSMACV, arrived in Washington without prior announcement for conferences with the President. Speculation was rife that he was to be named Westmoreland's successor. On the 26th he and the President huddled and Mr. Johnson probably informed him of his intentions, both with respect to force augmentations and the bombing restraint, and his intention to designate Abrams the new COMUSMACV. In the days that followed, the speech drafters took over, writing and rewriting the President's momentous address. Finally, it was decided that the announcement speech would be made on nation-wide television from the White House on the evening of March 31.

The night before the speech a cable under Katzenbach's signature, drafted by William Bundy, went out to US Embassies in Australia, New Zealand, Thailand, Laos, the Philippines and South Korea slugged "Literally Eyes Only for Ambassador or Charge." It instructed the addressees that they were to see their heads of government and inform them that:

After full consultation with GVN and with complete concurrence of Thieu and Ky, President plans policy announcement
Sunday night that would have following major elements:

a. Major stress on importance of GVN and ARVN
increased effectiveness, with our equipment and other support
as first priority in our own actions.

b. 13,500 support forces to be called up at once
in order to round out the 10,500 combat units sent in February.

c. Replenishment of strategic reserve by calling up
48,500 additional reserves, stating that these would be designed
for strategic reserve.

d. Related tax increases and budget cuts already
largely needed for non-Vietnam reasons.

...In addition, after similar consultation and concurrence,
President proposes to announce that bombing will be restricted

to targets most directly engaged in the battlefield area and
that this meant that there would be no bombing north of 20th
parallel. Announcement would leave open how Hanoi might
respond, and would be open-ended as to time. However, it would
indicate that Hanoi's response could be helpful in determining
whether we were justified in assumption that Hanoi would not
take advantage if we stopping bombing altogether. Thus, it
would to this extent foreshadow possibility of full bombing
stoppage at a later point. 64/

     The significance of the decision they were to communicate
to their respective heads of government could hardly have been lost on the
Ambassadors. Nevertheless, the cable dramatized the importance of preventing premature leaks by stating that the Ambassadors were to tell the
heads of Government to whom they were accreditted that they were "under
strictest injunction to hold it in total confidence and not to tell any one
repeat anyone until after announcement is made. This is vital. Similarly
you should tell no member of your staff whatever." 65/ It is important to
note that the cable defines the delimited area for the bombing halt as north
of 20°. This apparently was the intent of the President and his advisors
all along, but sometime before the speech was delivered any specific reference
to the geographic point of limitation was eliminated, for undetermined reasons,
if it ever had been included.

     The March 30 cable offered the Ambassadors some additional
explanatory rationale for the new course that they were to use at their discretion in conversations with their heads of government. These are important
because they represent the only available recorded statement by the Administration of its understanding of the purposes and expectations behind the new
direction in Vietnam policy. It is also significant that the points concerning the bombing halt are extremely close to those in Secretary Rusk's
draft points of March 5. Here, then, is how the Administration understood
the new policy, and wished to have understood by our allies:

    a. You should call attention to force increases that
would be announced at the same time and would make clear our
continued resolve. Also our top priority to re-equipping ARVN
forces.

    b. You should make clear that Hanoi is most likely to
denounce the project and thus free our hand after a short
period. Nonetheless, we might wish to continue the limitation
even after a formal denunciation, in order to reinforce its
sincerity and put the monkey firmly on Hanoi's back for whatever follows. Of course, any major military change could compel
full-scale resumption at any time.

    c. With or without denunciation, Hanoi might well feel
limited in conducting any major offensives at least in the

northern areas. If they did so, this could ease the pressure where it is most potentially serious. If they did not, then this would give us a clear field for whatever actions were then required.

d. In view of weather limitations, bombing north of the 20th parallel will in any event be limited at least for the next four weeks or so -- which we tentatively envisage as a maximum testing period in any event. Hence, we are not giving up anything really serious in this time frame. Moreover, air power now used north of 20th can probably be used in Laos (where no policy change planned) and in SVN.

e. Insofar as our announcement foreshadows any possibility of a complete bombing stoppage, in the event Hanoi really exercises reciprocal restraints, we regard this as unlikely. But in any case, the period of demonstrated restraint would probably have to continue for a period of several weeks, and we would have time to appraise the situation and to consult carefully with them before we undertook any such action. 66/

It is important to note that the Administration did not expect the bombing restraint to produce a positive Hanoi reply. This view apparently was never seriously disputed at any time during the long month of deliberations within the Government, except by ISA. The fact that the President was willing to go beyond the San Antonio formula and curtail the air raids at a time when few responsible advisors were suggesting that such action would produce peace talks is strong evidence of the major shift in thinking that took place in Washington about the war and the bombing after Tet 1968. The fact of anticipated bad weather over much of northern North Vietnam in the succeeding months is important in understanding the timing of the halt, although it can plausibly be argued that many advisors would have found another convenient rationale if weather had been favorable.

Finally, the message concluded with an invitation for the respective governments to respond positively to the announcement and with an apology for the tardiness with which they were being informed of this momentous action. "Vital Congressional timing factors" was the rather lame excuse offered, along with the need for "full and frank" consultation with the GVN before the decision (contradicting the impression the GVN put out after the announcement). The stage was thus finally set for the drama of the President's speech.

2. The Speech

At 9:00 p.m. Eastern Standard Time on Thursday March 31 Lyndon Johnson stepped before the TV cameras in the Oval Room of the White House and began, in grave and measured tones, one of the most

important speeches of his life. His first words struck the theme of what
was to come:

> Good Evening, my fellow Americans.

> Tonight I want to speak to you of peace in Vietnam
and Southeast Asia. 67/

Underscoring the peaceful motivations of past and present U.S. policy
in the area, he reviewed the recent history of U.S. attempts to bring
peace to Vietnam:

> For years, representatives of our government and others
have travelled the world -- seeking to find a basis for
peace talks.

> Since last September, they have carried the offer that
I made public at San Antonio.

> That offer was this:

> That the United States would stop its bombardment of
North Vietnam when that would lead promptly to productive
discussions -- and that we would assume that North Vietnam
would not take military advantage of our restraint.

> Hanoi denounced this offer, both privately and pub-
licly. Even while the search for peace was going on,
North Vietnam rushed their preparations for a savage
assault on the people, the government, and the allies of
South Vietnam.

> The President noted that the Viet Cong had apparently
decided to make 1968 the year of decision in Vietnam and their Tet offensive
had been the unsuccessful attempt to win a breakthrough victory. Although
they had failed, the President acknowledged their capability to renew the
attacks if they wished. He forcefully asserted, however, that the allies
would again have the power to repel their assault if they did decide to
attack. Continuing, he led up to his announcement of the bombing halt in
this way:

> If they do mount another round of heavy attacks, they
will not succeed in destroying the fighting power of South
Vietnam and its allies.

> But tragically, this is also clear: many men -- on
both sides of the struggle -- will be lost. A nation that
has already suffered 20 years of warfare will suffer once
again. Armies on both sides will take new casualties. And
the war will go on.

There is no need for this to be so.

There is no need to delay the talks that could bring an end to the long and this bloody war.

Tonight, I renew the offer I made last August -- to stop the bombardment of North Vietnam. We ask that talks begin promptly, that they be serious talks on the substance of peace. We assume that during those talks Hanoi will not take advantage of our restraint.

We are prepared to move immediately toward peace through negotiations.

So, tonight, in the hope that this action will lead to early talks, I am taking the first step to de-escalate the conflict. We are reducing -- substantially reducing -- the present level of hostilities.

And we are doing so unilaterally, and at once.

Tonight, I have ordered our aircraft and our naval vessels to make no attacks on North Vietnam, except in the area north of the DeMilitarized Zone where the continuing enemy build-up directly threatens allied forward positions and where the movements of their troops and supplies are clearly related to that threat.

The President then defined, albeit vaguely, the area within which the bombing would be restricted and suggested that all bombing could halt if the other side would reciprocate by scaling down hostilities.

The area in which we are stopping our attacks includes almost 90 percent of North Vietnam's population, and most of its territory. Thus there will be no attacks around the principal populated areas, or in the food-producing areas of North Vietnam.

Even this very limited bombing of the North could come to an early end -- if our restraint is matched by restraint in Hanoi. But I cannot in good conscience stop all bombing so long as to do so would immediately and directly endanger the lives of our men and our allies. Whether a complete bombing halt becomes possible in the future will be determined by events.

In the hope that the unilateral U.S. initiative would
"permit the contending forces to move closer to a political settlement,"
the President called on the UK and the Soviet Union to do what they could
to get negotiations started. Repeating his offer to meet at any time
and place he designated his representative should talks actually occur:

I am designating one of our most distinguished Americans, Ambassador Averell Harriman, as my personal representative for such talks. In addition, I have asked
Ambassador Llewellyn Thompson, who returned from Moscow
for consultation, to be available to join Ambassador Harriman
at Geneva or any other suitable place -- just as soon as
Hanoi agrees to a conference.

I call upon President Ho Chi Minh to respond positively,
and favorably, to this new step toward peace.

But if peace does not come now through negotiations,
it will come when Hanoi understands that our common resolve
is unshakable, and our common strength is invincible.

Turning his attention to other matters, the President outlined
the limited steps that the U.S. would take to strengthen its forces in South
Vietnam and the measures he would push to improve the South Vietnamese Army.
He then discussed the costs of the new efforts, the domestic frugality they
would require, and the balance of payments efforts necessary to their implementation. Next he outlined his own views of the unlikelihood of peace, in
an attempt to head off any false hope that the bombing cessation might
generate:

Now let me give you my estimate of the chances for
peace:

-- the peace that will one day stop the bloodshed in
South Vietnam,

-- that all the Vietnamese people will be permitted
to rebuild and develop their land,

-- that will permit us to turn more fully to our own
tasks here at home.

I cannot promise that the initiative that I have
announced tonight will be completely successful in achieving
peace any more than the 30 others that we have undertaken
and agreed to in recent years.

But it is our fervent hope that North Vietnam, after
years of fighting that has left the issue unresolved, will

now cease its efforts to achieve a military victory and will join with us in moving toward the peace table.

And there may come a time when South Vietnam -- on both sides -- are able to work out a way to settle their own differences by free political choice rather than by war.

As Hanoi considers its course, it should be in no doubt of our intentions. It must not miscalculate the pressures within our democracy in this election year.

We have no intention of widening this war.

But the United States will never accept a fake solution to this long and arduous struggle and call it peace.

No one can foretell the precise terms of an eventual settlement.

Our objective in South Vietnam has never been the annihilation of the enemy. It has been to bring about a recognition in Hanoi that its objective -- taking over the South by force -- could not be achieved.

We think that peace can be based on the Geneva Accords of 1954 -- under political conditions that permit the South Vietnamese -- all the South Vietnamese -- to chart their course free of any outside domination or interference, from us or from anyone else.

So tonight I reaffirm the pledge that we made at Manila -- that we are prepared to withdraw our forces from South Vietnam as the other side withdraws its forces to the North, stops the infiltration, and the level of violence thus subsides.

Our goal of peace and self-determination in Vietnam is directly related to the future of all of Southeast Asia -- where much has happened to inspire confidence during the past 10 years. We have done all that we knew now to do to contribute and to help build that confidence.

The President praised the progressive developments in much of Asia in recent years and offered the prospect of similar progress in Southeast Asia if North Vietnam would settle the war. He repeated the Johns Hopkins offer of assistance to North Vietnam to rebuild its economy. In his peroration he spoke with deep conviction and much feeling about the purposes and reasons for the U.S. involvement in Southeast Asia's

destiny which he had authorized. It represents perhaps our best insight
into the President's understanding and motivation in the war, as well
as his hopes and dreams:

> One day, my fellow citizens, there will be peace in
> Southeast Asia.

> It will come because the people of Southeast Asia
> want it -- those whose armies are at war tonight, and those
> who, though threatened, have thus far been spared.

> Peace will come because Asians were willing to work
> for it -- and to sacrifice for it -- and to die by the
> thousands for it.

> But let it never be forgotten: peace will come also
> because America sent her sons to help secure it.

> It has not been easy -- far from it. During the past
> four and a half years, it has been my fate and my responsi-
> bility to be commander-in-chief. I have lived -- daily and
> nightly -- with the cost of this war. I know the pain that
> it has inflicted. I know perhaps better than anyone the
> misgivings that it has aroused.

> Throughout this entire, long period, I have been sus-
> tained by a single principle:

> -- that what we are doing now, in Vietnam, is vital
> not only to the security of Southeast Asia, but it is
> vital to the security of every American.

> Surely we have treaties which we must respect.
> Surely we have commitments that we are going to keep.
> Resolutions of the Congress testify to the need to resist
> aggression in the world and in Southeast Asia.

> But the heart of our involvement in South Vietnam --
> under three Presidents, three separate Administrations --
> has always been America's own security.

> And the larger purpose of our involvement has always
> been to help the nations of Southeast Asia become inde-
> pendent and stand alone, self-sustaining as members of a
> great world community.

-- At peace with themselves, and at peace with all others.

With such an Asia, our country -- and the world -- will be far more secure than it is tonight.

I believe that a peaceful Asia is far nearer to reality, because of what America has done in Vietnam. I believe that the men who endure the dangers of battle -- fighting there for us tonight -- are helping the entire world avoid far greater conflicts, far wider wars, far more destruction, than this one.

The peace that will bring them home some day will come. Tonight I have offered the first in what I hope will be a series of mutual moves toward peace.

I pray that it will not be rejected by the leaders of North Vietnam. I pray that they will accept it as a means by which the sacrifices of their own people may be ended. And I ask your help and your support, my fellow citizens, for this effort to reach across the battlefield toward an early peace.

Listing the achievements of his administration and warning against the perils of division in America, the President ended his speech with his emotional announcement that he would not run for re-election.

Through all time to come, I think America will be a stronger nation, a more just society, and a land of greater opportunity and fulfillment because of what we have all done together in these years of unparalleled achievement.

Our reward will come in the life of freedom, peace, and hope that our children will enjoy through ages ahead.

What we won when all of our people united just must not now be lost in suspicion, distrust, selfishness, and politics among any of our people.

Believing this as I do, I have concluded that I should not permit the Presidency to become involved in the partisan divisions that are developing in this political year.

With America's sons in the fields far away, with America's future under challenge right here at home, with our hopes and the world's hopes for peace in the balance every day, I do not believe that I should devote an hour or a day of my time to any personal partisan causes or to

any duties other than the awesome duties of this office --
the Presidency of your country.

Accordingly, I shall not seek, and I will not accept,
the nomination of my Party for another term as your President.

But let men everywhere know, however, that a strong,
a confident, and a vigilant America stands ready tonight to
seek an honorable peace -- and stand ready tonight to defend
an honored cause -- whatever the price, whatever the burden,
whatever the sacrifices that duty may require.

Thank you for listening.

Good night and God bless all of you.

The speech had an electric effect on the U.S. and the whole
world. It completely upset the American political situation, spurred
world-wide hopes that peace might be imminent and roused fear and concern
in South Vietnam about the depth and reliability of the American commitment.
As already noted, no one in the Administration had seriously expected a
positive reaction from Hanoi, and when the North Vietnamese indicated three
days later that they would open direct contacts with the U.S. looking toward
discussions and eventual negotiation of a peaceful settlement of the conflict,
the whole complexion and context of the war was changed. To be sure, there
was the unfortunate and embarrassing wrangle about exactly where the northern
limit of the U.S. bombing would be fixed, with CINCPAC having sent extremely
heavy sorties to the very limits of the 20th parallel on the day after the
announcement only to be subsequently ordered to restrict his attacks below
19° on April 3. And there was the exasperatingly long public struggle
between the U.S. and the DRV about where their representatives would meet
and what title the contacts would be given, not finally resolved until May.
But it was unmistakably clear throughout all this time that a major corner
in the war and in American policy had been turned and that there was no
going back. The President's decision was enormously well received at home
and greeted with enthusiasm abroad where it appeared at long last there was
a possibility of removing this annoyingly persistent little war in Asia as
a roadblock to progress on other matters of world-wide importance involving
East and West.

The President's speech at the end of March was, of course,
not the end of the bombing much less the war, and a further history of the
role of the limited air strikes could and should be undertaken. But the
decision to cut back the bombing, the decision that turned American policy
toward a peaceful settlement of the war, is a logical and fitting place to
terminate this particular inquiry into the policy process that surrounded the
air war. Henceforth, the decisions about the bombing would be made primarily
in the Pacific by the field commanders since no vitally sensitive targets

requiring continuing Washington level political review were within the
reduced attack zone. A very significant chapter in the history of U.S.
involvement in the Vietnam war had come to a close.

     As those who struggled with the policy decisions about the
bombing came to learn, any dispassionate and objective appraisal of it is
almost impossible. As McGeorge Bundy noted in September 1967 after the
Stennis hearings, both its proponents and its opponents have been guilty
of excesses in their advocacy and criticism. As Bundy put it, "My own
summary belief is that both the advocates and the opponents of the bombing
continue to exaggerate its importance." 68/ To be sure, the bombing
had not been conducted to its fullest potential, but on the other hand it
had been much heavier and had gone on much longer than many if not most of
its advocates had expected at the outset. Whether more might have been
accomplished by different bombing policy decisions, at the start or along
the way -- in particular the fast full squeeze favored by the JCS -- would
necessarily remain an open question. What can be said in the end is that
its partial suspension in part did produce what most had least expected --
a breakthrough in the deadlock over negotiations. And that in the longer
view of history may turn out to be its most significant contribution.

FOOTNOTES

1. Broadcast on radio Hanoi, 1 Jan. 1968, emphasis added.

2. Kraslow and Loory, op. cit. p. 229.

3. JCS msg. to CINCPAC 6402, 032158Z Jan. 1968 & 6700, 062148Z Jan. 1968.

4. ASD/ISA Paul C. Warnke, Memorandum for the Secretary of Defense, Subject: "New NVN Bombing Proposal," 16 Jan. 1968. (TS-SENS).

5. New York Times, Jan. 18, 1968.

6. Background Information ..., op. cit. p. 56.

7. Testimony of Secretary of Defense (Designate) Clark M. Clifford, before the Senate Committee on Armed Services, Jan. 25, 1968. Excerpt from published hearings, pp. 20-21.

8. JCSM-78-68, 3 Feb. 1968 (TS).

9. Ibid.

10. ASD/ISA Paul C. Warnke, Memorandum for the Secretary of Defense, Subject: "Air Campaign Against North Vietnam (JCSM 78-68)," I-35128/68 (TS), 5 Feb. 1968.

11. Ibid.

12. Background Information..., op. cit. pp. 283-4.

13. Kraslow and Loory, op. cit., p. 232.

14. Background Information..., op. cit., pp. 57-58.

15. JCSM 91-68, 12 Feb. 1968 (TS).

16. JCS msg. 9926, 130218Z Feb. 1968 (TS).

17. "Report of Chairman, JCS on Vietnam Situation and MACV Force Requirements," 27 Feb. 1968 (TS).

18. CIA Memorandum, Subject: "Hanoi's Appraisal of its Strategic Position Prior to the Current Offensive," unnumbered, 27 Feb. 1968 (S), emphasis added.

19. The principle issue addressed in this re-evaluation was the level
of forces to be sent to Vietnam to meet MACV requirements for
augmentation resulting from TET. As such, the bulk of the papers
drafted and considered in the Clifford Group dealt only tangentially
with the air war. Since the problem of force deployments is treated
in Task Force paper IV.C.6, no attempt will be made here to furnish
the details of those papers. Only the sections dealing directly
with the air war will be treated. The broad outline of the policy
process, however, will be sketched to place the arguments about
bombing policy into perspective.

20. Handwritten notes by Morton Halperin from conversation with
Paul Warnke. (TS-EYES ONLY), no date.

21. Item in a package of materials sent to General Taylor and Mr. Warnke
by William P. Bundy on Feb. 29, 1968 (TS-NODIS).

22. CIA Memorandum (unnumbered), Subject: "Communist Alternatives in
Vietnam," 29 Feb. 1968 (S).

23. CIA Memorandum (unnumbered), Subject: "Questions Concerning the
Situation in Vietnam," 1 March 1968 (S).

24. Ibid.

25. CIA Intelligence Memorandum, Subject: "International Communist
Aid to North Vietnam," 2 March 1968 (S).

26. William P. Bundy Memorandum for Mr. Warnke, General Taylor,
Feb. 29, 1968 with attached memo, subject: "Alternative Courses
of Action," W.P. Bundy draft, Feb. 29, 1968 (TS-NODIS).

27. Ibid.,attachment, "Probably Soviet Responses to Various U.S.
Actions in Indochina -- Vietnam, Laos and Cambodia." (TS).

28. Ibid., attachment, "Probably Chinese Responses to Certain U.S.
Courses of Action in Indochina -- Vietnam, Laos, and Cambodia." (TS).

29. Memorandum signed "M.D.T.," Subject: "Viet-Nam Alternatives,"
undated but known to have been written sometime between Feb. 28
and March 3 with a copy sent to the President.

30. Ibid.

31. Draft Memorandum for the President, Subject: "An Alternative to
the MACV Request," March 3, 1968 (TS-NODIS).

32. OASD/SA/Southeast Asia Programs, Memorandum for the Secretary of Defense, 23 Feb. 1968 (S).

33. Draft Memorandum for the President, 4 March 1968 (TS-NODIS).

34. Ibid., Tab. E, "Negotiating Posture Options, and Possible Diplomatic Actions," (TS).

35. Ibid., Tab F, "Military Action Against North Vietnam," (TS-SENS)

36. Ibid., Tab F-1, "The Campaign Against North Vietnam," (TS-SENS)

37. Ibid.

38. Ibid.

39. Ibid.

40. Ibid.

41. Clark Clifford Memorandum for General Wheeler, 5 March 1968 with attached "Draft Statement" and "Points" by Dean Rusk, 5 March 1968 (TS-SENS--EYES ONLY).

42. William P. Bundy Letter to the Honorable Richard Helms, Director of Central Intelligence, March 8, 1968 (TS-NODIS).

43. Ibid.

44. Unsigned, undated Memorandum for the Director, CIA, in ISA files (TS), presumably not sent.

45. Secretary of the Air Force, Harold Brown, Memorandum for the Deputy Secretary of Defense, Subject: "SEA Alternative Strategies," 4 March 1968 (S).

46. Ibid.

47. Ibid.

48. Ibid.

49. Ibid.

50. Ibid.

51. Kraslow and Loory, op. cit., p. 233.

52. New York Times, March 10, 1968.

53. New York Times, March 18, 1968.

54. New York Times, March 17, 1968

55. Unsigned Memorandum for the Secretary of Defense, Subject: "Hanoi's Position on Settling the Conflict in Vietnam," March 11, 1968 (TS-SENS); the memo has "Dr. H" in the corner and was prepared by Halperin's Policy Planning Staff.

56. ASD/ISA Paul C. Warnke Memorandum for the Secretary of Defense, via the Deputy Secretary of Defense, Subject: "Vietnam Negotiations," March 14, 1968 (TS-SENS).

57. Ibid., emphasis added.

58. Ibid.

59. ASD/ISA Paul C. Warnke Memorandum for the Director of the Central Intelligence Agency, Subject: "North Vietnam Bombing Questions," 14 March 1968 (S); with the pencil notation, "not sent" at the top.

60. Draft Memorandu, Subject: "Vietnam Policy for the Next Six Months," 1st Draft/Dr. Halperin/16 March 68 (TS-SENS).

61. Ibid.

62. Ibid.

63. ASD/ISA Paul C. Warnke Memorandum for the Secretary of Defense, Subject: "New Bombing Targets," 19 Mar. 1968 (TS-SENS).

64. Department of State Msg. 139431, 30 Mar. 1968 (TS-NODIS-LITERALLY EYES ONLY FOR AMBASSADOR OR CHARGE), emphasis added.

65. Ibid.

66. Ibid.

67. White House Press Release, Mar. 31, 1968, "Remarks of the President to the Nation."

68. The Washington Post, Sept. 11, 1967.

IV.C Evolution of the War (26 Vols.)
Direct Action: The Johnson Commitments, 1964-1968
(16 Vols.)
8. Re-emphasis on Pacification: 1965-1967

TOP SECRET - SENSITIVE

UNITED STATES - VIETNAM RELATIONS
1945 - 1967

═══ VIETNAM TASK FORCE ═══

OFFICE OF THE SECRETARY OF DEFENSE

SET #13

TOP SECRET - SENSITIVE

IV. C. 8.

RE-EMPHASIS ON PACIFICATION:

1965 - 1967

0295

SUMMARY

IV. C. 11.   <u>TOP SECRET - Sensitive</u>

<u>The United States Re-Emphasizes Pacification - 1965 to Present</u>

<u>An Examination of a Major Trend in our Effort</u>

<u>SUMMARY</u>

By the summer of 1967, pacification had become a major ingredient
of American strategy in Vietnam, growing steadily in importance and the
amount of resources devoted to it. The U.S. Mission in Vietnam had been
reorganized three times in 15 months and each reorganization had been
designed primarily to improve the management of the pacification effort
and raise its priority within our overall effort.

Pacification -- or as it is sometimes called by Americans, Revolutionary Development (RD) -- had staged a comeback in priority from the
days in 1964 and 1965 when it was a program with little emphasis,
guidance, or support. It has by now almost equalled in priority <u>for the</u>
Americans the original priority given the Strategic Hamlet program in
1962-1963, although the Vietnamese have not yet convinced many people
that they attach the same importance to it as we do.

This study traces the climb in pacification's importance during the
last two years, until it reached its present level of importance, with
further growth likely.

This study concentrates on American decisions, American discussions,
American papers. It will be clear to the reader that, if this version
of events is accurate, the Vietnamese played a secondary role in the
move to re-emphasize pacification. It is the contention of this paper
that this was indeed the case, and that the Americans were the prime
movers in the series of events which led to the re-emphasis of pacification. This study does not cover many important events, particularly the
progress of the field effort, the CIA-backed PAT/Cadre program, and GVN
activity.

The process by which the American government came to increase its
support for pacification is disorderly and haphazard. Individuals like
Ambassador Lodge and General Walt and Robert Komer, seem in retrospect
to have played important roles, but to each participant in a story still
unfolding, the sequence may look different. Therefore, it is quite
possible that things didn't quite happen the way they are described here,
and someone else, whose actions are not adequately described in the files
available for this study, was equally important.

Nor was there anything resembling a conspiracy involved. Indeed,
the proponents of what is called so loosely in this paper "pacification"
were often in such violent disagreement as to what pacification meant

<u>TOP SECRET - Sensitive</u>

that they quarreled publicly among themselves and overlooked their common interests. At other times, people who disagreed strongly on major issues found themselves temporary allies with a common objective.

Moreover, there is the curious problem of the distance between rhetoric and reality. Even during the dark days of 1964-1965, most Americans paid lip service, particularly in official, on the record statements, to the ultimate importance of pacification. But their public affirmation of the cliches about "winning the hearts and minds of the people" were not related to any programs or priorities then in existence in Vietnam, and they can mislead the casual observer.

The resurgence of pacification was dramatically punctuated by three Presidential conferences on Pacific islands with the leaders of the GVN -- Honolulu in February, 1966, Manila in October, 1966 (with five other Chiefs of State also present), and Guam in March, 1967. After each conference the relative importance of pacification took another leap upward within the U.S. Government -- reflecting a successful effort within the U.S. Government by its American proponents -- and the U.S. tied the GVN onto Declarations and Communiques which committed them to greater effort.

In addition, each conference was followed by a major re-organization within the U.S. Mission, designed primarily to improve our management of the pacification effort. After Honolulu, Deputy Ambassador Porter was given broad new authority to run the civilian agencies. After Manila, Porter was directed to re-organize the components of USIA, CIA, and AID internally to create a single Office of Civil Operations (OCO). And after Guam, OCO -- redesignated as CORDS -- was put under the control of General Westmoreland, who was given a civilian deputy with the personal rank of Ambassador to assist him.

The low priority of pacification in 1965 was the understandable result of a situation in which battles of unprecedented size were taking place in the highlands and along the coast, the air war was moving slowly north towards Hanoi, and the GVN was in a continual state of disarray.

But a series of events and distinct themes were at work which would converge to give pacification a higher priority. They were to meet at the Honolulu conference in February, 1966.

I. Threads That Met At Honolulu

   A. Hop Tac

   The first was the hold-over program from 1964-1965 -- pacification's
one priority even then, the Hop Tac program. It had been suggested first
by Lodge on his way home from his first Ambassadorship, and Taylor and
Westmoreland had given it recognition as a high priority program. Although
Westmoreland judged it repeatedly as a partial success, it appears now to
have been a faultily conceived and clumsily executed program. It was conceptually unsound, lacked the support of the Vietnamese, created disagreements within the U.S. Mission which were never resolved, and then faded
away. So unsuccessful was it that during its life span the VC were able
to organize a regiment -- 165A -- in the Gia Dinh area surrounding Saigon,
and thus forced MACV in late 1966 to commit three U.S. infantry battalions
to Operation FAIRFAX to protect the capital. No one analyzed Hop Tac
before starting FAIRFAX. With the beginning of FAIRFAX, Hop Tac was buried
quietly and the United States proceeded to other matters.

   B. Ambassador Lodge and the True Believers

   Henry Cabot Lodge returned as Ambassador in August of 1965, and immediately began to talk of pacification as "the heart of the matter." In
telegrams and Mission Council meetings, Lodge told the President, the GVN,
and the Mission that pacification deserved a higher priority. Because he
saw himself as an advocate before the President for his beliefs rather
than as the overall manager of the largest overseas civil-military effort
in American history, * Lodge did not try, as Ambassador Maxwell Taylor had
done, to devise an integrated and unified strategy that balanced every
part of our effort. Instead, he declared, in his first month back in Vietnam (September, 1965), that "the U.S. military was doing so well now that
we face a distinct possibility that VC main force units will be neutralized,
and VC fortresses destroyed soon," and that therefore we should be ready to
give pacification a new push. While his involvement was irregular and
inconsistent, Lodge did nonetheless play a key role in giving pacification
a boost. His rhetoric, even if vague, encouraged other advocates of pacification to speak up. The man he brought with him, Edward Lansdale, gave
by his very presence an implicit boost to pacification.

   C. The III Marine Amphibious Force

   Meanwhile, to their own amazement, the Marines were discovering that
the toughest war for them was the war in the villages behind them near
the Da Nang air base, rather than the war against the main force, which
had retreated to the hills to build up. In the first 12 months of their
deployment, the Marines virtually reversed their emphasis, turning away

---

* No other American Ambassador has ever had responsibility and authority
  even close to that in Saigon; only military commands have exceeded it
  in size.

from the enemy to a grueling and painfully slow effort to pacify the
villages of the central coast in their three TAORs. It was a job that
Americans were not equipped for, and the Marine effort raised some basic
questions about the role of U.S. troops in Vietnam, but nonetheless, the
Marines began to try to sell the rest of the U.S. Government on the
success and correctness of their still unproved strategy. The result
was a major commitment to the pacification strategy by a service of the
U.S. Armed Forces, and influence on the other services, particularly the
Army.

D. Washington Grumbles About The Effort

When Lodge was Ambassador, there was widespread concern about the
management of the Mission. Lodge was admittedly not a manager. This
concern led to a major conference at Warrenton in January of 1966, during which increased emphasis on pacification and better organization
within the U.S. Mission were the main topics. Improving the Washington
organizational structure was raised, but not addressed candidly in the
final report; Washington seemed far readier to tell Saigon how to reorganize
than to set their own house in order. But Warrenton symbolizes the growing
dissatisfaction in Washington with the Mission as it was.

E. Presidential Emphasis on the "Other War" and Press Reaction

Finally, there was the need of the President, for compelling domestic
political reasons, to give greater emphasis to "the other war." With the
first full years of major troop commitment ending with victory not yet in
sight, there was a growing need to point out to the American public and to
the world that the United States was doing a great deal in the midst of
war to build a new Vietnam. While this emphasis did not necessarily have
to also become an emphasis on pacification, it did, and thus the President
in effect gave pacification his personal support -- an act which was
acutely felt by Americans in Vietnam.

F. Meanwhile, Back at the War...

A summary of the MACV Monthly Evaluations and other reports is contained here, showing how the U.S. command saw its own progress. The
summary suggests that MACV foresaw heavy fighting all through 1966, and
did not apparently agree with Ambassador Lodge's predictions and hopes
that a major pacification effort could be started, but the issue was not
analyzed before decisions were made.

II. Honolulu

A. The Conference - February 1966

The details of the working sessions at the Honolulu conference do
not appear, in retrospect, to be nearly as important on the future

emphasis on pacification as the public statements that came out of Honolulu, particularly the Declaration itself. The discussions and the Declaration are summarized, including the President's final remarks in plenary session.

    B. Public Impact...

The press reaction to the conference is summarized.

III. Honolulu to Manila

    A. Saigon: Porter in Charge

The first reorganization now took place, and Deputy Ambassador Porter was put in direct charge of the civilian agencies. His responsibility and his ability to carry out his responsibility were not equal from the outset, and Porter saw his role in different terms than those in Washington who had given him his difficult task. A major problem was the lack of full support that Porter received from Ambassador Lodge, who had never been fully in favor of the reorganization. Another problem was the lack of a parallel structure in Washington, so that Porter found himself caught between the Washington agencies and their representatives in Saigon, with Komer (see below) as a frequent participant. Nonetheless, Porter accomplished a great deal in the months this arrangement lasted; it just wasn't as much as Washington sought.

    B. Washington: Komer As The Blowtorch

In Washington, the President selected a McGeorge Bundy deputy, R. W. Komer, to be his Special Assistant on non-military activities in Vietnam. Komer did not have the same kind of authority over the Washington agencies that Porter, in theory, had over the Saigon extensions. Komer pushed pacification hard, and became the first senior official, with apparently ready access to the President, who put forward the pro-pacification position consistently in high level meetings. His mandate was contained in a loosely worded NSAM, 343, dated March 28, 1966. During the summer of 1966, Komer applied great pressure to both the Mission and the Washington agencies (thus earning from Ambassador Lodge the nickname of "Blowtorch"), with a series of cables and visits to Vietnam, often using the President's name.

    C. Study Groups and Strategists: Summer 1966

With Porter and Komer in their new roles, a series of Task Forces and Study Groups began to produce papers that gave a better rationale and strategy to pacification. These included the Army study called PROVN, the Priorities Task Force in Saigon, and the Roles and Missions Study Groups in Saigon. At the same time, Westmoreland, whose year end wrap-up message on January 1, 1966, had not even mentioned pacification, sent in a new long range strategy which emphasized pacification, to Lodge's pleasure. MACV also produced a new position on revamping ARVN, and briefed the Mission Council on it in August, 1966. The Honolulu emphasis was beginning to produce tangible results on the U.S. side.

D. The Single Manager

Despite the movement described in the above three sections, Washington wanted more, and was not satisfied with the rate of progress. Komer, therefore, in August of 1966 had produced a long paper which offered three possible changes in the management structure of the Mission. They were: (1) put all pacification responsibility and assets, including MACV Advisors, under Porter; (2) reorganize the civilian structure to create a single office of operations, and strengthen MACV internally, but leave the civilians and the military split; (3) give Westmoreland full pacification responsibility. The Mission rejected all these ideas, offering in their stead the proposal that Washington leave Saigon alone for a while, but the pressure for results and better management was too great, and the inadequacies of the Mission too obvious, to leave it alone. Secretary McNamara weighed in at this point with a draft Presidential memorandum proposing that Westmoreland be given responsibility for pacification. Komer and JCS concurred in it, but State, USIA, AID, and CIA nonconcurred. McNamara, Katzenbach, and Komer then went to Saigon to take a look at the situation. When they returned, Katzenbach, new to the State Department and previously uninvolved in the problem, recommended that Porter be told to reorganize the civilians along the lines previously discussed (similar to Komer's Alternative Number 2). The President agreed, discussing it with Lodge and Westmoreland at Honolulu. But he added a vital warning: he would give the civilians only about 90 to 120 days to make the new structure work, and then would reconsider the proposal to transfer responsibility for pacification to MACV.

E. The Manila Conference

The decision had not yet been transmitted to Saigon, but it had been made. At Manila, with six other heads of state in attendance, the discussion turned to other matters. At Manila, in the final Declaration, the GVN announced that they would commit half the armed forces to securing operations in support of pacification/RD. This had previously been discussed, but it was the public commitment that really mattered, and now it was on the record.

IV. OCO to CORDS

A. OCO on Trial: Introduction

The Office of Civil Operations was formed, creating confusion and resentment among the agencies, but also marking an immediate and major

TOP SECRET - Sensitive

step forward. The example of the civilians moving at this pace also
created pressure and conflict within MACV, which was for the first time
confronted with a strong civilian structure. The GVN indicated that it
understood and approved of the new structure.

B. OCO on Trial: Too Little Too Late -- Or Not Enough Time?

. Although it was slower than Washington desired, OCO did get off to
a start in December of 1966. Wade Lathram, who had been USAID Deputy
Director, was chosen to head up OCO -- a choice that was unfortunate,
because Lathram, a skilled and cautious bureaucrat, was not the kind of
driving and dynamic leader that OCO -- in a brink of disaster situation
from its inception -- needed.

Even worse, Porter was almost immediately diverted from OCO to pay
more attention to other matters. While the planners had hoped that
Porter would take OCO in hand and give Lathram direct guidance, instead
he left Lathram in control of OCO and was forced to turn his attentions
to running the Mission, during a long vacation (one month) by Lodge.

The most dramatic action that was taken was the selection of the
Regional Directors, a move which even attracted newspaper attention.
They included Henry Koren, formerly Porter's deputy; John Paul Vann,
the controversial former MACV advisor; and Vince Heymann of the CIA.

Slowly, the OCO then turned to picking its province representatives.
All in all, OCO accomplished many things that had never been done before;
given time it could no doubt have done much more. But it was plagued
from the outset by lack of support from the agencies and their representatives in Saigon, and Washington made higher demands than could be met
in Saigon.

C. Time Runs Out

It is not clear when the President made the decision to scrap OCO.
He communicated his decision to his field commanders at Guam, but there
was a two-month delay before the decision was announced publicly or discussed with the GVN.

D. The CORDS Reorganization

As Bunker took over the Mission, there was a considerable turnover
in key personnel. Bunker asked Lansdale and Zorthian to stay on, but
Porter, Habib, Wehrle, all left just as Locke, Komer, Calhoun, Cooper,
and General Abrams all arrived.

In the new atmosphere, Komer took the lead, making a series of recommendations which maintained the civilian position within MACV, and
Westmoreland accepted them.

TOP SECRET - Sensitive

TOP SECRET - Sensitive

An example of Komer's influence was the question of the role of the ARVN divisions in the RD chain of command, and here Westmoreland took Komer's suggestion even though it meant a reversal of the previous MACV position.

E. The Mission Assessment as CORDS Begins

The situation inherited by CORDS was not very promising. Measurements of progress had been irrelevant and misleading, and progress by nearly all standards has been slow or nonexistent. At this point, the study of CORDS and pacification becomes current events.

viii   TOP SECRET - Sensitive

TABLE OF CONTENTS

TOP SECRET - Sensitive

IV. C. 11.   RE-EMPHASIS ON PACIFICATION: 1965-1967

TABLE OF CONTENTS AND OUTLINE

I. THREADS THAT MET AT HONOLULU

TOP SECRET - Sensitive

I. Threads that Met at Honolulu

A. Hop Tac

While pacification received a low emphasis during troubled 1964-1965, there was one important exception: the Hop Tac program, designed to put "whatever resources are required" into the area surrounding Saigon to pacify it. The area was chosen by Ambassador Lodge in his last weeks as Ambassador in June, 1964, and Hop Tac deserves study because both its failures and limited achievements had many of the characteristics of our later pacification efforts -- and because, like all pacification efforts, there was constant disagreement within the Mission, the press, and the Vietnamese as to how well the program was doing.

Hop Tac -- an intensive pacification effort in the provinces ringing Saigon -- was formally proposed at a high level strategy session in Honolulu in July of 1964 by Lodge, then on his way home from his first assignment as Ambassador. In a paper presented to Secretaries Rusk and McNamara and incoming Ambassador Taylor at Honolulu (dated June 19, 1964), Lodge wrote:

> "A combined GVN-US effort to intensify pacification efforts
> in critical provinces should be made...The eight critical pro-
> vinces are: Tay Ninh, Binh Duong, Hau Nghia, Long An, Dinh Tuong,
> Go Cong, Vinh Long, and Quang Ngai. Top priority and maximum
> effort should be concentrated initially in the strategically
> important provinces nearest to Saigon, i.e., Long an, Hau Nghia,
> and Binh Duong. Once real progress has been made in these pro-
> vinces, the same effort should be made in the five others."[1]/

General Taylor and General Westmoreland began Hop Tac, setting up a new and additional headquarters in Saigon which was supposed to tie together the overlapping and quarrelsome commands in the Saigon area. The Vietnamese set up a parallel, "counterpart" organization, although critics of Hop Tac were to point out that the Vietnamese Hop Tac head-quarters had virtually no authority or influence, and seemed primarily designed to satisfy the Americans. (Ironically, Hop Tac is the Viet-namese word for "cooperation," which turned out to be just what Hop Tac lacked.)

Hop Tac had a feature previously missing from pacification plans: it sought to tie together the pacification plans of a seven-province area (expanded from Lodge's three provinces to include the adjacent pro-vinces of Phuoc Tuy, Bien Hoa, Phuoc Thanh, and Gia Dinh, which surround Saigon like a doughnut), into a plan in which each province subordinated its own priorities to the concept of building a "giant oil spot" around Saigon. In a phrase which eventually became a joke in the Mission, the American heading the Hop Tac Secretariat at its inception, Colonel

Jasper Wilson, briefed senior officials on the creation of "rings of
steel" which would grow outward from Saigon until the area from the
Cambodian border to the South China Sea was secure. Then, according
to the plan, Hop Tac would move into the Delta and North. Colonel
Wilson ordered his staff to produce a phased plan in which the area (Map 1)
to be pacified was divided into four circles around Saigon. Each ring
was to be pacified in four months, according to the original plan, which
never had any chance of success. But Wilson, under great pressure from
his superiors, ordered the plan produced, got his Vietnamese counterparts
to translate it, and issued it. The kickoff date for Hop Tac was to be
September 12, 1964: the operation, a sweep into the VC-controlled pine-
apple groves just west and southwest of the city of Saigon -- the VC
base nearest to the city, which had not been entered by the GVN since
the last outpost had been abandoned in 1960.

The operation began on schedule, with elements of the 51st Regiment
moving toward their objective west of Saigon. During the second day of
the operation, the unit ran into a minefield and took numerous casualties.
Shortly thereafter, instead of continuing the operation, the unit broke
off contact and, to the amazement of its advisors, turned back towards
the city of Saigon. When next located it was in the middle of Saigon
participating in the abortive coup d'etat of September 13, 1964.

From that point on, Hop Tac was a constant source of dispute within
the U.S. Mission. Almost to a man, the civilian agencies "supporting"
Hop Tac felt that the program was unnecessary, repetitive, and doomed.
They claimed that they preferred to work through existing channels, although these, in MACV's view, were inadequate. This view was not stated
openly, however, since the Ambassador and General Westmoreland had committed all U.S. agencies to full support. On October 6, 1964, for
example, General Taylor sent Washington an EXDIS cable in which he discussed and rejected a suggestion to decentralize the pacification effort,
and instead listed several actions that the Mission would take. First
among these was a "unanimous recommendation" that the Mission "give full
support to Hop Tac Plan, assuring it the necessary priority to give it
every chance to succeed...When Hop Tac priorities permit, concentrate on
selected weak areas." 2/ Thus there was a reluctance to criticize the
program directly.

Deadlines slipped continually; phase lines were readjusted; the
official count of "pacified" hamlets climbed steadily. But a special
study of the area made in October, 1964, by representatives of USOM,
USIS, and MACV concluded: "Generally speaking, Hop Tac, as a program,
does not appear to exist as a unified and meaningful operation." 3/

The official view of Hop Tac was that the new coordinating machinery
was doing some good. Thus, during a period in which cables on the general
situation were rather gloomy, Ambassador Taylor could tell the President

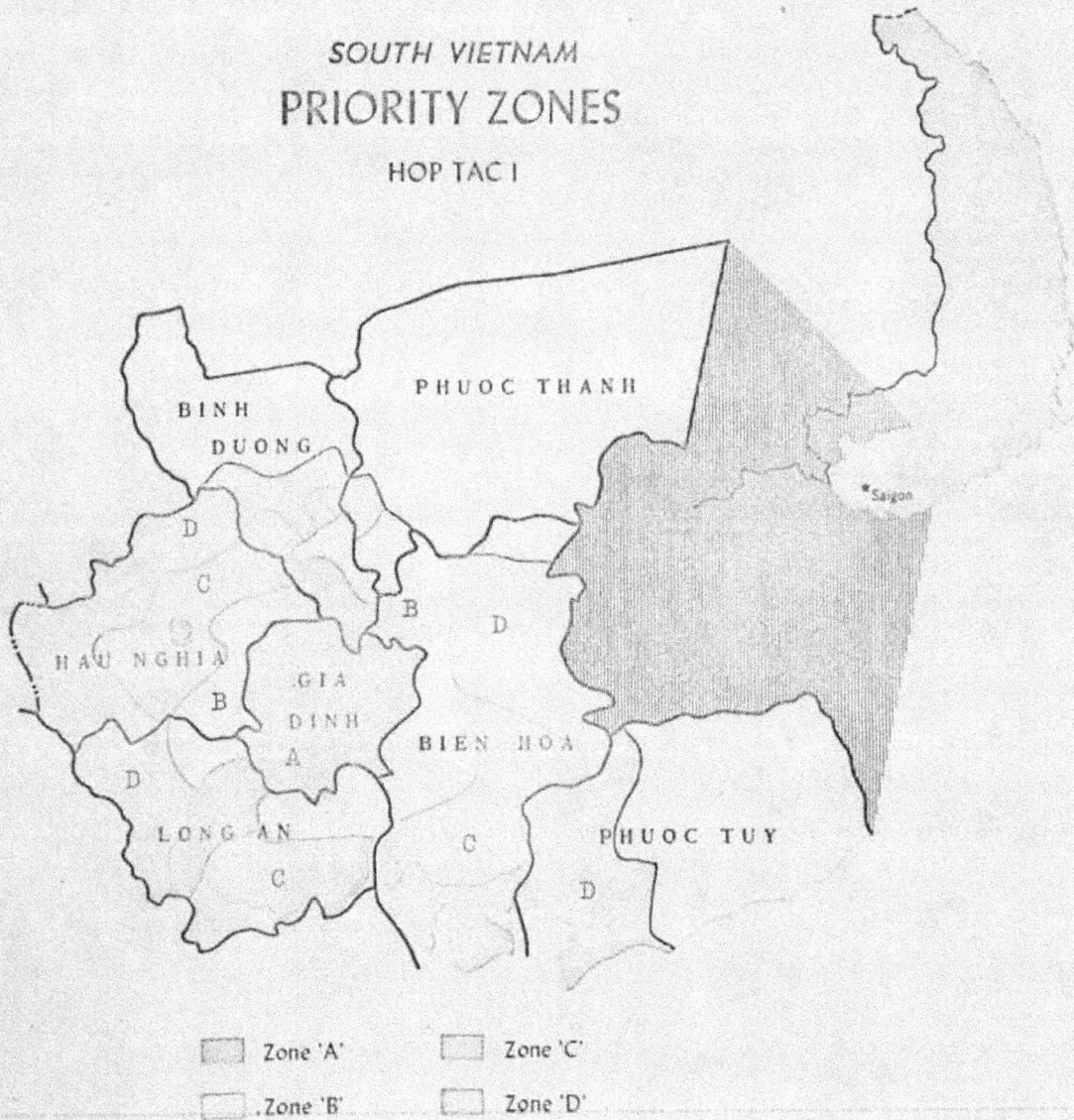

SOUTH VIETNAM
PRIORITY ZONES
HOP TAC I

BINH DUONG

PHUOC THANH

*Saigon

D

C

B

D

HAU NGHIA

GIA DINH

A

B

BIEN HOA

D

LONG AN

C

C

PHUOC TUY

D

Zone 'A'   Zone 'C'

Zone 'B'   Zone 'D'

MAP 1
SECRET
2A

Declassified per Executive Order 13526, Section 3.3
NND Project Number: NND 63316. By: NWD Date: 2011

in his weekly NODIS that while "pacification progress throughout the rest of Vietnam was minimal at best, largely because of the political climate...Some forward movement occurred in the Hop Tac effort growing out of U.S. Mission discussions with the Prime Minister on September 25. The number of operating checkpoints in the Hop Tac area increased markedly; command areas were strengthened; available troop strength increased." 4/ Minor statistical advances, taken out of context, were continually being used in the above manner to prove overall progress.

The MACV Command History for 1964 reflects the official view: "At the end of 1964, Hop Tac was one of the few pacification areas that showed some success and greater promise." 5/ But subsequent events in the area do not bear out this view. In February of 1966 for example -- 18 months after the birth of Hop Tac -- when the Hop Tac area was designated as one of the four "National Priority Areas," the briefers were unable to show Ambassadors Lodge and Porter any progress in the preceding year. They could not even produce a plan for the coming year. Originally Hop Tac was focused on cleaning out the nearest VC base areas, but by February of 1966 -- with the GVN unable to stop the growing VC build up, the emphasis was "placed on lines of communications, with special attention to be given vital installations including Bien Hoa and Tan Son Nhut air bases and ammunition and gasoline depots." 6/ The best the briefers could do, in the final briefing prior to the Honolulu Conference, was to say that they hoped to pacify 72 hamlets in the entire seven-province area, and "consolidate" 144 hamlets in Gia Dinh -- which meant the hamlets ringing Saigon, including many which were really part of the city. Lodge and Porter were told that day "there has been a lessening of security in Hau Nghia and Gia Dinh provinces. RF and PF units generally are not up to authorized strengths. The new cadre program should be helpful in solving the problem of continued hamlet security after pacification...The 1966 plan is not overly optimistic from a military standpoint." 7/ (The memorandum recording of this meeting, made by a member of General Lansdale's staff, shows as the only Ambassadorial guidance after this sobering report: "Maps drawn to depict progress of Rural Construction (Pacification) should show as the goal only that area to be pacified during the year...The U.S. Mission manpower committee should look into the use of refugees in the national labor force.") 8/

The Vietnamese were cynical about Hop Tac; it was something, speculation ran, that General Khanh had to do to keep the Americans happy, but it was clearly an American show, clearly run by the United States, and the Vietnamese were reluctant to give it meaningful support. It was one of the first major programs with which the United States became publicly identified (since Diem had always kept the United States in as much of a background role as possible -- and its shortcomings were in part derived from this fact.

All through Ambassador Taylor's tenure, Hop Tac was something on which he and the Mission Council pinned hope. General Westmoreland thought the program had been reasonably successful, when he told the Mission Council about Hop Tac's first year:

> "General Westmoreland said that while Hop Tac could be said only to have been about 50% successful, it had undoubtedly averted a VC seige of Saigon." 9/

This same view was reflected in McGeorge Bundy's comments in a memorandum to the President months earlier in February, 1965, when he said:

> "The Hop Tac program of pacification in this area has not been an unqualified success, but it has not been a failure, and it has certainly prevented any strangling seige of Saigon. We did not have a chance to form an independent judgment on Hop Tac, but we did conclude that whatever its precise measure of success, it is of great importance that this operation be pursued with full vigor. This is the current policy of the Mission." 10/

There were others who said that, as a matter of fact, Saigon was almost under seige and that the situation was deteriorating. Westmoreland's own headquarters, for example, sent to Washington in the June Monthly Evaluation from MACV, the following statement which seems to contradict Westmoreland's optimism:

> "The sealing off of Saigon from surrounding areas, no matter how incomplete the sealing may be, has had and will continue to have serious economic as well as military effects." 11/

Shortly after he arrived in Vietnam for his second tour, Lodge asked for a private assessment of Hop Tac from an Embassy officer, who reported to him in early September of 1965:

> "1. Hop Tac did not achieve its original goals primarily because they were completely unrealistic and did not take into account the difficulty of the task. These goals were set quite arbitrarily and with no regard for the available resources and the strength of the enemy.

> "2. The second reason for the failures of Hop Tac lies in its strategic concept. The idea of concentric circles outward from Saigon to be pacified in successive waves of clearing, securing and developing may be sound in macroscopic terms; when the Hop Tac area is looked at carefully, the viability of this strategy breaks down. The concentric phase lines around Saigon do not adequately take into account existing areas of GVN strength and existing Viet Cong base areas; rather

4

they commit the GVN to a continual expansionary effort
on all sides of Saigon simultaneously, an effort which
is beyond its capabilities. Above all, they ignore the
political structure of the area around Saigon.

"3. The U.S. Mission has two broad courses of action available in regard to Hop Tac. First, the Mission Council
may feel that the area encompassed by Hop Tac remains
the first pacification priority of the U.S. and the GVN.
If this is the considered judgment of the Mission Council,
then we must seek ways of re-emphasizing, re-invigorating
and reorienting Hop Tac in order to achieve a dramatic
and sustained success in pacification.

"4. There is an alternative open to the Mission Council.
Perhaps it would be politically unwise to attempt to
commit the GVN to re-emphasis of Hop Tac at this time.
There are several facts which support this view:

"A. The GVN has never considered Hop Tac its own plan
and its own number one priority. The staff planning
for the plan was done almost entirely by the United
States, and then translated into Vietnamese. It is,
in the eyes of many Vietnamese, 'the plan of the
Americans.'

"B. It is perhaps the most difficult area in the country
in which to attempt pacification. Since it surrounds
Saigon (but does not include it), every political
tremor in the capital is felt in the neighboring
area...the High Command has created chains of command
in the area which are clearly designed primarily to
prevent coups, and only secondarily to pacify the
countryside. Another example: in the last 11 months,
24 out of 31 district chiefs and five out of seven
province chiefs have been changed.

"C. Prime Minister Ky will never feel that Hop Tac is his
plan. If he is seeking a major public triumph, and
intends to devote his attention to achieving that
triumph, it is unlikely that he will choose Hop Tac,
which as mentioned above, is publicly considered an
American plan. Moreover, to the extent that any Vietnamese is publicly connected with Hop Tac, it is
Nguyen Khanh. For this reason, more than any other,
the dangers of re-emphasizing Hop Tac outweigh the
possible gains..."

"The situation in the Hop Tac area will not collapse if
Hop Tac is not revitalized now. With the available forces, and
particularly with the impending arrival of the 1st Infantry
Division to take up a position across the southern arc of Zone D,
Saigon itself is not going to be threatened any more than it
presently is. The threat -- which is substantial -- comes from
the enemy within, and the solution does not lie within the responsibility of the Hop Tac Council: it is a problem for the
Saigon police and intelligence communities. This threat, serious
as it is, is not directly affected by the presence of the Viet
Cong's 506th battalion 20 miles away in Hau Nghia, nor by Zone D.
The two problems can be dealt with separately, and solution of
the internal security problems of Saigon are not contingent on
the success of clearing Hau Nghia and Long An." 12/

In an effort to reconcile these opposing views about Hop Tac, Lodge
told the September 15 Mission Council that "the original reasons for the
emphasis placed on the area surrounding Saigon...were still valid, primarily because of the heavy density of population. Lodge noted, however,
lack of a clear commitment to Hop Tac on the part of the GVN, possibly
due to the fact that the Vietnamese consider the program an American
scheme. The view was also expressed that the trouble may also lie in
US/GVN differences over some fundamental concepts in Hop Tac. Finally,
Ambassador Lodge said it was essential that all interested American
agencies be agreed on concepts and tactics before an approach to the GVN
could be made." 13/ After this meeting, no significant action was taken,
and the matter lapsed.

The importance of Hop Tac is still difficult to assess; it is included here primarily because of its role as the one major pacification
program that was tried during the 1964-1965 period when pacification
was not receiving its present top-level emphasis. Whether or not it
averted a seige of Saigon, as General Westmoreland claimed, is a semantic question: what constitutes a seige in a guerrilla war? Saigon, of
course, never was under seige in the classic sense of the word, but it
is hard to conceive of it ever being literally cut off as Dien Bien Phu
or Makefing were -- this would not be a logical objective to the Viet
Cong, who wanted to put pressure on the capital but knew they couldn't
seal it off (nor would have wanted to, since they got supplies from it).

What is important is that the failures of Hop Tac were never adequately reported and analyzed prior to embarking on other pacification
efforts. Thus, at one point General Westmoreland told each of his Senior
Corps Advisors to start a Hop Tac in his area -- a strange request since
Hop Tac was designed to pull together a multiplicity of commands not
duplicated in any other area. Each Corps naturally responded by producing plans which concentrated their pacification assets around the
Corps headquarters -- Da Nang, and Can Tho or, in the case of II Corps,

6

TOP SECRET - Sensitive

Qui Nhon. This in turn led naturally to the later National Priority Area program, but had no other value.

With MACV reluctant to close down its Hop Tac Secretariat, with the civilian Americans giving Hop Tac only verbal support, and with the Vietnamese leaving a powerless staff at the headquarters, Hop Tac could well have survived as an appendix to the normal chain of command, as so many outdated structures survive in Vietnam because no one wants to admit their irrelevance. But General Westmoreland saw a way to dispose of Hop Tac cleanly and quietly in the summer of 1966, and he took it. At the Mission Council meeting of July 7, 1966:

> "General Westmoreland then turned to the subject of Hop
> Tac. He summarized the purpose of the Hop Tac concept, which
> was implemented two years ago, and said that -- while it has
> enjoyed only modest success over the past two years -- the
> situation in the area surrounding Saigon/Cholon would be com-
> paratively worse if we had not had the Hop Tac arrangement.
> He noted that recent organizational changes have taken place,
> which have resulted in the Capital Military Region becoming
> the Capital Military District (as part of the III Corps Tac-
> tical Zone) with Saigon remaining as an autonomous city. In
> view of these changes, there is some question of the validity
> of continuing with the original concept. More importantly,
> III Corps has a Revolutionary Development Council and a Hop
> Tac Council which results in some duplication of effort.
> Consequently, the General believes that these two councils
> should be merged, with the Revolutionary Development Council
> absorbing the Hop Tac Council. General Westmoreland asked
> the Mission Council to endorse this proposal for him to carry
> out. After brief discussion, Ambassador Lodge indicated his
> approval." 14/

By this time Hop Tac had long lost the "highest priority" which was supposed to justify it, and both the American and the Vietnamese had turned to other matters.

But Hop Tac was not adequately analyzed before embarking on other efforts, and its shortcomings were largely forgotten by the time that the still-deteriorating situation in Gia Dinh led MACV to commit three U.S. Army battalions to the inner area surrounding Saigon -- the original first phase of Hop Tac -- as part of Operation Fairfax in November of 1966. The Mission, with no institutional memory, forgot -- or never learned -- the lessons that Hop Tac could have offered.

B. Ambassador Lodge and the "True Believers"

Many senior American officials have paid varying degrees of lip
service to the pacification effort since 1962 -- a fact which makes it
extremely hard to determine who really pushed pacification and who
didn't. But about Ambassador Lodge, there can be little question. He
had repeatedly called pacification "the heart of the matter," and his
unfailing belief in the importance of the effort can be clearly shown
in his public and private statements and his cables.

His emphasis on pacification resumed the day he returned to Saigon
in August 1965, when in his arrival statement he said that the United
States supported the "true revolution" of the Vietnamese people. His
continual emphasis on the effort seems to have had a definite impact on
the mood in Washington and in the Mission, and played a role in the events
leading up to the Honolulu Conference in February 1966 -- where pacification was given (or so it seemed to Americans and Vietnamese alike in
Vietnam) the President's blessing.

It is true that Ambassador Taylor also felt that pacification was
important and that it would deserve high emphasis; his push on Hop Tac
clearly demonstrates this fact. But because Maxwell Taylor saw that it
was his responsibility as Ambassador to reconcile competing requirements
for limited resources, and develop a single overall strategy for the
effort, he never let pacification consume too many resources prematurely.
Lodge, on the other hand, did not see himself as an administrator or
manager of the U.S. Mission, but as the President's personal representative and advisor in Saigon. Thus, he felt no qualms about advocating a
certain course of action -- in this case, pacification. There is no
record of Ambassador Lodge worrying about the way his latest proposals
would affect the balance of the whole effort. He simply did not see himself as responsible for the actions of the operating agencies which
represented AID, USIA, and the CIA, let alone DOD, in Vietnam * -- not
even after receiving a strong letter of authority from President Johnson
in July of 1965: 15/

"As you take charge of the American effort in South
Vietnam, I want you to have this expression of my confidence,
and a reaffirmation of my desire that as Ambassador you exercise full responsibility for the work of the United States

---

* See for example, Lodge's NODIS to the President, February 1, 1966, in
which he said: "...I have learned of Zorthian's wire to Marks, which,
of course, he has the right to send, since I hold that Zorthian, like
U.S. agency chiefs here, has and should have an open channel to his
agency. It is a statement of Zorthian's opinion which, of course, was
sent without my approval or direction..." 16/ (The subject was apparently
a suggestion that Lodge address the United Nations General Assembly in
New York, although Lodge's cable cited does not explicitly state what
Zorthian's cable said.)

Government in South Vietnam. In general terms this authority
is parallel to that set forth in my letter to Ambassador Taylor
of July 2, 1964." * 17/

Given his belief in the fundamental importance of the pacification
effort, Lodge was ready to push it at any time he could. He did not
examine the possibility that certain times were more favorable than
others for an effort which needed the full participation of the Vietnamese in order to succeed, and, like many in the government, failed
to see that at certain times emphasis on pacification would not only
not work but would be harmful to GVN/US relations, and would reduce
the chances for a successful joint effort at some more propitious time.

Thus, it is not surprising that one of his last major documents at
the end of his first tour as Ambassador proposed Hop Tac (see I. A.) --
in the face of strong possibilities that the situation was not favorable
to it -- and that on his return in August 1965 he was advocating more
effort in pacification.

Thus, for example, meeting with his senior officers one month after
he arrived, Lodge "began the meeting by stating that in his opinion the
United States military was doing so well not that 'we face a distinct
possibility that VC main force units will be neutralized and that VC
fortresses will be destroyed soon. We should be ready to handle the VC
in small units. This gives counter-subversion/terrorism or pacification
or counterinsurgency -- I am not overly concerned with what we call it --
a new urgency for all of us here.'" 18/

It is likely that if Lodge had clarified his view of pacification
and repeated it continually in public and privately, as he did with
anything he believed in, his view would eventually have taken hold in
the United States Mission. But the problem of how pacification should
work was -- and is -- a very difficult one. It raises a number of extremely difficult questions on which the United States Government has
never reached a unified position.

Sensing that Lodge was receptive to ideas which emphasized pacification but that he had no set views on details, many groups and individuals
besieged him with a resurgence of ideas and philosophies on pacification.
They were all encouraged by his verbal support or his glowing cables to
Washington. The whole atmosphere in the Mission became more favorable
towards pacification and pacifiers; Lansdale, Colonel Serong (the
Australian who was to organize the Police Field Force with support from

---

* The letter to Taylor had said, among other points: "I wish it clearly
  understood that this overall responsibility includes the whole military effort in South Vietnam and authorizes the degree of command and
  control that you consider appropriate."

Lodge), Sir Robert Thompson (whose Malayan experiences had led him to
emphasize the police), Colonel Bohannon (who began as a Lansdale deputy,
but whose views took a different line), the Marines (with their pacification efforts and CAP's near Da Nang), the CIA (which produced, with
Lodge's strong support, the PAT's-turned RD cadre), USIA and AID (with
their small but growing field programs), the Army (which entered the
game late but elicited from Lodge on visits to the U.S. 25th Infantry
Division and then the 1st Infantry Division, some of his longest and
most glowing accounts of pacification in action. 19/)

These groups and individuals fought about details, sometimes
debating minor points like medieval monks but also disagreeing on
rather basic points -- such as whether the object was to gain the
population's support or to control them by force. (A popular Marine
saying, which tried to bridge the gap, went: "Get the people by the
balls, and their hearts and minds will follow.") But each group found
something that appealed to Lodge, and each in turn gained encouragement
from him. The slow change in mood also affected Washington.

In dealing with his role in the re-emphasis of pacification, we
must distinguish between Lodge's influence on our overall, or grand,
strategy -- on which he was ultimately to have considerable impact --
and his influence on the operational details of the policy. The latter
did not interest him on a continuing basis, and it is thus easy to underestimate his influence. There was, for example, a tendency in Saigon
during his Ambassadorship to minimize his importance, since each agency
could ignore him when he told them to do something and usually get away
with it. But this popular view overlooked Lodge's impact in encouraging all sorts of people to emerge from parts of the USG with renewed
hope for pacification. It overlooked the impact of his cables and statements, which added up to a massive endorsement of pacification. In his
NODIS weeklies to the President, for example, pacification receives more
attention than any other subject.

Alone, Lodge could have done little, if anything, to move the USG
around. But his influence seems clear, more so in retrospect than at
the time: at a time when frustrations were growing, he was emphasizing
a different rhetoric and strategy.

The best way to show his emphasis is simply to quote from the
cables and memoranda of the period. Each one shows Lodge, either
directly or indirectly, putting forth his general beliefs -- sometimes
contradictory. They form an important part of the background to
Honolulu, where pacification was to get its biggest push to that date:

1. Lodge at the end of his first tour in Vietnam, defining
   pacification in his paper proposing Hop Tac:

"The first priority after the military have cleared an
area is to bring about the selection of an able man for that area,

who will in turn go about creating a basically civilian
counter-terrorist organization on the 'precinct' level, or
equivalent thereof...Its prime purpose will be, notably with
police help, to create security for the local government and
free it from all intimidation by going through the precinct
with a fine-toothed comb...Once the local government feels
safer, it should move energetically to promote public safety
for the people; the people should then rally more to the
government; and this should create an upward spiral as
regards security organization...USOM and USIA will support
these local 'precinct' organizations, will actually work
through them, and will seek to make it attractive to be one
of those who builds such a counter-terrorism precinct organization...The military should take special precautions in their
operations not to injure in any way the non-combatants. It
must also behave itself so well that the people like the
Army..." 20/

2.   Lodge's Ten Point Program for Success:

"In each city precinct and each rural hamlet immediately adjacent to a thoroughly pacified city (i.e., the
smallest unit from a public safety standpoint) the following
program should be undertaken in the following order:

    "1. Saturate the minds of the people with some socially
conscious and attractive ideology, which is susceptible of
being carried out.

    "2. Organize the people politically with a hamlet chief
and committee whose actions would be backed by the police or
the military using police-type tactics. This committee should
have representatives of the political, military, economic and
social organizations and should have an executive who directs.

    "3. With the help of the police or military, conduct a
census.

    "4. Issue identification cards.

    "5. Issue permits for the movement of goods and people.

    "6. When necessary, hold a curfew.

    "7. Thanks to all these methods, go through each hamlet
with a fine-tooth comb to apprehend the terrorists.

    "8. At the first quiet moment, bring in agricultural
experts, school teachers, etc.

"9. The hamlet should also be organized for its own
defense against small Viet Cong attacks.

"10. After all these things have been accomplished, hold
elections for local office." 21/

COMMENT: Lodge began his second tour as Ambassador where he had left
off the year before. The above paper, which he also transmitted to the
President in a NODIS message, again represented no official U.S.
position. After writing it and giving it to everyone in the Mission,
he let the matter drop, and thus the paper did not assume any official
character. Since nothing was changed in the procedures of the Mission,
and since the old criteria for pacification still applied unchanged,
Lodge had, in typical fashion, failed to affect the operating Mission.

3.   The Assignment of Lansdale:

"Handpicked group of about ten experienced counter-
subversion/counter terrorism workers under direction of
Edward G. Lansdale will be going to Saigon to provide
Ambassador Lodge with special operating staff in field of
political action both at central level and also in connection
with rural programs." 22/

COMMENT: From the beginning, there was misunderstanding over Lansdale's
role in Lodge's Embassy. The first cable reflects this. The phrase
"counter-subversion/counter-terrorism workers," seems to contradict the
latter part of the sentence, about "political action." From the start
Lodge wanted him to "get pacification going." Thus, less than a
month later, Lodge told the President:

"I appointed Edward Lansdale, with his complete approval,
to be chairman of the U.S. Mission Liaison Group to the newly
created Vietnamese governmental body having to do with what we
call 'pacification,' what they call 'rural construction,' and
what means to me socially conscious practical politics, the
by-product of which is effective counter-subversion/terrorism.
I thought it was important for all concerned for him to have a
definite allocation where he would have the best chance of
bringing his talents to bear. I trust that the hopes of some
journalists that he is here in an adversarial relationship
with existing US agencies will be nipped in the bud by making
him the spokesman for the whole US Mission in this particular
regard." (underlining added) 23/

Thus, another action which served to strengthen the pacification priority,
although its primary reason probably was to get Lansdale working on
something other than Saigon politics.

4.   Lodge on the Use of U.S. Troops in Pacification:

"The presence of American troops does provide the opportunity for thorough pacification of the areas in which they are
stationed and full advantage should be taken of this opportunity. It is a very big dividend from our investment of men
and money. For example, the Third Marine Division has scored
impressive successes north, south, and west of Da Nang...If
our American troops can emulate this performance (of the proto-
CAC units) of 60 Americans and 150 Vietnamese, we ought to get
a tremendous amount of small unit nighttime effective pacification, and we would be neglecting an opportunity not to use
American troops for this purpose, thereby pacifying the country
and transforming the ARVN, making it into a much more vital and
effective element of Vietnamese society, able at some not too
remote date to carry on by themselves without outside help...
We are already discussing with the Vietnamese the possibility
of singling out areas that look like good prospects, that are
potentially pretty much over on our side, and then pacifying
them so as to get a little smell of across-the-board success in
the air...I am not ready to say, 'What areas would be chosen
for pacification, when should the plan be started, what objectives
would be best,' but hope to be able to do so soon. I am now
encouraging General Ky to concentrate GVN efforts and enthusiasm
on pacification so that this can have sustained, wholehearted
GVN participation...Development of popular electoral processes
is part of all our current planning for counter subversion/
terrorism in 'rural construction (pacification)'." 24/

COMMENT: Here, for the first time, Lodge addresses a key point: the
role of U.S. troops on pacification. The whole concept of the use of
U.S. troops was being worked out during this period (see following
section on Marines), and Lodge now began to weigh in with qualified
support for the Marine approach, based on an overly optimistic view of
the situation.

5.   Lansdale's Weekly Report, October 4, 1965:

"Past week devoted to getting GVN into sound start again
on pacification program...U.S. Mission Liaison Group shaping
up into realistic instrument for working level teamwork on
pacification by all U.S. Missions..." 25/

COMMENT: Lansdale was responding to the direction given him by Lodge.

6.   Lodge on the GVN's Attitude Towards Pacification:

"During my talk with General Co, the deputy Prime Minister
in charge of six ministries, I was impressed by the amount of

sustained analytical thought which he, with his colleagues, had
given to how to organize the government for the great new job
of pacification which confronts them -- and which is clearly
their government's most important single responsibility." 26/

COMMENT: Lodge had by this time let the GVN know clearly what tune he
wanted to hear, and with their usual skill the Vietnamese -- even
General Co, who turned out to be worthless on pacification -- were
playing the right song back.

7. "When the chance to win over the people was missed some
years ago, a situation came into being in which it was indispensable for the VC large units to be defeated before true
community building, with its mixture of political and security
measures, would be possible. Otherwise, the VC battalions,
emerging from untouchable sanctuaries, would destroy whatever
community building had painstakingly been achieved. Now it
looks as though the VC know this and has already begun to act
on the knowledge, transforming themselves into small units and
individual terrorists, and into subversive political operators." 27/

COMMENT: Lodge's sequence of events -- destroy the main force enemy
first, pacify second -- is hard to argue with, but his assessment of
VC capabilities and intentions falls short of accuracy.

As a final note to the examination of Lodge's emphasis on
pacification, it is worthwhile asking why he has so consistently put
such a high priority on the effort -- regardless of methodology -- to
gain control of the villages. The answer may lie in his strong views
on the way the war will end in Vietnam. Lodge doubted that there
would ever be meaningful negotiations with the Viet Cong. An old hand
at negotiating with the communists, Lodge felt that the most likely
end to the war was for the enemy to "fadeaway" after a prolonged
period of conflict. In his view, therefore, control of the population
became the best way to force the fadeaway. Furthermore, in the event
that there was some sort of pro forma discussions with the communists
at some future date, Lodge felt that there were certain minimum
conditions of a "satisfactory outcome" which must be met. An examination of his definition of a satisfactory outcome shows the overriding
importance of the pacification effort in his mind. The following is
from a telegram sent "For the President and the Secretary from Lodge"
on October 21, 1965, which Lodge considered one of his most important
cables:

"What we consider a satisfactory outcome to be would,
of course, be a very closely kept secret. It would include
the following, not necessarily in this order:

"1. The area around Saigon and south of Saigon (all of the Delta) must be pacified. This area includes about 55 to 60% of the population of Vietnam. 'Pacified' is defined as the existence of a state of mind among the people that they have a stake in the government as shown by the holding of local elections. It also means a proper local police force. In brief, a pacified area is economically, socially, and politically a part of the RVN.

"2. The thickly populated northeastern strip along the coast which includes 25% of the population would be completely pacified.

"3. The GVN would retain its present control of all cities and all provincial capitals.

"4. All principal roads would be open to the Vietnamese military day and night.

"5. Those areas not pacified would not be safe havens for the VC but would be contested by energetic offensive forays to prevent consolidation of a communist base.

"6. The VC disarms; and their weapons and explosives are removed from their hands. Their main force units broken up.

"7. North Vietnam stops its infiltration.

"8. Chieu Hoi rehabilitation would be extended to individual VC who are suitable...

"9. Hardcore VC to go to North Vietnam.

"10. GVN to approve.

"COMMENT: This means that we would not be insisting on the complete elimination of the VC although no safe haven would be allocated them. It would mean that we and the GVN would control 80 to 85% of the population and that the VC would be limited to the jungle and mountainous areas where they would go on as bandits, much as their counterparts in Malaya and Luzon -- and where the GVN would have the right to pursue them and try to destroy them." 28/

Lodge's formula for a satisfactory outcome is based on the absolute necessity of controlling the villages. In day-to-day terms this meant that, as Ambassador, Lodge had to push pacification as hard as possible. Thus, he was quite pleased with the emphasis that came out of the Honolulu conference in February of 1966.

C. III Marine Amphibious Force

To what extent the growing Marine emphasis on pacification was a factor during the period before the Honolulu conference is impossible to determine; the timing and evidence would suggest that the impact of the Marine strategy was greatest in the period after Honolulu, as they became more sure of the rightness of their approach, and as they garnered more and more publicity for it. Nonetheless, in the first eleven months of their mission in I Corps, the Marines had gotten deeply into the pacification program. The Marines thus became the most vocal advocates within the Armed Forces for emphasizing pacification more, and search and destroy less.

The Marine deployments and mission are covered in earlier decision studies in this series and will thus be treated only briefly here. The emphasis of this section is not on the influence the Marines had on the Honolulu conference, but on the way the Marines gradually moved into their new role, and the difficulties with it. The material here applied, therefore, equally to the pre- and post-Honolulu periods, throughout which the Marine successes, as they reported them, had a growing impact on the thinking of civilian and military alike, in Saigon, CINCPAC, and Washington.

The Marines landed their first troops -- two Battalion Landing Teams -- in Da Nang in March of 1965. Their original mission, "to secure enclaves in the northern region of Vietnam containing air and communications installations, was simplicity itself." 29/ (From "U.S. Marine Corps Civic Action Efforts in Vietnam, March 1965-March 1966, a study done by the USMC Historical Branch, SECRET; hereafter referred to as MC History; from unpaged draft.)

By the time of the Honolulu conference the Marines -- by now organized into the III Marine Amphibious Force -- had changed their mission considerably, and to a degree then unequalled among other American units was deeply engaged in pacification operations.

A monthly report issued by General Krulak, Commanding General, Fleet Marine Force, Pacific, indicates the evolution of Marine thinking on their mission. Reviewing the first seven months of their deployment in I Corps, the Fleet Marine Force, Pacific, wrote in September, 1965:

> "The Mission assigned III MAF was initially confined
> to airfield security. Subsequently, a limited offensive
> responsibility was added, which has gradually grown to an
> essentially unrestrained authority for offensive operations.
> Finally, and largely on its own, III MAF has entered the
> pacification program, with the bulk of its pacification
> efforts taking place since June." /Emphasis added/ 30/

One month later, after chronicling their successes, the report indicated the major shift in strategic thinking which was taking place at General Walt's headquarters in Da Nang, and at General Krulak's in Hawaii:

"While accomplishing all this the Marines were feeling,
with growing impact, a cardinal counterinsurgency principle:
that if local forces do not move in promptly behind the
offensive effort, then first line forces must be diverted to
provide the essential hamlet security, police and stabilization.
The alternative is to risk the development of vacua, into which
the VC guerrilla can flow. This condition grew during the
period. The Popular Forces and police were inadequate in
numbers and in quality to do their part of the job, as the
Marines did theirs. This operated to complicate the Marines'
problem by making the civic action effort more difficult,
by permitting harassment of our forces, and by making possible
a suicide attack on the Chu Lao and Marble Mountain areas.

"The end of the period saw the 676 square mile III MAF
area of influence more stable, more prosperous, and far more
hopeful, but it saw also an urgent need for efficient regional
or local forces to take up their proper burden, so the Marines
can maintain the momentum of their search/clear/pacification
efforts. It is plain that the most efficient way to bring this
about is to give III MAF substantial authority over the RF or
PF serving in this area, in order that they may be properly
trained and properly led." 31/

This summary, written in the headquarters of the man often regarded as
the philosopher of the Marine Corps, shows the Marines in the process
of swinging their emphasis around -- turning away from the offensive
against the enemy waiting in the nearby hills, and towards the people
and the VC guerrillas among the people inside their TAOR.

It was a crucial, difficult decision for the men who made it.
Significantly, the indications are strong that the decision was made
almost entirely inside Marine Corps channels, through a chain of
command that bypassed COMUSMACV and the civilian leaders of our
government, and ran from General Greene through General Krulak to
General Walt. The files do not reveal discussions of the implications,
feasibility, cost, and desirability of the Marine strategy among high-
ranking officials in the Embassy, MACV headquarters, the Defense and
State Departments. Yet in retrospect it seems clear that the strategy
the Marines proposed to follow, a strategy about which they made no
secret, was in sharp variance with the strategy of the other U.S. units
in the country, with far-ranging political implications that could even
affect the ultimate chances for negotiations.

It should be clear that the Marine concept of operations has a
different implicit time requirement than a more enemy-oriented
search and destroy effort. It is not within the scope of this paper
to analyze the different requirements, but it does appear that the
Marine strategy, which General Walt sometimes described as the

"wringing out of the VC from the land like you wring water out of a sponge," is slow and methodical, requires vast numbers of troops, runs the risk of turning into an occupation even while being called "pacification/civic action," and involves Americans deeply in the politics and traditions of rural Vietnam. The strategy can succeed, perhaps, but if it is to succeed, it must be undertaken with full awareness by the highest levels of the USG of its potential costs in manpower and time, and the exacting nature of the work. Instead, the documents suggest that the Marines determined their strategy basically on their own, deriving part of it from their own traditions in the "Banana Republics" and China (where Generals Walt, Krulak, Nickerson, and others had served in the 1930's), and partly from an attempt to solve problems of an unprecedented nature which were cropping up inside their TAORs, even on the edge of the great air base at Da Nang.

As it was, the Marine strategy was judged successful, at least by the Marines, long before it had even had a real test. It was applauded by many observers before the VC had begun to react to it, and as such, encouraged imitators while it was still unproven.

The Marine dilemma was how to support the pacification effort without taking it over. They thought they had succeeded in doing this by "self-effacing support for Vietnamese rural construction" after August of 1965, but there is much contradictory evidence on this point. The Marines themselves, according to the classified historical study they recently produced, understood that their pacification work had "to function through local Vietnamese officials. The tendency to produce Marine Corps programs or to work 'democratically' through individuals had to be strictly controlled. Only Vietnamese programs could be tolerated and support of these programs had to take place through Vietnamese governing officials..." 32/

But despite their good intentions to work through the existing GVN structure, the Marines found in many cases that the existing structure barely existed, except on paper, and in other cases that the existing structure was too slow and too corrupt for their requirements. And gradually the Marines got more deeply into the politics of rural Vietnam than they had intended, or presumably desired.

Their difficulties were greatest in the area of highest priority, the National Priority Area (as it was to be designated in October 1965) south of Da Nang. In a nine-village complex just south of the air base, the Marines urged upon the GVN successful completion of a special pacification program which had been designed by them in close conjunction with the Quang Nam Deputy Province Chief. The nine villages were divided into two groups, and the first phase, scheduled for completion first in December of 1965, included only five of the villages, with only 23,000 people living in them. By February, 1966, the plan had slipped considerably, and the projected completion date for the first

five villages was pushed back to April, 1966. The GVN and the Marines
considered their control to extend to over 16,000 of the 23,000 people
in the area, but, according to an Embassy evaluation of the area, only
682 were young men between the ages of 17 and 30. It was clear that
the Marines were trying to pacify an area in which the young men no
longer lived, having either been drafted, joined the VC, or gone to
Da Nang to work for the Americans. "The basic problem posed by this
lack of manpower must be solved before the area can be expected to
participate in its own defense," the Embassy report said. "Until it
is solved, the Marines and the ARVN will remain tied to defensive
mission involving them with the population. No one in Quang Nam sees
any immediate solution to this dilemma." The report concluded with a
description of how over-involved with local politics the Marines were
becoming, unintentionally, and said:

> "The plan, despite the valiant efforts of the Marines,
> is in trouble, caused by a confused and fragmented chain of
> command, a lack of skilled cadre, inability to recruit
> locally RF and PF -- and the open opposition of the VNQDD." 33/

The VNQDD, or Vietnam Quoc Dan Dang, was the political party
controlling the provinces of Quang Ngai, Quang Nam, and Quang Tin.
The Marines knew little about them, although, according to the study,
all the village chiefs in the area were VNQDD members. The VNQDD
were not supporting the priority area plan because they had not been
consulted in its formulation, and for this reason, and others, the
report predicted the failure of the plan, despite the heavy Marine
commitment.

Like Hop Tac, it was an unusually difficult situation, but it
illustrates the problems that the Marines, and any other U.S. troops
that got deeply involved in pacification, confronted in Vietnam.

D. Washington Grumbles About the Effort

Throughout the period of the buildup in Vietnam, there was a growing chorus of discontent in Washington over the management of the U.S. effort in Vietnam, most of it directed at the civilian agencies -- USIA, AID, and the CIA. Unhappiness with the way the Mission ran was to lead to three major reorganizations in the 15-month period from the Honolulu conference to the arrival of Ambassador Ellsworth Bunker. The first reorganization took place immediately after Honolulu, and assigned to the Deputy Ambassador, William J. Porter, specific duties and responsibilities which had previously been dispersed throughout the Mission and handled on an ad hoc basis. The second reorganization, which took place in November-December 1966, reorganized the internal components of AID, USIA, and the CIA so that the Deputy Ambassador could control directly a single Office of Civil Operation (OCO), by-passing the agency chiefs. The latest reorganization, which was announced in May 1967, transferred responsibility for OCO from the Deputy Ambassador to COMUSMACV, who in turn was given a civilian Deputy with the rank of Ambassador (R. W. Komer). This section outlines events leading to the first reorganization in March 1966, a reorganization which raised the priority of the pacification effort, but left most of the basic problems in the U.S. Mission unsolved. The actual reorganization, and its effects, will be covered in Part III. 1.

Efforts to reorganize the Saigon Mission are a recurring theme in recent history. The impetus for reorganization has consistently come from Washington, and the Mission has usually resisted. Its resistance is not hard to understand, since almost every reorganization scheme tended to diminish the authority and autonomy of senior members of the Mission Council such as the JUSPAO Director, the USAID Director, and the CIA Station Chief.

Skeptics have said that whenever things are going poorly, "Americans reorganize." But the opponents of various reorganization schemes have been unable to defend the existing Mission Council system, which must definitely be rated one of Vietnam's casualties. Not since the beginning of the "country team" concept in the 1950's ("Mission Council" being another term for the same structure) had the concept been tested the way it was to be tested in Vietnam. The pressure of events, the tension, the unprecedented size of the agencies and a host of other factors made the system shaky even under the strong manager Maxwell Taylor. Under the man who didn't want to manage, Lodge, it began to crumble. Each agency had its own ideas on what had to be done, its own communication channels with Washington, its own personnel and administrative structure -- and starting in 1964-65, each agency began to have its own field personnel operating under separate and parallel chains of command. This latter event was ultimately to prove the one which gave reorganization efforts such force, since it began to become clear to people in Washington and Saigon alike that the Americans in the provinces were not always working on the same team, and that they were receiving conflicting or over-lapping instructions from a variety of sources in Saigon and Washington.

Still, while General Taylor was Ambassador, reorganization was not something to be pushed seriously by Washington. With Lodge back in charge, it was a different story. As a matter of fact, so serious were Lodge's managerial deficiencies that even during his first tour, when the U.S. Mission was less than 20,000 men, and the entire civilian component under 1,000, there was talk of reorganization. In a personal message to Lodge on May 26, 1964, the President made the following prophetic statement:

> "I have received from /Mike7 Forrestal a direct account of your belief that there is need for change and improve-ment in the civilian side of the country team. We have reached a similar conclusion here, and indeed we believe it is essential for you to have a top-ranking officer who is wholly acceptable to you as chief of staff for country team operations. My own impression is that this should be either a newly appointed civilian of wide governmental experience and high standing, or General Westmoreland...." 34/

This message became irrelevant when Lodge suddenly resigned in June of 1964 to assist Governor Scranton's bid for the Republican nomination, but it shows that the President, Lodge, and apparently other people in Washington had deep concern with the structure of the Mission at this early date.

By sending Taylor and Alexis Johnson -- then the State Department's highest-ranking Foreign Service Officer -- to Saigon in July of 1964, the President in effect put off any Washington-initiated reorganiza-tions for the length of Taylor's tour, since no one in Washington could tell the former Chairman of the JCS how to run a mission.

Taylor organized the Mission Council -- not a new invention, but a formalization of the country team into a body which met once a week, with agendas, minutes, and records of decisions. Taylor was particularly concerned that the Mission Council should have a "satisfactory meshing with...counterpart activities on the GVN side." 35/ And while he was Ambassador the U.S. made a determined effort to make the system work without reorganization. In a letter to Elbridge Durbrow, who was once American Ambassador in Saigon himself, Alexis Johnson described the system:

> "Max and I dropped the title 'Country Team' and set up what we called the 'Mission Council' on a formalized basis. In addition to Max and myself, the members were General Westmoreland, Barry Zorthian as JUSPAO (Joint United States Public Affairs Office -- this covered both MACV and Embassy

info as well as psychological operations in the field and against
the DRV), the Director of USOM and the CAS Station Chief. We
established an Executive Secretary who was first Bill Sullivan
and later Jack Herfurt, who was charged with the preparation of
agenda, the recording of decisions, and, most importantly,
following up and monitoring of decisions that were taken.
We met regularly once a week (with occasional special meetings
as required), with paper circulated beforehand insofar as
possible. One of the responsibilities of the Executive Secretary was to see that issues were worked out beforehand at
staff level insofar as possible and the remaining issues
clearly defined....It was normally our practice to keep all
members of the Council fully informed and to discuss all questions,
regardless of their sensitivity....After an informal exchange
of views, we took up questions on the agenda, doing our best
to obtain the consensus of all members. When in rare cases
this was not achieved, the Ambassador of course took the
decision. We considered the full range of questions, including
such fundamental ones as when and under what circumstances we
should bomb the North...etc...Below the Mission Council level
we established a series of committees in problem areas involving
more than one agency of the mission, chaired by the agency of
primary interest. These committees were responsible directly
to the Mission Council....We persuaded the GVN, on its side,
to set up a similar organization that was first called the
'Pacification Council' and later the 'Rural Construction
Council.'....The GVN Council and the Mission Council met together once a week with an agenda prepared beforehand by the
two Executive Secretaries...One of my theories, and to a degree
I think it was borne out in Saigon, was that the Mission Council
and the Joint Council were important not so much for what was in
fact decided at the meetings but for the fact that their
existence, and the necessity of reporting to them, acted as a
spur to the staff people to get things done and to resolve
issues at their level. Organization structure of course does
not assure brilliant performance, but I do take some satisfaction in feeling that, due to the organizational structure
that we established, we established the habit of the Mission
elements and the GVN and the Mission, working together in a
more effective way." 36/

Whether or not the system described by Ambassador Johnson above
really worked the way he says it was supposed to is not the subject of
this study. But it appears that within a few months after Lodge
returned as Ambassador the people within the USG advocating reorganization as at least a partial solution to the problems of the Mission were
once again in full cry.

The relationship of the reorganizers to the pacifiers must be explained. Those who advocated restructuring the Mission for more effective management were not necessarily the same people advocating a higher emphasis for pacification. But usually, since the organization of the Mission was so obviously deficient, both groups of people would end up advocating some kind of change -- and even if they disagreed on the nature of the change, the most important fact was that they were generally pushing a similar mood of dissatisfaction with the Mission upon the high-ranking officials with whom they might come in contact. (It should be kept in mind that they were really not groups at all, in the normal sense of the word, but a shifting collection of individuals with varying degrees of loyalty to either their parent agency or their own sense of history; and on each individual issue a different set of allies and antagonists might well exist.)

The efforts of those advocating reorganization began to bear edible fruit in December 1965 and January 1966, when a conference was held at Warrenton, Va., to which the Mission sent an impressive collection of Mission Council members: Deputy Ambassador Porter, USAID Mission Director Mann, JUSPAO Director Zorthian, Political Counsellor Habib, General Lansdale, CIA Station Chief Jorgenson, and Brigadier General Collins, representing Westmoreland. From Washington came the second and third echelons of the bureaucracy: Leonard Unger, Deputy Assistant Secretary of State; Rutherford Poats, Assistant Administrator of AID; Major General Peers, SACSA; Alvin Friedman, ISA; William Colby and Peer da Silva, CIA; Chester Cooper, White House; and Sanford Marlowe, USIA. Other participants included: Major General Hutchins, CINCPAC; Rufus Phillips of Lansdale's group; Charles Zwick and Henry Rowen of BOB; George Lodge, the Ambassador's son; Desmond Fitzgerald, CIA; and Leon Goure, of RAND.

The purpose of the meeting was to "bring together senior representatives of the U.S. Mission, Saigon, the Vietnam Coordinating Committee, Washington, and several other individuals to (a) review the joint GVN-US pacification/rural construction program and seek to promote its more effective operation and (b) address the problem of the increasingly serious shortages and bottlenecks in manpower, materials, and transport in Vietnam and to designate priorities and machinery for resources control and allocation." The major unstated purpose, in addition to those mentioned above, was to discuss the organization of the U.S. Mission in Vietnam.

Warrenton was to turn out to be a prelude to Honolulu, and as such its recommendations never were to become an integral part of the Mission's plans and strategy. But the direction that was developed at Warrenton is significant, because it represents the clear and unmistakable thrust that existed at the time in the "working levels" of both Saigon and Washington. Given the normal time lag before individual thoughts can reach the stage of agreed-upon committee-produced papers,

Warrenton, we can assume, reflected the evolution of thinking that had been going on, particularly among the civilians, as the first year of U.S. combat troop and deployment began to end. Indeed, in its catch-all approach to pacification, Warrenton had something for everyone.

The final recommendations from the Warrenton conference were addressed to Secretaries Rusk and McNamara, Admiral Raborn, Mr. Bell, Mr. Marks, and Mr. McGeorge Bundy, from the meeting's co-chairmen, Ambassador Unger and Ambassador Porter. The conclusions included the following points (with comments as required):

> 1. "There was a consensus that the designation of priority rural construction areas for 1966 was important and that the modest goals set for these areas were realistic. However, it was emphasized that the contrast between the massive input of U.S. resources and the modest priority area goals made success in those areas imperative..." 37/

COMMENT: The National Priority Areas did not meet their 1966 goals.

> 2. "In view of the prime importance to the U.S. of success in the four National Priority Areas, there was discussion of the need for designating U.S. team chiefs to head the U.S. advisory effort in those areas. It was agreed that the U.S. Mission Council would consider this matter promptly and report its conclusions to the VNCC." 38/

COMMENT: The designation of team chiefs for the priority areas did not take place. Here is another example of the Washington effort to reorganize Saigon, with Saigon resisting.

> 3. "There was widespread recognition of the need to provide within the U.S. Mission a single focus of operational control and management over the full range of the pertinent U.S. efforts in order to gear all such U.S. activities and resources effectively into implementation or the rural construction concept. However, some concern was expressed that too drastic organizational changes within the U.S. Mission would create problems with the counterpart GVN organization and would not ensure success of rural construction programs. No agreement was reached on the precise form for organization changes but there was general consensus that the focal point of control and management had to rest just below the Ambassador and that there must be a senior Mission official solely concerned with this subject. Disagreement was registered as to: .(1) whether the Deputy Ambassador, assisted by a staff, should serve this function or whether another senior official

(perhaps a second Deputy Ambassador) should be appointed; and
(2) what extent individual agency personnel, funds, and operations devoted to rural construction could and should be broken
out of agency organizations and placed under the direction of
the single focal point..." 39/

COMMENT: Here was the compromise wording on the issue which concerned
the participants at Warrenton a great deal. Each representative at
Warrenton brought with him a proposed organization chart for the
Mission (see below), but no agreement could be reached at that time.
In the main body of the memorandum to the principals on January 13,
1966, Unger and Porter wrote:

"The optimum organization for the U.S. Mission for
its support of the rural construction/pacification
program -- a senior official with a supporting staff with
full-time responsibility in this field was considered
necessary. (Coordination is also required with Ambassador
Lodge and Mr. Bell on this point.) It would also be
desirable for such an official to have in Washington a
high-level point of liaison to assure the expeditious
discharge here of urgent Vietnam business in this field..." 40/

When he reported to the Mission Liaison Group on Warrenton
two weeks later, on January 27, 1966, Porter sharply downplayed the
move for reorganization which was coming from Washington and changed
the emphasis. He said:

"a. No decision was reached at Warrenton with
respect to a U.S. in-country organization for rural construction, although the possibility of a single manager
was discussed.

"b. The U.S. Mission will continue to support Rural
Construction with the same organizational structure it is now
using, placing particular reliance on the Mission Liaison Group.

"c. Officials in Washington were concerned about teamwork
among the U.S. agencies in Vietnam but not about ability to do
the job. Differences of opinion are expected, and machinery
exists to resolve them. Differences due to personalities cannot be tolerated.

"d. It is clearly understood in Washington that military
operations alone are not enough, and that effective Rural
Construction is imperative. The highest levels in the USG
are keenly aware of the importance of US/GVN work in Rural
Construction... " 41/ /Emphasis Added/

TOP SECRET - Sensitive

Although not much more than a footnote now, the reorganization schemes that were presented at Warrenton deserve brief mention. At Warrenton, the participants were still fishing for ways and means, and their proposals reveal to a limited extent the intent of each agency when faced, three months later, with a new structure in both Saigon and Washington -- with Porter in charge in Saigon and Komer in business in the White House (discussed in III, 1 & 2).

--Chester Cooper, working for McGeorge Bundy in the White House, proposed a second Deputy Ambassador for Pacification, with control over CIA, USAID, JUSPAO, and partial control (not clarified) over MACV's Rural Construction advisors. Cooper also wanted a "Washington representative" in Saigon to expedite resource allocation. He was ambiguous about Lansdale's role. Cooper advocated a unified field chain of command.

--Poats and Mann submitted a joint Washington-Saigon proposal on behalf of AID (another clear indication of the fact that the real chains of command ran through agency channels, rather than through the Ambassador to Washington). They advocated a complicated arrangement in which a Chief of Staff for Pacification would head up special task forces "drawn from operating agencies but staying in their operational job in their agencies." AID in effect wanted no major change in the Mission, and particularly opposed any change in the multiplicity of chains of command in the provinces. They also advocated a Theater CINC, a resources allocation committee chaired by the AID Mission Director, and a MACV advisory structure that is partially under the Ambassador and partially separate (not clarified).

Zorthian suggested that the Deputy Ambassador coordinate all pacification activities but made it clear that he would make no change in the chains of command. Indeed, he emphasized the direct access of each Mission Council member to the Ambassador, the separateness of each agency's field program.

SACSA proposed a division of MACV into a tactical unit command and a Pacification command. All civilian elements supporting pacification would be under the Deputy for Pacification, who in turn would report to the Ambassador and Deputy Ambassador. The advisory structure would have been split down the middle between tactical unit advisors and province/district advisors.

General Collins suggested no major change in the structure of the Mission, but advocated the formation of "Task Groups to deal with specific problems organized on an ad hoc

TOP SECRET - Sensitive

basis from personnel provided by interested agencies. The
Deputy Ambassador to be relieved of routine duties and to
spend substantially all his time on rural construction
duties...

The State Department proposed a "Central Pacification
Organization" which would have been not more than a
coordinating committee for the existing agencies. 42/

What these reorganization proposals seem to suggest, in light of
the ultimate direction that the Mission took, is that when agencies
are asked to produce suggestions which may reduce or inhibit their
prerogatives, they are unlikely to do so in a manner responsive to
the requirements of their politically-appointed chieftains. The
prerogatives and privileges of the agencies inevitably come first.
One does not reorganize voluntarily; the impetus comes from without.
This is also seen in the different attitude that the reorganizers
had towards Washington and Saigon. Although the same problem in
coordination existed (and still exists) in Washington as in Saigon,
the Washington officials always were ready to tell Saigon how to
clean up its house, but were slow to suggest self-improvements. At
Warrenton, perhaps prodded by the Saigon representatives, they did
take note of the matter, although they were reluctant to suggest a
clear solution:

"Note was also taken of the inadequacy of present
U.S. Government machinery to handle Vietnam problems
quickly and decisively. The need for referral of too
large a number of problems to the Secretarial level was
one of the problems mentioned. While the meeting did not
have time to come to any firm conclusions, there was a
view that the VNCC because of its coordinating, rather than
decision-cum-enforcement powers could not perform this task
except in part. If endowing the VNCC or its Chairman with
larger powers, and with a staff associated with no one agency,
is not a feasible solution, it was considered that the
required directing position might have to be set up at a
higher level, perhaps related to the National Security
Council." 43/

In the Warrenton report, then, all the events of the coming year
were foreshadowed, and, reading between the lines, one can now see
what was coming. Unfortunately, and obviously, this was not the
case at the time--particularly for the Mission in Saigon.

TOP SECRET - Sensitive

E.   Presidential Emphasis on "The Other War" and Press Reaction

At the end of 1965, with the bombing of the north in its tenth
month, and our ground forces growing steadily, the Administration was
making a determined effort to emphasize those American activities in
Vietnam which did not directly involve guns and fighting. This emphasis
on what came to be called the "Other War" reached a high point during
the conference at Honolulu in February of 1966. The emphasis on the
other war did not necessarily have to lead, as it did, to a re-emphasis
of pacification; that was a by-product, at least in part, of the renewed
support for pacification which had been coming from Ambassador Lodge, the
Marines, the CIA (with their cadre), and the advocates of organizational
reform (all covered in previous sections). But the two themes merged at
Honolulu, and thus, out of the conference, came the first clear statement
of Presidential support to pacification.

The need of the Administration to emphasize and publicize the non-
military aspects of the war needs little amplification. Few documents
show this emphasis in the pre-Honolulu period, since it was so obvious.
In an exception, a joint State-USIA message dated October 4, 1965,
Washington told the Saigon Mission:

"There is continuing concern at the highest levels
here regarding need to emphasize our non-military programs
in Vietnam and give them maximum possible public exposure
both in U.S. and abroad. /Emphasis Added/

"We recognize that the Mission is fully cognizant of
this problem and already has underway measures to broaden
public knowledge and understanding of non-military activities...
We are also conscious of difficulties involved in enlisting
greater press interest in these developments when it finds
military actions more dramatic and newsworthy. Nevertheless,
we hope will continue to give non-military programs increasing
priority..." 44/

It is useful to recall the situation which existed in February of 1966,
when the President went to Honolulu to meet with Ky and Thieu. On
January 30, 1966, the bombing of the North began again, after a 37-day
pause. There were 197,000 American servicemen in Vietnam by February 1.
The Washington Post -- which supported the Administration -- editorialized on February 1:

"It is to be hoped that a new look is being taken at
the military tactics in the South so that greater emphasis
can be put on the safety of civilians, the rehabilitation
of the countryside, the furtherance of economic growth....
Efforts behind the lines at economic and social programs
must be increased." 45/

28   TOP SECRET - Sensitive

Senator Fulbright had launched his public hearings on Vietnam, and on February 4 had subjected David Bell of AID to a nearly four-hour grilling in the committee. That same day, the conference was announced.

The emphasis at Honolulu was clear from before the conference started. In his press conference announcing the meeting, the President said that he would take Secretary Freeman and Secretary Gardner, not previously involved in Vietnam, as well as experts from their staffs. Freeman would go on to Saigon, the President added "to explore and inaugurate certain pacification programs in the fields of health, education, and agriculture." The President then added:

> "We are going to emphasize, in every way we can, in line with the very fine pronouncements that the Prime Minister /Ky/ has made concerning his desires in the field of education and health and agriculture. We want to be sure that we have our best planning and our maximum effort put into it. But we will, of course, go into the military briefing very thoroughly..." 46/

Even before the conference began, there were early reactions from the press to this emphasis. The New York Times editorialized on February 6:

> "Programs in health, education and agriculture of the kind President Johnson evidently has in mind, can make an important contribution. To combat the revolutionary idea the Communists have set loose in Vietnam, a better idea is needed. Vigorous social reform -- and particularly, land reform, which has received little more than lip-service so far -- could well be made the price of increased economic aid, which is now to be doubled.

> "But an effort to seek political 'victory' in South Vietnam is likely to prove as fruitless as the long attempt at military 'victory.' A more limited and realistic objective is essential." 47/

The conference itself, and its repercussions both in Washington and Vietnam, will be discussed in a following section, so there is little need to dwell on the pre-Honolulu period. In Saigon, where the word of the conference barely preceded the departure of the participants, the New York Times bureau chief wrote a perceptive article which reflected thinking of many junior and mid-level officials in both the U.S. Mission and the GVN. The theme it stated was not new then, and still has a very familiar ring today:

> "...There are now 230,000 to 250,000 pro-Communist troops in South Vietnam, including the Vietcong guerrillas

and about 11 tough regiments of the North Vietnamese Army.
That is at least twice as many enemy troops as there were at
the start of last year, despite the major United States
build-up since then.

"This does not mean that the American build-up has been
futile: the build-up was all that saved South Vietnam, in
the view of most experts. It does mean that no way has yet
been found to prevent the enemy from matching an American
build-up with a build-up of his own.

"About 200,000 American troops are now in South Vietnam
along with 550,000 South Vietnamese armed men, of whom about
half are well-trained army troops.

"American and South Vietnamese military officers have
asked for more American troops, requesting a force of about
400,000 men by the end of 1966. Not all of this strength
has been promised by President Johnson, but major reinforcements are already in the offing...

"But while 1966 will be an important year militarily,
one in which all generals assume that there will be bloodier
fighting, it will also be a year of increased emphasis on
the subtle political and social aspects of the struggle.

"The Honolulu conference will in fact concentrate
largely on economic, social and political problems,
according to informed sources.

"It is felt in Saigon, however, that the Johnson
Administration cannot, even with the best of intentions,
guarantee the allegiance of the Vietnamese to their Government merely by pumping more money and technical skill into
South Vietnam to give people the 'better life' of which
officials speak.

"At least 20 to 25 per cent of the country's area is
so firmly in control of the Vietcong guerrillas that no civic
and political programs are possible there at all. Other
large areas are so sharply contested that for the time being
pacification and rural-improvement workers cannot operate.

"Thus, rural-pacification work in 1966 is to be concentrated in one-third or fewer of the rural hamlets that the
Government already claims to control. The limitation implies
an admission that after five years of war the allies are
starting from scratch in this field, and that progress must
be slow.

TOP SECRET - Sensitive

"With American enthusiasm, the United States may wish
to speed the pace of pacification, but there will be serious
obstacles. Most of the sadder but wiser veterans of previous
programs in Vietnam seem convinced that pressure from
Washington for higher and more seductive statistical goals
is a major danger. They counsel 'slowly but surely.'

"As an example, the South Vietnamese Government is
trying to turn 23,000 rural-affairs workers, most of them
originally trained only in armed propaganda work, into
more rounded rural-construction workers.

"It then plans to recruit and train 19,000 more workers,
for a total of 42,000. In the opinion of some officials,
it will be very difficult even to reach this goal, and
any great expansion carries a risk of substituting numbers
for real training.

"The present pacification plan is considered imaginative and sound by experts with long experience in Vietnam,
but it is considered certain that the plan could be improved
at Honolulu.

"Experience has shown that the crucial matter in
Vietnam is always execution rather than planning. The
scarcest resources in the country are manpower and leadership.

"It is generally agreed that it would not be enough,
say, for the United States to offer help in improving
agriculture in the South Vietnamese countryside. The
Americans must also consider, it is felt, whether their
suggested plan is one that the South Vietnamese understand
and actually -- rather than merely politely -- approve, and
whether the badly strained South Vietnamese administration
can execute the plan.

"American experts in Saigon also assert that the highly
ideological Vietcong movement cannot be offset merely by
offers of a 'better life' for the peasants.

"The Vietcong have a loyal, dedicated and highly disciplined underground political structure that operates in
the heart of Saigon itself and in thousands of hamlets.
So far the peasants have shown little inclination to inform
on this structure and to help the Government activity.

"This is the central problem of the South Vietnamese
war..." 48/

                Charles Mohr

TOP SECRET - Sensitive

F. Meanwhile, Back at the War

The re-emphasis of pacification was, of course, a far more disorderly process than any written review can suggest, and unfortunately must overlook many events and recommendations which were not central to the re-emphasis of pacification. But it is useful and important to review briefly what the Mission was reporting to Washington about the overall effort during 1965, since Saigon's reports should have formed an important part of the background for decision.

This selection should be read not as the "objective" story of what was happening in Vietnam -- such an objective study is simply not possible at this time, even if we had access to enemy thinking -- but as a reflection of the beliefs of the Americans in Saigon, and as a reflection of what the Mission wanted Washington to believe.

This selection is entirely direct quotations from MACV's Monthly Evaluation Report. Each month this report began with a summary of the month's events, and the following items represent the running evaluation for 1965: /Emphasis Added/

"January, 1965: Review of military events in January tend to induce a decidedly more optimistic view than has been seen in recent months. Despite adverse influence exerted by national level political disorders and localized Buddhist/student rioting, the military experienced the most successful single month of the counterinsurgency effort...Pacification made little progress this month. Although some gains were made in the Hop Tac area, effort in the remainder of RVN was hampered by political activity and religious and student disorders...If the RVNAF capability can be underwritten by political stability and durability, a significant turning point in the war could be forthcoming.

"February, 1965: ...GVN forces continued to make progress in III and IV CTZ, maintained a tenuous balance over the VC in I CTZ, and suffered general regression in II CTZ...The indicators of RVNAF operational effort...all showed a decline. However, losses on both sides remained high due to the violence of encounters and VC tenacity...The long term effect of events in February is impossible to foretell. It is obvious that the complexion of the war has changed. The VC appear to be making a concerted effort to isolate the northern portion of RVN by seizing a salient to the sea in the northern part of II CTZ. Here RVNAF has lost the initiative, at least temporarily. However, US/GVN strikes against DRV and increased use of U.S. jet aircraft in RVN has had a salutary effect on

both military and civilian morale which may result in a greater
national effort and, hopefully, reverse the downward trend.

"March, 1965: Events in March were encouraging...RVNAF ground
operations were highlighted by renewed operational effort...VC
activity was considerably below the norm of the preceding six
months and indications were that the enemy was engaged in the
re-supply and re-positioning of units possibly in preparation
for a new offensive, probably in the II Corps area...In summary,
March has given rise to some cautious optimism. The current
government appears to be taking control of the situation and,
if the present state of popular morale can be sustained and
strengthened, the GVN, with continued U.S. support, should be
able to counter future VC offenses successfully.

"April, 1965: Friendly forces retained the initiative during
April and a review of events reinforces the feeling of optimism
generated last month...In summary, current trends are highly
encouraging and the GVN may have actually turned the tide at
long last. However, there are some disquieting factors which
indicate a need to avoid overconfidence. A test of these
trends should be forthcoming in the next few months if the
VC launch their expected counter-offensive and the period may
well be one of the most important of the war.

"May, 1965: The encouraging trends of the past few months did
not carry through into May and there were some serious setbacks.
However, it is hoped that the high morale and improved discipline and leadership which has developed during that period will
sustain future GVN efforts...

"June, 1965: During June the military situation in the RVN continued to worsen despite a few bright spots occasioned by RVNAF
successes. In general, however, the VC...retained the initiative
having launched several well-coordinated, savage attacks in
regimental strength...

"July, 1965: An overall analysis of the military situation at
the end of July reveals that GVN forces continued to make progress in IV Corps, maintained a limited edge in I Corps with the
increased USMC effort and suffered a general regression in the
northern portion of III Corps as well as in the central highlands
of II Corps. The VC monsoon offensive, which was so effective in
June, faltered during July as VC casualty figures reached a new
high...

"August, 1965: An evaluation of the overall military effort in
August reveals several encouraging facts. The most pronounced
is the steady increase in the number of VC casualties and the

number of VC "ralliers" to the GVN...In summary, the general increase in offensive operations by GVN, U.S. and Third Country forces and a correlative increase in enemy casualties have kept the VC off balance and prevented his interference with the build-up of U.S. forces. The often spoken of VC "monsoon offensive" has not materialized, and it now appears that the VC have relinquished the initiative in the conduct of the war.

"September, 1965: As the end of the monsoon season approached, the military situation appears considerably brighter than in May when the VC threatened to defeat the RVNAF. Since May the build-up of Free World Military Assistance Forces, coupled with aggressive combat operations, has thwarted VC plans and has laid the foundation for the eventual defeat of the VC...

"October, 1965: ...an increase in magnitude and tempo of engagements as the GVN/FWF maintained the initiative...In summary, the military situation during October continued to favor the Allies as the VC experienced heavy casualties from the overwhelming Allied fire power...

"November, 1965: The increasing tempo of the war was reflected in casualty totals which reached new highs for VC/PAVN and friendly forces...While keeping the enemy generally off balance, GVN/FWMAF were able to maintain and, to some degree, to increase the scope and intensity of friendly-initiated operations.

"December, 1965: Military activity in December was highlighted by an increase in the number of VC/PAVN attacks on isolated outposts, hamlets, and districts, towns, and the avoidance of contact with large GVN and Free World Forces. The effectiveness of this strategy was attested by the highest monthly friendly casualty total of the war, by friendly weapons losses in excess of weapons captured for the first time since July, and by 30% fewer VC casualties than in November...

"January, 1966: The Free World peace offensive, coupled with TET festivities and the accompanying cease-fire, resulted in a period of restricted military activities for both friendly and enemy forces...Despite this decrease in activity, GVN and Free World Forces continued to force inroads into areas long conceded as VC territory..." 49/ /Emphasis Added/

This is not the place for a detailed analysis of the reporting of the war, or of the implications of the above-cited evaluations. But several points do seem to emerge:

1. The reports are far too optimistic from January through April, 1965, and a big switch seems to come in June, 1965, when

General Westmoreland had already made his 44-battalion
request and warned of disaster if they were not forthcoming. May's report begins to show the change in mood,
but its ambiguous evaluation is in sharp contrast to the
brief backward look offered in September.

2. Pacification is mentioned in the January evaluation, but
   fades away to virtually nothing in the months of the build-
   up.

3. The evaluations do not suggest that the main force threat
   is in any way diminishing by the end of 1965. Indeed, they
   accurately predict larger battles in 1966. They do not
   suggest, therefore, that the time had come to start emphasizing pacification at the expense of exerting more
   pressure directly on the enemy. The evaluations do not
   address this question directly, of course, but they do
   suggest that if any greater emphasis was to be put on
   pacification, it could be done only if there was not a
   corresponding reduction in the attack effort against the
   VC. This, in turn, would imply that if pacification was
   to receive greater emphasis at the beginning of 1966, it
   would require either more Allied troops or else might
   lead to a lessening of pressure on the VC.

II. HONOLULU

II. Honolulu

   A. The Conference - February 1966

   The details of the closed meetings at Honolulu do not appear, in
retrospect, to be nearly as important on the future emphasis on pacification as the mere fact that the public statements of all participants
carried forward the theme that had been enunciated in the Declaration.
This may often be true of conferences; it certainly appears true of
this one, which was convened hastily and took place without any preparatory staff work on either side of the Pacific. In addition, the political
upheavals in the spring of 1966, which followed the conference closely,
contributed to a reduction in the importance of the details of the conference as it related to pacification.

   Pacification was discussed frequently during the closed sessions.
The first time came during the plenary session, when Ambassador Lodge
delivered his statement to the President.

   Speaking before a large audience which included General Thieu and
Air Vice Marshal Ky, Lodge made a general statement about what he called
"the subterranean war," and then discussed the four National Priority
Areas which the GVN and the U.S. had established in October 1965:

   "I would like to begin by saying that the successes and
   the sacrifices of the military, both the Vietnamese and the
   American military, have created a fresh opportunity to win
   the so-called 'subterranean war'...

   "...We can beat up North Vietnamese regiments in the high
   plateau for the next twenty years and it will not end the war
   -- unless we and the Vietnamese are able to build simple but
   solid political institutions under which a proper police can
   function and a climate created in which economic and social
   revolution, in freedom, are possible.

   "The GVN has organized itself to do this job and you will
   hear a presentation by General Thang, who is in charge. The
   American contribution consists of training and equipping of
   personnel; advice; and material...

   "Four priority areas have been chosen. Three are places
   of great importance and difficulty. The fourth is largely
   pacified and is the place where they want to get the economic
   and social development program going. We think the areas are
   well chosen. The three tough ones are close to the Vietnamese
   and American armies which means that the military presence
   helps pacification. And, as pacification gets going, it improves the base for the military.

"In the four priority areas are 192 hamlets, including
238,600 people, to be secured by the end of 1966. But GVN
efforts are not limited to these four priority areas. An
effort is underway which aims to raise the percentage of the
whole country which is pacified by about 14%; i.e., from the
current figure of about 52% to about 66% by the end of the
year..." * 1/

After the statements of Lodge and Westmoreland (who discussed only
military matters), the President said:

"I hope that out of this conference we will return with
clear views in our own minds as to how we can apply more military pressure and do it better, how we can build democracy in
Vietnam and what steps must be taken to do it better, how we
can search for peace in the world, honorable and just peace,
and do it better.

"If we can do the first, namely, develop better methods
for defeating the Viet Cong and better methods for developing
a democracy, I have no doubt but that the third will be much
easier to do because you can bargain much better from strength
than you can from weakness." 3/

---

* On March 4, 1966, Lodge transmitted the text and charts of this briefing to Secretary McNamara and apparently at the same time to the White
House, at the request of Jack Valenti. Lodge wrote:

"Dear Bob:

"At the request of Jack Valenti, I have put together a
book containing the text and maps used in my presentation at
the Honolulu Conference. It is intended to serve as a current
indicator of pacification progress being made within the 1966
National Priority Areas...

"I think I should call attention to the fact that for Americans, it is natural to set goals and then work to achieve them
by a specific date.

"This, however, is not the traditional Vietnamese way.
While they have set a goal of 190 hamlets in the four priority
areas, my guess would be that by the end of 1966, they may
have achieved somewhat more than this, but not necessarily the
ones which are listed here. In fact, if they ran into unexpectedly
heavy opposition in one place and find a particularly good and
unexpected opportunity elsewhere, they probably ought to change
the plan..." 2/

After a short recess, Secretary Rusk then discussed the reasons why Hanoi was not yet ready to negotiate, and said that if the GVN built "the kind of society which is indestructible," then Hanoi would probably come to the conference table more rapidly. "Anything that can move faster rather than more slowly on our side and your side," he said, "anything that can cause them to realize that an epidemic of confidence is building in the South and that momentum is gathering could hasten the time when Hanoi will decide to stop this aggression."4/

The President then said: "I hope that every person here from the U.S. side will bear in mind that before I take that plane back, I want to have the best suggestion obtainable as to how we can bring better military pressure on Hanoi and from the pacification side how we can bring a better program to the people of South Vietnam, and finally, third, what other efforts we can make to secure a just and honorable peace. Now, I want to have my little briefcase filled with those three targets -- a better military program, a better pacification program that includes everything, and a better peace program." 5/

General Thang then presented the GVN's pacification plans, in a briefing later made public. Thang said:

"The objective of the whole people of my country is a unified democratic and strong Vietnam...To reach this objective, our National Leadership Committee has promoted three main policies: first, military offenses; second, rural pacification; and third, democracy.

"...But it is necessary, Mr. President, to define what this means by pacification. In my opinion, that is a failure of the past government, not to define exactly what we mean by pacification...

"I think that it is necessary to...define pacification as an effort to restore the public security first, and carrying out a government policy which aims at improving the standard of living in this area in every respect -- political, economic, social.

"...the prerequisite is security...So our concept of pacification is based on four main points:

Point No. 1: The rural pacification operation can only implement through the real solidarity among the people, the armed forces, and the administration...

Point No. 2: Our government should be very clear when it says that it would like to build a new society for a better life in rural areas. That is meaningless to the peasant if you don't develop that in a concrete package.

/At this point, Thang launched into a lengthy explanation of what he meant by a new society. In a vague
discussion, he described the social, economic, and
political attributes of the new society, all of which
were general and idealized statements./

Point No. 3: The clear and realistic policy of the government contributing to a better life in a new society I just
mentioned should be widely known among the population and
the cadres...

Point No. 4: Rural pacification operations will open
lasting peace if the enemy infrastructure is destroyed
and permanently followed up, our own infrastructure created
and supported by the people...All provinces have promised
to the government that 75 percent of the following facts
maybe can be accomplished by the 1st of January 1967:

"Pacification of 963 new hamlets; pacification of 1,083
existing hamlets; building of 2251 classrooms; 913 kilometers
of roads; 128 bridges; 57 dams; and 119 kilometers of canals
...While we have selected four areas of priority, the pacification operation has been pushed forward as usual, but with
less efforts...

"Rural pacification will be a long-term operation. We
have modest and practical, rather than spectacular, goals for
1966..." 6/

After General Thang's remarks, the plenary session records show
repeated references to the pacification effort, although there is confusion as to what it means. General Thieu made additional summary
remarks on pacification, then Minister Ton gave a briefing on the economic situation, followed by David Bell on the same subject.

The next day, February 8, the working groups presented their findings
to the President. First, Secretary Rusk and Foreign Minister Do discussed
the session on negotiations. Then General Thang and Secretary Freeman
reported on their session on rural construction. The details of the
working groups session itself are covered below, but in plenary. Thang
emphasized the following points:

Our future should be developed mainly in four priority
areas...Handicraft should be introduced and developed
in those areas also...Rural electrification should be
developed and the number of generators increased in
1967...

39   TOP SECRET - Sensitive

Land reform efforts should be pushed forward...

We ask that construction material and cement be sent to
Vietnam as soon as possible so our school programs can
be developed...

The training of officials at hamlet and village levels
is vital... 7/

Secretary Freeman, who was about to make his first trip to Vietnam,
summarized for the Americans:

"Having spent a good deal of time yesterday listening to
the very eloquent presentations by the Chairman and the Prime
Minister, as well as by Minister Ton, this is pretty much what
we would call a nuts and bolts discussion session.

"One thing that was decided for United States purposes, for
purposes of phraseology, was that the word 'pacification' really
did not have the right tone. The term 'social construction'
might better be used...

"There was some discussion, considerable, about the selection
of province chiefs. It was strongly emphasized that it was important that the men be of integrity and ability, and that they
be selected and maintained and backed up.

"The Prime Minister, General Thieu, and then General Thang
both said that you /General Thieu/ were personally interested in
this, and that you were going to select them shortly, that they
would have a duration of at least a year, but would be carefully
reviewed and would be changed if they didn't do the job, but
wouldn't be changed for other reasons, which we thought was extremely important and we were gratified to find it out.

"You also explained to us, your associates General Ky and
General Thang, the change of command, saying in the past they
were confused, and that they were now clear, so that everyone
knew exactly what their function would be.

"Then you discussed the training of the cadre...

"I want to review the REA question and find out a bit more
about why that seemed to have some lag.

"Finally, we discussed the possibility of a joint training
program for the village and hamlet chiefs who presumably would
be elected, but that some background in the philosophy, purpose
and aims of government, and the techniques of governing and administration, were felt to be needed by those people. 8/

The President then responded to the remarks of Thang and Freeman by urging "all of you connected with our program...to give very special attention to refugee camps and the schools in the refugee camps." 9/ He then
turned to Minister Ton and David Bell for a discussion of the economic
situation. Then Secretary Gardner, who had co-chaired a working group
on health and education -- the distinction between rural construction and
the health/education programs was not clarified -- made his remarks. He
set out perhaps the most clearly-defined objectives of the session (except
for the economic negotiations), describing the new contract with the AMA
for training personnel, the new goal for provincial medical teams, and the
plans for a new medical logistics system. In large part his goals were
more specific than those of the other working group because the USAID
Public Health Chief in Saigon, Major General James Humphries, had already
laid groundwork for an excellent program of health services and assistance,
and Gardner was able to work from a specific plan.

Gardner went on to discuss education, where his goals and objectives
were less clear, and the President asked several detailed questions, concluding by asking General Ky to ask the Ambassador to request an educational team to go to Saigon after the agricultural team headed by Secretary
Freeman returned.

The Vietnamese then thanked the Americans for the conference, and in
turn some of the senior members of the American delegation -- in order,
Admiral Sharp, Leonard Marks, General Wheeler, Ambassador Lodge, Ambassador Harriman -- made brief statements about the meaning of the conference.
The President then made his final statement:

"...Preserve this communique, because it is one we don't
want to forget. It will be a kind of bible that we are going
to follow. When we come back here 90 days from now, or six
months from now, we are going to start out and make reference
to the announcements that the President, the Chief of State and
the Prime Minister made in paragraph 1, and what the leaders
and advisors reviewed in paragraph 2...You men who are responsible for these departments, you ministers, and the staffs
associated with them in both governments, bear in mind we are
going to give you an examination and the finals will be on just
what you have done.

"In paragraph 5; how have you built democracy in the rural
areas? How much of it have you built, when and where? Give us
dates, times, numbers.

"In paragraph 2; larger outputs, more efficient production
to improve credit, handicraft, light industry, rural electrification -- are those just phrases, high-sounding words, or have
you coonskins on the wall...

41

"Next is health and education, Mr. Gardner. We don't want
to talk about it; we want to do something about it. 'The
President pledges he will dispatch teams of experts.' Well, we
better do something besides dispatching. They should get out
there. We are going to train health personnel. How many? You
don't want to be like the fellow who was playing poker and when
he made a big bet they called him and said 'what have you got?'
He said, 'aces' and they asked 'how many' and he said 'one
aces'...

"Next is refugees. That is just as hot as a pistol in my
country. You don't want me to raise a white flag and surrender
so we have to do something about that...

"Growing military effectiveness: we have not gone in because
we don't want to overshadow this meeting here with bombs, with
mortars, with hand grenades, with 'Masher' movements. I don't
know who names your operations, but 'Masher.' I get kind of
mashed myself. But we haven't gone into the details of growing
military effectiveness for two or three reasons. One, we want
to be able to honestly and truthfully say that this has not been
a military build-up conference of the world here in Honolulu.
We have been talking about building a society following the outlines of the Prime Minister's speech yesterday.

"Second, this is not the place, with 100 people sitting
around, to build a military effectiveness.

"Third, I want to put it off as long as I can, having to
make these crucial decisions. I enjoy this agony...I don't
want to come out of this meeting that we have come up here and
added on X divisions and Y battalions or Z regiments or D
dollars, because one good story about how many billions are
going to be spent can bring us more inflation that we are
talking about in Vietnam. We want to work those out in the
quietness of the Cabinet Room after you have made your recommendations, General Wheeler, Admiral Sharp, when you come to
us..."10/ /Emphasis Added/

The President's remarks candidly indicated the type of pressure and
the expectations that he had for the effort.

But beyond the high-level interest so clearly demonstrated publicly
for the first time at Honolulu, what was accomplished? As mentioned
earlier, Honolulu's importance lay in two things: (1) the public support
shown for the "other war"; and (2) the sections of the Declaration which
committed the GVN to the electoral process. If nothing else was accomplished at Honolulu, that made the conference worthwhile. Thus, it is
perhaps petty to criticize the details of the conference. But they do

suggest an unfortunate failure to come to grips with any of the basic issues concerning pacification, and, moreover, a skillful performance by the GVN to please their American hosts. Thang's statement to the President after the working session, for example, with its emphasis on rural electrification, handicrafts, and the need for "materials and cement" -- none of which were major GVN concerns at that time -- can best be explained, in retrospect, by the Vietnamese desire to emphasize those things they felt the Secretary of Agriculture, the co-chairman of the American working group, was most interested in.

Although the inner workings of the conference do not seem to have had much importance on the development of the pacification effort, a record does remain of the "rural construction working group," and it deserves a brief summary. The meeting is useful to examine not because of its ultimate importance, which was marginal, but because it provides us with a record of a type of discussion between Americans and Vietnamese which has been replayed constantly since (and before). To some weary participants, the very words used have seemed to be unchanged since 1962.

A summary cannot, unfortunately, recapture the flavor of confusion which surrounds the memorandum for the record (A-2254, February 15, 1966). The meeting began with a discussion of terminology (see footnote on "revolutionary development") in which it was decided to use the phrase "social construction" in place of pacification in English. Then, according to the memorandum, everyone lapsed back into using the phrase "pacification."

The American representatives then pressed the issue of the role of the province chief, implying strongly that they thought the province chiefs should have more power and autonomy. The Vietnamese, led by General Co, neatly answered this issue, "referring to the establishment of Rural Construction Councils and Division and Corps levels, where such matters as the disposition and use of military forces are arbitrated and decided upon." When Leonard Unger, asked if the military commanders would be committed to providing the necessary military forces for the pacification effort, "General Co again responded, saying that in the past senior commanders tended to pull troops away from Provincial control for search and destroy operations. This is a natural desire on the part of these commanders who tend to feel that this is a more important role for such troops. Now, however, their missions have changed. These senior commanders are now directly involved in the pacification program, are members of the respective Rural Construction Councils...In other words, things have changed for the better. Ambassador Unger continued to pursue his point, stressing our concern that vestiges of the past may still remain. General Thang re-entered the discussion, explaining that the GVN now has a new chain of command, clear and clean from Saigon to the Corps to the Division to the Province to the District; there is only one channel in the country and it is a military channel...Still on the same subject,

Mr. Poats raised the question: What is the primary mission of the Division Commander? Is it pacification? General Thang answered in the affirmative."

The discussion continued along these lines, and the airgram candidly concludes: "Generals Co and Thang were being pressed by rather pointed questions at this juncture and seemed to be trying to indicate that pacification is a primary task, although other military tasks must continue to be performed. It was fairly apparent that troops charged with securing the pacification area are liable still to be withdrawn on a temporary basis to meet situations which ARVN senior commanders judge to be critical."

The meeting then discussed the cadre program; the renewed emphasis on village government; the role of the province chief (at this point General Co made his statement that the GVN would appoint province chiefs for one year minimum period, a decision which was never carried out); the introduction of troops; the cadre (again); the six areas where the effort needed improvement (agriculture, handicraft, land reform, rural electrification, construction materials, and training of local officials); land reform (with Minister Tri presenting his four-month old plan again, and Poats expressing "concern about the performance to date"); and the general question of pacification goals.

And then, after reporting back to the President in the meeting described earlier, the participants broke up, returning to Saigon and Washington to give "the other war" a new emphasis; to reorganize the Mission in Saigon; to appoint a new Special Assistant to the President in Washington; to start the quest for coonskins (the phrase was in common use in Saigon within a few days); to await the public and press reaction (see following section); and to walk without warning into a major political crisis which almost brought the government down, set back every time-schedule made at Honolulu, forced a postponement of the next scheduled conference from June-July until October, and -- through an ironic twist of fate -- left the GVN stronger than before, following a remarkably successful election.

B. Impact on Public in US, on US Mission in Vietnam, and on Vietnamese

"This week the word 'pacification' was on everyone's lips at the
Honolulu conference on Vietnam," wrote Charles Mohr in the New York
Times, February 13, 1966, "and many important members of the Johnson
Administration embraced the idea with all the enthusiasm of a horse
player with a new betting system. The main purpose of the Honolulu
conference was to dramatize this American enthusiasm for the 1966
rural pacification -- sometimes called 'rural construction' -- program
of the Government of South Vietnam and to pledge more American
assistance for the program."

Mohr's article may have been slightly exaggerated, but there can
be little doubt that the President's pledge on behalf of the U.S.
Government to the pacification effort began a new period for the U.S.
Government in Vietnam. From Honolulu on it was open and unmistakable
U.S. policy to support pacification and the "other war," and those who
saw these activities as unimportant or secondary had to submerge their
sentiments under a cloud of rhetoric. Despite this fact, of course,
many heated discussions still lay ahead of the Mission on program
after program, and many major battles remained to be fought. Porter
and Komer would fight them, as will be shown later.

This was the great impact of Honolulu -- on pacification. But
there were other ramifications of the Honolulu conference which over-
shadowed the emphasis on non-military activities in the months that
followed. Because of these events -- particularly the political upheavals that rocked Vietnam from March until June -- the follow-up
conference tentatively planned for June did not take place, and the
growth in pacification's importance was probably set back about six
months. While this study does not try to cover the concurrent events
of the period, it should be emphasized that the most important parts
of the Honolulu Declaration were not those dealing with pacification at
all, but rather the sections which committed the GVN to "formulate a
democratic constitution to the people for discussion and modification;
to seek its ratification by secret ballot; to create, on the basis of
elections rooted in that constitution, an elected government..." 11/
With these words, the GVN was openly committed, under U.S. pressure, to
a process which they probably did not desire or appreciate. In the
months that followed, the words of the Honolulu Declaration were used
against General Ky by his Buddhist Struggle Movement opponents, to
hoist him on his Honolulu petard; but then, in a remarkable about-
face, Ky simultaneously cracked down on the Buddhists and held successful elections for a Constitutional Assembly (September 11, 1966).

The following collection of newspaper items is selected to show
that there were differing opinions within the U.S. Mission and among
Vietnamese, but that in general the message from Honolulu did get
through to the Mission. Since almost every reporter in Saigon had
sources within some element of the Mission who were telling him their

honest feelings (the Saigon Mission, it was once said by Barry Zorthian, could not keep a secret 24 hours), the stories from Saigon do reflect what the Mission thought in the days just after Honolulu. The editorials and columnists from Washington indicate to what degree the Administration succeeded in convincing the press corps (which is not, of course, the U.S. public) that the emphasis at Honolulu was really on pacification.

EDITORIAL: The New York Herald Tribune, February 8:

"The meeting presents the prospect of our resuming the war in more favorable circumstances. The meeting of the heads of the American and South Vietnamese governments is a fresh and stronger demonstration of mutual confidence. On this basis they can now proceed to mount measures for dealing with the equally important military and civilian aspects of the war.

"The two are intimately related...the loyalty and support of the peasants in the interior are essential. President Johnson is bidding for them by offering some of the benefits of his Great Society program to the South Vietnamese. It will not be easy, in time of war,...but...they must be pursued with the same vigor as we press the war on the battlefield."

EDITORIAL: The Washington Evening Star, February 7:

"It is particularly significant that the American delegation included HEW Secretary Gardner and Orville Freeman, Secretary of Agriculture. Their presence certainly means that a greater 'pacification' effort will be made as the fighting goes on..."

COLUMNIST: Marquis Childs, February 9 (from Honolulu)

"This conference called by President Johnson is a large blue chip put on the survival value of the wiry, exuberant Air Vice Marshal Nguyen Cao Ky, and the generals who rule with him. It is expected that Ky will not only survive but that with massive economic help from the U.S. the national leadership committee will eventually win the support of the peasant in the countryside...Any sensible bookmaker would quote long odds against the bet paying off. But after so many false starts this seems to be the right direction -- a determined drive to raise the level of living in the countryside and close the gap of indifference and hostility between the peasant and the sophisticated city dweller...Over and over we have been told that only by winning the hearts and minds of the Vietnamese people will

we achieve a victory that has meaning beyond the grim choice of
pulverization of American occupation into the indefinite future
...This is the reason teams of American specialists in agriculture, health, and education are going to Vietnam..."

EDITORIAL: The New York Herald Tribune, February 9:

"Perhaps the most constructive part of the Honolulu
conference was the emphasis it placed on this hitherto
badly neglected aspect of the Viet Nam war /Pacification7.
It is unfortunate that Chief of State Thieu diverted attention
from it by heaping more fuel on the controversy over whether
the Viet Cong should or should not sit at a peace conference
table..."

EDITORIAL: The New York Times, February 9 and 13:

"The Honolulu conference has followed the classic pattern
of Summit meetings that are hastily called without thorough
preparation in advance; it has left confusion in its wake,
with more questions raised than answered...The one important
area of agreement at Honolulu, apart from continuation of
the military efforts, was on an expanded program of 'rural
construction.' The prospective doubling of American economic
aid, however, will be futile unless it is accompanied by a
veritable social revolution, including vigorous land reform.
Premier Ky cast some doubt in his emphasis on moving slowly.
His Minister of Rural Pacification envisages action in only
1,900 of South Vietnam's 15,000 hamlets this year.

"Vice President Humphrey evidently has his work cut out
for him in his follow-up visit to Saigon. Unless some way
can be found to give more momentum to this effort, the new
economic aid program may go down the same drain as all previous
programs of this kind.

"It would be a cruel deception for Americans to get the
idea that social reforms carried out by the Ky government
with American money are going to make any perceptible difference
in the near future to the Vietnamese people or to the course
of the war."

COLUMNIST: Ted Lewis, New York Daily News, February 10 (from
          Washington):

"Why, all of a sudden, has President Johnson begun to
come to grips with the 'other war' in South Vietnam?...
Johnson, with his typical oratorical flourishes, has given
the impression that he launched something totally new at

Honolulu...The fact is that for several years this problem of the 'other war' has been recognized as vital by the State Department, the Pentagon and even by the White House. But nobody did much about it, except in an offhand way...

"Johnson is a master of timing. He has definitely gained a political advantage over his Viet policy critics by stressing right now the need of winning over the peasants.../Senator Robert/ Kennedy complained in a Senate speech just ten days ago that there were 'many indications that we have not yet even begun to develop a program...It is absolutely urgent,' the Senator said, 'that we now act to institute new programs of education, land reform, public health, political participation...'."

NEWS ANALYSIS: Richard Critchfield in The Washington Evening Star, February 9 (from Saigon):

"President Johnson's historic decision at Honolulu backing an American-sponsored brand of social revolution as an alternative to communism in South Vietnam was warmly hailed today by veteran political observers. The Honolulu declaration was viewed as ending postwar era of American foreign policy aimed at stabilizing the status quo in Asia.

"The key phrase, in the view of many diplomats here, was the offer of full American 'support to measures of social revolution, including land reform based upon the principle of building upward from the hopes and purposes of all the people of Vietnam.

"...Johnson's decisions to put political remedies on a par with military action are also regarded here as a major personal triumph for Ambassador Henry Cabot Lodge and his top aide, Major General Edward G. Lansdale, the two main advocates of 'social revolution' in South Vietnam...The Honolulu declaration appears to signify a major shift away from the policy of primarily military support established by President Kennedy in 1961 and closely identified with General Maxwell Taylor, Defense Secretary McNamara, and Secretary of State Rusk...The Lodge-Lansdale formula was a striking departure in that it saw the eventual solution not so much in Hanoi's capitulation as in successful pacification in South Vietnam...The Honolulu declaration amounts to almost a point by point acceptance of this formula and both its phraseology and philosophy bear Lansdale's unmistakable imprint..."

EDITORIAL: The Baltimore Sun, February 10:

"Unless there was more substance to the Honolulu Conference than meets the eye, it could be summed up as much ado -- not

much ado about nothing but simply much ado...It was all
spectacular and diverting but so far as we can see the
problem of the war is where it was before the burst of
activity began...It is probably worthwhile to have a
reiteration of the social and economic measures needed in
South Vietnam...It is essential to underscore the political
nature of the war, along with the continuing military operations. But these matters were generally understood before
the Honolulu meetings. Perhaps events to come will make the
purpose of the meeting clearer."

EDITORIAL: The New York Post, February 9:

    "The Hawaii meetings were advertised as the beginning
of a vast new movement of economic and social reform in
Vietnam, President Johnson, we were told, went to Honolulu
to launch the new approach with maximum drama.

    "Instead, the session inadvertently underscored the
lack of interest of the junta in Saigon in anything but
military conquest of the Viet Cong, to be carried out by
stepped up U.S. armed efforts..."

NEWS STORY: AP, February 10 (from Honolulu):

    "Vice President Humphrey left for Saigon today with
South Vietnam's top leaders to spur action on programs
attacking hunger, disease, and ignorance in that war-torn
country..."

NEWS ANALYSIS: Charles Mohr, The New York Times, February 10
                (from Saigon):

    "In the atmosphere of Honolulu, there was much emphasis
on form, so much that in some ways it may have obscured
substance. The Americans appeared so delighted with
Marshal Ky's 'style' -- with his showing as a politically
salable young man with the right instincts rather than as
a young warlord -- that there seemed to be almost no
emphasis on the important differences between the Governments...What Marshal Ky told President Johnson was something
he had often said before: South Vietnamese society is still
riddled with social injustices and political weaknesses;
there is not one political party worthy of the name...The
South Vietnamese leaders believe that they could not survive
a 'peaceful settlement' that left the VC political structure
in place, even if the VC guerrilla units were disbanded.
Therefore, the South Vietnamese feel that 'rural pacification,' of which much was said at Honolulu, is necessary not

only to help them achieve military victory but also to prevent
a political reversal of that victory...As the Vietnamese see
pacification, its core is not merely 'helping the people to a
better life,' the aspect on which many American speakers
dwelled, it is rather the destruction of the clandestine VC
political structure and the creation of an ironlike system
of government political control over the population...

"But the two governments have never been closer than
they are in the aftermath of Honolulu, and the atmosphere
of good feeling seems genuine..."

NEWS ANALYSIS: Roscoe Drummond, February 14 (from Washington):

"...The decisions taken at Honolulu by President
Johnson and Premier Ky go to the heart of winning. They
were primarily social, economic, and political decisions.
They come at a malleable and perhaps decisive turn in the
war..."

NEWS ANALYSIS: Tom Wicker in The New York Times, February 13
(from Saigon):

"Vice President Humphrey...has left Saigon reverber-
ating with what he said was the 'single message' he had
come to deliver. The message was that the war in Vietnam
was a war to bring social justice and economic and political
progress to the Vietnamese people...Humphrey said at a
news conference here: 'Social and economic revolution
does not belong to the VC. Non-communist forces are the
ones forwarding the revolution.'

"The emphasis on social reform could also quiet
critics who contend that Washington has concentrated too
much on the military problem and not enough on civic
action to win the loyalty of the Vietnamese people..."

NEWS ANALYSIS: Charles Mohr, The New York Times, February 13
(from Saigon):

"By giving enormous emphasis and publicity to it,
an impression was left that pacification is something new.
In a sense, there was some truth in this. The men running the program, both Vietnamese and American, are new.
And the 1966 plan itself is a new one in many respects.

"Pacification is vitally important to success in the
guerrilla war in South Vietnam. Without it, purely military
success becomes empty even if all the battles are 'won'."

NEWS ANALYSIS: Joseph Alsop, February 14 (from Saigon):

"CART BEFORE HORSE...All that really mattered at Honolulu
was a Presidential decision to provide the forces needed to
keep the pressure on the enemy here in Vietnam. The odds
are heavy that the President, who seems to prefer doing good
by stealth, actually took this decision behind the electorate
smokescreen of talk about other matters. The question
remains whether the needed forces will be provided soon
enough. One must wait and see.

"But at the risk of sounding captious, and for the
sake of honesty and realism, it must be noted that there
was a big Madison Avenue element in all the talk about
'pacification' during the Hawaii meeting and Vice President
Humphrey's subsequent visit to Vietnam.

"This does not mean that pacification of the Vietnamese
countryside is an unimportant and/or secondary problem. On
the contrary, it will eventually be all-important and primary.
But one need only glance at the list of priority areas
marked for pacification now, to see the adman's touch in the
present commotion.

"There are: An Giang Province, which belongs to the
Hoa Hao sect and has been long since pacified by the Hoa
Hao; the Hop Tac region near Saigon, where General Harkins
experimented unhappily with the so-called oil spot technique;
parts of Binh Dinh Province along the north-south highway;
and the fringes of the Marine enclave at Da Nang.

"Each area differs from the others. In the case of the
nine villages on the fringes of the Marines' Da Nang enclave,
for instance, pacification is needed to insure airfield
security from mortar fire. Most of these villages have been
Viet Cong strongholds for over 20 years, and they could be
dangerous.

"...Pacification by the Marines looks very fine...But
it takes far too many Marines to do the job.

"Nonetheless, the real objections to making a big-
immediate show of pacification are quite different. The
Hop Tac experience tells the story. Here a great effort
was made by the Vietnamese authorities with the strong
support of General Harkins. A good deal was initially
accomplished. Boasts began to be heard. Whereat the
enemy sailed forth from the nearest redoubt area, knocked
down everything that had been built up, murdered all the

villagers who had worked with the government, and left things much worse than they had been before...An attempt to make a big immediate show of pacification needs to be warned against, because of the Washington pressure to do just that. A large element of the U.S. Mission was called home a month or so ago. And in effect, these men were commanded to produce a plan for making a show as soon as possible.

"Fortunately, they had the courage to point out that the cart was being put before the horse once again. Fortunately, Ambassador Lodge is well aware of the dangers of putting the cart before the horse. The pressure for something showy may continue, but it is likely to be resisted.

"If so, the pressure will not be altogether useless. The Vietnamese and the Americans here are getting ready for pacification on a big scale and in an imaginative way, partly because of that pressure.

"It is vital to have everything in readiness to do the job of pacification as soon as favorable circumstances arise. But it is also vital to bear in mind that really favorable circumstances cannot arise until the enemy's backbone of regular units is at last very close to the breaking point, if not actually beginning to break."

EDITORIAL: Christian Science Monitor, February 11:

"If Saigon and Washington fight South Vietnam's economic and social war as vigorously as they fight its military war, the Communist thrust against that country will fail. Yet this is the biggest 'if' of the war. Over and over lip-service has been paid to the inescapable need of winning over the peasantry. But time and again this has come to naught.

"We are cautiously encouraged by the latest steps being taken. The strong emphasis laid in the Honolulu Declaration on civic reforms is a commitment in the right direction. The sending of Vice-President Humphrey to study South Vietnamese reform programs on the spot is an even stronger earnest of America's intention not to let this program slip back into another do-nothing doldrum..."

III. Honolulu to Manila

A. Saigon: Porter in Charge

"Question. Mr. President, when you were in Los Angeles reporting
on the Honolulu Conference, you listed eleven items which you
said were discussed, and you said that in all these fields you
set targets, concrete targets. Would it be possible to get a list
of these concrete targets?

"Answer. I don't have any. I think what I had in mind there was
saying that we hoped to make certain progress in certain fields and
we expect to have another conference after a reasonable length of
time, in which we will take the hits, runs, and errors and see what
we have achieved and everybody would be answerable, so to speak, as
to the progress they have made and whether or not they are nearing
their goals...I hope to be in Honolulu in the next few months,
maybe in the middle of the year, and see what has been done. I
thought it was good that we could go there and have the Government
and the military leader, General Westmoreland, and the Ambassador
and the Deputy Ambassador, meet with the Vice President, the
Secretary of Agriculture and technicians, and try to expose to the
world for three days what this country is trying to do to feed the
hungry, and educate the people, and to improve the life span for
people who just live to be 35 now...A lot of our folks think it is
just a military effort. We don't think it should be that, and we
don't want it to be that..." 1/

As the President returned to Washington from Honolulu, the Vice
President, Secretary Freeman, and McGeorge Bundy headed up a large list
of high-ranking officials that went on to Saigon. Bundy, about to leave
the government, carried with him authority from the President to give
the Deputy Ambassador wide authority over all aspects of the rural construction program. On February 12, 1966, the President sent Ambassador
Lodge a NODIS telegram, which was designed to pave the way for Bundy's
reorganization effort:

"QUOTE. I hope that you share my own satisfaction with the
Honolulu Conference. The opportunity to talk face to face with
you, General Westmoreland and the Vietnamese leaders has given
me a much better appreciation of the problems each of you face,
but perhaps even more importantly the opportunities open to us.
I was particularly impressed with the apparent determination of
Thieu, Ky and the other Vietnamese Ministers to carry forward a
social policy of radical and constructive change. However, I
full well realize the tremendous job that they and we have in
putting this into practice. I intend to see that our organization back here for supporting this is promptly tightened and

strengthened and I know that you will want to do the same at
your end. I was impressed with Ambassador Porter and it seems
to me that he probably has the necessary qualifications to
give you the support you will need in this field. While I
know that he is already doing so, I suggest that your designation of him as being in total charge, under your supervision,
of all aspects of the rural construction program would constitute a clear and visible sign to the Vietnamese and to our own
people that the Honolulu Conference really marks a new departure
in this vital field of our effort there. We will of course be
glad to give prompt support with whatever additional personnel
or administrative rearrangement this might require within the
Mission or Embassy. Please let me know your own thoughts on
this.

"I hope that in June we can have a full report showing real
progress in our war on social misery in Viet Nam. In the meanwhile, I know that you will not hesitate to let me know how we
can be of help. UNQUOTE

"The President has instructed that a copy of this message
be given to McGeorge Bundy." 2/

The President also sent General Westmoreland a personal telegram that day,
which did not mention the matter of civilian organization. To Westmoreland he wrote:

"QUOTE. I want you to know that I greatly enjoyed the opportunity of talking directly with you at Honolulu and I hope you
share my own satisfaction on the outcome of that conference.
I was much encouraged by your presentation of the military
situation and now have even more pride and confidence in what
you and your men are doing. I feel that we are on the right
track and you can be sure of my continued support.

"I know that you share my own views on the equal importance of
the war on social misery, and hope that what we did at Honolulu
will help assure that we and the Vietnamese move forward with
equal vigor and determination on that front. As I have told
Ambassador Lodge and am telling Thieu and Ky, I hope that in
June I can have a report of real progress in that field. With
continued progress in the military field, we should by that
time be able to see ahead more clearly the road to victory over
both aggression and misery.

"You have my complete confidence and genuine admiration and
absolute support. I never forget that I have a lot riding on
you. UNQUOTE." 3/

After the mood at the Warrenton Conference, the push for reorganization should have come as no surprise to the higher ranking members of
the Mission. Discussions centering around the role of the Deputy Ambassador (and earlier, the DCM) as a manager for the mushrooming Civilian
Mission had been going on for a long time, as Lodge and Porter well knew.
With Bundy in Saigon to ease the issue, Lodge answered the President on
February 15, 1966:

> "I do indeed want to 'tighten and strengthen the organi-
> zation for support of the rural construction program at this
> end,' as you tell me you plan to do at yours. And I applaud
> your determination to treat 'rural construction' (for which
> there should be a better name) * as an end in itself and on a
> par with the military.

> "As you say, Ambassador Porter is already putting a great
> deal of effort into this work. I have never made a formal
> announcement of this fact because it seemed to me that the
> arrangement was working pretty well as it was and that public
> announcement was unnecessary. Also, I felt the U.S. Government

---

* Lodge had for some time been troubled by the phrase "rural construction"
-- the literal translation of the Vietnamese Xay Dung Nong Thon -- which
he felt suggested bricks and cement, rather than the entire program of
"revolutionary uplift" which he advocated. Right after the Honolulu
meeting, he asked each member of the Mission Council for suggestions on
how better to translate the Vietnamese phrase. Out of the suggestions
that he received (including Westmoreland's recommendation that we ought
to leave the phrase alone, just translating the literal meaning of the
Vietnamese as accurately as possible), Lodge chose the phrase "Revolutionary Development." At about the same time, the GVN dropped the word
"rural" from the name of the Ministry of Rural Construction (thus, Xay
Dung Nong Thon was replaced by Xay Dung). Lodge and Ky then announced
that henceforth the Vietnamese Ministry would be known in English as the
Ministry of Revolutionary Development, and the overall program called
Revolutionary Development (RD). To this day, the semantic gap remains
unbridged: the Vietnamese call it the Ministry of Construction (Bo Xay
Dung), except when they are talking in English to an American; the
Americans call it the MORD. The same applies to the program: moreover,
the confusion is often compounded by the fact that in most informal
discussions between Americans and Vietnamese, the term most often used
is still "pacification." See, for example, the Working Group session
at Honolulu, February 7, 1966: "It is perhaps significant that this was
the only time in the course of the meeting, i.e., at the outset, that
the newly adopted U.S. term was heard. Throughout the remainder of the
Working Group discussion, the term pacification was used almost exclusively.
In this connection, the Saigon U.S. representatives présent at the meeting
are inclined to doubt the actual appropriateness of the new term...)"

was getting really enthusiastic work without thought of self
from both Porter and Lansdale under present conditions. I felt
public announcements might make Lansdale feel less important
without any gain for Porter who does not need or want a sense
of importance. I believe that Americans are pulling together
here as never before and that there is a spirit here which is
worth more than organization charts.

"But I can see the merit of the idea that a public designation of Porter as being in total charge of the American
aspects of the rural construction program would 'constitute a
clear and visible sign to the Vietnamese and to our own people
that the Honolulu Conference really marks a new departure.'

"There are pitfalls to be avoided. For example, I assume
that if Porter's new allocation means that I am so taken up with
U.S. visitors that I am in effect separated from 'rural construction,' then we would take a new look at the whole thing.
Much of the most time-consuming job out here is not rural construction but is the handling and educating of U.S. visitors.
Although it must be done at the expense of the war effort within
Vietnam, it is vitally important. But it was not until the end
of January that I was free enough of visitors to start holding
meetings of U.S. 'rural construction' workers to probe and to
prod and to develop the 'check-up' maps which I showed you at
Honolulu.

"I suggest, therefore that I make the following announcement: 'I have today designated Deputy Ambassador William Porter
to take full charge, under my direction, of all aspects of work
of the United States in support of the programs of community
building, presently described as rural construction, agreed at
the Honolulu Conference. This includes overcoming by police
methods the criminal, as distinct from the military aspect of
Viet Cong violence; and the training and installation of health,
education and agricultural workers and of community organizers.
Ambassador Porter will have the support of a small staff drawn
from all elements of the U.S. Mission, and he and I will continue
to have the help of General Edward Lansdale as senior liaison
officer and adviser. Ambassador Porter will continue to serve
as my Deputy in the full sense of the word, but he will be relieved as far as possible of all routine duties not connected
with the Honolulu program. We are determined that this program
for peace and progress shall be carried forward with all the
energy and skill of a fully coordinated U.S. Mission effort,
always with full recognition that the basic task of nation-
building here belongs to the people of Viet Nam and to their
government.'

TOP SECRET - Sensitive

"I know that you appreciate that this is essentially a
Vietnamese program and that what Porter would be supervising
would be the American end of it. I recognize the existence of
the view that we must in effect impose detailed plans and somehow run the pacification effort ourselves. But I do not share
it. Nothing durable can be accomplished that way.

"As far as 'administrative rearrangement' is concerned,
I would like Sam Wilson to take the office now occupied by
Porter, with the rank of Minister, and to serve as Mission
coordinator. I intend to put Habib in the office now occupied
by Chadbourn with the rank of Minister....

"As soon as I receive word from you that this is satisfactory, I intend to make the announcement about Porter. The
other appointments can be announced later. LODGE" 4/

From the beginning, Lodge, who felt that "a public announcement was
unnecessary" except as a "clear and visible sign to the Vietnamese and
to our own people that the Honolulu conference really marks a new departure," 4/ was not overly enthusiastic about the public designation
of his deputy as being "in total charge" of something. The documentation
is virtually nonexistent on the question of whether Lodge's feelings on
this point acted as a constraint on Porter, but it is hard to escape the
strong impression that from the outset, Lodge was going along with the
new authority for Porter only with reluctance -- and that Porter had to
keep this in mind whenever he considered putting heavy pressure on an
agency.

Porter also had his reservations about his role. Whether these were
caused by a feeling that the Ambassador was not going to support him in
showdowns with the agencies, or whether his caution came from some more
basic feelings, there can be no doubt that he did not, in the period
between Honolulu and Manila, perform in his new role as the President
and his senior advisors had hoped. And thus once again, at Manila, a
reorganization was approved -- this time a much broader and far-reaching
one.

Porter's intentions were accurately foreshadowed in his first statement to the Mission Council on the subject, February 28, 1966. He sought
then to allay the fears which the announcement had raised in the minds of
the agency chiefs in Vietnam:

"Ambassador Porter described briefly his new responsibilities as he sees them in the pacification/rural development area.
He pointed out that the basic idea is to place total responsibility on one senior individual to pull together all of the civil

57   TOP SECRET - Sensitive

> aspects of revolutionary development. He sees this primarily as a coordinating effort and does not intend to get into the middle of individual agency activities and responsibilities. As he and his staff perceive areas which require attention and action by a responsible agency, he will call this to the attention of that agency for the purpose of emphasis; he intends to suggest rather than to criticize...Ambassador Porter noted that the non-priority areas are still getting the bulk of the resources, which means that we have not yet really concentrated on the priority areas and which also flags the necessity to bring the priority areas into higher focus. He will have a great interest in the allocation of resources such as manpower; yet he recognizes that under wartime conditions which prevail in Vietnam there will always be some inequity." 5/

It is important to emphasize that the appointment of Porter to his new role did indeed improve the organization of the Mission, and that Porter did accomplish some of the things that Washington had hoped he would -- but, under the constraints outlined below, he did not get enough done fast enough to satisfy the growing impatience in Washington with the progress of the effort. This impatience was to lead to the second reorganization and the formation of the Office of Civil Operations (OCO) after the Manila Conference. Although the impatience of Washington was justified, the fact is that under the new and limited mandate Porter had, he did begin the process of pulling together CIA, USAID, and JUSPAO, and forcing them to work more closely together. He also tried to focus General Lansdale's liaison efforts with General Thang more closely on items related to our operational objectives. He presented a new and vastly improved image of the civilian mission to the press, many of whom came to regard him as the most competent high official in the Mission. To one semi-official observer, Henry Kissinger, who visited Vietnam first in October of 1965, and then returned in July, 1966, the situation looked substantially improved:

> "The organization of the Embassy has been vastly improved since my last visit. The plethora of competing agencies, each operating their own program on the basis of partly conflicting and largely uncoordinated criteria, has been replaced by an increasingly effective structure under the extremely able leadership of Bill Porter. Porter is on top of his job. It would be idle to pretend that the previous confusion is wholly overcome. He has replaced competition by coordination; he is well on his way to imposing effective direction on the basis of carefully considered criteria. At least the basic structure for progress exists. Where eight months ago I hardly knew where to begin, the problem now is how to translate structure into performance -- a difficult but no insuperable task." 6/

Despite Kissinger's hopeful words, there was a growing tendency in Washington to demand more out of the Mission that it was then producing.

In a paper written in August, 1966, Robert W. Komer, whose role in the re-emphasis of pacification will be discussed in the next section, wrote:

> "There is a growing consensus that the US/GVN pacifica-
> tion effort needs to be stepped up, that management of our
> pacification assets is not yet producing an acceptable rate
> of return for our heavy support investments, and that paci-
> fication operations should be brought more abreast of our
> developing military effort against the NVA and VC main force.
> The President has expressed this view, and so has Ambassador
> Lodge among others." 7/

Why did Porter not live up to the expectations of Washington? While the documentation is weak on this point, the following reasons can be deduced from the available evidence, including discussions with people who worked in both Saigon and Washington:

1. The Ambassador was not fully backing his Deputy, and Porter
   was never sure of Lodge's support in Mission Council meetings,
   in telegrams, in discussions with the agencies. Many senior
   officials of the USG, including the President, had told Porter
   that he had their full support, and that they expected him to
   manage the Mission. But on a day-to-day basis, Porter had to
   get along with the Ambassador, who was still (and legitimately
   so) the boss. The result was a considerable gap between what
   high officials in Washington considered Porter's mandate, and
   what Porter felt he would be able to do without antagonizing
   the Ambassador. *

---

* This problem was foreshadowed in a remarkable way in 1963-1964. After
visiting Vietnam in December, 1963, the Secretary of Defense sent
President Johnson a memorandum in which he pointed out that the Mission
"lacks leadership...and is not working to a common plan...My impression
is that Lodge simply does not know how to conduct a coordinated administration... This has of course been stressed to him both by Dean Rusk
and myself (and also by John McCone), and I do not think he is con-
sciously rejecting our advice; he has just operated as a loner all his
life and cannot readily change now. Lodge's newly-designated deputy,
David Nes, was with us and seems a highly competent team player. I have
stated the situation frankly to him and he has said he would do all he
could to constitute what would in effect be an executive committee operating below the level of the Ambassador." It is fairly well established
that Nes, whatever his own ability and shortcomings was unable to
establish an "executive committee operating below the level of the Ambassador," and that, as a matter of fact his every attempt to move in
the direction indicated by the Secretary further alienated him from
the Ambassador. The presumed lesson in the incident was that it is
difficult and dangerous to tell one man's deputy that he has to assume
broad responsibility and authority if the top man does not want this
designation made.

2. The agencies involved -- AID, USIA, and CIA -- were hostile
to the new designation from the outset. Since every agency
paid lip-service to the new role of the Deputy Ambassador,
it is difficult to document this fact. But it is virtually
self-evident: since every agency was being told that its
chief representative in Saigon now worked for the Deputy
Ambassador, a career Foreign Service Officer, there was unhappiness with the system in both Saigon and Washington.
Men like the Director of JUSPAO, who had served in Vietnam
since January of 1964, and the CIA Station Chief, who retained a completely independent communications channel to
Washington, were not going to yield any portion of their
autonomy without some quiet grumbling and invisible foot-
dragging. To overcome this reluctance was not as easy for
Porter as Washington had perhaps hoped, particularly in
light of Lodge's attitude.

3. The Washington organization did not parallel the Saigon
structure it was supposed to support, and in fact actually
prevented strong and continuous support. With legitimate
legal and traditional responsibilities for programs overseas,
each agency in Washington was understandably reluctant to
channel their guidance through the Deputy Ambassador, whose
authority did not seem to be derived from the normal letter
of authority to all Chiefs of Mission sent by President
Kennedy in 1961. The agencies, moreover, also had a special
problem with regard to Vietnam: Congress was being far more
rigorous in its review of the Vietnam program than it was in
most other areas. The Moss Subcommittee on Overseas Governmental Operations, for example, was sending investigating
teams to Saigon regularly, and issuing well-publicized reports
criticizing the AID program across a broad front. The Sena-
torial group that reviews CIA programs was showing considerable
concern with the nature and size of the cadre and counter-
terror programs. And beyond that, there was the normal budgetary process, in which each agency generally handles its own
requests through an extremely complex and difficult process.
Each agency was bound to try to communicate as directly as
possible with their representatives in Saigon. Thus, while
some major conflicting policies which had previously existed
were ironed out through the new system (such as the role of
the cadre), many smaller, or second-level matters contained
to receive the traditional separate agency approach.

A good example of this was the vital issue of improving village/hamlet
government. Although consistently identified as a key element in any
successful pacification program, improving the war-torn village structure
seemed to escape the Mission organizationally. Responsibility for advice
and assistance to the GVN Ministry of Interior (later the Commissariat for

Administration), rested with the USAID Public Administration Division, which in turn was at the third level of the USAID, reporting to the USAID Director only through an Assistant Director for Technical Services. Within the Public Administration Division (PAD) itself, to make matters worse, improving village/hamlet government was only one of a large number of activities for which PAD was responsible -- and in the eyes of many traditionally-minded professional public administrators, it did not automatically come first.

Other issues of obvious importance -- such as budgeting, strengthening the Ministry, improving the National Institute of Administration, sending officials to the U.S. for participant training -- all came within the normal PAD program as outlined in the AID Country Assistance Program (CAP) for FY 67, and, moreover, they required more resources, more Americans, more attention at high levels of AID, than the village/hamlet government problem. When Ambassador Porter directed AID, in May of 1966, to begin massive efforts to improve village government, his orders were obeyed to the extent they could be within the context of previous AID commitments. The result was a further stretching of the already taut USAID/PAD staff, since no previous commitments or programs were cut back to provide man and/or money for village government.

At the same time, other sections of the Mission which were expected to support the renewed emphasis on local government were not producing as requested. JUSPAO, asked to support the effort with psychological operations, agreed in principle but found its existing list of priorities basically unchanged. The Embassy Political Section, which should have supported the effort at least to the extent of urging through its political contacts that the GVN revitalize the village structure, simply had better things to do. The CIA was also asked to support the effort; with their cadre assets, they were in a crucial position on the matter, particularly since some of the critics of the cadre had stated that the cadre actually undercut village government instead of strengthening it (as they claimed). Again, the CIA gave lip service to the idea, without making any significant change in their training of the cadre at Vung Tau.

In this situation, Ambassador Porter tried several times to get action, each time received enthusiastic, but generalized, words of agreement and support from everyone, and finally turned his attention to other matters; with the crush of business, there was always a more immediate crisis.

B. Washington: Komer as the Blowtorch

The Warrenton conference had discussed not only the reorganization
of the Mission in Saigon, but -- far more gingerly -- the need for a
more centralized management of the effort in Washington.

After the Honolulu conference the President decided to take action
to change the Washington structure on Vietnam, but not in quite the way
suggested at Warrenton. While many people at Warrenton, particularly the
State representative, had hoped that the President would designate one
man, with an interagency staff, as the overseer of an integrated political-
military-diplomatic-economic policy in Vietnam, the President decided to
reduce the scope of the job, and give one man responsibility for what was
coming to be called "The Other War." Thus, for the very first time, there
would be a high-ranking official -- a Special Assistant to the President
-- whose job would be to get the highest possible priority for non-military
activities. In effect, the President had assured a place at the decision
councils in Washington for someone with built-in pro-pacification, pro-
civil side bias. This was Robert W. Komer, whose strenuous efforts in the
next few months were to earn him the nickname of "The Blowtorch" (given
to him by Ambassador Lodge, according to Komer).

How much authority the President intended to give Komer is not clear.
It is quite likely that the issue was deliberately left vague, so as to
see what authority and what accomplishments Komer could carve out of an
ambiguous NSAM and his ready access to the President.

On March 23, 1966 -- six weeks after Manila -- Joseph Califano,
Special Assistant to the President, sent the Secretary of Defense an
EYES ONLY draft of the NSAM setting up Komer's authority. In the covering note, Califano said, "We would be particularly interested in whatever
suggestions you would have to strengthen Komer's authority." 8/ In response,
the Defense Department (the actual person making suggestion unidentified in
documents) suggested only one minor change, and approved the NSAM.

The other departments also suggested minor changes in other parts of
the NSAM, and on March 28, 1966, the President issued it as NSAM 343. It
said:

"In the Declaration of Honolulu I renewed our pledge of
common commitment with the Government of the Republic of Vietnam to defense against aggression, to the work of social
revolution, to the goal of free self-government, to the attack
on hunger, ignorance and disease, and to the unending quest for
peace. Before the Honolulu Conference and since, I have stressed
repeatedly that the war on human misery and want is as fundamental to the successful resolution of the Vietnam conflict, as our
military operations to ward off aggression... In my view, it is

essential to designate a specific focal point for the direction,
coordination and supervision in Washington of U.S. non-military
programs relating to Vietnam. I have accordingly designated
Mr. Robert W. Komer as Special Assistant to me for carrying out
this responsibility.

"I have charged him and his deputy, Ambassador William
Leonhart, to assure that adequate plans are prepared and coordinated covering all aspects of such programs, and that they are
promptly and effectively carried out. The responsibility will
include the mobilization of U.S. military resources in support
of such programs. He will also assure that the Rural Construc-
tion/Pacification program and the programs for combat force
employment and military operations are properly coordinated.

"His functions will be to ensure full and timely support
of the U.S. in Saigon on matters within his purview...

"In addition to working closely with the addressee Cabinet
officers he will have direct access to me at all times.

"Those CIA activities related solely to intelligence collection are not affected by this NSAM." 9/

Mr. Komer was in business, with a small staff and a mandate, as he
saw it, to prod people throughout the government, in both Washington and
Saigon. Combined with a personality that journalists called "abrasive,"
his mandate resulted in more pressure being put on the civilians associated
with Vietnam than ever before, and in some understandable frictions.

Komer's significance in the re-emphasis of pacification is important,
and must be dealt with briefly, although this section does not relate his
story in detail.

First, there was Komer's influence on AID. With little difficulty,
he established his ability to guide AID, and began to give them direct
instructions on both economic and pacification matters. AID, previously
with limited influence in the Mission's pacification policy, found its
influence diminished still further.

Of more significance was Komer's emphasis on the RD Cadre program,
run by the CIA. Together with Porter, he recommended a premature expansion of the program, in an effort to get the program moving faster. On
April 19, 1966, after his first trip to Vietnam, Komer told the President:

"Cadre Expansion. While the RD program has some questionable aspects, it seems the most promising approach yet developed.
The RD ministry led by General Thang is better than most, and
the Vung Tau and Montagnard training centers are producing 5500
trained men for insertion in 59-man teams into 93 villages
every 15 weeks.

"But Porter sees even this rate as insufficient to keep
up with 'the growing military capability to sweep the VC out
of key areas.' He urges rapid expansion via building another
training center (which he'd like to get Seabees to build).
The aim is roughly to double cadre output from 19,000 to
39,000 trained personnel per year. He thinks this rate could
be reached by end CY 1966. I agree with Porter and will press
this concept at the Washington end." 10/

Plans were approved, and construction began on the second training
center. But by the end of 1966 it was recognized that the attempt to
double cadre training would only weaken their quality, which was shaky
to begin with. The construction of the second center was abruptly halted.
Komer and Porter had miscalculated badly.

Komer also sought to influence the military in both Saigon and
Washington to give more attention to the pacification effort.

In cables to Saigon -- most of them slugged with his name, and thus
known as "Komergrams" -- Komer sought to prod the Mission forward on a
wide variety of programs. One of his most recurring themes was the Chieu
Hoi program * and in time his urgings did contribute to a more successful
program, with a high-ranking American official in Ambassador Porter's
office working on nothing else, in place of the previous ad hoc arrangement between JUSAPO and USAID.

Another recurring theme was refugees, but here he was less successful, particularly since the U.S. Mission was never able to determine
whether or not it desired to stimulate more refugees as means of denying
the VC manpower. His cables on this complex issue were characterized by
an absence of objective, but at least he was addressing frontally questions few other people would raise at all:

"For Porter from Komer: We here deeply concerned by growing number of refugees. Latest reports indicate that as of
31 August, a total of 1,361,288 had been processed...Of course,
in some ways, increased flow of refugees is a plus. It helps

---

* For example: "Porter from Komer: Highest authorities interested in
stepping up defection programs. While recognizing limitations Chieu
Hoi program and inadequacies GVN administration, program has achieved
impressive results and shown high return in terms modest U.S. support
costs. Greatly concerned by two recent administrative decisions taken
by GVN..." 11/ Or: "To Porter from Komer: USIA eager help maximize
success both Chieu Hoi and RD programs, in which highest authorities
vitally interested..." 12/ Or: "For Mann and Casler from Komer:
Would appreciate your following through on coordinated set of action
proposals to energize lagging Chieu Hoi program...We are concerned
about drop-off in returnees since April...Bell and Marks concur." 13/

deprive VC of recruiting potential and rice growers, and is
partly indicative of growing peasant desire seek security on
our side.

"Question arises, however, of whether we and GVN adequately set up to deal with increased refugee flow of this
magnitude. AID has programmed much larger refugee program
for FY 67, but is it enough?...Only Mission would have answers,
so intent this cable is merely to pose question, solicit bids
for increased support if needed, and assure you I would do all
possible generate such support." 14/

On another controversial issue, Land Reform, Komer repeatedly pressed
the Mission for public signs of progress, but by the time he went out to
Saigon as General Westmoreland's deputy in 1967, he -- and apparently the
President -- were still unsatisfied.

But perhaps the most important role Komer played was to keep the
general subject of pacification before the President, to encourage
Ambassador Lodge to talk pacification up, and to constitute a one-man,
full-time, nonstop lobby for pacification within the USG.

After his first trip to Vietnam, for example, Komer reported to the
President that "while our splendid military effort is going quite well,
our civil programs lag behind...To achieve the necessary results, we must
ourselves give higher priority to (and expand) certain key pacification
programs, especially cadres and police -- if necessary at some expense to
the military effort." 15/

Komer's memorandum constitutes only a small proportion of the information and suggestions reaching the President and his senior advisors on
Vietnam, and the intention of this paper is not to suggest that they were
in any sense definitive documents which show the direction of U.S. strategy
in Vietnam. But it seems clear that Komer was the first senior official
in Washington to make a major effort to put pacification near the top of
our combined civil-military effort, and that he had a particularly advantageous spot from which to try. He had authorized back-channel communications with the Ambassador and Deputy Ambassador in Saigon, apparent
access to the President, and the umbrella of the White House.

His memoranda to the President over his year in Washington showed
considerable change in thinking on many issues, but a consistent support
for more pacification. A small sample is revealing:

"Key aspects of pacification deserve highest priority --
and greater emphasis. Unless we and the GVN can secure and
hold the countryside cleared by military operations, we either
face an ever larger and quasi-permanent military commitment or
risk letting the VC infiltrate again...I personally favor more

attention to the Delta (IV Corps) region, which contains eight
out of Vietnam's 15 million people and is its chief rice bowl
...Clearly we must dovetail the military's sweep operations
and civil pacification. My impression is that, since the
military are moving ahead faster than the civil side we need
to beef up the latter to get it in phase. There's little
point in the military clearing areas the civil side can't
pacify. On the other hand, security is the key to pacification; people won't cooperate and the cadre can't function till
an area is secure...

"Somehow the civil side appears reluctant to call on military resources, which are frequently the best and most readily
available. I put everyone politely on notice that I would
have no such hesitations -- provided that the case was demonstrable -- and that this was the express request of the
Secretary of Defense." 15/ /Cited Supra./

In August of 1966, Komer produced the longest of his papers, and the
one he considered his most important. Its title was "Giving a New Thrust
to Pacification." In addition to discussing the substance of pacification,
the paper made some further organizational suggestions, which clearly foreshadowed the second reorganization of the Mission which took place after
the Manila conference. It is worth quoting in some length (all underlining
is part of the original):

"There is a growing consensus that the US/GVN pacification
effort needs to be stepped up, that management of our pacification assets is not yet producing an acceptable rate of return
for our heavy investments, and that pacification operations
should be brought more abreast of our developing military effort
against the NVA and VC main force. The President has expressed
this view, and so has Ambassador Lodge among others.

"I. What is pacification? In one sense, "pacification" can be
used to encompass the whole of the military, political, and civil
effort in Vietnam. But the term needs to be narrowed down for
operational purposes, and can be reasonably well separated out
as a definable problem area.

"If we divide the US/GVN problem into four main components,
three of them show encouraging progress. The campaign against
the major VC/NVA units is in high gear, the constitutional process seems to be evolving favorably, and we expect to contain
inflation while meeting most needs of the civil economy. But
there is a fourth problem area, that of securing the countryside and getting the peasant involved in the struggle against
the Viet Cong, where we are lagging way behind. It is this
problem area which I would term pacification...

          TOP SECRET - Sensitive

TOP SECRET - Sensitive

"At the risk of over-simplification, I see management of
the pacification problem as involving three main sub-tasks:
(1) providing local security in the countryside -- essentially
a military/police/cadre task; (2) breaking the hold of the
VC over the people; and (3) positive programs to win the active
support of the rural population.

"...Few argue that we can assure success in Vietnam without
also winning the 'village war.' Chasing the large units around
the boondocks still leaves intact the VC infrastructure, with
its local guerrilla capability plus the weapons of terror and
intimidation...So winning the 'village war' which I will loosely
call pacification, seems an indispensable ingredient of any high-
confidence strategy and a necessary precaution to close the
guerrilla option.

"...Yet another reason for stressing pacification is that
the U.S. is supporting a lot of assets in being which are at
the moment poorly employed. Even the bulk of ARVN, which increasingly sits back and watches the U.S. take over the more
difficult parts of the war against main enemy units and bases,
might be more effectively used for this purpose...Thus, even if
one contends that pacification as I have defined it is not vital
to a win strategy, stepping up this effort would add little to
present costs and might produce substantial pay offs.

"Beyond this, the time is psychologically ripe for greater
emphasis on pacification. South Vietnamese confidence is growing as the U.S. turns the tide. New US/FW military forces are
arriving to reinforce the campaign against the main force; their
presence will release much needed assets to pacification. The
GVN, fresh from success against the Buddhist led struggle and
confidently facing an election process leading toward a constitution, also has been making the kind of tough decisions --
devaluation, turnover of the Saigon port to military management,
etc. -- that will be needed in pacification, too.

"In sum, the assets are available, and the time is ripe for
an increased push to win the 'village war.'

"III. What is Holding Up the Pacification Efforts? The long
history of the Vietnam struggle is replete with efforts to secure
the countryside. Most of them, like Diem's strategic hamlet
program, proved abortive. ...Some of the chief difficulties we
confront are suggested below:

"A. We had to go after the major VC/NVA units first... It
was a matter of first things first...

TOP SECRET - Sensitive

"B. The VC/NVA have been able to select the weakest point in any embryonic GVN pacification effort and destroy it with a lightening attack...

"C. There are inherent difficulties in the pacification process itself...

"D. Lack of high quality assets. Pacification has also had to take a back seat in the sense that it generally gets only the lowest grade GVN assets -- and not enough of these...

"E. Last but not least, neither the U.S. nor the GVN have as yet developed an adequate plan, program, or management structure for dealing with pacification...

"1. The JCS and MACV are so preoccupied, however justifiably, with operations against the major VC/NVA units that they are not able to pay enough attention to the local security aspects of pacification...

"2. There is no unified civil/military direction within the GVN...

"3. A similar divided responsibility prevails on the U.S. side...

"4. Nor does there yet appear to be a well-understood chain of command from Porter even to the civilians operating in the field...

"5. There is no integrated civil/military plan for pacification on either the U.S. or GVN side...

"IV. How do we step up Pacification? ...It demands a multi-faceted civil-military response...

"A. Provide more adequate, continuous security for the locales in which pacification is taking place. This is the essential prerequisite. None of our civil programs in the countryside can be expected to be effective unless the area is reasonably secure. Nor, unless the people are protected, and their attitudes likely to change in favor of the GVN... To provide security requires the assignment on a long term basis of enough assets to defeat these resident VC companies and battalions, in addition to providing 24-hour security to the people until they are able to assist in providing their own protection. This is primarily the task of RF and PF, supported by the RD cadres and police...Some knowledgeable

TOP SECRET -Sensitive

experts contend that even if we improve the...RF, PF, police,
and cadre, they are together insufficiently to extend local
security much beyond existing secured areas. They feel that
lacking mobility and heavy firepower, these forces must be
thickened with a liberal sprinkling of regular ARVN units
working in the area outside the immediate area undergoing
pacification. I do not suggest that ARVN regulars gainfully
employed in battle against the enemy main forces be so diverted.
I do urge that those ARVN forces not now fully engaged -- a
substantial fraction of the total be used to contribute directly
to improving local security.

"B. We must devote more effort to breaking the hold of the
VC over the people...

"C. Carry out positive revolutionary development programs
to win active popular support. The cliche of winning support
by offering the people a better life through a series of interrelated RD programs has great relevance in Vietnam...

"D. Establish functioning priorities for pacification...

"E. Better Area Priorities... A greater stress on pacification logically means greater stress on the Delta...

"F. Concentrate additional resources on pacification...
Arguments made in the past that pacification is a delicate subject to be approached only with care and precision have lost
some of their relevance as the intensity of warfare has increased
...Increase:

> Police...
> RD Cadre...
> Material Support for Pacification...
> The U.S. Agricultural Effort...
> Chieu Hoi...
> Village/Hamlet Administration...

"G. Set more performance goals...

"H. Rapidly extend the security of key roads...

"I. Systematize the flow of refugees...

"J. Get better control over rice...

"V. How can Pacification be Managed More Effectively?

"A. Restructuring the GVN...

TOP SECRET - Sensitive

-- Place the RD and PF under the RD Ministry...

-- Establish a single line of command to the province chiefs...

-- Remove the Division from the pacification chain of command...

-- Strengthen the authority of the Province Chiefs...

-- Appoint civilian chiefs in selected provinces and districts...

"B. Parallel strengthening of the structure is essential. U.S. leadership has often sparked major pacification steps by the GVN. The structure for managing pacification advice to the GVN, and direct U.S. military/civilian support, have evolved slowly as the U.S. contributions have grown. Once it was possible to coordinate the U.S. pacification effort through an interagency committee for strategic hamlets. Later the Mission Council concept was used extensively. In the wake of the Honolulu Conference, the President appointed Ambassador Porter to take charge of the non-military effort in Vietnam. Several highly qualified people now give Porter the nucleus of a coordination and operations staff. However...the U.S. management structure must be strengthened considerably more.

"There are three basic alternatives, each building on the present structure, which could provide the needed result. Two of them are based on the principle of a 'single manager' over both civilian and military assets by assigning command responsibility either to Porter or Westmoreland. The third accepts a continued division between the civil and military sides for numerous practical reasons, but calls for strengthening the management structure of both.

"Alternative No. 1 -- Give Porter operational control over all U.S. pacification activity...

"Alternative No. 2 -- Retain the present separate civil and military command channels but strengthen the management structure of both MACV and the U.S. Mission. This option, recognizing the practical difficulties of putting U.S. civilian and military personnel under a single chief, would be to settle for improved coordination at the Saigon level.

"To facilitate improved coordination, however, it would require strengthening the organization for pacification within MACV and the U.S. Mission. MACV disposes of by far the greater number of Americans working on pacification in the field. It has advisory teams spending most of their time on pacification in 200 out of 230 districts and in all 43 provinces. These teams -- not counting

advisors at division, corps and all tactical units down to
battalion -- number about 2000 men compared with about one-
eighth this number from all other U.S. agencies combined.

"However, the senior officer in MACV dealing with pacification as his principal function is now a colonel heading the
J33 staff division. Moreover, with 400,000 U.S. troops soon
to be committed, General Westmoreland, his subordinate commanders, and his principal staff officers must spend increasing
time on military operations associated with defeating the
VC/NVA main formations. Therefore, management of the tremendous advisory resources with MACV inevitably suffers regardless
of General Westmoreland's personal effort to give balanced
attention to both.

"Hence there might be merit in COMUSMACV having a senior
deputy to manage pacification within MACV and pacification
advice to the JCS, as well as throughout the Vietnamese military
chain of command. Key staff sections, such as J33, Polwar Directorate, Senior Advisor for RF/PF, could be controlled by a chief
of staff for pacification responsive to the Deputy. Advisory
teams at corps and division would receive guidance and orders on
pacification from the Deputy. Province and district advisors
would receive all orders, except routine administrative instructions, through the pacification channel.

"To parallel the MACV organization and provide a single point
of liaison on the civil side, Ambassador Porter should have his
own field operations office formed by merging USAID Field Operations, JUSPAO Field Services and CAS Covert Action Branch. Control over the people assigned would be removed, as in Alternative
No. 1, from their parent agency. All civilian field personnel in
the advisory business would also receive their guidance and orders
from the Deputy Ambassador.

"For this dual civilian-military system to operate effectively,
the closest coordination would be required between the offices of
the MACV Deputy and the Deputy Ambassador. Since it is difficult
and dangerous to separate military and civilian aspects of pacification at the province level, most policy guidance and instructions to the provinces hopefully would be issued jointly and be
received by the senior military and civilian advisors who would
then develop their plans together.

"I would still favor a single civil/military team chief in the
province, even though he would have two bosses in Saigon talking
to him through different and parallel chains of command. Alternatively, since MACV already has a senior advisor in each province,
it would be possible similarly to assign a single civilian as the

Vietnamese province chief's point of contact on all non-military matters. All other civilians in the province would be under his control.

"Alternative No. 3 -- Assign responsibility for pacification civil and military, to COMUSMACV. This is not a new suggestion, and has a lot to recommend it. In 1964, General Westmoreland proposed that he be made "executive agent" for pacification. MACV at that time had an even greater preponderance of field advisors than it does today, and was devoting the bulk of its attention to pacification. Since the military still has by far the greatest capacity among U.S. agencies in Vietnam for management and the military advisors outnumber civilians at least 8 to 1 in the field, MACV could readily take on responsibility for all pacification matters.

"Turning over the entire pacification management task to COMUSMACV would require him to reorganize his staff to handle simultaneously the very large military operations business involving U.S., Free World and Vietnamese forces and the civil/military aspects of pacification at the same time. The USAID, JUSPAO, and CAS Covert Operations staffs would come under COMUSMACV's control where they would be used as additional "component commands." In this case, it might be desirable to have a civilian deputy to COMUSMACV for pacification.

"Also appropriate under this concept would be a single U.S. advisory team, under a team chief, at each subordinate echelon. The result would be a single chain of command to the field and coordinated civilian/military pacification planning and operations on the U.S. side. The U.S. Mission would speak to Vietnamese corps and division commanders, province chiefs and district chiefs with a single voice." 16/

In the latter part of this lengthy memorandum, Komer clearly foreshadowed both the formation of OCO after the Manila conference -- his Alternative No. 2 -- and the merger of OCO and MACV into MACCORDS after Guam -- his Alternative No. 3. But when he sent the paper to Saigon with his deputy in mid-August, the reaction from Lodge, Porter, and Westmoreland was uniformly negative: they asked him, in effect, to leave them alone since they were satisfied with their present organization.

But Komer had also distributed his paper around Washington, and was lobbying for another change in the structure of the Mission, although he remained, in August, vague as to which of the three alternatives he put forward he personally favored. When other senior officials of government began to voice feelings that additional organizational changes were necessary in the Mission in Saigon, the die was cast.

Another major attribute of Komer was his strong public and private optimism. He produced for any journalist willing to hear him out facts and figures that suggested strongly that the war was not only winnable, but being won at an accelerating pace.

To the President he sounded the same theme:

"After almost a year full-time in Vietnam, and six trips there, I felt able to learn a good deal more from my 11 days in country, 13-23 February. I return more optimistic than ever before. The cumulative change since my first visit last April is dramatic, if not yet visibly demonstrable in all respects. Indeed, I'll reaffirm even more vigorously my prognosis of last November (which few shared then) that growing momentum would be achieved in 1967 on almost every front in Vietnam." 17/

Komer believed in the concept of "sheer mass" -- that in time we would just overwhelm the Viet Cong:

"Wastefully, expensively, but nonetheless indisputably, we are winning the war in the South. Few of our programs -- civil or military -- are very efficient, but we are grinding the enemy down by sheer weight and mass. And the cumulative impact of all we have set in motion is beginning to tell. Pacification still lags the most, yet even it is moving forward.

"Indeed, my broad feeling, with due allowance for oversimplification, is that our side now has in presently programmed levels all the men, money and other resources needed to achieve success..." 18/

In summary, Komer's 13 months in Washington were spent steadily raising the priority of the pacification and other non-military efforts in Vietnam. While he never was in a controlling position within the Washington bureaucracy, he succeeded in making those who were more aware of the "other war" (a term he used continually until Ambassador Bunker announced in May of 1967 that he did not recognize that there was such a thing). While it can be no more than speculation, it would also appear that Komer played an important role in inserting into high-level discussions, including Presidential discussions, the pacification priority. Thus, when General Westmoreland visited the President at the LBJ ranch in August, 1966, Komer put before the President a series of pacification-related subjects to be used during the discussions. This happened again at Manila, where some of the points in final communique were similar to things Komer had been pushing earlier, as outlined in his August memorandum.

C. Study Groups and Strategists: Summer 1966

In the aftermath of Honolulu, task forces and study groups were suddenly assembling, producing papers on priorities, on organization of the Mission, on the role and mission of various forces. They were all manifestations of the new mood that had come over the Mission and Washington on pacification. The advocates of pacification -- with their widely differing viewpoints -- all saw their chance again to put forward their own concepts to a newly interested bureaucracy, starting with Komer and Porter.

The most important of the numerous studies were:

1. The Program for the Pacification and Long-Term Development of South Vietnam (Short Title: PROVN) -- commissioned by the Army Chief of Staff in July of 1965, completed and submitted in March 1966;

2. The Priorities Task Force -- formed in Saigon in April 1966 by Deputy Ambassador Porter, completed in July 1966;

3. The Inter-Agency "Roles and Missions" Study Group -- formed by Porter in July 1966, completed in August.

While the recommendations of these studies were never accepted in toto, they all play key roles in the development of strategic thinking in Washington and Saigon during the latter part of 1966, and they continue to be influential today.

PROVN -- As early as the summer of 1965, General Johnson saw the need to select a superior group of officers, and set them to work on a long-term study of the problem in Vietnam. The study was intended for internal Army use, and was for a while after its completion treated with such delicacy that Army officers were forbidden even to discuss its existence outside DOD. This was unfortunate, because in content it was far-ranging and thoughtful, and set a precedent for responsible forward planning and analysis which should be duplicated in other fields.

PROVN was charged with "developing new sources of action to be taken in South Vietnam by the United States and its allies, which will, in conjunction with current actions, modified as necessary, lead in due time to successful accomplishment of U.S. aims and objectives." With this broad mandate, PROVN staff spent eight months questioning returning officers from Vietnam, studying the history of the country, drawing parallels with other countries, analyzing the structure of the U.S. Mission; and making recommendations. In the end, the PROVN team decided that there was "no unified effective pattern" to the then-current efforts in Vietnam, and submitted a broad blueprint for action. Its thesis was simple:

"The situation in South Vietnam has seriously deteriorated. 1966 may well be the last chance to ensure eventual success. 'Victory' can only be achieved through bringing

the individual Vietnamese, typically a rural peasant, to
support willingly the GVN. The critical actions are those
that occur at the village, district, and provincial levels.
This is where the war must be fought; this is where that
war and the object which lies beyond it must be won. The
following are the most important specific actions required
now:

-- Concentrate U.S. operations on the provincial level
to include the delegation of command authority over
U.S. operations to the Senior U.S. Representative at
the provincial level.

-- Reaffirm Rural Construction as the foremost US/GVN
combined effort to solidify and extend GVN influence.

-- Authorize more direct U.S. involvement in GVN affairs
at those administrative levels adequate to ensure the
accomplishment of critical programs.

-- Delegate to the U.S. Ambassador unequivocal authority
as the sole manager of all U.S. activities, resources,
and personnel in-country.

-- Direct the Ambassador to develop a single integrated
plan for achieving U.S. objectives in SVN.

-- Reaffirm to the world at large the precise terms of
the ultimate U.S. objective as stated in NSAM 288:
A free and independent non-communist South Vietnam..." 19/

Beyond this frank and direct summary, the study had hundreds of recommendations, ranging from the specific and realizable to the vague and
hortatory.

In summary, the PROVN was a major step forward in thinking. Although
as mentioned above, its value was reduced for a long time by the restrictions placed on its dissemination, the candor with which it addressed
matters was probably possible only because it originated within a single
service, and thus did not require the concurrences of an inter-agency
study.

For example, the PROVN study addressed directly a point of such potential
embarrassment to the U.S. Government that it is quite likely an inter-agency
group would not have addressed it except perhaps in oblique terms:

"A PROVN survey...revealed that no two agencies of the U.S. Government viewed our objectives in the same manner. Failure to use that
unequivocal statement of our fundamental objective -- a free and
independent, non-communist South Vietnam -- set forth in NSAM 288,
hinders effective inter-agency coordination and the integrated application of U.S. support efforts." 20/

As for the study's "highest priority" activities, PROVN recommended:

"(1) Combat Operations -- the bulk of U.S. and FWMA Forces and designated RVNAF units should be directed against enemy base areas and against their lines of communication in SVN, Laos, and Cambodia as required; the remainder of Allied force assets must ensure adequate momentum to activity in priority Rural Construction areas.

"(2) Rural Construction -- in general, the geographic priorities should be, in order, the Delta, the Coastal Lowlands, and the Highlands; currently the highest priority areas are the densely populated and rich resource Delta provinces of An Giang, Vinh Long, Dinh Tuong, Go Cong, and the Hop Tac area surrounding Saigon.

"(3) Economic Stability -- current emphasis must be directed toward curbing inflation and reducing the excessive demands for skilled and semi-skilled labor imposed upon an over-strained economy..."

On the management of the United States effort -- which PROVN found extremely poor -- the recommendation was to create a single manager system, with the Ambassador in charge of all assets in Vietnam and the mission of producing a single integrated plan. PROVN suggested major steps in the direction of giving the Ambassador a stronger hold over the military.

Of greatest importance -- aside from the reorganizational suggestions -- was the PROVN conclusion on the supremacy of Rural Construction activities over everything else:

"Rural Construction must be designated unequivocally as the major US/GVN effort. It will require the commitment of a preponderance of RVNAF and GVN paramilitary forces, together with adequate U.S. support and coordination and assistance. Without question, village and hamlet security must be achieved throughout Vietnam...RC is the principal means available to broaden the allied base, provide security, develop political and military leadership, and provide necessary social reform to the people..." 21/

To this end, PROVN suggested a division of responsibility among the forces:

"The need to sustain security pervades every ramification of RC...The various forces capable of providing this environment must be unified...at the province level. They must include the ARVN as a major component -- as many of its battle-tested units as can possibly be devoted to this mission. These integrated national security forces must be associated

76

and intermingled with the people on a long-term basis.
Their capacity to establish and maintain public order and
stability must be physically and continuously credible.
The key to achieving such security lies in the conduct
of effective area saturation tactics, in and around populated areas, which deny VC encroachment opportunities." 22/

Finally, the study advocated a far stronger system of leverage for
American advisors in the field -- "mechanisms for exerting U.S. influence
must be built into the U.S. organization and its methods of operation." 23/

The PROVN study concluded with a massive "Blueprint for National Action"
which was never implemented. But the influence of the study was substantial. Within the Army staff, a responsible and select group of officers
had recommended top priority for pacification. Even if the Army staff
still rejected parts of the study, they were on notice that a study had
been produced within the staff which suggested a substantial revision
of priorities.

The PROVN study had some major gaps. Proceeding from the unstated
assumption that our commitment in Vietnam had no implicit time limits,
it proposed a strategy which it admitted would take years -- perhaps well
into the 1970's -- to carry out. It did not examine alternative strategies that might be derived from a shorter time limit on the war. In fact,
the report made no mention of one of the most crucial variables in the
Vietnam equation -- U.S. public support for the Administration.

Further, the report did little to prove that Vietnam was ready for
pacification. This "fact" was taken for granted, it seems -- a fault common to most American-produced pacification plans. While PROVN did suggest
geographic priorities, they were derived not even in part from the area's
receptivity to pacification but exclusively from the location and strategic importance of the area. Thus, the same sort of error made in Hop Tac
was being repeated in PROVN's suggestions.

MACV analyzed the report in May of 1966, calling it "an excellent overall approach in developing organization, concepts and policies..." In
a lengthy analysis of PROVN, MACV cabled:

"As seen here, PROVN recommends two major initiatives
essential to achieving U.S. objectives in South Vietnam:
creation of an organization to integrate total U.S. civil-
military effort, and exercise of greatly increased direct
U.S. involvement in GVN activities.

"MACV has long recognized need for the greatest possible unity of effort to gain U.S. objectives in South Vietnam.
MACV agrees with PROVN concept to achieve full integration
of effort in attaining U.S. objectives in South Vietnam.
Evolution of U.S. organization in Saigon is heading towards
this goal. Deputy Ambassador now has charge of revolutionary

and economic development programs and MACV is charged with
military programs. In addition, special task force has
been established by Deputy Ambassador to draft mission-
wide statement of strategy, objectives, and priorities. In
effect, this task force is engaged in integrated planning
which under PROVN concept would be performed by supra-agency
staff. PROVN proposal for designation of a single manager
with supra-staff is a quantum jump to achieve the necessary
degree of military-civil integration. This final step cannot be implemented by evolutions here in Saigon. It would
have to be directed and supervised from highest level in
Washington.

"MACV is in complete agreement with PROVN position that
immediate and substantially increased United States direct
involvement in GVN activities in form of constructive influence and manipulation is essential to achievement of U.S.
objectives in Vietnam. PROVN emphasizes that "leverage
must originate in terms of reference established by government agreement," and "leverage, in all its implications,
must be understood by the Vietnamese if it is to become an
effective tool." The direct involvement and leverage envisioned by PROVN could range from skillful diplomatic pressure to U.S. unilateral execution of critical programs.
MACV considers that there is a great danger that the extent
of involvement envisioned could become too great. A government sensitive to its image as champion of national sovereignty profoundly affected by the pressure of militant
minorities, and unsure of its tenure and legitimacy will
resent too great involvement by U.S. Excessive U.S. involvement may defeat objectives of U.S. policy: development
of free, independent non-communist nation. PROVN properly
recognizes that success can only be attained through support
of Vietnamese people, with support coming from the grass
roots up. Insensitive U.S. actions can easily defeat
efforts to accomplish this. U.S. manipulations could easily
become an American takeover justified by U.S. compulsion
to "get the job done." Such tendencies must be resisted.
It must be realized that there are substantial difficulties
and dangers inherent in implementing this or any similar
program.

"Several important aspects of proven concept require
comment, further consideration and resolution or emphasis.
Some of the more significant are:

"Regarding U.S. organization, MACV considers that any
major reorganization such as envisioned by PROVN must be
phased and deliberate to avoid confusion and slow-down in
ongoing programs...

"There appears to be an overemphasis on military control
in PROVN which may be undesirable. For instance, the study
states that all senior U.S. representatives (SUSREPs) initially will be U.S. military officers. This should not necessarily be stated policy. The senior U.S. representative,
particularly at province level, should be selected on basis
of major tasks to be performed, program emphasis in a particular area and other local considerations. PROVN also limits
U.S. single manager involvement in military activities. If
single manager concept of a fully integrated civil-military
effort is to be successful, military matters, such as roles
and missions, force requirements, and deployments must be
developed in full coordination and be integrated with civil
aspects.

"PROVN proposal for enlarged U.S. organization for
revolutionary development, particularly at sector and subsector levels, will require both military and civilian staff
increases. It will necessitate further civilian recruiting
and increased military input. Present shortage of qualified civilian personnel who desire duty in Vietnam must
be considered. It may fall to the military, as it is now
happening to some degree, to provide personnel not only for
added military positions, but also for many of civilian
functions as well.

"Regardless of what U.S. might desire, however, our
efforts to bring about new Vietnamese organizational structure must be tempered by continuous evaluation of the pressure such change places on Vietnamese leaders. Our goals
cannot be achieved by Vietnamese leaders who are identified
as U.S. puppets. The U.S. will must be asserted, but we
cannot afford to overwhelm the structure we are attempting
to develop.

"Accordingly, MACV recommends that PROVN, reduced primarily to a conceptual document, carrying forward the main
thrusts and goals of the study, be presented to National
Security Council for use in developing concepts, policies,
and actions to improve effectiveness of the American effort
in Vietnam." 24/

The "Priorities Task Force" -- This group was set up at Ambassador Porter's
direction in April 1966, following Komer's first trip to Vietnam, during
which Komer had strongly urged that the Mission try to establish a set of
interagency priorities. The actual work of this task force, which had
full interagency representation, was considered disappointing by almost
all its "consumers," particularly Komer, since it failed to come up with
a final list of priorities from which the Mission and Washington could
derive their programs. But it was by far the most ambitious task force
the Mission had ever set up, and it provoked considerable thought in the
Mission.

Its introductory section was a rather gloomy assessment of the situation. As such, it was at variance with the then current assessment of the situation -- but in retrospect, it is of far greater interest than the recommendations themselves!

"After some 15 months of rapidly growing U.S. military and political commitment to offset a major enemy military effort, the RVN has been made secure against the danger of military conquest, but at the same time it has been subjected to a series of stresses which threaten to thwart U.S. policy objectives...

"The enemy now has a broad span of capability for interfering with progress toward achievement of U.S. objectives. He can simultaneously operate offensively through employment of guerrilla and organized forces at widely separated points throughout the country, thus tying down friendly forces, while concentrating rehearsed surprise attacks in multi-battalion or even multi-regimental strength. ...The war will probably increase in intensity over the planning period (two years) though decisive military victory for either side is not likely. Guerrilla activity will make much of the countryside insecure. More of the rural population will be directly affected, and the number of refugees and civilian casualties on both sides seem bound to rise...

"Reasons for lack of success of the overall pacification program -- including all the stages from clear and secure operations to sustaining local government -- were varied. First, the primary hindrance to pacification was the low level of area security given active Viet Cong opposition. Second, political instability prevented continuing and coherent GVN direction and support of any pacification program. Third, pacification execution has been almost wholly Vietnamese and can be supported only indirectly by the U.S. This has made it less susceptible to American influence and more subject to political pressures and the weaknesses of Vietnamese administration and motivation. Fourth, no pacification concept since the strategic hamlet program has been sufficiently clear in definition to provide meaningful and consistent operational guidance to those executing the program. Fifth, given the pressure for success and the difficulty of measuring progress the execution of pacification failed to emphasize the political, social and psychological aspects of organizing the people and thus eliciting their active cooperation. The material aspects, being both visible and less difficult to implement, have received too much attention. Sixth, there was an absence of agreed, definitely stated pacification roles and missions not only within the GVN and the U.S. Mission but also between

the GVN and the U.S. Mission. This absence caused proliferation of various armed and unarmed elements not clearly related
to each other. Seventh, a quantitative and qualitative lack
of trained and motivated manpower to carry out pacification
existed. In addition, insufficient emphasis has been given
to training and orientation of local officials associated
with the pacification program. Eighth, lack of a well defined organizational structure in the U.S. Mission created
some confusion and conflicting direction of the pacification effort...

"During 1965, military plans were developed to support
revolutionary development; national priority areas were
selected where special emphasis would be placed on revolutionary development, and a structure was established by the
GVN extending an organizational framework for revolutionary
development from national to district levels. Meanwhile,
the U.S. Mission has begun action to centralize direction
for revolutionary development to ensure coordination of
all Mission activities in support of revolutionary development.

"A new approach was also taken in 1965 to bring coher-
ence to the use of cadre in the pacification process. Drawing on a concept of armed political action teams, whose
relative success locally was at least partly owing to direct
U.S. sponsorship and control, a combined cadre team approach
was developed. A new organization, the Revolutional Development Cadre, was established, which brought together and replaced a number of disparate cadre organizations. The combined cadre team approach includes armed units and special
skills of relating to and assisting the people. The combined
teams form the basis of the present pacification program.

"While these measures have helped to alleviate some of
the problem areas which previously frustrated pacification
efforts, some areas of major concern remain: First area
security where Revolutionary Development is being initiated
is not always adequate because of manpower problems; second,
continued existence of various overlapping security forces
further reduces effectiveness; third, approved pacification
concepts, roles, and missions agreed to by the U.S. and the
GVN are lacking; fourth, the effectiveness of the new RD
cadre teams remain to be tested and evaluated; fifth, extensive training of local and other officials associated with
RD still must be accomplished; sixth, emphasis on rapid
expansion and the desire for immediate visible and statistical progress would operate against lasting results; and,
seventh, organizational development and functioning on
both the GVN and U.S. sides are as yet incomplete. 25/

* * * * *

"The situation described above suggests that the course of events in Vietnam during the next two years will be significantly influenced by the following principal current trends.

"The war can be expected to increase in intensity, but decisive military victory should not be expected. It will be basically a war of attrition. Troop casualties should increase on both sides, and civilian casualties and refugees as well. The enemy can, if he chooses, increase still further the rate of his semi-covert invasion and the level of combat.

"The enemy will continue to build up his forces through infiltration from NVN and recruitment for main force VC units in SVN to achieve a favorable relationship of forces.

"At the same time, he will continue to reinforce his capabilities for political action in the urban areas, to exploit anticipated future political disturbances, to increase his terrorist acts in the cities, and to isolate the urban population from the countryside.

"GVN control of the countryside is not now being extended through pacification to any significant degree and pacification in the rural areas cannot be expected to proceed at a rapid rate. A new approach to pacification has been developed, but it is too early to judge its effectiveness. In addition, important problems requiring resolution remain...

"The Vietnamese will continue to face grave problems in creating an effective system of government. Under present conditions we cannot realistically expect a strong GVN to emerge over the planning period, nor can we expect political unity or a broadening of the base of popular support. The increased American presence, rising inflation and an image of considerable corruption are issues which will be increasingly exploited by unfriendly and opportunistic elements. U.S. influence on political events continues to be limited while our responsibility for Vietnam's future is increasing." 26/

The Task Force divided all activities in Vietnam into categories of importance, and assigned them priorities in groups. Unfortunately, the divisions were either too vague to be useful, or else they designated specific activities, such as agriculture, to such a low position that Washington found the selection unacceptable. In its first rank of importance the Task Force placed:

"1. Those activities designed to prepare a sound pacification program primarily through strengthening the human resources element of pacification, and through coordinated planning...

"2. Those activities which draw strength away from the enemy and add to GVN's strength and image of concern for all its citizens...

"3. Those psychological activities that support the war effort...

"4. Those activities that persuade the people that RVNAF is wholly on the side of the people and acting in their interests...

down through:

"16. Those activities which develop the leadership and organization of non-governmental institutions, particularly youth groups..." 27/

It was scarcely a list from which one could assemble a coherent program. Moreover, the above list of 16 "highest priority" tasks, was followed by a group of ten "high priority" tasks -- including strengthening provincial governments, autonomous municipal governments, better budgetary procedures, better refugee programs, minority programs, and so on. These, in turn, were followed by a nine-point list of "high priority programs." Into at least one of the 35 highest, high, or just plain priority activities, one could fit every program and project then being pursued in Vietnam. Furthermore, the proposal seemed to confuse inputs and outputs, placing in the same category "wishes" like "minimizing the adverse impact of and exploiting the opportunities provided by the American presence" (which was only "high priority") with "programs" like "creating a sound base for agricultural development."

The Priorities Task Force recommendations were used, unlike those of PROVN. In the FY 67 Country Assistance Program (CAP), submitted by AID to Congress that fall, the Task Force Strategy statement was used as a foreword, with Ambassador Lodge's approval. Moreover, the concept of priorities outlined in the final paper was applied to the AID program in Vietnam, with each activity being placed in one of the categories of priority. This did not result, however, in the original objective of reducing the size of the program and focusing it: instead, the AID program more than doubled in 1967, and a year later people were still complaining about the lack of clear-cut priorities. (As a matter of fact, when Deputy Ambassador Eugene Locke returned to Washington in September of 1967 with a "Blueprint for Vietnam," he was told that it lacked any sense of priorities, and was too much of a "shopping list.")

The "Roles and Missions" Study Group -- One of the Priority Task Force recommendations was that the Mission should establish another group to examine the question of the proper role of each military and paramilitary and police and civilian force in the country. This group was set up, under the chairmanship of Colonel George Jacobson in July of 1966, and submitted its final

report to the Mission Council on August 24. The group was once again
interagency, and it produced a paper of considerable value -- indeed, a
paper which could well have served as a basic policy document for the
Mission and Washington.

The Study Group made 81 recommendations, of which 66 were acceptable
to all agencies of the Mission. But even these 66 were not immediately
adopted as basic doctrine. Because of inertia and weariness, rather than
deliberate sabotage, the recommendations were never treated as basic policy,
and simply were carried out or not depending on the drive and desire of the
individual officials associated with each individual recommendation.

The report began, as almost all Vietnam studies seem to, with a definition:

"Revolutionary Development consists of those military
and civil efforts designed to liberate the population of
South Vietnam from communist coercion; to restore public
security; to initiate economic and political development;
to extend effective GVN authority throughout SVN; and to
win the willing support of the people to these ends." 28/

From there it developed the most logical and coherent approach to returning an area to GVN control and then gaining its support that had yet
been produced by a group in either the Mission or Washington. The report
was hailed by Porter, by Komer, and by various mid-level officials. Jacobson
himself was to be named Mission Coordinator four months later, a position
from which he could present his ideas directly to the Ambassadors.

While, as mentioned above, the recommendations were never issued as
Mission policy in a group, many of them found their way into the main
stream of the Mission through other means. Some of the more controversial
ones -- for example: "that Division be removed from the RD Chain of Command" -- remained as potent ideas to be discussed within the government and
with the Vietnamese, and to be acted on slowly.

Since the report foreshadowed several major developments in pacification, and since it still has today an intrinsic value of its own, it is
worth quoting some of its major points:

"High hopes are now pinned on the RD cadre, as the critical element of success in RD. Unfortunately, there is a
real danger it is being regarded as a panacea with curative
powers it does not, of and by itself, possess. The introduction of RD Cadre cannot alone achieve success in any of
the tasks discussed above. Even cadre such as may be available in six months...cannot compensate for the current fail-
ings and limitations of other fundamental elements bearing
directly on the RD process.

"...RD demands for its success radical reform within
the GVN including its Armed Forces. This reform must start

at the top...These radical changes in the GVN and RVNAF
seem most unlikely to occur without a strong, focused and
coordinated exertion of U.S. influence at high levels...

RECOMMEND: -- That FWMAF give increased emphasis to improving the performance and conduct of GVN military forces
through combined operations...

      -- That as the increase in FWMAF strength permits,
these forces engage with RVNAF in clearing operations in
support of RD with the primary objective of improving the
associated GVN forces...

      -- That in view of the deployment and capabilities
of FWMAF in Vietnam and recognizing the necessity for increased
security support to RD, the bulk of ARVN Divisional combat
battalions be assigned to Sector commanders with only those
Divisional battalions not so assigned to be under the control
of Divisions...

      -- That the Division be removed from the RD chain
of command...

      -- That Ranger units because of their frequently
intolerable conduct toward the populace, be disbanded with
individual Rangers reassigned * ...

      -- That RF and PF become Provincial and District
Constabulary...

      -- That the Constabulary be placed under the
Ministry of RD...

      -- That National Police (Special Branch) assume
primary responsibility for the destruction of the VC "infrastructure"...

      -- That Police Field Force be integrated into the
Constabulary...

      -- That the Vietnamese Information Service (VIS)
terminate its rural information cadre operations and assume
a supporting role...for RD Cadre, technical cadre, and hamlet
officials..." 29/

---

* This was a recommendation which MACV particularly opposed, arguing
that it "would seriously reduce ARVN combat strength." Westmoreland
added that he could not countenance the disbanding of units which had
just received a Presidential Unit Citation.

And so on. What lay behind each recommendation was an effort to unify the various GVN agencies and ministries working on pacification, streamline their operations, and, at the same time, increase U.S. influence over those operations.

While many items the Study Group recommended have still not been carried out, there has been growing acceptance of the bulk of the recommendations. In its initial reaction to the paper, MACV's Chief of Staff wrote to Ambassador Lodge "that many actions have been taken or are being considered by MACV which support and complement the overall objectives envisioned by the report. There are, however, certain recommendations with which we do not agree." 30/

The most important reservation that MACV had, concerned the allocation of resources for the RD effort:

"We are confronted with a determined, well-organized force operating in regimental and division strength. As long as this situation exists, it is imperative that the regular military forces retain first priority for the available manpower. Once the threat of the enemy's regular forces has diminished and the defeat of external aggression is accomplished, then other programs should have the first priority for recruiting...

In addition, MACV opposed the removal of Division from the RD chain of command; suggested a further task force to examine the Constabulary issue in detail; and opposed the suggestion that Special Branch Police -- which meant on the American side the CIA -- take over the anti-infrastructure effort. (On this latter point, the issue was finally resolved by an ingenious compromise structure under Westmoreland and Komer called ICEX -- Intelligence Coordination and Exploitation -- in July 1967.) Finally, Westmoreland rejected any internal changes in the MACV structure, as suggested by the Study Group. These had included:

" -- the establishment at MACV Division advisory level of a Deputy Senior Advisor for RD, at Corps a Deputy Senior Advisor for RD, and at COMUSMACV level a Deputy COMUSMACV for the entire MACV advisory effort and for RD...

" -- changes in the advisory rating system to emphasize the quality of the advice and the accuracy of reports, rather than the performance of the organization/Vietnamese they advise..." 31/

. USAID reacted favorably to the study. In his memo to Lodge, the Acting USAID Director said that the report "presents an antidote to our having been too indulgent with the GVN in the past to our peril and theirs." Once again, however, as with MACV, USAID added some reservations -- and the reservations all fell in areas in which USAID would have the action responsibility if something was to be done. USAID feared that the report recommended steps that would give the Ministry of RD too much strength, reflecting the worry of their Public Safety Division. The Constabulary recommendations, which had far-reaching implications, were given a particularly rough going-over. For example, to protect its own embryonic structure, the Police Field Force USAID made the following comment on the recommendation that the PFF be integrated as units into the Constabulary:

"USAID concurs with the reservation that PFF remain a separate entity with its essential police powers." 32/

The CIA also thought the report was "constructive and helpful," but listed a few "disagreements." Once again, these pertained to those items in which the ICA had a strong vested interest. They opposed strenuously, for example, the suggestion that the MACV subsector advisor -- the only American at the district level in almost every district -- "be given primary responsibility for monitoring the activities of the cadre." Using the argument that everything possible be done to retain the civilian nature of the cadre, the CIA refused to let the MACV subsector advisors do what they were already doing in many cases.

The CIA and MACV both opposed the suggestion that a single Director of Intelligence be appointed to command civilian and military intelligence structures. The CIA said that this was "unwieldly and unworkable" because "this is not a theater of war." 33/

The Political Section of the Embassy also thought the study was "valuable," but added that "it appears to neglect a number of political considerations." Beyond that, they supported every specific suggestion, while noting how hard it would be to carry some of them out.

JUSPAO shared the fears of USAID that the report would concentrate more power in the hands of the Ministry of RD than it could usefully employ. JUSPAO thought that the Constabulary should be created, therefore, but placed under the Ministry of Defense. JUSPAO also found the removal of the Division from the RD chain of command "hardly feasible or realistic at this juncture" -- begging the issue of whether or not the United States should seek this as a valuable objective.

When the exercise was over, there were many in the Mission in Saigon who felt that the Study Group recommendations should have formed a blueprint for action throughout the Mission. They pointed out that almost all the recommendations were concurred in by every agency, and that these could be carried out immediately. The remaining 15 which were still not unanimously accepted could then be discussed and perhaps resolved.

In Washington, at least one high official, R.W. Komer, felt the same way, and urged the Mission to use the recommendations as policy. But somewhere between August 24, when the paper was submitted, and the end of 1966, the paper was relegated to the useful but distinctly secondary role of another "study group," as its name suggests. While everyone was

complimentary about the paper, no machinery was set up in Ambassador
Porter's office to oversee the implementation of the recommendations.
While the agencies said that they agreed with most of the recommendations,
the all-important decisions as to how fast and how hard to push forward with
each recommendation was left to whichever agency "had the action" on it.
This in effect left some crucial decisions -- the variables in our effort --
outside the Deputy Ambassador's hands. He had no machinery for checking to
see what the agencies were doing to carry out the suggestions they said they
agreed with. He had virtually no staff to observe how the agencies were
actually handling each problem, although it was obvious that success or
failure on each item lay to a large extent in the method it was handled.
Indeed, Porter had no good way to even find out whether the agencies really
did accept the recommendations. He was reliant on a knowledgeable but small
staff which could only meddle in the internal matters of other agencies
to a limited degree.

It was these shortcomings in the new mandate to Porter that were becoming evident in the late summer of 1966, and pressure began to build
in Washington for another reorganization.

The pressure and emphasis on pacification was also producing visible
results in MACV. On August 8, 1966, the J-3 of MACV, Major General Tillson,
briefed the Mission Council on how MACV intended to "give maximum support
to RD." The briefing was general, simplistic, and shallow, but it was a
clear indication that General Westmoreland and MACV were beginning to respond to the pressure from outside their command that they should give
RD more support. As such, it marked a major step for MACV. Tillson said
that "military operations must be used to assure the security necessary
for RD to begin. All military operations are designed towards this goal..."

He then went on to trace the degree to which criticism of ARVN was justified, and examine the suggestion that ARVN be re-oriented to support RD --
something which was to become part of the Manila communique only two months
later:

"The ARVN has been at war continuously for a period of
over ten years...The fact that ARVN today even exists as an
organized fighting force is a tribute to its stamina and
morale.

"Since its inception, ARVN has been oriented, trained,
and led towards the task of offensive operations...It is difficult, in a short period of time, to redirect the motivation
and training of years, and to offset the long indoctrination
that offensive action against the VC is the reason for the
existence of the Army...

"In the 1967 campaign plan, we propose to assign ARVN
the primary mission of providing direct support to RD and
US/FW Forces the primary mission of destroying VC/NVA main
forces and base areas. Agreement has been reached between

General Westmoreland and General Vien that, in I, II and III
Corps areas, ARVN will devote at least 50% of its effort
directly in support of the RD program. In IV Corps, where
there are no U.S. forces, it was agreed that ARVN might have
to devote up to 75% of its effort to offensive operations...

"/General Vien has issued a directive that/ flatly states
that, while some progress has been made, desired results
are still lacking on RD. It emphasizes that RD efforts
must be on a par with efforts to destroy the enemy...These
directives of General Vien resulted from his conversations
with General Westmoreland..." 34/ /Emphasis Added/

This was by far the strongest verbal support that MACV had ever given
pacification, and it actually contained the kernel which developed into
the important passage in the Manila communique that committed the RVNAF
to support of RD.

The change in mood in Saigon among the Americans was reflected by
Ambassador Lodge in his Weekly NODIS to the President. On August 31, 1966,
he began his cable with:

"The biggest recent American event affecting Vietnam
was giving pacification the highest priority which it has
ever had -- making it, in effect, the main purpose of all
our activities...

"The above was brought about in several ways -- by word
in General Westmoreland's "Concept of Military Operations
in South Vietnam" of August 24, and by the deeds of the U.S.
1st and 25th Divisions and the III MAF. There has also been
the new MACV proposal to revamp ARVN and turn it into a
force better suited to pacification. Also at a special
meeting of the Mission Council a stimulating paper was presented by the "Interagency Roles and Mission Study Group"
which would take RF and PF, now a part of the Vietnamese
Armed Forces, make them into a "constabulary" and call it
that. Police Field Force would also be included in the
Constabulary under this concept." 35/

A week earlier, Westmoreland had sent forward to CINCPAC and JCS a
broad strategy statement for the coming year. He saw the time as "appropriate in light of the fact that we are on the threshold of a new phase
in the conflict resulting from recent battlefield successes and from the
continuing FWMAF buildup." After reviewing the course of battle since
the introduction of U.S. troops, Westmoreland projected his strategy over
the period until May 1, 1967, as "a general offensive with maximum practical support to area and population security in further support of RD."
He then added:

"The growing strength of US/FW Forces will provide the
shield and will permit ARVN to shift its weight of effort
to an extent not heretofore feasible to direct support of
RD. Also, I visualize that a significant number of US/FW
maneuver battalions will be committed to tactical areas of
responsibility (TAOR) missions. These missions encompass
base security and at the same time support RD by spreading
security radially from the bases to protect more of the
population...

"The priority effort of ARVN forces will be in direct
support of the RD program; in many instances the province
chief will exercise operational control over these units...
This fact notwithstanding, the ARVN division structure must
be maintained..." 36/

This long message, with its "new look" emphasis on pacification, was
sent apparently not for CINCPAC's routine consideration, as would be the
normal case in the military chain of command, but for the edification of
high-ranking civilian leaders in Washington. It ended with a comment
added by Ambassador Lodge -- an unusual procedure in a military message:

"I wish to stress my agreement with the attention paid
in this message to the importance of military support for
RD. After all, the main purpose of defeating the enemy
through offensive operations against the main forces and
bases must be to provide the opportunity through RD to get
at the heart of the matter, which is the population of SVN." 37/

The new emphasis on RD/pacification was thus coming from many sources
in the late summer of 1966. Porter and Komer, pushing the civilians
harder than they had ever been pushed before, had not only improved their
performance, but also to create pressures inside MACV for greater emphasis on RD. Westmoreland, responding to the pressure, and finding the
VC/NVA increasingly reluctant to give battle, was planning a two-pronged
strategy for late 1966-early 1967: attack and destroy enemy base areas,
and use more forces to protect and build up and expand the GVN population
centers.

D. The Single Manager

By the late summer of 1966, as has been shown in detail in the preceding
sections, the flaws in the structure of the U.S. Mission had been openly
criticized in studies or reports by the U.S. Army Staff (in PROVN), by
the Priorities Task Force and by the Roles and Missions Study Group in
Saigon, by Robert Komer in repeated memoranda, and by various other visitors
and observers. In addition to the written record, there were undoubtedly
numerous private comments being made both in Saigon and Washington, some
of which were reaching senior officials of the government.

The options before the USG were, in broad outline, fourfold. The Mission
could either remain unchanged, or else it could reorganize along one of
the three general lines which Komer had outlined in his August 7, 1966
memorandum:

    Alternative One -- Put Porter in charge of all advisory and
                       pacification activities, including the
                       military;

    Alternative Two -- Unify the civilian agencies into a single
                        civilian chain of command, and strengthen
                        the military internally -- but leave civilian
                        and military separate;

    Alternative Three -- Assign responsibility for pacification to
                         Westmoreland and MACV, and put the civilians
                         in the field under his command.

The Mission, as usual, argued for leaving the structure the way it was.
Their arguments in this direction were unfortunate, because in Washington
the mood was certainly in favor of some further changes, and by resisting
all suggestions uniformly, the Mission was simply causing friction with
Washington and reducing influence on the ultimate decisions.

The issue was joined more rapidly than anyone in Saigon had expected,
because in mid-September, 1966, the Secretary of Defense weighed in on the
issue in a direct way, producing a Draft Presidential Memorandum which
advocated handing over responsibility for pacification to COMUSMACV.

McNamara's draft said:

"Now that a Viet Cong victory in South Vietnam seems to
have been thwarted by our emergency actions taken over the
past 18 months, renewed attention should be paid to the
longer-run aspects of achieving an end to the war and building a viable nation in South Vietnam.

"Central to success, both in ending the war and in winning
the peace, is the pacification program. Past progress in

pacification has been negligible. Many factors have contributed, but one major reason for this lack of progress had been the existence of split responsibility for pacification on the U.S. side. For the sake of efficiency -- in clarifying our concept, focusing our energies, and increasing the output we can generate on the part of the Vietnamese -- this split responsibility on the U.S. side must be eliminated.

"We have considered various alternative methods of consolidating the U.S. pacification effort. The best solution is to place those activities which are primarily part of the pacification program, and all persons engaged in such activities, under COMUSMACV...In essence, the reorganization would result in the establishment of a Deputy COMUSMACV for Pacification who would be in command of all pacification staffs in Saigon and of all pacification activities in the field.

"It is recognized that there are many important aspects of the pacification problem which are not covered in this recommendation, which should be reviewed subsequent to the appointment of the Deputy COMUSMACV for Pacification to determine whether they should be part of his task -- for example, the psychological warfare campaign, and the Chieu Hoi and refugee programs. Equally important, is the question of how to encourage a similar management realignment of the South Vietnamese side, since pacification is regarded as primarily a Vietnamese task. Also not covered by this recommendation are important related national programs...Finally, there is the question of whether any organizational modification in Washington is required by the recommended change in Vietnam.

"I recommend that you approve the reorganization described in this memorandum as a first essential step toward giving a new thrust to pacification. Under Secretary Ball, Administrator Gaud, the Joint Chiefs of Staff, Director Helms, Director Marks, and Mr. Komer concur in this recommendation." 38/

This memorandum was apparently never sent to the President, but it was distributed, with a request for comments and concurrence, to Ball (Rusk being out of the country), Gaud, the JCS, Helms, Marks, and Komer. Only Komer and the JCS concurred, with the others producing alternate suggestions. The entire question was handled as an "EYES ONLY" matter.

The positions that were taken were:

State opposed the recommendation. In informal discussions with Komer, Alexis Johnson cited the failure of Hop Tac (which seems irrelevant), the

TOP SECRET - Sensitive

"optics" of militarizing the effort, and the need to check with Lodge as reasons against actions. 39/

AID agreed that the present program had its faults, but resisted the idea of a MACV takeover. Instead, they proposed a complex system of committees and deputies for RD, who would report to a Deputy Ambassador for Pacification. 40/

The JCS found that the proposal "provides an excellent rationale for an approach to the problem of appropriately integrating the civil and military effort in the important field of pacification" and concurred in the idea of a Deputy COMUSMACV for RD. 41/

CIA and USIA both opposed the reorganization, although their written comments are not in the files. 42/

Komer weighed in with a lengthy rationale supporting the idea. Although he may not have known it at the time, he was talking about the organizational structure he was going to fit into later. After agreeing that the need to get pacification moving was great, and that "the military are much better set up to manage a huge pacification effort," he said that 60-70% of "real job of pacification is providing local security. This can only be done by the military..." Komer then raised some additional points:

1. The Ambassador should remain in overall charge.

2. MACV should not assume responsibility for everything, only the high payoff war-related activities.

3. Logistic support should remain a multi-agency responsibility. 43/

As the discussions on the subject continued, Deputy Ambassador Porter arrived in the United States for a combined business-personal trip. When he found out what was being considered, he immediately made strong representations to McNamara, Komer, and Rusk. He also sent a personal cable back to Lodge, alerting him for the first time to what was afoot in Washington:

"Principal topic under discussion here is DOD proposal to bring both U.S. military and U.S. civilian resources needed to advance RD program under direction of Deputy COMUSMACV. This plan will be discussed with you during McNamara visit. It would detach all civilian field operations from direct control of Saigon civilian agencies and would place them under Deputy COMUSMACV for RD. In addition to controlling civilian field resources, latter would also manage U.S. military resources with view to increasing their effectiveness in furthering RD programs. Deputy COMUSMACV would be responsible to Ambassador or Deputy Ambassador through COMUSMACV. This at least is my understanding of proposal which is being strongly pushed here.

93   TOP SECRET - Sensitive

"I have taken position that this proposal and certain
counter proposals put forward by civilian agencies here
require careful field study. In its existing form, as
I understand it, it does not take into account the fact
that militarization of our approach to this important
civilian program runs counter to our aim of de-militarizing
GVN through constitutional electoral process...

"I have been stressing here that our military are already heavily loaded with responsibility for achieving
military measures required to further civilian RD programs,
such as evoking adequate cooperation from RVN...I have
emphasized need for MACV to grapple with problem of VC
guerrilla activity during night, as distinct from main
force activity during daytime which we now know can be
dealt with. These areas would appear to offer great possibilities for application of military talent and I repeat
that in my view question of burdening MACV further with
complex programs (cadre, police, etc.) requires careful
field study which I would have done promptly, if you agree,
by group similar to that which carried out 'Roles and Missions'
study." 44/

This was the background as Secretary McNamara, Under Secretary Katzenbach,
General Wheeler, and Mr. Komer went to Saigon in October. The issue had
been deferred, and when the visitors returned, they would make recommendations to the President. Katzenbach, making his first trip as Under Secretary,
was requested to look at the problem with a new eye and no prior prejudices.

When they came back from Saigon, Katzenbach and McNamara both sent the
President an important memorandum. Katzenbach argued for a strengthening
of Ambassador Porter's role, and a deferral of the question of turning
the RD effort over to MACV. McNamara concurred, but with a different emphasis. The memorandums were dated October 14 and 15, 1966, less than two
weeks before the Manila conference, and the recommendations were accepted
by the President. Katzenbach's memorandum was, for a first effort after
a short VIP trip, an unusually interesting one. Excerpts:

"...I believe decisive, effective RD depends on a clear
and precise common understanding of the security as we all
recognize to be the foundation of success in the 'other
war.'

"To illustrate the divergency of meanings, let me report
briefly on a conversation I had with a small group of reporters
in Saigon. It quickly degenerated into a debate, not between
the reporters and me, but between Ward Just of the Washington
Post and Charles Mohr of the New York Times.

"Just argued heatedly that RD could not begin to be effective unless security were first guaranteed both to the peasants

and to RD workers. 'An AID man cannot do his job,' he said, 'while being shot at by the VC.'

"Mohr responded just as heatedly, that security could not come first -- because security from guerrillas is meaningless and impossible until the peasant population is motivated to support the GVN and deprive the guerrillas of havens, secrecy, and resources.

"Obviously, the easy answer to this circular chicken-egg debate is to say that both are necessary -- military protection and public motivation against the VC. And yet even that answer is incomplete for it defines security only in the American frame of reference...

"I know of no one who believes we have begun effectively to achieve the goal of gaining the population's active support, despite a series of pacification programs and despite even the budding early efforts of Ambassador Porter's new program.

"The Military Aspect. Secretary McNamara, Mr. Komer, Ambassadors Johnson, Lodge, and Porter, Mr. Gaud, I, and all others who have approached the problem are perfectly agreed that the military aspect of RD has been spindly and weak." 45/

* * * * * * *

"This probably is the result of the entirely understandable preoccupation by MACV in recent months with the main force military emergency. However justifiable this has been, a major effect has nonetheless been our failure effectively to press RVNAF to even start meeting their crucial RD responsibilities.

"(I know of no one who believes that these should be met principally by American forces -- unless we should wish the whole RD effort to collapse once we leave.)

"The Civil Aspect. Similarly, the work of civilian agencies has fallen short -- largely, but not only because of the failure of RVNAF to provide a military screen behind which to work...

"Rather than engage in a civil-military debate, I think we should devote our efforts toward trying to devise an administrative structure that capitalizes on the assets each agency can offer to RD.

"What should be the elements of an ideal organization?

"1. It should have maximum leverage on RVNAF to engage in clear and hold operations in direct support of RDM efforts.

"2. It should have a single American "negative," anti-VC channel -- that is a single commander for all action against communist guerrilla forces. This commander would calibrate and choose among the various force alternatives -- depending on whether he believed the need to be military, para-military, or police.

"This command would include complete responsibility for all anti-VC intelligence -- that is, concerning all VC suspects either in the infrastructure or in guerrilla units.

"3. It should have a single, unified channel for all 'positive' pro-people aspects of RD, irrespective of the present lines of command within civilian agencies, allowing a single commander to calibrate and assign priorities to relevant positive programs on behalf of the peasantry.

"This, too, would include the immediate expansion of and control over all 'pro-people' intelligence -- that is, detailed district-by-district and province-by-province reporting on the particular gains most wanted by the populace (land reform, for example, in one province; or schools in another; or agricultural assistance in another).

"4. Sensitivity to political inputs and wise political guidance of the whole process are needed to ensure that military programs support rather than negate efforts to win public support and participation. Failure to assure this -- which characterized French efforts in Indochina and Algeria, in contrast to civil-led, successful, British efforts in Malaya and the Filipino campaign against the Huks -- means that the very process of gaining security would be weakened and prolonged, at increased cost in Vietnamese and American lives.

"Thus, overall civilian command of the RD program is needed for fundamental practical reasons, by no means for considerations of international image alone (though on the latter point, it must be observed that as soon as we put 'the other war' under obvious military control, it stops being the other war). In particular, it is, important not to block or reverse -- by the way we organize our efforts -- the current genuinely hopeful Vietnamese trend toward increased civilian influence and participation in government.

"In short, it is not the precise form of organization or the precise choice of flow chart that is important. What is important is:

"1. An immediate and effective military screen for RD efforts; and

"2. Authoritative and compelling administration of the efforts of civilian agencies.

"I believe we <u>can institute</u> effective administration of the RD program -- which Ambassador Lodge has aptly described as the heart of the matter -- achieving all of these ideals:

"1. Maintain the effect and the appearance of civilian control by immediately assigning overall supervision of all RD activities to Ambassador Porter (and assigning a second deputy to Ambassador Lodge to absorb the substantial other responsibilities now met by Ambassador Porter).

"2. That the several civilian lines of command within agencies be consolidated into one. Thus, USAID, JUSPAO, OSA, and the Embassy personnel assigned to RD all would continue under the nominal <u>administrative</u> control of their respective agencies but full, unified <u>operational</u> control would rest solely with Ambassador Porter.

"3. That Ambassador Porter's authority be made clear and full to each constituent agency of the RD team, including:

-- relocation of personnel;

-- the establishment of priorities irrespective of agency priorities;

-- and the apportionment of the funds allocated by each agency to Viet-Nam, bounded only by statutory limitations.

"4. That MACV immediately give highest-level command focus and consolidation to its RD concerns and staff, now that it is no longer so completely distracted from RD by the compelling requirements of main force combat. This would be organized around the thesis that the central need is the most effective persuasive power or leverage on RVNAF. This thesis is strengthened substantially by:

-- The firm intent, expressed to us in Saigon last week, of President Thieu and Prime Minister Ky to shift ARVN infantry to revolutionary development work starting in January;

-- The enhanced powers they intend to give to General Thang, already an able chief of RD for GVN.

"5. That the MACV effort embrace at least advisory control over all levels of force -- starting with ARVN but also including RF, PF, CIDG, and the para-military operations of the RD cadre, PFF, and PRV.

"These steps would greatly strengthen both the military and civil lines of command. They would contribute significantly to the success of RD. But not even these changes would be decisive without a strong link between them.

"The civil side requires the capacity to influence military movement which no organizational chart can provide. The MACV side requires the political and substantive expertise which a military organization does not -- and is not expected to -- possess.

"Thus the fundamental recommendation I would make is:

"6.   To appoint, as principal deputy and executive officer to Ambassador Porter, a general of the highest possible ability and stature -- of two, three or even four-star rank. To do so would win the following advantages:

"a.   Compelling indication of the seriousness with which the Administration regards RD.

"b.   The rank, and stature to insure optimum RD performance from MACV.

"c.   The rank and stature to afford maximum impact on GVN military leaders and capacity to persuade them properly to prod RVNAF when necessary.

"d.   Demonstrated command administrative capacities with which to assist Ambassador Porter, while bridging the inevitable institutional difficulties that might well otherwise develop from one arm of MACV's taking orders from a civilian.

"e.   A solution to the military control image problem, by which the advantages of close military support would be veiled by civilian control.

"f.   The capacity and position to formulate an effective qualitative plan encompassing both military and civil realities. Previous plans have focused on numbers of provinces, volume of RD cadre trained, and so on. They have put an unrealistic premium on quantitative, "statistical" success. Meaningful criteria, however, must be qualitative. I would envision such a qualitative plan intended to cover at least the next 12 months.

"There would be an additional prospective advantage as well. If it should later be found that dual lines of authority -- even given this strong link -- are not successful, then we could more readily fall back to a unitary, military command structure -- with the new RD general taking charge.

"He would have the benefit, in that situation, of having been under civilian control and his relationship to RD would already be evident, making the change to military control less abrupt and less susceptible to criticism." 46/

Secretary McNamara's memorandum -- sent the day before Katzenbach's -- was of greater importance, and stands out as one of the most far-reaching and thoughtful documents in the files. While this study concentrates on pacification, it is necessary to view McNamara's remarks about pacification in this memorandum within the context of the entire paper.

He said that the military situation had gone "somewhat better" than he had anticipated a year earlier, and that "we have by and large blunted the communist military initiative." But he found little cause for hope that the overall situation would turn dramatically in our favor within the next two years. "I see no reasonable way to bring the war to an end soon," he said, and described the enemy strategy as one of "keeping us busy and waiting us out (a strategy of attriting our national will)."

"Pacification is a basic disappointment. We have good grounds to be pleased by the recent elections, by Ky's 16 months in power, and by the faint signs of development of national political institutions and of a legitimate civil government. But none of this has translated itself into political achievements at Province level or below. Pacification has, if anything, gone backward..."

Thus, the Secretary found us "no better, and if anything worse off -- from the point of view of the important war (for the complicity of the people)."

He did not think at that time that major increases in U.S. force levels or bombing programs would make a big difference in the short run. Rather, he suggested a series of actions designed to emphasize to Hanoi that we were setting definite limits on the cost in men and money of the war, while settling down for the long haul -- "a posture that makes trying to 'wait us out' less attractive." His strategy was "five-pronged."

First, he suggested that we stabilize U.S. force levels in Vietnam, "barring a dramatic change in the war." The limit he proposed was the 470,000 total then under consideration. (CINCPAC had requested 570,000 by end 1967). This limit would "put us in a position where negotiations would be more likely to be productive, but if they were not we could pursue the all-important pacification task with proper attention and resources and without the spectre of apparently endless escalation of U.S. deployments."

Second, he recommended a barrier near the DMZ and "across the trails of Laos."

Third, he suggested that we "stabilize the Rolling Thunder program against the North." He thus recommended against the increase in the level

99

of bombing and the broader target systems that the JCS was then requesting.
Again, his reason was to "remove the prospect of ever-escalating bombing
as a factor complicating our political posture and distracting from the
main job of pacification in South Vietnam."

Fourth, he said, we should "pursue a vigorous pacification program."

"The large-unit operations war, which we know best how to
fight and where we have had our successes, is largely irrelevant to pacification as long as we do not lose it. By and
large, the people in rural areas believe that the GVN when
it comes will not stay but that the VC will; that cooperation with the GVN will be punished by the VC; that the GVN
is really indifferent to the people's welfare; that the low-
level GVN are tools of the local rich; and that the GVN is
ridden with corruption.

"Success in pacification depends on the interrelated
functions of providing physical security, destroying the
VC apparatus, motivating the people to cooperate, and establishing responsive local government. An obviously necessary
but not sufficient requirement for success of the RD cadre
and police is vigorously conducted and adequately prolonged
clearing operations by military troops who will 'stay' in
the area, who behave themselves decently and who show respect for the people.

"This elemental requirement of pacification has been
missing. In almost no contested area designated for pacification in recent years have ARVN forces actually 'cleared
and stayed' to a point where cadre teams, if available, could
have stayed overnight in hamlets and survived, let alone
accomplish their mission...

"Now that the threat of a communist main-force military victory has been thwarted by our emergency efforts,
we must allocate far more attention and a portion of the
regular military forces (at least half of ARVN and perhaps
a portion of the U.S. forces) to the task of providing an
active and permanent security system behind which the RD
teams and police can operate and behind which the political
struggle with the VC infrastructure can take place.

"The U.S. cannot do this pacification security job for
the Vietnamese. All we can do is 'massage the heart.' For
one reason, it is known that we do not intend to stay; if
our efforts worked at all, it would merely postpone the
eventual confrontation of the VC and GVN infrastructures.
The GVN must do the job, and I am convinced that drastic
reform is needed if the GVN is going to be able to do it.

"The first essential reform is in the attitude of GVN officials. They are generally apathetic, and there is corruption high and low. Often appointments, promotions, and draft deferments must be bought; and kickbacks on salaries are common. Cadre at the bottom can be no better than the system above them.

"The second needed reform is in the attitude and conduct of the ARVN. The image of the government cannot improve unless and until the ARVN improves markedly. They do not understand the importance (or respectability) of pacification nor the importance to pacification of proper, disciplined conduct. Promotions, assignments and awards are often not made on merit, but rather on the basis of having a diploma, friends, or relatives, or because of bribery. The ARVN is weak in dedication, direction and discipline.

"Not enough ARVN are devoted to area and population security, and when the ARVN does attempt to support pacification, their actions do not last long enough; their tactics are bad despite U.S. prodding (no aggressive small-unit saturation patrolling, hamlet searches, quick-reaction contact, or offensive night ambushes); they do not make good use of intelligence; and their leadership and discipline are bad.

"Furthermore, it is my conviction that a part of the problem undoubtedly lies in bad management on the American as well as the GVN side. Here split responsibility -- or 'no responsibility' -- has resulted in too little hard pressure on the GVN to do its job and no really solid or realistic planning with respect to the whole effort. We must deal with this management problem now and deal with it effectively.

"One solution would be to consolidate all U.S. activities which are primarily part of the civilian pacification program and all persons engaged in such activities, providing a clear assignment of responsibility and a unified command under a civilian relieved of all other duties. (If this task is assigned to Ambassador Porter, another individual must be sent immediately to Saigon to serve as Ambassador Lodge's deputy.) Under this approach, there would be a carefully delineated division of responsibility between the civilian-in-charge and an element of COMUSMACV under a senior officer, who would give the subject of planning for and providing hamlet security the highest priority in attention and resources. Success will depend on the men selected for the jobs on both sides (they must be among the highest rank and most competent administrators in the U.S. Government), on complete cooperation among the U.S.

101

---

elements, and on the extent to which the South Vietnamese can be shocked out of their present pattern of behavior. The first work of this reorganized U.S. pacification organization should be to produce within 60 days a realistic and detailed plan for the coming year.

"From the political and public-relations viewpoint, this solution is preferable -- if it works. But we cannot tolerate continued failure. If it fails after a fair trial, the only alternative in my view is to place the entire pacification program -- civilian and military -- under General Westmoreland. This alternative would result in the establishment of a Deputy COMUSMACV for Pacification who would be in command of all pacification staffs in Saigon and of all pacification staffs and activities in the field; one person in each corps, province and district would be responsible for the U.S. effort."

"(It should be noted that progress in pacification, more than anything else, will persuade the enemy to negotiate or withdraw.)"

Fifth, the Secretary recommended a renewed effort to get negotiations started, by taking steps "to increase our credibility" with Hanoi, by considering a shift in the pattern of our bombing program considering the possibility of cessation of bombing, by trying to "split the VC off from Hanoi," and by "developing a realistic plan providing a role for the VC in negotiations, postwar life, and government of the nation."

His summation was somber. While repeating his prediction that the next two years would not see a satisfactory conclusion by either large-unit action or negotiations, McNamara advocated pursuing both routes although "we should recognize that success from them is a mere possibility, not a probability."

"The solution lies in girding, openly, for a longer war and in taking actions immediately which will in 12 to 18 months give clear evidence that the continuing costs and risks to the American people are acceptably limited, that the formula for success has been found, and that the end of the war is merely a matter of time. All of my recommendations will contribute to this strategy, but the one most difficult to implement is perhaps the most important one -- enlivening the pacification program. The odds are less than even for this task, if only because we have failed so consistently since 1961 to make a dent in the problem. But, because the 1967 trend of pacification will, I believe, be the main talisman of ultimate U.S. success or failure in Vietnam, extraordinary imagination and effort should go into changing the stripes of that problem.

102

The memorandum closed with a comment on the thoughts of Thieu and Ky:

"They told me that they do not expect the enemy to negotiate or to modify his program in less than two years. Rather,
they expect the enemy to continue to expand and to increase
his activity. They expressed agreement with us that the key
to success is pacification and that so far pacification has
failed. They agree that we need clarification of GVN and
U.S. roles and that the bulk of the ARVN should be shifted
to pacification. Ky will, between January and July 1967,
shift all ARVN infantry divisions to that role. And he is
giving Thang, a good Revolutionary Development director,
added powers. Thieu and Ky see this as part of a two-year
(1967-1968) schedule, in which offensive operations against
enemy main force units are continued, carried on primarily
by the U.S. and other Free World forces. At the end of the
two-year period, they believe the enemy may be willing to
negotiate or to retreat from his current course of action." 47/

McNamara's memorandum marked a strong new emphasis on pacification
by him, and the ripples that this new emphasis set off were inevitably
to spread throughout the USG, changing emphasis and official rhetoric up
and down the line. His first reactions were official: comments on his
memorandum from George Carver, Helms' Special Assistant for Vietnamese
Affairs at the CIA; and from the JCS. Carver agreed with the evaluation
of the situation, but objected to some of the recommended actions, particularly the "press for negotiations" items which he felt would be "counter-
productive." Carver made the provocative statement that he considered
the prognosis "too gloomy." If the odds for enlivening the pacification
program are indeed "less than even, present U.S. objectives in Vietnam
are not likely to be achieved."

In his memorandum, Carver took issue with McNamara on pacification.
Carver felt that "despite the errors and administrative weaknesses of present
programs, in the concept of RD we have found the right formula, a catalyst
that is potentially capable of inspiring the Vietnamese into effective
action...Serious and systematic effort in this field is really a post-
Honolulu Conference development and it would be unrealistic to expect
dramatic, readily quantifiable progress in the short span of eight months."

Carver supported the new stress on pacification, adding that he would
support "wholeheartedly" a "real reorganizational change under which the
civilian director would have a joint staff of sufficient scope to enable
him to plan, control, and direct the U.S. effort and have operational control over all -- not just civilian -- elements engaged in RD..." He opposed
a "carefully delineated division between the civilian in charge and an element of COMUSMACV under a senior officer."

"A civilian pacification structure cannot be given a 'fair trial' unless
the civilian director has the necessary authority," Carver said. "Also, the

trial will not be fair if major quantifiable results are anticipated in a matter of months."

Carver's vision of pacification rested to a large degree on the idea of gaining the active support of the population. He seemed opposed to the use of troops to merely protect terrain and the people who lived on it, saying, "If an attempt is made to impose pacification on an unengaged populace by GVN or U.S. military forces, that attempt will fail."

He concluded, as he had begun:

"We agree with Secretary McNamara's prognosis that there is little hope for a satisfactory conclusion of the war within the next two years. We do not agree that "the odds are less than even" for enlivening the pacification program. If this were true, the U.S. would be foolish to continue the struggle in Vietnam and should seek to disengage as fast as possible. We think that if we establish adequate management and control on the U.S. side and ensure that the Vietnamese follow through on redirecting their military resources as promised, there are at least fair prospects for substantial progress in pacification over the next two years." 48/

The JCS review of McNamara's memorandum was far more severe. While agreeing that "There is no reason to expect that the war can be brought soon to a successful conclusion," the Chiefs made a strong case, as usual, for increased bombing, no predetermined force ceilings, and stated several times in different ways that the war was going very well indeed -- although this same point had been made by McNamara. The Chiefs also disagreed strongly with the move for negotiations which McNamara had suggested. Any bombing pause, they said, would be regarded by Hanoi, by the GVN, and by our Allies, as "renewed evidence of lack of U.S. determination to press the war to a successful conclusion."

On pacification, the JCS "adhered to their conclusion" that "to achieve optimum effectiveness, the pacification program should be transferred to COMUSMACV. However, if for political reasons a civilian type organization should be considered mandatory by the President, they would interpose no objection.

"Nevertheless, they are not sanguine that an effective civilian-type organization can be erected, if at all, except at the expense of costly delays. As to the use of a substantial fraction of ARVN for pacification purposes, the JCS concur. However, they desire to flag that adoption of this concept will undoubtedly elicit charges of a U.S. takeover of combat operations at increased cost in American casualties." 49/

The JCS requested that their views be brought to the attention of the President.

On the record, Secretary McNamara and Under Secretary Katzenbach had
been quite frank in telling the American public that they had found pacification lagging during their October trip to Vietnam. Katzenbach said
he was "concerned" and, after emerging from the meeting with the President,
told the White House press corps that "We have to do a good deal more to
get the 'other war' moving and I think we can." 50/ Even Komer, who remained
more optimistic than McNamara and Katzenbach, was quoted as "acknowledging"
that pacification was lagging.

While "military progress has exceeded our expectations," the Defense
Secretary said, progress in pacification has "been very slow indeed." His
trip also raised fears, for the first time, in Saigon that the military
would take over the pacification effort. Thus, at almost the very moment
that the President was hearing Katzenbach's recommendation that the civilians
be reorganized and given a last chance (see previous action), Ward Just
was writing from Saigon:

> "McNamara left behind the impression that his visit to
> South Vietnam last week marked the beginning of the end of
> civilian supremacy in the American effort...

> "Sources here were saying today that McNamara, a stickler
> for detail, was unimpressed with civilian descriptions of
> progress, or lack of it, in the pacification effort. The
> American who bears most of the authority for that, Deputy
> Ambassador William C. Porter, was in the U.S. during the
> McNamara visit.

> "There has always been, as one official here put it, a
> 'military component' to pacification. But it is understood
> now that that component will be increased and the military
> will more and more take control of pacification -- the task
> called nation-building.

> "...The other likely outcome of McNamara's four days in
> Vietnam is that the role of ARVN will change.

> "Informed sources said that McNamara heard no complaints
> whatsoever from American military sources regarding the per-
> formance of the ARVN, but the fact is that he did. It has
> been an open secret in Saigon that the role of the ARVN would
> change next year. Their work would be in pacification, not
> in striking at main force units...

> "There is now increased certainty that the war effort
> despite public homage to the 'other war' and the 'hearts and
> minds of the people' is more thoroughly military than ever --
> and more thoroughly American.

> "In the end, the military is thought to have carried the
> day not by force or logic or force of wisdom, although their

position here can be argued plausibly with both logic and wisdom, but by sheer weight of what one official called the juggernaut...

"'Westmoreland says do this, do that, and something happens,' one informed observer said. 'When Lodge says do this, do that, sometimes something happens, and sometimes it doesn't happen.'

"The men here who wanted to see one ideology beaten by a better one, to see the Vietnamese character (not to mention the countryside) preserved and not submerged by the war, who viewed the struggle as an exercise in counterinsurgency, have now certainly lost...

"It remains to be seen whether the problems of Vietnam lend themselves to military solutions and whether changing conditions in this war are better handled by colonels than diplomats." 51/

Just's article was wrong, of course, since the decision to give MACV responsibility for pacification had not been made. Indeed, within a few days this fact had also leaked to the press, and stories in the New York Times, datelined Saigon, spoke of the "abortive effort" by MACV to take over the effort. But the importance of the stories was not in their accuracy or inaccuracy, but in the fact that they indicated the emotions that had been raised by the subject during and after the McNamara-Katzenbach-Komer visit. In truth, no one in Saigon, not even Lodge and Westmoreland, knew at this time what the final decision was to be. But the subject was up for discussion, and the pressure from Washington had been measurably increased.

With the McNamara and Katzenbach memoranda in hand, the President apparently indicated tentative agreements to give the civilians a short trial period to get pacification moving. Then he left for his Asian tour, which was to climax with the Seven-Nation Conference at Manila. He left behind him instructions to prepare a message to Lodge and Porter and Westmoreland, instructing them in his decision. Since the message was drafted and sent on to the President in Wellington on October 18, before Manila, but not sent on to Lodge and Porter in Saigon until November 4, after Manila, there apparently remained some uncertainty as to his decision, which was not clarified until most of the principals were united briefly in Manila. But this is of marginal importance. The fact was that the President had approved the idea of giving the civilians a final chance.

The Cable Exchange: November, 1966

By October 18, McNamara, Katzenbach, and Komer had an agreed-upon telegram for the President to send Lodge. It was forwarded to Wellington, where the President had begun his Asian tour:

"State/Defense and Komer recommend your concurrence in the general plan recommended by both Secretary McNamara and

Under Secretary Katzenbach regarding reorganization on the American side of the administration of the Revolutionary Development (RD) program in Viet-Nam. We therefore recommend that you approve our sending the following State-Defense message to Ambassador Lodge:

BEGIN TEXT

"Personal For Lodge. You have described the RD program as the heart of the matter in SVN. We agree. Also, you have reported and we agree that progress in the RD program so far has been slight and unsatisfactory. We all agree that progress must be made in this crucial area if the war is to be won in the South and if the North is to be persuaded to negotiate. It is clear to us that some organizational changes are required on the American side to get RD moving -- to bring harder pressure on the GVN to do its job and to get solid and realistic planning with respect to the whole effort.

"We had considered putting the entire program under COMUSMACV to achieve these ends; and this may ultimately prove to be the best solution. But recognizing certain objections to this approach, we are prepared to try a solution which leaves the civilian functions under civilian management. As we see it, the trial organization would involve the following changes:

"1. The several civilian lines of command within U.S. agencies would be consolidated into one. Thus, line responsibility for all personnel assigned to RD civilian functions would rest solely with one high-ranking civilian. (We presume this man would be Ambassador Porter. If so, he would have to be relieved of all other duties, and you would have to have another deputy assigned to absorb the substantial other responsibilities now met by Ambassador Porter.) The authority of this civilian would be made clear and full to each constituent agency of the civilian RD team, including relocation of personnel, the establishment of priorities irrespective of agency priorities; and the apportionment of the funds allocated for RD by each agency to Viet-Nam (bounded only by statutory limitations).

"2. To strengthen Porter administratively, it might be well to assign him a competent Principal Deputy and Executive Officer -- a military officer of two or three-star rank. If this officer is desired, General Westmoreland can supply him or, if he requests, the officer can be provided from here. This officer would not be to command U.S. military forces or operations or to perform MACV's functions of advising and prodding the ARVN, but would be to provide administrative strength on the civilian side and to serve as a bridge to MACV, ensuring efficient interface between the civilian and military structures.

107

"3. We understand General Westmoreland is already considering
a MACV Special Assistant for Pacification or a Deputy for Pacification. We presume that the appointment of such a Special
Assistant or Deputy could be timed to coincide with the changes
on the civilian side, making possible the highest-level command
focus and consolidation to MACV's RD concerns and staff.

"4. Careful definition and delineation of responsibilities of the U.S. civilian and U.S. military sides would be
necessary in the whole RD establishment in South Viet-Nam to
ensure that nothing falls between the stools and that the two
efforts fully mesh.

"We are most anxious, as we know you are, to make progress
in RD. So this new organizational arrangement would be on
trial for 90-120 days, at the end of which we would take stock
of progress and reconsider whether to assign all responsibility
for RD to COMUSMACV." 52/

As mentioned above, this cable was not repeated to Saigon until after
the Manila Conference. Presumably, in the intervening period, the President
had had a chance to talk directly to Lodge and Westmoreland about the matter,
since they were both at Manila (Porter was not). In addition, Komer had
gone from Manila back to Saigon for a week's stay, and had given Porter a
clear warning that the reorganization was impending. When he left, Komer
left behind two members of his staff to assist Porter with the planning
for the reorganization, although Porter and Lodge, for some reason not
clear today, still seemed doubtful that the reorganization Washington was
pressing on them was really necessary, and really desired by the President.

The cable -- unchanged from the text cited above -- arrived in Vietnam
on November 4, 1966. 53/ It was slugged "Literally Eyes Only for Ambassador from Secretary, SecDef, and Komer," and because Lodge decided to interpret that slug line literally, the entire process was delayed one week --
a sorry spectacle and wholly unnecessary on all counts. When Lodge answered
the cable by requesting permission to discuss it with his assistants, there
was an understandable suspicion in Washington that he was simply doing so
to delay action a little while longer. But on the other hand, the cable
had received the highest slug normally available to State Department messages -- "Literally Eyes Only" -- and Lodge could say truthfully that he
was just following instruction.

In any event, Lodge sent his answer to Washington November 6:

"I agree that progress has been 'slight and unsatisfactory' and, undoubtedly some organizational changes can be
helpful. However, before commenting on that I would like
to set out some basic considerations.

"Crux of the problem is not defective organization. It
is security. Civilian reorganization can affect progress only

indirectly, because security will remain outside civilian
purview...

"To meet this need we must make more U.S. troops available
to help out in pacification operations as we move to concentrate ARVN effort in this work. U.S. forces would be the
catalyst; would lead by example, and would work with the
Vietnamese on the 'buddy' system. They would be the 10 percent of the total force of men under arms (90 percent of whom
would be Vietnamese) which would get the whole thing moving
faster.

"This has been done on a small scale already by elements
of the U.S. Marines, 1st and 25th U.S. Infantry Divisions,
and the Koreans. We think it can be made to work and the
gains under such a program, while not flashy, would hopefully
be solid. Everything depends on whether we can change ARVN
habits. Experiments already made indicate that U.S. casualties would be few. While it would take time, it would be
clear to everyone at home that time was working for us and it
might create a 'smell of victory.' It would eventually get
at Viet Cong recruiting -- surely an achievement which would
fundamentally affect the course of the war.

"I wonder whether the above result could not be achieved
if the phrase 'offensive operations' were to be redefined so
that instead of defining it as meaning 'seek out and destroy,'
which I understand is now the case, it would be defined as
'split up the Viet Cong and keep him off balance.'

"This new definition of the phrase 'offensive operations'
would mean fewer men for the purely 'military war, fewer U.S.
casualties and more pacification.

"It would also hasten the revamping of the ARVN, which
Ky says is now due to have been completed by normal Vietnamese
bureaucratic methods by July 1967 (which seems optimistic to
me). What I propose in this telegram would in effect revamp
the ARVN by 'on-the-job-training.' It is the only way that
I can think of drastically to accelerate the present pace.

* * * * *

"The question of transferring Revolutionary Development
civilian functions to COMUSMACV raises questions and I understand you recognize certain objections. I doubt whether it
would solve any existing problems, and it would certainly
create many new ones. I agree with your second paragraph
in which you say civilian functions should be left under
civilian management.

"I agree that civilian lines of command within U.S. agencies dealing with Revolutionary Development should be consolidated under Ambassador Porter. He should take unto himself the direct operation of the five categories of manpower now in the field. I refer to USAID public safety; USAID province reps; JUSPAO; CIA and the civil functions performed by the military advisers. They would all stay exactly where they are as far as rationing, housing and administration is concerned. Porter would have the operational authority and responsibility.

"I am not clear what another Deputy Ambassador would do and advise against such an unnecessary and unwieldy structure. Ambassador Porter does not now absorb 'substantial other responsibilities' which distract his attention from revolutionary development. Administrative matters involving the U.S. Mission as a whole are handled by the Mission Coordinator, and political affairs are handled by me with close support from the political counselor. Economic affairs, in which Porter as the man responsible for revolutionary development is intimately and necessarily involved, are well covered by AID and the Economic Counselor. Public affairs not connected with field operations associated with revolutionary development are well in hand and do not take Ambassador Porter's time.

"The only 'substantial other responsibility' which Porter carries outside of RD, is to take charge in my absence. I see no need, and would find it most inappropriate, for this to be changed.

"I think there is great merit in the idea of having a high-ranking military man involved in pacification work. He should be in charge of all the military aspects of pacification -- working with ARVN and selecting, expediting, and assigning the U.S. troops who would operate as suggested in para 3 above. He should be an officer with proper knowledge of and talent for the subject and I, of course, think of General Weyand. If the decision is made by all hands to put the military into pacification as suggested in para 3, the decision as to where to place such a general should not be too difficult.

"I agree that careful definition and delineation of responsibilities of the U.S. civilian and military sides is necessary. We intend that the two efforts fully mesh.

"Clearly there is very little that can be done economically, socially, psychologically, and politically for the 'hearts and minds' of men, if these men have knives sticking into their collective bellies. The knife must first be removed. It is

not the case -- as has so often been said -- of which came
first, the hen or the egg...

*   *   *   *   *

"This is obviously not reflected in our present organization
under which, nonetheless, much has been accomplished. When
Mac Bundy told me in February, after the Vice President's visit,
of the decision to relieve Porter of all of his duties as Deputy
(except that of being Charge d'Affaires in case of my absence)
so that he could take charge of the civilian aspects of pacification, I did not at first welcome the idea. I must, however,
recognize that under Porter a real asset has been built.

"To sum up, therefore, the first priority is more U.S.
troops to be allotted to pacification as set forth in paragraph
3; the second priority is better operation and tightening up
of the present organization; thirdly, are organizational changes.

"Considering that your message was "EYES ONLY," I request
authority to discuss it and my comments and plans with the
heads of the different Mission agencies involved here. We
are all anxious to make progress in RD, and the effort will
involve all of us. It requires security and time. Whatever
the trial period may be, I suggest we maintain a constant
taking stock of progress and of problems. Lodge." 54/

Back came Washington's answer on November 12, giving Lodge permission
to discuss the matter and show the cables to Porter, Westmoreland, and
"once plans mature, inform members Mission Council." With the civilians
in Washington already feeling that their trial period was underway, they
sought to get the Mission moving faster to reorganize. The cables became
a series of hints and threats and detailed guidance. The difficulty in
communication was quite high. Thus, the November 12 cable, drafted by
Ambassador Unger and cleared with McNamara, Helms, Gaud, Komer, Marks,
Katzenbach, and Rusk, and slugged "for Ambassador from Secretary, SecDef,
and Komer," laid out for Lodge and Porter a detailed description of how
the new structure should look -- although everyone knew that the plans
had already been drawn up and were sitting on Lodge and Porter's desks
in Saigon -- and began with this warning-hint:

"Following steps need to be taken promptly if we are, in
the time available, to give adequate test to organization
which is intended to keep RD civilian functions under civilian
management, an objective to which we know you attach considerable important." 55/

The cable went on to outline the organization, and discuss the question
of the use of U.S. troops:

"...We understand General Westmoreland plans use of limited number U.S. forces in buddy system principle to guide and motivate ARVN in RD/P. However, we have serious doubts about any further involvement U.S. troops beyond that in straight pacification operations. We fear this would tempt Vietnamese to leave this work more and more to us and we believe pacification, with its intimate contact with population, more appropriate for Vietnamese forces, who must after all as arm of GVN establish constructive relations with population. Hence we believe there should be no thought of U.S. taking substantial share of pacification. The urgent need is to begin effectively pressing ARVN." 56/

In Saigon, the Mission moved slowly. Three days later, with still no answer from Saigon, the State Department sent out the following very short and curt cable:

"Personal for Lodge and Porter from the Secretary

"Ref State 83699

"REFTEL was discussed today at highest levels, who wished to emphasize that this represents final and considered decision and who expressed hope that indicated measures could be put into effect just as rapidly as possible." 57/

This produced, at last, two long answers from Lodge and Porter, which laid out what the new structure was going to look like, and added some personal comments from Lodge:

"FOR THE SECRETARY, SECDEF AND KOMER

"NODIS

    "1. This is in reply to your 83699 as amended by your 85196 concerning which General Westmoreland, Porter and I have had extensive consultation.

    "2. We will, of course, carry out your instructions just as rapidly as possible, and our planning is already far advanced.

    "3. It is very gratifying that you feel as we do on the urgent need to revamp the ARVN, on the importance of putting all civilians in the field under Porter and of having single civilian responsibility in province and corps -- measures which we have long advocated. Doubt whether we can change over night habits and organization of ARVN acquired during the last ten years. Unless our success against main force daytime activity is equalled by success against guerrillas during the night, swift improvement cannot be expected to result simply by reorganization on the U.S. civilian side. It is our ability to infuse

courage and confidence into all the Vietnamese under arms who
are involved in pacification -- both military and police --
which is at stake.

"4. As regards your instruction for a military deputy for
Porter, General Westmoreland proposes Major General Paul Smith,
who is acceptable to Porter. Porter believes General Smith should
be attached to civilian agency (State Department - Embassy Saigon)
while on this duty, along lines precedents already established.
He could wear civilian or military garb as circumstances require.

* * *

"6. General Westmoreland does not wish to have a separate
deputy for Revolutionary Development, but has nominated Brigadier
General William Knowlton as Special Assistant for Pacification.

* * *

"8. Concerning paragraph 4(c). Mission directive will state
clearly that Deputy Ambassador Porter will be primarily occupied
with RD and that other Mission business will be handled by appropriate sections of Mission. There are certain other aspects to
consider, however. Porter has assumed charge when I have been
absent. Any change in that respect could only derogate from his
position in eyes of American community and GVN. He believes, and
I concur, that his assumption of charge cannot be 'nominal' without risk of downgrading him in local eyes. Additionally, it is
essential that there be a point of decision in Mission, without
ambiguity. In practice, Porter intends to leave routine functions
of Mission (political, protocol, administrative, personnel, con-
sular, visitors, etc.) to sections normally handling them. He
expects, however, to remain closely cognizant of political developments and together with political counselor and CAS chief
to consult and decide course of action to take or recommend to
department as circumstances dictate. I believe this is reasonable approach and have full confidence in his intention to concentrate on RD.

* * *

"10. Your paragraph 5. I have always believed that Revolutionary Development/Pacification must be carried out by Vietnamese
forces, who, as you say, must establish constructive relations
with the population. I have never advocated U.S. forces taking
on 'substantial' share of this task. I do believe, however,
that an American presence in this field amounting to a very
small percentage of the total manpower involved could induce
ARVN to take the proper attitude by 'on the job' training and
could give the necessary courage and confidence to the Vietnamese. Lodge" 58/

113

"FOR THE SECRETARY, SECDEF AND KOMER

"NODIS

"1. Herewith I transmit our recommendations carrying out
your 83699 and 85196. This is the best we can do in the immediate future and we think it is a forward step. But I believe
that you may wish to change it as we advance along this untrod
path and learn more about circumstances and people. Our proposal is as follows:

"a. The establishment of an office of operations,
headed by a Director of Operations. This headquarters office
of operations will include the present staff of: (1) USAID/
Field Operations; (2) USAID/Public Safety; (3) USAID/Refugees;
(4) JUSPAO/Field Services (minus North Viet-Nam branch); (5)
CAS/Cadre Operations Division. The Office of Operations will
be organized so that the above offices will not necessarily remain intact when they are merged into a single office. For
example, I intend to disband USAID/FO's cadre office, and put
those people now representing AID on cadre affairs directly under the cadre office. Thus there may be a net saving in manpower.

"b. All other divisions of AID and JUSPAO will remain
under the control of their respective directors -- MacDonald
and Zorthian -- who will be responsible to Porter, as they are
now, for their operations. (I exempt from this the special
question of press relations, on which Zorthian will continue
to report to me directly.) Thus, for example, MacDonald will
continue to oversee to Agriculture, Education, Health, Industry,
etc., Divisions, as well as continue, along with the economic
counselor Wehrle, to be responsible for the anti-inflation efforts. The Director of USAID will be freed from responsibilities
for the field operations, but his job continues to be one of
vast importance. I think it will now become more manageable.

* * *

"d. At province level we will select a single civilian
to be in charge of all other U.S. civilians in the province,
in same way as MACV senior advisor is responsible for the military involved in the advisory effort in the province. This
senior civilian representative will be the U.S. counterpart
for civilian affairs to the VN province chief and, together with
the MACV senior advisor (sector) and the province chief, will
form the provincial coordinating committee. The practice of
assaulting the province chief with a multiplicity of advisors,
often giving conflicting advice, should cease under this arrangement. The senior civilian representative will write the efficiency reports of the American civilians in the province,

114

regardless of their parent agency, and those reports will be
reviewed by Porter's office, which will also control transfers
and assignments.

* * *

"f. At the more complex region/corps level, we will consider
a similar system, with a senior civilian representative responsible for the overall U.S. civilian effort in the corps area.
He will work with the MACV senior advisor, and will in effect
be my agent (and Bill Porter's) at the corps. I have long believed in the need for a sophisticated politically-minded man
in charge of our effort with the politically volatile corps
commanders, and this is a step in that direction. Porter and
I will be looking carefully for the best men for these four difficult jobs...

"2. I do not want another deputy Ambassador. I intend to
provide office space for Porter in the new chancery (his present
office will remain at his disposal even after he moves). There
is simply no job for another deputy Ambassador, particularly
since the present political counselor works closely with me,
reporting directly.

"3. There is no doubt that the steps mentioned above are
major ones. Clearly I cannot predict now how long they will
take to achieve, or how much disruption they will cause in their
early stages. For one thing, I feel that a physical relocation
of certain offices now spread out across the city is vital, and
we are now studying the details of how to do this. Porter will
probably need to establish his offices in a building other than
the Chancery, in order to give the office of operations a firm
guiding hand. He will, however, keep an office close to me,
and he will be kept closely informed of policy developments.

* * *

"5. I will need your personal support during the period
which lies ahead. I am sure that all hands here, regardless
of agency affiliation, will support this effort to unify the
U.S. team. The same must be true of the agencies that must continue to backstop us in Washington. Personnel recruitment will
remain in your hands, and it ultimately determines the caliber
of our efforts. Porter will send you separate messages on the
question of personnel, so that new guidance and requirements
can be put into effect as quickly as possible.

"6. We look forward through reorganization to tightening
and simplifying contacts, advice and coordination with GVN
authorities reponsible for RD. 59/

E. The Manila Conference

President Johnson arrived in Manila on October 23, 1966, to attend
the seven-nation conference of troop contributing countries to the Vietnam
war. While the meeting was hectic and short, it did produce a communique
which contained some major statements about policy, strategy, and intentions. The three most important points in the communique of October 25
were:

a. The pledge that "allied forces...shall be withdrawn, after close
consultation, as the other side withdraws its forces to the North, ceases
infiltration, and the level of violence thus subsides. Those forces will
be withdrawn as soon as possible and not later than six months after the
above conditions have been fulfilled."

b. The announcement of a new program, which had been thought up in
Washington, for "National Reconciliation." Since the GVN was not in
genuine agreement with the idea, but under great pressure from the
Americans to commit themselves to it, the communique was quite vague on
what difference there was, if any, between the new National Reconciliation program and the old Chieu Hoi program.*

c. The formalization, in public, of the move towards getting ARVN
more deeply involved with the RD program: "The Vietnamese leaders stated
their intent to train and assign a substantial share of the armed forces
to clear-and-hold actions in order to provide a shield behind which a
new society can be built." This public confirmation of the tentative
steps that MACV had been taking was important. Classified documents
could not be used as the basis for a far-reaching reform of the ARVN;
they would never have received wide enough distribution, nor would they
have been fully accepted as doctrine by the doubters within both the
RVNAF and MACV. But here was a piece of paper signed by the President
and by General Thieu which said in simple language that a new direction
and mission was given to the ARVN. After Manila, MACV and the JCS began
in seriousness the formation of the mobile training teams which were designed to retrain every RVNAF unit so that it was more aware of the
importance of the population.

---

*Those Americans who hoped that National Reconciliation would become a
major new appeal to VC at middle and higher levels were to be in for a
disappointment in the year following Manila. The GVN did not agree with
the philosophy behind total forgiveness to the enemy, and continually
hedged its statements and invitations to the VC so that they resembled
surrender with amnesty rather than "national reconciliation." In fact,
the GVN did not make an internal announcement on the National Reconciliation program until Tet, 1967, almost four months after the Manila
conference, and three months after the GVN had "promised" the U.S. that
it would make the announcement. Then, when the Vietnamese finally did
make the announcement, they used the phrase "Doan Ket," which is accurately
translated as "National Solidarity," rather than "National Reconciliation."
The difference in meaning is, of course, significant, just as the earlier
mistranslation of "Xay Dung" into "Revolutionary Development" reflected
a divergence of views.

116

The reasoning behind the move to commit more troops to the relatively static missions involved in pacification had been laid out in documents and briefings by people as varied as Major General Tillson, in his August briefings of the Mission Council (cited in Section III.C.7) and Robert Komer, in his memorandum to the President. But a key assumption underlying the new emphasis on population control was the growing belief, in late 1966, that the main force war was coming to a gradual end. No other single factor played as great a role in the decision to commit troops to pacification as the belief that they were going to be less and less needed for offensive missions against main force units. The enemy-initiated large unit action statistics showed a sharp drop all through 1966, with a low point of less than two battalion sized or larger enemy initiated actions per month in the last quarter of 1966. There was increasing talk of the "end of the big battalion war," both in the press and in the Mission. Moreover, the first big U.S. push into VC base areas was getting under way, and it was possible to believe that when operations like Junction City and Cedar Falls were completed, the VC would have few placed left to hide within the boundaries of South Vietnam. Thus, some people were arguing in late 1966 and early 1967 that the number of troops that could be committed to RD was considerably higher than the amount that General Westmoreland was then contemplating; that the "substantial number" of the Manila communique could well be over half of all ARVN. These arguments were usually made orally and tentatively, rather than in formal written papers, since they usually raised the ire of the military. When military opposition to such a large RD commitment stiffened, the suggestions of civilians were often hedged or partially withdrawn. But nonetheless, the fact remains that the undeniable success against the main forces in 1966 was the major justifying factor for those advocating increased commitment of regular units -- even some U.S. units -- to pacification. At that time, officials were less worried about the possibility of a major resurgence of the enemy than about the possibility of a new guerrilla war phase. The fighting in and near the DMZ during Operations Hastings and Prairie (August-December 1966) had been the heaviest of the war, and had been judged not only as a major defeat for the enemy but as a possible turning point for the enemy, after which he "had begun to shift some of his effort away from conventional, or 'mobile warfare,' toward the more productive (from his standpoint) guerrilla tactics." 60/ The Marines considered Hastings and Prairie a foolhardy aberration on the enemy's part, although they noted that the region of the DMZ "is remote, favoring him with interior lines and working to our disadvantage through extension of our own supply lines." 61/

The Marines felt that the enemy attacks at the DMZ had been designed primarily to draw down resources from the Marine pacification efforts near Da Nang, an interesting example of how important they thought their embryonic pacification effort was. But, the Marines added, whenever the enemy probed or patrolled, he was "pursued by Marine infantry and pounded by air, artillery, and naval gunfire. The effort cost him an estimated 5,000 to 6,000 NVA troops killed or disabled and 414 weapons lost...and meant a severe loss of prestige, and a further erosion of the morale of his troops." 62/

Thus, the slowdown in large enemy actions, according to the Marine estimate, and signs that the future would see an increase in guerrilla activity -- "Major main force and NVA formations have been relatively inactive since September, as far as large unit actions are concerned. However, by the end of December, corresponding increases were already beginning to appear in rates of guerrilla activity." 63/

To what extent other military and civilian leaders accepted the Marine assessment of enemy capability and intentions is not clear from the documents, but the mood of the time was not far removed from the sentiments cited above. The end of the "big war" was coming, and pacification was the next step. It all fueled the proponents of greater pacification efforts by regular troops, and now, after Manila, the debate was already being conducted on terrain favorable for the first time to the pro-pacification advocates.

IV. DCO TO CORDS

IV. OCO to CORDS

A. OCO on Trial: Introduction

With the cable exchange completed, except for a few minor matters, Ambassador Lodge announced the formation of the Office of Civil Operations on November 26, 1966 -- one month after the original go-ahead signal had been given in Washington, and three weeks after the cable to Lodge telling him that the President wanted rapid action. While delays of this kind are common in government and do not normally affect events, in this case the delay got OCO off to a visibly slow start despite the fact that the President had clearly indicated to Lodge and Porter that he was putting OCO on trial and would review its accomplishments in a fairly short time.

The reasons for the Mission's slow start revealed again just how far apart Washington and its representatives in Saigon were in their philosophy and approach to the war.

Washington officials consistently underestimated the difficulty of the actions they wanted the Mission to do, and continually expected movement at speeds literally beyond the capability of the Mission. They held these ambitious expectations and exerted pressure accordingly -- not primarily because of the situation in the pacification program in South Vietnam (which was fairly static), but because of growing pressure from the public, the press, and Congress for visible progress in the war, because of growing American domestic dissatisfaction with the course of the war. If the American public could not see progress in Vietnam, the support the Administration had for the war would drop steadily.

In its efforts to show progress some members of the Administration were continually interpreting statistics and events in the most favorable light possible, and its critics -- particularly the press -- were interpreting the same events in the most unfavorable light possible. Since events in Vietnam were usually open to at least two different interpretations, the gap between the Administration and its critics over the basic question of How are We Doing? grew steadily during 1966 and 1967. But beyond the disagreements over facts and statistics, there was a continual effort by Washington officials to prod Saigon forward at a faster pace. Thus, if the Mission had just started a crash program at the highest speed ever achieved by the Mission, Washington officials, particularly Komer, acting (he said) in the President's name, would demand that the Mission redouble its efforts again. Komer, in a reflective moment, called it "creative tension."

The Saigon Mission responded to this pressure with resistance and hostility towards its Washington "backstops." When warned, for example, that the President was giving OCO 90 to 120 days to prove itself, Lodge and Porter both shot back pointed comments to the effect that this was an inadequate time period, and at the end of it results would probably not yet be visible. They were right, of course, but being right was not good enough. They fought the time deadline with too great a vehemence and did not do enough to "prove" OCO's worth. The result was the decision of March 1967 to put OCO under MACV.

The Mission thought that because they were "on the ground" they had a unique understanding of the problems of Vietnam, and that because they were on the ground they were the only accurate judges of the rate at which events needed to move. This point of view did not take into account domestic pressures in the United States; or, worse, it deliberately disregarded them. Thus, the Mission in Vietnam has generally tended to formulate strategy as though the United States will be fighting a slow war in Indochina for decades, while the Washington policymakers and strategists have tended to behave as though time runs out in November of 1968. (The mood of the Mission towards Washington is seen more clearly in press leaks than in cables. Thus, for example, the Evans and Novak column, from Saigon, on November 30, 1966, as OCO was being formed and the trial period beginning: "A note of quiet desperation is creeping into the top echelons of the U.S. Mission charged with winning the war in Vietnam. It grows partly out of frustration with what one top Embassy official describes as 'the hot blow torch on our rear ends' that comes from Washington, and, particularly, from the White House in search of ever-new victory proposals...Much of this frustration and gloom would vanish if attention in Washington were centered not on impossible trance tables for ending the war next month or next year but on a realistic projection of the modest gain now being made at great and painstaking effort." The difference in mood is reinforced by the climate of Vietnam, which is sluggish and humid, and by the influence of the Vietnamese, who after many years of war are rarely ready to race out and seek instant immortality on the field of battle or in the Ministries.

The one exception to this dangerous generalization has often been the individual American officer, usually military, serving in advisory or combat positions. There, with a 12-month tour standard, the Americans have pushed their Vietnamese counterparts hard, and often encountered great resistance. Indeed, the Americans in Vietnam often think they are already pushing the Vietnamese as hard as is desirable, and that Washington is asking the impossible when they send out instructions to get more out of the Vietnamese.

These were some of the background factors which were playing themselves out in late 1966 and early 1967. While tension between Washington and Saigon had existed before, and is inevitable between headquarters and the field, the pressure had by now reached a level higher than ever before. (It is ironic to note that the same tensions that exist between Washington and Saigon tend to exist between the Americans in Saigon and the Americans in the field. The phrase "Saigon commando" is used continually to castigate the uninformed officials in Saigon. There are too few people serving in Saigon with previous field experience, an unavoidable byproduct of the 12-month tour, and this increases the gap.)

120

TOP SECRET - Sensitive

So Washington officials talked about the lack of a sense of urgency in the Mission in Vietnam, and the Americans in Saigon talked about the dream world that Washington lived in, and the Americans in the provinces talked about the lack of understanding of the Americans in Saigon who had never seen the real war. Washington was dissatisfied with the progress in Vietnam, and since it could not influence the real obstacle, the Vietnamese, except through the American Mission, it deliberately put extra heat on the Mission. At least one high official involved in this period in Washington felt that it was a necessary and deliberate charade, and that only by overdoing its representations to the Mission could Washington assure that some fraction of its desires got through. More than one high-ranking official in Saigon felt that the only way to handle Washington was to hold out to them promises of progress and generally calm the home front down, or else run the risk of inflaming Washington and bringing still more reorganization down upon the Mission's head.

Rather than try to apportion responsibility for this sorry state of affairs, it would be useful to see the situation as the by-product of tensions produced by the Viet Cong strategy of survival and counter-punching at GVN weak spots, and the GVN's inability to be as good as we dream they should be. The United States could perhaps live with these problems in an age in which communications were not instantaneous, and publicity not so unrelenting.

Beyond this broad philosophical point, however, the fact is that the Mission in Vietnam was badly organized to conduct almost any kind of large and complex operation, let alone a war. Thus Washington was right to reorganize the Mission, and Saigon's reaction to each reorganization inevitably suggested that still more was needed.

Beyond that, the Mission in Vietnam did not have the full confidence of the Washington bureaucracy and Porter still lacked Lodge's full support.

TOP SECRET - Sensitive

B. OCO on Trial: Too Little Too Late -- Or Not Enough Time?

With the formation of OCO in late November the civilian mission began to move at a more rapid pace than it had in the post-Honolulu period. Most of this motion, of course, was internal to the U.S. Mission and could not produce visible results against the VC, an understandable fact when one considers the amount of work that the decision involved.

First, a Director of Civil Operations had to be chosen. Since Washington demanded rapid action, it was decided that the choice had to be someone already in Vietnam and ready to work, which sharply narrowed the list of possible men. The final selection was L. Wade Lathram, who had been the deputy director of USAID. Lathram was to prove to be the wrong man at the wrong time, a methodical and slow worker with strong respect for the very interagency system that he was supposed to supercede. In normal bureaucracies, Lathram could, and had, compiled excellent records, but OCO was demanding extraordinary results, and these required leadership and drive which Lathram did not possess.

It had been anticipated that Porter, a popular Ambassador and a knowledgeable and realistic man, would supply that leadership and drive, and that Lathram would simply run the OCO staff below Porter. But neither Porter nor Lathram saw their roles that way. Once OCO was formed, Porter to an unexpected degree stayed away from the day to day decisions, leaving them to Lathram. And Lathram simply did not have the position nor the stature to stand up to the full members of the Mission Council, whose assets he now partially controlled. (There was continued confusion over what was the responsibility of OCO and what remained under the control of the USAID, CIA and JUSPAO directors, and this confusion was never resolved -- and continues today under the CORDS structure.)

Moreover, Porter, who had not wanted a second Deputy Ambassador to come in to relieve him of all non-RD matters, soon found himself tied down in the business of the Embassy. Lodge went on a long leave shortly after the formation of OCO, taking about one month's vacation in Europe and the United States. This left Porter with responsibility for the full gamut of Ambassadorial activities, and he unavoidably became less and less concerned with the progress of OCO, even though it was in its first critical month. He had been given an office in the new OCO building (appropriated from AID), but he rarely used it, staying in the Embassy in another part of Saigon, and showing, in effect, by his failure to use his OCO office often that he could not devote much time to OCO.

The failure, therefore, to isolate Porter from all non-RD matters and provide Lodge with a full time DCM turned out to be a serious error. McNamara had clearly foreseen this in his 15 October memorandum to the President. In retrospect, we can see that Porter should have been given one job or the other, and the vacancy filled -- as Washington had suggested.

But Washington had just finished cramming an unpleasant action down the
Mission's throat, and it was felt that there were limits to how much
the Mission should be asked to take, especially since Lodge and Porter
were so adamant on the subject. 1/ Also, no one could foresee how
diverting other matters would become to Porter, or how much he would
delegate to Lathram.

The second major decision for OCO was the selection of the Regional
Directors -- men who would be given full control over all American
civilians in their respective regions. Here Porter presented Lathram
with three nominees (II Corps was left unfilled until a few weeks later)
and the choices appeared to be quite good ones: in I Corps, Porter's former
Assistant Deputy Ambassador, Henry Koren; in III Corps, the former MACV
Division Senior Advisor, then with AID, John Paul Vann; and in the Delta,
the CIA's former support chief, Vince Heymann. These were three respected
men, and they came from three different agencies, which emphasized the
interagency nature of OCO. In picking Vann, Porter had made a major
decision which involved possibly antagonizing both the CIA and MACV, for
Vann was without question one of the most controversial Americans in
Vietnam. He stood for impatience with the American Mission, deep and
often publicly-voiced disgust with the course of the past five years,
strong convictions on what needed to be done, driving energy and an
encyclopedic knowledge of recent events in Vietnam -- and was a burr in
the side of the CIA, with which he had frequently tangled, particularly
over the cadre program, and MACV, with which he had fought ever since
disagreeing publicly with General Harkins in 1963 (a fight which led to
his resignation from the Army and was extensively discussed in David
Halberstam's book, The Making of a Quagmire.)

The importance of the appointments was not lost on the Mission or
the press. While Lathram's appointment had stirred the bureaucracy but
not the press, the regional directors came as a surprise and a major
story. In a front-page story in The Washington Post, Ward Just described
Vann as "one of the legendary Americans in Vietnam," and said that Koren's
appointment indicated the great importance the Mission attached to the
jobs. Just added that "there were indications that, if OCO did not
succeed, the military command would take charge of pacification, or
'Revolutionary Development.'" 2/

Next came the selection of OCO Province Representatives, to be chosen
out of the available talent in each province. Here the slowness of the
civilians began to tell, and it was not until January that the appointments could be made for every province. Trying to pick men on the basis
of their knowledge and ability takes time and requires trips to each
province, consultations with other Mission Council members, etc., and
the civilians set out to do all this.

Meanwhile, a huge job which no one in Washington could fully appreciate
was underway -- the physical relocation of offices that Lodge had

described as necessary in his November 16 cable. Even in Washington it
may be difficult to get furniture and phones moved, except for very high-
ranking people; in Saigon a major relocation was more difficult to mount
than a military operation. While this was going on, involving literally
over one thousand people, work in OCO was even more confused and sporadic
than usual.

None of these minor organizational events would be of any importance
if it were not for the fact that they were eating away at the meager time
allotted to the civilians to prove that OCO should remain independent of
MACV. But they did consume time, and this was to prove to be a factor
in evaluating OCO.

The documents do not answer the question of whether or not OCO ever
really had a chance to survive, or whether it was just allowed to start
up by people who had already decided to turn RD over to MACV in a few
months. Both possibilities fit the available facts. An educated guess
would be that the decision to give Westmoreland control was tentatively
made by the President in the late fall of 1966, but that he decided he
would gain by allowing the civilians to reorganize first. If OCO proved
to be a major success, he could always continue to defer his decision.
If OCO fell short of the mark, then it still would be an organization in-
being ready to be placed into MACV without further internal changes, and
that in itself would be a major gain. Moreover, if the changes came when
Lodge and Porter were gone, there would be less difficulties.

If OCO moved too slowly for Washington's satisfaction, it nonetheless
accomplished many things which had previously been beyond the Mission's
ability:

-- Uniting personnel from AID, CIA, and JUSPAO into a single Plans
& Evaluations Section, OCO produced the first integrated plans for RD
on the U.S. side. These plans were ambitious and far-reaching, and
required MACV inputs. The fact that the civilians were asking MACV
for inputs to their own planning, rather than the reverse, so startled
MACV that MACV, in turn, began more intensive discussions or plans. The
planning effort involved several military officers on loan to OCO, a fact
which further heightened tension between OCO and MACV. When the plans
first formulated were presented to General Westmoreland, he indicated that
he was not going to be bound by any plans which reduced his flexibility
and ability to respond to military pressure whenever and wherever it
occurred; that is, he was reluctant to commit many military assets to
permanent RD support activities. But the relentless pressure from OCO,
from Komer in Washington, and even from the public attention focused on
the issue by Article 11 of the Manila communique ("The Vietnamese leaders
stated their intent to train and assign a substantial share of the armed
forces to clear-and-hold actions in order to provide a shield behind which
a new society can be built") all were working against General Westmoreland,
and towards the assignment of ARVN units to RD missions.

-- The civilians in the provinces spoke with a single voice for the first time. The province chiefs welcomed the change for this reason, according to most observers. Within the American team in each province, there was now a built-in obligation to consult with each other, instead of the previous situation in which more and more agencies were sending down to the provinces their own men who worked alone on their own projects.

-- The very act of physical relocation of the five major branches of OCO into a single building changed attitudes and behavior patterns in the civilian mission. Public Safety and the Special Branch advisors, for example, now were co-located, and began working together closely. Previously, they had both advised the same people through completely separate channels which met only at the top; i.e., when the chief of the Public Safety branch and the deputy CIA station chief had something specific and urgent they had to resolve. On the day-to-day matters, there had actually been a deliberate compartmentalization before OCO was formed.

These examples of gains could be repeated across a broad front. They were first steps in a direction which might ultimately have created a strong civilian mission, given time, better leaders, and more support from Washington. But even without these things, OCO was a definite plus.

The period between December and April was a period in which everyone paid lip service to the idea of supporting OCO, but in reality it was sniped at and attacked almost from the outset by the bureaucracies. In Saigon, Zorthian, and Hart, Directors of JUSPAO and CIA, respectively, made it clear that they wanted to remain very much involved in any decision affecting their respective fields of endeavor. While this was a reasonable point of view, it meant that CIA and even USIA officers in the field often refused to accept any guidance from the OCO representative, and cases began to come to light in which major actions were being initiated by the CIA without any consultation with OCO. (The CIA reasoning and defense rested on the fact that one of Hart's deputies was ostensibly an assistant director of OCO.)

In Washington, there was open skepticism to OCO from almost all quarters, particularly AID, which found itself footing most of the bill. USIA and CIA both indicated that they would continue to deal directly with their field personnel. In theory, everyone in Washington was to participate in the backstopping of the interagency OCO, but in practice, without a single voice in charge, this meant that no one was helping OCO, no one was trying to sell them as a going concern in Washington. Komer's role here was ambiguous; he supported OCO as long as it was in operation, and probably contributed more to its achievements than anyone else in Washington, but at the same time he was already on the record as favoring a military takeover, which was the very thing OCO sought to avoid.

125 .

Washington had decreed OCO, and had given Porter great responsibility. Unfortunately, they had failed to give him authority and stature needed to make the agencies work together.

As pointed out before, this might well have been overcome if time had not been so short. The slow methodical way of moving bureaucracies may be more effective than sweeping changes, anyway, if one has time. But in Vietnam no one was being given much time.

Shortly after OCO was formed, Komer's deputy, Ambassador William Leonhart, visited Vietnam, and when he returned, wrote the following penetrating assessment, which was sent to the President, Secretaries Rusk and McNamara, and Mr. Gaud and Mr. Helms:

"Whether Porter's new Office of Civil Operations (OCO) is viewed as a final organizational solution or as an inevitable intermediate step it is achieving a number of useful purposes. It establishes, on the civil side for the first time, unified interagency direction with a chain of command and communication from Saigon to the regions and provinces. It centralizes US-GVN field coordination of civil matters in one US official at each level. It affords a civil-side framework which can work more effectively with US military for politicomilitary coordination and more integrated pacification planning.

"At the time of my visit, OCO's impact had been felt mainly in Saigon. Its headquarters organization was largely completed. Three of the four Regional Directors had been named, all were at work, and one was in full time residence in his region. Regional staffs were being assembled but not yet in place. At province level, teams were being interviewed for the selection of Provincial Representatives. Porter expects them to be designated by January 1. Some slippage is possible, and it may be 90 days or so before the new organization is functioning. I participated in the initial briefings of the province teams I visited, passing along and emphasizing Bob Komer's admonitions against over-bureaucratization of effort and for fast and hard action. These were well-received. Morale was good. All the GVN Province Chiefs with whom I talked thought the new structure a great improvement." 3/

C. Time Runs Out

The decision to turn pacification over to MACV, with an integrated civil-military chain of command, was announced in Saigon on May 11, 1967, by Ambassador Ellsworth Bunker. In his announcement, Bunker said that the decision was entirely his.

But Bunker had been in Vietnam as Ambassador for less than two weeks, and he was therefore clearly acting under strong guidance, if not orders, from Washington. The decision to give MACV responsibility had actually stemmed from the clear and unmistakable fact that the President now considered such a reorganization highly desirable.

It is not clear when the President decided this in his own mind. The documents do not shed any light on this point, and, indeed, they simply fail to discuss the pros and cons of the decision in the early months of 1967, when the subject was a hot one in Washington and Saigon. This all suggests that whatever consideration of the issue was going on was confined strictly to private sessions between principals, and that the staff work previously done on a highly restricted basis was no longer considered necessary by the principals.

It has been suggested that the President had been strongly in favor of the move for months before he finally gave the go-ahead signal, and that he was held back by the strong opposition from Lodge and Porter, from Katzenbach, from the agencies in Washington -- and by the fact that it would appear to be a further "militarization" of the effort. This may well be the case; certainly nothing in the record disproves this possibility. But since there is no way that this study can answer the question, it must be left undecided.

Whenever the President made his decision in his own mind, he chose the Guam meeting as the place to discuss with a group of concerned officials outside his own personal staff. In a private meeting on March 20, or 21, 1967, with senior officials from Washington and Saigon, the President indicated that he felt the time had come to turn pacification over to MACV. The President enjoined those in the room at that meeting not to discuss the decision with anyone until it was announced, and he did not inform the GVN.

At the end of the Guam meeting, the President sent Komer back to Saigon with Westmoreland and Lodge, and Komer spent a week there, working out preliminary details of the reorganization. By this time Komer knew that he was to become Deputy to General Westmoreland, although many details remained to be ironed out.

When Komer returned to Washington, with the preliminary plans, a period followed during which no further action on the reorganization was taken. In all, nearly two months went by from the President's statement

at Guam to the public announcement, during which only a handful of people
in Washington and Saigon knew what was going to happen. The delays were
caused by a combination of factors: Bunker's understandable desire to
spend some time on personal business before going to Saigon, the President's desire to have Bunker make the final announcement himself after
he had reached Saigon, the need to work out final details. Since the
President was the man who had pressed everyone else working on Vietnam
to greater and greater effort, and since he stood to lose the most from
loss of time, it is surprising that he was now willing to see two months
lost, with a tired and lame-duck Mission in Vietnam, waiting for the new
team in a highly apprehensive state, and confusion at the higher levels.
But for reasons which are not readily apparent, the President did not push
his new team, and it was not until May 13, 1967, that Bunker made his
announcement (which had been drafted by Komer):

"Since being appointed U.S. Ambassador to Vietnam I have
been giving a great deal of thought to how to organize most
effectively the U.S. Advisory role in support of the Vietnamese
government's Revolutionary Development effort. Like my predecessor, I regard RD -- often termed pacification -- as close to
the heart of the matter in Vietnam.

"Support of Revolutionary Development has seemed to me and
my senior colleagues to be neither exclusively a civilian nor
exclusively a military function, but to be essentially civil-
military in character. It involves both the provision of continuous local security in the countryside -- necessarily a
primarily military task and the constructive programs conducted
by the Ministry of Revolutionary Development, largely through
its 59-member RD teams. The government of Vietnam has recognized the dual civil-military nature of the RD process by
assigning responsibility for its execution to the Corps/Region
Commanders and by deciding to assign the bulk of the regular
ARVN, as well as the Regional and Popular forces, to provide
the indispensable security so that RD can proceed in the countryside. As senior American official in Vietnam, I have concluded
that the U.S. Advisory and supporting role in Revolutionary
Development can be made more effective by unifying its civil
and military aspects under a single management concept. Unified
management, a single chain of command, and a more closely dove-
tailed advisory effort will in my opinion greatly improve U.S.
support of the vital RD program. Therefore, I am giving
General Westmoreland the responsibility for the performance of
our U.S. Mission field programs in support of pacification or
Revolutionary Development. To assist him in performing this
function, I am assigning Mr. Robert Komer to his headquarters
to be designated as a deputy to COMUSMACV with personal rank of
ambassador.

128

"I have two basic reasons for giving this responsibility to General Westmoreland. In the first place, the indispensable first stage of pacification is providing continuous local security, a function primarily of RVNAF, in which MACV performs a supporting advisory role. In the second place, the greater part of the U.S. Advisory and Logistic assets involved in support of Revolutionary Development belong to MACV. If unified management of U.S. Mission assets in support of the Vietnamese program is desirable, COMUSMACV is the logical choice.

"I have directed that a single chain of responsibility for advice and support of the Vietnamese Revolutionary Development program be instituted from Saigon down to district level. Just as Mr. Komer will supervise the U.S. Advisory role at the Saigon level as Deputy To General Westmoreland, so will the present OCO regional directors serve as deputies to U.S. field force commanders.

"At the province level, a senior advisor will be designated, either civilian or military, following analysis of the local situation.

"While management will thus be unified, the integrity of the Office of Civil Operations will be preserved. It will continue to perform the same functions as before, and will continue to have direct communication on technical matters with its field echelons. The present Revolutionary Development support division of MACV will be integrated into OCO, and its chief will serve as deputy to the Director of OCO. Such a unified civil/military U.S. advisory effort in the vital field of Revolutionary Development is unprecedented. But so too is the situation which we confront. RD is in my view neither civil nor military but a unique merging of both to meet a unique wartime need. Thus my resolution is to have U.S. civilian and military officials work together as one team in order more effectively to support our Vietnamese allies. Many further details will have to be worked out, and various difficulties will doubtless be encountered, but I am confident that this realignment of responsibilities is a sound management step and I count on all U.S. officers and officials concerned to make it work effectively in practice." 4/

Bunker outlined to Washington the line he proposed to take during a question and answer period with the press:

"Besides the above announcement, I intend to stress the following basic points in answer to press questions or in backgrounding: (a) I made this decision not because I think

129

that U.S. civilian support of RD has been unsatisfactory -- on
the contrary I am pleased with progress to date -- but because
I think it is essential to bring the U.S. military more fully
into the RD advisory effort and to pool our civil/military
resources to get optimum results: (b) indeed I regard all
official Americans in Vietnam as part of one team, not as
part of competing civilian and military establishments: (c)
as senior U.S. official in Vietnam, I intend to keep a close
eye on all U.S. activities, including pacification -- I am
not abdicating any of my responsibilities but rather am having
the entire U.S. pacification advisory effort report to me
through General Westmoreland rather than through two channels
as in the past: (d) during 34 years in the business world I have
learned that unified management with clear lines of authority is
the way to get the most out of large scale and highly diversified
programs: (e) since continuous local security, which RVNAF must
primarily provide, is the indispensable first stage of the pacification process, the MACV chain of command can obviously be
helpful to the RVNAF: and (f) I intend to see that the civilian
element of the U.S. effort is not buried under the military --
in many instances soldiers will end up working for civilians as
well as the reverse -- in fact Ambassador Komer will be General
Westmoreland's principal assistant for this function while
General Knowlton will be deputy to Mr. Lathram of OCO. I intend
to keep fully informed personally about all developments in this
field and to hold frequent meetings with General Westmoreland
and Ambassador Komer for the purpose of formulating policy." 5/

The reaction of the civilians in Vietnam to the announcement of
Ambassador Bunker was one of dismay. In the first confused days, before
details of the reorganization could be worked out and announced, the
press was able to write several articles which probably were accurate
reflections of the mood of most civilians:

"Civilian reactions today ranged from the bitter ('We
don't think they can do their own job -- how can they do ours?')
to the resigned ('I'll be a good soldier and go along') to the
very optimistic ('We've finally got a civilian in among the
generals'). Almost nowhere was there much enthusiasm for what
Bunker called 'a unique experiment in a unique situation.'

"Nor was there jubilation at the American military command.
Westmoreland, who wanted to take charge of the pacification program two years ago, is now reported to be deeply skeptical of
the possibility of producing the kind of quick results the White
House apparently wants.

"'I did not volunteer for the job,' he is reported to have
said privately this morning, 'but now that I've got it, I'll do
my best with it.'

"...Serious officials -- both civilian and military -- realize there are limitations on how far an officer will go in reporting 'negative' information, and how hard a civilian, now his subordinate, will fight for realism.

"...Officials today sought to mitigate the effect of the announcement by saying that Komer and his staff, physically located in the American Military Command in Saigon, will be in a far better position to influence the course of Pacification than he would among 'all the guys with glasses and sack suits' in the Office of Civil Operations." 6/

The Vietnamese reaction to the reorganization was more difficult to gauge. Ward Just, in the same story cited above, said "There was surprisingly little comment today from South Vietnamese, who have seen so many efforts at pacification and so many efforts to attempt to organize and reorganize themselves. One high American who professed to have spoken with the South Vietnamese command reported they are 'delighted.'" But Komer's talk with General Nguyen Duc Thang, the Minister for Construction (RD), did not reveal any delight on Thang's part. Indeed, Thang's first reaction was that the GVN should emulate the U.S. and turn pacification over to the Ministry of Defense -- an action which would have run directly counter to the U.S. objective of encouraging civilian government in Vietnam.

There is no telegraphic record of the first series of talks that Komer and Bunker had with Ky, Thieu, Vien, and Thang on the reorganization. Not until a Komer-Ky talk of May 15 does the cable traffic reflect the GVN reaction to the reorganization. By this time, it should be noted, the GVN knew that the U.S. did not want the GVN to follow suit, and it knew all our arguments and could play them back to us with ease:

"Ky said that General Thang had suggested that the RD effort be brought under Defense Ministry to conform to the U.S. reorganization. Ky and General Vien had demurred on grounds that such a reorganization on the GVN side would be far more complex than on U.S. side, would disrupt RD process, and would stretch General Vien and MOD too thin. Besides it would not be politically advisable at the very time when there was a hopeful trend toward a more civilianized and representative government. Komer agreed with Ky-Vien reasoning..." 7/

D. The CORDS Reorganization

With Bunker's announcement, the Mission began its second massive
reorganization in five months. This time, the reorganization was
accompanied by one of the periodic turnovers in Mission Council personnel which have characterized the Mission: for some reason, the
tours of many high-ranking officers seem to end at roughly the same
time, and thus, in 1964, 1965, and again in the spring of 1967,
several key members of the Mission Council all left within a few
weeks of each other. This time, in addition to Ambassador Lodge,
Porter, Habib, and Wehrle all left within a short period of time, and
only a high-level decision -- announced by Bunker at the same time as
the reorganization -- kept Zorthian and Lansdale on for extensions.
Into the Mission came Bunker, Locke, Komer, General Abrams, the new
Deputy COMUSMACV, and Charles Cooper, the new Economic Counselor, and
Archibald Calhoun, the new Political Counselor.

Despite the turnover, the reorganization seemed to proceed with
comparative ease. Perhaps the fact that OCO had already been formed
was critical here, since it meant that instead of MACV dealing with
three agencies simultaneously, the first discussions could be restricted
primarily to MACV and OCO. Moreover, because OCO was already a going
concern, the civilians were better organized than ever before to maintain their own position in dealings with the military.

But above all, it was the decision by Westmoreland and Bunker to
let Komer take the lead in the reorganization which was important.
Komer now made major decisions on how the new structure would look
which were usually backed up by Westmoreland. The result looked much
better than many people had dared hope.

The details of the reorganization are not worth detailed discussion
here. But one point can illustrate the way CORDS could resolve previously unresolved issues: the question of the role of the ARVN
Division in the chain of command.

As noted in an earlier section, study groups had over the years
advocated removing the ARVN Divisions from the chain of command on
Pacification/RD. But MACV had large advisory teams with the Divisions
and these teams controlled both the sector (Province) advisory teams
and Regimental advisory teams below them. The structure followed normal
military lines, and made good sense to most of the officers in the
higher levels of MACV.

The counter-argument was that Division was a purely military
instrument and could not adequately control the integrated civilian-
military effort that was needed at the Province level. Thus the Roles
and Missions Study Group, for example, had recommended that "Division
be Removed from the RD Chain of Command...that the role of the Province

132

Chief be upgraded...that Province Chiefs have operational control (as
a minimum) of all military and paramilitary forces assigned to operate
exclusively in their sector." 8/   The Study Group recognized that
"the power structure being what it is in the GVN, major progress toward
this goal will not be short range or spectacular." But, they urged,
the U.S. should begin to push forward on it.

MACV had nonconcurred in this recommendation. General Westmoreland,
in a memorandum to Lodge on September 7, 1966, had said that he did not
agree with the idea, and that, if carried out, "the Corps span of control
would be too large for effective direction." The suggestion, he added,
was "illogical." 9/

This was still the position of MACV when Komer arrived. In his
attempts to find a workable civilian-military chain of command, he
received two suggestions on the difficult question of the role of the
Division advisory teams. The first, and more routine, was to continue
the existing MACV system -- in which, no matter how good or bad the
GVN chain of command may be, the U.S. simply duplicates it on the advisory
side. This would mean that all American civilians and military at the
Province level would come under the Division-Corps chain of command.
The MACV staff assumed that this would happen.

John Paul Vann and a few colleagues had a different suggestion.
Vann maintained that the evidence suggested that when the Americans
made their desires known clearly to the Vietnamese, without the vague-
ness and contradictoriness which so often characterized them, then the
Vietnamese usually would follow suit after a suitable period of time.
Thus, said Vann, if the Americans remove the Division advisory team
from the U.S. chain of command, except for tactical matters and logistical
support, the GVN may follow, and reduce the power of their politically
potent Divisions.

The thesis Vann was putting forward -- that the GVN would follow
a strong U.S. example -- was untested and hotly disputed. Secondly,
there was the matter of MACV's stand against downgrading the role of
the ARVN Divisions. Few people observing the discussions thought that
the Vann suggestion had a chance of success.

But Komer, persuaded by the argument, did overrule many of his
staff and make the recommendation to Westmoreland. Westmoreland approved
it, and in June, 1967, the new chains of command were announced to the
U.S. Mission. After years of arguing, during all of which the trend
had been towards stronger ARVN Divisions, the U.S. had suddenly reversed
course on its own, without waiting for the Vietnamese to act. The change
was so complete that it even extended to that last (and, to career
officers, most important) question: who writes the efficiency report.
Under the new MACV guidance, the Senior Province Advisor would be rated

not by the Division Senior Advisor, but by the Deputy for CORDS and
the Corps level -- thus confirming the new command arrangements.

While it is still too early to tell if the GVN will completely
follow the U.S. lead, the early evidence suggests that the Vann
hypothesis was correct, and that following the U.S. action, the GVN
has begun to reduce the role of their Divisions in RD. There are now
indications that the GVN is seriously considering a plan in which the
Divisions would no longer have area responsibility but rather be
reduced to support of their forward units, and operational command on
large operations of troops.

E. The Mission Assessment as CORDS Begins

The situation that CORDS and Ambassador Komer inherited was not a very promising one. Despite all the lip service and all the "top priorities" assigned RD by the Americans in the preceding 18 months, progress in the field was not only not satisfactory, it was, according to many observers, nonexistent. The question of whether we were inching forward, standing still, or moving backward always seemed to the Mission and Washington to be of great importance, and therefore much effort was spent trying to analyze our "progress."

A strong case can be made for the proposition that we have spent too much time looking for progress in a program in which measurements are irrelevant, inaccurate, and misleading. But, nonetheless, the Mission did try to measure itself, and in May of 1967, as OCO turned into CORDS, produced the following assessment of RD for the first quarter of 1967.

"In truth, there has been little overall progress in RD activities, and the same must be said for the painful process of building a meaningful dialogue between the government and the people. A number of factors have been reported from Region III to account for this unhappy situation, but they might well apply to the rest of the country:

"a. The RD program for 1967 involved many new and different concepts, command arrangements, administrative and procedural functions and allocation of resources. Only recently have the majority of provincial officials involved become aware of the program.

"b. Many Ap Doi Moi (Real New Life Hamlets), through guidance from MORD, were located in fringe security areas. In most of these cases a great deal of military and jungle clearing operations were necessary. These take time, and, as a result, the deployment of the RD teams often were delayed.

"c. The hobbling effect of ineffectual officials has retarded the program.

"d. The people have had to develop new working relationships with the RD workers,* the ARVN, and the RF/PF. During this process, there has been a 'wait and see' attitude.

---

* "Workers" was another one of the special words the U.S. began using instead of accurate translations of the Vietnamese. This one was also Lodge's idea, as a more understandable word than "cadre" to describe the members of the 59-man teams.

"If, however, the picture is sombre, it is not unrelieved. The 1967 program may look at this point unencouraging statistically, but its progress is of a different and more important sort. In critical areas, progress has been registered. There has evolved an implicit understanding by many in the GVN that RD is a longer-term progress than hitherto believed, requiring a greater concentration of resources. In fact, there is increasing evidence that programming for 1967 has so concentrated scarce resources in the 11-point Ap Doi Moi that the GVN presence and services are spread very thin indeed in areas of lower priority. The fact that in general each RD team will remain in each hamlet for six months throughout the year, is a fundamental improvement in the program.

"As a result of the finer definition of the intent of RD and more interest in its possibilities, the 1967 program has become more vital than its predecessors. This vitality has produced new ideas, an increasing flexibility, which marks important progress in the program. Moreover, what the country has been engaged in is the process of laying a base for development; a long drawn out process which sees little initial reward, but without which nothing of permanence will be achieved. In other words, the first quarter of the year has not been witness to a vital social revolution, but has instead found evidence of a growing understanding of the nature of the revolution to come, and in so doing has taken a further step in the painful process of building a nation." 10/

---   ---   ---   ---   ---

With the formation of CORDS, this history becomes current events. CORDS is charged now with solving what have previously been unsolvable problems -- energizing the GVN to do things which it is not as interested in as we are; winning the hearts and minds of people who do not understand us or speak our language; working under intense pressure for immediate results in a field in which success -- if possible at all -- may require years. We have concentrated on the history of the United States bureaucracy in this study because that, in retrospect, seems to have been where the push for pacification came from -- not the Vietnamese. We have not been able to analyze properly the actual course of the effort in the field, where contradictory assessments of progress have plagued the U.S. In the final section which follows, we try to draw a few lessons from the course of events described in this study.

When completed, CORDS had produced a structure in which, regardless of civil-military tensions that cannot be wished away, all hands were working together under a single chain of command. The structure was massive, so massive that the Vietnamese were in danger of being almost

forgotten -- and for that there can be no excuse. But at least the
Mission was better run and better organized than it had ever been
before, and this fact may in time lead to a more efficient and successful effort. Without a unified voice in dealing with the Vietnamese, we
can never hope to influence the GVN to do the things we believe they
must do to save their own country.

VI. FOOTNOTES

TOP SECRET - Sensitive

VI. FOOTNOTES

I. THREADS THAT MET AT HONOLULU

1. Ambassador Lodge memorandum to Secretaries Rusk and McNamara, and Ambassador Taylor, June 19, 1964

2. Message, SAIGON 1035 to Washington, October 6, 1964, EXDIS

3. MACV Command History, 1964, p. 68

4. Message, SAIGON 1000, October 7, 1964

5. MACV Command History, 1964, p. 68

6. Memorandum, February 1966 - Report of Meetings on Rural Construction, February 1-4, 1966

7. Idem.

8. Idem.

9. Mission Council Minutes, September 15, 1965

10. McGeorge Bundy memorandum for the President, February 7, 1965

11. MACV Overall Monthly Evaluation, June 1965

12. Private Assessment of Hop Tac to Ambassador Lodge from Embassy Personnel, September 10, 1965

13. Mission Council Minutes, September 15, 1965

14. Mission Council Minutes, July 7, 1966

15. President Johnson's letter to Ambassador Lodge, July 1965

16. Message, SAIGON 2761, February 1, 1966, NODIS to the President

17. President Johnson letter to General Taylor, July 2, 1964

18. Ambassador Lodge quoted in memorandum for record, September 27, 1965; Special Meeting in Embassy Conference Room; p. 1

19. See, for example, SAIGON 4323, August 24, 1966, NODIS to the President

TOP SECRET - Sensitive

20. Ambassador Lodge memorandum dated June 19, 1964

21. Message, SAIGON 1100, September 30, 1965, NODIS to the President

22. Message, STATE 367, August 7, 1965, to Ambassador Lodge

23. Message, SAIGON 716, September 2, 1965, NODIS to the President

24. Message, SAIGON 952, September 18, 1965, NODIS to the President

25. Message, SAIGON 1059, October 4, 1965, NODIS to the President

26. Message, SAIGON 1190, October 6, 1967, NODIS to the President

27. Message, SAIGON 1273, October 13, 1965, NODIS to the President

28. Message, SAIGON 1377, October 21, 1965, NODIS to the President

29. USMC Historical Branch Study: "US Marine Corps Civic Action Efforts in Vietnam, March 1965-March 1966," (MC History), prepared in early 1967 (Draft with Unnumbered Pages).

30. General Krulak, CG of Fleet Marine Force, Pacific, Monthly Report on Activities of III MAF, September 1965, p. 4

31. General Krulak's report on III MAF, October 1965, p. 12

32. MC History (See Footnote 29)

33. Embassy POL Study of Quang Nam, February 15, 1966, p. 5

34. Message, STATE 2087, May 26, 1964, Personal from the President

35. Message, SAIGON 071010Z, July 7, 1964, to Secretary of State

36. Alexis Johnson letter to Ambassador Durbrow, November 26, 1965; Official-Informal

37. Warrenton Conference Study, January 22, 1965, Annex D, par.1

38. Ibid., Annex D, par. 2

39. Ibid., Annex D, par. 9

40. Ibid., Annex D, p. 4

41. Record of Mission Liaison Group Meeting, prepared by Colonel Sam Karrick, SLO, January 27, 1966

42. Warrenton Conference Report, Annex E, contains all the proposals brought to Warrenton

43. Warrenton Conference Report, Annex D, par. 14

44. Message, STATE 951, October 4, 1965, LIMDIS

45. The Washington Post editorial, February 1, 1966

46. President Johnson's Press Conference, February 4, 1966

47. The New York Times editorial, February 6, 1966

48. The New York Times, Charles Mohr, February 7, 1966

49. MACV Monthly Evaluation Report, 1965

II. HONOLULU

1. Ambassador Lodge's briefing to Honolulu Conference, February 1966

2. Ambassador Lodge's letter to Secretary McNamara, March 4, 1966

3. President Johnson's comments to Honolulu Conference, February 1966

4. Secretary Rusk's comments to Honolulu Conference, February 1966

5. President Johnson's comments to Honolulu Conference, February 1966

6. General Thang briefing to Honolulu Conference, February 7, 1966

7. Honolulu Conference, Plenary Documents, February 8, 1966

8. Secretary Freeman's comments to Honolulu Conference, February 8, 1966

9. President Johnson's comments to Honolulu Conference, February, 1966

10. President Johnson's final statement to Honolulu Conference, Plenary Documents, February 9, 1966

11. Declaration of Honolulu, Part II, February 8, 1966

III. HONOLULU TO MANILA

1. President Johnson's Press Conference in Saigon, February 11, 1966

2. Message, STATE 2368, February 12, 1966, NODIS

3. Message, SAIGON 2365, February 12, 1966, NODIS

4. Message, SAIGON 2959, February 15, 1966, NODIS

5. Mission Council Minutes, February 28, 1966

6. Henry Kissinger letter to Robert W. Komer, August 8, 1966,
    EYES ONLY

7. Robert W. Komer paper, "Giving a New Thrust to Pacification,"
    August 7, 1966

8. Joseph Califano memorandum to Secretary of Defense, March 23, 1966
    EYES ONLY

9. NSAM 343, March 28, 1966

10. Robert W. Komer memorandum to the President, April 19, 1966, p. 3

11. Message, STATE 3214, April 26, 1966

12. Message, STATE 3344, May 7, 1966

13. Message, STATE 3760, June 4, 1966

14. Message, STATE 83089, November 10, 1966

15. Robert W. Komer memorandum to the President, April 19, 1966

16. Robert W. Komer paper, "Giving a New Thrust to Pacification,"
    August 7, 1966

17. Robert W. Komer memorandum to the President, February 28, 1967

18. Idem.

19. PROVN Study Team Summary Statement, March 1966, pp. 1-2

20. Ibid., pp. 46-47

21. Ibid., p. 67

22. Ibid.

23. Ibid.

24. Message, MACJ33 18244, May 12, 1966

25. Priorities Task Force Summary, July 1966

26. Ibid.

27. Ibid.

28. Roles and Missions Study Group Report, p. 1

29. Ibid.

30. Roles and Missions Study Group memorandum to Ambassador Lodge
    September 7, 1966

31. Roles and Missions Study Group Report, Section V, pp. 2-4,
    August 1966

32. USAID memorandum to Ambassador Lodge, September 8, 1966

33. CIA comments on Roles and Missions Study Group Recommendations

34. Major General Tillson (J-3, MACV) briefing to Mission Council,
    August 8, 1966

35. Message, SAIGON 4923, August 31, 1966, NODIS to the President

36. Message, COMUSMACV to CINCPAC 260242Z, August 1966

37. Ibid.

38. Draft Presidential memorandum by Secretary of Defense,
    September 15, 1966

39. Ibid., State Department's opposition

40. Ibid., AID's recommendation

41. Ibid., JCS concurrence in idea of a Deputy COMUSMACV for RD

42. Ibid., CIA and USIA opposition

43. Robert W. Komer memorandum to Secretary McNamara, September 22,
    1966

44. Message, STATE 61251, October 6, 1966 to Ambassador Lodge

45. Mr. Katzenbach's memorandum to the President, October 15, 1966, "Administration of Revolutionary Development"

46. Ibid.

47. Secretary McNamara's memorandum to the President, October 14, 1966

48. Mr. George Carver's memorandum to Richard Helms (Director of CIA), October 15, 1966, Reference Footnote 47.

49. JCSM-572-66, October 14, 1966

50. The Washington Evening Star article on President Johnson's meeting with White House Press Corps, October 15, 1966

51. Ward Just article, The Washington Post, October 17, 1966

52. Message, STATE 68390, October 20, 1966, NODIS

53. Message, STATE 78865, November 4, 1966

54. Message, SAIGON 10204, November 6, 1966, NODIS to the President

55. Message, STATE 83699, November 12, 1966, to Ambassador Lodge

56. Ibid.

57. Message, STATE 85196, November 15, 1966

58. Message, SAIGON 11124, November 17, 1966, NODIS

59. Message, SAIGON 11125, November 17, 1966, NODIS

60. III MAF Summary of 1966 Operations by FMF/Pacific, December 1966, p. 22

61. Ibid., p. 21

62. Ibid., p. 21

63. Ibid., p. 22

IV. OCO to CORDS

1. Messages, SAIGON 11124 and 11125, 1966 (See Footnotes 58 and 59, of III., above)

2. The Washington Post article by Ward Just, December 3, 1966

3. Wiliam Leonhart memorandum for the President, December 30, 1966

4. Ambassador Bunker statement in Saigon, May 13, 1967

5. Ambassador Bunker Press Conference in Saigon, May 13, 1967

6. Ward Just, The Washington Post, May 12, 1967

7. Message, SAIGON 25839, May 16, 1967

8. Roles and Missions Study Group, Appendix A, August 1966 (Saigon)

9. General Westmoreland memorandum to Ambassador Lodge, September 7, 1966

10. U.S. Mission Assessment of RD for 1st Quarter of 1967 (A-662, May 12, 1967)

www.ingramcontent.com/pod-product-compliance
Lightning Source LLC
Chambersburg PA
CBHW050352110426
42812CB00008B/2436